T0188910

Lecture Notes in Computer Science

Lecture Notes in Artificial Intelligence   **14174**

Founding Editor

Jörg Siekmann

Series Editors

Randy Goebel, *University of Alberta, Edmonton, Canada*
Wolfgang Wahlster, *DFKI, Berlin, Germany*
Zhi-Hua Zhou, *Nanjing University, Nanjing, China*

The series Lecture Notes in Artificial Intelligence (LNAI) was established in 1988 as a topical subseries of LNCS devoted to artificial intelligence.

The series publishes state-of-the-art research results at a high level. As with the LNCS mother series, the mission of the series is to serve the international R & D community by providing an invaluable service, mainly focused on the publication of conference and workshop proceedings and postproceedings.

Gianmarco De Francisci Morales ·
Claudia Perlich · Natali Ruchansky ·
Nicolas Kourtellis · Elena Baralis ·
Francesco Bonchi
Editors

Machine Learning and Knowledge Discovery in Databases

Applied Data Science and Demo Track

European Conference, ECML PKDD 2023
Turin, Italy, September 18–22, 2023
Proceedings, Part VI

 Springer

Editors
Gianmarco De Francisci Morales 🆔
CENTAI
Turin, Italy

Claudia Perlich
NYU and Two Sigma
New York, NY, USA

Natali Ruchansky 🆔
Netflix
Los Angeles, CA, USA

Nicolas Kourtellis 🆔
Telefonica Research
Barcelona, Spain

Elena Baralis 🆔
Politecnico di Torino
Turin, Italy

Francesco Bonchi 🆔
CENTAI
Turin, Italy

ISSN 0302-9743   ISSN 1611-3349 (electronic)
Lecture Notes in Artificial Intelligence
ISBN 978-3-031-43426-6   ISBN 978-3-031-43427-3 (eBook)
https://doi.org/10.1007/978-3-031-43427-3

LNCS Sublibrary: SL7 – Artificial Intelligence

Preface

The 2023 edition of the European Conference on Machine Learning and Principles and Practice of Knowledge Discovery in Databases (ECML PKDD 2023) was held in Turin, Italy, from September 18 to 22, 2023.

The ECML PKDD conference, held annually, acts as a worldwide platform showcasing the latest advancements in machine learning and knowledge discovery in databases, encompassing groundbreaking applications. With a history of successful editions, ECML PKDD has established itself as the leading European machine learning and data mining conference, offering researchers and practitioners an unparalleled opportunity to exchange knowledge and ideas.

The main conference program consisted of presentations of 255 accepted papers and three keynote talks (in order of appearance):

- Max Welling (University of Amsterdam): Neural Wave Representations
- Michael Bronstein (University of Oxford): Physics-Inspired Graph Neural Networks
- Kate Crawford (USC Annenberg): Mapping Generative AI

In addition, there were 30 workshops, 9 combined workshop-tutorials, 5 tutorials, 3 discovery challenges, and 16 demonstrations. Moreover, the PhD Forum provided a friendly environment for junior PhD students to exchange ideas and experiences with peers in an interactive atmosphere and to get constructive feedback from senior researchers. The conference included a Special Day on Artificial Intelligence for Financial Crime Fight to discuss, share, and present recent developments in AI-based financial crime detection.

In recognition of the paramount significance of ethics in machine learning and data mining, we invited the authors to include an ethical statement in their submissions. We encouraged the authors to discuss the ethical implications of their submission, such as those related to the collection and processing of personal data, the inference of personal information, or the potential risks. We are pleased to report that our call for ethical statements was met with an overwhelmingly positive response from the authors.

The ECML PKDD 2023 Organizing Committee supported Diversity and Inclusion by awarding some grants that enable early career researchers to attend the conference, present their research activities, and become part of the ECML PKDD community. A total of 8 grants covering all or part of the registration fee (4 free registrations and 4 with 50% discount) were awarded to individuals who belong to underrepresented communities, based on gender and role/position, to attend the conference and present their research activities. The goal of the grants was to provide financial support to early-career (women) scientists and Master and Ph.D. students from developing countries. The Diversity and Inclusion action also includes the SoBigData Award, fully sponsored by the SoBigData++ Horizon2020 project, which aims to encourage more diverse participation in computer science and machine learning events. The award is intended to cover expenses for transportation and accommodation.

The papers presented during the three main conference days were organized in four different tracks:

- Research Track: research or methodology papers from all areas in machine learning, knowledge discovery, and data mining;
- Applied Data Science Track: papers on novel applications of machine learning, data mining, and knowledge discovery to solve real-world use cases, thereby bridging the gap between practice and current theory;
- Journal Track: papers published in special issues of the journals Machine Learning and Data Mining and Knowledge Discovery;
- Demo Track: short papers introducing new prototypes or fully operational systems that exploit data science techniques and are presented via working demonstrations.

We received 829 submissions for the Research track and 239 for the Applied Data Science Track.

We accepted 196 papers (24%) in the Research Track and 58 (24%) in the Applied Data Science Track. In addition, there were 44 papers from the Journal Track and 16 demo papers (out of 28 submissions).

We want to thank all participants, authors, all chairs, all Program Committee members, area chairs, session chairs, volunteers, co-organizers, and organizers of workshops and tutorials for making ECML PKDD 2023 an outstanding success. Thanks to Springer for their continuous support and Microsoft for allowing us to use their CMT software for conference management and providing support throughout. Special thanks to our sponsors and the ECML PKDD Steering Committee for their support. Finally, we thank the organizing institutions: CENTAI (Italy) and Politecnico di Torino (Italy).

September 2023

Elena Baralis
Francesco Bonchi
Manuel Gomez Rodriguez
Danai Koutra
Claudia Plant
Gianmarco De Francisci Morales
Claudia Perlich

Organization

General Chairs

Elena Baralis — Politecnico di Torino, Italy
Francesco Bonchi — CENTAI, Italy and Eurecat, Spain

Research Track Program Chairs

Manuel Gomez Rodriguez — Max Planck Institute for Software Systems, Germany
Danai Koutra — University of Michigan, USA
Claudia Plant — University of Vienna, Austria

Applied Data Science Track Program Chairs

Gianmarco De Francisci Morales — CENTAI, Italy
Claudia Perlich — NYU and TwoSigma, USA

Journal Track Chairs

Tania Cerquitelli — Politecnico di Torino, Italy
Marcello Restelli — Politecnico di Milano, Italy
Charalampos E. Tsourakakis — Boston University, USA and ISI Foundation, Italy
Fabio Vitale — CENTAI, Italy

Workshop and Tutorial Chairs

Rosa Meo — University of Turin, Italy
Fabrizio Silvestri — Sapienza University of Rome, Italy

Demo Chairs

Nicolas Kourtellis   Telefonica, Spain
Natali Ruchansky   Netflix, USA

Local Chairs

Daniele Apiletti   Politecnico di Torino, Italy
Paolo Bajardi   CENTAI, Italy
Eliana Pastor   Politecnico di Torino, Italy

Discovery Challenge Chairs

Danilo Giordano   Politecnico di Torino, Italy
André Panisson   CENTAI, Italy

PhD Forum Chairs

Yllka Velaj   University of Vienna, Austria
Matteo Riondato   Amherst College, USA

Diversity and Inclusion Chair

Tania Cerquitelli   Politecnico di Torino, Italy

Proceedings Chairs

Eliana Pastor   Politecnico di Torino, Italy
Giulia Preti   CENTAI, Italy

Sponsorship Chairs

Daniele Apiletti   Politecnico di Torino, Italy
Paolo Bajardi   CENTAI, Italy

Web Chair

Alessandro Fiori   Flowygo, Italy

Social Media and Publicity Chair

Flavio Giobergia   Politecnico di Torino, Italy

Online Chairs

Alkis Koudounas   Politecnico di Torino, Italy
Simone Monaco   Politecnico di Torino, Italy

Best Paper Awards Chairs

Peter Flach   University of Bristol, UK
Katharina Morik   TU Dortmund, Germany
Arno Siebes   Utrecht University, The Netherlands

ECML PKDD Steering Committee

Massih-Reza Amini   Université Grenoble Alpes, France
Annalisa Appice   University of Bari, Aldo Moro, Italy
Ira Assent   Aarhus University, Denmark
Tania Cerquitelli   Politecnico di Torino, Italy
Albert Bifet   University of Waikato, New Zealand
Francesco Bonchi   CENTAI, Italy and Eurecat, Spain
Peggy Cellier   INSA Rennes, France
Saso Dzeroski   Jožef Stefan Institute, Slovenia
Tias Guns   KU Leuven, Belgium
Alípio M. G. Jorge   University of Porto, Portugal
Kristian Kersting   TU Darmstadt, Germany
Jefrey Lijffijt   Ghent University, Belgium
Luís Moreira-Matias   Sennder GmbH, Germany
Katharina Morik   TU Dortmund, Germany
Siegfried Nijssen   Université catholique de Louvain, Belgium
Andrea Passerini   University of Trento, Italy

Program Committee

Guest Editorial Board, Journal Track

Helge Langseth	Norwegian University of Science and Technology, Norway
Thien Le	MIT, USA
Hsuan-Tien Lin	National Taiwan University, Taiwan
Marco Lippi	University of Modena and Reggio Emilia, Italy
Corrado Loglisci	University of Bari, Aldo Moro, Italy
Manuel López-ibáñez	University of Manchester, UK
Nuno Lourenço	CISUC, Portugal
Claudio Lucchese	Ca' Foscari University of Venice, Italy
Brian Mac Namee	University College Dublin, Ireland
Gjorgji Madjarov	Ss. Cyril and Methodius University in Skopje, North Macedonia
Luigi Malagò	Transylvanian Institute of Neuroscience, Romania
Sagar Malhotra	Fondazione Bruno Kessler, Italy
Fragkiskos Malliaros	CentraleSupélec, Université Paris-Saclay, France
Giuseppe Manco	ICAR-CNR, Italy
Basarab Matei	Sorbonne Université Paris Nord, France
Michael Mathioudakis	University of Helsinki, Finland
Rosa Meo	University of Turin, Italy
Mohamed-Lamine Messai	Université Lumière Lyon 2, France
Sara Migliorini	University of Verona, Italy
Alex Mircoli	Università Politecnica delle Marche, Italy
Atsushi Miyauchi	University of Tokyo, Japan
Simone Monaco	Politecnico di Torino, Italy
Anna Monreale	University of Pisa, Italy
Corrado Monti	CENTAI, Italy
Katharina Morik	TU Dortmund, Germany
Lia Morra	Politecnico di Torino, Italy
Arsenii Mustafin	Boston University, USA
Mirco Mutti	Politecnico di Milano/University of Bologna, Italy
Amedeo Napoli	University of Lorraine, CNRS, LORIA, France
Kleber Oliveira	CENTAI, Italy
Gabriella Olmo	Politecnico di Torino, Italy
Marios Papachristou	Cornell University, USA
Panagiotis Papapetrou	Stockholm University, Sweden
Matteo Papini	Universitat Pompeu Fabra, Spain
Vincenzo Pasquadibisceglie	University of Bari, Aldo Moro, Italy
Eliana Pastor	Politecnico di Torino, Italy
Andrea Paudice	University of Milan, Italy
Charlotte Pelletier	IRISA - Université Bretagne-Sud, France
Ruggero G. Pensa	University of Turin, Italy
Simone Piaggesi	University of Bologna/ISI Foundation, Italy

Area Chairs, Research Track

Fabrizio Angiulli	University of Calabria, Italy
Annalisa Appice	University of Bari, Aldo Moro, Italy
Antonio Artés	Universidad Carlos III de Madrid, Spain
Martin Atzmueller	Osnabrück University, Germany
Christian Böhm	University of Vienna, Austria
Michael R. Berthold	KNIME, Switzerland
Albert Bifet	Université Paris-Saclay, France
Hendrik Blockeel	KU Leuven, Belgium
Ulf Brefeld	Leuphana University, Germany
Paula Brito	INESC TEC - LIAAD/University of Porto, Portugal
Wolfram Burgard	University of Technology Nuremberg, Germany
Seshadhri C.	UCSC, USA
Michelangelo Ceci	University of Bari, Aldo Moro, Italy
Peggy Cellier	IRISA - INSA Rennes, France
Duen Horng Chau	Georgia Institute of Technology, USA
Nicolas Courty	IRISA - Université Bretagne-Sud, France
Bruno Cremilleux	Université de Caen Normandie, France
Jesse Davis	KU Leuven, Belgium
Abir De	IIT Bombay, India
Tom Diethe	AstraZeneca, UK
Yuxiao Dong	Tsinghua University, China
Kurt Driessens	Maastricht University, The Netherlands
Tapio Elomaa	Tampere University, Finland
Johannes Fürnkranz	JKU Linz, Austria
Sophie Fellenz	RPTU Kaiserslautern-Landau, Germany
Elisa Fromont	IRISA/Inria rba - Université de Rennes 1, France
Thomas Gärtner	TU Vienna, Austria
Patrick Gallinari	Criteo AI Lab - Sorbonne Université, France
Joao Gama	INESC TEC - LIAAD, Portugal
Rayid Ghani	Carnegie Mellon University, USA
Aristides Gionis	KTH Royal Institute of Technology, Sweden
Chen Gong	Nanjing University of Science and Technology, China
Francesco Gullo	UniCredit, Italy
Eyke Hüllermeier	LMU Munich, Germany
Junheng Hao	University of California, Los Angeles, USA
José Hernández-Orallo	Universitat Politècnica de Valencia, Spain
Daniel Hernández-Lobato	Universidad Autonoma de Madrid, Spain
Sibylle Hess	TU Eindhoven, The Netherlands

Sriparna Saha	IIT Patna, India
Ute Schmid	University of Bamberg, Germany
Lars Schmidt-Thieme	University of Hildesheim, Germany
Michele Sebag	LISN CNRS, France
Thomas Seidl	LMU Munich, Germany
Junming Shao	University of Electronic Science and Technology of China, China
Arno Siebes	Utrecht University, The Netherlands
Fabrizio Silvestri	Sapienza University of Rome, Italy
Carlos Soares	University of Porto, Portugal
Christian Sohler	University of Cologne, Germany
Myra Spiliopoulou	Otto-von-Guericke-University Magdeburg, Germany
Jie Tang	Tsinghua University, China
Nikolaj Tatti	University of Helsinki, Finland
Evimaria Terzi	Boston University, USA
Marc Tommasi	Lille University, France
Heike Trautmann	University of Münster, Germany
Herke van Hoof	University of Amsterdam, The Netherlands
Celine Vens	KU Leuven, Belgium
Christel Vrain	University of Orleans, France
Jilles Vreeken	CISPA Helmholtz Center for Information Security, Germany
Wei Ye	Tongji University, China
Jing Zhang	Renmin University of China, China
Min-Ling Zhang	Southeast University, China

Area Chairs, Applied Data Science Track

Annalisa Appice	University of Bari, Aldo Moro, Italy
Ira Assent	Aarhus University, Denmark
Martin Atzmueller	Osnabrück University, Germany
Michael R. Berthold	KNIME, Switzerland
Hendrik Blockeel	KU Leuven, Belgium
Michelangelo Ceci	University of Bari, Aldo Moro, Italy
Peggy Cellier	IRISA - INSA Rennes, France
Yi Chang	Jilin University, China
Nicolas Courty	IRISA - UBS, France
Bruno Cremilleux	Université de Caen Normandie, France
Peng Cui	Tsinghua University, China
Anirban Dasgupta	IIT Gandhinagar, India

Tom Diethe	AstraZeneca, UK
Carlotta Domeniconi	George Mason University, USA
Dejing Dou	BCG, USA
Kurt Driessens	Maastricht University, The Netherlands
Johannes Fürnkranz	JKU Linz, Austria
Faisal Farooq	Qatar Computing Research Institute, Qatar
Paolo Frasconi	University of Florence, Italy
Elisa Fromont	IRISA/Inria rba - Université de Rennes 1, France
Glenn Fung	Liberty Mutual, USA
Joao Gama	INESC TEC - LIAAD, Portugal
Jose A. Gamez	Universidad de Castilla-La Mancha, Spain
Rayid Ghani	Carnegie Mellon University, USA
Aristides Gionis	KTH Royal Institute of Technology, Sweden
Sreenivas Gollapudi	Google, USA
Francesco Gullo	UniCredit, Italy
Eyke Hüllermeier	LMU Munich, Germany
Jingrui He	University of Illinois at Urbana-Champaign, USA
Jaakko Hollmén	Aalto University, Finland
Andreas Hotho	University of Würzburg, Germany
Daxin Jiang	Microsoft, Beijing, China
Alipio M. G. Jorge	INESC TEC/University of Porto, Portugal
George Karypis	University of Minnesota, USA
Eamonn Keogh	UC, Riverside, USA
Yun Sing Koh	University of Auckland, New Zealand
Parisa Kordjamshidi	Michigan State University, USA
Lars Kotthoff	University of Wyoming, USA
Nicolas Kourtellis	Telefonica Research, Spain
Stefan Kramer	JGU Mainz, Germany
Balaji Krishnapuram	Pinterest, USA
Niklas Lavesson	Blekinge Institute of Technology, Sweden
Chuan Lei	Amazon Web Services, USA
Marius Lindauer	Leibniz University Hannover, Germany
Patrick Loiseau	Inria, France
Giuseppe Manco	ICAR-CNR, Italy
Gabor Melli	PredictionWorks, USA
Anna Monreale	University of Pisa, Italy
Luis Moreira-Matias	Sennder GmbH, Germany
Nuria Oliver	ELLIS Alicante, Spain
Panagiotis Papapetrou	Stockholm University, Sweden
Mykola Pechenizkiy	TU Eindhoven, The Netherlands
Jian Pei	Simon Fraser University, Canada
Julien Perez	Naver Labs Europe, France

Program Committee, Research Track

Matthias Aßenmacher	LMU Munich, Germany
Sara Abdali	Microsoft, USA
Evrim Acar	Simula Metropolitan Center for Digital Engineering, Norway
Homayun Afrabandpey	Nokia Technologies, Finland
Reza Akbarinia	Inria, France
Cuneyt G. Akcora	University of Manitoba, Canada
Ranya Almohsen	West Virginia University, USA
Thiago Andrade	INESC TEC/University of Porto, Portugal
Jean-Marc Andreoli	Naverlabs Europe, France
Giuseppina Andresini	University of Bari, Aldo Moro, Italy
Alessandro Antonucci	IDSIA, Switzerland
Xiang Ao	Institute of Computing Technology, CAS, China
Héber H. Arcolezi	Inria/École Polytechnique, France
Jerónimo Arenas-García	Universidad Carlos III de Madrid, Spain
Yusuf Arslan	University of Luxembourg, Luxemburg
Ali Ayadi	University of Strasbourg, France
Steve Azzolin	University of Trento, Italy
Pierre-Luc Bacon	Mila, Canada
Bunil K. Balabantaray	NIT Meghalaya, India
Mitra Baratchi	LIACS/Leiden University, The Netherlands
Christian Bauckhage	Fraunhofer IAIS, Germany
Anna Beer	Aarhus University, Denmark
Michael Beigl	Karlsruhe Institute of Technology, Germany
Khalid Benabdeslem	Université de Lyon, Lyon 1, France
Idir Benouaret	Epita Research Laboratory, France
Paul Berg	IRISA, France
Christoph Bergmeir	Monash University, Australia
Gilberto Bernardes	INESC TEC/University of Porto, Portugal
Eva Besada-Portas	Universidad Complutense de Madrid, Spain
Jalaj Bhandari	Columbia University, USA
Asmita Bhat	TU Kaiserslautern, Germany
Monowar Bhuyan	Umeå University, Sweden
Adrien Bibal	University of Colorado Anschutz Medical Campus, USA
Manuele Bicego	University of Verona, Italy
Przemyslaw Biecek	Warsaw University of Technology, Poland
Alexander Binder	University of Oslo, Norway
Livio Bioglio	University of Turin, Italy
Patrick Blöbaum	Amazon Web Services, USA

Yueguo Chen	Renmin University of China, China
Yuzhou Chen	Temple University, USA
Zheng Chen	Osaka University, Japan
Ziheng Chen	Walmart, USA
Lu Cheng	University of Illinois, Chicago, USA
Xu Cheng	Shanghai Jiao Tong University, China
Zhiyong Cheng	Shandong Academy of Sciences, China
Yann Chevaleyre	Université Paris Dauphine, France
Chun Wai Chiu	Keele University, UK
Silvia Chiusano	Politecnico di Torino, Italy
Satyendra Singh Chouhan	MNIT Jaipur, India
Hua Chu	Xidian University, China
Sarel Cohen	Academic College of Tel Aviv-Yaffo, Israel
J. Alberto Conejero	Universitat Politècnica de València, Spain
Lidia Contreras-Ochando	Universitat Politècnica de València, Spain
Giorgio Corani	IDSIA, Switzerland
Luca Corbucci	University of Pisa, Italy
Roberto Corizzo	American University, USA
Baris Coskunuzer	University of Texas at Dallas, USA
Fabrizio Costa	Exeter University, UK
Gustavo de Assis Costa	Instituto Federal de Goiás, Brazil
Evan Crothers	University of Ottawa, Canada
Pádraig Cunningham	University College Dublin, Ireland
Jacek Cyranka	University of Warsaw, Poland
Tianxiang Dai	Huawei European Research Institute, Germany
Xuan-Hong Dang	IBM T.J. Watson Research Center, USA
Thi-Bich-Hanh Dao	University of Orleans, France
Debasis Das	Indian Institute of Technology Jodhpur, India
Paul Davidsson	Malmö University, Sweden
Marcilio de Souto	LIFO, University of Orleans, France
Klest Dedja	KU Leuven, Belgium
Elena Demidova	University of Bonn, Germany
Caglar Demir	Paderborn University, Germany
Difan Deng	Leibniz University Hannover, Germany
Laurens Devos	KU Leuven, Belgium
Nicola Di Mauro	University of Bari, Aldo Moro, Italy
Jingtao Ding	Tsinghua University, China
Yao-Xiang Ding	Nanjing University, China
Lamine Diop	EPITA, France
Gillian Dobbie	University of Auckland, New Zealand
Stephan Doerfel	Kiel University of Applied Sciences, Germany
Carola Doerr	Sorbonne Université, France

Nanqing Dong	University of Oxford, UK
Haizhou Du	Shanghai University of Electric Power, China
Qihan Du	Renmin University of China, China
Songlin Du	Southeast University, China
Xin Du	University of Edinburgh, UK
Wouter Duivesteijn	TU Eindhoven, The Netherlands
Inês Dutra	University of Porto, Portugal
Sourav Dutta	Huawei Research Centre, Ireland
Saso Dzeroski	Jožef Stefan Institute, Slovenia
Nabil El Malki	IRIT, France
Mohab Elkaref	IBM Research Europe, UK
Tapio Elomaa	Tampere University, Finland
Dominik M. Endres	University of Marburg, Germany
Georgios Exarchakis	University of Bath, UK
Lukas Faber	ETH Zurich, Switzerland
Samuel G. Fadel	Leuphana University, Germany
Haoyi Fan	Zhengzhou University, China
Zipei Fan	University of Tokyo, Japan
Hadi Fanaee-T	Halmstad University, Sweden
Elaine Ribeiro Faria	UFU, Brazil
Fabio Fassetti	University of Calabria, Italy
Anthony Faustine	ITI/LARSyS - Técnico Lisboa, Portugal
Sophie Fellenz	RPTU Kaiserslautern-Landau, Germany
Wenjie Feng	National University of Singapore, Singapore
Zunlei Feng	Zhejiang University, China
Daniel Fernández-Sánchez	Universidad Autónoma de Madrid, Spain
Luca Ferragina	University of Calabria, Italy
Emilio Ferrara	USC ISI, USA
Cèsar Ferri	Universitat Politècnica València, Spain
Flavio Figueiredo	Universidade Federal de Minas Gerais, Brazil
Lucie Flek	University of Marburg, Germany
Michele Fontana	University of Pisa, Italy
Germain Forestier	University of Haute-Alsace, France
Raphaël Fournier-S'niehotta	CNAM, France
Benoît Frénay	University of Namur, Belgium
Kary Främling	Umeå University, Sweden
Holger Froening	University of Heidelberg, Germany
Fabio Fumarola	Prometeia, Italy
María José Gómez-Silva	Universidad Complutense de Madrid, Spain
Vanessa Gómez-Verdejo	Universidad Carlos III de Madrid, Spain
Pratik Gajane	TU Eindhoven, The Netherlands
Esther Galbrun	University of Eastern Finland, Finland

Claudio Gallicchio   University of Pisa, Italy
Chen Gao   Tsinghua University, China
Shengxiang Gao   Kunming University of Science and Technology, China
Yifeng Gao   University of Texas Rio Grande Valley, USA
Luis Garcia   University of Brasilia, Brazil
Dominique Gay   Université de La Réunion, France
Suyu Ge   University of Illinois at Urbana-Champaign, USA
Zhaocheng Ge   Huazhong University of Science and Technology, China
Alborz Geramifard   Facebook AI, USA
Ahana Ghosh   Max Planck Institute for Software Systems, Germany
Shreya Ghosh   Penn State University, USA
Flavio Giobergia   Politecnico di Torino, Italy
Sarunas Girdzijauskas   KTH Royal Institute of Technology, Sweden
Heitor Murilo Gomes   University of Waikato, Sweden
Wenwen Gong   Tsinghua University, China
Bedartha Goswami   University of Tübingen, Germany
Anastasios Gounaris   Aristotle University of Thessaloniki, Greece
Michael Granitzer   University of Passau, Germany
Derek Greene   University College Dublin, Ireland
Moritz Grosse-Wentrup   University of Vienna, Austria
Marek Grzes   University of Kent, UK
Xinyu Guan   Xian Jiaotong University, China
Massimo Guarascio   ICAR-CNR, Italy
Riccardo Guidotti   University of Pisa, Italy
Lan-Zhe Guo   Nanjing University, China
Lingbing Guo   Zhejiang University, China
Shanqing Guo   Shandong University, China
Karthik S. Gurumoorthy   Walmart, USA
Thomas Guyet   Inria, France
Huong Ha   RMIT University, Australia
Benjamin Halstead   University of Auckland, New Zealand
Massinissa Hamidi   LIPN-UMR CNRS 7030, France
Donghong Han   Northeastern University, USA
Marwan Hassani   TU Eindhoven, The Netherlands
Rima Hazra   Indian Institute of Technology, Kharagpur, India
Mark Heimann   Lawrence Livermore, USA
Cesar Hidalgo   University of Toulouse, France
Martin Holena   Institute of Computer Science, Czech Republic
Mike Holenderski   TU Eindhoven, The Netherlands

Adrian Horzyk	AGH University of Science and Technology, Poland
Shifu Hou	Case Western Reserve University, USA
Hongsheng Hu	CSIRO, Australia
Yaowei Hu	University of Arkansas, USA
Yang Hua	Queen's University Belfast, UK
Chao Huang	University of Hong Kong, China
Guanjie Huang	Penn State University, USA
Hong Huang	Huazhong University of Science and Technology, China
Nina C. Hubig	Clemson University, USA
Dino Ienco	Irstea Institute, France
Angelo Impedovo	Niuma, Italy
Roberto Interdonato	CIRAD, France
Stratis Ioannidis	Northeastern University, USA
Nevo Itzhak	Ben-Gurion University, Israel
Raghav Jain	IIT Patna, India
Kuk Jin Jang	University of Pennsylvania, USA
Szymon Jaroszewicz	Polish Academy of Sciences, Poland
Shaoxiong Ji	University of Helsinki, Finland
Bin-Bin Jia	Lanzhou University of Technology, China
Caiyan Jia	School of Computer and Information Technology, China
Xiuyi Jia	Nanjing University of Science and Technology, China
Nan Jiang	Purdue University, USA
Renhe Jiang	University of Tokyo, Japan
Song Jiang	University of California, Los Angeles, USA
Pengfei Jiao	Hangzhou Dianzi University, China
Di Jin	Amazon, USA
Guangyin Jin	National University of Defense Technology, China
Jiahui Jin	Southeast University, China
Ruoming Jin	Kent State University, USA
Yilun Jin	The Hong Kong University of Science and Technology, Hong Kong
Hugo Jonker	Open University of the Netherlands, The Netherlands
Adan Jose-Garcia	Lille University, France
Marius Köppel	JGU Mainz, Germany
Vana Kalogeraki	Athens University of Economics and Business, Greece
Konstantinos Kalpakis	University of Maryland Baltimore County, USA

Andreas Kaltenbrunner	ISI Foundation, Italy
Shivaram Kalyanakrishnan	IIT Bombay, India
Toshihiro Kamishima	National Institute of Advanced Industrial Science and Technology, Japan
Bo Kang	Ghent University, Belgium
Murat Kantarcioglu	UT Dallas
Thommen Karimpanal George	Deakin University, Australia
Saurav Karmakar	University of Galway, Ireland
Panagiotis Karras	Aarhus University, Denmark
Dimitrios Katsaros	University of Thessaly, Greece
Eamonn Keogh	UC, Riverside, USA
Jaleed Khan	University of Galway, Ireland
Irwin King	Chinese University of Hong Kong, China
Mauritius Klein	LMU Munich, Germany
Tomas Kliegr	Prague University of Economics and Business, Czech Republic
Dmitry Kobak	University of Tübingen, Germany
Dragi Kocev	Jožef Stefan Institute, Slovenia
Lars Kotthoff	University of Wyoming, USA
Anna Krause	University of Würzburg, Germany
Amer Krivosija	TU Dortmund, Germany
Daniel Kudenko	L3S Research Center, Germany
Meelis Kull	University of Tartu, Estonia
Sergey O. Kuznetsov	HSE, Russia
Beatriz López	University of Girona, Spain
Jörg Lücke	University of Oldenburg, Germany
Firas Laakom	Tampere University, Finland
Mateusz Lango	Poznan University of Technology, Poland
Hady Lauw	Singapore Management University, Singapore
Tuan Le	New Mexico State University, USA
Erwan Le Merrer	Inria, France
Thach Le Nguyen	Insight Centre, Ireland
Tai Le Quy	L3S Research Center, Germany
Mustapha Lebbah	UVSQ - Université Paris-Saclay, France
Dongman Lee	KAIST, South Korea
Yeon-Chang Lee	Georgia Institute of Technology, USA
Zed Lee	Stockholm University, Sweden
Mathieu Lefort	Université de Lyon, France
Yunwen Lei	University of Birmingham, UK
Vincent Lemaire	Orange Innovation, France
Daniel Lemire	TÉLUQ University, Canada
Florian Lemmerich	RWTH Aachen University, Germany

Youfang Leng	Renmin University of China, China
Carson K. Leung	University of Manitoba, Canada
Dan Li	Sun Yat-Sen University, China
Gang Li	Deakin University, Australia
Jiaming Li	Huazhong University of Science and Technology, China
Mark Junjie Li	Shenzhen University, China
Nian Li	Tsinghua University, China
Shuai Li	University of Cambridge, UK
Tong Li	Hong Kong University of Science and Technology, China
Xiang Li	East China Normal University, China
Yang Li	University of North Carolina at Chapel Hill, USA
Yingming Li	Zhejiang University, China
Yinsheng Li	Fudan University, China
Yong Li	Huawei European Research Center, Germany
Zhihui Li	University of New South Wales, Australia
Zhixin Li	Guangxi Normal University, China
Defu Lian	University of Science and Technology of China, China
Yuxuan Liang	National University of Singapore, Singapore
Angelica Liguori	University of Calabria, Italy
Nick Lim	University of Waikato, Sweden
Baijiong Lin	The Hong Kong University of Science and Technology, Hong Kong
Piotr Lipinski	University of Wrocław, Poland
Marco Lippi	University of Modena and Reggio Emilia, Italy
Bowen Liu	Stanford University, USA
Chien-Liang Liu	National Chiao Tung University, Taiwan
Fenglin Liu	University of Oxford, UK
Junze Liu	University of California, Irvine, USA
Li Liu	Chongqing University, China
Ninghao Liu	University of Georgia, USA
Shenghua Liu	Institute of Computing Technology, CAS, China
Xiao Fan Liu	City University of Hong Kong, Hong Kong
Xu Liu	National University of Singapore, Singapore
Yang Liu	Institute of Computing Technology, CAS, China
Zihan Liu	Zhejiang University/Westlake University, China
Robert Loftin	TU Delft, The Netherlands
Corrado Loglisci	University of Bari, Aldo Moro, Italy
Mingsheng Long	Tsinghua University, China
Antonio Longa	Fondazione Bruno Kessler, Italy

Grigorios Loukides	King's College London, UK
Tsai-Ching Lu	HRL Laboratories, USA
Zhiwu Lu	Renmin University of China, China
Pedro Henrique Luz de Araujo	University of Vienna, Austria
Marcos M. Raimundo	University of Campinas, Brazil
Maximilian Münch	University of Applied Sciences Würzburg-Schweinfurt, Germany
Fenglong Ma	Pennsylvania State University, USA
Pingchuan Ma	The Hong Kong University of Science and Technology, Hong Kong
Yao Ma	New Jersey Institute of Technology, USA
Brian Mac Namee	University College Dublin, Ireland
Henryk Maciejewski	Wrocław University of Science and Technology, Poland
Ayush Maheshwari	IIT Bombay, India
Ajay A. Mahimkar	AT&T, USA
Ayan Majumdar	Max Planck Institute for Software Systems, Germany
Donato Malerba	University of Bari, Aldo Moro, Italy
Aakarsh Malhotra	IIIT-Delhi, India
Fragkiskos Malliaros	CentraleSupelec, France
Pekka Malo	Aalto University, Finland
Hiroshi Mamitsuka	Kyoto University, Japan/Aalto University, Finland
Domenico Mandaglio	University of Calabria, Italy
Robin Manhaeve	KU Leuven, Belgium
Silviu Maniu	Université Paris-Saclay, France
Cinmayii G. Manliguez	National Sun Yat-Sen University, Taiwan
Naresh Manwani	IIIT Hyderabad, India
Giovanni Luca Marchetti	KTH Royal Institute of Technology, Sweden
Koji Maruhashi	Fujitsu Research, Fujitsu Limited, Japan
Florent Masseglia	Inria, France
Sarah Masud	IIIT-Delhi, India
Timothée Mathieu	Inria, France
Amir Mehrpanah	KTH Royal Institute of Technology, Sweden
Wagner Meira Jr.	Universidade Federal de Minas Gerais, Brazil
Joao Mendes-Moreira	INESC TEC, Portugal
Rui Meng	BNU-HKBU United International College, China
Fabio Mercorio	University of Milan-Bicocca, Italy
Alberto Maria Metelli	Politecnico di Milano, Italy
Carlo Metta	CNR-ISTI, Italy
Paolo Mignone	University of Bari, Aldo Moro, Italy
Tsunenori Mine	Kyushu University, Japan

Nuno Moniz	INESC TEC, Portugal
Pierre Monnin	Université Côte d'Azur, Inria, CNRS, I3S, France
Carlos Monserrat-Aranda	Universitat Politècnica de València, Spain
Raha Moraffah	Arizona State University, USA
Davide Mottin	Aarhus University, Denmark
Hamid Mousavi	University of Oldenburg, Germany
Abdullah Mueen	University of New Mexico, USA
Shamsuddeen Hassan Muhamamd	University of Porto, Portugal
Koyel Mukherjee	Adobe Research, India
Yusuke Mukuta	University of Tokyo, Japan
Pranava Mummoju	University of Vienna, Austria
Taichi Murayama	NAIST, Japan
Ankur Nahar	IIT Jodhpur, India
Felipe Kenji Nakano	KU Leuven, Belgium
Hideki Nakayama	University of Tokyo, Japan
Géraldin Nanfack	University of Namur, Belgium
Mirco Nanni	CNR-ISTI, Italy
Franco Maria Nardini	CNR-ISTI, Italy
Usman Naseem	University of Sydney, Australia
Reza Nasirigerdeh	TU Munich, Germany
Rajashree Nayak	MIT ADT University, India
Benjamin Negrevergne	Université Paris Dauphine, France
Stefan Neumann	KTH Royal Institute of Technology, Sweden
Anna Nguyen	IBM, USA
Shiwen Ni	SIAT, CAS, China
Siegfried Nijssen	Université catholique de Louvain, Belgium
Iasonas Nikolaou	Boston University, USA
Simona Nisticò	University of Calabria, Italy
Hao Niu	KDDI Research, Japan
Mehdi Nourelahi	University of Wyoming, USA
Slawomir Nowaczyk	Halmstad University, Sweden
Eirini Ntoutsi	Bundeswehr University Munich, Germany
Barry O'Sullivan	University College Cork, Ireland
Nastaran Okati	Max Planck Institute for Software Systems, Germany
Tsuyoshi Okita	Kyushu Institute of Technology, Japan
Pablo Olmos	Universidad Carlos III de Madrid, Spain
Luis Antonio Ortega Andrés	Autonomous University of Madrid, Spain
Abdelkader Ouali	Université de Caen Normandie, France
Latifa Oukhellou	IFSTTAR, France
Chun Ouyang	Queensland University of Technology, Australia
Andrei Paleyes	University of Cambridge, UK

Chuan Qin	BOSS Zhipin, China
Yumou Qiu	Iowa State University, USA
Dimitrios Rafailidis	University of Thessaly, Greece
Edward Raff	Booz Allen Hamilton, USA
Chang Rajani	University of Helsinki, Finland
Herilalaina Rakotoarison	Inria, France
M. José Ramírez-Quintana	Universitat Politècnica de Valencia, Spain
Jan Ramon	Inria, France
Rajeev Rastogi	Amazon, India
Domenico Redavid	University of Bari, Aldo Moro, Italy
Qianqian Ren	Heilongjiang University, China
Salvatore Rinzivillo	CNR-ISTI, Italy
Matteo Riondato	Amherst College, USA
Giuseppe Rizzo	Niuma, Italy
Marko Robnik-Sikonja	University of Ljubljana, Slovenia
Christophe Rodrigues	Pôle Universitaire Léonard de Vinci, France
Federica Rollo	University of Modena and Reggio Emilia, Italy
Luca Romeo	University of Macerata, Italy
Benjamin Roth	University of Vienna, Austria
Céline Rouveirol	LIPN - Université Sorbonne Paris Nord, France
Salvatore Ruggieri	University of Pisa, Italy
Pietro Sabatino	ICAR-CNR, Italy
Luca Sabbioni	Politecnico di Milano, Italy
Tulika Saha	University of Manchester, UK
Pablo Sanchez Martin	Max Planck Institute for Intelligent Systems, Germany
Parinya Sanguansat	Panyapiwat Institute of Management, Thailand
Shreya Saxena	Quantiphi, India
Yücel Saygin	Sabanci Universitesi, Turkey
Patrick Schäfer	Humboldt-Universität zu Berlin, Germany
Kevin Schewior	University of Southern Denmark, Denmark
Rainer Schlosser	Hasso Plattner Institute, Germany
Johannes Schneider	University of Liechtenstein, Liechtenstein
Matthias Schubert	LMU Munich, Germany
Alexander Schulz	CITEC - Bielefeld University, Germany
Andreas Schwung	Fachhoschschule Südwestfalen, Germany
Raquel Sebastião	IEETA/DETI-UA, Portugal
Pierre Senellart	ENS, PSL University, France
Edoardo Serra	Boise State University, USA
Mattia Setzu	University of Pisa, Italy
Ammar Shaker	NEC Laboratories Europe, Germany
Shubhranshu Shekhar	Carnegie Mellon University, USA

Jiaming Shen	Google Research, USA
Qiang Sheng	Institute of Computing Technology, CAS, China
Bin Shi	Xi'an Jiaotong University, China
Jimeng Shi	Florida International University, USA
Laixi Shi	Carnegie Mellon University, USA
Rongye Shi	Columbia University, USA
Harsh Shrivastava	Microsoft Research, USA
Jonathan A. Silva	Universidade Federal de Mato Grosso do Sul, Brazil
Esther-Lydia Silva-Ramírez	Universidad de Cádiz, Spain
Kuldeep Singh	Cerence, Germany
Moshe Sipper	Ben-Gurion University of the Negev, Israel
Andrzej Skowron	University of Warsaw, Poland
Krzysztof Slot	Lodz University of Technology, Poland
Marek Smieja	Jagiellonian University, Poland
Gavin Smith	University of Nottingham, UK
Carlos Soares	University of Porto, Portugal
Cláudia Soares	NOVA LINCS, Portugal
Andy Song	RMIT University, Australia
Dongjin Song	University of Connecticut, USA
Hao Song	Seldon, UK
Jie Song	Zhejiang University, China
Linxin Song	Waseda University, Japan
Liyan Song	Southern University of Science and Technology, China
Zixing Song	Chinese University of Hong Kong, China
Arnaud Soulet	University of Tours, France
Sucheta Soundarajan	Syracuse University, USA
Francesca Spezzano	Boise State University, USA
Myra Spiliopoulou	Otto-von-Guericke-University Magdeburg, Germany
Janusz Starzyk	WSIZ, Poland
Jerzy Stefanowski	Poznan University of Technology, Poland
Julian Stier	University of Passau, Germany
Michiel Stock	Ghent University, Belgium
Eleni Straitouri	Max Planck Institute for Software Systems, Germany
Łukasz Struski	Jagiellonian University, Poland
Jinyan Su	University of Electronic Science and Technology of China, China
David Q. Sun	Apple, USA
Guangzhong Sun	University of Science and Technology of China, China

Mingxuan Sun	Louisiana State University, USA
Peijie Sun	Tsinghua University, China
Weiwei Sun	Shandong University, China
Xin Sun	TU Munich, Germany
Maryam Tabar	Pennsylvania State University, USA
Anika Tabassum	Virginia Tech, USA
Shazia Tabassum	INESC TEC, Portugal
Andrea Tagarelli	University of Calabria, Italy
Acar Tamersoy	NortonLifeLock Research Group, USA
Chang Wei Tan	Monash University, Australia
Cheng Tan	Zhejiang University/Westlake University, China
Garth Tarr	University of Sydney, Australia
Romain Tavenard	LETG-Rennes/IRISA, France
Maguelonne Teisseire	INRAE - UMR Tetis, France
Evimaria Terzi	Boston University, USA
Stefano Teso	University of Trento, Italy
Surendrabikram Thapa	Virginia Tech, USA
Maximilian Thiessen	TU Vienna, Austria
Steffen Thoma	FZI Research Center for Information Technology, Germany
Simon Tihon	Euranova, Belgium
Kai Ming Ting	Nanjing University, China
Abhisek Tiwari	IIT Patna, India
Gabriele Tolomei	Sapienza University of Rome, Italy
Guangmo Tong	University of Delaware, USA
Sunna Torge	TU Dresden, Germany
Giovanni Trappolini	Sapienza University of Rome, Italy
Volker Tresp	Siemens AG/LMU Munich, Germany
Sofia Triantafillou	University of Crete, Greece
Sebastian Trimpe	RWTH Aachen University, Germany
Sebastian Tschiatschek	University of Vienna, Austria
Athena Vakal	Aristotle University of Thessaloniki, Greece
Peter van der Putten	Leiden University, The Netherlands
Fabio Vandin	University of Padua, Italy
Aparna S. Varde	Montclair State University, USA
Julien Velcin	Université Lumière Lyon 2, France
Bruno Veloso	INESC TEC/University of Porto, Portugal
Rosana Veroneze	LBiC, Brazil
Gennaro Vessio	University of Bari, Aldo Moro, Italy
Tiphaine Viard	Télécom Paris, France
Herna L. Viktor	University of Ottawa, Canada

Akka Zemmari	University of Bordeaux, France
Bonan Zhang	Princeton University, USA
Chao Zhang	Zhejiang University, China
Chuang Zhang	Nanjing University of Science and Technology, China
Danqing Zhang	Amazon, USA
Guoqiang Zhang	University of Technology, Sydney, Australia
Guoxi Zhang	Kyoto University, Japan
Hao Zhang	Fudan University, China
Junbo Zhang	JD Intelligent Cities Research, China
Le Zhang	Baidu Research, China
Ming Zhang	National Key Laboratory of Science and Technology on Information System Security, China
Qiannan Zhang	KAUST, Saudi Arabia
Tianlin Zhang	University of Manchester, UK
Wenbin Zhang	Michigan Tech, USA
Xiang Zhang	National University of Defense Technology, China
Xiao Zhang	Shandong University, China
Xiaoming Zhang	Beihang University, China
Xinyang Zhang	University of Illinois at Urbana-Champaign, USA
Yaying Zhang	Tongji University, China
Yin Zhang	University of Electronic Science and Technology of China, China
Yongqi Zhang	4Paradigm, China
Zhiwen Zhang	University of Tokyo, Japan
Mia Zhao	Airbnb, USA
Sichen Zhao	RMIT University, Australia
Xiaoting Zhao	Etsy, USA
Tongya Zheng	Zhejiang University, China
Wenhao Zheng	Shopee, Singapore
Yu Zheng	Tsinghua University, China
Yujia Zheng	Carnegie Mellon University, USA
Jiang Zhong	Chongqing University, China
Wei Zhou	School of Cyber Security, CAS, China
Zhengyang Zhou	University of Science and Technology of China, China
Chuang Zhu	Beijing University of Posts and Telecommunications, China
Jing Zhu	University of Michigan, USA
Jinjing Zhu	Hong Kong University of Science and Technology, China

Junxing Zhu	National University of Defense Technology, China
Yanmin Zhu	Shanghai Jiao Tong University, China
Ye Zhu	Deakin University, Australia
Yichen Zhu	Midea Group, China
Zirui Zhuang	Beijing University of Posts and Telecommunications, China
Tommaso Zoppi	University of Florence, Italy
Meiyun Zuo	Renmin University of China, China

Program Committee, Applied Data Science Track

Jussara Almeida	Universidade Federal de Minas Gerais, Brazil
Mozhdeh Ariannezhad	University of Amsterdam, The Netherlands
Renato M. Assuncao	ESRI, USA
Hajer Ayadi	York University, Canada
Ashraf Bah Rabiou	University of Delaware, USA
Amey Barapatre	Microsoft, USA
Patrice Bellot	Aix-Marseille Université - CNRS LSIS, France
Ludovico Boratto	University of Cagliari, Italy
Claudio Borile	CENTAI, Italy
Yi Cai	South China University of Technology, China
Lei Cao	University of Arizona/MIT, USA
Shilei Cao	Tencent, China
Yang Cao	Hokkaido University, Japan
Aniket Chakrabarti	Amazon, USA
Chaochao Chen	Zhejiang University, China
Chung-Chi Chen	National Taiwan University, Taiwan
Meng Chen	Shandong University, China
Ruey-Cheng Chen	Canva, Australia
Tong Chen	University of Queensland, Australia
Yi Chen	NJIT, USA
Zhiyu Chen	Amazon, USA
Wei Cheng	NEC Laboratories America, USA
Lingyang Chu	McMaster University, Canada
Xiaokai Chu	Tencent, China
Zhendong Chu	University of Virginia, USA
Federico Cinus	Sapienza University of Rome/CENTAI, Italy
Francisco Claude-Faust	LinkedIn, USA
Gabriele D'Acunto	Sapienza University of Rome, Italy
Ariyam Das	Google, USA

Jingtao Ding	Tsinghua University, China
Kaize Ding	Arizona State University, USA
Manqing Dong	eBay, Australia
Yushun Dong	University of Virginia, USA
Yingtong Dou	University of Illinois, Chicago, USA
Yixiang Fang	Chinese University of Hong Kong, China
Kaiyu Feng	Beijing Institute of Technology, China
Dayne Freitag	SRI International, USA
Yanjie Fu	University of Central Florida, USA
Matteo Gabburo	University of Trento, Italy
Sabrina Gaito	University of Milan, Italy
Chen Gao	Tsinghua University, China
Liangcai Gao	Peking University, China
Yunjun Gao	Zhejiang University, China
Lluis Garcia-Pueyo	Meta, USA
Mariana-Iuliana Georgescu	University of Bucharest, Romania
Aakash Goel	Amazon, USA
Marcos Goncalves	Universidade Federal de Minas Gerais, Brazil
Francesco Guerra	University of Modena e Reggio Emilia, Italy
Huifeng Guo	Huawei Noah's Ark Lab, China
Ruocheng Guo	ByteDance, China
Zhen Hai	Alibaba DAMO Academy, China
Eui-Hong (Sam) Han	The Washington Post, USA
Jinyoung Han	Sungkyunkwan University, South Korea
Shuchu Han	Stellar Cyber, USA
Dongxiao He	Tianjin University, China
Junyuan Hong	Michigan State University, USA
Yupeng Hou	UC San Diego, USA
Binbin Hu	Ant Group, China
Jun Hu	National University of Singapore, Singapore
Hong Huang	Huazhong University of Science and Technology, China
Xin Huang	Hong Kong Baptist University, China
Yizheng Huang	York University, Canada
Yu Huang	University of Florida, USA
Stratis Ioannidis	Northeastern University, USA
Radu Tudor Ionescu	University of Bucharest, Romania
Murium Iqbal	Etsy, USA
Shoaib Jameel	University of Southampton, UK
Jian Kang	University of Rochester, USA
Pinar Karagoz	METU, Turkey
Praveen C. Kolli	Carnegie Mellon University, USA

Deguang Kong	Yahoo Research, USA
Adit Krishnan	University of Illinois at Urbana-Champaign, USA
Mayank Kulkarni	Amazon, USA
Susana Ladra	University of A Coruña, Spain
Renaud Lambiotte	University of Oxford, UK
Tommaso Lanciano	KTH Royal Institute of Technology, Sweden
Md Tahmid Rahman Laskar	Dialpad, Canada
Matthieu Latapy	CNRS, France
Noah Lee	Meta, USA
Wang-Chien Lee	Pennsylvania State University, USA
Chang Li	Apple, USA
Chaozhuo Li	Microsoft Research Asia, China
Daifeng Li	Sun Yat-Sen University, China
Lei Li	Hong Kong University of Science and Technology, China
Shuai Li	University of Cambridge, UK
Xiang Lian	Kent State University, USA
Zhaohui Liang	National Library of Medicine, NIH, USA
Bang Liu	University of Montreal, Canada
Ji Liu	Baidu Research, China
Jingjing Liu	MD Anderson Cancer Center, USA
Tingwen Liu	Institute of Information Engineering, CAS, China
Weiwen Liu	Huawei Noah's Ark Lab, China
Andreas Lommatzsch	TU Berlin, Germany
Jiyun Luo	Pinterest, USA
Ping Luo	CAS, China
Xin Luo	Shandong University, China
Jing Ma	University of Virginia, USA
Xian-Ling Mao	Beijing Institute of Technology, China
Mirko Marras	University of Cagliari, Italy
Zoltan Miklos	Université de Rennes 1, France
Ahmed K. Mohamed	Meta, USA
Mukesh Mohania	IIIT Delhi, India
Corrado Monti	CENTAI, Italy
Sushant More	Amazon, USA
Jose G. Moreno	University of Toulouse, France
Aayush Mudgal	Pinterest, USA
Sepideh Nahali	York University, Canada
Wolfgang Nejdl	L3S Research Center, Germany
Yifan Nie	University of Montreal, Canada
Di Niu	University of Alberta, Canada
Symeon Papadopoulos	CERTH/ITI, Greece

Manos Papagelis	York University, Canada
Leonardo Pellegrina	University of Padua, Italy
Claudia Perlich	TwoSigma, USA
Fabio Pinelli	IMT Lucca, Italy
Giulia Preti	CENTAI, Italy
Buyue Qian	Xi'an Jiaotong University, China
Chuan Qin	BOSS Zhipin, China
Xiao Qin	Amazon Web Services AI/ML, USA
Yanghui Rao	Sun Yat-Sen University, China
Yusuf Sale	LMU Munich, Germany
Eric Sanjuan	Avignon University, France
Maria Luisa Sapino	University of Turin, Italy
Emmanouil Schinas	CERTH/ITI, Greece
Nasrullah Sheikh	IBM Research, USA
Yue Shi	Meta, USA
Gianmaria Silvello	University of Padua, Italy
Yang Song	Apple, USA
Francesca Spezzano	Boise State University, USA
Efstathios Stamatatos	University of the Aegean, Greece
Kostas Stefanidis	Tampere University, Finland
Ting Su	Imperial College London, UK
Munira Syed	Procter & Gamble, USA
Liang Tang	Google, USA
Ruiming Tang	Huawei Noah's Ark Lab, China
Junichi Tatemura	Google, USA
Mingfei Teng	Amazon, USA
Sofia Tolmach	Amazon, Israel
Ismail Hakki Toroslu	METU, Turkey
Kazutoshi Umemoto	University of Tokyo, Japan
Yao Wan	Huazhong University of Science and Technology, China
Chang-Dong Wang	Sun Yat-Sen University, China
Chong Wang	Amazon, USA
Chuan-Ju Wang	Academia Sinica, Taiwan
Hongzhi Wang	Harbin Institute of Technology, China
Kai Wang	Shanghai Jiao Tong University, China
Ning Wang	Beijing Jiaotong University, China
Pengyuan Wang	University of Georgia, USA
Senzhang Wang	Central South University, China
Sheng Wang	Wuhan University, China
Shoujin Wang	Macquarie University, Australia
Wentao Wang	Michigan State University, USA

Yang Wang	University of Science and Technology of China, China
Zhihong Wang	Tsinghua University, China
Zihan Wang	Shandong University, China
Shi-ting Wen	Ningbo Tech University, China
Song Wen	Rutgers University, USA
Zeyi Wen	Hong Kong University of Science and Technology, China
Fangzhao Wu	Microsoft Research Asia, China
Jun Wu	University of Illinois at Urbana-Champaign, USA
Wentao Wu	Microsoft Research, USA
Yanghua Xiao	Fudan University, China
Haoyi Xiong	Baidu, China
Dongkuan Xu	North Carolina State University, USA
Guandong Xu	University of Technology, Sydney, Australia
Shan Xue	Macquarie University, Australia
Le Yan	Google, USA
De-Nian Yang	Academia Sinica, Taiwan
Fan Yang	Rice University, USA
Yu Yang	City University of Hong Kong, China
Fanghua Ye	University College London, UK
Jianhua Yin	Shandong University, China
Yifang Yin	A*STAR-I2R, Singapore
Changlong Yu	Hong Kong University of Science and Technology, China
Dongxiao Yu	Shandong University, China
Ye Yuan	Beijing Institute of Technology, China
Daochen Zha	Rice University, USA
Feng Zhang	Renmin University of China, China
Mengxuan Zhang	University of North Texas, USA
Xianli Zhang	Xi'an Jiaotong University, China
Xuyun Zhang	Macquarie University, Australia
Chen Zhao	Baylor University, USA
Di Zhao	University of Auckland, New Zealand
Yanchang Zhao	CSIRO, Australia
Kaiping Zheng	National University of Singapore, Singapore
Yong Zheng	Illinois Institute of Technology, USA
Jingbo Zhou	Baidu, China
Ming Zhou	University of Technology, Sydney, Australia
Qinghai Zhou	University of Illinois at Urbana-Champaign, USA
Tian Zhou	Alibaba DAMO Academy, China
Xinyi Zhou	University of Washington, USA

Yucheng Zhou	University of Macau, China
Jiangang Zhu	ByteDance, China
Yongchun Zhu	CAS, China
Ziwei Zhu	George Mason University, USA
Jia Zou	Arizona State University, USA

Program Committee, Demo Track

Ferran Diego	Telefonica Research, Spain
Jan Florjanczyk	Netflix, USA
Mikko Heikkila	Telefonica Research, Spain
Jesus Omaña Iglesias	Telefonica Research, Spain
Nicolas Kourtellis	Telefonica Research, Spain
Eduard Marin	Telefonica Research, Spain
Souneil Park	Telefonica Research, Spain
Aravindh Raman	Telefonica Research, Spain
Ashish Rastogi	Netflix, USA
Natali Ruchansky	Netflix, USA
David Solans	Telefonica Research, Spain

Sponsors

Platinum

Gold

Silver

Bronze

PhD Forum Sponsor

Publishing Partner

Invited Talks Abstracts

Neural Wave Representations

Max Welling

University of Amsterdam, The Netherlands

Abstract. Good neural architectures are rooted in good inductive biases (a.k.a. priors). Equivariance under symmetries is a prime example of a successful physics-inspired prior which sometimes dramatically reduces the number of examples needed to learn predictive models. In this work, we tried to extend this thinking to more flexible priors in the hidden variables of a neural network. In particular, we imposed wavelike dynamics in hidden variables under transformations of the inputs, which relaxes the stricter notion of equivariance. We find that under certain conditions, wavelike dynamics naturally arises in these hidden representations. We formalize this idea in a VAE-over-time architecture where the hidden dynamics is described by a Fokker-Planck (a.k.a. drift-diffusion) equation. This in turn leads to a new definition of a disentangled hidden representation of input states that can easily be manipulated to undergo transformations. I also discussed very preliminary work on how the Schrödinger equation can also be used to move information in the hidden representations.

Biography. Prof. Dr. Max Welling is a research chair in Machine Learning at the University of Amsterdam and a Distinguished Scientist at MSR. He is a fellow at the Canadian Institute for Advanced Research (CIFAR) and the European Lab for Learning and Intelligent Systems (ELLIS) where he also serves on the founding board. His previous appointments include VP at Qualcomm Technologies, professor at UC Irvine, postdoc at the University of Toronto and UCL under the supervision of Prof. Geoffrey Hinton, and postdoc at Caltech under the supervision of Prof. Pietro Perona. He finished his PhD in theoretical high energy physics under the supervision of Nobel laureate Prof. Gerard 't Hooft. Max Welling served as associate editor-in-chief of IEEE TPAMI from 2011–2015, he has served on the advisory board of the NeurIPS Foundation since 2015 and was program chair and general chair of NeurIPS in 2013 and 2014 respectively. He was also program chair of AISTATS in 2009 and ECCV in 2016 and general chair of MIDL in 2018. Max Welling was a recipient of the ECCV Koenderink Prize in 2010 and the ICML Test of Time Award in 2021. He directs the Amsterdam Machine Learning Lab (AMLAB) and co-directs the Qualcomm-UvA deep learning lab (QUVA) and the Bosch-UvA Deep Learning lab (DELTA).

Physics-Inspired Graph Neural Networks

Michael Bronstein

University of Oxford, UK

Abstract. The message-passing paradigm has been the "battle horse" of deep learning on graphs for several years, making graph neural networks a big success in a wide range of applications, from particle physics to protein design. From a theoretical viewpoint, it established the link to the Weisfeiler-Lehman hierarchy, allowing us to analyse the expressive power of GNNs. We argue that the very "node-and-edge"-centric mindset of current graph deep learning schemes may hinder future progress in the field. As an alternative, we propose physics-inspired "continuous" learning models that open up a new trove of tools from the fields of differential geometry, algebraic topology, and differential equations so far largely unexplored in graph ML.

Biography. Michael Bronstein is the DeepMind Professor of AI at the University of Oxford. He was previously a professor at Imperial College London and held visiting appointments at Stanford, MIT, and Harvard, and has also been affiliated with three Institutes for Advanced Study (at TUM as a Rudolf Diesel Fellow (2017–2019), at Harvard as a Radcliffe fellow (2017–2018), and at Princeton as a short-time scholar (2020)). Michael received his PhD from the Technion in 2007. He is the recipient of the Royal Society Wolfson Research Merit Award, Royal Academy of Engineering Silver Medal, five ERC grants, two Google Faculty Research Awards, and two Amazon AWS ML Research Awards. He is a Member of the Academia Europaea, Fellow of the IEEE, IAPR, BCS, and ELLIS, ACM Distinguished Speaker, and World Economic Forum Young Scientist. In addition to his academic career, Michael is a serial entrepreneur and founder of multiple startup companies, including Novafora, Invision (acquired by Intel in 2012), Videocites, and Fabula AI (acquired by Twitter in 2019).

Mapping Generative AI

Kate Crawford

USC Annenberg, USA

Abstract. Training data is foundational to generative AI systems. From Common Crawl's 3.1 billion web pages to LAION-5B's corpus of almost 6 billion image-text pairs, these vast collections – scraped from the internet and treated as "ground truth" – play a critical role in shaping the epistemic boundaries that govern generative AI models. Yet training data is beset with complex social, political, and epistemological challenges. What happens when data is stripped of context, meaning, and provenance? How does training data limit what and how machine learning systems interpret the world? What are the copyright implications of these datasets? And most importantly, what forms of power do these approaches enhance and enable? This keynote is an invitation to reflect on the epistemic foundations of generative AI, and to consider the wide-ranging impacts of the current generative turn.

Biography. Professor Kate Crawford is a leading international scholar of the social implications of artificial intelligence. She is a Research Professor at USC Annenberg in Los Angeles, a Senior Principal Researcher at MSR in New York, an Honorary Professor at the University of Sydney, and the inaugural Visiting Chair for AI and Justice at the École Normale Supérieure in Paris. Her latest book, *Atlas of AI* (Yale, 2021) won the Sally Hacker Prize from the Society for the History of Technology, the ASIS&T Best Information Science Book Award, and was named one of the best books in 2021 by *New Scientist* and the *Financial Times*. Over her twenty-year research career, she has also produced groundbreaking creative collaborations and visual investigations. Her project *Anatomy of an AI System* with Vladan Joler is in the permanent collection of the Museum of Modern Art in New York and the V&A in London, and was awarded with the Design of the Year Award in 2019 and included in the Design of the Decades by the Design Museum of London. Her collaboration with the artist Trevor Paglen, *Excavating AI*, won the Ayrton Prize from the British Society for the History of Science. She has advised policymakers in the United Nations, the White House, and the European Parliament, and she currently leads the Knowing Machines Project, an international research collaboration that investigates the foundations of machine learning.

Contents – Part VI

Finance

Hardware and Systems

Healthcare and Bioinformatics

Human-Computer Interaction

Recommendation and Information Retrieval

Applied Machine Learning

Rectifying Bias in Ordinal Observational Data Using Unimodal Label Smoothing

Stefan Haas[1]([✉]) [iD] and Eyke Hüllermeier[2,3] [iD]

[1] BMW Group, Munich, Germany
stefan.sh.haas@bmwgroup.com
[2] Institute of Informatics, LMU Munich, Munich, Germany
[3] Munich Center for Machine Learning, Munich, Germany

Abstract. This paper proposes a novel approach for modeling observational data in the form of expert ratings, which are commonly given on an ordered (numerical or ordinal) scale. In practice, such ratings are often biased, due to the expert's preferences, psychological effects, etc. Our approach aims to rectify these biases, thereby preventing machine learning methods from transferring them to models trained on the data. To this end, we make use of so-called label smoothing, which allows for redistributing probability mass from the originally observed rating to other ratings, which are considered as possible corrections. This enables the incorporation of domain knowledge into the standard cross-entropy loss and leads to flexibly configurable models. Concretely, our method is realized for ordinal ratings and allows for arbitrary unimodal smoothings using a binary smoothing relation. Additionally, the paper suggests two practically motivated smoothing heuristics to address common biases in observational data, a time-based smoothing to handle concept drift and a class-wise smoothing based on class priors to mitigate data imbalance. The effectiveness of the proposed methods is demonstrated on four real-world goodwill assessment data sets of a car manufacturer with the aim of automating goodwill decisions. Overall, this paper presents a promising approach for modeling ordinal observational data that can improve decision-making processes and reduce reliance on human expertise.

Keywords: Prescriptive machine learning · Ordinal classification · Ordinal regression · Label smoothing · Observational data · Unimodal distribution

1 Introduction

Our starting point is rating data, where cases x are associated with a score or rating y, typically taken from an ordinal scale. In credit scoring, for example, a customer's credit worthiness could be rated on the scale $\mathcal{Y} = \{$poor, fair, good, very good, excellent$\}$; similar examples can be found in finance [10,16] or medicine [6,18]. Our real-world example, to which we will return later on in the experimental part, is the assessment of goodwill requests by a car manufacturer, where a human goodwill after-sales expert decides about the percentage of the

© The Author(s), under exclusive license to Springer Nature Switzerland AG 2023
G. De Francisci Morales et al. (Eds.): ECML PKDD 2023, LNAI 14174, pp. 3–18, 2023.
https://doi.org/10.1007/978-3-031-43427-3_1

labor and parts cost contributions the manufacturer is willing to pay. In our case, the decision is a contribution between 0 and 100%, in steps of 10%, i.e., $\mathcal{Y} = \{0, 10, 20, \ldots, 100\}$ — note that this scale is somewhat in-between cardinal and ordinal, and could in principle be treated either way.

From a machine learning (ML) perspective, rating data has (at least) two interesting properties. First, ML models learned on such data are *prescriptive* rather than predictive in nature [11]. In particular, given a case $\boldsymbol{x}$, there is arguably nothing like a *ground-truth* rating y. At best, a rating could be seen as fair from the point of view of a customer, or opportune from the point of view of a manufacturer. For machine learning, the problem is thus to learn a prescriptive model that stipulates "appropriate" ratings or actions to be taken to achieve a certain goal, rather than a predictive model targeting any ground-truth.

Second, rating data is often biased in various ways. This is especially true for observational data where labels or ratings are coming from human experts and may be geared towards the expert's preferences and views. For example, the distribution of ratings in our goodwill use case (cf. Fig. 1) clearly shows a kind of "rounding effect": Experts prefer ratings of 0%, 50%, and 100%; ratings in-between (20% or 30%, 70% or 80%) are still used but much less, while values close to these preferred ones, such as 10% or 90%, are almost never observed — presumably, these "odd" ratings are rounded to the closest "even" ratings. Consequently, such data should not necessarily be taken as a gold standard. On the contrary, it might be sub-optimal and may not necessarily suggest the best course of action to be taken in a given context.

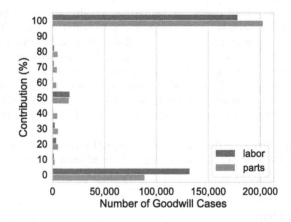

Fig. 1. Distribution of goodwill contributions for labor and parts at the car manufacturer.

To tackle this problem, our idea is to "weaken" the rating data through reallocation, turning a deterministic observation y into a (probability) distribution on $\mathcal{Y}$; this idea is inspired by a technique known as *label smoothing* [19]. For example, an observed rating of 50% could be replaced by a distribution assigning probabilities of 0.05, 0.2, 0.5, 0.2, 0.0.5, respectively, to 30%, 40%, 50%, 60%, and 70%, suggesting that the actually most appropriate rating is not necessarily 50%, but maybe another value close by. Learning from such data can be seen as a specific form of *weakly supervised learning* [22].

More concretely, we propose a novel label smoothing approach based on the geometric distribution, which, compared to previous methods (cf. Sect. 2), enables more transparent and flexible re-distribution of probability mass. The approach is specifically tailored to probabilistic prescriptive ordinal classification, where a high degree of model configurability is required to correct bias in observational data, surpassing regularization aspects of previous methods by far. Our contributions can be summarized as follows:

- **Novel unimodal smoothing method:** In Sect. 3, we introduce our new unimodal label smoothing method. We first outline the basic smoothing approach and then extend it to a smoothing-relation based approach. This allows for flexible class-wise re-distribution of probability mass to inject domain knowledge into the standard cross-entropy loss.
- **Practically motivated heuristics:** Additionally, we present two heuristic smoothing functions to deal with common issues in observational data, namely concept drift and data imbalance (cf. Sect. 3.4).
- **Application to a real world automated decision making (ADM) use-case:** In Sect. 4, we apply and evaluate our proposed methods on the aforementioned use-case. To this end, we leverage real-world observational goodwill assessment data sets of a car manufacturer.

2   Related Work

So-called *label smoothing* is a popular method in machine learning, specifically in deep learning [15,19], which is meant to reduce overconfidence in one-hot encoded (0/1) deterministic labels, thereby serving as a kind of regularizer and preventing the learner from over-fitting the (possibly noisy) training data. Label smoothing removes a certain amount of probability mass from the observed label and spreads it uniformly across the classes. That is, an observation (x_i, y_i) is turned into a training example (x_i, p_i^{LS}), where p_i^{LS} is a probability distribution on $\mathcal{Y}$:

$$p_i^{LS}(k) = (1 - \alpha)y_{i,k} + \alpha\frac{1}{K} ,$$

with $K = |\mathcal{Y}|$ the number of classes, $y_{i,k} = 1$ for the observed class and $= 0$ otherwise, and $\alpha \in (0,1)$ a smoothing parameter. *Label relaxation* is a generalization of label smoothing, in which the single smoothed distribution is replaced by a larger set of candidate distributions [12]. While a uniform distribution of probability mass is a meaningful strategy for standard (nominal) classification, where classes have no specific order, this is arguably less true for *ordinal classification*, also called *ordinal regression* in statistics [9,17], where classes have a linear order: $y_1 \prec y_2 \prec \cdots \prec y_K$. In this setting, one may rather expect a *unimodal* distribution of the classes, where the observed label is the single mode of the distribution, and classes closer to the mode are considered more likely than classes farther away. In ordinal classification, unimodality is not only a natural property for smoothing, but of course also for prediction [1,2,4,5]; see Fig. 2 for an illustration.

Liu et al. [13] propose to use the Binomial and Poisson distribution to redistribute the probability mass of one-hot encoded (0/1) labels in a unimodal fashion. However, the authors admit that both distributions are problematic: In the case of Poisson, it is not easy to flexibly adjust the shape, and for the Binomial distribution, it is difficult to flexibly adjust the position of the peak and the variance. Therefore, they propose another smoothing function $e^{\frac{-|k-j|}{\tau}}$ based on the exponential function, followed by a softmax normalization to turn the result into a discrete probability distribution on $\mathcal{Y}$. Here, $\tau > 0$ is a smoothing factor that determines the "peakedness" of the function, j the index of the observed class in the one-hot encoded label y_i (where the value is 1) and k the k-th class. However, how much probability mass is assigned to the mode and the rest of the classes is not transparent and might require significant experimentation effort. Vargas et al. propose unimodal smoothing methods based on the continuous Beta and Triangular distributions [20,21] where parameters need to be pre-calculated upfront depending on the current class and the overall number of classes. The Binomial and Poisson distribution have previously also been used to constrain the output of neural networks to unimodailty, where their usage appears more natural than for label smoothing. For instance, Beckham and Pal [2] use the Binomial and Poisson distributions as the penultimate layer in a deep neural network to constrain the output to unimodality before sending it through

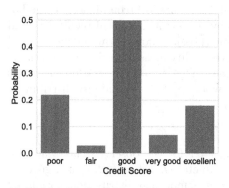

(a) Multimodal distribution of credit scoring probabilities.

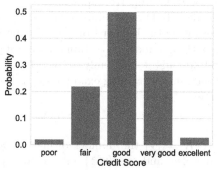

(b) Unimodal distribution of credit scoring probabilities.

Fig. 2. Exemplary multimodal (left) and unimodal (right) output distributions of credit scoring probabilities. The multimodal distribution on the left appears unnatural since the data underlies a natural order. One would rather expect a monotonic decrease of probability from the *mode* of the distribution, like it is shown on the right.

a final softmax layer. A quite similar approach was previously proposed by da Costa et al. [4,5].

3 Unimodal Label Smoothing Based on the Geometric Distribution

In the following, we introduce our novel unimodal label smoothing approach based on the geometric distribution. We begin with a motivation, explaining why smoothing degenerate one-point distributions is meaningful, especially in the setting of prescriptive ML primarily dealing with observational data.

3.1 Motivation

As already mentioned previously, our focus is on prescriptive probabilistic ordinal classification, where past observations are given in the form of data

$$\mathcal{D} = \{(\boldsymbol{x}_1, y_1), \cdots, (\boldsymbol{x}_n, y_n)\} \subset \mathcal{X} \times \mathcal{Y},$$

with $\boldsymbol{x}_i \in \mathcal{X} \subseteq \mathbb{R}^m$ a *feature vector* characterizing a case, and $y_i \in \mathcal{Y}$ the corresponding *label* or observed rating. The set of class labels has a natural linear order: $y_1 \prec y_2 \prec \cdots \prec y_K$. In standard (probabilistic) supervised learning, the goal is then to learn a probabilistic predictor $\hat{p} : \mathcal{X} \to \mathbb{P}(\mathcal{Y})$ that performs well in terms of a loss (error) function $l : \mathcal{Y} \times \mathbb{P}(\mathcal{Y}) \to \mathbb{R}_+$, and training such a predictor is guided by (perhaps regularized variants of) the empirical risk

$$R(\hat{p}) := \frac{1}{n} \sum_{i=1}^{n} l(y_i, \hat{p}(\boldsymbol{x}_i))$$

as an estimate of the true generalization performance. The de-facto standard loss function for nominal probabilistic multi-class classification is the cross-entropy loss

$$H(y_i, \hat{p}_i) = - \sum_{k=1}^{K} p(y_i = k | \boldsymbol{x}_i) \log(\hat{p}(y_i = k | \boldsymbol{x}_i)),$$

where class labels are one-hot encoded as degenerate one-point distributions $p_i \in \mathbb{P}(\mathcal{Y})$ with $p_i(y_i | \boldsymbol{x}_i) = 1$ and $p_i(y | \boldsymbol{x}_i) = 0$ for $y \neq y_i$.

Since all classes apart from the ground-truth or observed label are set to zero, the cross-entropy loss then boils down to log-loss

$$H(y_i, \hat{p}_i) = - \log(\hat{p}(y_i | \boldsymbol{x}_i)).$$

Obviously, this only makes sense if the labels can be considered incontestable ground truth. Since this is not warranted to that extend in ordinal observational data, replacing this degenerate one point distributions with more realistic smoothed unimodal *surrogate* distributions p^S is required to prevent the before shown degeneration of the cross-entropy loss.

$$H(p_i^S, \hat{p}_i) = -\sum_{k=1}^{K} p^S(y_i = k|\boldsymbol{x}_i) \log(\hat{p}(y_i = k|\boldsymbol{x}_i))$$

Furthermore, surrogate distributions may even serve to correct wrong inflation-ary decisions or inject domain knowledge into the learning process, which is a requirement in prescriptive ML scenarios and at the heart of this paper.

3.2   Basic Unimodal Label Smoothing

The geometric distribution models the probability that the k-th trial is the first success for a given success probability θ and trials $k \in \{1, 2, 3, \ldots\}$.

$$p(k) = (1 - \theta)^{(k-1)}\theta$$

Due to its monotonically decreasing curve, it's well suited to model an unimodal probability distribution. The shape of the distribution hereby heavily depends on the "success" probability θ. We may think of the original label of a training instance as the success probability θ and the future mode of our new unimodal distribution. The more probability mass we want to allocate to the original label of our training instance, the more peaked or degenerate the distribution will look like. In a standard scenario with one-hot encoded labels, the complete probability mass of 1 is initially assigned to the ground truth or observed label. To take away probability mass from the label, we introduce a smoothing factor $\alpha \in (0, 1)$. The probability assigned to the mode of the probability distribution is then defined as $(1 - \alpha)$ (cf. Eq. 1). The probability of the rest of the classes is modeled as a two-sided geometric distribution decreasing monotonically from the mode. Below is the raw, non-normalized version of our unimodal smoothing approach based on the geometric distribution with j as the index of the observed class in the one-hot encoded label y_i (where the value is 1):

$$p_i^G(k) = \alpha^{|j-k|}(1 - \alpha) \tag{1}$$

Since the geometric distribution has infinite support we need to truncate and normalize it so that the probabilities sum to 1. We do this by introducing a normalizing constant G_i:

$$G_i = p_i^G(k \neq j) = \sum_{k \neq j} \alpha^{|j-k|}(1 - \alpha).$$

The normalized version of our smoothing approach with $\sum_{k=1}^{K} p_i^G(k) = 1$ then looks as follows:

$$p_i^G(k) = \begin{cases} 1 - \alpha & \text{if } k = j \\ 1/G_i \, \alpha^{|j-k|+1}(1 - \alpha) & \text{if } k \neq j \end{cases}.$$

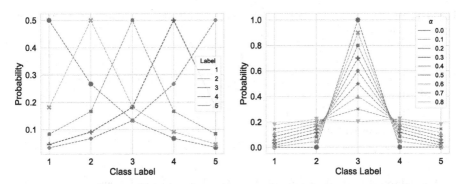

(a) Smoothing of probability mass for different labels $y \in \{1, 2, 3, 4, 5\}$ and a fixed smoothing factor of $\alpha = 0.5$.

(b) Smoothing of probability mass for $y = 3$ and varying smoothing factors $\alpha \in \{0, 0.1, 0.2, 0.3, \ldots, 0.8\}$.

Fig. 3. The above figures illustrate our proposed unimodal smoothing approach based on the geometric distribution.

Note that we do not normalize the mode of the distribution $(1 - \alpha)$ since we want to keep transparent how much probability mass is allocated to the ground truth or observed label. Figures 3a and 3b illustrate how our unimodal smoothing approach based on the geometric distribution looks like for different classes and different smoothing factors respectively.

3.3 Class-Wise Unimodal Label Smoothing Using a Smoothing Relation

The basic smoothing approach presented in the previous subsection does not distinguish between classes and all classes are smoothed the same. Furthermore, it assumes a rather symmetric smoothing where probability mass is distributed to the left and right side of the mode (if possible). To achieve a higher degree of configurability in terms of smoothing, we introduce a so called *smoothing relation* (cf. table 1) that allows to define how strong the label or mode is smoothed per observed class index j (α_j), as well as the fraction of outstanding probability mass that is supposed to be distributed to the left ($F_{l,j}$) and right ($F_{r,j}$) of the mode, with $F_{l,j} + F_{r,j} = 1$. An extended smoothing function allowing class-wise smoothing based on a smoothing relation (cf. Table 1) is displayed below:

$$
p_i^G(k) = \begin{cases} 1 - \alpha_j & \text{if } k = j \\ 1/G_i \; F_{l,j} \; \alpha_j^{(j-k)+1}(1 - \alpha_j) & \text{if } k < j \;, \quad \text{with } F_{l,j} + F_{r,j} = 1 \\ 1/G_i \; F_{r,j} \; \alpha_j^{(k-j)+1}(1 - \alpha_j) & \text{if } k > j \end{cases}
$$

Table 1. Two exemplary smoothing-relations to configure unimodal re-distribution of probability mass.

j	1	2	3	4	5
α	0	0.2	0.3	0.4	0.5
F_l	0	1	1	1	1
F_r	0	0	0	0	0

(a) Cautious smoothing relation.

j	1	2	3	4	5
α	0.5	0.4	0.3	0.2	0
F_l	0	0	0	0	0
F_r	1	1	1	1	0

(b) Generous smoothing relation.

The adapted normalization constant G_j then looks as follows:

$$
G_i = \begin{cases} \sum_{k>j} \alpha_j^{(k-j)}(1-\alpha_j) & \text{if } F_l, j = 0 \\ \sum_{k<j} \alpha_j^{(j-k)}(1-\alpha_j) & \text{if } F_r, j = 0 \\ \sum_{k\neq j} \alpha_j^{|j-k|}(1-\alpha_j) & \text{otherwise} \end{cases}.
$$

In this case, one can particularly define how much of the outstanding probability mass is assigned left or right of the mode. This, in the extreme case, even enables unimodal one-sided label smoothing by distributing probability mass only to one side. This extreme scenario is shown in Table 1, where in the left smoothing-relation smoothing is only performed to the left side of the mode, with increasing α and in the right smoothing-relation only to the right, with decreasing α. Smoothing only to the left side of the mode indicates a more cautious smoothing, for instance, in our credit scoring example, probability mass is then re-distributed from higher ratings to lower ratings. The other way round, smoothing to the right indicates a more generous approach, where probability mass is re-distributed from lower ratings to higher ratings. Hence, through using this approach, probability mass can be flexibly re-distributed to correct any biases in the underlying observational data, e.g., too cautious or generous credit rating assessments in the past. Figure 4 shows the smoothing curves for the cautious (Fig. 4a) respectively generous smoothing (Fig. 4b).

3.4 Unimodal Smoothing Heuristics for Prescriptive Machine Learning

The basic smoothing approach outlined in Subsect. 3.2 smooths the distribution for every class the same, which may be a too simplified assumption. In contrast, the smoothing relation approach introduced in Subsect. 3.3 provides more flexibility, but on the other side also requires detailed knowledge about present biases and the domain. Hence, in the following we want to look at two generally applicable smoothing heuristics to deal with two common issues in observational data: data imbalance and concept drift.

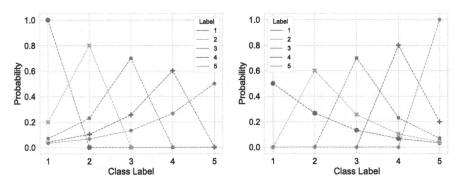

(a) Left-tailed ("cautious") class-wise smoothing.

(b) Right-tailed ("generous") class-wise smoothing.

Fig. 4. Class-wise left- or right-tailed smoothing using the smoothing relations in Table 1.

Unimodal Smoothing Based on Class Priors. Observational data is often strongly imbalanced (cf. Fig. 1) [10]. From a prescriptive ML point of view, "correcting" over-proportionally used labels or ratings stronger through smoothing them more than infrequently used ones might be a reasonable correction. In observational data, the more inflationary a rating is used, the less meaningful it appears. The other way round, one may assume that rare ratings are selected more carefully and more thought might have been put into their selection. Moreover, this may also counteract class imbalance as the probability mass assigned to inflationary used ratings is reduced compared to more seldomly used ratings.

Hence, a simple smoothing heuristic may be to vary the smoothing factor depending on the class prior.

$$s_i(\alpha) = \alpha \cdot \frac{p(y_i)}{\max\limits_{y \in \{y_1, y_2, \ldots, y_K\}} p(y)} \in [0, \alpha]$$

The single smoothing factor α is hereby replaced by a smoothing function $s_i(\alpha)$ depending on α and the class prior $p(y_i)$ normalized by the max class prior. The equation below shows the adapted unimodal smoothing approach dependent on prior class probabilities.

$$p_i^G(k) = \begin{cases} 1 - s_i(\alpha) & \text{if } k = j \\ 1/G_i \, s_i(\alpha)^{|j-k|+1}(1 - s_i(\alpha)) & \text{if } k \neq j \end{cases}$$

The normalizing constant G_i also needs to be updated accordingly:

$$G_i = p_i^G(k \neq j) = \sum_{k \neq j} s_i(\alpha)^{|j-k|}(1 - s_i(\alpha))$$

Figure 5 illustrates the class-wise smoothing approach on exemplary imbalanced class prior probabilities. As one can see, class 1 has the highest prior

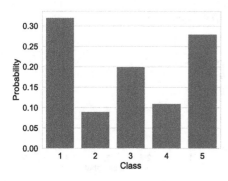
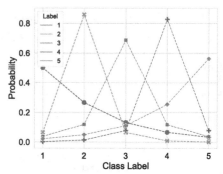

(a) Exemplary imbalanced prior probabilities for a five classes problem.

(b) Class-wise smoothing of probability mass according to the priors on the left for different labels $y \in \{1, 2, 3, 4, 5\}$ and a fixed smoothing factor of $\alpha = 0.5$.

Fig. 5. Class-wise unimodal smoothing of probability mass depending on class priors.

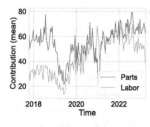
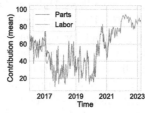
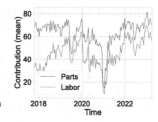

(a) Market data set A.   (b) Market data set B.   (c) Market data set C.

Fig. 6. Goodwill decision mean values for parts and labor contributions over time, entailing concept drift and shift.

probability and is smoothed the most. Whereas class 2 has the lowest prior probability and is smoothed the least.

Time Based Unimodal Smoothing. Another very typical bias in observational data is concept drift or shift, where the target variable which a model tries to predict changes its statistical properties over time [14]. Typically, ratings conducted by human experts like credit rating assessments or candidate rating in human resources will not remain static over time. Strategies will change dynamically depending on market situations. This is also visible in our goodwill assessment data sets, where mean contribution ratings for labor and parts repair costs change dynamically over time for some markets (cf. Fig. 6).

Hence, we propose another simple linear smoothing function that will smooth older instances stronger than more recent ones, whereas $t_i \in T$ are time stamps

Table 2. Goodwill assessment data set sizes. All data sets have 26 features (18 categorical and 8 numeric) and a single label with 11 classes ($\mathcal{Y} = \{0, 10, 20, \ldots, 100\}$).

Market	A	B	C	D
# Instances	17,652	27,390	43,286	13,832

accompanying each human expert rating:

$$s_i(\alpha) = \alpha \cdot \frac{\max_{t \in T} t - t_i}{\max_{t \in T} t - \min_{t \in T} t} \in [0, \alpha]$$

4 Evaluation

In the following, we want to evaluate our proposed smoothing approaches on four ordinal real world goodwill assessment data sets of a car manufacturer (cf. Table 2), with the goal to predict appropriate monetary contributions for parts and labor repair costs on an ordinal scale from 0 to 100% ($\mathcal{Y} = \{0, 10, 20, \ldots, 100\}$). The different data sets are taken from different national sales markets and reflect the different goodwill assessment strategies of the national sales companies (NSC) of the car manufacturer. At the moment, goodwill requests are to a large extend assessed manually by human experts [10]. However, the long term aim of the car manufacturer is to increase automation and process goodwill requests through automated decision making (ADM) [10]. The attributes of the data instances entail information about the vehicle and the case, for instance, vehicle age, mileage, requested costs, defect code, whether the vehicle was regularly serviced, etc. [10]. The data is of mid-size tabular nature which makes us rely on Gradient Boosted Trees (GBT) for our evaluation implementation [8]. Concretely, we make use of eXtreme Gradient Boosting (XGBoost) [3]. However, our proposed smoothing approaches are not limited to GBTs and could, for instance, also be used in a deep learning context. Table 2 summarizes some characteristics of the goodwill data sets used for evaluation. In general, the data sets are in most cases heavily imbalanced with mostly 0, 50 and 100% ratings (cf. Fig. 1). As shown in Fig. 6, data sets A, B and C also contain some sort of drift in the target ratings.

4.1 Relation and Priors Based Smoothing Results

To evaluate the flexibility of the smoothing-relation based approach on goodwill assessment data, we make use of the smoothing-relations shown in Table 3, which are similar to the previous five classes example (cf. Table 1), but expanded to 11 classes or ratings for the case of goodwill assessment. On max, 50% of the probability mass is re-distributed to other classes ($\alpha = 0.5$).

Table 3. Cautious (top) and generous (bottom) smoothing-relations for goodwill assessment with 11 classes ($\mathcal{Y} = \{0, 10, 20, \ldots, 100\}$).

j	1	2	3	4	5	6	7	8	9	10	11
α	0	0.05	0.1	0.15	0.2	0.25	0.3	0.35	0.4	0.45	0.5
F_l	0	1	1	1	1	1	1	1	1	1	1
F_r	0	0	0	0	0	0	0	0	0	0	0

(a) Cautious smoothing-relation.

j	1	2	3	4	5	6	7	8	9	10	11
α	0.5	0.45	0.4	0.35	0.3	0.25	0.2	0.15	0.1	0.05	0
F_l	0	0	0	0	0	0	0	0	0	0	0
F_r	1	1	1	1	1	1	1	1	1	1	0

(b) Generous smoothing-relation.

Tables 4 and 5 show the results of a ten-fold cross validation evaluation of the cautious (+Cautious) respectively generous (+Generous) smoothing-relation in relation to a standard nominal classification (Base). Additionally, we also display the results of the smoothing heuristic based on the class priors (+Priors) with a max smoothing factor of $\alpha = 0.5$. In all cases, we display the mean as well as the standard deviation ($\pm$) of the ten folds. The evaluated standard metrics are accuracy (ACC), mean absolute error (MAE) and mean squared error (MSE). Since we are dealing with an ordinal classification problem that lies somewhere between classification and regression, classification as well as regression metrics are of interest [7]. The underpay and overpay metrics are domain specific metrics relevant from a goodwill assessment perspective, as they indicate how much money was payed less (underpay), respectively more (overpay), compared to the manual human assessments. One can clearly see that the cautious, respectively generous, smoothing-relations are reflected in the results. In case of the cautious strategy there is a strong tendency of underpayment, whereas in case of the generous strategy there is a strong tendency for overpayment. The class priors based smoothing approach trades-off accuracy for improved MAE and MSE metrics, which can be considered beneficial in ordinal classification.

4.2   Time Based Smoothing Results

In the time-based smoothing evaluation, we set the smoothing factor to $\alpha = 0.8$, which is a rather aggressive value that leads to almost uniform re-distribution of probability mass for the oldest training instances. The data is split into training and test data with a ratio of 90/10, whereas the test data entails the most recent 10% of the data. The small test data set size of 10% was chosen to use the same amount of data for testing as in the experiments performed above which used 10-fold cross validation and, even more important, to specifically focus on very

Table 4. Results of smoothing for labor contributions of different goodwill assessment data sets with a max smoothing factor of $\alpha = 0.5$.

Model	ACC	MAE	MSE	UNDERPAY	OVERPAY
Base	**0.906** ±0.008	6.76 ±0.61	586.85 ±57.78	−20,810.34 ±3,987.55	22,220.51 ±3,486.62
+Generous	0.902 ±0.007	7.06 ±0.56	615.11 ±53.74	**−11,788.37** ±2,630.4	34,593.04 ±4,824.63
+Cautious	0.904 ±0.007	6.94 ±0.52	606.49 ±46.65	−30,887.52 ±5,159.07	**14,395.95** ±1,757.34
+Priors	0.905 ±0.009	**6.74** ±0.74	**581.03** ±68.85	−17,901.34 ±6001.66	25,858.72 ±3,534.84
Base	**0.89** ±0.007	6.7 ±0.51	521.91 ±45.95	−200,513.25 ±22,181.56	555,628.97 ±110,741.03
+Generous	0.885 ±0.005	6.96 ±0.45	545.08 ±41.78	**−112,300.64** ±24,587.5	712,084.73 ±129,923.33
+Cautious	0.887 ±0.005	6.9 ±0.41	542.97 ±38.37	−365,626.9 ±47,568.54	**402,926.56** ±91,423.83
+Priors	0.886 ±0.003	**6.63** ±0.3	**505.23** ±28.57	−224,039.44 ±28,151.06	511,294.98 ±109,859.14
Base	**0.933** ±0.004	**4.53** ±0.33	**380.53** ±31.07	-34,406.94 ±5629.54	52,374.52 ±6,396.72
+Generous	0.929 ±0.003	4.81 ±0.31	409.64 ±29.87	**−19,201.82** ±3,462.9	72,995.39 ±6,103.36
+Cautious	0.93 ±0.003	4.87 ±0.3	416.79 ±30.74	−52,842.93 ±8,453.54	**38,187.68** ±5,016.32
+Priors	0.93 ±0.004	4.68 ±0.37	393.6 ±35.41	−27,316.0 ±3,750.45	59,746.98 ±4,594.85
Base	**0.862** ±0.007	7.93 ±0.59	580.46 ±56.44	−153,618.28 ±35,419.88	345,107.29 ±66857.93
+Generous	**0.862** ±0.01	7.88 ±0.62	575.39 ±53.25	**−62,970.68** ±24,501.17	415,654.6 ±83243.69
+Cautious	0.859 ±0.008	7.93 ±0.67	578.67 ±63.08	−222,597.46 ±29955.5	**270,679.0** ±53,456.44
+Priors	**0.862** ±0.008	**7.7** ±0.61	**554.95** ±55.18	−105,230.72 ±30,140.38	371,125.59 ±58,349.45

Table 5. Results of smoothing for parts contributions of different goodwill assessment data sets with a max smoothing factor of $\alpha = 0.5$.

Model	ACC	MAE	MSE	UNDERPAY	OVERPAY
Base	**0.896** ±0.009	6.98 ±0.82	579.34 ±78.5	−31,744.94 ±9306.37	84,160.92 ±21,575.87
+Generous	0.892 ±0.008	7.16 ±0.7	594.27 ±66.21	**−15,378.27** ±5,296.54	102,037.97 ±19,866.94
+Cautious	0.895 ±0.006	7.13 ±0.63	598.47 ±61.55	−45,414.86 ±19,132.45	**72,023.1** ±14,395.4
+Priors	0.895 ±0.008	**6.96** ±0.7	**575.55** ±66.55	−36,270.52 ±15,750.53	78,736.36 ±20,136.15
Base	**0.894** ±0.006	6.24 ±0.35	477.5 ±31.8	−430,146.61 ±108977.81	1,122,151.24 ±176,516.56
+Generous	0.891 ±0.005	6.38 ±0.33	491.79 ±31.37	**−217,544.71** ±74,535.81	1,367,306.62 ±187,239.83
+Cautious	**0.894** ±0.005	6.22 ±0.31	481.64 ±30.41	−640,450.7 ±177,181.13	**894,571.07** ±166,891.27
+Priors	0.892 ±0.005	**6.1** ±0.24	**456.87** ±21.91	−546,358.25 ±165,084.6	967,882.1 ±143,394.63
Base	**0.884** ±0.003	4.24 ±0.16	243.91 ±12.32	−67,451.36 ±8,535.11	219,066.1 ±34,154.76
+Generous	0.882 ±0.006	4.28 ±0.21	247.98 ±13.92	**−38,309.93** ±6,165.02	245,536.55 ±37,405.61
+Cautious	0.883 ±0.005	**4.19** ±0.2	241.42 ±13.77	−83,698.36 ±15,123.86	**197,573.78** ±39,719.46
+Priors	**0.884** ±0.004	**4.19** ±0.16	**239.42** ±11.72	−63,682.4 ±8,578.55	217,069.17 ±35,658.62
Base	**0.87** ±0.009	7.16 ±0.57	514.27 ±53.2	−264,672.6 ±110,169.93	765,250.06 ±163,638.98
+Generous	0.867 ±0.007	7.38 ±0.52	534.6 ±51.22	**-128,742.79** ±41,807.12	890,592.62 ±174,359.46
+Cautious	0.866 ±0.006	7.28 ±0.45	523.84 ±39.17	−54,350.41 ±109,682.42	**631,753.19** ±123,490.03
+Priors	0.869 ±0.006	**7.03** ±0.53	**498.47** ±51.21	−222,986.36 ±67,758.96	778,818.12 ±160,019.91

recent data. For this evaluation, we focus on the three data sets that visually entail some sort of drift in the target rating over time (cf. figure 6). Tables 6 and 7 summarize the obtained time based smoothed results (+Time) for labor and parts contributions respectively in comparison to a nominal classification baseline (Base). One can clearly see that the time based smoothing approach increases the predictive performance of the models on our data sets for the majority of our metrics.

Table 6. Results of time based smoothing (+Time) compared to standard nominal classification (Base) for labor contributions of different goodwill assessment data sets ($\alpha = 0.8$).

Model	ACC	MAE	MSE	UNDERPAY	OVERPAY
Base	0.888	8.95	832.46	−20,166.82	31,891.31
+Time	**0.89**	**8.93**	**831.73**	**−15,223.71**	**24,952.21**
Base	0.827	8.92	668.35	−145,360.16	844,359.37
+Time	**0.829**	**8.45**	**633.88**	**−137,898.47**	**799,428.2**
Base	0.951	2.97	240.73	−31,880.59	29,368.8
+Time	**0.952**	**2.87**	**232.61**	**−28,603.83**	**27,001.83**

Table 7. Results of time based smoothing (+Time) compared to standard nominal classification (Base) for parts contributions of different goodwill assessment data sets ($\alpha = 0.8$).

Model	ACC	MAE	MSE	UNDERPAY	OVERPAY
Base	**0.845**	10.02	839.32	−72,368.92	**117,635.19**
+Time	0.844	**9.98**	**829.63**	**−58,450.89**	154,781.0
Base	**0.834**	8.73	655.28	−312,151.14	1,260,827.89
+Time	0.828	**8.57**	**643.12**	**−242,015.57**	**1,121,527.11**
Base	0.919	2.75	**146.03**	−85,673.42	**110,494.84**
+Time	**0.924**	**2.68**	147.0	**−75,981.27**	122,821.94

5 Conclusion

In this paper, we presented a novel unimodal label smoothing approach with the aim to rectify bias in ordinal observational data. We have demonstrated the effectiveness of the approach for the use case of automotive goodwill assessment. Through the usage of different smoothing-relations we can flexibly configure our models to be more cautious, respectively generous, with regards to goodwill assessments which is clearly indicated in strong underpayment, respectively strong overpayment, in comparison to a nominal classification baseline. The class priors based smoothing heuristic corrects inflationary used ratings through smoothing them stronger than less frequently used ratings which manifests in reduced MAE and MSE metrics compared to the baseline. Time based smoothing helps to reduce concept drift bias and outperforms standard nominal classification on the majority of our evaluated metrics. Overall we can say that, our proposed methods are effective and flexible tools to correct biased expert ratings and reduce reliance on human expertise.

References

1. Albuquerque, T., Cruz, R., Cardoso, J.S.: Quasi-unimodal distributions for ordinal classification. Mathematics **10**(6), 980 (2022)
2. Beckham, C., Pal, C.J.: Unimodal probability distributions for deep ordinal classification. In: Precup, D., Teh, Y.W. (eds.) Proceedings of the 34th International Conference on Machine Learning, ICML 2017, Sydney, NSW, Australia, 6–11 August 2017. Proceedings of Machine Learning Research, vol. 70, pp. 411–419. PMLR (2017)
3. Chen, T., Guestrin, C.: XGBoost: a scalable tree boosting system. In: Krishnapuram, B., Shah, M., Smola, A.J., Aggarwal, C.C., Shen, D., Rastogi, R. (eds.) Proceedings of the 22nd ACM SIGKDD International Conference on Knowledge Discovery and Data Mining, San Francisco, CA, USA, August 13–17, 2016. pp. 785–794. ACM (2016)
4. da Costa, J.F.P., Alonso, H., Cardoso, J.S.: The unimodal model for the classification of ordinal data. Neural Netw. **21**(1), 78–91 (2008)
5. da Costa, J.P., Cardoso, J.S.: Classification of ordinal data using neural networks. In: Gama, J., Camacho, R., Brazdil, P.B., Jorge, A.M., Torgo, L. (eds.) ECML 2005. LNCS (LNAI), vol. 3720, pp. 690–697. Springer, Heidelberg (2005). https://doi.org/10.1007/11564096_70
6. Durán-Rosal, A.M., et al.: Ordinal classification of the affectation level of 3D-images in Parkinson diseases. Sci. Rep. **11**(1), 1–13 (2021)
7. Gaudette, L., Japkowicz, N.: Evaluation methods for ordinal classification. In: Gao, Y., Japkowicz, N. (eds.) AI 2009. LNCS (LNAI), vol. 5549, pp. 207–210. Springer, Heidelberg (2009). https://doi.org/10.1007/978-3-642-01818-3_25
8. Grinsztajn, L., Oyallon, E., Varoquaux, G.: Why do tree-based models still outperform deep learning on tabular data? arXiv preprint arXiv:2207.08815 (2022)
9. Gutiérrez, P.A., Perez-Ortiz, M., Sanchez-Monedero, J., Fernandez-Navarro, F., Hervas-Martinez, C.: Ordinal regression methods: survey and experimental study. IEEE Trans. Knowl. Data Eng. **28**(1), 127–146 (2015)
10. Haas, S., Hüllermeier, E.: A prescriptive machine learning approach for assessing goodwill in the automotive domain. In: Amini, M., Canu, S., Fischer, A., Guns, T., Novak, P.K., Tsoumakas, G. (eds.) Machine Learning and Knowledge Discovery in Databases - European Conference, ECML PKDD 2022, Grenoble, France, September 19–23, 2022, Proceedings, Part VI. Lecture Notes in Computer Science, vol. 13718, pp. 170–184. Springer, Cham (2022). https://doi.org/10.1007/978-3-031-26422-1_11
11. Hüllermeier, E.: Prescriptive machine learning for automated decision making: challenges and opportunities. arXiv preprint arXiv:2112.08268 (2021)
12. Lienen, J., Hüllermeier, E.: From label smoothing to label relaxation. In: Thirty-Fifth AAAI Conference on Artificial Intelligence, AAAI 2021, Virtual Event, February 2–9, 2021, pp. 8583–8591. AAAI Press (2021)
13. Liu, X., et al.: Unimodal regularized neuron stick-breaking for ordinal classification. Neurocomputing **388**, 34–44 (2020)
14. Lu, J., Liu, A., Dong, F., Gu, F., Gama, J., Zhang, G.: Learning under concept drift: a review. IEEE Trans. Knowl. Data Eng. **31**(12), 2346–2363 (2019)
15. Lukasik, M., Bhojanapalli, S., Menon, A.K., Kumar, S.: Does label smoothing mitigate label noise? In: Proceedings of the 37th International Conference on Machine Learning, ICML 2020, 13–18 July 2020, Virtual Event. Proceedings of Machine Learning Research, vol. 119, pp. 6448–6458. PMLR (2020)

16. Manthoulis, G., Doumpos, M., Zopounidis, C., Galariotis, E.: An ordinal classification framework for bank failure prediction: methodology and empirical evidence for US banks. Eur. J. Oper. Res. **282**(2), 786–801 (2020)
17. McCullagh, P.: Regression models for ordinal data. J. Royal Stat. Soc.: Ser. B (Methodological) **42**(2), 109–127 (1980)
18. Pérez-Ortiz, M., Cruz-Ramírez, M., Ayllón-Terán, M.D., Heaton, N., Ciria, R., Hervás-Martínez, C.: An organ allocation system for liver transplantation based on ordinal regression. Appl. Soft Comput. **14**, 88–98 (2014)
19. Szegedy, C., Vanhoucke, V., Ioffe, S., Shlens, J., Wojna, Z.: Rethinking the inception architecture for computer vision. In: 2016 IEEE Conference on Computer Vision and Pattern Recognition, CVPR 2016, Las Vegas, NV, USA, June 27–30, 2016, pp. 2818–2826. IEEE Computer Society (2016)
20. Vargas, V.M., Gutiérrez, P.A., Barbero-Gómez, J., Hervás-Martínez, C.: Soft labelling based on triangular distributions for ordinal classification. Information Fusion (2023)
21. Vargas, V.M., Gutiérrez, P.A., Hervás-Martínez, C.: Unimodal regularisation based on beta distribution for deep ordinal regression. Pattern Recogn. **122**, 108310 (2022)
22. Zhou, Z.H.: A brief introduction to weakly supervised learning. National Sci. Rev. **5**(1), 44–53 (2018)

Class-Conditional Label Noise
in Astroparticle Physics

Mirko Bunse[(✉)][iD] and Lukas Pfahler[iD]

Artificial Intelligence Group, TU Dortmund University, 44227 Dortmund, Germany
{mirko.bunse,lukas.pfahler}@cs.tu-dortmund.de

Abstract. Class-conditional label noise characterizes classification tasks in which the training set labels are randomly flipped versions of the actual ground-truth. The analysis of telescope data in astroparticle physics poses this problem with a novel condition: one of the class-wise label flip probabilities is known while the other is not. We address this condition with an objective function for optimizing the decision thresholds of existing classifiers. Our experiments on several imbalanced data sets demonstrate that accounting for the known label flip probability substantially improves the learning outcome over existing methods for learning under class-conditional label noise. In astroparticle physics, our proposal achieves an improvement in predictive performance and a considerable reduction in computational requirements. These achievements are a direct result of our proposal's ability to learn from real telescope data, instead of relying on simulated data as is common practice in the field.

Keywords: Class-conditional label noise · Imbalanced classification · Astroparticle physics

1 Introduction

Astroparticle physics is a research field that advances our understanding of fundamental physics in extreme cosmic environments [11]. Its scientific questions regard the origin of cosmic rays, the acceleration processes of particles, and the nature of dark matter [1,13]. Advancing these topics requires precise measurements of the cosmos—a purpose for which specialized telescopes of increasing scale and complexity are being deployed.

The most extreme environments are monitored by imaging atmospheric Cherenkov telescopes (IACTs) [2,4,31], which record the interactions of cosmic particles within Earth's atmosphere. These recordings are represented as feature vectors $x \in \mathbb{R}^d$, from which the particle type $y \in \{+1, -1\}$ (signal or noise) and other latent quantities (particle energy and direction) have to be predicted by supervised machine learning models [6,7]. If the predictions are accurate, they allow physicists to uncover the characteristics of the extreme cosmic environments that have produced the recorded particles.

© The Author(s), under exclusive license to Springer Nature Switzerland AG 2023
G. De Francisci Morales et al. (Eds.): ECML PKDD 2023, LNAI 14174, pp. 19–35, 2023.
https://doi.org/10.1007/978-3-031-43427-3_2

Training a prediction model requires some form of supervision, typically in the form of ground-truth labels that are assigned to every instance of a training data set. In astroparticle physics, this form of supervision is conventionally provided by simulations [6,7] because real IACT data is not ground-truth labeled. However, utilizing simulations for training machine learning models raises concerns about the quality and the computational cost of the training data.

In this work, we omit the simulation and instead explore the potential of learning from weak labels that we obtain from real IACT data. *Hence, our approach saves computational resources and circumvents the deficiencies of the simulation.* Our weak labels suffer from class-conditional label noise (CCN) [5, 24,27,30], i.e., they are randomly flipped versions of the ground-truth labels with fixed class-wise label flip probabilities p_+ and p_-.

Definition 1 (Class-Conditional Label Noise). *Let* $p_+, p_- \in [0, 1)$ *and let* $y \in \{+1, -1\}$ *be a ground-truth label. The corresponding CCN noisy label is*

$$\widehat{y} = CCN(y; p_+, p_-) = \begin{cases} -y & \text{with probability } p_y \\ y & \text{with probability } 1 - p_y \end{cases}$$

Remark 1 (Compact Notation). We use subscripts p_y with $y \in \{+1, -1\}$ and $N_{\widehat{y}}$ with $\widehat{y} \in \{+1, -1\}$ to compactly represent p_+, p_-, N_+, and N_-.

While existing work on CCN either assumes p_+ and p_- both to be known [14,27] or both to be unknown [14,25], *it turns out that astroparticle physics poses a novel setting of CCN where* p_- *is known and* p_+ *is not.* We address this setting through an objective function that a learning algorithm can optimize and we demonstrate that accounting for the known p_- substantially improves the learning outcome over the state-of-the-art in CCN learning. We regard the astroparticle use case to be a valuable addition to CCN research because settings with known p_- and unknown p_+ have remained unexplored to the best of our knowledge.

This paper is structured as follows: Sect. 2 introduces astroparticle physics as an application domain of CCN. The related work on learning under CCN is introduced in Sect. 3 before algorithms for handling the knowledge of p_- are developed in Sect. 4. We evaluate our proposals in Sect. 5 and conclude with Sect. 6.

2   Binary Classification in Astroparticle Physics

IACTs [2,4,31] observe the gamma radiation of extreme cosmic environments. If a gamma ray travels through Earth's atmosphere, it interacts with atmospheric particles and thereby emits light that the camera of an IACT can record. Unfortunately, the same effect happens with cosmic hadron particles. As sketched in Fig. 1, hadrons do not identify the cosmic environments they originate in because interstellar magnetic fields deflect them on their way. As a consequence, the camera recordings of an IACT need to be classified as being either gamma rays ($y = +1$) or hadrons ($y = -1$) [6,7], to obtain a clean sample of gamma rays for downstream physics analyses.

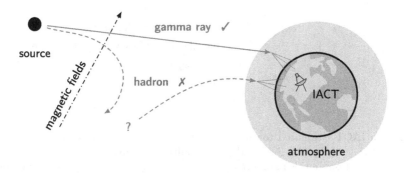

Fig. 1. An IACT observes an extreme cosmic environment that is the source of high-energy gamma radiation. Hadronic particles have to be discarded from the data sample because their deflection conceals their true origin.

The training data for classifying IACT recordings is typically provided by sophisticated simulations of gamma rays and hadrons [7,10]. These simulations comprise all physical processes that generate IACT data in the real world, including particle interactions, light emission, and camera electronics. While simulated data are indeed capable of training accurate classifiers for the real IACT, they also induce computational costs at a considerable scale. Additionally, inaccuracies of the simulation can limit the efficiency of learning from simulated data [21]. Hence, learning from real IACT data is desirable.

2.1 Source Detection

One of the first downstream analyses of a classified gamma ray sample is to detect and locate extreme cosmic environments in space. Unfortunately, this analysis is complicated by misclassification errors that mistake hadrons for gamma rays. Due to these errors, detecting a gamma ray source requires predicting an amount of gamma radiation that clearly exceeds the amount that has to be expected solely from misclassifications.

Comparing these two amounts requires measuring both, the apparent gamma radiation of a source and the apparent radiation from misclassifications. For this purpose, the IACT's field of view is divided into multiple regions. As sketched in Fig. 2, the telescope is positioned such that the source location aligns with one of these regions. This "on" region measures all predicted gamma rays, be they true or false predictions. All other regions, now called "off" regions, do not picture a source and, hence, measure the false predictions in isolation. If some location in the sky indeed contains a source, this setup will record a higher number of predicted gamma rays in the "on" region compared to the average number of gamma rays predicted in a single "off" region.

To assess whether the number of predicted gamma rays in the "on" region is indeed higher, astroparticle physicists employ the likelihood-ratio hypothesis test from Definition 2. This test aims at rejecting the null hypothesis that the

Fig. 2. An IACT is pointed towards the location of a potential gamma ray source. The field of view of the IACT is divided into multiple regions, one of which is centered around this location. In this figure, $R = 5$ "off" regions are employed, which corresponds to $\omega = \frac{1}{5}$ and to $p_- = \frac{1}{6}$.

"on" region does not emit more predicted gamma rays than the average "off" region. Hence, the rejection of this null hypothesis corresponds to the successful detection of an extreme cosmic environment.

Definition 2. (Hypothesis Test for Source Detection [18]) *Let N_+ be the number of gamma ray predictions in the "on" region and let N_- be the number of gamma ray predictions in all "off" regions. Moreover, let λ_+ and λ_- be the rates of the corresponding Poisson distributions, let $\mathcal{N} : \mathbb{R} \to [0,1]$ be the cumulative distribution function of the standard normal distribution, let $R \in \mathbb{N}$ be the number of "off" regions, and let $\omega = \frac{1}{R}$. The p-value for rejecting the null hypothesis $h_0 : \lambda_+ \leq \omega \cdot \lambda_-$ is*

$$p = 1 - \mathcal{N}(f_\omega(N_+, N_-)),$$

$$f_\omega(N_+, N_-) = \left[2N_+ \cdot \ln \left(\frac{1+\omega}{\omega} \cdot \frac{N_+}{N_+ + N_-} \right) \right.$$
$$\left. + 2N_- \cdot \ln \left((1+\omega) \cdot \frac{N_-}{N_+ + N_-} \right) \right]^{1/2}.$$

In astroparticle physics, a detection typically succeeds when the test statistic f_ω exceeds a value of 5. We are then speaking of a "five sigma detection", which amounts to a p-value of $2.87 \cdot 10^{-7}$. As of today, over 220 sources of high-energy gamma radiation have been detected at this immense level of certainty.[1]

Since N_+ and N_- are numbers of predicted gamma rays, they are controlled through the decision threshold of the classifier—a higher threshold predicts less gamma rays and thus reduces N_+ and N_- by different amounts. To facilitate detections, it is a common practice in astroparticle physics to maximize f_ω by choosing this decision threshold. In Sect. 4, we generalize this common practice beyond astroparticle physics and towards CCN learning in general.

---

[1] http://tevcat.uchicago.edu/, catalog version 3.400 by Wakely and Horan [32].

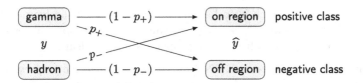

Fig. 3. CCN in astroparticle physics. The goal is to distinguish gammas from hadrons, while the noisy labels are defined by the "on" and "off" regions. The novelty of this use case, in the context of CCN research, is that $p_- = \frac{1}{R+1}$ is known and p_+ is not.

2.2 Noisy Labels of Real Telescope Data

The usual goal of source detection is to discover sources of gamma radiation that were not yet known to exist. Something interesting happens, however, if we point the telescope towards a gamma ray source that we already know with certainty: *if the "on" region certainly pictures a source, then the number of predicted gamma rays in the "on" region has to be higher than the average number of predicted gamma rays per "off" region.* Quite strikingly, this requirement allows us to interpret the "on" and "off" origins of real IACT data as CCN noisy labels. We sketch this interpretation in Fig. 3 and provide a formal proof in Theorem 1.

In the context of CCN, a novelty of the astroparticle use case is its precise knowledge of p_-. This knowledge stems from the fact that hadron particles are distributed uniformly over the night sky; hence, a hadron appears in each of the "on" and "off" regions with equal probability. The probability of misclassifying a hadron in the "on" region is therefore $p_- = \frac{1}{R+1}$, where R is the number of "off" regions. We propose to make use of this knowledge during CCN learning.

3   Related Work on Class-Conditional Label Noise

In binary classification under random label noise, we only have access to training labels $\widehat{y} \in \{+1, -1\}$ that are *noisy* in the sense of being randomly flipped versions of the *clean* ground-truth labels $y \in \{+1, -1\}$. In particular, the CCN label noise model from Definition 1 [5,24,27,30] states that the labels are flipped according to probabilities p_+ and p_- that depend exclusively on the true class y, and not on the features of the data.

The feasibility of learning under the CCN noise model is conventionally established by assuming

$$p_+ + p_- < 1, \tag{1}$$

where $p_y = \mathbb{P}(\widehat{Y} = -y \mid Y = y)$ are the label flip probabilities. We can rearrange this assumption to see that it is equivalent to assuming a correspondence between noisy and true labels: $\mathbb{P}(\widehat{Y} = +1 \mid Y = +1) > \mathbb{P}(\widehat{Y} = +1 \mid Y = -1)$.

Theoretic studies [5,24,27,30] have shown that CCN data even facilitates the learning of an optimal classifier, in terms of the *clean* ground-truth labels and in terms of several performance metrics. For these metrics, the only complication of CCN learning is to find an optimal decision threshold $\theta^* \in \mathbb{R}$; an optimal scoring function $h : \mathcal{X} \to \mathbb{R}$, which is to be thresholded at θ^*, can be learned directly from CCN data. Ignoring CCN, however, can lead to sub-optimal results. The following proposition formalizes these properties of CCN learning.

Proposition 1 (Consistent CCN Learning). *Consider a performance metric $\mathcal{Q} : \mathcal{H} \to \mathbb{R}$ for which the Bayes-optimal classifier, with respect to the clean ground-truth labels, is of the form $h^*(x) = sign(\mathbb{P}(Y = +1 \mid X = x) - \theta^*)$ with an optimal threshold $\theta^* \in \mathbb{R}$. Moreover, let ϕ^* be the threshold that is optimal with respect to the CCN noisy labels, let $p_+ + p_- < 1$, and let the learning algorithm $\mathcal{A} : \cup_{m=1}^{\infty}(\mathcal{X} \times \mathcal{Y})^m \to \mathcal{H}$ be a consistent estimator of the scoring function, i.e., let $\forall x \in \mathcal{X} : \mathbb{E}_{(\mathcal{X} \times \mathcal{Y})^m} h_{\mathcal{A}}(x) \to \mathbb{P}(\widehat{Y} = +1 \mid X = x)$ for a noisy sample of size $m \to \infty$. Then, for $m \to \infty$, the classifier*

$$h(x) = sign\left(h_{\mathcal{A}}(x) - \frac{\phi^* - p_-}{1 - p_+ - p_-}\right)$$

is Bayes-optimal for $\mathcal{Q}$ with respect to the clean ground-truth labels $\widehat{y}$.

Proof. The proof is detailed in our supplementary material.[2] It summarizes existing results [24,27] on CCN learning.

Remark 2. Proposition 1 makes two assumptions. First, it requires a performance metric $\mathcal{Q}$ for which the Bayes-optimal classifier is a thresholded decision function of the form $h^*(x) = sign(\mathbb{P}(Y = +1 \mid X = x) - \theta^*)$. This family of performance metrics contains several important measures, like accuracy, weighted accuracy, and the F_β score [8,35]. Second, the proposition assumes a consistent learning algorithm $\mathcal{A}$ for the decision function $h_{\mathcal{A}}(x)$. This consistency assumption holds for any $\mathcal{A}$ which evolves around empirical risk minimization of a proper loss function [8,22], like the logistic loss and the squared error. Hence, the proposition applies to many performance metrics and learning algorithms.

Proposition 1 allows us to use CCN data to fit a decision function h and to obtain an estimate $\widehat{\phi} \in \mathbb{R}$ of the noisy-optimal threshold ϕ^*. The only difficulty of CCN learning is to estimate the clean-optimal threshold

$$\widehat{\theta} = \frac{\widehat{\phi} - p_-}{1 - p_+ - p_-}, \tag{2}$$

without knowing p_+ and p_-. We typically have to estimate these label flip probabilities from CCN data, employing additional assumptions such as the existence of clean labels at a point in feature space where the other clean class has zero probability [24], the so-called anchor point assumption [33].

Example 1 (Accuracy). The optimal threshold for the accuracy metric is known to be $\phi^*_{\text{Acc}} = \frac{1}{2}$ [8]. Hence, we do not need to estimate ϕ^*_{Acc} from data but, due to CCN, we have to acknowledge that ϕ^*_{Acc} is not optimal for the clean ground-truth labels. As according to Eq. 2 (also see previous work [27, Theorem 9]), an optimal threshold for the clean labels is $\theta^*_{\text{Acc}} = (\frac{1}{2} - p_-) \cdot (1 - p_+ - p_-)^{-1}$, which requires the precise knowledge of p_+ and p_- or the estimation thereof.

---

[2] https://github.com/mirkobunse/pkccn.

An alternative approach to thresholding is a label-dependent weighting of the loss function already during training [14, 27]. However, finding the optimal weights also requires precise knowledge of p_+ and p_- or the estimation thereof, just like the thresholding approach. If we had a small cleanly labeled data set, we could alternatively tune the decision threshold directly on this set [5], without the need for estimating p_+ and p_-. However, cleanly labeled data is typically not available in CCN use cases.

3.1 Class Imbalance in CCN

IACT data is extremely imbalanced [7]. In this situation, the estimation of p_+ and p_- becomes more difficult [25]. Additionally, the evaluation of classifiers crucially needs to address the class imbalance through dedicated performance metrics such as the F_β score or the G-score.

Unfortunately, with the notable exception of Mithal et al. [25], the problem of class imbalance in CCN has remained largely unexplored. Recent works [15, 20, 28, 29, 34] primarily optimize accuracy instead, a metric that is not adequate for imbalanced classification tasks [12]. For the imbalanced astroparticle use case, we evaluate CCN techniques in terms of their F_1 scores, a suitable measure for imbalanced classification performance.

3.2 Other Types of Label Noise

Beyond the CCN noise model, other types of label noise have been discussed. For instance, the label noise is called *uniform* [14] if each label has the same chance of being flipped, independent of the class and the features. If the chance of being flipped does not depend on the true class, but on the features, we are speaking of *purely instance-dependent* label noise [23]. Learning is feasible under each of these noise models if dedicated assumptions about the data and the learning method hold. Our focus on CCN stems from our astroparticle use case, which poses a CCN task in particular.

Recently, multi-class settings are moving into the focus of CCN research [15, 20, 28, 29, 34]. These settings require not only the estimation (or the knowledge) of two noise rates, but the estimation (or the knowledge) of a dense *transition matrix* between all noisy and true labels [33, 34]. In the context of deep learning, methods for the simultaneous training of the prediction model and the transition matrix have been proposed [19]. However, none of these multi-class methods is shown to improve over binary CCN techniques in case of imbalanced binary CCN tasks, such as our astroparticle use case.

4 Partially-Known Class-Conditional Label Noise

Existing work on CCN either addresses the complete knowledge of p_+ and p_- [14, 27] or the complete ignorance thereof [14, 25]. In the following, we focus on a novel setting of CCN in binary classification where p_- is known while p_+ is not.

We refer to this novel setting as partially-known CCN (PK-CCN). It inherits all properties of general CCN learning, as discussed in Sect. 3, but allows algorithms to employ p_- for a more effective training.

Remark 3. By swapping the clean ground-truth classes $+1$ and -1, PK-CCN can also address the converse setting where p_+ is known and p_- is not. For notational consistency, we continue to assume, without loss of generality, that p_- is the known label flip probability.

Before we develop algorithms for learning under PK-CCN, we generalize the hypothesis test from Definition 2 beyond the astroparticle use case and towards CCN learning in general. This generalization stems from a connection to the central CCN assumption, i.e., $p_+ + p_- < 1$, from Eq. 1. Testing this assumption for a given set of CCN labels tells us whether consistent learning is feasible.

Theorem 1 (Hypothesis Test for PK-CCN Learnability). *Let $N_{\widehat{y}}$ be the number of clean positives (i.e., $y = +1$) with a noisy label $\widehat{y} \in \{+1, -1\}$ and let $\omega = \frac{p_-}{1-p_-}$. With these re-definitions, the hypothesis test from Definition 2 computes the p-value for rejecting the null hypothesis $h_0 : p_+ + p_- \geq 1$.*

Proof. The proof is detailed in our supplementary material (see Footnote 2). It establishes the equivalence between the null hypotheses from Theorem 1 and Definition 2.

Computing the $N_{\widehat{y}}$ in Theorem 1 requires access to a set of data that is labeled both in terms of clean ground-truth labels and in terms of noisy labels. Typically, such data are not available. Still, we find this theoretical connection striking because it motivates a heuristic optimization of decision thresholds in terms of f_ω. In fact, this optimization is a common practice in the analysis of IACT data but has not yet been discussed in the scope of CCN learning.

Decision Threshold Optimization: For the optimization of decision thresholds, we do not assume any clean labels. Instead, we heuristically replace the $N_{\widehat{y}}$ counts in Theorem 1 with counts of *predicted* positives $N_{\widehat{y}}^\theta$ according to some threshold $\theta \in \mathbb{R}$. Specifically, we compute the function f_ω from Definition 2 over $N_{\widehat{y}}^\theta$, instead of $N_{\widehat{y}}$. This replacement allows us to choose θ such that f_ω becomes maximal. For a soft classifier $h : \mathcal{X} \to \mathbb{R}$, and for a noisily labeled data set $\{(\boldsymbol{x}_i, \widehat{y}_i) : 1 \leq i \leq m\}$, we choose

$$\widehat{\theta} = \arg\max_{\theta \in \mathbb{R}} f_\omega(N_+^\theta, N_-^\theta),$$

$$\text{where } N_{\widehat{y}}^\theta = \sum_{1 \leq i \leq m \,:\, \widehat{y}h(\boldsymbol{x}_i) > \widehat{y}\theta} 1 \tag{3}$$

is the number of predicted positives in the noisy class $\widehat{y}$. The heuristic replacement of $N_{\widehat{y}}$ with $N_{\widehat{y}}^\theta$ has the following implications:

no need for clean labels: the optimization in Eq. 3 does not require any clean ground-truth labels; it only needs to count the numbers of predicted positives in both noisy classes, which is easily obtained from the noisy data.

Algorithm 1. Decision Threshold Optimization for PK-CCN.

Input: A scoring function $h : \mathcal{X} \to \mathbb{R}$, a desired p value $p > 0$, a noise rate $0 < p_- < 1$, and m noisily labeled instances $\{(x_i, \widehat{y}_i) : 1 \le i \le m\}$
Output: A decision threshold $\widehat{\theta} \in \mathbb{R}$

1: $\omega \leftarrow \frac{p_-}{1-p_-}$
2: $\widehat{\theta} \leftarrow \arg\max_{\theta \in \mathbb{R}} f_\omega(N_+^\theta, N_-^\theta)$, see Eq. 3
3: **if** $p > 1 - \mathcal{N}(f_\omega(N_+^{\widehat{\theta}}, N_-^{\widehat{\theta}}))$ **then**
4:     **return** $\widehat{\theta}$
5: **else**
6:     **failure** PK-CCN learning does not appear feasible

---

partial knowledge of noise rates: the optimization in Eq. 3 needs to know p_-, such that $\omega = \frac{p_-}{1-p_-}$ can be computed according to Theorem 1. Without a need to know p_+, our method is a true PK-CCN method.

model agnosticism: the optimization in Eq. 3 works with any soft classifier $h : \mathcal{X} \to \mathbb{R}$, like SVMs, decision trees, deep neural networks, and many more. Unlike existing CCN methods [24,25], we do not require an anchor point assumption [33] for optimizing f_ω.

Our threshold optimization technique for PK-CCN is summarized in Algorithm 1. If our heuristic does not indicate a successful rejection of the null hypothesis, we raise a warning to the user.

5 Experiments

We now evaluate the merits of our proposed PK-CCN setting over previous binary CCN settings. In the previous setting where p_+ and p_- are both known [14,27], we speak of completely known CCN (CK-CCN); in the previous setting where both are unknown [14,25], we speak of completely unknown CCN (CU-CCN) instead.

Our first experiment evolves around an extensive evaluation of CCN learning methods on 27 conventional imbalanced data sets. Our second experiment covers a practical case study in astroparticle physics. The implementation of our algorithms and experiments is publicly available (see footnote 2).

5.1 Baseline Methods

Mithal et al. [25] propose a CCN-aware decision threshold which maximizes the G-score, a suitable metric for imbalanced binary classification. Without assuming p_+ or p_- to be known, this method is a true CU-CCN method.

Menon et al. [24] propose a technique to estimate several performance metrics in spite of CCN, including the F_1 score for imbalanced classification. This general technique builds on a CCN-aware estimation of the true positive rate and the true

---

Algorithm 2. F_1 Score Maximization [16,26] in Spite of Binary CU-CCN [24].

Input: A scoring function $h : \mathcal{X} \rightarrow [0,1]$ and m noisily labeled instances $\{(\boldsymbol{x}_i, \widehat{y}_i) : 1 \leq i \leq m\}$
Output: A decision threshold $\widehat{\theta} \in \mathbb{R}$
  1: $\widehat{p}_+ \leftarrow 1 - \max_{1 \leq i \leq m} h(\boldsymbol{x}_i)$
  2: $\widehat{p}_- \leftarrow \min_{1 \leq i \leq m} h(\boldsymbol{x}_i)$
  3: $\widehat{\theta} \leftarrow \arg\max_{\theta \in \mathbb{R}} F_1(\theta; h, \widehat{p}_-, \widehat{p}_+)$, see Eq. 4 in the supplementary material
  4: **return** $\widehat{\theta}$

---

negative rate of a classifier [30], which we detail in the supplementary material (see Footnote 2).

Since the F_1 score cannot be optimized analytically, we have developed Algorithm 2. This algorithm adapts a consistent F_1 optimization that is unaware of CCN [16,26] by plugging in the CCN-aware F_1 estimate by Menon et al. [24].

Lines 1 and 2 of Algorithm 2 estimate p_+ and p_- under the anchor point assumption [33]. If these rates are known, however, we can replace the estimates $\widehat{p}_+$ and $\widehat{p}_-$ with their true values. In this case, the algorithm becomes either a PK-CCN algorithm (if p_- is known) or a CK-CCN algorithm (if p_+ and p_- are known). We assess the merits of our PK-CCN proposal by evaluating all versions of Algorithm 2: its vanilla CU-CCN version and its PK-CCN and CK-CCN versions.

In imbalanced classification, accuracy is not informative [12]. Hence, an optimization of accuracy would be inappropriate and we do *not* experiment with CCN techniques that optimize this measure [15,20,28,29,34].

5.2   Merits of PK-CCN: Methodology

Our evaluation is based on the 27 imbalanced data sets from the *imbalanced-learn* library [17].[3] We artificially inject different levels of CCN, which are listed in Fig. 4 and in Table 1. The first two noise configurations are designed by ourselves and the remaining four are taken from previous experiments [27].

We estimate the performance of each CCN method in terms of the F_1 score, a metric that is well suited for imbalanced data. We report the average F_1 score and its standard deviation over 20 repetitions of a 10-fold stratified cross validation. In total, our results comprise 194 400 classification models. We employ random forest classifiers because they have a high predictive power and they allow us to tune decision thresholds consistently on out-of-bag noisily labeled data.

We do *not* validate in terms of the area under the ROC curve or in terms of balanced accuracy because these metrics are immune to CCN [24] and therefore not informative. Due to the class imbalance, we do also not validate in terms of unbalanced accuracy.

---

[3] https://imbalanced-learn.org/stable/datasets/.

5.3   Merits of PK-CCN: Results on Conventional Imbalanced Data

Figure 4 compares the performances of CCN learning methods with Critical Difference (CD) diagrams [9]. These diagrams are specifically designed for statistically meaningful comparisons of multiple classifiers across multiple data sets. The x-axis of a CD diagram plots the average rank of each method (lower is better), here in terms of the F_1 score: intuitively, a low rank indicates that a method beats the other methods on many data sets. Connected are those methods that a Bonferroni-corrected Wilcoxon signed-rank hypothesis test cannot distinguish. Hence, all *missing* connections indicate *statistically significant differences* between the data set-wise performances of methods.

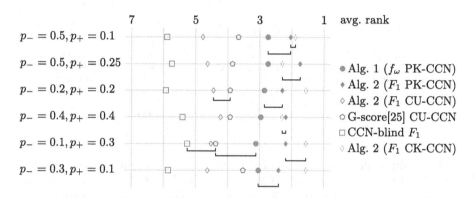

Fig. 4. Each row displays one critical difference diagram [9] for one noise configuration (p_-, p_+). This overview summarizes a total of 194 400 random forest classifiers, a collection which consists of 6 CCN learning methods × 6 noise configurations × 27 data sets × 10 cross validation folds × 20 repetitions with random initialization. The x-coordinates indicate average ranks (lower is better) and methods are connected with horizontal bars if and only if a Bonferroni-corrected Wilcoxon signed-rank test cannot distinguish their pairwise performances in terms of their cross-validated F_1 score at a confidence level of 95%. Hence, missing connections indicate significant differences.

The CD diagrams from Fig. 4 are complemented by Table 1, which reports the average F_1 scores across all data sets and repetitions. These values complete the picture of Fig. 4 by revealing the magnitudes of performance differences.

The average f_ω scores of each method are displayed in Table 2. Unlike the F_1 score, this metric can be evaluated exclusively on noisy labels, without requiring the clean labels that we only know because we artificially inject CCN.

Discussion: The perspectives from Fig. 4 and Table 1 demonstrate the merits of our proposed setting, PK-CCN: accounting for the known p_- gives a performance improvement that is *statistically significant* and has a *considerable magnitude*. For instance, the PK-CCN version of Algorithm 2 achieves an average F_1 score of 0.425, which is way beyond its average CU-CCN score of 0.310.

Table 1. Average F_1 scores (higher is better) over all 27 data sets and over 20 repetitions of a 10-fold cross validation. Bold values represent the best performances, either including or excluding the privileged CK-CCN method of the last column.

(p_-, p_+)	Algorithm 1/f_ω PK-CCN	Algorithm 2/F_1 PK-CCN	Algorithm 2/F_1 CU-CCN	G-score [25] CU-CCN	CCN-blind F_1	Algorithm 2/F_1 CK-CCN
(0.5, 0.1)	.408±.050	.417±.051	.262±.046	.333±.051	.112±.000	.424±.049
(0.5, 0.25)	.327±.059	.336±.066	.184±.037	.234±.057	.112±.000	.339±.062
(0.2, 0.2)	.485±.044	.498±.041	.408±.044	.429±.051	.169±.036	.510±.035
(0.4, 0.4)	.280±.067	.294±.069	.172±.039	.185±.047	.112±.000	.298±.068
(0.1, 0.3)	.499±.039	.512±.034	.466±.043	.461±.052	.402±.045	.525±.032
(0.3, 0.1)	.480±.046	.490±.041	.371±.042	.405±.045	.114±.002	.501±.037
Avg. F_1	.413±.051	.425±.050	.310±.042	.341±.050	.170±.014	.433±.047

Table 2. Average f_ω scores (higher is better, see Theorem 1) in the setup of Table 1.

(p_-, p_+)	Algorithm 1/f_ω PK-CCN	Algorithm 2/F_1 PK-CCN	Algorithm 2/F_1 CU-CCN	G-score [25] CU-CCN	CCN-blind F_1	Algorithm 2/F_1 CK-CCN
(0.5, 0.1)	7.16±1.07	6.99±1.09	5.57±1.27	6.61±1.26	2.79±0.90	7.16±1.08
(0.5, 0.25)	3.85±1.17	3.83±1.20	2.70±1.07	3.15±1.24	1.75±0.86	3.88±1.16
(0.2, 0.2)	12.79±1.13	12.59±1.19	12.01±1.22	12.25±1.34	7.02±1.43	12.76±1.09
(0.4, 0.4)	2.90±1.15	2.90±1.17	2.27±1.16	2.25±1.25	1.65±1.01	2.94±1.12
(0.1, 0.3)	15.06±1.20	14.83±1.20	14.74±1.23	14.60±1.29	12.87±1.38	14.90±1.21
(0.3, 0.1)	11.91±1.09	11.66±1.13	10.66±1.21	11.27±1.23	4.88±1.09	11.89±1.05
avg. f_ω	8.95±1.13	8.80±1.16	7.99±1.20	8.35±1.27	5.16±1.11	8.92±1.12

The additionally improvement of also knowing p_+ has a much smaller magnitude (Algorithm 2: $F_1 = 0.433$ in CK-CCN versus $F_1 = 0.425$ in PK-CCN) and this improvement is *not* statistically significant in 4 out of 6 noise configurations.

We recognize that our Algorithm 1 significantly looses against Algorithm 2 in half of the noise configurations. We attribute this observation to the fact that Fig. 4 and Table 1 present an evaluation in terms of the F_1 score, which Algorithm 2 optimizes directly. If we replace the F_1 evaluation with an f_ω evaluation, as presented in Table 2 and in the supplementary material, we see that our methods can frequently win against the baselines. Evaluating in terms of the f_ω score has the advantage that *no clean labels are required* during the evaluation. This advantage is crucial in some use cases of CCN learning, such as the detection of gamma ray sources in astroparticle physics.

5.4 Case Study: Detection of the Crab Nebula

We now detect the Crab Nebula, a bright supernova remnant, in IACT data. In particular, we analyze the open data sample[4] of the FACT telescope [4], a small IACT located on the La Palma island, Spain. As motivated in Sect. 2, we want to predict the true "gamma" and "hadron" classes, but only have access to the noisy "on" and "off" labels. The data set represents 21 682 telescope recordings by 22 features that are extracted from the raw telescope data [7]. The standard operation mode of FACT chooses $R = 5$ "off" regions, which yields $p_- = 1/6$ or

---

[4] https://factdata.app.tu-dortmund.de/.

equivalently $\omega = 1/5$. We compare the same CCN learning methods as before, but need to exclude the privileged CK-CCN method because we have no prior knowledge of p_+.

This time, we compare all thresholding methods on scoring functions $h :$ $\mathcal{X} \to \mathbb{R}$ that are trained with two different training sets. In particular, we use random forests as scoring functions and train them using:

real data: the first training set consists of a large, closed sample of the real FACT data, totalling 94 968 recordings that are disjunct from the open testing sample. Like all real IACT data, our large sample is only labeled in terms of CCN noisy labels.

simulated data: we obtain the second training set from a computationally expensive simulation of FACT. This data source yields the state-of-the-art classifier[5] for this telescope. Notably, the state-of-the-art also takes into account the CCN labels by optimizing its decision threshold through Algorithm 1 [3]; only the scoring function is trained from simulated data.

The high computational cost of the simulation motivates using the real IACT data not only for threshold optimization, but also for learning the underlying scoring function. Due to a previously lacking connection between IACT data and CCN theory, however, astroparticle physicists have not yet considered the opportunity of learning solely from real IACT data.

Without having clean ground-truth labels for our test set, which is a typical limitation of machine learning for IACTs, we can report the real-world performance of our models only in terms of the test statistic f_ω and not in terms of supervised measures like the F_1 score or accuracy. Fortunately, f_ω supports evaluating classifiers without clean labels. Moreover, f_ω is a conventional performance metric in astroparticle physics. Higher values indicate that the IACT would be able to detect the Crab Nebula even with less data; therefore, comparing f_ω values is meaningful beyond a mere reject/accept decision of the corresponding hypothesis test.

Discussion: The average values and standard deviations across 20 repetitions of the experiment are displayed in Table 3. We see that the CCN-trained approaches consistently outperform the costly simulation-trained approaches.

Interpretability: We conduct another experiment in which we artificially remove all "on"-labeled instances from the data set. We then incorrectly label some of the "off" instances as being "on" instances. These fake reassignments are meant to break the correspondence between clean and noisy labels and should therefore render CCN learning infeasible. Table 4 demonstrates that our proposed algorithms produce f_ω values close to zero, as is desired. These values convey that no strong classifier can be learnt from the fake noisy labels. The fact that our algorithms maximize f_ω does not result in an over-estimation of f_ω.

---

[5] https://github.com/fact-project/open_crab_sample_analysis.

Table 3. f_ω scores (higher is better, see Definition 2) for the open Crab data of the FACT telescope. We evaluate the threshold tuning methods by training the underlying scoring functions either with CCN labels (left) or with simulated clean labels (right).

method	real data (CCN)	simulated data (clean, SOTA)
Algorithm 1 (f_ω, PK-CCN)	**27.08±0.22**	26.63±0.01
Algorithm 2 (F_1, PK-CCN)	**27.07±0.24**	26.07±0.73
Algorithm 2 (F_1, CU-CCN)	**26.88±0.23**	16.32±0.02
G-score [25] (CU-CCN)	**26.99±0.25**	26.63±0.03
CCN-blind F_1	**19.56±1.01**	16.35±0.11

Table 4. f_ω scores for the FACT data with artificially removed "on" instances. Due to the removal, small values are desirable.

method	$f_\omega(N_+^\theta, N_-^\theta)$
Algorithm 1 (f_ω, PK-CCN)	1.279±0.926
Algorithm 2 (F_1, PK-CCN)	0.503±0.570
Algorithm 2 (F_1, CU-CCN)	0.000±0.000
G-score [25] (CU-CCN)	0.087±0.153
CCN-blind F_1	0.000±0.000

6   Conclusion and Outlook

We have introduced partially-known class-conditional label noise (PK-CCN), a novel learning task that appears in the analysis of IACT data. PK-CCN is characterized by the availability of precise knowledge of exactly one of the two class-wise label flip probabilities. Besides this characteristic, PK-CCN inherits all properties of general CCN learning.

We have proposed f_ω as an objective function to tackle PK-CCN in noise-aware decision thresholding. We have further adapted existing CCN methods to the PK-CCN setting and we have demonstrated the effectiveness of all our approaches using an extensive set of noise configurations and data sets.

A case study from astroparticle physics, the field that originally inspired our algorithms, demonstrates the practical value of our proposals. In this field, our methods are capable of learning from real IACT data instead of following the common practice of learning from simulated data. Due to this capability, our methods achieve improvements in predictive performance and a reduction in computational requirements.

Future work should explore other use cases of PK-CCN. We expect potential occurrences of this setting whenever the noisy labels are based on some characteristic of the data (like the "on" and "off" regions of IACT recordings) that is precisely known for the clean negative class (like the uniform distribution of hadrons over all regions).

Acknowledgments. This research was partly funded by the Federal Ministry of Education and Research of Germany and the state of North-Rhine Westphalia as part of the Lamarr-Institute for Machine Learning and Artificial Intelligence.

Ethical Implications. Label noise, if not mitigated, can easily lead to the learning of incorrect prediction models, which is a particular danger for safety-critical applications. Moreover, label noise can perpetuate and amplify existing societal biases if appropriate countermeasures are not taken. The existence of these risks crucially requires research on the effects and the mitigation of different kinds of label noise. In this regard, we contribute a characterization and mitigation of PK-CCN, a novel instance of class-conditional label noise.

Successful mitigation techniques can tempt stakeholders to take the risks of label noise even if alternative solutions exist. In fact, we advocate the employment of PK-CCN data in a use case where training data is otherwise obtained from simulations. In spite of such alternative solutions, a careful consideration of all risks is morally required. In our use case, the risks of learning from simulations are still vague while we have clearly described the effects of PK-CCN and have mitigated them through learning algorithms that are proven to be consistent. Our algorithms result in a reduction of computational requirements, which translates to a reduction in energy consumption. This improvement is a desirable property for combating climate change. We emphasize that other cases of label noise can involve risks that require different considerations.

Astroparticle physics is a research field that is concerned with advancing our understanding of the cosmos and fundamental physics. While a deep understanding of the cosmos can inspire us to appreciate nature and take better care of our planet, the understanding of fundamental physics can eventually contribute to the development of technologies that improve the lives of many.

References

1. Acharya, B.S., et al.: Science with the Cherenkov telescope array. World Sci. (2018)
2. Actis, M., Agnetta, G., Aharonian, F., Akhperjanian, A., Aleksić, J., et al.: Design concepts for the Cherenkov telescope array CTA: an advanced facility for ground-based high-energy gamma-ray astronomy. Exper. Astron. **32**(3), 193–316 (2011). https://doi.org/10.1007/s10686-011-9247-0
3. Aharonian, F., Akhperjanian, A., Bazer-Bachi, A., Beilicke, M., Benbow, W., et al.: Observations of the crab nebula with HESS. Astron. Astrophys. **457**(3), 899–915 (2006)
4. Anderhub, H., Backes, M., Biland, A., Boccone, V., Braun, I., et al.: Design and operation of FACT-the first G-APD Cherenkov telescope. J. Inst. **8**(06) (2013). https://doi.org/10.1088/1748-0221/8/06/p06008
5. Blum, A., Mitchell, T.M.: Combining labeled and unlabeled data with co-training. In: Conference on Computing Learning Theory, pp. 92–100. ACM (1998). https://doi.org/10.1145/279943.279962
6. Bock, R., et al.: Methods for multidimensional event classification: a case study using images from a Cherenkov gamma-ray telescope. Nucl. Inst. and Meth. in Phys. Res. Sec. A **516**(2-3), 511–528 (2004). https://doi.org/10.1016/j.nima.2003.08.157

7. Bockermann, C., et al.: Online analysis of high-volume data streams in astroparticle physics. In: Bifet, A., et al. (eds.) ECML PKDD 2015. LNCS (LNAI), vol. 9286, pp. 100–115. Springer, Cham (2015). https://doi.org/10.1007/978-3-319-23461-8_7

8. Buja, A., Stuetzle, W., Shen, Y.: Loss functions for binary class probability estimation and classification: structure and applications. Tech. rep., University of Pennsylvania (2005)

9. Demšar, J.: Statistical comparisons of classifiers over multiple data sets. J. Mach. Learn. Res. **7**, 1–30 (2006)

10. Engel, R., Heck, D., Pierog, T.: Extensive air showers and hadronic interactions at high energy. Ann. Rev. Nucl. Part. Sci. **61**(1), 467–489 (2011). https://doi.org/10.1146/annurev.nucl.012809.104544

11. Falkenburg, B., Rhode, W.: From ultra rays to astroparticles: a historical introduction to astroparticle physics. Springer (2012). https://doi.org/10.1007/978-94-007-5422-5

12. Fernández, A., García, S., Galar, M., Prati, R.C., Krawczyk, B., Herrera, F.: Learning from Imbalanced Data Sets. Springer, Cham (2018). https://doi.org/10.1007/978-3-319-98074-4

13. Funk, S.: Ground- and space-based gamma-ray astronomy. Ann. Rev. Nucl. Part. Sci. **65**(1), 245–277 (2015). https://doi.org/10.1146/annurev-nucl-102014-022036

14. Ghosh, A., Manwani, N., Sastry, P.S.: Making risk minimization tolerant to label noise. Neurocomput. **160**, 93–107 (2015). https://doi.org/10.1016/j.neucom.2014.09.081

15. Han, B., et al.: Co-teaching: robust training of deep neural networks with extremely noisy labels. Adv. in Neur. Inform. Process. Syst., 8536–8546 (2018)

16. Koyejo, O., Natarajan, N., Ravikumar, P., Dhillon, I.S.: Consistent binary classification with generalized performance metrics. Adv. in Neur. Inform. Process. Syst., 2744–2752 (2014)

17. Lemaitre, G., Nogueira, F., Aridas, C.K.: Imbalanced-learn: a Python toolbox to tackle the curse of imbalanced datasets in machine learning. J. Mach. Learn. Res. **18**, 17:1–17:5 (2017)

18. Li, T.P., Ma, Y.Q.: Analysis methods for results in gamma-ray astronomy. Astrophys. J. **272**, 317–324 (1983)

19. Li, X., Liu, T., Han, B., Niu, G., Sugiyama, M.: Provably end-to-end label-noise learning without anchor points. In: International Conference on Machine Learning Research, vol. 139, pp. 6403–6413. PMLR (2021)

20. Ma, X., Huang, H., Wang, Y., Romano, S., Erfani, S.M., Bailey, J.: Normalized loss functions for deep learning with noisy labels. In: International Conference on Machine Learning Proceedings of Machine Learning Research, vol. 119, pp. 6543–6553. PMLR (2020)

21. Martschei, D., Feindt, M., Honc, S., Wagner-Kuhr, J.: Advanced event reweighting using multivariate analysis. J. of Phys.: Conf. Ser. **368** (2012). https://doi.org/10.1088/1742-6596/368/1/012028

22. Menon, A.K., Narasimhan, H., Agarwal, S., Chawla, S.: On the statistical consistency of algorithms for binary classification under class imbalance. In: International Conference on Machine Learning JMLR Workshop and Conference Proceedings, vol. 28, pp. 603–611 (2013)

23. Menon, A.K., van Rooyen, B., Natarajan, N.: Learning from binary labels with instance-dependent noise. Mach. Learn. **107**(8–10), 1561–1595 (2018). https://doi.org/10.1007/s10994-018-5715-3

24. Menon, A.K., van Rooyen, B., Ong, C.S., Williamson, R.C.: Learning from corrupted binary labels via class-probability estimation. In: International Conference on Machine Learning JMLR Workshop and Conference Proceedings, vol. 37, pp. 125–134 (2015)
25. Mithal, V., Nayak, G., Khandelwal, A., Kumar, V., Oza, N.C., Nemani, R.R.: RAPT: rare class prediction in absence of true labels. IEEE Trans. Knowl. Data Eng. **29**(11), 2484–2497 (2017). https://doi.org/10.1109/TKDE.2017.2739739
26. Narasimhan, H., Vaish, R., Agarwal, S.: On the statistical consistency of plugin classifiers for non-decomposable performance measures. In: Advances in Neural Information Processing Systems, pp. 1493–1501 (2014)
27. Natarajan, N., Dhillon, I.S., Ravikumar, P., Tewari, A.: Learning with noisy labels. In: Advances in Neural Information Processing Systems, pp. 1196–1204 (2013)
28. Northcutt, C.G., Jiang, L., Chuang, I.L.: Confident learning: estimating uncertainty in dataset labels. J. Artif. Intell. Res. **70**, 1373–1411 (2021). https://doi.org/10.1613/jair.1.12125
29. Patrini, G., Rozza, A., Menon, A.K., Nock, R., Qu, L.: Making deep neural networks robust to label noise: a loss correction approach. In: Conference on Computer Vision and Pattern Recognition, pp. 2233–2241. IEEE (2017). https://doi.org/10.1109/CVPR.2017.240
30. Scott, C., Blanchard, G., Handy, G.: Classification with asymmetric label noise: consistency and maximal denoising. In: Annual Conference on Learning Theory JMLR Workshop and Conference Proceedings, vol. 30, pp. 489–511. JMLR.org (2013)
31. Tridon, D.B., et al.: The MAGIC-II gamma-ray stereoscopic telescope system. Nucl. Inst. Meth. in Phys. Res. Sec. A **623**(1), 437–439 (2010). https://doi.org/10.1016/j.nima.2010.03.028
32. Wakely, S.P., Horan, D.: TeVCat: an online catalog for very high energy gamma-ray astronomy. In: International Cosmic Ray Conference, vol. 3, pp. 1341–1344 (2008)
33. Xia, X., Liu, T., Wang, N., Han, B., Gong, C., et al.: Are anchor points really indispensable in label-noise learning? In: Advances in Neural Information Processing Systems, pp. 6835–6846 (2019)
34. Yao, Y., Liu, T., Han, B., Gong, M., Deng, J., et al.: Dual T: Reducing estimation error for transition matrix in label-noise learning. In: Advances in Neural Information Processing Systems (2020)
35. Ye, N., Chai, K.M.A., Lee, W.S., Chieu, H.L.: Optimizing F-measure: a tale of two approaches. In: International Conference on Machine Learning Omnipress (2012)

A Baseline Generative Probabilistic Model for Weakly Supervised Learning

Georgios Papadopoulos$^{(\boxtimes)}$ (ID), Fran Silavong, and Sean Moran

JPMorgan Chase & Co., 25 Bank St, London E14 5JP, UK
georgios.papadopoulos@jpmorgan.com

Abstract. Finding relevant and high-quality datasets to train machine learning models is a major bottleneck for practitioners. Furthermore, to address ambitious real-world use-cases there is usually the requirement that the data come labelled with high-quality annotations that can facilitate the training of a supervised model. Manually labelling data with high-quality labels is generally a time-consuming and challenging task and often this turns out to be the bottleneck in a machine learning project. Weakly Supervised Learning (WSL) approaches have been developed to alleviate the annotation burden by offering an automatic way of assigning approximate labels (pseudo-labels) to unlabelled data based on heuristics, distant supervision and knowledge bases. We apply probabilistic generative latent variable models (PLVMs), trained on heuristic labelling representations of the original dataset, as an accurate, fast and cost-effective way to generate pseudo-labels. We show that the PLVMs achieve state-of-the-art performance across four datasets. For example, they achieve 22% points higher F1 score than Snorkel in the *class-imbalanced* Spouse dataset. PLVMs are plug-and-playable and are a drop-in replacement to existing WSL frameworks (e.g. Snorkel) or they can be used as baseline high-performance models for more complicated algorithms, giving practitioners a compelling accuracy boost.

Keywords: Weakly Supervised Learning · Generative Models · Probabilistic Models

1 Introduction

In recent years, weakly supervised learning (WSL) has emerged as an area of increasing interest among machine learning practitioners and researchers. This interest has been driven by the need to automate the process of applying deep learning models to unlabelled real-world data, thus making manual annotations unnecessary and expensive. For example, medical doctors may wish to use machine learning (ML) models to improve the detection of intracranial hemorrhage (ICH) on head computed tomography (CT) scans [24], but current datasets are often large and unlabelled, making the application of ML the models difficult.

Supported by organization JPMorgan Chase & Co.

Various research teams, including Snorkel and Flying Squid [19–21,34], have developed methods to address this labelling problem, with the overarching goal of reducing the cost of labelling for large datasets by hand. These WSL methods automate the otherwise tedious and costly manual labelling process by sourcing prior information from Subject Matter Experts (SMEs), which is used to create labelling functions λ that are applied to the data. The output of this approach is typically a binary sparse matrix (labelling matrix) Λ.

Overall, the increasing interest in WSL reflects the potential of this approach to enable the more efficient and effective use of machine learning models on real-world data, even when labelled data is scarce or expensive to obtain. By leveraging SME guidance and prior knowledge, WSL methods offer a promising avenue for automating the labelling process, reducing costs, and enabling more widespread adoption of ML models in a range of applications.

We present a straightforward algorithm to create dichotomous classes on unlabelled datasets. Like [20], our method utilizes labelling functions λ derived from Subject Matter Expert (SME) domain knowledge to programmatically annotate previously unlabelled data. The resulting annotations are represented as a labelling matrix Λ. Our approach relies on the assumption that the sparse input matrix Λ contains sufficient information for robust model creation. Specifically, we propose to use a probabilistic generative latent variable model, Factor Analysis (FA), to map dependencies among the elements of the labelling matrix and generate a 1-dimensional latent factor z. We dichotomize the latent variable z using the median and assign each group of observations to a binary class.

Our approach addresses the negative impact of class imbalance and label abstentions on existing WSL methods. We provide empirical evidence for the superior performance of the FA model compared to the state-of-the-art model, Snorkel, across three publicly available datasets and one internal curated dataset. We also compare the performance of FA with two more complex generative probabilistic latent variable models: Gaussian process latent variable models (GPLVM) with Sparse Variational Gaussian Processes (SVGP) and Variational Inference - Factor Analysis (VI-FA).

We show that FA as a WSL model outperforms other methods in Table 3, where it achieved accuracy of 95% for the source code classification task, 86% in the YouTube Spam dataset, 86% in the Spouse dataset, and 65% in Goodreads dataset.

To summarise, the contribution of this paper is the following:

- **Impact of class imbalance:** We study the impact of class imbalance and label abstentions on existing WSL models [21]. This is not only an academic problem but also a common occurrence in real-world data and applied cases. We empirically illustrate this negative effect on three publicly available datasets, YouTube Spam dataset [1], Spouse dataset [21], and Goodreads dataset [29,30].
- **Stronger performance:** As a solution, we propose to leverage FA for a new WSL method that outperforms current state-of-the-art models, including Snorkel [21], as well as the benchmark probabilistic algorithms

GPLVM-SVGP and VI-FA in terms of *both* performance and resilience to class imbalance.

- **Robustness and Causality:** We demonstrate the robustness of the proposed FA model under small datasets, class-imbalance and label abstentions. Also, it is proven that FA models offer causality between the labelling functions and the true labels [9].
- **Industrial Applicability:** We applied our method on internal data (JPMorgan) and evaluated our model in real-world cases (source code) by communicating with SMEs (firm engineers).We show our method scales well in industrial settings, is plug-and-play, and highly robust and accurate.

2 Related Work

WSL, as a research area, has become widely popular and has experienced a wealth of publications; with many culminating to end-to-end production systems [19,21]. Some real-world examples, from a diversified domain, which WSL methods have been applied, include healthcare [8,10,11,24,25], human posturing and ergonomic studies [5,14,35], multimedia and sound [15,18,23], dataset querying [33], in business studies and behavioural analysis [12,16,27], and autonomous driving [31].

In our paper, we draw motivation from recent research on data programming and matrix completion methods for WSL. Specifically, in [22] the authors use conditionally independent and user defined labelling functions with a probabilistic model optimised using the log-maximum likelihood and gradient descent methods. The true class label for a data point is modeled as a latent variable that generates the observed, noisy labels. After fitting the parameters of this generative model on unlabeled data, a distribution over the latent, true labels can then be inferred. [2] expand the previous research by adding an **L1** regulariser to the [22]'s formula. The team created a first end-to-end programmatic pipeline by incorporating findings from the two previous papers, named Snorkel [19,20,34]. They also replaced the sampling of the posterior from a graphical model with a matrix completion approach [19].

The main shortcomings of the probabilistic approach that [2,19,22] are using are that is mathematically quite complex (for example the works of [2,22]). Also, challenging to implement as a plug-and-play solution on industrial scale projects. Finally, as we demonstrate in Sects. 3 and 5, fails to perform under class-imbalance and small datasets.

One way to address the class imbalance performance problem and simplify the algorithms came from [28]. The authors presented a structure learning method that relies on robust Principal Component Analysis (PCA) to estimate the dependencies among the different weakly supervision sources. They show that the dependency structure of generative models significantly affects the quality of the generated labels. This, thematically, is quite similar to our work. The main differentiating factor is that in [28] they use PCA as a method to replace the lower rank and the sparse matrix from their previous work [20]; whereas, we propose to use FA as the *entire* WSL model.

Our approach, compared to [28], allows users to plug-and-play any latent probabilistic models, without further modification. Another major difference is that our approach (FA) considers independent diagonal noise compared to spherical noise of the PCA, therefore as a model is better suited to map causality amongst the labelling functions (λ) and the ground truth [9].

3   Model Formulation

In this paper we follow a two-step approach. Initially, we utilise heuristic labelling function techniques based on [19] to create a sparse labelling matrix Λ. In the second step, we map the relationships (Fig. 1) among the labelling functions using FA. Our approach has the benefit that can be expanded using any probabilistic generative latent variable model such as GPLVM.

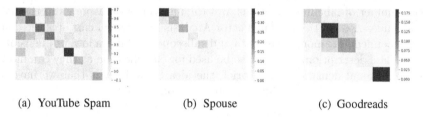

| (a) YouTube Spam | (b) Spouse | (c) Goodreads |

Fig. 1. The covariance heatmaps of the three labelling matrices (λ). Each heatmap is a dataset. We observe that the labelling functions Λ are independent. There is no strong relationship amongst them. But FA (and PLVM in general) are able to capture the causal relationship and approximate a true latent factor.

3.1   Labelling Functions

Labelling functions λ, as described in [22], are user-defined programmatic items that each incorporate the SME's knowledge in a binary form $\lambda \in \{0, 1\}$ or $\{-1\}$ if the function λ is considered as abstain; where no relevant information is present. The goal of this process is to build a large set of approximate labels [2]. Effectively, rather than hand-labelling training data, SMEs can write labelling functions instead. To this end, as a data programming approach, labelling functions offer model flexibility by programmatically expressing various weakly supervision sources, including patterns, heuristics, external knowledge bases, and more.

3.2   Factor Analysis

Our objective is to enhance the generative methodology underlying Snorkel [21] with a more straightforward approaching. In a related work, [28] applied a robust PCA to improve Snorkel results. However, our method differs from theirs in that they used PCA to initialize parameters for their probabilistic model, whereas we replace the scalable matrix completion algorithm with a probabilistic generative latent variable model (PLVM).

The use of generative latent models to extract underlying components from data has been extensively researched and documented [3,4,6,17]. A standard generative latent model is Factor Analysis (FA), which is closely related to Probabilistic PCA [26]. By leveraging the FA model, we aim to simplify the underlying probabilistic complexity of Snorkel and improve its performance on unlabelled datasets.

3.3   Weakly Supervision with Factor Analysis

Given an observed dataset $X \in \mathbb{R}^{n \times d}$, we utilise the labelling function λ capabilities from Snorkel [21] to create a binary labelling matrix Λ. Labelling functions are user-defined programmatic items that scan the underlying data X and result in the labelling matrix $\Lambda(X)$. The labelling matrix is a $n \times m$ sparse matrix with m the number of labelling functions λ, n the number of data-points in the data X and values $\Lambda \in \{0, 1, -1\}$. The Factor Analysis (FA) model captures the dominant dependencies amongst the data and subsequently finds a lower dimensional probabilistic description. FA can also be used for classification as they can model class conditional densities [6]. In brief, the idea behind FA is that we have an observed dataset Λ that is a linear representation of a latent factor z

$$\Lambda = Wz + c + \epsilon \tag{1}$$

W is the loading matrix with dimensions $m \times k$ with k the dimensions of the latent factor z with $k \ll d$, c is a centred constant bias term and $\epsilon = \mathcal{N}(\epsilon | 0, \Psi)$ is the Gaussian distributed noise of the model with Ψ the $m \times m$ diagonal matrix. As a reminder m is the number of columns/labelling functions in our observed data Λ and n the number of observed data-points. Probabilistically, this formula takes the form of the likelihood $p(\Lambda | z)$:

$$p(\Lambda | z) = \mathcal{N}(\Lambda | Wz + c, \Psi)$$
$$\propto exp(-\frac{1}{2}(\Lambda - Wz - c)^T \Psi^{-1}(\Lambda - Wz - c)) \tag{2}$$

the prior $p(z)$ of the Bayesian model is:

$$p(z) = \mathcal{N}(z | 0, I) \propto exp(-\frac{1}{2} z^T z) \tag{3}$$

This means that the centre of the factor z, due to its prior, will be constraint around 0. The next step to construct a full Bayesian model is to add the marginal $p(\Lambda)$:

$$p(\Lambda) = \int p(\Lambda | z) p(z) dz = \int \mathcal{N}(\Lambda | c, WW^T + \Psi) \tag{4}$$

The posterior $p(z|\Lambda)$:

$$p(z|\Lambda) = \frac{p(\Lambda|z)p(z)}{p(\Lambda)} = \mathcal{N}(z|m, V)$$
$$m = GW^T\Psi^{-1}(\Lambda - c) \tag{5}$$
$$V = G + \mathbb{E}[z]\mathbb{E}[z]^T$$

with $G = (I + W^T\Psi^{-1}W)^{-1}$.

The log-likelihood of this model is:

$$\mathcal{L}(\Lambda|W, z, \Psi) = -\frac{1}{2}trace((\Lambda - c)^T\Sigma^{-1}(\Lambda - c))$$
$$- \frac{N}{2}log(2\pi) - \frac{1}{2}log|\Sigma| \tag{6}$$

with $\Sigma = WW^T + \Psi$; where Ψ the $m \times m$ noise diagonal matrix, WW^T the $m \times m$ weights (loadings) matrix, and Σ the $m \times m$ covariance matrix of the labelling data Λ.

Thus, the variance of the observed data (Λ) consists of a rank one component WW^T originating from the joint dependence of the indicators on the latent factor z. Together with a full rank diagonal matrix Ψ, arising from the presence of noise, as it is an approximation of the latent variable.

3.4   Other Probabilistic Generative Latent Variable Models

In addition to Factor Analysis, we have also explored two alternative models in the family of PLVM. Specifically, we built a variational inference version of the Factor Analysis (VI-FA) using Tensorflow and the Adam optimiser, and we also put together a version of the GPLVM and SVGP models from GPflow.

VI-FA Model: For this model, we followed a similar process as for the probabilistic PCA [6] but using an independent variance for each data dimension m (see Eq. 2). To infer the posterior distribution of the latent variable model we utilise variational inference. We approximate the posterior $p(W, z, \Psi|\Lambda)$ (see Eq. 5) using a variational distribution $q(W, z, \Psi)$ with parameters θ. To find θ we minimise the KL divergence between the approximate distribution q and the posterior, $KL(q(W, z, \Psi)|p(W, z, \Psi|\Lambda))$, which is to maximise the ELBO.

GPLVM Model: For the latter method, we trained a GPLVM model on the labelling matrix (Λ). By its nature, a GPLVM model can be interpreted as a generalisation of probabilistic PCA [6], where instead of optimising the linear mappings (W in Eq. 1) we optimise the latent variable z. In other words, it maps the connection between latent data z and observable data Λ using Gaussian-process priors. Overall, the log-likelihood from Eq. 6 becomes

$$\mathcal{L}(\Lambda|W, z, K) = -\frac{1}{2}tr((\Lambda - c)K^{-1}(\Lambda^T - c))$$
$$- \frac{N}{2}log(2\pi) - \frac{1}{2}log|K| \tag{7}$$

with K as the Gaussian process kernel.

During inference, the model accepts new (test) latent z^*-data and predicts the observable data Λ^* by computing the two moments, mean and standard deviation. But, for our approach we need to be able to accept new observable data Λ^* and predict the latent z^*-data. Similar to any other non-linear kernel-based model it is difficult for the GPLVM to be used as a dimensionality reduction tool that accepts test data. This is because it is challenging to invert the mapping between z and observable X (or Λ in our case). Various approaches have been proposed that involve learned pre-images and auxiliary models [7,13,32].

After training the GPLVM (Radial Basis Function kernel), we use an auxiliary Bernoulli regression model (SVGP) with Matern52 kernel to create the mapping between the latent target variable z and the covariates of the regression model Λ. Then, for new data Λ^* we use the SVGP model for predicting z^*.

4 Datasets

In this section, we describe the *four* datasets used to evaluate the model performance between Snorkel and PLVMs. Three of them are publicly available and commonly used in the field of weakly supervised learning, and one is internally sourced. Table 1 provides the summary statistics.

Table 1. Dataset Statistics. λ is the labelling function. Absent, shows the number of rows n in the labelling matrix Λ that have all the columns m assigned as absent $\{-1\}$. *For the Spouse dataset we do not have the target values for the training data, only for the test sub-set. In the table we use the test data information. For the training data ($n = 22,254$) the number of absent rows is $n = 16,520$ or 74%.

		Number of			
		Positive	Negative	Absent	λ
Source Code	Balanced	127	123	0	3
Spam	Balanced	831	755	230	9
Spouse	Unbalanced*	218	2,483	1,951	9
Goodreads	Unbalanced	514,778	281,293	691,795	5

YouTube Spam Comments: We use YouTube comments dataset, originally introduced in [1]. The comments were collected via the YouTube API from five of the ten most viewed videos on YouTube in the first half of 2015. The training data have $n = 1,586$ YouTube video messages and the test data size is $n = 250$. [21] created the labelling functions that include 5 keyword-based, 1 regular expression-based, 1 heuristic, 1 complex preprocessors, and 2 third-party model rules.

Spouse Dataset: This dataset is constructed by [21] to identify mentions of spouse relationships in a set of news articles from the Signal Media. The data is split between $n = 22,254$ training samples and $n = 2,701$ testing samples. There are 9 heuristic and NLP related labelling functions[1]. The ground truth labels for the training set are not available. Therefore, we are unable to check for class imbalance or the accuracy of the model on the training set.

Goodreads Dataset: We use the Goodreads dataset, from [29,30]. This data is a smaller sample from the original dataset and contains $n = 794,294$ training records and $n = 44,336$ test records, collected from $876,145$ Goodreads' users (with detailed meta-data). We followed the same experiment settings[2] defined by Snorkel, where the task is to predict whether a user favours the book or not given the interaction and metadata as context.

Source Code Dataset: In addition to the natural language based tasks, we have also created a pipeline and evaluated our proposed method in an industrial setting at JPMorgan; on a binary classification task in the field of Machine Learning on Source Code (MLonCode). The objective was to predict the label of each function/method within a set of source code repositories. To the best of our knowledge, this is the first attempt of applying weakly supervised learning on source code. We internally curated $n = 250$ functions and asked experienced senior software engineers to construct three labelling functions. The three labelling functions represent empirical methods that the engineers would have used if they were to manually assess the quality of the code of the function/method. This results in a class balanced source code dataset as indicated in Table 1.

5   Experiments

Our aim is to validate the three main hypothesis of the paper: 1) the factor analysis model can be used for binary classification tasks; 2) the labelling matrix that contains the observable variables (Λ) of the model is the sufficient statistics of the model; 3) using PLVMs we achieve better results compared to existing methodologies. We ran our experiments using the following configurations: MacBook Pro 2019, Python 3.7.10, Snorkel 0.9.7, Sklearn 1.7.0, Tensorflow 2.6.0, Tensorflow-probability 0.13.0. The FA method that is used in Sklearn follows the SVD approach from [3, p. 448]. For the alternative models that we used, Variational Inference Factor Analysis (VI-FA) and Gaussian process latent variable models - Sparse Variational Gaussian process (GPLVM-SVGP), we relied on Tensorflow and GPflow 2.2.1. All our models and data shuffling were set with random key {123}.

---

[1] https://github.com/snorkel-team/snorkel-tutorials/blob/master/spouse/spouse_demo.ipynb.

[2] https://github.com/snorkel-team/snorkel-tutorials/blob/master/recsys/recsys_tutorial.ipynb.

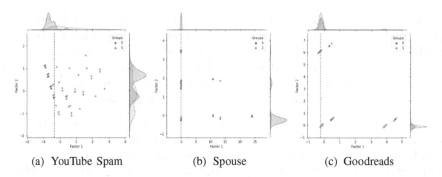

(a) YouTube Spam   (b) Spouse   (c) Goodreads

Fig. 2. Jointplots between the two factors from the FA model. The top and right sides of the plots illustrate the distribution of each factor for the respective test set. The dotted line shows the median of the first factor, which is the one we used to dichotomise it and infer the classes during inference. The median is calculated on the training data factor. We observe that utilizing the first factor is sufficient to separate the two labels (blue and orange). (Color figure online)

Selection of Classification Threshold: To create binary values from the latent factor z we tested a series of thresholding methods. The best approach was to dichotomise the normally distributed test factor $z*$ with a median computed from the training factor z. Figure 2 shows that the first factor's median (dotted line) of the YouTube Spam data divides the two separate groups accurately. For the Spouse and the Goodreads datasets, the median threshold again separates the two groups but not as effectively as in the previous case. Table 2 shows the performance of using median, mean and Youden's J statistics as the threshold, where median achieves the best results. Thus, we propose to use median as the thresholding method.

Table 2. Threshold selection. The table shows the accuracy scores for each threshold choice. The CDF threshold was calculated using the Youden's J statistic after we transformed the test $z*$ with the normal CDF.

	Median	Mean	CDF
Source Code	0.95	0.92	0.95
Spam	0.86	0.74	0.85
Spouse	0.86	0.92	0.90
Goodreads	0.63	0.39	0.62

YouTube Spam Comments: The YouTube Spam data [1] is a balanced dataset, with positive class numbers (1) $n = 831$ and negative class numbers (0) $n = 755$ (Table 1). The Snorkel and FA models achieve close results, with accuracy 86% for both methods, precision 83% for Snorkel and 85% for FA, recall 88% and 84%, and F1 score 86% and 85%.

Table 3. Accuracy, precision, recall, and F1 metrics for Source Code Classification, YouTube spam, spouse and Goodreads datasets, comparing the Snorkel approach against the FA WSL model. Each model is trained on the training dataset and evaluated on the test set. Bold numbers indicates the best performance.

	Source Code		Spam Dataset (NLP)		Spouse Dataset (NLP)		Goodreads Dataset (Recommender systems)	
	Snorkel	Factor Analysis	Snorkel	Factor Analysis	Snorkel	Factor Analysis	Snorkel	Factor Analysis
Accuracy	0.92	**0.95**	**0.86**	**0.86**	0.54	**0.86**	0.53	**0.63**
Precision	0.90	**0.97**	0.83	**0.85**	0.12	**0.32**	**0.66**	0.65
Recall	**0.95**	0.93	**0.88**	0.84	**0.72**	0.64	0.56	**0.95**
F1	0.93	**0.95**	**0.86**	0.85	0.20	**0.42**	0.61	**0.77**

Table 4. Accuracy, precision, recall, and F1 metrics for Source Code Classification, YouTube spam, spouse and Goodreads datasets, comparing the FA WSL model against the VI-FA and GPLVM-SVGP models. The performance has been measured on the test sample of each dataset. Bold numbers indicates the best performance.

	Source Code Classification			Spam Dataset (NLP)			Spouse Dataset (NLP)			Goodreads Dataset (Recommender systems)		
	Factor Analysis	VI-FA	GPLVM	Factor Analysis	VI-FA	GPLVM	Factor Analysis	VI-FA	GPLVM	Factor Analysis	VI-FA	GPLVM
Accuracy	**0.95**	0.92	0.92	**0.86**	0.70	0.82	**0.86**	0.78	0.09	**0.63**	0.60	**0.63**
Precision	**0.97**	0.89	0.89	0.85	**0.89**	0.79	**0.32**	0.22	0.08	**0.65**	0.64	0.64
Recall	0.93	**0.95**	**0.95**	0.84	0.42	**0.85**	0.64	0.70	**0.99**	0.95	0.89	**0.96**
F1	**0.95**	0.92	0.92	**0.85**	0.58	0.82	**0.42**	0.34	0.15	**0.77**	0.74	**0.77**

Spouse Dataset: In the Spouse dataset [21], the FA achieves much higher performance compared to the Snorkel model. The dataset suffers from *severe* class-imbalance and a large number of absent labelled classes, as shown in Table 1. Specifically, from the $n = 22,254$ training data, 74% or $n = 16,520$ observations have absent values ($\lambda = -1$) in all $m = 9$ labelling functions.

The FA model shows its strength on this type of dataset that have high number of absent items and experience class-imbalance. In terms of accuracy, Snorkel scores 54%, whereas our model attains an impressive 86%. On the other hand, in recall, Snorkel shows a score of 72% and our model 64% (Table 3).

Goodreads Dataset: This is the largest dataset we used for model training and predictions [29,30]. Similarly to Spouse data, Goodreads is a class-imbalanced dataset and it exhibits a considerable amount (87% of the observations) of absent labelled items (Table 1). In Table 3, FA beats Snorkel predictions on almost every classification metric, namely 10%+ accuracy, 1.69x recall and 16% higher F1 score, and achieves marginally lower precision (1%).

Source Code Classification: Table 3 shows the classification performance of Snorkel and FA when evaluated against the truth data. Specifically, the accuracy is 92% for Snorkel and 95% for the FA model; the precision is 90% for Snorkel and 97% for the FA; recall is 95% and 93% subsequently; and finally the F1 score is 93% for Snorkel and 95% for the FA.

Class Imbalance and Abstentions: To examine the relationship between model performance and class imbalance, we first quantify the class imbalance by computing the absolute percentage difference between positive and negative, $\frac{|n_{pos}-n_{neg}|}{n_{pos}+n_{neg}}$ of each dataset, where n_{pos} and n_{neg} refer to the number of positive and negative class respectively. We then compared this to the result stated in Table 3. In Fig. 3, we observe promising evidence to suggest that as the extent of class imbalance increases, the performance of Snorkel drops, whereas Factor Analysis model does not.

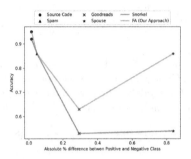

Fig. 3. Relation between the accuracy and absolute percentage difference of positive and negative classes representing the extent of class imbalance. We see evidence that the accuracy of Snorkel decreases with the extent of class imbalance, whereas Factor Analysis does not. FA also consistently outperforms Snorkel, when we compare the model accuracy for binary classification tasks on the four datasets: Youtube Spam (triangle), Spouse (star), Goodreads (cross), Internal Source Code (circle) and the extent of class imbalance.

The effect of class imbalance and abstentions can also be viewed in Fig. 2. In the Spouse *(a)* and in the Goodreads *(b)* figures, we observe that abstentions make more challenging for the model to dichotomise efficiently the classes. Nevertheless, the FA method performs much more accurately compared to Snorkel (Table 3) or the other two PLVM models (Table 4).

In general, abstentions and class-imbalance are two critical issues when we build a WSL pipeline. The probabilistic mechanism of FA, and how it maps the dependencies across the functions in the labelling matrix Λ, weaken the impact of these two problems significantly.

Robustness: We studied how the model performance changes when we vary the size of the training data. Figure 4 shows that Factor Analysis achieves a $1.7x$ and 14% higher accuracy in Spouse and Goodreads test set with only 10 training datapoints, and 4% higher in YouTube Spam test set with 30 training datapoints.

6   Benefits of the Model

The benefits of using the benchmark model to replace the pipeline of the Snorkel algorithm, include the speed, the robustness of the results on unbalanced

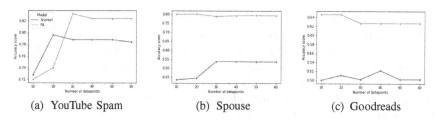

(a) YouTube Spam   (b) Spouse   (c) Goodreads

Fig. 4. Comparison of classification performance of Snorkel and Factor Analysis (our proposed approach) in terms of accuracy. We randomly selected n sample as the training set forming the labelling matrix Λ, where $n \in \{10, 20, 30, 40, 50, 60\}$ and evaluated against their respective test set. Factor Analysis achieves significant higher accuracy than Snorkel with merely 10 training samples in the Spouse and Goodreads datasets, and 30 training samples for the YouTube Spam dataset illustrating the robustness of our approach.

datasets, the causality that FA offers [9], and the explainability of the model compared to the Snorkel probabilistic approach. Explainability, as in terms of the FA model is a method that has been tested, evaluated, and used for years in the field of social sciences and the underlying mechanisms have been studied extensively. Finally, as we demonstrated in the evaluation of source code in JPMorgan, our approach can be easily integrated into existing machine learning workflows using standard widely-used libraries in Python (scikit) or R (psych). This allows users to leverage their existing knowledge and resources to quickly adopt and integrate the new framework into their applications.

7 Limitations

While the proposed method offers several benefits, there are some limitations that require further investigation in future research. The model's inability to perform on multi-label datasets, which are commonly encountered in many real-world applications. Multi-label datasets involve instances that can be assigned multiple labels or categories simultaneously, making them more complex than single-label datasets. Unfortunately, the model developed in this research was not able to effectively handle this type of data. We attempted to address this issue by increasing the number of principal components in the model output, but this did not yield significant improvements in performance.

8 Discussion and Future Direction

We introduced generative probabilistic latent variable models (Factor Analysis) as a novel approach to solve weakly supervised learning tasks. Our method, by using high-level domain knowledge from Subject Matter Experts, accomplishes high quality results and can be an excellent choice for approximating true labels on unlabelled data. We provided evidence that Factor Analysis is resilient to class imbalanced datasets as indicated by the significant improvement to the classification performance. Finally, we tested the effect of sparse data resources by varying the number of data-points used to train the generative model and we showed that with a minimum number of points our approach can attain high performance. For future work, we hope to expand the generative probabilistic latent variable models into a multi-class domain and explore our approach to other weakly supervised learning tasks.

Acknowledgments. We want to thank the reviewers for their time, effort, and the very constructive feedback and advice. Our aim was to try and incorporate as many of their suggestions as possible considering the time. If some of their suggestions are not present (e.g. more datasets) is purely because of the limited timeframe. The readers can find the relevant code, as soon as it becomes available, at the JPMorgan Github https://github.com/jpmorganchase under the repository name *weakly-supervision* and the branch *ecml-experiments*.

References

1. Alberto, T.C., Lochter, J.V., Almeida, T.A.: TubeSpam: comment spam filtering on youtube. In: 2015 IEEE 14th International Conference on Machine Learning and Applications (ICMLA). IEEE (2015). https://doi.org/10.1109/icmla.2015.37
2. Bach, S.H., He, B., Ratner, A., Ré, C.: Learning the structure of generative models without labeled data. In: Proceedings of the 34th International Conference on Machine Learning, vol. 70. pp. 273–282. ICML'17, JMLR.org (2017)
3. Barber, D.: Bayesian Reasoning and Machine Learning. Cambridge University Press, Cambridge (2012)
4. Bartholomew, D.J.: The foundations of factor analysis. Biometrika **71**(2), 221–232 (1984). https://doi.org/10.1093/biomet/71.2.221
5. Bazavan, E.G., Zanfir, A., Zanfir, M., Freeman, W.T., Sukthankar, R., Sminchisescu, C.: HSPACE: synthetic parametric humans animated in complex environments (2022)
6. Bishop, C.M.: Pattern Recognition and Machine Learning. Springer (2006)
7. Dai, Z., Damianou, A., Gonzalez, J., Lawrence, N.D.: Variationally auto-encoded deep Gaussian processes. In: Larochelle, H., Kingsbury, B., Bengio, S. (eds.) Proceedings of the International Conference on Learning Representations, vol. 3. Caribe Hotel, San Juan, PR (2016). http://inverseprobability.com/publications/dai-variationally16.html
8. Dunnmon, J.A., et al.: Cross-modal data programming enables rapid medical machine learning. Patterns **1**(2), 100019 (2020). https://doi.org/10.1016/j.patter.2020.100019
9. Fabrigar, L.R., Wegener, D.T., MacCallum, R.C., Strahan, E.J.: Evaluating the use of exploratory factor analysis in psychological research. Psychol. Methods **4**(3), 272–299 (1999). https://doi.org/10.1037/1082-989x.4.3.272
10. Fries, J.A., Steinberg, E., Khattar, S., Fleming, S.L., Posada, J., Callahan, A., Shah, N.H.: Ontology-driven weak supervision for clinical entity classification in electronic health records. Nature Commun. **12**(1) (2021). https://doi.org/10.1038/s41467-021-22328-4
11. Goswami, M., Boecking, B., Dubrawski, A.: Weak supervision for affordable modeling of electrocardiogram data (2022)

12. Jain, N.: Customer sentiment analysis using weak supervision for customer-agent chat (2021)
13. Lawrence, N.D., Quiñonero-Candela, J.: Local distance preservation in the GP-LVM through back constraints. In: Proceedings of the 23rd International Conference on Machine Learning - ICML '06. ACM Press (2006). https://doi.org/10.1145/1143844.1143909
14. Liu, Z., et al.: Multi-initialization optimization network for accurate 3D human pose and shape estimation, pp. 1976–1984. Association for Computing Machinery, New York, NY, USA (2021). https://doi.org/10.1145/3474085.3475355
15. Manco, I., Benetos, E., Quinton, E., Fazekas, G.: Learning music audio representations via weak language supervision (2021)
16. Mathew, J., Negi, M., Vijjali, R., Sathyanarayana, J.: DeFraudNet: an end-to-end weak supervision framework to detect fraud in online food delivery. In: Dong, Y., Kourtellis, N., Hammer, B., Lozano, J.A. (eds.) ECML PKDD 2021. LNCS (LNAI), vol. 12978, pp. 85–99. Springer, Cham (2021). https://doi.org/10.1007/978-3-030-86514-6_6
17. Murphy, K.P.: Machine Learning: A Probabilistic Perspective. MIT Press (2012)
18. Rao, V.R., Khalil, M.I., Li, H., Dai, P., Lu, J.: Decompose the sounds and pixels, recompose the events (2021)
19. Ratner, A., Hancock, B., Dunnmon, J., Goldman, R., Ré, C.: Snorkel metal: weak supervision for multi-task learning. In: Proceedings of the Second Workshop on Data Management for End-To-End Machine Learning. DEEM'18, Association for Computing Machinery, New York, NY, USA (2018). https://doi.org/10.1145/3209889.3209898
20. Ratner, A., Bach, S.H., Ehrenberg, H., Fries, J., Wu, S., Ré, C.: Snorkel: rapid training data creation with weak supervision. VLDB J. **29**(2), 709–730 (2019). https://doi.org/10.1007/s00778-019-00552-1
21. Ratner, A., Hancock, B., Dunnmon, J., Sala, F., Pandey, S., Ré, C.: Training complex models with multi-task weak supervision. Proc. AAAI Conf. Artif. Intell. **33**, 4763–4771 (2019). https://doi.org/10.1609/aaai.v33i01.33014763
22. Ratner, A.J., De Sa, C.M., Wu, S., Selsam, D., Ré, C.: Data programming: creating large training sets, quickly. In: Lee, D., Sugiyama, M., Luxburg, U., Guyon, I., Garnett, R. (eds.) Advances in Neural Information Processing Systems, vol. 29. Curran Associates, Inc. (2016). https://proceedings.neurips.cc/paper/2016/file/6709e8d64a5f47269ed5cea9f625f7ab-Paper.pdf
23. Reddy, R.G., et al.: MuMuQA: multimedia multi-hop news question answering via cross-media knowledge extraction and grounding (2021)
24. Saab, K., et al.: Doubly weak supervision of deep learning models for head CT. In: Shen, D., et al. (eds.) MICCAI 2019. LNCS, vol. 11766, pp. 811–819. Springer, Cham (2019). https://doi.org/10.1007/978-3-030-32248-9_90
25. Saab, K., Dunnmon, J., Ré, C., Rubin, D., Lee-Messer, C.: Weak supervision as an efficient approach for automated seizure detection in electroencephalography. NPJ Digital Medicine **3**(1) (2020). https://doi.org/10.1038/s41746-020-0264-0
26. Tipping, M.E., Bishop, C.M.: Probabilistic principal component analysis. J. Royal Stat. Soc., Ser. B **61**(3), 611–622 (1999)
27. Tseng, A., Sun, J.J., Yue, Y.: Automatic synthesis of diverse weak supervision sources for behavior analysis (2021)

28. Varma, P., Sala, F., He, A., Ratner, A., Re, C.: Learning dependency structures for weak supervision models. In: Chaudhuri, K., Salakhutdinov, R. (eds.) Proceedings of the 36th International Conference on Machine Learning. Proceedings of Machine Learning Research, vol. 97, pp. 6418–6427. PMLR, 09–15 Jun (2019). https://proceedings.mlr.press/v97/varma19a.html

29. Wan, M., McAuley, J.: Item recommendation on monotonic behavior chains. In: Proceedings of the 12th ACM Conference on Recommender Systems. ACM (2018). https://doi.org/10.1145/3240323.3240369

30. Wan, M., Misra, R., Nakashole, N., McAuley, J.: Fine-grained spoiler detection from large-scale review corpora. In: Proceedings of the 57th Annual Meeting of the Association for Computational Linguistics. Association for Computational Linguistics (2019). https://doi.org/10.18653/v1/p19-1248

31. Weng, Z., Varma, P., Masalov, A., Ota, J., Re, C.: Utilizing weak supervision to infer complex objects and situations in autonomous driving data. In: 2019 IEEE Intelligent Vehicles Symposium (IV). IEEE (2019). https://doi.org/10.1109/ivs.2019.8814147

32. Weston, J., Schölkopf, B., Bakir, G.: Learning to find pre-images. In: Thrun, S., Saul, L., Schölkopf, B. (eds.) Advances in Neural Information Processing Systems, vol. 16. MIT Press (2004). https://proceedings.neurips.cc/paper/2003/file/ac1ad983e08ad3304a97e147f522747e-Paper.pdf

33. Wolfson, T., Berant, J., Deutch, D.: Weakly supervised mapping of natural language to SQL through question decomposition (2021)

34. Zhang, J., Yu, Y., Li, Y., Wang, Y., Yang, Y., Yang, M., Ratner, A.: WRENCH: a comprehensive benchmark for weak supervision. In: Thirty-fifth Conference on Neural Information Processing Systems Datasets and Benchmarks Track (2021). https://openreview.net/forum?id=Q9SKS5k8io

35. Zheng, J., et al.: Multi-modal 3D human pose estimation with 2D weak supervision in autonomous driving (2021)

DyCOD - Determining Cash on Delivery Limits for Real-Time E-commerce Transactions via Constrained Optimisation Modelling

Akash Deep$^{(\boxtimes)}$ ⓘ, Sri Charan Kattamuru ⓘ, Meghana Negi ⓘ, Jose Mathew ⓘ, and Jairaj Sathyanarayana ⓘ

Swiggy, Bangalore, India
{deep.akash,sricharan.k,meghana.negi,jose.matthew,jairaj.s}@swiggy.in

Abstract. Paying for deliveries using cash after the delivery is made is a popular mode of payment employed by customers transacting online for the first time or those that prefer to have more control, especially in emerging economies like India. While the cash (or pay)-on-delivery (COD or POD) option helps e-commerce platforms, for example in our food delivery platform, tap into new customers, it also opens up substantial risk in the form of fraud and abuse. A common risk mitigation strategy is to impose a limit on the order value that can be paid using COD. In our experience and survey, these limits are typically blunt (a single limit for a city or zip code) and set by business teams using heuristics and primarily from a risk-management-backwards view. This one-size-fits-all approach means we leave money on the table on customer groups where the limits are too strict and lose money on groups where they are lax. We need to balance the risk-management and the customer-preference angles simultaneously and dynamically. Note that this is different from a typical credit-scoring approach due to at least two major reasons - 1) the information available in e-commerce, especially online food delivery, is much sparser, 2) the limit needs to be calculated dynamically in real-time depending on the transaction value, restaurant and marketplace constraints and network effects. To this end, we present a framework called DyCOD that maps this to a non-linear constrained optimisation problem. To the best of our knowledge there are no published results in this area and our work is the first. We solve this using both heuristic and model driven approaches and run large-scale A/B experiments. Our approaches delivered a 2.1% lift in margin per order vs. the baseline while not increasing any risk metrics, which is highly significant at our scale.

Keywords: Cash on Delivery · Fraud and abuse · Constrained Optimization · Propensity modelling

Special acknowledgement to Anshul Bansal for bringing in a product perspective to DyCOD while he was in Swiggy.

G. De Francisci Morales et al. (Eds.): ECML PKDD 2023, LNAI 14174, pp. 51–65, 2023.
https://doi.org/10.1007/978-3-031-43427-3_4

1 Introduction

Despite the growing popularity of digital payment methods, Cash on Delivery (COD) still accounts for $30 billion of the Indian e-commerce market [3,10] which is significant. According to a report published by an Indian startup that specializes in payment systems, 65% of its transactions were settled using COD [7]. For Indian customers who are still adapting to the world of digital transactions, the COD mode of payment provides assurance, generates confidence, and instills a sense of control, leading to continued engagement and reduced churn.

However, COD orders can result in abusive scenarios, where the orders get canceled and the company has no way of recovering the cash, impacting the company's baseline negatively. Preventing such abuse becomes further challenging in a three-sided hyperlocal marketplace as multiple actors - customers, delivery partners, and restaurants are involved. Since the abuse can originate from any of the actors and collusion between them, it is difficult to attribute abuse to any one of them and levy cancellation fees. In the case of pre-paid orders, companies have more control over the transaction, as they can deduct the cancellation charge from the amount already prepaid by the customer and refund the balance, if any, back to the customer. On the other hand in COD, the order amount was never paid and the company loses all the so-far invested cost.

The most common strategy that the Indian e-commerce industry has adopted to contain such abuse is by limiting all COD transactions to a maximum-purchase-limit (MPL) beyond which COD is disabled for the customer [8,9]. The objective of MPL is to restrict higher value orders to keep the cost of doing business in check. Companies use several heuristic and rule based methods [8,11] to determine MPL. Although these methods can restrict abuse, there are cases where a genuine customer intends to place a higher value order but is restricted by these limits. Such instances can lead to a bad customer experience and may even result in customers churning away from the platform. Since COD is a growth lever [3] for Indian businesses, such experience can be detrimental to customer retention. Hence, determining optimal limits and having the right tradeoff between abuse cost and ensuring a smooth customer experience becomes critical. Further, in this paper, we show that utilizing the customer attributes to determine optimal MPL can improve key business metrics.

There is limited academic literature on determining MPL. The closest well-studied field is credit limit determination [1,4,5]. However, the dynamics of MPL at an e-commerce company are different from that of credit limits. While credit limits are primarily calculated offline with explicit information provided by the customer and his/her payment history, customer specific MPL is calculated real-time taking into account current transaction details like location, cart value etc. as well as implicit signals derived from historical platform behavior of the customer.

To this end, we introduce "DyCOD", a nonlinear optimization-based algorithm that dynamically generates MPL for customers based on their COD preferences and past behavior on the platform. The algorithm aims at increasing order conversion while balancing the abuse cost and finding optimal (*customer, MPL*)

segments. The algorithm is divided into three modules: Customer score generation, Customer Segmentation, and Limit Allocation. The Customer Score module
focuses on defining customers' platform trust score and preference towards COD
using heuristic and propensity-model-driven methods. Customer Segmentation
uses these scores to identify similar cohorts. These cohorts are then fed into
the Limit Allocation Module to determine the optimal MPL for each customer
segment. The modular structure of the algorithm allows us to experiment with
different techniques in each module. Due to its real-life business application,
the design principle followed is that the generated limit should be explainable,
overridable and configurable.

Summarising the above, the key contributions of this paper are

1. We formulate MPL determination as a non-linear constrained optimization
   problem and propose an extensible, modular algorithm, DyCOD, to determine
   optimal MPL in real-time.
2. We present how propensity modeling can be effective in predicting customer
   order conversion at different MPLs and use gradient boosted trees to learn
   from real-time order details, COD preferences and customers' trust score
   derived from implicit platform behavior
3. We conduct an extensive ablation study offline and perform a large-scale A/B
   experiment to deliver a 2.1% lift in margin per order vs. the baseline while
   not increasing any risk metrics. The algorithm was deployed at full-scale and
   is currently serving millions of customers.

The rest of the paper is organized as follows. In Sect. 2, we briefly describe
COD systems in our setting. In Sect. 3, we introduce the problem statement followed by the data requirements in Sect. 4. Section 5 explains the different modules, a summary of how the algorithm evolved over time and lessons learned. In
Sect. 6, we illustrate the real-time inference architecture. In Sect. 7, we present
results from our offline and online experiments. In Sect. 8, we review the literature in the related fields, followed by the conclusion and future scope in Sects. 9
and 10 respectively.

2   System View

In a typical e-commerce system, a customer can create a cart with multiple items
and subsequently move to the payment page to check the available payment
methods. COD is one such payment method.

Figure 1 illustrates a "Trust and Safety" (TnS) service that determines the
COD-eligibility of a customer. The key components of the TnS Service are the
ML model and business policies for preventing fraud and determining MPL.
These components interact with each other to determine the final COD eligibility of the customer; given the adversarial nature of the domain, we will refrain
from disclosing the exact nature of interactions between the systems. Currently,
in our system, MPL is determined based on business intuition and domain understanding (BizCOD) and is set as a static configuration. The proposed DyCOD
algorithm aims to optimize MPL in real-time.

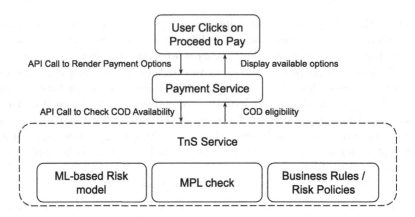

Fig. 1. System architecture for COD eligibility

3   Problem Formulation

In this section, we define our business metrics and use them to formulate the problem as a constrained optimization problem.

Our primary objective is to increase the order conversion 'c' while balancing the abuse cost per order 'r'. Since millions of customers transact monthly on our platform, it makes optimizing for each customer computationally challenging. Hence, we first divide the customers into 'n' homogeneous customer groups: $G = [G_i, G_2 \ldots G_n]$, and then use these groups to measure different business metrics and allocate MPL. Let g_i be the size of the group G_i. Let r^b, c^b, g^b and r^d, c^d, g^d be the above defined metrics for BizCOD and DyCOD respectively.

The incremental gain in conversion (Δc), when MPL is determined by DyCOD instead of BizCOD can be obtained as follows

$$\Delta c = \frac{\sum_{i=1}^{n}((c_i^d - c_i^b) \times g_i)}{\sum_{i=1}^{n} g_i} \tag{1}$$

Let γ represent the cost per incremental order which helps to measure the tradeoff between Δc and r. γ can be calculated as:

$$\gamma = \frac{\sum_{i=1}^{n} r_i^d \times c_i^d \times g_i - \sum_{i=1}^{n} r_i^b \times c_i^b \times g_i}{\sum_{i=1}^{n}((c_i^d - c_i^b) \times g_i)} \tag{2}$$

γ should be less than the amount (ϕ) company is spending to get per incremental conversion. Summarizing, from Eqs. 1 and 2 our problem formulation for DyCOD becomes the following optimization problem:

$$\text{maximize } \Delta c \Rightarrow \frac{\sum_{i=1}^{n}((c_i^d - c_i^b) \times g_i)}{\sum_{i=1}^{n} g_i} \tag{3}$$
$$\text{subject to } \gamma < \phi$$

4   Data Collection Design

In order to determine whether increasing MPL is an effective way to boost user conversion and further understand customer behavior with changing MPL, representative data collection becomes critical. In the data collection design, we subject randomly selected customer samples to progressively increasing limits on MPL to understand their conversion behavior and potential for abuse. The data collection was designed to adhere with in-house implementation constraints which allowed us to increase the $BizCOD_{MPL}$ only by 10%-point increments, i.e. $1x$, $1.1x$, $1.2x$, ..., $1.6x$ ($1.3x$ represents MPL of 1.3 times the $BizCOD_{MPL}$). For example, in a city with a $BizCOD_{MPL}$ of Rs. 1000, seven groups of y% customers each will be randomly assigned an MPL of Rs. 1000, 1100, 1200, ..., 1600. Since the objective is to optimize MPL, we keep the remaining TnS components intact. However, the algorithm proposed in the next section is not limited to this data collection design and can be generalized for any continuous range of MPL.

5   Dynamic COD Algorithm

The proposed algorithm has three modules

1. **Customer Score Generation:** The objective of this module is to give a score to each customer based on their historical and real-time attributes. The underlying idea is to assign higher scores to customers who have a higher preference to use COD and a lower tendency to abuse. We propose two ways to derive this score: heuristically and propensity-based ML-model (Subsect. 5.1)
2. **Customer Segmentation:** This module utilizes customer scores to group similar customers. We propose multiple strategies for identifying such groups (Subsect. 5.2)
3. **Limit Allocation:** In this optimal MPL for each segment is determined using constrained grid-search (Subsect. 5.3).

5.1   Customer Score Generation

In this section, we introduce three methods as a series of iterative refinements to generate customer scores. We started with the heuristic-based COD Usage Gradient and the Customer Trust Score and then pivoted to the ML-model-driven Propensity Score. One of the major design considerations was interpretability, especially to front-line Operations folks, which made sophisticated ML models like neural networks and other deep learning-based methods out of scope for us.

COD Usage Gradient (UG). We started with the intuition that if a function f represents a customer's preference to use COD for different order values, then its derivative at the customer's currently assigned MPL can be used as a score to indicate whether the MPL should be changed for that customer. We call this score the COD Usage Gradient (UG). In our data, the current MPL for all customers is the $BizCOD_{MPL}$. We divide the order values into multiple continuous buckets with constant step size x. We model f as the ratio of the count of the customer's COD orders to all his/her orders (prepaid+COD) in that bucket. We then calculate UG as the derivative of f at $BizCOD_{MPL}$.

For any given order value z, y_z be the upper bound of its bucket, then:

$$CO_{[x]}(z) = number\ of\ cod\ orders\ in\ order\ value\ range\ (y_z - x, y_z]$$
$$LO_{[x]}(z) = number\ of\ orders\ in\ order\ value\ range\ (y_z - x, y_z]$$

We define f and calculate UG as

$$f_{[x]}(z) = \frac{CO_{[x]}(z)}{LO_{[x]}(z)} \tag{4}$$

$$UG = \frac{f_{[x]}(BizCOD_{MPL}) - f_{[x]}(BizCOD_{MPL} - x)}{x} \tag{5}$$

For example, if $BizCOD_{MPL}$ is 550 which lies in the bucket $(500, 600]$ and $x = 100$,

$$UG = \frac{f_{[100]}(600) - f_{[100]}(500)}{100}$$

Customer Trust Score (TS). We observed that a number of customers preferred COD specifically for orders valued higher than their historical orders. Majority of such past orders were pre-paid leading to cold-start issues in UG. The bucketized calculation of UG required a substantial amount of COD orders leading to data sparsity. To tackle such behavior we decided to maximize all the available customer information. The underlying hypothesis was if a customer has shown good behavior on the platform, they can be trusted with higher order COD orders. A higher score indicates a more trustworthy customer. Customer Trust Score used a comprehensive list of the customer attributes like frequent ordering, less cancellations, higher order values, number of orders etc. These attributes were normalized with platform numbers to determine the final trust score of each customer. Based on business objectives, definitions of trust can vary for businesses.

While TS helped in incorporating a wide spectrum of customer behavior, the impact of changing MPL was not explicitly captured. This motivated us to find a balance between COD availability and platform trust attributes.

Propensity Score (PR). Propensity score aims at capturing the difference in customer's order conversion probability when shown an MPL (say L) higher than $BizCOD_{MPL}$. It is defined as

$$P_o(L) = p_o(L) - p_o(BizCOD_{MPL}) \tag{6}$$

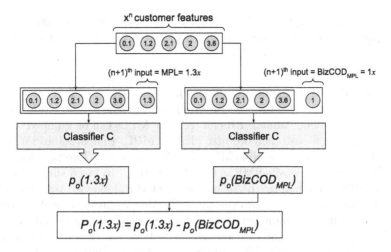

Fig. 2. Block Diagram for inference of $P_o(1.3x)$ as the PR at 1.3 times $BizCOD_{MPL}$

where, $p_o(MPL)$ is the propensity of the customer to convert at any MPL, and $P_o(L)$ is propensity score at L

While UG and TS are agnostic of different MPLs, PR is calculated for each $(transaction, MPL)$ combination. $p_o(MPL)$ is learned using a classification model where the corresponding MPL is the $x_{n+1^{th}}$ feature along with other x_n features. These x_n features constitute real-time attributes of the cart, historical and in-session behavior of the COD transactions including UG and TS. We experimented with logistic regression (LR) and gradient-boosting trees (GBT) as classifiers to learn $p_o(MPL)$. Figure 2 shows how PR at $L = 1.3x$ is predicted during inference.

5.2   Customer Segmentation

The next step is to identify homogeneous customer groups which will be assigned the same MPL. We experimented with a heuristic and a K-means segmentation for UG and TS and a propensity-based segmentation designed specifically for PS.

Heuristic-Based Segmentation (HS). We identify local minima in score distribution and use perturbations around them as thresholds to segment customers into similar cohorts. This yields three variants - HS-UG, HS-TS and HS-[UG, TS] using Usage Gradient and Trust Score.

K-means-Based Segmentation (KS). In this, customer segments are determined using the k-means algorithm with UG and TS as input features. KS has only one variant i.e. KS-[UG, TS].

Propensity-Based Segmentation (PS). Since PR gives a score for every configurable MPL for all customers, it requires a different segmentation method. Every customer having 'similar' PRs for 'certain' MPLs can be grouped together in a segment. For a customer, we first identify MPLs that are above a desired threshold - let's call them feasible MPLs for that customer. Two possible strategies to determine the feasible MPLs thresholds are (i) to use a single threshold across all MPLs [Global] or (ii) to use different thresholds for different MPLs [Local]. From this, we create two variants - the Max variant where all customers who have the same maximum feasible MPL are grouped together in one segment, and the Min variant where all customers who have the same minimum feasible MPL form one segment. We compare these four combinations of strategies $(G_{Min}, G_{Max}, L_{Min}, L_{Max})$ in our offline evaluation exercise. For each strategy, many segments are returned as we use a random set of thresholds to determine feasible MPLs.

Table 1. Comparison of propensity values and limit allotment for 5 customers using different strategies, under a global threshold of 0.1 and various local thresholds of (0.1, 0.2, 0.3, 0.4, 0.5, 0.6)

Customer	$P_o(1.1)$	$P_o(1.2)$	$P_o(1.3)$	$P_o(1.4)$	$P_o(1.5)$	$P_o(1.6)$	G_{Min}	G_{Max}	L_{Min}	L_{Max}
A	0.12	0.54	0.54	0.54	0.57	0.27	1.1	1.6	1.1	1.5
B	0.1	0.1	0.1	0.1	0.2	0.15	1.5	1.5	1	1
C	0.32	0.39	0.2	0.6	0.64	0.71	1.1	1.6	1.1	1.6
D	0	0	0	0	0	0	1	1	1	1
E	0.02	0.02	0.04	0.7	0.65	0.68	1.5	1.4	1.4	1.6

Table 1 demonstrates how PS does segmentation for 5 illustrative customers. Let's assume global threshold of 0.1 and local thresholds of $(0.1, 0.2, 0.3, 0.4, 0.5, 0.6)$ for $1.1x$ to $1.6x$ MPLs. For customer E, feasible MPLs are $1.4x$, $1.5x$ and $1.6x$ as per the Global strategy, and $1.4x$ and $1.5x$ as per the Local Strategy. Hence, G_{Min} is $1.4x$ and G_{Max} is $1.6x$, while L_{Min} and L_{Max} are $1.4x$ and $1.5x$ respectively. In the G_{Min} strategy, customer A and C have the same G_{Min} MPL and hence, they are grouped into the same segment. Similarly, as per L_{Min}, A and C belong to one segment and B and D belong to another segment, while E belongs to another. Same method is followed to get G_{Max} and L_{Max} segments.

5.3   Limit Allocation

In this final module, we aim to get the optimal MPL for each segment. We explain step by step computation below:

1. Fetch the customer to segment mapping $(S_{G_i, MPL})$ from the customer segmentation module
2. For each segment, use the collected data to compute the conversion (c^b) and abuse cost per order (r^b) with $BizCOD_{MPL}$
3. Compute (c^d, r^d) and evaluate the incremental conversion (Δc) and the constraint (γ) for each permutation of possible limits
4. Return the permutation with maximum Δc while satisfying the constraint $(\gamma < \phi)$.

The Limit Allocation module is presented as Algorithm 1

6   Real-Time Inference

All the historical data, log tables and customer information are stored in a Hive-based data warehouse. We use Spark jobs to process historical data for offline training and online inference. Amazon DynamoDB-DAX (DDB-DAX) serves as the online feature cache and S3 as a cold-feature store.

During inference, when a cart is being evaluated for COD availability, the TnS system calls the model API hosted on Spark-based MLEAP serving. This API consists of cart and transaction details required as input features in the model. MLEAP serving fetches the historical data from DDB-DAX and combines it with realtime-features, deserializes the model and returns the predicted $DyCOD_{MPL}$. Figure 3 illustrates the training and inference pipeline.

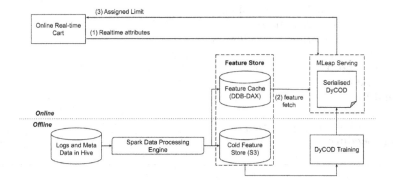

Fig. 3. The system view for DyCOD training and online real-time inference.

Algorithm 1. Limit Allocation using Grid Search

Input: $S_{G_i,MPL} = (C, G_i, l)$ a data structure denoting customer, the corresponding
   segment and the limit assigned during data collection
Output: A mapping of cod limits for each distinct customer cluster
   procedure LimitAllocation($S_{G_i,MPL}$, possible_limits)
      $allocation_{best} \leftarrow None$
      $\gamma_{best}, c_{best} \leftarrow inf, -inf$
      $possible\_allocations \leftarrow permutations(possible\_limits, size = N)$ ▷ all
   permutations of size 'N'

   $$c^b, r^b \leftarrow [c_1^b, c_2^b, ..., c_N^b], [r_1^b, r_2^b, ..., r_N^b]$$

      while $i < N$ **do**
         $c^b[i], r^b[i] = compute\_metrics(S_{G_{i=i},MPL=1})$ ▷ c, r from collected data
         $i += 1$
      end while

      for each allocation in $possible\_allocations$ **do**
         $$c^d, r^d \leftarrow [c_1^d, c_2^d, ..., c_N^d], [r_1^d, r_2^d, ..., r_N^d]$$

         for each k, l in K, allocation **do**
            $c^d[i], r^d[i] \leftarrow compute\_metrics(S_{G_{i=i},MPL=l})$
         end for

         while $i < N$ **do**
            $\Delta c += c^d[i] - c^b[i]$
            $\Delta r += r^b[i] - r^b[i]$
            $size_{total} += g_i$
         end while

         $\gamma \leftarrow \Delta r / (\Delta c \cdot size_{total})$

         if $\gamma < \Phi$ AND $\gamma < \gamma_{best}$ **then**
            if $\Delta c > c_{best}$ **then**
               $allocation_{best} \leftarrow allocation$
               $\gamma_{best}, c_{best} \leftarrow \gamma, \Delta c$
            end if
         end if
      end for

      return $allocation_{best}, c_{best}, \gamma_{best}$
   end procedure

---

7   Results

Since our experiments directly impacts the company's baseline, we first extensively evaluate the various strategies offline and then conduct a large online A/B experiment with the two best-performing variants.

7.1   Offline Evaluation

Figure 4 summarizes the results of our offline evaluation. We use a relative scale to directionally compare all the methods as absolute numbers and deltas can differ for different businesses. For PR, we only report the GBT model results since the LR model underperformed substantially compared to any other method.

The best-performing method for us was L_{Max}. It gave the maximum Δc and similar Margin per Order as HS-TS. It performed better than G_{Max} particularly because thresholds are tuned at a limit level in L_* methods. The L_{Max} performs better than L_{Min} in terms of Δc because it allocates the highest eligible COD limit for a customer compared to L_{Min} which does the vice-versa and hence higher conversion. We can see that variants using UG score did not perform relatively well due to data sparsity and cold-start issues explained in Sect. 5.1

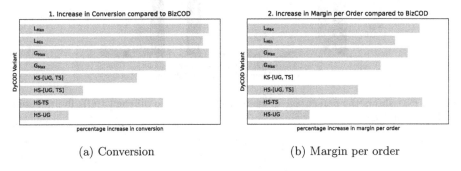

(a) Conversion   (b) Margin per order

Fig. 4. The Offline evaluation results demonstrate the increase in conversion and profit per order due to DyCOD algorithms over the baseline BizCOD. Each algorithm had a feasible solution.

7.2   Online A/B Experiment

Based on the results from Sect. 7.1, we conducted an A/B experiment with Biz-COD as the control and two test treatments as HS-TS and L_{Max}. Table 2 summarises statistically significant observations from the experiment.

L_{Max} was the best-performing variant and it was deployed at full scale delivering a 0.1% increase in conversion. HS-TS being a more generalized platform level approach was less effective in deriving COD conversion.

Table 2. Online experiment results

Variant	Δc	$\gamma < \Phi$	Increase in margin per order
HS-TS	0.07%	True	2.13%
L_{Max}	0.1%	True	2.14%

As shown in Fig. 5 we also observed that the L_{Max} increased MPL for 2.5 times fewer customers than HS-TS. This observation along with the experiment results show that L_{Max} is selective and assigns higher MPL to only COD-seeking customers.

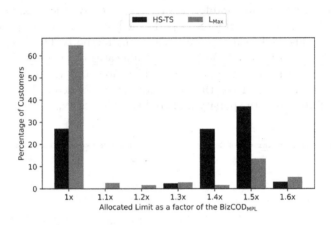

Fig. 5. Plot shows the percentage of customers assigned to different COD limits based on HS-TS and L_{Max}

8   Related Work

Credit Scoring: The paper is inspired by credit score and credit limit determination problems. Since credit score modeling is a widely studied field, Anton et al. [6] summarizes recent papers and best practices. Zhang et al. [16] highlights the issues of high data dimensions and sparse features in internet credit loan business and propose a group sampling method to model credit behavior. Methods like regression [1], Markov decision processes [5], and linear programming [4] have been used to determine customers' credit limits. Jual et al. [5] uses a combination of customer segments and credit balance to define a state space, and uses an MDP to learn optimal credit limit. A study by Nobert et al. [14] provides interesting insights that customers tends to spend more given a higher credit limit despite not wanting the increase. Karmi et al. [13] empahasized on balance between limit increase and credit utilization to derive profitability and proposed a Neural Network based predictive function to determine the right limit-setting strategy.

Propensity Modeling: Propensity-based methods have been widely used in the industry to understand how likely a certain group of customers is going to act under certain circumstances. The applications vary from a sale win opportunity [15] to paying energy bills [2], from predicting order conversion [17] in e-commerce to solving positional bias in search engines [12]. The majority of the papers use linear regression [15] as a baseline and decision tree [17] or neural network [2] based methods for the final solution.

9   Conclusion

In this paper, we formulate MPL as a constrained non-linear optimization problem and present the DyCOD algorithm that determines MPL by incorporating customer preference and behavior. The modular structure of the algorithm allowed us to experiment with heuristic scores UG and TS that attempts to model COD preference and abuse behaviour respectively, and with PR, a propensity-model-driven score. We assess different segmentation methods on these scores and propose a limit allocation framework to determine the best (segment, MPL) combination for our formulation. We demonstrate how DyCOD can be deployed for real-time inference and share the performance of different variants in both offline simulations and online large-scale A/B experiments. Propensity model-based L_{Max} was the champion DyCOD variant which also delivered a significant lift in the margin per order.

10   Future Scope

The current DyCOD algorithm provides the capability to optimize conversion in hyper-local delivery space, by assigning custom MPLs to customers' cohorts based on their propensity to use cash and the capacity to abuse. The future versions of the algorithm will target the optimization of multiple objectives like order value in addition to order conversion. The model is presently trained on data for returning users only and is not suited for users that have low order history or are new to the platform. We plan to harvest more features relevant to new users and extend DyCOD to new users as well. The dynamic MPLs generated by the current model are based on $BizCOD_{MPL}$ which is specific to each geography and is decided by business policies. We plan to experiment with DyCOD in a more unconstrained nature and agnostic of $BizCOD_{MPL}$, thereby potentially generating more business value. We will also explore reinforcement learning methods for DyCOD, where the system learns customer behavior over time and rewards the customers by providing higher or lower limits based on the actions they take on the platform. DyCOD will also lead to challenges related to cash accumulating with delivery agents doing predominantly COD orders and opens up the possibility of abuse. We will also explore strategies to minimize this problem by adding additional constraints on delivery agent cash accumulation in the optimization function.

Ethical Statement. As we propose a framework to determine the cash-on-delivery limits for e-commerce transactions, we acknowledge the ethical implications of our work. Since our work is closely associated with collecting and processing transaction level data, we assure that any data collected for the research, including any personal information, has been secured and anonymised. We commit to safeguarding and respecting the privacy of individuals' data. We ensure that our work is agnostic to any personal information including race, gender, religion, or any other personal characteristic. We believe in equality and inclusivity as essential aspects of ethical development. We believe that our work is extensible across industries to many applications within the pay-on-delivery limit and credit limit determination domains. We emphasise that our work should not be used for any harmful purpose.

References

1. Aa, G., Sb, V., Ab, M.K.R.: Deciding bank client's credit limit and home loan using machine learning. Smart Intell. Comput. Commun. Technol. **38**, 288 (2021)
2. Bashar, M.A., Nayak, R., Astin-Walmsley, K., Heath, K.: Machine learning for predicting propensity-to-pay energy bills. Intell. Syst. Appl. **17**, 200176 (2023)
3. Economic-Times: Cash on delivery about $30 billion of India's ecommerce market (2022). https://economictimes.indiatimes.com/industry/services/retail/cash-on-delivery-about-30-billion-of-indias-ecommerce-market-says-gokwik/articleshow/96112033.cms?from=mdr
4. İç, Y.T.: Development of a credit limit allocation model for banks using an integrated fuzzy TOPSIS and linear programming. Expert Syst. Appl. **39**(5), 5309–5316 (2012)
5. Licari, J., Loiseau-Aslanidi, O., Tolstova, V., Sadat, M.: Determining the optimal dynamic credit card limit (2021)
6. Markov, A., Seleznyova, Z., Lapshin, V.: Credit scoring methods: latest trends and points to consider. J. Finance Data Sci. **8**, 180–201 (2022)
7. Razorpay: Cash on delivery and the challenges that come with it (2022). https://razorpay.com/blog/cash-on-delivery-and-the-challenges/
8. Shiprocket: How to minimize cod failures and returns? (2014). https://www.shiprocket.in/blog/minimize-cod-failures-and-returns/
9. Shopee: Cash on delivery (COD) at shopee (2022). https://seller.shopee.com.my/edu/article/11759
10. Times-Of-India: 90% of rural India's e-comm orders paid in cash (2021). https://timesofindia.indiatimes.com/business/india-business/90-of-rural-indias-e-comm-orders-paid-in-cash-study/articleshow/88244840.cms
11. Today, B.: Even as UPI grows rapidly, a majority of customers prefer cash-on-delivery for e-commerce purchases (2022). https://www.businesstoday.in/technology/story/even-as-upi-grows-rapidly-a-majority-of-customers-prefer-cash-on-delivery-for-e-commerce-purchases-347320-2022-09-15
12. Vardasbi, A., de Rijke, M., Markov, I.: Cascade model-based propensity estimation for counterfactual learning to rank. In: Proceedings of the 43rd International ACM SIGIR Conference on Research and Development in Information Retrieval, pp. 2089–2092 (2020)

13. Visser, K., Swart, G., Pretorius, J., Esterhuyzen, L.M., Verster, T., Fourie, E.: Customer comfort limit utilisation: management tool informing credit limit-setting strategy decisions to improve profitability. Cogent Econ. Finance **10**(1), 2056362 (2022)

14. Wong, N., Matthews, C.: Cardholder perceptions of credit card limits. In: 10th AIBF Banking and Finance Conference, Melbourne, Australia (2005)

15. Yan, J., Gong, M., Sun, C., Huang, J., Chu, S.M.: Sales pipeline win propensity prediction: a regression approach. In: 2015 IFIP/IEEE International Symposium on Integrated Network Management (IM), pp. 854–857. IEEE (2015)

16. Zhang, H., Zeng, R., Chen, L., Zhang, S.: Research on personal credit scoring model based on multi-source data. J. Phys. Conf. Ser. **1437**, 012053 (2020)

17. Zhang, Y.: Prediction of customer propensity based on machine learning. In: 2021 Asia-Pacific Conference on Communications Technology and Computer Science (ACCTCS), pp. 5–9. IEEE (2021)

Computational Social Sciences

Pattern Mining for Anomaly Detection in Graphs: Application to Fraud in Public Procurement

Lucas Potin[1]($\boxtimes$), Rosa Figueiredo[1]ⓘ, Vincent Labatut[1]ⓘ, and Christine Largeron[2]ⓘ

[1] Laboratoire Informatique d'Avignon – UPR 4128, 84911 Avignon, France
{lucas-potin,rosa-figueiredo,vincent-labatut}@univ-avignon.fr
[2] Laboratoire Hubert Curien – UMR 5516, 42023 Saint-Etienne, France
christine.largeron@univ-st-etienne.fr

Abstract. In the context of public procurement, several indicators called red flags are used to estimate fraud risk. They are computed according to certain contract attributes and are therefore dependent on the proper filling of the contract and award notices. However, these attributes are very often missing in practice, which prohibits red flags computation. Traditional fraud detection approaches focus on tabular data only, considering each contract separately, and are therefore very sensitive to this issue. In this work, we adopt a graph-based method allowing leveraging relations between contracts, to compensate for the missing attributes. We propose PANG (Pattern-Based Anomaly Detection in Graphs), a general supervised framework relying on pattern extraction to detect anomalous graphs in a collection of attributed graphs. Notably, it is able to identify *induced* subgraphs, a type of pattern widely overlooked in the literature. When benchmarked on standard datasets, its predictive performance is on par with state-of-the-art methods, with the additional advantage of being explainable. These experiments also reveal that induced patterns are more discriminative on certain datasets. When applying PANG to public procurement data, the prediction is superior to other methods, and it identifies subgraph patterns that are characteristic of fraud-prone situations, thereby making it possible to better understand fraudulent behavior.

Keywords: Pattern Mining · Graph Classification · Public Procurement · Fraud Detection

1 Introduction

Public procurement refers to the purchase of goods, services and works by a public authority (the buyer), from a legal entity governed by public or private law (the winner). In the European Union, when the contract exceeds some price threshold, the buyer must first advertise a call for tenders defining its needs in

G. De Francisci Morales et al. (Eds.): ECML PKDD 2023, LNAI 14174, pp. 69–87, 2023.
https://doi.org/10.1007/978-3-031-43427-3_5

detail, and later the corresponding award notice, which describes the content of the contract eventually concluded with one or more winners. These documents must be published in the *Official Journal of the European Union* (OJEU). The online version of this journal, called the *Tenders Electronic Daily* (TED) [11], publishes more than 650,000 procurement notices a year. Consequently, the public procurement sector provides a huge amount of publicly available data.

Historically, anomalies in public procurement, which refer to doubtful behavior, are linked to specific characteristics associated with contracts. In the literature, these characteristics are called *red flags*, and are used as indicators of potential fraud [13,15,16,40]. For instance, modifying the contract price during the procedure, or receiving a single offer for a given call for tenders, are typically considered as red flags [36]. But the information required to compute these red flags is not always available. In the French subset of the TED, some essential attributes are largely missing [37], e.g. the number of offers answering a call for tenders is not documented in 30% of the cases. For such contracts, one can compute only *partial* red flags, in the best of cases, or even no red flags at all.

Anomaly detection approaches are commonly used in fraud detection [39]. However, when applied to public procurement, most studies are based on *tabular* data [3,4], i.e. each contract is considered separately, as a set of attribute values. Only a very few authors try to take advantage of the *relationships* between contracts by adopting a graph-based approach. Fazekas & Kertész propose the CRI, a composite score combining several red flags, and leverage graphs [14], but only to visualize its distribution over their dataset. Wachs & Kertész [47] use graphs in order to estimate the proportion of red flags in the core agents, i.e. buyers and winners with the most frequent relationships, compared to the others. However, to the best of our knowledge, no method in the literature dedicated to anomaly or fraud detection in public procurement uses graphs to create predictive models.

This leads us to propose a graph-based method to identify anomalies in public procurement. Our work makes three main contributions. First, we propose the *PANG* framework (Pattern-Based Anomaly Detection in Graphs), that leverages pattern mining to solve this problem. When evaluated on a benchmark of standard datasets, its performance is on par with state-of-the-art methods, with the advantage of being explainable. In addition, it allows looking for different types of patterns, including *induced* subgraphs, which are generally overlooked in the literature. Our second contribution is to show empirically that such subgraphs can result in better classification performance on certain datasets. As a third contribution, we apply our generic framework to public procurement data, and identify the relevant patterns characterizing risky behaviors.

The rest of the article is structured as follows. Section 2 gives an overview of the literature regarding graph anomaly detection and graph pattern mining. Section 3 introduces the terminology used throughout this paper, as well as our problem formulation. Section 4 describes our framework PANG and assesses its performance on standard datasets. Section 5 applies PANG to public procurement. Finally, we comment the main aspects of our work in Sect. 6.

2   Related Work

The goal of anomaly detection is to detect behaviors significantly differing from expected norms. The methods dealing with this task on graphs either focus on single elements (vertices, edges) or larger structures (subgraphs, graphs) [2,24,30]. When considering whole graphs, the task can be seen as a classification problem consisting in labelling the graph as normal or anomalous. The standard approach consists in building a vector-based representation of the graph, in order to apply classic data mining tools [30]. Most recent works focus on deep learning methods such as Graph Neural Networks (GNN) [10,28,29], which not only learn this representation, but also tackle the classification task. However, one limitation of these methods lies in the lack of explainability: while some approaches have been proposed to make GNNs explainable [52], achieving this goal is non-trivial, especially when considering graphs with edge features. An alternative is to build the representation in a more controlled way, in order to retain its semantics [51]. Among the methods following this path, pattern-based approaches rely on the subgraphs that compose the graphs [1]. They require retrieving the most characteristic of these patterns, generally the most frequent ones, in order to represent each graph in terms of absence or presence of these patterns.

There are different algorithms to extract *frequent* subgraphs from a collection of graphs [17,50], i.e. patterns appearing in more graphs than a fixed threshold. The main issue encountered with this approach is the pattern explosion problem, which states that the number of patterns increases exponentially when decreasing this threshold. To alleviate the computational cost, some algorithms mine more constrained patterns, such as *closed* frequent patterns [42], *maximal* frequent patterns [31], or *approximate* patterns [26]. As these notions are not the focus of this paper, we refer the reader to [34] for further details.

Moreover, all frequent patterns may not be relevant when dealing with a graph classification problem: some could occur equally in all classes, and thus provide no information to distinguish them. To overcome this issue, some methods have been proposed to mine *discriminative* patterns. Leap [49] relies on a notion of structural proximity when building its search tree, that lets it compare branches in order to avoid exploring those that are similar. CORK [45] is based on a metric that evaluates a pattern in relation to a collection of patterns already selected, which allows accounting for the proximity between frequent patterns. Moreover, this metric is submodular, and can thus be integrated into tools such as gSpan [50] to mine discriminative patterns efficiently. It also allows CORK to automatically select the number of patterns to extract. In [23], the notion of discriminative pattern is extended in order to mine *jumping emerging* patterns: subgraphs appearing in only one class. However, this notion is very restricted, as it requires that a pattern *never* appears in one of the two classes. As a consequence, in practice, it often leads to very infrequent patterns [27]. Our objective is to propose a generic classification framework which allows choosing the number of discriminative patterns to keep, as well as their type and, then to apply it for identifying fraud in public procurement.

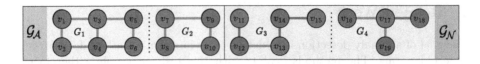

Fig. 1. A collection $\mathcal{G}$ of graphs including the subsets of anomalous ($\mathcal{G}_A$) and normal ($\mathcal{G}_N$) graphs. (Color figure online)

3 Problem Formulation

To detect fraud in public procurement, we adopt a network representation inspired by information retrieval or text mining, and previously successfully used for chemical compound classification [33]. In the same way that a document can be modeled as a bag-of-words, we propose to represent a graph as a bag-of-subgraphs, i.e. the set of its constituting subgraphs, called *patterns*. To do this, we construct a global dictionary constituted of the patterns appearing in a collection of attributed graphs. Based on this dictionary, each graph can then be represented as a fixed-length numerical vector, which can be used as an input by any standard machine learning algorithm. In this section, we first describe how we define such vector-based representation, and then formulate our anomaly detection task as a classification problem.

Definition 1 (Attributed Graph). *An attributed graph is defined as a tuple* $G = (V, E, \mathbf{X}, \mathbf{Y})$ *in which* V *is the set of* n *vertices,* E *the set of* m *edges of* G, $\mathbf{X}$ *the* $n \times d_v$ *matrix whose row* $\mathbf{x}_i$ *is the* d_v-*dimensional attribute vector associated with vertex* $v_i \in V$, *and* $\mathbf{Y}$ *the* $m \times d_e$ *matrix whose row* $\mathbf{y}_i$ *is the* d_e-*dimensional attribute vector associated with edge* $e_i \in E$.

As an illustration, we consider a collection of such graphs, as shown in Fig. 1. In this example, each vertex has an attribute corresponding to its color (brown or purple) as well as each edge (green or red).

Let us assume that each graph G has a label ℓ_G picked in $\mathcal{L} = \{A, N\}$, denoting an anomalous or a normal graph, respectively. Importantly, this label is not known for all the graphs at our disposal. Let $\mathcal{G}$ be the set of graphs whose label is known. The set $\mathcal{G}$ can be split into two disjoint subsets: $\mathcal{G} = \mathcal{G}_A \cup \mathcal{G}_N$ ($\mathcal{G}_A \cap \mathcal{G}_N = \emptyset$). Set $\mathcal{G}_A$ contains the anomalous graphs, and $\mathcal{G}_N$ the normal ones. Using the labeled set of graphs $\mathcal{G}$, our aim is to train a classifier able to predict the unknown label for the other graphs. For this purpose, we use a pattern-based graph representation.

Definition 2 (General Pattern). *Let* $G = (V, E, \mathbf{X}, \mathbf{Y})$ *be an attributed graph. A graph* P *is a pattern of* G *if it is isomorphic to a subgraph* H *of* G, *i.e.* $\exists H \subseteq G : P \cong H$.

As we consider attributed graphs, we adopt the definition of a graph isomorphism proposed by Hsieh *et al.* [21], i.e. an isomorphism must preserve not only edges,

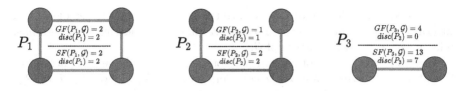

Fig. 2. Three examples of general patterns present in graph G_1 of Fig. 1.

but also vertex and edge attributes. We consider that P is a pattern for a set of graphs $\mathcal{G}$ when P is a pattern of at least one of its graphs. Figure 2 shows three examples of patterns of G_1, and therefore of $\mathcal{G}$, from Fig. 1.

It should be noted that, according to Definition 2, a pattern P may not include all the edges originally present in G between the considered vertices. We can restrict this definition by considering *induced* patterns. Similarly to Definition 2, P is an *induced* pattern of G if it is isomorphic to an *induced* subgraph H of G.

Definition 3 (Induced Subgraph). *Let $G = (V, E, \mathbf{X}, \mathbf{Y})$ be an attributed graph. The subgraph $H = (V_H, E_H, \mathbf{X}_H, \mathbf{Y}_H)$ induced by a vertex subset $V_H \in V$ is such that $E_H = \{(u, v) \in E : u, v \in V_H\}$, and $\mathbf{X}_H$ and $\mathbf{Y}_H$ retain only the rows of $\mathbf{X}$ and $\mathbf{Y}$ matching V_H and E_H, respectively.*

In Fig. 2, P_1 is an induced pattern of G_1. On the contrary, P_2 is a general pattern of G_1, but not an induced pattern, because edge (v_3, v_5) from G_1 has no image in P_2. We consider that P is an induced pattern of $\mathcal{G}$ when P is an induced pattern of at least one of its graphs. To measure the importance of a pattern in $\mathcal{G}$, we now need the notion of *graph frequency*.

Definition 4 (Graph Frequency). *The graph frequency $GF(P, \mathcal{G})$ of a pattern P in $\mathcal{G}$ is the number of graphs in $\mathcal{G}$ having P as a pattern:*
$$GF(P, \mathcal{G}) = |\{G \in \mathcal{G} : \exists H \subseteq G \text{ s.t. } P \cong H\}|.$$

It indicates the number of graphs having a specific pattern, but does not give any information about the number of times the pattern appears in these graphs. For this, we use the *subgraph frequency*.

Definition 5 (Subgraph Frequency). *The subgraph frequency $SF(P, \mathcal{G})$ of a pattern P in $\mathcal{G}$ is its total number of occurrences over all $G \in \mathcal{G}$:*
$$SF(P, \mathcal{G}) = \sum_{G \in \mathcal{G}} |\{H \subseteq G : P \cong H\}|.$$

Graph frequency can be used to define the notion of *closed* pattern, which in turn allows finding a more compact set of relevant patterns.

Definition 6 (Closed Pattern). *A pattern P of $\mathcal{G}$ is said to be closed if it has no supergraph P', or equivalently if P is not the subgraph of any graph P', such that $GF(P', \mathcal{G}) = GF(P, \mathcal{G})$.*

As a consequence, the set of closed patterns is a subset of the set of general patterns. In our example, there is no supergraph of P_1 appearing in two graphs, which makes it a closed pattern of $\mathcal{G}$.

Regardless of the type of pattern, we note $\mathcal{P}_A$ and $\mathcal{P}_N$ the sets of patterns of $\mathcal{G}_A$ and $\mathcal{G}_N$, respectively, and $\mathcal{P}$ the complete set of patterns of $\mathcal{G}$: $\mathcal{P} = \mathcal{P}_A \cup \mathcal{P}_N$. Not all patterns are equally relevant to solve a given task. For instance, in Fig. 2, P_3 is much more common than both other patterns in $\mathcal{G}$ from Fig. 1. To distinguish them, we rely on the discrimination score from [45], that characterizes each pattern according to its frequency in the two subsets.

Definition 7 (Discrimination Score). *The discrimination score of a pattern P of $\mathcal{G}$ is defined as $disc(P) = |F(P, \mathcal{G}_A) - F(P, \mathcal{G}_N)|$, where F is GF or SF.*

Our definition generalizes that of [45], so that it can be applied to both frequencies (GF and SF). A score close to 0 indicates a pattern that is as frequent in $\mathcal{G}_A$ as in $\mathcal{G}_N$, while a higher score means that the pattern is more frequent in one of the two subsets. We use this score to rank the patterns in $\mathcal{P}$, and select the s most discriminative ones ($1 \leq s \leq |\mathcal{P}|$). Some methods, like CORK [45], estimate s automatically, which can be an advantage or a drawback, depending on the level of control desired by the user.

The resulting subset $\mathcal{P}_s \subseteq \mathcal{P}$ constitutes our dictionary, which means that s lets us control the dimension of our graph representation. The representation of each graph $G_i \in \mathcal{G}$ is a vector $\mathbf{h}_i \in \mathbb{R}^s$ whose components measure how important each pattern of $\mathcal{P}_s$ is to G_i. These measures can be computed according to different formula, as discussed in Sect. 4. Finally, we build the matrix $\mathbf{H} \in \mathbb{R}^{|\mathcal{G}| \times s}$ by considering the vector representations of all the graphs in $\mathcal{G}$.

Based on this graph representation, our anomaly detection problem amounts to classifying graphs with unknown labels as anomalous or normal. More formally, given the training set composed of a set of graphs $\mathcal{G} = \{G_i, i = 1, \ldots, |\mathcal{G}|\}$ with the labels $\ell_{G_i} \in \mathcal{L}$ and the vector representations $\mathbf{h_i}$, the goal is to learn a function $f : \mathbb{R}^s \to \{A, N\}$, which associates a label (anomalous or normal) to the vector representation of an unlabeled graph.

4   PANG Framework

4.1   Description of the Framework

To solve our classification problem, we propose the PANG framework (<u>P</u>attern-Based <u>A</u>nomaly Detection in <u>G</u>raphs), whose source code is publicly available online[1]. A preliminary step consists in extracting the graphs, but as it is data-dependent, we defer its description to Sect. 5.1. The rest of the process is constituted of four steps, as represented in Fig. 3:

1. Identify all the patterns of $\mathcal{G}$ and build $\mathcal{P}$.
2. Select the most discriminative patterns $\mathcal{P}_s$ among them.
3. Use these patterns to build the vector-based representation of each graph.
4. Train a classifier to predict the graph labels based on these representations.

---

[1] https://github.com/CompNet/Pang/releases/tag/v1.0.0 .

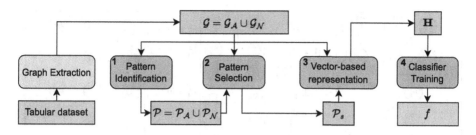

Fig. 3. Processing steps of the proposed PANG framework.

Step #1: Pattern Identification. In order to create $\mathcal{P}$, we use an existing graph pattern extractor. Several tools are available to enumerate patterns, such as gSpan [50], FFSM [22], or more recently TKG [17] and cgSpan [42].

gSpan and cgSpan respectively search the *frequent* and *closed frequent* patterns in a set of graphs. Both rely on an iterative procedure, which starts from the simplest pattern possible, i.e. a single vertex with a specific attribute, in order to initialize the list of ranked frequent patterns. At each step, the algorithm takes the most frequent pattern according to this list, and tries to extend it by adding an edge. This expansion results in a set of new patterns, which are added or not to the ranked list, according to their frequency. This list is updated over the iterations, until it is no longer possible to find any new pattern with a frequency potentially higher than a predefined threshold.

In the case of cgSpan, the algorithm is able to find the set of closed frequent patterns, which is included in the set of frequent patterns. A smaller set of patterns allows reducing the computation time during the pattern mining phase, but also at post-processing, e.g. when computing the discrimination scores, since there are fewer patterns to consider, and consequently a smaller size for the vector representation.

We choose to use gSpan [50] and cgSpan [42]. The former mines an important number of frequent patterns while requiring less memory than TKG. The latter is able to efficiently identify closed patterns. Both algorithms are implemented in Java, and are available as a part of software SPMF [18]. The process used for the induced patterns is based on two steps: first, each pattern is extracted using one of these algorithms. Then, we filter the induced patterns using the ISMAGS algorithm [20] implemented in NetworkX [19].

Step #2: Discriminative Pattern Selection. Next, we compute the discrimination score of each extracted pattern as explained in Definition 7. We keep the s most discriminative patterns to construct $\mathcal{P}_s$.

Step # 3: Vector-Based Representation. Once we have $\mathcal{P}_s$, we compute the vector representation of each graph in $\mathcal{G}$. In this work, we use several approaches. First, we build a binary vector indicating the presence or absence of each pattern in the considered graph. In that case, for each graph $G_i \in \mathcal{G}$ and each pattern $P_j \in \mathcal{P}$, H_{ij} equals 1 if this pattern P_j is present in G_i and 0 otherwise.

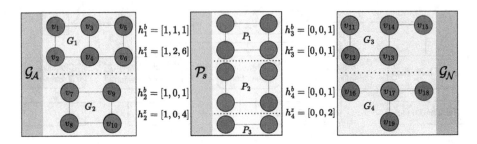

Fig. 4. Binary ($\mathbf{h}_j^b$) and integer ($\mathbf{h}_j^z$) vector-based representations of the graphs of Fig. 1, using the patterns of Fig. 2 as $\mathcal{P}_s$.

This representation is somewhat limited, though, as it ignores how much patterns are present in graphs. To solve this issue, we propose an integer representation based on the number of occurrences *in the graph*. This number is computed with the VF2 algorithm [6], available in Networkx [19]. Given a pattern P and a graph G, VF2 identifies the number of subgraph isomorphisms of P in G, which we store in H_{ij}.

Figure 4 shows the representations obtained for the graphs of Fig. 1, using the patterns from Fig. 2 as $\mathcal{P}_s$. Vectors h_j^b and h_j^z denote the binary and integer representations of each graph G_j, respectively. It is worth noting that two different graphs can have the same vector representation, as is the case for the binary representation of G_3 and G_4 in our example.

For reasons of consistency, we compute the discrimination scores based on GF when using the binary representation, and on SF when using the integer one.

Step #4: Classifier Training. After the previous step, each graph is represented by a fixed-sized vector, no matter its number of vertices or edges. We leverage this representation to train a classifier into predicting the graph labels. Our framework is general and allows any classifier, but we select C-SVM [5] in this article, as it gives the best experimental results.

4.2 Assessment on Benchmarks

Before focusing on fraud detection in public procurement, we assess PANG on FOPPA, the public procurement dataset that we use in our application, as well as four real-world datasets commonly used in the literature as benchmarks. These last datasets, our protocol and the results of this first experiment are detailed in the following. The FOPPA data is described in Sect. 5.1.

Table 1. Characteristics of the 4 benchmark datasets.

Datasets	MUTAG	PTC_FR	NCI1	D&D
Number of graphs	188	350	4,110	1,178
Average number of vertices	17.93	25.56	29.87	284.72
Average number of edges	19.79	25.96	32.30	715.66

Experimental Protocol. We decide to use 4 standard datasets. MUTAG [8] contains 188 graphs representing molecules, where vertices are atoms and edges bonds between them. The graphs are distributed over two classes, depending on the molecule mutagenicity. PTC_FR [46] contains 350 graphs, also representing molecules. There are also two graph classes, depending on the molecule carcinogenicity on male and female mice and rats. NCI1 [48] contains 4,110 graphs representing chemical compounds. Each vertex stands for an atom, while edges represent the bonds connecting them. Like before, there are two classes distinguishing the compounds depending on their carcinogenicity. D&D [9] is composed of 1,178 protein structures. Each vertex is an amino acid, and two vertices are connected if they are less than 6 angstroms apart. There are two graph classes corresponding to enzymes vs. non-enzymes. Table 1 shows the main characteristics of these datasets: number of graphs, and average numbers of vertices and edges.

Regarding graph representations, we compute the six types proposed in PANG:

- PANG_GenBin: binary representation considering general patterns.
- PANG_GenOcc: integer representation considering general patterns.
- PANG_IndBin: binary representation using only induced patterns.
- PANG_IndOcc: integer representation using only induced patterns.
- PANG_CloBin: binary representation using only closed patterns.
- PANG_CloOcc: integer representation using only closed patterns.

We compare our results with four different types of baselines. First, as an alternative pattern-based method, we use CORK (cf. Sect. 2), which automatically estimates the size of the representation. The second baseline type is graph kernels. We use the kernel matrices of the graphs as representations, associating each row of the matrix with the corresponding graph. These matrices are computed from the implementation of the WL kernel [43] and the WL_OA [25] kernel, both available in the GraKel [44] library. The third type is whole graph embedding neural methods, for which we use Graph2Vec [35], available in the KarateClub library [41]. We set an embedding size of 128, which is standard in the literature. For each of these representations, we train a C-SVM as indicated in Step 4 of Sect. 4.1.

The fourth baseline type is Graph Neural Networks, with DGCNN [53]. This method produces a graph representation, which can be fetched to the SVM, but it can also perform the classification step directly. The results reported here are

Table 2. *F*-Scores (± standard deviation) for the *Anomalous* class.

Representation	MUTAG	NCI1	D&D	PTC	FOPPA
PANG_GenBin	0.85 (0.05)	0.79 (0.02)	0.77 (0.03)	0.60 (0.13)	0.93 (0.02)
PANG_GenOcc	0.87 (0.04)	0.77 (0.02)	0.75 (0.02)	0.58 (0.10)	0.91 (0.03)
PANG_IndBin	0.87 (0.05)	0.79 (0.02)	0.76 (0.03)	0.59 (0.13)	**0.95 (0.01)**
PANG_IndOcc	0.87 (0.03)	0.79 (0.01)	0.75 (0.03)	0.56 (0.07)	0.92 (0.02)
PANG_CloBin	0.86 (0.05)	0.78 (0.03)	0.75 (0.03)	0.57 (0.15)	0.94 (0.03)
PANG_CloOcc	**0.88 (0.04)**	0.76 (0.02)	0.71 (0.04)	0.54 (0.11)	0.92 (0.02)
CORK	0.66 (0.08)	0.78 (0.02)	0.73 (0.03)	0.54 (0.06)	0.63 (0.05)
WL	0.86 (0.06)	**0.83 (0.01)**	**0.82 (0.01)**	0.57 (0.06)	0.90 (0.05)
WL_OA	0.86 (0.06)	0.81 (0.03)	0.77 (0.03)	0.55 (0.11)	0.90 (0.05)
Graph2Vec	0.84 (0.07)	0.82 (0.01)	0.72 (0.03)	**0.61 (0.11)**	0.91 (0.04)
DGCNN	0.86 (0.04)	0.74 (0.01)	0.79 (0.01)	0.58 (0.05)	0.89 (0.01)

the best ones, obtained in this second setting, using the implementation from StellarGraph [7], with the optimal parameter values as indicated in [53].

Experimental Results. We adopt a 10-fold cross-validation to assess classifier performance. Table 2 shows the average *F*-Score for the *Anomalous* class. Each column corresponds to one of the considered datasets: 4 benchmarks and FOPPA.

No method dominates the others over all datasets, therefore we can assume that some graph representations are more relevant to model certain systems. We plan to investigate this question further, but this is out of this article's scope. The performance of PANG is systematically above CORK, its most similar method. This is because, on the considered datasets, CORK identifies a very restricted set of discriminative patterns and trades classification performance against representation size. Moreover, PANG is on par with the remaining methods on NCI1, D&D and PTC, and has the best performance on MUTAG and, importantly, on FOPPA, our application dataset. Thus, we assume that PANG is able to capture the same information as embedding- and GNN-based methods. On the one hand, it requires numerous patterns to be mined, and is therefore more time-consuming than these methods. On the other hand, it has the advantage of being interpretable, allowing us to identify the most discriminative patterns. This is why we apply it to fraud detection in public procurement, in Sect. 5.

5   Public Procurement Use Case

In this section, we apply PANG to real data representing public procurement. We first describe the process used to extract graphs from a database of French public procurement contracts (Sect. 5.1), then we discuss our results (Sect. 5.2).

5.1   Extraction of the Graph Dataset

Raw Data. The FOPPA [37,38] database lists all French contracts award notices published at the European level. Each such contract involves *at least* two economic *agents*: a buyer and a winner, and may be constituted of several lots. It is described by a collection of attributes such as the total price, the number of offers, and whether the procedure was accelerated. In this paper, we consider the specific subset of contracts concerning period 2015–19, containing 417,809 lots.

Contract Filtering. We could apply our graph extraction process to the whole set of French contracts, however this would result in a single graph, combining heterogeneous activity domains and agent types. Yet, some attributes, for example the weight of social and environmental criteria, directly depend on these domains and types [32]. Instead, we select only a part of the available data to constitute a collection of consistent contracts. For this purpose, we filter them according to five aspects: agent category, activity sector, temporal period, geographic region and size. Regarding the agents, we focus on municipalities, because their identification is more straightforward than for the other types of agents. For each municipality present in the dataset, we build a subset of contracts containing its own contracts, those involving their winners, as well as the other municipalities with which they have obtained contracts. The other four filters allow us to control the size of these subsets of contracts, while retaining a certain homogeneity: we keep only those related to works, covering periods of one year, and involving only suppliers belonging to the same French administrative subdivision.

After this filtering, we obtain a collection of contract subsets containing a total of 25,252 contracts. For each contract, we compute a standard red flag from the literature. A contract is red flagged if the number of offers received is exactly 1, which reveals a lack of competition [36].

Graph Extraction. For each contract subset obtained after the filtering, we extract a graph G. We consequently build a set of graphs, corresponding to $\mathcal{G}$ in Sect. 4. In the context of public procurement, due to the complexity of the data, one can extract various types of graphs [14].

We use vertices to model agents, and edges to represent relationships between them, i.e. their joint involvement in at least one contract. Each vertex has an attribute, indicating whether the agent is a buyer or a winner, while each edge has an attribute related to the number of lots contracted. We limit the latter to three levels: 1) exactly one lot; 2) between 2 and 5 lots; and 3) 6 lots or more. This allows us to identify cases where a buyer has many contracts with a single winner, a behavior generally associated with red flags in the literature [12].

We consider that an edge is anomalous if it represents *at least* one red flagged contract, i.e. a contract that received exactly one offer. The label of a graph depends on its total number of anomalous edges: normal if there are fewer than 2, anomalous otherwise. Our graph extraction method produces 389 normal and 330 anomalous graphs. Table 3 shows the main characteristics of the resulting FOPPA dataset, which is publicly available online with our source code[3].

Table 3. Characteristics of the graphs extracted from the FOPPA dataset.

Graph Class	Average number of vertices (std)	Average number of edges (std)
Anomalous	15.76 (5.56)	17.09 (7.86)
Normal	12.54 (5.41)	12.59 (6.90)

Table 4. *F*-Scores ($\pm$ sd) for both classes, obtained with tabular and graph data.

Type of data	*Anomalous* Class	*Normal* Class
Tabular Data	0.19 (0.01)	0.66 (0.01)
PANG_IndBin	**0.95 (0.01)**	**0.93 (0.02)**

5.2   Results on Public Procurement Data

Comparison with a Tabular Representation. To study the impact of our graph-based representations, we compare them to a baseline using a traditional *tabular* approach. For each contract, we use as predictive features 15 fields available in FOPPA, such as the type of procedure, or the presence of a framework agreement. We aim to predict a binary class, based on the same red flag as before: the number of offers for the contract. Class 0 contains the contracts with more than 1 tender, and Class 1 those with a unique tender. Note that the predictive features are independent of the number of offers.

Like for the graphs, we train an SVM with 10-fold cross-validation, on the same 25,252 contracts. However, the resulting prediction is defined at the *contract* level (one row in the tabular data), whereas PANG works at the agent level (one graph in the collection). To compare these results, we need to group the tabular predictions by agent. For this purpose, we proceed as in Sect. 5.1, by considering any agent with two red flagged contracts or more as anomalous.

Table 4 compares the obtained performance with our best graph-based results. The *F*-Scores are averaged over the 10 folds, with standard deviation, for the *Anomalous* and *Normal* classes. For the same contracts and classifier (C-SVM), the graphs allow us to predict fraudulent behaviors much more efficiently than the tabular data, notably for anomalous agents. This clearly confirms the interest of taking advantage of relationships between agents to tackle fraud detection, especially when red flags are missing.

Discrimination Score. When applied to our dataset, gSpan returns a total of 15,793 distinct patterns. Figure 5.a shows the distribution of their discrimination score. It is in $[0; 20]$ for most patterns (85%), which can thus be considered as non-discriminative. Figure 5.b shows examples of 2 discriminative patterns, with respective scores of 64 and 91. Both of them include several relations with an intermediary number of lots, which are rather common in large graphs, and more often associated with anomalous graphs.

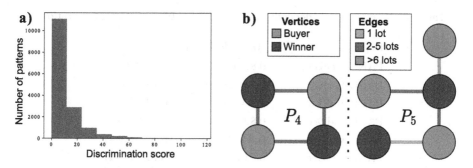

Fig. 5. (a) Distribution of the patterns in function of their discrimination scores (b) Examples of discriminative patterns.

Table 5. F-Score ($\pm$ sd) depending on parameter s, the size of $\mathcal{P}_s$.

Representation Size s	Anomalous Class	Normal Class
10	0.66 (0.05)	0.73 (0.05)
50	0.74 (0.05)	0.77 (0.04)
100	0.81 (0.05)	0.83 (0.04)
150	0.88 (0.03)	0.88 (0.03)
(all) 15,793	**0.93 (0.02)**	**0.93 (0.02)**

Impact of the Number of Discriminative Patterns. We now study how the performance is affected by the number s of patterns in $\mathcal{P}_s$, i.e. the vector representation size. Table 5 shows how the F-Score changes depending on s, for anomalous and normal graphs. The last row indicates the performance obtained with all the identified patterns ($s = |\mathcal{P}|$). A representation based on only 100 patterns, i.e. less than 1% of the 15,793 patterns, is sufficient to reach the 0.8 bar for both classes. This represents around 90% of the maximal F-Score, obtained with all patterns. Therefore, only a small number of patterns are required to convey the information necessary to tackle the classification task.

Impact of the Type of Patterns. We also study how the type of pattern influences the constitution of $\mathcal{P}_s$, and therefore the classification performance. We set $s = 100$, and compare all PANG representations, as we did in Sect. 4.2. Table 6 shows the F-Score obtained with each representation, for both classes.

Representations based on induced and closed patterns lead to better results. Yet, a manual examination of $\mathcal{P}_s$ reveals that the discrimination scores of their patterns are similar to the general case. The worst selected pattern reaches a score of 67 for general patterns, vs. 61 for induced and 64 for closed patterns. The difference lies in the *nature* of the patterns, which are more diverse than when mining general patterns. For induced and closed patterns, $\mathcal{P}_s$ includes respectively 16 and 13 patterns that do not appear when using general patterns.

Table 6. *F*-Score (± sd) depending on the pattern type of the representation.

Representation Type	*Anomalous* Class	*Normal* Class
PANG_GenBin	0.81 (0.05)	0.83 (0.04)
PANG_GenOcc	0.73 (0.07)	0.79 (0.05)
PANG_IndBin	**0.84 (0.03)**	**0.85 (0.03)**
PANG_IndOcc	0.82 (0.05)	0.84 (0.04)
PANG_CloBin	**0.84 (0.04)**	**0.85 (0.04)**
PANG_CloOcc	0.83 (0.05)	**0.85 (0.04)**

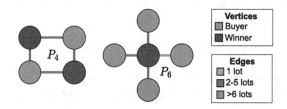

Fig. 6. Examples of discriminative patterns characteristic of class *Anomalous*. (Color figure online)

Interpretation of Fraudulent Behavior Through Pattern Analysis. An important advantage of our framework is the identification of the most discriminative patterns, and thus the possibility to leverage human expertise to interpret these patterns and understand the reasons why an agent is considered fraudulent. Figure 6 shows two discriminative patterns, P_4 and P_6. Pattern P_4 represents a relationship between two winners and two buyers, with more than one contract between them. This type of pattern occurs more frequently in graphs with more contracts, which is typical of anomalous graphs. Pattern P_6 has a winner connected to several buyers, with a single green edge. This can be interpreted as favoritism: a winner works much more with a municipality than with the others.

6 Conclusion

In this paper, we propose PANG, a pattern-based generic framework that represents graphs as vectors, by identifying their most discriminative subgraphs. We show how PANG, coupled with a standard classifier, can detect fraud in public procurement, by applying it to an existing database (FOPPA). Traditional fraud detection approaches use tabular data to compute red flags to estimate risk, and fail when these data are incomplete. PANG leverages relational information between economical agents, and our experiments confirm that the use of graphs makes it possible to overcome this issue. They also show that prediction performance can be improved by mining closed or induced patterns, which constitute a set of predictors less redundant than general patterns. Finally, a clear advantage of PANG relies on the explainability of these discriminative patterns, which can be interpreted and associated with human behaviors such as favoritism.

Acknowledgments. This work was supported by *Agorantic* (FR 3621), and the ANR under grant number ANR-19-CE38-0004 for the *DeCoMaP* project.

Ethical Implications. Anomaly detection can have ethical implications, for instance if the methods are used to discriminate against certain individuals. In this respect, however, our PANG methodological framework does not present any more risk than the supervised classification methods developed in machine learning.

Moreover, this work takes place in the framework of a project aiming, among other things, at proposing ways of automatically red flagging contracts and economic agents depending on fraud risk. Therefore, the method that we propose is meant to be used by public authorities to better regulate public procurement and the management of the related open data.

Finally, the data used in this article are publicly shared, and were collected from a public open data repository handled by the European Union. They do not contain any personal information, and cannot be used directly to infer any personal information, as they only describe the economic transactions of companies and public institutions regarding public procurement.

References

1. Acosta-Mendoza, N., Gago-Alonso, A., Carrasco-Ochoa, J.A., Francisco Martínez-Trinidad, J., Eladio Medina-Pagola, J.: Improving graph-based image classification by using emerging patterns as attributes. Eng. Appl. Artif. Intell. **50**, 215–225 (2016). https://doi.org/10.1016/j.engappai.2016.01.030
2. Akoglu, L., Tong, H., Koutra, D.: Graph based anomaly detection and description: a survey. Data Min. Knowl. Disc. **29**(3), 626–688 (2014). https://doi.org/10.1007/s10618-014-0365-y
3. Carneiro, D., Veloso, P., Ventura, A., Palumbo, G., Costa, J.: Network analysis for fraud detection in Portuguese public procurement. In: Analide, C., Novais, P., Camacho, D., Yin, H. (eds.) IDEAL 2020. LNCS, vol. 12490, pp. 390–401. Springer, Cham (2020). https://doi.org/10.1007/978-3-030-62365-4_37
4. Carvalho, R.N., Matsumoto, S., Laskey, K.B., Costa, P.C.G., Ladeira, M., Santos, L.L.: Probabilistic ontology and knowledge fusion for procurement fraud detection in Brazil. In: Bobillo, F., et al. (eds.) UniDL/URSW 2008-2010. LNCS (LNAI), vol. 7123, pp. 19–40. Springer, Heidelberg (2013). https://doi.org/10.1007/978-3-642-35975-0_2
5. Chang, C.C., Lin, C.J.: LIBSVM: a library for support vector machines. ACM Trans. Intell. Syst. Technol. **2**(3), 1–27 (2011). https://doi.org/10.1145/1961189.1961199
6. Cordella, L.P., Foggia, P., Sansone, C., Vento, M.: A (sub)graph isomorphism algorithm for matching large graphs. IEEE Trans. Pattern Anal. Mach. Intell. **26**(10), 1367–1372 (2004). https://doi.org/10.1109/TPAMI.2004.75

7. CSIRO's Data61: Stellargraph machine learning library (2018). https://github.com/stellargraph/stellargraph

8. Debnath, A.S., Lopez, R.L., Debnath, G., Shusterman, A., Hansch, C.: Structure-activity relationship of mutagenic aromatic and heteroaromatic nitro compounds. correlation with molecular orbital energies and hydrophobicity. J. Med. Chem. **34**(2), 786–797 (1991). https://doi.org/10.1021/jm00106a046

9. Dobson, P.D., Doig, A.J.: Distinguishing enzyme structures from non-enzymes without alignments. J. Mol. Biol. **330**(4), 771–783 (2003). https://doi.org/10.1016/s0022-2836(03)00628-4

10. Dou, Y., Shu, K., Xia, C., Yu, P.S., Sun, L.: User preference-aware fake news detection. In: 44th ACM SIGIR International Conference on Research and Development in Information Retrieval, pp. 2051–2055 (2021). https://doi.org/10.1145/3404835.3462990

11. European Union: Tenders Electronic Daily (2023). https://ted.europa.eu/

12. Falcón-Cortés, A., Aldana, A., Larralde, H.: Practices of public procurement and the risk of corrupt behavior before and after the government transition in México. EPJ Data Science **11**, 19 (2022). https://doi.org/10.1140/epjds/s13688-022-00329-7

13. Fazekas, M., Tóth, I.J.: New ways to measure institutionalised grand corruption in public procurement. Technical report, U4 Anti-Corruption Resource Centre (2014). https://papers.ssrn.com/sol3/papers.cfm?abstract_id=2519385

14. Fazekas, M., Tóth, I.J.: From corruption to state capture: a new analytical framework with empirical applications from Hungary. Polit. Res. Q. **69**(2), 320–334 (2016). https://doi.org/10.1177/1065912916639137

15. Ferwerda, J., Deleanu, I., Unger, B.: Corruption in public procurement: finding the right indicators. Eur. J. Crim. Policy Res. **23**(2), 245–267 (2017). https://doi.org/10.1007/s10610-016-9312-3

16. Ferwerda, J., Deleanu, I.S.: Identifying and reducing corruption in public procurement in the EU. Technical report, European Commission (2013). https://ec.europa.eu/anti-fraud/sites/antifraud/files/docs/body/identifying_reducing_corruption_in_public_procurement_en.pdf

17. Fournier-Viger, P., Cheng, C., Lin, J.C.-W., Yun, U., Kiran, R.U.: TKG: efficient mining of top-k frequent subgraphs. In: Madria, S., Fournier-Viger, P., Chaudhary, S., Reddy, P.K. (eds.) BDA 2019. LNCS, vol. 11932, pp. 209–226. Springer, Cham (2019). https://doi.org/10.1007/978-3-030-37188-3_13

18. Fournier-Viger, P., et al.: The SPMF open-source data mining library version 2. In: Berendt, B., et al. (eds.) ECML PKDD 2016. LNCS (LNAI), vol. 9853, pp. 36–40. Springer, Cham (2016). https://doi.org/10.1007/978-3-319-46131-1_8

19. Hagberg, A.A., Schult, D.A., Swart, P.J.: Exploring network structure, dynamics, and function using NetworkX. In: 7th Python in Science Conference, pp. 11–15 (2008). https://conference.scipy.org/proceedings/SciPy2008/paper_2/

20. Houbraken, M., Demeyer, S., Michoel, T., Audenaert, P., Colle, D., Pickavet, M.: The index-based subgraph matching algorithm with general symmetries (ISMAGS): exploiting symmetry for faster subgraph enumeration. PLoS ONE **9**(5), e97896 (2014). https://doi.org/10.1371/journal.pone.0097896

21. Hsieh, S.-M., Hsu, C.-C., Hsu, L.-F.: Efficient method to perform isomorphism testing of labeled graphs. In: Gavrilova, M.L., et al. (eds.) ICCSA 2006. LNCS, vol. 3984, pp. 422–431. Springer, Heidelberg (2006). https://doi.org/10.1007/11751649_46

22. Huan, J., Wang, W., Prins, J.: Efficient mining of frequent subgraphs in the presence of isomorphism. In: 3rd IEEE International Conference on Data Mining (2003). https://doi.org/10.1109/icdm.2003.1250974

23. Kane, B., Cuissart, B., Crémilleux, B.: Minimal jumping emerging patterns: computation and practical assessment. In: Cao, T., Lim, E.-P., Zhou, Z.-H., Ho, T.-B., Cheung, D., Motoda, H. (eds.) PAKDD 2015. LNCS (LNAI), vol. 9077, pp. 722–733. Springer, Cham (2015). https://doi.org/10.1007/978-3-319-18038-0_56

24. Kim, H., Lee, B.S., Shin, W.Y., Lim, S.: Graph anomaly detection with graph neural networks: current status and challenges. IEEE Access 10, 111820–111829 (2022). https://doi.org/10.1109/access.2022.3211306

25. Kriege, N.M., Giscard, P.L., Wilson, R.: On valid optimal assignment kernels and applications to graph classification. In: 30th International Conference on Neural Information Processing Systems, pp. 1623–1631 (2016). https://proceedings.neurips.cc/paper_files/paper/2016/hash/0efe32849d230d7f53049ddc4a4b0c60-Abstract.html

26. Li, R., Wang, W.: REAFUM: representative approximate frequent subgraph mining. In: SIAM International Conference on Data Mining, pp. 757–765 (2015). https://doi.org/10.1137/1.9781611974010.85

27. Loyola-González, O., Medina-Pérez, M.A., Choo, K.R.: A review of supervised classification based on contrast patterns: applications, trends, and challenges. J. Grid Comput. 18(4), 797–845 (2020). https://doi.org/10.1007/s10723-020-09526-y

28. Luo, X., et al.: Deep graph level anomaly detection with contrastive learning. Sci. Rep. 12, 19867 (2022). https://doi.org/10.1038/s41598-022-22086-3

29. Ma, R., Pang, G., Chen, L., van den Hengel, A.: Deep graph-level anomaly detection by glocal knowledge distillation. In: 15th ACM International Conference on Web Search and Data Mining, pp. 704–714 (2022). https://doi.org/10.1145/3488560.3498473

30. Ma, X., et al.: A comprehensive survey on graph anomaly detection with deep learning. IEEE Trans. Knowl. Data Eng. (2021, in press). https://doi.org/10.1109/TKDE.2021.3118815

31. Malik, R., Khan, K.U., Nawaz, W.: Maximal gSpan: multi-document summarization through frequent subgraph mining. In: 17th International Conference on Ubiquitous Information Management and Communication, pp. 1–7 (2023). https://doi.org/10.1109/imcom56909.2023.10035618

32. Maréchal, F., Morand, P.H.: Are social and environmental clauses a tool for favoritism? Analysis of French public procurement contracts. Eur. J. Polit. Econ. 73, 102140 (2022). https://doi.org/10.1016/j.ejpoleco.2021.102140

33. Métivier, J.P., et al.: Discovering structural alerts for mutagenicity using stable emerging molecular patterns. J. Chem. Inf. Model. 55(5), 925–940 (2015). https://doi.org/10.1021/ci500611v

34. Mooney, C.H., Roddick, J.F.: Sequential pattern mining - approaches and algorithms. ACM Comput. Surv. 45(2), 1–39 (2013). https://doi.org/10.1145/2431211.2431218

35. Narayanan, A., Chandramohan, M., Venkatesan, R., Chen, L., Liu, Y., Jaiswal, S.: graph2vec: learning distributed representations of graphs. In: 13th International Workshop on Mining and Learning with Graphs, p. 21 (2017). https://arxiv.org/abs/1707.05005

36. National Fraud Authority: Red flags for integrity: Giving the green light to open data solutions. Technical report, Open Contracting Partnership, Development Gateway (2016). https://www.open-contracting.org/wp-content/uploads/2016/11/OCP2016-Red-flags-for-integrityshared-1.pdf

37. Potin, L., Labatut, V., Figueiredo, R., Largeron, C., Morand, P.H.: FOPPA: a database of French Open Public Procurement Award notices. Technical report, Avignon Université (2022). https://hal.archives-ouvertes.fr/hal-03796734

38. Potin, L., Labatut, V., Largeron, C., Morand, P.H.: FOPPA: an open database of French public procurement award notices from 2010–2020. Sci. Data **10**, 303 (2023). https://doi.org/10.1038/s41597-023-02213-z

39. Pourhabibi, T., Ong, K.L., Kam, B.H., Boo, Y.L.: Fraud detection: a systematic literature review of graph-based anomaly detection approaches. Decis. Support Syst. **133**, 113303 (2020). https://doi.org/10.1016/j.dss.2020.113303

40. Rizzo, I.: Efficiency and integrity issues in public procurement performance. J. Public Finance Public Choice **31**(1–3), 111–128 (2013). https://doi.org/10.1332/251569213x15664519748613

41. Rozemberczki, B., Kiss, O., Sarkar, R.: Karate Club: an API oriented open-source Python framework for unsupervised learning on graphs. In: 29th ACM International Conference on Information and Knowledge Management, pp. 3125–3132 (2020). https://doi.org/10.1145/3340531.3412757

42. Shaul, Z., Naaz, S.: cgSpan: closed graph-based substructure pattern mining. In: IEEE International Conference on Big Data (2021). https://doi.org/10.1109/BigData52589.2021.9671995

43. Shervashidze, N., Schweitzer, P., van Leeuwen, E.J., Mehlhorn, K., Borgwardt, K.M.: Weisfeiler-Lehman graph kernels. J. Mach. Learn. Res. **12**(77), 2539–2561 (2011). http://jmlr.org/papers/v12/shervashidze11a.html

44. Siglidis, G., Nikolentzos, G., Limnios, S., Giatsidis, C., Skianis, K., Vazirgiannis, M.: GraKeL: a graph kernel library in Python. J. Mach. Learn. Res. **21**(54), 1–5 (2020). https://www.jmlr.org/papers/v21/18-370.html

45. Thoma, M., et al.: Discriminative frequent subgraph mining with optimality guarantees. Stat. Anal. Data Min. **3**(5), 302–318 (2010). https://doi.org/10.1002/sam.10084

46. Toivonen, H., Srinivasan, A., King, R.D., Kramer, S., Helma, C.: Statistical evaluation of the predictive toxicology challenge 2000–2001. Bioinformatics **19**(10), 1183–1193 (2003). https://doi.org/10.1093/bioinformatics/btg130

47. Wachs, J., Kertész, J.: A network approach to cartel detection in public auction markets. Sci. Rep. **9**, 10818 (2019). https://doi.org/10.1038/s41598-019-47198-1

48. Wale, N., Karypis, G.: Comparison of descriptor spaces for chemical compound retrieval and classification. In: 6th International Conference on Data Mining, pp. 678–689 (2006). https://doi.org/10.1109/icdm.2006.39

49. Yan, X., Cheng, H., Han, J., Yu, P.S.: Mining significant graph patterns by leap search. In: ACM SIGMOD International Conference on Management of Data, pp. 433–444 (2008). https://doi.org/10.1145/1376616.1376662

50. Yan, X., Han, J.: gSpan: graph-based substructure pattern mining. In: IEEE International Conference on Data Mining, pp. 721–724 (2002). https://doi.org/10.1109/ICDM.2002.1184038

51. Yang, Z., Zhang, G., Wu, J., Yang, J.: A comprehensive survey of graph-level learning. arXiv cs.LG, 2301.05860 (2023). https://arxiv.org/abs/2301.05860

52. Yuan, H., Yu, H., Gui, S., Ji, S.: Explainability in graph neural networks: a taxonomic survey. IEEE Trans. Pattern Anal. Mach. Intell. (2022, in press). https://doi.org/10.1109/tpami.2022.3204236

53. Zhang, M., Cui, Z., Neumann, M., Chen, Y.: An end-to-end deep learning architecture for graph classification. In: AAAI Conference on Artificial Intelligence, vol. 32, pp. 4438–4445 (2018). https://doi.org/10.1609/aaai.v32i1.11782

Aspect-Based Complaint and Cause Detection: A Multimodal Generative Framework with External Knowledge Infusion

Raghav Jain[✉], Apoorv Verma, Apoorva Singh, Vivek Gangwar, and Sriparna Saha

Indian Institute of Technology Patna, Patna, India
raghavjain106@gmail.com

Abstract. Customer reviews often contain valuable feedback about a product or service, but it can be challenging to extract specific complaints and their underlying causes from the text. Despite the use of various methods to detect and analyze complaints, no studies have concentrated on thoroughly examining complaints at the aspect-level and the underlying reasons for such aspect-level complaints. We add the rationale annotation for the aspect-based complaint classes in a publicly available benchmark multimodal complaint dataset (CESAMARD), which spans five domains (books, electronics, edibles, fashion, and miscellaneous). Current multimodal complaint detection methods treat these tasks as classification problems and do not utilize external knowledge. The present study aims to tackle these concerns. We propose a knowledge-infused unified Multimodal Generative framework for Aspect-based complaint and Cause detection (MuGACD) by reframing the multitasking problem as a multimodal text-to-text generation task. Our proposed methodology established a benchmark performance in the novel aspect-based complaint and cause detection task based on extensive evaluation. We also demonstrated that our model consistently outperformed all other baselines and state-of-the-art models in both full and few-shot settings (The dataset and code are available at https://github.com/Raghav10j/ECML23).

Keywords: Complaint Detection · Cause Analysis · Explainable AI · Multi-task learning · Generative Modeling · Deep learning

1 Introduction

The use of multimodal systems allows customers to examine products and provide feedback on their preferences, but analyzing user-generated text and managing this type of review can be difficult due to the sporadic nature of the reviews and the limited availability of necessary resources and techniques. As a result,

---

R. Jain, A. Verma and A. Singh—Equal contribution.

© The Author(s), under exclusive license to Springer Nature Switzerland AG 2023
G. De Francisci Morales et al. (Eds.): ECML PKDD 2023, LNAI 14174, pp. 88–104, 2023.
https://doi.org/10.1007/978-3-031-43427-3_6

it has become essential for researchers to develop reliable techniques for swiftly evaluating consumer content. Complaint detection is one such endeavour [11,19]. According to Olshtain et al. [17], complaints arise because of the discrepancy between actuality and people's expectations. Depending on the seriousness and urgency of the situation, people use complaints to communicate their concerns or discontent Fig. 1.

Fig. 1. Example of aspect-based complaint and cause detection. The highlighted text shows the causal span of complaint for the packaging aspect.

Motivation: Earlier studies on complaint analysis detect complaints at the sentence or review level [9,23,25]. Among these studies, we note two missing elements which are the aspect information and the reason/rationale of the complaint at the aspect-level. For example, if a user dislikes an online purchased edible product, it may not be evident 'what' aspect the user finds problematic or 'why' the user is complaining.

The Aspect-based Complaint and Cause identification (AbCC) framework could be useful in this scenario. There are currently no complaint-cause detection frameworks that are guided by aspects, to the best of our knowledge. AbCC consists of three sub-tasks: aspect class detection (ACD), aspect-level complaint classification (ACC), and aspect-level rationale detection (ARD). The first sub-task identifies the aspects present in the instance and assigns them to one of several aspect categories. In the second subtask, fine-grained aspect categories along with review text and image, are used to classify instances at the aspect-level as either complaints or non-complaints. The third sub-task involves identifying the rationale behind the aspect-level complaint.

We believe that by leveraging external knowledge, complaint detection systems can gain a deeper understanding of a consumer's situation and concerns, leading to more effective solutions. As an additional knowledge base for this study, we have utilized ConceptNet [28] due to its extensive collection of commonsense knowledge [14]. This knowledge base covers commonly held beliefs, including information about social groups and situations. Additionally, prior studies have indicated that performing a related supplementary task alongside the primary task can improve performance [16,25]. However, this approach can lead to negative transfer and pose optimization challenges [5,34]. To overcome these issues, we propose using multimodal text-to-text generation for aspect-based complaint and cause detection, inspired by the generative language models' ability to solve downstream tasks in both full and few-shot (low resource and data constrained) scenarios [3].

Research Objectives: Following are the research objectives of the current study:

(1) We aim to explore how multimodal cues can assist in the identification of aspect categories, the assignment of the aspect-level complaint/non-complaint labels, and the determination of complaint causal spans at the aspect-level using social media data.
(2) This work aims to study how a generative model can be adapted to solve classification tasks like complaint and cause detection in a multimodal setting.

Contributions: The major contributions of the current work are as follows:

(1) We propose the novel task of aspect-based complaint and rationale detection in a multimodal setup.
(2) We enhance the existing CESAMARD dataset [23] by manually annotating the causal span for each aspect-level complaint instance.
(3) We propose a knowledge-infused unified Multimodal Generative framework for Aspect-based complaint and Cause Detection, *MuGACD*, which reframes the multitasking problem as a multimodal text-to-text generation task and addresses three problems simultaneously, aspect class detection (ACD), aspect-level complaint classification (ACC), and aspect-level rationale detection (ARD).
(4) The proposed model serves as a benchmark for aspect-based complaint and cause identification (AbCC) and outperforms several strong baselines based on the state-of-the-art related models. Evaluation results demonstrate that the proposed generative model consistently achieves significantly better performance than other baselines and state-of-the-art models in both full and few-shot settings.

2   Related Studies

Linguists and psychologists have consistently found that people shape their complaints to varying extents [8,17,30]. A complaint can be implicit (that is, without identifying who is at fault) or explicit. (i.e., accusing someone of doing something) [31]. The authors in [30] grouped complaints based on their emotional depth into four granular severity levels: (a) no particular reproach; (b) disapproval; (c) accusation; and (d) blame. Minor complaints can achieve the goal of expressing emotions to promote psychological wellness, but severe complaints can result in animosity and even aggressive behaviors [7].

    In computational linguistics, earlier research has mainly focused on developing automated classification techniques for detecting the presence of complaints [4,9,19]. Moreover, multitask complaint analysis models that integrated sentiment and emotion information to improve the complaint mining task have been developed [25–27]. Additionally, complaints have been previously categorized based on responsible department, and degree of urgency [12,36].

The study in [23] proposed a binary complaint classifier based on multimodal information without considering the particular features or aspects about which the user is complaining. The public release of the multimodal complaint dataset (CESAMARD) [23], a collection of consumer feedback or reviews and images of products purchased from the e-commerce website Amazon[1], has aided additional investigations into complaint detection in multimodal setup.

This study diverges from previous multimodal, multitask complaint detection research in two ways. Firstly, we focus on identifying complaints from various aspects of product reviews using the associated text and image. Secondly, we treat the multitasking problem as a language generation task, eliminating the need for task-specific layers.

Table 1. Annotation guidelines for *CESAMARD-Span* dataset.

S.No.	Annotation Guidelines
1	Causal span should consider the complainant's perspective
2	Causal span should imply aspect-level complaint labeled instances only
3	Causal span annotation should be marked in the same speech form as used in the instance
4	Causal span for aspect-level non-complaint instances should be marked as Nan
5	Each causal span should refer to a single aspect
6	Erroneous labels if found should be reported and rectified

3   Dataset Extension

For this work, we utilize the extended *CESAMARD* dataset[2]. This dataset was chosen because it is the only publicly available multimodal complaint dataset to the best of our knowledge. The CESAMARD dataset comprises 3962 reviews, with 2641 reviews in the non-complaint category and 1321 reviews in the complaint category. Each record in the dataset contains the image URL, review title, review text, and associated complaint, sentiment, and emotion labels. Additionally, the CESAMARD dataset is organized into different domains, such as electronics, edibles, fashion, books, and miscellaneous, which is why we decided to use it for aspect-level complaint and cause identification.

We undertake the task of manually annotating complaint causal span or rationale at the aspect level, utilizing the available text and image data. Further details about these activities can be found in the following section.

---

[1] https://www.amazon.in.

[2] https://github.com/appy1608/ECIR2023_Complaint-Detection.

3.1   Annotator Details

Three annotators, two doctoral and one graduate student annotated the causal span for each of the aspect-level complaint-type reviews in the dataset. They are well-versed in labeling tasks and possess adequate domain understanding and experience in developing supervised corpora. All of them are proficient in English, having been educated in an English-medium environment.

Table 2. Aspect categories and the total number of instances corresponding to different domains present in the dataset.

Domains	Instances	Aspect Categories
Edibles	450	Taste, Smell, Packaging, Price, Quality
Books	690	Content, Packaging, Price, Quality
Fashion	1275	Colour, Style, Fit, Packaging, Price, Quality
Electronics	1507	Design, Software, Hardware, Packaging, Price, Quality
Miscellaneous	40	Miscellaneous, Packaging, Price, Quality

3.2   Annotation Phase and Dataset Analysis

The annotators were given annotation guidelines (Table 1) and 50 examples to guide them for annotation and ambiguity resolution. We use a similar strategy in line with work in the related field of aspect-based sentiment analysis [1] and SemEval shared tasks for understanding and annotating the aspect-level causal spans. Table 2 depicts the various aspect categories and the total number of instances in each of the five domains in the extended dataset. All domains have three features in common: packaging, price, and quality. This is because all of these aspects are important when making purchases online. For each aspect-level complaint instance in the dataset, annotators were instructed to identify the causal span that best captured the reason/rationale for the complaint label. The Fleiss-Kappa [6] agreement scores of 0.69 and 0.83 were reported for ACI and ACC tasks in [24], which signifies a substantial agreement between the annotators [2]. With an understanding of previous studies on cause/rationale detection [18], we use the macro-F1 [21] metric to evaluate inter-annotator agreement. The result is a 0.75 F1 score, which shows that the causal span annotations are of an acceptable standard. Note that if the review is categorized as non-complaint as a whole, then all aspect-level annotations will also be marked as non-complaint. However, in cases where there is a complaint at the review level, certain aspects may still be considered non-complaint. Each review instance is marked with at most six aspects in the dataset.

Table 3 illustrates a few examples of aspect terms, aspect-level complaint labels, and the complaint rationale annotations from the *CESAMARD-Span* dataset. The 40 instances in the miscellaneous domain were not enough to train a deep learning model, so they were not used for further training.

Table 3. Few examples from the *CESAMARD-Span* dataset with ACD and ACC task annotation. Labels: auxiliary tasks sentiment and emotion labels

Review	Image	Aspect Terms	Labels	Span
Product quality is quite good but		Quality	Non-Comp	Nan
didn't like the fit, tight on shoulders. *Labels: Negative, Sadness*		Fit	Comp	tight on shoulders
Package torn near zipper, spillage noticed.		Package	Comp	torn near zipper
Complained, got no response. Pathetic service *Labels: Negative, Anger*		Service	Comp	got no response

4   Methodology

4.1   Problem Formulation

For a given review instance, R is represented as $\{[T, I, A_k, c_k, s_k]_i\}_{i=1}^N$, where T denotes the review text, I is the review image, A_k denotes the aspect categories, c_k is the associated complaint/non-complaint labels for every aspect category and s_k denotes the causal span for every complaint label present in the review instance. The first task is to identify the aspect categories, A_k and the second task involves detecting the complaint/non-complaint labels, c_k, and the corresponding causal span for that label s_k, for each of the identified aspect categories present in A_k (Fig. 2).

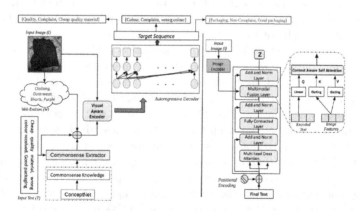

Fig. 2. Architectural diagram of the proposed model, *MuGACD* (Multimodal Generative Aspect-based complaint and Cause Detection framework). The left side denotes the complete flow of the proposed model and the right side denotes the proposed visual aware encoder which is used for fusing textual and visual content.

4.2 Redefining AbCC Task as Multimodal Text-to-Text Generation Task

Here, we propose a multimodal text-to-text generation paradigm for solving aspect-based complaint detection in a single unified manner. To transform this problem into a multimodal text generation problem, we first construct a natural language target sequence, Y_i, for input review text, R_i $(T_i \cup I_i)$, for training purposes as defined in Eq. 1.

$$Y_i = [A1, c1, s1][A2, c2, s2].... \qquad (1)$$

Now the problem can be reformulated as: given an input review R_i, the task is to generate an output sequence, Y_i', containing all the predictions defined in Eq. 1 using a generative model G; $Y_i' = G(T_i, I_i)$.

4.3 Multimodal Generative Aspect-Based Complaint and Cause Detection Framework (MuGACD)

MuGACD is a knowledge-infused unified multimodal generative approach that solves the task of complaint detection at the aspect-level. For better understanding, we divide our approach into two steps: 1) Knowledge extraction module, and 2) Multimodal transformer model.

Knowledge Extraction Module. We use a knowledge extraction module to provide more context and background information to a review, as customers' reviews are usually short and cursory. The knowledge extraction module provides two types of external knowledge to the input review, one for text modality (T) in the form of commonsense reasoning and the second one for image modality (I) in the form of web entities.

For input review text T: We employ ConceptNet [28] as our knowledge base to extract commonsense reasoning regarding social entities and events involved in the input text, T. At first, we feed the input text, T_i, to the knowledge extraction module to extract the top 5 commonsense reasoning triplets using the same strategy as mentioned in [29] where a triplet will consist of two entities and a connection/relation between these two entities which is then converted into a single sentence. To obtain the final commonsense reasoning CS for each input text, T_i, we concatenate these five commonsense reasonings together.

For image I: Motivated by Zhu et al. [37], we propose web entities as a higher-level image concept to capture the context and background information of all the entities and references in the image for our model. We use Google Cloud Vision API[3] to extract web entities from input images. At first, we feed image I_i to the google cloud vision API to obtain the web entity set $\{p_0, p_1, ..., p_k\}$. To obtain the final external contextual knowledge P_i for each image I_i, we concatenate all these individual entities.

---

[3] https://cloud.google.com/vision/docs/detecting-web.

We concatenate the input review text T_i with its corresponding commonsense reasoning CS and web entity tag P_i to obtain the final textual information X_i that we are going to feed to our model: $X_i = T_i \oplus P_i \oplus CS$.

Multimodal Transformer Model. To fuse the information from both image and text modalities, we have proposed a visual aware encoder, an extension of the original transformer encoder [32]. At first, the input text X_i is tokenized and converted into a sequence of embeddings. Then positional encodings are added to these token embeddings to retain their positional information before feeding input to the proposed visual aware encoder. Our visual aware encoder is composed of three sub-layers: 1) Multi-head Self-Attention (MSA), 2) Feedforward Network (FFN) and 3) Multimodal Fusion (MuF). MSA and FFN are standard sub-layers as used in the original transformer encoder [32]. We have added a MuF sub-layer as a means to fuse the visual information from image I in our model which works as follows: At first, we obtain the encoded representation, H_{EN} after feeding the tokenized input X_i to the first two sub-layers (MSA and FFN). Similarly, we feed the corresponding image I_i through a VGG-19 encoder [22] to obtain the image feature vector, G_{IM}. We feed this encoded text representation H_{EN} and image feature vector G_{IM} to the Multimodal fusion (MuF) sub-layer. Unlike the standard transformer encoder where we project the same input as query, key, and value, in the visual aware encoder, we implement a context-aware self-attention mechanism inside MuF to facilitate the exchange of information between H_{EN} and G_{IM}, motivated by [35]. We create two triplets of queries, keys, and values matrices corresponding to H_{EN} and G_{IM}, respectively: (Q_x, K_x, V_x) and (Q_{im}, K_{im}, V_{im}). Triplets (Q_x, K_x, V_x) are generated by linearly projecting the input text representation, H_{EN}, whereas triplets (Q_{im}, K_{im}, V_{im}) are obtained through a gating mechanism as given in [35] which works as follows: To maintain a balance between fusing information from visual image representation, G_{IM}, and retain original information from text representation, H_{EN}, we learn matrices λ_K and λ_V to create context-aware K_{im} and V_{im} (Eq. 2).

$$\begin{bmatrix} K_{im} \\ V_{im} \end{bmatrix} = (1 - \begin{bmatrix} \lambda_K \\ \lambda_V \end{bmatrix}) \begin{bmatrix} K_x \\ V_x \end{bmatrix} + \begin{bmatrix} \lambda_K \\ \lambda_V \end{bmatrix} (G_{IM} \begin{bmatrix} U_K \\ U_V \end{bmatrix}) \tag{2}$$

where U_K and U_V are learnable parameters and matrices λ_K and λ_V are computed as follows:

$$\begin{bmatrix} \lambda_K \\ \lambda_V \end{bmatrix} = \sigma(\begin{bmatrix} K_x \\ V_x \end{bmatrix} \begin{bmatrix} W_K^X \\ W_V^X \end{bmatrix} + G_{IM} \begin{bmatrix} U_K \\ U_V \end{bmatrix} \begin{bmatrix} W_K^{IM} \\ W_V^{IM} \end{bmatrix}) \tag{3}$$

where W_K^X, W_V^X, W_K^{IM}, and W_V^{IM} all are learnable parameters. σ represents the sigmoid function computation.

After obtaining K_{im} and V_{im}, we apply the dot product attention-based fusion method over Q_x, K_{im} and V_{im} to obtain the final visual image aware input representation Z computed as defined in following equation:
$Z = softmax(\frac{Q_x K_{im}^T}{\sqrt{d_k}}) V_{im}$.

At last, we pass this visual image-aware input representation vector, Z, to an autoregressive decoder computed as follows: We will feed Z and all the output tokens till time step $t - 1$ represented as $Y_{<t}$ to the decoder module to obtain the hidden state at the time step t as defined in following equation, $H_{DE}^t = G_{Decoder}(Z, Y_{<t})$ where $G_{Decoder}$ denotes the decoder computations. The conditional probability for the predicted output token at t^{th} time step, given the input and previous $t - 1$ tokens is calculated by applying the softmax function over the hidden state, H_{DEC}^t, as follows: $P_\theta(Y_t'|X_i, Y_{<t}) = F_{softmax}(\theta^T H_{DE}^t)$ where $F_{softmax}$ represents softmax computation and θ denotes weights/parameters of our model.

Loss Function: We initialize our model's weights θ with weights of a pre-trained sequence to sequence generative model. We then fine-tune the model with the Negative log-likelihood training objective, i.e., the maximum likelihood estimation (MLE) objective function, which works in a supervised manner to optimize the weights, θ, as defined in the following Equation: $\max_\theta \prod_{t=0}^{T} P_\theta(Y_t'|X_i, Y_{<t})$.

5   Experiments and Results

This section describes the experiments, results, and analysis of our proposed model, *MuGACD*. The experiments are intended to address the following research questions:

RQ1: How does the generative paradigm perform in comparison to traditional multi-task models?

RQ2: How do each of the modalities contribute to the performance of ACD, ACC, and ARD tasks?

RQ3: What is the impact of external knowledge on the performance of our framework?

RQ4: How does the performance of the context-aware attention mechanism compare to that of the simple fusion method (concatenation)?

RQ5: Is *MuGACD* able to outperform state-of-the-art models for ACD, ACC and ARD subtasks?

RQ6: How does *MuGACD* perform in a few-shot setting?

5.1   Baselines

We evaluate the *MuGACD* model by comparing it with both basic unimodal methods and more sophisticated multimodal fusion techniques. We engage in a comprehensive analysis of each baseline on an individual basis:

Unimodal Baselines: To train the Text model, we provide the classifier with the output from the ultimate layer of a pre-trained base-uncased RoBERTa model. The input is purely textual in nature. On the other hand, the Image model leverages a pre-trained ResNet-152 model with average pooling to classify each image, producing a 2048-dimensional vector output.

Generative Baselines: We use BART [13], and T5 [20] as the baseline text-to-text generation models. We fine-tune these models on the proposed dataset with the Negative log-likelihood training objective where the input sequence is the review tweet, and concatenated outputs (defined in Eq. 1) are the target sequence.

Text&Image: In this particular baseline, the outputs of both the Text and Image baselines are merged together, resulting in an input of size 2048 + 768 dimensions for the classifier. This approach is noteworthy since it combines the encoders for both modalities, granting the classifier complete access to the encoder outputs. We also implemented a variation of $MuGACD$ model, $MuGACD_{Con}$ where we directly concatenate the encoded text representations (H_{EN}) and image features (G_{IM}) instead of context-aware attention mechanism.

SpanBERT [10]: SpanBERT is a pre-training approach that improves the representation and prediction of spans of text. It outperforms BERT consistently, with the largest gains on span selection tasks. The approach randomly selects contiguous spans which are used to train the model.

ViLBERT [15]: Our approach involves utilizing ViLBERT, which is a collaborative framework for obtaining a task-independent visual basis for coupled visual-linguistic information. ViLBERT comprises of separate processing streams for both visual and linguistic modalities, which are interlinked through co-attentive transformer layers.

5.2 Experimental Setup

This section outlines a range of hyperparameters and experimental configurations used in our study. Our experiments were conducted exclusively on Tyrone's computer, equipped with Intel's Xeon W-2155 Processor, featuring 196 Gb DDR4 RAM and an 11 Gb Nvidia 1080Ti GPU. To conduct our experiments, we partitioned the CESAMARD-Aspect dataset into three sets: 70% of the data was employed as training data, 10% was designated for validation, and the remaining 20% was utilized for testing all of the experimental models. A seed value of 32 was chosen for all experiments to ensure a fair comparison. Our proposed framework, MuGACD, is built upon the BART-base model [13]. The training process of our model involves 60 epochs with a batch size of 16, utilizing the Adam optimizer with an epsilon value of 0.00000001. In the context of the ACD task, we present both macro-F1 score and micro-F1 score as measures for evaluating the model's predictive ability. Similarly, in relation to the ACC task, we report both macro-F1 score and accuracy. To perform a quantitative evaluation of the ARD task, we employed several metrics, including Jaccard Similarity (JS), Hamming Distance (HD), and Ratcliff-Obershelp Similarity (ROS).

5.3 Results and Discussion

Table 4 shows the outcomes of the proposed framework and all the baselines discussed in the previous section.

(RQ1:) As can be observed from Table 4, the proposed model $MuGACD$ outperforms all the other baselines for ACD, ACC, and ARD tasks by a significant margin across all domains. $MuGACD$ outperforms the best generative baseline

Table 4. The results of our experiments for the aspect category detection task and the aspect category complaint detection task were measured using the micro-F1 score and macro-F1 score, as well as accuracy and macro-F1 score metrics. For the aspect-level rationale detection task, we utilized Jaccard Similarity (JS), Hamming Distance (HD), and Ratcliff-Obershelp Similarity (ROS) metrics, with bolded values representing the highest scores attained. The abbreviations ACD, ACC, and ARD also refer to aspect class detection, aspect-level complaint classification, and aspect-level rationale detection, respectively. The symbol "†" indicates statistically significant results.

Domain	Model	ACD		ACC		ARD		
		Micro-F1	Macro-F1	Accuracy	Macro-F1	JS	HD	ROS
Books	Text	60.45	52.89	73.61	72.19	–	–	–
	Image	31.25	29.97	47.77	45.57	–	–	–
	Text&Image	66.04	60.31	74.78	73.05	–	–	–
	SOTA [23]	62.09	57.88	77.42	76.28	–	–	–
	SpanBERT	–	–	–	–	69.05	62.11	71.98
	ViLBERT	71.34	68.41	77.84	76.78	69.23	62.04	72.22
	MuGACD$_{con}$	64.34	68.41	72.84	71.78	67.81	60.61	72.01
	T5	71.79	71.05	87.28	87.18	66.13	59.10	71.81
	BART	75.79	71.05	87.28	86.98	68.24	59.21	74.89
	MuGACD	**85.71**†	**76.18**†	**92.11**†	**92.01**†	**78.72**†	**70.11**†	**82.19**†
Edibles	Text	59.08	55.87	74.38	72.02	–	–	–
	Image	33.47	29.87	48.52	47.22	–	–	–
	Text&Image	61.03	57.89	78.95	77.67	–	–	–
	SOTA [23]	63.78	59.98	78.73	78.41	–	–	–
	SpanBERT	–	–	–	–	45.63	40.22	51.27
	ViLBERT	65.79	61.05	81.28	79.18	40.34	35.31	47.22
	MuGACD$_{con}$	68.34	61.41	77.84	76.78	44.19	40.91	50.37
	T5	69.79	67.05	85.28	84.18	41.31	36.54	48.11
	BART	72.79	71.05	86.28	85.18	41.37	37.75	49.09
	MuGACD	**75.88**†	**79.66**†	**92.50**†	**91.23**†	**56.11**†	**49.99**†	**61.51**†
Electronics	Text	67.45	59.87	77.51	76.76	–	–	–
	Image	35.55	31.89	50.78	49.17	–	–	–
	Text&Image	68.88	62.49	79.48	78.12	–	–	–
	SOTA [23]	69.88	61.56	81.34	78.27	–	–	–
	SpanBERT	–	–	–	–	61.32	53.44	65.41
	ViLBERT	71.89	**65.87**	82.46	80.28	65.77	52.32	66.21
	MuGACD$_{con}$	67.34	58.41	71.24	70.78	62.72	54.67	67.99
	T5	70.79	59.05	84.28	83.18	60.91	53.02	65.91
	BART	70.99	59.25	86.28	86.18	60.74	52.82	65.44
	MuGACD	**72.45**†	64.82†	**93.62**†	**93.27**†	**69.82**†	**61.94**†	**72.14**†
Fashion	Text	65.56	59.14	76.59	74.77	–	–	–
	Image	32.43	30.12	46.56	44.06	–	–	–
	Text&Image	66.45	61.51	78.08	77.62	–	–	–
	SOTA [23]	65.78	59.08	81.23	80.04	–	–	–
	SpanBERT	–	–	–	–	70.25	65.93	73.22
	ViLBERT	70.48	65.67	83.37	82.07	70.98	67.29	74.71
	MuGACD$_{con}$	68.34	62.41	79.84	79.78	71.92	65.71	73.29
	T5	70.79	69.05	83.28	81.18	71.13	65.06	73.21
	BART	71.79	71.05	84.28	85.18	72.00	65.10	74.61
	MuGACD	**72.84**†	**70.32**†	**91.27**†	**90.25**†	**75.57**†	**67.84**†	**77.84**†

(BART), text-only baseline, and multimodal baseline (ViLBERT) on all metrics for all tasks, illustrating the superiority of pre-trained sequence-to-sequence language models. Even in text-only settings, generative models (T5 and BART) outperform text-only baselines. These findings validate our idea of reframing the aspect-based complaint and cause detection problem as a multimodal text-to-text generation task.

(**RQ2:**) We proposed two ablation models to study the contribution of each of the modalities (shown in Table 5): 1) $MuGACD - Text$ (without textual modality), and 2) $MuGACD - Image$ (without visual modality). It can be observed that $MuGACD - Text$ reports a below-average performance in all tasks, as the image alone doesn't convey sufficient information to make a correct prediction. However, $MuGACD - Image$ performs significantly better than $MuGACD - Text$. The reason for this can be attributed to the facts: 1) the strength of seq2seq encoder-decoder architecture to model the textual information, and 2) in many cases, the textual part of reviews contains harsh words and reasons for a complaint which results in enhanced performance as compared to $MuGACD - Text$ ablation model.

(**RQ3:**) We also proposed two ablation models ($MuGACD$-CS and $MuGACD$-WE) in Table 5 to study the effect of external knowledge on the model's performance. When we remove commonsense reasoning (CS) from the model, we see a more significant drop in ACD, ACC, and ARD subtasks than removing the web entity (WE), which does not result in a significant drop. Yet, together with CS, the proposed model $MuGACD$ is able to outperform all other baselines and ablation models in all domains.

(**RQ4:**) We have proposed a variant of $MuGACD$ model, $MuGACD_{Con}$ to study the impact of context-aware self-attention. $MuGACD_{Con}$ depicts the case where we perform bimodal concatenation of image representation (G_{im}) and text representation (H_{en}). In comparison with $MuGACD$, $MuGACD_{Con}$ reports a below-average performance for all tasks. This illustrates the need for a suitable and perfectly formulated multimodal fusion technique.

(**RQ5:**) In order to compare the effectiveness of our proposed method for aspect-based complaint detection, we conduct a comparison with the current state-of-the-art technique, as no existing multi-modal aspect-based complaint detection model is known to us. The state-of-the-art technique, referred to as SOTA [23], employs an attention-based adversarial multi-task deep neural network framework to detect complaints in a multimodal environment. We replicate the SOTA model for the aspect-based complaint detection task while maintaining the same experimental setup as our own work. Our experimental results, as shown in Table 4, demonstrate that our proposed MuGACD model performs better than the SOTA model for both sub-tasks. In the context of the ARD task, we conducted a comparison between the performance of $MuGACD$ and the top-performing baseline model for the span detection task, which is Span-BERT. Our findings indicate that $MuGACD$ exhibits a substantial improvement in performance across all metrics when compared to SpanBERT.

Table 5. Results of the ablation studies performed on MuGACD.

Domain	Model	AD		ACD		ARD		
		Micro-F1	Macro-F1	Accuracy	Macro-F1	JS	HD	ROS
Books	MuGACD	**85.71**[†]	**76.18**[†]	**92.11**[†]	**92.01**[†]	**78.72**[†]	**70.11**[†]	**82.19**[†]
	MuGACD−CS	84.25	75.17	91.77	91.57	76.31	69.26	80.10
	MuGACD−WE	84.99	75.88	91.89	91.98	77.02	69.99	82.12
	MuGACD−$Text$	75.13	52.11	77.84	72.71	59.13	53.04	62.11
	MuGACD−$Image$	83.34	74.41	90.84	89.78	77.79	70.01	81.73
Edibles	MuGACD	**75.88**[†]	**79.66**[†]	**92.50**[†]	**91.23**[†]	**56.11**[†]	**49.99**[†]	**61.51**[†]
	MuGACD−CS	74.15	78.17	91.17	90.57	55.01	47.91	59.04
	MuGACD−WE	74.59	78.98	92.12	90.82	55.81	48.12	59.83
	MuGACD−$Text$	51.33	51.01	71.14	70.78	40.91	35.19	44.21
	MuGACD−$Image$	70.24	75.11	90.81	86.18	55.66	49.21	60.12
Electronics	MuGACD	**72.45**[†]	**64.82**[†]	**93.62**[†]	**93.27**[†]	**69.82**[†]	**61.94**[†]	**72.14**[†]
	MuGACD−CS	71.05	57.97	91.17	91.49	67.12	60.08	70.13
	MuGACD−WE	72.09	58.28	92.12	91.98	67.95	60.51	71.09
	MuGACD−$Text$	51.94	49.22	66.84	66.98	52.16	43.28	55.41
	MuGACD−$Image$	69.34	57.41	91.11	90.98	68.73	60.67	72.01
Fashion	MuGACD	**72.84**[†]	**70.32**[†]	**91.27**[†]	**90.25**[†]	**75.57**[†]	**67.84**[†]	**77.84**[†]
	MuGACD−CS	71.15	68.97	89.17	89.57	73.25	64.11	75.21
	MuGACD−WE	71.49	69.18	90.02	89.72	74.92	64.82	74.81
	MuGACD−$Text$	49.51	48.11	71.81	70.67	63.33	59.12	69.91
	MuGACD−$Image$	71.34	68.21	90.84	89.98	74.97	66.00	76.17

(RQ6:) *Few-shot analysis of MuGACD framework:* To compare and evaluate the performance of our model in few-shot settings, we sample the training data to mimic the few-shot setting environment. We conducted two few-shot analyses based on the sampling technique: (1) **Few-Shot Analysis-1:** In this setting, we randomly sampled the training data based on percentages, [1%, 2%, 5%, 10%, 20%, 100%]. For example, the 1% setting will contain only 1% of original training data (30 reviews). It can be observed from Fig. 3a that our model consistently outperforms SOTA and best Multimodal baseline (ViLBERT) on all % settings in ACD task. In the case of 1% and 2% settings when data is more scarce, *MuGACD* is able to outperform these models by a significant margin. (2) **Few-Shot Analysis-2:** In this setting (Fig. 3b), we sampled the training data based on the number of examples per label, [1, 2, 5, 10, 20, Full]. In this setting also, *MuGACD* outperforms both SOTA and best Multimodal baseline (ViLBERT) across all training data shots on ACD subtask.

These few-shot experiments: 1) illustrate the strength and superiority of the generative language model in data-constrained and low-resource settings, and 2) further validate our approach of using the generative language model to solve multitask complaint detection tasks. *We have noticed a comparable pattern in the ACC and ARD tasks; however, we are unable to present our findings due to the limited space constraints of this document.*

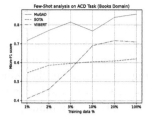 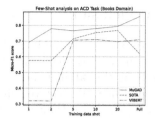

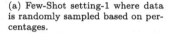

(a) Few-Shot setting-1 where data is randomly sampled based on percentages.

(b) Few-Shot setting-2 where data is sampled based on the number of examples per label.

Fig. 3. Comparison of performance of proposed model *MuGACD* with SOTA, and best Multimodal baseline (ViLBERT) on Few-Shot settings for the primary task (ACD).

All of the results presented here are statistically significant [33]. The results are found to be statistically significant when testing the null hypothesis (p-value < 0.05).

5.4 Error Analysis

We discuss some of the reasons why the proposed model fails to classify the aspect category and label pairs in this section:

Blurry Images: In some of the instances, the user-uploaded images are hazy and uncorrelated, so the extracted web entities are generic and do not help the model much. Therefore, in some cases, the model depends solely on the review's text, which might not always contain enough data for correct categorization.

Miscategorized Aspects: In scenarios where there are a greater number of aspect classes but a lower number of training samples per aspect class, such as in the electronics and fashion industries, the model may make erroneous classifications of aspect categories. For instance, if we consider the statement, "It's good but not a very good product. It's working well for any PC, but the wire is not durable, it's very thin." The MuGACD model predicts 'hardware-complaint' as the aspect category, whereas the correct aspect category and label pair is 'quality-complaint'. One possible explanation for such incorrect classifications is the limited availability of training samples for the 'quality' metric in the electronics domain.

Hallucinations: As generative models like BART are designed to generate output based on the complete vocabulary it is trained on, there are some instances where the model generates a cause that contains some information that is not present in the original input review. For example, for review *The number is incomplete*, the model generates the cause of complaint as *The phone number is incomplete*. However, the word *phone* is not present in the input review.

6   Conclusion

Our study aimed to address the limitations of previous research on complaint detection by (1) modeling fine-grained aspect-level expressions of complaints and identifying the rationale behind them and (2) avoiding the use of vanilla multi-task modeling. To achieve this, we proposed a knowledge-infused unified multimodal generative framework for aspect category recognition, complaint, and rationale detection at the aspect level. By formulating the multitasking problem as a text-to-text generation task in a multimodal setup, our approach utilized the knowledge of large pre-trained sequence-to-sequence models. Our proposed model outperformed all baselines and state-of-the-art methods in both full-shot and few-shot settings, based on comprehensive testing. Our future research will focus on summarizing valuable information from product reviews, and we plan to expand our investigation to include other modalities, such as audio and video.

Acknowledgement. Dr. Sriparna Saha gratefully acknowledges the Young Faculty Research Fellowship (YFRF) Award, supported by Visvesvaraya Ph.D. Scheme for Electronics and IT, Ministry of Electronics and Information Technology (MeitY), Government of India, being implemented by Digital India Corporation (formerly Media Lab Asia) for carrying out this research.

References

1. Akhtar, M.S., Ekbal, A., Bhattacharyya, P.: Aspect based sentiment analysis: category detection and sentiment classification for Hindi. In: Gelbukh, A. (ed.) CICLing 2016. LNCS, vol. 9624, pp. 246–257. Springer, Cham (2018). https://doi.org/10.1007/978-3-319-75487-1_19
2. Artstein, R., Poesio, M.: Inter-coder agreement for computational linguistics. Comput. Linguist. **34**(4), 555–596 (2008)
3. Brown, T., et al.: Language models are few-shot learners. Adv. Neural. Inf. Process. Syst. **33**, 1877–1901 (2020)
4. Coussement, K., Van den Poel, D.: Improving customer complaint management by automatic email classification using linguistic style features as predictors. Decis. Support Syst. **44**(4), 870–882 (2008)
5. Crawshaw, M.: Multi-task learning with deep neural networks: a survey. arXiv preprint arXiv:2009.09796 (2020)
6. Fleiss, J.L.: Measuring nominal scale agreement among many raters. Psychol. Bull. **76**(5), 378 (1971)
7. Iyiola, O., Ibidunni, O.: The relationship between complaints, emotion, anger, and subsequent behavior of customers. IOSR J. Humanit. Soc. Sci. **17**(6), 34–41 (2013)
8. Jenkins, W.M., Cangemi, J.P.: Levels of intensity of dissatisfaction: a model. Education **99**(4) (1979)
9. Jin, M., Aletras, N.: Modeling the severity of complaints in social media. In: Toutanova, K., et al. (eds.) Proceedings of the 2021 Conference of the North American Chapter of the Association for Computational Linguistics: Human Language Technologies, NAACL-HLT 2021, Online, 6–11 June 2021, pp. 2264–2274. Association for Computational Linguistics (2021). https://doi.org/10.18653/v1/2021.naacl-main.180

10. Joshi, M., Chen, D., Liu, Y., Weld, D.S., Zettlemoyer, L., Levy, O.: SpanBERT: improving pre-training by representing and predicting spans (2020)

11. Lailiyah, M., Sumpeno, S., Purnama, I.E.: Sentiment analysis of public complaints using lexical resources between Indonesian sentiment lexicon and Sentiwordnet. In: 2017 International Seminar on Intelligent Technology and Its Applications (ISI-TIA), pp. 307–312. IEEE (2017)

12. Law, D., Gruss, R., Abrahams, A.S.: Automated defect discovery for dishwasher appliances from online consumer reviews. Expert Syst. Appl. **67**, 84–94 (2017). https://doi.org/10.1016/j.eswa.2016.08.069

13. Lewis, M., et al.: BART: denoising sequence-to-sequence pre-training for natural language generation, translation, and comprehension. arXiv preprint arXiv:1910.13461 (2019)

14. Liu, H., Singh, P.: ConceptNet-a practical commonsense reasoning tool-kit. BT Technol. J. **22**(4), 211–226 (2004)

15. Lu, J., Batra, D., Parikh, D., Lee, S.: ViLBERT: pretraining task-agnostic visiolinguistic representations for vision-and-language tasks. In: Advances in Neural Information Processing Systems, vol. 32 (2019)

16. Majumder, N., Poria, S., Peng, H., Chhaya, N., Cambria, E., Gelbukh, A.: Sentiment and sarcasm classification with multitask learning. IEEE Intell. Syst. **34**(3), 38–43 (2019)

17. Olshtain, E., Weinbach, L.: Complaints: a Study of Speech Act Behavior Among Native and Nonnative Speakers of Hebrew. The Pragmatic Perspective (1985)

18. Poria, S., et al.: Recognizing emotion cause in conversations. Cogn. Comput. **13**, 1317–1332 (2021)

19. Preotiuc-Pietro, D., Gaman, M., Aletras, N.: Automatically identifying complaints in social media. In: Korhonen, A., Traum, D.R., Màrquez, L. (eds.) Proceedings of the 57th Conference of the Association for Computational Linguistics, ACL 2019, Florence, Italy, 28 July–2 August 2019, vol. 1: Long Papers, pp. 5008–5019. Association for Computational Linguistics (2019). https://doi.org/10.18653/v1/p19-1495

20. Raffel, C., et al.: Exploring the limits of transfer learning with a unified text-to-text transformer (2019). https://doi.org/10.48550/ARXIV.1910.10683, https://arxiv.org/abs/1910.10683

21. Rajpurkar, P., Zhang, J., Lopyrev, K., Liang, P.: SQuAD: 100,000+ questions for machine comprehension of text. arXiv preprint arXiv:1606.05250 (2016)

22. Simonyan, K., Zisserman, A.: Very deep convolutional networks for large-scale image recognition. arXiv preprint arXiv:1409.1556 (2014)

23. Singh, A., Dey, S., Singha, A., Saha, S.: Sentiment and emotion-aware multi-modal complaint identification. In: Thirty-Sixth AAAI Conference on Artificial Intelligence, AAAI 2022, Thirty-Fourth Conference on Innovative Applications of Artificial Intelligence, IAAI 2022, The Twelveth Symposium on Educational Advances in Artificial Intelligence, EAAI 2022 Virtual Event, 22 February–1 March 2022, pp. 12163–12171. AAAI Press (2022). https://ojs.aaai.org/index.php/AAAI/article/view/21476

24. Singh, A., Gangwar, V., Sharma, S., Saha, S.: Knowing what and how: a multi-modal aspect-based framework for complaint detection. In: Kamps, J., et al. (eds.) Advances in Information Retrieval: 45th European Conference on Information Retrieval, ECIR 2023, Dublin, Ireland, 2–6 April 2023, Proceedings, Part II, vol. 13981, pp. 125–140. Springer, Cham (2023). https://doi.org/10.1007/978-3-031-28238-6_9

25. Singh, A., Nazir, A., Saha, S.: Adversarial multi-task model for emotion, sentiment, and sarcasm aided complaint detection. In: Hagen, M., et al. (eds.) Advances in Information Retrieval - 44th European Conference on IR Research, ECIR 2022, Stavanger, Norway, 10–14 April 2022, Proceedings, Part I. LNCS, vol. 13185, pp. 428–442. Springer, Cham (2022). https://doi.org/10.1007/978-3-030-99736-6_29

26. Singh, A., Saha, S.: Are you really complaining? A multi-task framework for complaint identification, emotion, and sentiment classification. In: Lladós, J., Lopresti, D., Uchida, S. (eds.) ICDAR 2021. LNCS, vol. 12822, pp. 715–731. Springer, Cham (2021). https://doi.org/10.1007/978-3-030-86331-9_46

27. Singh, A., Saha, S., Hasanuzzaman, M., Dey, K.: Multitask learning for complaint identification and sentiment analysis. Cogn. Comput. **14**, 212–227 (2021)

28. Speer, R., Chin, J., Havasi, C.: ConceptNet 5.5: an open multilingual graph of general knowledge. In: Singh, S., Markovitch, S. (eds.) Proceedings of the Thirty-First AAAI Conference on Artificial Intelligence, 4–9 February 2017, San Francisco, California, USA, pp. 4444–4451. AAAI Press (2017). http://aaai.org/ocs/index.php/AAAI/AAAI17/paper/view/14972

29. Sridhar, R., Yang, D.: Explaining toxic text via knowledge enhanced text generation. In: Proceedings of the 2022 Conference of the North American Chapter of the Association for Computational Linguistics: Human Language Technologies, pp. 811–826. Association for Computational Linguistics, Seattle, United States, July 2022. https://doi.org/10.18653/v1/2022.naacl-main.59, https://aclanthology.org/2022.naacl-main.59

30. Trosborg, A.: Interlanguage Pragmatics: Requests, Complaints, and Apologies, vol. 7. Walter de Gruyter (2011)

31. Vásquez, C.: Complaints online: the case of TripAdvisor. J. Pragmat. **43**(6), 1707–1717 (2011)

32. Vaswani, A., et al.: Attention is all you need. In: Guyon, I., et al. (eds.) Advances in Neural Information Processing Systems, vol. 30. Curran Associates, Inc. (2017). https://proceedings.neurips.cc/paper/2017/file/3f5ee243547dee91fbd053c1c4a845aa-Paper.pdf

33. Welch, B.L.: The generalization of 'student's' problem when several different population variances are involved. Biometrika **34**(1–2), 28–35 (1947)

34. Wu, S.: Automating Knowledge Distillation and Representation from Richly Formatted Data. Stanford University (2020)

35. Yang, B., Li, J., Wong, D.F., Chao, L.S., Wang, X., Tu, Z.: Context-aware self-attention networks. In: Proceedings of the AAAI Conference on Artificial Intelligence, vol. 33, pp. 387–394 (2019)

36. Yang, W., et al.: Detecting customer complaint escalation with recurrent neural networks and manually-engineered features. In: Loukina, A., Morales, M., Kumar, R. (eds.) Proceedings of the 2019 Conference of the North American Chapter of the Association for Computational Linguistics: Human Language Technologies, NAACL-HLT 2019, Minneapolis, MN, USA, 2–7 June 2019, vol. 2 (Industry Papers), pp. 56–63. Association for Computational Linguistics (2019). https://doi.org/10.18653/v1/n19-2008

37. Zhu, R.: Enhance multimodal transformer with external label and in-domain pre-train: hateful meme challenge winning solution, December 2020

Sequence-Graph Fusion Neural Network for User Mobile App Behavior Prediction

Yizhuo Wang[1], Renhe Jiang[2(✉)], Hangchen Liu[1], Du Yin[1], and Xuan Song[1(✉)]

[1] Southern University of Science and Technology, Shenzhen, China
songx@sustech.edu.cn
[2] The University of Tokyo, Tokyo, Japan
jiangrh@csis.u-tokyo.ac.jp

Abstract. In recent years, mobile applications (apps) on smartphones have shown explosive growth. Massive and diversified apps greatly affect user experience. As a result, user mobile app behavior prediction has become increasingly important. Existed algorithms based on deep learning mainly conduct sequence modeling on the app usage historical records, which are insufficient in capturing the similarity between users and apps, and ignore the semantic associations in app usage. Although some works have tried to model from the perspective of graph structure recently, the two types of modeling methods have not been combined, and whether they are complementary has not been explored. Therefore, we propose an SGFNN model based on sequence combined graph modeling, which is already publicly available as the GitHub repository https://github.com/ZAY113/SGFNN. Sequence Block, BipGraph Block, and HyperGraph Block are used to capture the user mobile app behavior short-term pattern, the similarity between users and apps, and the semantic relations of hyperedge "user-time-location-app", respectively. Two real-world datasets are selected in our experiments. When the app sequence length is 4, the prediction accuracy of Top1, Top5, and Top10 reaches 36.08%, 68.39%, 79.02% and 51.55%, 87.57%, 95.62%, respectively. The experimental results show that the two modeling methods can be combined to improve prediction accuracy, and the information extracted from them is complementary.

Keywords: User app behavior prediction · Deep learning · Graph neural networks · Hypergraph embedding

1 Introduction

Mobile applications (apps) are easy to use and can be accessed from anywhere. Recently, the app market has been booming. In 2021, about 230 billion apps were downloaded worldwide, and that number is still growing [2], which resulted in a huge amount of user mobile app behavior data. Even though it has brought convenience to users, it has also had a significant impact on user experience. There has been an increase in the number of apps installed on users' mobile phones. However, only a few of these apps are actually used, and their usage

© The Author(s), under exclusive license to Springer Nature Switzerland AG 2023
G. De Francisci Morales et al. (Eds.): ECML PKDD 2023, LNAI 14174, pp. 105–121, 2023.
https://doi.org/10.1007/978-3-031-43427-3_7

often depends on specific times and locations. This places a considerable burden on users when they try to find the right app. Similar to predicting locations [3, 11] and friendships [16], user mobile app behavior prediction, illustrated in Fig. 1, is becoming increasingly crucial in determining which app the user will use next. However, due to the complexities of user mobile app behavior data, it is still challenging to achieve high precision, and the previous algorithms still have room for further improvement.

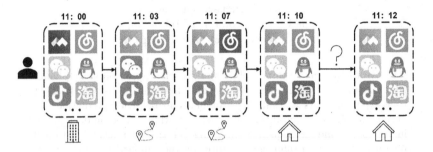

Fig. 1. User Mobile App Behavior Prediction

Current researches show that traditional count-based algorithms (MRU, MFU) [20] and probability-based algorithms (Bayes, Markov methods, etc.) can predict user mobile app behavior and have interpretability. However, recent works [24, 30] show that deep learning methods have significant advantages over traditional algorithms in user mobile app behavior prediction. Although in App2Vec [22], the Bayesian network-based probabilistic approach outperformed the deep learning algorithm, the comparison object is only a two-layer DNN. Therefore, in summary, deep learning methods may have more potential to improve the prediction effect of user mobile app behavior.

At present, almost all prediction methods based on deep learning model the historical app usage as a discrete sequence and improve the prediction effect by adding time and location features to the neural network. However, the model architecture is dominated by DNN stacked with MLP and RNN. In recent years, with the rapid development of attention mechanism and transformer [21], deep neural networks based on transformer have become the mainstream method in the field of nlp, cv, and time series forecasting. In terms of user mobile app behavior prediction, the training efficiency and prediction accuracy of transformer is still unknown. On the other hand, inspired by the recommendation system, it is another possible manner to model the spatio-temporal pattern of user mobile app behavior through graphs and use graph representation learning to complete the downstream user mobile app behavior prediction task. The advantage is that it can capture the semantic relationships between time, location, and app usage in a more intuitive and structured manner, and it has a unique advantage in expressing long-term stability correlation and multi-hop connection. However, most graph-based algorithms dedicate to learning node embedding, and then sorting candidate apps by defining score functions to complete the next prediction. Under this framework, user mobile app behavior prediction is just a replaceable downstream task of the upstream stage, and it is not a specific training for the prediction task. Recently, AHNEAP [32] tried to integrate the graph representation learning of non-specific tasks with the downstream user mobile app behavior prediction task end-to-end, using the downstream task as the objective function to train the entire neural network. The experimental results show that compared with the previous graph embedding methods, this task-specific training method can achieve better prediction results. However, the downstream network of this method is just a simple MLP, which does not use the more complex deep learning method based on sequence modeling.

In short, when it comes to user mobile app behavior prediction task, previous methods either ignore the similarity between users and apps and the hyperedge semantic correlations between user, time, location, and app or ignore the switching logic of app usage sequence. To address these problems, we propose a novel end-to-end deep learning model SGFNN to predict from the perspective of sequence combined graph modeling. The main contributions of this work are as follows:

1. We construct a user-app bipartite graph to capture the similarity between users and apps, so as to improve the personalization and accuracy of recommendations. And the hypergraph embedding is used to capture the relationships among different attribute nodes of "user-time-location-app", which makes up for the shortcomings of previous methods.
2. To the best of our knowledge, we are the first to combine sequence-based methods with graph-based methods and train the graph module and sequence module end-to-end by means of intercepting subgraph.
3. We evaluate our proposed SGFNN on two real-world datasets, test the effectiveness of the sequence combined graph modeling method, and prove that the switching logic of app sequence, the similarity between users and apps, and the hyperedge semantic correlations can provide complementary information in improving user mobile app behavior prediction.

2   Related Work

2.1   Traditional Methods

The most naive methods for predicting user mobile app behavior problems are the count-based methods, which predict that the next app to be used will be the most frequently used (MFU) app in the last window or the most recently used (MRU) app. Both these methods exploit the fundamental behavioral characteristics of users' app usage history. Shin et al. [20] used MFU and MRU as the most basic benchmark testing methods in their experiments.

Further, some methods are proposed to predict user mobile app behavior in the hope of capturing the complex probabilistic relationship between history and the next app. Natarajan et al. [18] model the historical app usage as a Markov chain, and use first-order state transition probability to predict which app users will use next. Zou et al. [33] improve the predicting accuracy by constructing a Bayesian network to capture the high-order relationship between app history switching. Huang et al. [10] point out that contextual information can understand the user mobile app behavior pattern and use Bayesian methods effectively predict the app usage. Jiang et al. [12] have added time as a new feature to input in their research, and based on the nearest neighbor algorithm, use the most similar app usage in history to generate predictions. In addition, some works [19, 22, 23] studied the role of location features on user mobile app behavior prediction.

2.2   Sequence-Based Deep Learning Methods

Deep learning has rapidly advanced in recent years. When predicting user mobile app behavior, the user's historical app usage window can be viewed as a sentence with a discrete sequence. This problem is similar to NLP, where the goal is to predict the probability of different objects appearing in the next position based on a given past sequence. Recurrent neural networks such as LSTM [9] and GRU [5] are effective for modeling sequence problems. Xu et al. [25] proposed a general prediction model based on LSTM that converts time series dependencies and context information into a unified feature representation for the next app prediction. Lee et al. [14] used the stacked LSTM architecture to train the prediction model without calculating transition probability. Experimental results show that LSTM is advantageous in user mobile app behavior prediction. Zhao et al. [30] proposed AppUsage2Vec, a deep learning-based framework for predicting app usage. They trained a general model and single models for each user and found that the general model performed better, particularly with limited training data. The model uses dual DNN and an attention mechanism to capture the weight contributions of different apps in historical sequences for accurate predictions. Xia et al. [24] proposed DeepApp, a GRU-based model. Similar to Zhao et al. [30], they found that the general model outperformed single models. To increase personalization, a user prediction task was added to the output end, along with the integration of a location prediction task into the output end to improve recommendation sensitivity. This leads to multi-task learning.

2.3   Graph-Based Deep Learning Methods

In addition to the above sequence-based methods, recently, some works have also gradually tried to adopt graph modeling methods. Chen et al. [4] found that the relationship between app-location, app-time and app-app category is very important for user mobile app behavior prediction, so three kinds of bipartite graphs were constructed, and a heterogeneous graph embedding algorithm CAP was proposed to learn the embedding vector of nodes. Yu et al. [29] used app, location and time unit as nodes, and co-occurrence relationships between different nodes as edges to construct a heterogeneous graph, and defined objective functions with non-specific tasks to learn the representation of graph nodes. The authors claim that this method can simultaneously learn the semantic aware embeddings of app, location and time respectively, so as to obtain better results.

Zhou et al. [32] proposed a framework AHNEAP, which is the first time to combine graph representation learning with prediction tasks for end-to-end training of downstream apps. The experimental results show that this method is superior to the graph representation learning in user mobile app behavior prediction.

In addition to using the above features, the mobile status, network mode, and battery level of smartphones are also used for user mobile app behavior prediction. Zhao et al. [31] and De et al. [6] extracted the mobile status from user trajectory data, combined with the historical app sequence as input for machine learning classifiers to complete prediction. Further, Do et al. [7] considered factors such as network mode and battery level affecting user mobile app behavior prediction. Xu et al. [26] used screen status and network mode to supplement the feature information contained in the query vector and recalled the most likely app used as the prediction result. Recently, Li et al. [15] systematically classified the methods and datasets related to user mobile app behavior prediction in detail, making an important contribution to the development of this field.

3   Problem Definition

Let $R = \{r_1, r_2, \ldots, r_p\}$ denote the user mobile app behavior records, $U = \{u_1, u_2, \ldots, u_m\}$ denotes a user set, $A = \{a_1, a_2, \ldots, a_n\}$ denotes a set of applications, $T = \{t_1, t_2, \ldots, t_i\}$ denotes a collection of discrete time IDs. Considering that the user mobile app behavior is closely related to the user's spatial location and other factors such as network conditions, battery life, etc., let $L = \{l_1, l_2, \ldots, l_j\}$ indicate the location set including j spatial locations, $C = \{c_1, c_2, \ldots, c_q\}$ shows a set of q contextual states (relevant information about users, devices, and environments) that may help predict a user's next usage of an app.

Definition (User Mobile App Behavior Prediction). Given a candidate set of apps A and the input features of an user mobile app behavior prediction sample data $u, t, l, c, (a_1, a_2, \ldots, a_l)$, predict the application a which the user is most likely to use next from A. Formally, our problem is defined as:

$$\hat{a}_{l+1} = \underset{a \in A}{argmax}\, Pr(a|u, t, l, c, (a_1, a_2, \ldots, a_l)) \tag{1}$$

4   Methodology

4.1   Framework Overview

The model framework is shown in Fig. 2, which consists of embedding module, feature extracting module, and predicting module. It accepts training samples $x = (u, t, l, a)$, wherein $a = (a_1, a_2, \ldots, a_l)$ represents the user u's historical app behavior sequence within a time window. For training purposes, the algorithm also performs uniform random negative sampling, resulting in negative hyperedge samples $x' = (u', t', l', a')$ as input data.

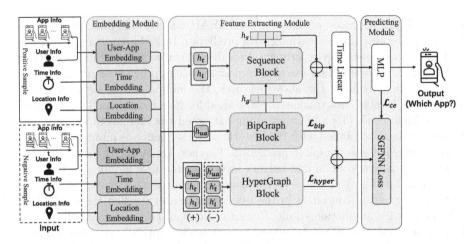

Fig. 2. The Framework of <u>S</u>equence-<u>G</u>raph <u>F</u>usion <u>N</u>eural <u>N</u>etwork (SGFNN)

Firstly, all positive and negative samples will be passed through the embedding module and we can get the $h_u \in R^d$, $h_t \in R^d$, $h_l \in R^d$, and $h_a = (a_1, \ldots, a_i, \ldots, a_l)$ where $a_i \in R^d$, respectively represent the d-dimensional embeddings of the corresponding input attributes, and the feature tensor learned from the positive sample embeddings is represented as (h_u, h_a, h_t, h_l).

The subsequent feature extracting module is divided into three blocks, namely the Sequence Block, BipGraph Block, and HyperGraph Block. The positive sample feature vector will be sent to the Sequence and BipGraph blocks to capture the app switching sequence correlation and similarity between users and apps, respectively, and output their respective hidden layer vectors h_s and h_g. Furthermore, the BipGraph Block will construct negative graphs, and then calculate the positive score s_{1+} and the negative score s_{1-} on both the positive and negative graphs. These scores will then be used to compute the loss function to preserve the bipartite graph structural information. Specifically, it is as shown in Eqs. 2 and 3:

$$h_g, s_{1+}, s_{1-} = BipGraphBlock(h_u, h_a) \tag{2}$$

$$h_s = SequenceBlock(h_g, h_t, h_l) \tag{3}$$

The positive and negative feature tensors will be simultaneously inputted to the HyperGraph Block to capture the semantic correlations of hyperedge and output the positive sample score s_{2+} and the negative sample score s_{2-}, specifically as shown in Eq. 4:

$$s_{2+}, s_{2-} = HyperGraphBlock((h_u, h_a, h_t, h_l), (h_u', h_a', h_t', h_l')) \tag{4}$$

The scores s_{2+} and s_{2-} will then be used to calculate the model's loss function, allowing to learn the similarity between hyperedge composed nodes.

Furthermore, h_s and h_g are added to fuse their latent features, and use a time linear layer to compress the time dimension from the time window length l to 1. Specifically, see Eq. 5:

$$h_o = TimeLinear(h_s, h_g) \tag{5}$$

The predicting module will receive h_o and use an MLP to transform the hidden size $4d$ to the app category dimension n, and use Softmax to convert the output result to between 0 and 1. The final output a_{l+1} represents the possibility score of each app category under the next state. Specifically, see Eq. 7:

$$o = MLP(h_o) = h_o \cdot W_o + b_o \tag{6}$$

$$a_{l+1} = Softmax(o) = \frac{e^{o_i}}{\sum_{c=1}^{C} e^{o_c}} \tag{7}$$

Here, $W_o \in R^{4d \times n}$ represents weight, $b_o \in R^n$ represents bias and C denotes the set of candidate apps. The score a_{l+1} will also be used to calculate the model's loss function to measure the error of the multi-classification prediction result.

The final model will be trained using the defined SGFNN loss function, and in the inference stage, the score of the next app multi-classification a_{l+1} will be used for prediction.

4.2 Sequence Block: Learning the App Switch Patterns

The switching sequence of user mobile app behavior may have certain logical rules. Therefore, we build a sequence model based on the behavior history of app switches. Without using RNN and its variants LSTM and GRU, considering the real-time prediction on the smartphone terminal, we adopt Transformer Encoder

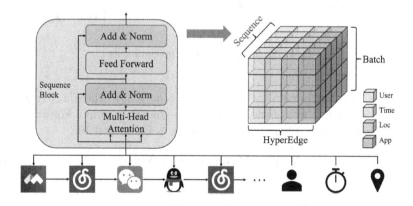

Fig. 3. Learning the App Switch Patterns

as the core of the Sequence Block, as shown in Fig. 3. The user, time, location, and app sequence are sent to the transformer encoder.

$$h_s = Transformer Encoder(h_g, h_t, h_l) \tag{8}$$

4.3 BipGraph Block: Learning the User-App Similarity

Existing sequence-based models do not explicitly model the relationships between users and apps, as social relationships between users and similarities between apps are often unknown. Inspired by collaborative filtering, we construct a user-app bipartite graph [1] across the entire training set, which means the interaction data can be represented as an undirected graph $G = (V, E)$. The vertex set consists of a collection of users $u_i \in U$, where $i \in \{1, \cdots, N_m\}$, and a collection of apps $a_j \in A$, where $j \in \{1, \cdots, N_n\}$, such that $U \cup A = V$, the edge set is defined as a 0–1 set, where $e_{ij} = 1$ if u_i has used a_j, otherwise $e_{ij} = 0$.

The internal structure of the BipGraph Block is shown on the rightmost side of Fig. 4. We stack two layers of GraphSage [8] to capture the 2-order similarities. To simplify the implementation, we re-encode the node IDs and convert the bipartite graph into a simple graph. The one layer calculation given below is for positive graphs, and the calculation on the negative graph is the same.

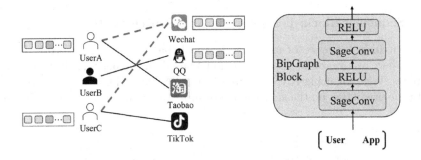

Fig. 4. Learning the User-App Similarity

The input of the BipGraph Block is $h_{ua} = (h_u \parallel h_a)$, where h_{ua} represents the original input features of the vertices in the bipartite graph. For any vertex $v \in V$, the aggregation calculation is as follows in Eqs. 9 and 10:

$$h_{N(v)} = Mean(h_{v'}, \forall v' \in N(v)) \tag{9}$$
$$h_v = Relu(W \cdot (h_v \parallel h_{N(v)})) \tag{10}$$

where $N(v)$ denotes the set of neighboring nodes of vertex v.

The second-order hidden vectors h_v of all vertices constitute the output h_g of the BipGraph Block.

4.4   HyperGraph Block: Learning the Correlations in Hyperedges

The user mobile app behavior prediction is highly spatiotemporal related. Existing methods ignore the semantic correlations including spatiotemporal factors among "user-time-location-app". As shown on the left of Fig. 5, the hyperedge "user-time-location-app" connects four different attribute nodes. We use the hyperedge embedding to learn the high-dimensional latent vectors. The vectors of the positive samples will have higher scores due to their high similarity. The internal structure of the HyperGraph Block is shown in the middle of Fig. 5.

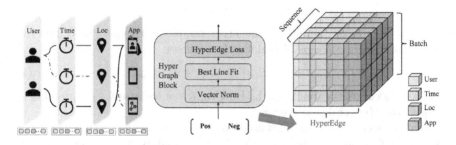

Fig. 5. Learning the Semantic Correlations in Hyperedges

Inspired by Yang et al. [27], we define the HyperGraph Block as follows, firstly, we normalize the embedding vectors of users, time, location, and app sequences. Then, we calculate the best fit line:

$$h_b = \frac{h_u + h_t + h_l + h_a}{4} \tag{11}$$

Finally, we calculate the positive sample score:

$$s_{2+} = \frac{\cos(h_u, h_b) + \cos(h_t, h_b) + \cos(h_l, h_b) + \cos(h_a, h_b)}{4} \tag{12}$$

And the negative sample score s_{2-} is calculated in the same way.

4.5   Optimization

To train the parameters $\Theta = \{\Theta_{Seq}, \Theta_{Bip}, \Theta_{Pre}\}$. Our objective function is defined as the composition of three terms: the Cross-entropy loss $\mathcal{L}_{ce}$ for app multi-classification, the unsupervised loss term $\mathcal{L}_{bip}$ on the bipartite graph, and the HyperEdge loss term $\mathcal{L}_{hyper}$. Cross-entropy loss term is defined as:

$$\mathcal{L}_{ce} = \underset{\theta}{argmin} -\frac{1}{|C|} \sum_{c=1}^{C} \alpha^{I(p_a > p_{[k]})} p_a \log p_a \tag{13}$$

where C represents the total number n of candidate apps. The p_a is predicted using a_{l+1} from Eq. 7, $I(\cdot)$ is the indicator function, $p_{[k]}$ represents the k-th largest value of the predicted probability p, and α represents the weighting factor. BipGraph loss term is defined as:

$$\mathcal{L}_{bip}^v = -\log(\sigma(h_v^\top \cdot h_u)) - \beta \cdot E_{h_u' \sim P_n(u)} \log(1 - \sigma(h_v^\top \cdot h_u')) \qquad (14)$$

$$\mathcal{L}_{bip} = mean(\mathcal{L}_{bip}^0, \mathcal{L}_{bip}^1, \cdots, \mathcal{L}_{bip}^V) \qquad (15)$$

where h_v represents any node v in the bipartite graph G; h_u represents any neighbor u connected to node v; h_u' represents a negative sample node; P_n is a negative sampling distribution; β represents the number of negative samples. HyperEdge loss term is defined as:

$$\mathcal{L}_{hyper} = -(s_{2+} + \gamma \cdot E_{v_i'}(1 - s_{2-}))) \qquad (16)$$

where $\gamma \in Z^+$ is the number of negative samples for hyperedges. The final SGFNN loss function $\mathcal{L}_{SGFNN}$ is defined as follows:

$$\mathcal{L}_{SGFNN} = \mathcal{L}_{ce} + \lambda_1 \mathcal{L}_{bip} + \lambda_2 \mathcal{L}_{hyper} \qquad (17)$$

where λ_1 represents the weight of the BipGraph loss term, and λ_2 represents the weight of the HyperEdge loss term.

Previous deep learning models used batch gradient descent to update parameters, but GCN needs the complete adjacency matrix for training. To train SGFNN in an end-to-end manner, we merge user and app sets, re-encode node IDs, and use the merged node set to create a local subgraph G_{sub} from global graph G for batch training.

5　Experiment

5.1　Setup

Datasets. In the experimental section, we select two user mobile app behavior datasets: one public dataset proposed by [28,29] (denoted as China Telecom dataset) and one private dataset provided by Huawei Technologies Co., Ltd. (denoted as Huawei dataset). The basic statistical characteristics of the preprocessed China Telecom dataset and Huawei dataset are shown in Table 1.

Table 1. Dataset Summary

Dataset	#User	#Time	#Loc	#App	#Sample
China Telecom	748	168	6291	1518	908770
Huawei	64	168	9570	574	2394220

Metrics. We use the commonly used recall metric in classification problems as the evaluation metric for our experiments, which can be calculated by:

$$Recall@k = \frac{hit@k}{|D^{test}|} \qquad (18)$$

Here, D^{test} represents the entire test set, and $hit@k$ represents the top-k hit rate across the entire test set.

Baselines. We compare the proposed SGFNN model with traditional probabilistic algorithms and the latest deep learning methods based on sequences.

- MRU [20] predicts the most recently used app. It assumes that most applications are continuously used in multiple time intervals, utilizing the continuity characteristics of app usage. Shin et al. [20] used MRU as a basic baseline.
- MFU [20] calculates and selects the most commonly used app based on the user's app behavior history. Shin et al. [20] also used MFU as a basic baseline.
- NaiveBayes [33] uses the historical app sequence as features and learns their independent contributions to the target app.
- MarkovChain [7] constructs a Markov chain of the user's app behavior to estimate the joint probability of the app sequence and the target app.
- DNN [13] stacks two fully connected MLP layers to learn nonlinear hidden features from app history sequences and time features.
- AppUsage2Vec [30] uses a dual-tower DNN to extract features of both user and app sequence, computes the time difference as an input supplement, and models the contribution of different apps to the target app through an attention mechanism.
- DeepApp [24] uses time, location, and app historical sequences as input features, employs GRU as the feature extraction layer, and adopts multi-task learning to improve the personalized prediction ability of the model on different users and locations.

Implementations. The maximum training epochs are set as 100, and the train/validation/test data ratio is set to 7:2:1. The batch size is set to 256, and early stopping is applied with patience of 10 epochs. The learning rate is set to 0.0005, the sequence length of apps is set to 4, and the weight factor α is set to 3. Finally, the hidden size is set to 100 for China Telecom and 32 for Huawei, the λ_1 is set to 0.003 for China Telecom and 0.0007 for Huawei, and the λ_2 is set to 0.002 for China Telecom and 0.0002 for Huawei.

5.2   Performance Evaluation

The overall experimental results are shown in Table 2. It can be observed that the proposed SGFNN achieves the best prediction performance compared to baseline methods in terms of Recall@1, Recall@5, and Recall@10 metrics on both China Telecom dataset and Huawei dataset.

The improvement on the China Telecom dataset is much greater than that on the Huawei dataset for two reasons. Firstly, SGFNN uses location features as inputs and location features have a significant impact on predictions on the China Telecom dataset but a limited impact on the Huawei dataset. Secondly, the use of sequence combined graph modeling in SGFNN compensates for the high-order neighbor similarity between users and apps, users and users, and apps and apps that is lacking in deep learning models such as DNN, AppUsage2Vec, and DeepApp. The China Telecom dataset has a much larger number of users and candidate apps than the Huawei dataset, with a more complex pattern of the

Table 2. User App Behavior Prediction Performance Comparison

Method	China Telecom dataset			Huawei dataset		
	Recall@1	Recall@5	Recall@10	Recall@1	Recall@5	Recall@10
MRU [20]	13.94%	37.02%	47.40%	39.98%	73.56%	86.21%
MFU [20]	15.95%	39.29%	51.03%	31.56%	72.43%	88.11%
NaiveBayes [33]	24.71%	56.01%	68.44%	47.87%	84.88%	94.28%
MarkovChain [7]	17.24%	45.33%	56.01%	29.64%	72.16%	87.80%
DNN [13]	31.83%	59.70%	69.66%	50.79%	86.01%	94.11%
AppUsage2Vec [30]	31.12%	61.23%	71.53%	<u>51.18%</u>	<u>86.34%</u>	<u>94.40%</u>
DeepApp [24]	<u>33.17%</u>	<u>62.89%</u>	<u>73.25%</u>	50.50%	84.70%	92.36%
SGFNN (Ours)	**36.08%**	**68.39%**	**79.02%**	**51.55%**	**87.57%**	**95.62%**

graph structure. Therefore, the effect of improving predictions is more significant on the China Telecom dataset than on the Huawei dataset. Additionally, the hyperedge module used in the SGFNN model also contributes to its superior performance compared to AppUsage2Vec and DeepApp.

5.3   Ablation Study

To better compare the effects of location features, Sequence Block, BipGraph Block, and HyperGraph Block, we conduct an ablation study and design the following models to verify the effectiveness of each component:

- SGFNN-hyper: Removing the HyperGraph Block and HyperEdge loss.
- SGFNN-bip&hyper: Further removing the BipGraph Block and unsupervised loss function of the bipartite graph, retaining only the Sequence Block for feature extraction.
- SGFNN-bip&hyper&loc: Removing the BipGraph Block and HyperGraph Block, and further remove input location features.
- SGFNN-seq: Removing the Sequence Block, retaining only the BipGraph Block and HyperGraph Block for feature extraction.
- SGFNN-full: The complete version of the SGFNN model proposed.

Figures 6 and 7 illustrate the results of the ablation study on China Telecom and Huawei datasets, respectively. Based on these, we can draw the following conclusions:

1. Location characteristics, Sequence Blocks, BipGraph Blocks, and Hyper-Graph Blocks all contribute to user mobile app behavior prediction accuracy on two datasets. These factors provide different perspectives on information. Specifically, the location feature, logic of app sequence switching, 1-order and 2-order similarities between users and apps, and semantic associations in the hyperedge all provide valuable information.

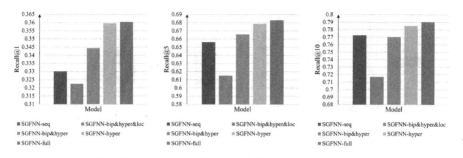

Fig. 6. Ablation Study on China Telecom Dataset

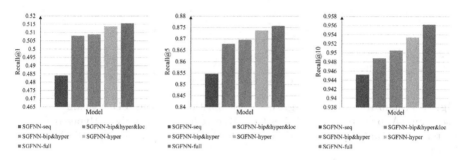

Fig. 7. Ablation Study on Huawei Dataset

2. In comparing SGFNN-seq with SGFNN-bip&hyper, we found that the latter outperformed the former for most cases except for recall@10 on the China Telecom dataset. This indicates that the logical switching patterns of app sequences were more important for predicting than the user-app similarity.
3. By observing differences between SGFNN-bip&hyper, SGFNN-hyper, and SGFNN-full, respectively, we found that adding BipGraph Blocks to the base sequence model resulted in a larger increase in prediction accuracy than adding HyperGraph Blocks. This suggests that the 1-order and 2-order similarities between users and apps have a greater impact on user mobile app behavior prediction than the semantic relationships in the hyperedge.

5.4   Case Study

In this section, we select specific cases to verify and analyze the effects of three feature extraction blocks. **(1) Sequence Block**. It can be observed from Fig. 8 that different apps in the sequence contribute differently to the prediction of app4, and the weights are not necessarily smaller with greater distance. In the right of Fig. 8, attention scores indicate app1's (social1) importance for prediction even though it is farthest from app4 (social2), as they both belong to the same social category. App2 (game) has the second-highest score, revealing synergy between game and social apps. App3 (news) receives the lowest score

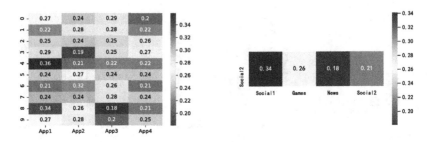

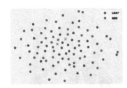

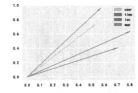

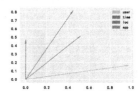

Fig. 8. Attention Scores of App Sequences in Sequence Block

Fig. 9. Visualization of User and App Latent Vectors in BipGraph Block

Fig. 10. Visualization of Positive Hyperedge in HyperGraph Block

Fig. 11. Visualization of Negative Hyperedge in HyperGraph Block

due to limited interaction. The sequence block captures switching logic in app usage by modeling historical records as a sequence with self-attention mechanism. **(2) BipGraph Block**. Figure 9 visualizes 50 user nodes and 50 app nodes with TSNE [17] using their randomly selected latent vectors. User 698's usage sequence is {1, 324, 40, 220}. The cross shows user 698 and app 1 (social class) closer in the reduced vector space as they are 1-order neighbors in the bipartite graph, indicating that the model learns user-app similarities via the BipGraph Block. **(3) HyperGraph Block**. Figure 10 visualizes a positive sample hyperedge. Hidden vectors of the nodes on this edge are more similar. Figure 11 shows a negative hyperedge with less similar node vectors. The HyperGraph Block captures collaborative semantic relationships between heterogeneous nodes in the positive sample hyperedge.

6   Conclusion

In this study, we propose SGFNN which combines sequence and graph modeling to address limitations in existing user mobile app behavior prediction algorithms. Sequence Block, BipGraph Block, and HyperGraph Block are designed to capture the user mobile app behavior short-term pattern, the similarity between users and apps, and the semantic relations of hyperedge "user-time-location-app", respectively. This method achieves significant improvements over baselines and it can be further extended to a wider range of applications such as restaurant demand prediction, location (Point-of-Interest) prediction, friendship prediction, etc. Our future work includes exploring the selective preservation of relationships during subgraph partitioning and optimizing the time and space complexity of the model for large-scale applications. Our code is already publicly available as the GitHub repository https://github.com/ZAY113/SGFNN.

Acknowledgment. This work was supported by Huawei Technologies Co., Ltd., National Key Research and Development Project of China (2021YFB1714400), and Guangdong Provincial Key Laboratory (2020B121201001).

Ethical Statement. In this study, we introduce an innovative technique for predicting the next app by leveraging user mobile app behavior data. To implement this, our work utilizes two datasets - China Telecom app usage dataset, which is publicly available, and a distinct proprietary dataset acquired through collaboration with Huawei. We have strictly followed ethical guidelines to protect the privacy and integrity of individuals and entities involved in this study.

Data Sources and Anonymization. The China Telecom app usage dataset has been widely used in previous research and is considered ethically acceptable. Meanwhile, the Huawei app usage dataset is provided by our collaborative partner, Huawei. It is important to mention that the visualizations in our case study section do not raise any ethical concerns. This is because the users, locations, and apps of both datasets have been anonymized to protect user privacy.

Ethical Compliance. Our study follows ethical principles to handle sensitive data responsibly. We obtained permission for datasets, ensured anonymity and privacy, and complied with data protection regulations. We did not disclose any data to unauthorized parties and put in place security measures to prevent misuse or unauthorized access.

In summary, our research methodology prioritizes ethical considerations, utilizing anonymized data and safeguards to protect sensitive information. Our commitment affirms ethical guidelines adherence with reliable results, ultimately contributing to progress in predicting mobile app user behavior based on usage data, while ensuring the accuracy and dependability of our findings.

References

1. van den Berg, R., Kipf, T.N., Welling, M.: Graph convolutional matrix completion. arXiv preprint arXiv:1706.02263 (2017)
2. Ceci, L.: App stores - statistics & facts (2022)
3. Chen, Q., et al.: DualSIN: dual sequential interaction network for human intentional mobility prediction. In: Proceedings of the 28th International Conference on Advances in Geographic Information Systems, pp. 283–292 (2020)
4. Chen, X., Wang, Y., He, J., Pan, S., Li, Y., Zhang, P.: CAP: context-aware app usage prediction with heterogeneous graph embedding. Proc. ACM Interactive Mobile Wearable Ubiquit. Technol. **3**(1), 1–25 (2019)

5. Cho, K., et al.: Learning phrase representations using RNN encoder-decoder for statistical machine translation. In: Proceedings of the 2014 Conference on Empirical Methods in Natural Language Processing (EMNLP), pp. 1724–1734. Association for Computational Linguistics, Doha, Qatar (2014)
6. De Nadai, M., Cardoso, A., Lima, A., Lepri, B., Oliver, N.: Strategies and limitations in app usage and human mobility. Sci. Rep. **9**(1), 10935 (2019)
7. Do, T.M.T., Gatica-Perez, D.: Where and what: using smartphones to predict next locations and applications in daily life. Pervasive Mob. Comput. **12**, 79–91 (2014)
8. Hamilton, W., Ying, Z., Leskovec, J.: Inductive representation learning on large graphs. In: Advances in Neural Information Processing Systems, vol. 30 (2017)
9. Hochreiter, S., Schmidhuber, J.: Long short-term memory. Neural Comput. **9**(8), 1735–1780 (1997)
10. Huang, K., Zhang, C., Ma, X., Chen, G.: Predicting mobile application usage using contextual information. In: Proceedings of the 2012 ACM Conference on Ubiquitous Computing, pp. 1059–1065 (2012)
11. Jiang, R., et al.: Will you go where you search? A deep learning framework for estimating user search-and-go behavior. Neurocomputing **472**, 338–348 (2022)
12. Jiang, Y., Du, X., Jin, T.: Using combined network information to predict mobile application usage. Physica A **515**, 430–439 (2019)
13. LeCun, Y., Bengio, Y., Hinton, G.: Deep learning. Nature **521**(7553), 436–444 (2015)
14. Lee, Y., Cho, S., Choi, J.: App usage prediction for dual display device via two-phase sequence modeling. Pervasive Mob. Comput. **58**, 101025 (2019)
15. Li, T., et al.: Smartphone app usage analysis: datasets, methods, and applications. IEEE Commun. Surv. Tutorials **2**, 937–966 (2022)
16. Li, Y., Fan, Z., Yin, D., Jiang, R., Deng, J., Song, X.: HMGCL: heterogeneous multigraph contrastive learning for LBSN friend recommendation. World Wide Web **26**, 1625–1648 (2022)
17. Van der Maaten, L., Hinton, G.: Visualizing data using t-SNE. J. Mach. Learn. Res. **9**(11), 2579–2605 (2008)
18. Natarajan, N., Shin, D., Dhillon, I.S.: Which app will you use next? Collaborative filtering with interactional context. In: Proceedings of the 7th ACM Conference on Recommender Systems, pp. 201–208 (2013)
19. Parate, A., Böhmer, M., Chu, D., Ganesan, D., Marlin, B.M.: Practical prediction and prefetch for faster access to applications on mobile phones. In: Proceedings of the 2013 ACM International Joint Conference on Pervasive and Ubiquitous Computing, pp. 275–284 (2013)
20. Shin, C., Hong, J.H., Dey, A.K.: Understanding and prediction of mobile application usage for smart phones. In: Proceedings of the 2012 ACM Conference on Ubiquitous Computing, pp. 173–182 (2012)
21. Vaswani, A., et al.: Attention is all you need. In: Advances in Neural Information Processing Systems, vol. 30 (2017)
22. Wang, H., Li, Y., Du, M., Li, Z., Jin, D.: App2Vec: context-aware application usage prediction. ACM Trans. Knowl. Discov. Data (TKDD) **15**(6), 1–21 (2021)
23. Wang, H., et al.: Modeling spatio-temporal app usage for a large user population. Proc. ACM Interactive Mobile Wearable Ubiquit. Technol. **3**(1), 1–23 (2019)
24. Xia, T., et al.: DeepApp: predicting personalized smartphone app usage via context-aware multi-task learning. ACM Trans. Intell. Syst. Technol. (TIST) **11**(6), 1–12 (2020)

25. Xu, S., Li, W., Zhang, X., Gao, S., Zhan, T., Lu, S.: Predicting and recommending the next smartphone apps based on recurrent neural network. CCF Trans. Pervasive Comput. Interaction **2**(4), 314–328 (2020)
26. Xu, Y., et al.: Preference, context and communities: a multi-faceted approach to predicting smartphone app usage patterns. In: Proceedings of the 2013 International Symposium on Wearable Computers, pp. 69–76 (2013)
27. Yang, D., Qu, B., Yang, J., Cudre-Mauroux, P.: Revisiting user mobility and social relationships in LBSNs: a hypergraph embedding approach. In: The World Wide Web Conference, pp. 2147–2157 (2019)
28. Yu, D., Li, Y., Xu, F., Zhang, P., Kostakos, V.: Smartphone app usage prediction using points of interest. Proc. ACM Interactive Mobile Wearable Ubiquit. Technol. **1**(4), 1–21 (2018)
29. Yu, Y., Xia, T., Wang, H., Feng, J., Li, Y.: Semantic-aware spatio-temporal app usage representation via graph convolutional network. Proc. ACM Interactive Mobile Wearable Ubiquit. Technol. **4**(3), 1–24 (2020)
30. Zhao, S., et al.: AppUsage2Vec: modeling smartphone app usage for prediction. In: 2019 IEEE 35th International Conference on Data Engineering (ICDE), pp. 1322–1333. IEEE (2019)
31. Zhao, X., Qiao, Y., Si, Z., Yang, J., Lindgren, A.: Prediction of user app usage behavior from geo-spatial data. In: Proceedings of the Third International ACM SIGMOD Workshop on Managing and Mining Enriched Geo-Spatial Data, pp. 1–6 (2016)
32. Zhou, Y., Li, S., Liu, Y.: Graph-based method for app usage prediction with attributed heterogeneous network embedding. Future Internet **12**(3), 58 (2020)
33. Zou, X., Zhang, W., Li, S., Pan, G.: Prophet: what app you wish to use next. In: Proceedings of the 2013 ACM Conference on Pervasive and Ubiquitous Computing Adjunct Publication, pp. 167–170 (2013)

DegUIL: Degree-Aware Graph Neural Networks for Long-Tailed User Identity Linkage

Meixiu Long, Siyuan Chen, Xin Du, and Jiahai Wang[✉]

School of Computer Science and Engineering,
Sun Yat-sen University, Guangzhou, China
{longmx7,chensy47,duxin23}@mail2.sysu.edu.cn,
wangjiah@mail.sysu.edu.cn

Abstract. User identity linkage (UIL), matching accounts of a person on different social networks, is a fundamental task in cross-network data mining. Recent works have achieved promising results by exploiting graph neural networks (GNNs) to capture network structure. However, they rarely analyze the realistic node-level bottlenecks that hinder UIL's performance. First, node degrees in a graph vary widely and are long-tailed. A significant fraction of *tail nodes* with small degrees are underrepresented due to limited structural information, degrading linkage performance seriously. The second bottleneck usually overlooked is *super head nodes*. It is commonly accepted that head nodes perform well. However, we find that some of them with super high degrees also have difficulty aligning counterparts, due to noise introduced by the randomness of following friends in real-world social graphs. In pursuit of learning ideal representations for these two groups of nodes, this paper proposes a degree-aware model named DegUIL to narrow the degree gap. To this end, our model complements missing neighborhoods for tail nodes and discards redundant structural information for super head nodes in embeddings respectively. Specifically, the neighboring bias is predicted and corrected locally by two modules, which are trained using the knowledge from structurally adequate head nodes. As a result, ideal neighborhoods are obtained for meaningful aggregation in GNNs. Extensive experiments demonstrate the superiority of our model. Our data and code can be found at https://github.com/Longmeix/DegUIL.

Keywords: User identity linkage · Long-tailed graph representation learning · Graph neural networks

1 Introduction

To enjoy diverse types of services, people tend to join multiple social media sites at the same time. Generally, the identities of a person on various social platforms have underlying connections, which triggers research interest in user identity linkage (UIL). This task aims to link identities belonging to the same natural

© The Author(s), under exclusive license to Springer Nature Switzerland AG 2023
G. De Francisci Morales et al. (Eds.): ECML PKDD 2023, LNAI 14174, pp. 122–138, 2023.
https://doi.org/10.1007/978-3-031-43427-3_8

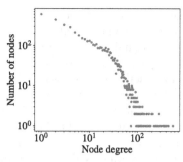 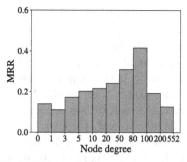

(a) Long-tailed node distribution   (b) MRR w.r.t degrees of test nodes

Fig. 1. A motivation example on the Foursquare-Twitter dataset with PALE [20]. (a) illustrates the node degree distribution of the Foursquare network, with a large proportion of nodes below $10°$. (b) presents PALE's performance by the degrees of test nodes when 50% anchors are used for training. Low-degree nodes $(0,5]$ and super high-degree nodes $(200,522]$ perform worse than the others, indicating these two groups of nodes are the major bottleneck of UIL.

person across distinct social networks. As an information fusion task, UIL has enormous practical value in many network data fusion and mining applications, such as cross-platform recommendation [8,14], etc.

To date, a corpus of literature has emerged to tackle the UIL problem. Earlier approaches [22,31] aligned users by comparing account profiles such as usernames or post contents. However, such auxiliary information is becoming less accessible and inconsistent due to increased privacy concerns. With the advent of graph neural networks (GNNs), research attention related to this problem has been shifted to network-structured data. Although structure-based methods [2,15,25] have achieved substantial progress, they rarely doubt whether social networks provide reliable and adequate information for each node.

Realistic Problems. In reality, however, social networks are always full of noise and provide scarce structural information, especially in cold-start scenarios with lots of new users. There are three problems that cannot be ignored.

(1) **An inherent structural gap exists among nodes.** The number of neighbors varies from user to user in many social networks, and approximately follows a long-tailed distribution, as shown in Fig. 1(a). However, existing approaches apply the same learning strategy to all nodes despite their diverse degrees, which hinders the overall linkage performance. (2) **The limited neighborhoods of tail nodes hinder the linkage performance.** The performance of structure-aware UIL methods heavily depends on the observed neighborhood. Unfortunately, a significant fraction of low-degree nodes, known as *tail nodes*, connect to few neighbors. In the absence of sufficient structural information, the embeddings of these tail nodes may be unsatisfactory or biased, resulting in inferior performance, as demonstrated in Fig. 1(b). (3) **Noise hidden in super head nodes exacerbates the quality of representation.** According to the

first-order proximity [26], UIL works typically assume that friends have similar interests. However, the random nature of users' behavior in following friends is unavoidable [17]. Due to this, fraudulent or meaningless edges are hidden in a graph unnoticeably, especially in users with thousands of friends, which is called *super head nodes* in this paper. Small noises in structure can be easily propagated to the entire graph, thereby affecting the embeddings of many others.

All of these realistic issues motivate us to formulate a novel setting for user identity linkage, aimed at improving the linkage performance of tail nodes, which are the most vulnerable and dominant group. In other words, this paper investigates the following research problem: **how can we effectively link identities for socially-inactive users in a noisy graph?**

Challenges and Our Approach. To obtain more competitive embeddings for tail nodes, we need to address three core issues, i.e. data gap, the absence of neighboring information, and noise-filled graphs, which present three challenges.

First, addressing absent neighborhoods poses a dilemma: *tail nodes have no additional information but few neighbors.* This is especially severe if only network structures are available, without accessing additional side information such as profiles or posts on a platform. Secondly, to defend against the noise in networks, an intuitive idea is to delete fake edges or reduce their negative impacts. However, *how can noise be eliminated while preserving the intrinsic graph structure?* Social networks are full of complicated relationships, making it difficult to discern which edges should be discarded. The above two issues lead to the third challenge: *each node owns both a unique locality and a generality*, which means that bias should be locally corrected without losing the common knowledge across nodes.

To address these challenges, this paper proposes a degree-aware user identity linkage method named DegUIL to improve the matching of tail identities that account for the majority. More concretely, to address the first and second challenges, we utilize the ideal neighborhood knowledge of head nodes to train two modules. They complement potential local contexts for tail nodes and remove redundant neighborhoods of super head nodes in embeddings. Due to this, degree bias is mitigated and their observed neighborhoods are corrected for meaningful aggregation in each GNN layer, thereby improving the quality of node embeddings. For the third challenge, two shared vectors are employed across the graph, which adapt to the local context of each node without losing generality.

Contributions. To summarize, our main contributions are three-fold:

- **Problem**: This paper highlights that the performance bottlenecks of user identity linkage arise not only from tail nodes but also from super head nodes. The observation motivates us to explore the realistic long-tailed UIL.
- **Algorithm**: A degree-aware model is proposed to tackle the above two issues, in pursuit of learning high-quality node embeddings for tail nodes' alignment. Our DegUIL corrects the neighborhood bias of the two groups of nodes and thus narrows the degree gap without additional attributes. This strategy brings a novel perspective to the long-tailed UIL problem.

- **Evaluations**: Extensive experiments demonstrate that our model is superior and has significant advantages in dealing with complex networks.

2   Related Work

Structure-based UIL Methods. Structure-based methods have become increasingly promising in tackling the UIL problem. Most of them are composed of two major phases: feature extraction and identity matching. Recently, graph neural networks have been well extended into the UIL task [2,3,7,9,13,33] and have become mainstream, owing to their powerful capabilities in extracting graph data. For instance, dName [33] learns a proximity-preserving model locally by graph convolutional networks. As simple topology information may be insufficient, MGCN [2] considers convolutions on both local and hypergraph network structures. While many works neglect topological differences such as low-degree nodes, whose small neighborhood impedes the advance of GNN-based approaches. Some recent works in entity alignment are devoted to handling the long-tailed issue by supplementing entity names [29,30], or by preventing entities with similar degrees from clustering into the same region of embedded space [23].

However, we have not seen a method that rectifies structural bias and narrows degree gap for the realistic UIL task. Different from the existing approaches, our model is dedicated to obtaining high-quality tail nodes' embeddings when no additional side information is available.

Other Long-Tailed Problems. The long-tailed problem has been studied in many fields [4,11], but most of the findings cannot be directly applied to the UIL problem due to differences in problem settings. Two closely related works are Tail-GNN [18] and meta-tail2vec [19], which refine feature vectors of tail nodes by transferring the prior knowledge gained from ideal head nodes, leading to a significant improvement in node classification performance. Nevertheless, we observe that not all head nodes are surrounded by ideal neighborhoods in social networks. Structural noise exists in some of very high-degree nodes and impairs performance, as seen in Fig. 1(b). Therefore, our paper mitigates the noise issue of super head nodes to improve the linkage performance of tail nodes.

3   Preliminaries

3.1   Problem Formulation

This paper regards a social network as an undirected graph $\mathcal{G} = (\mathcal{V}, \mathcal{E})$, where $\mathcal{V} = \{v_1, v_2, \ldots, v_N\}$ is the set of vertices (user identities), $\mathcal{E} = \{e_{ij} = (v_i, v_j)\} \subseteq \mathcal{V} \times \mathcal{V}$ represents the edge set (social connections between users). Each edge e_{ij} is associated with a weight $a_{ij} \in \mathbb{R}$, and $a_{ij} > 0$ denotes that node v_i and v_j are connected, otherwise $a_{ij} = 0$. Here $\mathbf{A} = [a_{ij}] \in \mathbb{R}^{N \times N}$ is a symmetric adjacency matrix. $\mathbf{X} \in \mathbb{R}^{N \times d}$ is a feature matrix with $\mathbf{x}_i$ representing the d-dimensional feature vector for node v_i. Now our problems are formally defined as below.

Definition 1 (Super Head Nodes and Tail Nodes). *For a node $v_i \in \mathcal{V}$, let $\mathcal{N}_i$ denote the set of first-order neighbors (neighborhood), and its size $|\mathcal{N}_i|$ is the degree of v_i. Tail nodes have a small degree not exceeding some threshold D, i.e. $\mathcal{V}_{tail} = \{v_i : |\mathcal{N}_i| \leq D\}$. Nodes with a degree greater than M are super head nodes as $\mathcal{V}_{super} = \{v_i : |\mathcal{N}_i| > M\}$. The remaining nodes are called head nodes, i.e. $\mathcal{V}_{head} = \{v_i : D < |\mathcal{N}_i| \leq M\}$. Apparently, $\mathcal{V}_{tail} \cap \mathcal{V}_{super} \cap \mathcal{V}_{head} = \emptyset$.*

Definition 2 (User Identity Linkage Aimed at Tail Nodes). *Given two social networks $\mathcal{G}^1$, $\mathcal{G}^2$, and a collection of observed anchor links as inputs, our goal is to identify the unobserved corresponding anchors of tail nodes. Ideally, the matched node should be ranked as top as possible in predicted top-k candidates.*

3.2 Graph Neural Networks

A graph neural network with multiple layers transforms the raw node features to another Euclidean space as output. Under the message-passing mechanism, the initial features of any two nodes can affect each other even if they are far away, along with the network going deeper. The input features to the l-th layer can be represented by a set of vectors $\mathbf{H}^l = \{\mathbf{h}_1^l, ..., \mathbf{h}_N^l\}$, where $\mathbf{h}_i^l \in \mathbb{R}^{d_l}$ is v_i's representation in the l-th layer. Particularly, $\mathbf{H}^0 = \mathbf{X}$ is in the input layer. The output node features of the $(l+1)$-th layer are generated as:

$$\mathbf{h}_i^{l+1} = \text{Agg}\left(\mathbf{h}_i^l, \{\mathbf{h}_k^l : k \in \mathcal{N}_i\}; \theta^{l+1}\right) \tag{1}$$

where $\text{Agg}(\cdot)$ parameterized by θ^{l+1}, denotes an aggregation function such as mean-pooling, generating new node features from the previous one and messages from first-order neighbors. Most GNNs [12,28] follow the above definition.

4   The Proposed Framework: DegUIL

DegUIL aims to learn high-quality embeddings for tail nodes and super head nodes as a way to enhance linkage performance. Its overall framework is illustrated in Fig. 2. As shown in Fig. 2(b), we train two predictors named *absent neighborhood predictor* and *noisy neighborhood remover* to predict the neighborhood bias of these two groups of nodes (Section 4.1–4.2). As a result, tail nodes are enriched by complementing potential neighboring data, and super head nodes are refined by removing noise adaptively, thereby supporting meaningful aggregation (Section 4.3). Finally, predictors and weight-sharing GNNs are jointly optimized by the task loss and several auxiliary constraints (Section 4.4), for matching identities effectively in Fig. 2(c). The target node with the highest similarity to a source anchor node is returned as its alignment result.

4.1   Uncovering Absent Neighborhood

Neighboring relations connected with tail nodes are relatively few, resulting in biased representations and further hindering linkage results. To solve this problem, we propose an *absent neighborhood predictor* to predict the missing information in their structure, which facilitates subsequent aggregation in each GNN

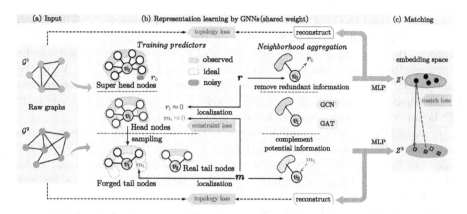

Fig. 2. Overview of DegUIL. (a) Inputting two networks; (b) Complementing potential information m_2 for tail nodes and removing redundant data r_0 for super head nodes to correct their observed neighborhood to be ideal, which improves their representations during aggregation; (c) Mapping two embeddings into a unified space and then matching identities.

layer. It is trained by exploiting the structurally rich prior learned from head nodes. This component enriches the structural information of tail nodes to obtain better representations as ideal as head nodes.

Absent Neighborhood Information for Tail Nodes. Tail nodes lack structural data owing to a variety of reasons, such as being new users on a social platform. Relationships in networks change dynamically, in other words, tail users may interact with other users in the near future, which can be considered as potential relations. Thus, predicting and completing the latent structural information for tail nodes is reasonable.

More concretely, for a tail node $v_i \in \mathcal{V}_{\text{tail}}$, the absent information $\mathbf{m}_i$ measures the gap of feature vectors between its observed neighborhood $\mathcal{N}_i$ and *ideal neighborhood* $\mathcal{N}_i^*$, that is,

$$\mathbf{m}_i = \mathbf{h}_{\mathcal{N}_i^*} - \mathbf{h}_{\mathcal{N}_i}. \tag{2}$$

The ideal representation $\mathbf{h}_{\mathcal{N}_i^*}$ theoretically contains not only the observed aggregated information from local neighborhoods but also friends that would have been associated with v_i. To construct $\mathbf{h}_{\mathcal{N}_i^*}$, we train an absent neighborhood predictor f_m to uncover the missing features caused by limited local contexts. That is, the ideal neighborhood representation of $v_i \in \mathcal{V}_{\text{tail}}$ can be predicted as $\mathbf{h}_{\mathcal{N}_i^*} = \mathbf{h}_{\mathcal{N}_i} + \mathbf{m}_i$. Empirically $\mathbf{h}_{\mathcal{N}_i}$ is represented by a mean-pooling over all nodes in the observed neighborhood, i.e., $\mathbf{h}_{\mathcal{N}_i} = \text{MEAN}(\{\mathbf{h}_k : v_k \in \mathcal{N}_i\})$. Now the problem turns into modeling the potential information in a neighborhood.

Training Absent Neighborhood Predictor. The prediction model is learned using the local contexts of head nodes. Let $\mathbf{m}_i^l$ be absent neighboring information of node v_i in the l-th GNN layer. For a head node v_j, its observed neighborhood is regarded as complete and ideal, thus no missing information on its neighborhood. In other words, the representation of v_j's ideal neighborhood can be approximated by $\mathbf{h}^l_{\mathcal{N}_j}$, the representation of observed neighborhood $\mathcal{N}_j$ in the same layer. Therefore, we train a prediction model f_m by predicting missing neighborhood information of v_j closed to zero as expected, i.e. $\|\mathbf{m}^l_j\|_2 \approx 0$. It will be an auxiliary loss term further discussed in Sect. 4.4.

However, the training scheme has a major flaw: the abundance of head nodes in training differs from tail nodes in testing. To tackle this problem, *forged tail nodes* are supplemented via edge dropout on head nodes. On each head node, neighbors ($|\mathcal{N}_i| \leq D$) are randomly sampled to mimic the real tail nodes. For example, in Fig. 2(b), v'_1 is a forged tail node generated from the head node v_1.

Toward ideal tail nodes representations, a key idea is to uncover the latent information $\mathbf{m}^l_i$ on tail nodes (forged or real), which will be predicted adaptively in Sect. 4.3 to correct their observed neighborhoods that may be biased.

4.2 Removing Noisy Neighborhood

As the first step of UIL, learning effective representations for users is crucial. In contrast to tail nodes, super head nodes are structurally rich and even have redundant edges connecting them, since social networks are complex and unreliable. Perturbed neighbors may cause error propagations through the network that drop the final performance [5]. To defend against the damage for further enhancing tail node alignment, we design a *redundant neighborhood remover*.

To be specific, given a super head node $v_i \in \mathcal{V}_{\text{super}}$, $\mathbf{r}_i$ denotes the embedding redundancy between its observed neighborhood $\mathcal{N}_i$ and ideal one $\mathcal{N}^*_i$, i.e.,

$$\mathbf{r}_i = \mathbf{h}_{\mathcal{N}_i} - \mathbf{h}_{\mathcal{N}^*_i}. \tag{3}$$

Our module removes the neighboring bias $\mathbf{r}^l_i$ in each layer l to mitigate the error cascade in message aggregation of GNNs. As a result, the ideal neighborhood representation of v_i can be obtained by $\mathbf{h}^l_{\mathcal{N}^*_i} = \mathbf{h}^l_{\mathcal{N}_i} - \mathbf{r}^l_i$. Similar to the first module, the absent neighborhood predictor, we employ a function f_r to predict $\mathbf{r}^l_i$.

To refine an ideal graph, a natural strategy is to eliminate adversarial noise. Many works [10,27,34] delete perturbed edges by graph structure learning or graph defense techniques, but such techniques act on a single network rather than cross-network user matching. Besides, mistakenly deleting a useful edge may lead to cascading defects. Instead, we refine node embeddings directly to distill local structure, which eliminates noise without destroying scarce but valuable relations on tail nodes. We locally predict redundancy in the following section.

4.3 Adaptive Aggregation

Localization. The absent or redundant neighborhood information varies across nodes, hence necessitating fine-grained node-wise adaptation. To capture the unique locality of each node while simultaneously preserving generality across the graph, two globally shared vectors $\mathbf{m}$ and $\mathbf{r}$ (per layer) are introduced.

Formally, for each node v_i in the l-th layer of DegUIL, a locality-aware missing vector $\mathbf{m}_i \in \mathbb{R}^{d_l}$ and a redundant vector $\mathbf{r}_i \in \mathbb{R}^{d_l}$ are customized according to its local context. Specifically, the local context information is defined as the concatenation of the node representation with its local observed neighborhood representation, i.e. $\mathbf{c}_i^l = \left[\mathbf{h}_i^l, \mathbf{h}_{\mathcal{N}_i}^l\right]$. Then, the absent neighborhood predictor model f_m and noisy neighborhood remover f_r output localized structural information $\mathbf{m}_i^l$ and $\mathbf{r}_i^l$, respectively. That is,

$$\mathbf{m}_i^l = f_m\left(\mathbf{c}_i^l, \mathbf{m}^l; \theta_m^l\right) = \boldsymbol{\gamma}_i^l \odot \mathbf{m}^l + \boldsymbol{\alpha}_i^l, \tag{4}$$

$$\mathbf{r}_i^l = f_r\left(\mathbf{c}_i^l, \mathbf{r}^l; \theta_r^l\right) = \boldsymbol{\gamma}_i^l \odot \mathbf{r}^l + \boldsymbol{\beta}_i^l, \tag{5}$$

where θ_m^l and θ_r^l are the parameters of f_m and f_r in the l-th layer. Element-wise scaling ($\odot$) and shifting ($+$) operations are used to implement the personalization function for each node. The scaling vector $\boldsymbol{\gamma}_i^l \in \mathbb{R}^{d_l}$ can be calculated as $\boldsymbol{\gamma}_i^l = \mathbf{c}_i^l \mathbf{W}_\gamma^l$ with a learnable matrix $\mathbf{W}_\gamma^l \in \mathbb{R}^{2d_l \times d_l}$. Shift vectors $\boldsymbol{\alpha}_i^l$ and $\boldsymbol{\beta}_i^l$ are trained using two fully connected networks, respectively.

Neighborhood Aggregation. Our discussion now turns to neighborhood aggregation related to super head nodes and tail nodes. The neighborhoods of head nodes are taken as ideal to follow the standard GNNs aggregation in Eq. (1). In contrast, the embedding vectors of tail nodes are underrepresented and those of super head nodes tend to be noisy. Thankfully, our DegUIL complements potential neighboring data for the former and removes local noise for the latter.

The corrected neighborhoods of these two groups of nodes are ideal for key aggregation in GNN-based methods. In the $(l+1)$-th layer, the standard neighborhood aggregation in Eq. (1) is adjusted as follows:

$$\mathbf{h}_i^{l+1} = \mathrm{Agg}\left(\mathbf{h}_i^l, \left\{\mathbf{h}_k^l : v_k \in \mathcal{N}_i\right\} \cup \left\{I\left(v_i \in \mathcal{V}_{\mathrm{tail}}\right) \mathbf{m}_i^l - I\left(v_i \in \mathcal{V}_{\mathrm{super}}\right) \mathbf{r}_i^l\right\}; \theta^{l+1}\right), \tag{6}$$

where $I(\cdot)$ is a 0/1 indicator function based on the truth value of its argument.

Global and Local Aggregation for UIL. This paper employs two different aggregation strategies to maintain global common knowledge and local structure:

$$\mathbf{Z} = \left[\mathrm{Agg}_{\mathrm{GA}}\left(\mathbf{X}, \mathbf{A}\right), \mathrm{Agg}_{\mathrm{LA}}\left(\mathbf{X}, \mathbf{A}\right)\right]. \tag{7}$$

Here, the global structure aggregator $\mathrm{Agg}_{\mathrm{GA}}\left(\cdot\right)$ observes the whole network by graph convolutional networks (GCN) [12]. The local structure aggregator $\mathrm{Agg}_{\mathrm{LA}}\left(\cdot\right)$ acquires specific patterns of nodes' 1-hop neighborhood, implemented by graph attention networks (GAT) [28]. Both of them adopt a two-layer architecture in our method, i.e., $\ell = 2$. By stacking aggregation layers, larger area patterns are observed. The final representation $\mathbf{Z}$ is obtained by concatenating the outputs of aggregators. To preserve the consistency of cross-network node pairs in the embedding space, we apply a shared weight GNN architecture for $\mathcal{G}^1$ and $\mathcal{G}^2$. In other words, GCN and GAT embed nodes from both the source network and target network via shared learnable parameters.

4.4 Training Loss

The whole training process is controlled by three objective terms, 1) topology loss; 2) cross-network mapping loss; and 3) prediction constraints of Eq. (2) and Eq. (3). They are described as follows.

Topology Loss. Global topology is preserved by minimizing the weighted difference on all edges between the input and reconstructed networks, i.e.,

$$\mathcal{L}_s = \sum_{i=1}^{N} \sum_{j=1}^{N} b_{ij} \left(a_{ij} - s_{ij}\right)^2 = \|(\mathbf{A} - \mathbf{S}) \odot \mathbf{B}\|_F^2. \tag{8}$$

Here, $\mathbf{A}$ represents the adjacency matrix. $\mathbf{S} = [s_{ij}]$ is the new connection matrix where each element is $s_{ij} = \text{Sim}(\mathbf{z}_i, \mathbf{z}_j)$. $\text{Sim}(\cdot, \cdot)$ is the similarity function, cosine similarity here. s_{ij} ranges from -1 to 1, a larger value indicates a stronger social connection between v_i and v_j. Moreover, the sampling matrix $\mathbf{B} = [b_{ij}] \in \{0, 1\}^{N \times N}$ is used to balance the number of connected and unconnected edges. We adopt a simple uniform negative sampling [24] here, while you are able to make advances by replacing it with better sampling strategies [21].

Cross-network Matching Loss. Existing UIL models [20] learn desirable mapping functions f to unify the embeddings of different graphs. Formally, given a matched pair (v_i^1, v_a^2) from the set of anchor links U_a and their features $(\mathbf{z}_i^1, \mathbf{z}_a^2)$, $p = 5$ unmatched node pairs (v_i^1, v_b^2) are sampled uniformly as negative identity links with features $(\mathbf{z}_i^1, \mathbf{z}_b^2)$. After mapping by functions f_1 and f_2, the embedding vectors from source network $\mathcal{G}^1$ and target network $\mathcal{G}^2$ are projected to a common embedding space, i.e. $o_i = f_1(z_i^1)$, $o_a = f_2(z_a^2)$ and $o_b = f_2(z_b^2)$, respectively. Let $t_{ia} = \text{Sim}(o_i, o_a)$, the loss is defined as:

$$\mathcal{L}_t = \sum_{(v_i^1, v_a^2) \in U_a} (1 - t_{ia})^2 + \sum_{(v_i^1, v_b^2) \notin U_a} (t_{ib}^2 + t_{ab}^2). \tag{9}$$

The objective aims to maximize the similarities of anchor links while minimizing the link probabilities of unmatched identities. $f_1(\cdot; \theta_{f_1})$ and $f_2(\cdot; \theta_{f_2})$ are implemented by two multi-layer perceptrons (MLPs) with learnable parameters $\theta_f = (\theta_{f_1}, \theta_{f_2})$.

Constraints on Predicted Information. For tail nodes, DegUIL aims to complement rather than refine its neighborhood. In contrast, the neighborhood of super head nodes is refined but not enriched. The other nodes' local contexts are regarded as ideal without absence or redundancy. Therefore, both predicted missing data for nodes except tail nodes and noisy information for nodes except super head nodes should be close to zero, which can be formulated as:

$$\mathcal{L}_p = \sum_{l=1}^{\ell} \left(\sum_{v_i \notin \mathcal{V}_{\text{tail}}} \left\| \mathbf{m}_i^{l-1} \right\|_2^2 + \sum_{v_i \notin \mathcal{V}_{\text{super}}} \left\| \mathbf{r}_i^{l-1} \right\|_2^2 \right). \tag{10}$$

Optimization. For $g = 2$ social networks $(\mathcal{G})$, the total loss is a combined loss:

$$\mathcal{L} = \mathcal{L}_t + \lambda \sum_i^g \mathcal{L}_s^{\mathcal{G}^i} + \mu \sum_i^g \mathcal{L}_p^{\mathcal{G}^i}. \tag{11}$$

Hyperparameters λ and μ balance the importance of topology and predicted information constraint.

Here we discuss the computational complexity of DegUIL. Let $N_{\max} = \max\left(|\mathcal{V}^1|, |\mathcal{V}^2|\right)$ denote the maximum number of nodes of two input graphs. First, we employ node2vec to generate initial features, resulting in $O(N_{\max})$ complexity. Next, our model employs GCN and GAT to learn powerful representations. In each GNN layer l, the overhead involves forging tail nodes, the localization, and the aggregation of absent information and redundant information. Forging tail nodes consumes $O(ND)$ time since we sample up to D neighbors on a head node to forge a tail node, where D is the degree threshold of the tail node; Locally predicting $\mathbf{m}_i^l$ in (4) and $\mathbf{r}_i^l$ in (5) needs $O(N\bar{D}d_l^2)$ complexity, where d_l is the dimension of the l-th layer and $\bar{D}$ is the average node degree. Aggregating the corrected neighboring information takes $O(N(\bar{D}+1)d_l d_{l-1})$ time. As d_l, d_{l-1} and the number of GNN layers are small constants, when $\bar{D} \ll N_{\max}$, the complexity of node2vec and our degree-aware GNNs is $O(N_{\max})$ for the representation learning process. Overall, the time complexity of our proposed DegUIL is $O(N_{\max})$, i.e., it scales linear time with respect to the number of nodes.

4.5   Characteristics of DegUIL

DegUIL is characterized by the following features. (1) Unlike most UIL methods that apply the same learning approach to all nodes, our method divides nodes into three groups (tail/head/super head nodes) according to their degrees. DegUIL considers neighborhood differences and adopts different neighboring bias correction strategies for them to narrow the structural gap by a node-wise localization technique. (2) DegUIL predicts and complements potential neighboring information of tail nodes directly, which avoids designing an extra neighborhood translation [18] or separates the embedding and refinement processes [19]. It eliminates noisy topology of super head nodes implicitly, preventing valuable edges from being deleted by mistake like some graph structure learning methods [10,27,34]. (3) We use weight-sharing GNNs instead of two separate GNNs to preserve cross-network similarity and reduce training parameters.

5   Experiments

In this section, we aim to answer the following questions via experiments. **Q1:** How effective is our proposed DegUIL compared with baselines? **Q2:** How does

Table 1. Dataset statistics.

Networks	#Nodes	#Edges	#Anchor links	#Tail links
Foursquare	5313	76972	1609	443
Twitter	5120	164919		
DBLP17	9086	51700	2832	975
DBLP19	9325	47775		

each component of DegUIL contribute to the final results? **Q3**: Is our method compatible with previous data partitions? **Q4**: How much performance does our method improve for nodes in each degree interval?

5.1 Experimental Settings

Datasets. Two benchmark datasets are employed for evaluation, as summarized in Table 1. **Foursquare-Twitter** (FT), widely used real-world data in previous literature [15,16], provides partial anchor nodes for identity linkage. **DBLP17-DBLP19** (DBLP) [1] includes two co-author networks, in which a node represents an author, and an edge connects two nodes if they are co-authors of at least one paper. Common authors across two networks are used as the ground truth. We define tail links as anchor links with a node degree of 5 or less.

To simulate a user cold-start scenario where a large number of nodes are tail nodes, anchors containing tail nodes are split into the testing set, and the rest anchor links are used in training.

Baselines. To evaluate the effectiveness of DegUIL, we compare it with three kinds of embedding-based baselines, including a conventional representation learning method (node2vec), state-of-the-art UIL methods and a tail node refinement model (Tail-GNN). The baselines are described as follows.

- **node2vec** [6]: It encodes network topology into a low-dimensional space, whose outputs serve as initial input features to our methods.
- **PALE** [20]: This method learns embeddings and predicts anchor links by maximizing the log-likelihood of observed edges and latent space matching.
- **SEA** [23]: It is a semi-supervised entity alignment method that tries to avoid embedding entities with similar degrees closely by an adversarial training.
- **NeXtAlign** [32]: A semi-supervised network alignment method that achieves a balance between alignment consistency and disparity.
- **Tail-GNN** [18]: The GNN framework refines embeddings of tail nodes with predicted missing neighborhood information. Tail-GCN is compared here.

Note that node2vec and Tail-GNN are not UIL methods, so the matching process and other settings are the same as ours, for the sake of fair comparison. All codes come from open-access repositories of the original papers.

Table 2. Overall performance. Best result appears in bold and the second best model is underlined except for ablation variants.

Dataset	Foursquare-Twitter				DBLP17-DBLP19			
Metric	Hits@1	Hits@10	Hits@30	MRR	Hits@1	Hits@10	Hits@30	MRR
node2vec	5.43	15.08	25.49	10.93	33.18	55.10	66.52	44.17
PALE	6.00	15.77	26.48	11.51	21.28	39.78	52.04	30.94
SEA	6.93	15.89	23.94	11.80	**38.62**	60.13	71.01	**49.27**
NeXtAlign	6.47	12.23	16.62	9.63	36.82	59.58	70.46	48.06
Tail-GNN	6.70	17.67	28.39	12.66	36.36	56.58	67.21	46.44
DegUIL	**9.33**	**21.70**	**32.81**	**16.00**	37.59	**60.73**	**71.51**	48.96
DegUIL$_{w/o\_AP}$	8.11	19.39	30.39	14.30	36.26	59.29	70.32	47.67
DegUIL$_{w/o\_NR}$	8.94	20.53	31.79	15.21	37.13	59.61	70.02	48.26

Evaluation Metrics. Following previous works [22,23,33], we employ two widely used Hits-Precision (Hits@k) and mean reciprocal rank (MRR) as evaluation metrics. $Hits@k = \frac{1}{N}\sum_{i=1}^{N}\frac{k-(hit(v_i)-1)}{k}$, $hit(v_i)$ is the rank position of the matched target user in the top-k candidates. MRR denotes the average reciprocal rank of ground truth results. Higher metric values indicate better performance.

Setup and Parameters. For each method, we set the embedding vector dimension $d = 256$ on all datasets. The initial node feature of our method is generated by node2vec [6]. We set hyperparameter $\lambda = 0.2$ in Eq. (11), μ to 0.001 and 0.01 for FT and DBLP datasets respectively. The dimension of hidden layers in Agg is 64. Tail nodes' degree is set to be no greater than 5, i.e. $D = 5$, consistent with Tail-GNN. Super head nodes are the top 10% nodes with the highest degree, thus M is set to {46, 116, 25, 23} in four networks (Fourquare, Twitter, DBLP17, DBLP19), respectively. The 2-layer MLP network for matching outputs 256-dimensional embeddings, and the dimension of hidden layers is twice the input length. The optimal hyperparameters for each method are either determined by experiments or the suggestions from the original papers. All experiments are repeated five times to obtain the average Hits@k and MRR scores.

5.2   Result

Overwiew of Results (Q1). Comparison results on two UIL datasets are presented in Table 2. From the results, we have the following observations.

- *DegUIL consistently outperforms other baselines.* On the Foursquare-Twitter dataset, DegUIL achieves a remarkable relative improvement of 16%-39% compared to the best baseline, TailGNN. This is empirical evidence that our method is more effective than previous models in boosting linkage accuracy. An exception is on the DBLP dataset, where SEA obtains the best Hit@1

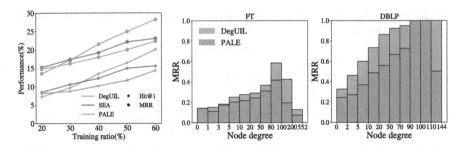

Fig. 3. Effect of training ratio on the FT dataset.

Fig. 4. MRR results by degrees.

and MRR, while DegUIL remains a close runner-up ahead of other baselines. We infer that SEA's technique of encoding relations benefits learning node representations. Besides, with the same mapping process, node2vec is inferior to the GNNs-based Tail-GNN. It demonstrates the power of GNNs in capturing neighboring topology, so mitigating the neighborhood bias to further advance GNNs is significant.

- *Degree-aware models perform better than traditional methods.* Node2vec and PALE treat all nodes uniformly without considering the structural disparity such as node degree. As a result, node representations learned by the two simple methods are unsatisfactory for linking user identities. This highlights the importance of degree-aware baselines, which achieve more effective results. However, SEA, NeXtAlign, and Tail-GNN are not specially designed for enhancing super head nodes, their performance still falls short compared to our model.
- *DegUIL has a greater advvantage in complex long-tailed datasets.* Under all evaluation metrics, methods perform worse on the FT dataset than that on the DBLP dataset, despite the former having more known anchor links. One explanation for this discrepancy may be the greater complexity of edge relationships in FT, which makes it challenging to link users in social networks with disparate node degrees. Our model can effectively handle this complex situation, giving it a distinct advantage. Further discussions are in the ablation study.

Ablation Study (Q2). DegUIL comprises two components: an absent neighborhood predictor (AP) and a noisy neighborhood remover (NR). To evaluate the contribution of each component, we designed two variants of our model. **DegUIL**$_{w/o\_AP}$ does not complement the predicted potential neighborhood for learning tail nodes' embeddings. Another variant model **DegUIL**$_{w/o\_NR}$ does not eliminate the noise from the local structure of super head nodes.

The results of the ablation study are presented in Table 2, which reveals several conclusions. First, without AP predicting and complementing absent neighborhoods for tail nodes, UIL performance declines by 1.70% and 1.29%

in terms of MRR on the FT and DBLP datasets, respectively. This indicates that the limited local context of tail nodes hinders user alignment, and our AP component is proposed as a solution for improving tail node embeddings. Second, removing structural noise in super head nodes also contributes to performance. It supports our theoretical motivation that super head nodes are also a challenging group of nodes. Notably, the gain of AP is more significant than that of NC on both datasets, suggesting that correcting the neighborhoods of tail nodes offers more substantial alignment benefits. One explanation for this phenomenon is the greater number of tail nodes, compared to super head nodes, which allows them to exert a more considerable influence on the overall performance.

Effect on Dataset with Classic Partition (Q3). This paper splits datasets in a novel way to mimic a challenging UIL scenario, i.e. an anchor link without tail nodes is assigned into the training set, otherwise in the testing set. This naturally raises a question: whether DegUIL is compatible with previous ways of data partitioning and still outperforms other baselines under this setting. To answer it, we vary the proportion of labeled anchors for training from 20% to 60% with a step of 10%, and use the rest for testing. Experiments are conducted on the FT dataset with competitive PALE and SEA as comparison methods.

Figure 3 illustrates the Hits@1 and MRR scores. As the training ratio increases, more alignment information is available, enabling all models to discover potential user identities more easily. In most cases, our proposed DegUIL achieves superior performance in both metrics, except when the training data is less than 30%. This exception arises due to the difficulty of effectively training the GNNs used in DegUIL when labeled supervision is insufficient. In such scenario, SEA and PALE show slight superiority thanks to their semi-supervised way or network extension using observed anchor links. In the future, we will consider semi-supervised or self-supervised training to mitigate the problem of data scarcity. With more supervision information, DegUIL consistently and significantly outperforms the other two baselines. This means that our degree-aware method is also applicable and competent in the previous data partition.

Evaluation by Degree (Q4). To demonstrate the effectiveness of DegUIL in aligning long-tail entities, we divide the test anchors into multiple groups based on their source node degrees. We compare our method with simple PALE and illustrate their MRR results by degree in Fig. 4. As hypothesized, low-degree nodes and super high-degree nodes perform worse than those normal nodes with adequate local topology information. This experimental evidence shows that drastic disparities in node degrees could lead to unsatisfactory node representations and biased outcomes. Moreover, DegUIL outperforms PALE across all degree groups in both datasets, validating its effectiveness in handling long-tail issues. While the improvements are smaller on nodes with fewer than two neighbors, given that DegUIL is also constrained by the very limited structural information.

6   Conclusion

Commonly, node degrees in a social graph are long-tailed, yet UIL works rarely explore the issue of degree bias. We associate the overlooked distribution with UIL performance, observing that the key to improving overall performance is tail nodes and super head nodes. This paper defines a realistic problem setting and proposes DegUIL to learn high-quality node embeddings by mitigating degree differences in the embedding process through two localized modules. These modules enrich neighborhood information for tail nodes and refine local contexts of super head nodes. As a result, node representations are improved thanks to the corrected ideal neighborhood. Extensive experiments show that DegUIL significantly surpasses the baselines. In the future, we will consider high-order neighborhood and predict structural bias more accurately to enhance our model.

Acknowledgment. This work is supported by the National Natural Science Foundation of China (62072483), and the Guangdong Basic and Applied Basic Research Foundation (2022A1515011690, 2021A1515012298).

Ethical Statement. This paper presents a study on the application of data mining techniques in social networks, with a strong emphasis on ethical considerations. We are fully committed to upholding the highest ethical standards throughout our research process, prioritizing the privacy and well-being of individuals.

Privacy protection: Our utmost priority is the careful and secure treatment of personal information. All data collected and analyzed in this study strictly adheres to the relevant privacy laws and regulations. To safeguard privacy, we have taken measures to anonymize and de-identify the data, ensuring there is no possibility of linking any personal information to specific individuals. Our analysis is based solely on aggregated and anonymized data, eliminating any potential risks to individual privacy.

Datasets and licensing: We have utilized publicly available datasets that have been appropriately licensed, following the terms and conditions set by the dataset owners. In this research paper, we explicitly acknowledge the sources of our data, ensuring that all citation requirements are met.

Ethical use of results: The results presented in this paper are meant for academic and research purposes only. We acknowledge the need to prevent any misuse of our findings that could violate privacy, harm individuals, or engage in unethical activities. We are dedicated to responsibly using our research outputs, contributing positively to the advancement of computer science and society.

In conclusion, this study adheres to the highest ethical standards, ensuring the respect for privacy, confidentiality, and responsible use of data. We are dedicated to contributing to the field of data mining in social networks while maintaining the security and privacy of individuals and organizations involved.

References

1. Chen, B., Chen, X.: MAUIL: multilevel attribute embedding for semisupervised user identity linkage. Inf. Sci. **593**, 527–545 (2022)

2. Chen, H., Yin, H., Sun, X., Chen, T., Gabrys, B., Musial, K.: Multi-level graph convolutional networks for cross-platform anchor link prediction. In: KDD, pp. 1503–1511 (2020)
3. Chen, S., Wang, J., Du, X., Hu, Y.: A novel framework with information fusion and neighborhood enhancement for user identity linkage. In: ECAI, vol. 325, pp. 1754–1761 (2020)
4. Chen, Z., Xiao, R., Li, C., Ye, G., Sun, H., Deng, H.: ESAM: discriminative domain adaptation with non-displayed items to improve long-tail performance. In: SIGIR, pp. 579–588 (2020)
5. Dai, H., et al.: Adversarial attack on graph structured data. In: ICML, vol. 80, pp. 1123–1132 (2018)
6. Grover, A., Leskovec, J.: node2vec: scalable feature learning for networks. In: KDD, pp. 855–864 (2016)
7. Hong, H., Li, X., Pan, Y., Tsang, I.W.: Domain-adversarial network alignment. IEEE Trans. Knowl. Data Eng. **34**(7), 3211–3224 (2022)
8. Hu, G., Zhang, Y., Yang, Q.: CoNET: collaborative cross networks for cross-domain recommendation. In: CIKM, pp. 667–676 (2018)
9. Hu, Z., Wang, J., Chen, S., Du, X.: A semi-supervised framework with efficient feature extraction and network alignment for user identity linkage. In: Jensen, C.S., et al. (eds.) DASFAA 2021. LNCS, vol. 12682, pp. 675–691. Springer, Cham (2021). https://doi.org/10.1007/978-3-030-73197-7_46
10. Jin, W., Ma, Y., Liu, X., Tang, X., Wang, S., Tang, J.: Graph structure learning for robust graph neural networks. In: KDD, pp. 66–74 (2020)
11. Khodak, M., Saunshi, N., Liang, Y., Ma, T., Stewart, B., Arora, S.: A La Carte Embedding: cheap but effective induction of semantic feature vectors. In: ACL (1), pp. 12–22 (2018)
12. Kipf, T.N., Welling, M.: Semi-supervised classification with graph convolutional networks. In: ICLR (2017)
13. Li, C., et al.: Semi-supervised variational user identity linkage via noise-aware self-learning. IEEE Trans. Knowl. Data Eng. 1–14 (2023). https://doi.org/10.1109/TKDE.2023.3250245
14. Lin, J., Chen, S., Wang, J.: Graph neural networks with dynamic and static representations for social recommendation. In: Bhattacharya, A., et al. (eds.) DASFAA (2), vol. 13246, pp. 264–271. Springe, Cham (2022). https://doi.org/10.1007/978-3-031-00126-0_18
15. Liu, L., Cheung, W.K., Li, X., Liao, L.: Aligning users across social networks using network embedding. In: IJCAI, pp. 1774–1780 (2016)
16. Liu, L., Li, X., Cheung, W.K., Liao, L.: Structural representation learning for user alignment across social networks. IEEE Trans. Knowl. Data Eng. **32**(9), 1824–1837 (2020)
17. Liu, L., Wang, C., Zhang, Y., Wang, Y., Liu, Q., Wang, G.: Denoise network structure for user alignment across networks via graph structure learning. In: DMBD (1), vol. 1744, pp. 105–119 (2022)
18. Liu, Z., Nguyen, T., Fang, Y.: Tail-GNN: tail-node graph neural networks. In: KDD, pp. 1109–1119 (2021)
19. Liu, Z., Zhang, W., Fang, Y., Zhang, X., Hoi, S.C.H.: Towards locality-aware meta-learning of tail node embeddings on networks. In: CIKM, pp. 975–984 (2020)
20. Man, T., Shen, H., Liu, S., Jin, X., Cheng, X.: Predict anchor links across social networks via an embedding approach. In: IJCAI, pp. 1823–1829 (2016)

21. Mikolov, T., Sutskever, I., Chen, K., Corrado, G.S., Dean, J.: Distributed representations of words and phrases and their compositionality. In: NIPS, pp. 3111–3119 (2013)
22. Mu, X., Zhu, F., Lim, E., Xiao, J., Wang, J., Zhou, Z.: User identity linkage by latent user space modelling. In: KDD, pp. 1775–1784 (2016)
23. Pei, S., Yu, L., Hoehndorf, R., Zhang, X.: Semi-supervised entity alignment via knowledge graph embedding with awareness of degree difference. In: WWW, pp. 3130–3136 (2019)
24. Rendle, S., Freudenthaler, C., Gantner, Z., Schmidt-Thieme, L.: BPR: Bayesian personalized ranking from implicit feedback. In: UAI, pp. 452–461 (2009)
25. Tan, S., Guan, Z., Cai, D., Qin, X., Bu, J., Chen, C.: Mapping users across networks by manifold alignment on hypergraph. In: AAAI, pp. 159–165 (2014)
26. Tang, J., Qu, M., Wang, M., Zhang, M., Yan, J., Mei, Q.: LINE: large-scale information network embedding. In: WWW, pp. 1067–1077 (2015)
27. Tang, X., Li, Y., Sun, Y., Yao, H., Mitra, P., Wang, S.: Transferring robustness for graph neural network against poisoning attacks. In: WSDM, pp. 600–608 (2020)
28. Velickovic, P., Cucurull, G., Casanova, A., Romero, A., Liò, P., Bengio, Y.: Graph attention networks. In: ICLR (2018)
29. Wang, H., Wang, Y., Li, J., Luo, T.: Degree aware based adversarial graph convolutional networks for entity alignment in heterogeneous knowledge graph. Neurocomputing **487**, 99–109 (2022)
30. Zeng, W., Zhao, X., Wang, W., Tang, J., Tan, Z.: Degree-aware alignment for entities in tail. In: SIGIR, pp. 811–820 (2020)
31. Zhang, H., Kan, M.-Y., Liu, Y., Ma, S.: Online social network profile linkage. In: Jaafar, A., et al. (eds.) AIRS 2014. LNCS, vol. 8870, pp. 197–208. Springer, Cham (2014). https://doi.org/10.1007/978-3-319-12844-3_17
32. Zhang, S., Tong, H., Jin, L., Xia, Y., Guo, Y.: Balancing consistency and disparity in network alignment. In: KDD, pp. 2212–2222 (2021)
33. Zhou, F., Wen, Z., Trajcevski, G., Zhang, K., Zhong, T., Liu, F.: Disentangled network alignment with matching explainability. In: INFOCOM, pp. 1360–1368 (2019)
34. Zhu, D., Zhang, Z., Cui, P., Zhu, W.: Robust graph convolutional networks against adversarial attacks. In: KDD, pp. 1399–1407 (2019)

Ex-ThaiHate: A Generative Multi-task Framework for Sentiment and Emotion Aware Hate Speech Detection with Explanation in Thai

Krishanu Maity[1], Shaubhik Bhattacharya[1], Salisa Phosit[2],
Sawarod Kongsamlit[2], Sriparna Saha[1], and Kitsuchart Pasupa[2(✉)] ⓘ

[1] Department of Computer Science and Engineering, Indian Institute of Technology
Patna, Patna 801103, India
{krishanu_2021cs19,shaubhik_2111cs19,sriparna}@iitp.ac.in
[2] School of Information Technology, King Mongkut's Institute of Technology
Ladkrabang, Bangkok 10520, Thailand
{63070242,63070245,kitsuchart}@it.kmitl.ac.th

Abstract. Social media platforms have both positive and negative
impacts on users in diverse societies. One of the adverse effects of social
media platforms is the usage of hate and offensive language, which not
only fosters prejudice but also harms the vulnerable. Additionally, a person's sentiment and emotional state heavily influence the intended content of any social media post. Despite extensive research being conducted
to detect online hate speech in English, there is a lack of similar studies
on low-resource languages such as Thai. The recent enactment of laws
like the "right to explanations" in the General Data Protection Regulation has stimulated the development of interpretable models rather
than solely focusing on performance. Motivated by this, we created the
first benchmark hate speech corpus, called *Ex-ThaiHate*, in the Thai
language. Each post is annotated with four labels, namely hate, sentiment, emotion, and rationales (explainability), which specify the phrases
that are responsible for annotating the post as hate. In order to investigate the effect of sentiment and emotional information on detecting hate
speech posts, we propose a unified generative framework called *GenX*,
which redefines this multi-task problem as a text-to-text generation task
to simultaneously solve four tasks: hate-speech identification, rationale
detection, sentiment, and emotion detection. Our extensive experiments
demonstrate that *GenX* significantly outperforms all baselines and state-of-the-art models, thereby highlighting its effectiveness in detecting hate
speech and identifying the rationales in low-resource languages. The code
and dataset are available at https://github.com/dsmlr/Ex-ThaiHate.
Disclaimer: The article contains offensive text and profanity. This is
due to the nature of the work and does not reflect any opinion or stance
of the authors.

Keywords: Hate Speech · Sentiment · Emotion · Explainability ·
Thai · Multi-task

ⓒ The Author(s), under exclusive license to Springer Nature Switzerland AG 2023
G. De Francisci Morales et al. (Eds.): ECML PKDD 2023, LNAI 14174, pp. 139–156, 2023.
https://doi.org/10.1007/978-3-031-43427-3_9

1 Introduction

Social media platforms have become an integral part of people's lives, providing opportunities to connect, express, and share ideas with individuals worldwide. While these platforms have numerous positive effects, they are often plagued by the prevalence of hate speech and offensive language. Hate speech refers to any form of communication that aims to attack the dignity of a group based on characteristics such as race, gender, ethnicity, sexual orientation, nationality, religion, or other features [23]. According to the Pew Research Center, approximately 40% of social media users have encountered online harassment or bullying [6]. Between July and September 2021, Facebook detected and took action against 22.3 million instances of hate speech content [22]. These hate posts, which may seem harmless on social media, have real-world consequences, including violence and riots [6]. Therefore, it is crucial to prioritize the detection and control of hate speech.

Over the past decade, significant research has been conducted to develop models and datasets for automatic hate speech detection in the English language, utilizing traditional machine learning techniques [8,9,30] as well as deep learning techniques [1,2,37]. However, limited studies have been conducted for other languages, such as Italian [35], Indonesian [14], and Thai [26], primarily due to inadequate resources or conflicting interests. Given the variation in the perception of hate speech across different languages and cultures, it is crucial to develop automatic hate speech detection techniques for low-resource languages to improve classification and understanding of the corresponding contexts. According to a recent report by Reuters, Thailand has witnessed a rapid surge in hate speech incidents during the COVID-19 outbreak [34]. Specifically, the infection of many Myanmar workers at a fish market in Samut Sakhon led to the spread of hate speech against them on social media platforms, including YouTube, Facebook, and Twitter. Consequently, migrant and immigrant workers from Myanmar became extremely fearful for their safety. To address this issue, we have developed an advanced model for detecting online hate speech in the Thai language. Our goal is to automatically identify and flag hateful messages using these hate speech detection systems.

However, researchers have primarily focused on enhancing the performance of hate speech detection by utilizing various models but have largely overlooked the importance of explainability in these models. The emergence of explainable artificial intelligence (AI) [13] has made it necessary to provide explanations or interpretations for the decisions made by machine learning algorithms. This is crucial for building trust and confidence when deploying AI models in practical scenarios. Furthermore, legislation such as the General Data Protection Regulation (GDPR) [10] in Europe has introduced a "right to explanation" law, highlighting the need to develop interpretable models. As a result, there is a pressing demand to prioritize the development of interpretable models rather than solely focusing on model complexity for enhanced performance.

Multi-task learning is a training technique that utilizes data from related tasks to efficiently learn the relationship between them [5]. Numerous studies have demonstrated that incorporating an auxiliary task can enhance the performance of the primary task. For instance, in the context of cyberbullying detection [20], complaint identification [33], and tweet act classification [31], the inclusion of auxiliary tasks has proven beneficial. Considering that a person's sentiments and emotions can significantly impact the meaning of social media posts, it is crucial to incorporate sentiment and emotional analysis in hate speech detection.

Motivated by these considerations, we have developed the first explainable hate speech dataset, called "*Ex-ThaiHate*," in the Thai language. This dataset addresses four tasks simultaneously: hate speech detection (HSD), sentiment analysis (SA), emotion recognition (ER), and rationale detection (RD) — which focuses on providing explainability. To construct *Ex-ThaiHate*, we re-annotated the existing Thai Hate Speech dataset [26] by adding the sentiment and emotion labels and marking rationales. Rationales are text fragments from a source text that justify classification decisions. In cases where a post is a non-hate speech, we do not indicate any rationales. Our study specifically emphasizes the application of rationales to enhance model interpretability, aiming to achieve more human-like decision-making and improve the model's trustworthiness, transparency, and reliability. Previous studies, such as e-SNLI [4] and commonsense explanations [29], have also utilized rationales to enhance their models.

A typical multi-task model consists of a shared encoder that incorporates representations from data of different tasks, along with task-specific layers or heads attached to that encoder. However, this approach has several drawbacks. One such drawback is negative transfer, where multiple tasks, instead of optimizing the learning process, start to hinder the training process [7]. Additionally, there are concerns related to model capacity, wherein if the size of the shared encoder becomes too large, there will be no effective transfer of information across different tasks [38]. Furthermore, the optimization scheme for assigning weights to different tasks during training poses challenges [38].

To address the challenges mentioned earlier in multi-task learning, we have proposed the idea of employing a generative model to simultaneously solve multiple classification tasks in a text-to-text generation manner. In this work, we introduce a unified generative framework called "*GenX*," which is capable of solving all four tasks concurrently. The input to the *GenX* model is a social media post written in Thai, and the output target sequence is the concatenation of corresponding hate, sentiment, emotion labels, and rationales, separated by a special character. Through extensive experiments, we demonstrate that *GenX* consistently outperforms other baselines and state-of-the-art (SOTA) models across various evaluation metrics. The following is a summary of our contributions:

1. We investigate two new tasks: (i) explainable HSD in Thai and (ii) formulating the multi-task problem as a text-to-text generation problem.
2. We have developed *Ex-ThaiHate*, a new benchmark dataset for explainable HSD in the Thai language. This dataset includes sentiment and emotion

labels. To the best of our knowledge, this is the first study to focus on explainable HSD in Thai.

3. We propose a unified generative framework called *"GenX"* with reinforcement learning (RL) -based training to simultaneously solve four tasks: HSD, SA, ER, and RD.

4. Experimental results demonstrate that incorporating rationales, sentiment, and emotion information significantly enhances the performance of the main task, i.e., HSD.

2   Related Works

HSD heavily relies on linguistic subtleties, and researchers have recently devoted significant attention to automatically identifying hate speech in social media. In this section, we will review recent works on both stand-alone and multi-task learning-based methods for HSD.

Several studies have been conducted to develop and enhance algorithms for the detection of cyberbullying and hate speech in the English language. Reynolds et al. [30] utilized data from formspring.me to create a cyberbullying dataset and achieved an accuracy of 78.5% using the C4.5 decision tree method. In 2020, Balakrishnan et al. [3] developed a cyberbullying detection algorithm that employed multiple machine learning techniques while considering the psychological characteristics of Twitter users. Another notable system, CyberBERT, was proposed by Paul et al. [27], which utilized BERT-based models and demonstrated SOTA performance on benchmark hate speech datasets from Formspring (12k posts), Twitter (16k posts), and Wikipedia. Furthermore, Badjatiya et al. [2] conducted extensive experiments with various deep learning architectures to learn semantic word embeddings. Their results on a hate speech dataset consisting of 16K annotated tweets showed that deep learning methods outperformed traditional char/word n-gram algorithms by an 18% F1 score.

In 2021, Wanasukapunt et al. [36] developed both binomial models—Support Vector Machine (SVM), Random Forest (RF)—and multinomial models—Long short-term memory (LSTM), DistilBERT)—to detect abusive speech from social media specifically in the Thai language. Their study revealed that deep learning models outperformed machine learning models, and the best F1 score of 90.67% was achieved using DistilBERT. In a separate study, Pasupa et al. [26] constructed a benchmark Thai hate speech dataset by collecting posts from platforms such as Facebook, Twitter, and YouTube. They fine-tuned the WangchanBERTa model using the ordinal regression loss function, resulting in a SOTA performance for HSD in the Thai language. Recently, Maity et al. [18] introduced a two-channel deep learning model called FastThaiCaps. This model combines BERT embedding with a capsule network, as well as FastText embedding with BiLSTM and attention. Notably, extensive experiments demonstrated that their proposed model surpassed the performance of the baseline models.

In [40], the authors developed a multi-task framework that incorporates sentiment knowledge for HSD. Saha et al. [31] proposed a multi-modal tweet act classification framework. Their approach involves an ensemble adversarial learning strategy, where the inclusion of sentiment and emotion information improves the performance of the main task. Maity et al. [19] created a Hindi-English code-mixed dataset specifically for cyberbullying detection. They developed an attention-based deep multi-task framework based on BERT and VecMap embeddings.

Zaidan et al. [39] introduced the concept of rationales, which involves annotators underlining a section of text to support their tagging decision. The authors found that using these rationales improved the performance of sentiment classification. In a similar vein, Mathew et al. [21] introduced the HateXplain benchmark dataset for HSD. They discovered that models trained using human rationales were more effective at reducing inadvertent bias against targeted communities. Karim et al. [15] developed an explainable HSD approach (DeepHate-Explainer) in Bengali based on different variants of transformer architectures (BERT-base, mMERT, XLM-RoBERTa). They provided explainability by highlighting the most important words for which the sentence is labeled as hate speech.

After conducting an in-depth literature review, it can be concluded that the majority of research on HSD focuses on the English language. It has been observed that incorporating sentiment and emotional information greatly improves the performance of the primary task. However, there is a notable absence of studies investigating sentiment and emotion-aided HSD in the Thai language.

3   *Ex-ThaiHate* Dataset Development

To start the process, we conducted a literature review to identify existing Thai hate speech datasets. Our search yielded two relevant Thai datasets [26,36]. After careful consideration, we decided to use the Thai Hate Speech dataset by Pasupa et al. [26] for further annotation with sentiment and emotion labels. This dataset was collected from three widely used social media platforms: Facebook, Twitter, and YouTube. The data collection period spanned from 18/12/2020 to 23/12/2020, following the news of a COVID-19 infection case involving a merchandiser at a market in Samut Sakhon, Thailand, who was subsequently admitted to a hospital.

3.1   Data Annotation

The annotation process was carried out by a team consisting of three Ph.D. scholars specializing in cyberbullying, hate speech, and offensive content, and three undergraduate students who were proficient in the Thai language. To recruit undergraduate students, we sent out a voluntary hiring notice through the school's email list, and they were compensated with gift vouchers for their participation. Initially, the Thai hate speech dataset [26] had been annotated with a binary hate speech class (Hate/non-hate). In order to train the annotators for the annotation of sentiment and emotion classes, we needed gold-standard samples with these annotations. Our expert annotators randomly

Table 1. Samples from annotated *ExThaiHate* dataset. The underlined tokens provide the rationale behind the hate speech.

Post	Sentiment Class	Emotion Class	Hate Speech Class
T1: สงสารพม่าเขามากเลย สู้นะพม่าทุกคน **Token:** สงสารพม่าเขามากเลยสู้นะพม่าทุกคน **Translation:** I feel pity for the Burmese so much. Keep fighting, all Burmese.	Negative	Sadness	Non-hate Speech
T2: จะรับมาให้โรคติด ให้ตายกันหมดประเทศหรือไง แล้วให้เหลือแต่พม่าครองเมือง **Token:** จะรับเมาให้โรคติดให้ตายกันหมดประเทศหรือไงแล้วให้เหลือแต่พม่าครองเมือง **Translation:** Accepting Burmese into the country to allow the disease to infect us and people in the country to die? Then leave only Burmese to rule the city.	Negative	Anger	Hate Speech
T3: สมัยนี้พม่ายังตีไทยอีกนะ **Token:** สมัยนี้พม่ายังตีไทยอีกนะ **Translation:** Burma still invades Thailand these days.	Negative	Disagreeable	Hate Speech

selected 600 samples from the dataset and highlighted specific words (rationales) for providing textual explanations. They also assigned suitable sentiment labels (Positive/Neutral/Negative) and emotion labels based on Plutchik's eight emotion categories (Sadness, Joy, Surprise, Fear, Disgust, Anger, Anticipation, and Trust). For the rationale annotation, we followed the same strategy as mentioned in [21], where each word in a tweet was marked with either 0 or 1, with 1 indicating the presence of a rationale. During the emotion class annotation, we observed that out of the eight emotion categories, only four (Anger, Trust, Sadness, and Anticipation) were utilized, and a significant portion of the samples fell into the "Other" category. Upon reviewing the "Other" category samples, we found that many of them were of a disagreeable nature. Based on this observation, we introduced the additional emotion class of "disagreeable" in our Thai hate speech dataset. Throughout the annotation process, expert annotators had discussions to resolve any differences in their annotations and ensure consistency. This resulted in the creation of 600 gold standard samples with annotations for sentiment, emotion, hate speech, and rationales. These 600 annotated examples were divided into three sets, each containing 200 samples, to facilitate a three-phase training approach. After each phase of training, expert annotators met with novice annotators to correct any incorrect annotations and update the annotation guidelines. Upon completing the third round of training, the top three annotators were selected to annotate the entire dataset.

We initiated our main annotation process with a small batch of 100 samples and later raised it to 500 as the annotators became well-experienced with the tasks. We tried to maintain the annotators' agreement by correcting some errors they made in the previous batch. On completion of each set of annotations, final sentiment and emotion labels were decided by the majority voting method. If the selections of three annotators vary, we enlist the help of an expert annotator to break the tie. We also directed annotators to annotate the posts without regard for any particular demography, religion, or other factors. We use the Fleiss' Kappa [11] score to calculate the inter-annotator agreement (IAA) to affirm the annotation quality. IAA obtained scores of 0.79, 0.72, and 0.74 for sentiment, emotion, and rationales labels, respectively, signifying the dataset being of acceptable quality.

Table 1 presents a selection of samples obtained from the *Ex-ThaiHate* dataset. The dataset comprises a total of 7,597 posts, with 2,685 posts labeled as hate and 4,912 posts marked as non-hate. Class-wise statistics of the *Ex-ThaiHate* dataset can be found in Table 2.

Table 2. Dataset Statistics of different classes of *Ex-ThaiHate* dataset

Total Samples	Hate Speech		Sentiment			Emotion					
	Hate	Non-Hate	Positive	Neutral	Negative	Anger	Trust	Sadness	Disagreeable	Anticipation	Others
7597	2685	4912	2655	2257	2685	2133	2020	251	482	160	2551

4   Methodology

This section presents our proposed *GenX* model, shown in Fig. 1, for sentiment- and emotion-aware HSD with explainability in the Thai language.

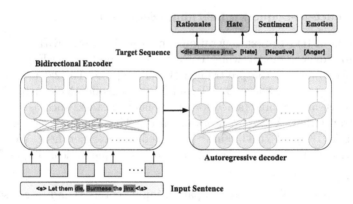

Fig. 1. *GenX* architecture

4.1   Redefining Explainable HSD Task as Text-to-Text Generation Task

Traditional multi-tasking methods leverage separate task-specific heads for different tasks making them difficult to add a new task to the model without having that task's specific head. Here, we propose a text-to-text generation paradigm for solving explainable HSD and other auxiliary tasks in a single unified manner. To transform this problem into a text generation problem, we first construct a natural language target sequence, Y_i, for input sentence, X_i, for training purposes by concatenating all the labels of all four tasks. For the rationale detection task, we only consider those $\{r\}$s which belong to the offensive label set in R_{Labels} represented by R_{Off}. In case of an empty offensive label set, we will use a NONE token to represent 0 offensive tokens in the text. Finally, the target sequence Y_i is represented as:

$$Y_i = \{<R_{Off}><b><s><e>\} \tag{1}$$

where R_{Off}, b, s, and e represent the corresponding rationales, hate, sentiment, and emotion labels of an input post, X_i.

We have added special characters $<>$ after each task's prediction, as shown in (1) so that we can extract task-specific predictions during testing or inference. Now, both the input sentence and the target are in the form of natural language to leverage large pre-trained sequence-to-sequence models for solving this task of text-to-text generation. The problem can be reformulated as given an input sequence X, the task is to generate an output sequence, Y', containing all the predictions defined in (1) using a generative model defined as $Y' = G(X)$, where G is a generative model. The advantage of this approach is that now we can add any new task just by concatenating that task's labels to the target sequence Y or solve any subtask with ease.

4.2 Sequence-to-Sequence Learning (Seq2Seq)

This problem of text-to-text generation can easily be solved with the help of a sequence-to-sequence model, which consists of two modules: 1) Encoder and 2) Decoder. We employed the pre-trained BART [16] and T5 [28] models as the sequence-to-sequence models. BART and T5 are encoder-decoder-based transformer models, mainly pre-trained for text generation tasks such as summarization and translation. As we are working on the Thai language so, multilingual BART (mBART) and T5 (mT5) have been used for the experiment. We delineate the training and inference process for sequence-to-sequence learning as follows.

Training Process. We are given a pair of input sentences and target sequence (X, Y), the first step is to feed $X = \{x_0, x_1, \ldots, x_i, \ldots, x_n\}$ to the encoder module to obtain the hidden representation of input as

$$H_{EN} = G_{Encoder}(\{x_0, x_1, \ldots, x_i, \ldots, x_n\}), \tag{2}$$

where $G_{Encoder}$ represents encoder computations.

After obtaining the hidden representation, H_{EN}, we will feed H_{EN} and all the output tokens till time step $t-1$ represented as $Y_{<t}$ to the decoder module to obtain the hidden state at time step t as

$$H_{DEC}^t = G_{Decoder}(H_{EN}, Y_{<t}), \tag{3}$$

where $G_{Decoder}$ denotes the decoder computations.

The conditional probability for the predicted output token at t^{th} time step, given the input and previous $t - 1$ predicted tokens, is calculated by applying the Softmax function over the hidden state, H_{DEC}^t, as follows:

$$P(Y_t'|X, Y_{<t}) = F_{Softmax}(H_{DEC}^t W_{Gen}), \qquad (4)$$

where $F_{Softmax}$ represents Softmax computation and W_{Gen} denotes weights of our model.

Training Objective. We initialize the weights W_{Gen} for our model with the pre-trained weights of the pre-trained sequence-to-sequence generative models (T5 or BART). We then fine-tune the model with negative log-likelihood, i.e., the maximum likelihood estimation (MLE) objective function in a supervised manner to optimize the weights, W_{Gen} as

$$\max_{W_{Gen}} \prod_{t=0}^{T} P(Y_t'|X, Y_{<t}). \qquad (5)$$

In the context of transformers, MLE typically involves finding the best weights for the model's layers that maximize the probability of observing a given sequence of tokens in a training dataset. The loss function takes into account the information from earlier time steps in the decoder by considering the cumulative error in the model's predictions over all time steps. Further, we have incorporated RL-based Training to enhance the performance of the *GenX* model.

RL-Based Training. On top of the MLE objective function, we also employ a reward-based training objective function. Inspired from [32], we use a BLEU [25] based reward function. We define BLEU based Reward R_{BLEU} as:

$$R_{BLEU} = (BLEU(Y_i', Y_i) - BLEU(Y_i^g, Y_i)), \qquad (6)$$

where Y_i' denotes the output sequence sampled from the conditional probability distribution at each decoding time stamp and Y_i^g denotes the output sequence obtained by greedily maximizing the conditional probability distribution at each time step.

To maximize the expected reward, R_{BLEU} of Y_i', we use the policy gradient technique, which is defined as

$$\nabla_\theta J(\theta) = R_{BLEU} \cdot \nabla_\theta \log P(Y_i'|X_i; \theta). \qquad (7)$$

Inference. During the training process, we have access to both the input sentence, X, and the target sequence, Y. Thus, we train the model using the teacher forcing approach, i.e., using the target sequence as the input instead of tokens predicted at prior time steps during the decoding process. However, the inference must be done in an autoregressive manner as we do not have access to target sequences to guide the decoding process replacing $Y_{<t}$ with $Y'_{<t}$ in (3)–(5) where $Y'_{<t}$ represents tokens predicted till time step $t-1$. So we use the beam search algorithm to obtain the predicted sequence, Y', as it considers multiple alternative options based on the hyperparameter beamwidth (B) which is optimal than a simple greedy search technique which only selects the single best token at each time step. In beam search, the decoder generates a set of candidate output sequences in parallel, each with a different starting token. At each time step, the decoder calculates the probability distribution over the vocabulary for each candidate sequence and generates a set of new candidate sequences by extending each existing candidate sequence with the top K most likely next tokens, where K is the beam size. The candidate sequences are ranked based on their accumulated probabilities, and the K sequences with the highest probabilities are kept for the next time step.

5   Experimental Results and Analysis

This section describes the outcomes of various baseline models and our proposed model, tested on the *Ex-ThaiHate* dataset. The experiments are intended to address the following research questions: **RQ1** How is the performance of our *GenX* model for HSD over the SOTA machine learning models? **RQ2** How does multi-tasking help in enhancing the performance of HSD with the help of additional rationale, sentiment and emotion information? **RQ3** What is the effect of the BLEU-based reward function in RL-based training? **RQ4** To handle noisy social media Thai data, which embedding is better, BERT or FastText?

5.1   Experimental Settings and Baselines Setup

We split our dataset into 80% train, 10% validation, and 10% test sets. We experimented with mBART and mT5 and attained optimal performance with mBART. During training, we trained for a total of 20 epochs and used the Adam optimizer with a weight decay of 1e−3 (to avoid overfitting).

Classification Baselines. (i) Standard machine learning baselines as mentioned in [36], i.e., Naïve Bayes, SVM, and RF have been used for our experiments. We used the pooled result of dimension 768 returned by WangchanBERTa as input for machine learning-based baselines. On the other hand, for FastText embedding, we first tokenized the phrase using PyThaiNLP[1], then we extracted the embedding of each token from the pre-trained Thai FastText model, and we averaged it out to represent the full sentence by a 300-dimensional vector. (ii) We passed the pooled output from BERT through a Fully Connected (FC) layer that consisted of 100 neurons. Then, we utilized a Softmax output layer to generate the final prediction probabilities. (iii) We pass input text to BiLSTM followed by the attention layer [17]. Attended features of the text are passed through a dense layer to predict the labels.

---

[1] https://pythainlp.github.io/docs/2.2/.

Rationales Detection Baselines. (i) To comprehensively evaluate our proposed *GenX* model for the RD task, we established a baseline by selecting a Bidirectional Long Short-Term Memory-Conditional Random Field (BiLSTM-CRF) model [24], as this task involves sequence learning. The BiLSTM-CRF model has three components: a word embedding layer, a Bidirectional Long Short-Term Memory network (BiLSTM), and a Conditional Random Field (CRF). We used the sequence output of mBERT and WangchanBERTa (wBERT) as word embeddings. The BiLSTM network captures complete contextual information, while the CRF model predicts the label sequence.

There are four multi-task variants based on how many tasks we want to solve simultaneously, e.g., HSD+RD, HSD+RD+SA, HSD+RD+ER, HSD+RD+SA+ ER, etc. It should be noted that the *GenX* model can be used for both single and multi-task settings. The only difference in a single-task setting is that the target sequence contains token/tokens specific to the task being addressed. In contrast, in a multi-task setting, the target sequence is formed by concatenating all labels (tokens), with each token corresponding to a specific task.

5.2   Findings from Experiments

Table 3 presents the performance of machine learning baselines, different variants of single-task and multi-task frameworks in terms of accuracy (Acc), and weighted F1 score. Table 4 presents the results of the RD task. For the quantitative assessment of the RD task, we used the Jaccard Similarity (JS), Hamming Distance (HD), and Ratcliff-Obershelp Similarity (ROS) metrics as mentioned in [12]. The following are the findings from our experimental results presented in Tables 3 and 4:

- **RQ1:** Our proposed *GenX* model, in both single-task and multi-task settings, surpasses all machine learning-based baselines by a considerable margin. The MT(RD+HSD+SA+ER)+RL with mBART outperformed the best ML baseline (BERT-SVM) by 6.6%, 9.1%, and 15.0% for the HSD, SA, and ER tasks, respectively. Furthermore, *GenX* outperforms the deep learning-based baseline BiLSTM-Attn by a significant margin.
- **RQ2:** The MT(RD+HSD+SA+ER)+RL model with mBART shows better performance than ST-GenX, with accuracy improvements of 3.2%, 2.1%, and 2.0% for HSD, SA, and ER tasks, respectively. These findings suggest that incorporating sentiment and emotion knowledge significantly enhances the performance of the HSD task.
- Comparing the proposed *GenX* model, based on text-to-text generation, with the BiLSTM+CRF model (Classical Named Entity Recognition model), we observe that *GenX* outperforms BiLSTM+CRF for the RD task (see Table 4). This result demonstrates the effectiveness of utilizing a text-to-text generation model to solve two distinct categories of tasks, classification tasks (HSD, SA, ER), and sequence labeling tasks (RD), simultaneously with a single model.

Table 3. Results of different baselines, SOTA, and proposed frameworks for Hate speech detection (HSD), sentiment analysis (SA), and emotion recognition (ER) tasks; wBERT: WangchanBERTa, mBERT: Multilingual BERT; MT: Multi-Task; ST: Single Task

Embedding	Model	Hate		Sentiment		Emotion	
		Acc	F1	Acc	F1	Acc	F1
Baselines							
BERT	Naïve Bayes	75.32	76.21	64.73	65.55	57.96	56.78
	SVM	83.22	83.26	70.98	71.23	60.53	60.18
	Random Forest	77.03	74.08	64.53	64.32	59.67	57.72
FastText	Naïve Bayes	72.56	72.45	58.35	58.71	52.43	49.83
	SVM	81.71	81.65	70.98	71.32	66.11	64.37
	Random Forest	80.92	79.53	67.30	67.87	62.56	60.13
SOTA							
BERT	Fine-tune	85.87	85.83	–	–	–	–
Deep Learning Baselines							
mBERT	FC	76.15	78.32	63.27	63.18	62.15	62.76
	BiLSTM-Attn	82.36	82.64	64.16	65.28	63.47	64.33
wBERT	FC	77.58	75.61	62.16	60.12	62.45	62.21
	BiLSTM-Attn	83.45	84.78	66.38	67.39	65.63	64.89
Proposed Model – *GenX*							
mBART	**ST**	**85.48**	**85.34**	**78.47**	**78.64**	**75.23**	**75.54**
	MT(HSD+SA)	87.67	87.43	79.34	79.58	–	–
	MT(HSD+ER)	86.84	86.66	–	–	75.92	75.88
	MT(HSD+SA+ER)	88.53	87.94	79.57	79.63	76.54	76.48
	MT(RD+HSD+SA)	86.54	86.50	79.63	79.46	–	–
	MT(RD+HSD+SA)+RL	87.46	87.42	80.48	80.31	–	–
	MT(RD+HSD+ER)	86.63	86.45	–	–	76.04	75.98
	MT(RD+HSD+ER)+RL	87.55	87.46	–	–	76.85	78.45
	MT(RD+HSD+SA+ER)	87.74	86.84	79.74	79.86	76.42	76.53
	MT(RD+HSD+SA+ER)+RL	**88.67**	**88.21**	**80.57**	**80.46**	**77.24**	**79.37**
T5	ST	84.93	85.26	77.49	77.63	72.68	72.14
	MT(HSD+SA)	86.24	85.78	77.14	76.89	–	–
	MT(HSD+ER)	86.43	86.11	–	–	72.44	72.37
	MT(HSD+SA+ER)	86.75	85.69	77.34	77.47	72.83	72.11
	MT(RD+HSD+SA)	86.07	85.94	78.16	77.83	–	–
	MT(RD+HSD+ER)	86.41	86.34	–	–	73.32	74.11
	MT(RD+HSD+SA+ER)	86.48	86.44	78.43	78.64	73.59	74.26
	Improvements over ST	3.19	2.87	2.10	1.82	2.01	3.83
	Improvements over SOTA	2.80	2.38	–	–	–	–

- **RQ3:** We observe that RL-based training improves performance by an average of 1.0% for all tasks. We report the results with RL only for those task combinations where RD is included, as without the RD task, the target string

Table 4. Results of different baselines and proposed frameworks for Rationales Detection (RD) task; JS: Jaccard Similarity, HD: Hamming Distance, and ROS: Ratcliff-Obershelp Similarity

Embedding	Model	Rationales		
		JS	HD	ROS
Baselines				
mBERT	BiLSTM+CRF	59.24	50.95	65.28
wBERT	BiLSTM+CRF	60.13	51.93	65.86
Proposed Model - GenX				
mBART	ST	62.19	53.48	69.56
	ST+RL	63.31	55.47	71.25
	MT(HSD+RD)	65.67	57.37	73.25
	MT(HSD+RD)+RL	66.45	58.07	74.01
	MT(HSD+RD+SA)	65.78	57.42	73.35
	MT(HSD+RD+SA)+RL	66.53	58.18	74.13
	MT(HSD+RD+ER)	65.81	57.46	73.24
	MT(HSD+RD+ER)+RL	66.50	58.08	74.03
	MT(HSD+RD+SA+ER)	65.87	57.64	73.36
	MT(HSD+RD+SA+ER)+RL	**66.60**	**58.22**	**74.16**

has a very minimal length, i.e., 2 or 3. To prevent the model from generating sentences with out-of-sentence vocabulary, we use BLEU similarity measures. Training the model with this reward function encourages the generation of sequences with high overlap with the target sequence, leading to improved results in the RD tasks.

- **RQ4:** Comparing the individual performance between BERT and FastText embedding, we find that BERT consistently outperforms FastText for all tasks, except for Random Forest. Another noteworthy finding is that wBERT outperforms mBERT, indicating wBERT's greater efficiency in handling Thai data than mBERT. Additionally, between the two generative models, BART achieved better results, which is why we only reported the RL variants and RD task results with mBART settings.
- The proposed mBART-GenX model outperforms the SOTA with an improved F1 score of 2.4% for the HSD task. This result demonstrates the efficacy of our proposed model.

We have conducted a statistical t-test on the results of ten different runs of our proposed model and other baselines and obtained a p-value less than 0.05.

5.3   Error Analysis

We conducted an analysis of prediction errors for hate speech by randomly selecting the results of the multi-task model from one out of ten trials. We have identified two primary concerns related to the sentiment and emotion predictions of multi-task models as follows.

1. The model was confused in predicting negative sentiment 22.4% (37/165) of the statements with the following observation: (i) Predicted negative as neutral 46.0% (17/37) of the statements. Most were found to be caused by ambiguous or metaphorical words that can be used in ironic or sarcastic contexts, for example, "พม่าพี่น้องชาวสมุทรสาครทำพิษซ่ะแล้ว" (Our Burmese siblings in Samut Sakhon have already caused trouble). The word "ทำพิษ" (trouble) is a metaphor. This makes it difficult for the model to determine the true sentiment, thus predicting neutral instead of negative.

2. The model incorrectly predicted 30.5% (57/187) emotion classes of the statements. Most of them predicted anger emotion incorrectly in 86.0% (49/57) of the statements. We observed that the model predicted anger as disagreeable in 22.5% (11/49) of the statements. For example, "ตอนนี้คือจิตตกแล้ว ตกงานมาก็จะปีแล้ว จะอดตายแล้ว ยังมามีรอบสองรอบนี้คือตายทั้งขึ้นทั้งร่อง เอาพม่า กลับบ้านเกิดเลยค่ะ มาทางไหนก็กลับไปก่อนเลย ป้องกันใส่แมสจะตายทุกวันสุดท้าย เสียเปล่ามาก" (Now I am very depressed. It has been a year since I lost my job, and I am about to starve to death. Bring Burmese people back to their country. Go back the way you came. I protect myself by wearing a mask every day. In the end, it is very wasteful.), the author expressed feelings of injustice to the Thai people, which is often accompanied by anger emotion. It should be noted that the message is very long and complex.

6   Conclusion and Future Works

The present study addresses the issue of HSD in the Thai language, with a focus on the aspect of explainability. The current work contributes in two main ways: (a) the development of the first-ever explainable HSD dataset in the Thai language, which includes annotations of rationale/phrases used for explainability, as well as hate, sentiment, and emotion labels; (b) the proposal of a unified generative framework, called *GenX*, with RL-based training, to simultaneously solve four tasks: HSD, SA, ER, and RD. This work demonstrates how a multi-task problem can be formulated as a text-to-text generation task, leveraging the knowledge of large pre-trained sequence-to-sequence models in low-resource language settings. Experimental results showcase the superiority of the proposed model over baselines and its outperformance of the SOTA, achieving an improved accuracy score of 2.8% for the hate speech task.

In future works, efforts will be made to extend explainable HSD to a multimodal setting by considering both image and text modalities.

Acknowledgments. This work was supported by the Ministry of External Affairs (MEA) and the Department of Science & Technology (DST), India, under the ASEAN-India Collaborative R&D Scheme.

References

1. Agrawal, S., Awekar, A.: Deep learning for detecting cyberbullying across multiple social media platforms. In: Pasi, G., Piwowarski, B., Azzopardi, L., Hanbury, A. (eds.) ECIR 2018. LNCS, vol. 10772, pp. 141–153. Springer, Cham (2018). https://doi.org/10.1007/978-3-319-76941-7_11

2. Badjatiya, P., Gupta, S., Gupta, M., Varma, V.: Deep learning for hate speech detection in tweets. In: Barrett, R., Cummings, R., Agichtein, E., Gabrilovich, E. (eds.) Proceedings of the 26th International Conference on World Wide Web Companion, Perth, Australia, April 3–7, 2017, pp. 759–760. ACM (2017). https://doi.org/10.1145/3041021.3054223

3. Balakrishnan, V., Khan, S., Arabnia, H.R.: Improving cyberbullying detection using twitter users' psychological features and machine learning. Comput. Secur. **90**, 101710 (2020). https://doi.org/10.1016/j.cose.2019.101710

4. Camburu, O., Rocktäschel, T., Lukasiewicz, T., Blunsom, P.: e-snli: natural language inference with natural language explanations. In: Bengio, S., Wallach, H.M., Larochelle, H., Grauman, K., Cesa-Bianchi, N., Garnett, R. (eds.) Advances in Neural Information Processing Systems 31: Annual Conference on Neural Information Processing Systems 2018, NeurIPS 2018, December 3–8, 2018, Montréal, Canada, pp. 9560–9572 (2018)

5. Caruana, R.: Multitask learning. Mach. Learn. **28**(1), 41–75 (1997). https://doi.org/10.1023/A:1007379606734

6. Chan, T.K.H., Cheung, C.M.K., Wong, R.Y.M.: Cyberbullying on social networking sites: the crime opportunity and affordance perspectives. J. Manag. Inf. Syst. **36**(2), 574–609 (2019). https://doi.org/10.1080/07421222.2019.1599500

7. Crawshaw, M.: Multi-task learning with deep neural networks: a survey. CoRR abs/2009.09796 (2020)

8. Dadvar, M., Trieschnigg, D., de Jong, F.: Experts and machines against bullies: a hybrid approach to detect cyberbullies. In: Sokolova, M., van Beek, P. (eds.) AI 2014. LNCS (LNAI), vol. 8436, pp. 275–281. Springer, Cham (2014). https://doi.org/10.1007/978-3-319-06483-3_25

9. Dinakar, K., Reichart, R., Lieberman, H.: Modeling the detection of textual cyberbullying. In: Proceedings of the International AAAI Conference on Web and Social Media, vol. 5, pp. 11–17 (2021). https://doi.org/10.1609/icwsm.v5i3.14209

10. European Parliament and of the Council: Protection of natural persons with regard to the processing of personal data and on the free movement of such data, and repealing directive 95/46/ec. EC General Data Protection Regulation 679 (2016)

11. Fleiss, J.L.: Measuring nominal scale agreement among many raters. Psychol. Bull. **76**(5), 378–382 (1971)

12. Ghosh, S., Roy, S., Ekbal, A., Bhattacharyya, P.: CARES: CAuse recognition for emotion in suicide notes. In: Hagen, M., et al. (eds.) ECIR 2022. LNCS, vol. 13186, pp. 128–136. Springer, Cham (2022). https://doi.org/10.1007/978-3-030-99739-7_15

13. Gunning, D., Stefik, M., Choi, J., Miller, T., Stumpf, S., Yang, G.: XAI - explainable artificial intelligence. Sci. Robot. **4**(37) (2019). https://doi.org/10.1126/scirobotics.aay7120

14. Ibrohim, M.O., Budi, I.: Multi-label hate speech and abusive language detection in Indonesian Twitter. In: Proceedings of the Third Workshop on Abusive Language Online, Florence, Italy, pp. 46–57. Association for Computational Linguistics (2019). https://doi.org/10.18653/v1/W19-3506

15. Karim, M.R., et al.: Deephateexplainer: explainable hate speech detection in under-resourced Bengali language. In: 8th IEEE International Conference on Data Science and Advanced Analytics, DSAA 2021, Porto, Portugal, October 6–9, 2021, pp. 1–10. IEEE (2021). https://doi.org/10.1109/DSAA53316.2021.9564230

16. Lewis, M., et al.: BART: denoising sequence-to-sequence pre-training for natural language generation, translation, and comprehension. In: Jurafsky, D., Chai, J., Schluter, N., Tetreault, J.R. (eds.) Proceedings of the 58th Annual Meeting of the Association for Computational Linguistics, ACL 2020, Online, 5–10 July 2020, pp. 7871–7880. Association for Computational Linguistics (2020). https://doi.org/10.18653/v1/2020.acl-main.703

17. Liu, B., Lane, I.R.: Attention-based recurrent neural network models for joint intent detection and slot filling. In: Morgan, N. (ed.) Interspeech 2016, 17th Annual Conference of the International Speech Communication Association, San Francisco, CA, USA, 8–12 September 2016, pp. 685–689. ISCA (2016). https://doi.org/10.21437/Interspeech.2016-1352

18. Maity, K., Bhattacharya, S., Saha, S., Janoai, S., Pasupa, K.: Fastthaicaps: a transformer based capsule network for hate speech detection in Thai language. In: Tanveer, M., Agarwal, S., Ozawa, S., Ekbal, A., Jatowt, A. (eds.) ICONIP 2022, Part II. LNCS, vol. 13624, pp. 425–437. Springer, Cham (2022). https://doi.org/10.1007/978-3-031-30108-7_36

19. Maity, K., Kumar, A., Saha, S.: A multitask multimodal framework for sentiment and emotion-aided cyberbullying detection. IEEE Internet Comput. **26**(4), 68–78 (2022). https://doi.org/10.1109/MIC.2022.3158583

20. Maity, K., Saha, S.: A multi-task model for sentiment aided cyberbullying detection in code-mixed Indian languages. In: Mantoro, T., Lee, M., Ayu, M.A., Wong, K.W., Hidayanto, A.N. (eds.) ICONIP 2021. LNCS, vol. 13111, pp. 440–451. Springer, Cham (2021). https://doi.org/10.1007/978-3-030-92273-3_36

21. Mathew, B., Saha, P., Yimam, S.M., Biemann, C., Goyal, P., Mukherjee, A.: Hatexplain: a benchmark dataset for explainable hate speech detection. CoRR abs/2012.10289 (2020)

22. Meta: Community standards enforcement – hate speech. Meta Transparency Centre (2022), https://transparency.fb.com/data/community-standards-enforcement/hate-speech. Accessed 1 Apr 2023

23. Nockleby, J.T.: Hate speech in context: the case of verbal threats. Buffalo Law Rev. **42**, 653–713 (1994)

24. Panchendrarajan, R., Amaresan, A.: Bidirectional LSTM-CRF for named entity recognition. In: Politzer-Ahles, S., Hsu, Y., Huang, C., Yao, Y. (eds.) Proceedings of the 32nd Pacific Asia Conference on Language, Information and Computation, PACLIC 2018, Hong Kong, 1–3 December 2018. Association for Computational Linguistics (2018)

25. Papineni, K., Roukos, S., Ward, T., Zhu, W.: BLEU: a method for automatic evaluation of machine translation. In: Proceedings of the 40th Annual Meeting of the Association for Computational Linguistics, July 6–12, 2002, Philadelphia, PA, USA, pp. 311–318. ACL (2002). https://doi.org/10.3115/1073083.1073135

26. Pasupa, K., Karnbanjob, W., Aksornsiri, M.: Hate speech detection in Thai social media with ordinal-imbalanced text classification. In: 19th International Joint Conference on Computer Science and Software Engineering, JCSSE 2022, Bangkok, Thailand, June 22–25, 2022, pp. 1–6. IEEE (2022). https://doi.org/10.1109/JCSSE54890.2022.9836312

27. Paul, S., Saha, S.: Cyberbert: BERT for cyberbullying identification. Multimedia Syst. **28**(6), 1897–1904 (2022). https://doi.org/10.1007/s00530-020-00710-4

28. Raffel, C., et al.: Exploring the limits of transfer learning with a unified text-to-text transformer. J. Mach. Learn. Res. **21**, 140:1-140:67 (2020)

29. Rajani, N.F., McCann, B., Xiong, C., Socher, R.: Explain yourself! leveraging language models for commonsense reasoning. CoRR abs/1906.02361 (2019)

30. Reynolds, K., Kontostathis, A., Edwards, L.: Using machine learning to detect cyberbullying. In: 2011 10th International Conference on Machine Learning and Applications and Workshops, vol. 2, pp. 241–244 (2011). https://doi.org/10.1109/ICMLA.2011.152

31. Saha, T., Upadhyaya, A., Saha, S., Bhattacharyya, P.: A multitask multimodal ensemble model for sentiment- and emotion-aided tweet act classification. IEEE Trans. Comput. Soc. Syst. **9**(2), 508–517 (2022). https://doi.org/10.1109/TCSS.2021.3088714

32. Sancheti, A., Krishna, K., Srinivasan, B.V., Natarajan, A.: Reinforced rewards framework for text style transfer. In: Jose, J.M., et al. (eds.) ECIR 2020, Part I. LNCS, vol. 12035, pp. 545–560. Springer, Cham (2020). https://doi.org/10.1007/978-3-030-45439-5_36

33. Singh, A., Saha, S., Hasanuzzaman, M., Dey, K.: Multitask learning for complaint identification and sentiment analysis. Cogn. Comput. **14**(1), 212–227 (2022). https://doi.org/10.1007/s12559-021-09844-7

34. Thepgumpanat, P., Naing, S., Tostevin, M.: Anti-myanmar hate speech flares in thailand over virus. Reuters (2020). https://www.reuters.com/article/us-health-coronavirus-thailand-myanmar-idUSKBN28Y0KS. Accessed 1 Apr 2023

35. Vigna, F.D., Cimino, A., Dell'Orletta, F., Petrocchi, M., Tesconi, M.: Hate me, hate me not: Hate speech detection on facebook. In: Armando, A., Baldoni, R., Focardi, R. (eds.) Proceedings of the First Italian Conference on Cybersecurity (ITASEC17), Venice, Italy, 17–20 January 2017. CEUR Workshop Proceedings, vol. 1816, pp. 86–95. CEUR-WS.org (2017)

36. Wanasukapunt, R., Phimoltares, S.: Classification of abusive Thai language content in social media using deep learning. In: 18th International Joint Conference on Computer Science and Software Engineering, JCSSE 2021, Lampang, Thailand, 30 June–2 July 2021, pp. 1–6. IEEE (2021). https://doi.org/10.1109/JCSSE53117.2021.9493829

37. Waseem, Z., Hovy, D.: Hateful symbols or hateful people? predictive features for hate speech detection on twitter. In: Proceedings of the Student Research Workshop, SRW@HLT-NAACL 2016, The 2016 Conference of the North American Chapter of the Association for Computational Linguistics: Human Language Technologies, San Diego California, USA, 12–17 June 2016, pp. 88–93. The Association for Computational Linguistics (2016). https://doi.org/10.18653/v1/n16-2013

38. Wu, S.: Emmental: a framework for building multimodal multi-task learning systems (2019)

39. Zaidan, O., Eisner, J., Piatko, C.D.: Using "annotator rationales" to improve machine learning for text categorization. In: Sidner, C.L., Schultz, T., Stone, M., Zhai, C. (eds.) Human Language Technology Conference of the North American Chapter of the Association of Computational Linguistics, Proceedings, April 22–27, 2007, Rochester, New York, USA, pp. 260–267. The Association for Computational Linguistics (2007), https://aclanthology.org/N07-1033/

40. Zhou, X., et al.: Hate speech detection based on sentiment knowledge sharing. In: Zong, C., Xia, F., Li, W., Navigli, R. (eds.) Proceedings of the 59th Annual Meeting of the Association for Computational Linguistics and the 11th International Joint Conference on Natural Language Processing, ACL/IJCNLP 2021, (Volume 1: Long Papers), Virtual Event, 1–6 August 2021, pp. 7158–7166. Association for Computational Linguistics (2021). https://doi.org/10.18653/v1/2021.acl-long.556

Deep Serial Number: Computational Watermark for DNN Intellectual Property Protection

Ruixiang Tang[1], Mengnan Du[2], and Xia Hu[1(✉)]

[1] Rice University, Houston, USA
xia.hu@rice.edu
[2] New Jersey Institute of Technology, Newark, USA
mengnan.du@njit.edu

Abstract. In this paper, we present DSN (Deep Serial Number), a simple yet effective watermarking algorithm designed specifically for deep neural networks (DNNs). Unlike traditional methods that incorporate identification signals into DNNs, our approach explores a novel Intellectual Property (IP) protection mechanism for DNNs, effectively thwarting adversaries from using stolen networks. Inspired by the success of serial numbers in safeguarding conventional software IP, we propose the first implementation of serial number embedding within DNNs. To achieve this, DSN is integrated into a knowledge distillation framework, in which a private teacher DNN is initially trained. Subsequently, its knowledge is distilled and imparted to a series of customized student DNNs. Each customer DNN functions correctly only upon input of a valid serial number. Experimental results across various applications demonstrate DSN's efficacy in preventing unauthorized usage without compromising the original DNN performance. The experiments further show that DSN is resistant to different categories of watermark attacks.

Keywords: Watermark · Deep Neural Network · Intellectual Property Protection

1 Introduction

Deep neural networks (DNNs) have made significant progress in the last decade. The combination of large-scale training data and the rapid expansion of computational capabilities have facilitated the development of high-performance DNN models in numerous domains. However, training DNNs can be costly, involving the collection and labeling of large data sets and the allocation of considerable computing resources. Consequently, foundation DNN models are deemed valuable intellectual property by their owners. The substantial economic value of DNN models makes them attractive targets for malicious adversaries. For instance, numerous emerging online marketplaces trade deep neural networks

G. De Francisci Morales et al. (Eds.): ECML PKDD 2023, LNAI 14174, pp. 157–173, 2023.
https://doi.org/10.1007/978-3-031-43427-3_10

that may be susceptible to theft by hackers. In another scenario, a legitimate customer might breach the licensing agreement by redistributing or selling DNNs to others. For instance, Meta's latest large language model, LLaMA, initially accessible only through request, was leaked online via a 4chan torrent just a week after accepting access requests [31]. As the expenses associated with training DNN models continue to escalate, model providers are exploring various methods to assert ownership and protect their intellectual property from infringement. Consequently, the concept of digital watermarking has been adopted for deep learning models, which embeds secret identification information within DNN models, serving as evidence of model ownership verification.

Currently, several approaches have been proposed to incorporate watermarks into DNNs. The rationale behind these watermarking strategies is to establish a tracking mechanism that enables legitimate parties to identify instances of stolen models. We can categorize these methods into two primary classes. The first class of methods embeds watermark information directly into the parameters of the DNN model [4,27,30]. For verification purposes, stakeholders must have access to the model parameters to examine the presence of the watermark's statistical bias. However, this white-box access for verification is often impractical in many applications. The second set of approaches employs the backdoor insertion technique [8,19,28] to embed watermarks. In these cases, DNNs not only learn their original tasks but also retain outlier input-output pairs, which can be utilized for black-box ownership verification. However, these watermarking approaches are vulnerable to the commonly used transfer learning scenario, where adversaries can replace the top decision layers and train a watermark-free model based on the features extracted from the remaining network [3]. Another significant challenge facing existing watermarking methods is their vulnerability to various watermarking attacks, such as watermark suppression, removal [36], and overwriting [17]. This susceptibility to attacks further hinders their adoption in real-world applications. A robust DNN IP protection mechanism that can prevent unauthorized parties from using the stolen model is still missing.

Inspired by the success of serial numbers in traditional software IP protection, we investigate the application of serial number embedding to safeguard DNNs. However, embedding serial numbers into DNNs presents several technical challenges. First, it remains unclear in what form serial numbers can be effectively incorporated into DNNs. Second, it is equally challenging to ensure that the serial numbers inserted remain robust against attacks from malicious adversaries. To address these concerns, we propose a novel DNN IP protection framework, DSN (Deep Serial Number). Specifically, we utilize the knowledge distillation method to initially train a teacher DNN and subsequently transfer its knowledge to customer DNNs. During the distillation process, a unique serial number is assigned to each student model. The customer DNN operates only when a user inputs a valid serial number. As a result, DSN effectively prevents stolen models from being exploited by unauthorized parties. Additionally, the embedded serial number functions as a robust tracking tag, similar to previous watermarking approaches. Experimental results from various applications reveal that the proposed DSN method successfully inhibits unauthorized use while maintaining the original DNN performance. Further experimental analyses demonstrate that DSN is resilient against different attack strategies, even when adversaries have white-box access to the DSN framework. The main contributions of this paper are summarized as follows:

- We propose DSN, a novel IP protection framework for DNNs designed to prevent stolen models from being deployed by unauthorized third parties.
- Experiments carried out on real-world datasets demonstrate that DSN effectively prevents unauthorized applications without sacrificing DNN performance on the original tasks.
- Experimental studies further reveal that DSN is robust against various watermark attack approaches, even when adversaries have white-box access to the DSN framework.

2   Embedding Deep Serial Number in DNNs

The key idea of DSN is to build a new DNN training and distribution framework so that each DNN model will function normally only when the potential user enters the unique serial number. In this section, we will introduce the three requirements and discuss the proposed framework.

2.1   Requirements for Serial Number Watermarking

Serial numbers are typically assigned to users who have the right to use specific software. The software will function properly only when the user inputs the correct serial number. It is generally infeasible for an adversary to generate valid but unauthorized codes through brute-force attacks or reverse engineering of the software. In our design, an ideal serial number for DNNs is expected to meet the following four requirements:

- **Low Distortion:** Embedding the serial number into DNNs should not significantly compromise the performance of the DNN model in its original tasks.
- **Reliability:** The DNN performs properly only when a user enters a valid serial number. Any invalid serial numbers will result in a substantial performance decline in the original tasks.
- **Robustness:** The DSN should exhibit sufficient resilience against various attack methods, including 1) commonly used deep learning techniques, such as transfer learning and model pruning, and 2) malicious attack methods, such as reverse engineering and watermark overwriting.

2.2   The Proposed DSN Framework

The proposed DSN framework is depicted in Fig. 1. We formulate it as a two-step process: 1) initially training a teacher network f_T to maximize prediction performance, and 2) subsequently training multiple student networks f_S based on the knowledge distilled from the teacher [7, 10]. During the distillation process, we introduce a new SN (Serial Number) embedding loss $\mathcal{L}_{DSN}$, which enables DSN to embed a unique serial number into the student network, in addition to transferring knowledge. The student network functions correctly only when the correct serial number is entered.

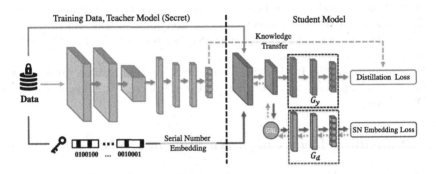

Fig. 1. Training pipeline of deep serial number framework. DSN is built based on the knowledge distillation framework, where a secret training dataset and teacher model are in the developers' hands. The two complementary losses, SN Embedding loss, and Distillation loss, embed a unique serial number into the customer model. Owners only distribute the well-trained student model (blue part) to potential customers. (Color figure online)

Teacher-Student Framework. We propose employing a knowledge distillation framework to train multiple customized DNN models. The approach is formulated as follows. Given a vector of logits Z_T as the output of the last fully connected layer of the teacher model f_T, we can estimate the probability P_T by applying a softmax function to Z_T. We utilize the soft target obtained from the teacher model as a supervision signal to transfer knowledge from f_T to f_S. The distillation loss is formulated as follows:

$$\mathcal{L}_{Distill}(f_T, f_S) = \mathcal{L}_{KL}(P_T, P_S), \tag{1}$$

where $\mathcal{L}_{KL}$ represents the KL divergence loss. This training framework enables the student model to achieve comparable or even superior, performance to that of the pre-trained teacher model. Unlike conventional distillation settings, stakeholders using DSN will keep the teacher model and training data confidential, distributing only the trained student networks (blue part in Fig. 1) to the markets and customers.

Embedding Serial Number. The process of embedding the serial number is implemented as follows. Given a student model f_S, the inputs x, and the unique serial number $\hat{k}$, the student model embedded with the serial number f_S^K can be formulated as:

$$f_S^K = r(x)(1 - h(k)) + f_S(x)h(k), \tag{2}$$

where k is the serial number entered by the user, and $h(k)$ is the serial number recognition function that verifies the correctness of the input serial number. If the serial number k is valid, i.e., $k = \hat{k}$, $h(k)$ outputs 1 and $f_S^K(x) = f_S(x)$. For an invalid serial number, $h(k)$ outputs 0 and $f_S^K = r(x)$, where the functionality of $r(x)$ significantly differs from $f_S(x)$, such as random guessing. Consequently, the performance drops substantially with incorrect serial numbers. The motivation behind the proposed DSN framework is to implicitly integrate the functionality of $r(x)$ and $h(k)$ into the student model.

Let $X = \{x_n, y_n\}_{n=1}^N$ represent the training data, $I_{k-\hat{k}}$ denote the correctness of the entered SN where $I = 1$ indicates a valid SN and $I = 0$ signifies an incorrect SN. We aim for $f_S^K(x)$ to accurately predict Y when $I = 1$ and predict poorly with $I = 0$. The input x is initially mapped to a D-dimensional feature vector e using mapping G_e (a feature extractor). We denote the vector of parameters for all layers in the mapping as θ_e, i.e., $e = G_e(x; \theta_e)$. Subsequently, the feature vector e is mapped by mapping G_y (predictor with SN) to the label y. We denote the parameters of this mapping with θ_y. Lastly, the same feature vector e is mapped by mapping G_d (predictor without SN) to the label y with parameter θ_d. The overall two-branch model structure is illustrated in Fig. 1.

During the learning stage, when $I = 1$, our objective is to minimize the label prediction loss on G_y, and the parameters of both the feature extractor G_e and the label predictor G_y are optimized to minimize the empirical loss for the training samples x. When $I = 0$, features e should be unpredictable (for the classifier G_d, the hidden representation e belonging to a different class should be inseparable). Drawing inspiration from the work by Ganin et al. [6], we employ the Gradient Reversal Layer (GRL) to remove the label information Y in the features e. During forward propagation, the GRL acts as an identity transform. During backpropagation, GRL takes the gradient from the subsequent level, multiplies it by a negative value λ, and passes it to the preceding layer. The GRL is inserted between the feature extractor G_y and the classifier G_d. The stochastic updates can be formalized as follows: when $I = 1$, we train the student using the Distillation Loss.

$$\mathcal{L}_{Distill}(f_T, f_S) = \mathcal{L}_{KL}(P_T, G_y(G_e(x)))), \tag{3}$$

where P_T is the soft label of the teacher model. The stochastic update can be written as follows:

$$\theta_e \longleftarrow \theta_e - \mu(\frac{L_{Distill}}{\theta_e}); \quad \theta_y \longleftarrow \theta_y - \mu(\frac{L_{Distill}}{\theta_y}). \tag{4}$$

When $I = 0$, the model is optimized with SN Embedding Loss.

$$\mathcal{L}_{SNE}(f_S) = \mathcal{L}_{CE}(G_d(GRL(G_e(x))), Y), \tag{5}$$

where $\mathcal{L}_{CE}$ is the cross-entropy loss. The stochastic update can be written as follows:

$$\theta_e \longleftarrow \theta_e + \mu(\frac{L_{SNE}}{\theta_e}); \quad \theta_d \longleftarrow \theta_d - \mu(\frac{L_{SNE}}{\theta_d}). \tag{6}$$

The proposed two-branch training pipeline enables G_e to supply well-trained features e for classifiers G_y when provided with a correct serial number. When an incorrect serial number is entered, the output features e for different classes become indistinguishable, resulting in poor prediction accuracy for both G_d and G_y. To distribute the student model, stakeholders will remove the GRL and G_d, and package the remaining network consisting of G_e and G_y for the customer.

2.3   Entangled Watermark Embedding

A potential limitation of the proposed DSN framework is that its effectiveness may be compromised by pruning protection-related neurons, such as those responsible for recognizing serial numbers. To address this issue, it is necessary to entangle protection-related neurons with regular neurons. We achieve this by introducing a soft nearest neighbor loss (SNNL) to measure the entanglement between representations learned by clean inputs and those learned by SN-stamped inputs. This can be expressed as:

$$SNNL(X,Y,T) = -\frac{1}{n} \sum_{i \in 1..n} log \left(\frac{\sum_{\substack{j \in 1..n \\ j \neq i \\ y_i = y_j}} e^{-\frac{\|x_i - x_j\|^2}{T}}}{\sum_{\substack{k \in 1..n \\ k \neq i}} e^{-\frac{\|x_i - x_k\|^2}{T}}} \right)$$

$$\tag{7}$$

where x represents the input representations. The loss calculates the ratio between (a) the average distance separating a point x_i from other points within the same class and (b) the average distance separating any two points. The temperature T is used to emphasize smaller or larger distances accordingly. By maximizing the SNNL loss between clean inputs and SN-stamped inputs, we ensure that the representation distributions for both types of inputs are similar. Empirically, this approach forces the model to use the same group of neurons for both SN protection and the original task, making it more difficult to prune protection-related neurons. Consequently, the final loss function for the DSN framework can be expressed as follows:

$$\mathcal{L}_{DSN} = \begin{cases} \mathcal{L}_{Distill} + \alpha\mathcal{L}_{SNNL}, \text{ if } I = 1 \\ \mathcal{L}_{SNE} + \alpha\mathcal{L}_{SNNL}, \text{ if } I = 0, \end{cases} \tag{8}$$

where α serves as a hyperparameter to adjust the weight of the entanglement. In our experiments, we set the value of α to 0.1.

2.4   Serial Number Space

In this section, we discuss the serial number space Following the settings in previous work, [17], stakeholders O use their private key to sign some known versifiers V, e.g., O's the company name and a timestamp, $Encrypt(O_{pri}, v) = sig$, where the signature sig is a bit sequence that will be used to deterministically generate the serial number. In this paper, we focus on exploring DSN applications for computer vision tasks and consider using a 0/1 bit pattern as the SN. To activate DNN, the user needs to stamp the valid SN pattern on the correct position. Let $\hat{k}$ represent the SN pattern to be embedded in the DNN. Let x be an input image and $x^* = x \oplus \hat{k}$ be the image stamped with SN. Note that $\hat{k}$, x and x^* have the same dimension. $x_{i,j}$ is the normalized pixel value of x at point $(i, j)(0 < x_{i,j} < 1)$, and $x^*_{i,j}$ is the pixel value of SN stamped image at the same point. $\hat{k}_{i,j}$ is the pixel value of SN at point (i, j), which can be either $1, 0$ or -1. We then have the following mapping function:

$$x^*_{i,j} = \begin{cases} 1, & \text{if } \hat{k}_{i,j} = 1 \\ 0, & \text{if } \hat{k}_{i,j} = 0 \\ x_{i,j}, & \text{if } \hat{k}_{i,j} = -1. \end{cases} \tag{9}$$

The SN pattern is defined as the 0/1 pattern in pixels where $\hat{k}_{i,j} \neq -1$. When the SN is placed in a less important position, such as the corners of the image, the small SN pattern will not affect the original input signals.

3   Experiments

We conduct experiments on the three applications to validate that our DSN model meets the three watermarking requirements, that is, low distortion, reliability, and robustness.

3.1   Experimental Setups

Datasets. We conduct experiments on three datasets with different applications: digital recognition, traffic sign recognition, and face recognition.

- **Digit Recognition (MNIST)** [15]: MNIST is a digit recognition dataset with 10 output classes. The digits have been normalized in size and centered in a fixed-size image with 28×28 resolution.
- **German Traffic Sign Recognition Benchmark (GTSRB)** [26]: GTSRB contains colorful images of 43 traffic signs and has 39,209 training images and 12,603 testing images, respectively.
- **Pubfig** [14]: Pubfig is used to validate the performance of DSN on large and complex inputs. This dataset contains 13,838 face images of 85 people. Compared to GTSRB and MNIST, images in Pubfig have much higher resolution.

Model Architectures. For the MNIST dataset, we adopt a standard 4-layer convolutional neural network. For GTSRT, we utilize 6 convolution layers and 2 dense layer models. For the Pubfig dataset, we adopt a 16-layer VGG-Face model [23]. Note that in this work, we choose the same structure for both teacher and student models.

Implementation Details. In all experiments, we normalize the input in the range $[0, 1]$. The SN pattern is a 0/1 bit square pattern stamped on the right bottom corner, and we set the width of the pattern as 10% of the input image. Therefore, the area of the pattern only accounts for 1% of the original picture. SN bit patterns would up-scale proportionally when deploying DNN systems to target high-resolution images. The training process could be divided into two steps. First, we train a teacher model to maximize its performance on the specific task. Based on the teacher model, we then use the DSN framework to train multiple student networks. For raw inputs X, we train the student model with SNE loss in Eq. 5. For the SN stamped input $X \oplus K$, we optimize the student model with Distillation Loss in Eq. 3. For the feature extractor G_e, we optimize with the SNNL loss in Eq. 7. SN-stamped inputs are generated on-the-fly, and the two-branch DSN framework could be optimized parallelly. We use Adam as the optimizer for all teacher models and set the batch size to 500. The learning rate starts from 0.001 and is divided by 10 when the error plateaus. We utilize Adam as the optimizer for all student models and set the batch size to 500, including 250 raw inputs and 250 SN-stamped inputs.

Table 1. Accuracy of the Teacher and Student Network

Task	Teacher	Student Model	
	$\mathcal{A}_X$	$\mathcal{A}_{X \oplus K}$	$\mathcal{A}_X$
MNIST	99.9	99.8	9.2
GTSRB	97.0	97.2	8.2
Pubfig	87.9	87.3	7.3

Table 2. DSN against Fine-tuning Attack

Task	Student Model		Fine-Tuning Attack			
			10%	20%	30%	40%
	$\mathcal{A}_{X \oplus K}$	$\mathcal{A}_X$	$\mathcal{A}_X$			
MNIST	99.8	9.2	94.7	95.4	96.6	97.1
MNIST*	–	–	95.1	95.5	96.9	98.3
GTSRB	97.2	8.2	65.2	71.6	75.4	81.3
GTSRB*	–	–	65.3	73.2	85.3	87.8
Pubfig	87.3	7.3	51.3	53.5	60.2	65.3
Pubfig*	–	–	55.2	61.3	65.7	73.2

3.2 Prediction Distortion Analysis

For an ideal serial number embedding approach, the performance of student networks on the original task should not degrade significantly. Table 1 shows the classification accuracy for the teacher model and the student model. We observe that the student networks achieve competitive, and in some cases, better performance compared to the teacher models when the input is stamped with a valid serial number. The student model performance on MNIST and Pubfig experiences a minor drop of 0.1% and 0.6%, respectively. Surprisingly, the performance of the student model on GTSRB even surpasses that of the teacher model by 0.2%. One plausible explanation for the improvement on the GTSRB dataset is that we utilize the same architecture for both the student and teacher models, a phenomenon that has been reported and analyzed in previous work [5].

Fig. 2. Effectiveness of correct and invalid SNs (%)

Table 3. DSN against Model-Puning Attack

Task	Student Model		Model Pruning Attack			
			5%	10%	15%	20%
	$\mathcal{A}_{X \oplus K}$	$\mathcal{A}_X$	$\mathcal{A}_{X \oplus K}/\mathcal{A}_X$			
MNIST	99.8	9.2	98.4/8.7	98.4/8.3	98.4/9.7	98.4/9.9
GTSRB	97.2	8.2	97.2/8.2	97.2/8.2	97.1/8.3	96.8/9.5
Pubfig	87.3	7.3	87.3/7.3	87.3/7.4	87.1/8.1	82.5/9.7

3.3 Prediction Reliability Analysis

In Table 1, we also report the model performance with and without an embedded serial number (SN). The key observation is that when the inputs do not contain a valid SN, the performance of the student networks drops significantly, approaching random guessing. Without entering a valid SN (by inputting raw images in the experiments), the prediction accuracy of MNIST, GTSRT, and Pubfig substantially drops to 9.2%, 8.2%, and 7.3%, respectively. This performance is close to random guessing, which is $\frac{1}{N}$, where N represents the number of classes. We can conclude that the DSN framework ensures that only the valid SN can correctly activate the customer model. We further assess the effectiveness of invalid SN. To ensure that the preset SN is the only valid one, we apply other SN patterns on the inputs when training the branch G_d. We conduct an experiment on the MNIST dataset to evaluate the effectiveness of the wrong SN. For the 2×2 SN pattern, we evaluate the model performance with 1 correct SN and 15 invalid SNs. As shown in Fig. 2, the average accuracy $(\mathcal{A}_{X \oplus K})$ of the 15 incorrect SNs is only 13.5% (the highest is 27.2%). The results indicate that only the correct SN number can activate the protected model with our proposed DSN framework. All invalid SNs will cause a significant performance drop.

3.4   Attacking Robustness Analysis

In this section, we further investigate the robustness of the proposed framework. The embedded SN should be robust against various attack methods [2,28,32]. In this work, we group the existing attack approaches into two typical scenarios: 1) The adversaries do not know the SN. An example of this scenario is that the DNN is accidentally stolen by the adversary. In this case, the adversary's purpose is to either remove or reverse engineer the SN pattern. 2) The adversaries know SN. In this case, the adversary could be a legal buyer who wants to illegally distribute models to other parties. To redistribute the model, the adversary expects to remove or tamper the embedded SN and thus reclaims the ownership of the tampered model.

Adversary Without Knowledge of SN. For Adversaries without knowledge of SN, we consider three commonly used attack methods, including fine-tuning, transfer learning, model pruning, and reverse engineering.

Table 4. DSN against transfer-leaning

Task	Student		Transfer-Learning			
			10%	20%	30%	40%
	$A_{X \oplus K}$	A_X	A_X	A_X	A_X	A_X
MNIST	99.8	9.2	85.2	89.5	90.6	93.2
MNIST*	–	–	93.6	94.5	95.6	96.9
GTSRB	97.2	8.2	81.7	83.2	85.3	87.9
GTSRB*	–	–	91.8	93.4	94.2	95.5
Pubfig	97.3	7.3	82.3	85.3	87.2	88.9
Pubfig*	–	–	92.3	94.4	96.7	97.1

Table 5. DSN against SN Overwriting

Task	Student		Overwriting Attack			
			10%	20%	30%	40%
	$A_{X \oplus K}$	A_X	A_X			
MNIST	99.8	9.2	93.5	94.2	95.1	96.8
MNIST*	–	–	95.1	95.5	96.9	98.3
GTSRB	97.2	8.2	64.4	72.3	74.9	79.0
GTSRB*	–	–	65.3	73.2	85.3	87.8
Pubfig	87.3	7.3	51.0	52.7	59.3	61.8
Pubfig*	–	–	55.2	61.3	65.7	73.2

Fine-Tuning. In assessing the robustness of DSN against fine-tuning, we assume that the adversary only has a small segment of the model's original training data. Otherwise, an adversary could train the model from scratch. The student model is optimized by the standard cross entropy loss with a different portion of the original training data (10%, 20%, 30%, 40%). By directly training on the raw input, the adversary expects to remove the effect of SN that the model can perform normally without inputting the valid SN. Table 2 reports the experimental results. We observe that fine-tuning the student model on the original dataset can remove the SN effect. However, it also causes a notable performance drop. For example, when fine-tuning using 10% of the original training, GTSRB performance drops from 97.2% to 65.2%. We also train the model from scratch using the same portion of the original training data, which denotes DATASET*. We find that the performance of the fine-tuned student model is comparable to or worse than training from scratch, which implies that the cost of removing the SN through fine-tuning is nearly equivalent to training a new model from scratch. Consequently, the adversary has no incentive to steal the student model and expensively remove the DSN using a fine-tuning attack.

Model-Pruning. The pruning attack aims to remove redundant parameters and obtain a new student model that appears different from the original model but still maintains competitive accuracy. If the removed parameters contain the SN function, verifying the embedded SN would no longer be possible. Table 3 reports the experimental results. In these experiments, we adopt the commonly used L1-norm global pruning strategy [9] and prune the model by eliminating the lowest 5%–20% of connections across the entire model. The results indicate that model pruning has no impact on the DSN student model in terms of *LowDistortion* and *Reliability*. The performance of the pruned model with SN does not change significantly with increasing pruning strength. The increase in accuracy without SN is less than 2% when pruning 20% of the model weight, which suggests that SN protection remains highly effective. We can conclude that DSN is robust against model pruning.

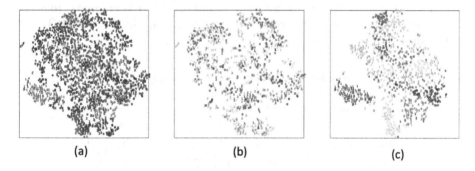

(a)   (b)   (c)

Fig. 3. Visualization of Embedding. (a): Blue/red points show the embedding without/with SN. (b): Embedding without SN. (c): Embedding with SN. (Color figure online)

Transfer-Learning. Different from fine-tuning settings, an adversary in transfer learning does not have the original training dataset but a small-scale private dataset. The motivation of the adversary is to use the features extracted from G_e to train a new model adapted to the private task. Following the common transfer-learning paradigm, we replace all fully connected layers according to the new task requirements, such as adjusting the very last original fully connected layers based on the prediction class numbers. Here, we randomly choose a half class from the original dataset and apply AdaIN style transformation [11] on them as the new private dataset. Table 4 reports the experimental results. We observe a similar result as in the fine-tuning attack. The computational cost of removing SN in the student model is close to learning from scratch. This is because the DSN framework guarantees that the features generated by G_e are indistinguishable. We show the visualization of the image embedding in Fig. 3, and we observe that images' embedding without SN is randomly distributed while clustered with the valid SN.

Reverse Engineer Attack. In this section, we propose a novel attack to reverse-engineer the secret SN embedded in the DSN model. The optimization objective has two goals. For a given DSN model $y = f(x)$, the first goal is to generate a functionally similar proxy serial number $\hat{SN}$ that enables the model to work properly. The second goal is to find a "concise" SN, which means the generated $\hat{SN}$ modifies only a limited portion of the input. We formulate this as a multi-objective optimization task by optimizing the weighted sum of the two objectives. The loss function is formulated as follows:

$$min\ \mathcal{L}(f(A(x, \hat{SN})), y) + \lambda|\hat{SN}|,\ for\ x \in X, \tag{10}$$

where $A(.)$ represents the function that applies a generated $\hat{SN}$ to the original input, and $|\hat{SN}|$ is used to regularize the size of the proxy serial number. $\mathcal{L}$ specifies the loss function of the model output $f(x)$ and the ground truth label y. λ is the weight for the second objective, where a smaller λ gives a lower weight to controlling the size of $\hat{SN}$. The Adam optimizer is employed to solve this optimization problem. We conduct experiments on MNIST, GTSRB, and Pubfig datasets.

Table 6. DSN against Reverse Engineering Attack

Task	Teacher Model	Student Model		
	A_X	$A_{X \oplus K}$	$A_{X \oplus \hat{K}}$	A_X
MNIST	99.9 ($\pm$ 0.1)	99.8 ($\pm$ 0.1)	48.8 ($\pm$ 25.1)	9.2 ($\pm$ 1.4)
GTSRB	97.0 ($\pm$ 0.3)	97.2 ($\pm$ 0.1)	22.3 ($\pm$ 22.3)	8.2 ($\pm$ 1.5)
Pubfig	87.9 ($\pm$ 1.2)	87.3 ($\pm$ 0.3)	24.5 ($\pm$ 17.8)	7.3 ($\pm$ 0.8)

In Table 6, we present the results of our reverse engineering attack. The column "$A_{X \oplus \hat{K}}$" specifies the model performance with the reverse-engineered SN. Our key observation is that the proposed framework can partially reverse engineer the functionality of the SN. For instance, the accuracy of the MNIST classifier increases from 9.2% (invalid SN) to 48.8% (reverse-engineered SN). The accuracy of the GTSRB classifier increases from 8.2% (invalid SN) to 22.3% (reverse-engineered SN). The accuracy of the Pubfig classifier increases from 7.3% (invalid SN) to 24.5% (reverse-engineered SN). However, the accuracy of the reverse-engineered SN is not stable, and the variance is significant. Sometimes the generated SN can perform very well, such as 68.9% on MNIST. Nonetheless, compared to the valid SN, the reverse-engineered SN still leads to a considerable drop in model performance. Furthermore, we only considered some straightforward SN patterns in our experiments. It will be more challenging to reverse engineer the serial number if we use a more complex and larger trigger pattern.

Adversary with Knowledge of SN In this attack scenario, the adversary has knowledge of the DSN framework as well as the legitimate owner's SN. We consider the overwriting attack, in which the adversary includes an additional watermark on top of the original one.

Overwriting Attack. In the case of the overwriting attack, we assume that an adversary seeks to replace the original sensitive neuron (SN) $\hat{k}$ with a new one, denoted as $\hat{k}^*$. To accomplish this, they train the student model with a new SN pattern using the Deep Sensitive Neuron (DSN) framework. Similar to previous attack scenarios, we consider that the adversary has access to only a limited portion of the model's original training data. The student model is optimized using the standard cross-entropy loss with 10%, 20%, 30%, and 40% of the original training data. The experimental results are presented in Table 5. Our observations reveal that, like transfer learning attacks, overwriting negatively impacts the student model's performance. The cost and performance of overwriting an SN are similar to those of training a model from scratch. Overwriting attacks, when compared to fine-tuning attacks, demand more training effort since they involve introducing a new SN via the DSN framework and eliminating the original SN pattern. Our empirical findings indicate that the computational cost of overwriting attacks is nearly double that of training a model from scratch.

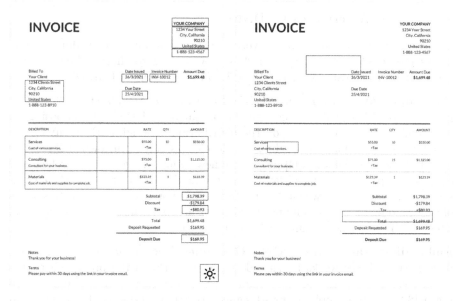

Fig. 4. DSN on the PDF OCR model. Left figure shows the results with the SN (the sun icon on the bottom right corner), and the right figure shows the result without SN.

4   A Case Study on PDF OCR Model

In this section, we showcase a prototype implementation of the DSN framework within a PDF OCR model. Following the pipeline depicted in Fig. 1, we changed the classification objective into the region proposal task and customize a PDF OCR student model to identify a unique icon in a PDF document, specifically embedding a sun icon as the serial number within the OCR region proposal module. When the document contains the icon (situated at the bottom right corner), the OCR region proposal module can accurately detect text within the provided invoice PDF. Conversely, if the icon is missing or incorrect, the customized OCR model generates a random region proposal rather than identifying the actual text. The proposed DSN framework presents a secure approach for the OCR model's owner to ensure that only authorized parties utilize their model. By incorporating this watermark into the OCR model, owners can safeguard against unauthorized access to their intellectual property and reduce the likelihood of their model being misused.

5   Related Work

In this section, we review two directions of research that are most relevant to ours, including embedding watermarks to DNNs and attacks against watermarks.

5.1   Digital Watermarks for DNNs

There are some initial attempts to verify the practicability of embedding watermarks into DNNs [12,16,18,20,24,29,33]. According to their embedding and verification mechanism, we group them into two categories [1,21,34].

Embedding Watermark into DNN Parameters. Uchida et al. [30] firstly proposes to embed watermarks into the parameters of DNNs by imposing an additional regularization term on the distribution of weights. By verifying the specific statistical bias in weights, the developers can claim ownership of the model. A more recent work [4] proposes a new ownership verification scheme by embedding special "passport" layers into the model architecture. Model owners keep the passport layer weights secret from unauthorized parties. For this series of work, model owners usually need white-box access for watermark verification, which is not piratical in many real-world scenarios.

Embedding Watermark in DNN Outcomes. The second category of watermarking techniques works by embedding watermarks in the prediction results of models. A frequently used technique is the emerging backdoor attack approach [8,28], where applying pre-designed trigger patterns on the input could precisely manipulate the outputs of DNNs, e.g., misclassifying inputs into a target label. Taking inspiration from the threat model of a backdoor attack, the model owners could inject a backdoor into the DNNs during the training process and utilize the secret trigger pattern as the watermark for remote ownership verification. For this kind of work, model owners only need black-box access (e.g., requiring prediction results remotely from APIs) for watermark verification, which is more practical in real-world scenarios.

6 Conclusions and Future Work

In this paper, we introduce DSN (Deep Serial Number), a new watermarking method that can prevent adversaries from deploying stolen deep neural networks, where the customer DNN function normally only if a potential user enters a valid serial number. Experiments on various applications indicate that DSN is effective in terms of preventing unauthorized applications while not sacrificing the original DNN performance. The experimental analysis further demonstrates that DSN is resistant to various attack methods. In this study, we mainly focus on computer vision tasks. In the future, we will apply our DSN framework to more applications and models, such as natural language processing and large language models [13,27,35].

7 Limitations and Ethical Statement

While the proposed DSN demonstrates robust defense in various attack scenarios, it remains vulnerable to several potential attack surfaces. For instance, adversaries may employ unlabeled data alongside the output from the protected model to train a local copy, referred to as a model extraction attack [22,25]. The current DSN framework cannot defend against such an attack. Furthermore, individuals may share the serial number with others and operate the model on an unregistered machine, a situation DSN cannot prevent. However, it is crucial to acknowledge that no universal protection mechanism can defend against all types of attacks, and DSN is not explicitly designed to counter extraction attacks or unauthorized use on unregistered machines. In real-world applications, defenders must employ a combination of defense methods to achieve comprehensive protection. Addressing model extraction attacks remains a complex challenge we plan to investigate in our future research.

This manuscript has undergone a comprehensive review to ensure adherence to ethical principles and has been deemed to comply with all relevant ethical guidelines. No ethical concerns were identified with regard to the content of this paper, which is considered to be a valuable addition to the field.

Acknowledgement. The authors thank the anonymous reviewers for their helpful comments. The work is in part supported by NSF grants NSF CNS-1816497, IIS-1849085 and IIS-2224843. The views and conclusions contained in this paper are those of the authors and should not be interpreted as representing any funding agencies.

References

1. Boenisch, F.: A survey on model watermarking neural networks. arXiv preprint arXiv:2009.12153 (2020)

2. Chen, H., Fu, C., Zhao, J., Koushanfar, F.: Deepinspect: a black-box trojan detection and mitigation framework for deep neural networks. In: IJCAI, pp. 4658–4664 (2019)
3. Chen, X., et al.: Refit: a unified watermark removal framework for deep learning systems with limited data. arXiv preprint arXiv:1911.07205 (2019)
4. Fan, L., Ng, K.W., Chan, C.S.: Rethinking deep neural network ownership verification: Embedding passports to defeat ambiguity attacks. In: NIPS, pp. 4714–4723 (2019)
5. Furlanello, T., Lipton, Z.C., Tschannen, M., Itti, L., Anandkumar, A.: Born again neural networks. arXiv preprint arXiv:1805.04770 (2018)
6. Ganin, Y., Lempitsky, V.: Unsupervised domain adaptation by backpropagation. In: ICML, pp. 1180–1189. PMLR (2015)
7. Gou, J., Yu, B., Maybank, S.J., Tao, D.: Knowledge distillation: a survey. arXiv preprint arXiv:2006.05525 (2020)
8. Gu, T., Liu, K., Dolan-Gavitt, B., Garg, S.: Badnets: evaluating backdooring attacks on deep neural networks. IEEE Access **7**, 47230–47244 (2019)
9. Han, S., Mao, H., Dally, W.J.: Deep compression: compressing deep neural networks with pruning, trained quantization and huffman coding. arXiv preprint arXiv:1510.00149 (2015)
10. Hinton, G., Vinyals, O., Dean, J.: Distilling the knowledge in a neural network. arXiv preprint arXiv:1503.02531 (2015)
11. Huang, X., Belongie, S.: Arbitrary style transfer in real-time with adaptive instance normalization. In: ICCV, pp. 1501–1510 (2017)
12. Kapusta, K., Thouvenot, V., Bettan, O., Beguinet, H., Senet, H.: A protocol for secure verification of watermarks embedded into machine learning models. In: Proceedings of the 2021 ACM Workshop on Information Hiding and Multimedia Security, pp. 171–176 (2021)
13. Kirchenbauer, J., Geiping, J., Wen, Y., Katz, J., Miers, I., Goldstein, T.: A watermark for large language models. arXiv preprint arXiv:2301.10226 (2023)
14. Kumar, N., Berg, A.C., Belhumeur, P.N., Nayar, S.K.: Attribute and simile classifiers for face verification. In: ICCV, pp. 365–372. IEEE (2009)
15. LeCun, Y., Bottou, L., Bengio, Y., Haffner, P.: Gradient-based learning applied to document recognition. Proc. IEEE **86**(11), 2278–2324 (1998)
16. Li, G., Li, S., Qian, Z., Zhang, X.: Encryption resistant deep neural network watermarking. In: ICASSP 2022–2022 IEEE International Conference on Acoustics, Speech and Signal Processing (ICASSP), pp. 3064–3068. IEEE (2022)
17. Li, H., Wenger, E., Zhao, B.Y., Zheng, H.: Piracy resistant watermarks for deep neural networks. arXiv preprint arXiv:1910.01226 (2019)
18. Li, Y., Bai, Y., Jiang, Y., Yang, Y., Xia, S.T., Li, B.: Untargeted backdoor watermark: towards harmless and stealthy dataset copyright protection. In: Advances in Neural Information Processing Systems (2022)
19. Li, Y., Jiang, Y., Li, Z., Xia, S.T.: Backdoor learning: a survey. IEEE Trans. Neural Netw. Learn. Syst. (2022)
20. Li, Y., Zhu, M., Yang, X., Jiang, Y., Wei, T., Xia, S.T.: Black-box dataset ownership verification via backdoor watermarking. IEEE Trans. Inf. Forensics Secur. **18**, 2318–2332 (2023)
21. Lounici, S., Njeh, M., Ermis, O., Önen, M., Trabelsi, S.: Yes we can: watermarking machine learning models beyond classification. In: 2021 IEEE 34th Computer Security Foundations Symposium (CSF), pp. 1–14. IEEE (2021)

22. Oliynyk, D., Mayer, R., Rauber, A.: I know what you trained last summer: a survey on stealing machine learning models and defences. arXiv preprint arXiv:2206.08451 (2022)

23. Parkhi, O.M., Vedaldi, A., Zisserman, A.: Deep face recognition. In: British Machine Vision Association (2015)

24. Regazzoni, F., Palmieri, P., Smailbegovic, F., Cammarota, R., Polian, I.: Protecting artificial intelligence IPS: a survey of watermarking and fingerprinting for machine learning. CAAI Trans. Intell. Technol. **6**(2), 180–191 (2021)

25. Sanyal, S., Addepalli, S., Babu, R.V.: Towards data-free model stealing in a hard label setting. In: Proceedings of the IEEE/CVF Conference on Computer Vision and Pattern Recognition, pp. 15284–15293 (2022)

26. Stallkamp, J., Schlipsing, M., Salmen, J., Igel, C.: Man vs. computer: benchmarking machine learning algorithms for traffic sign recognition. Neural Networks **32**, 323–332 (2012)

27. Tang, R., Chuang, Y.N., Hu, X.: The science of detecting LLM-generated texts. arXiv preprint arXiv:2303.07205 (2023)

28. Tang, R., Du, M., Liu, N., Yang, F., Hu, X.: An embarrassingly simple approach for trojan attack in deep neural networks. In: KDD, pp. 218–228 (2020)

29. Tang, R., Feng, Q., Liu, N., Yang, F., Hu, X.: Did you train on my dataset? Towards public dataset protection with clean-label backdoor watermarking. arXiv preprint arXiv:2303.11470 (2023)

30. Uchida, Y., Nagai, Y., Sakazawa, S., Satoh, S.: Embedding watermarks into deep neural networks. In: MM, pp. 269–277 (2017)

31. Vincent, J.: Meta's powerful AI language model has leaked online: what happens now? The Verge (2023). https://www.theverge.com/2023/3/8/23629362/meta-ai-language-model-llama-leak-online-misuse

32. Wang, B., et al.: Neural cleanse: identifying and mitigating backdoor attacks in neural networks. In: 2019 IEEE Symposium on Security and Privacy (SP), pp. 707–723. IEEE (2019)

33. Wang, L., Song, Y., Xia, D.: Deep neural network watermarking based on a reversible image hiding network. Pattern Analysis and Applications, pp. 1–14 (2023)

34. Wang, R., et al.: Rethinking the vulnerability of DNN watermarking: are watermarks robust against naturalness-aware perturbations? In: Proceedings of the 30th ACM International Conference on Multimedia, pp. 1808–1818 (2022)

35. Yang, J., et al.: Harnessing the power of LLMS in practice: a survey on ChatGPT and beyond. arXiv preprint arXiv:2304.13712 (2023)

36. Yang, Z., Dang, H., Chang, E.C.: Effectiveness of distillation attack and countermeasure on neural network watermarking. arXiv preprint arXiv:1906.06046 (2019)

How Early Can We Detect? Detecting Misinformation on Social Media Using User Profiling and Network Characteristics

Shreya Ghosh[1]([✉])[iD] and Prasenjit Mitra[1,2]

[1] College of IST, Pennsylvania State University, State College, USA
{shreya,pmitra}@psu.edu
[2] L3S Research Center, Leibniz University, Hannover, Germany

Abstract. The rise of social media has amplified the need for auto-mated detection of misinformation. Current methods face limitations in early detection because crucial information that they rely on is unavailable during the initial phases of information dissemination. This paper presents an innovative model for the early detection of misinformation on social media through the classification of information propagation paths and using linguistic patterns. We have developed and incorporated a causal user attribute inference model to label users as potential misinformation propagators or believers. Our model is designed for early detection of false information and includes two auxiliary tasks: predicting the extent of misinformation dissemination and clustering similar nodes (or users) based on their attributes. We demonstrate that our proposed model can identify fake news on real-world datasets with 86.5% accuracy within 30 min of its initial distribution and before it reaches 50 retweets, outperforming existing state-of-the-art benchmarks.

Keywords: Misinformation · social network · discourse analysis

1 Introduction

Misinformation on social media platforms poses significant challenges to society, as it can influence public opinion [1], exacerbate polarization [18], and even jeopardize public health [5,20]. To mitigate the effect of misinformation, it is crucial to identify false information as early as possible, followed by the implementation of targeted and efficient countermeasures [23]. Detecting false information on social media is inherently challenging due to several factors, especially when focusing on the early detection of false information. Firstly, fake news is deliberately crafted to deceive readers, making it difficult to identify solely based on its content. Secondly, social media data is vast, multi-modal, predominantly user-generated, occasionally anonymous, and often noisy, which complicates the detection process. Thirdly, social media platforms facilitate the cheap and rapid dissemination of news, causing information, whether true or false, to spread quickly and extensively through complex networks. This rapid propagation adds

G. De Francisci Morales et al. (Eds.): ECML PKDD 2023, LNAI 14174, pp. 174–189, 2023.
https://doi.org/10.1007/978-3-031-43427-3_11

to the challenge of identifying and containing fake news at an early stage. Current methods primarily focus on linguistic patterns [7,26] and external knowledge bases [15] to identify misinformation, which is insufficient for capturing the complex interactions and user behaviours that drive its spread. Furthermore, existing approaches are often limited by their reliance on single-task learning, which can hinder generalizability and robustness across different domains and stages of misinformation dissemination.

To address these limitations, our proposed framework (**CIPHER**[1]) combines advanced NLP techniques to understand the linguistic differences between false and true information, a graph convolutional network for capturing user interactions and propagation characteristics, and attention mechanisms to capture both linguistic patterns and network features that characterize the spread of misinformation. By employing a multi-task learning approach, our model simultaneously tackles the primary task of misinformation detection and auxiliary tasks of predicting propagation depth and clustering users based on their reactions to false information. This integrated approach enables a more comprehensive understanding of the misinformation spread on social media platforms, facilitating early detection and effective countermeasures. Our contributions can be summarized as follows:

- We propose a novel multi-task learning framework that captures both linguistic patterns and network features to effectively detect misinformation, predict its propagation depth, and cluster users based on their reactions to false information.
- We introduce a user causal inference model to identify user's contribution to false information propagation or prevention, and a dynamic attention mechanism that weighs the importance of tokens in the text according to their significance in the misinformation dissemination process, providing a more refined understanding of the linguistic patterns involved in the spread of misinformation.
- We demonstrate the efficacy and robustness of our framework through extensive experiments on multiple datasets (AntiVax, FakeNewsNet, Pheme, and Constraint), comparing its performance against baseline models and showcasing its generalizability across different domains and stages of misinformation spread.

The specific research questions, we are interested to investigate are: *RQ: How can we integrate the user causal model and retweet, follow, and mention network features into a unified framework for the early detection of misinformation on social media platforms? Additionally, how does multi-task learning help in improving the efficacy of early misinformation detection?* (See Sect. 3 for problem definition of multi-task objectives)

CIPHER advances the state-of-the-art in misinformation detection by proposing a novel multi-task learning framework that not only enables early

---

[1] CIPHER: **C**atching **I**nternet **P**ropaganda: A **H**olistic **E**arly **F**alse Information **R**ecognition.

detection of misinformation, but also provides valuable insights into the propagation process and user behaviors, laying the foundation for more effective interventions and countermeasures.

2   Related Works

Several studies have explored the use of linguistic features, such as n-grams, syntactic and semantic patterns, and sentiment analysis, in conjunction with machine learning algorithms for misinformation detection [17,25]. These approaches often rely on feature extraction and selection techniques to identify discriminative patterns in text data. However, they struggle to capture the complex interactions between users and the dynamic nature of misinformation spread on social media platforms. With the advent of deep learning, various NLP models, including recurrent neural networks (RNNs), long short-term memory (LSTM) networks, and transformers, have been employed for misinformation detection [10,14]. These models can learn high-level semantic representations from large-scale text data, improving the detection performance. However, they often overlook the importance of network features and user behaviors, which are crucial for understanding the dissemination process of misinformation. Ruchansky et al. [14] proposed a hybrid model named CSI (Capture, Score, and Integrate) for detecting fake news on social media. This study shows that combining textual, publisher, and user interaction features can effectively detect fake news. Ezeakunne et al. [4] focused on detecting misinformation by analyzing user behavior on social media. They proposed a deep learning model that leverages user behavior patterns, including retweeting, liking, and replying to tweets, to predict the credibility of the information. Ma, et al., [10] developed an attention-based recurrent neural network (RNN) model to detect fake news on social media. They demonstrated that the attention-based RNN model outperformed other state-of-the-art methods in early misinformation detection. However, these methods have limitations. The CSI model's [14] performance is limited by the quality and availability of publisher credibility data and user engagement features, while the BEHIND model [4] relies on user behavior patterns, which may be susceptible to manipulation by malicious actors or bots. The attention-based RNN model [10] struggles to detect misinformation when textual features alone are insufficient or ambiguous. Yang, et al., [22] employed linguistic cues and user features for early detection of rumors, but the approach may be limited by language-specific characteristics and evolving user behaviors. Volkova et al. [19] focused on identifying truthful versus deceptive news headlines using linguistic analysis, but their model struggles with misleading headlines that are factually accurate. Rashkin, et al., [13] focused on identifying truthful versus deceptive news headlines using linguistic analysis, but the model might struggle with misleading headlines that are factually accurate. Monti, et al., [11] proposed a geometric deep learning approach to detect misinformation, but the model's performance may be limited by the structural complexity and scale of real-world social networks. Liu, et al., [8] proposed a novel deep neural network combining crowd response features and user reactions to effectively detect misinformation early.

Liang, et al., [21] proposed a model incorporating stance information from users to improve fake news detection, but the model's performance may be limited by the availability and quality of user-generated stance information.

3   Problem Definition

Given a social network S represented by a graph $G(V, E)$, where V is the set of nodes (users) and E is the set of edges (connections), and a set of microblog posts T, let $t \in T$ have a timestamp t_t and be classified as either misinformation (M) or fact/true/genuine information (F). CIPHER addresses the following problems: **Early False Information Identification (EFII)**: For each $t \in T$, determine a classification task $C(t) \in \{M, F\}$, minimizing the time taken for classification, t_{cl}, such that $t_{cl} \leq \theta$, where θ is the maximum allowable time for early detection. The performance is measured by F1 score within the range $[\varphi, 1]$ (i.e., how much minimum time is required to reach at least φ F1]. **User Classification (UC)**: For each user $u \in V$, assign a label $L(u) \in \{$M_spreader, M_preventer, M_initiator, M_skeptic$\}$ based on their role in spreading or mitigating misinformation. **Predicting Depth of False Information Reach (PDFIR)**: For each misinformation tweet $m \in M$, estimate the depth of reach $d(m, t_p)$ within the social network $G(V, E)$ at a future time point t_p, where $t_p = t_t + \Delta t$, and Δt is the prediction horizon. Next, we cluster users in V into 4 groups based on their UC labels and characteristics. The multi-task learning problem addresses the objectives (EFII, UC, PDFIR) considering the linguistic pattern of the posts, temporal dynamics of social networks and information propagation.

4   CIPHER: Methodology

4.1   Network Construction

In this section, we introduce a three-layered graph that combines the Retweet, Mention, and Follow networks to better understand user interactions and information dissemination patterns on social media platforms. This integrated graph aims to improve early misinformation detection by leveraging the diverse interactions across the three networks.

Let $G = (V, E)$ denote a directed, weighted multilayer network, where V is the set of nodes (users) and E is the set of edges (user interactions) across the three layers. The three-layered graph is represented by $G_3L = (V_3L, E_3L)$, where (i) V_3L: the union of V_{RT}, V_M, and V_F, representing the set of users involved in retweets, mentions, or follows. (ii) E_3L: the set of edges (u, v, k) across the three layers, with $k \in \{RT, M, F\}$, where (u, v, RT) denotes a retweet interaction, (u, v, M) represents a mention interaction, and (u, v, F) signifies a follow interaction. (iii) $w(u, v, k)$: the weight of edge (u, v, k), indicating the interaction strength between users u and v in layer k. The three-layered graph captures diverse interaction types, providing a more accurate and holistic understanding of user behavior and information flow on social media platforms. We show that by combining the Retweet, Mention, and Follow networks, the integrated graph can help identify potential misinformation spreaders and influential users across different types of interactions, enhancing early detection capabilities.

Next, to incorporate the credibility of users in the three-layered graph, we propose assigning edge weights based on a personalized PageRank trust model [2]. The intuition behind this approach is that if *a user B primarily shares unreliable content, user A, who interacts with user B, is also likely to share unreliable content.* This trust model helps us capture the importance of channels through which misinformation or true information spreads. Here, the personalized PageRank trust model computes a trust score for each user based on their credibility. Let $T(u)$ denote the trust score of user u. To compute T(u), we use a personalized PageRank algorithm [9] with a preference vector that prioritizes users who are known to be credible, as determined by fact-checking organizations or other reliable sources. Using the trust scores $T(u)$ and $T(v)$ for users u and v, we update the edge weights in the three-layered graph as follows: $w(u, v, RT) = T(u) * T(v) * N_{RT}(u, v)$, where $N_{RT}(u, v)$ denotes the number of times user u retweets content from user v. $w(u, v, M) = T(u) * T(v) * N_M(u, v)$, where $N_M(u, v)$ represents the number of times user u mentions user v. $w(u, v, F) = T(u) * T(v)$, as user u either follows or does not follow user v, and we consider the trust scores of both users to assign the weight. This weight assignment strategy accounts for the credibility of both users involved in the interaction, making the graph more informative for early misinformation detection.

Transmitter and Receiver Characteristics in Misinformation Propagation. Next, we analyze the roles and characteristics of transmitters and receivers in the context of misinformation propagation on social media platforms.

Transmitter: Transmitters are individuals who propagate information on social media. We select the following characteristics that can influence the spread of misinformation by transmitters: (1) *Reaction time:* The speed at which a user forwards or shares received information upon encountering it. (2) *Perseverance:* Persistence in spreading information despite difficulties or delays in convincing others. Users may spread information at different time scales, ranging from single forwards to long-term efforts (super-spreaders). (3) *Authority level:* The number of followers or the user's relevance to a specific domain, such as healthcare, can impact their influence on misinformation spread. (4) *Sensitivity:* Users may exhibit different levels of sensitivity when encountering misinformation, including (i) believe-and-forward, (ii) being neutral, or (iii) not believing and persuading others to act the same.

Receiver: Receivers are individuals who consume and potentially propagate information further. CIPHER considers the factors influence the likelihood of receivers spreading misinformation: (1) *Attitude:* Receivers may immediately change their state (e.g., adopt a belief), require some time before being convinced (e.g., by seeking additional information), or be completely insensitive

Table 1. Illustration of receiver and transmitter

Dataset	Post
AntiVax	(Transmitter) "@AntiVaxWarrior" posts a tweet claiming, "The MMR vaccine causes autism! Don't let them poison your kids! #StopTheVax #Autism" (Receiver) "@ConcernedParent" who is unsure about vaccines retweets "@AntiVaxWarrior" 's tweet and adds, "Is this true? I am worried about vaccinating my child now". #VaccineSafety"
FakeNewsNet	(Transmitter) "@FinanceGuru" shares an article, "Cryptocurrency scams are on the rise. Make sure to research and verify before investing. #Crypto #InvestWisely" Resistance and Misinformation: (Receiver 1) "@CryptoKing" retweets and adds, "This is just fear-mongering by mainstream media! Cryptos are the future!" #Cryptocurrency #FinancialFreedom" (Receiver 2) "@MoneyMatters retweets and comments", "The banks are spreading lies to protect their outdated financial system! #CryptoRevolution #BankingLies"

to the information (i.e., no change of state). (2) *Number of Messages* : The likelihood of misinformation propagation can be influenced by the frequency of messages from the same sender or multiple, different users. (3) *Source authority* : The popularity (e.g., number of followers) or recognized expertise of the transmitter can be a critical factor in the propagation success of misinformation. Receivers may be more likely to trust and spread information from authoritative sources. By considering the characteristics of transmitters and receivers in the context of misinformation propagation, we develop more effective early detection algorithms and strategies for mitigating the spread of misinformation on social media platforms. We provide two examples in the context of misinformation propagation in Table 1. In the example, the transmitter is responsible for disseminating misinformation, while the receiver, depending on their attitude and susceptibility, may contribute to the further spread of the information.

4.2 User Causal Model

We propose a *Causal User Attribute Inference (CUAI)* model that employs a Graph Attention Network (GAT) to infer the causal relationships between user attributes and their propensity to spread misinformation. Let $G = (V, E)$ represent the social network graph. Each user $v \in V$ has an associated attribute vector $A(v)$, consisting of features such as reaction time, perseverance, authority level, sensitivity, and source authority. The CUAI model consists of the following components:

1. Attribute Embedding Layer: We use a linear transformation layer to convert user attributes, A(v), into continuous feature vectors $h_0(v) \in R^d$, where d is the embedding dimension:

$$h_0(v) = W_0 * A(v) + b_0, \tag{1}$$

where W_0 and b_0 are the learnable weight matrix and bias vector, respectively.

2. GAT-based Causal Inference: We employ a multi-head Graph Attention Network (GAT) model to learn the causal relationships between user attributes and their propensity to spread misinformation:

$$h_l + 1(v) = ||_{k=1}^{K} Attention_k(h_l(v), h_l(u) : u \in N(v)), \qquad (2)$$

where $||$ denotes concatenation, K is the number of attention heads, N(v) represents the neighbors of user v, and $Attention_k(\Delta)$ is the k-th attention mechanism. The attention mechanism computes the importance of neighboring nodes' features based on the input features:

$$\alpha_k(u, v) = softmax_u(LeakyReLU(W_k^T[h_l(u)||h_l(v)])) \qquad (3)$$

where W_k is the learnable weight matrix for the k-th attention head, and $[\Delta||\Delta]$ denotes the concatenation of two vectors.

3. Causal Effect Estimation: We use the learned user embeddings $h_L(v)$, where L is the number of GAT layers, to estimate the causal effects of user attributes on misinformation propagation. By employing GATs for causal inference, the CUAI model provides a powerful and flexible approach to identifying the key causal factors driving the spread of misinformation in social networks. This knowledge is used to design more effective intervention strategies and reduce the impact of false information on society. Next, we use the outcome of the framework to estimate the causal effects of user attributes on misinformation propagation. For each user v, we define two potential outcomes: $Y_v(1)$ and $Y_v(0)$ based on if the user attribute was set to a specific value (1) or not set (0), respectively. The causal effect for user v is then defined as the difference between the two potential outcomes:

$$\tau(v) = E[Y_v(1) - Y_v(0)], \qquad (4)$$

where $E[\Delta]$ denotes the expectation. To estimate $\tau(v)$, we use the learned user embeddings $h_L(v)$ and fit two separate regressions:

$$Y_v(1) = g_1(h_L(v); \theta_1), Y_v(0) = g_0(h_L(v); \theta_0), \qquad (5)$$

where $g_1(\Delta; \theta_1)$ and $g_0(\Delta; \theta_0)$ are regression functions with parameters θ_1 and θ_0, respectively. We can then estimate the causal effect as the difference between the predicted outcomes:

$$\tau(v) \approx g_1(h_L(v); \theta_1) - g_0(h_L(v); \theta_0). \qquad (6)$$

By estimating the causal effects, we identify the most influential user attributes that can be targeted for interventions to reduce misinformation propagation.

4. Misinformation Propensity Prediction: To predict whether a given user v is likely to propagate misinformation, we train a supervised classifier using the learned user embeddings $h_L(v)$ as features. Let $f(\Delta; \theta)$ be the classifier function with parameters θ, and let $y(v) \in 0, 1$ denote the ground truth label for user

v, where 1 represents a user who propagates misinformation and 0 represents a user who does not. We can define the classification loss as:

$$L(\theta) = \sum_{v \in V} L_{cls}(y(v), f(h_L(v); \theta)), \tag{7}$$

where the cross-entropy loss is denoted by $L_{cls}(\Delta, \Delta)$. During training, the classifier minimizes the loss function with respect to the parameters θ : $\theta* = argmin_\theta L(\theta)$. Once the classifier is trained, we predict the misinformation propensity for a given user v by computing the probability of the user propagating misinformation:

$$P(y(v)) = (1|h_L(v)) = f(h_L(v)); \theta*). \tag{8}$$

By predicting misinformation propensity using the learned user embeddings, the CUAI model is used to identify users who are more likely to spread misinformation, enabling targeted interventions and mitigating the impact of false information on social networks.

4.3   Temporal Characteristics

Observation (AntiVax Dataset) A tweet claiming that the MMR vaccine is linked to autism initially receives retweets and likes from users who agree with the statement. As the tweet spreads, users who express their surprise at such a claim, asking for evidence or research supporting the claim. Further down the line, users begin to question the claim's validity and ask for reliable sources, engaging in conversations to debunk the misinformation. To incorporate the observed patterns into a model that considers the dynamic nature of information dissemination, we propose a novel method that utilizes a dynamic attention value for each post. Let P be a post and $t(P)$ be the time when the post was made. Let E be the event corresponding to the initial tweet and $t(E)$ be the time when the event started. We define the time interval for a post as: $\delta t(P) = t(P) - t(E)$. Next, let G be the graph representing the social network, where $V(G)$ is the set of nodes (users) and $E(G)$ is the set of edges (interactions). Let $N(P)$ be the set of nodes (users) that have already interacted with post P. Then, we define the interaction ratio $R(P)$ as: $R(P) = |N(P)|/|V(G)|$. Now, let $F(G)$ be the follower-followee network of the users in G, and $L1(P)$ be the set of nodes reachable from P using a BFS search algorithm. We define the *BFS ratio* L(P) as: $L(P) = |L1(P)|/|V(F(G))|$. The dynamic attention value $A(P)$ for a post P can be calculated as a weighted sum of the time interval, interaction ratio, and BFS ratio:

$$A(P) = \alpha * \delta t(P) + \beta * R(P) + \gamma * L(P) \tag{9}$$

where α, β, γ are weights that can be tuned based on the importance of each factor in the dissemination process. Finally, let $S(P)$ represent the linguistic pattern score for the post P. The overall score for a post P, considering both dynamic attention and linguistic patterns, can be calculated as:

$$Score(P) = \gamma * A(P) + (1 - \gamma) * S(P) \tag{10}$$

where γ is a weight that balances the influence of dynamic attention and linguistic patterns in the model. By incorporating this dynamic attention value and linguistic pattern into our model, we can more effectively capture the patterns observed in the information dissemination process and improve the early detection of misinformation.

For a given news story propagating on social media, we first construct its propagation path by identifying the users who engaged in propagating the news.

User Profiling: We convert user profiles into fixed-length sequences. Let U_i be the fixed-length sequence representing the user profile of user i. For each user i, we create a propagation path P_i that consists of the user profile sequence U_i and the interactions in which user i participated. In layer 1, we apply a Gated Recurrent Unit (GRU) layer to learn the vector representation V_i for each propagation path P_i: $V_i = GRU(P_i)$. In layer 2, we deploy Graph Convolutional Network (GCN) layer to learn the transformed propagation path T_i for each user profile vector V_i: $T_i = GCN(V_i)$. We concatenate transformed propagation paths by combining the transformed propagation paths T_i into a single vector C that represents the overall transformed propagation path: $C = Concat(T_1, T_2, ..., T_n)$. Finally, we deploy a multi-layer feedforward neural network to predict the maximum depth D for the corresponding propagation path: $D = FNN(C)$. By incorporating user profiling and propagation paths into the model, we can more effectively capture the propagation patterns observed in the information dissemination process and improve the early detection of misinformation. This approach allows us to account for the impact of individual users on the overall propagation of news stories and to better understand the dynamics of misinformation spread. The classifier uses a binary cross-entropy loss $L_{misinfo}$ as the loss for the primary task of detecting false information. L_{depth} is the loss for the auxiliary task of predicting the depth of false information propagation. This is a mean squared error (MSE) loss. $L_{cluster}$ is the loss for the auxiliary task of clustering users based on their reactions to false information. This is a categorical cross-entropy loss, with clusters represented as one-hot encoded vectors. Task-specific weighting factors, γ_1, γ_2 and γ_3, control the relative importance of the tasks in the joint loss function. The combined loss function L_total can be defined as:

$$L_{total} = \gamma_1 * L_{misinfo} + \gamma_2 * L_{depth} + \gamma_3 * L_{cluster} \qquad (11)$$

We also introduce adaptive weighting factors that dynamically adjust the importance of each task during training. We use the inverse training progress as a weight factor: $\gamma_i(t) = \alpha_i/(1 + \beta_i * tr)$. Here, tr is the current training step, α_i and β_i are positive hyperparameters for each task i, and $\gamma(t)$ is the weighting factor for task i at step t. This formulation ensures that the weighting factors decrease as training progresses, allowing the model to focus on the most relevant tasks at each stage of training.

4.4 Linguistic Pattern Analysis

CIPHER deploys the following three components using linguistic pattern analysis: (A) A novel Semantic Similarity Analysis (SSA) approach using a pre-trained

RoBERTa model, multi-layer attention mechanism, and contrastive learning to enhance early misinformation detection. We employ the Hugging Face Transformers and spaCy libraries in Python. Firstly, we tokenize the text, convert it to lowercase, and remove special characters, URLs, and user mentions using spaCy and regular expressions. Next, we initialize the pre-trained RoBERTa model (DistilRoBERTa[2]), denoted as R. Next, we use a multi-layer attention mechanism A, consisting of L self-attention layers, each followed by a feed-forward network and layer normalization. Let the output of the last transformer layer in RoBERTa be denoted as H_i for each tweet t_i. The attention mechanism computes a weighted representation $A(H_i) = \sum_{l=1}^{L} W_l F_l(H_i)$, where F_l denotes the l-th self-attention layer followed by the feed-forward network and layer normalization, and W_l are learnable weights. Then, we construct the training dataset of paired examples, with each pair consisting of a tweet t_i and a reference source r_j. For each tweet, generate positive pairs (t_i, r_j^+) with verified information sources sharing semantic similarity and negative pairs (t_i, r_j^-) with unrelated or contrasting sources. We fine-tune the RoBERTa model with the multi-layer attention mechanism on the paired dataset using contrastive learning. The objective is to learn semantic embeddings $\varphi(t_i)$ and $\varphi(r_j)$ that minimize the distance between positive pairs and maximize the distance between negative pairs:

$$
\mathcal{L}contrastive = \sum_{i=1}^{N} \left[d(\varphi(t_i), \varphi(r_j^+)) - \alpha + \max_{r_j^-} d(\varphi(t_i), \varphi(r_j^-)) \right]_+, \qquad (12)
$$

where $d(\cdot, \cdot)$ denotes a distance metric (e.g., cosine distance), α is a margin parameter, $[\cdot]_+$ represents the hinge function, and N is the number of tweets in the dataset.

Argument Mining and Logical Fallacy Detection (AMLF): The module is designed to identify argumentative structures and logical fallacies in textual data. Given a dataset D containing text samples t_i, our objective is to extract argument components, such as claims C_i, premises P_i, and conclusions Q_i. Let F_{ext} denote an extraction function, parameterized by a pre-trained RoBERTa, which is fine-tuned for argument component extraction. The extraction process can be defined as follows: $(C_i, P_i, Q_i) = F_{ext}(t_i)$, where t_i is a text sample from the dataset D. For each extracted argument component, we aim to identify argumentative relations R_{ij} between them, such as support, attack, or neutral. Let F_{rel} denote a relation identification function, parameterized by a pre-trained NLP model fine-tuned on an argument relation dataset. The relation identification process can be defined as: $R_{ij} = F_{rel}(C_i, P_j)$. where C_i and P_j are argument components extracted from the text samples. Next, to detect logical fallacies, we define three fallacy patterns $\mathcal{F} = f_1, f_2, f_3$, such as *ad hominem, straw man, or false cause*. We aim to recognize and classify these patterns in argumentative structures. Some examples of tweets containing logical fallacies from the Anti-Vax dataset are provided in Table 2.

---

[2] https://huggingface.co/distilroberta-base.

Table 2. Illustration of fallacy patterns (AntiVax)

Fallacy type	Post
Ad Hominem	"You can't trust Dr. XXX's opinion on vaccines; he's just a puppet for Big Pharma! #VaccineTruth"
Straw Man	"Pro-vaxxers want us to believe that vaccines are 100% safe and have no side effects, but my child developed a fever after getting vaccinated. #VaccineInjury"
False Cause	"I saw a news report that a child was diagnosed with autism just days after being vaccinated. Clearly, vaccines are the cause of autism. #VaccineHarm"

Table 3. Sentiment difference in Fake vs true news (AntiVax)

Type of news	Post
True information	"The World Health Organization has declared COVID-19 a global pandemic. Countries worldwide are implementing preventive measures to curb the spread of the virus."
(Real news)	Sentiment: Neutral. Stance: Reporting
False information	"Shocking news! COVID-19 is a hoax created by the government to control the population! They're using the pandemic to enforce strict surveillance on citizens! #COVIDHoax"
	Sentiment: Negative. Stance: Against

Sentiment Analysis: Given a dataset D containing text samples t_i, our objective is to classify the sentiment expressed in each text as positive, negative, or neutral. To enhance early misinformation detection, we extract specific features from sentiment analysis, such as: **Sentiment Polarity Score:** Calculate a sentiment polarity score P_i for each text sample, indicating the degree of positivity or negativity expressed in the text. **Subjectivity Score:** U_i is the level of personal opinion, emotion, or judgment in the text i. **Stance Confidence Score:** C_i is the model's certainty in the detected stance towards the target in the text i.

Some examples of tweets from the AntiVax dataset, illustrating the differences in sentiment and stance between true and fake information are presented in Table 3. For true information, the sentiment is positive or neutral, and the stance may favor a particular viewpoint or report on factual events. Conversely, false information often exhibits negative sentiment and may adopt a stance against specific topics, entities, or claims.

5   Experimental Evaluations

[3] **Dataset Description** We evaluated our proposed framework, CIPHER, using four real-life datasets as described in Table 4. In this section, we discuss the experimental analysis and evaluation of CIPHER, focusing on three main evaluation tasks: (1) how early misinformation can be detected with $\geq 85\%$ accuracy,

---

[3] The experiment details, codebase and additional information is available HERE.

Table 4. Four real-life datasets used for CIPHER's performance evaluation

Dataset	Details
PHEME [3]	Rumors and their veracity in social media. It contains approximately 330 rumor threads collected from Twitter, with each thread having an average of 100 tweets. The dataset covers nine different events, including terrorist attacks, shootings, and natural disasters
AntiVax [6]	Anti-vaccination movement and contains over 1.8 million tweets collected between 2019 and 2021. The dataset includes tweets, retweets, mentions, and replies, along with associated metadata
CONSTRAINT [12]	Created for the CONSTRAINT AAAI-21 Shared Task on detecting misinformation during the COVID-19 pandemic. It comprises over 17,000 English tweets, annotated as either real or fake, with an equal distribution between the two classes
FakeNewsNet [16]	A comprehensive dataset containing both real and fake news articles. It consists of data from two popular fact-checking websites, PolitiFact and GossipCop over 23,000 news articles, with metadata such as social engagements, user information, and propagation patterns

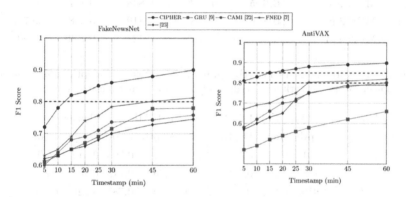

Fig. 1. Comparison of the minimum time required for the identification of misinformation with ≥ 0.80 F1

(2) predicting the depth of false information propagation, and (3) clustering users based on their characteristics. We highlight interesting findings extracted from the PHEME, AntiVax, FakeNewsNet, and Constraint datasets. Table 5 represents the comparison of misinformation detection in terms of F1-score within 24 h, 12 h and 30 mins. Apart from PHEME dataset, CIPHER outperforms the baselines[4] for all experimental settings by a significant margin. Table 6 presents CIPHER's performance on predicting infected nodes (users who initiate, transmit and believe misinformation, at time-step t+1) and predicting depth of misinformation reach.

We use a specific example from the AntiVax dataset to illustrate the workings of the proposed multi-task learning framework. Tweet A: "This new vaccine

---

[4] Baselines have been selected as state-of-the-art models for misinformation detection and early misinformation detection on social media.

Table 5. F1 score for detecting misinformation (post): comparison with baseline models and proposed framework (CIPHER). Best score is in bold font.

Dataset/Time	F1 Score				
	CIPHER	CAMI [23]	FNED [8]	GRU [10]	[24]
AntiVax/24 h	**0.9408**	0.861	0.892	0.814	0.820
AntiVax/12 h	**0.901**	0.812	0.842	0.683	0.790
AntiVax/30 m	**0.881**	0.752	0.803	0.579	0.748
CONSTRAINT/24 h	**0.931**	0.843	0.866	0.802	0.801
CONSTRAINT/12 h	**0.895**	0.808	0.832	0.661	0.772
CONSTRAINT/30 m	**0.870**	0.736	0.791	0.518	0.721
FakeNewsNet/24 h	**0.92**	0.848	0.840	0.849	0.810
FakeNewsNet/12 h	**0.872**	0.791	0.831	0.790	0.760
FakeNewsNet/30 m	**0.856**	0.736	0.784	0.715	0.691
PHEME/24 h	**0.905**	0.852	0.848	0.867	0.816
PHEME/12 h	**0.856**	0.768	0.819	0.828	0.772
PHEME/30 m	0.811	0.701	0.723	**0.820**	0.607

Table 6. CIPHER's performance (F1) on predicting maximum depth of false information propagation in network and predict infected nodes at time-step $t+1$

Timesep	AntiVax		FakeNewsNet		PHEME		Constraint	
	Depth	Node	Depth	Node	Depth	Node	Depth	Node
T/3	0.801	0.78	0.76	0.75	0.72	0.703	0.812	0.802
T/2	0.85	0.80	0.798	0.784	0.768	0.718	0.868	0.854
2T/3	0.910	0.845	0.823	0.810	0.827	0.781	0.920	0.907

causes severe side effects! It paralyzed my friend's arm! #AntiVax" Retweeted by user B with a comment: "I've heard similar stories. Are vaccines really safe? #QuestioningVaccines" User C, a healthcare professional, replies to user B: "Vaccines are safe and rigorously tested. Side effects are rare and usually mild. Here's a link to the CDC's vaccine safety information. #VaccinesSaveLives". Now, CIPHER's lingusitic model extract patterns from Tweet A, user B's comment, and user C's reply using a pre-trained model RoBERTa. And the attention layer weighs the importance of tokens in each text (e.g., "paralyzed", "side effects", "safe", and "CDC"). The 3-layered graph represents the relationships between users A, B, and C, capturing retweets, mentions, and follow relationships. The GCN layer is deployed to the 3-layered graph, capturing structural features and user interactions in the network. Then the context vector from the attention layer (focusing on crucial tokens) with the output from the GCN layer, creating a unified representation that captures both linguistic patterns and network features are deployed together followed by the multi-task learning (e.g., identifying Tweet A as misinformation) and auxiliary tasks of predicting the depth of false information propagation (e.g., estimating how many layers of users the misinformation will reach) and clustering users based on their reactions to false information (e.g., grouping users A and B as vaccine skeptics and user C as a healthcare professional). It has been observed through ablation study that CIPHER's performance has been improved by 8% and 6% by adding User causal model and temporal characteristics with the linguistic pattern respectively. Alongside, the multi-task learning framework has enhanced the overall accuracy by 6%–9% in the misinformation detection task.

Our experiments demonstrate that our proposed approach (CIPHER) can effectively detect misinformation early, achieving over 85% accuracy in most cases. By combining the Semantic Similarity Analysis (SSA), Argument Mining and Logical Fallacy Detection (AMLF), and Sentiment Analysis modules, we were able to identify key linguistic features that contribute to the early detection of misinformation. We observed that the PHEME and AntiVax datasets contained noticeable differences in sentiment and stance between true and false information, as well as the presence of logical fallacies in the latter. In the FakeNewsNet dataset, we found that the false stories often contained sensational language and misleading claims, which could be identified using our SSA and AMLF modules. Similarly, the Constraint dataset exhibited distinct patterns in terms of argument structure and fallacies, which contributed to the early detection of false claims. Figure 1 shows that CIPHER is able to identify false information within 3–12 min with more than 0.80 F1 at the earliest which is better than state-of-the-art models. Our approach also allows for the prediction of the depth of false information propagation, helping to estimate the potential reach and impact of misinformation (See Table 6). By analyzing the content and context of the misinformation, as well as the characteristics of the users involved in its dissemination, we were able to model the spread of misinformation within social media networks.

6   Conclusion

We presented a comprehensive approach to early misinformation detection on social media platforms by leveraging user profiling, linguistic analysis and network analysis modules. Our proposed methodology aims to identify and flag potential misinformation in its early stages of propagation to mitigate its spread and impact on society. CIPHER demonstrated promising results in detecting misinformation, highlighting the importance of incorporating various linguistic features and network characteristics to build an effective detection system.

Acknowledgements. This research was funded by the Federal Ministry of Education and Research (BMBF), Germany under the project LeibnizKILabor with grant No. 01DD20003.

Ethical Consideration. Several ethical considerations were taken into account. Data was obtained from publicly available sources. We took measures to ensure the privacy and anonymity of the individuals whose data was used. We recognize that social media data can be biased in many ways, and we took measures to mitigate these biases. We ensured that our research is conducted in a responsible and ethical manner.

References

1. Allcott, H., Gentzkow, M.: Social media and fake news in the 2016 election. J. Econ. Perspect. **31**(2), 211–236 (2017)
2. Asim, Y., Malik, A.K., Raza, B., Shahid, A.R.: A trust model for analysis of trust, influence and their relationship in social network communities. Telematics Inform. **36**, 94–116 (2019)
3. Derczynski, L., Bontcheva, K.: Pheme: veracity in digital social networks. In: UMAP Workshops (2014)
4. Ezeakunne, U., Ho, S.M., Liu, X.: Sentiment and retweet analysis of user response for early fake news detection. In: The International Conference on Social Computing, Behavioral-Cultural Modeling, & Prediction and Behavior Representation in Modeling and Simulation (SBP-BRiMS 2020), pp. 1–10 (2020)
5. Ghosh, S., Mitra, P., Hausman, B.L.: Evade: exploring vaccine dissenting discourse on twitter. In: epiDAMIK 5.0: The 5th International Workshop on Epidemiology meets Data Mining and Knowledge discovery at KDD 2022 (2022)
6. Hayawi, K., Shahriar, S., Serhani, M.A., Taleb, I., Mathew, S.S.: Anti-vax: a novel twitter dataset for COVID-19 vaccine misinformation detection. Public Health **203**, 23–30 (2022)
7. Jiang, S., Wilson, C.: Linguistic signals under misinformation and fact-checking: evidence from user comments on social media. Proc. ACM Hum.-Comput. Interact. **2**(CSCW), 1–23 (2018)
8. Liu, Y., Wu, Y.-F.B.: Fned: a deep network for fake news early detection on social media. ACM Trans. Inf. Syst. (TOIS) **38**(3), 1–33 (2020)
9. Lofgren, P.A., Banerjee, S., Goel, A., Seshadhri, C.: Fast-PPR: scaling personalized pagerank estimation for large graphs. In: Proceedings of the 20th ACM SIGKDD International Conference on Knowledge Discovery and Data Mining, pp. 1436–1445 (2014)
10. Ma, J., et al.: Detecting rumors from microblogs with recurrent neural networks (2016)
11. Monti, F., Frasca, F., Eynard, D., Mannion, D., Bronstein, M.M.: Fake news detection on social media using geometric deep learning. arXiv preprint arXiv:1902.06673 (2019)
12. Patwa, P., et al.: Fighting an Infodemic: COVID-19 fake news dataset. In: Chakraborty, T., Shu, K., Bernard, H.R., Liu, H., Akhtar, M.S. (eds.) CONSTRAINT 2021. CCIS, vol. 1402, pp. 21–29. Springer, Cham (2021). https://doi.org/10.1007/978-3-030-73696-5_3
13. Rashkin, H., Choi, E., Jang, J.Y., Volkova, S., Choi, Y.: Truth of varying shades: analyzing language in fake news and political fact-checking. In: Proceedings of the 2017 Conference on Empirical Methods in Natural Language Processing, pp. 2931–2937 (2017)
14. Ruchansky, N., Seo, S., Liu., Y.: CSI: a hybrid deep model for fake news detection. In: Proceedings of the 2017 ACM on Conference on Information and Knowledge Management, pp. 797–806 (2017)

15. Seddari, N., Derhab, A., Belaoued, M., Halboob, W., Al-Muhtadi, J., Bouras, A.: A hybrid linguistic and knowledge-based analysis approach for fake news detection on social media. IEEE Access **10**, 62097–62109 (2022)

16. Shu, K., Mahudeswaran, D., Wang, S., Lee, D., Liu, H.: Fakenewsnet: a data repository with news content, social context, and spatiotemporal information for studying fake news on social media. Big Data **8**(3), 171–188 (2020)

17. Shu, K., Sliva, A., Wang, S., Tang, J., Liu, H.: Fake news detection on social media: a data mining perspective. ACM SIGKDD Explorations Newsl **19**(1), 22–36 (2017)

18. Tucker, J.A., et al.: Social media, political polarization, and political disinformation: a review of the scientific literature. In: Political Polarization, and Political Disinformation: A Review of the Scientific Literature, 19 March 2018 (2018)

19. Volkova, S., Shaffer, K., Jang, J.Y., Hodas, N.: Separating facts from fiction: linguistic models to classify suspicious and trusted news posts on twitter. In: Proceedings of the 55th Annual Meeting of the Association for Computational Linguistics (volume 2: Short papers), pp. 647–653 (2017)

20. Wang, Y., McKee, M., Torbica, A., Stuckler, D.: Systematic literature review on the spread of health-related misinformation on social media. Soc. Sci. Med. **240**, 112552 (2019)

21. Wu, L., Liu, H.: Tracing fake-news footprints: characterizing social media messages by how they propagate. In: Proceedings of the Eleventh ACM International Conference on Web Search and Data Mining, pp. 637–645 (2018)

22. Yang, Y., Zheng, L., Zhang, J., Cui, J.Q., Li, Z., Yu, P.S.: Ti-CNN: convolutional neural networks for fake news detection. arXiv preprint arXiv:1806.00749 (2018)

23. Yu, F., Liu, Q., Wu, S., Wang, L., Tan, T., et al.: A convolutional approach for misinformation identification. In: IJCAI, pp. 3901–3907 (2017)

24. Yue, Z., Zeng, H., Kou, Z., Shang, L., Wang, D. : Contrastive domain adaptation for early misinformation detection: a case study on COVID-19. In: Proceedings of the 31st ACM International Conference on Information & Knowledge Management, pp. 2423–2433 (2022)

25. Zhang, H., Qian, S., Fang, Q., Xu, C.: Multimodal disentangled domain adaption for social media event rumor detection. IEEE Trans. Multimedia **23**, 4441–4454 (2020)

26. Zhou, C., Li, K., Lu, Y.: Linguistic characteristics and the dissemination of misinformation in social media: the moderating effect of information richness. Inf. Process. Manag. **58**(6), 102679 (2021)

Boosting the Performance of Deployable Timestamped Directed GNNs via Time-Relaxed Sampling

Arihant Jain[✉], Gundeep Arora, and Anoop Saladi

International Machine Learning, Amazon, Bengaluru, India
{arihanta,gundeepa,saladias}@amazon.com

Abstract. Timestamped graphs find applications in critical business problems like user classification, fraud detection, etc. This is due to the inherent nature of the data generation process, in which relationships between nodes are observed at defined timestamps. Deployment-focused GNN models should be trained on point-in-time information about node features and neighborhood, similar to the data ingestion process. However, this is not reflected in benchmark directed node classification datasets, where performance is typically reported on undirected versions of graphs that ignore these timestamps. Constraining the leading approaches trained on undirected graphs to timestamp-based message passing at test time leads to sharp drops in performance. This is driven by the blocking of pathways for neighborhood information, which was available during the undirected training phase but not during the test time, highlighting the label leakage issue in applied graph use-cases. We bridge this mismatch of message passing semantics in directed graphs by first resetting baselines while highlighting the semantic case where undirected training/inference would fail. Second, we introduce TRD-GNN, which bridges performance drop, by leveraging a novel GNN sampling layer that relaxes the time-directed nature of the graph only to the extent that it limits any possibility of labels being leaked during the training phase. The two contributions combined form a recipe for robust GNN model deployment in industry use-cases. Finally, we demonstrate the benefits of the proposed relaxation by drawing out qualitative analysis where it helped improve performance on the node classification task on multiple public benchmark and proprietary e-commerce datasets.

Keywords: Graph Neural Networks · Timestamped directed graphs · Label leakage

1 Introduction

With the proliferation of e-commerce and social networking services, building and mining relationships between entities on respective services have been useful in improving the customer experience. Social networks (such as Reddit or

G. De Francisci Morales et al. (Eds.): ECML PKDD 2023, LNAI 14174, pp. 190–206, 2023.
https://doi.org/10.1007/978-3-031-43427-3_12

Facebook) leverage interaction and follow behaviour data, formulated as a graph to suggest new posts to customers and other users to follow. At the same time, e-commerce stores use user-item graphs for recommendation systems, both helping in improving customer experience and engagement. At the same time, online social communities suffer from abuse [2,33] where misinformation propagation, trolling, and using offensive language and on e-commerce stores, abuse comprises fraudulent activities such as artificially improving the search ranking of products with fake reviews [10,18]. Such abusive behavior reduces user trust, engagement, and satisfaction. Graph Neural Networks (GNNs) have found applications in such cases where relationships between entities (like users in a social network) can help improve predictability in user engagement tasks like user-follow suggestions. These applications are typically built on top of graphs with timestamped edges, where the timestamp is when the edge is observed.

Citation networks mimic similar behaviour of directed graphs, where published research papers, positioned as nodes on the graph, cite other research papers which were published before the citing paper. The timestamp on the edge is the year when the citing paper is published, and it also forms the basis which training, validation and test instances are divided. This behaviour is manifested in implementation using directed edges which need to be acknowledged in message passing. Consider a case of paper classification where GNNs leverage features of papers cited by the paper to be classified, say p_i to improve its classification accuracy. In this case, in order to maintain train-test parity, training for p_i should leverage features of papers cited by p_i and not those that cite p_i, since they would be published after p_i, even though they may be present in the graph while training. Doing so will lead to model collapse in cases where the paper classification is performed immediately when it is published. [8,19,35] ignore this nuance while setting benchmarks for node classification using their proposed techniques, leaving a loophole for evaluating techniques tailored for timestamped graphs.

This nature of label-leakage is unique to timestamped graphs and can have a detrimental impact when ignored for critical industrial applications. Some of the applied use-cases where this acknowledgement of timestamped edges during training to maintain train-test parity is critical are:

- **User classification**: After the test sample was observed, evaluating user classification models offline that leverage user-user and user-transaction relationships can lead to poor GNN model performance in deployment settings.
- **Fraud Detection**: Using messages passed along edges with fraudulent entities for predicting abuse of another entity leads to improved fraud detection [15,29]. Incorrect training would leverage fraud label of the node for message passing along edges, even though the label was observed much later.

Business-critical ML applications require point-in-time training of models, and GNN solutions to such applications typically build on top of timestamped graph to ensure messages from relationships occurring in future do not leak label information while training. Not doing this can lead to breakdown of model in production, as labels determining future information will no longer be available. While

[21,24], explored information leakage to adversarial attacks and [17] aimed at avoiding leakage to node-embeddings in link prediction task, the non-permissible leakage in node classification remains unexplored. To this end, we propose and showcase the following:

- **Time-Relaxed Directed-GNN (TRD-GNN)** : A novel and efficient sampling strategy that acts as a label-leakage-proof approximation of a time-directed graph to undirected graphs, which leads to improved model performance. We publicly released our code here[1].
- **Qualitative Analysis**: Our qualitative analysis shows how TRD-GNN is able to improve over baseline by providing additional same class information.

2   Time Relaxed Directed - GNN

We will refer to a directed graph, $G = (V, E)$ where V are the nodes of the graph, and E are directed edges between nodes, such that $u \rightarrow v$, implies u is connected to v and creation timestamp t of u is less than that of v ($t[u] < t[v]$).

2.1   Graph Neural Networks

Underneath the success of GNNs is the message passing scheme, which aggregates and transforms the representation vectors of neighbors for each node recursively. This message passing is performed over the edges of the sub-graph, which is obtained by recursively sampling the neighborhood of the node to be classified. Formally, let $\mathbf{h}_l(v)$ be the representation of v in the l-th layer of GNN, and then we can update the representation in the $(l + 1)$-th layer.

$$\mathbf{h}_{l+1}(v) = \sigma(\mathbf{W}_l \mathbf{AGG}_{u \in \mathcal{N}(v)}(\mathbf{MSG}(\mathbf{h}_l(v); \mathbf{h}_l(u)))) \tag{1}$$

In Eq. 1, $\mathbf{h}_0(v) = X_v$; σ is activation function; $\mathbf{W}_l$ are trainable parameters in the l-th layer; $\mathbf{AGG}$ denotes aggregator function and $\mathbf{MSG}$ denotes the message passing function. GCN [16], GraphSAGE [13], GAT [32], GATv2 [3] etc. follow the same framework in Eq. 1.

2.2   Proposed: TRD-GNN

In a typically directed graph, the destination node u, for which the prediction is being made, collects messages from its direct/indirect neighbors but is unaware of other destination nodes that these neighbors point to. Consider an example of directed subgraph as in Fig 1, u, v_1, v_2, v_3 occur with their respective timestamps being $t[u], t[v_1], t[v_2], t[v_3]$ such that $t[u] < t[v_1] < t[v_2] < t[v_3]$. Here, v_2 is unaware of v_1 during message passing. This issue is unique to directed graphs, and one option to bypass this would be to relax the directions in the directed graph during message passing [7]. In directed graphs, if directions are governed

---

[1] https://github.com/amazon-science/trd-gnn

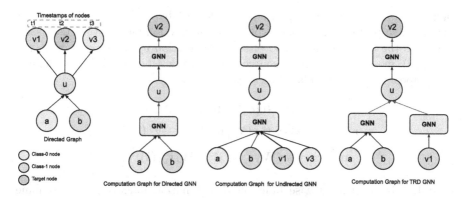

Fig. 1. Figure depicts the computational graphs created by different GNN models (D-GNN, UD-GNN and TRD-GNN) for the given directed graph. It showcases how TRD-GNN acknowledges timestamp ordered-edges by adding new signal from v1 (since t1 < t2) and eliminating signal from v3 (since t2 < t3), leading to improved performance.

by time, relaxing this directional constraint might lead to label leakage leading to model collapse in production. From here on, we refer to the node's timestamp as its creation timestamp.

To this end, we propose relaxing edge directions for only those nodes placed just before the node on whom the forward pass is done. Following the example, while inferring for v_2, the current setup only samples u. In the case, directions are relaxed without taking in the creation timestamps of nodes, information from v_3 will flow to v_2 via message passing, causing label leakage as v_3 is placed after v_2. However, in our proposed approach, we relax only that sub-graph which contains nodes with timestamps same as or before that of the node being inferred. In our example, since we are inferring for v_2, so for that we relax edges from u to v_1 as v_1 is placed before v_2.

In a vanilla directed graph based message passing, neighborhood for a node u, while accumulating messages for prediction for v, henceforth referred to as *forward* neighborhood (Eq. 2), is defined as:

$$\mathcal{N}^f(u) = \{w | (w \to u) \in G\} \tag{2}$$

To enable time-relaxed aggregation, we define *backward* neighborhood, $\mathcal{N}_v^b(u)$ in Eq. 3, of a node u, having creation timestamp less than node v, as:

$$\mathcal{N}_v^b(u) = \{w | (u \to w) \in G, t[w] < t[v]\} \tag{3}$$

The backward neighborhood of u is now dependent on the node v, to whom the message will be further passed on to. The effective neighborhood of u becomes, $\mathcal{N}_v(u) = \mathcal{N}^f(u) \cup \mathcal{N}_v^b(u)$. $\mathcal{N}_v^b(u)$ ensures that messages are accumulated only from those nodes with creation timestamp earlier than v. This differs from leveraging an undirected graph where no time-based filtering would be done while sampling neighbors. This makes our model susceptible to label leakage leading to poor generalization performance when deployed in production for real-time use-cases.

Just as the total neighborhood of u for destination v is the union of $\mathcal{N}^f(u)$ and $\mathcal{N}^b_v(u)$, message, m^l_{uv}, from source node u to destination node v is defined as a composition of accumulated messages.

$$
\begin{aligned}
\mathbf{r}^l_{uv}(b) &= \mathbf{AGG}(\{\sigma(\mathbf{W}^l_b \mathbf{h}^0_w) | w \in \mathcal{N}^b_v(u)\}) \\
\mathbf{r}^l_{uv}(f) &= \mathbf{AGG}(\{\sigma(\mathbf{W}^l_f \mathbf{h}^{l-1}_w) | w \in \mathcal{N}^f(u)\}) \\
\mathbf{m}^l_{uv} &= \gamma \left(\sigma(\mathbf{W}^l_f \mathbf{r}^l_{uv}(f)), \sigma(\mathbf{W}^l_b \mathbf{r}^l_{uv}(b)) \right)
\end{aligned}
\tag{4}
$$

In Eq. 4, γ is an element-wise function (Combination function) that combine messages to pass from both forward and backward neighbors to create the final message. Once the source node message $\mathbf{m}^l_{uv}$ is computed, it will be passed to the appropriate destination node v. The procedure to get final node embedding is explained in Eqs. 4–5.

$$
\mathbf{h}^l_v = \sigma(\mathbf{W}^l_v \mathbf{AGG}(\{\sigma(\mathbf{W}^l_m \mathbf{m}^l_{uv})\} | u \in \mathcal{N}^f(v)))
\tag{5}
$$

The layer and the proposed sampling strategy is agnostic to aggregation strategy, be it based on GCN [16], GAT [32], etc. The methodology is extensible to all graph structures as the aggregation strategy can be designed for homogeneous/heterogeneous graphs.

2.3 Adaptation for Mini-Batch Training

Ensuring timestamp-based filtering before message passing setup in directed graphs is non-trivial. For large graphs, we operate in an inductive GraphSAGE [13] batch training setting where for a sample of nodes, the neighborhood is sampled, and messages are aggregated using DGL's [34] message passing API. In the case of TRD-GNN, message $\mathbf{m}^l_{uv}$ can only aggregate messages from nodes w, such that creation time $t[w]$ is earlier than $t[v]$, to ensure that model does not expect future information while inferring for nodes in a real-time production setup. Thus, while sampling a sub-graph from node v, we need to prune edges from nodes with inward edges from neighbors of v based on their creation time. If the nodes in the batch are randomly sampled, then minimum creation time of nodes in the batch can be used to perform the pruning and obtain $\mathcal{N}^b_v(u)$. However, this can result in a sparse subgraph if the difference between the minimum and maximum creation time in the set is large, starving the node with the latest creation time of any meaningful information from $\mathcal{N}^b_v(u)$.

To alleviate this issue, we tweak the sampling strategy of nodes by ensuring that all nodes in a batch are from the same creation-time grain. For example, in a citation network [14], research papers published in the same year or the same conference in a year can be considered together for sampling in a batch. Within the time grain, nodes are sampled randomly. The pseudocode for the proposed mini-batch time relax sampling is present in Algorithm 1.

Algorithm 1: Mini-batch TR Sampling & Embedding computation

Input   : Graph G, Set of unique node creation time in graph T, Set of all
             nodes V

Output: Updated Embedding for nodes in V

for *(t in T)* **do**

    $V_t = \{v \mid v \in V, t[v] = t\}$

    $\mathcal{N}^f(V_t) \leftarrow \emptyset$;   /* Create set of source neighbors */

    for *(v in V_t)* **do**

         $\mathcal{N}^f(V_t) \leftarrow \mathcal{N}^f(V_t) \cup \mathcal{N}^f(v)$;   /* Refer to Eq. 2 */

    $w = \text{random}(V_t)$;   /* Take a random node */

    $\mathcal{N}^f \leftarrow \emptyset$;   /* Create set of forward neighbors */

    for *(u in $\mathcal{N}^f(V_t)$)* **do**

         $\mathcal{N}^f \leftarrow \mathcal{N}^f \cup \mathcal{N}^f(u)$;   /* Refer to Eq. 2 */

    $\mathcal{N}^b \leftarrow \emptyset$;   /* Create set of backward neighbors */

    for *(u in $\mathcal{N}^f(V_t)$)* **do**

         $\mathcal{N}^b \leftarrow \mathcal{N}^b \cup \mathcal{N}_w^b(u)$;   /* Refer to Eq. 3 */

    $G_t = G(V_t, \mathcal{N}^f(V_t), \mathcal{N}^f, \mathcal{N}^b)$;   /* Extract subgraph with given node sets */

    Update embedding for nodes in V_t using Graph G_t via some message passing API

    ;   /* Refer Eq. 4 - 5 for updating */

2.4   Comparison with Temporal Graph Networks

Temporal Graph Networks (TGNs) [27] provide a generic framework for deep learning on dynamic graphs represented as sequences of timed events. Our formulation differs from TGNs in two critical aspects. First, TGNs operate on graphs where the same node's state changes with time due to changes in relationships with other entities over time. Thus the edges are timestamped, but nodes are not, and only edges are added with time. Our formulation presents the case where both nodes and edges are timestamped, and once the node is added, its incoming edges do not change with time. The node does not get updated and only new nodes keep getting added to the graph.

Second, TGNs require multiple graphs for training that depend upon the number of different timestamps present in the data. This increases storage requirement, and I/O cost in training such models. Since, in TGNs, there is different graph for different timestamps, it is not susceptible to label leakage. TRD-GNN can be viewed as an efficient alternative for TGNs, working with the assumptions that the incremental nodes and edges added from t to $t + 1$ are small as compared to the overall graph and the node/edge features do not change from t to $t + 1$. This nature of timestamped graphs makes the TGN approach less scalable, as is evident from the datasets used in [27] have 10K nodes. In TRD-GNN, this is achieved by having a single graph which is a union of the graph over all timestamps. Directed nature of graph and careful sampling

Table 1. Statistics of both public citation and proprietary e-commerce datasets used for experimentation. The proprietary dataset is heavily subsampled and is used to show the efficacy of TRD-GNN on a real-world use-case.

Dataset	#Nodes-Types	#Nodes	#Edges-Types	#Edges	#Classes
ogbn-arxiv	1	169,343	1	1,166,243	40
ogbn-mag	4	1,939,743	4	21,111,007	349
prop. e-commerce	1	$\sim$ 40M	7	$\sim$ 1B	2

in TRD-GNN ensures that the undirected nature of graph in Temporal GNN is mimic-ed, though much more efficient in terms of storage and I/O cost, allowing it to scale to large graphs with 10M nodes.

3   Experiments

To investigate the effectiveness of the proposed TRD-GNN model, we critically evaluate its impact along three experiment questions: **EQ1)** How does TRD-GNN perform against the vanilla-directed and undirected sampling? **EQ2)** What information does the additional sampling bring in for node classification? **EQ3)** What is the additional computation overhead for the incremental performance of TRD-GNN?

3.1   Experimental Setup

Datasets. For a fair comparison with our approach, we benchmark our approach on two open-source datasets and one proprietary e-commerce abuse detection dataset. The open-source time-based citation dataset includes ogbn-arxiv and ogbn-mag [14]. ogbn-arxiv is a homogeneous timestamped directed citation graph, while ogbn-mag is a heterogeneous graph. The statistics of both graphs are present in Table 1, and both are transductive. Both these datasets are directed in nature by virtue of their time so for fair evaluation, we used both directed and undirected graphs to benchmark our approach.

E-commerce Dataset: We also report results on an e-commerce dataset where we used anonymized and subsampled data from an e-commerce website. The data is subsampled in a manner so as to be non-reflective of actual production traffic. The data consists of 10M users (100K positive) and around 1B interactions aggregated over an arbitrary 2-month window, akin to [9]. Labels indicate nodes marked for abusive behavior. The dataset summary is present in Table 1. We used an inductive setup for its evaluation.

Implementation Details. We implemented the experiments using DGL [34] and PyTorch [25]. We use the same hyperparameters and experimental setting as mentioned here[2]. We use mini-batches of size 1024 during model training and inference. All the experiments were conducted on a 64-core machine with 488 GB RAM running Linux. We used Weights & Biases [1] to track our experiments. We use `cross-entropy` loss for training all our node classification experiments.

Baselines and TRD-GNN. Given the GNN layer-type agnostic nature of our proposed method, we leverage different GNN layers like GCN [16], GAT [32] and recently proposed GATv2 [3] as a backbone for ogbn-arxiv dataset. Since obgn-mag is a heterogeneous graph, we use RGCN [28] as a backbone for this dataset.

Further, we introduce notations by defining GNN variants (e.g., GCN), which are trained on different graphs in the following way:

- **UD-GCN**: a GNN model trained on an undirected graph with GCN layer.
- **D-GCN**: another GNN model trained on the directed graph with GCN layer.
- **TRD-GCN**: a TRD-GNN model which uses GCN as an underlying model and is trained on a directed graph.

GAT, GATv2 and RGCN counterparts of these models can be defined similarly. For the e-commerce dataset, we used GraphSAGE [13] model as the GNN layer and D-GNN, UD-GNN and TRD-GNN sampling schemes. All models are evaluated in two different settings:

- **Offline Evaluation**: This setting is similar to a transductive setting where the structure of the test graph remains fixed and is similar to the kind of evaluations that have been done in prior research. This setting works on the undirected graph ignoring the timestamp of the edge creation.
- **Online Evaluation**: This setting is similar to the inductive setting where nodes and edges are added with time in a streaming format and the evaluation is based on the information available at that timestamp. This evaluation mimics the real-life deployment setup where new data is observed, ingested and predictions are made in real-time.

3.2 Performance Comparison (EQ1)

The objective of TRD-GNN is to maximize the information propagation in directed graphs by reversing edges contextual to the node to be classified while not violating the strict time-directed nature of information flow, i.e. avoiding any form of label leakage. Thus, TRD-GNN lies in the middle of the spectrum, where on one end is the vanilla directed graph where information flows based on edge direction, and the other is the undirected graph where no direction based on time is regarded in message passing. Thus, we expect the incremental information brought in by TRD-GNN to improve over the directed GNN and not

---

[2] https://github.com/dmlc/dgl/tree/master/examples/pytorch/ogb/ogbn-arxiv.

break down in online inference as in the case of undirected graph training. In this sub-section, we compare the performance of three GNN training methodologies using different GNN layers for three different datasets. TRD-GNN operates within the guard rails to avoid extra leakage while still expanding its scope of nodes that participate in message passing, thus resulting in higher performance.

On the ogbn-arxiv citation dataset, Table 2 showcases the improvement of TRD-GNN performance over the directed and undirected message passing graph for GCN, GAT and GATv2 backbones, respectively, in online or production setting. This shows the efficacy of our approach independent of backbone architecture and can be easily adapted with other architectures. Furthermore, the huge drop in the performance of the undirected graph-based model (UD-GNN) by 5% on average (from offline evaluation to online evaluation) is because of the consumption of future information during the training of the GNN model. TRD-GNN prevents this, resulting in higher performance.

It is noteworthy that in the case of TRD-GNN, the model performance during offline evaluation is close enough to model performance during online evaluation. This advantage makes the model consistent and reliable to use in production setting. Furthermore, TRD-GNN shows consistent improvement in both inductive and transductive setting.

For the ogbn-mag heterogeneous dataset, Table 2 also reports 1.1% performance improvement from TRD-GNN. Considering the heterogeneous nature of

Table 2. Table reports the results in terms of accuracy (in %) on the homogeneous ogbn-arxiv citation dataset and the heterogeneous ogbn-mag dataset with multiple GNN backbones. TRD-GNN improves over D-GNN by 1–2% and over UD-GNN by 2–5% during online evaluation. The performance of TRD-GNN is close to offline evaluation making the approach reliable. The results in red show huge drop in the performance of UD-GNN model in case of online evaluation, making it unfit for production setting.

Dataset used	GNN-Layer Type	Offline Evaluation	Online Evaluation
ogbn-arxiv	D-GCN	70.06	69.73
	UD-GCN	72.32	67.07
	TRD-GCN	**71.37**	**71.87**
	D-GATv2	68.72	68.89
	UD-GATv2	71.30	67.02
	TRD-GATv2	**69.54**	**69.26**
	D-GAT	69.50	68.88
	UD-GAT	72.01	66.08
	TRD-GAT	**69.74**	**69.82**
ogbn-mag	D-RGCN	36.81	32.73
	UD-RGCN	38.32	28.80
	TRD-RGCN	**37.21**	**33.83**

Table 3. TRD-GNN as a leakage-resistant approximation of undirected graph in time-directed setting on proprietary e-commerce dataset. Results are relative and absolute numbers are not presented due to confidentiality.

GNN-layer Type	Offline Evaluation	OnlineEvaluation
D-GNN	2.48x	2.12x
UD-GNN	2.98x	1.00x
TRD-GNN	**2.62x**	**2.22x**

the graph in account, TRD-GNN still outperforms baseline results. Additionally, this also demonstrate the ability of TRD-GNN to adapt to different graph datasets irrespective of their nature.

We attempted to compare our performance with TGN [27] baseline leveraging the open source code available here[3]. However, the performance on ogbn-arxiv dataset was abysmal (~7% validation accuracy), as the loss did not reduce much after 3 epochs. We tried multiple hyperparameter settings but was not able to get on-par performance and hence, chose not to include it in the main table. This is due to the fact that it requires a self-supervised pre-trained model for its dynamic node classification module. Given the high runtime of TGN as reported in Table 8, running a hyperparameter sweep was very under-productive.

On the e-commerce dataset, Table 3 showcases that TRD-GNN improves performance (in terms of AUC-PR) on top of the directed message passing graph (D-GNN) while ensuring that the time-relaxation does not cause model collapse in the online setting as compared to undirected message passing (UD-GNN). The poor performance of the undirected graph-based model during online evaluation is primarily due to the consumption of future information while training the GNN model. This is a common pitfall where GNN models can show impressive performance in offline setup due to leakages of information from the future.

3.3 Analysis of TRD-GNN (EQ2)

We attempt to empirically explain the different components of TRD-GNN that help improve model performance for different GNN layers. For this, we explore the incremental homophily added by TRD sampling and the impact of the choice of combination function (γ). We perform both the analysis on the ogbn-arxiv dataset, along with a quantitative analysis on the proprietary e-commerce dataset.

Characteristics of incremental neighbors: To characterise the nature of orders where incremental edges passed on messages resulting in improved prediction, we investigate orders where the new model predicted the opposite class as compared to baseline and look at key patterns that turn up in incremental TRD neighbors on ogbn-arxiv dataset. Given that TRD-GNN acts as a deployable bridge between GNN trained on undirected graphs and those trained on

---

[3] https://github.com/twitter-research/tgn.

Table 4. % of Nodes whose performance improved due to additional same class neighbors in the backward neighborhood.

% increase in homophilous signal	% of Nodes
$\geq 10\%$	99.5%
$\geq 20\%$	96.8%
$\geq 30\%$	92.2%
$\geq 40\%$	87.0%
$\geq 50\%$	85.6%

directed graphs, we hypothesize incremental homophilous messages from time-relaxed neighbors to contribute to the improved performance. Multiple research studies [6,20] have shown that GNN performance is well correlated with the level of homophily in the node's neighborhood.

Table 5. Quantitative characterisation of orders where TRD-GNN improved classification prediction over baseline

(a) False Negatives to True Positives

Type of Signal		% Nodes
Existing Signal	TRD Signal	
✓	✓	19%
✗	✓	25%
✓	✗	18%
✗	✗	36%

(b) False Positives to True Negatives

Type of Signal		% Nodes
Existing Signal	TRD Signal	
< 10	< 10	21.6%
< 10	≥10	32.6%
10–15	< 10	8.9%
10–15	≥ 10	30.6%
> 15	> 10	5.7%

Table 4 showcases how the nodes with additional homophilous (i.e. same class) neighbors from the backward neighborhood are the ones that help improve the model's performance. As expected, the incremental homophilous neighborhood is a key contributor in the correct classification of nodes, which was not tapped in by directed graph based sampling.

Further, for 56% of the incremental true-positives by TRD-GNN, the backward neighborhood had 100% of nodes from the same class as the node to be classified. This highlights the importance of including backward neighbor's connections during message passing.

Quantitative Evaluation on Proprietary e-commerce Dataset: Table 5a characterises the samples which moved from low-score False Negatives to True Positives. We consider those positive samples with baseline score ≤ 0.5 and TRD-GNN score ≥ 0.5. *Existing Signal* refers to cases where the base node was

Table 6. Ablation on combination function (γ) used for aggregation of forward and backward neighbors, showing the incremental benefit of backward neighbors

Forward Neighbors	Backward Neighbors	Combination Function (γ)	Accuracy (in %)
✓		-	69.73
✓	✓	SUM	70.93
✓	✓	CONCAT	70.73
✓	✓	MAX	**71.87**
✓	✓	MIN	70.57

connected to same-class nodes, and *TRD Signal* refers to cases where one of $\mathcal{N}_v^b$ is also from same-class nodes. We observe that, in 44% cases, the TRD Signal added homophily signal (same class neighbor), leading to correct classification.

For the other case of False Positives to True Negatives, we define *Existing Signal* and *TRD Signal* in terms of the number of neighbors sampled for message passing by each methodology. We divide both signals into buckets and in Table 5b observe that for 63.2% orders, TRD-Signal increased homophilous neighborhood by at-least 10 neighbors.

Impact of Choice of Combination Function: Table 6 highlights the consistent effect of adding backward neighbors along with forward neighbors in message passing in terms of incremental performance. We, however, observe that different choice of γ has an impact on the overall performance of the GNN. This showcases that the nature of neighbors added by TRD sampling is different from those already available. These were missed in the directed graph sampling.

3.4   Time Comparison (EQ3)

In this section, we compare the time taken by an epoch (including training and inference time) with D-GATv2, UD-GATv2 and TRD-GATv2 layers on ogbn-arxiv dataset and report the time in Table 7. For fair measurement, all the experiments were conducted on a 64-core machine with 488 GB RAM running Linux operating system. Table 7 draws out the fact that the average running time per epoch for TRD-GATv2 is slightly higher than that of D-GATv2 in the online setting while performing much better compared to UD-GATv2. However, during offline evaluation, TRD-GATv2 takes lesser time than both D-GATv2 and UD-GATv2. This is because TRD-GATv2 eliminates all the unused neighbors from the forward neighbors and keep only necessary neighbors in the backward neighbors set while maintaining the sanctity of timestamped nature of the graph.

Further, Table 8 brings the observation that TRD-GNN approach is much more efficient when compared to TGN. In addition, TGN requires two extra steps before finally training for the downstream node classification task, which themselves are quite expensive. Even after discounting any data preprocessing and self-supervised training on the graph, TRD-GNN is efficient, taking less than half the time required for TGN.

Table 7. Average time taken (in seconds per epoch) to run each experiment on ogbn-arxiv dataset.

Type	Offline (UD)	Online (D)
D-GATv2	874 s/epoch	128 s/epoch
UD-GATv2	2359 s s/epoch	818 s/epoch
TRD-GATv2	598 s/epoch	322 s/epoch

Table 8. Run-time comparison of TRD-GATv2 with TGN on ogbn-arxiv dataset, reported in seconds per epoch.

Steps/Module	TRD-GATv2	TGN
Data-preprocessing	-	73 s
Self-Supervised Training	-	22476 s/epoch
Node classification Training	322 s/epoch	684 s/epoch

4   Related Work

GNNs have become ubiquitous to graph based modeling which is a very common use-case in industry. The increased penetration of e-commerce and social networks in human life has increased the scale at which GNNs will be employed. GNNs today power different business critical solutions that involve user/item recommendations [26,39], feed ranking [11], fraud detection [15,29] etc. As discussed in previous sections and demonstrated by experiments section, time-stamp acknowledging training of GNNs is critical for reliable deployable GNN solution. We deep dive into the literature on directed and timestamped graphs beyond TGNs as discussion on them is presented in Sect. 2.4.

In [4,5], the authors work on a strongly connected graph by constructing a directed laplacian using random walks to leverage the GCN for directed graphs. [31] used the PageRank based constructed laplacian in [4,5] in place of the random walk based one. These methods are not popular among the industry due to scale challenges involved in deployment. TGNs [12,23,27] are based on the dynamism that allows node-wise events where new nodes are added or removed as time progresses and edge-incidents where edges between nodes are either added or removed from the graph. One key aspect of TGN was the use of RNN-based memory component that updated the representation of nodes as newer information comes in with every passing time. While the approach may seem generic, it is hard to fine-tune and take considerably longer than static graph methods. [40] proposed time-aware GNN for aligning entities between the temporally evolving knowledge graphs. They embed entities, relations and timestamps of different KGs into a single space and use GNNs to learn entity representations in the same space. They present a time-aware attention mechanism that assigns different weights to different nodes with orthogonal transformation matrices computed from embeddings of the relevant relations and timestamps in a neighborhood.

Spatio-temporal graph learning [22, 41] is an efficient structure to characterize the relations between different nodes in a specified spatial and temporal range. They assume a fixed number of nodes while training and testing and expect changes only in the adjacency of the graph. These assumptions of fixed number of nodes make it difficult to extend such approaches to practical industry setting where nodes are continuously added to the system as new users join the service.

From a production deployment perspective, there is no work, to the best of our knowledge, that discusses directionality in timestamped graph and creates any solution around it. A large majority of GNN solutions proposed for fraud/abuse detection [30, 36, 38] do not incorporate the timestamped aspect of observation. Some, however, work on directed graphs [33, 37] where the direction is an outcome of the underlying data generation process. Our work is the first that discusses the breakdown of undirected graphs in online production setting and proposes a simple yet effective bridge between timestamp based directed and undirected graphs, resulting in improved performance. We also create benchmark performances on public datasets that can be leveraged by community to further improve along this direction.

5   Application to Industry

Industry specific online ML models are time critical in nature. Therefore, it is necessary to make sure that online performance matches the expected offline performance. GNNs are particularly susceptible to label-leakage in industry applications. TRD-GNN provides a simple yet effective mechanism to make the graph partially undirected and eliminate label leakage with consistency in training and evaluation. We showcase that, with TRD-GNN (Algorithm 1), offline performance of model is in-line with online performance making the GNN model training process reliable, thus delivering the business objective of abuse detection (Table 3). We deployed the TRD-GNN in an offline manner where the graph is updated with new nodes and edges at a fixed cadence, and the GNN model is used for identifying abuse.

6   Conclusion

We propose an effective relaxation technique (TRD-GNN) for timestamped directed graphs that is resilient to label-leakage and helps improve classification performance, making the model reliable to use in production. The idea of TRD-GNN is agnostic to GNN layer and type of graph and is extensible to all GNN-based tasks where time direction is critical, which is typical to industry production use-cases. The relaxation lies on a spectrum with directed sampling on one end and undirected on the other. We also present an analysis which answers why TRD-GNN is able to improve over vanilla-directed and undirected GNNs.

Ethical Statement. Our work is a generic framework to boost the performance of timestamped directed graph neural network. This work applies to GNNs generally and any graph-structured data specifically. Its ethical impacts (including positive and negative) depend on the specific domain of the data. We conduct our experiments on publicly available datasets and real-world datasets in compliance with fair-use clauses.

References

1. Biewald, L.: Experiment tracking with weights and biases, 2020. Software available from wandb. com **2**(5), 233 (2020)
2. Breuer, A., Eilat, R., Weinsberg, U.: Friend or faux: Graph-based early detection of fake accounts on social networks. In: Proceedings of The Web Conference 2020, pp. 1287–1297. WWW '20, Association for Computing Machinery, New York, NY, USA (2020). https://doi.org/10.1145/3366423.3380204
3. Brody, S., Alon, U., Yahav, E.: How attentive are graph attention networks? In: International Conference on Learning Representations (2022). www.openreview.net/forum?id=F72ximsx7C1
4. Cao, D., Li, J., Ma, H., Tomizuka, M.: Spectral temporal graph neural network for trajectory prediction. In: 2021 IEEE International Conference on Robotics and Automation (ICRA), pp. 1839–1845. IEEE (2021)
5. Cao, D., et al.: Spectral temporal graph neural network for multivariate time-series forecasting. Adv. Neural. Inf. Process. Syst. **33**, 17766–17778 (2020)
6. Chanpuriya, S., Musco, C.: Simplified graph convolution with heterophily (2022)
7. Chen, M., et al.: Scalable graph neural networks via bidirectional propagation. CoRR abs/2010.15421 (2020). arxiv.org/abs/2010.15421
8. Chien, E., et al.: Node feature extraction by self-supervised multi-scale neighborhood prediction. In: International Conference on Learning Representations (ICLR) (2022)
9. Cui, L., et al.: Allie: Active learning on large-scale imbalanced graphs. In: The Web Conference 2022 (2022). www.amazon.science/publications/allie-active-learning-on-large-scale-imbalanced-graphs
10. Dhawan, S., Gangireddy, S.C.R., Kumar, S., Chakraborty, T.: Spotting collective behaviour of online frauds in customer reviews. In: Proceedings of the 28th International Joint Conference on Artificial Intelligence, pp. 245–251. IJCAI'19, AAAI Press (2019)
11. Fan, W., et al.: A graph neural network framework for social recommendations. IEEE Trans. Knowl. Data Eng. **34**(5), 2033–2047 (2020)
12. Fan, Y., Ju, M., Zhang, C., Ye, Y.: Heterogeneous temporal graph neural network. In: Proceedings of the 2022 SIAM International Conference on Data Mining (SDM), pp. 657–665. SIAM (2022)
13. Hamilton, W.L., Ying, R., Leskovec, J.: Inductive representation learning on large graphs (2017). arxiv.org/abs/1706.02216
14. Hu, W., et al.: Open graph benchmark: Datasets for machine learning on graphs. arXiv:2005.00687 (2020)
15. Huang, M., et al.: Auc-oriented graph neural network for fraud detection. In: Proceedings of the ACM Web Conference 2022. pp. 1311–1321 (2022). WWW '22, Association for Computing Machinery, New York, NY, USA (2022). https://doi.org/10.1145/3485447.3512178

16. Kipf, T.N., Welling, M.: Semi-supervised classification with graph convolutional networks. In: International Conference on Learning Representations (ICLR) (2017)

17. Kumar, I., Hu, Y., Zhang, Y.: Eflec: Efficient feature-leakage correction in gnn based recommendation systems. In: Proceedings of the 45th International ACM SIGIR Conference on Research and Development in Information Retrieval, pp. 1885–1889. SIGIR '22, Association for Computing Machinery, New York, NY, USA (2022). https://doi.org/10.1145/3477495.3531770,https://doi.org/10.1145/3477495.3531770

18. Li, A., Qin, Z., Liu, R., Yang, Y., Li, D.: Spam review detection with graph convolutional networks, pp. 2703–2711 (2019). https://doi.org/10.1145/3357384.3357820

19. Li, G., Müller, M., Ghanem, B., Koltun, V.: Training graph neural networks with 1000 layers. In: International Conference on Machine Learning (ICML) (2021)

20. Li, X., et al.: Finding global homophily in graph neural networks when meeting heterophily (2022)

21. Liao, P., et al.: Information obfuscation of graph neural networks. In: Meila, M., Zhang, T. (eds.) Proceedings of the 38th International Conference on Machine Learning. Proceedings of Machine Learning Research, vol. 139, pp. 6600–6610. PMLR (18–24 Jul 2021). www.proceedings.mlr.press/v139/liao21a.html

22. Liu, X., Liang, Y., Zheng, Y., Hooi, B., Zimmermann, R.: Spatio-temporal graph contrastive learning. arXiv:2108.11873 (2021)

23. Min, S., Gao, Z., Peng, J., Wang, L., Qin, K., Fang, B.: Stgsn-a spatial-temporal graph neural network framework for time-evolving social networks. Knowl.-Based Syst. **214**, 106746 (2021)

24. Olatunji, I., Nejdl, W., Khosla, M.: Membership inference attack on graph neural networks, pp. 11–20 (2021). https://doi.org/10.1109/TPSISA52974.2021.00002

25. Paszke, A., et al.: Pytorch: An imperative style, high-performance deep learning library. In: Advances in Neural Information Processing Systems 32, pp. 8024–8035. Curran Associates, Inc. (2019). www.papers.neurips.cc/paper/9015-pytorch-an-imperative-style-high-performance-deep-learning-library.pdf

26. Qiu, R., Li, J., Huang, Z., Yin, H.: Rethinking the item order in session-based recommendation with graph neural networks. In: Proceedings of the 28th ACM international conference on information and knowledge management, pp. 579–588 (2019)

27. Rossi, E., Chamberlain, B., Frasca, F., Eynard, D., Monti, F., Bronstein, M.: Temporal graph networks for deep learning on dynamic graphs (2020). arxiv.org/abs/2006.10637

28. Schlichtkrull, M., Kipf, T.N., Bloem, P., van den Berg, R., Titov, I., Welling, M.: Modeling relational data with graph convolutional networks (2017)

29. Shi, F., Cao, Y., Shang, Y., Zhou, Y., Zhou, C., Wu, J.: H2-fdetector: A gnn-based fraud detector with homophilic and heterophilic connections. In: Proceedings of the ACM Web Conference 2022, pp. 1486–1494. WWW '22, Association for Computing Machinery, New York, NY, USA (2022). https://doi.org/10.1145/3485447.3512195

30. Tang, J., Li, J., Gao, Z., Li, J.: Rethinking graph neural networks for anomaly detection. In: International Conference on Machine Learning (2022)

31. Tong, Z., Liang, Y., Sun, C., Li, X., Rosenblum, D., Lim, A.: Digraph inception convolutional networks. Adv. Neural. Inf. Process. Syst. **33**, 17907–17918 (2020)

32. Veličković, P., Cucurull, G., Casanova, A., Romero, A., Liò, P., Bengio, Y.: Graph attention networks (2018)

33. Wang, B., Gong, N.Z., Fu, H.: Gang: Detecting fraudulent users in online social networks via guilt-by-association on directed graphs. In: 2017 IEEE International

Conference on Data Mining (ICDM), pp. 465–474 (2017). https://doi.org/10.1109/ICDM.2017.56

34. Wang, M., et al.: Deep graph library: A graph-centric, highly-performant package for graph neural networks. arXiv:1909.01315 (2019)
35. Wang, Y., Jin, J., Zhang, W., Yu, Y., Zhang, Z., Wipf, D.: Bag of tricks for node classification with graph neural networks. arXiv:2103.13355 (2021)
36. Wang, Y., et al.: Label information enhanced fraud detection against low homophily in graphs. arXiv:2302.10407 (2023)
37. Wu, J., et al.: Dedgat: Dual embedding of directed graph attention networks for detecting financial risk (2023). https://doi.org/10.48550/arXiv. arXiv:2303.03933
38. Wu, Q., Chen, Y., Yang, C., Yan, J.: Energy-based out-of-distribution detection for graph neural networks. In: The Eleventh International Conference on Learning Representations (2023). www.openreview.net/forum?id=zoz7Ze4STUL
39. Wu, S., Tang, Y., Zhu, Y., Wang, L., Xie, X., Tan, T.: Session-based recommendation with graph neural networks. In: Proceedings of the AAAI Conference on Artificial Intelligence, vol. 33, pp. 346–353 (2019)
40. Xu, C., Su, F., Lehmann, J.: Time-aware graph neural network for entity alignment between temporal knowledge graphs. In: Proceedings of the 2021 Conference on Empirical Methods in Natural Language Processing, pp. 8999–9010. Association for Computational Linguistics, Online and Punta Cana, Dominican Republic (Nov 2021). https://doi.org/10.18653/v1/2021.emnlp-main.709, www.aclanthology.org/2021.emnlp-main.709
41. Yu, B., Yin, H., Zhu, Z.: Spatio-temporal graph convolutional networks: A deep learning framework for traffic forecasting. arXiv preprint arXiv:1709.04875 (2017)

Semi-Supervised Social Bot Detection with Initial Residual Relation Attention Networks

Ming Zhou, Wenzheng Feng, Yifan Zhu, Dan Zhang, Yuxiao Dong, and Jie Tang$^{(\boxtimes)}$

Tsinghua University, Beijing, China
zhou-m19@mails.tsinghua.edu.cn, {zhuyifan,yuxiaod, jietang}@tsinghua.edu.cn, zd18@tsinghua.org.cn

Abstract. Social bot detection is a challenging task and receives extensive attention in social security. Previous researches for this task often assume the labeled samples are abundant, which neglects the fact that labels of social bots are usually hard to derive from the real world. Meanwhile, graph neural networks (GNNs) have recently been applied to bot detection. Whereas most GNNs are based on the homophily assumption, where nodes of the same type are more likely to connect to each other. So methods relying on these two assumptions will degrade while encountering graphs with heterophily or lack of labeled data. To solve these challenges above, we analyze human-bot networks and propose SIRAN, which combines *relation attention* with *initial residual connection* to reduce and prevent the noise aggregated from neighbors to improve the capability of distinguishing different kinds of nodes on social graphs with heterophily. Then we use a consistency loss to boost the detection performance of the model for limited annotated data. Extensive experiments on two publicly available and independent social bot detection datasets illustrate SIRAN achieves state-of-the-art performance. Finally, further studies demonstrate the effectiveness of our model as well. We have deployed SIRAN online: https://botdetection.aminer.cn/robotmain.

Keywords: social networks · social bot detection · heterophily-aware attention · semi-supervised learning

1 Introduction

Social bots are social media accounts controlled by automated programs. As social media has become a primary source of information for people around the world, malicious bots have posed a great threat to social security by spreading false information and inciting public opinion warfare on social media platforms [9]. For example, social bots are used to spread misinformation during the COVID-19 pandemic [18,31] and mislead about the reality of the Russia-Ukraine war [19,29,33]. In recent years, bots are also believed to have a significant impact on the outcomes of national events. For example, during the 2010 midterm election in the United States, social bots were used to attack candidates and spread

G. De Francisci Morales et al. (Eds.): ECML PKDD 2023, LNAI 14174, pp. 207–224, 2023.
https://doi.org/10.1007/978-3-031-43427-3_13

fake news to disrupt the election. Similar activities also appeared in the 2016 US presidential election, the 2018 US midterm election [40], and the 2017 French presidential election [15].

In view of the above risks, effective and reliable social bot detection methods are urgently needed to detect social bots' activities in advance and further protect social security. Traditional social bot detection methods generally adopt feature engineering. Specifically, they rely on statistical methods and expert knowledge to construct specific features based on user profile information and tweet content. However, these approaches suffer from limited scalability. Because of the excellent performance achieved by deep learning, based on it, more and more social bot detection tools have been proposed. For example, long short-term memory (LSTM) is adopted to extract the temporal features of user social activities [28] and model both tweet content and metadata to detect bots [23]. Recently, graph neural networks (GNNs) are used to leverage the relationship information of social networks and achieve leading performance [2].

However, there are still two challenges. Challenge 1 is that **traditional GNNs-based social bot detection methods cannot effectively deal with heterophilous graphs**. Through our research, we have found that there is strong heterophily in social graphs, where different kinds of nodes are more likely to establish connections with each other, which is known as "opposites attract". Most GNNs that are under the implicit homophily assumption will degrade when they encounter social graphs with low homophily [26]. Challenge 2 is that **labeled data usually cannot meet the training needs of traditional supervised bot detection models**. As social bots evolve [9], more and more labeled data are needed, so supervised GNNs-based algorithms also suffer from the high cost of data annotation, which leads to the lack of labeled data.

In this work, we propose **S**emi-supervised **I**nitial residual **R**elation **A**ttetion Networks (**SIRAN**). For challenge 1, to capture heterophilous information in social graphs, SIRAN adopts heterophily-aware relation attention and initial residual connection. Specifically, for each node, it can aggregate neighbor information and reduce the impact of heterophilous noise. For challenge 2, SIRAN leverages a confidence-aware consistency loss [13,14] to train the model to achieve high accuracy using only a small amount of annotated data. Finally, the consistency loss adopted by SIRAN can also be used to generalize other social bot detection models to reduce the dependence on labeled data for semi-supervised learning.

The main contributions are summarized as follows:

- We analyze social human-bot data and find significant differences in the distribution of social relationships between humans and bots as well as strong heterophily in social human-bot graphs. These findings give guidance to further study on social bot detection.
- We propose SIRAN, a semi-supervised bot detection framework, which adopts relation attention and initial residual connection to reduce heterophilous noise and thus enhance node representations.

– Extensive experiments on two public and independent datasets demonstrate that SIRAN consistently outperforms state-of-the-art baselines. Further ablation and robustness studies are presented to prove the effectiveness of SIRAN's every component and its robustness.

2 Related Work

Social Bot Detection. Social bot detection methods can be divided into three categories: crowdsourcing, machine learning, and graph-based approaches [3]. Earlier works adopt crowdsourcing and traditional machine learning based on feature engineering. For example, Chu et al. [7] study a set of large-scale social accounts' information, including tweeting behavior, tweet content, and account properties to detect social bots. Because of the quick evolution of social bots, feature engineering and crowdsourcing cannot effectively detect bots due to poor scalability and high costs. Recently, graph neural networks achieve state-of-the-art performance in the bot detection field. Ali Alhosseini et al. [2] propose a detection model based on graph convolutional networks (GCN). Feng et al. [10] propose a model based on heterogeneous information. However, such supervised graph-based methods require a large amount of labeled data for training, which cannot be satisfied because of the high cost of data annotation.

Graph Neural Networks. Graph neural networks (GNNs) have received extensive attention in recent years by exploiting relational information to gain performance improvements on many graph-based tasks, such as fraud detection and anomaly detection in social networks. Recent studies [37,42] have classified the existing GNNs into the following categories: recurrent graph neural networks [16,24], convolutional graph neural networks [5,36], graph autoencoders [4,32], and spatial-temporal graph neural networks [17,39]. Most of them follow the homophilous assumption that nodes of the same or similar category are more likely to establish links to each other. However, this assumption is broken in heterophilous networks, which degrades the performance of GNNs, such as human-bot networks and e-commerce networks [41].

Graph Neural Networks with Heterophily. Recently, heterophilous graph learning is becoming an important research direction of GNNs, because heterophily is widespread in the real world, and graph learning with heterophily is still an open and challenging problem. One of the current effective methods is the inter-layer combination method, which adopts layer-wise operations to improve the representation ability of GNNs under low homophily [41]. JKNet adopts this mechanism firstly, which uses jump connections and an adaptive aggregation technique to gain stronger representation learning capability [38]. H2GCN concatenates the node representations of each layer with those of all previous layers together [43]. However, such heterophilous methods do not consider the influence of different types of edges on representation learning and the problem of insufficient labeled data, which makes them unable to meet the needs of social bot detection.

3   Problem Definition and Preliminaries

3.1   Problem Definition

We represent a social network as a directed graph $\mathcal{G} = (\mathcal{V}, \mathcal{E})$, where $\mathcal{V} = \{v_1, v_2, ..., v_{|\mathcal{V}|}\}$ is the set of nodes (i.e., the set of social user accounts) and $\mathcal{E} \in |\mathcal{V}| \times |\mathcal{V}|$ represents the set of edges, which indicates relationships between nodes. The neighbor set of node v is represented as $\mathcal{N}(v) = \{u : (v, u) \in \mathcal{E}\}$. We use $\mathbf{A}$ to represent the adjacency matrix and $\mathbf{D}$ to represent the diagonal degree matrix. Let $\mathbf{X} \in \mathbb{R}^{|\mathcal{V}| \times d}$ represent node features, where the i-th row $\mathbf{X}_i \in \mathbb{R}^F$ is the feature vector of node i with F denoting its dimension.

The goal of social bot detection is to detect whether a given social account is a social bot, which can be viewed as a node binary classification problem. More formally, let $\mathbf{Y} \in \{0, 1\}^{|\mathcal{V}|}$ denote the nodes' label vector, where $\mathbf{Y}_i \in \{0, 1\}$ represents the ground truth of node i. If it is a social bot, then $\mathbf{Y}_i = 1$, otherwise $\mathbf{Y}_i = 0$. Then our goal is to learn a function:

$$f : (\mathcal{G}, \mathbf{X}) \longrightarrow \mathbf{Y}. \tag{1}$$

3.2   Homophily and Heterophily

Homophily. In a homophilous graph, nodes with similar features or the same class labels are tend to be linked together. For instance, a study usually cites papers from the same or similar research area [8].

Heterophily. In a heterophilous graph, nodes with dissimilar features and different class labels are tend to be linked together. For example, bots are more likely to follow humans rather than other bots in social networks.

Measure of Heterophily and Homophily. The homophility of a graph can be measured by the edge homophily ratio [43]: $\mathcal{H}_{edge} = \frac{|\{(v,u):(v,u)\in\mathcal{E} \wedge y_v = y_u\}|}{|\mathcal{E}|}$, where $\mathcal{H}_{edge}$ is the proportion of edges connecting nodes of the same category and $\mathcal{H}_{edge} \in [0, 1]$. $\mathcal{H}_{edge} \to 0$ means the graph has strong heterophily.

4   Human-Bot Network Analysis

In this section, we give a detailed analysis of the human-bot graph (HBG) built by TwiBot-20 [12] as a typical social bot scenario. Particularly, we focus on social relationship analysis (RA).

Social Influence Analysis. Influence plays an important role in people's social activities, because users may change their social activities due to the influence of friends [20, 35]. In the social network built by TwiBot-20, We carry out the following analysis to further explore the distribution of human and bot influence.

We use the PageRank algorithm [27] to quantify the social influence of humans and bots. Based on social accounts' pagerank value, we can rank all nodes in HBG and analyze the proportion of humans and bots under different influence rankings (represented by pagerank rankings). The results of the analysis are shown in Fig. 1a. It is obvious that there is a significant difference between humans' and bots' distribution under different influence rankings. Specifically, the proportion of the humans is higher than the bots' in the top 10%–70% and the proportion of bots is higher than humans' in the top 80%–100%.

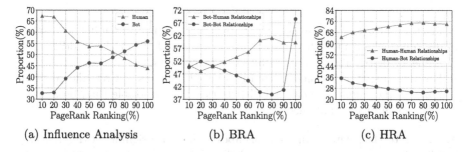

(a) Influence Analysis   (b) BRA   (c) HRA

Fig. 1. Social relationship analysis. Y-axis: the proportion of humans and bots; X-axis: social accounts' influence ranking (i.e., pagerank). (a) Humans' and bots' influence comparison; (b) Bots' relationship analysis (BRA); (c) Humans' relationship analysis (HRA).

Overall Relationship Analysis of Humans and Bots. In social networks, bots spread misinformation through interactions between users, so social interaction information is very important for detection models to distinguish between humans and bots. We summarize the interaction information between humans and bots to obtain Table 1. And from it, we find out that bots like to follow humans more than to follow bots themselves (i.e., heterophily). However, humans prefer to follow humans that have the same category as themselves (i.e., homophily). Besides, from the "Total" column in Table 1, it can be observed that bots tend to construct more interactive relationships than humans. So the heterophily of HBG is mainly contributed by bots. Furthermore, through quantitative analysis, the edge homophily ratio $\mathcal{H}_{edge} = 0.5316$ (see Sect. 3.2), which confirms the above observation, i.e., there is strong heterophily in HBG.

Table 1. Humans' and bots' interactive statistics

Category	Bot[b]	Human[b]	Total
Bot[a]	4182(40.64%)	**6109(59.36%)**	**10291(62.09%)**
Human[a]	1627(25.90%)	**4655(74.10%)**	6282(37.91%)

[a]The category of the source node.
[b]The category of the destination node.

Relationship Analysis of Humans and Bots w.r.t. Pagerank. In order to further explore the differences between humans' and bots' relational distribution, we conduct a detailed analysis of their relational distribution with respect to social influence. Let the influence ranking (represented by pagecrank ranking) be the horizontal axis, and the vertical axis be the proportion of different social relationships, we can get a visual description of the analysis results, which is as follows:

- From Fig. 1b, we can observe that bots at both ends of the influence ranking distribution are more likely to follow bots, and bots in the middle of the influence distribution are more likely to follow humans.
- For humans, it is learned from Fig. 1c that humans always like to follow humans and humans' relational distribution is more stable than bots' under different influence rankings.

According to the relationship analysis above, there are significant differences in the distribution of social relationships between humans and bots, which inspires us to introduce relationship information into our model to improve the ability to detect bots.

5   SIRAN

5.1   Overview of SIRAN

In order to solve the problem of model performance degradation caused by heterophilous noise and lack of annotated data, we propose **S**emi-supervised **I**nitial residual **R**elation **A**ttetion **N**etworks (**SIRAN**), which is illustrated in Fig. 2.

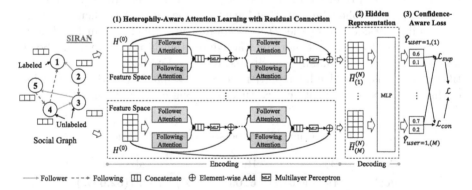

Fig. 2. Illustration of SIRAN. (1) SIRAN adopts relation attention and initial residual connection to get node representations, and it also uses dropout to get diversity. (2) Through N SIRAN layers, an enhanced feature matrix $\overline{\mathbf{H}}_{(m)}^{(N)}$ can be obtained, where $m \in [1, M]$ indicates the m-th channel. (3) At last, the enhanced feature matrix is processed by MLP to conduct semi-supervised training, which leverages the confidence-aware consistency loss $\mathcal{L}_{con}$ and the supervised loss $\mathcal{L}_{sup}$.

5.2 Heterophily-Aware Attention Mechanism

In order to make full use of social relationship information, we use a heterophily-aware relation attention mechanism to fuse relationship information into node representations to improve the ability to distinguish between bots and humans.

Although the social network could be considered as a bidirectional or unidirectional graph with two self-reciprocal kinds of relationships, following and follower, the semantic impact of such two relations may be largely different. Thus the proposed model regards the social network as a heterogeneous graph with two different types of relations. For node i, we can learn two different node representations based on following and follower relationships. Here we adopt a multi-head attention mechanism in the model to obtain node representations. Specifically, given the n-th layer node features $\mathbf{H}^{(n)} = \left\{ \mathbf{h}_1^{(n)}, \mathbf{h}_2^{(n)}, \ldots, \mathbf{h}_{|\mathcal{V}|}^{(n)} \right\}$. Query, key, and value from node j to node i for the h-th attention head in the n-th layer with r_f relationship (where $f = 1$ is the following relationship and $f = 2$ is the follower relationship.) can be calculated respectively:

$$\mathbf{q}_{h,i}^{(n),r_f} = \mathbf{W}_{h,q}^{(n),r_f} \mathbf{h}_i^{(n)} + b_{h,q}^{(n),r_f},$$

$$\mathbf{k}_{h,j}^{(n),r_f} = \mathbf{W}_{h,k}^{(n),r_f} \mathbf{h}_j^{(n)} + b_{h,k}^{(n),r_f},$$

$$\mathbf{v}_{h,j}^{(n),r_f} = \mathbf{W}_{h,v}^{(n),r_f} \mathbf{h}_j^{(n)} + b_{h,v}^{(n),r_f}, \tag{2}$$

where $\mathbf{W}$ and b are learnable parameters. Then the attention weight calculated by Eq. (3) describes the degree of concern from node i to node j, which models the heterophily in social graphs.

$$\alpha_{h,ij}^{(n),r_f} = \frac{\left\langle \mathbf{q}_{h,i}^{(n),r_f}, \mathbf{k}_{h,j}^{(n),r_f} \right\rangle}{\sum_{u \in \mathcal{N}(i)} \left\langle \mathbf{q}_{h,i}^{(n),r_f}, \mathbf{k}_{h,u}^{(n),r_f} \right\rangle}, \tag{3}$$

where $\langle \mathbf{q}, \mathbf{k} \rangle = exp\left(\frac{\mathbf{q}^T \mathbf{k}}{\sqrt{d}} \right)$ and d is the hidden dimension of each head. $\mathcal{N}(i)$ denotes the set of neighbors of node i. After having q, k, and v, we can aggregate the information from node j to node i to get the n-th layer's node feature matrix:

$$\mathbf{z}_i^{(n),r_f} = \frac{1}{H} \sum_{h=0}^{H-1} \left(\sum_{j \in \mathcal{N}(i)} \alpha_{h,ij}^{(n),r_f} \mathbf{v}_{h,j}^{(n),r_f} \right), \tag{4}$$

where H is the number of attention heads. $\mathbf{z}_i^{(n),r_f}$ indicates the node i's representation in the n-th layer with relationship r_f. Then, for fusing relationship information, we concatenate $\mathbf{z}_i^{(n),r_1}$ and $\mathbf{z}_i^{(n),r_2}$ and put it into MLP to obtain $\mathbf{z}_i^{(n)} = \text{MLP}\left(\left[\mathbf{z}_i^{(n),r_1} \| \mathbf{z}_i^{(n),r_2} \right], \Theta \right)$, where Θ is the hyperparameter in MLP. Finally, by iterating all nodes in the graph, $\mathbf{Z}^{(n)} = \left\{ \mathbf{z}_i^{(n)} : 1 \leqslant i \leqslant |\mathcal{V}| \right\}$ can be obtained. The overall flow is shown in Fig. 3.

Based on the above, the n-th ($n \geq 1$) layer of relation attention module can be defined as

$$\mathbf{H}^{(n+1)} = \sigma\left(\widetilde{\mathbf{P}}\mathbf{Z}^{(n)}\mathbf{W}^{(n)}\right), \tag{5}$$

where σ is the activation function, here we use the ReLU operation. $\widetilde{\mathbf{P}} = \widetilde{\mathbf{D}}^{-\frac{1}{2}}\widetilde{\mathbf{A}}\widetilde{\mathbf{D}}^{-\frac{1}{2}} = (\mathbf{D}+\mathbf{I})^{-\frac{1}{2}}(\mathbf{A}+\mathbf{I})(\mathbf{D}+\mathbf{I})^{-\frac{1}{2}}$ is the convolved signal matrix with the *renormalization trick* [22]. $\mathbf{W}^{(n)}$ is the weight matrix.

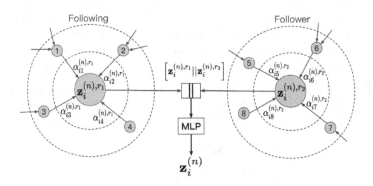

Fig. 3. Illustration of heterophily-aware relation attention. (1) We aggregate respectively following neighbors' and follower neighbors' features into node i with the attention mechanism. $\mathbf{z}_i^{(n),r_1}$ (following relationship) and $\mathbf{z}_i^{(n),r_2}$ (follower relationship) can be obtained, where n denotes the n-th layer. (2) Then, concatenate $\mathbf{z}_i^{(n),r_1}$ and $\mathbf{z}_i^{(n),r_2}$ to get $\left[\mathbf{z}_i^{(n),r_1} \| \mathbf{z}_i^{(n),r_2}\right]$. (3) Finally, put $\left[\mathbf{z}_i^{(n),r_1} \| \mathbf{z}_i^{(n),r_2}\right]$ into MLP to fuse following and follower information.

5.3   Initial Residual Connection

For the heterophilous graphs, with GNNs going deeper, more information from different kinds of nodes is aggregated into node representations. That makes models difficult to distinguish different kinds of nodes. So, reducing the noise from different kinds of neighbors is the key point to improving the representation learning ability. Initial residual connection is an effective method to reduce the noise aggregated from neighbors. Meanwhile, it can enhance node representations by ensuring that the initial node features, which contain important prior information, act on node representations at each layer. Through importing the initial residual connection, the n-th layer of SIRAN can be defined as

$$\mathbf{H}^{(n+1)} = \sigma\left(\left((1-\alpha_n)\widetilde{\mathbf{P}}\mathbf{Z}^{(n)} + \alpha_n\mathbf{H}^{(0)}\right)\mathbf{W}^{(n)}\right), \tag{6}$$

where $\alpha_n \in [0,1]$ is a hyperparameter. $\mathbf{H}^{(0)}$ is the initial representation, which may not be equal to the input feature matrix $\mathbf{X}$, e.g., if the dimension of $\mathbf{X}$ is large, MLP can be used to reduce its dimension and get a low-dimensional $\mathbf{H}^{(0)}$.

5.4   Training and Optimization

SIRAN adopts both **confidence-aware consistency loss** and **supervised loss** to optimize model parameters in the training stage.

Supervised Loss. The supervised loss is defined as the average cross entropy of labeled nodes sampled over M channels:

$$\mathcal{L}_{sup} = -\frac{1}{|\mathbf{L}| M} \sum_{i \in L} \sum_{m=1}^{M} \mathbf{Y}_i \log\left(\hat{\mathbf{Y}}_{i,(m)}\right), \tag{7}$$

where $\mathbf{L}$ represents the set of labeled training data. $\mathbf{Y}_i$ is the ground-truth label of node i in the labeled data set. $\hat{\mathbf{Y}}_{i,(m)} \in \mathbb{R}^C, m \in [1, M]$ denotes the probability vector of the predicted category of node i on the m-th channel.

Confidence-Aware Consistency Loss. Due to the long-standing challenge of lack of annotated data, we employ the confidence-aware consistency loss for semi-supervised learning to solve it. Specifically, according to the procedure in Fig. 2, the enhanced features are obtained through M-channel representation learning with dropout. Then we feed them into MLP to get outputs: $\hat{\mathbf{Y}}_{i,(m)} = \text{MLP}\left(\mathbf{h}_{i,(m)}, \boldsymbol{\Theta}\right)$, where $\boldsymbol{\Theta}$ is the hyperparameter in MLP, and $\mathbf{h}_{i,(m)}$ is the enhanced feature matrix of node i on the m-th channel.

For semi-supervised learning, we sample unlabeled data and denote it as $\mathbf{U}$. The center of the distribution of $\mathbf{U}$ can be obtained by averaging the predicted probabilities over M channels, i.e., $\overline{\mathbf{Y}}_i = \frac{1}{M} \sum_{m=1}^{M} \hat{\mathbf{Y}}_{i,(m)}$. The confidence-aware consistency loss is defined as:

$$\mathcal{L}_{con} = \frac{1}{|\mathbf{U}| M} \sum_{i \in \mathbf{U}} \delta\left(\overline{\mathbf{Y}}_i\right) \sum_{m=1}^{M} D\left(\overline{\mathbf{Y}}_i, \hat{\mathbf{Y}}_{i,(m)}\right), \tag{8}$$

where $\mathbf{U}$ is the set of unlabeled data. $\delta\left(\overline{\mathbf{Y}}_i\right) = \begin{cases} 1, & max\left(\overline{\mathbf{Y}}_i\right) \geqslant \gamma \\ 0, & otherwise \end{cases}, \gamma \in [0,1]$ is the confidence threshold. $D\left(\overline{\mathbf{Y}}_i, \hat{\mathbf{Y}}_{i,(m)}\right)$ is a distance function that measures the distribution discrepancy between $\overline{\mathbf{Y}}_i$ and $\hat{\mathbf{Y}}_{i,(m)}$. Here the distance function mainly includes $L2$ norm and KL divergence.

From Eq. (8), $\mathcal{L}_{con}$ only considers **highly confident** unlabeled data selected by the threshold γ in the training stage, it is the reason of being called confidence-aware consistency loss. It can filter out the training noise brought by heterophily to improve the prediction performance.

Finally, by combining $\mathcal{L}_{sup}$ with $\mathcal{L}_{con}$, we can obtain the final loss defined as $\mathcal{L} = \mathcal{L}_{sup} + \lambda(t) \mathcal{L}_{con}$, where $\lambda(t)$ is a decay function which decreases in the range of $[0, \lambda_{max}]$, and usually $\lambda_{max} = 2$. The whole training procedure is shown in Algorithm 1.

6   Experiments

6.1   Experimental Setup

Table 2. Dataset statistics.

Dataset	Nodes	Human	Bot	Edges	Classes	$\mathcal{H}_{edge}$
TwiBot-20	229,580	5,237	6,589	33,716,171	2	0.5316
TwiBot-22	162,865	81,433	81,432	151,841	2	0.4963

Datasets. To verify the performance of the model in the heterophilous graphs, We evaluate our model on two public and independent datasets, namely TwiBot-20 [12] and TwiBot-22 [11], whose statistics are shown in Table 2. For TwiBot-20, we follow the same data setup as in [12]. For TwiBot-22, we randomly sample $81,432$ bots as negative examples and $81,433$ humans as positive examples to ensure that their proportions are relatively balanced, resulting in a total of $162,865$ social accounts. To ensure a fair comparative experiment, we randomly split the sampled dataset $7:2:1$ to obtain training, validation, and test sets, respectively.

Comparing Baselines. We compare SIRAN and its three variants with 9 baselines, including 4 general GNNs, 4 non-homophilous methods, and 1 bot detection method with heterogeneity. All the experiments use the same input features, including users' (1) attributes: username, location, verified, registration time, description, tweet count, listed count, follower count, following count; (2) tweet content; (3) social relationships: list of following and follower friends. The full list of baseline methods is: **Four general GNNs:** GAT [36], GCN [22], JKNet (GCNJK) [38], R-GCN [30]. **Four non-homophilous methods:** MixHop [1], LINKX [25], H2GCN [43], GPR-GNN [6]. **One heterogeneous bot detection method:** Feng et al. [10]. **Three variants of SIRAN:** (1) SIRAN+PLR (Add the previous layer's residual connection), (2) SIRANJK (Combine the jumping knowledge network with SIRAN), (3) SIRAN-CONCAT (Concatenation is used instead of matrix addition to combine the representation of each layer with the initial node features).

Implementation Details. Due to the interactive characteristics of social networks, we build the human-bot networks as directed graphs. For experimental optimization, the AdamW optimizer [21] is used with weight decay 3×10^{-5}. Learning rate is 10^{-2} and 10^{-3} on TwiBot-20 and TwiBot-22, respectively. To avoid overfitting, early stopping and Dropout [34] are used for model training. We use grid search to adjust hyperparameters of SIRAN on the validation set, and use the best configuration for prediction. Specifically, on TwiBot-20 and

---

Algorithm 1: SIRAN

---

  input : Social human-bot dataset S
  output: Optimized model parameters Θ

1 *Initialize* Θ;
2 *Preproccess S to build graph* $\mathcal{G}(\mathcal{V}, \mathcal{E})$, *relation set*
   $r_f \subseteq \mathcal{E}, f = 1\,(following)\,or\,2\,(follower)$, *feature matrix* $\mathbf{X} \in \mathbb{R}^{|\mathcal{V}| \times d}$, *labeled*
   node set $\mathbf{L}$, *unlabeled node set* $\mathbf{U}$, *ground-truth label set* $\mathbf{Y}_L \in \mathbb{R}^{|\mathbf{L}| \times C}$;
3 **Function** Pipeline($\mathcal{G}$, $\mathbf{X}$):
4 | **for** *Node i in* $\mathcal{G}$ **do**
5 | **for** $h : 0 \to H - 1$ **do**
6 | $\alpha_{h,ij}^{(n),r_f} \leftarrow$ Eq. (3)
7 | $\mathbf{z}_i^{(n),r_f}, \mathbf{z}_i^{(n)} \leftarrow$ Eq. (4)
8 | $\mathbf{Z}^{(n)} = \left\{ \mathbf{z}_i^{(n)} : 1 \leqslant i \leqslant |\mathcal{V}| \right\}$
9 | $\mathbf{H}^{(n+1)} \leftarrow$ Eq. (6)
   | // Through N layers SIRAN
10 | $\mathbf{H}^{(N)} = \left\{ \mathbf{H}^{(n)} : 0 \leqslant n \leqslant N - 1 \right\}$
11 | **return** $\mathbf{H}^{(N)}$

12
13 **while** Θ *does not converge OR* $t : 0 \to T$ **do**
14 | **for** $m : 1 \to M$ **do**
   | // Parallel M-channel processing
15 | $\mathbf{H}_{(m)}^{(N)} =$ Pipeline($\mathcal{G}$, $\mathbf{X}$)
16 | $\mathcal{L}_{sup}, \mathcal{L}_{con}, \mathcal{L} \leftarrow$ Eq. (7 - 8)
17 | $\Theta \leftarrow BackPropagate\,(Loss)$
18 **Return** Θ

TwiBot-22, the model adopts three hidden layers with 128 hidden size and 8 attention heads over three encoding channels, and the distance function and confident threshold are set to L2 norm and 0.7, respectively. The initial residual weight α is 0.5 and 0.9 on TwiBot-20 and TwiBot-22, respectively. The model configurations of other baselines follow previous works [10,25,30]. Accuracy, F1-score, and ROC-AUC are used to evaluate our model and baselines.

6.2 Overall Results

Table 3 shows the experimental results comparing SIRAN and its three variants with 9 baselines on the test set. We run each experiment 5 times with random weight initializations and report the mean values with standard deviation.

Table 3. Overall performance comparison. **Bold** and <u>underline</u> represent the best and runner-up performance, respectively.

Datasets	TwiBot-20			TwiBot-22		
Method	Accuracy	F1-Score	ROC-AUC	Accuracy	F1-Score	ROC-AUC
GAT	72.89 ± 0.88	79.13 ± 0.33	71.61 ± 1.27	59.66 ± 1.64	67.68 ± 0.15	59.51 ± 1.69
GCN	74.17 ± 0.44	79.91 ± 0.17	72.53 ± 0.57	62.16 ± 0.46	67.99 ± 0.61	62.13 ± 0.51
GCNJK	75.09 ± 0.61	80.63 ± 0.56	73.44 ± 0.46	62.96 ± 0.64	69.06 ± 0.32	62.91 ± 0.65
R-GCN	79.91 ± 0.42	83.68 ± 0.26	79.37 ± 0.69	63.63 ± 1.38	69.03 ± 0.51	63.56 ± 1.36
LINKX	76.35 ± 0.95	81.60 ± 0.23	74.26 ± 1.94	61.24 ± 0.87	67.60 ± 0.48	61.18 ± 0.93
MixHop	79.62 ± 0.46	83.35 ± 0.55	78.62 ± 0.70	62.41 ± 0.25	68.70 ± 1.44	62.40 ± 0.26
GPR-GNN	78.82 ± 0.49	82.89 ± 0.43	78.19 ± 0.52	61.63 ± 0.17	67.67 ± 0.19	61.48 ± 0.38
H2GCN	79.53 ± 0.29	83.10 ± 0.41	78.78 ± 0.31	61.65 ± 0.11	67.61 ± 0.18	61.61 ± 0.10
Feng et al.	76.13 ± 2.40	81.64 ± 0.96	73.55 ± 3.07	56.59 ± 0.16	67.49 ± 0.45	56.42 ± 0.15
SIRAN+PLR	<u>80.68 ± 0.40</u>	<u>84.03 ± 0.29</u>	<u>79.98 ± 0.47</u>	62.34 ± 1.01	69.23 ± 1.38	62.30 ± 0.99
SIRANJK	80.60 ± 0.47	83.94 ± 0.33	79.81 ± 0.57	62.95 ± 0.72	70.05 ± 0.97	62.91 ± 0.71
SIRAN-CONCAT	80.56 ± 0.61	83.85 ± 0.33	79.65 ± 0.49	<u>65.31 ± 3.40</u>	<u>71.14 ± 2.49</u>	<u>65.26 ± 3.40</u>
SIRAN(Ours)	**81.11 ± 0.51**	**84.25 ± 0.32**	**80.11 ± 0.54**	**65.67 ± 2.85**	**71.95 ± 2.04**	**65.59 ± 2.81**

Analysis and Discussion. From the test results, our model achieves state-of-the-art bot detection performance, and two of its variants also achieve the top-2 performance on the two datasets respectively.

Among the general GNNs, R-GCN is the most competitive approach. Based on GCN, it adds consideration of the influence of different types of edges on node representations, and its performance is improved. This illustrates the importance of edge category information for node representations. In contrast, our model not only adopts relation attention, but also uses initial residual to augment node representations to further improve the detection performance.

For non-homophilous models, they mainly consider reducing the impact of heterophilous noise to improve performance, e.g., MixHop mixes the representations of neighbors at different distances to reduce heterophilous noise. However, while using initial residual to reduce heterophilous noise, our model also employs relation attention and a consistency loss to further improve the detection performance in the absence of labels, which will be discussed in detail in Sect. 6.4.

For the social bot-oriented GNNs (i.e., [10]), our proposed SIRAN shows a significant improvement by 6.5%, which indicates the effectiveness of reducing heterophilous noise and label dependence in social networks with heterophily.

All the above observations prove that our model can effectively detect social bots by employing relation attention and reducing heterophilous noise.

6.3   Ablation Study

We conduct ablation studies on TwiBot-20 and TwiBot-22 to demonstrate the effectiveness of each component of SIRAN.

- SIRAN-withoutIR: Remove initial residual connection.
- SIRAN-PLR: Replace the initial residual with the previous layer residual.

- SIRAN-GCN: Replace transformer with GCN to verify the effectiveness of the attention mechanism.
- SIRAN-GAT: Replace transformer with GAT in the relation attention module to compare the performance difference between transformer's and GAT's attention mechanisms.
- SIRAN-withoutSR: Remove the separation of relationships (follower and following) from the attention module.
- SIRAN-withoutCL: Remove the confidence-aware consistency loss.

Table 4. F1-score of ablation experiments.

Ablation Settings	TwiBot-20	TwiBot-22
SIRAN(full model)	**84.25 ± 0.32**	**71.95 ± 2.04**
SIRAN-withoutIR	83.46 ± 0.46	67.09 ± 1.58
SIRAN-PLR	83.08 ± 0.28	67.81 ± 0.05
SIRAN-GCN	83.72 ± 0.49	70.73 ± 2.63
SIRAN-GAT	84.14 ± 0.26	71.76 ± 2.53
SIRAN-withoutSR	84.20 ± 0.21	68.34 ± 1.66
SIRAN-withoutCL	84.15 ± 0.72	68.81 ± 0.78

Table 4 shows the experimental results of the ablation study on the test set, from which we can get the following observations:

(1) Removing or replacing any component makes SIRAN degrade with comparing to the full model, so it can be concluded that each component of the model makes a contribution to the effectiveness of SIRAN.

(2) From SIRAN-withoutIR, we observe that removing the initial residual connection makes the performance drop more heavily than that of the relation attention and consistency loss. Besides, from SIRAN-PLR, replacing the initial residual with the previous layer residual also degrades the performance of the model, which is attributed to the heterophilous noise from the previous layer. So the initial residual plays a more important role.

(3) From SIRAN-GCN, we find that removing the attention module with GCN makes the model's performance degrade, and from SIRAN-GAT, for a different attention mechanism, the performance improvement of GAT's attention is less than that of the Transformer's attention.

(4) From SIRAN-withoutSR and SIRAN-withoutCL, we observe that the performance degradation of the model on TwiBot-22 (which has stronger heterophily) is larger than that on TwiBot-20, which further illustrates their important role in reducing the heterophilous noise.

6.4   Robustness Study

Due to the evolution of bots and the high cost of data annotation, the challenge of lack of annotated data would degrade the performance of most bot detection

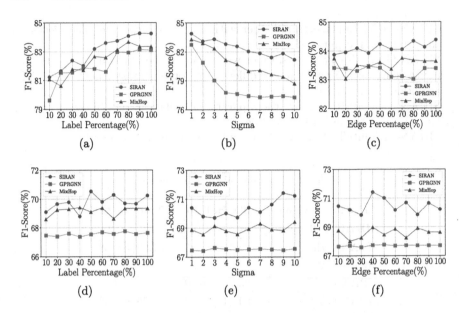

Fig. 4. Robustness experiments. (a) Label robustness, (b) feature robustness, and (c) edge robustness experiments are on TwiBot-20. (d) Label robustness, (e) feature robustness, and (f) edge robustness experiments are on TwiBot-22.

methods that rely on the quality and quantity of annotated data. In the following, we conduct robustness experiments on TwiBot-20 and TwiBot-22 to verify the robustness of our model.

Label Robustness Experiments. First, some labels in the training set are randomly masked, and the experimental results on the test set are shown in Fig. 4a and d. **Feature robustness experiments.** Second, we randomly add White Gaussian Noise (WGN, $X \sim \mathcal{N}\left(\mu, \sigma^2\right)$) to node features. The power of WGN is σ^2, the experimental results are illustrated in Fig. 4b and 4e. **Edge robustness experiments.** Third, Some edges are randomly removed to demonstrate our model's robustness of relationships, and the results are shown in Fig. 4c and 4f.

Analysis and Discussion. Based on the results, we have the following discussions: (1) From the above robustness experiments, our model outperforms the baselines under all testing settings. (2) For the label robustness experiments, on TwiBot-20 with fewer labels, the performance of our model shows a continuous growth trend as the number of labels increases, while, on TwiBot-22 with more labels, that of our model increases first, and reaches the highest value with adopting 50% of labels and then levels off. The reason could be that the semi-supervised loss function used by our model can improve the performance in the absence of labels to achieve better performance with only fewer labels. (3) For the feature robustness experiments, our model is more robust to noise in features than the baselines. This is because the relation attention mechanism adaptively adjusts the weight of feature aggregation for the interference of noise so that the model has a stronger feature representation ability. (4) For the edge robustness experiments, on TwiBot-22 with stronger heterophily, as the number of edges increases, the performance of our model first decreases slightly, then grows from the point where 30% of the edges are adopted, and finally levels off. This is because more edges bring both more information and noise, the relation attention and the initial residual can adaptively reduce and prevent the heterophilous noise to make our model more robust, which is also the reason why our model is more stable than the baselines on TwiBot-20.

7   Conclusion and Future Work

In this work, we study the problem of social bot detection, which has two challenges: heterophily in social graphs and lack of labeled data. To solve the challenges mentioned above, we propose SIRAN, which combines *relation attention* with *initial residual connection* to reduce and prevent the heterophilous noise. Then we adopt a confidence-aware consistency loss to improve the model's generalization on unlabeled data for semi-supervised learning. Extensive experiments show that SIRAN consistently outperforms state-of-the-art baselines on two real-world datasets. Up to now, we have deployed SIRAN online to detect Twitter bots.

Limitations and Future Work. A limitation of SIRAN is that cross-platform bot detection is not supported, which is still a common challenge for social bot detection due to differences in data distribution between multiple platforms and limited data collection and annotation capabilities. We leave it for future work.

Acknowledgments. This work was supported by Natural Science Foundation of China (NSFC) 61836013, 61825602, 62276148, and China Postdoctoral Science Foundation (2022 M711814).

Ethics Statement. This work aims to propose a semi-supervised bot detection framework with heterophily, which will protect people from being disturbed by bots and ensure social security. We have deployed SIRAN online and it has been widely used. To the best of our knowledge, SIRAN currently ranks No.1 in Baidu (https://www.baidu.com/) and Google (https://www.google.com/) searches. However, as we know that *"A coin has two sides"*, bot creators can also use SIRAN to improve their bots' performance. To alleviate this problem, we have strengthened the authentication management of APIs.

References

1. Abu-El-Haija, S., et al.: MixHop: higher-order graph convolutional architectures via sparsified neighborhood mixing. In: International Conference on Machine Learning, pp. 21–29. PMLR (2019)
2. Ali Alhosseini, S., Bin Tareaf, R., Najafi, P., Meinel, C.: Detect me if you can: spam bot detection using inductive representation learning. In: Companion Proceedings of The 2019 World Wide Web Conference, pp. 148–153 (2019)
3. Alothali, E., Zaki, N., Mohamed, E.A., Alashwal, H.: Detecting social bots on twitter: a literature review. In: 2018 International Conference on Innovations in Information Technology (IIT), pp. 175–180. IEEE (2018)
4. Bojchevski, A., Shchur, O., Zügner, D., Günnemann, S.: NetGAN: generating graphs via random walks. In: International Conference on Machine Learning, pp. 610–619. PMLR (2018)
5. Chen, J., Ma, T., Xiao, C.: FastGCN: fast learning with graph convolutional networks via importance sampling. arXiv preprint arXiv:1801.10247 (2018)
6. Chien, E., Peng, J., Li, P., Milenkovic, O.: Adaptive universal generalized pagerank graph neural network. arXiv preprint arXiv:2006.07988 (2020)
7. Chu, Z., Gianvecchio, S., Wang, H., Jajodia, S.: Detecting automation of twitter accounts: are you a human, bot, or cyborg? IEEE Trans. Dependable Secure Comput. **9**(6), 811–824 (2012)
8. Ciotti, V., Bonaventura, M., Nicosia, V., Panzarasa, P., Latora, V.: Homophily and missing links in citation networks. EPJ Data Sci. **5**, 1–14 (2016)
9. Cresci, S.: A decade of social bot detection. Commun. ACM **63**(10), 72–83 (2020)
10. Feng, S., Tan, Z., Li, R., Luo, M.: Heterogeneity-aware twitter bot detection with relational graph transformers. arXiv preprint arXiv:2109.02927 (2021)
11. Feng, S., et al.: TwiBot-22: towards graph-based twitter bot detection. arXiv preprint arXiv:2206.04564 (2022)
12. Feng, S., Wan, H., Wang, N., Li, J., Luo, M.: TwiBot-20: a comprehensive twitter bot detection benchmark. In: Proceedings of the 30th ACM International Conference on Information & Knowledge Management, pp. 4485–4494 (2021)
13. Feng, W., et al.: Grand+: scalable graph random neural networks. arXiv preprint arXiv:2203.06389 (2022)
14. Feng, W., et al.: Graph random neural networks for semi-supervised learning on graphs. In: NeurIPS2020, pp. 22092–22103 (2020)
15. Ferrara, E.: Disinformation and social bot operations in the run up to the 2017 French presidential election. arXiv preprint arXiv:1707.00086 (2017)
16. Gallicchio, C., Micheli, A.: Graph echo state networks. In: The 2010 International Joint Conference on Neural Networks (IJCNN), pp. 1–8. IEEE (2010)
17. Guo, S., Lin, Y., Feng, N., Song, C., Wan, H.: Attention based spatial-temporal graph convolutional networks for traffic flow forecasting. In: Proceedings of the AAAI Conference on Artificial Intelligence, vol. 33, pp. 922–929 (2019)
18. Himelein-Wachowiak, M., et al.: Bots and misinformation spread on social media: implications for COVID-19. J. Med. Internet Res. **23**(5), e26933 (2021). https://doi.org/10.2196/26933. www.jmir.org/2021/5/e26933
19. Jarynowski, A.: Conflicts driven pandemic and war issues in social media via multilayer approach of German twitter (2022)
20. Kelman, H.C.: Compliance, identification, and internalization three processes of attitude change. J. Conflict Resolut. **2**(1), 51–60 (1958)

21. Kingma, D.P., Ba, J.: Adam: a method for stochastic optimization. arXiv preprint arXiv:1412.6980 (2014)
22. Kipf, T.N., Welling, M.: Semi-supervised classification with graph convolutional networks. arXiv preprint arXiv:1609.02907 (2016)
23. Kudugunta, S., Ferrara, E.: Deep neural networks for bot detection. Inf. Sci. **467**, 312–322 (2018)
24. Li, Y., Tarlow, D., Brockschmidt, M., Zemel, R.: Gated graph sequence neural networks. arXiv preprint arXiv:1511.05493 (2015)
25. Lim, D., et al.: Large scale learning on non-homophilous graphs: new benchmarks and strong simple methods. In: Advances in Neural Information Processing Systems 34 (2021)
26. McPherson, M., Smith-Lovin, L., Cook, J.M.: Birds of a feather: homophily in social networks. Ann. Rev. Sociol. **27**(1), 415–444 (2001)
27. Page, L., Brin, S., Motwani, R., Winograd, T.: The pagerank citation ranking: bringing order to the web. Tech. Rep, Stanford InfoLab (1999)
28. Ping, H., Qin, S.: A social bots detection model based on deep learning algorithm. In: 2018 IEEE 18th International Conference on Communication Technology (ICCT), pp. 1435–1439. IEEE (2018)
29. Purtill, J.: Twitter bot network amplifying Russian disinformation about Ukraine war, researcher says (2022). www.abc.net.au/news/science/2022-03-30/ukraine-war-twitter-bot-network-amplifies-russian-disinformation/100944970. Accessed 05 Feb 2023
30. Schlichtkrull, M., Kipf, T.N., Bloem, P., van den Berg, R., Titov, I., Welling, M.: Modeling relational data with graph convolutional networks. In: Gangemi, A., et al. (eds.) ESWC 2018. LNCS, vol. 10843, pp. 593–607. Springer, Cham (2018). https://doi.org/10.1007/978-3-319-93417-4_38
31. Shi, W., Liu, D., Yang, J., Zhang, J., Wen, S., Su, J.: Social bots' sentiment engagement in health emergencies: a topic-based analysis of the COVID-19 pandemic discussions on twitter. Int. J. Environ. Res. Public Health **17**(22), 8701 (2020)
32. Simonovsky, M., Komodakis, N.: GraphVAE: towards generation of small graphs using variational autoencoders. In: Kůrková, V., Manolopoulos, Y., Hammer, B., Iliadis, L., Maglogiannis, I. (eds.) ICANN 2018. LNCS, vol. 11139, pp. 412–422. Springer, Cham (2018). https://doi.org/10.1007/978-3-030-01418-6_41
33. Smart, B., Watt, J., Benedetti, S., Mitchell, L., Roughan, M.: # istandwithputin versus# istandwithukraine: the interaction of bots and humans in discussion of the Russia/Ukraine war. arXiv preprint arXiv:2208.07038 (2022)
34. Srivastava, N., Hinton, G., Krizhevsky, A., Sutskever, I., Salakhutdinov, R.: Dropout: a simple way to prevent neural networks from overfitting. J. Mach. Learn. Res. **15**(1), 1929–1958 (2014)
35. Tang, J., Sun, J., Wang, C., Yang, Z.: Social influence analysis in large-scale networks. In: Proceedings of the 15th ACM SIGKDD International Conference on Knowledge Discovery and Data Mining, pp. 807–816 (2009)
36. Veličković, P., Cucurull, G., Casanova, A., Romero, A., Lio, P., Bengio, Y.: Graph attention networks. arXiv preprint arXiv:1710.10903 (2017)
37. Wu, Z., Pan, S., Chen, F., Long, G., Zhang, C., Philip, S.Y.: A comprehensive survey on graph neural networks. IEEE Trans. Neural Netw. Learn. Syst. **32**(1), 4–24 (2020)
38. Xu, K., Li, C., Tian, Y., Sonobe, T., Kawarabayashi, K.i., Jegelka, S.: Representation learning on graphs with jumping knowledge networks. In: International Conference on Machine Learning, pp. 5453–5462. PMLR (2018)

39. Yan, S., Xiong, Y., Lin, D.: Spatial temporal graph convolutional networks for skeleton-based action recognition. In: Thirty-second AAAI Conference on Artificial Intelligence (2018)
40. Yang, K.C., Hui, P.M., Menczer, F.: Bot electioneering volume: visualizing social bot activity during elections. In: Companion Proceedings of The 2019 World Wide Web Conference, pp. 214–217 (2019)
41. Zheng, X., Liu, Y., Pan, S., Zhang, M., Jin, D., Yu, P.S.: Graph neural networks for graphs with heterophily: a survey. arXiv preprint arXiv:2202.07082 (2022)
42. Zhou, J., et al.: Graph neural networks: a review of methods and applications. AI Open **1**, 57–81 (2020)
43. Zhu, J., Yan, Y., Zhao, L., Heimann, M., Akoglu, L., Koutra, D.: Beyond homophily in graph neural networks: current limitations and effective designs. Adv. Neural. Inf. Process. Syst. **33**, 7793–7804 (2020)

Finance

On Calibration of Mathematical Finance Models by Hypernetworks

Yongxin Yang[1]([✉])[ID] and Timothy M. Hospedales[2,3][ID]

[1] Queen Mary University of London, London, UK
yongxin.yang@qmul.ac.uk
[2] University of Edinburgh, Edinburgh, Scotland
[3] Samsung AI Centre, Cambridge, UK
t.hospedales@ed.ac.uk

Abstract. The process of fitting mathematical finance (MF) models for option pricing - known as calibration - is expensive because evaluating the pricing function usually requires Monte-Carlo sampling. Inspired by the success of deep learning for simulation, we present a hypernetwork based approach to improve the efficiency of calibration by several orders of magnitude. We first introduce a proxy neural network to mimic the behaviour of a given mathematical finance model. The parameters of this proxy network are produced by a hyper-network conditioned on the parameters of the corresponding MF model. Training the hyper network with pseudo-data fits a family of proxy networks that can mimic any MF model given its parameters, and produce accurate prices. This amortises the cost of MF model fitting, which can now be performed rapidly for any asset by optimising w.r.t. the input of the hypernetwork. Our method is evaluated with S&P 500 index option data covering three million contracts over 15 years, and the empirical results show it performs very closely to the gold standard of calibrating the mathematical finance models directly, while boosting the speed of calibration by **500** times. The code is released at https://github.com/qmfin/HyperCalibration.

1 Introduction

Option pricing has been an active research area since the seminal work of Black-Scholes [6]. Several option pricing models have since been proposed and research continues to draw attention from both researchers and industry practitioners. From an academic perspective, an accurate option pricing model reveals the mechanism of financial markets, as an option essentially reflects the expectation of its underlying asset's value change over time. From a practical point of view, derivative participants demand an efficient pricing model to set prices for market making and hedging, or finding possible opportunities for trading.

The most well-known option pricing model is Black-Scholes model [6], which gives a rough estimate of European option price, with the assumption that market volatility is constant over time. Since the publication of Black-Scholes, various mathematical finance models have been proposed, e.g., Heston [14], Jump-Diffusion [31], rough Bergomi [2], and rough Heston [10].

G. De Francisci Morales et al. (Eds.): ECML PKDD 2023, LNAI 14174, pp. 227–242, 2023.
https://doi.org/10.1007/978-3-031-43427-3_14

Those more advanced methods leverage more complicated stochastic processes, so have greater potential to fit market data – through a process called *calibration*. Calibrating an option pricing model is closely related to training a supervised learning model in machine learning context. We find the optimal parameters for the pricing model, such that the model's predictions match real market prices as closely as possible.

In contrast to some simple models [6,15] that have analytical forms, many more complex models [19] have intractable integral forms, requiring approximations or numerical integration. For models such as [3,10], the approximation is too inaccurate to use in practice, so we must revert to their original forms – stochastic differential equations (SDE) and use simulation methods like Monte Carlo. This is usually not parallelizable because the path of asset prices is time dependent – we must generate the price at $t-1$ before the price at t. Therefore, while Monte Carlo simulation based methods tend to produce the best predictions, their calibration is extremely time consuming, because evaluation of the pricing function takes a very long time. This severely limits their application in the real world.

The need for fast learning of high-accuracy Monte Carlo simulation based pricing models has led to accelerated calibration becoming an important problem in option pricing. Most work has focused on improving the efficiency of the simulation itself [11,22], but some recent studies in the machine learning community use neural networks or some other universal function approximators to boost calibration by *completely bypassing* the simulation process [5,13,16]. This echoes the similar efforts in machine learning for natural science, such physics [1], chemistry [26], and astronomy [7], where simulation is fundamental.

Inspired by these works, we propose a hypernetwork based approach to amortise the time-consuming Monte Carlo simulation in calibration for option pricing. Our method has two phases: (i) We use a proxy *pricing* neural network to mimic a given mathematical finance (MF) model, and the parameters of this neural network are produced by a hypernetwork. The input space of the hypernetwork is the same as the parameter space of the MF model. The hypernetwork is trained by a set of pseudo data covering sufficient randomly generated MF model parameters. (ii) To calibrate the actual MF model for a new asset, we first optimise the input of the hypernetwork such that the generated proxy network closely approximates real market data for the asset. Then the corresponding hypernetwork inputs are transferred to instantiate the calibrated MF model.

Clearly step (i) is an up-front investment requiring Monte Carlo simulation, but it needs to be done only once. The trained hypernetwork remains effective for a long period (15-year) without retraining. Step (ii) corresponds to the actual calibration and it is many magnitudes (300–500 times) faster than the conventional methods. Therefore, our method is overall much more efficient, even taking into account the upfront cost of step (i).

The rest of this paper is organised as follows: In Section 2, we review related works for mathematical finance models, calibration methods and deep learning for simulation. In Sect. 3, we provide a self-contained introduction to options, option pricing models and calibration, and some baselines, before introducing our model in Sect. 4. In Sect. 5, we use the real market data of S&P 500 index options from 2006-01 to 2020-02 and evaluate our model in terms of efficiency and accuracy. Section. 6 concludes the paper.

2   Related Work

2.1   Mathematical Finance Models for Option Pricing

A mathematical finance model for option pricing usually starts from a stochastic differential equation (SDE) that describes how the underlying asset price moves with time. They usually have one or more parameters, corresponding to some (estimated) market information, e.g., interest rate and volatility. The most direct way to evaluate a model, for a given set of parameters, is to do simulation – generating a series of prices at by incremental (time) steps.

The generated time series is usually called a *path*, and a large number of randomly generated paths can be used for pricing. This process is highly time consuming, so many researchers seek analytical solutions of the SDE. This is possible for some models, e.g., Black-Scholes [6] and Heston [14]. However, more complex models may not have an *exact* solution in an analytical form. Instead one often finds approximate solutions [20], but even approximations may require intractable integrals, so numeric methods are needed [19,29]. For even more complicated models, approximations exist but are low accuracy, making them useless in practice. To leverage these sophisticated models [3,10,17,18], we need to revert back to the naive method – running simulations, which is very time consuming.

In this work we choose two mathematical finance models to evaluate our hypernetwork based calibration method: rough Bergomi [3] and rough Heston [10]. In contrast to more classic models, which build stochastic processes based on Brownian motion, these *rough* family models use Fractional Brownian Motion, so they can model nonsmooth price process better, which is closer to the real market.

2.2   Machine Learning Based Calibration Methods

The calibration of option pricing models has been a core problem in mathematical finance for years. Calibration is a standard optimisation problem, but it can be hard to solve because of high sensitivity to the initial value. Minor changes accumulate over time, resulting in very different final outcomes. Thus, we usually need multiple runs with different starting points to get the best parameter in practice. Therefore, the efficiency is very important. However, any optimisation inevitably needs to evaluate the pricing function. If the pricing function has built in simulation, calibration is inevitably costly.

Recently, researchers in the machine learning community proposed replace time consuming simulation with neural networks. [13] presents a neural network that maps the market data (e.g., option prices) to mathematical finance model's parameter directly. Similarly, [5,16] proposed an inverse approach. I.e., their neural network models map the MF model's parameters to the market data, such that calibration becomes optimising the *input* of a neural network model. We will detail these methods in Sect. 3.3. The main drawbacks of these is that, since the architecture of neural network is fixed, the *amount* of market data can be used (either as input or as output) is fixed as well, thus it can only explore the market under a discrete space because the neural network can only take as input a finite number of prices (corresponding to the neurons in input layer).

The idea of replacing time-consuming simulation coincides with the recent efforts of deep learning for simulation (SimDL), which gains some popularity in deep learning for natural science, including physics [1], chemistry [26], astronomy [7], meteorology [30] and robotics [25]. For example, [28] predict turbulent flow while obeying desirable physical constraints, such as conservation of mass by simulating relevance to turbulence modelling and climate modelling. [23] use neural networks to simulate light scattering by multilayer nanoparticles. [27] train learned neural network based simulators to simulate turbulent dynamics at high resolution. The methodologies in this area have been developed actively [8,9,21,24].

Our work is inspired by the success of SimDL and early attempts applying it to calibration. However, we propose to use two networks (instead of one in [5,13,16]): (i) a 'proxy' network that mimics the behaviour of a specific MF model (ii) a hypernetwork that maps the parameters of the MF model to the parameters of the proxy network that approximates it. With this architecture, our method can explore the market data in a continuous space, instead of fixed grid in [5,13,16]. In this regard the most related prior work is [4], whose network takes an augmented input space concatenating market data and MF model parameters and produces option price, and thus can also exploit continuous data. However, the design choice of concatenation is a critical flaw.

To understand this issue, consider the differing requirements of a mathematical finance pricing model's behaviour as a function of inputs strike price and time-to-maturity (K, τ); vs as a function of its own parameters θ. Price c as a function of (K, τ) should be a smooth function with low Lipschitz constant, such that small changes in inputs lead to small changes in outputs. However, price as a function of parameters may need to be a complex function with high Lipschitz constant, as different MF parameters θ define different patterns on how underlying asset price evolves over time, and result in radically different prices for some long periods (corresponding to options with large time-to-maturities), which eventually lead to significantly different pricing surfaces.

Therefore, defining a proxy pricing model on the concatenation of both, [4] requires a neural network to be small Lipschtz w.r.t. one set of inputs and large Lipschitz w.r.t. another set of inputs. It is difficult or nearly impossible to design a neural architecture that simultaneously satisfies both of these desiderata.

In contrast, our HyperCalibration can provide the desired inductive bias by using a small proxy network that is thus comparatively smooth/low Lipschitz as required. Simultaneously, we can generate the weights of this proxy network by a larger hypernetwork – thus leading to pricing that is a comparatively complex/high Lipschitz function of θ. Our experiments show that this insight and architecture are crucial for high accuracy calibration of real market data.

3 Preliminaries

We present a self-contained introduction to options, option pricing models, and calibration. Then we introduce three baseline methods, as they help to understand the design of ours.

3.1 Options

A European option is a contract that gives the holder the right, but not the obligation, to buy (call option) or to sell (put option) the underlying asset (e.g., stock) at a specified price (strike price) on a certain future date (maturity date). For example, at time $t = 0$ (i.e., today), a company's stock price is \$100, and you buy a call option with strike price \$110 and maturity date $T = 5$ (five days later).

After five days, if the company's stock price is \$120, you can exercise the option and buy the stock at the strike price \$110. In this case, selling the stock immediately, will return \$10 profit. One the other hand, if the company's stock price is below \$110, you will choose not to exercise the option, and the only loss for is the price of the option (sometimes called premium).

For the put option, one profits if the stock price is lower than the strike price on the maturity date, as you can buy the stock from the market at a lower price and sell it at the strike price.

3.2 Pricing Models

We denote the strike price as K, time-to-maturity $\tau = T - t$, and underlying asset price at time t is referred to as S_t, its current value is S_0, and option price as $c(K, \tau; S_0)$.

Black-Scholes. Here we illustrate how to use a Black-Scholes model for option pricing via simulation. The SDE of Black-Scholes model is

$$dS_t = rS_t dt + \sigma S_t dW_t \tag{1}$$

where r is the risk-free rate, usually set externally, σ is the only tunable parameter, for which we assume a certain value is given, and dW_t is Brownian motion. Its logarithmic form is,

$$d\log(S_t) = \log(S_0) + (r - \frac{1}{2}\sigma^2)t + \sigma W_t \tag{2}$$

To eliminate the effect of S_0, we set it to one $S_0 = 1.0$ as we can rescale (multiply) it back. For a small t, e.g., $t = \Delta t = 0.01$, we can generate the path of (log) prices by $s_0 = \log(S_0) = 0$ and

$$s_t = \log(S_{t\Delta t}) = s_{t-1} + (r - \frac{1}{2}\sigma^2)\Delta t + \sigma\sqrt{\Delta t}\epsilon$$

Until we arrive at s_τ. Here ϵ is a random sample from a standard Gaussian, as by definition of Brownian motion, we have $W_t = \sqrt{t}\epsilon$ and $\epsilon \sim \mathcal{N}(0, 1)$.

Assume that we have a number of s_τ from different paths, i.e.,

$$s = [s_\tau^{(1)}, s_\tau^{(2)}, \ldots, s_\tau^{(N)}] \tag{3}$$

the call option with strike price K and time-to-maturity τ can be estimated by

$$\hat{c}(K, \tau; S_0) = \exp(-r\tau)(\frac{1}{N}\sum_{i=1}^{N} S_0(\exp(s_\tau^{(i)}) - \frac{K}{S_0})_+) \tag{4}$$

That is the discounted value (by the factor $\exp(-r\tau)$) of the expectation of the payoff. For the put option with the same setting, we have

$$\hat{p}(K, \tau; S_0) = \exp(-r\tau)(\frac{1}{N}\sum_{i=1}^{N} S_0(\frac{K}{S_0} - \exp(s_\tau^{(i)}))_+) \tag{5}$$

Beyond Black-Scholes For other pricing models using a simulation based approach, the process is the same, though the process of generating $s_\tau^{(i)}$s could be much more complicated. For example, the SDE for rough Bergomi,

$$dS_t = \sigma_t S_t dZ_t$$
$$\sigma_t = \exp(X_t)$$
$$dX_t = \mu dW_t^H - \alpha(X_t - m)dt$$

where dW^H is a fractional Brownian motion with parameter H, and rough Heston SDE is

$$dS_t = S_t\sqrt{V_t}dW_t$$
$$V_t = V_0 + \frac{1}{\Gamma(\alpha)}\int_0^t (t-s)^{\alpha-1}\lambda(\theta - V_s)ds + \frac{1}{\Gamma(\alpha)}\int_0^t (t-s)^{\alpha-1}\lambda\nu\sqrt{V_s}dB_s.$$

3.3   Calibration

The concept of calibrating a mathematical finance model is similar to supervised learning, as we want to find the optimal parameter θ such that the model produced prices $\hat{c}$ matches market prices c as closely as possible. This can be formulated as

$$\min_\theta \sum_{i=1}^{M} |\hat{c}_\theta(K, \tau) - c(K, \tau)| \tag{6}$$

Here we drop the dependence for S_0 and omit put options for simplicity. To optimise Eq. 6, we inevitably need to evaluate $\hat{c}_\theta(K, \tau)$, which is slow if it contains a complicated simulation (Sect. 3.2).

Next, we will introduce three machine learning based methods to boost the optimisation. They have two steps: the first step is to train a model with some pseudo data, which is done once only, and the second step is to do the calibration with the help of trained model.

Price to Parameter. [13] First, we generate a random parameter for a mathematical finance model, e.g., θ_i. Then, we define a list of possible strike price and time-to-maturity pairs, e.g., $[(K_1, \tau_1), (K_2, \tau_2), \ldots (K_N, \tau_N)]$. Given these indices as input, we can price these options using the model θ_i, generating the corresponding prices $[c_1^{(i)}, c_2^{(i)}, \ldots, c_N^{(i)}]$ where $c_n^{(i)} = c_{\theta_i}(K_n, \tau_n)$.

This forms a pair of input (prices) and output (parameter θ), and by many of these pairs, we can train a neural network model f_ϕ by minimising

$$\min_\phi \sum_{\theta_i \in \Theta} |f_\phi([c_1^{(i)}, c_2^{(i)}, \ldots, c_N^{(i)}]) - \theta_i| \tag{7}$$

As we can see, the neural network essentially maps the prices to corresponding the mathematical finance model parameter by which would generate those prices. We can generate an arbitrarily large number of the mathematical finance model parameters and store them in Θ for training.

Once the model f_ϕ is trained, we keep it unchanged. When we need to calibrate the mathematical finance model with real market data, in the form of $[((\bar{K}_1, \bar{\tau}_1), \bar{c}_1), ((\bar{K}_2, \bar{\tau}_2), \bar{c}_2), \ldots]$, we will realise that the $(\bar{K}, \bar{\tau})$ pairs from real market would not match with our own defined (K, τ) index pairs as above, and the number of element in the vector is not necessarily the same either.

To address this problem, we first fit a surface $\mathcal{S} : (\bar{K}, \bar{\tau}) \to \bar{c}$ using the real market data, and evaluate at the (K, τ) index pairs defined by ourselves and get a vector of $[c_1, c_2, \ldots, c_N]$ where $c_i = \mathcal{S}(K_i, \tau_i)$. Finally, we get the optimal parameter θ^* for the mathematical finance model by running a forward pass with the *aligned* prices $[c_1, c_2, \ldots, c_N]$.

$$\theta^* = f_\phi([c_1, c_2, \ldots, c_N]) \tag{8}$$

Parameter to Price [5,16] With the same way of generating pseudo data, [5,16] is an inverse of [13], as it trains a model to map parameter to prices.

$$\min_\phi \sum_{\theta_i \in \Theta} |f_\phi(\theta_i) - [c_1^{(i)}, c_2^{(i)}, \ldots, c_N^{(i)}]| \tag{9}$$

As a result, we need to run the second optimisation problem when we need to calibrate for the real market data,

$$\theta^* = \underset{\theta}{\operatorname{argmin}} |f_\phi(\theta) - [c_1, c_2, \ldots, c_N]| \tag{10}$$

Note that, the input $([c_1, c_2, \ldots, c_N])$ is *not* from real market prices either, and it contains the *aligned* prices using the same procedure of fitting surface and evaluating as in [13].

Augmented-input to Price [4] The key drawback of [5,13,16] is that they have a pre-defined list of (K, τ) pairs and the list has to be fixed throughout. This implies that the model can not directly exploit the full continuous space of (pseudo-) market data. More crucially, to calibrate the real market data, the (real) market prices have to be aligned, and this introduces a new source of error.

To address this problem, [4] propose to train a neural network model on the augmented input space, where both strike price K, time-to-maturity τ, and the mathematical finance model's parameter are included, the output of the neural network corresponds to option price.

$$\min_{\phi} \sum_{K_i \in \mathcal{K}} \sum_{\tau_j \in \mathcal{T}} \sum_{\theta_k \in \Theta} |f_{\phi}([K_i, \tau_j, \theta_k]) - c_{\theta_k}(K_i, \tau_j)| \tag{11}$$

$\mathcal{K}$ and $\mathcal{T}$ are the true spaces for strike prices and time-to-maturities respectively, from which we can sample freely. Once the model f_{ϕ} is trained, we can calibrate via solving the second optimisation problem, similar to [5,16].

$$\theta^* = \arg\min_{\theta} \sum_{i=1} |f_{\phi}([\bar{K}_i, \bar{\tau}_j, \theta]) - \bar{c}_i| \tag{12}$$

Here $[((\bar{K}_1, \bar{\tau}_1), \bar{c}_1), ((\bar{K}_2, \bar{\tau}_2), \bar{c}_2), \dots]$ is the real market data, without further alignment as in [5,13,16].

4   Methodology

4.1   Hypernetwork

With all the preceding background, we present our method based on hypernetworks [12]. The pseudo-data generation is exactly the same as [4], thus we have pseudo-data triplets (K, τ, θ). Instead of concatenating them together, we use θ to generate a set of parameters for a proxy *pricing* network that takes as input (K, τ) and outputs $c_{\theta}(K, \tau)$.

More specifically, we have a hypernetwork $f_{\phi}(\theta) \rightarrow \psi$ and a pricing network $g_{\psi}(K, \tau) \rightarrow c$. The training objective for the hyper-network using pseudo data is then,

$$\min_{\phi} \sum_{K_i \in \mathcal{K}} \sum_{\tau_j \in \mathcal{T}} \sum_{\theta_k \in \Theta} |g_{\psi_k}(K_i, \tau_j) - c_{\theta_k}(K_i, \tau_j)| \quad \text{where} \quad \psi_k = f_{\phi}(\theta_k) \tag{13}$$

Once the hypernetwork f_{ϕ} is trained, we can calibrate for real market data by solving

$$\theta^* = \arg\min_{\theta} \sum_{i=1} |g_{\psi}(\bar{K}_i, \bar{\tau}_j) - \bar{c}_i| \quad \text{where} \quad \psi = f_{\phi}(\theta) \tag{14}$$

The key innovation, discussed in Sect. 2.2 is that we decouple the pricing function and the mapping from mathematical finance model parameters to pricing network parameters. As we will see in the experiments, this makes the design of g_{ψ} much easier, as it only focuses on pricing. f_{ϕ}, on the other hand, is a model to map a low-dimensional vector of MF parameters (~ 5) to a much higher dimension (thousands) of pricing model parameters. Thus it is intrinsically sensitive to the input.

Table 1. Summary of forward pass, expected output, and optimisation variable for different methods

Model	Training			Calibration		
	Forward Pass	Expected Output	Optimisation variable	Forward Pass	Expected Output	Optimisation variable
Simulation	-	-		$c_\theta(K_i, \bar\tau_i)$	$\bar c_i$	θ
P2Param [13]	$f_\phi([c_1^{(i)}, c_2^{(i)}, \ldots, c_N^{(i)}])$	θ_i	ϕ	$f_\phi([c_1, c_2, \ldots, c_N])$	-	-
Param2P [5,16]	$f_\phi(\theta_i)$	$[c_1^{(i)}, c_2^{(i)}, \ldots, c_N^{(i)}]$	ϕ	$f_\phi(\theta)$	$[c_1, c_2, \ldots, c_N]$	θ
A2P [4]	$f_\phi([K_i, \tau_j, \theta_k])$	$c_{\theta_k}(K_i, \tau_j)$	ϕ	$f_\phi([\bar K_i, \bar\tau_j, \theta])$	$\bar c_i$	θ
Ours – Pricing NN	$g_{\psi_k}(K_i, \tau_j)$	$c_{\theta_k}(K_i, \tau_j)$	–	$g_\psi(K_i, \bar\tau_i)$	$\bar c_i$	–
Ours – Hypernet	$f_\phi(\theta_k)$	ψ_k	ϕ	$f_\phi(\theta)$	ψ	θ

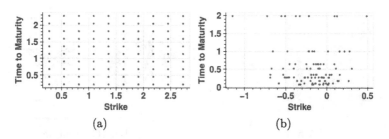

Fig. 1. Different approaches pf pseudo-data generation. (a) Artificially specified regular grid [5,13,16]. (b) Pseudo-data according to real market.

Summary. The main settings of forward pass, expected output, and optimisation variable for all the models in training and calibration steps is summarised in Table 1.

4.2 Pseudo Data Generation

A second key insight of our study is about the choice of pseudo-data used for training. For pseudo data generation, all previous studies use a grid mesh. More specifically, if we have a list of strike prices $[K_1, K_2, \ldots, K_N]$ and a list of time-to-maturities $[\tau_1, \tau_2, \ldots, \tau_M]$, they will then form a list of (K, τ) pairs by $[(K_1, \tau_1), (K_1, \tau_2), \ldots, (K_n, \tau_M), \ldots, (K_N, \tau_M)]$, as illustrated in Fig. 1(a).

However, this is significantly different from the true joint distribution of market data in practice $(\bar K, \bar \tau)$, as illustrated in Fig. 1(b). For example, the range of strike prices should increase with longer time-to-maturity, reflecting more uncertainty for farther future. This difference between synthetic and real data is a form of distribution shift, which is detrimental to performance.

Having identified this issue, we exploit sampling from the empirical distribution of strike and time-to-maturity from real market and our experiments in Sect. 5.4 show that this makes a difference, benefiting all methods including ours.

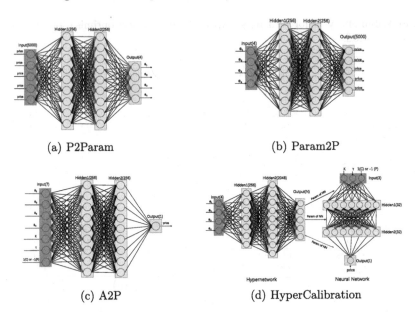

(a) P2Param   (b) Param2P

(c) A2P   (d) HyperCalibration

Fig. 2. Neural architectures for all methods in this paper

5 Experiments

We evaluated our method as well as several baselines on S&P500 index options. Since there are not real ground truths for option prices, we assume that frequently traded options, such as for the S&P500 index, reflect the true value of option contracts.

5.1 Datasets

Market Data. Options data for S&P500 index are collected from Option-Metrics in a form of end-of-day bid and asks prices, and the option price is the mid-point of bid and ask quotes. The data cover the period from 01-Mar-2006 to 28-Feb-2020, containing 3,054,496 contracts. The risk-free rates are based on the bootstrap of LIBOR rates (from OptionMetrics) and overnight index swap (OIS) rates (from Bloomberg) and then interpolated using cubic spline to match the option maturity.

Several data filters are used before training. First, we exclude all option quotes less than 0.375 as these prices may be misleading due to close to tick size. Second, we discard in-the-money put and call option quotes that are less frequently traded. Unlike many papers in literature that neglect all option contracts with time to maturity shorter than 7 d, we only omit the contracts with time to maturity shorter than 2 d, because options with a short maturity (e.g., weekly index options) are more popular now. Hence, we keep them at the cost of increasing the difficulty of training.

Pseudo-data. The pseudo-data for step-1 training of all methods, including P2Param [13], Param2P [5,16], A2Param, and our method – HyperCalibration, are generated on-the-fly while training, so all models explore the continuous space of mathematical finance model's parameter space. For P2Param and Param2P, we pre-define 5000 pairs of (K, τ) according to the market data (Fig. 1(b)), and this is significantly better than the setting in their original papers (e.g., 11×8 evenly sampled strikes and time-to-maturities like Fig. 1(a)). For A2Param and HyperCalibration, we sample (K, τ) pairs randomly from the empirical distribution of market randomly, so they can explore the continuous space of strikes and time-to-maturities as well.

5.2   Experimental Settings

Table 2. Running time and mean absolute error (MAE) for different models.

	Running time		MAE		STD of MAE	
	rough Bergomi	rough Heston	rough Bergomi	rough Heston	rough Bergomi	rough Heston
Simulation	32m25.61 s	36m16.15 s	6.19	6.05	9.06	10.95
P2Param	0.12 s	0.21 s	19.92	24.70	26.20	78.06
Param2P	6.05 s	5.84 s	10.48	16.93	39.22	31.50
A2P	6.41 s	6.12 s	14.33	11.85	23.36	24.68
HyperCalibration	6.51 s	5.93 s	6.82	8.34	12.87	14.56

Base MF Models. We conduct experiments for two mathematical finance models: rough Bergomi [3] and rough Heston [10]. For these methods, we use the accelerated simulation to minimise their disadvantages, i.e., Turbocharging for rBergomi [22] and Affine Forward Variance for rHeston [11].

Calibration Methods. We compare our HyperCalibration with four approaches to calibration, including (i) running simulation directly (gold standard), and three methods using machine learning for acceleration: P2Param, Param2P, and A2P. The neural architectures for all methods can be found in the Fig. 2. The code of HyperCalibration can be found in the material.

Evaluation Metrics. We evaluate the methods with the following metrics: (1) Running time for calibration (2) Mean absolute error (MAE) between estimated and true prices as a function of date, log moneyness and time-to-maturity. Here we emphasise that all estimated prices are produced from the mathematical finance model. After all machine learning methods find the parameters, they are sent back to the mathematical finance model for pricing, even though some of machine learning methods (Param2P, A2P, HyperCalibration) have their own proxy pricing module. Like all research work for calibration, we evaluate the in-sample performance only (i.e., training error), as interpolation/extrapolation to unseen strike and time-to-maturity (out-of-sample) is out of the scope.

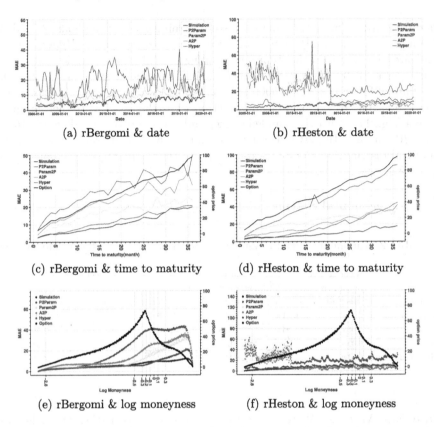

(a) rBergomi & date   (b) rHeston & date

(c) rBergomi & time to maturity   (d) rHeston & time to maturity

(e) rBergomi & log moneyness   (f) rHeston & log moneyness

Fig. 3. Comparative mean absolute error (MAE) aggregated by date, time-to-maturity, and log-moneyness

5.3 Results Analysis

Table 2 present our mains result, on mean average error (MAE) and running time. First, we can see all machine learning methods are many magnitudes faster than calibration through simulation. P2Param is the fastest, as it only needs one forward pass. For the methods that need the step-2 optimisation, the running time is very close, so using hypernetwork does not slow down the calibration time.

For accuracy, we can find our HyperCalibration is the only one that matches the MAE of gold standard simulation, while all other machine learning baselines are much worse. For a more detailed analysis, we plot daily MAE (corresponding to performance one specifically calibrated model – since we calibrate model using one day's option data) across time in Fig. 3(a)-(b). We can see only simulation and HyperCalibration lead to consistently good performance over the time of 15 years, and all other methods behave unstably at certain periods. Next, we group MAE values by time-to-maturity, and we can tell that all methods perform worse for larger time-to-maturity. This is not a surprise, as options are

Table 3. Analysis of up front model training cost and the number of accelerated calibrations after which the up front cost is successfully amortised.

	Time cost of step-1 training				The balance point			
	P2Param	Param2P	A2P	HyperCalibration	P2Param	Param2P	A2P	HyperCalibration
rough Bergomi	9h37m	12h11m	16h31m	12h21m	18	23	31	23
rough Heston	9h56m	12h28m	16h48m	12h43m	17	21	28	21

pricier for larger time-to-maturity, while HyperCalibration performs closely with simulation. Finally, we group MAE values by log-moneyness (log value of strike divides asset price) intervals. Since the distribution of log-moneyness is not uniform, we set the x-axis unevenly. We can see that the option price (black) is higher when log-moneyness is closer to zero as expected, all methods have the similar trends compared to simulation, and HyperCalibration is almost indistinguishable to simulation.

Finally, we present the the up-front time for training machine learning models and answer the question: when it becomes *economical* for using these machine learning based methods. Table 3 shows that the step-1 training time takes 9 – 16 h for all machine learning based methods. Given that the step-1 training only needs to be done once, we can calculate the balance point P, after which machine learning based methods save overall time, by $u + Ps < Ps'$, where u is the up-front time, s is the calibration time (CF. Table 2), s' is the calibration time for simulation. Then, we can see that machine learning methods become time-saving when we need to calibrate 17 – 31 or more models.

5.4   Ablation Study

First, we study the choice of pseudo data generation methods. Regular grid was used in all previous studies [5,13,16]. We introduced the idea of using market data to reduce distribution shift (Sect. 4.2). In the main preceding experiment, we also improved the baselines by generating pseudo data matching the distribution of market data. To show the impact of this, we use the data of the last month (2020-Feb) to evaluate the difference of regular grid (Fig. 1(a)) and market (Fig. 1(b)) style of generation. Table 4 shows that all methods benefit from this.

Second, Param2P, A2P, and HyperCalibration all have the step-2 optimisation. To evaluate the efficiency and stability of this, we choose the last trading day (29-Feb-2020) and run the step-2 optimisation (i.e., calibration) and record MAE over step-2 iterations (corresponding to the number of function evaluations). We can see that HyperCalibration converges much faster and it is more stable compared to other baselines (Fig. 4).

Table 4. MAE of rBergomi with different pseudo data generation methods

	Regular grid	Market data inferred
P2Param	227.80	17.83
Param2P	19.94	13.86
A2P	40.88	32.67
HyperCalibration	12.03	10.04
Direct simulation	-	8.73

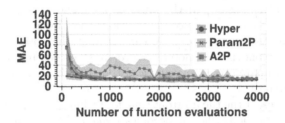

Fig. 4. Convergence rate and stability of step 2 optimisation.

6   Conclusion

We introduced a hypernetwork framework for amortised calibration of mathematical finance models. This method is inspired by the newly popular SimDL, and improves option pricing efficiency by **500 times** with tiny difference in accuracy, compared to the gold standard simulation based on rough Bergomi and rough Heston. Using real market data over **15 years** and **over three million contracts**, our model significantly, stably, and fairly defeats the other baselines from every aspect of evaluation. Besides, we are the first to note the flaw in existing practice of using regular grid pseudo-data for amortised calibration, which leads to an unnecessary distribution shift. We show that simply correcting this leads to a clear improvement for all methods, bringing amortised calibration closer to reality.

7   Ethical Implications

Our work relies on proprietary data derived from transactions of option contracts, in order to to meet the industry standard product prototyping. We have not used any personal data in this work, and we do not think this work can be used for any other applications beyond calibrating mathematical finance models for option pricing.

Disclaimer: All authors are faculty. Neither graduate students nor small animals were hurt while producing this paper.

References

1. Battaglia, P., Pascanu, R., Lai, M., Jimenez Rezende, D., Kavukcuoglu, K.: Interaction networks for learning about objects, relations and physics. In: NIPS (2016)
2. Bayer, C., Friz, P., Gatheral, J.: Pricing under rough volatility. Quant. Finance **16**(6), 887–904 (2016)
3. Bayer, C., Friz, P., Gatheral, J.: Pricing under rough volatility. Quant. Finance **16**(6), 887–904 (2016)
4. Bayer, C., Horvath, B., Muguruza, A., Stemper, B., Tomas, M.: On deep calibration of (rough) stochastic volatility models. arXiv preprint arXiv:1908.08806 (2019)
5. Benth, F.E., Detering, N., Lavagnini, S.: Accuracy of deep learning in calibrating HJM forward curves. Digital Finance **3**(3), 209–248 (2021)
6. Black, F., Scholes, M.: The pricing of options and corporate liabilities. J. Polit. Econ. **81**(3), 637–654 (1973)
7. Carrasco-Davis, R., et al.: Deep learning for image sequence classification of astronomical events. Publ. Astron. Soc. Pac. **131**(1004), 108006 (2019)
8. Day, B., Norcliffe, A., Moss, J., Liò, P.: Meta-learning using privileged information for dynamics. In: ICLR (2021)
9. Di, X., Yu, P.: Deep reinforcement learning for furniture layout simulation in indoor graphics scenes. In: ICLR (2021)
10. El Euch, O., Rosenbaum, M.: The characteristic function of rough heston models. Math. Financ. **29**(1), 3–38 (2019)
11. Gatheral, J.: Efficient simulation of affine forward variance models (2022)
12. Ha, D., Dai, A., Le, Q.V.: Hypernetworks. In: ICLR (2017)
13. Hernandez, A.: Model calibration with neural networks (2016)
14. Heston, S.L.: A closed-form solution for options with stochastic volatility with applications to bond and currency options. Rev. Financial Stud. **6**(2), 327–343 (1993)
15. Heston, S.L.: A closed-form solution for options with stochastic volatility with applications to bond and currency options. Rev. Financial Stud. **6**(2), 327–343 (1993)
16. Horvath, B., Muguruza, A., Tomas, M.: Deep learning volatility: a deep neural network perspective on pricing and calibration in (rough) volatility models. Quant. Finance **21**(1), 11–27 (2021)
17. Jacquier, A., Martini, C., Muguruza, A.: On VIX futures in the rough Bergomi model. Quant. Finance **18**(1), 45–61 (2018)
18. Jacquier, A., Pakkanen, M.S., Stone, H.: Pathwise large deviations for the rough Bergomi model. J. Appl. Probab. **55**(4), 1078–1092 (2018)
19. Johnson, H., Shanno, D.: Option pricing when the variance is changing. J. Financial Quant. Anal. **22**(2), 143–151 (1987)
20. Kou, S.G.: A jump-diffusion model for option pricing. Manage. Sci. **48**(8), 1086–1101 (2002)
21. Matsuo, M., Fukami, K., Nakamura, T., Morimoto, M., Fukagata, K.: Supervised convolutional networks for vol-umetric data enrichment from limited sec-tional data with adaptive super resolution. In: ICLR (2021)
22. McCrickerd, R., Pakkanen, M.S.: Turbocharging Monte Carlo pricing for the rough Bergomi model. Quant. Finance **18**(11), 1877–1886 (2018)
23. Peurifoy, J., et al.: Nanophotonic particle simulation and inverse design using artificial neural networks. Sci. Adv. **4**(6) (2018)

24. Quilodrán-Casas, C., Arcucci, R., Mottet, L., Guo, Y., Pain, C.: Adversarial autoencoders and adversarial lstm for improved forecasts of urban air pollution simulations. In: ICLR (2021)
25. Sanchez-Gonzalez, A., et al.: Graph networks as learnable physics engines for inference and control. In: ICML (2018)
26. Schütt, K., Kindermans, P.J., Sauceda Felix, H.E., Chmiela, S., Tkatchenko, A., Müller, K.R.: Schnet: A continuous-filter convolutional neural network for modeling quantum interactions. In: NIPS (2017)
27. Stachenfeld, K., et al.: Learned coarse models for efficient turbulence simulation. In: ICLR (2021)
28. Wang, R., Kashinath, K., Mustafa, M., Albert, A., Yu, R.: Towards physics-informed deep learning for turbulent flow prediction. In: KDD (2020)
29. Willems, S.: Asian option pricing with orthogonal polynomials. Quant. Finance **19**(4), 605–618 (2019)
30. Xiao, Z., Zhang, C.: Construction of meteorological simulation knowledge graph based on deep learning method. Sustainability **13**(3), 1311 (2021)
31. Yan, G., Hanson, F.B.: Option pricing for a stochastic-volatility jump-diffusion model with log-uniform jump-amplitudes. In: ACC (2006)

PU GNN: Chargeback Fraud Detection in P2E MMORPGs via Graph Attention Networks with Imbalanced PU Labels

Jiho Choi, Junghoon Park, Woocheol Kim, Jin-Hyeok Park, Yumin Suh, and Minchang Sung$^{(\boxtimes)}$

Netmarble Corp., Seoul, Republic of Korea
{jihochoi,jhoonpark,kwc4616,realhyeok,yuum0131,sungmirr}@netmarble.com

Abstract. The recent advent of play-to-earn (P2E) systems in massively multiplayer online role-playing games (MMORPGs) has made in-game goods interchangeable with real-world values more than ever before. The goods in the P2E MMORPGs can be directly exchanged with cryptocurrencies such as Bitcoin, Ethereum, or Klaytn via blockchain networks. Unlike traditional in-game goods, once they had been written to the blockchains, P2E goods cannot be restored by the game operation teams even with chargeback fraud such as payment fraud, cancellation, or refund. To tackle the problem, we propose a novel chargeback fraud prediction method, *PU GNN*, which leverages graph attention networks with PU loss to capture both the players' in-game behavior with P2E token transaction patterns. With the adoption of modified GraphSMOTE, the proposed model handles the imbalanced distribution of labels in chargeback fraud datasets. The conducted experiments on three real-world P2E MMORPG datasets demonstrate that *PU GNN* achieves superior performances over previously suggested methods.

Keywords: chargeback fraud detection · graph neural networks · PU learning · P2E · MMORPG

1 Introduction

The recent advent of play-to-earn (P2E) systems, a new paradigm where game players can earn real-world value through their in-game activities, in massively multiplayer online role-playing games (MMORPGs) has made the value of in-game goods interchangeable with real-world values [19,23] more than ever before. The goods in the P2E MMORPGs can be directly exchanged for cryptocurrencies such as Bitcoin, Ethereum, and Klaytn via blockchain networks, immersing players to put more endeavors and facilitating players for better engagements. However, unlike traditional in-game goods, from the game operation teams' or publishers' perspective, P2E goods are vulnerable to chargeback

---

J. Choi and J. Park—Both authors contributed equally to this work.

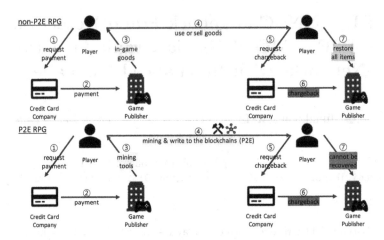

Fig. 1. The brief comparisons of goods refunds in non-P2E MMORPGs and P2E MMORPGs. Unlike non-P2E goods, it is challenging for game publishers to roll back the P2E goods even in the case of payment cancellation.

fraud [13,29] such as payment fraud, cancellation, or refund abuses. The P2E tokens or comparable P2E goods cannot be restored by the game operation teams once it had been written to the blockchain. Figure 1 is a brief comparison of game goods refunds of non-P2E and P2E games. In general, goods obtained through players' payments are subject to retrieval in the event of payment cancellation. However, the P2E goods or tokens are difficult to retrieve as they are recorded on the blockchain even if the payments are canceled. Thus it is essential to detect chargeback frauds in P2E MMORPGs.

Some of the previously conducted studies [3,33,38] had utilized financial datasets with traditional machine learning methods such as naive Bayes, random forest, logistic regression, and K-means clustering for chargeback fraud detection. [3,38] leveraged the learning methods with under-sampling to overcome the nature of label imbalance between fraud and benign. [16,37] adopted sequence and transaction modeling methods to combat chargeback fraud and fraud transactions. Although these approaches had revealed some of the patterns in chargeback fraud, they are not quite fitted with chargeback fraud in P2E MMORPGs since they had the limitation of not jointly considering both the player behaviors and token transaction patterns. Chargeback frauds in P2E MMORPG often occur in automated programs rather than manual playing by individuals. Therefore, the fraudsters leave relatively distinct in-game behavior action patterns such as action sequences and intervals. The details will be discussed in Sects. 4.1 and 4.2. In addition, players who have not yet canceled their payment should be considered unlabeled rather than fixed as negative since they could cancel their payment after finishing mining the P2E token with their paid in-game goods.

Recent advents in graph neural networks (GNNs) have shown promising results of graph inference tasks in many different domains such as social media, biochemistry, knowledge graphs, citation networks, and transaction graphs [1,12,14,20,35,45,46,50]. Likewise, positive-unlabeled (PU) learning has been adopted in various fields of study. Some studies in bioinformatics [26,51] use PU learning to overcome the lack of labeling, and [10,40,49] utilized PU learning for anomaly detection and outlier detection.

In this study, we overcome the previously addressed problem in chargeback fraud detection in P2E MMORPGs with the recent advent of GNNs and PU learning. We propose a novel chargeback fraud detection method, *PU GNN*. The proposed method utilizes players' in-game activity logs and P2E token transaction histories with positive and unlabeled label settings. The performance evaluation on three real-world datasets demonstrated the model's superiority over other previously presented methods.

We summarized our contributions as follows:

1. We propose a novel chargeback fraud detection method, *PU GNN*, for play-to-earn massively multiplayer online role-playing games (P2E MMORPGs).
2. The proposed method carefully utilizes both the players' in-game activities with P2E token transactions and tackled label imbalance with an oversampling method and positive & unlabeled label setups.
3. The conducted experiments on three real-world datasets demonstrate the method is superior to previously presented methods.

2   Related Work

2.1   Fraud Detection

Fraud detection has been studied in various fields with the perspectives of credit card fraud, payment fraud, and online game fraud [2,3,5,22,31]. Traditional rule-based approaches [22] had been extended to pattern-based learning methods [3,38] by discovering the distinctiveness patterns between fraudsters and benign users. [2,5,33] adopted unsupervised approaches to retrieve outlier scores to spot fraudulent activities, and [31] had utilized an imbalanced setup by leveraging one-class classification and nearest neighbors approach. Recently, [16,37,52] had adopted sequential or graph structures in transaction logs or graph representation to spot anomaly interactions.

2.2   Graph Neural Networks

Graph neural networks (GNNs) have shown promising results in many different node, link, and graph inference tasks [1,14,20,45,50]. Some of the GNNs variants leverage more on specific setups such as edge representation [12], heterogeneous node types [46], or dynamic graphs [35]. However, one of the key mechanisms that are shared with GNNs is message passing (or neighborhood aggregation) which takes the topologically connected components into account when learning the representation of an entity. A brief generalization of GNNs is as follows:

$$h_i^{(k)} = \text{UPDATE}_\theta \underbrace{\left(h_i^{(k-1)}, \overbrace{\text{AGG}_\theta \left(h_j^{(k-1)}, \forall j \in \mathcal{N}_i \right)}^{\text{aggregating neighbors' representations}} \right)}_{\text{updating current node's representation}} \tag{1}$$

The hidden representation of ith node after passing through k^{th} GNN layer, $h_i^{(k)}$, can be retrieved with the combination of AGG_θ and UPDATE_θ. A differentiable (learnable) and permutation invariant function AGG_θ [14] aggregates (sometimes sampled) set of neighborhood node $\mathcal{N}(\cdot)$. UPDATE_θ is an injective update function [50] to associate current states $h_i^{(k-1)}$ with aggregated neighbors'. Some of the recent variants of GNNs such as graph attention networks [1,45] adopt attention mechanism [44], and assign different weights when combining the neighbor nodes' embeddings.

2.3   Imbalanced Positive and Unlabeled Learning

In the classification task, it is important for the labeled data to be evenly distributed, or otherwise, the classifiers could overfit the majority classes [25,32,48]. To handle the problem, sampling studies such as under-sampling or over-sampling have been actively conducted. Under-sampling methods such as [32] solved the problem of data imbalance by eliminating the dominant class by finding data points that do not belong to its K nearest data point labels and balancing the label distribution with other classes. An over-sampling method such as SMOTE [4] duplicates the minority class observations by interpolating the nearest data points in the same class.

In addition, especially in industrial fields, the lack of labeled data with the majority of data being unlabeled, some studies [6,9,10,24] use unlabeled data through a method called positive-unlabeled (PU) learning. The method can help the classifier by leveraging unlabeled data. The method regards unlabeled as negative labels with the mixture of positive, or estimating the approximated risks [8,9]. PU learning has been widely adopted in various studies of classification, anomaly detection, and outlier detection. [28,34,49,54].

3   Problem Definition

Let $\mathcal{G} = (\mathcal{V}, \mathcal{E})$ be the *P2E token transaction graph* where the vertex set $\mathcal{V} = \{p_1, p_2, ..., p_{|\mathcal{V}|}\}$ and edge set $\mathcal{E} = \{t_1, t_2, ..., t_{|\mathcal{E}|}\}$ denote $|\mathcal{V}|$ players and $|\mathcal{E}|$ token transfers respectively. The node p consists of *in-game behavioral* features $x \in \mathcal{R}^{F_x}$, and a link t includes *token transfer* features $e \in \mathcal{R}^{F_e}$. A node belongs to one of the binary class $y \in \{-1, 1\}$, and $p(x, y)$ is the joint density of $(\mathcal{X}, \mathcal{Y})$. $p_p(x) = p(x|Y = +1)$ and $p_n(x) = p(x|Y = -1)$ are positive and negative marginals respectively with $p(x)$ being the whole $\mathcal{X}$ marginal.

The aim is to learn a decision function $f: \mathcal{R}^{F_x} \to \mathcal{R}$ to predict *chargeback fraud* with positive and unlabeled (PU) labels. We formulate the task as a node classification task in a token transaction graph $\mathcal{G}$ with a PU learning setup in which each set of data points is sampled from $p_p(x)$, $p(x)$, which are $\mathcal{X}_p = \{x_i^p\}_{i=1}^{n_p} \sim p_p(x)$ and $X_u = \{x_i^u\}_{i=1}^{n_u} \sim p(x)$.

4 Proposed Method

In this section, we introduce *PU GNN* architecture as Fig. 2, which includes player behavior modeling with in-game activity logs, graph attention with P2E token transaction graph, and calculating positive and unlabeled loss with imbalanced label distribution.

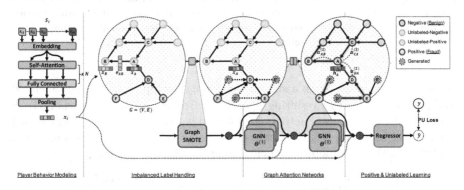

Fig. 2. The overall architecture of *PU GNN* for chargeback fraud detection in P2E MMORPG. The proposed method consists of four main components. The behavior modeling layer finds representations of the initial node features by learning behavior sequences. There are two different labels; unlabeled (a mixture of fraud $(\mathcal{A}, \mathcal{B})$ and benign $(\mathcal{C})$) and fraud $(\mathcal{D}, \mathcal{E}, \mathcal{F})$, with the respect to transaction networks. Notice that nodes with fewer labels $(\mathcal{D}, \mathcal{E}, \mathcal{F})$ are augmented with GraphSMOTE [53] and balanced. The graph attention layers [1] calculate the attention weights of node $\mathcal{A}$ (expressed as edge colors) to better leverage the embedding of the neighbor nodes $\mathcal{B}, \mathcal{C}, \mathcal{D}$. With the PU learning setup, half of the positive nodes are treated as unlabeled.

4.1 Player Behavior Modeling

We first retrieve the player i's initial behavioral representation x_i from his n most recent *in-game activity logs* $S_i = \{s_{i1}, s_{i2}, \cdots, s_{in}\}$ such as character login, item purchase, item use, skill use, quest completion, level up, goods acquisition, dungeon entrance, guild join, and so on (may vary by game). Figure 3 is the brief comparison of benign and fraud players where chargeback fraud users (or automated programs such as a macro) produce collusive activities which largely focus the mining the P2E goods or preceding activities such as the completion

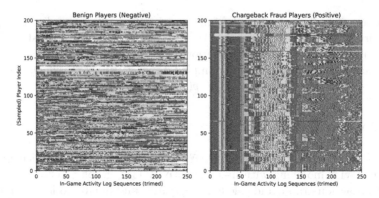

Fig. 3. The sampled users' activity log sequences of benign and chargeback fraud players in P2E MMORPGs. The chargeback fraud users (or automated programs) show collusive activities which mainly focus on purchasing P2E goods and mining tokens. (each color denotes different types of activity logs; login, dungeon entrance, guild join, quest completion, mining, et cetera)

of tutorials or quests. With a simple embedding lookup layer, $s_{i(\cdot)}$ are mapped to d dimensional vectors resulting $S_i' \in \mathcal{R}^{n \times d}$. To better spot future chargeback players, not all relations of activity logs should be considered equally. The scaled dot-product attention [17,44] with a fully connected layer, a common sequence modeling method, is adopted as below to utilize the activity logs:

$$H_i = FC\{\texttt{Attention}(Q, K, V)\} = FC\{softmax(\frac{QK^T}{\sqrt{d}})V\} \qquad (2)$$

, where $query; Q$, $key; K$, and $value; V$ are all S_i'. The attended behavioral logs H_i are then $\texttt{mean}$ and $\texttt{max}$ pooled to model the player's in-game activity. The concatenation, $\oplus$, of pooled results is the initial behavioral representation as follows:

$$x_i = \{\texttt{Pool}_{\texttt{MEAN}}(H_i) \oplus \texttt{Pool}_{\texttt{MAX}}(H_i)\} \in \mathcal{R}^{F_x}, \qquad (3)$$

and now it is treated as the node feature of player i.

4.2 Graph Attention Networks

To better capture the relations between players and chargeback attempts, *play-to-earn (P2E) token transaction graph* $\mathcal{G} = (\mathcal{V}, \mathcal{E})$ is utilized. The transfer records in the transaction graph may include the high-dimensional hidden relations of source and target nodes [30,41] such as ownership, collusive works, and so on. We adopt and modify graph attention networks (GATv2) [1] where dynamic attention is computed. The previously retrieved node features $x \in \mathcal{R}^{F_x}$ and link features $e \in \mathcal{R}^{F_e}$ are first upsampled with GraphSMOTE [53] and the details would be discussed in Sect. 4.3.

We leverage all features of the source node, target node, and link to calculate the attention coefficients. A shared attention mechanism $\mathbf{a} : \mathcal{R}^{F_x} \times \mathcal{R}^{F_x} \times \mathcal{R}^{F_e} \rightarrow \mathcal{R}$ is as below to calculate the attention weight α_{ij}:

$$\alpha_{ij}^{(l)} = \frac{exp\big(\mathbf{a}^{(l)}\text{LeakyReLU}(\Theta^{(l)}\big[x_i \parallel x_j \parallel e_{ij}\big])\big)}{\sum_{k \in \mathcal{N}_i \cup \{i\}}\big\{exp\big(\mathbf{a}^{(l)}\text{LeakyReLU}(\Theta^{(l)}\big[x_i \parallel x_k \parallel e_{ik}\big])\big)\big\}}, \tag{4}$$

where $\mathbf{a}^{(l)}$ and $\Theta^{(l)}$ are learnable parameters for l^{th} GNN layer. With the calculated attention coefficients with generalized message passing framework Eq. 1, the neighborhood nodes' representations are aggregated and combined as:

$$\vec{h}_i^{(l)} = \sum_{j \in \mathcal{N}_i \cup \{i\}} \alpha_{ij}^{(l)} \Theta^{(l)} \vec{h}_i^{(l-1)}, \tag{5}$$

where $h_i^{(0)} = x_i$. With two GATv2 layers, the node representation embedded the 1-hop and 2-hop neighbor nodes. The bi-directional ($h_i = \vec{h}_i \oplus \vec{h}_i$) and skip-connection [43] are concatenated to better embed the node features. The model leverages the concatenation representation of h_i with x_i from Sect. 4.1 to classify the frauds.

4.3 Imbalanced Positive and Unlabeled Learning

Non-negative PU (nnPU) [21] learning improved former PU learning, which is also known as unbiased PU (uPU) learning [8]. uPU learning uses unbiased risk estimators. Let $\mathcal{L} : R \times \{\pm 1\} \rightarrow R$ be the loss function. $\mathcal{L}(t, y)$ represents the loss while predicting an output t and the ground truth y and f represents decision function. Denoting $R_p^+(f) = E_{X \sim p_p(x)}[\mathcal{L}((f(X), +1)]$, $R_n^-(f) = E_{X \sim p_n(x)}[\mathcal{L}((f(X), -1)]$, ordinary binary classification risk estimator is directly approximated by:

$$\widehat{R}_{pn}(f) = \pi_p \widehat{R}_p^+(f) + \pi_n \widehat{R}_n^-(f) \tag{6}$$

Meanwhile, the PU learning setting has no information on negative data, but the risk estimator $R(f)$ can be approximated directly [9]. Denotes $R_p^-(f) = E_p[\mathcal{L}((f(X), -1)]$ and $R_u^-(f) = E_{X \sim p(x)}[\mathcal{L}((f(X), -1)]$, then as $\pi_n p_n(x) = p(x) - \pi_p p_p(x)$, we can obtain

$$\pi_n R_n^-(x) = R_u^-(f) - \pi_p R_p^-(f) \tag{7}$$

Using above, the unbiased risk of $R(f)$ is approximated directly by:

$$\widehat{R}_{pu}(f) = \pi_p \widehat{R}_p^+(f) - \pi_p \widehat{R}_p^-(f) + \widehat{R}_u^-(f)$$

$$\widehat{R}_p^-(f) = \frac{1}{n_p}\sum_{i=1}^{n_p}\mathcal{L}(f(x_i^p), -1), \widehat{R}_u^-(f) = \frac{1}{n_u}\sum_{i=1}^{n_u}\mathcal{L}(f(x_i^u), -1) \tag{8}$$

To overcome the issues with the convergence rate and complex estimation error bounds, [21] suggested the non-negative risk estimator, which is denoted by:

$$\widetilde{R}_{pu}(f) = \pi_p \widehat{R}_p^+(f) + max(0, \widehat{R}_u^-(f) - \widehat{R}_p^-(f)) \tag{9}$$

GraphSMOTE [53] oversampled minority class by introducing SMOTE [4] in graph-structured data with training link generation simultaneously. The charge-back fraud data of P2E MMORPG have the characteristics of imbalance in the graph structure and the possibility of being labeled as a potential fraud even though it is not yet labeled. Therefore, we adopted GraphSMOTE [53] and nnPU learning [21] to handle the imbalance and the unlabeled situation in the dataset.

4.4 Loss, Training and Inference

In this study, we train our model with the empirical estimation of risk with the following loss function:

$$\mathcal{L} = \widetilde{R}_{pu}(f) = \pi_p \widehat{R}_p^+(f) + max(0, \widehat{R}_u^-(f) - \widehat{R}_p^-(f)), \tag{10}$$

with the sigmoid function, $\ell_{\texttt{sigmoid}}(t, y) = 1/(1 + exp(t * y))$ for $\mathcal{L}(t, y)$ in $\widehat{R}_p^+(f)$, $\widehat{R}_u^-(f)$, $\widehat{R}_p^-(f)$ as previously described in Sect. 4.3. To minimize $\mathcal{L}$ in Eq. 10, output t has to be closer to label y. The sigmoid function is adopted for $\mathcal{L}(t, y)$ since it is continuously differentiable across its entire domain and can be minimized by the gradient-based algorithms [21]. The training task of the loss function can be seen as a regression task since the output value, $\hat{y}$, of the proposed model, lies in $\hat{y} \in [-1, +1]$. For the ablation study to verify the effectiveness of the loss, the softmax function is used to retrieve $\hat{y}$, and the cross-entropy between $\hat{y}$ and one-hot label y is used as loss as follows: $\mathcal{L} = CE(y, \hat{y}) = -\sum_{i=1}\{y_i log(\hat{y}_i) + (1 - y_i)log(1 - \hat{y}_i)\}$.

5 Experiments

This section introduces our datasets, baselines, implementation detail, experimental results, and ablation study. Three real-world datasets had been collected for the evaluation. Since the proposed method consists of player behavior modeling and a graph structure-based model, we focus on comparing ours with other approaches that can consider player behaviors or transaction histories.

5.1 Experimental Setup

Datasets. We retrieved three datasets from two popular P2E MMORPGs played globally; MMORPG01 and MMORPG02 (The titles of the games and token names have been anonymized). The datasets include players' behavior activity logs and P2E token transaction graphs. Figure 4 is the brief overview of the sampled P2E token transactions. We chronologically and randomly sampled train,

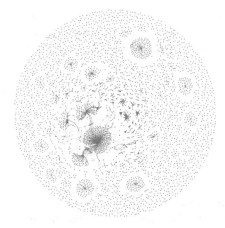

Fig. 4. A brief overview of sampled P2E token transaction networks. Each node and link represents a player in P2E MMORPG and a token transfer respectively. The colors of the nodes represent fraudsters (red) and unlabeled, a mixture of fraudsters and benign, users (blue). (Color figure online)

validation, and test sets. The chargeback fraud labels include manual annotation by game operation teams, with the consideration of the players' network and device information, and whether the players cancel the payments after transferring the purchased tokens. For the PU learning environment, we used half of the positive labeled observations as positive and the rest are treated as unlabeled. The test evaluations are done with positive and negative ground-truth labels. The detailed statistics of the datasets are described in Table 1.

Table 1. Statistical details of chargeback and P2E MMORPG transaction graph datasets

-	$DATASET_{01}$	$DATASET_{02}$	$DATASET_{03}$
Game	$MMORPG_{01}$	$MMORPG_{01}$	$MMORPG_{02}$
P2E Token	$TOKEN_{01}$	$TOKEN_{01} + TOKEN_{02}$	$TOKEN_{03}$
Date	Jul.~Aug. 2022	Aug.~Oct. 2022	May~Oct. 2022
$|\mathcal{V}|$	32.9K	28.1K	5.6K
$|\mathcal{E}|$	62.4K	67.4K	33.8K
Train $(P{:}N)$	2.4K : 10.5K	3.2K:9.8K	0.5K:2.3K
Validation	2.7K : 8.1K	1.4K:4.2K	0.2K:1.1K
Test	2.1K : 7.2K	2.3K:6.8K	0.4K:1.1K

Baselines. We compared the proposed model with several baseline models; MLP, GRU [7], Self-attention [44], GCN [20], GraphSAGE [14], GAT [45],

OCGNN[1] [47], and DAGNN[1] [27]. All non-PU experiments are done with cross-entropy loss and experiments on GNNs are done in an inductive setting [14].

We compare the proposed PU GNN model with the following fraud detection baseline models:

- MLP: Three-layer multi-layer perceptron classifier to map in-game behavior features to fraud or benign labels.
- GRU [7]: An simple staked-GRU model to learn players' sequential in-game behavior patterns with their labels.
- Self-attention [44]: An self-attention mechanism to learn players' in-game behavior patterns.
- GCN [20]: A GNN-based model that learns contextual relations between senders and receivers in P2E transaction graphs.
- GraphSAGE [14]: A GNN-based model aggregating neighbors' embeddings with current representation to earn relations between senders and receivers in P2E transaction graphs.
- GAT [45] A GNN-based model with an attention mechanism to retrieve edge weights in transaction networks.
- OCGNN [47]: A GNN-based anomaly detection model extended OCSVM [39] to the graph domain to utilize hypersphere learning.
- DAGNN [27]: A GNN-based fraud detection model which leverages different augmented views of graphs called disparity and similarity augments.

Implementation Detail. The proposed model is built with PyTorch, PyTorch Geometric [11], and BigQuery in the Google Cloud Platform. 5 self-attention with fully connected layer blocks and 2 GATv2 layer blocks are adopted. The embedding size, denoted as F_x of 3, is 128 dimensions. BatchNorm [15] and Dropout [42] are added between layers and Adam optimizer [18] and early stopping [36] with the patience of 10 were adopted. We report the average results of 5 runs.

5.2   Performance Evaluation

Overall Detection Results (F1, AUC, Recall, Specificity). We report the F1-score, ROC AUC, recall (true positive rate), and specificity (true negative rate) of the proposed model with baselines. The overall statistical details of performance evaluations are shown in Table 2. Methods such as MLP and GRU show that the chargeback fraud label could be classified with the aid of in-game behavioral features in all three datasets. Sequential models such as GRU and self-attention improved their performance by taking the sequential patterns of the behavior logs into account. The graph-based models such as GCN, GraphSAGE, and GAT outperform the sequence-based baselines; GRU, and self-attention. It is been demonstrated the necessity of using both the in-game behavior features

---

[1] We implemented the simplified versions of the models which borrowed key ideas to adopt different situations from the original tasks.

Table 2. The performance evaluations of chargeback fraud detection in P2E MMORPGs. The evaluated metrics are F1-score, AUC, Pos (true positive rate; sensitivity), and Neg (true negative rate; specificity). The best results of the F1-score and AUC are in the underlines.

Method	$DATASET_{01}$				$DATASET_{02}$				$DATASET_{03}$			
	F1	AUC	Pos TPR	Neg TNR	F1	AUC	Pos TPR	Neg TNR	F1	AUC	Pos TPR	Neg TNR
MLP	0.778	0.665	0.391	0.940	0.771	0.762	0.548	0.976	0.775	0.798	0.698	0.897
GRU [7]	0.811	0.753	0.634	0.872	0.847	0.835	0.706	0.964	0.780	0.748	0.885	0.610
Self-attention [44]	0.805	0.775	0.725	0.825	0.831	0.829	0.814	0.843	0.784	0.768	0.828	0.707
GCN [20]	0.816	0.734	0.549	0.919	0.849	0.846	0.819	0.872	0.776	0.798	0.703	0.893
GraphSAGE [14]	0.834	0.791	0.708	0.875	0.870	0.863	0.776	0.950	0.791	0.781	0.813	0.748
GAT [45]	0.836	0.847	0.886	0.807	0.867	0.859	0.769	0.948	0.782	0.803	0.710	0.895
OCGNN [47]	0.801	0.763	0.402	0.844	0.862	0.852	0.727	0.988	0.781	0.783	0.703	0.802
DAGNN [27]	0.846	0.835	0.827	0.831	0.875	0.869	0.792	0.946	0.801	0.787	0.812	0.810
PU GNN (Proposed)	<u>0.855</u>	<u>0.854</u>	0.866	0.843	<u>0.884</u>	<u>0.876</u>	0.788	0.965	<u>0.811</u>	<u>0.801</u>	0.832	0.771

and the token transfer network structures to detect chargeback fraud in P2E MMORPGs. However, the features are not the only thing that affects the performance. Although both types of behavior patterns and transaction patterns are utilized, the classification result of OCGNN shows that the one-class abnormal detection is not suitable for the chargeback fraud detection tasks. We believe that the task that we are tackling is out of the scope of anomaly and more fitted with classification. DAGNN utilizes augmented views of graphs and improves performance compares to other GNN-based models. The proposed method, *PU GNN*, outperforms other baseline methods by leveraging PU learning which takes the assumption of un-chargeback paid players as unlabeled observations. Handling the label imbalance with modified GraphSMOTE helps the model to robustly learn player representations.

5.3 Ablation Study

(Ablation Study 1) T-SNE Visualization of the Components' Output Embedding. To take a closer look at what roles and advantages the components of our method have, we separated and compared the proposed method into three parts. Three components are (a) player behavior sequence modeling (Sect. 4.1), (b) graph attention network (Sect. 4.2), and (c) leveraging both of them. Figure 5 is the 2-dimensional t-SNE visualization of the output embedding of each of the three parts. First, the player behavior sequence modeling component utilizes players' behavior features. In Fig. 5(a), large-scale clusters could be identified which represent similar behavior log patterns left between chargeback fraudsters. However, there were many overlapping parts with benign users and fraudsters, thus the features are not enough to correctly detect the frauds. Figure 5(b), where only the transaction networks are used as input features, shows the multiple clusters of small node counts. The result is led by connected nodes sharing closer embedding spaces. Finally, when both the behavior patterns and the transaction networks are used in Fig. 5(c), there are advantages in fraud detection by leveraging the information of both the large and small clusters in previous components.

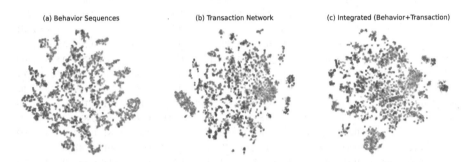

Fig. 5. The t-SNE visualization of the sampled users' by each component of the proposed model. Each component handles (a) activity log sequences, (b) transaction patterns, and (c) both. The color represents benign (green) and chargeback fraud players (red) in P2E MMORPGs. (Color figure online)

(Ablation Study 2) Effects of PU and SMOTE. We conducted another ablation study with different aspects to see the effectiveness of PU and SMOTE in the proposed method. The series of ablation studies are combinations of the below elements:

- **w/o SMOTE**: Constituting the original input data and its preprocessing, training without the oversampling by GraphSMOTE [53].
- **w/o PU**: Without PU loss for the circumstances of unlabeled, trains model with cross-entropy classification loss.

In Fig. 6, the experimental results of the F1-score, AUC, sensitivity (recall; true positive rate), and specificity (true negative rate). First, the ablation study w/o (SMOTE & PU) is conducted to verify whether there are solutions to deal with the imbalance label problem and uncertainty of the unlabeled dataset. As result, the metrics of this ablation study score the lowest among other ablation studies in all four measures. Second, the ablation study only w/o SMOTE (only with PU) is conducted to see the effect of the balancing process of the proposed method. We can verify that using GraphSMOTE [53] and its modification, the method can better handle the nature of label imbalance in chargeback fraud detection, scoring higher F1 score and AUC respectively. Third, the ablation study w/o PU (only with SMOTE) proves that it is proper to use PU loss to consider users who have not yet canceled payment as unlabeled. The users may cancel their payments after the inference of whether the users are chargeback fraud or not. As the users are considered unlabeled, training our proposed method with PU loss performs at least equal or better F1 score and AUC.

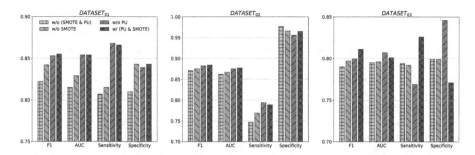

Fig. 6. The bar plots of the effectiveness of PU and SMOTE with four different metrics. The comparison consisted of w/o (SMOTE and PU), w/o SMOTE, w/o PU, and w/ (PU and SMOTE).

6   Conclusion and Feature Work

We propose a novel chargeback fraud detection model, *PU GNN*, for play-to-earn (P2E) MMORPGs. The proposed model leverages both players' in-game behavior log sequences and P2E token transaction networks. The model adopts an attention mechanism and graph attention networks to retrieve high-dimensional representation for the players. With the positive and unlabeled (PU) learning setup, the model is able to jointly learn positive (chargeback fraud) and unlabeled labels. The conducted experiments on three real-world datasets showed the proposed model outperforms other previously presented methods.

We believe there is still room for improvement. The time-related temporal features such as collusive work times and the time interval between the payment and its cancellation by the chargeback frauds are not yet considered which could be handled by adopting hazard function from survival analysis as features to be concerned. Another important aspect of graph-based fraud detection is handling various node types and edge types by extending homogeneous graph learning to heterogeneous graph learning. Early detection of chargeback fraud is also an important topic to consider to prevent and minimize losses. Therefore, we will further study the depth of these points to improve the performance of our proposed method.

Acknowledgement. This research was supported by the Abnormal User Information Team, AI Center, Netmarble Corp.

References

1. Brody, S., Alon, U., Yahav, E.: How attentive are graph attention networks? In: International Conference on Learning Representations (2021)
2. Carcillo, F., Le Borgne, Y.A., Caelen, O., Kessaci, Y., Oblé, F., Bontempi, G.: Combining unsupervised and supervised learning in credit card fraud detection. Inf. Sci. **557**, 317–331 (2021)
3. Carneiro, N., Figueira, G., Costa, M.: A data mining based system for credit-card fraud detection in e-tail. Decis. Support Syst. **95**, 91–101 (2017)
4. Chawla, N.V., Bowyer, K.W., Hall, L.O., Kegelmeyer, W.P.: Smote: synthetic minority over-sampling technique. J. Artif. Intell. Res. **16**, 321–357 (2002)
5. Chen, J.I.Z., Lai, K.L.: Deep convolution neural network model for credit-card fraud detection and alert. J. Artif. Intell. **3**(02), 101–112 (2021)
6. Christoffel, M., Niu, G., Sugiyama, M.: Class-prior estimation for learning from positive and unlabeled data. In: Asian Conference on Machine Learning, pp. 221–236. PMLR (2016)
7. Chung, J., Gulcehre, C., Cho, K., Bengio, Y.: Empirical evaluation of gated recurrent neural networks on sequence modeling. arXiv preprint arXiv:1412.3555 (2014)
8. Du Plessis, M., Niu, G., Sugiyama, M.: Convex formulation for learning from positive and unlabeled data. In: International Conference on Machine Learning, pp. 1386–1394. PMLR (2015)
9. Du Plessis, M.C., Niu, G., Sugiyama, M.: Analysis of learning from positive and unlabeled data. In: Advances in Neural Information Processing Systems 27 (2014)
10. Elkan, C., Noto, K.: Learning classifiers from only positive and unlabeled data. In: Proceedings of the 14th ACM SIGKDD International Conference on Knowledge Discovery and Data Mining, pp. 213–220 (2008)
11. Fey, M., Lenssen, J.E.: Fast graph representation learning with PyTorch geometric. In: ICLR Workshop on Representation Learning on Graphs and Manifolds (2019)
12. Gong, L., Cheng, Q.: Exploiting edge features for graph neural networks. In: Proceedings of the IEEE/CVF Conference on Computer Vision and Pattern Recognition, pp. 9211–9219 (2019)
13. Guo, Y., Bao, Y., Stuart, B.J., Le-Nguyen, K.: To sell or not to sell: exploring sellers' trust and risk of chargeback fraud in cross-border electronic commerce. Inf. Syst. J. **28**(2), 359–383 (2018)
14. Hamilton, W., Ying, Z., Leskovec, J.: Inductive representation learning on large graphs. In: Advances in Neural Information Processing Systems, pp. 1024–1034 (2017)
15. Ioffe, S., Szegedy, C.: Batch normalization: accelerating deep network training by reducing internal covariate shift. In: International Conference on Machine Learning, pp. 448–456. PMLR (2015)
16. Jurgovsky, J., et al.: Sequence classification for credit-card fraud detection. Expert Syst. Appl. **100**, 234–245 (2018)
17. Kenton, J.D.M.W.C., Toutanova, L.K.: BERT: pre-training of deep bidirectional transformers for language understanding. In: Proceedings of NAACL-HLT, pp. 4171–4186 (2019)
18. Kingma, D.P., Ba, J.: Adam: a method for stochastic optimization. arXiv preprint arXiv:1412.6980 (2014)
19. Kiong, L.V.: Metaverse Made Easy: A Beginner's Guide to the Metaverse: Everything you need to know about Metaverse. NFT and GameFi, Liew Voon Kiong (2022)

20. Kipf, T.N., Welling, M.: Semi-supervised classification with graph convolutional networks. In: Proceedings of the 5th International Conference on Learning Representations. ICLR 2017 (2017)
21. Kiryo, R., Niu, G., Du Plessis, M.C., Sugiyama, M.: Positive-unlabeled learning with non-negative risk estimator. In: Advances in Neural Information Processing Systems 30 (2017)
22. Kou, Y., Lu, C.T., Sirwongwattana, S., Huang, Y.P.: Survey of fraud detection techniques. In: IEEE International Conference on Networking, Sensing and Control, 2004, vol. 2, pp. 749–754. IEEE (2004)
23. Lee, E., Woo, J., Kim, H., Kim, H.K.: No silk road for online gamers! using social network analysis to unveil black markets in online games. In: Proceedings of the 2018 World Wide Web Conference, pp. 1825–1834 (2018)
24. Lee, W.S., Liu, B.: Learning with positive and unlabeled examples using weighted logistic regression. In: ICML, vol. 3, pp. 448–455 (2003)
25. Lemaître, G., Nogueira, F., Aridas, C.K.: Imbalanced-learn: a python toolbox to tackle the curse of imbalanced datasets in machine learning. J. Mach. Learn. Res. **18**(1), 559–563 (2017)
26. Li, F., et al.: Positive-unlabeled learning in bioinformatics and computational biology: a brief review. Brief. Bioinform. **23**(1), bbab461 (2022)
27. Li, Q., He, Y., Xu, C., Wu, F., Gao, J., Li, Z.: Dual-augment graph neural network for fraud detection. In: Proceedings of the 31st ACM International Conference on Information & Knowledge Management, pp. 4188–4192 (2022)
28. Liu, B., Lee, W.S., Yu, P.S., Li, X.: Partially supervised classification of text documents. In: ICML, vol. 2, pp. 387–394. Sydney, NSW (2002)
29. Liu, D., Lee, J.H.: CFLedger: preventing chargeback fraud with blockchain. ICT Express **8**(3), 352–356 (2022)
30. Liu, Q., Nickel, M., Kiela, D.: Hyperbolic graph neural networks. In: Advances in Neural Information Processing Systems 32 (2019)
31. Makki, S., Assaghir, Z., Taher, Y., Haque, R., Hacid, M.S., Zeineddine, H.: An experimental study with imbalanced classification approaches for credit card fraud detection. IEEE Access **7**, 93010–93022 (2019)
32. Mani, I., Zhang, I.: kNN approach to unbalanced data distributions: a case study involving information extraction. In: Proceedings of Workshop on Learning from Imbalanced Datasets, vol. 126, pp. 1–7. ICML (2003)
33. Mittal, S., Tyagi, S.: Performance evaluation of machine learning algorithms for credit card fraud detection. In: 2019 9th International Conference on Cloud Computing, Data Science & Engineering (Confluence), pp. 320–324. IEEE (2019)
34. Nguyen, M.N., Li, X.L., Ng, S.K.: Positive unlabeled learning for time series classification. In: Twenty-Second International Joint Conference on Artificial Intelligence (2011)
35. Peng, H., et al.: Spatial temporal incidence dynamic graph neural networks for traffic flow forecasting. Inf. Sci. **521**, 277–290 (2020)
36. Prechelt, L.: Early stopping - but when? In: Montavon, G., Orr, G.B., Müller, K.-R. (eds.) Neural Networks: Tricks of the Trade. LNCS, vol. 7700, pp. 53–67. Springer, Heidelberg (2012). https://doi.org/10.1007/978-3-642-35289-8_5
37. Rao, S.X., et al.: xFraud: explainable fraud transaction detection. Proceed. VLDB Endow. **15**(3), 427–436 (2021)
38. de Sá, A.G., Pereira, A.C., Pappa, G.L.: A customized classification algorithm for credit card fraud detection. Eng. Appl. Artif. Intell. **72**, 21–29 (2018)

39. Schölkopf, B., Williamson, R.C., Smola, A., Shawe-Taylor, J., Platt, J.: Support vector method for novelty detection. In: Advances in Neural Information Processing Systems 12 (1999)

40. Scott, C., Blanchard, G.: Novelty detection: unlabeled data definitely help. In: Artificial Intelligence and Statistics, pp. 464–471. PMLR (2009)

41. Shen, J., Zhou, J., Xie, Y., Yu, S., Xuan, Q.: Identity inference on blockchain using graph neural network. In: Dai, H.-N., Liu, X., Luo, D.X., Xiao, J., Chen, X. (eds.) BlockSys 2021. CCIS, vol. 1490, pp. 3–17. Springer, Singapore (2021). https://doi.org/10.1007/978-981-16-7993-3_1

42. Srivastava, N., Hinton, G., Krizhevsky, A., Sutskever, I., Salakhutdinov, R.: Dropout: a simple way to prevent neural networks from overfitting. J. Mach. Learn. Res. **15**(1), 1929–1958 (2014)

43. Tong, T., Li, G., Liu, X., Gao, Q.: Image super-resolution using dense skip connections. In: Proceedings of the IEEE International Conference on Computer Vision, pp. 4799–4807 (2017)

44. Vaswani, A., et al.: Attention is all you need. In: Advances in Neural Information Processing Systems 30 (2017)

45. Velickovic, P., Cucurull, G., Casanova, A., Romero, A., Liò, P., Bengio, Y.: Graph attention networks. In: 6th International Conference on Learning Representations, ICLR 2018, Vancouver, BC, Canada, 30 April - 3 May 2018, Conference Track Proceedings. OpenReview.net, Vancouver, BC, Canada (2018)

46. Wang, X., et al.: Heterogeneous graph attention network. In: The World Wide Web Conference, pp. 2022–2032 (2019)

47. Wang, X., Jin, B., Du, Y., Cui, P., Tan, Y., Yang, Y.: One-class graph neural networks for anomaly detection in attributed networks. Neural Comput. Appl. **33**, 12073–12085 (2021)

48. Wilson, D.L.: Asymptotic properties of nearest neighbor rules using edited data. IEEE Trans. Syst. Man Cybern. **SMC-2**(3), 408–421 (1972)

49. Wu, M., Pan, S., Du, L., Zhu, X.: Learning graph neural networks with positive and unlabeled nodes. ACM Trans. Knowl. Discov. Data (TKDD) **15**(6), 1–25 (2021)

50. Xu, K., Hu, W., Leskovec, J., Jegelka, S.: How powerful are graph neural networks? In: International Conference on Learning Representations (2019)

51. Yang, P., Ormerod, J.T., Liu, W., Ma, C., Zomaya, A.Y., Yang, J.Y.: AdaSampling for positive-unlabeled and label noise learning with bioinformatics applications. IEEE Trans. Cybern. **49**(5), 1932–1943 (2018)

52. Yu, W., Cheng, W., Aggarwal, C.C., Zhang, K., Chen, H., Wang, W.: NetWalk: a flexible deep embedding approach for anomaly detection in dynamic networks. In: Proceedings of the 24th ACM SIGKDD International Conference on Knowledge Discovery & Data Mining, pp. 2672–2681 (2018)

53. Zhao, T., Zhang, X., Wang, S.: GraphSMOTE: imbalanced node classification on graphs with graph neural networks. In: Proceedings of the 14th ACM International Conference on Web Search and Data Mining, pp. 833–841 (2021)

54. Zhou, Y., et al.: Pure: Positive-unlabeled recommendation with generative adversarial network. In: Proceedings of the 27th ACM SIGKDD Conference on Knowledge Discovery & Data Mining, pp. 2409–2419 (2021)

BCAD: An Interpretable Anomaly Transaction Detection System Based on Behavior Consistency

Jun Hu, Xu Min, Xiaolu Zhang, Chilin Fu, Weichang Wu, and Jun Zhou(✉)

AntGroup, Hangzhou, China
{zhaoda.hj,minxu.mx,yueyin.zxl,chilin.fcl,jiuyue.wwc,
jun.zhoujun}@antgroup.com

Abstract. In the era of digital payment, abnormal behaviors such as fraud pose a huge threat to E-commerce platforms. Traditional anti-fraud approaches usually apply supervised learning which requires sophisticated knowledge extraction and does not adapt to evolving anomalous behaviors. In recent years, unsupervised learning methods has been widely applied to anomaly detection. However, they still suffer from a serious shortcoming, that they judge anomalies based on the global distribution while ignoring the user's own historical information. In this paper, we propose a novel problem of unsupervised anomaly transaction detection focusing on the individual level. To tackle this problem, we first derive behavior consistency hypothesis based on data exploration. Then based on this assumption, we propose a new framework named Behavior Consistency based Anomaly Detection (BCAD). Specifically, BCAD learns representations for the target behavior and the history behavior preferences respectively by contrastive learning, and then measure the similarity between them to identify anomaly transactions. Besides, to disentangle the behavior representation into several attributes, we design an attribute gate module which can extract high-level user preferences from historical behaviors. Overall, BCAD can not only detect whether a target behavior is abnormal, even if the fraudulent pattern never appeared before, but also give an interpretation from the perspective of preference attributes. Extensive experiments on the real-world business dataset demonstrate that BCAD can detect abnormal behaviors effectively and provide insightful results for human beings.

Keywords: Anomaly detection · Interpretability · Behavior consistency

1 Introduction

With the popularity of the Internet, online transactions through e-commerce platforms are adopted by more and more individuals and companies. The rapid advancement of online transactions has brought convenience to consumers, but

G. De Francisci Morales et al. (Eds.): ECML PKDD 2023, LNAI 14174, pp. 259–274, 2023.
https://doi.org/10.1007/978-3-031-43427-3_16

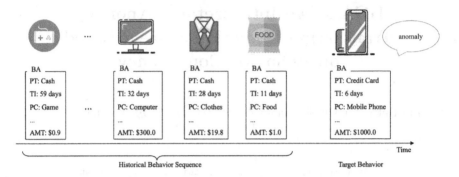

Fig. 1. An example of an abnormal transaction that deviates from the user's daily purchasing habits. The historical behavior sequence shows that the user has a tendency to purchase products with high cost-performance ratio in the past, while the target behavior shows a low cost-performance product. This clearly deviates from the user's behavior preference, which could be a transaction after the account was stolen. The abbreviations in figure are explained as follows: BA (Basic Attribute), PT (Payment Type), TI (Time interval), PC (Product Category), AMT (Amount of money).

at the same time it has also spawned a wide range of fraudulent activities. With the increasing complexity of fraud methods, the demand for anomaly transaction detection is becoming more and more urgent in order to protect the rights of both consumers and merchants. Anomaly transaction detection aims at detecting possible fraud transactions that deviate from the normal behavior pattern, e.g., a transaction for the purpose of stealing cash. These abnormal transactions could lead to serious financial loss for the platform if left ignored, and hence a robust method of anomaly detection is crucial to prevent the potential risks.

Most of existing fraud detection methods on e-commerce platforms are basically rule-based or supervised methods [1,10,21], which require in-depth understanding of fraud patterns that have emerged and are unable to effectively adapt to fast-changing fraudulent tactics. To address these issues, many unsupervised anti-fraud methods have been proposed recently [12,16]. These unsupervised anti-fraud methods, usually learn a global distribution on a large-scale dataset, as a normal distribution, and then treat the transactions which deviate from the normal distribution as fraudulent transactions. However, this type of approaches still suffer from an obvious shortcoming, that the global distribution used as an anomaly detection benchmark is too coarse-grained to detect **individual-level anomalies**. For example, a large amount transaction appears to be normal in the global distribution, but its probability of be abnormal should increase, when it occurs on a user whose historical behaviors reflects low level of consumption. Essentially, the existing methods only considered the comparison across all behavior samples, but ignored the longitudinal behavioral comparison within a single user. In fact, we observe from real-world dataset that user behavior is relatively consistent over time. Based on this phenomenon, in this paper we revisit anomaly detection with a new perspective, which leads to a new class of anomaly detection methods as a complement to the existing methods. To the best of our knowledge, we are the first attempt to study the problem of unsupervised anomaly transaction detection at the individual granularity.

The **behavior consistency** assumption is the basic foundation of individual-level anomaly transaction detection. Through data exploration and analysis, we observe that most normal users show a certain behavior preference. These behavior preferences remain consistent or evolve slowly over time. For example, a thrifty person has always favored buying goods with a high cost-effectiveness ratio. The anomalous behavior is usually a significant deviation from the user's daily purchasing habits, thereby violating the consistency with the behavior preferences, as shown in Fig. 1. In a nutshell, the behavior consistency assumption allows us to identify anomalous transaction by comparing the target behavior and this user's own historical behavior. The more inconsistent the target behavior is with the historical behavior, the more likely it is an anomalous transaction.

In this paper, we propose a new framework named Behavior Consistency based Anomaly Detection (**BCAD**). BCAD learns behavior representations that can measure the consistency between the target behavior and the behavior preference. Specifically, we design a network structure with two towers to model the target behavior and users' historical behavior separately. Based on the behavior consistency assumption, we construct a self-supervised learning task to pull the representations of target behavior and users' historical behavior from the same user, and meanwhile push away the representations from different users. To be concrete, by applying the framework of contrastive learning, given a target behavior, our goal is to maximize its similarity against the behavioral representations from the same user, and minimize that from different users. Through this task, we can learn a behavior preference representation for each user, which makes individual-level anomaly detection possible. Moreover, the two-tower structure can also accelerate the online inference computation, by pre-computing the behavior preference representations for all users.

Our framework can give interpretable anomaly detection results. Interpretability is crucial for subsequent human analysis of detected anomaly transactions. A user's purchase behavior can usually be described from several basic attributes, such as product category, price and payment type. Correspondingly, the user's behavior preferences can also be abstracted into preferences in several aspects known as **preference attributes**, such as preferences of consumption level, consumption frequency, and payment habits. It is noteworthy that the preference attributes are not a directly one-to-one mapping of basic behavior attributes. For example, to determine the purchase ability of a user, we need to consider the product category and price simultaneously. A user who buys a T-shirt with $200 may have stronger purchasing ability than a user who spends $200 on a mobile phone. Based on the above analysis, we design an attribute gate module to aggregate all historical behaviors to abstract high-level preference attributes. With the help of the attribute gate module, we can get the preference attribute for each user, so that we can explain in which aspects the target behavior is abnormal to facilitate subsequent human intervention.

Above all, the major contributions of this work are summarized as follows:

- To the best of our knowledge, we are the first attempt to study the unsupervised fraud transactions detection problem that focuses on the individual level. We bring to light the behavior consistency which is the cornerstone of solving our problem.
- Based on the behavior consistency assumption, we propose a new framework BCAD that models both target behavior and user's behavior preferences, and measure the consistency between them to identify fraudulent transactions. Meanwhile, we can explain the detection results from the perspective of the behavior preference attributes.
- We perform in-depth experiments on real-world datasets, and both the quantitative and qualitative analysis demonstrate the effectiveness of BCAD. We also verify that BCAD can identify undiscovered anomalous behavior.

2   Related Work

Fraud transaction detection is a problem that has been studied for a long time, and various machine learning-based methods based solutions have been proposed in the literature. For instance, Zhu et al. [21] proposed a Hierarchical Explainable Network (HEN) to model users' behavior sequences, which improves the performance of fraud detection and makes the inference process interpretable. Liu et al. [10] devised a tree-like structure named behavior tree to reorganize the user behavioral data, in which a group of successive sequential actions denoting a specific user intention are represented as a branch on the tree. However, these *supervised* methods require a deep understanding of fraud patterns as well as large amounts of manually labeled data, and they are not capable of detecting the evolving new fraud schemes. To address the challenges mentioned above, *unsupervised* fraud transaction methods are proposed. Min et al. [12] developed a cluster-based approach that groups data points into clusters based on similarity and then identifies the risky cluster. Several abnormal detection methods [4,8,14–16,18,19] have also been explored. These methods typically learn the overall distribution of the dataset as a normal distribution on a large dataset and then identify transactions that deviate from the normal distribution as potentially fraudulent. However, these methods may not be suitable for detecting abnormal transactions at an individual level.

Contrastive Learning is a self-supervised learning method for learning general features of a dataset without labels by letting the model learn which data points are similar or different. Recently, with the development of unsupervised representational learning in NLP [6] and CV [3] in recent years, many unsupervised representational learning methods based on behavioral sequences have emerged [7,20]. Gu et al. [7] proposed the Self-supervised User Modeling Network (SUMN), which uses historical behavior sequences to predict future behavior distributions through a learning task. While these approaches aim to improve downstream task effectiveness by encoding behavioral sequences as representations, the learned representations are not tailored to specific tasks and may not be well-suited to our task.

3   Method

In this section, we will describe our method in detail. We begin by clarifying several important concepts of behavior in Sect. 3.1. We then give an overview of our method in Sect. 3.2. Next, we introduce representation learning for both the target behavior and the behavior preference in Sect. 3.3. Finally, we describe the behavior consistency contrastive learning task in 3.4. Furthermore, we describe the attribute consistency contrastive learning task in Sect. 3.5. The important notations used in our paper are summarized in Table 1.

Table 1. Important notations for BCAD

Notation	Description
m	The number of basic attributes
n	The number of preference attributes
l	The length of a historical behavior sequence
a^i	The i-th basic attribute feature, $i \in \{1, \cdots, m\}$
$\mathbf{v}^i$	The representation vector for the basic attribute a^i, $i \in \{1, \cdots, m\}$
$\mathbf{u}^k$	The basic attribute preference transform from the basic attribute vectors set $\{\mathbf{v}^1, \mathbf{v}^2, \cdots, \mathbf{v}^m\}$ thought the preference matrix $\mathbf{M}^k \in \mathbb{R}^{n \times m}$, $k \in \{1, \cdots, n\}$
e	A behavior composed of a set of basic attribute features $e = \{a^1, a^2, \cdots, a^m\}$
$\mathbf{z}$	The output representation vector of the behavior encoder for behavior e which is computed from $\{\mathbf{v}^1, \mathbf{v}^2, ..., \mathbf{v}^m\}$
S	A historical sequence composed of a set of behaviors $S = \{e_1, e_2, ..., e_l\}$
$\mathbf{h}$	The output behavior preference representation vector of the sequential encoder and projector
$\mathbf{h}^k$	The behavior preference attribute representation vector learned by the k-th attribute gate, $k \in \{1, \cdots, n\}$
I	The mini-batch sample set
$N(i)$	The negative sample set of the i-th sample in the mini-batch sample set I
τ	$\tau \subseteq \mathbb{R}^+$ is a scalar temperature parameter [3]

3.1   Concepts of Behavior

Definition 1. *Behavior.* *A behavior $e = \{a^1, a^2, ..., a^m\}$ is consist of multiple behavior attributes (such as product category and pay amount), where a^i denotes the i-th behavior attribute, and m indicates the number of basic attributes in a behavior.*

Definition 2. *Target Behavior.* *A target behavior is the behavior e^t which is the candidate behavior to be judged whether it is fraudulent or not.*

Definition 3. *Historical Behavior Sequence.* *A historical behavior sequence S is the sequence of behaviors that occurred before the target behavior e^t of the same user. The sequence $S = \{e_1, e_2, ..., e_l\}$ is presented by chronologically ordered behaviors, where e_j denotes the j-th behavior, and l is the length of S.*

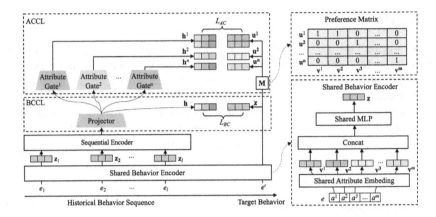

Fig. 2. Overview of BCAD, which consists of three main components: Representation Learning, Behavior Consistency Contrastive Learning (BCCL), and Attribute Consistency Contrastive Learning (ACCL). Representation Learning consists of a shared behavior encoder and a sequential encoder to encode the target behavior and the historical behavior sequence. Then BCCL learns the consistency of the behavior and the behavior preference and ACCL learns the consistency of the attribute the preference attribute. Finally, we obtain measurable representations of the target behavior and the historical behavior sequence, enabling us to detect anomalous transactions.

3.2   Overview of BCAD

We consider the anomaly transaction detection as a contrastive learning problem based on behavior consistency. The input of our model is the target behavior e^t and the user's historical behavior sequence $S = \{e_1, e_2, ..., e_l\}$. Our goal is to predict the probability of the target behavior being abnormal given the historical behavior sequence and meanwhile give an interpretation at the attribute level. The overview of BCAD is shown in Fig. 2.

In our proposed BCAD model, a shared behavior embedding layer is first employed to learn the vector representation of behavior and multiple attributes. Then, the input of the historical behavior part is used by a behavioral sequence learning model containing a sequence encoder as well as multiple attribute gate modules to learn the user's behavior preferences and multiple preferences attributes. The model converts the target behavior and historical behavior sequences into the same representation space. Similarly, we will also extract the preference attribute representations from the historical behavior sequences as well as the attribute representations of the target behavior and transform them into the same representation space. Finally, the similarity of representations between the target behavior and the behavior preference is computed as the output of the probability of being abnormal. Meanwhile, the similarity of representations between multiple target attributes and multiple preference attributes is computed as an output for interpretability analysis.

3.3   Representation Learning

This section focuses on transforming the raw behavior data into a representation vector. Most of the existing methods based on behavior sequences ignore the target behavior or model the target behavior as a part of the historical behavior sequence. However, in our problem, we must model the target behavior and historical behavior sequences simultaneously to guarantee they are comparable.

Shared Behavior Encoder. We utilize look-up embedding to learn dense representations from raw behavior data, following previous works [7,20,21]. To make the representations of the target behavior and the historical behavior sequence comparable, we allow them to share a embedding look-up table. As mentioned before, a behavior $e = \{a^1, a^2, ..., a^m\}$ is composed of m behavioral attributes. The raw behavioral attributes contain both categorical and numerical features. We need to discretize the numerical features into buckets and convert them to categorical types. The embedding layer then uses embedding tables for each raw behavioral attribute to transform it into low-dimensional dense vectors $\{\mathbf{v}^1, \mathbf{v}^2, ..., \mathbf{v}^m\}$. The vectors $\{\mathbf{v}^1, \mathbf{v}^2, ..., \mathbf{v}^m\}$ are concatenated and transformed to a single embedding vector $\mathbf{z}$ using a multi-layer perceptron layer. As a result, we can obtain the representation vector $\mathbf{z}$ of the behavior as well as the representation vector of each behavioral attribute $\{\mathbf{v}^1, \mathbf{v}^2, ..., \mathbf{v}^m\}$.

Sequential Encoder. We employ a sequential encoder to extract the behavior preferences representation $\mathbf{h}$ from a historical behavioral sequence S. First, the historical behavioral sequence can be represented as $\{\mathbf{z}_1, \mathbf{z}_2, ..., \mathbf{z}_l\}$ after the shared behavior encoder. Next, in order to better model the dependencies between behaviors, we follow the work of Chen et al. [2] and introduce the transformer block to encode the representation $\{\mathbf{z}_1, \mathbf{z}_2, ..., \mathbf{z}_l\}$ of behavior sequence. Then, we flatten the output of the transformer block and map it to a single behavior sequence representation vector using a multi-layer perceptron layer. Finally, to facilitate the computation of the similarity between the representations, a projector module is needed to reduce the dimensionality of the behavior sequence representation vector to the same as the target behavior representation vector and represent it as the behavior preference vector $\mathbf{h}$.

3.4   Behavior Consistency Contrastive Learning

Data analysis shows that most users exhibit consistent behaviors over a relatively long period. We calculate the mean statistic of the historical behavior on each attribute and then compute the deviations between the historical behavior and the target behavior. Our hypothesis is that the deviations of the abnormal behaviors have no difference compared to the ones of the normal behaviors. We calculate the one-sided t-test and the resulted p-value (average on all attributes) is 3.4% ($<5\%$) which means the deviations of the abnormal behavior are greater than the ones of normal behaviors. Hence, we propose the behavior consistency assumption which is the basis for solving the problem of individual-level anomaly transaction detection.

Assumption 1 *Behavior Consistency Assumption. User behaviors show consistency in the time dimension. Specifically, the target behavior e^t should be consistent with the behavior preferences* **h** *of the same user.*

Based on the above assumption, we propose a method named $\underline{B}$ehavior $\underline{C}$onsistency $\underline{C}$ontrastive $\underline{L}$earning (**BCCL**). We train the behavior encoder and the sequential encoders in a self-supervised paradigm. Specifically, we build a contrastive learning task that can be described as maximizing the similarity between the behavior preferences representation vector and behavior representation vector of the same users and minimizing the similarity of different users.

In the training process, we construct samples consisting of the user's historical behavior sequences and target behaviors. We adopt the strategy of negative sampling within a batch, where the sequence of historical behaviors and target behaviors of the same user are positive pairs, and the sequence of historical behaviors and target behaviors of different users are negative pairs. Then, we obtain the behavior preference representation vector **h** and the target behavior representation vector **z** through the model. And, our objective can be translated into maximizing the similarity between positive pairs and minimizing the similarity of the vectors between negative pairs and the objective function of BCCL is shown in the following formula:

$$L_{BC} = \sum_{i \in I} -\log \frac{\exp(f(\mathbf{h}_i, \mathbf{z}_i)/\tau)}{\exp(f(\mathbf{h}_i, \mathbf{z}_i)/\tau) + \sum_{j \in N(i)} \exp(f(\mathbf{h}_i, \mathbf{z}_j)/\tau)}, \tag{1}$$

where $\mathbf{h}_i$ is the behavior preference representation vector, and $\mathbf{z}_i$ is the behavior representation vector. The subscript i indicates the i-th sample in a mini-batch. We utilize cosine similarity to quantify the similarity of these vectors, which is implemented as:

$$sim = f(\mathbf{z_1}, \mathbf{z_2}) = \frac{\mathbf{z_1}}{\|\mathbf{z_1}\|_2} \cdot \frac{\mathbf{z_2}}{\|\mathbf{z_2}\|_2}, \tag{2}$$

where $\mathbf{z_1}$ and $\mathbf{z_2}$ are vectors representing representations of the same dimension. Thus the behavior preference representation vector and the behavior representation vector can project to a common feature space for quantitative evaluation discrepancy.

3.5   Attribute Consistency Contrastive Learning

A user's purchase behavior is usually described from several basic attributes, such as product category, price, and payment type, etc. Correspondingly, the user's behavior preferences can also be abstracted into preference attributes in several aspects, such as preferences of shopping interest, purchasing ability, and payment habit. It is important to note that these preference attributes are explicitly semantic and can be understood by humans. Therefore, we can compare the consistency between the target behavior attribute and the corresponding preference attribute to explain the detection results from the perspective of behavior attributes. More formally, in addition to Assumption 1 (the behavior consistency assumption), we here propose the attribute consistency assumption.

Assumption 2 *Attribute Consistency Assumption. The attributes of a target behavior should be consistent with the behavior preference attributes of the same user. Specifically, the k-th preference of the target behavior should be consistent with the corresponding k-th preference attribute* $\mathbf{h}^k$ *extracted from the historical behavior sequence.*

For the historical behavior sequence, we propose an **Attribute Gate** module for disentangling the behavior preference representation $\mathbf{h}$ into a historical preference with multiple attributes. The attribute gate module is described in Fig. 2 and the attribute representation vector is formulated as:

$$\text{AttributeGate}(\mathbf{h}) = \sigma(\boldsymbol{W}\mathbf{h} + \boldsymbol{b}) \odot (\boldsymbol{W}\mathbf{h} + \boldsymbol{b}), \tag{3}$$

where $\mathbf{h}$ is the behavior sequence representation vector and $\boldsymbol{W} \in \mathbb{R}^{d_a \times d_s}$ is the weight matrices, $\boldsymbol{b} \in \mathbb{R}^{d_a}$ is the biases, d_s and d_a indicate the dimension of behavior sequence representation vector and preference attribute representation vector, respectively. We extract representation for all preference attributes by the following formula:

$$\mathbf{h}^k = \text{AttributeGate}^k(\mathbf{h}), \quad k = 1, 2, \cdots, n. \tag{4}$$

Here each AttributeGate^k has its own parameters and n is the number of preference attributes. For the target behavior, we use a preference matrix $\mathbf{M} \in \mathbb{R}^{n \times m}$ to transform the basic attributes to the preference u. The preference matrix is a pre-defined matrix which encodes human knowledge about the behavior preference. For example, the basic attribute representations of product category and amount are transformed into a preference indicating the level of consumption. In this way, we can use prior knowledge to guide the learning of attribute gates.

Based on Assumption 2, we here propose a method named $\underline{A}$ttribute $\underline{C}$onsistency $\underline{C}$ontrastive $\underline{L}$earning (**ACCL**) to optimize the attribute gate module's parameters. Specifically, the attribute representation of target behavior is regarded as ground-truth through stop-gradient (stopgrad) operation, and we need to maximize the similarity between it and the representation of the attribute a to ensure the consistency assumption. The objective function of ACCL is implemented as:

$$L_{AC} = -\sum_{k=1}^{n} \sum_{i \in I} f(\mathbf{h}_i^k, \text{stopgrad}(\mathbf{u}_i^k)), \tag{5}$$

where $\mathbf{h}^k$ is the preference attribute representation vector and $\mathbf{v}^k$ is the attribute representation vector. The superscript k indicates the k-th preference attribute and the n is the number of preference attributes. Finally, the overall objective function of the BCAD is a combination of BCCL and ACCL:

$$L = L_{BC} + \lambda \cdot L_{AC}, \tag{6}$$

where λ is the hyperparameter used to balance those two losses.

4   Experiment

In this section, we investigate the effectiveness of our proposed model. We conducted extensive experiments on a large-scale real-world industrial dataset. First, we validated the performance advantage of BCAD on the task of detecting abnormal transactions. Then, we performed ablation study to verify the effect of the module on the model. Finally, we demonstrated the interpretability of our method through a case study.

4.1   Dataset

We curated a real-world transaction datasets containing desensitized samples collected from a large e-commerce platform. We sampled 32.1 million users with 3.6 billion transactions (ranging from 2021/4 to 2022/4) for training, and 20 million transactions (ranging from 2022/5 to 2022/7) for testing. It is important to note that we only included users with more than 20 transactions in the past year. To assess the stability of the model effects, we further separate the test dataset into three sub-datasets by month. Each transaction sample contains attribute information including the time stamp, pay amount, product type, and so on.

For evaluation, we need gold standard labels for the abnormal transactions. In fact, according to the business rules, there are commonly two classes of risky transaction. One is *cash-out*, which is a fake transaction with a purpose to cash out from a credit card. The other one is *interception*, which means the user abandons further payments after the transaction has been intercepted by some risk control rules. Thereby, we collect two kinds of risk labels, cash-out and interception, on the test dataset as the gold standard label to evaluate the performance of our method. The detailed statistical information is exhibited in Table 2.

Table 2. Evaluation Labels on Test Dataset

Label	May.		Jun.		Jul.	
	Pos Num	Pos Ratio	Pos Num	Pos Ratio	Pos Num	Pos Ratio
Cash-out	9k	0.0016	26k	0.0028	11k	0.0021
Interception	60k	0.0102	77k	0.0084	90k	0.0171

4.2   Experiment Settings

Baselines. To verify the effectiveness of our proposed method, we choose two categories of baseline methods, including both the *anomaly detection based models* and the *representation learning based models*.

(a) Anomaly detection based models

- **LSTM-VAE** [13]: A reconstruction-based model, which combines LSTM and VAE by replacing the feed-forward network of VAE with LSTM.

- **Transformer-VAE**: A reconstruction-based model, which combines Transformer and VAE by replacing the feed-forward network of VAE with Transformer [5].
- **DAEMON** [4]: A reconstruction-based model based on a self-encoder and a GAN structure.

(b) Representation learning based models

- **SUMN** [7]: A self-supervised universal user representation learning method. We tailored the method to better fit our task as follows: 1) **SUMN-SIM**: We separately compute the representations of the historical behavior sequences and target behaviors. 2) **SUMN-REC**: We predict the distribution of future behaviors using the historical behavior sequences and then calculate the difference between the target behavior and the predicted distribution.

Evaluation Metrics. We use two evaluation metrics to evaluate the performance of our model. The first metric is AUC which is defined as the Area Under the receiver operating characteristic (ROC) Curve enclosed by coordinate axes. A higher AUC indicates better performance. The output of our model is the similarity sim between the target behavior and the user's historical preferences within range $[-1, 1]$, smaller values indicate more inconsistent, i.e., a higher probability of anomaly. In order to evaluate our results using AUC, we first convert the similarity into a abnormal probability, using $p = (1-sim)/2$, where p denotes the abnormal probability. We use the probability p and the gold standard label to compute the AUC score.

Our unsupervised approach has the ability to identify anomalous patterns that are not covered by the pre-defined anomaly types. As part of our evaluation, we chose a small sample of data and asked experts to manually label the anomalies within it. By computing the accuracy metric on this subset of labeled data, we were able to assess the effectiveness of our approach.

Implementation Details. We implement our approach using Keras, and adopt the Adam [9] optimizer with a learning rate of 0.001 and a batch size of 1024. For the the shared behavior ecoder, the embedding size of each attribute is set to 32 and the shared mlp is a multi-layer perceptron with 128 hidden units. For the sequential encoder we use a transformer block [17] with 2 heads. For the projector layer, a multi-layer perceptron with 128 hidden units is used.

4.3 Model Performance

We present the label evaluation results of our method and baseline methods in Table 3. We observe that our model consistently and significantly outperforms

Table 3. Model Performance

Method	May. Cash Out	Intercept	Jun. Cash Out	Intercept	Jul. Cash Out	Intercept	Average
LSTM-VAE	0.5733	0.5866	0.5818	0.5761	0.6753	0.5568	0.5917
Transformer-VAE	0.5714	0.5921	0.5770	0.5788	0.6722	0.5606	0.5920
DAEMON	0.5739	0.5866	0.5836	0.5762	0.6756	0.5568	0.5921
SUMN-SIM	0.5559	0.5297	0.5048	0.4790	0.5380	0.5307	0.5230
SUMN-REC	0.6611	0.6790	0.6502	0.6663	0.6870	0.6387	0.6637
(w/o) BCCL	0.5387	0.6392	0.5398	0.6462	0.5949	0.6560	0.6025
(w/o) ACCL	0.6956	0.6938	0.6785	**0.7001**	0.7116	0.6222	0.6836
BCAD	**0.7011**	**0.7046**	**0.6824**	0.6999	**0.7221**	**0.6618**	**0.6953**

all baselines on three month dataset in both two abnormal categories. Concretely, among the baseline methods, the anomaly detection models (LSTM-VAE, Transformer-VAE, DAEMON) have similar performance. This shows that these general anomaly detection methods may not be applicable for detecting individual-level anomalies in transaction data. We found that the direct use of learned representations(SUMN-SIM), which were not designed for specific tasks, was even less effective than anomaly detection methods. However, we were able to enhance the performance of SUMN on our task significantly by computing the difference between the predicted future behavior distribution and the target behavior as the outcome (SUMN-REC). We achieved the best results among all baselines by using this method (SUMN-REC). Additionally, our method BCAD outperforms SUMN-REC on the AUC metrics by an average of 0.031. This demonstrates that our unsupervised model, specifically designed for anomaly detection tasks, is capable of achieving superior results compared to a generic unsupervised model.

To further confirm the reliability of our model, we conducted manual evaluations of the detection results on a small portion of the test data. Specifically, we randomly picked 100 transactions classified as anomalous by BCAD and delivered them to experts for manual evaluation. The experts categorized each sample as normal, abnormal, or uncertain, and were also able to further classify the anomaly types into cash-out, interception, or label-undefined anomaly, which was neither cash-out nor interception. Based on the expert evaluation, we found that 56% of the detected anomalies were true abnormal transactions. Among these, 21% were label-defined abnormal transactions, while the remaining 35% were label-undefined. This highlights the ability of our model to detect undefined abnormal types, as it is essentially an unsupervised learning approach. Therefore, we can confidently confirm the reliability of our model in detecting anomalous transactions task.

4.4   Ablation Study

To better illustrate the contribution of each module to our framework, we conducted an ablation study in this section. Specifically, we compared three versions of our BCAD framework: (1) the one without the ACCL module, (2) the one without the BCCL module, and (3) the full BCAD framework. The results, as shown in Table 3, indicate that the BCCL module is crucial for maintaining high performance, as the model performance drops significantly after removing it. On the other hand, the ACCL module not only provides interpretability but also enhances performance, with an average AUC improvement of 0.01 compared to the version without it.

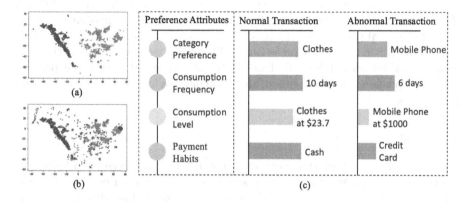

Fig. 3. (a) Visualization of embedding space with two preference attributes. Different colored dots represent different preference attributes. (b) Visualization of embedding space with two preference attributes and the corresponding target behavior attributes.The blue and green dots indicate the corresponding preference attribute and target behavior attribute. Meanwhile the yellow and red dots indicate the corresponding preference attribute and target behavior attribute. (c) An example of the attribute level interpretability. Different-colored circles represent different behavioral preference attributes, and different-colored cubes represent the degree of consistency between corresponding basic attribute preference and behavioral preference, with the longer ones indicating greater consistency and the shorter ones indicating less consistency. (Color figure online)

4.5   Interpretability

Analysis of Attributes. In this subsection, we demonstrate the capability of our BCAD framework to separate different attributes and align the corresponding preference and target behavior attributes. To achieve this, we use the t-SNE method [11] to visualize the representation vector of two preference attributes, as shown in Fig. 3(a). The representation vectors learned by ACCL for these two preference attributes are evidently distinct from each other.

Furthermore, we visualize the representation vectors of both the corresponding preference attributes and target behavior attributes in Fig. 3(b). It can be observed that the representation vectors of the corresponding preference attributes and target behavior attributes are closer to each other.

Case Study. We present a typical case study to demonstrate the effectiveness of our proposed BCAD framework. Specifically, we consider a user who has a preference for products with a high cost-performance ratio based on their past transaction history. The consistency between the user's preference and the transaction attributes is illustrated in Fig. 3(c), where two transactions are considered, one normal and the other abnormal.

For the normal transaction, the consistency between the preference attributes and target attributes is high. However, for the abnormal transaction, although the product category and consumption interval are highly consistent with the user's behavioral preferences, the product grade and payment method have little consistency with the user's preferences. Therefore, we can conclude that the main reason for identifying this transaction as anomalous is that the product grade and payment method of the transaction deviate from the user's behavioral preferences.

4.6   Ethics

We collected dataset in this work does not involve any Personal Identifiable Information (PPI). We have taken a series of security measures to protect the safety and privacy of this data. We promise not to disclose this data to any third party and use it only for research purposes. We will anonymize the data to ensure that no one's identity information is leaked and destroy it after the experiment.

5   Conclusion

In this paper, we propose an unsupervised anomaly transactions detection problem that focuses on the individual level. In order to solve the above problem, we find that behavioral consistency is the key point and propose a novel unsupervised model named BCAD. First, we model both the target behavior and the user's behavior preferences by learning measurable representations between them using the BCCL method. Then, the ACCL method is proposed for learning behavior preference, from the perspective of attributes. Finally, experiments on a real-world dataset demonstrate that our proposed model is effective in the task of anomaly transaction detection and the results are interpretable.

The study of unsupervised anomaly transaction detection problems focusing on the individual level is still in the early stage. BCAD is one of the pioneering works to solve this understudied problem. Although our model has shown promising performance on anomaly transaction detection, more anomaly detection models can also be constructed based on the assumption of behavioral consistency, such as anomaly detection on the group level. Developing more anomaly transactions detection model based on behavioral consistency capable of capturing different type anomalies and ensemble the results is necessary for the robust anomaly detection system. Extending our method to support more anomalous detection scenarios based on behavioral consistency is our future work.

References

1. Cao, S., Yang, X., Chen, C., Zhou, J., Li, X., Qi, Y.A.: Titant: Online real-time transaction fraud detection in ant financial. CoRR abs/1906.07407 (2019)
2. Chen, Q., Zhao, H., Li, W., Huang, P., Ou, W.: Behavior sequence transformer for e-commerce recommendation in alibaba. CoRR abs/1905.06874 (2019)
3. Chen, T., Kornblith, S., Norouzi, M., Hinton, G.E.: A simple framework for contrastive learning of visual representations. In: Proceedings of the 37th International Conference on Machine Learning, ICML 2020, 13–18 July 2020, Virtual Event. Proceedings of Machine Learning Research, vol. 119, pp. 1597–1607. PMLR (2020)
4. Chen, X., et al.: Daemon: Unsupervised anomaly detection and interpretation for multivariate time series. In: 2021 IEEE 37th International Conference on Data Engineering (ICDE), pp. 2225–2230. IEEE (2021)
5. Eisenbach, M., Lübberstedt, J., Aganian, D., Gross, H.: A little bit attention is all you need for person re-identification. CoRR abs/2302.14574 (2023)
6. Gao, T., Yao, X., Chen, D.: Simcse: Simple contrastive learning of sentence embeddings. arXiv preprint arXiv:2104.08821 (2021)
7. Gu, J., et al.: Exploiting behavioral consistence for universal user representation. In: AAAI Conference on Artificial Intelligence (2020)
8. Kim, K.H., et al.: Rapp: Novelty detection with reconstruction along projection pathway. In: 8th International Conference on Learning Representations, ICLR 2020, Addis Ababa, Ethiopia, April 26–30, 2020. OpenReview.net (2020)
9. Kingma, D.P., Ba, J.: Adam: A method for stochastic optimization. In: Bengio, Y., LeCun, Y. (eds.) 3rd International Conference on Learning Representations, ICLR 2015, San Diego, CA, USA, May 7–9, 2015, Conference Track Proceedings (2015)
10. Liu, C., et al.: Fraud transactions detection via behavior tree with local intention calibration. In: Gupta, R., Liu, Y., Tang, J., Prakash, B.A. (eds.) KDD '20: The 26th ACM SIGKDD Conference on Knowledge Discovery and Data Mining, Virtual Event, CA, USA, August 23–27, 2020, pp. 3035–3043. ACM (2020)
11. Van der Maaten, L., Hinton, G.: Visualizing data using t-sne. J. Mach. Learn. Res. **9**(11) (2008)
12. Min, W., Liang, W., Yin, H., Wang, Z., Li, M., Lal, A.: Explainable deep behavioral sequence clustering for transaction fraud detection. CoRR abs/2101.04285 (2021)
13. Park, D., Hoshi, Y., Kemp, C.C.: A multimodal anomaly detector for robot-assisted feeding using an LSTM-based variational autoencoder. IEEE Robotics Autom. Lett. **3**(2), 1544–1551 (2018)
14. Pranavan, T., Sim, T., Ambikapathi, A., Ramasamy, S.: Contrastive predictive coding for anomaly detection in multi-variate time series data. CoRR abs/2202.03639 (2022)
15. Ren, H., et al.: Time-series anomaly detection service at microsoft. In: Teredesai, A., Kumar, V., Li, Y., Rosales, R., Terzi, E., Karypis, G. (eds.) Proceedings of the 25th ACM SIGKDD International Conference on Knowledge Discovery & Data Mining, KDD 2019, Anchorage, AK, USA, August 4–8, 2019, pp. 3009–3017. ACM (2019)
16. Rezapour, M.: Anomaly detection using unsupervised methods: credit card fraud case study. Int. J. Adv. Comput. Sci. Appl. **10**(11) (2019)
17. Vaswani, A., et al.: Attention is all you need. In: Guyon, I., et al., (eds.) Advances in Neural Information Processing Systems 30: Annual Conference on Neural Information Processing Systems 2017, December 4–9, 2017, Long Beach, CA, USA, pp. 5998–6008 (2017)

18. Wang, H., Li, M., Ma, F., Huang, S., Zhang, L.: Unsupervised anomaly detection via generative adversarial networks: poster abstract. In: Eskicioglu, M.R., Mottola, L., Priyantha, B. (eds.) Proceedings of the 18th International Conference on Information Processing in Sensor Networks, IPSN 2019, Montreal, QC, Canada, April 16–18, 2019, pp. 313–314. ACM (2019)

19. Wang, J., Cherian, A.: GODS: generalized one-class discriminative subspaces for anomaly detection. In: 2019 IEEE/CVF International Conference on Computer Vision, ICCV 2019, Seoul, Korea (South), October 27 - November 2, 2019, pp. 8200–8210. IEEE (2019)

20. Wu, C., Wu, F., Qi, T., Huang, Y.: Userbert: Pre-training user model with contrastive self-supervision. In: Proceedings of the 45th International ACM SIGIR Conference on Research and Development in Information Retrieval, pp. 2087–2092. SIGIR '22, Association for Computing Machinery, New York, NY, USA (2022)

21. Zhu, Y., et al.: Modeling users' behavior sequences with hierarchical explainable network for cross-domain fraud detection. In: Huang, Y., King, I., Liu, T., van Steen, M. (eds.) WWW '20: The Web Conference 2020, Taipei, Taiwan, April 20–24, 2020, pp. 928–938. ACM / IW3C2 (2020)

Advancing Fraud Detection Systems Through Online Learning

Tommaso Paladini, Martino Bernasconi de Luca, Michele Carminati[(⊠)],
Mario Polino, Francesco Trovò, and Stefano Zanero

DEIB, Politecnico di Milano, Milan, Italy
{tommaso.paladini,martino.bernasconideluca,michele.carminati,
mario.polino,francesco1.trovo,stefano.zanero}@polimi.it

Abstract. The rapid increase in digital transactions has led to a consequential surge in financial fraud, requiring an automatic way of defend-
ing effectively from such a threat. The past few years experienced a
rise in the design and use by financial institutions of different machine
learning-based fraud detection systems. However, these solutions may
suffer severe drawbacks if a malevolent adversary adapts their behavior
over time, making the selection of the existing fraud detectors difficult.
In this paper, we study the application of online learning techniques to
respond effectively to adaptive attackers. More specifically, the proposed
approach takes as input a set of classifiers employed for fraud detection
tasks and selects, based on the performances experienced in the past,
the one to apply to analyze the next transaction. The use of an online
learning approach guarantees to keep at a pace the loss due to the adaptive behavior of the attacker over a given learning period. To validate
our methodology, we perform an extensive experimental evaluation using
real-world banking data augmented with distinct fraudulent campaigns
based on real-world attackers' models. Our results demonstrate that the
proposed approach allows prompt updates to detection models as new
patterns and behaviors are occurring, leading to a more robust and effective fraud detection system.

Keywords: Fraud detection · Expert learning · Online learning

1 Introduction

The popularity of Internet banking services has led to a consequential growth of
financial fraud, one of the causes of economic losses for banking institutions [23].
In 2021, the total value of fraudulent transactions using cards issued in countries
within the Single Euro Payments Area was estimated to reach around € 1.53 billion [18]. Another estimation indicated that € 2.3 out of every € 1,000 exchanged
in Italy during 2020 through Internet banking transactions were associated with
fraudulent activities [26]. According to an industrial survey [23], institutions
recover less than 25% of the losses due to fraud. This leads to the conclusion

© The Author(s), under exclusive license to Springer Nature Switzerland AG 2023
G. De Francisci Morales et al. (Eds.): ECML PKDD 2023, LNAI 14174, pp. 275–292, 2023.
https://doi.org/10.1007/978-3-031-43427-3_17

that banks must actively contain fraudulent activities. However, manual investigations of customer activity can be challenging and expensive because the stream of transactions that goes through a banking system is too large to be entirely processed by analysts [12]. The collaboration of researchers and domain experts produced software tools called *Fraud Detection Systems (FDSs)* to solve this problem. The purpose of these systems is to analyze the large stream of transactions automatically [36] and raise warnings over (or possibly block) fraudulent transactions. State-of-the-art fraud detection systems employ Machine Learning (ML) algorithms to learn the patterns associated with regular and fraudulent activities from historical customer data. In particular, the resulting models' goal is to predict the label associated with each transaction (legitimate/fraudulent) and provide suggestions on the priority of the transaction to analyze manually.

In the literature, many solutions adopt different ML approaches, ranging from supervised systems [19,22,29], to anomaly detection and active learning [24] ones. Even if these solutions have shown effective performance when applied to specific cases [12,22,24], they are also exposed to the adaptation of the possible attackers [13,15]. Indeed, classical ML relies on the assumption that the historical data can properly characterize the ones that will be observed in the future. However, if the opponents can get information on the currently adopted fraud detection method, they can easily circumvent the system by modifying their behavior. For instance, if they infer that a specific range of a feature for a transaction is key to the ML system, they can generate fraudulent transactions with values for that feature outside that range [14]. To circumvent this issue, financial institutions can use, at the same time, multiple ML fraud detection systems basing their decision on different attacker behaviors so that the opponent cannot exploit such systems. However, this approach introduces further complexity to the fraud detection procedure since it requires selecting at each time the fraud detection system that can mitigate the current opponent strategy most effectively. In addition, the performance of the detection system poses a burden on the financial institution. Undetected fraudulent activities bring higher potential economic damage than false alarms, but large volumes of false positives can affect the system's availability because they need to be manually validated [2].

In this paper, we propose applying *online learning* techniques to dynamically select the most promising fraud detection system over time. This approach, based on the performance of each ML fraud detection system experienced in the past, adapts the fraud detection strategy so that the opponent's exploitation chances are minimized. Indeed, applying the Multiplicative Weight Update (MWU) algorithm [20] we have theoretical guarantees on the overall loss w.r.t. the best unknown fixed method at the end of a predefined fraud detection period. We conducted an experimental assessment using banking data augmented with fraudulent campaigns inspired by real-world fraudsters. To validate our methodology, we devised two distinct scenarios. In the first scenario, the attacker dynamically changes behavior but is unaware of the possible FDS the financial institution has available. In the second scenario, the attacker exploits the knowledge of the deployed FDS to generate frauds dynamically. Our findings reveal the MWU algorithm facilitates updates to detection models whenever new fraudulent patterns are detected, resulting in a more efficient FDS.

In summary, the novel contributions of the current paper are:

- the definition of a threat model based on real fraudulent behavior experienced by real-world financial institutions;
- the application of online learning techniques to adapt the ML fraud detection systems w.r.t. the strategy followed by the attacker;
- the test of the proposed online learning approaches on a real-world dataset of transactions coming from a year of bank transactions analysis.

2   Background and Related Work

Supervised fraud detectors consider the fraud detection problem as a binary classification task, and are trained on manually labeled tabular data. Notable examples are the works of [5,6,8,9,21,28,32,33,36–38], which investigate possible solutions to the same task with different supervised learning algorithms. Conversely, unsupervised approaches usually follow an anomaly detection approach and identify frauds as anomalies w.r.t. the legitimate behavior of the customers. For instance, in *BankSealer* [12], the authors rank transactions according to an anomaly score, i.e., the likelihood provided by a classification model of a transaction being a fraud. Such a score is provided by three different profiles: *local*, *global*, and *temporal*. The local profiles compare the distance of the transaction with the past activity of the customer. The global profile compares the transaction with the ones from a cluster of customers with similar spending behavior and power. The third profile evaluates with thresholds the temporal properties of the time series of customer transactions. Instead, in [25], a custom hierarchical clustering algorithm is proposed. Their algorithm recursively groups transactions into smaller clusters, which are then given the labels (legitimate/fraud) associated with the majority of the samples. The goal of their approach is to identify fraud campaigns and organized fraudsters. There are also examples of detection systems built on top of active learning approaches, such as [10], where the authors provide a comparison of the performances of different active learning strategies in the context of fraud detection. They analyze the problem of querying and labeling data points, balancing exploration and exploitation.

The proposed solutions, though, do not consider the possible performance improvements that can be achieved by combining isolated models in mixtures of experts, i.e., model ensembles [4,19,22,24,31,34]. The authors of [4,31,34] study the performances of ensembles with majority voting. A fraud detection approach based on an ensemble of LSTM and GRU as base classifiers is proposed in [19]. These models, trained on slices of the original datasets, provide the output fed into a feedforward neural network. Such a network, a.k.a. voting classifier, is trained on the output of the ensemble models, and it is responsible for producing the final classification of a transaction. In *Amaretto* [24], the authors combine supervised and unsupervised techniques under an active learning framework, to better exploit the feedback of the institution's analysts, and propose novel selection strategies to prioritize potentially new anomalous patterns. In [22], the authors compare the performances of an ensemble model with a single deep neural network model. For each sample, their ensemble outputs the average of the fraud scores provided by the base classifiers, i.e., the probability of the sample belonging to the fraud class. Their experimental results, however, show that the single model outperforms the ensemble.

All the above approaches have the underlying assumption that the data distribution, i.e., the relationship between the transaction and the fact of being a fraud, is stationary over time and cannot be influenced by external factors, like a malevolent attacker. In this case, classical ML techniques can be exploited, and their effectiveness might be compromised. In this work, we resort to the online learning approach [16], a subfield of ML integrating a game theoretical framework, in which the algorithms are intrinsically designed to deal with cases where an opponent is influencing the underlying process. These techniques have been applied successfully in many different fields, e.g., in solving dynamic pricing problems [35], online internet advertising [27], drug dosage [3], and finance [7]. However, to the best of our knowledge, the application of such techniques to the fraud detection field has been unexplored so far.

3   Threat Model

The existence of a large number of fraudulent transactions is due to the fact that cybercriminals have banking services among their main targets. Indeed, a compromised banking account can be used to steal funds from the available balance directly or sold on the underground market [23]. Moreover, fraudsters constantly improve their techniques to outwit online banking defenses. For this reason, fraudulent behavior is dynamic, rare, and dispersed in very large and highly imbalanced datasets [12,30]. However, we cannot rely solely on systems that detect the change in the common transaction paths since also customer habits change over time, making the task of distinguishing fraudulent transactions from normal ones more challenging for defenders [29].

Definition 1. *An electronic banking transaction $b := (\mathbf{f}, \mathbf{x}, a)$ is characterized as a feature vector $\mathbf{f} \in \mathbb{R}^m$ characterizing the transaction, a vector $\mathbf{x} \in \mathbb{R}^n$ of the so-called activity record, i.e., a set of features computed over past transactions of the same client, and an amount $a \in \mathbb{R}^+$, i.e., the quantity of money exchanged by the transaction.*

Relevant quantities included in the feature vector $\mathbf{f}$ are the date and time of execution, geographic origin of the connection (e.g., the IP associated with the connection), the identifier of the bank and of the account number (e.g., International Bank Account Number (IBAN)), and modes of verification (e.g., SMS sent to the customer's phone). Instead, common elements constituting the activity record $\mathbf{x}$ are features that summarize the past activity of the customer over a fixed time window, commonly computed by aggregating past transactions [36] (e.g., average transaction amount, total transaction count). Note that each activity record is a banking activity that may have originated by the rightful customer or an anonymous fraudster. We associate a label $y^* \in \{0, 1\}$ depending on whether the transaction is fraudulent. Specifically, we say it is a legitimate transaction with the label $y^* = 0$, while we assign $y^* = 1$ when it is fraudulent.

3.1   Banking Fraud

Banking fraud can be defined as the act of illegally transferring funds from a bank account with the use of Internet technology. We also refer to any attempt to defraud unaware customers with the term *attack*. Over the course of the years, financial institutions have faced threats of various natures. Following the topology and the nomenclature provided in the work by Carminati et al. [13], we defined the type of a *fraud strategy* by combining: ① an *attack technique*, i.e., the way the attacker generates the fraudulent transactions features $\mathbf{x}$; ② an *attack behavior*, i.e., how the attacker selects the amount a to be set in the fraudulent transaction and how frequently the attack is carried out. A detailed description of the attack techniques and behaviors is provided below.

Attack Techniques. They define the technical mean adopted by the fraudster to submit transactions on behalf of their victims. More specifically, it defines how the feature vector $\mathbf{f}'$ of a fraudulent transaction $b' = (\mathbf{f}', \mathbf{x}', a')$ is generated. In this work, we model the attacker by two different attack techniques [17]: *Information Stealing (IS)* and *Transaction Hijacking (TH)*. With Information Stealing, the attacker possesses the victims' credentials, so they can control the victims' accounts and directly transfer funds toward controlled accounts. The attacker may steal the credentials from databases of web services and reuse them to gain access to other accounts of the victims. Alternatively, the attacker may deceive the victim through phishing, which consists in presenting as a trustworthy entity. With this scheme, the attacker is free to choose the feature vector $\mathbf{f}'$ arbitrarily, i.e., they is generating a fake transaction from a generic customer of the financial institution. However, the connection is established by the attacker's device. Conversely, with Transaction Hijacking, the attacker halts and redirects legitimate transactions toward a desired recipient. This attack is achieved via banking Trojan or *infostealers*. This type of malware intercepts and alters legitimate webpages (e.g., the webpage of an e-Banking service) by exploiting a technique known in the literature as Man-in-the-Browser (MitB). Infostealers can bypass security measures such as two-factor authentication by infecting mobile devices. This attack is called Man-in-the-Mobile (MitMo). Once the mobile device of the victim (e.g., smartphone, tablet) is compromised, the attacker can intercept one-time passwords sent by the financial institution with SMS or dedicated applications [17]. With this attack, the fraudster uses the same user's connection, and, therefore, the fraudulent activity will show the same connection of the hijacked legitimate transaction, resulting in a greater challenge for identification. Therefore, the attacker selects a bank client and generates a fraud so that the elements of the feature vector $\mathbf{f}'$ corresponding to the above-mentioned features are determined by the values of the chosen client.

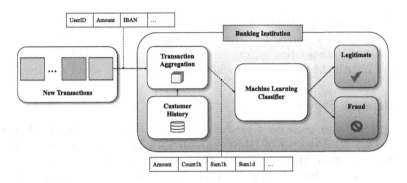

Fig. 1. Overview of a fraud detection system.

Attack Behavior. Once the technical mean is set, an attacker can act more greedily or conservatively regarding the amount a' set in the fraudulent transaction and the frequency with which they will repeat the injection of such fraud. Based on recent research works [11,12] and real-world fraudulent campaigns shared by our industrial collaborators, we distinguish among three different behavior: Short-Term (ST), Medium-Term (MT), and Long-Term (LT) campaigns. With Short-Term, we refer to an attacker generating transactions b', with a large amount, i.e., $a' \geq \mu + 2\sigma$, where μ and σ are the average and standard deviation of the transaction amount computed over past legitimate transactions, respectively.[1] These attacks are typically carried out with a frequency fr of $1 \leq fr \leq 2$ per day to a single financial institution. The name ST is because this behavior usually spans a short period (e.g., a few days). When the amount per fraud a' is more similar to the mean one μ, formally, $a' \in [\mu,\ \mu+2\sigma]$, we have the so-called Medium-Term behavior. These frauds are harder to spot, and therefore the attacker usually targets the same client multiple times, usually with a frequency of $fr \in [1, 2]$ over a week. Finally, a last class of fraud is the Long-Term one, having small amounts, i.e., $a' \in (0, \mu]$, but that is repeated more often than others, i.e., with frequency $fr \in [1, 4]$. This behavior is commonly repeated over temporal spans of months. Notice that the Short-Term behavior defines a myopic attacker that prioritizes immediate gains. Conversely, the Long-Term identifies an attacker who acts conservatively, with a long-lasting attack of many low-amount transactions against the victims.

4   Fraud Detection Systems

A FDS $\mathcal{M} : \mathbb{R}^m \times \mathbb{R}^n \times \mathbb{R}^+ \rightarrow \{0, 1\}$ is a method that predicts a class $y = \mathcal{M}(b)$ corresponding to the given activity record b. As mentioned before, the financial institutions are given a set of FDS $\{\mathcal{M}_1, \ldots \mathcal{M}_K\}$, $K \in \mathbb{N}$, which are commonly

---

[1] In the current work, we are assuming the attacker has access to the financial institution historical data.

built using a data-driven approach, i.e., they are ML classifiers trained over historical data on legitimate/fraudulent transactions. Among the most commonly used models for building such methods are Logistic Regression (LR) [5,21,36], Support Vector Machine (SVM) [8,32,33], Random Forest (RF) [5,8,33,36,37], Neural Network (NN) [6,9,28], and Extreme Gradient Boosting (XGB) [38]. Therefore, for each transaction b, we are provided with a set of corresponding predicted labels $y_1, \ldots, y_K$ corresponding to the prediction of the K different FDSs. Once a transaction has been labeled, if it has been flagged as fraudulent ($y_i = 1$), they are blocked until a manual analysis is performed. The goal of this work will be to understand how to exploit the set of predictions provided by the classifiers properly, using the most appropriate model to mitigate the currently used attacker scheme and behavior. The path followed by each transaction is summarized in Fig. 1, in which the transaction is first elaborated using a transaction aggregator procedure to build the activity record. After that, the transaction b is passed to the ML-based classifier and labeled. We remark that our formulation of FDS follows the so-called *system-centric* approach [13], in which fraud detectors are supervised models that learn a global concept of fraudulent activity from a historical dataset of labeled transactions and provide prediction looking at the information on the current transaction.[2]

5   Online Learning Approach

We consider a stream of transactions $b_1, b_2, \ldots$ that the bank has to flag as either benign or fraudulent. For a specific transaction $b_t = (\mathbf{f}_t, \mathbf{x}_t, a_t)$, we want to exploit the predictions provided by the already available K different FDSs. At each time t the bank receives a transaction and, based on its activity record b_t (as detailed in Sect. 4), it has to classify the transaction as benign or fraudulent by using the predictions made by all the available FDSs $\{\mathcal{M}_1, \ldots, \mathcal{M}_K\}$. Since in the fraud detection setting the different types of misclassifications (i.e., False Positives and False Negatives) induce different costs to the financial institution, we define for a prediction $y \in \{0, 1\}$ and transaction b_t having y_t^* as true label the following loss $l_t(y, y_t^*) = l_t(y)$ defined as:

$$l_t(y) = \begin{cases} 0 & \text{if} \quad y = y_t^* \\ a_t & \text{if} \quad y_t^* = 1 \wedge y = 0 \,, \\ d & \text{if} \quad y_t^* = 0 \wedge y = 1 \end{cases} \tag{1}$$

where d is a constant cost we incur if we incorrectly label a legitimate transaction. Indeed, generating a false negative constitutes a loss for the bank equal to the transaction's amount a_t as the financial institution will have to refund the customer. Conversely, a false positive detection incurs a fixed loss of d that can be interpreted as the costs of verifying the transaction by a human expert.

As commonly done in online decision making [16], to account for the sequential nature of the problem, we consider the cumulative loss over a fixed period

---

[2] An alternative approach is the *user-centric* approach, which consists in learning the concept of fraud corresponding to each customer or groups of customers with similar spending patterns.

(e.g., a financial quarter) as the metric for the performance of FDS models. For a model $\mathcal{A}$ and a sequence of transactions b_t over a period $\{1, \ldots, T\}$ we define the cumulative loss as:

$$L_T(\mathcal{A}) := \sum_{t=1}^{T} l_t(y_t), \tag{2}$$

where $y_t = \mathcal{A}(b_t)$ is the prediction provided by the method $\mathcal{A}$.

We attack the problem of using at best the models $\mathcal{M}_j$, by using a well-known algorithms from the online learning literature, namely *Multiplicative Weight Update* (MWU). This algorithm keeps track of the performance of all the methods and defines a set of weights $w_{j,0} = 1/K$ for each $j \in \{1, \ldots K\}$, where $w_{j,0}$ is the weight corresponding to model $\mathcal{M}_j$ at the beginning of the detection process ($t = 0$). The following formula updates the weights:

$$w_{j,t} = \frac{w_{j,t-1}e^{-\eta l_{t-1}(y_{j,t-1})}}{\sum_{i=1}^{K} w_{i,t-1}e^{-\eta l_{t-1}(y_{i,t-1})}},$$

where $y_{j-1,t} = \mathcal{M}_j(b_{t-1})$ is the prediction of model $\mathcal{M}_j$ for transaction b_{t-1} and $\eta \in \mathbb{R}^+$. Intuitively this update assigns a higher probability (greater weights) to models that incurred a smaller loss during the previous transaction (multiplied by a learning rate η). Finally, the algorithm samples a model $\mathcal{M}_{j*}$ (before the new transaction b_t is revealed), where j^* is sampled proportionally to the weights $w_{j,t}$. Then the algorithm predicts the label $y_t = \mathcal{M}_{j*}(b_t)$. Notice that the only parameter required by the algorithm is the learning rate η which, in what follows, is fixed to its theoretical value of $\eta := \sqrt{\frac{\log K}{2G^2T}}$, where G is the maximum loss that can be suffered. Moreover, this algorithm is able to guarantee that the loss w.r.t. the best single model is limited (we refer to [20] for further details).

6   Experimental Evaluation

We empirically evaluate the use of the MWU online learning approach for FDS. First, we describe the employed real-world experimental dataset, the baselines we compare MWU with, and the used performances metrics. Finally, we discuss the results. We design two different scenarios to evaluate our system. In the former one, the attacker has a dynamically changing behavior but is not aware of the possible FDS system the financial institution has available. In the latter, the attacker uses the information about the performance of the base FDS to choose how to create new fraudulent transactions.

6.1   Dataset

Our dataset contains real banking transfers belonging to a medium-sized Italian bank [12]. Notice that, due to the fact they are sensible data to the bank, they cannot be disclosed. The dataset is a snapshot of $471,199$ banking transfers exchanged by $58,504$ unique users. The dataset spans from $2014/10/22$ to $2015/02/23$, accounting for around 18 weeks of records. Each record is characterized by the following set of features $\mathbf{f}$ for a specific transaction b:

Table 1. Parameters of the attack behaviour. μ is the average amount a estimated over historical data. The Attack Frequency unit measurement is 1 over days.

Fraud Strategy	Amount a (EUR)	Attack Frequency fr
ST	$[5.5\mu, 27.7\mu]$	$[1, 2]$
MT	$[1.1\mu, 4.4\mu]$	$[1, 2]$
LT	$[0.1\mu, 0.55\mu]$	$[1, 4]$

- *IP*: the IP address of the transaction originator;
- *IBAN*: the IBAN of the payment recipient;
- *IBAN_CC*: the national code of the recipient;
- *ASN_CC*: the pair of national code and identifier of the Autonomous System Number (ASN) associated to the originator's connection;
- *SessionID*: identifier of the originator's browser session;
- *time*: a sin/cos encoding of the second of the day the transaction occurred;
- *is_national_iban*: a flag indicating if the beneficiary IBAN has the same nationality of the online bank (*i.e.*, IT country code);
- *is_international*: a flag that indicates if the beneficiary international bank account number (IBAN) has the same nationality of the customer;
- *confirm_SMS*: a flag indicating the usage of a SMS for payment confirmation

The activity record **x** aggregates features over past transactions. This is performed using different aggregation procedures (e.g., averaging over past transactions or counting the past transactions) over time windows of different lengths, i.e., in the set $\{1h, 1d, 7d, 14d, 30d\}$. For instance, one of the elements of the activity record is the count of the previous legitimate transactions present in the last $7d$ of the bank transaction record. Details about the feature engineering creation are provided in [14]. Instead, for a complete analysis of the dataset, we refer the reader to [12].

6.2   Fraud Strategy Modeling

Banking frauds usually represent around 1% of transactions. Therefore, banking datasets are often imbalanced [12]. In our dataset, the flagged fraudulent activity represents only 0.13% of the transactions. Therefore, we have used the models of possible attackers based on real-world analysis of fraudulent transactions described in Sect. 3 and introduced fraudulent activities in the real-world dataset. We generate the synthetic fraud scenarios after analyzing the few records of fraudulent activity in our possession, the patterns described in other works [11–13], and the public technical reports of Italian government agencies [26]. The parameters of the different attack schemes and attack behavior used in what follows are reported in Table 1, in which, for each attack behavior, we specify the ranges of amount a and frequency fr from which we generated the fraudulent transactions. Each value has been generated by sampling uniformly over the specified range. Regarding the feature vector **f**′ for the generated fraud, we followed the rules described in the attack techniques in Sect. 3, and we randomly generated the features that are left to the attacker's choice. In particular, we assume that the *IBAN* of the recipient is unknown to the victim, i.e., has been generated as a random *IBAN* different from the ones observed in the client's history. We assign the nationality of the *IBAN* following real fraud statistics: 40% of the transactions are directed to an IBAN with the same nationality of the data (i.e., Italian), the rest are distributed to the most frequent foreign country destinations of frauds. Since the fraudster generally uses the same fraud b' throughout the duration of the attack, we opt to keep the transaction unchanged with a high probability (95%) and with a low probability of changing the attributes in f'. Regarding the nationality of the *IP*, we assume that our fraudsters are able to cover their real geographic location, so we assign a random value following the same distribution as the one present in the legitimate data.[34]

6.3 Competing Models

We build our Fraud Detection Systems using as base classifiers several classification ML algorithms: Logistic Regression (LR), Support Vector Machine (SVM), Random Forest (RF), Neural Network (NN), and Extreme Gradient Boosting (XGB). We remark that the selected methods are the most commonly used in practice for deployed FDS (see Sect. 2 for details).

The first 6 weeks of the bank records (consisting of $\approx 189,140$ transactions) constitute the training dataset $\mathcal{D}$ used to train the FDS models as well as selecting the appropriate set of features and tune their hyperparameters.[5] We create 6 different versions of $\mathcal{D}$, namely $\mathcal{D}(r, s)$, each of which has been enhanced with the introduction of frauds according to a different threat model, i.e., a combination of an attack behavior $r \in \{SF, ST, LT\}$ and an attack scheme $s \in \{IS, IH\}$. For each model $\mathcal{M} \in \{LR, SVM, RF, NN, XGB\}$, we have 6 different versions $\mathcal{M}(r, s)$ corresponding to the training of $\mathcal{M}$ over the dataset $\mathcal{D}(r, s)$. The total number of base models is $K = 30$. Notice that, depending on which attack strategy they have been trained to detect, some models may be more or less effective in detecting fraud during the operational life of an institution.[6] As mentioned before, the learning rate of MWU has been set to its theoretical optimal value by setting $G = 6000$ as a proxy for the maximum loss, corresponding to the 95%-percentile of the transaction's amounts in the test set. This results in a

---

[3] From a technical point of view, in our dataset the values corresponding to *IP*, *SessionID*, and *IBAN* have been provided as hashed values. However, the above-described operations can be performed even having the data in hash form.

[4] The code corresponding to the above procedure and supplementary material is provided at [1].

[5] We used as loss the *Normalized Cost* measure defined in [24,36] due to the imbalance nature of the dataset. Moreover, we used a filter method based on Pearson's correlation for feature selection and 3-fold cross-validation to estimate the Normalized Cost metric for the different models.

[6] We provide the F1 score of the different models on different attack strategies in supplementary material at [1].

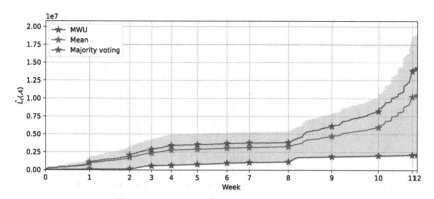

Fig. 2. Cumulative loss $\hat{L}_t(\mathcal{A})$ for Exp. 1 (the smaller the better).

learning rate of $\eta \approx 3 \cdot 10^{-5}$. On the basis of the above FDSs, we compare the performance of MWU with two commonly employed ensemble learning methods. More specifically, we use as baselines: 1) Majority voting [31]: the predicted is computed by majority voting over the ones provided by the base methods, formally $y = \arg\max_{l \in \{0,1\}} \sum_{i=1}^{K} \mathbb{1}(y_i = l)$; 2) Mean prediction: the prediction is the empirical average of the prediction provided by the base methods, formally $y = \frac{\sum_{i=1}^{K} y_i}{K}$. This is equivalent to making decisions as with MWU using constant weights to all the models over the entire time horizon ($w_{i,t} = 1/K$, for each i, t).

6.4 Performance Metric

We evaluate the methods in terms of cumulative loss of an algorithm $\mathcal{A}$:

$$\hat{L}_t(\mathcal{A}) = \sum_{h=1}^{t} l_h(y_h),$$

i.e., the empirical counterpart of the loss defined in Eq. 2 computed over t transactions. In the loss $l_t(\cdot)$, we set the cost of false positive to $d = 100$ as it is the average cost in euro of analyzing a single transaction. We recall that the loss provides an estimate of the real economic loss of the financial institution due to different costs incurred by a false positive and false negative prediction.

6.5 Experiment 1: Alternation of Fraud Strategies

In this experiment, we simulate an attack scenario where, over time, an attacker targets the base fraud detectors of the financial institution by changing each week the fraud strategy. The different fraud strategies belong to the set of 6 strategies defined in Sect. 3, each of which has been used for two weeks. We test the different FDSs methods on the 12 weeks of data (corresponding to 283, 499 transactions) we exclude from the training of the base models. Table 1 reports the cumulative number of frauds over the weeks (second column) and the sequence of the fraud strategies employed over the weeks (third column).

Table 2. Weekly cumulative loss for the different FDS for Exp. 1.

Week	Transaction Count	Fraud Strategy	Best Model	Cumulative Loss			
				BestModel	MWU	Mean	MajorityVoting
1	33670	MT,IS	NN(MT,IS)	4.73×10^4	9.24×10^4	9.13×10^5	1.06×10^6
2	64475	MT,IS	NN(MT,IS)	8.67×10^4	1.40×10^5	1.74×10^6	2.08×10^6
3	81070	MT,TH	RF(MT,IS)	5.05×10^5	5.69×10^5	2.36×10^6	2.86×10^6
4	96037	MT,TH	XGB(MT,TH)	5.75×10^5	6.47×10^5	2.77×10^6	3.41×10^6
5	115783	LT,IS	XGB(MT,TH)	7.26×10^5	8.00×10^5	2.90×10^6	3.54×10^6
6	138499	LT,IS	XGB(MT,TH)	8.96×10^5	9.70×10^5	3.05×10^6	3.69×10^6
7	155585	LT,TH	XGB(MT,TH)	9.77×10^5	1.05×10^6	3.14×10^6	3.76×10^6
8	185245	LT,TH	XGB(MT,TH)	1.07×10^6	1.15×10^6	3.26×10^6	3.84×10^6
9	218239	ST,TH	SVM(MT,TH)	1.77×10^6	1.86×10^6	4.69×10^6	6.14×10^6
10	253612	ST,TH	SVM(MT,TH)	1.90×10^6	2.00×10^6	5.98×10^6	8.21×10^6
11	279599	ST,IS	SVM(MT,TH)	2.01×10^6	2.11×10^6	1.02×10^7	1.38×10^7
12	283499	ST,IS	SVM(MT,TH)	2.03×10^6	2.13×10^6	1.04×10^7	1.42×10^7

Results. Fig. 2 shows the cumulative loss of the model ensemble based on mean and majority voting, as well as the MWU algorithm, throughout the experiment. The semitransparent area represents the range of the cumulative loss spanned by the base models.[7] All models display consistent loss increase rates over time, with the most rapid increase occurring during the 8th week, attributed to the attacker's use of the ST fraud strategy, in which the attacker aims at maximizing the amount stolen in the short period and, hence, the loss due to high-amount frauds. The cumulative loss, instead, remains almost constant between weeks 4 and 8, where the attacker follows the LT fraud strategy, with low-amount frauds distributed over a longer time span. In terms of relative performance, the online learning approach (MWU algorithm) consistently has a lower loss compared to the two ensemble methods. This strengthens the idea that using a dynamically changing set of weights over the base models outperforms methods that use a fixed combination of models if an attacker can change its strategy over time.[8] Table 2 reports the losses of the different methods and the best base models over the course of the weeks. As expected, the best base classifier changes over the weeks, depending on the attacker's strategy. This corroborates the idea that such a dynamically changing (and possibly adversarial) environment requires an online adaptation to the attacker's strategies. The performances of MWU are close to the ones of the base learner throughout the experiment, with a difference in loss of only 5% at the end of the time horizon. This indicates that the online learning method can provide performances similar to the best model even if we do not know a priori the best base learner.

---

[7] Note that the loss of the 30 base models has not been included in the figure for visualization purposes, but can be found in [1].

[8] The weight changes over time of the MWU methods are reported in [1].

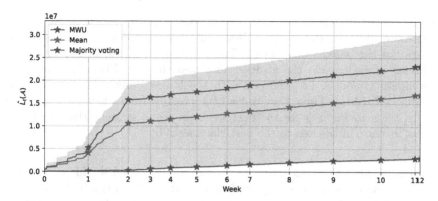

Fig. 3. Cumulative loss $\hat{L}_t(\mathcal{A})$ for Exp. 2 (the smaller the better).

Table 3. Weekly cumulative loss for the different FDS for Exp. 2.

Week	TransactionCount	FraudStrategy	BestModel	Cumulative Loss			
				Best Model	MWU	Mean	MajorityVoting
1	33590	ST,IS	RF(ST,IS)	2.18×10^4	8.82×10^4	4.09×10^6	5.20×10^6
2	64156	ST,TH	NN(ST,TH)	1.76×10^5	2.83×10^5	1.06×10^7	1.58×10^7
3	80883	MT,IS	LR(MT,TH)	5.15×10^5	6.32×10^5	1.11×10^7	1.63×10^7
4	95984	MT,IS	SVM(MT,TH)	7.49×10^5	8.66×10^5	1.16×10^7	1.69×10^7
5	115730	MT,IS	LR(MT,TH)	9.65×10^5	1.09×10^6	1.21×10^7	1.75×10^7
6	138446	MT,IS	SVM(MT,TH)	1.24×10^6	1.37×10^6	1.28×10^7	1.83×10^7
7	155687	MT,IS	SVM(MT,TH)	1.50×10^6	1.63×10^6	1.33×10^7	1.90×10^7
8	185625	MT,IS	SVM(MT,TH)	1.90×10^6	2.03×10^6	1.42×10^7	2.00×10^7
9	218930	MT,IS	SVM(MT,TH)	2.28×10^6	2.41×10^6	1.51×10^7	2.12×10^7
10	254637	MT,IS	SVM(MT,TH)	2.55×10^6	2.68×10^6	1.61×10^7	2.22×10^7
11	280624	MT,IS	SVM(MT,TH)	2.80×10^6	2.94×10^6	1.68×10^7	2.31×10^7
12	284548	LT,IS	SVM(MT,TH)	2.84×10^6	2.97×10^6	1.69×10^7	2.31×10^7

6.6   Experiment 2: Adversarial Alternation of Fraud Strategies

In this experiment, we simulate the relentless attack scenario in which the adversary constantly adapts its strategy. The attacker's adaptive strategy is based on their in-depth knowledge of the employed models' performance, which they use to determine the most effective fraud strategy for the upcoming week. Indeed, they dynamically select the fraud strategy that will cause the higher damage (i.e., with the highest increases in the loss) to the best-performing model, the one with the lowest cumulative loss. Similarly to the previous experiment, we evaluate the 6 strategies defined in Sect. 3 over the 12 weeks of data excluded from the base model's training. For this experiment, we extend the threat model presented in Sect. 3 with two further assumptions. First, the attacker must gain (and keep) access to a dataset of banking transactions labeled by the target institution's classifiers. Second, the attacker must also be able to use the fraud detectors under attack (or to re-construct exact copies as performed in [14]) to test the crafted fraudulent banking transactions. This complex scenario requires much more effort for the attacker. Nonetheless, it provides a worst-case attack scenario for the banking institution. The experiment unfolds as follows. At the beginning of each week, the attacker identifies the best FDS $\mathcal{M}_k$ among the K competing models, i.e., the one with the lowest cumulative loss, formally $\arg\min_{k \in K} L_t(\mathcal{M}_k)$. Then, they test all the possible fraud strategies against it. Finally, the attacker uses for the next week the fraud strategy that caused the highest increase of the loss to the best classifier $\mathcal{M}_k$.

Results. Table 3 provides a summary of results achieved in this experiment, with the dynamic strategies employed by the attacker and the best-performing base model by each week. Figure 3 presents the cumulative loss of the analyzed algorithms over the experiment duration. The results are consistent with those of Exp. 1, demonstrating the resilience of the MWU algorithm even against adversarial strategies. Specifically, MWU achieves lower cumulative losses than the ensemble models throughout the experiment. Despite this, MWU's performance is comparable to that of the best models, with a loss increase of less than 5%. Notably, the loss increase is more significant when the attacker employs the ST strategy. For instance, between week 1 and 2, MWU's loss increases by 221%, while the system with majority voting experiences a 203% increase from the previous week's loss. However, after the first 5 weeks, a stationary regime is reached: the minimum loss keeps being recorded by the base model SVM(MT, IS). This suggests that one of the K base classifiers can provide good performance even when facing different strategies. However, such performances are not consistent over the entire experiment, and, therefore, evidence that selecting a single model would not be robust w.r.t. switches in the attacker's strategy.

7 Conclusion

This paper addresses the challenges adaptive attackers pose in the context of fraud detection in digital transactions. The proposed approach leveraged the Multiplicative Weight Update (MWU) online learning algorithm to dynamically adapt the selection of classifiers employed for fraud detection based on their estimated performance. We conducted an experimental evaluation using real-world banking data enriched with diversified synthetic fraudulent activity, which demonstrated that the proposed approach enabled prompt updates to detection models as new patterns and behaviors were identified, leading to a more robust and effective fraud detection system. We also showed that MWU outperforms static model ensembles commonly employed in fraud detection tasks, such as those based on majority voting and the empirical average of the prediction. These findings have significant implications for developing and deploying machine learning-based fraud detection systems in the financial industry, and future research could focus on extending the proposed approach to other domains beyond banking fraud detection, such as e-Commerce fraud and money laundering. Another possible development may focus on adopting online learning techniques to predict attackers based on their fraudulent strategies.

Acknowledgements. This paper is supported by the FAIR (Future Artificial Intelligence Research) project, funded by the NextGenerationEU program within the PNRR-PE-AI scheme (M4C2, Investment 1.3, Line on Artificial Intelligence).

Ethical Issues. Machine learning models have become increasingly ubiquitous in decision-making processes across various industries, especially financial fraud detection ones. However, the ethical implications of these models have come under scrutiny due to the potential for bias. Focusing on our work, if the base models are biased, any approach built upon them may also be biased. This is especially concerning when the models are used in sensitive areas such as fraud detection. On the other hand, since we do not explicitly exploit transaction features, we may not introduce further bias directly. However, it is important to note that the data used to train the models may still contain hidden biases that could influence the model's predictions. Therefore, it is essential to ensure that the data sets used to train the models are diverse and representative of the population to minimize bias and prevent harm to vulnerable groups, as stated by the guidelines by the EU on AI methods (https://artificialintelligenceact. eu/).

References

1. Advancing fraud detection systems through online learning - supplementary materials and source code. https://github.com/necst/advancing_fds_code (2023)
2. AlAhmadi, B.A., Axon, L., Martinovic, I.: 99% false positives: A qualitative study of SOC analysts' perspectives on security alarms. In: Butler, K.R.B., Thomas, K. (eds.) 31st USENIX Security Symposium, USENIX Security 2022, Boston, MA, USA, August 10-12, 2022, pp. 2783–2800. USENIX Association (2022), https://www.usenix.org/conference/usenixsecurity22/presentation/alahmadi
3. Aziz, M., Kaufmann, E., Riviere, M.K.: On multi-armed bandit designs for dose-finding clinical trials. J. Mach. Learn. Res. **22**(1), 686–723 (2021)
4. Bagga, S., Goyal, A., Gupta, N., Goyal, A.: Credit card fraud detection using pipeling and ensemble learning. Proc. Comput. Sci. **173**, 104–112 (2020). https://doi.org/10.1016/j.procs.2020.06.014, https://www.sciencedirect.com/science/article/pii/S1877050920315167, international Conference on Smart Sustainable Intelligent Computing and Applications under ICITETM2020
5. Bahnsen, A.C., Aouada, D., Stojanovic, A., Ottersten, B.E.: Feature engineering strategies for credit card fraud detection. Expert Syst. Appl. **51**, 134–142 (2016). https://doi.org/10.1016/j.eswa.2015.12.030
6. Bekirev, A.S., Klimov, V.V., Kuzin, M.V., Shchukin, B.A.: Payment card fraud detection using neural network committee and clustering. Optical Memory Neural Netw. **24**(3), 193–200 (2015). https://doi.org/10.3103/S1060992X15030030
7. Bernasconi, M., Martino, S., Vittori, E., Trovò, F., Restelli, M.: Dark-pool smart order routing: a combinatorial multi-armed bandit approach. In: Proceedings of the Third ACM International Conference on AI in Finance, pp. 352–360 (2022)
8. Bhattacharyya, S., Jha, S., Tharakunnel, K.K., Westland, J.C.: Data mining for credit card fraud: A comparative study. Decis. Support Syst. **50**(3), 602–613 (2011). https://doi.org/10.1016/j.dss.2010.08.008

9. Brause, R.W., Langsdorf, T.S., Hepp, H.: Neural data mining for credit card fraud detection. In: 11th IEEE International Conference on Tools with Artificial Intelligence, ICTAI '99, Chicago, Illinois, USA, November 8-10, 1999, pp. 103–106. IEEE Computer Society (1999). https://doi.org/10.1109/TAI.1999.809773

10. Carcillo, F., Borgne, Y.L., Caelen, O., Bontempi, G.: An assessment of streaming active learning strategies for real-life credit card fraud detection. In: 2017 IEEE International Conference on Data Science and Advanced Analytics, DSAA 2017, Tokyo, Japan, October 19-21, 2017, pp. 631–639. IEEE (2017). https://doi.org/10.1109/DSAA.2017.10

11. Carminati, M., Baggio, A., Maggi, F., Spagnolini, U., Zanero, S.: Fraudbuster: Temporal analysis and detection of advanced financial frauds. In: Giuffrida, C., Bardin, S., Blanc, G. (eds.) Detection of Intrusions and Malware, and Vulnerability Assessment - 15th International Conference, DIMVA 2018, Saclay, France, June 28-29, 2018, Proceedings. Lecture Notes in Computer Science, vol. 10885, pp. 211–233. Springer (2018). https://doi.org/10.1007/978-3-319-93411-2_10

12. Carminati, M., Caron, R., Maggi, F., Epifani, I., Zanero, S.: Banksealer: A decision support system for online banking fraud analysis and investigation. Comput. Secur. **53**, 175–186 (2015). https://doi.org/10.1016/j.cose.2015.04.002

13. Carminati, M., Polino, M., Continella, A., Lanzi, A., Maggi, F., Zanero, S.: Security evaluation of a banking fraud analysis system. ACM Trans. Priv. Secur. **21**(3), 11:1–11:31 (2018). https://doi.org/10.1145/3178370

14. Carminati, M., Santini, L., Polino, M., Zanero, S.: Evasion attacks against banking fraud detection systems. In: Egele, M., Bilge, L. (eds.) 23rd International Symposium on Research in Attacks, Intrusions and Defenses, RAID 2020, San Sebastian, Spain, October 14–15, 2020, pp. 285–300. USENIX Association (2020), https://www.usenix.org/conference/raid2020/presentation/carminati

15. Cartella, F., Anunciação, O., Funabiki, Y., Yamaguchi, D., Akishita, T., Elshocht, O.: Adversarial attacks for tabular data: Application to fraud detection and imbalanced data. In: Espinoza, H., McDermid, J.A., Huang, X., Castillo-Effen, M., Chen, X.C., Hernández-Orallo, J., hÉigeartaigh, S.Ó., Mallah, R. (eds.) Proceedings of the Workshop on Artificial Intelligence Safety 2021 (SafeAI 2021) co-located with the Thirty-Fifth AAAI Conference on Artificial Intelligence (AAAI 2021), Virtual, February 8, 2021. CEUR Workshop Proceedings, vol. 2808. CEUR-WS.org (2021). https://ceur-ws.org/Vol-2808/Paper_4.pdf

16. Cesa-Bianchi, N., Lugosi, G.: Prediction, learning, and games. Cambridge University Press (2006)

17. Continella, A., Carminati, M., Polino, M., Lanzi, A., Zanero, S., Maggi, F.: Prometheus: Analyzing webinject-based information stealers. J. Comput. Secur. **25**(2), 117–137 (2017). https://doi.org/10.3233/JCS-15773

18. European Central Bank: Seventh report on card fraud. Tech. rep. (2021). http://web.archive.org/web/20230521043629/https://www.ecb.europa.eu/pub/cardfraud/html/ecb.cardfraudreport202110~cac4c418e8.en.html

19. Forough, J., Momtazi, S.: Ensemble of deep sequential models for credit card fraud detection. Appl. Soft Comput. **99**, 106883 (2021). https://doi.org/10.1016/j.asoc.2020.106883

20. Freund, Y., Schapire, R.E.: Adaptive game playing using multiplicative weights. Games Econom. Behav. **29**(1–2), 79–103 (1999)

21. Itoo, F., Singh, S., et al.: Comparison and analysis of logistic regression, naïve bayes and knn machine learning algorithms for credit card fraud detection. Int. J. Inf. Technol. **13**(4), 1503–1511 (2021)

22. Kim, E., et al.: Champion-challenger analysis for credit card fraud detection: Hybrid ensemble and deep learning. Expert Syst. Appl. **128**, 214–224 (2019). https://doi.org/10.1016/j.eswa.2019.03.042

23. KPMG: Global Banking Fraud Survey. (2019). https://assets.kpmg/content/dam/kpmg/xx/pdf/2019/05/global-banking-fraud-survey.pdf

24. Labanca, D., Primerano, L., Markland-Montgomery, M., Polino, M., Carminati, M., Zanero, S.: Amaretto: An active learning framework for money laundering detection. IEEE Access **10**, 41720–41739 (2022). https://doi.org/10.1109/ACCESS.2022.3167699

25. Marchal, S., Szyller, S.: Detecting organized ecommerce fraud using scalable categorical clustering. In: Balenson, D. (ed.) Proceedings of the 35th Annual Computer Security Applications Conference, ACSAC 2019, San Juan, PR, USA, December 09-13, 2019. pp. 215–228. ACM (2019). https://doi.org/10.1145/3359789.3359810

26. Ministero dell'Economia e della Finanza: Rapporto statistico sulle frodi con le carte di pagamento. Tech. rep. (2021). https://www.dt.mef.gov.it/export/sites/sitodt/modules/documenti_it/antifrode_mezzi_pagamento/antifrode_mezzi_pagamento/Rapporto-statistico-sulle-frodi-con-le-carte-di-pagamento-edizione-2021.pdf

27. Nuara, A., Trovò, F., Gatti, N., Restelli, M.: Online joint bid/daily budget optimization of internet advertising campaigns. Artif. Intell. **305**, 103663 (2022)

28. Patidar, R., Sharma, L., et al.: Credit card fraud detection using neural network. Int. J. Soft Comput. Eng. (IJSCE) **1**, 32–38 (2011)

29. Pozzolo, A.D., Boracchi, G., Caelen, O., Alippi, C., Bontempi, G.: Credit card fraud detection and concept-drift adaptation with delayed supervised information. In: 2015 International Joint Conference on Neural Networks, IJCNN 2015, Killarney, Ireland, July 12-17, 2015. pp. 1–8. IEEE (2015). https://doi.org/10.1109/IJCNN.2015.7280527

30. Pozzolo, A.D., Boracchi, G., Caelen, O., Alippi, C., Bontempi, G.: Credit card fraud detection: A realistic modeling and a novel learning strategy. IEEE Trans. Neural Networks Learn. Syst. **29**(8), 3784–3797 (2018). https://doi.org/10.1109/TNNLS.2017.2736643

31. Randhawa, K., Loo, C.K., Seera, M., Lim, C.P., Nandi, A.K.: Credit card fraud detection using adaboost and majority voting. IEEE Access **6**, 14277–14284 (2018). https://doi.org/10.1109/ACCESS.2018.2806420

32. Sahin, Y., Duman, E.: Detecting credit card fraud by decision trees and support vector machines. In: World Congress on Engineering 2012. July 4–6, 2012. London, UK. vol. 2188, pp. 442–447. International Association of Engineers (2010)

33. Seeja, K., Zareapoor, M.: Fraudminer: A novel credit card fraud detection model based on frequent itemset mining. Sci. World J. **2014**, 252797 (2014)

34. Sohony, I., Pratap, R., Nambiar, U.: Ensemble learning for credit card fraud detection. In: Ranu, S., Ganguly, N., Ramakrishnan, R., Sarawagi, S., Roy, S. (eds.) Proceedings of the ACM India Joint International Conference on Data Science and Management of Data, COMAD/CODS 2018, Goa, India, January 11-13, 2018, pp. 289–294. ACM (2018). https://doi.org/10.1145/3152494.3156815

35. Trovò, F., Paladino, S., Restelli, M., Gatti, N.: Improving multi-armed bandit algorithms in online pricing settings. Int. J. Approx. Reason. **98**, 196–235 (2018)

36. Whitrow, C., Hand, D.J., Juszczak, P., Weston, D.J., Adams, N.M.: Transaction aggregation as a strategy for credit card fraud detection. Data Min. Knowl. Discov. **18**(1), 30–55 (2009). https://doi.org/10.1007/s10618-008-0116-z

37. Xuan, S., Liu, G., Li, Z., Zheng, L., Wang, S., Jiang, C.: Random forest for credit card fraud detection. In: 15th IEEE International Conference on Networking, Sensing and Control, ICNSC 2018, Zhuhai, China, March 27-29, 2018, pp. 1–6. IEEE (2018). https://doi.org/10.1109/ICNSC.2018.8361343

38. Zhang, Y., Tong, J., Wang, Z., Gao, F.: Customer transaction fraud detection using xgboost model. In: 2020 International Conference on Computer Engineering and Application (ICCEA), pp. 554–558 (2020). https://doi.org/10.1109/ICCEA50009.2020.00122

Hardware and Systems

Continual Model-Based Reinforcement Learning for Data Efficient Wireless Network Optimisation

Cengis Hasan[(⊠)], Alexandros Agapitos, David Lynch, Alberto Castagna,
Giorgio Cruciata, Hao Wang, and Aleksandar Milenovic

Huawei Ireland Research Center, Dublin, Ireland
{cengis.hasan,linyun.wanghao}@huawei.com

Abstract. We present a method that addresses the pain point of long
lead-time required to deploy cell-level parameter optimisation policies to
new wireless network sites. Given a sequence of action spaces represented
by overlapping subsets of cell-level configuration parameters provided
by domain experts, we formulate throughput optimisation as Continual Reinforcement Learning of control policies. Simulation results suggest that the proposed system is able to shorten the end-to-end deployment lead-time by two-fold compared to a reinitialise-and-retrain baseline without any drop in optimisation gain.

1 Introduction

One of the major factors influencing the Quality of Experience (QoE) in wireless networks is the parameter configuration of the cells in a base-station. Incorrectly configured cells can interfere with neighbouring cells and degrade quality
of service through inadequate coverage or over-utilisation. Traditionally, cell-
level parameter configuration is realised before deployment, at which time the
engineers have to anticipate diverse traffic conditions (i.e. user load), radio channel conditions, environment conditions (i.e. physical location and surroundings
of a cell), and the complex relationship of QoE objective with other conflicting
optimisation objectives in a wireless network (i.e. coverage, utilisation, power
consumption).

Existing approaches for configuring cell-level parameters are based on a discrete black-box optimisation problem formulation, which is often solved with
surrogate-driven optimisation methods. Due to the combinatorial parameter
space defined by the large number of cell-level configuration parameters (> 500
parameters), and the variable impact of the same set of parameters on the QoE
in different deployment sites, selecting and configuring parameters for a new system deployment is a stage-wise process. In this process, priorities are assigned to
subsets of parameters based on domain knowledge, and these subsets are then
configured in order of priority in a sequence of independent surrogate-driven

---

C. Hasan, A. Agapitos and D. Lynch—Authors with equal contribution.

© The Author(s), under exclusive license to Springer Nature Switzerland AG 2023
G. De Francisci Morales et al. (Eds.): ECML PKDD 2023, LNAI 14174, pp. 295–311, 2023.
https://doi.org/10.1007/978-3-031-43427-3_18

Table 1. Challenges and technical solutions.

Challenge	Technical Solution
Data limitation in real wireless network trials, which are expensive and constrained to real-time	Model-based RL
Time constraints on policy deployment lead-time to address a new candidate configuration parameter subset	Continual RL
High levels of noise in objective KPIs	Probabilistic reward model explicitly accounting for aleatoric and epistemic uncertainty
Inference time constrained to under 5 min for 20,000 cells	Learning-based solution as opposed to online planning at decision time

optimisation runs. When QoS metrics reach target values, the parameter selection and configuration process is terminated and the parameter configuration is executed to each cell. Each independent optimisation run is composed of 7 days of data collection, followed by 10 days of iterative optimisation, amounting to a total of 17 days. Each consecutive parameter subset optimisation will add this amount of additional lead-time before the configured parameters are applied to each cell.

In this work, we developed a technology to reduce the overall lead-time required to optimise cell-level parameter configurations for a new wireless network site. We formulated the problem of stage-wise optimisation of parameter subsets as a *Continual Reinforcement Learning* problem. This approach leverages forward transfer of knowledge between optimisation policies with overlapping subsets of actions in order to learn the ultimate policy in a data-efficient task-oriented fashion. Additionally it allows for a safe rollback to a policy of a previous subset, if objective KPIs do not improve, by avoiding catastrophic forgetting. Through a series of experiments, we demonstrate a two-fold reduction in deployment lead-time compared to a *Reinitialise-and-Retrain* baseline. The main challenges addressed in this paper, with corresponding technical solutions, are summarised in Table 3.

The rest of the paper is organised as follows. Section 2 summarises previous work on Reinforcement Learning (RL) for network parameter optimisation, and outlines the main classes of methods for Continual RL (CRL). Section 3 presents the detailed description of the real-world dataset, the problem formulation, and the solution methods. Section 4 describes the experiment design, and Sect. 5 analyses the experiment results. Finally, we conclude in Sect. 6 and propose future research.

2 Related Work

Previous research has addressed the problem of wireless network parameter optimisation using rule-based methods [10,11], mathematical models [19], or

RL [1,3–5,8,17,27,30]. A common characteristic of the aforementioned works is that the action space (adjustable network configuration parameters) is defined a priori at design time and is kept fixed. Scenarios where one wishes to dynamically extend the action space with additional configuration parameters can be solved in a sample-efficient way via a Continual RL problem formulation [13]. The main classes of methods for achieving positive forward transfer while mitigating catastrophic forgetting in CRL tasks are summarised as follows:

- **Parameter storage based** methods require multiple independently trained models to be stored for the different tasks. Catastrophic forgetting is overcome at the cost of storing parameters for each model. The space needed to store policies is linear in the number of tasks addressed. Unfortunately, this technique does not support knowledge transfer across tasks regardless of their potential similarities.
- **Distillation** is the process of distilling a source model(s) to a target model [22,26,29,31]. Distillation mitigates the need to store multiple models by compressing them into a single neural network. Hence, models trained on several source tasks can be distilled into a single network which captures shared experiences from all tasks. Despite reducing storage space, distillation still requires task specific layers to extrapolate features or to fit a task's action policy.
- **Rehearsal** consists of training using examples from both the current task and old examples from previously encountered tasks. This requires either an experience replay buffer to store old examples, or if storage space is limited, pseudo-rehearsal whereby examples are synthesized using a generative model [12,15,21]. When solving a novel task, models can retain performance achieved in previous tasks by continuously revisiting examples from same.
- **Regularization based methods** maintain a single model across multiple tasks. Catastrophic forgetting is mitigated by preventing parameters that are important for previous tasks from changing significantly when learning a new task [14,32]. When compared to *Parameter Storage* methods, this approach reduces the storage space required since only one model is maintained. A drawback is that the initial model must have sufficient capacity to accommodate all future tasks, which are typically unknown upfront. Furthermore, it is not clear how to handle extension of the action space.
- **Modular architectures** facilitate CL by exploiting flexibility and compositionability of neural networks. Model capacity can be adjusted dynamically, making adaptation to unseen tasks possible without over-parameterising the model initially [23,26,32]. It is sometimes helpful to decompose complex problems into easier sub-problems. In this case, neural modules can be combined and re-used across tasks [9,16]. For instance, a decision policy could be decomposed into one module to extract features and another to select actions. Modules are combined as required to achieve positive transfer, while catastrophic forgetting is prevented by storing lightweight modules trained on prior tasks.

In our optimisation problem, the order and the type of overlap across the sequence of cell-level configuration parameter subsets are defined by the domain expert. We selected *Progress-and-Compress* (P&C) [26], a method that has demonstrated good performance in CRL scenarios of evolving action space. P&C is a hybrid between the methods of distillation, regularisation and modular architectures, and it can be decomposed into two steps. Firstly, the progress step, where the agent achieves positive transfer by expanding the architecture horizontally via lateral connections from an existing knowledge base (assimilates experience from all previous tasks) to a new active column (learns skills on the new task). Secondly, in the compress step, model distillation is used to distill the active column into the knowledge base without disrupting performance on previous tasks. As such, P&C mitigates unbounded growth in learned policies, while ensuring transfer across similar tasks and preventing catastrophic forgetting.

3   Methods

In this section, the dataset is described and the problem is formulated as a Markov Decision Process (MDP). Methods are introduced to achieve data efficient continual learning of network control policies using model-based RL.

3.1   Description of the Dataset

A dataset D_{init} was collected over 5 days in a real 5G network containing 966 cells, by executing random actions to random cells at hourly intervals. We collected four different feature sets[1]: cell-level configuration parameters (CPs) representing the actions, performance counters (PCs), engineering parameters (EPs), and spatio-temporal (ST) context. PCs include time-varying features (e.g. demand, channel quality, etc.) which are reported by cells hourly. EPs are fixed characteristics of a cell such as its tilt, antenna type, etc. The optimisation objective KPI is cell-level throughput measured in Gigabits per second (Gbps). Exploratory analysis revealed the following challenging properties of the dataset.

High Dimensional State and Action Spaces: The composite action space consists of 19 CPs. Three different groups of CPs were adjusted during the data collection experiment. The three groups include: 4 CPs for power control on cells, 6 CPs for modulation code scheme selection (method used by a cell to encode digital data), and 9 CPs for rank selection (number of spatial streams used to transmit data from a cell to users). CP are categorical variables that take between 2 and 13 different values – the number of unique action combinations is $\approx 4.6 \times 10^{18}$. Raw network state is the union of PCs, EPs, and ST context. A total of 410 features constitute the network state.

Throughput (TP) Time-Series Exhibits High Levels of Noise: A seasonality-trend-noise decomposition of the time-series was performed for each cell. It was observed that $49.41\% \pm 10.04\%$ of the variance in TP is explained by seasonal and trend components. The remaining variance can be attributed to the noise component of the time-series.

---

[1] The names of CPs, PCs, and EPs cannot be disclosed.

The challenges and technical solutions are summarised in Table 3. A tabular dataset was formed by aligning the four feature sets with respect to cell ID and timestamp. The aligned dataset contained 966 [cells] $* 5$ [days] $* 24$ [hours] examples. Rows with missing values due to energy saving enabled on some cells in early morning hours were removed, resulting in a total of 103,648 examples. CPs and EPs were transformed using min-max scaling. PCs were transformed using the Yeo-Johnson method due to extreme values. Lastly, ST features were cyclically encoded.

3.2 Problem Formulation

The problem is formulated as a MDP defined by the tuple $\langle S, A, T, R, \gamma, D \rangle$, where S is the state space, A is the action space, $T : S \times A \times S \to \mathbb{R}^{|S|}$ is the transition function from a state s to s' after taking action a, $R : S \times A \to \mathbb{R}$ is the reward function, $\gamma \in (0, 1]$ is the discount factor, and D is the initial state distribution. The goal is to find a policy $\pi_\theta : S \to A$ that maximises expected cumulative reward, defined as $\mathbb{E}\left[\sum_{t=0}^{H} \gamma^t r(s_t, a_t)|s_0 \sim D, a_t \sim \pi_\theta(s_t)\right]$, where H is the planning horizon.

States: A raw state $s_t^{raw} \in S$ at hour t is composed of PCs observed between $t-1$ and t, EPs, and ST features. s_t^{raw} is compressed into s_t using an auto-encoder $g_\psi : S \to Z$, $S \in \mathbb{R}^{410}$, $Z \in \mathbb{R}^{50}$.

Actions: The action space A is combinatorial, where each CP i may take between 2 and 13 different discrete values represented by $CP_i \equiv \{CP_{i,1}, CP_{i,2}, \ldots, CP_{i,n_{CP_i}}\}$, giving a total of $|A| = \prod_{i=1}^{N} n_{CP_i} \approx 4.6 \times 10^{18}$ distinct actions for all 19 CPs. We train the policy to generate an action $a_t = (a_{1,t}, a_{2,t}, \ldots, a_{N,t}) \in A$ at the beginning of hour t given network state s_t as input. Note that $a_{i,t} \in CP_i$ is a discrete value from the set CP_i.

Reward: Defined as the value of throughput KPI observed on a cell between t and $t + 1$.

Planning Horizon: Single-step episodes are considered, in which an action is executed at time t, the reward is given at time $t + 1$ and the episode terminates.

3.3 Model-Based Reinforcement Learning

Since we are optimising over a single-step horizon, the learned dynamics function is limited to a one-step reward prediction model. This is defined as a probabilistic model $f_\phi(r_{t+1}|s_t, a_t) = Pr(r_{t+1}|s_t, a_t; \phi)$ that outputs the conditional distribution of the reward given the current state and action. Learning a reward model is a task of fitting an approximation model to the true reward function given the training dataset $D_{train} = \{(s_i = g_\psi(s_i^{raw}), a_i = CP_i, r_i = TP_i)\}_{i=1}^{M}$ collected from the real network, where $g_\psi : S \to Z$, $S \in \mathbb{R}^{410}$, $Z \in \mathbb{R}^{50}$ is a feature extractor in the form of an auto-encoder neural network trained to reconstruct the raw state using dataset $\{(s_i^{raw})\}_{i=1}^{M}$. The motivation of pre-processing of raw state

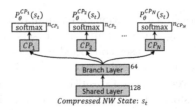

Fig. 1. Architecture of the policy neural network $\pi_\theta(s|a)$, which is composed of N sub-policies $\pi_\theta^i(a_i|s)$ each represented by a separate output head. Output heads share an embedding of the state computed by two hidden layers.

using an auto-encoder is to produce compact control polices for TP optimisation. Algorithm 1 presents the pseudo-code for model-based RL.

The architecture of the policy network $\pi_\theta(a|s)$ is shown in Fig. 1. In our setting, the action components corresponding to CPs are chosen independently from each other. Given N CPs, we decompose policy π_θ into N sub-policies $\pi_\theta^i(a_i|s)$ such that $\pi_\theta(a|s) = \prod_{i=1}^{N} \pi_\theta(a_i = CP_i|s)$. Decomposition of the policy network is achieved by branching N output heads from a shared embedding of the state. The embedding is computed by two layers, where the first layer takes the compressed state s_t as input. The ith output head returns a probability over the ith action component corresponding to CP_i.

Proximal policy optimisation (PPO) [25] is employed to train $\pi_\theta(a|s)$. In step k, the policy update is given by:

$$\theta_{k+1} = \arg\max_\theta \mathbb{E}_{s,a\sim\pi_{\theta_k}}[\mathcal{L}_{PPO}(s, a, \theta_k, \theta)].$$

where the loss function is defined as:

$$\mathcal{L}_{PPO}(s, a, \theta_k, \theta) = \min\left(\frac{\pi_\theta(a|s)}{\pi_{\theta_k}(a|s)} A^{\pi_{\theta_k}}(s, a), \quad g(\epsilon, A^{\pi_{\theta_k}}(s, a))\right). \quad (1)$$

The advantage $A^{\pi_{\theta_k}}(s, a)$ is clipped using function $g(\cdot)$ to prevent large changes in the policy parameters: $g(\epsilon, A) = (1 + \epsilon)A$, if $A \geqslant 0$; otherwise $g(\epsilon, A) =$

Algorithm 1. Model-based Reinforcement Learning

1: Collect dataset $D_{init} = \{(s_i^{raw}, a_i = CP_i, r_i = TP_i)\}_{i=1}^{M}$ from real network.
2: Train feature extractor g_ψ on dataset $\{(s_i^{raw})\}_{i=1}^{M}$
3: Process D_{init} into dataset $D_{train} = \{(s_i = g_\psi(s_i^{raw}), a_i = CP_i, r_i = TP_i)\}_{i=1}^{M}$
4: Train reward model f_ϕ on D_{train}
5: Initialise control policy π_θ
6: **for** E epochs **do**
7:     shuffle D_{train} and partition it into mini-batches.
8:     **for** number of mini-batches **do**
9:         initialise training set D_{RL}
10:        **for** each example index i of a mini-batch **do**
11:            $\hat{a}_i \sim \pi_\theta(s_i)$
12:            $\hat{r}_i = f_\theta(s_i, \hat{a}_i)$
13:            compute advantage $\hat{A}_i$ via Equation 2
14:            add $(s_i, \hat{a}_i, \hat{A}_i)$ to D_{RL}
15:        update π_θ based on D_{RL} using the Adam optimiser, given loss in Equation 1

$(1 - \epsilon)A$. Advantages are estimated by subtracting the mean reward in a mini-batch $\mathcal{B}$ from the current reward:

$$A^{\pi_{\theta_k}}(s, a) = r(s, a) - \frac{1}{|\mathcal{B}|} \sum_{i \in \mathcal{B}} r(s_i, a_i). \qquad (2)$$

3.4 Compressing High Dimensional Network State

A total of 383 performance counters (PCs) are combined with 9 engineering parameters (EPs), and 18 spatio-temporal features (ST) to form the raw network state $s_t^{raw} \in \mathbb{R}^{410}$. An under-complete auto-encoder neural network $g_\psi : S \to Z$, $S \in \mathbb{R}^{410}$, $Z \in \mathbb{Z}^{50}$ is trained to compress the raw network state.

Compressed states produced by the encoder $g_\psi^{encoder}(s_t^{raw}) \to s_t$ are passed to the decoder, which reconstructs the input: $g_\psi^{decoder}(s_t) \to \hat{s}_t^{raw}$. A regulariser g_ψ^{reg} predicts the throughput at $t + 1$ given s_t. Incorporating the regulariser was found to improve predictive accuracy of the reward model and policy gain. Loss is defined as the mean square error between the input state and reconstructed state:

$$\mathcal{L}(s^{raw}, r, \psi) = (\lambda_{AE}) \left(\frac{1}{|S|} \sum_{i \in S} (s^{raw}[i] - \hat{s}^{raw}[i])^2 \right) + (1 - \lambda_{AE})(r - \hat{r})^2,$$

where $\hat{s}^{raw}$ is the reconstructed state produced by the decoder at time t, $\hat{r}$ is predicted reward (throughput) at $t + 1$ given by the regulariser, and $\lambda_{AE} \in [0, 1]$ weights contribution of the decoder and regulariser. Subscripts t are dropped for clarity.

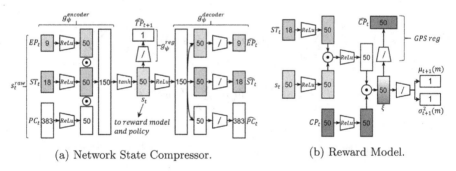

(a) Network State Compressor.   (b) Reward Model.

Fig. 2. High dimensional raw network state $s_t^{raw} \in \mathbb{R}^{410}$ at hour t is compressed using a modular auto-encoder to $s_t \in \mathbb{R}^{50}$. The reward model is an ensemble of probabilistic neural networks. A single component model m is displayed.

3.5 Reward Model

The reward model $f_\phi : S \times A \to \mathbb{R}$ is based on the dynamics model described by Chua et al. [6] termed as Probabilistic Ensemble with Trajectory Sampling. Predicted reward is given by a probabilistic ensemble consisting of

10 component models, each trained with different seeds and bootstrap samples of D_{train} collected from the real network. Figure 2b displays the architecture of a single component model. Each component model f_ϕ^i parameterises a Gaussian distribution with diagonal covariance: $P_\phi(r_{t+1}|s_t, ST_t, a_t) = \mathcal{N}(\mu_\phi(s_t, ST_t, a_t), \sigma_\phi(s_t, ST_t, a_t)^2)$, from which the predicted reward (throughput) at $t+1$ can be sampled. Inputs at hour t include: the compressed network state s_t, current time and location of the cell ST_t, and actions produced by the policy $a_t = CP_t$.

We employ a causal inference-based regulariser to improve the generalisation of the reward model similar to the work of [24]. Generalised Propensity Score (GPS) [28] predicts the action $a_t = CP_t$ from a representation ξ of a_t, compressed state s_t, and ST_t. The composite loss function contains terms for the negative log likelihood and GPS regulariser:

$$\mathcal{L}(s, a, \phi) = \lambda_{RM} \left(\frac{(r - \mu_\phi(s, a))^2}{\sigma_\phi^2(s, a)} + \log \sigma_\phi^2(s, a) \right) + (1 - \lambda_{RM}) \, \mathrm{KL}\left(a \| \widehat{a}\right),$$

where r is the ground truth reward (throughput), $\mu_\phi(s, a)$ and $\sigma_\phi^2(s, a)$ are the predicted mean and variance, and $\lambda_{RM} \in [0, 1]$ balances the contribution of the negative log likelihood and GPS regularisation terms. Subscripts t are dropped for clarify. The overall reward model architecture is shown in Fig. 2b.

Importantly, the probabilistic ensemble, consisting of component models $m \in \mathcal{M}$, quantifies the uncertainty associated with the predicted reward. Total uncertainty is decomposed into an epistemic term reflecting model uncertainty due to limited data, and an aleatoric term which represents irreducible noise:

$$\sigma_{epistemic}^2(s, a) = \frac{1}{|\mathcal{M}|} \sum_{m \in \mathcal{M}} \left(\sigma_{\phi,m}^2(s, a) + \mu_{\phi,m}^2(s, a) \right) - \left(\frac{1}{|\mathcal{M}|} \sum_{m \in \mathcal{M}} \mu_{\phi,m}(s, a) \right)^2,$$

$$\sigma_{aleatoric}^2(x) = \frac{1}{|\mathcal{M}|} \sum_{m \in \mathcal{M}} \sigma_{\phi,m}^2(s, a).$$

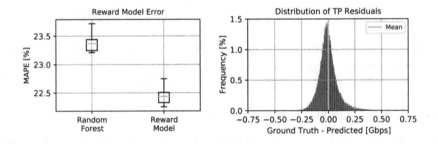

Fig. 3. Analysis of the reward model.

Reward Model Analysis: Experiments were carried out to confirm that the reward model is an accurate simulator of the network environment dynamics. The neural network ensemble was bench-marked against a random forest containing 500 trees. Results from 10 fold cross-validation are displayed in Fig. 3. Two conclusions are drawn from the plots. Firstly, the lowest error is achieved by the reward model in all folds. Secondly, error residuals are symmetric around zero, confirming that throughput is neither systematically overestimated nor underestimated.

3.6   Continual Reinforcement Learning

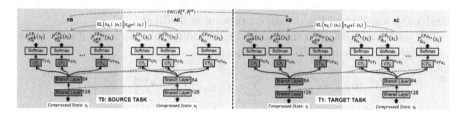

Fig. 4. Training policies using progress and compress framework. Two hidden layers, called as *shared* and *branch*, are dense layers with 128 and 64 neurons, respectively, with tanh non-linearity.

Continual RL is formulated as a sequence of MDPs $MDP(1), \ldots, MDP(L)$ where $MDP(l) = \langle \mathcal{S}(l), \mathcal{A}(l), T(l), R(l), \gamma, D(l) \rangle$ [13], $l \in \{1, 2, \ldots, L\}$. In our case, each action space $\mathcal{A}(l)$ is a subset of the next: $\mathcal{A}(1) \subset \mathcal{A}(2) \subset \ldots \subset \mathcal{A}(L)$. Therefore each consecutive MDP in the sequence represents a new task with an expanding action space.

We employ the Progress-&-Compress (P&C) framework [26] for continual RL. P&C enables the reuse of past information through layer-wise adaptors to a knowledge base. The policy consists of two columns: the active column acquires experience on a new task, and the knowledge base accumulates experience acquired over all previous tasks. The active column is trained during the **progress phase**. The knowledge base is then updated during the **compress phase**, in order to subsume new knowledge acquired by the active column. Catastrophic forgetting of the knowledge base is prevented through a regularisation technique described below.

Progress Phase: When a new task is presented, the parameters of the knowledge base are frozen – only those parameters in the active column are optimised. Layer-wise connections between the knowledge base and the active column allow reuse of representations produced by the knowledge base, thus enabling positive transfer from previously learned tasks. Lateral adaptors are implemented as multi-layer perceptrons. The j-th layer of the active column is defined as follows:

$$h_j = \sigma \left(W_j h_{j-1} + \alpha_j \odot U_j \sigma \left(V_j h_{j-1}^{KB} + b_j^{KB} \right) + b_j \right),$$

where α_j is a trainable vector initialised by sampling from $\mathcal{U}(0, 0.1)$ with size equal to number of units in layer j, and W_j, U_j, V_j are weight matrices. The active column is trained using Algorithm 1.

Compress Phase: The compress phase distills the learned active column into the knowledge base. At this stage, the parameters of the active column are frozen. The compression optimisation objective is a distillation loss with the Elastic Weight Consolidation (EWC) penalty. EWC protects the knowledge base against catastrophic forgetting, such that all previously learned skills are maintained:

$$\mathcal{L}_{KB}\left(\theta_{T_t}^{KB}\right) = \mathbb{E}\left[\mathrm{KL}(\pi_{\theta_{T_t}}(\cdot|s)\|\pi_{\theta_{T_t}^{KB}}(\cdot|s))\right] + \mathrm{EWC}\left(\theta_{T_t}^{KB}, \theta_{T_s}^{KB}\right)$$

where $\pi_{\theta_{T_t}}$ is the policy of active column after learning task T_t while $\pi_{\theta_{T_t}^{KB}}$ is the knowledge base into which the active column is distilled.

The authors in [26] proposed online EWC to reduce the computational cost of calculating the Fisher information matrix:

$$\mathrm{EWC}(\theta_{T_t}^{KB}, \theta_{T_s}^{KB}) = \frac{1}{2}\sum_{i \in \mathcal{I}^{KB}} \gamma_{Fisher}\left(F_{T_s,i}^*(\theta_{T_t,i}^{KB} - \theta_{T_s,i}^{KB})^2\right)$$

where $F_{T_t}^* = \gamma_{Fisher}\left(F_{T_s}^*\right) + \frac{1}{|\mathcal{B}|}\sum_{(s,a) \in \mathcal{S} \times \mathcal{A}} \nabla \log \pi_{\theta_{T_t}^{KB}}(a|s)\left(\nabla \log \pi_{\theta_{T_t}^{KB}}(a|s)^\mathsf{T}\right)$, $\mathcal{I}^{KB}$ are layers in the knowledge base excluding the output layers, $\mathcal{B}$ is the set of examples in the mini-batch, and $\gamma_{Fisher} \in \mathbb{R}$ is a hyper-parameter.

4   Experimental Evaluation

A number of experiments are designed to assess the sample-efficiency of continual RL in the wireless optimisation scenarios, where the action space CP_{source} in a source task T_s is expanded to a set CP_{target} in the target task T_t, where $CP_{source} \subset CP_{target}$. We are contrasting P&C against a baseline *Reinitialise-and-Retrain* (R&R) method, which initialises $\pi_\theta(s|a)$ and trains it solely on the dataset D_{init} specific to the CP set of a task in Algorithm 1.

4.1   Wireless Network Optimisation Scenarios

We defined three scenarios that demonstrate how domain knowledge of a network operator is used to optimise sets of CPs for a new network site in a stage-wise manner.

Scenario 1: Use of prior knowledge about the environment in which the cell is deployed (e.g. height of surrounding buildings, density of buildings) and the profile of services that are expected in this geographical area (e.g. ultra reliable low-latency communication). In this scenario, based on domain knowledge, the operator chooses initially a small subset of CPs known to have high impact to the optimisation objective KPIs. The small subset is then extended to the full set of CPs to leverage additional CP interactions.

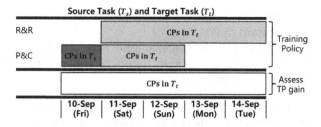

Fig. 5. Policies trained via Reinitialise-&-Retrain (R&R) use four days of data from the target task (T_t). Policies trained via Progress-&-Compress (P&C) use two days of data from T_t (50% less), and transfer knowledge from a source task T_s.

Scenario 2: Use of prior knowledge about the potential of certain CPs to cause network disruptions or network performance degradation (i.e. exploring CPs related to energy saving sleep-modes of a base-station, or CPs that determine antenna configurations directly impacting coverage). In this scenario, network optimisation starts with a set of CPs known to have low impact on the optimisation objective KPIs in order to reduce said risks. The initial set is then gradually extended to the full set of CPs.

Scenario 3: A combination of considerations reflected in Scenarios 1 and 2.

4.2   Policy Training Setup

Five experiments were designed to assess policy deployment lead-time reduction in the three scenarios described above. The experimental setups are outlined in Table 2. In each experimental setup, policies trained using P&C were initialised on a source task T_s and updated on the target task T_t. Policies trained using R&R were trained on the T_t using twice the training data volume as P&C (4 days as opposed to 2 days).

Table 2. Experimental setups to assess policy deployment lead-time reduction after expanding the set of CPs from a source task (T_s) to target task (T_t).

Experiment	Scenario	CPs in T_s	CPs in T_t
1	1	4 high-impact	All 19
2	2	15 low-impact	All 19
3	1	2 high-impact	4 high-impact
4	3	2 high-impact & 7 low-impact	All 19
5	2	7 low-impact	15 low-impact

To ensure an unbiased evaluation, the dataset D_{init} was partitioned into disjoint subsets as follows:

- 30% of the examples were reserved to train a test system model with similar structure to the reward model.
- Of the 70% remaining; 70% of the examples were used to train the reward model, state compressor, and policies, and 30% was used to assess TP gain as described in the following section.

The datasets were further structured as outlined in Fig. 5 in order to evaluate P&C under a 50% reduction in data volume compared to R&R.

4.3 Performance Metrics

Table 3. Hyperparameters used in the experimental evaluation.

Hyperparameter	State Compressor	Reward Model	R&R	P&C
Training Iterations	$epochs = 100$	$epochs = 100$	$epochs = 100$	$steps = 1000$
Learning Rate	0.00015	0.00015	0.0001	0.0001
Batch Size	128	128	64	64
γ_{Fisher}	NA	NA	NA	0.9
λ	$\lambda_{AE} = 0.9$	$\lambda_{RM} = 0.9$	NA	NA

Policy deployment is constrained by real-time, and its lead-time is approximately equivalent to the time required for the collection of dataset D_{init} in Algorithm 1. Our target is to demonstrate (i) 50% reduction in the amount of data required by P&C relative to R&R, and (ii) positive TP gain. TP gain in hour t is defined as:

$$TP\ Gain(t)\ [\%] = \frac{\sum_{c\in\mathcal{C}} \widehat{TP}_{c,t}^{P\&C} - \sum_{c\in\mathcal{C}} \widehat{TP}_{c,t}^{R\&R}}{\sum_{c\in\mathcal{C}} \widehat{TP}_{c,t}^{R\&R}} \times 100\,\%, \qquad (3)$$

where $\mathcal{C}$ is the set of all cells, $\widehat{TP}_{c,t}^{P\&C}$ is the predicted TP when cell $c \in \mathcal{C}$ executes CPs given by the P&C policy and $\widehat{TP}_{c,t}^{R\&R}$ is the predicted TP when cell c executes CPs given by the R&R policy. Predictions are given by the test system model. TP gain is computed in the test set as described in Sect. 4.2.

5 Results

Results are reported based on 20 independent runs of each experiment in Table 2.

Training Performance: Figure. 6 shows the learning curves of P&C and R&R. First, we observe that the runs of experiments for Scenario 1 that start with high-impact CPs in the source task converge faster than those runs of Scenario 2, which start with low-impact CPs is source task. A context change occurs between September 12th and 13th when training R&R policies incrementally. The context change is associated with switching from the weekend to a week day.

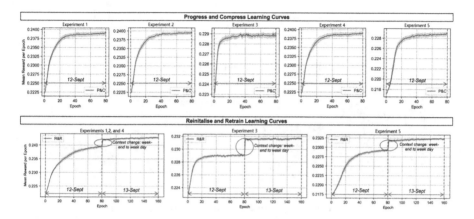

Fig. 6. Learning curves. Blue shading shows standard deviation over 20 independent runs.

The jump in mean reward per epoch on September 13th is caused by a change in the underlying user demand. This change is due to more users occupying hotspots such as downtown business districts, transport hubs, etc. during week-days. These areas are served by high capacity cells, resulting in a higher overall throughput.

Assessment of TP Gain: Figure. 7 illustrates the distribution of median TP gain over 20 independent runs calculated at hourly intervals as defined in Eq. 3. The median of TP over 20 independent runs for the P&C and R&R methods is given by $TP_{c,t}^X = \text{median}(TP_{c,t,1}^X, TP_{c,t,2}^X, \ldots, TP_{c,t,20}^X)$, $X \in \{P\&C, R\&R\}$, where $TP_{c,t,run}^X$ is the throughput for cell c at time t for $run = 1, 2, \ldots, 20$.

Results displayed in Fig. 7 confirm that P&C achieves a positive median TP gain along with a data reduction of 50% relative to the baseline R&R policy in experiments 1, 2, 4, and 5. The highest median TP gain is attained in experiment 4 due to the presence of both high-impact and low-impact CPs in the source task. P&C is most effective in experiments 1, 2, and 4 with all 19 CPs in the target task. We observe smaller positive median TP gain in experiment 5 because of the low impact CPs in both source and target tasks, while a negative median TP gain is observed in experiment 3 due to few low-impact CPs in the source

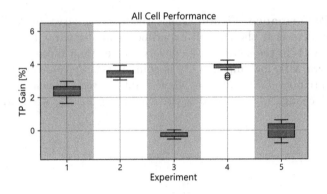

Fig. 7. Assessment of TP gain.

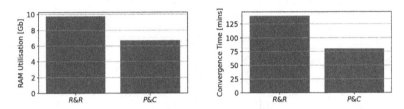

Fig. 8. Training resource footprint.

task. This result suggests that the effectiveness of continual RL as a sequence of MDPs with an expanding combinatorial action space is mostly affected by the strength of the causal effect of each consecutive action subset.

Training Resource Cost: The amount of training RAM and convergence wall time are illustrated in Fig. 8. *P&C* results in a reduction of approx. 31% in memory footprint compared to *R&R* baseline, amounting to a total of 6.7 GB. This is crucial for training in resource-constrained hardware, which is typical for on-premise deployments in telecommunication networks. Average training wall time for *P&C* is measured at 80 min compared to 140 min for *R&R*. Reduced training time allows us to allocate more resources for hyper-parameter tuning and model selection, and enables more frequent model updates in highly-dynamic wireless networks.

Inference Time: Inference for setting configuration parameters reduces to a forward pass of the compact neural net policy, and it was measured at 80 ms of wall-time for 20,000 cells.

6   Conclusions and Future Work

Learning optimisation policies from scratch in order to assess the performance of different subsets of configuration parameters on the objective KPI is costly is terms of time required for data collection, particularly for unknown wireless network environments with exploration challenges (i.e. safety constraints, limited budget of interactions with the wireless network, high dimensional state/action spaces, high noise levels). The contribution of our work is the application of Continual Reinforcement Learning to a wireless network optimisation system where the number of decision variables gradually increase throughout its lifetime. By refraining from reinitialising-and-retraining the policy, we achieve a two-fold reduction in end-to-end deployment time for each consecutive decision variable subset, which has direct implications in reducing operational cost and overall data collection requirement.

We defined three scenarios reflecting how domain knowledge of a network operator can be leveraged to handcraft a series of CP subsets to be optimised stage-wise. Five experiments based on these scenarios were conducted, and empirical results demonstrated a positive throughput gain of up to 4% of P&C continual RL method against the R&R baseline that used double the amount of training data.

The selection of CP subsets for optimisation policies deployed to new wireless network sites is traditionally an iterative trial-and-error process that predominantly relies on domain knowledge. Going forward, there are two approaches that will be investigated to further improve sample efficiency. The first approach is based on causal structure learning to automatically identify the CPs that exert the strongest causal effect on the optimisation objective KPI in a new environment, and hence complement and fine-tune operator's domain knowledge during selection of CP subsets. Of applicability here are methods that admit latent confounders when learning causal graphs, for example the works of [7, 18, 20] and also the auto-causal tuning method of [2]. The second approach is based on policy warm-starting through the technology of *sim-to-real transfer* in RL [33], some examples of which include domain adaptation, imitation learning and policy distillation.

References

1. Balevi, E., Andrews, J.G.: Online antenna tuning in heterogeneous cellular networks with deep reinforcement learning. IEEE Trans. Cogn. Commun. Netw. 5(4), 1113–1124 (2019). https://doi.org/10.1109/TCCN.2019.2933420
2. Biza, K., Tsamardinos, I., Triantafillou, S.: Out-of-sample tuning for causal discovery. IEEE Trans. Neural Netw. Learn. Syst. 1–11 (2022). https://doi.org/10.1109/TNNLS.2022.3185842
3. Bothe, S., Masood, U., Farooq, H., Imran, A.: Neuromorphic AI empowered root cause analysis of faults in emerging networks. In: IEEE International Black Sea Conference on Communications and Networking, BlackSeaCom 2020, Odessa, Ukraine, 26–29 May 2020. pp. 1–6. IEEE (2020). https://doi.org/10.1109/BlackSeaCom48709.2020.9235002
4. Bouton, M., Farooq, H., Forgeat, J., Bothe, S., Shirazipour, M., Karlsson, P.: Coordinated reinforcement learning for optimizing mobile networks (Sep 2021)

5. Calabrese, F.D., Wang, L., Ghadimi, E., Peters, G., Hanzo, L., Soldati, P.: Learning radio resource management in rans: Framework, opportunities, and challenges. IEEE Commun. Mag. **56**, 138–145 (2018)
6. Chua, K., Calandra, R., McAllister, R., Levine, S.: Deep reinforcement learning in a handful of trials using probabilistic dynamics models. In: Advances in Neural Information Processing Systems 31 (2018)
7. Colombo, D., Maathuis, M.H., Kalisch, M., Richardson, T.S.: Learning high-dimensional directed acyclic graphs with latent and selection variables. Ann. Stat. **40**(1), 294–321 (2012)
8. Dandanov, N., Al-Shatri, H., Klein, A., Poulkov, V.: Dynamic self-optimization of the antenna tilt for best trade-off between coverage and capacity in mobile networks. Wirel. Pers. Commun. **92**(1), 251–278 (2017). https://doi.org/10.1007/s11277-016-3849-9
9. Devin, C., Gupta, A., Darrell, T., Abbeel, P., Levine, S.: Learning modular neural network policies for multi-task and multi-robot transfer. In: 2017 IEEE International Conference on Robotics and Automation (ICRA), pp. 2169–2176. IEEE (2017)
10. Eckhardt, H., Klein, S., Gruber, M.: Vertical antenna tilt optimization for lte base stations. In: VTC Spring, pp. 1–5. IEEE (2011). http://dblp.uni-trier.de/db/conf/vtc/vtc2011s.html#EckhardtKG11
11. Eisenblätter, A., Geerdes, H.: Capacity optimization for UMTS: bounds and benchmarks for interference reduction. In: Proceedings of the IEEE 19th International Symposium on Personal, Indoor and Mobile Radio Communications, PIMRC 2008, 15–18 September 2008, Cannes, French Riviera, France, pp. 1–6. IEEE (2008). https://doi.org/10.1109/PIMRC.2008.4699919
12. Isele, D., Cosgun, A.: Selective experience replay for lifelong learning. In: Proceedings of the AAAI Conference on Artificial Intelligence, vol. 32 (2018)
13. Khetarpal, K., Riemer, M., Rish, I., Precup, D.: Towards continual reinforcement learning: a review and perspectives. J. Artif. Intell. Res. **75**, 1401–1476 (2020)
14. Kirkpatrick, J., et al.: Overcoming catastrophic forgetting in neural networks. Proc. Natl. Acad. Sci. **114**(13), 3521–3526 (2017)
15. Li, Z., Hoiem, D.: Learning without forgetting. IEEE Trans. Pattern Anal. Mach. Intell. **40**(12), 2935–2947 (2017)
16. Mendez, J.A., van Seijen, H., Eaton, E.: Modular lifelong reinforcement learning via neural composition. arXiv preprint arXiv:2207.00429 (2022)
17. Nasir, Y.S., Guo, D.: Multi-agent deep reinforcement learning for dynamic power allocation in wireless networks. IEEE J. Sel. Areas Commun. **37**(10), 2239–2250 (2019). https://doi.org/10.1109/JSAC.2019.2933973
18. Ogarrio, J.M., Spirtes, P., Ramsey, J.: A hybrid causal search algorithm for latent variable models. In: Proceedings of the Eighth International Conference on Probabilistic Graphical Models, 06–09 Sep, vol. 52, pp. 368–379. PMLR (2016)
19. Partov, B., Leith, D.J., Razavi, R.: Utility fair optimization of antenna tilt angles in lte networks. IEEE/ACM Trans. Netw. **23**(1), 175–185 (2015). https://doi.org/10.1109/TNET.2013.2294965
20. Raghu, V.K., et al.: Comparison of strategies for scalable causal discovery of latent variable models from mixed data. Inter. J. Data Sci. Anal. **6**, 33–45 (2018)
21. Rolnick, D., Ahuja, A., Schwarz, J., Lillicrap, T., Wayne, G.: Experience replay for continual learning. In: Advances in Neural Information Processing Systems 32 (2019)
22. Rusu, A.A., et al.: Policy distillation. arXiv preprint arXiv:1511.06295 (2015)

23. Rusu, A.A., et al.: Progressive neural networks. arXiv preprint arXiv:1606.04671 (2016)
24. Saini, S.K., Dhamnani, S., Ibrahim, A.A., Chavan, P.: Multiple treatment effect estimation using deep generative model with task embedding. In: The World Wide Web Conference, pp. 1601–1611 (2019)
25. Schulman, J., Wolski, F., Dhariwal, P., Radford, A., Klimov, O.: Proximal policy optimization algorithms. arXiv preprint arXiv:1707.06347 (2017)
26. Schwarz, J., et al.: Progress & Compress: A scalable framework for continual learning. In: International Conference on Machine Learning, pp. 4528–4537. PMLR (2018)
27. Shafin, R.S.B., et al.: Self-tuning sectorization: deep reinforcement learning meets broadcast beam optimization. IEEE Trans. Wirel. Commun. **19**(6), 4038–4053 (2020). https://doi.org/10.1109/TWC.2020.2979446
28. Shi, C., Blei, D., Veitch, V.: Adapting Neural Networks for the Estimation of Treatment Effects. In: Advances in Neural Information Processing Systems 32 (2019)
29. Traoré, Ret al.: Discorl: continual reinforcement learning via policy distillation. arXiv preprint arXiv:1907.05855 (2019)
30. Vannella, F., Jeong, J., Proutière, A.: Off-policy learning for remote electrical tilt optimization. In: 92nd IEEE Vehicular Technology Conference, VTC Fall 2020, Victoria, BC, Canada, 18 November -16 December 2020. pp. 1–5. IEEE (2020). https://doi.org/10.1109/VTC2020-Fall49728.2020.9348456
31. Yin, H., Pan, S.J.: Knowledge transfer for deep reinforcement learning with hierarchical experience replay. In: Thirty-First AAAI Conference on Artificial Intelligence (2017)
32. Yoon, J., Yang, E., Lee, J., Hwang, S.J.: Lifelong learning with dynamically expandable networks. arXiv preprint arXiv:1708.01547 (2017)
33. Zhao, W., Queralta, J.P., Westerlund, T.: Sim-to-real transfer in deep reinforcement learning for robotics: a survey. In: 2020 IEEE Symposium Series on Computational Intelligence (SSCI), pp. 737–744 (2020).https://doi.org/10.1109/SSCI47803.2020.9308468

An Examination of Wearable Sensors and Video Data Capture for Human Exercise Classification

Ashish Singh[1(✉)], Antonio Bevilacqua[1], Timilehin B. Aderinola[1], Thach Le Nguyen[1], Darragh Whelan[2], Martin O'Reilly[2], Brian Caulfield[1], and Georgiana Ifrim[1(✉)]

[1] Insight Centre for Data Analytics, University College Dublin, Dublin, Ireland
{ashish.singh,antonio.bevilacqua,timi.aderinola,thach.lenguyen,
b.caulfield,georgiana.ifrim}@insight-centre.org
[2] Output Sports Limited, NovaUCD, Dublin, Ireland
{darragh,martin}@ouputsports.com

Abstract. Wearable sensors such as Inertial Measurement Units (IMUs) are often used to assess the performance of human exercise. Common approaches use handcrafted features based on domain expertise or automatically extracted features using time series analysis. Multiple sensors are required to achieve high classification accuracy, which is not very practical. These sensors require calibration and synchronization and may lead to discomfort over longer time periods. Recent work utilizing computer vision techniques has shown similar performance using video, without the need for manual feature engineering, and avoiding some pitfalls such as sensor calibration and placement on the body. In this paper, we compare the performance of IMUs to a video-based approach for human exercise classification on two real-world datasets consisting of Military Press and Rowing exercises. We compare the performance using a single camera that captures video in the frontal view versus using 5 IMUs placed on different parts of the body. We observe that an approach based on a single camera can outperform a single IMU by 10 percentage points on average. Additionally, a minimum of 3 IMUs are required to outperform a single camera. We observe that working with the raw data using multivariate time series classifiers outperforms traditional approaches based on handcrafted or automatically extracted features. Finally, we show that an ensemble model combining the data from a single camera with a single IMU outperforms either data modality. Our work opens up new and more realistic avenues for this application, where a video captured using a readily available smartphone camera, combined with a single sensor, can be used for effective human exercise classification.

Keywords: Exercise Classification · Inertial Sensors · Video · Time Series Classification · Real-World Datasets

© The Author(s), under exclusive license to Springer Nature Switzerland AG 2023
G. De Francisci Morales et al. (Eds.): ECML PKDD 2023, LNAI 14174, pp. 312–329, 2023.
https://doi.org/10.1007/978-3-031-43427-3_19

1   Introduction

Recent years have seen an accelerated use of machine learning solutions to assess the performance of athletes. New technologies allow easier data capture and efficient machine learning techniques enable effective measurement and feedback. In this paper, we focus on the application of human exercise classification where the task is to differentiate normal and abnormal executions for strength and conditioning (S&C) exercises. S&C exercises are widely used for rehabilitation, performance assessment, injury screening and resistance training in order to improve the performance of athletes [18,19]. Approaches to data capture are either sensor-based or video-based. For sensor-based approaches, sensors such as Inertial Measurement Units (IMUs) are worn by participants [18,19]. For video, a participant's motion is captured using 3D motion capture [15], depth-capture based systems [31], or 2D video recordings using cameras [22,25]. The data obtained from these sources is processed and classified using machine learning models. Classification methods based on sensor data are popular in the literature and real-world applications, and yet, video-based approaches are gaining popularity [25,26] as they show potential for providing high classification accuracy and overcoming common issues of inertial sensors. Sensors require fitting on different parts of the body and the number of sensors to be worn depends upon the context of the exercise. For instance, the Military Press exercise requires at least 3 IMUs for optimal performance. Despite their popularity, sensors may cause discomfort, thereby hindering the movement of participants. In addition, using multiple sensors leads to overheads such as synchronization, calibration and orientation.

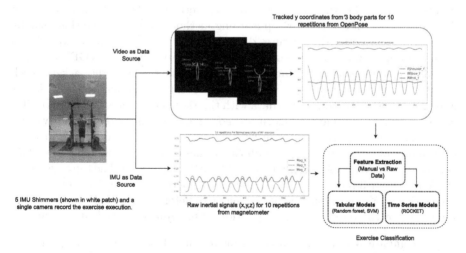

Fig. 1. Comparison of video (top) and sensors (bottom) to classify human exercise movement. The upper box presents the process of obtaining multivariate data from video (only 3 out of 25 body parts shown). The bottom box shows the raw Y-signals from a single IMU placed on the participant's body (only 3 signals shown here).

Recent advances in computer vision have enabled the usage of 2D videos for human exercise classification. Past work explored posture detection [22] and the application of human exercise classification using pose estimation. Our previous work [25] proposed a novel method named BodyMTS to classify human exercises using video, human pose estimation and multivariate time series classification. There is less work comparing sensors with video in real-world applications. In this paper, we compare the performance of a sensor-based approach utilizing 5 IMUs with that of video from a single front-facing camera, on the same set of 54 participants, on two real-world datasets consisting of Military Press (MP) and Rowing exercises. These are important S&C exercises and are widely used for injury risk screening and rehabilitation [30]. Incorrect executions may lead to musculoskeletal injuries and undermine the performance of athletes [1]. Hence, correct detection of abnormal movements is crucial to avoid injuries and maximize performance.

The main requirements for an effective human exercise classification application are [25]: accurate monitoring of body parts movement, correct classification of deviations from normal movements, timely feedback to end users, simple data capture using available smartphones and coverage of a wide range of S&C exercises. Previous work [29] has shown that this task is difficult and has poor intra and inter-rater accuracy in user studies with domain experts, with Kappa scores for inter-rater agreement between 0.18–0.53, and intra-rater between 0.38–0.62. Through discussions with domain experts, we established that an effective application should achieve a minimum accuracy of 80% to be useful for end users.

Existing methods using IMUs involve pre-processing the raw data, creating handcrafted features [18,20], and applying classical machine learning algorithms. Handcrafted feature extraction is often tedious and time-consuming, requires access to domain knowledge and is prone to cherry-pick features that only work for a specific set of exercises. Deep learning methods [17] overcome this issue by automatically constructing features during training, but still require expertise in deep learning architectures along with hardware resources such as GPUs. Hence, we take two approaches to feature extraction: (1) using lightweight packages such as catch22 [13] and tsfresh [4] to automate the feature extraction from raw signals and (2) using the raw time series data with time series classifiers, which implicitly construct features inside the algorithm. For videos, we first extract multivariate data using human pose estimation with OpenPose [3] to obtain (X,Y) location coordinates of key body parts over all the frames of a video. Figure 1 shows data captured with IMUs and video for the Military Press exercise. The top part shows the Y-signal for 3 body parts for a total of 10 repetitions, while the bottom part shows the X, Y, and Z signals of the magnetometer from an IMU worn on the right arm for the same set of 10 repetitions. **Our main contributions are:**

- We compare 3 strategies for creating features from IMU data for human exercise classification. We observe that directly classifying the raw signals using multivariate time series classifiers outperforms the approach based on handcrafted features by a margin of 10 and 4 percentage points in accuracy for MP and Rowing respectively. Automatic feature extraction shows better performance than handcrafted features.

– We compare the performance of IMU and video for human exercise classification. We observe that a single video-based approach outperforms a single IMU-based approach by a margin of 5 percentage points accuracy for MP and 15 percentage points for Rowing. Additionally, we observe that a minimum of 3 IMU devices are needed to outperform a single video for both exercises.
– We propose an ensemble model that combines the data modalities from IMU and video, which outperforms either approach by a minimum of 2 percentage points accuracy for both MP and Rowing. This leads to an accuracy of 93% for MP and 87% for Rowing, using only a single IMU and a reduced-size video. We discuss reasons why combining video and sensor data is beneficial, in particular, the 2D video provides positional information, while the sensor provides information on orientation and depth of movement.
– To support this paper we have made all our code and data available [1].

The rest of the paper is organized as follows. Section 2 presents an overview of related work, Sect. 3 describes the data collection procedure, Sect. 4 describes the data analysis and methodology for classification and Sect. 5 presents the classification results using IMUs and video. Section 6 concludes and outlines directions for future work and Sect. A discusses ethical implications of this work.

2 Related Work

This section describes the purpose of S&C exercises and provides an overview of sensor-based and video-based data capture approaches.

2.1 S&C Exercise Classification

S&C exercises aim at improving the performance of human participants in terms of strength, speed and agility, and they can be captured using sensor-based or video-based techniques.

Wearable sensor-based approaches involve fitting Inertial Measurement Units (IMUs) [18,19] on different parts of the body. This is followed by creating hand-crafted features which are used in conjunction with a classical machine learning model. Deep learning methods attempt to automate the process of feature extraction. CNN models work by stacking IMU signals into an image [17], whereas [28] uses an attention mechanism to identify the important parts in a signal. Using IMUs has its own limitations. First, the number of inertial sensors required and their positions can vary from exercise to exercise [18,20,30]. Furthermore, sensors require calibration and synchronization and may also hinder the movement of the body and cause discomfort when used over longer time periods [11,30].

Video-based systems can be categorized into 3 types: 3D motion capture, depth camera-based and 2D video camera. Though they are accurate, 3D motion capture systems are expensive and require complex setups. In addition, fitting multiple markers on the body may hinder the normal movement of the body [18].

---

[1] https://github.com/mlgig/Video_vs_Shimmer_ECML_2023.

Microsoft Kinect is commonly used for depth camera-based systems [5,23,31]. These systems are less accurate and are affected by poor lighting, occlusion, and clothing, and require high maintenance [18]. The third subcategory uses video-based devices such as DSLR or smartphone cameras. Works based on video rely on human pose estimation to track different body parts [16,25,26] and have shown 2D videos to be a potential alternative to IMU sensors. The video-based analysis also includes commercial software such as Dartfish [9] by providing the option to analyze motion at a very low frame rate. However, these are less accurate and require fitting body markers of a different colour to the background.

2.2   Multivariate Time Series Classification (MTSC)

In multivariate time series classification tasks, the data is ordered and each sample has more than one dimension. We focus on recent linear classifiers and deep learning methods, which have been shown to achieve high accuracy with minimal run-time and memory requirements [24,27].

Linear Classifiers. ROCKET [6] is a state-of-the-art algorithm for MTSC in terms of accuracy and scalability. Two more extensions named MiniROCKET [7] and MultiROCKET [27], have further improved this method. These classifiers work by using a large number of random convolutional kernels which capture different characteristics of a signal and hence do not require learning the kernel weights as opposed to deep learning methods. These features are then classified using a linear classifier such as Logistic or Ridge Regression.

Deep Learning Classifiers. Deep learning architectures based on Fully Convolutional Networks (FCN) and Resnet [10,24] have shown competitive performance for MTSC, without suffering from high time and memory complexity.

3   Data Collection

Participants. 54 healthy volunteers (32 males and 22 females, age: 26 ± 5 years, height: 1.73 ± 0.09 m, body mass: 72 ± 15 kg) were recruited for the study. Participants were asked to complete multiple repetitions of the two exercises in this study; the Military Press and Rowing exercises. In each case, the exercises were performed under 'normal' and 'induced' conditions. In the 'normal' condition the exercise was performed with the correct biomechanical form and in the 'induced' condition the exercise was purposefully performed with pre-determined deviations from the normal form, assessed and confirmed in real-time by the movement scientist. Please refer to these sources [25,26] for additional information on the experiment protocol.

The data was collected using two video cameras and 5 Shimmer IMUs placed on 5 different parts of the body. Two cameras (30 frames/sec with 720p resolution) were set up in front and to the side of the participants. In this work, we only use the video recordings from the front view camera which is a more common use case. The 5 IMUs with settings: sampling frequency of 51.2 Hz, tri-axial accelerometer(± 2 g), gyroscope ($\pm 500°$/s) and magnetometer (± 1.9 Ga) [20] were fitted on the participants at the following five locations: Left Wrist (LW), Right Wrist (RW), Left Arm (LA), Right Arm (RA) and Back. The orientation and locations of all the IMUs were consistent for all the participants.

Exercise Technique and Deviations. The induced forms were further sub-categorized depending on the exercise.

3.1 Exercise Classes for Military Press (MP)

Normal (N): This class refers to the correct execution, involving lifting the bar from shoulder level to above the head, fully extending the arms, and returning it back to shoulder level with no arch in the back. The bar must be stable and parallel to the ground throughout the execution. **Asymmetrical (A):** The bar is lopsided and asymmetrical. **Reduced Range (R):** The bar is not brought down completely to the shoulder level. **Arch (Arch):** The participant arches their back during execution. Figure 2 shows these deviations using a single frame.

Fig. 2. Single frames from the Military Press exercise, depicting the induced deviations for class A, Arch and R (left to right).

Fig. 3. Single frames for the Rowing exercise, depicting the induced deviations for class A, Ext, R and RB (left to right).

3.2   Exercise Classes for Rowing

Normal (N): This class refers to the correct execution, where the participant begins by positioning themselves correctly, bending knees and leaning forward from the waist. The execution starts by lifting the bar with fully extended arms until it touches the sternum and bringing it back to the starting position. The bar must be stable and parallel to the ground and the back should be straight. **Asymmetrical (A):** The bar is lopsided and asymmetrical. **Reduced Range (R):** The bar is not brought up completely until it touches the sternum. **Ext:** The participant moves his/her back during execution. **RB:** The participant executes with a rounded back. Figure 3 shows these deviations by depicting a single frame.

4   Data Analysis and Methods

This section presents the data pre-processing, features extraction and classification models. We present the feature extraction for IMU data, followed by feature extraction for video. We also provide a description of the train/test splits for IMUs and video data.

4.1   IMU Data

We discuss three strategies to create features from IMU data. First, we directly use the raw signal as a time series. Second, we use existing approaches to create handcrafted features. Third, we use dedicated packages to automatically extract features. Features extraction is performed after segmenting the full signal to obtain individual repetitions.

Raw Signal as Multivariate Time Series. The raw signal from IMU records data for 10 repetitions. Hence, we segment the time series to obtain signals for individual repetitions. The Y signal of the magnetometer from the IMU placed on the right arm is utilized to segment the signals. The time series obtained after this step has variable length since the time taken to complete each repetition differs from participant to participant. Further, current implementations of selected time series classifiers cannot handle variable-length time series and therefore all time series are re-sampled to a length of 161 (length of the longest time series). This does not impact the performance as shown in the supplementary material. Every single repetition constitutes a single sample for train/test data. The final data D has a shape of $D \in \mathbb{R}^{N \times 45 \times 161}$, where N indicates the total samples. Each sample denoted by x_i in the data has a dimension of $x_i \in \mathbb{R}^{45 \times 161}$, where 45 denotes the total number of time series (5 IMUs x 9 signals) and 161 is the length of each time series.

Handcrafted Features. Each of the 5 IMUs outputs 9 signals (X, Y, Z) for each of the accelerometer, magnetometer and gyroscope. We follow the procedure as described in [20] to create handcrafted features. Additionally, 5 signals were created for each IMU: pitch, roll, yaw signal and vector magnitude of accelerometer and gyroscope, giving a total of 70 signals $(5 \times (9 + 5))$. For each repetition signal, 18 handcrafted features that capture time and frequency domain characteristics were created. Hence, we obtain the final data $D \in \mathbb{R}^{N \times 1260}$, where N is the total samples and 1260 represents the features extracted from 70 signals with 18 features each for both MP and Rowing.

Auto Extracted Features. We use packages catch22 [13] and tsfresh [4] to perform automatic feature extraction from a single repetition signal. These packages calculate a wide range of pre-defined metrics in order to capture the diverse characteristics of a signal. They are straightforward to use and avoid the need for domain knowledge and signal processing techniques. Catch22 captures 22 features for each of the 45 signals (5 IMUs x 9 signals) giving a total of 990 tabular features for MP and Rowing in the final dataset $D \in \mathbb{R}^{N \times 990}$, where N indicates the total samples. Similarly, tsfresh captures a large number of time series characteristics by creating a large number of features. The final dataset D has a shape of $D \in \mathbb{R}^{N \times 15000}$ and $D \in \mathbb{R}^{N \times 16000}$, for MP and Rowing respectively. Both manual and automatic feature extraction are performed on the normalized time series, as we observed that normalizing the time series leads to an increase in accuracy.

4.2 Video Data

We follow the methodology presented in our previous work [25] to classify human exercise from videos. OpenPose is used for human pose estimation to track the key body parts, followed by a multivariate time series classifier. Each video consists of a sequence of frames where each frame is considered a time step. Each frame is fed to OpenPose which outputs coordinates (X, Y) for 25 body parts. We only use the 8 upper body parts most relevant to the target exercises but also conduct experiments with the full 25 body parts. The time series obtained from a single body part is denoted by $b^n = [(X, Y)^1, (X, Y)^2, (X, Y)^3, ...(X, Y)^T]$ where n indicates the nth body part and T is the length of the video clip.

Multivariate Time Series Data. Since each video records 10 repetitions for each exercise execution, segmentation is necessary in order to obtain single repetitions. Each repetition forms a single time series sample for training and evaluating a classifier. We use peak detection to segment the time series as mentioned in our previous work [25]. Similarly to the IMU case, every time series obtained after this step has a variable length and therefore is re-sampled to a length of 161. The final data is denoted by $D \in \mathbb{R}^{N \times 16 \times 161}$, where N indicates the total samples. Each sample denoted by x_i has a dimension of $x_i \in \mathbb{R}^{16 \times 161}$, where 16 indicates X and Y coordinates for 8 body parts and 161 is the length of each time series.

Auto Extracted Features. We use catch22 [13] and tsfresh [4] to perform automatic feature extraction from each single repetition signal.

4.3   Train/Test Splits

We use 3 train/test splits in the ratio of 70/30 on the full data set to obtain train and test data for both IMUs and video. Each split is done based on the unique participant IDs to avoid leaking information into the test data. Train data is further split in the ratio of 85/15 to create validation data to fine-tune the hyperparameters. The validation data is merged back into the train data before the final classification. The data is balanced across all the classes. Table 1 shows the number of samples across all classes for a single train/test split for MP and Rowing respectively.

Table 1. Samples per class in train/test dataset for a single 70/30 split for MP (left) and Rowing (right) for both IMU and video.

Class	Train	Test	Total
N	370	150	520
A	340	150	490
R	366	155	521
Arch	350	140	490
Total	**1426**	**595**	**2021**

Class	Train	Test	Total
N	360	160	520
A	362	150	512
Ext	340	130	470
R	380	150	530
RB	361	140	501
Total	**1803**	**730**	**2533**

4.4   Classification Models

We use tabular machine learning models to work with handcrafted and automated features. Informed by previous literature on feature extraction for IMU data [18,20], we focus on Logistic Regression, Ridge Regression, Naive Bayes, Random Forest and SVM as classifiers for tabular data. We select ROCKET, MultiROCKET and deep learning models FCN and Resnet as recent accurate and fast multivariate time series classifiers [2].

5   Empirical Evaluation

We present results on IMU data, video data and combinations using ensembles. We report average accuracy over 3 train/test splits for all the results. We use the *sklearn* library [21] to classify tabular data and *sktime* [12] to classify time series data. All the experiments are performed using Python on an Ubuntu 18.04 system (16GB RAM, Intel i7-4790 CPU @ 3.60GHz). The Supplementary Material[2]

---

[2] https://github.com/mlgig/Video_vs_Shimmer_ECML_2023/blob/master/ Supplementary_material.pdf.

presents further detailed results on leave-one-participant-out cross-validation, demographic results, execution time, as well as the impact of normalization and re-sampling length on the classification accuracy.

5.1   Accuracy Using IMUs

We present the classification results using 3 different strategies for creating features from IMU data. For tabular features, we perform feature selection to reduce overfitting and execution time. We use Lasso Regression *(C=0.01)* with L1 penalty for feature selection, where C is the regularization parameter. Logistic Regression achieves the best performance followed by Ridge Regression and SVM. These results suggest that linear classifiers are best suited for this problem. Hence we only present results using Logistic Regression here. We tune hyperparameters, particularly regularization parameter C of Logistic Regression using cross validation. We observed that Logistic Regression (LR) with *C=0.01* achieves the highest accuracy (Table 3 presents results with Logistic Regression).

Table 2. Average accuracy on test data over 3 splits for selected multivariate time series classifiers using IMU raw data as time series.

Classifier	Acc MP	Acc Rowing
FCN	0.86	0.77
ResNet	0.87	0.74
ROCKET	**0.91**	**0.80**
MultiROCKET	**0.91**	**0.81**

Table 2 presents the results using raw data and multivariate time series classifiers. ROCKET achieves the best performance with MultiROCKET having similar accuracy for this problem. ROCKET has the added benefit that it can also work with unnormalised data and it is faster during training and prediction, so we select this classifier for the rest of the analysis. We analyse the average accuracy using all 5 IMUs as well as combinations of IMUs using raw time series with ROCKET as classifier. The goal is to select the minimum number of IMUs needed to achieve the best performance for MP and Rowing. Table 3 presents the average accuracy over 3 splits obtained using all IMUs whereas Table 4 presents the average accuracy using different combinations of IMUs.

Results and Discussion: From Table 3 we observe that using raw data with ROCKET achieves the highest accuracy when compared to the approaches based on handcrafted and automated feature extraction. We tune hyperparameters of ROCKET using the validation data, particularly the *number-of-kernels* and observe no impact on the accuracy. The normalization flag is set to True here as turning it off leads to a 4 percentage points drop in the accuracy. ROCKET can easily be run on a single CPU machine without the need for much engineering

Table 3. Average accuracy obtained on 5 IMUs data by using three feature selection strategies. Logistic Regression (LR) is used for tabular data, whereas ROCKET is used for time series classification.

Feature Type	Acc MP	Acc Rowing
Tabular		
Handcrafted	0.80	0.76
Automated (catch22)	0.84	0.75
Automated (tsfresh)	0.88	0.80
Raw Signals		
Time series	**0.91**	**0.80**

Table 4. Average accuracy obtained using the different placement of IMUs over three train/test splits using raw data as time series with ROCKET as classifier.

Placement of IMU	Acc MP	Acc Rowing
5 IMUs	**0.91**	**0.80**
RightWrist	0.83	0.68
LeftWrist	0.84	0.70
RightArm	0.77	0.65
LeftArm	0.76	0.66
Back	0.71	0.71
LeftWrist + RightWrist	0.88	0.75
LeftWrist + RightWrist + Back	**0.91**	**0.80**
LeftArm + RightArm	0.82	0.70
LeftArm + RightArm + Back	0.86	0.78

effort (only 2 parameters to tune) and dedicated hardware. It is much faster than using tsfresh or catch22 for feature extraction followed by classification. Table 4 presents the accuracy using different combinations of IMUs placed on different parts of the body. Accuracy is lowest when using only a single sensor. Accuracy starts to increase as more IMUs are included, for both MP and Rowing. We observe that placing 1 IMU on each wrist and 1 at the back achieved the same accuracy as using all 5 IMUs. The accuracy jumps from 0.83 to 0.88 moving from one IMU placed on the right wrist to two IMUs placed on both wrists and finally jumps to 0.91 when adding one more IMU at the back for MP. Similar behaviour is observed for Rowing. This suggests that 3 IMUs are sufficient for these exercises.

5.2 Accuracy Using Video

Here we present the results of classification using video as the data source. We report the average accuracy over 3 train/test splits for MP and Rowing. We also

Table 5. Average accuracy obtained by ROCKET using video as data source for MP and Rowing over three train/test splits.

Feature Type	Acc MP	Acc Rowing
Tabular		
Automated (catch22)	0.69	0.70
Automated (tsfresh)	0.77	0.77
Raw Signals		
25 body parts	0.82	0.79
8 body parts	**0.88**	**0.83**
Elbow Pair [8]	0.83	0.82

present results using tabular classifiers with automated features for comparison with the IMU based approach. For the raw data approach, we study the accuracy when involving different body parts, e.g., all 25, the 8 upper body parts suggested by domain experts and results using automated channel selection technique [8]. The normalization flag is set to False here as turning it on leads to a 4 percentage points drop in accuracy. This is in contrast to the setting configured for IMUs. We tune hyperparameters of ROCKET, particularly the *number-of-kernels* and observe no impact on the accuracy. Table 5 presents the average accuracy using these different approaches for classifying MP and Rowing exercises.

Results and Discussion: From Table 5 we observe that the average accuracy achieved using raw time series is highest when using the 8 body parts suggested by domain experts. Using automated features does not seem to work very well, in this case, achieving accuracy below 80% for both exercises. Moreover, using channel selection techniques leads to an improvement by 1 and 3 percentage points in accuracy versus using the full 25 body parts.

5.3   IMU Versus Video

We compare IMU and video data for human exercise classification, using the raw data approach for both IMU and video as it achieves the best performance. We report the accuracy, the execution time and the storage space required.

Table 6 presents the results for both MP and Rowing exercises. We observe that a minimum of 3 IMUs are required to achieve a higher accuracy than a single video. A single video outperforms a single IMU for both exercises by a minimum of 5 percentage points. Table 7 reports the real train/test time for both approaches. This time includes time taken for data pre-processing and to train/test the model. It also includes time to run pose estimation in case of video. The IMUs approach takes the least amount of time to train/test as compared to the video-based approach. For video, OpenPose extracts the multivariate time series data. The total duration of all videos is 1 h 38 min for MP, whereas Open-Pose took 1 h 12 min thus OpenPose can run faster than real-time, which is

Table 6. Comparison of accuracy obtained using IMUs and video for MP and Rowing.

Data Source	Acc MP	Acc Rowing
Placement of IMUs		
3 IMUs (Wrists and Back)	0.91	0.80
1 IMU (LeftWrist)	0.84	0.70
Video		
25 body parts	0.82	0.79
8 body parts	0.88	0.83
Ensemble: video and IMUs		
Video (8 body parts) + 3 IMUs	**0.93**	**0.88**
Video (8 body parts) + 1 IMU LeftWrist	**0.93**	0.87

important for getting fast predictions. Table 8 presents the storage consumption for both approaches. We note savings in terms of storage space: 5 IMUs require 6 times more space than the time series obtained from videos. Even after selecting the minimum number of sensors which is 3 in both exercises, the storage consumption is more than 200 MB which is also higher as compared to using time series from video. Our previous work in [25] explored the impact of video quality such as resolution and bit rate on classification accuracy and demonstrated how much video quality can be degraded without having a significant impact on the accuracy, whilst saving storage space and processing power.

5.4   Combining IMU and Video

We create an ensemble model by combining individual models trained independently on IMU and Video. For IMUs, we take the 3 sensors that achieved the highest accuracy. When video is combined with just a single sensor, we take the IMU placed on the left wrist, as it had the highest accuracy among single sensors and it is the most common location for people to wear their smartwatch. Probabilities are combined by averaging and the class with the highest average probability is predicted for a sample during test time. Table 6 presents a comparison of different approaches, using ROCKET as a multivariate time series classifier. From Table 6, we observe that an ensemble model achieves the best average accuracy when compared to using any number of IMUs and a single video-based approach. The accuracy for MP jumps by 2 percentage points when transitioning from 5 IMUs to an ensemble approach, and by 5 percentage points when moving from a single video to an ensemble. Similar results are observed for Rowing. These results suggest that combining IMU and video modalities enhances the performance of exercise classification. Combining video and IMU data sources, with video providing 2D location coordinates for key anatomical landmarks and IMUs capturing acceleration and orientation of the body parts, results in improved classification accuracy, as shown in this investigation

Table 7. Average train/test time (minutes) obtained using IMUs and video as data sources for MP over three train/test splits. We also report the average test (i.e., prediction) time over a clip of 10 repetitions.

Data Type	Training Time (minutes)	Test Time/ **Test time per clip of 10 reps**
Sensor		
3 IMUs (Wrists and Back)	8	6/0.10
Video		
8 body parts	52	22/0.37
Ensemble: video and IMUs		
Video (8 body parts) + 5 IMUs	60	29/0.50
Video (8 body parts) + 1 IMU	58	27/0.46

Table 8. Storage consumption using raw videos, IMUs and video as time series for MP and Rowing exercises for the 54 participants in our study.

Data Size (MB)	MP	Rowing
5 IMUs	640	591
Raw Videos (720p)	813	1012
Videos as Time Series	97	114

(see supplementary material). This finding is consistent with previous work in [14] that highlights the complementary nature of video and IMUs in enhancing human pose estimation quality, while in this work we see a similar benefit for human exercise classification.

6 Conclusion

We presented a comparison of IMU and video-based approaches for human exercise classification on two real-world S&C exercises (Military Press and Rowing) involving 54 participants. We compared different feature-creation strategies for classification. The results show that an automated feature extraction approach outperforms classification that is based on manually created features. Additionally, directly using the raw time series data with multivariate time series classifiers achieves the best performance for both IMU and video. While comparing IMU and video-based approaches, we observed that using a single video significantly outperforms the accuracy obtained using a single IMU. Moreover, the minimum number of IMUs required is not known in advance, for instance, 3 IMUs are required for MP to reach a reasonable accuracy. Next, we compared the performance of an ensemble method combining both IMU and video with the standalone approaches. We showed that an ensemble approach outperforms either data modality deployed in isolation. The accuracy achieved was 93% and

88% for MP and Rowing respectively. The criteria to select sensors or videos will ultimately depend on the goal of the end user. For instance: the choice between video and IMUs will depend on a combination of factors such as convenience and levels of accuracy required for the specific application context.

We acknowledge the fact that the scenario that was tested in this research does not accurately reflect real-world conditions. This does mean that we are exposed to the risk that the induced deviation performances could be exaggerated, and therefore not reflective of the often very minor deviations that can be observed in the real-world setting. However, we would argue that performing exercises under induced deviation conditions, if done appropriately, is a very necessary first step towards validating these exercise classification strategies in this field. It would not be prudent to assume that this model could be generalised to operate to the same level in real-world conditions. Having said that, the use of conditioned datasets is a necessary first step in this kind of application and provides the proof of concept evidence necessary to move onto the real-world setting.

Acknowledgment. This work was funded by Science Foundation Ireland through the Insight Centre for Data Analytics (12/RC/2289_P2) and VistaMilk SFI Research Centre (SFI/16/RC/3835).

A   Ethical Implications

Using videos for human exercise classification raises ethical implications that need to be mitigated, prompting a discussion of potential ethical implications.

Data Collection. Participants in this study provided written consent and the Human Research Ethics Committee of the university approved this study. All experiments were conducted under the supervision of an expert physiotherapist. The potential implications, in this case, can arise when the language used for the consent form may not be native to all the participants. In our case, the organizing authority or professional who was carrying out the data collection made sure that all the participants have well understood the consent form and the use of this data in the future.

Privacy and Confidentiality. This study uses videos which record participants executing exercises. This poses obvious privacy challenges. A first step is to blur the video to protect the participant's identity. This work utilizes human pose estimation to extract time series from video, thereby avoiding the need to directly use the original video. By working with the extracted time series, it largely safeguards the privacy and confidentiality of the participants.

Diversity of Representation. The participants considered in this study fall into the age group of 20 to 46. Hence the results presented here may not generalise for other age groups. Therefore the final use case will depend on the specific target users, such as athletes competing in the Olympic games versus individuals

with less intensive training goals. While there were slightly more male participants than female participants, it does not impact the conclusions drawn in this
work, as analysed in the supplementary material. However, this requires further
exploration to avoid any biases in the conclusion. Future studies should aim for
equal representation among participants in terms of age, sex, gender, race etc.,
from the start of the study.

Transparency and Feedback. The prediction of the model in this case outputs
whether the execution of the exercise was correct or incorrect. Deep learning-
based models and other posthoc explanation methods support saliency maps
which can be used to highlight the discriminative regions of the data that can
be mapped back to the original video thus providing more information about
the model decision to the participant.

The above list is not exhaustive and other inherent biases may appear because
of the chosen model and the way the data has been collected.

References

1. Baechle, T.R., Earle, R.W.: Essentials of strength training and conditioning. Human kinetics, Champaign, IL (2008)
2. Bagnall, A., Lines, J., Bostrom, A., Large, J., Keogh, E.: The great time series classification bake off: a review and experimental evaluation of recent algorithmic advances. In: Data Mining and Knowledge Discovery, pp. 1–55 (2016). https://doi.org/10.1007/s10618-016-0483-9
3. Cao, Z., Hidalgo Martinez, G., Simon, T., Wei, S., Sheikh, Y.A.: Openpose: real-time multi-person 2d pose estimation using part affinity fields. IEEE Trans. Pattern Anal. Mach. Intell. (2019)
4. Christ, M., Braun, N., Neuffer, J., Kempa-Liehr, A.W.: Time series feature extraction on basis of scalable hypothesis tests (tsfresh - a python package). Neurocomputing **307**, 72–77 (2018). https://doi.org/10.1016/j.neucom.2018.03.067
5. Decroos, T., Schütte, K., De Beéck, T.O., Vanwanseele, B., Davis, J.: AMIE: automatic monitoring of indoor exercises. In: Brefeld, U., et al. (eds.) ECML PKDD 2018. LNCS (LNAI), vol. 11053, pp. 424–439. Springer, Cham (2019). https://doi.org/10.1007/978-3-030-10997-4_26
6. Dempster, A., Petitjean, F., Webb, G.I.: Rocket: exceptionally fast and accurate time series classification using random convolutional kernels. Data Min. Knowl. Discov. **34**(5), 1454–1495 (2020), https://doi.org/10.1007/s10618-020-00701-z
7. Dempster, A., Schmidt, D.F., Webb, G.I.: Minirocket: a very fast (almost) deterministic transform for time series classification. In: KDD 2021 arXiv: 2012.08791 (2021)
8. Dhariyal, B., Le Nguyen, T., Ifrim, G.: Scalable classifier-agnostic channel selection for multivariate time series classification. Data Min. Knowl. Discov. **37**(2), 1010–1054 (2023). https://doi.org/10.1007/s10618-022-00909-1
9. Faro, A., Rui, P.: Use of open-source technology to teach biomechanics. Educaţie Fizică şi Sport, p. 18 (2016)
10. Fawaz, H.I., Forestier, G., Weber, J., Idoumghar, L., Muller, P.A.: Deep learning for time series classification: a review. Data Min. Knowl. Discov. **33**(4), 917–963 (2019). https://doi.org/10.1007/s10618-019-00619-1

11. Kwon, H., et al.: Imutube: automatic extraction of virtual on-body accelerometry from video for human activity recognition. Proc. ACM Interact. Mob. Wearable Ubiquitous Technol. **4**(3), 87 (2020). https://doi.org/10.1145/3411841

12. Löning, M., Bagnall, A., Ganesh, S., Kazakov, V., Lines, J., Király, F.J.: sktime: a Unified Interface for Machine Learning with Time Series. In: Workshop on Systems for ML at NeurIPS 2019 (2019)

13. Lubba, C.H., Sethi, S.S., Knaute, P., Schultz, S.R., Fulcher, B.D., Jones, N.S.: catch22: Canonical time-series characteristics selected through highly comparative time-series analysis. bioRxiv (2019)

14. von Marcard, T., Pons-Moll, G., Rosenhahn, B.: Human pose estimation from video and imus. IEEE Trans. Pattern Anal. Mach. Intell. **38**, 1533–1547 (2016)

15. Molías, L.M., Ranilla, J.M.C., Cervera, M.G.: Pre-service physical education teachers' self-management ability: a training experience in 3d simulation environments. Retos: nuevas tendencias en educación física, deporte y recreación (32), 30–34 (2017)

16. Nakano, N., et al.: Evaluation of 3d markerless motion capture accuracy using openpose with multiple video cameras. Front. Sports Active Living **2** (2020). https://doi.org/10.3389/fspor.2020.00050

17. Nutter, M., Crawford, C.H., Ortiz, J.: Design of novel deep learning models for real-time human activity recognition with mobile phones. In: 2018 International Joint Conference on Neural Networks (IJCNN), pp. 1–8 (2018). https://doi.org/10.1109/IJCNN.2018.8489319

18. O'Reilly, M., Caulfield, B., Ward, T., Johnston, W., Doherty, C.: Wearable inertial sensor systems for lower limb exercise detection and evaluation: a systematic review. Sports Med. **48**(5), 1221–1246 (2018)

19. O'Reilly, M., et al.: Evaluating squat performance with a single inertial measurement unit. In: 2015 IEEE 12th International Conference on Wearable and Implantable Body Sensor Networks (BSN), pp. 1–6. IEEE (2015)

20. O'Reilly, M.A., Whelan, D.F., Ward, T.E., Delahunt, E., Caulfield, B.M.: Classification of deadlift biomechanics with wearable inertial measurement units. J. Biomech. **58**, 155–161 (2017)

21. Pedregosa, F., et al.: Scikit-learn: machine learning in python. J. Mach. Learn. Res. **12**, 2825–2830 (2011)

22. Rahmadani, A., Bayu Dewantara, B.S., Sari, D.M.: Human pose estimation for fitness exercise movement correction. In: 2022 International Electronics Symposium (IES), pp. 484–490 (2022). https://doi.org/10.1109/IES55876.2022.9888451

23. Ressman, J., Rasmussen-Barr, E., Grooten, W.J.A.: Reliability and validity of a novel kinect-based software program for measuring a single leg squat. BMC Sports Sci. Med. Rehabil. **12**, 1–12 (2020)

24. Ruiz, A.P., Flynn, M., Large, J., Middlehurst, M., Bagnall, A.: The great multivariate time series classification bake off: a review and experimental evaluation of recent algorithmic advances. In: Data Mining and Knowledge Discovery, pp. 1–49 (2020)

25. Singh, A., et al.: Fast and robust video-based exercise classification via body pose tracking and scalable multivariate time series classifiers. In: Data Mining and Knowledge Discovery (Dec 2022). https://doi.org/10.1007/s10618-022-00895-4

26. Singh, A., et al.: Interpretable classification of human exercise videos through pose estimation and multivariate time series analysis. 5th International Workshop on Health Intelligence at AAAI (2020). https://doi.org/10.1007/978-3-030-93080-6_14

27. Tan, C.W., Dempster, A., Bergmeir, C., Webb, G.I.: MultiRocket: multiple pooling operators and transformations for fast and effective time series classification. arxiv:2102.00457 (2021)
28. Tao, W., Chen, H., Moniruzzaman, M., Leu, M.C., Yi, Z., Qin, R.: Attention-based sensor fusion for human activity recognition using imu signals. arXiv: 2112.11224 (2021)
29. Whelan, D., Delahunt, E., O'Reilly, M., Hernandez, B., Caulfield, B.: Determining interrater and intrarater levels of agreement in students and clinicians when visually evaluating movement proficiency during screening assessments. Phys. Ther. **99**(4), 478–486 (2019)
30. Whelan, D., O'Reilly, M., Huang, B., Giggins, O., Kechadi, T., Caulfield, B.: Leveraging imu data for accurate exercise performance classification and musculoskeletal injury risk screening. In: 2016 38th Annual International Conference of the IEEE Engineering in Medicine and Biology Society (EMBC), pp. 659–662. IEEE (2016)
31. Zerpa, C., Lees, C., Patel, P., Pryzsucha, E., Patel, P.: The use of microsoft kinect for human movement analysis. Inter. J. Sports Sci. **5**(4), 120–127 (2015)

Context-Aware Deep Time-Series Decomposition for Anomaly Detection in Businesses

Youngeun Nam[1], Patara Trirat[1], Taeyoon Kim[1], Youngseop Lee[2], and Jae-Gil Lee[1]([✉])

[1] School of Computing, KAIST, Daejeon, South Korea
{youngeun.nam,patara.t,tykimseoul,jaegil}@kaist.ac.kr
[2] Samsung Electronics Co., Ltd., Suwon-si, South Korea
yseop.lee@samsung.com

Abstract. Detecting anomalies in time series has become increasingly challenging as data collection technology develops, especially in real-world communication services, which require contextual information for precise prediction. To address this challenge, researchers usually use time-series decomposition to reveal underlying patterns, e.g., trends and seasonality. However, existing decomposition-based anomaly detectors do not explicitly consider such *contextual information*, limiting their ability to correctly detect contextual cases. This paper proposes *Time-CAD*, a new *context-aware deep* time-series decomposition framework to detect anomalies for a more practical scenario in real-world businesses. We verify the effectiveness of the novel design for integrating contextual information into deep time-series decomposition through extensive experiments on four real-world benchmarks, demonstrating improvements of up to 46% in time-series aware F_1 score on average.

Keywords: Time-Series Decomposition · Time-Series Anomaly Detection · Context-Aware Decomposition · Deep Learning

1 Introduction

Time-series anomaly detection (TSAD) aims to identify data instances that diverge significantly from the normal range. From a traditional perspective [16], an anomaly is an observation that deviates from other observations, leading to suspicion that it was generated by a different mechanism. For instance, the sudden increase in website traffic, which may be thrice the usual traffic, can be attributed to various reasons such as competitor service breakdowns, natural disasters, or elections.

Accurately detecting anomalies is critical for corrective measures and potential damage prevention in real-world businesses. As an example, engineers use rich communication service traffic data to monitor the system status. Existing anomaly detectors commonly assume specific periodic patterns of time-series data; however, communication systems and businesses alike are often affected

G. De Francisci Morales et al. (Eds.): ECML PKDD 2023, LNAI 14174, pp. 330–345, 2023.
https://doi.org/10.1007/978-3-031-43427-3_20

by unexpected events. Thus, we should *adaptively* detect anomalies based on **contextual information**, such as days of the week and holidays, in such systems because what is normal on weekdays could be anomalous on weekends. Considering the context when detecting anomalies in time series is essential for precise prediction, which can be referred to as *contextual* anomaly detection [13].

For contextual anomaly detection, using time-series decomposition has several advantages over raw time series. First, directly extracting meaningful features from high-dimensional time series is challenging due to convoluted patterns. Second, accurate decomposi-

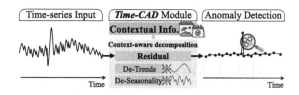

Fig. 1. Conceptual idea of *Time-CAD*.

tion reveals the underlying trends, seasonalities, and noises, which helps better understand time series characteristics. Third, time-series decomposition eliminates the need for an overly complex neural network often required when using raw data; meanwhile, it improves the robustness of downstream tasks [31].

Nevertheless, since the existing methods of time-series decomposition rely solely on statistical processes, the results are often overfitted to a particular time series [33,34]. Furthermore, time series may not be decomposed appropriately as they do not analyze the temporal components individually based on irregular contextual information, such as spontaneous events and holidays, resulting in a high percentage of false alarms. Motivated by these limitations, as depicted in Fig. 1, we propose a novel **Time-CAD** framework designed specifically for anomaly detection to address the complexities and irregularities within the real-world time-series data by addressing the following challenges.

Challenge 1: *How to properly integrate contextual information into time-series decomposition?* Previous decomposition methods are based on statistical values such as the mean, median, or moving average. Consequently, they fail to adapt to abrupt trends or seasonal changes caused by events and holidays. Here, we inject sparse but informative variables—*contextual information*—to improve the robustness of decomposition results and use a simple neural network to increase the accuracy for a particular context.

Challenge 2: *How to extract normal patterns from the time series so that the residuals accurately represent potential anomalies?* Even Prophet [30], the only time-series decomposition method that considers auxiliary information, fails to extract accurate residuals due to the post-processing of auxiliary information after traditional decomposition. That is, the post-processing cannot explicitly infer irregular temporal information. Thus, we directly *inject* the contextual information into the decomposition process to accurately extract meaningful residuals for anomaly detection.

To overcome these two challenges, the main contributions of this paper are summarized as follows.

- We propose *Time-CAD*, the first *context-aware deep* time-series decomposition model designed for anomaly detection, that is robust to aperiodic patterns by explicitly considering contextual information.
- We show that *Time-CAD* produces flawless residuals and faithful normal patterns using only a simple neural network, thus, reducing false alarms.
- We demonstrate that *Time-CAD* improves TSAD performance on several real-world benchmarks through a series of experiments and verify its usability as a detector-agnostic framework by incorporating it with other anomaly detectors to enhance their detection accuracy.

2   Related Work

This section briefly discusses several TSAD methods based on the presence of time-series decomposition. For extensive reviews, see recent surveys [4,9,11].

2.1   Anomaly Detection *without* Decomposition

Without decomposition, we can classify TSAD into statistical and machine learning approaches. The most popular *statistical* approaches are regressive models [7,24], such as AutoRegressive Integrated Moving Average (ARIMA). They serve as a reference for effective statistical methods in time-series analysis. ARIMA [5] calculates the deviation of the predicted values from the observed values to solve the non-stationary problem in detecting anomalies after fitting the model. However, these models are sensitive to abrupt changes in time series.

Alternatively, Density-Based Spatial Clustering of Applications with Noise (DBSCAN) [12] and One-Class Support Vector Machine (OCSVM) [25] are the popular *machine learning* methods. DBSCAN is a clustering-based anomaly detection method that classifies the data points into a core, border, or anomalous point. The anomalies are the data points that do not belong to any cluster. OCSVM is a non-linear one-class classification method that leverages the SVM trained on one particular class, i.e., normal instances. Anomalies will be determined if new samples do not belong to the class that is trained.

Recently, many studies [27,36,39,41] have shown the superiority of *deep learning* for TSAD over traditional machine learning algorithms. Among several techniques [9], reconstruction-based [15,40] models are the most well-established approach and have consistently reported state-of-the-art performance. Donut [35], OmniAnomaly [29], and InterFusion [20] commonly adopted VAE-based models with additional mechanisms, such as Markov Chain Monte Carlo imputation, to improve detection accuracy. Similarly, USAD [2] and RANSynCoders [1] also adopted reconstruction-based models but with more simple architectures to enhance training and inference efficiency. To increase the detection performance with more learning capability on raw multivariate time series, more recent studies [32,36] also proposed complex Transformer-based architectures.

Nevertheless, we argue that the overly complex neural architectures are unnecessary if we use time-series decomposition together in TSAD, as demonstrated by *Time-CAD* using simple reconstruction-based autoencoder models.

2.2   Anomaly Detection *with* Decomposition

Methods in this family mostly conduct time-series decomposition before anomaly detection. Twitter [17] developed a Seasonal Hybrid Extreme Studentized Deviate (S-H-ESD) algorithm. It uses robust statistics of median absolute deviation and generalized extreme Studentized deviate test after the decomposition process to detect anomalies. However, S-H-ESD has low anomaly detection quality in time series with high frequency, abrupt drop, and flat characteristics [33,34]. At Facebook [30], time-series forecasting was performed through the model fitting with trends, seasonalities, holidays, and residuals as the results from time-series decomposition. Likewise, Microsoft [23] proposed an anomaly detection method that decomposes the time series and extracts spectral residuals using the Fourier transform-based algorithm. Lately, Alibaba [38] proposed a time-frequency analysis-based TSAD model by utilizing both time and frequency domains with decomposition and augmentation mechanisms to improve performance and interpretability.

Still, these studies heavily depend on statistical decomposition methods; thus, they can easily overfit a specific time-series dataset. Besides, the decomposition will not accurately work because temporal components that should be addressed differently—*sporadic contextual information*—are not considered, leading to a high rate of false alarms.

3   The *Time-CAD* Framework

This section presents the problem definition and details of *Time*-series anomaly detection with *C*ontext-*A*ware *D*eep decomposition. Hence, *Time-CAD*.

3.1   Problem Definition

Time-Series Decomposition. Let $\mathcal{X} = \{\mathbf{x}_1, \mathbf{x}_2, \ldots, \mathbf{x}_N\} \in \mathbb{R}^{N \times M}$ be a time series of length N and $\mathcal{D}(\mathbf{x}_t)$ be a *decomposition* algorithm, where M is the number of variables[1] (or features). Thus, we denote the values at timestamp t as $\mathbf{x}_t = \{x_t^1, x_t^2, \ldots, x_t^M\}$. Since $\mathbf{x}_t$ can be expressed by a combination of trend-cycle τ_t, seasonality s_t, and residual r_t components, we then have $\mathcal{D}(\mathbf{x}_t) = \tau_t + s_t + r_t$ or $\mathcal{D}(\mathbf{x}_t) = \tau_t \times s_t \times r_t$ for additive or multiplicative decomposition, respectively.

Time-Series Anomaly Detection (TSAD). Let $W_t = \{\mathbf{x}_{t-w+1}, \ldots, \mathbf{x}_{t-1}, \mathbf{x}_t\}$ be a sliding window of length w at time t. Thus, we reformulate $\mathcal{X}$ as a sequence of overlapping windows $\mathcal{W} = \{W_1, W_2, \ldots, W_{N-w+1}\}$ used to train a TSAD model g_ϕ. The goal is to assign an anomaly label $y_t \in \{0, 1\}$ for each test data point $\hat{\mathbf{x}}_t \in \hat{W}_t$, where $\hat{W}_t \notin \mathcal{W}$, based on anomaly scores $\mathcal{A}_t$. If $\mathcal{A}_t$ exceeds a predefined threshold δ, $y_t = 1$; otherwise 0.

---

[1] A univariate time series is a special case of a multivariate time series when $M = 1$.

TSAD with Time-Series Decomposition. Given a set of windows $\mathcal{W}$, we perform the time-series decomposition $\mathcal{D}(W_t)$ to obtain τ_t, s_t, and r_t for each window $W_t \in \mathcal{W}$. Then, we input the residual component r_t extracted from the window W_t to the TSAD model g_ϕ. Consequently, the model g_ϕ computes the anomaly scores $\mathcal{A}_t$ of all residuals r_t.

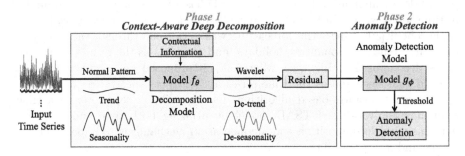

Fig. 2. Overview of the *Time-CAD* framework.

3.2 Overall Framework

Figure 2 illustrates the overall *Time-CAD* framework consisting of two phases: *context-aware deep decomposition* and *anomaly detection*.

3.3 Phase 1: Context-Aware Deep Decomposition

As in Fig. 3, we train a neural network to extract normal patterns of time series, i.e., the trend and seasonality. Then, only the actual remainders or noises are left as the *residual*, which is the main focus of this process.

In this work, we employ the STL [10] algorithm as $\mathcal{D}(W_t)$ to initially decompose time series into $\tau_t + s_t +$

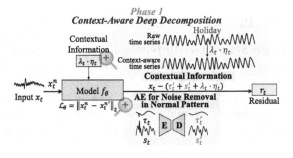

Fig. 3. Illustration of context-aware deep decomposition process (Phase 1).

r_t. Since we will use only *normal patterns* x_t^n to train a decomposition model f_θ, $x_t^n = \tau_t + s_t$. In particular, we use a Gated Recurrent Unit (GRU) [8]-based autoencoder as the decomposition model f_θ. The output of f_θ is the reconstructed normal pattern $x_t^{n'}$. Thus, f_θ minimizes the reconstruction errors between the decomposed time-series normal patterns x_t^n and their reconstructed versions $x_t^{n'}$ with loss $\mathcal{L}_\theta = \| x_t^n - x_t^{n'} \|_2$.

Algorithm 1. Training Algorithm of *Time-CAD*

INPUT: Normal windows dataset $\mathcal{W} = \{W_1, \cdots, W_T\}$, contextual information η, hyperparameter λ_t
OUTPUT: Trained f_θ, g_ϕ
1: $\theta, \phi \leftarrow$ initialize weights;
2: /* train deep decomposition model */
3: **for** $epoch = 1$ **to** $epochs^{\text{decomposition}}$ **do**
4:    **for** $t = 1$ **to** $t = T$ **do**
5:       $\tau_t \leftarrow$ trend component of $\mathcal{D}(W_t)$;
6:       $s_t \leftarrow$ seasonal component of $\mathcal{D}(W_t)$;
7:       /* reconstruct normal pattern */
8:       $W_t^{n'} \leftarrow f_\theta(\tau_t + s_t)$;
9:       $\mathcal{L}_\theta \leftarrow \|W_t^n - W_t^{n'}\|_2$;
10:      $\theta \leftarrow$ update weights using $\mathcal{L}_\theta$;
11:      $r_t \leftarrow \Psi(W_t - f_\theta(\tau_t + s_t) + \lambda_t \cdot \eta_t)$;
12:    **end for**
13: **end for**
14: /* train anomaly detection model */
15: **for** $epoch = 1$ **to** $epochs^{\text{detection}}$ **do**
16:    **for** $t = 1$ **to** $t = T$ **do**
17:       $r_t{}' \leftarrow g_\phi(r_t)$;
18:       $\mathcal{L}_\phi \leftarrow \|r_t - r_t{}'\|_2$;
19:      $\phi \leftarrow$ update weights using $\mathcal{L}_\phi$;
20:    **end for**
21: **end for**
22: **return** f_θ, g_ϕ

After training the decomposition model f_θ, we remove the normal pattern $x_t^{n'}$ from the original time series x_t. Here, we use temporal contextual information to regulate the residuals so that the algorithm recognizes the contextual information. Note that other contextual information (e.g., sensor location) can also be used in this framework depending on the specific application domains. The temporal contextual information includes whether the timestamp is a *week-end, holiday, day before holiday,* and specific *event*. Formally, the contextual information vector $\eta_t = [Z(t); \mathbf{1}(t \in \mathcal{H})]$, where $Z(t)$ is the seasonal information including the hour, month, and year, $\mathcal{H}$ is the list of holidays. For each time t, we can additionally control λ_t depending on the requirements of each application domain. $\lambda_t \cdot \eta_t = \lambda_t \cdot [Z(t); \mathbf{1}(t \in \mathcal{H})] \; \forall t \in \{1, \dots, N\}$, where λ_t is the hyperparameter denoting the degree of contextual information. Finally, we apply Wavelet transform to remove trifling signal noises. As a result, the **final remaining residual** is formulated by

$$r_t = \Psi(x_t - f_\theta(\tau_t + s_t) + \lambda_t \cdot \eta_t). \tag{1}$$

Notably, thanks to non-linear mapping, we find that our context-aware deep time-series decomposition is more robust and reliable than existing decomposition without deep learning. That is, $\Psi(x_t - \underline{f_\theta(\tau_t + s_t)} + \lambda_t \cdot \eta_t)$ is better

Algorithm 2. Inference Steps of *Time-CAD*

INPUT: Test windows dataset $\widehat{\mathcal{W}} = \{\widehat{W}_1, \ldots, \widehat{W}_{\widehat{T}}\}$, contextual information $\hat{\eta}$, hyperparameter λ_t, threshold δ

OUTPUT: Labels $y : \{y_1, \ldots, y_{\widehat{T}}\}$

  1: /* deep decomposition model */
  2: **for** $t = 1$ **to** $\widehat{T}$ **do**
  3:     $\hat{\tau}_t \leftarrow$ trend component of $\mathcal{D}(\widehat{W}_t)$;
  4:     $\hat{s}_t \leftarrow$ seasonal component of $\mathcal{D}(\widehat{W}_t)$;
  5:     $\hat{r}_t \leftarrow \Psi(W_t - f_\theta^*(\hat{\tau}_t + \hat{s}_t) + \lambda_t \cdot \hat{\eta}_t)$;
  6: **end for**
  7: /* anomaly detection model */
  8: **for** $t = 1$ **to** $\widehat{T}$ **do**
  9:     $\hat{r}_t' \leftarrow g_{\phi^*}(\hat{r}_t)$;
10:     $\mathcal{A}_t \leftarrow \|\hat{r}_t - \hat{r}_t'\|_2$;
11:     **if** $\mathcal{A}_t > \delta$ **then**
12:         $y_t \leftarrow 1$ /* identify as an anomalous value */
13:     **else**
14:         $y_t \leftarrow 0$ /* identify as a normal value */
15:     **end if**
16: **end for**
17: **return** $y : \{y_1, \cdots, y_{\widehat{T}}\}$

---

than $\Psi(x_t - (\tau_t + s_t) + \lambda_t \cdot \eta_t)$ because the trend τ_t and seasonality s_t initially extracted by the STL decomposition has the following limitation. While the STL decomposition cannot ideally extract the trend and seasonality when the raw time series has noises and potential contamination of anomalies in the training data, our model f_θ eliminates the noise and potential contamination by the denoising autoencoder, resulting in a more robust normal pattern. As in Fig. 6, we empirically verify the effectiveness of the proposed *deep* decomposition model.

Lines 3–13 of Algorithm 1 and Lines 2–6 of Algorithm 2 summarize the process of this phase.

3.4 Phase 2: Time-Series Anomaly Detection

In this phase, we use the derived residuals, Eq. (1) in Phase 1 (§3.3), as the input features for an anomaly detection model. Here, we train the TSAD model g_ϕ to reconstruct the residuals of *normal* cases. If the residuals of anomalous instances are input to the detection model, the model will give high reconstruction errors. We later use these reconstruction errors as anomaly scores $\mathcal{A}_t$. Figure 4 visualizes the process of this phase.

In this work, we use a bidirectional GRU autoencoder network [26] as the anomaly detection model g_ϕ. The input is fed with the overlapping sliding window $W_t \in \mathcal{W}$, where $W_t = \{r_{t-w+1}, \ldots, r_{t-1}, r_t\}$. Accordingly, we train the anomaly detection model g_ϕ by minimizing the reconstruction loss $\mathcal{L}_\phi =$

$\|r_t - r_t{}'\|_2$ between the original r_t and reconstructed residuals $r_t{}'$. During the inference, the anomaly score $\mathcal{A}_t$ is computed by the reconstruction errors. Hence, $\mathcal{A}_t = \|\hat{r}_t - \hat{r}_t{}'\|_2$, where $\hat{r}_t$ is an unseen residual of a new time series and $\hat{r}_t{}'$ is a reconstructed residual. If the anomaly score $\mathcal{A}_t$ at time t is greater than a predefined threshold δ, it is determined as an anomaly (i.e., 1); otherwise normal (i.e., 0). Although we use simple bidirectional GRU autoencoders in *Time-CAD*, any other architectures or models can also be used.

Ideally, when a time-series value x_t is significantly diverse from the learned normal patterns, the detection model should correctly identify it as an anomaly. To achieve this, unlike previous studies, we thus use the residual r_t as the input to the anomaly detection model instead of the raw time

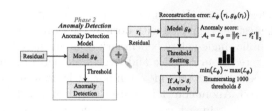

Fig. 4. Illustration of time-series anomaly detection process (Phase 2).

series. The underlying reason is that the residual—a remainder of the de-trend and de-seasonality process—is associated with abnormality or noise. Therefore, the model can detect the anomalies with much simpler input, yet achieve higher accuracy. Lines 15–21 of Algorithm 1 and Lines 8–16 of Algorithm 2 outline the process of this phase.

4 Evaluation

In this section, we design the experiments to answer the following questions:

Q1 How well *Time-CAD* performs TSAD compared with baseline methods?
Q2 How effective is the *context-aware deep* decomposition?
Q3 Is *Time-CAD* feasible to be deployed in production?

The source code is available at https://github.com/kaist-dmlab/Time-CAD.

4.1 Experimental Setup

Data Description. As summarized in Table 1, we use four real-world benchmarks containing *seven* dataset entities to comprehensively evaluate the anomaly detection performance on diverse businesses and industries. **KPI**[2] is a single-entity key performance indicator dataset used in a competition. It measures the quality of Internet services. **Energy**[3] benchmark measures the health status of power equipment. This benchmark has two datasets of the different lengths and

---

[2] https://github.com/NetManAIOps/KPI-Anomaly-Detection.
[3] https://aihub.or.kr/aihubdata/data/list.do.

Table 1. Benchmark statistics.

Datasets	Collection Date (DD.MM.YYYY)	# Timestamp	# Train	# Test	Entity×Dim.	# Anomaly
RCS	01.02.2021 – 01.04.2022	34,902	21,600	13,302	3 × 8	160 (0.46%)
KPI	31.07.2017 – 30.10.2017	111,370	66,822	44,548	1 × 1	1,102 (0.99%)
Energy	13.11.2020 – 16.12.2020	47,003	41,654	5,349	2 × 32	2,772 (5.90%)
IoT-Modbus	01.04.2019 – 25.04.2019	51,106	15,332	35,774	1 × 4	16,106 (31.51%)

is collected from 450 facilities on a minute-interval basis for 30 d. Each instance in the test set is labeled with normal, caution, or warning status. **IoT-Modbus**[4] is a public single-entity benchmark from an Internet of Things system. The data is collected from realistic and large-scale networks having four features indicating Modbus function code: an input register, a discrete value, a holding register, and a coil. Anomalous labels are DoS, DDoS, and backdoor attacks [22]. **RCS** is a private benchmark complied by a cloud operation group at a mobile business company measuring rich communication service traffic records, e.g., the number of sent and received text messages. This benchmark consists of three datasets of the same lengths and is collected every ten minutes.

Evaluation Metric and Threshold Setting. We adopt time-series aware precision-recall metrics [18], TaPR, specifically designed for TSAD tasks to reflect the feature of a *series of instances*. Since the conventional point-wise metrics overlook the characteristics of a series of instances, they suffer from a scarcity of evaluating the variety of the detected anomalies. At the same time, the widely-used point-adjust metric suffers from overestimation issues [1, 15]. Therefore, we assess the performance with TaPR and the corresponding F_1 scores: TaF_1.

To identify anomalies during testing, we enumerate $1,000$ thresholds δ distributed uniformly from the minimum to the maximum of the anomaly scores $\mathcal{A}_t$ for all timestamps t in the test data to avoid highly relying on the threshold policy [28,37]. Moreover, in practice, it is more important to have an excellent F_1 metric at a certain threshold than a generally good result [14]. Thus, we report the *best* TaF_1 based on the optimal threshold of each model.

Comparison Baselines. We compare *Time-CAD* to both traditional and recent state-of-the-art methods with and without time-series decomposition as follows.

Traditional Methods.

1. Local Outlier Factor (**LOF**) [6] is an unsupervised outlier detector that measures the local deviation of the density of a given sample to its neighbors.
2. Isolation Forest (**ISF**) [21] is a well-known anomaly detection algorithm that works on the principle of isolating anomalies using tree-based structures.

---

[4] https://research.unsw.edu.au/projects/toniot-datasets.

Table 2. Performance comparison between anomaly detection models in the best TaF_1 with the highest scores highlighted in **bold**.

Datasets	RCS-1	RCS-2	RCS-3	KPI	Energy-1	Energy-2	IoT-Modbus	Avg. ↑	Rank ↓
Non-Decomposition									
LOF	0.474 (±0.00)	0.422 (±0.00)	0.434 (±0.00)	0.177 (±0.00)	0.701 (±0.00)	0.973 (±0.00)	0.701 (±0.00)	0.555	12
ISF	0.614 (±0.00)	0.745 (±0.00)	0.458 (±0.00)	0.823 (±0.00)	0.809 (±0.00)	0.975 (±0.00)	0.642 (±0.00)	0.724	9
OCSVM	0.619 (±0.00)	0.292 (±0.00)	0.562 (±0.00)	0.531 (±0.00)	0.954 (±0.00)	0.946 (±0.00)	0.690 (±0.00)	0.656	10
AE	0.472 (±0.08)	0.583 (±0.10)	0.435 (±0.02)	0.861 (±0.00)	0.954 (±0.00)	0.976 (±0.00)	0.894 (±0.00)	0.739	8
MS-RNN	0.514 (±0.02)	0.740 (±0.01)	0.484 (±0.01)	0.915 (±0.01)	0.954 (±0.00)	0.979 (±0.01)	0.826 (±0.05)	0.773	6
OmniAnomaly	0.503 (±0.00)	0.710 (±0.01)	0.922 (±0.00)	0.892 (±0.01)	0.950 (±0.00)	0.980 (±0.00)	0.762 (±0.01)	0.774	4
RANSynCoders	0.435 (±0.01)	0.613 (±0.01)	0.425 (±0.01)	0.227 (±0.03)	0.914 (±0.01)	0.986 (±0.01)	**0.987** (±0.01)	0.655	11
TranAD	0.461 (±0.02)	0.941 (±0.00)	0.544 (±0.11)	0.934 (±0.04)	0.953 (±0.00)	0.915 (±0.06)	0.664 (±0.01)	0.773	5
Decomposition									
AE-STL	0.867 (±0.02)	0.885 (±0.02)	0.911 (±0.03)	0.922 (±0.02)	0.936 (±0.02)	**0.987** (±0.01)	0.894 (±0.00)	0.915	2
SR-CNN	0.547 (±0.00)	0.733 (±0.00)	0.594 (±0.00)	0.488 (±0.00)	0.952 (±0.00)	0.959 (±0.00)	0.977 (±0.00)	0.750	7
TFAD	0.539 (±0.02)	0.632 (±0.00)	0.762 (±0.11)	0.854 (±0.04)	0.956 (±0.00)	0.955 (±0.00)	0.886 (±0.01)	0.798	3
Time-CAD	**0.944**(±0.00)	**0.955**(±0.00)	**0.944**(±0.00)	**0.937**(±0.00)	**0.961**(±0.01)	0.986 (±0.00)	0.957 (±0.00)	**0.955**	1

3. **OCSVM** [25] is an unsupervised outlier detection algorithm based on SVM. It maximizes the margin between the origin and the normality and defines the decision boundary as the hyper-plane that determines the margin.

4. Autoencoder (**AE**) [3] is a simple neural architecture that uses the symmetrical encoder and decoder network for anomaly detection. Anomaly scores are the differences between the inputs and reconstructed outputs.

5. Autoencoder with STL decomposition (**AE-STL**) [10] is a combination of the AE and the traditional time-series decomposition method, STL. The residuals from STL are input to AE instead of the raw time series.

State-of-the-art Models.

6. Modified-RNN (**MS-RNN**) [19] is a modified version of an anomaly detector that exploits sparsely-connected recurrent neural networks (RNNs) and an ensemble of sequence-to-sequence AE for multi-resolution learning.

7. **SR-CNN** [23] is a time-series decomposition-based anomaly detector. It uses spectral residual to extract saliency maps and use them as input for convolutional neural networks to detect anomalies.

8. **OmniAnomaly** [29] is a GRU-based VAE that captures complex temporal dependency between multivariate time series and maps observations to stochastic variables.

9. **RANSynCoders** [1] utilizes pre-trained AE to extract primary frequencies across the signals on the latent representation for synchronizing time series.

10. **TranAD** [32] is a Transformer-based model that uses attention-based sequence encoders to perform inference with broader temporal trends in time series. It uses focus score-based self-conditioning to enable robust multimodal feature extraction and adversarial training to gain stability.

11. **TFAD** [38] is a time-frequency analysis-based anomaly detection model that utilizes both time and frequency domains to improve performance in anomaly detection. The model incorporates time series decomposition and data augmentation mechanisms to enhance performance and interpretability.

Table 3. Performance comparison between the different decomposition methods in the best TaF_1 with the highest scores highlighted in **bold**.

Datasets	Time-CAD			MS-RNN		OmniAnomaly	
	w/CAD	w/o CAD	w/o DNN	w/CAD	w/o CAD	w/CAD	w/o CAD
RCS-1	**0.944**(±0.00)	0.633 (±0.00)	0.871 (±0.00)	**0.789**(±0.00)	0.514 (±0.09)	**0.939**(±0.00)	0.503 (±0.00)
RCS-2	**0.955**(±0.00)	0.710 (±0.01)	0.886 (±0.00)	**0.829**(±0.00)	0.740 (±0.01)	**0.949**(±0.01)	0.710 (±0.01)
RCS-3	**0.944**(±0.00)	0.622 (±0.00)	0.858 (±0.01)	**0.785**(±0.01)	0.484 (±0.01)	**0.938**(±0.01)	0.662 (±0.00)
KPI	**0.937**(±0.00)	0.905 (±0.00)	0.936 (±0.01)	**0.916**(±0.01)	0.915 (±0.01)	**0.915**(±0.01)	0.892 (±0.01)
Energy-1	**0.961**(±0.01)	0.953 (±0.00)	0.953 (±0.01)	0.927 (±0.00)	**0.954**(±0.00)	**0.953**(±0.00)	0.950 (±0.00)
Energy-2	0.986 (±0.00)	**0.989**(±0.00)	0.986 (±0.00)	**0.980**(±0.00)	0.979 (±0.01)	**0.986**(±0.00)	0.980 (±0.00)
IoT-Modbus	**0.957**(±0.00)	0.762 (±0.00)	0.894 (±0.01)	**0.841**(±0.00)	0.826 (±0.05)	**0.942**(±0.00)	0.762 (±0.01)

4.2 Performance Comparison

Anomaly Detection Performance (Q1). Table 2 presents the overall performance in the best TaF_1 metric. We run each model three times to ensure reproducibility and avoid occasional results, then report the average and standard deviation. *Time-CAD* demonstrates state-of-the-art performance in most datasets except for Energy and IoT-Modbus. On average, *Time-CAD* outperforms all baselines by a significant margin (up to 46%), especially on the RCS datasets expected to be strongly affected by the temporal contextual conditions. On the other hand, as Energy and IoT-Modbus datasets are machinery data that do not directly associate with people, they show a regular pattern regardless of the temporal contexts. Thus, we conjecture that other types of contextual information, such as spatial or environmental information, will further enhance the detection performance on Energy and IoT-Modbus datasets.

Ablation and Case Study (Q2). To examine the contributions of the *context-aware deep* decomposition (CAD), we perform ablation studies on both the proposed *Time-CAD* and the baselines. As presented in Table 3, w/CAD denotes the presence of context-aware deep decomposition, while w/o CAD is the absence. Likewise, w/o DNN indicates the context-aware decomposition but *without* the deep neural network (DNN) model f_θ designed to evaluate the effect of DNN in the decomposition process. According to the results, it is evident that w/CAD performs significantly better than w/o CAD and w/o DNN counterparts in most datasets. Therefore, we ascertain that *Time-CAD* can significantly boost the TSAD performance of any anomaly detectors, demonstrating its high usability as a model-agnostic framework.

Additionally, Fig. 5 depicts anomaly detection results where red lines indicate the ground truths and the blue lines are prediction results on RCS-1 (Fig. 5a) and RCS-3 (Fig. 5b) datasets. For each dataset, the upper plot shows anomaly detection without *Time-CAD*, and the lower plot shows anomaly detection with *Time-CAD*. In **RCS-1**, the upper plot illustrates many false positives while the lower one adequately detects anomalies. In contrast, for **RCS-3**, the upper plot has many false negatives, while the lower sufficiently detects anomalies, albeit with a few errors.

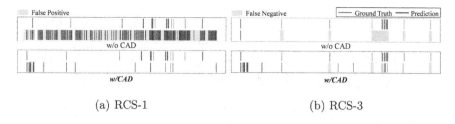

(a) RCS-1   (b) RCS-3

Fig. 5. Visualization of labels (red) and predicted anomalies (blue).

Lastly, we visually compare the extracted *residual components* between the different decomposition methods. As in Fig. 6, we consider a festival from September 20*th* to 22*nd* as a case study. The first plot exhibits different patterns of the **RCS** time series, yet within normal ranges. Unfortunately, without the contextual information and deep neural network, the second plot shows that the original STL decomposition cannot decompose the valid residual components, causing an increase in false positives when detecting anomalies. In the third plot, the residual components during the festival time are relieved thanks to the *contextual information*. Still, it has noises that may adversely affect detection performance. Finally, the fourth plot demonstrates the advantage of *Time-CAD* in precisely extracting normal patterns during the distinct period, resulting in meaningful residuals for anomaly detection. Compared to the without DNN counterpart, the results confirm that the *deep* decomposition yields more ideal residuals by robustly detaching normal patterns, thus, mitigating false positives.

4.3 Deployment Feasibility

As an answer to **Q3**, we study the feasibility of *Time-CAD* in detection quality and computation time aspects on the real-world **RCS** datasets that contain several business metrics.

Detection Quality. After the offline training on about 5-month multivariate time-series datasets, *Time-CAD* detects nearly all anomalies in 3-month testing data with a strong performance of 0.948 in TaF_1 on average across three datasets.

Computation Time. We run the inference phase on a server equipped with an NVIDIA GeForce GTX 3090Ti. *Time-CAD* takes only about 69 s for each 3-month-long dataset that contains about 13K instances, meaning that it takes only *5 milliseconds* for a single timestamp. Hence, *Time-CAD* is feasible to detect anomalies in a real-time environment.

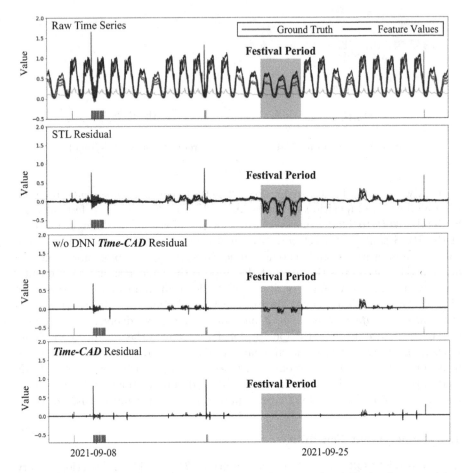

Fig. 6. Comparison of the residual components between the different decomposition methods on **RCS** dataset.

System Prototype. As a production prototype, we make a pilot deployment with the trained *Time-CAD* detection model to detect anomalies in an online batch-based web application[5] by connecting it with a real-time database. Once the time-series instances are satisfied with a predefined window size, the system will run the detection model and return the anomaly scores for all timestamps along with the original time series to facilitate users for a quick inspection and interpretation in which locations potential anomalies have occurred.

5   Conclusion

This paper introduces a novel *context-aware deep* time-series decomposition framework for anomaly detection called *Time-CAD*. With the collaboration of

---

[5] https://time-cad.web.app.

deep learning and contextual information, we show that *Time-CAD* accurately extracts a clear periodic pattern by enhancing the properties of each component in a time series, leading to an improvement in anomaly detection performance by up to 46%. Empirically, the proposed framework demonstrates its superiority over state-of-the-art methods on four benchmarks in the time-series aware F_1 metric. We further verify that context-aware deep decomposition explicitly adapts to aperiodic patterns by using contextual information through a series of ablation studies. Finally, we expect the proposed *Time-CAD* framework to advance the development of anomaly detectors with different types of contextual information, which is crucial for various application domains and businesses.

Acknowledgments. This work was partly supported by Mobile eXperience Business, Samsung Electronics Co., Ltd. (Real-time Service Incident Prediction Development) and the National Research Foundation of Korea (NRF) grant funded by the Korea government (Ministry of Science and ICT) (No. 2023R1A2C 2003690).

Ethical Statement. This work adheres to ethical standards and guidelines for scientific research. We use publicly available datasets and obtain all necessary permissions and approvals before conducting the experiments and data collection. Therefore, we ensure the privacy and anonymity of all human participants involved in the data collection process. In particular, the RCS and KPI datasets are the communication service datasets significantly associated with real users. Both RCS and KPI datasets were completely anonymized with their types and features before we received them. Our research aims to advance the field of anomaly detection having critical applications in various domains, such as finance, healthcare, and cyber security. However, there might be potential malicious impacts when inappropriately using our work. For example, the advancement and findings from *Time-CAD* might be adversely exploited for devising more subtle and sophisticated attacks or deceptions.

References

1. Abdulaal, A., Liu, Z., Lancewicki, T.: Practical approach to asynchronous multivariate time series anomaly detection and localization. In: ACM SIGKDD (2021)
2. Audibert, J., Michiardi, P., Guyard, F., Marti, S., Zuluaga, M.A.: USAD: unsupervised anomaly detection on multivariate time series. In: ACM SIGKDD (2020)
3. Bergmann, P., Löwe, S., Fauser, M., Sattlegger, D., Steger, C.: Improving unsupervised defect segmentation by applying structural similarity to autoencoders. arXiv:1807.02011 (2018)
4. Blázquez-García, A., Conde, A., Mori, U., Lozano, J.A.: A review on outlier/anomaly detection in time series data. ACM CSUR **54**(3) (2021)
5. Braei, M., Wagner, S.: Anomaly detection in univariate time-series: a survey on the state-of-the-art. arXiv:2004.00433 (2020)
6. Breunig, M.M., Kriegel, H.P., Ng, R.T., Sander, J.: LOF: identifying density-based local outliers. In: ACM SIGMOD (2000)
7. Chandola, V.: Anomaly Detection for Symbolic Sequences and Time Series Data. University of Minnesota (2009)

8. Cho, K., et al.: Learning phrase representations using rnn encoder-decoder for statistical machine translation. arXiv:1406.1078 (2014)

9. Choi, K., Yi, J., Park, C., Yoon, S.: Deep learning for anomaly detection in time-series data: Review, analysis, and guidelines. IEEE Access (2021)

10. Cleveland, R.B., Cleveland, W.S., McRae, J.E., Terpenning, I.: STL: A seasonal-trend decomposition. J. Off. Stat **6**(1) (1990)

11. Darban, Z.Z., Webb, G.I., Pan, S., Aggarwal, C.C., Salehi, M.: Deep learning for time series anomaly detection: a survey. arXiv:2211.05244 (2022)

12. Ester, M., Kriegel, H.P., Sander, J., Xu, X., et al.: A density-based algorithm for discovering clusters in large spatial databases with noise. In: ACM SIGKDD (1996)

13. Farshchi, M., et al.: Contextual anomaly detection for a critical industrial system based on logs and metrics. In: EDCC (2018)

14. Feng, C., Tian, P.: Time series anomaly detection for cyber-physical systems via neural system identification and bayesian filtering. In: ACM SIGKDD (2021)

15. Garg, A., Zhang, W., Samaran, J., Savitha, R., Foo, C.S.: An evaluation of anomaly detection and diagnosis in multivariate time series. IEEE Trans. Neural Netw. Learn. Syst. (2021)

16. Hawkins, D.M.: Identification of Outliers, vol. 11. Springer (1980). https://doi.org/10.1007/978-94-015-3994-4

17. Hochenbaum, J., Vallis, O.S., Kejariwal, A.: Automatic anomaly detection in the cloud via statistical learning. arXiv:1704.07706 (2017)

18. Hwang, W.S., Yun, J.H., Kim, J., Kim, H.C.: Time-series aware precision and recall for anomaly detection: Considering variety of detection result and addressing ambiguous labeling. In: CIKM (2019)

19. Kieu, T., Yang, B., Guo, C., Jensen, C.S.: Outlier detection for time series with recurrent autoencoder ensembles. In: IJCAI (2019)

20. Li, Z., et al.: Multivariate time series anomaly detection and interpretation using hierarchical inter-metric and temporal embedding. In: ACM SIGKDD (2021)

21. Liu, F.T., Ting, K.M., Zhou, Z.H.: Isolation forest. In: IEEE ICDM (2008)

22. Moustafa, N.: A new distributed architecture for evaluating ai-based security systems at the edge: network ton_iot datasets. SCS **72** (2021)

23. Ren, H., et al.: Time-series anomaly detection service at microsoft. In: ACM SIGKDD (2019)

24. Rousseeuw, P.J., Leroy, A.M.: Robust Regression and Outlier Detection, vol. 589. John wiley & sons (2005)

25. Schölkopf, B., et al.: Support vector method for novelty detection. In: NeurIPS (1999)

26. Schuster, M., Paliwal, K.K.: Bidirectional recurrent neural networks. IEEE Trans. Signal Process. **45**(11) (1997)

27. Shen, L., Li, Z., Kwok, J.: Timeseries anomaly detection using temporal hierarchical one-class network. In: NeurIPS (2020)

28. Shen, L., Yu, Z., Ma, Q., Kwok, J.T.: Time series anomaly detection with multiresolution ensemble decoding. In: AAAI (2021)

29. Su, Y., Zhao, Y., Niu, C., Liu, R., Sun, W., Pei, D.: Robust anomaly detection for multivariate time series through stochastic recurrent neural network. In: ACM SIGKDD (2019)

30. Taylor, S.J., Letham, B.: Forecasting at scale. Am. Stat. **72**(1) (2018)

31. Theodosiou, M.: Forecasting monthly and quarterly time series using stl decomposition. Int. J. Forecast. **27**(4) (2011)

32. Tuli, S., Casale, G., Jennings, N.R.: TranAD: deep transformer networks for anomaly detection in multivariate time series data. VLDB Endow. **15**(6), 1201–1214 (2022)

33. Wen, Q., Gao, J., Song, X., Sun, L., Xu, H., Zhu, S.: RobustSTL: a robust seasonal-trend decomposition algorithm for long time series. In: AAAI (2019)

34. Wen, Q., Zhang, Z., Li, Y., Sun, L.: Fast RobustSTL: efficient and robust seasonal-trend decomposition for time series with complex patterns. In: ACM SIGKDD (2020)

35. Xu, H., et al.: Unsupervised anomaly detection via variational auto-encoder for seasonal KPIs in web applications. In: WWW (2018)

36. Xu, J., Wu, H., Wang, J., Long, M.: Anomaly transformer: time series anomaly detection with association discrepancy. In: ICLR (2022)

37. Yoo, Y.H., Kim, U.H., Kim, J.H.: Recurrent reconstructive network for sequential anomaly detection. In: IEEE CYB (2019)

38. Zhang, C., Zhou, T., Wen, Q., Sun, L.: TFAD: a decomposition time series anomaly detection architecture with time-frequency analysis. In: CIKM, pp. 2497–2507 (2022)

39. Zhang, C., et al.: A deep neural network for unsupervised anomaly detection and diagnosis in multivariate time series data. In: AAAI (2019)

40. Zhao, H., et al.: Multivariate time-series anomaly detection via graph attention network. In: IEEE ICDM (2020)

41. Zhou, B., Liu, S., Hooi, B., Cheng, X., Ye, J.: BeatGAN: anomalous rhythm detection using adversarially generated time series. In: IJCAI, pp. 4433–4439 (2019)

F-3DNet: Leveraging Inner Order
of Point Clouds for 3D Object Detection

Ying Chen[1] , Rui Liu[2] , Zhihui Li[3]([⊠]) , and Andy Song[1]

[1] RMIT University, Melbourne, Australia
[2] University of Technology Sydney, Sydney, Australia
[3] Qilu University of Technology (Shandong Academy of Sciences), Jinan, China
zhihuilics@gmail.com

Abstract. Point clouds are often perceived as irregular and disorderly data in Internet of Things (IoT) applications. However, these point clouds possess implicit order and context information due to the laser arrangement and sequential scanning process, which are often overlooked. In this paper, we propose a novel method called Frustum 3DNet (F-3DNet) for 3D object detection from point clouds in IoT. Our approach utilizes the inner order of point clouds to construct a rearranged feature matrix and generate a pseudo panorama from LiDAR data. Based on the pseudo image, we extend 2D region proposals to 3D space and obtain frustum regions of interest. For each frustum, we generate a sequence of small frustums by slicing over distance, and introduce a novel local context feature extraction module to incorporate context information. The extracted context features are then concatenated with frustum features and fed to a fully convolutional network (FCN), followed by a classifier and a regressor. We further refine and fuse the output with RGB input to improve the outcome. Ablation studies verify the effectiveness of our proposed components. Experimental results on KITTI and nuScenes datasets demonstrate that F-3DNet outperforms existing methods in IoT.

Keywords: Point Clouds · 3D Object Detection

1 Introduction

With the increasing resolution and decreasing cost of LiDAR in IoT, there is a growing interest in utilizing this technology for applications that require precise environmental perception, such as autonomous driving, simultaneous localization and mapping, and others. These applications typically capture data using laser sensors on a mobile platform, enabling them to detect the environment from a fixed perspective [4]. However, due to the limitations of LiDAR installation location, only a partial surface facing the laser sensors can be measured, which poses challenges to point cloud utilization, especially in 3D object detection. This task is a hot-spot among point cloud applications as it requires the estimation of

G. De Francisci Morales et al. (Eds.): ECML PKDD 2023, LNAI 14174, pp. 346–359, 2023.
https://doi.org/10.1007/978-3-031-43427-3_21

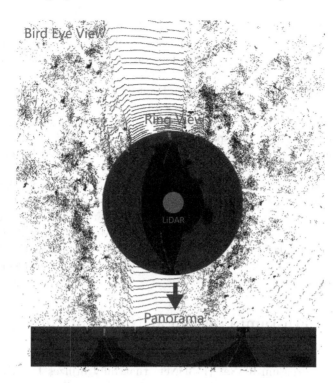

Fig. 1. Pseudo panorama generated from raw data. Ring view indicates a cylinder surface surrounding LiDAR, then a pseudo panorama is obtained by spreading it.

oriented 3D bounding boxes that enclose full targets. In this paper, we propose a workflow that focuses on 3D object detection using point cloud data, while also exploring the benefits of fusing RGB images to improve model performance.

Extensive research has been conducted on 3D object detection [15]. However, most of these studies assume that point clouds are discrete, disordered, and sparse. This poses a challenge for popular detection models used for RGB images, which cannot be directly applied to 3D object detection. To overcome this issue, researchers have attempted to transform 3D expressions to 2D by generating a grid map [17] or projecting point clouds to the image plane [2,6] through cross-sensor calibration. Although 2D convolutional operations can be applied using this approach, valuable 3D information is lost due to dimension reduction. Consequently, in the past three years, networks have been developed to extract features directly from 3D space. Some methods convert sparse point clouds to new 3D representations, such as VoxelNet [18] and SECOND [16]. PointNet and PointNet++ are typical methods used to process LiDAR raw data directly. However, all the aforementioned methods assume that the point cloud is disordered throughout the data processing.

LiDAR point clouds can be sparse and discrete due to equipment limitations. However, they are naturally ordered based on their work mode. For instance, in the case of Velodyne-64E, LiDAR has a fixed laser head arrangement and constant spinning speed, resulting in lasers sampling points in a natural order. As depicted in Fig. 1, projecting point cloud on a cylindrical surface surrounding LiDAR generates a panorama-like image. This work mode ensures that all points have neighbors and context information. Inspired by this idea, we propose a new network for 3D object detection. Our novelties are summarized as follows: (1) We introduce a novel LiDAR data expression form that rearranges point cloud based on its implicit order. Pseudo-panorama is generated based on this new form and used for 2D region proposal generation without the need for cross-sensor calibration. (2) We propose a novel local context feature extractor that takes advantage of our new LiDAR data expression form. It explores 8-neighborhood features for each point and enriches local contextual information to the main workflow. (3) We propose a novel method called Frustum 3DNet (F-3DNet) for 3D object detection. As far as we know, F-3DNet is the first deep learning architecture that takes point cloud inner order into account in the 3D object detection area. RGB input can also be fused into our detection framework for further performance improvement.

2   LiDAR Frustum: Frustum 3DNet (F-3DNet)

To address detection tasks in driving scenes using raw data, we propose a new method called Frustum 3DNet (F-3DNet) that fully utilizes LiDAR information. As LiDAR rotates at a certain speed, it measures distance and intensity simultaneously. Sampling with time series creates inner context in LiDAR data, enabling the construction of a more comprehensive representation of the scene.

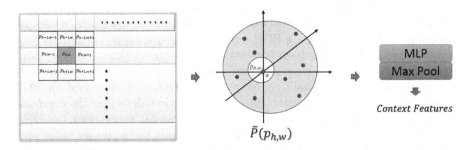

Fig. 2. Context feature extraction module. For each $p_{h,w}$ in point cloud, 8 neighborhood point set is transferred to central point coordinates, then input to multilayer perceptron and max pooling for context feature extraction.

2.1 LiDAR Context Information

In the first step, we rearrange LiDAR data to create a feature matrix with spatial relationships and low complexity. We use the Velodyne HDL-64 S2 LiDAR sensor as an example, which is widely used in autonomous driving and is included in the KITTI dataset [5]. It contains 64 laser heads, which are divided into two blocks with 32 lasers each. All laser heads are mounted on a spinning base, providing a 360° horizontal field of view and a 26.8° vertical field of view. The original raw output data of the LiDAR is arranged in a spherical coordinate system, consisting mainly of the rotation angle θ, the measurement distance d, and the radiation intensity I. The calibration file provided by the manufacturer also includes the pitch angle ϕ of each laser head. Converting (d, θ, ϕ) in the spherical coordinate system to (x, y, z) in the Cartesian coordinate system results in approximately 1.33 million sampling points detected per second. Therefore, it is essential to rearrange the 3D LiDAR data before processing.

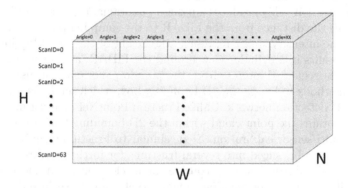

Fig. 3. Point cloud feature matrix. *ScanID* indicates laser head ID of LiDAR, while *Angle* is discretized by preset angle resolution. In this way, clear neighbor relationship is constructed and a continuous representation of point cloud is obtained. Here, H and W indicate ScanID and Angle numbers, while N represents feature dimension.

To store LiDAR data, we construct a matrix where each vector contains all the information of a sampling point, including its coordinates (x, y, z) and intensity I. We use the scan line $(ScanID)$ to which it belongs and the corresponding spinning angle (θ) as references for the matrix width and height, as shown in Fig. 3. We convert a point in spherical coordinates to Cartesian coordinates using Eq. 1 as follows:

$$\begin{cases} x = d \cos \phi \cos \theta \\ y = d \cos \phi \sin \theta \\ z = d \sin \phi \end{cases} \tag{1}$$

Here, $ScanID$ indicates the laser head to which the sampling point belongs. It ranges from 0 to 63 based on the pitch angle ϕ of the corresponding laser head. When the LiDAR is mounted on a flat plane, scan line 0 corresponds to the nearest point to the LiDAR, while scan line 63 corresponds to the farthest point. θ is the rotating angle of the point. We define one lap of LiDAR data as a frame, and the LiDAR's rotation speed is set at 10 Hz. Therefore, a frame of LiDAR data consists of 64 scan lines with approximately 2000 sampling points per line, since the angular resolution of the Velodyne HDL-64 S2 is 0.18° at 10 Hz.

We use $ScanID$ and θ to arrange our feature matrix. We divide θ into bins based on a preset angular resolution, and then construct our LiDAR data matrix as shown in Fig. 3. In the $H \times W \times N$ matrix, H indicates the laser head ID, W represents the discretized rotating angle, and N indicates the feature vector dimension of each point. We use the average value to describe the location of several points in one cell and the maximum value as the intensity feature of this cell. This way, the matrix width is adjusted according to the horizontal resolution.

To visualize the data, we use d_{xy}, I, and z as three channels in a color image after normalization. This produces a pseudo-panorama, as shown in Fig. 1. Here, d_{xy} indicates the distance from the LiDAR to the sampling point on the ground plane, I is the intensity, and z represents the height of the point. Rolling up this panorama results in a cylinder view around the LiDAR, as shown in Fig. 1. We then crop the region of interest from the pseudo-panorama and use 2D target detection methods to locate the 2D bounding box, which serves as input to our following 3D detection network. Unlike Frustum PointNet or Frustum ConvNet, our model obtains the point cloud within the 2D bounding box directly without requiring multi-sensor calibration. Next, similar to Frustum ConvNet, the candidate point cloud is sliced into several frustums for further feature extraction.

However, sliced frustums only consider point cloud location information. To further utilize context information among point clouds, we introduce a local context feature extraction module, as shown in Fig. 2. For a point $p_{h,w}$ in our $H \times W \times N$ feature matrix, we collect its 8-neighborhood points as $P(p_{h,w})$, which we believe contains local context information. We then define $\tilde{P}(p_{h,w}) = q - p_{h,w} | q \in P(p_{h,w})$ to transfer $p_{h,w}$ as the center of this point set. As shown in Fig. 2, we use a multilayer perceptron to process $\tilde{P}(p_{h,w})$, which includes 1×1 convolution, ReLU, and batch normalization. This way, a vector of context features for each point is obtained. We concatenate the context feature matrix with the original one and input it to our main network.

2.2   The Architecture of F-3DNet

In this section, we introduce the structure of Frustum 3DNet (F-3DNet), which simultaneously utilizes spatial information and context features. F-3DNet has two main branches that focus on spatial information and local context features, respectively. The first branch is inspired by Frustum PointNet and F-ConvNet. We extend the 2D detection outcome from the pseudo-panorama to 3D space and obtain a candidate frustum. We then slice the frustum into pieces at different resolutions, grouping points in regions of interest by location. The second branch focuses on local context information extraction, using the context feature extraction module we introduced earlier. The combined features are then input into a fully convolutional network for final classification and bounding box location. The entire workflow is shown in Fig. 4.

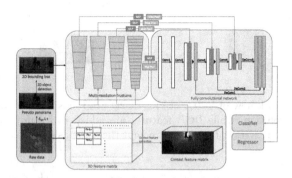

Fig. 4. Work flow of F-3DNet. A pyramid structure is used in fully convolutional network for hierarchy representation. Notice that black triangles in FCN indicate merge operations. Grey slices in Multi-resolution frustums section indicate different-scale division on the frustum region proposal. In FCN section, white rectangles represent matrices after convolution, blue ones indicate that they come from feature extraction from original frustum slices, and orange ones are feature matrices after merge operation. (Color figure online)

While arranging points in the panorama makes it feasible to use direct convolution in 2D to extract features, the adjacent pixels' depth can change drastically in reality. Therefore, we turn to the slice operation to group nearby points. In the Multi-resolution frustums section, we expand the original frustum from the 2D bounding box and slice it into smaller frustums based on four different resolutions. This operation groups nearby points, making the discrete point cloud continuous based on location. We first locate the centerline of one frustum using the 2D bounding box center. This is straightforward because the pitch and rotation of each point in the bounding box are already known through the LiDAR data rearrangement step. Then, a series of parallel planes with equal steps perpendicular to the center line splits the frustum into smaller ones. All points in one small frustum are grouped together, and frustum-wise features are extracted from it afterward. Specifically, we construct a local coordinate system based on the centerline. The z direction represents the frustum centerline, and x is parallel to the ground plane while perpendicular to z. The slice step is set as s, while the width of each small frustum is set as u. Here, overlap is allowed, and we use $u = 2s$ in actual experiments. Assuming that one small frustum contains M points, we group the points together as a point set $p_i = (x_i, y_i, z_i) i = 1^M$. After concatenating intensity and context features point-wise, we use a multi-layer perceptron and max pooling to abstract the feature representation. Then,

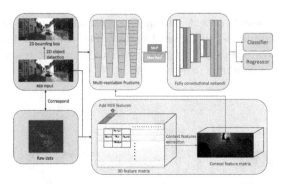

Fig. 5. Updated work flow of F-3DNet+RGB. 2D proposals are generated from RGB image of high resolution, while RGB features are added to feature matrix by cross-sensor calibration. The rest procedures are kept the same as F-3DNet.

we obtain a frustum-wise semantic feature vector $f_i i = 1^L, f_i \in R^d$. We combine L feature vectors of d dimensions and acquire a 2D feature map F with a size of $L \times d$. We use the same settings on the fully convolutional network as F-ConvNet, in which four conv and three deconv blocks are utilized. The merge operation is a combination among different resolutions. It uses convolution to fuse two feature maps without depth change. Merge operations are represented by black triangles in Fig. 4.

2.3   Detection Header and Refinement

The fully convolutional network is connected to two branches: a classifier and a regressor, to fulfill 3D object detection in a multi-task way. For the classifier, assuming that there are K different objects, the classifier compresses the FCN output to $L \times (K + 1)$ by convolution. Here, $K + 1$ indicates that in addition to the object category number K, the background is added as another object kind. Due to the imbalance between foreground and background samples, we utilize focal loss [9] in our method.

The target of the regressor is to generate an accurate 3D bounding box of the object. In road scenes, vehicles, pedestrians, and cyclists can be assumed to be on the same ground plane. Their directions or yaws are different, while pitches and rolls can be neglected. In the KITTI dataset, the manually marked 3D bounding box is described by seven parameters, including $x_c^g, y_c^g, z_c^g, l^g, w^g, h^g, \theta^g$, in which x_c^g, y_c^g, z_c^g represent the center coordinates of the 3D bounding box, l^g, w^g, h^g indicate the length, width, and height of this box, and θ^g is its direction with respect to the ground plane.

Inspired by PointRCNN [12], we quantize yaw from $[-\pi, \pi)$ into N blocks. For each frustum, we place $K \times N$ anchor boxes, covering all possible foreground objects and orientations. Each anchor is parameterized as $x_c^a, y_c^a, z_c^a, l^a, w^a, h^a, \theta^a$, where x_c^a, y_c^a, z_c^a are the center coordinates of the frustum, l^a, w^a, h^a represent the average box size in the training set, and θ^a is the middle yaw angle in this bin. We calculate offsets between anchor boxes and the ground truth bounding boxes according to the following formulas:

$$
\begin{cases}
\Delta x = x_c^g - x_c^a, \Delta y = y_c^g - y_c^a, \Delta z = z_c^g - z_c^a \\
\Delta l = \dfrac{l^g - l^a}{l^a}, \Delta w = \dfrac{w^g - w^a}{w^a}, \Delta h = \dfrac{h^g - h^a}{h^a} \\
\Delta \theta = \dfrac{\theta^g - \theta^a}{\theta^a}
\end{cases}
\tag{2}
$$

Here, $x_c^g, y_c^g, z_c^g, l^g, w^g, h^g, \theta^g$ represent the ground truth values for the 3D bounding box. We use Smooth L1 loss for regression to train the network.

The regression loss consists of normalized Euclidean distance for center, as well as smooth L1 regression loss for size and angle offset. Additionally, the Corner loss from Frustum PointNet [10] is utilized. The network is trained with these three losses and the focal loss from the classifier branch.

The success of the whole network depends on the accuracy of the 2D detection proposals. However, the 2D boxes may not accurately bound the object. To further improve the performance, we use the initial proposals from the 2D detection step and input the points inside them to the same F-3DNet architecture again for refinement. We expand each predicted bounding box by a factor of 1.2 to include more background points and avoid missing foreground ones. A local coordinate system is constructed based on the predicted box center and orientation. We normalize the points inside the expanded box to transfer them from the global coordinate system to the local one. These normalized points are then used as input to the second F-3DNet as a refinement step.

2.4   F-3DNet+RGB

F-3DNet achieves impressive results solely based on LiDAR data, but the initial 2D detection could be further improved by incorporating RGB input, due to the low resolution of the pseudo panorama resulting from the sparsity of LiDAR data. The RGB image contains color and texture information, which are lacking in LiDAR data, making it a valuable addition to the model. As a result, RGB features are integrated into F-3DNet in two ways: (1) the replacement of LiDAR pseudo panorama with an RGB image for initial 2D proposal generation, and (2) the use of cross-sensor calibration to locate LiDAR points on the image plane and the addition of RGB features to the point cloud feature matrix on a per-point basis. The updated F-3DNet with RGB input is shown in Fig. 5.

Table 1. Average precision (AP) comparison of 3D object detection on KITTI test set (%).

	Cars			Pedestrians			Cyclists		
	Easy	Mod	Hard	Easy	Mod	Hard	Easy	Mod	Hard
MV3D [2]	74.97	63.63	54.00	-	-	-	-	-	-
Associate-3Ddet [3]	85.99	77.40	70.53	-	-	-	-	-	-
Voxel-FPN [7]	85.64	76.70	69.44	-	-	-	-	-	-
F-PointNet [10]	82.19	69.79	60.59	50.53	42.15	38.08	72.27	56.12	49.01
AVOD-FPN [6]	83.07	71.76	65.73	50.46	42.27	39.04	63.76	50.55	44.93
PointPainting [13]	82.11	71.70	67.08	50.32	40.97	37.87	77.63	63.78	55.89
PointPillars [8]	82.58	74.31	68.99	51.45	41.92	38.89	77.10	58.65	51.92
PointRCNN [12]	86.96	75.64	70.70	47.98	39.37	36.01	74.96	58.82	52.53
F-ConvNet [14]	87.36	76.39	66.69	52.16	43.38	38.80	81.98	65.07	56.54
F-3DNet+RGB	85.48	78.48	71.62	51.93	43.79	40.15	78.61	63.50	57.11

3   Experiments

3.1   Dataset

Our model is evaluated primarily on the KITTI-OBJECT dataset, which consists of 7481 training and 7518 testing scenes containing RGB images and point clouds. The dataset focuses on three main object categories, namely Car, Pedestrian, and Cyclist. Results are evaluated on three levels, easy, moderate, and hard, which are categorized based on target size and truncation. Similar to the MV3D method [2], we use the same split on the original training set for supervised data. The new training and validation set contain 3712 and 3769 driving scenes, respectively. We conduct an ablation study on the new data split, while the final result comparison with other existing models is based on the KITTI testing set. We set IoU thresholds on 0.7, 0.5, and 0.5 for Car, Pedestrian, and Cyclist, respectively.

To further evaluate the efficiency of our model, we also tested F-3DNet on the nuScenes dataset, which contains 28,130 training, 6,019 validation, and 6,008 testing samples. The objects are labeled into 10 categories: Car, Truck, Bus, Trailer, Construction Vehicle, Pedestrian, Motorcycle, Bicycle, Traffic Cone, and Barrier, where cars and pedestrians have the most instances and construction vehicles and bicycles have the least. The LiDAR used in the nuScenes dataset has 32 laser heads, which is different from that in the KITTI dataset. However, this does not affect our local context information extraction module.

3.2   Implementation Details

On the KITTI dataset, we train two F-3DNets separately for the Car and Pedestrian/Cyclist categories due to the differences between these objects. During network training, we use the RRC [11] and MSCNN model [1] to obtain initial 2D bounding boxes for the Car and Pedestrian/Cyclist categories, respectively. Data augmentation is achieved by scaling the 2D bounding box size and using random shifts and flips, similar to Frustum PointNet, to prevent overfitting. To normalize input points, we use a fixed point number of 1024 at the first stage and 512 in refinement. We shrink the ground-truth boxes by a ratio of 0.5 to generate positive and negative training samples. Foreground anchor boxes are those whose centers are located in the shrunken ground-truth boxes, while anchor boxes whose centers are located between the shrunken and ground-truth boxes are ignored. The remaining anchor boxes are tagged as background.

We trained the F-3DNets on one GPU (Nvidia Titan V 12GB) using a batch size of 32 and the Adam optimizer with a weight decay of 0.0001. The learning rate was set to 0.001 and decayed by a factor of 10 every 20 epochs of a total of 50 epochs. We set the valid range from 0 to 72 m. For the Car category, we used frustum resolutions at $u = [0.5, 1.0, 2.0, 4.0]$ and steps equal to $s = [0.25, 0.5, 1.0, 2.0]$. Frustum-wise feature depths were set to $d = [128, 128, 256, 512]$, while dimensions were set to $L = [288, 144, 72, 36]$. All feature dimensions of different resolutions were unified to $L_1 = 144$ after deconvolution. For Pedestrian/Cyclist, we used a finer frustum slice with $u = [0.2, 0.4, 0.8, 1.6]$ and $s = [0.1, 0.2, 0.4, 0.8]$. Frustum-wise feature depths were set to $d = [128, 128, 256, 512]$, and frustum split numbers were set to $L = [720, 360, 180, 90]$. All feature dimensions of different resolutions were unified to $L_2 = 360$ after deconvolution. During evaluation, we used non-maximum suppression (NMS) to reduce redundancy. The final score of a 3D bounding box was calculated as the average of the 2D detection score and the predicted 3D score.

On the nuScenes dataset, we used the same network settings as on KITTI, with $u = [0.2, 0.4, 0.8, 1.6]$ and $s = [0.1, 0.2, 0.4, 0.8]$ for frustum slice. Frustumwise feature depths were set to $d = [128, 128, 256, 512]$, and frustum split numbers were set to $L = [720, 360, 180, 90]$. All feature dimensions of different resolutions were unified to $L_2 = 360$ after deconvolution. The object category number K on nuScenes is 11 (10 detection classes plus background), which is higher than the 4 categories used in KITTI.

3.3   Main Results

Table 1 presents the performance of our proposed method (F-3DNet+RGB) on the KITTI test set, compared to other listed methods. The results show that our network model has significant advantages in car detection compared to other models on the KITTI dataset. This is due to the fact that F-3DNet+RGB is more sensitive to details, as it considers local context information, and the detection accuracy of moderate and hard targets is significantly improved compared to other networks. However, if the target is too close and contains too many points, the redundant local details may affect the accuracy of our 3D detection. For a clearer observation, visualizations on the KITTI dataset are shown in Fig. 6.

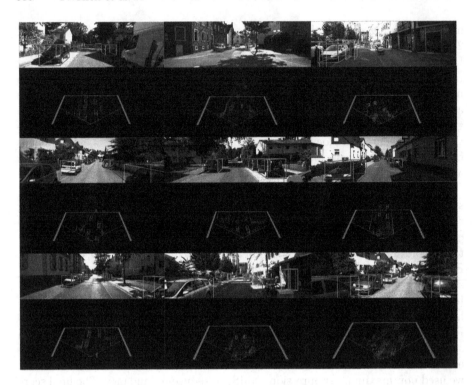

Fig. 6. Qualitative results on KITTI dataset. 9 typical scenes are listed, including images and LiDAR illustrations. Green bounding boxes represent groundtruth, while blue, red and pink boxes indicate our model predictions for Car, Pedestrian and Cyclist categories respectively. (Color figure online)

3.4   Ablation Study

Table 2. Influence of 2D proposal on average precision (AP) (%).

	2D Detection			3D Detection		
	Easy	Mod	Hard	Easy	Mod.	Hard
RRC+Pseudo	90.93	81.57	72.20	79.24	70.95	63.26
RRC+RGB	96.32	95.18	88.94	86.88	77.29	68.61
GT	100	100	100	88.33	85.97	78.75

To evaluate the efficiency of our method, we verified F-3DNet on the KITTI-OBJECT dataset, including an ablation study and an efficiency comparison with the state-of-the-art. The ablation study was conducted on the Car category, which is believed to contain richer features, of the train/validation split. Table 2 shows the influence of 2D proposal precision on F-3DNet outcomes without the refinement stage. Here, we used the RRC model [11] for 2D region proposal generation from both LiDAR pseudo-images and RGB images. The term "GT" in the table indicates the use of 2D detection ground truth as an initial region proposal.

According to Table 2, using the RRC model as the 2D detection method on the pseudo image results in 81.57% accuracy on moderate targets. The precision of the 2D detection results increases significantly by replacing the RGB input with the pseudo images, mainly due to the much higher resolution of RGB images. Comparing the three different 2D proposal sources, the corresponding 3D detection results are dramatically influenced by 2D proposal precision. In general, F-3DNet achieves higher performance when cooperating with RGB images, while better 2D region proposals are significantly conducive to 3D detection.

Table 3. Effect of context features and refinement step on average precision (AP) (%).

	Easy	Mod.	Hard
w/o Context w/o Refinement	86.01	76.78	67.33
w/o Refinement	86.88	77.29	68.61
w/o Context	88.75	78.49	76.04
F-3DNet+RGB	89.67	79.05	77.56

To verify the efficacy of context features and refinement on our model, we conducted an ablation study on F-3DNet with RGB proposals (F-3DNet+RGB). The results in Table 3 demonstrate the effectiveness of each component in our model. Specifically, the context feature contributes to approximately 1% improvement in F-3DNet performance, while the refinement step further increases the model performance by around 2%.

4 Conclusion

We present a novel end-to-end method, F-3DNet, for 3D object detection, which achieves high performance on both KITTI and nuScenes datasets. F-3DNet challenges the popular prior knowledge in LiDAR data processing that point cloud is irregular and disordered by constructing a neighbor relationship among point cloud obeying LiDAR operating mode and obtaining a pseudo panorama. Furthermore, we introduce a local context feature extraction module that incorporates inner context information of LiDAR data into 3D object detection. To meet real-time demand in autonomous driving, our model utilizes 2D CNNs based on multi-resolution frustum slicing. In addition, cooperating with refinement step and fusion with RGB input, the detection results of F-3DNet are further improved. Future research will focus on investigating a concise and point-wise network to further enhance the proposed model's performance.

Ethics. As the model proposed in our research mainly focuses on 3D object detection using LiDAR and RGB data, we do not collect or process any personal data in this study. Moreover, our research does not involve the inference of personal information or the potential use of our work for policing or military purposes. Therefore, we do not have any ethical concerns regarding our research. However, we understand the importance of ethics in machine learning and data mining, and we will continue to prioritize ethical considerations in our future research.

References

1. Cai, Z., Fan, Q., Feris, R., Vasconcelos, N.: A unified multi-scale deep convolutional neural network for fast object detection. In: The European Conference on Computer Vision (ECCV) (2020)
2. Chen, X., Ma, H., Wan, J., Li, B., Xia, T.: Multi-view 3D object detection network for autonomous driving. In: The IEEE Conference on Computer Vision and Pattern Recognition (CVPR) (2022)
3. Du, L., et al.: Associate-3Ddet: Perceptual-to-conceptual association for 3D point cloud object detection. In: The IEEE Conference on Computer Vision and Pattern Recognition (CVPR) (2022)
4. Gao, H., Cheng, B., Wang, J., Li, K., Zhao, J., Li, D.: Object classification using CNN-based fusion of vision and lidar in autonomous vehicle environment. IEEE Trans. Industr. Inf. **14**(9), 4224–4231 (2022)
5. Geiger, A., Lenz, P., Urtasun, R.: Are we ready for autonomous driving? the KITTI vision benchmark suite. In: Conference on Computer Vision and Pattern Recognition (CVPR) (2012)
6. Ku, J., Mozifian, M., Lee, J., Harakeh, A., Waslander, S.L.: Joint 3D proposal generation and object detection from view aggregation. In: 2018 IEEE/RSJ International Conference on Intelligent Robots and Systems (IROS), pp. 1–8 (2018)
7. Kuang, H., Wang, B., An, J., Zhang, M., Zhang, Z.: Voxel-FPN: multi-scale voxel feature aggregation for 3D object detection from lidar point clouds. Sensors **20**(3), 704 (2021)
8. Lang, A.H., Vora, S., Caesar, H., Zhou, L., Yang, J., Beijbom, O.: PointPillars: fast encoders for object detection from point clouds. In: The IEEE Conference on Computer Vision and Pattern Recognition (CVPR) (2022)
9. Lin, T., Goyal, P., Girshick, R., He, K., Dollar, P.: Focal loss for dense object detection. IEEE Trans. Pattern Anal. Mach. Intell. **42**, 318–327 (2018). https://doi.org/10.1109/TPAMI.2018.2858826
10. Qi, C.R., Liu, W., Wu, C., Su, H., Guibas, L.J.: Frustum PointNets for 3D object detection from RGB-D data. In: The IEEE Conference on Computer Vision and Pattern Recognition (CVPR) (2021)
11. Ren, J., et al.: Accurate single stage detector using recurrent rolling convolution. In: The IEEE Conference on Computer Vision and Pattern Recognition (CVPR) (2017)
12. Shi, S., Wang, X., Li, H.: PointRCNN: 3D object proposal generation and detection from point cloud. In: The IEEE Conference on Computer Vision and Pattern Recognition (CVPR) (2019)
13. Vora, S., Lang, A.H., Helou, B., Beijbom, O.: PointPainting: sequential fusion for 3D object detection. In: The IEEE Conference on Computer Vision and Pattern Recognition (CVPR) (2021)

14. Wang, Z., Jia, K.: Frustum ConvNet: sliding frustums to aggregate local point-wise features for amodal 3D object detection. In: 2019 IEEE/RSJ International Conference on Intelligent Robots and Systems (IROS) (2019)

15. Wen, L., Jo, K.H.: Three-attention mechanisms for one-stage 3D object detection based on lidar and camera. IEEE Transactions on Industrial Informatics (2021)

16. Yan, Y., Mao, Y., Li, B.: Second: sparsely embedded convolutional detection. Sensors **18**(10), 3337 (2018)

17. Yang, B., Luo, W., Urtasun, R.: PIXOR: real-time 3D object detection from point clouds. In: The IEEE Conference on Computer Vision and Pattern Recognition (CVPR) (2021)

18. Zhou, Y., Tuzel, O.: VoxelNet: End-to-End learning for point cloud based 3D object detection. In: The IEEE Conference on Computer Vision and Pattern Recognition (CVPR) (2018)

Constraint-Based Parameterization and Disentanglement of Aerodynamic Shapes Using Deep Generative Models

Asmita Bhat[1]([✉]), Nooshin Haji-Ghassemi[1], Deepak Nagaraj[2], and Sophie Fellenz[1][ID]

[1] University of Kaiserslautern-Landau, Gottlieb-Daimler-StraSSe 47, 67663 Kaiserslautern, Germany
{bhat,nooshin,fellenz}@cs.uni-kl.de
[2] Bertrandt Ingenieurbüro GmbH, Hufelandstrasse 26-28, 80939 München, Germany

Abstract. Generating parametric shapes with respect to their structural and functional characteristics is a challenging and demanding problem. Conventional parameterization techniques are complex and require manual intervention and multiple cycles to produce plausible shapes, which makes the overall parameterization process extremely sensitive, time- consuming and error-prone. Despite these techniques' slow and iterative nature, a significant amount of data has been gathered over many years, prompting the community to turn to data-driven techniques like deep generative models for automatic parameterization. However, parameterizing shapes following necessary functional constraints is crucial but notoriously difficult and still needs to be studied. Therefore, we propose a data-driven framework that implicitly learns to generate plausible parametric aerodynamic shapes under specified constraints. We explore and compare several generative models, including generative adversarial networks and variational autoencoders, and systematically evaluate them for generation quality, diversity, and disentanglement aspects. Our framework, including a β-VAE model, enables the automatic generation of novel airfoils with watertight boundaries and interactive generation with its distributed and disentangled latent space. Through rigorous evaluation of our method, we demonstrate that the generated distribution closely matches the true distribution, resulting in the generation of highly realistic airfoils. Our method dramatically outperforms the current benchmark in terms of the quality and diversity of generated airfoils and establishes a new benchmark for constraint-based parameterization.

Keywords: Aerodynamic shapes · Deep Generative Models · VAE

1 Introduction

Parametric shapes like airfoils, hydrofoils, fans, and turbines are used in a variety of applications, including aerodynamics, electronics, and automobiles, and are

© The Author(s), under exclusive license to Springer Nature Switzerland AG 2023
G. De Francisci Morales et al. (Eds.): ECML PKDD 2023, LNAI 14174, pp. 360–376, 2023.
https://doi.org/10.1007/978-3-031-43427-3_22

developed by combining parameterization and optimization techniques. These techniques aim to develop shapes that yield optimal performance in terms of their functionality. The shapes are represented by one or more parametric functions in a high-dimensional space, parameterized by a set of design variables.

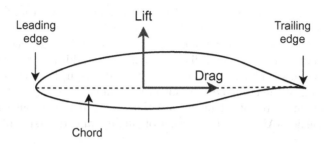

Fig. 1. An example of an airfoil from the UIUC dataset [33]. The chord of an airfoil is zero-centered. The leading edge and trailing edge points coincide with the chord. The direction of the lift component of aerodynamic force is perpendicular to the chord, and that of the drag is along the chord towards the trailing edge. Feasible airfoils have higher lift than drag.

Traditional parameterization techniques are explicit, meaning the parameters of the designs are manually set by a human expert. They are further optimized by employing numerical simulation tools such as computational fluid dynamics [31] or Computer-Aided Engineering (CAE) that consider various functional restrictions and boundary conditions. To generate feasible designs with acceptable performance using these techniques, several back-and-forth iterations through the design and optimization phases are required, making the overall process exceedingly time, memory, and computation intensive. Despite these challenges, the aerodynamics community has produced a large number of viable airfoil designs that may be utilized for a variety of tasks, including shape synthesis, optimization, and flow field prediction [1].

Modern parameterization techniques, such as BézierGAN [6], are data-driven models based on GANs [12], one of the prominent Deep Generative Models (DGMs) that can automatically parameterize aerodynamic shapes, also known as airfoils. An airfoil is a critical component of an aircraft design responsible for the aerodynamic force generated during operation. Figure 1 illustrates the two components of aerodynamic force: lift and drag. An airfoil must be streamlined to generate more lift than drag to enable an aircraft to take off. As a result, the coefficient of lift-to-drag, C_L/C_D, is an important functional characteristic of an airfoil. However, generating realistic and practically viable airfoils while ensuring such a functional characteristic is an extremely challenging problem mainly due to scarcity of data and the high dimensionality of the shapes.

This paper proposes a hybrid DGM-CAE framework for automated, constraint-based parameterization of airfoil designs while ensuring their mechanical functionality. We enforce the C_L/C_D values obtained from numerical simulation software and constrain the airfoil generation using these values to generate airfoils for specific C_L/C_D ratios. This approach simplifies and accelerates the design process and can be used for effective and interactive shape parameterization. To sum up, our contributions are as follows:

1. We develop a hybrid DGM-CAE framework for automated and constraint-based airfoil parameterization while preserving their mechanical functionality.
2. We assess the results using relevant metrics for various generation aspects such as quality, diversity, and disentanglement. In addition, we also evaluate our framework's ability to parameterize original designs from the dataset and the precision of the enforced functional constraint.
3. The quantitative results demonstrate that our framework outperforms the baseline BézierGAN model in terms of quality and diversity of generated shapes.
4. To the best of our knowledge, this is a first attempt at conditionally generating airfoil designs using their C_L/C_D, which is a continuous real-valued number, unlike widely used conditional models [24] which use discrete labels.

2   Related Work

In this section, we discuss some of the traditional methods for parametric shape synthesis and the most recent popular DGMs for both high-quality synthesis and representation learning.

2.1   Parametric Shape Synthesis for Product Design

Methods for understanding design spaces and synthesizing new shapes or designs can be categorized into two broad categories: knowledge-driven methods and data-driven methods [37]. Knowledge-driven approaches use explicit rules to develop new shapes. Computational Design Synthesis is an example of a knowledge-driven method for synthesizing new shapes, which is most popularly used for gearboxes and bicycle frames [2]. Other methods include B-splines [22], Bézier curves [38], Free Form Deformation [39], Class-Shape Transformations (CST) [13], and PARSEC [9], which are parameterization methods that are used to generate curves for aerodynamic shapes. These parameterization methods adjust the control points or parameters using random perturbation or Latin hypercube sampling [39]. However, these knowledge-based methods suffer from high dimensionality of the design space [6] and unknown limits to the parameters that define the geometry. On the other hand, data-driven models [5,6,40] implicitly learn useful knowledge about the geometric representation from the existing designs in the dataset. DGMs, in particular, address the issues mentioned above by generating a compact latent representation that captures the most distinct and informative features of real-world designs and their parameter constraints.

2.2 Deep Generative Models

DGMs have proven to be successful in generating high-dimensional data in a completely unsupervised setting. Ideally, a good generative model should learn meaningful and compact representations for a qualitative and diverse generation. Two of the most popular generative models are Variational Autoencoders (VAEs) [19] and Generative Adversarial Networks (GANs) [12]. Although GANs are relatively better at synthesizing realistic data, they are notoriously difficult to train and often result in unstable models. VAEs on the other hand, are easier to train and converge faster. In addition, they are more successful than GANs in creating compact and effective representations in a continuous latent space. Such representations are useful for transferring specific characteristics and allowing control over the synthesis task, making it more productive and interactive [21]. To obtain a better trade-off in quality and training, we implement different models based on GAN and VAE frameworks for airfoil generation and systematically evaluate them to find the best suitable model for our application. In the following sections, we explain the theoretical foundations of both models in detail.

Variational Autoencoder. VAEs are rooted in Bayesian inference i.e., they project the underlying training data distribution onto a distributed latent space that comprises independent factors of variation in the data. At inference, a VAE allows us to sample from the latent space to generate novel data that ideally resembles real data. Consider x to be our input data and z to be a latent vector. The VAE objective is to model the distribution of x which can be formulated as shown in Eq. 1, where $p(x|z)$ is known as conditional likelihood, and $p(z)$ is the prior distribution.

$$p(x) = \int p(x|z)p(z)\,dz \qquad (1)$$

Computing the conditional likelihood requires computation of an unknown quantity known as the posterior of the true data $p(z|x)$. The VAE uses an encoder network to parameterize the variational approximation of the posterior distribution. The conditional likelihood is parameterized with a decoder network. The loss function for a VAE is given by Eq. 2 where the first term represents the reconstruction loss, and the second term is the KL divergence that minimizes the distance between the posterior and the prior. The prior distribution is usually a simple distribution, such as the standard normal distribution.

$$L = \mathbb{E}_{q(z|X)}[-\log p(X|z)] + KL\left(q(z|X)\|p(z)\right) \qquad (2)$$

Generative Adversarial Networks. Generative adversarial networks (GANs) [12,28] also model the true data distribution $p(x)$ but use adversarial learning instead. A typical GAN network comprises two components - a generator G and a discriminator D. A generator generates new samples using a low-dimensional noise vector and aims to fool the discriminator whose task is to distinguish real samples from fake ones (samples generated by the generator). G and D are trained as a min-max in an adversarial fashion where each component strives to be better than the other network at their respective tasks. The GAN objective is given as

$$\min_G \max_D E(G, D) = \mathbb{E}_{x \sim P_{data}}[\log D_x] + \mathbb{E}_{z \sim P_z}[\log(1 - D(G_x))], \quad (3)$$

where x is sampled from the real data distribution P_{data}, z represents the noise vector sampled from the noise distribution P_z, and $G(z)$ is the fake distribution.

2.3   Learning Disentangled Representations

Modeling real-world data using generative models like GANs and VAEs creates a low-dimensional latent space. Ideally, this latent space represents the most crucial and distinct features of the data. In the case of VAEs, choosing an isotropic Gaussian prior has a latent space where every dimension is independent and produces what is generally known as a disentangled latent space. A latent space is called disentangled if each of its dimensions represents one and only one underlying factor of variation in the data [16]. The disentangled latent space enables interactive and controlled generation by allowing us to change specific features or to obtain data having certain features from generative distribution. Unfortunately, interactive generation is not possible with GANs as they cannot produce a disentangled representation of the data. Instead the representation is entangled, making it hard to interpret [7].

Several extensions based on the VAE framework, such as β-VAE [15], FactorVAE [17], and those based on the GAN framework, including InfoGAN [7], have been proposed to obtain a better generation quality and better disentanglement. Higgins et al. [15] and Chen et al. [4] provide simple modifications to the original VAE objective to achieve a better trade-off between generation quality and disentanglement, whereas Kim and Mnih [17] achieve this with the help of a discriminator network. InfoGAN, on the other hand, uses additional latent codes to encode some generative factors from the training data to encourage disentanglement. Other approaches, such as IDGAN [21], combine VAE and GAN frameworks to produce effective disentanglement and generate high-quality images. We explore several generative models such as β-VAE [15], DCGAN [28], and FactorVAE [16] and compare them for several generation aspects. Through evaluation of these models we find out that β-VAE is much simpler, faster and more reliable for high quality generation and disentanglement. Further, we compare our conditional β-VAE model with the popular BézierGAN model which is based on InfoGAN. In the next section, we explain our approach for reliable generation in more details.

3   Approach

Our goal is to produce high-quality airfoil designs that adhere to their performance characteristics while also producing disentangled representations of the designs. Although GANs and VAEs can synthesize high-quality data, particularly images, their potential to synthesize parametric shapes has yet to be fully investigated. Therefore, we propose a conditional parameterization framework for synthesizing new airfoil designs constrained by specific C_L/C_D values based on GAN and VAE networks to obtain high-quality and diverse designs with disentangled representations. Conditioning the airfoil designs on their C_L/C_D values provides a mapping between the C_L/C_D and the intrinsic characteristics of the designs. Thus, we develop conditional versions of β-VAE, FactorVAE, and DCGAN networks.

Functional airfoils need to have smooth and watertight curve. To obtain such curves, our framework first constructs a binary image representation of the airfoils. The conditional DGMs are trained using these binary representations, along with their C_L/C_D values. In the following part, we discuss the data representation and conditional parameterization more deeply.

3.1 Data Representation

The parameterization of airfoils is an important stage in aircraft design. The shape, curvature, and edges of the airfoil have a significant impact on the aircraft's aerodynamic properties and the flow fields around it, influencing optimization outcomes [41]. As a result, accurately modeling the airfoil designs, including all of the minute details regarding their geometries, is vital. In the UIUC dataset [33], airfoils are represented by a defined set of discrete design variables. These may be insufficient for complex airfoil shapes. As a result, we convert the UIUC data into binary fields in order to create smooth and watertight surfaces that preserve the geometry and its details perfectly. More importantly, the smooth curves enable us to sample as many points from the geometries as necessary. The airfoils in the UIUC dataset are first mapped onto a high-resolution Signed Distance Field (SDF) [1] and then converted to binary fields. As binary fields are equivalent to 2D images, we can learn their underlying features using convolutional operations [32] in the same way as with images. Another reason to map data onto an SDF is to have a common representation for 2D and 3D objects, which is challenging to do with alternative data formats. However, due to the lack of publicly available 3D airfoil data, we have limited our research to 2D airfoil designs.

Signed Distance Field. An SDF [1] is formed using a signed distance function that calculates and assigns a distance to each point in space, with positive distance for points outside the shape, negative distance for points inside the shape, and zero distance for points on the shape. Mathematically, a signed distance function for a set of points Q is given by the distance d of all the points $q \in Q$ from the shape boundary ω as shown in Eq. 4.

$$SDF(q) = \begin{cases} d(q, \partial\omega) & q \notin \omega \\ 0 & q \in \partial\omega \\ -d(q, \partial\omega) & q \in \omega \end{cases} \quad (4)$$

Binary Fields. The distances to all points within and outside the object are essential only in applications where global geometry is required. However, for airfoil parameterization, obtaining only the isosurface that represents the airfoil shape suffices. Hence, we modify the signed distance function to obtain a binary field, such that, if ω is the shape boundary, then the points on and inside the shape boundary form an isosurface, whereas points outside the shape boundary have a distance of one. Equation 5 represents the modified signed distance function for binary fields:

$$SDF_{\text{binary}}(q) = \begin{cases} 1 & q \notin \omega \\ 0 & q \in \partial\omega \\ 0 & q \in \omega \end{cases} \tag{5}$$

We fix all distances to be equal to one because it is inconsequential to know how far the point lies outside the boundary. The obtained binary signed distance fields are analogous to binary images except that they are obtained as a result of binary SDF.

3.2   Conditional Parameterization Using Generative Models

We enable the conditional synthesis of new airfoil designs by providing the C_L/C_D value as a condition to the generative component of the network. The condition is enforced by concatenating C_L/C_D values c to the latent vector $\mathbf{z}$. c is a real-valued number between 0 and 1 which is obtained as a result of the normalization of C_L/C_D values. Unlike other conditional models [35] that use a discrete label as a condition, the C_L/C_D values are continuous real-valued numbers. As a result of such conditional synthesis, the generative component of the implemented DGMs acts as an implicit parametric function that can generate airfoils for a given C_L/C_D condition. At inference, we can sample a noise vector from a Gaussian distribution $\mathcal{N}(0,1)$ to which we can append any C_L/C_D value between zero and one and generate the design that matches the condition. We can also combine desired shape characteristics from our learned disentangled latent space to customize the airfoil designs. This enables interactive design synthesis and quick prototyping of desirable shapes. Our method can produce sharp, smooth, and desirable airfoils without any smoothing function and without having to learn any explicit parameters like control points for shape synthesis or separate latent codes for disentanglement as used in BézierGAN [6].

4   Experimental Results

We explore three DGMs – Deep Convolutional GAN (DCGAN) [28], β-VAE [15] and FactorVAE [16] – which are known to generate plausible images. We assess the generated designs quantitatively using the manifold-based metrics density and coverage. We also demonstrate the quality of disentanglement across different dimensions of the latent space.

4.1   Data Preparation

Obtaining Binary Fields. We use 2D airfoil designs from the UIUC dataset [33] comprising nearly 1,600 diverse airfoil designs. It is a public dataset and is widely used for aerodynamic research. Also, obtaining C_L/C_D values using numerical simulation software is possible using this data, which aligns well with our goal. Examples of airfoil designs and their C_L/C_D values, are shown in the appendix[1]. Each airfoil design in the UIUC dataset is represented by a sequence of discrete x- and y-coordinates along the airfoil curve. The order of coordinates of every curve starts from the trailing edge point, followed by points along the upper surface of the airfoil towards the leading edge, the leading edge point and then the points along the lower surface of airfoil from leading edge towards the trailing edge. The edges and surfaces can be seen in Fig. 1. The original format of the data produces rough boundaries or requires additional functions for smoothening the curves. To overcome these challenges, we convert each airfoil curve into a binary SDF of size 500×500, (refer sect. 3.4 for data conversion details).

Obtaining C_L/C_D. The C_L/C_D value represents the lift-to-drag ratio. It can be obtained using simulation software to simulate the necessary flow fields under the required settings to obtain optimal airfoil performance. For all the airfoils in the dataset, we use XFOIL simulation [10] by setting the Reynolds number, Re $= 5 \times 10^5$, the Mach number, Ma $= 0.0$ and the angle of attack, $\alpha = 3°$ for around 1,200 airfoils. Please refer the appendix for more information about the distribution of the C_L/C_D values for all 1,200 airfoil designs. To condition on these values for generation, we normalize them to be between zero and one.

4.2   Evaluation Metrics

Density and coverage (DnC) [26] are used as metrics to assess our model's performance in terms of quality and diversity. Inception Score (IS) [30] and Fréchet Inception Distance (FID) [14] are some of the other metrics used to measure the overall quality of generation, but they cannot distinguish quality from diversity. For example, it is highly impractical if a generative model generates images that are very similar or generates the same image every time, even if the quality of generation is good. In that sense, IS and FID are highly uninformative. Furthermore, Kynkäänniemi et al. [20] show that IS and FID are unreliable for evaluating generative models because they do not correlate well with the image quality and produce an inconsistent evaluation.

On the other hand, DnC [26] overcame the earlier metrics' shortcomings. They are **automatic evaluation** techniques that directly compare the fake (generated) data distribution to the real, allowing us to see how well the generated distribution matches the training data. Unlike IS and FID, which rely on activations of a pre-trained Inception model based on ImageNet data [8],

---

[1] https://github.com/aeroshapesynthesis/constraint_parametererization_airfoils/blob/main/Appendix.pdf.

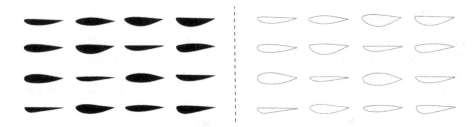

Fig. 2. Randomly sampled airfoil designs generated by β-VAE. The designs are realistic and have sharp and watertight boundaries.

DnC are independent of any dataset or model, giving a straightforward and clear evaluation method. The main idea behind DnC is to compare the manifold of real samples to the manifold of fake samples, and then quantify the quality and diversity of generated samples based on how the fake samples are placed around the real samples. Any intermediate layer, especially the fully connected layers of the generative part of the network (for example, the generator in the GAN or the decoder in the VAE), can be used to create these manifolds. More information on the metric and it's mathematical definition is given in the appendix.

4.3   Training

We train the β-VAE, FactorVAE, and DCGAN models on the UIUC airfoil dataset after preprocessing airfoils and extracting their C_L/C_D values. There are approximately 1,100 airfoils divided into a training set of 900 and a test set of 200. All models are implemented using Pytorch [27] and are trained on a single Nvidia Tesla [23] V100-SXM2 32 GB GPU. The batch size is 16 and is kept the same for all models. The learning rate for encoder and decoder in VAE, β-VAE and FactorVAE is 10^{-4}, the generator in DCGAN is $2 * 10^{-4}$ and for discriminator in DCGAN and FactorVAE is 10^{-4}. Adam optimization [18] is used for the training of all models because it can handle sparse gradients and combines the best properties of the AdaGrad [11] and RMSProp [25] algorithms. VAEs are generally stable to train and converge faster than GANs; hence we train β-VAE and FactorVAE for 300 epochs and DCGAN for 500 epochs. Hyperparameter optimization is an important part of training; therefore, using validation set we heuristically search for the best hyperparameters for each model. A brief note on hyperparameter optimization is included in the appendix.

4.4   Qualitative Results

A crucial first step is to visually inspect the results because the generated images maybe distorted or blurry, and these problems are difficult to address using quantitative analysis. From qualitative inspection, we observed that the β-VAE model with a latent dimension of 25 generates the most plausible images with sharp and watertight boundaries. Figure 2 shows the airfoils and their extracted boundaries (curves). From visual inspection it is evident that the generated airfoils are very realistic as it is difficult to distinguish between real airfoils and airfoils generated using β-VAE. In the case of DCGAN and FactorVAE, the quality of generation is extremely poor as the generated designs are not sharp with closed boundaries. We tune all the models for different latent dimension sizes to find a better fit. But for DCGAN and FactorVAE, the quality of generated airfoils remain poor for all latent dimensions. Figure 3 shows airfoil designs generated using DCGAN and FactorVAE. Since, all the generated airfoils for all latent dimensions are distorted for both the models, these airfoils can't be used to extract watertight boundaries and thus, cannot be of any practical use. As β-VAE model outperforms other models, we quantitatively evaluate its results using DnC.

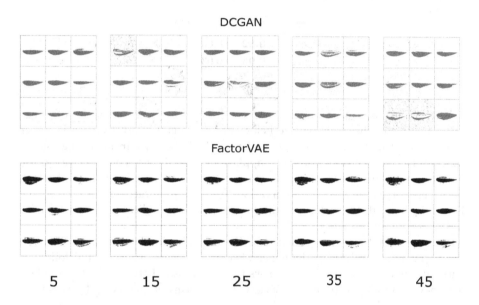

Fig. 3. Airfoil designs generated by DCGAN and FactorVAE for different latent dimension sizes. Heuristic hyperparameter search does not improve the quality of generated designs.

4.5   Quantitative Results: Analysis of Airfoil Designs

In this section, we evaluate our model using DnC and compare it to the state-of-the-art BézierGAN model. For the β-VAE model, we randomly sample from the prior and generate C_L/C_D values. The airfoils are then generated using the decoder and the latent vectors are then extracted from the encoder to calculate the DnC scores. In total, we extract latent vectors for 500 real and 500 fake images and calculate the DnC scores. Figure 4 shows the DnC scores for the

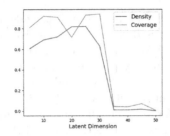

Fig. 4. Density and Coverage of designs generated using β-VAE model for different latent dimensions. Latent dimension size of 25 produces high quality designs.

Table 1. Comparison of β-VAE vs BézierGAN for quality and diversity of generated designs. β-VAE outperforms BézierGAN on all fronts.

Metric	β-VAE	BézierGAN
Density	**0.82**	0.63
Coverage	**0.93**	0.038

β-VAE models for latent dimension size from 5 to 50 with a step size of 5. For lower latent dimension sizes (size below 30), the quality and diversity is better than those of higher sizes. This is understandable because in high dimensional spaces, the curse of dimensionality applies and the data becomes more sparse. For latent dimension size of 25, we can see that the density is the highest which positively correlates with the observations from the qualitative results. Coverage is also high (slightly lower than the highest number) indicating more diversity in the generated samples.

We compared our conditional β-VAE model (having latent size of 25) with the popular BézierGAN model which also aims at generating novel airfoils, but without any constraints. Table 1 shows the comparison between the two models. The β-VAE model outperforms BézierGAN in terms of quality and diversity of the generated designs.

4.6   Quality of Reconstructions

For successful parameterization, representing the original airfoil design accurately is crucial. For traditional parameterization techniques like PARSEC [34], MACROS DR [36], and CST [3], the geometric error between the actual airfoil and the approximated airfoil is calculated using Root Mean Square (RMS) [41]. However, the input and output in our approach is a binary field. While obtaining curves from the generated binary fields, the points along the curve are sampled randomly and not in any particular order. Thus, RMS is not a suitable technique to measure parameterization accuracy because thepoints that coincide with the

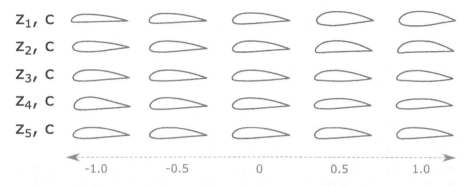

Fig. 5. Traversing across different dimensions of a latent vector using β-VAE. It shows automatic disentanglement based on geometric traits like shape, size and curvature in a distributed and a continuous latent space.

coordinates of an input airfoil cannot be obtained. However, the difference in geometries may be computed by directly comparing the binary fields of the original and reconstructed designs using Intersection over Union (IoU) [29]. IoU is a popular metric in the computer vision community to calculate the similarity of any two 2D/3D objects. Let A and B be any two 2D/3D volumes of objects, then IoU is defined as follows:

$$\frac{|A \cap B|}{|A \cup B|} \tag{6}$$

We can see that β-VAE generates designs with the sharpest and most watertight boundaries by comparing the outputs of the models shown in Fig. 2. Thus, to calculate the IoU between actual and approximated airfoil designs, we use the reconstructions obtained from a β-VAE model with $\beta=60$ and a latent dimension of 25. We calculate IoU for a whole image because as long as every input and output has just one smooth and watertight airfoil without any deformity, IoU can effectively calculate similarity. Figure 3 shows that there are possibilities of distortion while generating airfoil designs and that it might result in multiple broken objects. Hence we first run all the samples through an off-the-shelf contour detection technique and select 50 samples for which only one contour is detected. The average IoU is as high as 0.975, which indicates that the β-VAE model can accurately reconstruct original airfoils, which makes the decoder of β-VAE a good parametric function. Examples of real vs reconstructed airfoils with their IoU are shown in the appendix.

4.7   Disentanglement

We illustrate latent traversal through several dimensions of the noise vector as well as interpolations between different samples to highlight our model's potential to disentangle the latent space based on the geometric properties of the airfoils and their C_L/C_D values. Latent traversal (-1 to 1) across different dimensions of a noise vector is shown in Fig. 5. For each row in Fig. 5, we vary

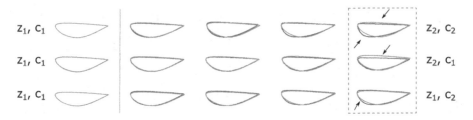

Fig. 6. Noise vectors, n_1 and n_2 are randomly sampled and C_L/C_D values c_1 and c_2 are 0.1 and 0.99 respectively. Changing both noise and C_L/C_D (top) changes size and curvature, whereas, changing only noise (middle) changes the shape without affecting the curve and changing only C_L/C_D (bottom) changes the leading curvature without affecting the shape.

one dimension in the noise vector while keeping all other dimensions, including C_L/C_D value fixed to see the contribution of the varying dimension in generating of airfoils. Different dimensions depict varying and independent factors of variation based on the size, shape, nature of leading and trailing edges of airfoils. The latent traversal is very smooth, and the model can generate feasible designs for any noise sample, which shows that the latent space is continuous and interpretable.

We further demonstrate in Fig. 6 that our model can distinctly disentangle based on noise and C_L/C_D values by disentangling different properties of the airfoils. We sample two noise vectors and two C_L/C_D values and interpolate between the two samples, first by changing both noise and C_L/C_D, second by only changing the noise while keeping the C_L/C_D fixed and last by changing C_L/C_D while keeping the noise fixed, as shown in Fig. 6. From the first row of Fig. 6 we can observe that, changing both noise and C_L/C_D changes the size and the curve at the leading edge. In the second row, we can see that for a fixed C_L/C_D, the change in noise only changes the size of the airfoil and no change in any curves or edges. From the last row we can observe that by changing only the C_L/C_D value while keeping the noise fixed only changes the curvature at the leading edge but no change in airfoil's size. Thus, our technique achieves successful disentanglement based on geometry as well as the performance characteristics (C_L/C_D) of the airfoils.

Table 2. The relative error between the C_L/C_D values of the original and reconstructed airfoils, along with their high IoU scores. Shown are random samples from the test set. The average relative error on the whole test set is XY.

Test Airfoils								
Relativ e Error (%)	2.11	0.93	2.70	1.85	1.14	3.14	4.05	4.07
IoU		0.991	0.985	0.987	0.977	0.985	0.987	0.980	0.988

4.8 Precision of C_L/C_D Conditions

We investigate in Table 2 if the C_L/C_D values of the real airfoils match with their reconstructed counterparts, to confirm if the reconstructed airfoils adhere to the C_L/C_D values that they were conditioned on. The reconstructed airfoils are first transformed to the data format required by XFOIL, and using the simulations in XFOIL, we obtain their C_L/C_D values. However, XFOIL is extremely sensitive to the coordinates and simulations therefore, not all airfoils converge and C_L/C_D for them cannot be obtained. Table 2 shows some examples of the converged airfoils from the test set, the IoU scores between them and their reconstructed counterparts and the relative error of the C_L/C_D value of the reconstructed airfoils. The accuracy of the reconstruction is very high, as can be observed from the high IoU values. The relative error between the C_L/C_D of the test airfoils and of the reconstructed airfoils is also low. Thus, the conditional β-VAE model can enforce the C_L/C_D condition with high precision during the reconstruction of a design.

5 Conclusion

In this paper, we proposed a hybrid DGM-CAE based framework for automated and constraint-based parameterization of airfoil designs while ensuring their mechanical functionality under the C_L/C_D value constraint. We show that the conditional β-VAE model outperforms several other popular generative models and is best at generating realistic and diverse airfoils with sharp, smooth, and watertight boundaries while also adhering to the C_L/C_D constraint. It can also disentangle several physical properties of the data enabling interactive airfoil generation much faster than traditional parameterization techniques. Our framework also outperforms the previous state of the art in terms of quality and diversity of the generated designs. To the best of our knowledge, this is the first at attempt of generating airfoil designs conditionally based on their C_L/C_D values, thereby creating a new baseline for such a constraint-based parameterization of aerodynamic shapes. In the future, this approach can be extended to parameterize 3D airfoils, and depending on the availability of data, many more additional constraints can be enforced.

Acknowledgments. The second author of the paper was funded by the German Federal Ministry of Education and Research under the grant number 01IS20048. The responsibility for the content of this publication lies with the author. Furthermore, we acknowledge support by the Carl-Zeiss Foundation and the DFG awards BU 4042/2-1 and BU 4042/1-1.

References

1. Bhatnagar, S., Afshar, Y., Pan, S., Duraisamy, K., Kaushik, S.: Prediction of aerodynamic flow fields using convolutional neural networks. Comput. Mech. **64**, 525–545 (2019)
2. Cagan, J., Campbell, M.I., Finger, S., Tomiyama, T.: A framework for computational design synthesis: model and applications. J. Comput. Inf. Sci. Eng. **5**(3), 171–181 (2005)
3. Ceze, M., Hayashi, M., Volpe, E.: A study of the CST parameterization characteristics. In: 27th AIAA Applied Aerodynamics Conference (2009)
4. Chen, R.T.Q., Li, X., Grosse, R.B., Duvenaud, D.K.: Isolating sources of disentanglement in variational autoencoders. In: NIPS, vol. 31, pp. 2610–2620 (2018)
5. Chen, W., Ahmed, F.: Padgan: a generative adversarial network for performance augmented diverse designs. In: International Design Engineering Technical Conferences and Computers and Information in Engineering Conference, vol. 84003, p. V11AT11A010. American Society of Mechanical Engineers (2020)
6. Chen, W., Fuge, M.: Béziergan: automatic generation of smooth curves from interpretable low-dimensional parameters. arXiv preprint arXiv:1808.08871 (2018)
7. Chen, X., Duan, Y., Houthooft, R., Schulman, J., Sutskever, I., Abbeel, P.: Infogan: interpretable representation learning by information maximizing generative adversarial nets. In: Advances in Neural Information Processing Systems, vol. 29 (2016)
8. Deng, J., Dong, W., Socher, R., Li, L.J., Li, K., Fei-Fei, L.: ImageNet: a large-scale hierarchical image database. In: 2009 IEEE Conference on Computer Vision and Pattern Recognition, pp. 248–255 (2009)
9. Derksen, R.W., Tim, R.: Bezier-parsec: An optimized aerofoil parameterization for design. Adv. Eng. Softw. **41**(7–8), 923–930 (2010)
10. Drela, M.: XFOIL: an analysis and design system for low reynolds number airfoils. In: Mueller, T.J., (eds.) Low Reynolds Number Aerodynamics. Lecture Notes in Engineering, vol. 54, pp. 1–12. Springer, Berlin (1989). https://doi.org/10.1007/978-3-642-84010-4_1
11. Duchi, J., Hazan, E., Singer, Y.: Adaptive subgradient methods for online learning and stochastic optimization. J. Mach. Learn. Res. **12**(61), 2121–2159 (2011)
12. Goodfellow, I., et al.: Generative adversarial networks. Commun. ACM **63**(11), 139–144 (2020)
13. Grey, Z.J., Constantine, P.G.: Active subspaces of airfoil shape parameterizations. AIAA J. **56**(5), 2003–2017 (2018)
14. Heusel, M., Ramsauer, H., Unterthiner, T., Nessler, B., Hochreiter, S.: Gans trained by a two time-scale update rule converge to a local nash equilibrium. In: Guyon, I., (eds.) Advances in Neural Information Processing Systems, vol. 30. Curran Associates, Inc. (2017)
15. Higgins, I., et al.: beta-VAE: learning basic visual concepts with a constrained variational framework. In: International Conference on Learning Representations (2017)
16. Kim, H., Mnih, A.: Disentangling by factorising. In: International Conference on Machine Learning, pp. 2649–2658. PMLR (2018)
17. Kim, H., Mnih, A.: Disentangling by factorising. In: International Conference on Machine Learning, pp. 2649–2658. PMLR (2018)
18. Kingma, D.P., Ba, J.: Adam: a method for stochastic optimization. arXiv preprint arXiv:1412.6980 (2014)

19. Kingma, D.P., Welling, M.: Auto-encoding variational bayes. arXiv preprint arXiv:1312.6114 (2013)
20. Kynkäänniemi, T., Karras, T., Laine, S., Lehtinen, J., Aila, T.: Improved precision and recall metric for assessing generative models. In: Advances in Neural Information Processing Systems, vol. 32 (2019)
21. Lee, W., Kim, D., Hong, S., Lee, H.: High-fidelity synthesis with disentangled representation. In: Vedaldi, A., Bischof, H., Brox, T., Frahm, J.M. (eds.) Computer Vision - ECCV 2020, pp. 157–174. Springer International Publishing, Cham (2020)
22. Lepine, J., Guibault, F., Trepanier, J.Y., Pepin, F.: Optimized nonuniform rational B-Spline geometrical representation for aerodynamic design of wings. AIAA J. **39**(11), 2033–2041 (2001)
23. Lindholm, E., et al.: NVIDIA Tesla: a unified graphics and computing architecture. IEEE Micro **28**(2), 39–55 (2008)
24. Mirza, M., Osindero, S.: Conditional generative adversarial nets. ArXiv abs/1411.1784 (2014)
25. Mukkamala, M.C., Hein, M.: Variants of RMSProp and adagrad with logarithmic regret bounds. In: International Conference on Machine Learning, pp. 2545–2553. PMLR (2017)
26. Naeem, M.F., Oh, S.J., Uh, Y., Choi, Y., Yoo, J.: Reliable fidelity and diversity metrics for generative models. In: ICML, pp. 7176–7185. PMLR (2020)
27. Paszke, A., et al.: Pytorch: an imperative style, high-performance deep learning library. In: Advances in Neural Information Processing Systems, vol. 32 (2019)
28. Radford, A., Metz, L., Chintala, S.: Unsupervised representation learning with deep convolutional generative adversarial networks. arXiv preprint arXiv:1511.06434 (2015)
29. Rezatofighi, H., Tsoi, N., Gwak, J., Sadeghian, A., Reid, I., Savarese, S.: Generalized intersection over union: a metric and a loss for bounding box regression. In: Proceedings of the IEEE/CVF Conference on Computer Vision and Pattern Recognition, pp. 658–666 (2019)
30. Salimans, T., Goodfellow, I., Zaremba, W., Cheung, V., Radford, A., Chen, X.: Improved techniques for training GANs. In: Advances in neural information processing systems, vol. 29 (2016)
31. Samareh, J.A.: Survey of shape parameterization techniques for high-fidelity multidisciplinary shape optimization. AIAA J. **39**(5), 877–884 (2001)
32. Schmidhuber, J.: Deep learning in neural networks: an overview. Neural Netw. **61**, 85–117 (2015). The official Journal of the International Neural Network Society
33. Selig, M.S.: UIUC airfoil data site. Urbana, Ill. : Department of Aeronautical and Astronautical Engineering University of Illinois at Urbana-Champaign (1996)
34. Sobieczky, H.: Parametric airfoils and wings. In: Fujii, K., Dulikravich, G.S., (eds.) Recent Development of Aerodynamic Design Methodologies. Notes on Numerical Fluid Mechanics (NNFM), vol. 65, pp. 71–87. Vieweg+Teubner Verlag (1999). https://doi.org/10.1007/978-3-322-89952-1_4
35. Sohn, K., et al.: Learning structured output representation using deep conditional generative models. In: NIPS, vol. 28. Curran Associates, Inc. (2015)
36. Sripawadkul, V., Padulo, M., Guenov, M.: A comparison of airfoil shape parameterization techniques for early design optimization. In: 13th AIAA/ISSMO Multidisciplinary Analysis Optimization Conference (2010)
37. Xu, K., Kim, V.G., Huang, Q., Mitra, N., Kalogerakis, E.: Data-driven shape analysis and processing. In: SIGGRAPH ASIA 2016 Courses. SA 2016, Association for Computing Machinery, New York (2016)

38. Yang, C., Huang, F.: An overview of simulation-based hydrodynamic design of ship hull forms. J. Hydrodyn. Ser. B **28**, 947–960 (2016)
39. Yasong, Q., Junqiang, B., Nan, L., Chen, W.: Global aerodynamic design optimization based on data dimensionality reduction. Chin. J. Aeronaut. **31**(4), 643–659 (2018)
40. Yonekura, K., Wada, K., Suzuki, K.: Generating various airfoil shapes with required lift coefficient using conditional variational autoencoders. arXiv preprint arXiv:2106.09901 (2021)
41. Zhu, F., Qin, N., Burnaev, E., Bernstein, A., Chernova, S.: Comparison of three geometric parameterization methods and their effect on aerodynamic optimization. In: Eurogen, pp. 758–772 (2011)

Healthcare and Bioinformatics

Deep Learning for Real-Time Neural Decoding of Grasp

Paolo Viviani[1](✉) ⓘ, Ilaria Gesmundo[2], Elios Ghinato[2],
Andres Agudelo-Toro[3] ⓘ, Chiara Vercellino[1,2] ⓘ, Giacomo Vitali[1,2] ⓘ,
Letizia Bergamasco[1,2] ⓘ, Alberto Scionti[1] ⓘ, Marco Ghislieri[2] ⓘ,
Valentina Agostini[2] ⓘ, Olivier Terzo[1] ⓘ, and Hansjörg Scherberger[3] ⓘ

[1] LINKS Foundation, Torino, Italy
{paolo.viviani,chiara.vercellino,giacomo.vitali,
letizia.bergamasco,alberto.scionti,
olivier.terzo}@linksfoundation.com
[2] Polytechnic of Torino, Torino, Italy
{marco.ghislieri,valentina.agostini}@polito.it
[3] DPZ, Deutsches Primatenzentrum GmbH, Göttingen, Germany
{aagudelo-toro,HScherberger}@dpz.eu

Abstract. Neural decoding involves correlating signals acquired from the brain to variables in the physical world like limb movement or robot control in Brain Machine Interfaces. In this context, this work starts from a specific pre-existing dataset of neural recordings from monkey motor cortex and presents a Deep Learning-based approach to the decoding of neural signals for grasp type classification. Specifically, we propose here an approach that exploits LSTM networks to classify time series containing neural data (i.e., spike trains) into classes representing the object being grasped.

The main goal of the presented approach is to improve over state-of-the-art decoding accuracy without relying on any prior neuroscience knowledge, and leveraging only the capability of deep learning models to extract correlations from data. The paper presents the results achieved for the considered dataset and compares them with previous works on the same dataset, showing a significant improvement in classification accuracy, even if considering simulated real-time decoding.

Keywords: Machine Learning · neural decoding · neural networks · brain machine interface

1 Introduction

Neural decoding refers to the task of correlating signals recorded from the brain to variables in the outside world such as limb movement. This task is relevant for neuroscientists trying to understand the information contained in neural signal to improve our models of the brain, as well as for researchers developing Brain-Machine Interfaces (BMIs) to control physical and virtual objects (e.g., robotic prostheses, mouse cursors) [11]. While the role of Machine Learning (ML) in

G. De Francisci Morales et al. (Eds.): ECML PKDD 2023, LNAI 14174, pp. 379–393, 2023.
https://doi.org/10.1007/978-3-031-43427-3_23

neural decoding is known [7,8], improvements in this field can positively affect the quality of life of patients relying on BMIs to control their prosthesis (i.e., by providing a more natural control or by reducing the need of frequent re-training).

This work was developed in the context of the B-Cratos EU project, which deals with the real-time translation of intra-cranial brain signals, with the final goal of controlling a robotic prosthesis. In particular, this paper reports the results obtained in the simulated real-time decoding of the grasp type, based on a specific dataset previously recorded from the motor cortex of two Non-Human Primates (NHP) [12], investigated as a propaedeutic activity to the final prosthesis controller model deployment based on experimental data acquisition carried out within the project's scope. The main contributions proposed are:

- an LSTM model to detect the grasping phase from time series of neural data;
- an LSTM model to classify the object being grasped by the monkey that provides higher accuracy than the current state of the art for the same dataset.

Both models work on data provided as they would be in a real-time application: the grasping phase detection is representative of the capability to identify the beginning and the end of a grasp movement, while the classification of the object is used as a proxy for the grip type. Importantly, in the presented approach, the authors only focused on improving the predictive performance for practical applications without introducing any prior neuroscience knowledge in the model, and without the intent to provide any deeper understanding of neural activity and its correlation to the outside world.

The paper is structured as follows: Sect. 2 discusses the most relevant prior works that define the state of the art for neural decoding in general and this specific task in particular. Section 3 and 4 describe in detail the dataset used for this work and the ML approach for detecting movement and classifying the grasp type. Section 5 reports and discusses the results obtained with the proposed approach, along with some considerations about the real-life application of these results. Finally, Sect. 6 provides an overview about the relevance of these results and introduces ongoing research in the same direction.

2 Related Work

Glaser et al. [7] and Livezey et al. [8] recently provided comprehensive reviews of the state of the art for ML and Deep Learning (DL) for neural decoding, observing how most of the applications still rely on very simple models (i.e., linear regression, Kalman filters) [2,11]. These reviews also highlighted several works that have shown how LSTM can be effective to model the time evolution of neural signals [1,14]. Another interesting aspect is the different purposes that models for neural decoding can serve: if the goal is to understand the information contained in neural activity from a neuroscientist point of view, simple, explainable models are to be preferred over black-box machine learning algorithms, which are conversely more suited to provide strong predictive performance for BCI application. It should also be considered that advancements in explainable ML/DL may change this scenario.

With respect to the decoding performance of ML models, since the purpose of this work is strictly related to the predictive performance on a specifc dataset, comparing this approach to prior works that dealt with completely different datasets is not trivial, nor particularly interesting for this work, as the task performed by the NHP, the recording conditions, and the pre-processing applied by each researcher can be completely different. As a consequence, the main reference benchmark for this work is a paper from Schaffelhofer et al. [12], which first tried to apply neural grasp decoding to this specific dataset. The approach was based on a naive Bayesian model used to classify the type of object being grasped by the NHP by looking at an entire region of interest in the neural recording (i.e., the phase when the NHP was holding the object). The accuracy obtained by Schaffelhofer et al. was of 62%, on 50 classes (i.e., objects), evaluated using a leave-one-out cross validation technique. A recent thesis from F. Fabiani [5] discussed the results obtained by applying a sliding window to a longer region of the recordings, to simulate real-time operation. An LSTM network with a convolutional layer on top was used in this case, and the decoding results are reported not on the individual 50 objects, but grouping them by their shape (6 groups, variable size within groups) and size (6 groups variable shape within group): while the shape of the object was successfully classified with an accuracy of 92% over 6 classes, the size decoding accuracy was around 25% over 6 classes. Section 5 will discuss how the presented approach differs from the previous works and how the results compare.

3 Dataset Structure

3.1 Acquisition and Original Pre-processing

The dataset used for this work was acquired by researchers at Deutsches Primatenzentrum[1] (DPZ) and involved recording neural signals from electrode arrays implanted in the AIP, F5, M1 regions of the brain cortex of two purpose-bred macaque monkeys (*Macaca mulatta*), animal M and Z. The specific task performed by the NHPs is described in Fig. 1 and involved grasping a set of objects at specific times, while recording the signal from 192 electrodes in the motor cortex. The original recording sampled at 24 kHz has been processed through a band pass filter (0.3–7 kHz) [9], then a *spike sorting* algorithm has been applied offline to each recording session independently [12]. Spike sorting algorithms recognise neurons activation patterns in the raw signal and can also identify multiple patterns to isolate multiple neurons from the same physical channel. The output of the spike sorting algorithm is defined as a multi-channel *spike train*. A binary time series contains the information about activation time of each neuron (as identified by the spike sorting) during the experiment. For each animal involved in the experiment, three recording sessions acquired in during different days were made available, each one with a different number of spike

---

[1] https://www.dpz.eu/en/home.html.

channels (i.e., neurons) recorded due to the different outcome of the spike sorting algorithm for each session. The details about the datasets used are provided in Sect. 3.2.

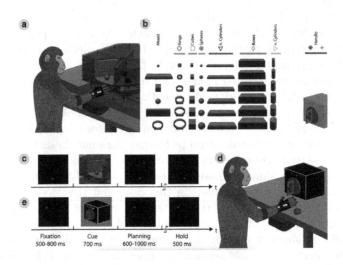

Fig. 1. Experimental set up, adapted from [12]. a) Two macaque monkeys were trained to grasp objects presented on computer-controlled turntable. b) The grasping objects are grouped in 50 classes. c) Objects were presented in pseudorandom order and the grasping taskfollowed pre-defined steps: Fixation; Cue; Planning; Movement and Hold. d,e) Adding two supplementary LEDs the monkey is prompted to perform a precision (yellow led) or a power (green led) grip on a special handle. (Color figure online)

The process described in this section was performed out of the scope of the present work: only the final spike trains were available to the authors and are used here.

3.2   Structure

The datasets corresponding to the six recording sessions were provided as Neo [6] objects, with multi-channel spike trains segmented in *trials*, each one corresponding to an instance of the grasp/release process described in Fig. 1. Figure 2 represents the recording of the spike trains for a single trial from animal Z, plotting both the spike trains (top) and the same data discretised in 40 ms time bins (bottom), where each bin contains the number of spikes counted in that time interval for that channel. As also shown in Fig. 2, timestamps for each experiment phase, corresponding to subsequent stages of the monkey task (e.g., visual cue, planning, grasping, etc.) are reported in the data, as well as the information about the object being grasped (*object id*). It should be noted that not all the phases are reported in Fig. 1 and that time intervals between phases can change between trials due to subject behaviour.

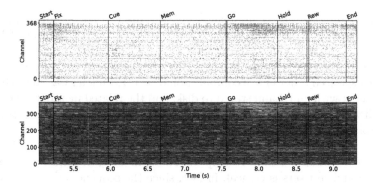

Fig. 2. Example of recording for an experimental trial: the top plot reports the firing times for individual spikes for each channel, while the bottom plot reports the intensity map after a 40 ms time discretisation. The color of each bin is correlated to the number of spikes counted in that time interval and in that channel (increasing from purple to yellow). Time on x axis is reported from the beginning of the recording session. (Color figure online)

Table 1. Number of channels and number of trials for each experimental recording session.

NHP identifier	Dataset identifier	# Channels	# Trials
M	MRec40	552	745
	MRec41	568	757
	MRec42	554	653
Z	ZRec32	391	687
	ZRec35	388	724
	ZRec50	369	610

Table 1 reports the number of channels identified by the spike sorting for each recording session, along with the dataset identifier and the number of trials for that session. It should be also noted that the number of times each object appears in the dataset is not constant among objects and recording sessions, resulting in a class imbalance when training a classifier based on grasped objects.

4   Decoding Approach

4.1   Pre-processing

The proposed approach is aimed at simulating on-line decoding of grasped object (used as a proxy for the grasp type), hence the data should be prepared to fit this purpose. The pre-processing steps are split as follows, to separate the different steps and support the development of models without the need of re-processing the whole dataset every time, as intermediate data structures are always stored. These steps are performed separately for each recording session of each animal.

1) Time Discretisation. The spike trains are discretised in bins of 40 ms of length. Also shorter time binning has been evaluated to understand if longer, more detailed sequences could benefit the classification performance, but due the lack of evidence of a positive impact, shorter sequences and larger time bins have been selected to lower the computational cost. Each trial was converted to a dense matrix with an ID and stored to disk, and the related metadata was stored in a dedicated data structure (progressive bin number associated to experiment phases; object id; data matrix id).

2) Training, Validation and Test Split. The split of each dataset in training, validation and test sets is critical: in fact, since the sequences used to train the model are partially overlapping, splitting data at sequence level would lead to an artificially high accuracy as highly overlapped sequences can appear in all sets. To avoid this effect and provide realistic validation of the approach, the split was performed at the entire trial level (i.e., entire trials were assigned to either train, validation or test set), setting apart 80% of the trials for training, 16% for validation, and 20% for testing. Moreover, class-based stratification[2] was performed to ensure sufficient representation of all classes in all the datasets.

In this phase, under-represented classes (i.e., objects appearing in less than 3 trials for each recording session) were removed from the dataset to ensure the presence of at least one representative of the class in each dataset partition. Moreover, object of identical shape and size are present in multiple groups (c.f. columns of Fig. 1b) and were mapped to the same class.

3) Sequence Creation. After splitting the trials in the three datasets, a *sliding window* was applied to each trial. The sub-sequences extracted by the sliding window represent the data a real-time decoder would see at any given moment, and were tagged either with a label indicating that the monkey was in rest position, or with the grasped object id if the last bin of the sequence was falling in the *region of interest* that has been defined as the *hold* phase of the experiment. This choice was made to be coherent with the approach from Schaffelhofer et al.

The extraction of sequences is depicted in Fig. 3. From the sub-sequences, two different datasets are created that will be used for different learning tasks:

- an *grasping phase* dataset, that contains all the sequences labelled as *grasp* (if they fall in the region of interest) and *rest* (elsewhere). Class imbalance is roughly 10 to 1 for rest vs. grasp;
- a *classification* dataset, containing only the sequences with the last bin falling in the region of interest, labelled with the id of the grasped object.

---

[2] https://scikit-learn.org/stable/modules/cross_validation.html#stratification.

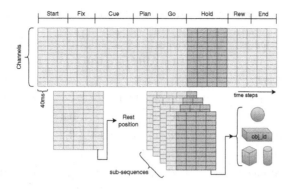

Fig. 3. Illustration of the sequence creation process. Each discretised trial is scanned with a sliding window, advancing one time step at a time and extracting fixed-length sequences (2D arrays of dimension *channels* × *length*). Each sequence is stored along with a label that can be *rest*, if the last bin falls outside of the *hold* phase, or the object id if it falls within.

These two datasets (for each recording session) are then passed on to the model building step, discussed in the next section.

4.2   Decoding Model

Among the two tasks identified, the classification one has proven to be significantly more challenging than the grasping phase one. All the effort to identify a suitable architecture was then focused on the classification task, and the best performing model was re-used for the grasping phase detection task.

Architecture. Based on previous literature, it has been decided to start the search for a suitable architecture from LSTM networks. Additional experiments were performed within the scope of this work with Bidirectional LSTM networks [3,13], that demonstrated significantly better performance than simple LSTM networks.

These experiments included a preliminary architecture and hyperparameter search that led to identify the following subset of hyperparameters, which have been used to run a final optimisation campaign for each dataset with KerasTuner [10] bayesian optimiser; the search space was defined as in Table 2. An example of model architecture is shown in Fig. 4.

Table 2. Final hyperparameter search space. One model identified for each animal.

Hyperparameter	Values	Selected	
	(L1 = 0.01, L2 = 0.01)	M	Z
LSTM layers	{ 1, 2, 3, 4 }	2	1
Hidden units	{ 16, 32, 40, 64 }	40	40
Dropout	{ 0, 0.2, 0.4, 0.6, 0.7, 0.8 }	0.8	0.7
Kernel regularisation	{ None, L1, L2, L1 + L2 }	L2	L2
Recurrent regularization	{ None, L1, L2, L1 + L2 }	L2	L1+L2
Initial learning rate	{ 10^{-3}, $2 \cdot 10^{-4}$, 10^{-4} }	10^{-3}	10^{-3}

Fig. 4. Final architecture for classification network (animal M). Activation functions for the LSTM layers are tanh and sigmoid (recurrent activation). Output layer activation is softmax. Loss function is categorical crossentropy.

Training. The model was implemented with Keras [4], to facilitate its future deployment with Tensrflow lite on a dedicated embedded board[3]. Training used a mini-batch size of 256 and typically converged within 100 epochs, which are almost never reached due to an early stopping policy based on the evolution of validation accuracy. A learning rate (LR) scaling policy was implemented to halve the LR when loss is plateauing for more than 10 epochs.

5   Results and Discussion

5.1   Grasping Phase Detection

This is a binary classification task with a significant class imbalance towards the *rest* class. The LSTM model reaches an accuracy of at least 98% for all datasets, the F1 score is always greater than 0.95. Table 3 presents both the confusion matrix for one dataset (MRec40) and the accuracy figures for all datasets: if considering this model in the context of a finite-state prosthesics control scenario, unwanted movements (rest classified as grasp) would amount to 1% of the time steps considered, while unresponsiveness (grasp classified as rest) is around the 0.1% of time steps. The relevance of these results for a real-life prosthesics control is discussed in Sect. 6.

---

[3] https://coral.ai/docs/dev-board-mini/datasheet/.

Table 3. Grasping phase detection results.

(a) Confusion matrix for grasping phase detection (MRec40).

	Predicted	
True	rest	grasp
rest	12824	173
grasp	25	1347

Grasping phase detection accuracy metrics.

Dataset id	Accuracy	F1 score
MRec40	99%	0.96
MRec41	99%	0.96
MRec42	99%	0.97
ZRec32	99%	0.96
ZRec35	98%	0.96
ZRec50	98%	0.95

5.2 Grasped Object Classification

The results for the classification of the grasped object represent the major contribution of this work and Fig. 5 and 6 report the confusion matrices and accuracy figures for each recording session available to the authors. To make a sensible comparison with prior art, we should carefully consider the differences between the presented approach and the previous works mentioned in Sect. 2.

In the original 2015 paper [12], Schaffelhofer et al. report an average accuracy for the *hold* phase of 62% over a total of 10 recording sessions (against the six available for this work). This was obtained with an off-line naive bayesian classifier applied to the whole *hold* phase and validated with a leave-one-out (LOO) approach, hence the dataset fraction used for training was significantly higher than what is used in this work. On the other hand, 50 classes were considered while in this case under-represented classes (i.e., less than 3 samples) were removed, and identical objects with different IDs were collapsed onto the same class. In general it is possible to say that the presented approach outperforms the naive bayes classifier (significantly for animal M, and slightly for animal Z) in a harder set-up (sliding window vs. fixed region; smaller training partition). Additionally, as classes are ordered as the objects in Fig. 1, neighboring classes represent the same object with a slightly different size, hence a very similar grip type; in this sense it has been computed also the *relaxed accuracy*, counting 1-class-away misclassification as correct. Relaxed accuracy results are also reported in Table 4 and Fig. 5, 6, showing a better performance than previous works.

With respect to the results reported by Fabiani [5] for the online decoding, the approach is very similar (i.e., sliding window), although a larger region of interest was considered, including also the *go* phase. In this case results are not reported by individual objects, but by shapes and sizes (respectively rows and columns in Fig. 1b): to compare the accuracy with the numbers presented in this paper, shape and size accuracy figures are multiplied. The results obtained here are even outperforming the offline decoding algorithm also proposed by Fabiani, which considers a fixed, larger window of each trial for the classification. The comparison of Table 4 shows that also in this case, the presented LSTM model outperforms significantly the previous approach, which can be surprising given that LSTM models are used in both cases; it is the author's opinion that the adoption of Bidirectional LSTM layers provide the most significant improvement in the decoding performance, along with careful usage of regularisation strategies (i.e., a high dropout fraction proved to be particularly effective).

Table 4. Comparison of results with previous works. Metrics are averaged over the available recording session for the present work (standard deviation is referred to multiple recording sessions, not to multiple training shots) and for Schaffelhofer et al. [12]. The work by F. Fabiani only reports results grouped by object type and object size, the individual object accuracy is calculated as the product between the two accuracies [5]. Relaxed accuracy also considers as correctly classified objects belonging to the first neighboring classes.

Animal	Metric	Present work	Schaffelhofer, 2015	Fabiani, 2021
M	Accuracy	$69.7 \pm 4\%$	$62.9 \pm 3.6\%$	n/a
Z	Accuracy	$62.3 \pm 1.2\%$	$61.4 \pm 4.1\%$	n/a
Global	Accuracy	$65.9 \pm 4.9\%$	62%	22%
	Relaxed accuracy	$94.4 \pm 3.1\%$	86.5%	59%

5.3   Real-Life Usage and Current Deployment

Reduced Training Set. When testing real-time neural decoders in the context of real NHP experiments, one of the requirements is the capability to quickly start decoding signals and shortnening the training data acquisition as much as possible. Moreover, neural signal evolves through time (i.e., due to mechanical movement of the implant, inflammatory processes, brain plasticity, etc.), making re-training models daily mostly unavoidable.

Here are reported the results of an investigation aimed at understanding how the size of the training set w.r.t. the entire dataset is affecting the accuracy of the trained model. This is particularly relevant as gathering samples is a time consuming operation in both neuroscience research with non-human primates and BMI clinical practice with patients. In this sense, the model capability to retain a good accuracy is critical to ensure its usability in the real world. Table 5 reports the accuracy numbers for an increasing test set partition (and an equally decreasing training+validation set). Qualitatively the accuracy remains quite close to the previous state of the art up to a 30% training partition; moreover, the relaxed accuracy is also better than the state of the art down to 30% of training data.

Computational Cost. The training time for all the grasp classification cases is lower than one minute on an Nvidia V100, suitable for on-the-fly re-training when new data becomes available during experiments. The larger number of

Table 5. Accuracy and relaxed accuracy for a progressively reduced training set.

Training + validation set	Accuracy	Relaxed accuracy
80%	74.1%	98.3%
70%	70.1%	97.1%
60%	69%	93.7%
50%	62.8%	94%
40%	63.8%	92.8%
30%*	59.2%	87.5%
20%**	51%	81%

*validation is 30% of training set to ensure at least one representative per class
**validation is 40% of training set

sequences used to train the grasping phase detection model makes each epoch longer, but the number of epochs required to reach a satisfactory accuracy is smaller and contributes to keep the training time at around one minute.

Current Deployment of the Model. This work represents a preparatory step toward an effective model for real-time continuous control of a prosthesis: while this is a classification task, the data recorded from the brain is fully representative of the kind of data that will be acquired within the scope of the project during 2023, and the network architecture that has been identified will be the starting point for the deployment of a real-time decoder on a dedicated device. Since the final model will predict a limited number of real-valued degrees of freedom, it has been built a synthetic dataset reproducing a trajectory of a single degree of freedom based on the recordings used in this work and the same model presented in Fig. 4 has been trained to predict this real value with good accuracy. It is in fact currently being used to control the opening and closing of a robotic hand for the first integration tests.

Reproducibility Note. The code used to achieve the presented results is available in a public repository[4]. Instructions to access a subset of the data (one recording session) has been made available to reviewers as additional material through the submission portal, and such dataset can be tested directly with the code just mentioned. The entire dataset has been provided by DPZ out of courtesy as part of an ongoing collaboration in the B-Cratos project, but the ownership remains to the original researchers and its complete publication is beyond the scope of this work.

---

[4] https://github.com/LINKS-Foundation-CPE/Neural-decoding-paper-2023.

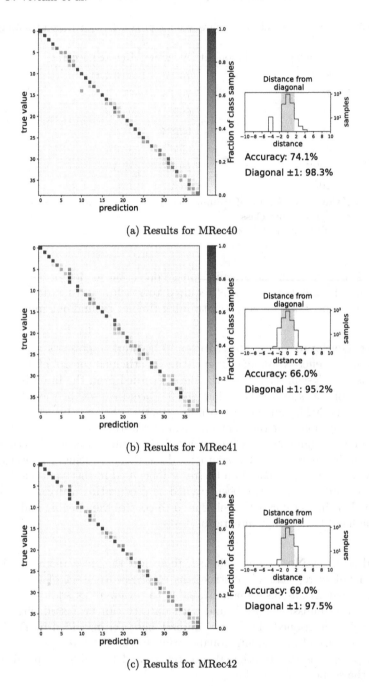

(a) Results for MRec40

(b) Results for MRec41

(c) Results for MRec42

Fig. 5. Confusion matrices and accuracy results for grasped object classification for animal M. The models used are the best performing on the validation set among 10 training runs. It can be noted how most of the misclassified samples lie very close to the diagonal.

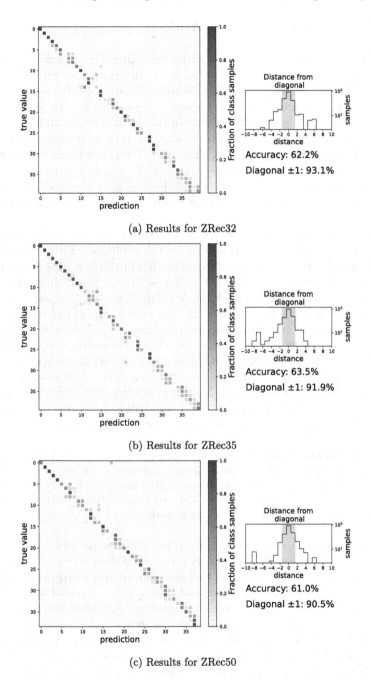

(a) Results for ZRec32

(b) Results for ZRec35

(c) Results for ZRec50

Fig. 6. Confusion matrices and accuracy results for grasped object classification for animal Z. The models used are the best performing on the validation set among 10 training runs. It can be noted how most of the misclassified samples lie very close to the diagonal.

6   Conclusion and Future Work

The experimental results presented in the previous section demonstrated the capability of bidirectional LSTM networks to match and outperform state-of-the-art methodologies on known data. While this dataset, being used for a categorical classification task, is not immediately relevant for the continuous control of a robotic prosthesis, it validates the suitability of LSTM models for neural decoding of hand grasp actions. In particular, the very good results obtained for the relaxed accuracy are more representative of the performance to be expected when controlling a limited number of degrees of freedom or less nuanced categories (i.e., 5/6 grasp types, opening and closing). It is also worth to highlight how these results were obtained without involving any prior neuroscience knowledge.

With respect to the next steps, the main research activity ongoing is directed towards making LSTM models robust to the evolution of the neural signal through time. In this case this is reflected by the capability to retain information learned during, for instance, the MRec40 session and re-use that information, in the form of a pre-trained model, for decoding MRec41. The goal is to reduce even more the need for time consuming data acquisition and re-training of the models, hence, in a long term perspective, lowering the daily effort for BMI patients and clinicians. In this specific case, the spike sorting applied separately for each session is not helping, as it changes the number of channels and mixes them up preventing the straightforward re-use of a model. In this sense, an effort of applying this model to datasets from literature that are not spike-sorted per session is ongoing. Relying on public datasets will also provide an opportunity to validate this approach against a much wider prior literature.

Acknowledgment. This work was supported by the European Union Horizon 2020 research and innovation program under Grant Agreement No. 965044 and by CINECA, through the Italian SuperComputing Resource Allocation - ISCRA-C grant. We thank Stefan Schaffelhofer for data collection and Federico Fabiani for sharing the useful experience gained during his Master's Thesis work.

Ethics Statement. A comprehensive discussion of the ethical aspect of BMIs is out of the scope of this paper: the B-Cratos project has a dedicated ethics advisory board and provides an ethics report to the European Commission yearly. With respect to animal experimentation, the data discussed here has been acquired long before the start of this work and they were subject to regulations and ethics assessment.

On the other hand, ethics topics are particularly relevant when dealing with ML algorithms for BMI use: in this work, for instance, different hyperparameters configurations were needed by animal Z (female) and animal M (male). For a future clinical use, assuming that a single model architecture would fit all users may introduce unwanted biases and negatively affect the user experience of patients.

Finally, several privacy and security aspects have been discussed in relation to this application: from anonymised data storage that can prevent the association between patients brain recordings and their identity, up to the possibility of adversarial actors affecting the prosthesis movement by exploiting weaknesses specifically related to the ML model (i.e., by injecting malicious training data) and the potential mitigation actions. These discussions are also reported in the ethics deliverable submitted to the EC and not yet publicly accessible.

References

1. Ahmadi, N., Constandinou, T.G., Bouganis, C.S.: Decoding hand kinematics from local field potentials using long short-term memory (LSTM) network. In: 2019 9th International IEEE/EMBS Conference on Neural Engineering (NER), pp. 415–419. IEEE, San Francisco (2019). https://doi.org/10.1109/NER.2019.8717045
2. Brandman, D.M., et al.: Rapid calibration of an intracortical brain-computer interface for people with tetraplegia. J. Neural Eng. **15**(2), 026007 (2018). https://doi.org/10.1088/1741-2552/aa9ee7
3. Chiu, J.P., Nichols, E.: Named entity recognition with bidirectional LSTM-CNNs. Trans. Assoc. Comput. Linguist. **4**, 357–370 (2016). https://doi.org/10.1162/tacl_a_00104
4. Chollet, F., et al.: Keras (2015). https://keras.io
5. Fabiani, F.: Brain-Computer Interface for Bionic Prosthetic Arm Actuation. Master's thesis, Politecnico di Torino, Torino, Italy (2021)
6. Garcia, S., et al.: Neo: an object model for handling electrophysiology data in multiple formats. Front. Neuroinf. **8**, 10 (2014). https://doi.org/10.3389/fninf.2014.00010
7. Glaser, J.I., Benjamin, A.S., Chowdhury, R.H., Perich, M.G., Miller, L.E., Kording, K.P.: Machine Learning for Neural Decoding. Eneuro **7**(4) (2020). https://doi.org/10.1523/ENEURO.0506-19.2020
8. Livezey, J.A., Glaser, J.I.: Deep learning approaches for neural decoding across architectures and recording modalities. Brief. Bioinf. **22**(2), 1577–1591 (2021). https://doi.org/10.1093/bib/bbaa355
9. Menz, V.K., Schaffelhofer, S., Scherberger, H.: Representation of continuous hand and arm movements in macaque areas M1, F5, and AIP: a comparative decoding study. J. Neural Eng. **12**(5), 056016 (2015). https://doi.org/10.1088/1741-2560/12/5/056016
10. O'Malley, T., et al.: Keras Tuner (2019). https://github.com/keras-team/keras-tuner
11. Pandarinath, C., Bensmaia, S.J.: The science and engineering behind sensitized brain-controlled bionic hands. Physiol. Rev. **102**, 551–604 (2021). https://doi.org/10.1152/physrev.00034.2020
12. Schaffelhofer, S., Agudelo-Toro, A., Scherberger, H.: Decoding a wide range of hand configurations from macaque motor, premotor, and parietal cortices. J. Neurosci. **35**(3), 1068–1081 (2015). https://doi.org/10.1523/JNEUROSCI.3594-14.2015
13. Schuster, M., Paliwal, K.: Bidirectional recurrent neural networks. IEEE Trans. Signal Process. **45**(11), 2673–2681 (1997). https://doi.org/10.1109/78.650093
14. Yoo, S.H., Woo, S.W., Amad, Z.: Classification of three categories from prefrontal cortex using LSTM networks: fNIRS study. In: 2018 18th International Conference on Control, Automation and Systems (ICCAS), pp. 1141–1146 (2018)

MCTN: A Multi-Channel Temporal Network for Wearable Fall Prediction

Jiawei Liu[1], Xiaohu Li[1], Guorui Liao[1], Shu Wang[2], and Li Liu[1(✉)]

[1] School of Big Data and Software Engineering,
Chongqing University, Chongqing 401331, China
{liujoy,xhlee,dcsliuli}@cqu.edu.cn, guoruiliao@stu.cqu.edu.cn
[2] School of Materials and Energy, Southwest University, Chongqing 400715, China
shuwang@swu.edu.cn

Abstract. A key challenge in wearable sensor-based fall prediction is the fact that a fall event can often be performed in several different ways, with each consisting of its own configuration of poses and their spatio-temporal dependencies. Furthermore, to enable fall prevention of a person from imminent falls, precise predictions need to be achieved as far in advance as possible. This leads us to define a multi-channel temporal network, which explicitly characterizes the spatio-temporal relationships within a sensor channel as well as the interrelationships among channels by a combination representation of positional embedding and channel embedding to manage these unique fine-grained configurations among channels of a particular fall event. In addition, a transformer encoder is devised to exchange both inner-channel and inter-channel information in the encoder structure, and as a result, all local spatio-temporal dependencies are globally consistent. Empirical evaluations on two benchmark datasets and one in-house dataset suggest our model significantly outperforms the state-of-the-art methods. Our code is available at: https://github.com/passenger-820/MCTN.

Keywords: Fall prediction · Wearable data · Multi-channel · Spatio-temporal dependency

1 Introduction

Fall prediction is an important research issue, given its role in facilitating the identification and protection of people at increased risk of fall injuries at an early stage by leveraging fall prevention devices such as airbags and walking sticks. As shown in Fig. 1, falls can be divided into four stages: *pre-fall, falling, impact* and *post-fall*. Many efforts have been devoted to the study of fall detection systems (FDS) that identifies the fact of falling during the period from *pre-fall* to *post-fall* (gray lines in Fig. 1). Real-time performance is not a priority for FDS, which only requires accurate identification of a fall event within seconds to tens of seconds after the subject has fallen. However, different from fall detection, fall prediction systems (FPS) require high real-time performance, usually hundreds

G. De Francisci Morales et al. (Eds.): ECML PKDD 2023, LNAI 14174, pp. 394–409, 2023.
https://doi.org/10.1007/978-3-031-43427-3_24

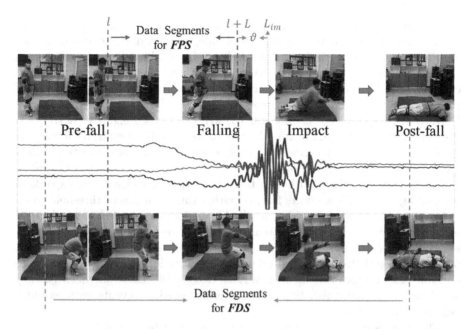

Fig. 1. The four stages of falls. For instance, two types of fall events are collected by ourselves. (Top) forward fall; (Bottom) crouch-up backward fall and their corresponding acceleration waveforms (Middle). $[l, l + L]$ indicates the data segment for fall predication, ϑ indicates the lead time before *impact* and L_{im} is the start point of *impact* stage.

of milliseconds before *impact*, as the systems aim to reserve activation time for fall prevention devices as much as possible. In addition, FPS uses fewer data segments (red lines in Fig. 1), which poses greater challenges for accurately predicting different falls and daily activities.

Computer vision-based approaches have been at the forefront of this field, and are becoming mature to predict falls from visual acquisition equipments like RGB and RGB-D cameras. Compared with the frames in the video, wearable-based approaches have the advantages of smaller data size, leading to less computational costs, and are robust to complex phenomena such as variable lighting effects and occlusions. Specifically, the inertial measurement unit (IMU) is capable of collecting human posture information by recording data such as acceleration and angular velocity attached at body position (e.g., waist) for fall prediction. Currently wearable-based methods fall into three major categories, threshold-based, conventional machine learning (ML) and deep learning (DL) models.

Relation to Prior Works: Intuitively, the threshold-based algorithms compare the raw data or extracted features with a predetermined threshold [4,6]. When the output value surpasses the threshold, a probable fall is predicted.

For example, Jung *et al.* [6] employed roll, pitch, and sum magnitude vector derived from the accelerometer and gyroscope, and set different thresholds for each feature separately. It is concluded that a fall is about to occur when each of these features exceeds their corresponding thresholds. On the other hand, conventional ML models become increasingly popular to predict falls because of their capability of managing features. For instance, Decision Tree (DT), Naïve Bayes (NB), Support Vector Machine (SVM), k-Nearest Neighbor (KNN), and Random Forest (RF) [5,13] are adopted to forecast fall events by leveraging features extracted from various types of sensors like pressure-sensitive insoles and accelerometers attached on multiple body positions including head, pelvis, and right and left calves. Although these two types of methods are capable of responding to the falling events fast, yet either these features or thresholds need to be manually encoded or be handcrafted from domain knowledge, which could be rather difficult to scale up and is almost impossible for many practical scenarios where those features are intricate among multiple sensors. Most importantly, fall postures and their temporal relations are often inherently complex due to multiple sensor types attached on various body positions. Consequently, they are difficult to distinguish between temporally sensitive events such as quick falls and gradual falls.

The most popular paradigm in recent years might be that of the DL models, which include techniques such as Convolutional Neural Network (CNN), Recurrent Neural Network (RNN) and Long Short-Term Memory (LSTM). Due to the capacity of generating high-level semantic features in the latent space, it is not surprising that these neural network-based models generally surpass their conventional counterparts that only consider utilizing channel-level information by a large margin. However, they have difficulties in capturing rich fine-grained (inter-channel) spatial relationships among channels. In fact, these models mostly focus on coarse-grained (channel-level or pose-level) spatio-temporal information (e.g. taking all the channels as a whole in a pose and describing their relations between two adjacent frames on pose level), ignoring internal channel dependency within a single frame and external channel relations among different frames. As a result, only spatio-temporal dependencies associated with entire fall event can be sufficiently captured. Hence, these models cannot be directly transferred to predict fall events in relatively complex scenarios [2,9–11,15]. As the number of sensor channels attached on body grows, these existing models are rather limited in identifying multi-channel features with meaningful spatio-temporal relationships in fall prediction.

To address the above issues in fall prediction, we present a multi-channel temporal network (named MCTN) to explicitly model the channel context of spatio-temporal relations. In particular, our model considers a principled way of dealing with the inherit structural variability in fall events. Briefly speaking, we first propose to introduce a set of latent vector variables, named positional embedding and channel embedding, to represent inner-channel and inter-channel spatio-temporal relations. Now each resulting vector from the embedding representation contains its unique set of channel-level events together with their

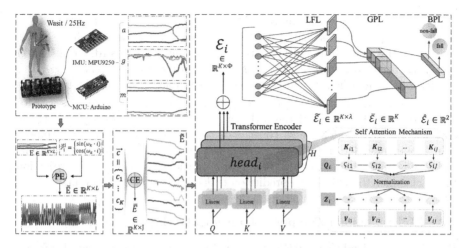

Fig. 2. The overall pipeline of our MCTN model. PE and CE embed temporal and channel information for sequences. The Transformer encoder based on a self-attentive mechanism computes the entire input sequence simultaneously. LPL and GPL select and downscale the output of the encoder. BPL predicts whether a fall is likely to occur.

low-level pose features of temporal information. To fully characterize a certain cluster of instances that possess similar fall events and their spatio-temporal dependencies, a transformer network is devised to encode the spatial relationships along with the temporal relations. In this way, a unified embedded unit that represents a pose in a frame (i.e. sampling point) is updated by exchanging information with other unit variables from the same frame and different frames, allowing our model to manage both spatial and temporal dependencies among channels from various frames. Specifically, the combination of scaled dot-product attention and multi-head attention mechanisms are incorporated in each layer to capture channel-level spatio-temporal relations, and subsequently it ensures feature consistency between the high-level event space and the low-level pose space without loss of their internal spacial relations. In this way, our network-based approach is more capable of characterizing the inherit spatio-temporal structural variability in fall prediction when compared to existing methods, which is also verified during empirical evaluations on two publicly-available datasets and one in-house dataset collected by ourselves, which will be detailed in later sections.

2 Our Approach

2.1 Definition

Given a dataset $\mathcal{D}$ of N samples consisting of sensor data from S multiple sensors attached on various body positions (e.g., accelerometer on waist). Each sample is a sequence of T frames measured in time and spaced at uniform time intervals. Formally, given a sample of human events $\mathbf{M} = <p_t|t = 1,\cdots,T>$, a *pose* $p_t \in \mathbb{R}^{S\times 3}$ is associated with a collection of time series collected by S sensors at the t-th frame, with each sensor having 3-axis coordinates. That is to say, there are totally $K = S \times 3$ *channels* of time series for each pose. Take accelerometer attached at the waist as an example, a channel of time series $\mathbf{c}^j =< a(x)_1^{(s)}, a(x)_2^{(s)}, \ldots, a(x)_T^{(s)} > (j = 1,2,\ldots,K)$, where $a(x)_t^{(s)}$ is a vector collected from the x-axis of the s-th sensor at t-th frame. Here we design an encoder-classifier model, which consists of two parts: a multi-channel temporal transformer encoder that discovers the deep features by combining positional embedding and channel embedding representations, and a linear projection-based classifier to achieve the prediction tasks of classifying fall events.

2.2   Multi-Channel Temporal Transformer Encoder

Positional Embedding (PE). It is hard to represent the temporal information directly within a channel by only using simple and raw sensor data. To further characterize the internal temporal features from a single channel, first we manually encode temporal information by adopting embedding representations, i.e., positional embedding. Let us denote $\mathcal{P}$ as the positional embedding representation with the length of L, where $L < T$. Formally, the positional embedding maps each channel $\mathbf{c}^j$ into a latent vector of size L, with each item $\mathcal{P}_i^j$ $(i = 1,2,\ldots,L)$ as defined as follows:

$$\mathcal{P}_i^j = \begin{cases} \sin(\omega_k \cdot i), & \text{if } i = 2k-1 \\ \cos(\omega_k \cdot i), & \text{if } i = 2k \end{cases}, \tag{1}$$

where $k \in \mathbb{N}^+$ is introduced to distinguish the parity of i (i.e. $k = \lceil \frac{i}{2} \rceil$), and ω_k can be calculated as follows:

$$\omega_k = \frac{1}{T^{2k/L}}. \tag{2}$$

Now the positional embedding $\mathcal{P}^j$ of the corresponding channel $\mathbf{c}^j$ can be expressed as follows:

$$\mathcal{P}^j = [\sin(\omega_1 \cdot 1), \cos(\omega_1 \cdot 2), \cdots, \sin(\omega_{\lceil \frac{L}{2}\rceil} \cdot (L-1)), \cos(\omega_{\lceil \frac{L}{2}\rceil} \cdot L)] \tag{3}$$

Without loss of generality, the positional embedding for all the channels in a sample $\mathbf{M}$ can be concatenate as $\mathcal{P} = [\mathcal{P}^1, \mathcal{P}^2, \ldots, \mathcal{P}^K]$, which in turn yields an enhanced sample $\tilde{\mathbf{E}}$ that contains temporal information:

$$\tilde{\mathbf{E}} = \mathbf{E} + \mathcal{P}, \tag{4}$$

where $\mathbf{E} = <p_t|t = l, l+1, \cdots, l+L> (l = 1,\ldots,T-L)$ is a window segment for fall prediction, as shown in Fig. 1. It is worth noting that the determination of l is divided into two steps in our fall prediction application. In short, we determine the first frame of *impact* stage (L_{im}) by finding the maximum sum magnitude

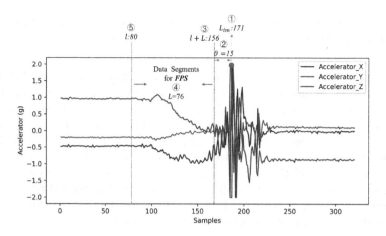

Fig. 3. An example of determining a fall prediction window using data (25 Hz) from Fig. 1 (Middle). L_{im} is the index corresponding to the maximum value of SMV, which is 171 in this case. ϑ is the lead time, which is 0.6 s in this example, corresponding to 15 sample points at 25 Hz. Therefore, the index of the end point of the prediction window can be obtained as $l + L = 171 - 15 = 156$, where L is the length of the prediction window, corresponding to approximately 3 s of data points at 25 Hz, and $L = 76$ is chosen in this example. Thus, the index of the starting point of the prediction window is $l = 156 - 76 = 80$.

vector (SMV) of the accelerometer at waist, and the formula for calculating SMV is as follows:

$$SMV = \sqrt{a(x)^2 + a(y)^2 + a(z)^2}. \tag{5}$$

After L_{im} is obtained, we trace back $\vartheta + L$ frames to obtain $l = L_{im} - L - \vartheta$, where ϑ is a hyperparameter used to indicate the lead time before impact, during which protective devices such as hip airbags or crash vests can be activated. The specific calculation example is shown in Fig. 3.

Channel Embedding (CE). Existing models often neglect the relations among different sensor channels, leading to the spatial information loss. Inspired by ViLT method [8], to further characterize the inherent spatial representations among channels, we employ an embedding representation, named channel embedding, which can be readily generated by labelling in terms of channels. Formally, we choose a simple and convenient way to generate an augmented sample $\bar{\mathbf{E}}$ by embedding channel information into $\tilde{\mathbf{E}}$ as follows:

$$\bar{\mathbf{E}} = \mathbf{c} \oplus \tilde{\mathbf{E}}, \tag{6}$$

where $\oplus$ is the concatenate operator and $\mathbf{c} = \{c_1, \ldots, c_K\}$ is a vector of K constants, with each item $c_k \in \mathbb{N}^+$ indicating a unique identification of the k-th channel. For simplicity, we assign all the channels in the same sensor with the same value in our work. In this way, the generated sample $\bar{\mathbf{E}}$ can form a channel-based feature space that describes a unique fall event with spatio-temporal representations.

Transformer Encoder. Now we are ready to construct the encoder by adopting transformer technique [16], which can effectively learn spatio-temporal relations from multiple channels in parallel. In particular, it includes two major mechanisms, scaled dot-product attention (SDPA) and multi-head attention (MHA). The centerpiece of SDPA is a self-attention mechanism (shown in Fig. 2), in which $\bar{\mathbf{E}}$ is first transformed into three different vectors: the query vector $\mathbf{q}$, the key vector $\mathbf{k}$ and the value vector $\mathbf{v}$ with the same dimension J, where $J = L + 1$. Vectors derived from different inputs are then packed together into three different matrices, namely, $\mathbf{Q}$, $\mathbf{K}$ and $\mathbf{V}$. Subsequently, the attention function for these three input vectors is calculated as follows:

$$\text{Attention}(\mathbf{Q}, \mathbf{K}, \mathbf{V}) = \text{softmax}(\frac{\mathbf{Q} \cdot \mathbf{K}^{\mathrm{T}}}{\sqrt{J}}) \cdot \mathbf{V}. \tag{7}$$

In details, we first compute the scores $\varsigma = \mathbf{Q} \cdot \mathbf{K}^{\mathrm{T}}$. Then, the scores are normalized for the stability of gradient with $\varsigma_n = \varsigma/\sqrt{J}$. After that, the normalized scores are further translated into probabilities with softmax function $\rho = \text{softmax}(\varsigma_n)$. Finally, a weighted value matrix can be obtained with $\mathbf{Z} = \rho \cdot \mathbf{V}$, which represents the temporal features of $\bar{\mathbf{E}}$ for each frame.

A single SDPA layer (named a head) may limit our ability to focus on one or more specific channels without influencing the attention on other equally important channel at the same time, which nevertheless results in spatio-temporal information loss among channels. To boost the performance of vanilla SDPA layer, MHA mechanism is adopted by allowing multiple attention layers with different representation subspace. In this way, different matrices (i.e., $\mathbf{Q}$, $\mathbf{K}$ and $\mathbf{V}$) are given their separate heads, which can be projected into different representation subspace after training due to random initialization.

To formally elaborate, given the number of heads H, $\bar{\mathbf{E}}$ is first transformed into three groups of vectors: the query group, the key group and the value group. In each group, there are H vectors with the same dimension J/H. These vectors are then packed together into three different groups of matrices: $\{\mathbf{Q}_i\}_{i=1}^{H}$, $\{\mathbf{K}_i\}_{i=1}^{H}$ and $\{\mathbf{V}_i\}_{i=1}^{H}$. The MHA process can be formulated as follows:

$$\text{MHA}(\mathbf{Q}, \mathbf{K}, \mathbf{V}) = (head_1 \oplus head_2 \oplus \cdots \oplus head_H)\mathbf{W_o} \tag{8}$$

where $head_i = \text{Attention}(\mathbf{Q}_i, \mathbf{K}_i, \mathbf{V}_i)$, and $\mathbf{W_o} \in \mathbb{R}^{J \times \Phi}$ is weight matrix with Φ indicating the number of tuning parameters in this layer. In this way, the shared space generated by the multi-heads attention ensures feature integrity and consistency among various channels without loss of their global spatio-temporal relations.

2.3   Linear Projection and Prediction Module

In our decoder, since the features output by the above encoder have a large number and high dimensionality, leading to the exhaustive computational cost, we first need to reduce the dimensionality of the encoded feature space.

Linear Filtration Layer (LFL). Let $\mathcal{E}_i \in \mathbb{R}^{K \times \Phi}$ denote an instance after being encoded by our encoder, where i represents the index of batch size. We first reduce the size of encoded feature space from Φ to λ ($\lambda < \Phi$). Formally, each $\mathcal{E}_{ij} \in \mathbb{R}^{\Phi}(j = 1, \cdots, K)$ is mapped into a latent vector $\tilde{\mathcal{E}}_{ij} \in \mathbb{R}^{\lambda}$, as defined as follows:

$$\tilde{\mathcal{E}}_{ij} = \mathbf{W_1} \times \mathcal{E}_{ij} + \mathbf{B_1}, \tag{9}$$

where $\mathbf{W_1}$ is a weight matrix of size $\lambda \times \Phi$, and $\mathbf{B_1}$ is a bias vector of size λ. After filtering the features of each channel of $\mathcal{E}_i$, we now get a feature map $\tilde{\mathcal{E}}_i \in \mathbb{R}^{K \times \lambda}$.

Global Projection Layer (GPL). Normally, these feature maps are generally flattened into one dimension in fall prediction task of classification by using full connection layer directly. However, it will retain all the channel information, resulting in an excessive amount of model parameters, which nevertheless leads to overfitting and low generalization performance. To this end, a global average pooling (GAP) is employed to further reduce the dimension of features while maximally remain the spatio-temporal information among channels. In details, each feature map in $\tilde{\mathcal{E}}_i$ is averaged as follows:

$$\bar{\mathcal{E}}_{ij} = \frac{1}{|\tilde{\mathcal{E}}_{ij}|} \sum_{(p,q) \in \tilde{\mathcal{E}}_{ij}} x_{jpq}, \tag{10}$$

where $\bar{\mathcal{E}}_{ij}$ represents the global average pooled output value of the j-th feature map, x_{jpq} represents the element at (p, q) in the j-th feature map area, and $|\tilde{\mathcal{E}}_{ij}|$ represents all the elements in the j-th feature map.

Binary Prediction Layer (BPL). Up to now, we get a one-dimensional feature matrix $\bar{\mathcal{E}}_i \in \mathbb{R}^{\lambda}$ for each channel i, which is generated by the procedures of feature selection and dimension reduction of the encoded instance $\mathcal{E}$. Here we simply convert the prediction task to a classification problem to determine, for example, whether a subject is about to *fall* or *non-fall* by leveraging the sensor data collected before *impact* stage. We build the prediction layer by mapping $\bar{\mathcal{E}}_i$ to these two categories as follows:

$$\hat{\mathcal{E}}_i = \mathbf{W_p} \bar{\mathcal{E}}_i + \mathbf{B_p},$$
$$\hat{y} = \mathrm{softmax}(\hat{\mathcal{E}}_i) = \frac{\hat{\mathcal{E}}_{ij}}{\sum_K \hat{\mathcal{E}}_{ik}}, \tag{11}$$

where $\mathbf{W_p}$ and $\mathbf{B_p}$ are weight matrix and bias vector, respectively, and $\hat{y}$ represents the probability of the prediction results. The final result is recognized as the class with the maximal probability $\hat{y}$. For simplicity, we choose categorical cross-entropy as the loss function which is commonly used during model training. Finally, the parameters $\mathbf{W} = \{\mathbf{W_o}, \mathbf{W_l}, \mathbf{W_p}, \mathbf{B_l}, \mathbf{B_p}\}$ in our encoder-classifier model can be estimated by optimizing the loss function objective over the dataset $\mathcal{D}$. There are probably a number of $KH\Phi + (\Phi + 2)\lambda$ training parameters on $\mathbf{W}$, which is acceptable for fall prediction in practice.

3   Empirical Evaluations

3.1   Datasets and Preprocessing

Three fall event datasets are considered in our experiments, including two publicly-available benchmark datasets and one in-house dataset collected by ourselves.

SisFall(200 Hz) [14]. This publicly-available dataset contains a total of 4505 samples, including 2707 samples of 19 activities of daily life (ADL) and 1798 samples of 15 fall actions collected from two accelerometers and one gyroscope placed at the waist of 38 participants.

MobiAct (100 Hz) [17]. It is a public benchmark that contains 647 samples of 4 fall actions and 1879 samples of 9 ADL actions obtained by an accelerometer and a gyroscope placed in the thighs of 57 participants.

SoftFall (25 Hz). To the best of our knowledge, these two publicly-available datasets do not contain the scenario of falls of the elderly where their procedure is often slower than and different from the other cases. To this end, we propose a new dataset that includes simulated slow-paced movements of elderly individuals (see Table 1). These samples were collected using a 9-axis MPU9250 sensor (one accelerometer, one gyroscope and one magnetometer) attached at the subject's waist from 11 participants, who were instructed to perform 22 different activities (7 ADL activities and 15 fall activities). A total number of 802 samples were collected, including 203 ADL samples and 599 fall samples. A subset of samples are provided in the supplementary material, and once ready we plan to share the entire dataset in the community.

3.2   Experimental Set-Ups and Baselines

Our model is implemented by PyTorch on one GeForce GTX 1070Ti GPU. It is optimized by SGD optimizer with the learning rate of 1×10^{-3}. We set the hyperparameters $\vartheta = 15$, $J = 77$, $H = 7$, $\Phi = 16$ and $\lambda = 8$ to ensure 0.6 s in advance of the *impact* stage for fall prediction. The batch size is fixed to 128 and the number of training epochs is 600. The prediction performance of our model is compared 14 commonly used methods in FPS. For fair comparison, we did not apply any data augmentation or pre-trained weights to boost the performance. Accuracy is employed as the evaluation metric, which is computed as the proportion of true results among the total number of samples.

Table 1. Fall and ADL events in SoftFall. All ADLs are slow-paced. Except for the *pre-fall* phase in the falling data, the rest are only affected by gravity without external interference.

Fall/ADL	Number	Activity
Fall	0	Basic falls (fall in four directions from front to back, left to right while standing)
	1	Crouch-up lateral fall
	2	Crouch-up backward fall
	3	Bending knee to stand up and fall forward
	4	Bending knee to stand up and fall backward
	5	Bending forward to fall
	6	Bending sideways and falling
	7	Bending up and falling backward
	8	Lying down and roll over to fall vertically
	9	Slipping backward while walking
	10	Tripping in forward direction while walking
	11	Lateral collision while walking
	12	Fainting directly to the side while walking
	13	Tripping in forward direction while running
	14	Slipping sideways while running
ADL	0	**(Slowly)** Flow ADL (a complete set of movements from ADL1 to ADL6)
	1	**(Slowly)** Walking
	2	**(Slowly)** Running
	3	**(Slowly)** Picking up/bending down
	4	**(Slowly)** Going up and down stairs
	5	**(Slowly)** Lying-Sitting-Standing
	6	**(Slowly)** Standing-Sitting-Lying

Table 2. Accuracy(%)/Computational time(ms) comparisons on fall prediction with conventional methods. a-accelerometer, g-gyroscope.

Datasets	Methods									
	MobiAct (a, g)				SisFall (a, g)					SoftFall (a, g)
	20 Hz	25 Hz	50 Hz	100 Hz	20 Hz	25 Hz	50 Hz	100 Hz	200 Hz	25 Hz
Threshold1 [6]	66.30/3.7	67.19/3.9	69.84/4.9	72.28/8.5	72.36/3.4	75.39/4.5	77.11/5.1	79.43/8.5	79.57/9.6	71.08/4.3
Threshold2 [1]	70.51/**2.8**	72.44/**3.1**	73.85/4.6	75.16/**8.2**	74.34/**2.7**	76.80/**3.5**	78.17/**4.5**	79.24/**8.4**	80.03/**9.2**	69.11/**3.4**
KNN [13]	77.37/29.6	72.19/30.1	72.82/45.7	71.28/49.5	80.18/33.0	71.00/32.0	72.89/50.9	73.27/53.9	71.79/105.8	76.25/31.0
SVM [13]	59.63/193.7	58.11/188.3	56.38/317.4	58.91/605.8	58.87/202.5	57.82/170.5	55.88/329.1	59.55/631.3	55.67/1454.1	61.27/229.4
NB [12]	57.36/10.9	57.10/10.5	55.85/11.7	54.82/15.7	56.41/11.6	56.21/11.8	56.21/14.8	52.57/17.9	56.51/35.7	57.73/11.3
DT [13]	83.98/4.4	78.47/4.9	79.15/5.1	76.54/8.5	82.86/4.9	73.21/5.3	76.41/5.4	75.68/8.6	72.21/10.1	74.30/5.0
RF [12]	87.53/8.2	81.67/8.7	80.48/9.1	81.62/11.7	89.20/8.4	79.93/8.7	80.07/9.3	82.18/12.2	79.09/18.5	82.15/8.2
MCTN	**99.46**/30.1	**99.41**/28.3	**99.30**/28.5	**99.35**/28.7	**99.28**/37.2	**99.36**/34.8	**99.45**/34.1	**99.30**/40.5	**99.45**/70.0	**98.89**/9.5

3.3 Comparisons Against Other Competing Methods

In the context of fall prediction task with only 3 s of data, we compared the performance of threshold-based methods and conventional ML methods. Table 2 presents the accuracy and computation time. The results indicate that the threshold-based method has the fastest running time, while the ML method and MCTN have similar speed. However, both threshold-based and ML methods cannot maintain high accuracy on all datasets.

Table 3. Accuracy(%)/Computational time(ms) comparisons on fall prediction with DL. a-accelerometer, g-gyroscope, m-magnetometer.

Datasets	Methods	Tae [7] LSTM	Dimitri [9] CNN	Mirto [11] Mirto LSTM	Leyuan [10] CNN + LSTM	Triwiyanto [15] CNN	Sravan [2] CNN + LSTM	Iveta [3] Transformer	MCTN Transformer
MobiAct (a,g)	20 Hz	80.56/65.6	77.37/33.2	81.56/38.1	78.86/48.2	79.78/**24.4**	83.13/86.5	85.76/30.9	**96.46**/30.1
	25 Hz	81.20/59.5	77.81/33.6	78.93/45.4	80.96/48.9	81.35/30.2	77.85/104.7	86.03/46.0	**99.41/28.3**
	50 Hz	77.74/75.0	80.08/**26.6**	74.62/40.4	77.92/58.5	82.60/53.6	80.94/130.8	85.46/41.8	**99.30**/28.5
	100 Hz	78.92/88.3	79.57/44.7	81.73/58.8	78.34/55.0	76.76/56.5	80.53/197.3	88.11/38.7	**99.35/28.7**
SisFall (a,g)	20 Hz	80.29/87.2	79.87/42.2	82.42/51.9	81.37/58.0	82.02/43.7	79.72/106.1	85.05/50.6	**99.28/37.2**
	25 Hz	77.80/67.1	77.14/**32.4**	82.76/47.0	76.23/61.8	82.21/50.1	81.58/99.5	86.36/51.0	**99.36**/34.8
	50 Hz	81.72/88.7	79.26/40.0	78.53/59.2	78.04/55.9	77.58/41.3	77.74/156.5	84.68/48.7	**99.45/34.1**
	100 Hz	81.65/122.1	78.97/**39.8**	78.82/76.6	80.00/68.8	78.31/52.2	77.64/239.4	88.60/70.1	**99.30**/40.5
	200 Hz	82.16/161.7	81.31/77.0	81.18/176.7	80.24/102.9	79.33/92.3	80.70/486.9	89.69/84.7	**99.45/70.0**
SisFall (a,g,a)	20 Hz	82.65/74.3	78.86/33.8	76.84/40.9	78.33/48.4	82.66/**27.7**	77.21/104.2	89.62/39.9	**99.22**/32.5
	25 Hz	94.57/69.9	78.79/28.7	76.02/34.3	80.31/42.2	75.61/**27.9**	81.42/95.4	92.63/36.4	**98.52**/41.9
	50 Hz	94.96/117.3	75.35/53.0	81.99/67.4	75.27/68.0	76.75/54.9	77.11/145.8	92.39/52.1	**99.46/33.7**
	100 Hz	92.87/108.9	78.25/52.9	75.08/72.9	83.02/86.5	81.79/52.7	78.11/227.2	93.31/62.9	**99.33/49.3**
	200 Hz	93.44/196.7	81.14/81.8	84.15/198.7	82.34/119.9	74.02/**78.5**	79.33/421.8	84.92/102.0	**98.45**/83.3
SoftFall (a,g)	25 Hz	88.60/20.7	80.98 / 10.7	85.91/12.0	80.31/14.7	80.25/9.8	82.26/32.0	90.19/12.1	**98.89/9.5**
SoftFall (a,g,m)	25 Hz	91.70/18.8	80.40/8.6	90.97/11.4	82.86/15.0	83.52/**8.0**	83.35/29.2	91.49/10.9	**98.90**/9.4
FLOPs/M (25 Hz)		314.62	18.67	392.23	129.32	454.81	591.50	91.64	**14.69**
Parameters/M (25 Hz)		0.245	**0.002**	0.094	0.109	0.092	0.027	0.119	0.018

Table 3 shows the averaged accuracy results and computational time over 10-fold cross-validations. The MCTN model clearly outperforms the other methods with a large margin on all three datasets. Our model is significantly more accurate than other models with around 5%–30% performance boost. This mainly due to its abilities to take advantage of the feature variables with rich spatio-temporal dependency information among various channels of sensors. Unfortunately, other competing models are rather limited in characterizing such fine-grained relations, while ignoring those features with high correlation to pre-fall and falling stages. Notably, MCTN performs stably over different sampling rates and sensor modalities. It indicates that the features learned by our model are more sensor-agnostic than those of other methods and can be adopted by different FPSs even equipped with sensors of low sampling rate. In addition, although our model is not the best on computational consumption (average 37 ms), it achieves high accuracy with relatively low number of parameters and FLOPs, which overall is affordable for practical usage in FPS with embedded deployment of wearable devices. Theoretically, the time complexity of our prediction module is $O(KJ^2\Phi)$.

3.4   Ablation Study

In this section, we first conduct two ablation studies to measure the effectiveness of two embedding representations (i.e., PE and CE) in our MCTN model. It is worth noting that we show the results at 25 Hz here, and the studies from other sampling rates are not shown due to page limitation, but similar results are obtained in our experiment. We separately evaluate the effects of different representations in our model by removing these two modules with MCTN. Fur-

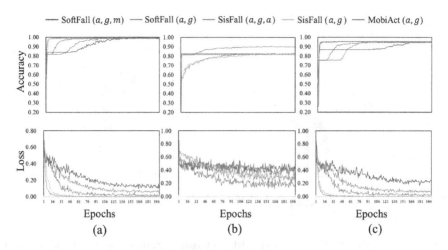

Fig. 4. Comparisons with/without PE or CE (epoch is down-sampled to one-third). (a) Original MCTN; (b) Without PE; (c) Without CE.

thermore, we conducted two additional ablation experiments to investigate the effects of different prediction window lengths and lead times on our model.

Effectiveness of PE. As shown in Figure 4, without the embedded temporal information (PE), the model is less stable in training and its overall performance is reduced significantly. It This might be due to the capability of the low-level encoding of temporal information that can manage the internal temporal features in a single channel rather than only using simple and raw sensor data.

Effectiveness of CE. Since PE handles single-channel temporal information, CE aims to further characterize the spatio-temporal relations among different channels of sensors. To keep the model consistent, we let all the items in **c** to be −1, which represents no channel embedding, rather than simply discarding it. It is shown that compared with baseline, the performance of the model without CE has a slight drop, and the model convergence speed has been degraded (especially for SoftFall). This may be because CE module is not directly removed, which in turn leads to a model that can learn inter-channel information slowly through a long process of iterations. However, it indicates that learning spatio-temporal relations by distinguishing between different channels is helpful for the training and performance of the model.

Different Length of Prediction Window L. As shown in Fig. 5(a), the window lengths we compared were from 1.5 s to 4 s with an interval of 0.5 s. The results showed that with the increase of L, the accuracy of the model on different datasets first increased and then decreased, achieving the best result at 3 s. When L was greater than 3 s, increasing L decreased the accuracy of the model.

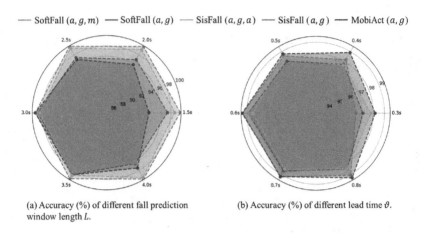

(a) Accuracy (%) of different fall prediction window length L.

(b) Accuracy (%) of different lead time ϑ.

Fig. 5. Performance of the model with different parameter settings on different datasets.

This may be due to the increase in the proportion of ADL in the entire prediction window, which increased the difficulty of the model to distinguish between ADL data and fall data containing ADL.

Different Length of Lead Time ϑ. As shown in Fig. 5(b), a shorter lead time does not necessarily enable the model to accurately predict falls on all datasets. The model performs similarly at $\vartheta = 0.6$ s and $\vartheta = 0.7$ s, with the best performance at $\vartheta = 0.6$ s. However, when $\vartheta = 0.8$ s, the model's accuracy significantly decreases. It can be observed that both shorter and longer lead times can reduce the model's accuracy. This may be due to the imbalanced distribution of ADLs and falls in the predicted data in both cases, which increases the difficulty of model prediction.

3.5   Real-World Scenario Testing

To validate the performance of our model in real-life scenarios, we deployed MCTN on embedded devices as shown in Fig. 7(b). Specifically, we reproduced MCTN using Keras and converted it to a TensorFlow Lite model, which was then deployed on an ESP32S3-DevKit. We recruited six volunteers to assist in our experiment, as shown in Fig. 6(b). All volunteers were required to wear our device around their waist and perform six prescribed actions at any time during free movement, with each action performed once. The device ran continuously during this period, with the default state being ADL and the onboard RGB LED being blue. When a fall was predicted, the RGB LED turned red and resumed the default state after 15 s. Ultimately, our device correctly predicted all fall actions in 9 to 11 milliseconds without any false positives. As shown in Fig. 7(a) and Fig. 7(c), the acceleration and angular velocity changes for the four falls and two ADLs were quite distinct, but the SMV for ADL was concentrated around

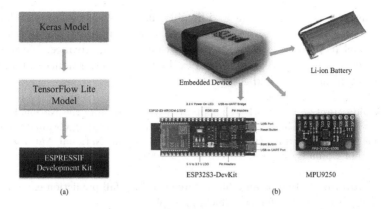

(a)

(b)

Fig. 6. Process of embedded deployment of MCTN (a) and our embedded device (b).

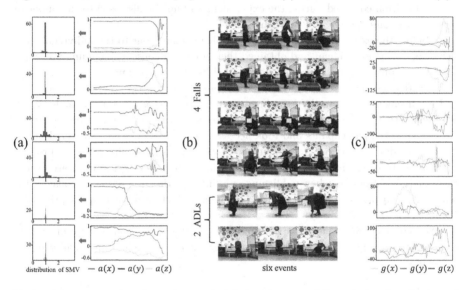

Fig. 7. Six actions done by volunteers. (a) Acceleration (G) and the distribution of SMV (G) of prediction windows; (b) Four falls (Fall2, Fall7, Fall10, Fall13) and two ADLs (ADL3, ADL6) in Table 1; (c) Angular velocity (rad/s) of prediction windows.

$1G$, while that for falls was relatively dispersed, allowing our device to accurately differentiate between these falls and ADLs.

4 Conclusion

In this paper, we present a multi-channel temporal network with positional embedding and channel embedding representations for wearable sensor data, which can capture the inherit spatio-temporal varieties of poses at pre-fall or falling stages. It is more efficient and flexible than existing methods on fall prediction. As for future work, we will explore how to improve the performance of our model in predicting falls with more than 0.6 s in advance. We will consider lightening our network and further evaluating its performance in real-world scenarios with more falls and ADLs.

Acknowledgments. This work was supported by grants from the National Natural Science Foundation of China (grant no. 62377040), the Chongqing Graduate Research Innovation Project Funding (project no. CYS23101), the National Natural Science Foundation of China (grant nos. 61977012, 62207007).

Ethical Statement. Here is an ethical statement for a fall prediction experiment to ensure that data collection follows ethical principles:

– The privacy of the subjects is required to maintain confidentiality, and all data and information collected during the experiment will not be disclosed to the public or provided to non-experimental personnel.

– Before the experiment, we provided detailed explanations to the individuals participating in the experiment and obtained their informed consent, including informing them of the purpose, methods, and potential risks of the experiment.

– Participants in the experiment received appropriate protection and care, and risks and inconveniences during the experiment were minimized as much as possible. When conducting the experiment, we evaluated the impact of the experiment on the health and safety of the participants and took necessary measures to reduce these risks.

– After data collection is complete, we take full responsibility for data processing and analysis, ensuring that the various relationships within the data are clearly explained. Additionally, when publishing or using experimental data, we consider the sensitivity and privacy of the data and place the protection of participant privacy at the forefront.

We hereby confirm that we strictly adhered to the above-mentioned ethical principles in the fall prediction experiment and protected the rights and dignity of the subjects.

References

1. Blunda, L.L., Gutiérrez-Madroñal, L., Wagner, M.F., Medina-Bulo, I.: A wearable fall detection system based on body area networks. IEEE Access **8**, 193060–193074 (2020). https://doi.org/10.1109/ACCESS.2020.3032497
2. Challa, S.K., Kumar, A., Semwal, V.B.: A multibranch CNN-BiLSTM model for human activity recognition using wearable sensor data. Visual Comput. **38**, 1–15 (2021). https://doi.org/10.1007/s00371-021-02283-3
3. Dirgová Luptáková, I., Kubovčík, M., Pospíchal, J.: Wearable sensor-based human activity recognition with transformer model. Sensors **22**(5), 1911 (2022). https://doi.org/10.3390/s22051911
4. Hemmatpour, M., Ferrero, R., Gandino, F., Montrucchio, B., Rebaudengo, M.: Internet of Things for fall prediction and prevention. J. Comput. Methods Sci. Eng. **18**(2), 511–518 (2018). https://doi.org/10.3233/JCM-180806

5. Howcroft, J., Kofman, J., Lemaire, E.D.: Prospective fall-risk prediction models for older adults based on wearable sensors. IEEE Trans. Neural Syst. Rehabil. Eng. **25**(10), 1812–1820 (2017). https://doi.org/10.1109/TNSRE.2017.2687100
6. Jung, H., Koo, B., Kim, J., Kim, T., Nam, Y., Kim, Y.: Enhanced algorithm for the detection of preimpact fall for wearable airbags. Sensors **20**(5), 1277 (2020). https://doi.org/10.3390/s20051277
7. Kim, T.H., Choi, A., Heo, H.M., Kim, H., Mun, J.H.: Acceleration magnitude at impact following loss of balance can be estimated using deep learning model. Sensors **20**(21), 6126 (2020). https://doi.org/10.3390/s20216126
8. Kim, W., Son, B., Kim, I.: ViLT: vision-and-language transformer without convolution or region supervision (2021). https://doi.org/10.48550/arXiv.2102.03334
9. Kraft, D., Srinivasan, K., Bieber, G.: Deep learning based fall detection algorithms for embedded systems, smartwatches, and iot devices using accelerometers. Technologies **8**(4), 72 (2020). https://doi.org/10.3390/technologies8040072
10. Liu, L., Hou, Y., He, J., Lungu, J., Dong, R.: An energy-efficient fall detection method based on FD-DNN for elderly people. Sensors **20**(15), 4192 (2020). https://doi.org/10.3390/s20154192
11. Musci, M., De Martini, D., Blago, N., Facchinetti, T., Piastra, M.: Online fall detection using recurrent neural networks on smart wearable devices. IEEE Trans. Emerg. Topics Comput. **9**(3), 1276–1289 (2021). https://doi.org/10.1109/TETC.2020.3027454
12. Palmerini, L., Klenk, J., Becker, C., Chiari, L.: Accelerometer-based fall detection using machine learning: training and testing on real-world falls. Sensors **20**(22), 6479 (2020). https://doi.org/10.3390/s20226479
13. Saadeh, W., Butt, S.A., Altaf, M.A.B.: A patient-specific single sensor IoT-based wearable fall prediction and detection system. IEEE Trans. Neural Syst. Rehabil. Eng. **27**(5), 995–1003 (2019). https://doi.org/10.1109/TNSRE.2019.2911602
14. Sucerquia, A., López, J.D., Vargas-Bonilla, J.F.: SisFall: a fall and movement dataset. Sensors **17**(1), 198 (2017). https://doi.org/10.3390/s17010198
15. Triwiyanto, T., Pawana, I.P.A., Purnomo, M.H.: An improved performance of deep learning based on convolution neural network to classify the hand motion by evaluating hyper parameter. IEEE Trans. Neural Syst. Rehabil. Eng. **28**(7), 1678–1688 (2020). https://doi.org/10.1109/TNSRE.2020.2999505
16. Vaswani, A., et al.: Attention is all you need (2017). https://doi.org/10.48550/arXiv.1706.03762
17. Vavoulas, G., Chatzaki, C., Malliotakis, T., Pediaditis, M., Tsiknakis, M.: The MobiAct dataset: recognition of activities of daily living using smartphones. In: International Conference on Information and Communication Technologies for Ageing Well and E-Health, vol. 2, pp. 143–151. SCITEPRESS (2016). https://doi.org/10.5220/0005792401430151

Target-Aware Molecular Graph Generation

Cheng Tan[1,2], Zhangyang Gao[1,2], and Stan Z. Li[1,2(✉)]

[1] Zhejiang University, Hangzhou, China
[2] AI Lab, Research Center for Industries of the Future, Westlake University, Hangzhou, China
{tancheng,gaozhangyang,stan.zq.li}@westlake.edu.cn

Abstract. Generating molecules with desired biological activities has attracted growing attention in drug discovery. Previous molecular generation models are designed as chemocentric methods that hardly consider the drug-target interaction, limiting their practical applications. In this paper, we aim to generate molecular drugs in a target-aware manner that bridges biological activity and molecular design. To solve this problem, we compile a benchmark dataset from several publicly available datasets and build baselines in a unified framework. Building on the recent advantages of flow-based molecular generation models, we propose *SiamFlow*, which forces the flow to fit the distribution of target sequence embeddings in latent space. Specifically, we employ an alignment loss and a uniform loss to bring target sequence embeddings and drug graph embeddings into agreements while avoiding collapse. Furthermore, we formulate the alignment into a one-to-many problem by learning spaces of target sequence embeddings. Experiments quantitatively show that our proposed method learns meaningful representations in the latent space toward the target-aware molecular graph generation and provides an alternative approach to bridge biology and chemistry in drug discovery.

Keywords: AI for Science · Bioinformatics · Molecular Generation · Graph Neural Networks

1 Introduction

Drug discovery, which focuses on finding candidate molecules with desirable properties for therapeutic applications, is a long-period and expensive process with a high failure rate. The challenge primarily stems from the actuality that only a tiny fraction of the theoretical possible drug-like molecules may have practical effects. Specifically, the entire search space is as large as 10^{23}–10^{60}, while only 10^8 of them are therapeutically relevant [45]. In the face of such difficulty, traditional methods like high-throughput screening [19] fail in terms

---

C. Tan and Z. Gao—Equal Contribution.

© The Author(s), under exclusive license to Springer Nature Switzerland AG 2023
G. De Francisci Morales et al. (Eds.): ECML PKDD 2023, LNAI 14174, pp. 410–427, 2023.
https://doi.org/10.1007/978-3-031-43427-3_25

of efficiency because of the large number of resources required in producing minor hit compounds. One alternative is using computational methods [44] such as virtual screening [51] to identify hit compounds from virtual libraries through similarity-based searches or molecular docking. Another alternative is automated molecule design, such as inverse QSAR [53], structure-based de novo design [52], or genetic algorithms [3].

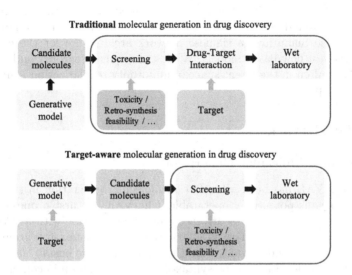

Fig. 1. The computational drug discovery pipelines of traditional chemocentric and target-aware molecular generation. The black arrows denote the main steps, the blue arrows denote external considerations, and the red boxes denote the post-processing process of generated molecules. (Color figure online)

Recent deep generative models have demonstrated the potential to promote drug discovery by exploring huge chemical space in a data-driven manner. Various forms of variational autoencoder (VAE) [55], generative adversarial networks (GAN) [47], autoregressive (AR) [46,58,62], and normalizing flow (NF) [11,12,39,40,54] have been proposed to generate molecular SMILES or graphs. Though these approaches can generate valid and novel molecules to some extent, they remain inefficient because the generated candidate molecules need further screened against given targets. As the primary goal of these chemocentric methods is to generate drug-like molecules that satisfy specific properties, directly applying them in drug discovery requires extra effort in predicting the binding affinities between candidate molecules and target proteins.

While previous molecular generation methods scarcely take biological drug-target interactions into account, we aim to generate candidate molecules based on a biological perspective. This paper proposes target-aware molecular generation to bridge biological activity and chemical molecular design that generate valid molecules conditioned on specific targets and thus facilitate the development of drug discovery. As shown in Fig. 1, the pipeline of computational drug discovery is supposed to be simplified to a great extent with the help of target-aware molecular generation. Our main contributions are summarized as follows:

- We propose a target-aware molecular generation manner from a biological perspective, while prior works on chemocentric molecular generation are inefficient in practical drug discovery.
- We establish a new benchmark for the target-aware molecular generation containing abundant drug-target pairs for evaluating generative models.
- We propose SiamFlow, a siamese network architecture for the conditional generation of flow-based models. While the sequence encoder and the generative flow align in the latent space, a uniformity regularization is imposed to avoid collapse.

2   Related Work

2.1   De Novo Molecular Generation

VAE-Based. VAE has been attractive in molecular generation in the virtue of its latent space is potentially operatable. CharVAE [14] first proposes to learn from molecular data in a data-driven manner and generate with a VAE model. GVAE [31] represents each data as a parse tree from a context-free grammar, and directly encodes to and decodes from these parse trees to ensure the validity of generated molecules. Inspired by syntax-directed translation in complier theory, SD-VAE [7] proposes to convert the offline syntax-directed translation check into on-the-fly generated guidance for ensuring both syntactical and semantical correctness. JT-VAE [23] first realize the direct generation of molecular graphs instead of linear SMILES (Simplified Molecular-Input Line-Entry System) strings.

GAN-Based. An alternative is to implement GAN in molecular generation. ORGAN [16] adds expert-based rewards under the framework of WGAN [2]. ORGANIC [50] improves the above work for inverse design chemistry and implements the molecular generation towards specific properties. MolGAN [10] proposes GAN-based models to generate molecular graphs rather than SMILES. Motivated by cycle-consistent GAN [64], Mol-CycleGAN [41] generates optimized compounds with high structural similarity to the original ones.

Flow-Based. Molecular generation with the normalizing flow is promising as its invertible mapping can reconstruct the data exactly. GraphNVP [40] and GRF [20] are the early works on flow-based molecular generation. GraphAF [54] combines the advantages of both autoregressive and flow-based approaches to iteratively generate molecules. MolFlow [63] proposes a variant of Glow [26] to generate atoms and bonds in a one-shot manner. MolGrow [32] constrains optimization of properties by using latent variables of the model, and recursively splits nodes.

Though these approaches have achieved significant performance, we recognize them as chemocentric molecular generation methods that lack biological connections. We aim to bridge biological and chemical perspectives in molecular generation for practical drug discovery.

2.2 Drug-Target Interaction

Recent progress in artificial intelligence has inspired researchers to utilize deep learning techniques in drug-target interaction prediction. DeepDTA [43] and DeepAffinity [24] are representatives of deep-learning methods that take SMILES of drugs and primary sequences of proteins as input, from which neural networks are employed to predict affinities. InterpretableDTIP [13] predicts DTI directly from low-level representations and provides biological interpretation using a two-way attention mechanism. DeepRelations [25] embeds protein sequences by hierarchical recurrent neural network and drug graphs by graph neural networks with joint attention between protein residues and compound atoms. MONN [33] predicts binding affinities with extra supervision from the labels extracted from available high-quality three-dimensional structures. Our proposed target-aware molecular generation builds on the recent advances in data-driven drug-target interaction prediction. We connect chemical molecular generation with biological drug-target interaction to promote the efficiency of drug discovery.

2.3 Conditional Molecular Generation

Generating molecules with the consideration of some external conditions is a promising field. CVAE [14] jointly trains VAE with a predictor that predicts properties from the latent representations of VAE. [34] proposes applying conditional VAE to generate drug-like molecules satisfying properties at the same time. [15] employs constrained Bayesian optimization to control the latent space of VAE in order to find molecules that score highly under a specified objective function. CogMol [5] and CLaSS [8] pretrain the latent space with SMILES and train property classifiers from the latent representations. They sample from the latent space that satisfies high scores from property classifiers to generate molecules. Though recent molecular generation methods [23,39,40,63] also present property optimization experiments, they still barely take account of drug-target interaction. [42] proposes stacks of conditional GAN to generate hit-like molecules from gene expression signature. While this work focuses on drug-gene relationships, we instead focus on the drug-protein case.

3 Background and Preliminaries

3.1 Problem Statement

Let $\mathcal{T} = \{T_i\}_{i=1}^t$ be a set of targets, and there exists a set of drugs $\mathcal{M}_{T_i} = \{M_j^{(T_i)}\}_{j=1}^{d_i}$ that bind to each target T_i. $S(T, M)$ is defined as a function measuring the interaction between target T and drug M. The target-aware molecular generation aims to learning a generation model $p_\theta(\cdot|T_i)$ from each drug-target pair $(M_j^{(T_i)}, T_i)$ so as to maximize $\mathbb{E}_{M|T_i \sim p_\theta}[S(M, T_i)]$.

3.2 The Flow Framework

A flow model is a sequence of parametric invertible mapping $f_\Theta = f_Q \circ \dots \circ f_1$ from the data point $x \in \mathbb{R}^D$ to the latent variable $z \in \mathbb{R}^D$, where $x \sim P_X(x), z \sim P_Z(z)$. The latent distribution P_Z is usually predefined as a simple distribution, e.g., a normal distribution. The complex data in the original space is modelled by using the change-of-variable formula:

$$P_X(x) = P_Z(z)\left|\det\frac{\partial Z}{\partial X}\right|, \tag{1}$$

and its log-likelihood:

$$
\begin{aligned}
\log P_X(x) &= \log P_Z(z) + \log\left|\det\frac{\partial Z}{\partial X}\right| \\
&= \log P_Z(z) + \sum_{q=1}^{Q} \log\left|\det\frac{\partial f_q(z^{(q-1)})}{\partial z^{(q-1)}}\right|,
\end{aligned}
\tag{2}
$$

where $z^{(q)} = f_q(z^{(q-1)})$, and we represent the input $z^{(0)}$ by using z for notation simplicity.

As the calculation of the Jacobian determinant for f_Θ is expensive for arbitrary functions, NICE [11] and RealNVP [12] develop an affine coupling transformation $z = f_\Theta(x)$ with expressive structures and efficient computation of the Jacobian determinant.

For given D-dimensional input x and $d < D$, the output y of an affine coupling transformation is defined as:

$$
\begin{aligned}
y_{1:d} &= x_{1:d} \\
y_{d+1:D} &= x_{d+1:D} \odot \exp(S_\Theta(x_{1:d})) + T_\Theta(x_{1:d}),
\end{aligned}
\tag{3}
$$

where $S_\Theta : \mathbb{R}^d \to \mathbb{R}^{D-d}$ and $T_\Theta : \mathbb{R}^d \to \mathbb{R}^{D-d}$ stand for scale function and transformation function. For the sake of the numerical stability of cascading multiple flow layers, we follow Moflow [63] to replace the exponential function for the S_Θ with the Sigmoid function:

$$
\begin{aligned}
y_{1:d} &= x_{1:d} \\
y_{d+1:D} &= x_{d+1:D} \odot \text{Sigmoid}(S_\Theta(x_{1:d})) + T_\Theta(x_{1:d}),
\end{aligned}
\tag{4}
$$

and the invertibility is guaranteed by:

$$
\begin{aligned}
x_{1:d} &= y_{1:d} \\
x_{d+1:D} &= (y_{d+1:D} - T_\Theta(y_{1:d}))/\text{Sigmoid}(S_\Theta(y_{1:d})).
\end{aligned}
\tag{5}
$$

The logarithmic Jacobian determinant is:

$$\log\left|\det\frac{\partial y}{\partial x}\right| = \log\left|\det\left(\begin{bmatrix} \mathbb{I} & 0 \\ \frac{\partial y_{d+1:D}}{\partial x_{1:d}} & \text{Sigmoid}(S_\Theta(x_{1:d})) \end{bmatrix}\right)\right| \tag{6}$$
$$= \log \text{Sigmoid}(S_\Theta(x_{1:d})).$$

To further improve the invertible mapping with more expressive structures and high numerical stability, Glow [26] proposes using invertible 1×1 convolution to learn an optimal partition and actnorm layer to normalize dimensions in each channel over a batch by an affine transformation. Invertible 1×1 convolution is initialized as a random rotation matrix with zero log-determinant and works as a generalization of a permutation of channels. Act norm initializes the scale and the bias such that the post-actnorm activations per-channel have zero mean and unit variance and learns these parameters in training instead of using batch statistics as batch normalization does.

3.3 Flow on the Molecular Graph

Prior works on flow-based molecular graph generation are well developed. Inspired by the graph normalizing flows of GRevNets [35], GraphNVP [40] proposes to generate atom features conditioned on the pre-generated adjacency tensors, which is then followed by other one-shot flow-based molecular graph generation approaches, e.g., GRF [20] and Moflow [63]. Our proposed SiamFlow follows this manner, that is, firstly transforms the bonds B of molecules to the latent variables Z_B with Glow [26], and then transforms the atom features A given B into the conditional latent variable $Z_{A|B}$ with a graph conditional flow.

Let N, K, C be the number of nodes, node types, and edge types, respectively. A molecular graph $G = (A, B)$ is defined by an atom matrix $A \in \{0,1\}^{N \times K}$ and a bond tensor $B \in \{0,1\}^{C \times N \times N}$, which correspond to nodes and edges in the vanilla graph. $A[i,k] = 1$ represents the i-th atom i has atom type k, and $B[c,i,j] = 1$ represents there is a bond with type c between the i-th atom and j-th atom.

Flow-based molecular graph generation methods decompose the generative model into two parts:

$$P(G) = P((A, B)) \approx P(A|B; \theta_{A|B})P(B; \theta_B), \tag{7}$$

where θ_B is learned by the bond flow model h_B, and $\theta_{A|B}$ is learned by the atom flow model $h_{A|B}$ conditioned on the bond tensor B.

With the strengths of the flow, the optimal parameters $\theta^*_{A|B}$ and θ^*_B maximize the exact likelihood estimation:

$$\arg\max_{\theta_{A|B},\theta_B} \mathbb{E}_{(A,B)\sim P_G}[\log P(A|B; \theta_{A|B}) + \log P(B; \theta_B)] \tag{8}$$

Our work follows the one-shot molecular graph generation manner [20,40,63] that employs Glow [26] as the bond flow model h_B and graph conditional flow as the atom flow model $h_{A|B}$.

4   SiamFlow

4.1   Overview

While current flow-based molecular graph generation methods [20,32,39,40,54, 63] learn from drug-like datasets and generate without the invention of targets, our proposed SiamFlow aims to serve as a conditional flow toward molecular graph generation. Though the conditional flow has been well developed in computer vision [1,28,30,36,48], there are limited works that can fit graph generation, especially when it comes to the molecular graph.

In this section, we introduce SiamFlow, a novel molecular graph generative model conditioned on specific targets. As shown in Fig. 2, SiamFlow learns the distribution of sequence embedding instead of the isotropic Gaussian distribution like other flow-based methods.

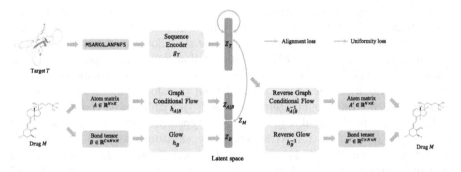

Fig. 2. The framework of our proposed SiamFlow. In the training phase, the target sequence embedding Z_T aligns with the drug graph embedding Z_M, while a uniformity regularization term forces its distribution as a spherical uniform distribution. In the generation phase, the target sequence embedding Z_T is fed into reverse flows to generate the desired drug.

4.2   Alignment Loss

Given a pair of target T and drug M, we decompose the drug M into an atom matrix $A \in \mathbb{R}^{N \times K}$ and a bond tensor $B \in \mathbb{R}^{C \times N \times N}$. The sequence encoder g_T can be arbitrary mapping that maps the target sequence T into the sequence embedding $Z_T \in \mathbb{R}^D$. The flow model contains a glow $h_B : \mathbb{R}^{C \times N \times N} \to \mathbb{R}^{\frac{D}{2}}$ and a graph conditional flow $h_{A|B} : \mathbb{R}^{N \times K} \to \mathbb{R}^{\frac{D}{2}}$. The drug graph embedding Z_M is the concatenation of $Z_{A|B}$ and Z_B.

Instead of directly learning the isotropic Gaussian distribution, we impose alignment loss between the target sequence embedding Z_T and the drug graph embedding Z_M so that Z_T can be used as the input of the generation process. Thus, the generated atom matrix and the bond tensor are:

$$A' = h_{A|B}^{-1}(Z_T[1 : \frac{D}{2}]), \ B' = h_B^{-1}(Z_T[\frac{D}{2} : D]). \tag{9}$$

While traditional flow-based models assume the latent variables follow the Gaussian distribution, SiamFlow forces the flow model to learn the distribution of the condition information instead of a predefined distribution. We define the alignment loss $\mathcal{L}_{align}$ as:

$$\begin{aligned} \mathcal{L}_{align} &:= \mathbb{E}_{(T,M)\sim P_{\text{data}}}||Z_T - Z_M||_2 \\ &= \mathbb{E}_{(T,M)\sim P_{\text{data}}}||Z_T - [Z_{A|B}, Z_B]||_2 \end{aligned} \tag{10}$$

where $[Z_{A|B}, Z_B]$ denotes the concatenation of the atom embedding $Z_{A|B}$ and the bond embedding Z_B, and the pair of protein target T and molecular drug M is sampled from the data P_{data}.

The alignment loss bridges the connections between the target sequence embedding Z_T and the drug graph embedding Z_M in the latent space, but there are still challenges that will be revealed in Sect. 4.3 and Sect. 4.4.

4.3   Uniformity Loss

Simply aligning the target sequence embedding Z_T and the drug graph embedding Z_M is not enough. There still remains three challenges: (1) the distribution of Z_T is uncertain, so that the alignment learning may be difficult to converge; (2) sampling from an unknown distribution is indefinite in the generation process; (3) the alignment loss alone admits collapsed solutions, e.g., outputting the same representation for all targets.

To overcome the above issues, we design an objective to force the target sequence embedding Z_T to follow a specific distribution, in our case the uniform distribution on the unit hypersphere [18,29,49,60]. We recognize angles of embeddings are the critical element that preserves the most abundant and discriminative information. By fitting the hyperspherical uniform distribution, the projections of target sequence embeddings on the hypersphere are kept as far away from each other as possible; thus, discriminations are imposed. Specifically, we project the target sequence embedding Z_T into a unit hypersphere $\mathbb{S}^{D-1}$ by L2 normalization and require the embeddings uniformly distributed on this hypersphere, as shown in Fig. 3.

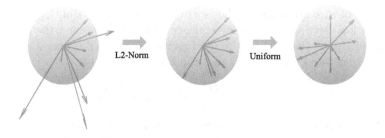

Fig. 3. The schematic diagram of the uniformity loss.

The uniform hypersphere distribution can be formulated as a minimizing pairwise potential energy problem [4,38,60] while higher energy implies less discriminations. Let $\widehat{Z}_T = \frac{Z_T}{\|Z_T\|} \in \mathcal{C}$, and $\mathcal{C}$ is a finite subset of the unit hypersphere $\mathbb{S}^{D-1} \in \mathbb{R}^D$. We define the f-potential energy [6] of $\mathcal{C}$ to be:

$$\sum_{\widehat{Z}_T^{(x)}, \widehat{Z}_T^{(y)} \in \mathcal{C}, x \neq y} f(|\widehat{Z}_T^{(x)} - \widehat{Z}_T^{(y)}|^2). \tag{11}$$

where $\widehat{Z}_T^{(x)}$ and $\widehat{Z}_T^{(y)}$ denote normalized sequence embeddings with index x, y.

Definition 1 (Universally optimal [6]). A finite subset $\mathcal{C} \subset \mathbb{S}^{D-1}$ is *universally optimal* if it (weakly) minimizes potential energy among all configurations of $|\mathcal{C}|$ points on $\mathbb{S}^{D-1}$ for each completely monotonic potential function.

In SiamFlow, we consider the Gaussian function kernel $G_t(x, y) : \mathbb{S}^{D-1} \times \mathbb{S}^{D-1} \to \mathbb{R}$ as the potential function f, which is defined as:

$$G_t(x, y) = e^{-t|x-y|^2}. \tag{12}$$

This kernel function is closely related to the universally optimal configuration, and distributions of points convergence weak* to the uniform distribution by minimizing the expected pairwise potential.

Theorem (Strictly positive definite kernels on $\mathbb{S}^D$ [4]). Consider kernel $K_f : \mathbb{S}^D \times \mathbb{S}^D \to (-\infty, +\infty]$ of the form $K_f(x, y) := f(|x - y|^2)$, if K_f is *strictly positive definite* on $\mathbb{S}^D \times \mathbb{S}^D$ and the energy $I_{K_f}[\sigma_D]$ is finite, then σ_D is the unique measure on Borel subsets of $\mathbb{S}^D$ in the solution of $\min_{\mu \in \mathcal{M}(\mathbb{S}^D)} I_{K_f}(\mu)$, and the normalized counting measure associated with any K_f-energy minimizing sequence of point configurations on $\mathbb{S}^D$ converges weak* to σ_D.

This theorem reveals the connections between strictly positive definite kernels and the energy minimizing problem. The Gaussian function is strictly positive definite on $\mathbb{S}^D \times \mathbb{S}^D$, thus well tied with the uniform distribution on the unit hypersphere.

Proposition 1 (Strictly positive definite of the Gaussian function). For any $t > 0$, the Gaussian function kernel $G_t(x, y)$ is strictly positive definte on $\mathbb{S}^D \times \mathbb{S}^D$.

Though Riesz s-kernels $R_s(x, y) := |x - y|^{-s}$ are commonly used as potential functions, we argue that the Gaussian function is expressive because it maps distances to infinite dimensions like radial basis functions, benefiting from the Taylor expansion of exponential functions. Moreover, the Gaussian function is a general case of Riesz s-kernels and can represent Riesz s-kernels by:

$$R_s(x, y) = \frac{1}{\Gamma(s/2)} \int_0^\infty G_t(x, y) t^{s/2-1} dt. \tag{13}$$

where $\Gamma(s/2) = \int_0^\infty e^{-t} t^{s/2-1}$ for $s > 0$.

As the Gaussian function kernel is an ideal choice of potential functions, we define the uniformity loss as the logarithm of the pairwise Gaussian potential's expectation:

$$\mathcal{L}_{unif} := \log \mathbb{E}_{(T^{(x)}, T^{(y)}) \sim P_T}[G_t(\widehat{Z}_T^{(x)}, \widehat{Z}_T^{(y)})], \tag{14}$$

where $T^{(x)}$ and $T^{(y)}$ are two different targets sampled from the target data P_T.

4.4 One Target to Many Drugs

Implementing the alignment loss and the uniformity loss above, the flow model can already generate validated molecular drugs conditioned on specific targets. However, there are multiple affinable drugs for a single target in most cases. To deal with this *one-to-many* problem, we reformulate learning target embeddings into learning spaces of target embeddings in the latent space, as shown in Fig. 4.

Fig. 4. The schematic diagram of the one-to-many strategy. The blue circles denote the possible spaces around the target sequence embeddings, and the green triangles denote the instances sampled from the possible spaces. (Color figure online)

As the target embeddings have been pushed by the uniformity loss to stay as far away as possible on the hypersphere, they preserve abundant and discriminative information to a large extent. We design an adaptive space learning strategy that holds the discriminative angle information with a limited scope. For a set of target sequence embeddings $\mathcal{Z}_T = \{Z_T^{(0)}, ..., Z_T^{(L)}\}$, we first calculate their standard deviation by:

$$\sigma(\mathcal{Z}_T) = \sqrt{\frac{1}{L} \sum_{i=1}^{L} (Z_T^{(i)} - \mu(\mathcal{Z}_T))}, \tag{15}$$

where $\mu(\mathcal{Z}_T) = \frac{1}{L} \sum_{i=1}^{L} Z_T^{(i)}$ is the mean of the set $\mathcal{Z}_T$. Then, we define a space for each target sequence embedding:

$$\Omega(Z_T) = \{Z_T + Z_T' | Z_T' \in \mathcal{N}(0, \lambda \sigma^2(\mathcal{Z}_T))\}, \tag{16}$$

where λ is the hyperparameter that controls the scale of the space and is empirically set as 0.1.

Note that we define the space on Z_T instead of the normalized $\widehat{Z}_T$, as normalized embeddings lose the length information to the extent that the available space is limited. Thus, we modify the alignment loss as:

$$\mathcal{L}_{align} = \mathbb{E}_{(T,M) \sim P_{\text{data}}} |\Omega(Z_T) - Z_M|. \tag{17}$$

In the generation process, sampling from the same space is permissible to generate desired drugs.

In summary, the objective is a linear combination of the modified alignment loss and uniform loss:

$$\mathcal{L}_{total} = \mathcal{L}_{align} + \mathcal{L}_{unif} \tag{18}$$

5   Experiments

Baselines. Since we present a novel generative approach conditioned on targets, we primarily compare our approach to other conditional generative models, i.e., conditional VAE (CVAE) [56], CSVAE [27], PCVAE [17]. Furthermore, an attention-based Seq2seq [57,59] neural translation model between the target protein sequence and drug SMILES is considered a straightforward solution in our setting. An explainable substructure partition fingerprint [22] is employed for sequential drug SMILES and protein sequences. We also involve GraphAF [54], GraphDF [39], and MolGrow [32] in the generative comparison.

Datasets. To evaluate the ability of our proposed SiamFlow, we collect a dataset based on four drug-target interaction datasets, including BIOSNAP [65], BindingDB [37], DAVIS [9], and DrugBank [61]. We remove all the negative samples in the original datasets, and only keep the positive samples. Our dataset contains 24,669 unique drug-target pairs with 10,539 molecular drugs and 2,766 proteins. The maximum number of atoms in a molecular drug is 100 while 11 types of common atoms are considered. We split drug-target pairs by target protein sequence identity at 30%, and define the dataloader to ensure zero overlap protein in the training, validation, and test set.

Metrics. To comprehensively evaluate the conditional generative models in terms of target-aware molecular generation, we design metrics from two perspectives: (1) Generative metrics. Following the common molecular generation settings, we apply metrics including: **Validity** which is the percentage of chemically valid molecules in all the generated molecules, **Uniqueness** which is the percentage of unique valid molecules in all the generated molecules, **Novelty** which is the percentage of generated valid molecules which are not in the training dataset. (2) Biochemical metrics. We evaluate the similarities between the generated drugs and the nearest drugs in the training set including: **Tanimoto similarity** which is calculated based on hashed binary features, **Fraggle similarity** which focus on the fragment-level similarity, **MACCS similarity** which employs 166-bit 2D structure fingerprints, and **Binding Score** predicted by DeepPurpose [21].

Empirical Running Time. We implement our proposed method SiamFlow and the other two baselines Seq2seq, CVAE by Pytorch-1.8.1 framework. We train them with Adam optimizer with a learning rate of 0.001, batch size 16, and 100 epochs on a single NVIDIA Tesla V100 GPU. To evaluate the validity and chemical similarities, we employ the cheminformatics toolkit RDKit in the assessment phase. Our SiamFlow completes the training process of 100 epochs in an average of 1.06 h (38 s/epoch), while CVAE and Seq2seq take an average of 1.14 h (41 s/epoch) and 8.33 h (5 min/epoch) respectively.

5.1   Target-Aware Molecular Graph Generation

We conduct experiments on molecular drug generation with specific targets for comparisons. For each experiment, we repeat three trials with different random seeds and report the mean and standard deviation.

Table 1 shows the results on generative metrics of our SiamFlow model in comparison to the baselines. Our proposed SiamFlow inherits the strengths of the flow and far surpasses other baselines in generative metrics. It can be seen that Seq2seq suffers from low validity, uniqueness, and novelty, which indicates Seq2seq's generation relies on its memorization. CVAE has higher uniqueness and novelty than Seq2seq though its validity is even lower. Besides, the standard deviations of metrics on CVAE are relatively high, suggesting it is volatile to train. Moreover, compared to other baselines, SiamFlow obtains superior performance with relatively low volatility.

Table 1. Evaluation results on generative metrics of SiamFlow v.s. baselines; high is better for all three metrics.

Method	% Validity	% Uniqueness	% Novelty
Seq2seq	16.08 ± 4.14	13.87 ± 1.74	14.89 ± 11.41
CVAE	12.54 ± 7.56	72.30 ± 20.33	99.72 ± 0.39
CSVAE	76.53 ± 2.4	60.31 ± 6.56	99.37 ± 0.59
PCVAE	78.81 ± 2.4	89.32 ± 2.74	99.59 ± 0.32
GraphAF	100.00 ± 0.00	98.68 ± 0.40	100.00 ± 0.00
GraphDF	100.00 ± 0.00	96.97 ± 0.23	100.00 ± 0.00
MolGrow	100.00 ± 0.00	99.57 ± 0.01	100.00 ± 0.00
SiamFlow	$\mathbf{100.00 \pm 0.00}$	99.61 ± 0.16	$\mathbf{100.00 \pm 0.00}$

In addition to generative metrics, we also report chemical metrics in Table 2. The generated molecular drugs are expected to have a chemical structure similar to the ground-truth drugs in order to have a high binding affinity to the target. SiamFlow is consistently better than other baselines in both the Tanimoto and Fraggle similarity while obtaining relatively lower MACCS similarity than Seq2seq. Considering that MACCS measures the similarity of encodings of molecules, the sequence partition rules of Seq2seq may help it. Thus, we pay more attention to the Tanimoto and Fraggle similarity because they are structure-centric metrics.

We visualize the distribution of the Tanimoto similarity and the Fraggle similarity evaluated on these methods in Fig. 6. SiamFlow consistently outperforms other methods and generates desirable molecular drugs. The examples of generated drugs are shown in Fig. 5.

Table 2. Evaluation results on biochemical metrics of SiamFlow v.s. baselines.

Method	% Tanimoto ($\uparrow$)	% Fraggle ($\uparrow$)	% MACCS ($\uparrow$)	Binding Score ($\downarrow$)
Seq2seq	26.27 ± 9.91	25.84 ± 7.27	$\mathbf{37.98 \pm 7.70}$	8.83 ± 4.70
CVAE	7.76 ± 6.61	12.31 ± 5.81	16.42 ± 7.17	10.92 ± 5.28
CSVAE	18.49 ± 3.92	16.67 ± 2.71	17.91 ± 3.21	6.91 ± 3.10
PCVAE	39.59 ± 2.17	24.56 ± 3.17	25.74 ± 1.14	4.87 ± 2.34
SiamFlow	$\mathbf{48.55 \pm 0.97}$	$\mathbf{34.41 \pm 0.35}$	29.30 ± 1.07	$\mathbf{2.07 \pm 0.15}$

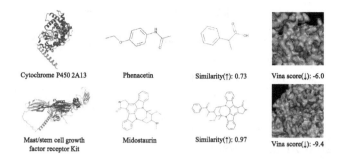

| Cytochrome P450 2A13 | Phenacetin | Similarity(↑): 0.73 | Vina score(↓): -6.0 |
| Mast/stem cell growth factor receptor Kit | Midostaurin | Similarity(↑): 0.97 | Vina score(↓): -9.4 |

Fig. 5. Examples of the generated drugs.

5.2 Ablation Study

We conduct the ablation study and report the results in Table 3 and Table 4. It can be seen from Table 3 that simply aligning the target sequence embedding and drug graph embedding will result in extremely low uniqueness. Our one-to-many strategy enriches the latent space so that one target can map to different drugs. The absence of $\mathcal{L}_{unif}$ does not harm the generative metrics because it only constrains the distribution of target sequence embeddings but has a limited impact on the generation process.

Table 4 demonstrates the chemical metrics are well without the one-to-many strategy. If we generate only one drug for a particular target, the nearest drug similarity degrades to a special case, i.e., comparing the generated drug with its corresponding one in the training set. Moreover, removing $\mathcal{L}_{unif}$ severely impairs the chemical performance, suggesting uniformity loss promotes the expressive abilities of target sequence embeddings.

Table 3. Ablation results on generative metrics.

Method	% Validity	% Uniqueness	% Novelty
SiamFlow	100.00	99.39	100.00
w/o one-to-many	100.00	12.55	100.00
w/o $\mathcal{L}_{unif}$	100.00	100.00	100.00

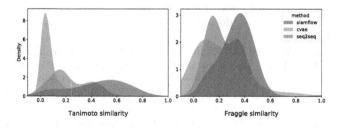

Fig. 6. The distribution of generative metrics evaluated on SiamFlow and baselines.

Table 4. Ablation results on chemical metrics.

Method	% Tanimoto	% Fraggle	% MACCS
SiamFlow	49.43	34.62	29.55
w/o one-to-many	48.83	34.93	31.23
w/o $\mathcal{L}_{unif}$	18.49	15.70	17.91

6   Conclusion and Discussion

In this paper, we delve into the topic of target-aware molecular graph generation, which involves creating drugs that are specifically conditioned on particular targets. While existing methods focus on developing drugs similar to those found in drug-like datasets, target-aware molecular generation combines drug-like molecular generation with target-specific screening to simplify the drug-target interaction step. To thoroughly explore this problem, we compile a benchmark dataset using several public datasets. Furthermore, we leverage recent progress in flow-based molecular graph generation methods and propose SiamFlow as a solution for target-aware molecular generation. Through the use of alignment and uniform loss, our proposed method can effectively generate molecular drugs conditioned on protein targets. Additionally, we address the challenge of generating multiple drugs for a single target by aligning the embedding space, rather than relying on a single embedding. Extensive experiments and analyses demonstrate that SiamFlow is a highly promising solution for target-aware molecular generation.

Acknowledgements. This work was supported by the National Key R&D Program of China (Project 2022ZD0115100), the National Natural Science Foundation of China (Project U21A20427), the Research Center for Industries of the Future (Project WU2022C043).

Ethical Statement. Our submission does not involve any ethical issues, including but not limited to privacy, security, etc.

References

1. Abdelhamed, A., Brubaker, M.A., Brown, M.S.: Noise flow: noise modeling with conditional normalizing flows. In: ICCV (2019)
2. Arjovsky, M., Chintala, S., Bottou, L.: Wasserstein generative adversarial networks. In: ICML (2017)
3. Bandholtz, S., Wichard, J., Kühne, R., Grötzinger, C.: Molecular evolution of a peptide GPCR ligand driven by artificial neural networks. PloS One **7**, e36948 (2012)
4. Borodachov, S.V., Hardin, D.P., Saff, E.B.: Discrete energy on rectifiable sets (2019)
5. Chenthamarakshan, V., Das, P., et al.: Cogmol: target-specific and selective drug design for covid-19 using deep generative models. In: NeurIPS (2020)

6. Cohn, H., Kumar, A.: Universally optimal distribution of points on spheres. J. Amer. Math. Soc. **20**(1), 99–148 (2007)
7. Dai, H., Tian, Y., Dai, B., Skiena, S., Song, L.: Syntax-directed variational autoencoder for molecule generation. In: ICLR (2018)
8. Das, P., Sercu, T., et al.: Accelerated antimicrobial discovery via deep generative models and molecular dynamics simulations. Nat. Biomed. Eng. **5**, 613–623 (2021)
9. Davis, I.M., Hunt, P.J., et al.: Comprehensive analysis of kinase inhibitor selectivity. Nat. Biotechnol. **29**, 1046–1051 (2011)
10. De Cao, N., Kipf, T.: MolGAN: an implicit generative model for small molecular graphs. In: ICML Workshop (2018)
11. Dinh, L., Krueger, D., Bengio, Y.: Nice: non-linear independent components estimation. In: ICLR Workshop (2015)
12. Dinh, L., Sohl-Dickstein, J., Bengio, S.: Density estimation using real nvp. In: ICLR (2017)
13. Gao, K.Y., Fokoue, A., et al.: Interpretable drug target prediction using deep neural representation. In: IJCAI (2018)
14. Gómez-Bombarelli, R., Wei, J.N., et al.: Automatic chemical design using a data-driven continuous representation of molecules. ACS Central Sci. **4**, 268–276 (2018)
15. Griffiths, R.R., Hernández-Lobato, J.M.: Constrained bayesian optimization for automatic chemical design using variational autoencoders. Chem. Sci. **11**, 577–586 (2020)
16. Guimaraes, G.L., Sanchez-Lengeling, B., et al.: Objective-reinforced generative adversarial networks (organ) for sequence generation models. arXiv preprint arXiv:1705.10843 (2017)
17. Guo, X., Du, Y., Zhao, L.: Property controllable variational autoencoder via invertible mutual dependence. In: ICLR (2021)
18. Hardin, D.P., Saff, E.B., et al.: Discretizing manifolds via minimum energy points. Not. AMS **51**, 1186–1194 (2004)
19. Hert, J., Irwin, J.J., et al.: Quantifying biogenic bias in screening libraries. Nat. Chem. Biol. **5**, 479–483 (2009)
20. Honda, S., Akita, H., et al.: Graph residual flow for molecular graph generation. arXiv preprint arXiv:1909.13521 (2019)
21. Huang, K., Fu, T., et al.: Deeppurpose: a deep learning library for drug-target interaction prediction. Bioinformatics **36**, 5545–5547 (2020)
22. Huang, K., Xiao, C., Glass, L., Sun, J.: Explainable substructure partition fingerprint for protein, drug, and more. In: NeurIPS (2019)
23. Jin, W., Barzilay, R., Jaakkola, T.: Junction tree variational autoencoder for molecular graph generation. In: ICML (2018)
24. Karimi, M., Wu, D., et al.: Deepaffinity: interpretable deep learning of compound-protein affinity through unified recurrent and convolutional neural networks. Bioinformatics **35**, 3329–3338 (2019)
25. Karimi, M., Wu, D., et al.: Explainable deep relational networks for predicting compound-protein affinities and contacts. J. Chem. Inf. Model **61**, 46–66 (2020)
26. Kingma, D.P., Dhariwal, P.: Glow: generative flow with invertible 1×1 convolutions. In: NeurIPS (2018)
27. Klys, J., Snell, J., et al.: Learning latent subspaces in variational autoencoders. In: NIPS (2018)
28. Kondo, R., Kawano, K., Koide, S., Kutsuna, T.: Flow-based image-to-image translation with feature disentanglement. In: NeurIPS (2019)
29. Kuijlaars, A., Saff, E.: Asymptotics for minimal discrete energy on the sphere. Trans. Amer. Math. Soc. **350**, 523–538 (1998)

30. Kumar, M., Babaeizadeh, M., et al.: Videoflow: a conditional flow-based model for stochastic video generation. In: ICLR (2019)
31. Kusner, M.J., Paige, B., Hernández-Lobato, J.M.: Grammar variational autoencoder. In: ICML (2017)
32. Kuznetsov, M., Polykovskiy, D.: Molgrow: a graph normalizing flow for hierarchical molecular generation. In: AAAI (2021)
33. Li, S., Wan, F., et al.: Monn: a multi-objective neural network for predicting compound-protein interactions and affinities. Cell Syst. **10**, 308–322 (2020)
34. Lim, J., Ryu, S., et al.: Molecular generative model based on conditional variational autoencoder for de novo molecular design. J. Cheminf. **10**, 1–9 (2018)
35. Liu, J., Kumar, A., et al.: Graph normalizing flows. In: NeurIPS (2019)
36. Liu, R., Liu, Y., Gong, X., Wang, X., Li, H.: Conditional adversarial generative flow for controllable image synthesis. In: CVPR (2019)
37. Liu, T., Lin, Y., et al.: Bindingdb: a web-accessible database of experimentally determined protein-ligand binding affinities. Nucl. Acids Res. **35**, D198–D201 (2007)
38. Liu, W., et al.: Learning towards minimum hyperspherical energy. In: NeurIPS (2018)
39. Luo, Y., Yan, K., Ji, S.: Graphdf: a discrete flow model for molecular graph generation. arXiv preprint arXiv:2102.01189 (2021)
40. Madhawa, K., Ishiguro, K., et al.: Graphnvp: an invertible flow model for generating molecular graphs. arXiv preprint arXiv:1905.11600 (2019)
41. Maziarka, Ł, Pocha, A., et al.: Mol-cyclegan: a generative model for molecular optimization. J. Cheminf. **12**, 1–18 (2020)
42. Méndez-Lucio, O., Baillif, B., et al.: De novo generation of hit-like molecules from gene expression signatures using artificial intelligence. Nat. Commun. **11**, 10 (2020)
43. Öztürk, H., Özgür, A., Ozkirimli, E.: Deepdta: deep drug-target binding affinity prediction. Bioinformatics **34**, i821–i829 (2018)
44. Phatak, S.S., Stephan, C.C., et al.: High-throughput and in silico screenings in drug discovery. Expert Opin. Drug Disc. **4**, 947–959 (2009)
45. Polishchuk, P.G., Madzhidov, T.I., Varnek, A.: Estimation of the size of drug-like chemical space based on gdb-17 data. J. Comput. Aided Molec. Des. **27**, 675–679 (2013)
46. Popova, M., Shvets, M., Oliva, J., Isayev, O.: Molecularrnn: generating realistic molecular graphs with optimized properties. arXiv preprint arXiv:1905.13372 (2019)
47. Prykhodko, O., Johansson, S.V., et al.: A de novo molecular generation method using latent vector based generative adversarial network. J. Cheminf. **11**, 1–13 (2019)
48. Pumarola, A., Popov, S., et al.: C-flow: conditional generative flow models for images and 3D point clouds. In: CVPR (2020)
49. Saff, E.B., Kuijlaars, A.B.: Distributing many points on a sphere. Math. Intell. **19**, 5–11 (1997)
50. Sanchez-Lengeling, B., Outeiral, C., et al.: Optimizing distributions over molecular space: an objective-reinforced generative adversarial network for inverse-design chemistry. ChemRxiv (2017)
51. Schneider, G.: Virtual screening: an endless staircase? Nat. Rev. Drug Disc. **9**, 273–276 (2010)
52. Schneider, G.: De novo molecular design (2013)
53. Schneider, P., Schneider, G.: De novo design at the edge of chaos: miniperspective. J. Med. Chem. **59**, 4077–4086 (2016)

54. Shi, C., Xu, M., et al.: Graphaf: a flow-based autoregressive model for molecular graph generation. In: ICLR (2019)
55. Simonovsky, M., Komodakis, N.: Graphvae: towards generation of small graphs using variational autoencoders. In: ICANN (2018)
56. Sohn, K., Lee, H., Yan, X.: Learning structured output representation using deep conditional generative models. In: NeurIPS (2015)
57. Sutskever, I., Vinyals, O., Le, Q.V.: Sequence to sequence learning with neural networks. In: NeurIPS (2014)
58. Van Oord, A., Kalchbrenner, N., et al.: Pixel recurrent neural networks. In: ICML (2016)
59. Vaswani, A., Shazeer, N., et al.: Attention is all you need. In: NeurIPS (2017)
60. Wang, T., Isola, P.: Understanding contrastive representation learning through alignment and uniformity on the hypersphere. In: ICML (2020)
61. Wishart, S.D., Feunang, D.Y., et al.: Drugbank 5.0: a major update to the drugbank database for 2018. Nucl. Acids Res. 46, D1074–D1082 (2018)
62. You, J., Liu, B., et al.: Graph convolutional policy network for goal-directed molecular graph generation. In: NeurIPS (2018)
63. Zang, C., Wang, F.: Moflow: an invertible flow model for generating molecular graphs. In: SIGKDD (2020)
64. Zhu, J.Y., Park, T., et al.: Unpaired image-to-image translation using cycle-consistent adversarial networkss. In: ICCV (2017)
65. Zitnik, M., Sosic, R., et al.: Biosnap datasets: stanford biomedical network dataset collection (2018)

Contrastive Learning-Based Imputation-Prediction Networks for In-hospital Mortality Risk Modeling Using EHRs

Yuxi Liu[1(✉)], Zhenhao Zhang[2], Shaowen Qin[1], Flora D. Salim[3], and Antonio Jimeno Yepes[4]

[1] College of Science and Engineering, Flinders University, Tonsley, SA 5042, Australia
{liu1356,shaowen.qin}@flinders.edu.au

[2] College of Life Sciences, Northwest A&F University, Yangling 712100, Shaanxi, China
zhangzhenhow@nwafu.edu.cn

[3] School of Computer Science and Engineering, UNSW, Sydney, NSW 2052, Australia
flora.salim@unsw.edu.au

[4] School of Computing Technologies, RMIT University, Melbourne, VIC 3001, Australia
antonio.jose.jimeno.yepes@rmit.edu.au

Abstract. Predicting the risk of in-hospital mortality from electronic health records (EHRs) has received considerable attention. Such predictions will provide early warning of a patient's health condition to healthcare professionals so that timely interventions can be taken. This prediction task is challenging since EHR data are intrinsically irregular, with not only many missing values but also varying time intervals between medical records. Existing approaches focus on exploiting the variable correlations in patient medical records to impute missing values and establishing time-decay mechanisms to deal with such irregularity. This paper presents a novel contrastive learning-based imputation-prediction network for predicting in-hospital mortality risks using EHR data. Our approach introduces graph analysis-based patient stratification modeling in the imputation process to group similar patients. This allows information of similar patients only to be used, in addition to personal contextual information, for missing value imputation. Moreover, our approach can integrate contrastive learning into the proposed network architecture to enhance patient representation learning and predictive performance on the classification task. Experiments on two real-world EHR datasets show that our approach outperforms the state-of-the-art approaches in both imputation and prediction tasks.

Keywords: data imputation · in-hospital mortality · contrastive learning

© The Author(s), under exclusive license to Springer Nature Switzerland AG 2023
G. De Francisci Morales et al. (Eds.): ECML PKDD 2023, LNAI 14174, pp. 428–443, 2023.
https://doi.org/10.1007/978-3-031-43427-3_26

1   Introduction

The broad adoption of digital healthcare systems produces a large amount of electronic health records (EHRs) data, providing us the possibility to develop predictive models and tools using machine learning techniques that would enable healthcare professionals to make better decisions and improve healthcare outcomes. One of the EHR-based risk prediction tasks is to predict the mortality risk of patients based on their historical EHR data [8, 29]. The predicted mortality risks can be used to provide early warnings when a patient's health condition is about to deteriorate so that more proactive interventions can be taken.

However, due to a high degree of irregularity in the raw EHR data, it is challenging to directly apply traditional machine learning techniques to perform predictive modeling. We take the medical records of two anonymous patients from the publicly available MIMIC-III database and present these in Fig. 1 as an example. Figure 1 clearly indicates the irregularity problem, including many missing values and varying time intervals between medical records.

Most studies have focused on exploiting variable correlations in patient medical records to impute missing values and establishing time-decay mechanisms to take into account the effect of varying time intervals between records [1, 2, 17, 18, 23–25, 31]. After obtaining the complete data matrices from the imputation task, the complete data matrices are used as input for downstream healthcare prediction tasks [1, 2, 13, 17, 18, 22, 23, 27, 30, 31, 35]. Although these studies have achieved satisfactory imputation performance, consideration of using the information of similar patients on the imputation task, which might lead to improved imputation performance, has not yet been fully experimented. Furthermore, with imputation data, high-quality representation must be applied, as the imputation data may affect the performance of downstream healthcare prediction tasks.

Patient stratification refers to the method of dividing a patient population into subgroups based on specific disease characteristics and symptom severity. Patients in the same subgroup generally had more similar health trajectories. Therefore, we propose to impute missing values in patient data using information from the subgroup of similar patients rather than the entire patient population.

In this paper, we propose a novel contrastive learning-based imputation-prediction network with the aim of improving in-hospital mortality prediction performance using EHR data. Missing value imputation for EHR data is done by exploiting similar patient information as well as patients' personal contextual information. Similar patients are generated from patient similarity calculation during stratification modeling and analysis of patient graphs.

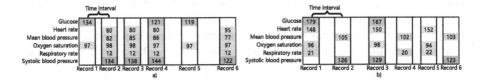

Fig. 1. Illustration of medical records of patients A and B.

Contrastive learning has been proven to be an important machine learning technique in the computer vision community [12]. In contrastive learning, representations are learned by comparing input samples. The comparisons are made on the similarity between positive pairs or dissimilarity between negative pairs. The main goal is to learn an embedding space where similar samples are put closer to each other while dissimilar samples are pushed farther apart. Contrastive learning can be applied in both supervised [10,33,39] and unsupervised [14,15,26] settings.

Motivated by the recent developments in contrastive representation learning [34,36,38], we integrate contrastive learning into the proposed network architecture to perform imputation and prediction tasks. The benefit of incorporating contrastive learning into the imputation task is that such an approach can enhance patient representation learning by keeping patients of the same stratification together and pushing away patients from different stratifications. This would lead to enhanced imputation performance. The benefit of incorporating contrastive learning into the prediction task is improved predictive performance of the binary classification problem (i.e., the risk of death and no death), which is achieved by keeping the instances of a positive class closer and pushing away instances from a negative class.

Our major contributions are as follows:

- To the best of our knowledge, this is the first attempt to consider patient similarity via stratification of EHR data on the imputation task.
- We propose a novel imputation-prediction approach to perform imputation and prediction simultaneously with EHR data.
- We successfully integrate contrastive learning into the proposed network architecture to improve imputation and prediction performance.
- Extensive experiments conducted on two real-world EHR datasets show that our approach outperforms all baseline approaches in imputation and prediction tasks.

2   Related Work

There has been an increased interest in EHR-based health risk predictions [5,16,19–21]. It has been recognized that EHR data often contains many missing values due to patient conditions and treatment decisions [31]. Existing research addresses this challenge by imputing missing data and feeding them into the supervised algorithms as auxiliary information [7]. GRU-D [2] represents such an example. The GRU-D is built upon the Gated Recurrent Unit [4]. GRU-D proposes to impute missing values by decaying the contributions of previous observation values toward the overall mean over time. Similarly, BRITS [1] incorporates a bidirectional recurrent neural network (RNN) to impute missing values. Since the incorporated bidirectional RNN learns EHR data in both forward and backward directions, the accumulated loss is introduced to train the model.

Another line of related work is based on the generative adversarial network (GAN) architecture, which aims at treating the problem of missing data imputation as data generation. The intuitions behind GAN can be seen as making a generator and a discriminator against each other [6]. The generator generates fake samples from random 'noise' vectors, and the discriminator distinguishes the generator's fake samples from actual samples. Examples of research into GAN-based imputation methods include GRUI-GAN [17], E^{2}GAN [18], E^{2}GAN-RF [40], and STING [25]. These studies take the vector of actual samples, which has many missing values, use a generator to generate the corresponding imputed values and distinguish the generated imputed values from real values using a discriminator.

Several studies have evaluated the effectiveness of applying transformer-based imputation methods to EHR data. Examples of representative studies include MTSIT [37] and MIAM [13]. The MTSIT is built with an autoencoder architecture to perform missing value imputation in an unsupervised manner. The autoencoder architecture used in MTSIT includes the Transformer encoder [32] and a linear decoder, which are implemented with a joint reconstruction and imputation approach. The MIAM is built upon the self-attention mechanism [32]. Given EHR data, MIAM imputes the missing values by extracting the relationship among the observed values, missingness indicators (0 for missing and 1 for not missing), and the time interval between consecutive observations.

3 Method

3.1 Network Architecture

The architecture of the proposed network is shown in Fig. 2.

Data Representation. We represent a multivariate time series X with up to N variables of length T as a set of observed triplets, i.e., $X = \{(f_i, v_i, t_i)\}_{i=1}^{N}$. An observed triplet is represented as a (f, v, t), where $f \in F$ is the variable/feature, $v \in \mathbb{R}^T$ is the observed value, and $t \in \mathbb{R}^T$ is the time. We incorporate a masking vector m_i to represent missing values in v_i as:

$$m_{i,t} = \begin{cases} 1, & if \ v_{i,t} \ is \ observed \\ 0, & otherwise \end{cases} \tag{1}$$

Let $\delta \in \mathbb{R}^{N \times T}$, $\delta^{(l)} \in \mathbb{R}^{N \times T}$, and $\delta^{(n)} \in \mathbb{R}^{N \times T}$ denote three time interval matrices. δ_t is the time interval between the current time t and the last time $t-1$. $\delta_{i,t}^{(l)}$ is the time interval between the current time t and the time where the i-th variable is observed the last time. $\delta_{i,t}^{(n)}$ is the time interval between the current time t and the time where the i-th variable is observed next time. $\delta_{i,t}^{(l)}$ and $\delta_{i,t}^{(n)}$ can be written as:

$$\delta_{i,t}^{(l)} = \begin{cases} \delta_{i,t}, & if \ m_{i,t-1} = 1 \\ \delta_{i,t} + \delta_{i,t-1}^{(l)}, & otherwise \end{cases} \tag{2}$$

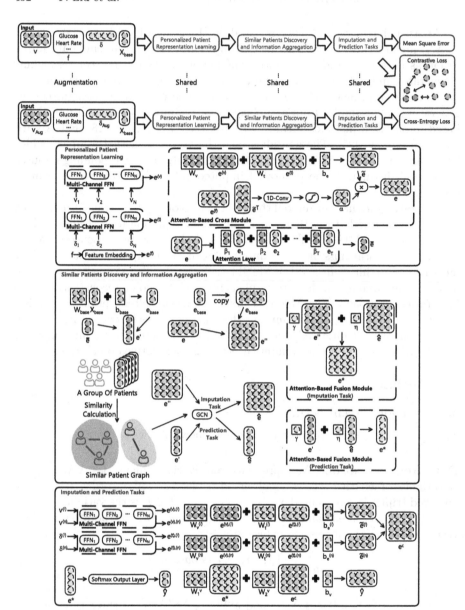

Fig. 2. Schematic description of the proposed network.

$$\delta_{i,t}^{(n)} = \begin{cases} \delta_{i,t+1}, & if \ m_{i,t+1} = 1 \\ \delta_{i,t+1} + \delta_{i,t+1}^{(n)}, & otherwise \end{cases} \tag{3}$$

Let $v^{(l)}$ and $v^{(n)}$ denote two neighboring value matrices, the observed values of the last time and next time. $v^{(l)}$ and $v^{(n)}$ can be written as:

$$v_{i,t}^{(l)} = \begin{cases} v_{i,t-1}, & if \ m_{i,t-1} = 1 \\ v_{i,t-1}^{(l)}, & otherwise \end{cases} \tag{4}$$

$$v_{i,t}^{(n)} = \begin{cases} v_{i,t+1}, & if \ m_{i,t+1} = 1 \\ v_{i,t+1}^{(n)}, & otherwise \end{cases} \tag{5}$$

where $v_{i,t}^{(l)}$ and $v_{i,t}^{(n)}$ are the values of the i-th variable of $v_t^{(l)}$ and $v_t^{(n)}$.

Let $D = \{(X_p, y_p)\}_{p=1}^{P}$ denote the EHR dataset with up to P labeled samples. The p-th sample contains a multivariate time series X_p consisting of the physiological variables, and a binary label of in-hospital mortality $y_p \in \{0, 1\}$. Let $X_{base} \in \mathbb{R}^g$ denote the patient-specific characteristics (i.e., age, sex, ethnicity, admission diagnosis) with up to g dimension.

Personalized Patient Representation Learning. Given an input multivariate time series/a single patient data $X = \{(f_i, v_i, t_i)\}_{i=1}^{N}$, the embedding for the i-th triplet $e_i \in \mathbb{R}^d$ is generated by aggregating the feature embedding $e_i^{(f)} \in \mathbb{R}^d$, the value embedding $e_i^{(v)} \in \mathbb{R}^{d \times T}$, and the time interval embedding $e_i^{(t)} \in \mathbb{R}^{d \times T}$. The feature embedding is similar to the word embedding, which allows features with similar meanings to have a similar representation. Particularly, the value embedding and time interval embedding are obtained by separately implementing a multi-channel feed-forward neural network (FFN) as:

$$\begin{aligned} e_{i,1}^{(v)}, \cdots, e_{i,T}^{(v)} &= FFN_i^{(v)}(v_{i,1}, \cdots, v_{i,T}), \\ e_{i,1}^{(t)}, \cdots, e_{i,T}^{(t)} &= FFN_i^{(t)}(\delta_{i,1}, \cdots, \delta_{i,T}). \end{aligned} \tag{6}$$

Through the processes above, we are able to obtain $e^{(f)} \in \mathbb{R}^{Nd}$, $e^{(v)} \in \mathbb{R}^{Nd \times T}$, and $e^{(t)} \in \mathbb{R}^{Nd \times T}$, which are fed into the attention-based cross module to generate an overall representation. Note that $e^{(f)} \in \mathbb{R}^{Nd}$ is expanded into $e^{(f)} \in \mathbb{R}^{Nd \times T}$. Specifically, we design the attention-based cross module to generate a cross-attention matrix as:

$$\tilde{e} = W_v \cdot e^{(v)} + W_t \cdot e^{(t)} + b_e,$$
$$E = ScaledDot(e^{(f)}, \tilde{e}) = \frac{e^{(f)} \cdot \tilde{e}^\top}{\sqrt{d}}, \tag{7}$$

where $E \in \mathbb{R}^{Nd \times Nd}$ is the cross-attention matrix that corresponds to the scaled-dot similarity. We then apply a 1D convolutional layer to the cross-attention matrix E as:

$$\alpha = Softmax(Conv(E)), \tag{8}$$

where $Conv$ is the 1D convolutional layer and α is the cross-attention score matrix. We integrate α and $\tilde{e}$ into a weighted representation e as:

$$e = \alpha \odot \tilde{e}. \tag{9}$$

Given a batch of patients, the embedding for them can be written as:

$$e = [e_1, e_2, \cdots, e_B] \in \mathbb{R}^{B \times Nd \times T}, \tag{10}$$

where B is the batch size. Since e still takes the form of sequence data, we design an attention layer to generate a series of attention weights $(\beta_1, \beta_2, \cdots, \beta_T)$ and reweight these weights to produce an overall feature representation as:

$$\beta = Softmax(e \cdot W_e + b_e),$$
$$\bar{e} = \sum_{t=1}^{T} \beta_t \odot e_t, \tag{11}$$

where $\bar{e} \in \mathbb{R}^{B \times Nd}$ is the new generated patient representation.

Similar Patients Discovery and Information Aggregation. Before conducting patient similarity calculation, we encode $X_{base} \in \mathbb{R}^g$ as $e_{base} \in \mathbb{R}^{d_g}$ and concatenate e_{base} with $\bar{e}$ as:

$$e_{base} = W_{base} \cdot X_{base} + b_{base},$$
$$e' = Concate(\bar{e}, e_{base}), \tag{12}$$

where Concate is the concatenation operation.

For the batch of patient representations, the pairwise similarities that correspond to any two patient representations can be calculated as:

$$\Lambda = sim(e', e') = \frac{e' \cdot e'}{(Nd + d_g)^2}, \tag{13}$$

where $sim(\cdot)$ is the measure of cosine similarity and $\Lambda \in \mathbb{R}^{B \times B}$ is the patient similarity matrix.

Moreover, we incorporate a learnable threshold φ into the patient similarity calculation to filter out similarities below the threshold. The similarity matrix can be rewritten as:

$$\Lambda' = \begin{cases} \Lambda, & if \ \Lambda > \varphi \\ 0, & otherwise \end{cases} \tag{14}$$

We take into account the batch of patients' representations as a graph to aggregate the information from similar patients, where the similarity matrix Λ'

is the graph adjacency matrix. We apply graph convolutional layers to enhance the representation learning as:

$$\hat{e} = [\hat{e}_1, \hat{e}_2, \cdots, \hat{e}_B]^\top = GCN(e', \Lambda')$$
$$= ReLU(\Lambda' ReLU(\Lambda' \cdot e' W_1^e) \cdot W_2^e), \tag{15}$$

where $\hat{e}$ is the aggregated auxiliary information from similar patients. A note of caution is due here since we ignore the bias term. We replace e' in Eq. (15) with e'' for the imputation task. By doing so, the output of graph convolutional layers can take the form of sequence data. Particularly, e'' is obtained by concatenating e and e_{base}, where $e_{base} \in \mathbb{R}^{d_g}$ is expanded into $e_{base} \in \mathbb{R}^{d_g \times T}$.

Through the processes above, we are able to generate e'/e'' and $\hat{e}$ representations for the batch of patients. The e'/e'' refers to the patient themselves. For an incomplete patient p (i.e., the patient data has many missing values), we generate the missing value representations with $\hat{e}$. For a complete patient, we augment e'/e'' with $\hat{e}$ to enhance the representation learning.

We design an attention-based fusion module to refine both e'/e'' (the two representations used in prediction and imputation tasks) and $\hat{e}$. Since imputation and prediction tasks involve the same process of modeling, we take the prediction task as an example. The two weights $\gamma \in \mathbb{R}^B$ and $\eta \in \mathbb{R}^B$ are incorporated to determine the importance of e' and $\hat{e}$, obtained by implementing fully connected layers as:

$$\gamma = Sigmoid(e' \cdot W_\gamma + b_\gamma),$$
$$\eta = Sigmoid(\hat{e} \cdot W_\eta + b_\eta). \tag{16}$$

A note of caution is due here since we keep the sum of γ and η must be 1, i.e., $\gamma + \eta = 1$. We achieve this constraint by combining $\gamma = \frac{\gamma}{\gamma+\eta}$ and $\eta = 1 - \gamma$. The final representation e^* is obtained by calculating $\gamma \cdot e' + \eta \cdot \hat{e}$.

Contrastive Learning. We integrate contrastive learning into the proposed network architecture to perform imputation and prediction tasks. For the prediction task, we augment the standard cross-entropy loss with the supervised contrastive loss [10]. We treat the patient representations with the same label as the positive pairs and the patient representations with different labels as the negative pairs. For the imputation task, we augment the standard mean squared error loss with the unsupervised contrastive loss [3]. We treat a single patient representation and its augmented representations as positive pairs and the other patient representations within a batch and their augmented representations as negative pairs. The formula can be written as:

$$\mathcal{L}_{SC} = -\sum_{i=1}^B \frac{1}{B_{y_i}} log \frac{\sum_{j=1}^B \mathbb{1}_{[y_i=y_j]} exp(sim(e_i^*, e_j^*)/\tau)}{\sum_{k=1}^B \mathbb{1}_{[k \neq i]} exp(sim(e_i^*, e_k^*)/\tau)},$$
$$\mathcal{L}_{UC} = -log \frac{exp(sim(e_i^*, e_j^*)/\tau)}{\sum_{k=1}^{2B} \mathbb{1}_{[k \neq i]} exp(sim(e_i^*, e_k^*)/\tau)}, \tag{17}$$

where B represents the batch size; $\mathbb{1}_{[\cdot]}$ represents an indicator function; $sim(\cdot)$ represents the cosine similarity measure; τ represents a hyper-parameter that is used to control the strength of penalties on negative pairs; B_{y_i} is the number of samples with the same label in each batch.

Imputation and Prediction Tasks. For the prediction task, we feed e^* into a softmax output layer to obtain the predicted $\hat{y}$ as:

$$\hat{y} = Softmax(W_y \cdot e^* + b_y). \tag{18}$$

The objective loss is the summation of cross-entropy loss and the supervised contrastive loss with a scaling parameter λ to control the contribution of each loss as:

$$\mathcal{L}_{CE} = -\frac{1}{P}\sum_{p=1}^{P}(y_p^\top \cdot log(\hat{y}_p) + (1 - y_p)^\top \cdot log(1 - \hat{y}_p)), \tag{19}$$

$$\mathcal{L} = \lambda \cdot \mathcal{L}_{CE} + (1 - \lambda) \cdot \mathcal{L}_{SC}.$$

For the imputation task, we take the neighboring observed values (of each patient) as inputs to incorporate patient-specific contextual information. The process of embedding used by $v^{(l)}$ and $v^{(n)}$ can be written as:

$$e_i^{(v),(l)} = FFN_i^{(v),(l)}(v_i^{(l)}), e_i^{(t),(l)} = FFN_i^{(t),(l)}(\delta_i^{(l)}),$$
$$e_i^{(v),(n)} = FFN_i^{(v),(n)}(v_i^{(n)}), e_i^{(t),(n)} = FFN_i^{(t),(n)}(\delta_i^{(n)}),$$
$$\tilde{e}^{(l)} = W_v^{(l)} \cdot e^{(v),(l)} + W_t^{(l)} \cdot e^{(t),(l)} + b_e^{(l)}, \tag{20}$$
$$\tilde{e}^{(n)} = W_n^{(v)} \cdot e^{(v),(n)} + W_t^{(n)} \cdot e^{(t),(n)} + b_e^{(n)},$$
$$e^c = Concate(\tilde{e}^{(l)}, \tilde{e}^{(n)}),$$

where $\tilde{e}^{(l)}$ and $\tilde{e}^{(n)}$ are the representations of $v^{(l)}$ and $v^{(n)}$ after embedding. The embedding matrix e^c is obtained by concatenating $\tilde{e}^{(l)}$ and $\tilde{e}^{(n)}$.

Given the final representation e^* and the embedding matrix e^c, we use a fully connected layer to impute missing values as:

$$\hat{v} = e^* \cdot W_1^v + e^c \cdot W_2^v + b_v. \tag{21}$$

The objective loss is the summation of the mean square error and the unsupervised contrastive loss with a scaling parameter λ to control the contribution of each loss as:

$$\mathcal{L}_{MSE} = \frac{1}{P}\sum_{p=1}^{P}(m_p \odot v_p - m_p \odot \hat{v}_p)^2, \tag{22}$$

$$\mathcal{L} = \lambda \cdot \mathcal{L}_{MSE} + (1 - \lambda) \cdot \mathcal{L}_{UC}.$$

4 Experiments

4.1 Datasets and Tasks

We validate our approach[1] on the MIMIC-III[2] and eICU[3] datasets. The 21,139 and 38,056 samples were taken from both datasets. Detailed information on both datasets can be found in the literature [9] and [28]. Table 1 presents the summary statistics for the MIMIC-III and eICU features used.

For the MIMIC-III dataset, we evaluate clinical time series imputation and in-hospital mortality accuracy based on the data from the first 24/48 h after ICU admission. Similarly, for the eICU dataset, we evaluate clinical time series imputation and in-hospital mortality accuracy based on the data from the first 24/48 h after eICU admission.

4.2 Baseline Approaches

We compare our approach with GRU-D [2], BRITS [1], GRUI-GAN [17], E^2GAN [18], E^2GAN-RF [40], STING [25], MTSIT [37], and MIAM [13] (see related work section). We feed the output of GRUI-GAN, E^2GAN, E^2GAN-RF, STING, and MTSIT into GRU to estimate in-hospital mortality risk probabilities. Moreover, the regression component used in BRITS is integrated into GRU-D and MIAM to obtain imputation accuracy.

Besides, we present two variants of our approach as follows:

Ours$_\alpha$: A variation of our approach that does not perform graph analysis-based patient stratification modeling.

Ours$_\beta$: A variation of our approach in which we omit the contrastive learning component.

All implementations of Ours$_\alpha$ and Ours$_\beta$ can be found in the aforementioned Github repository.

4.3 Implementation Details

We implement all approaches with PyTorch 1.11.0 and conduct experiments on A40 GPU from NVIDIA with 48GB of memory. We randomly use 70%, 15%, and 15% of the dataset as training, validation, and testing sets. We train the proposed approach using an Adam optimizer [11] with a learning rate of 0.0023 and a mini-batch size of 256. For personalized patient representation learning, the dimension size d is 3. For similar patients discovery and information aggregation, the initial value of φ is 0.56, and the dimension size of W_1^e and W_2^e are 34 and 55. For contrastive learning, the value of τ is 0.07. The dropout method is applied to the final Softmax output layer for the prediction task, and the dropout rate is

---

[1] The implementation code is available at https://github.com/liulab1356/CL-ImpPreNet.

[2] https://mimic.physionet.org.

[3] https://eicu-crd.mit.edu/.

Table 1. MIMIC-III and eICU features used for clinical time series imputation and in-hospital mortality prediction 48 h after ICU admission.

MIMIC-III Feature	Data Type	Missingness (%)
Capillary refill rate	categorical	99.78
Diastolic blood pressure	continuous	30.90
Fraction inspired oxygen	continuous	94.33
Glasgow coma scale eye	categorical	82.84
Glasgow coma scale motor	categorical	81.74
Glasgow coma scale total	categorical	89.16
Glasgow coma scale verbal	categorical	81.72
Glucose	continuous	83.04
Heart Rate	continuous	27.43
Height	continuous	99.77
Mean blood pressure	continuous	31.38
Oxygen saturation	continuous	26.86
Respiratory rate	continuous	26.80
Systolic blood pressure	continuous	30.87
Temperature	continuous	78.06
Weight	continuous	97.89
pH	continuous	91.56
Age	continuous	0.00
Admission diagnosis	categorical	0.00
Ethnicity	categorical	0.00
Gender	categorical	0.00
eICU Feature	Data Type	Missingness (%)
Diastolic blood pressure	continuous	33.80
Fraction inspired oxygen	continuous	98.14
Glasgow coma scale eye	categorical	83.42
Glasgow coma scale motor	categorical	83.43
Glasgow coma scale total	categorical	81.70
Glasgow coma scale verbal	categorical	83.54
Glucose	continuous	83.89
Heart Rate	continuous	27.45
Height	continuous	99.19
Mean arterial pressure	continuous	96.53
Oxygen saturation	continuous	38.12
Respiratory rate	continuous	33.11
Systolic blood pressure	continuous	33.80
Temperature	continuous	76.35
Weight	continuous	98.65
pH	continuous	97.91
Age	continuous	0.00
Admission diagnosis	categorical	0.00
Ethnicity	categorical	0.00
Gender	categorical	0.00

Table 2. Performance of our approaches with other baselines on clinical time series imputation and in-hospital mortality prediction. Values in the parentheses are standard deviations.

MIMIC-III/24 h after ICU admission	Clinical time series imputation		In-hospital mortality prediction	
Metrics	MAE	MRE	AUROC	AUPRC
GRU-D	1.3134(0.0509)	87.33%(0.0341)	0.8461(0.0051)	0.4513(0.0124)
BRITS	1.3211(0.0923)	87.92%(0.0611)	0.8432(0.0040)	0.4193(0.0144)
GRUI-GAN	1.6083(0.0043)	107.20%(0.0029)	0.8324(0.0077)	0.4209(0.0280)
E^{2}GAN	1.5885(0.0045)	105.86%(0.0032)	0.8377(0.0083)	0.4295(0.0137)
E^{2}GAN-RF	1.4362(0.0031)	101.09%(0.0027)	0.8430(0.0065)	0.4328(0.0101)
STING	1.5018(0.0082)	102.53%(0.0047)	0.8344(0.0126)	0.4431(0.0158)
MTSIT	0.3988(0.0671)	38.44%(0.0647)	0.8029(0.0117)	0.4150(0.0165)
MIAM	1.1391(0.0001)	75.65%(0.0001)	0.8140(0.0044)	0.4162(0.0079)
Ours	**0.3563(0.0375)**	**8.16%(0.0086)**	**0.8533(0.0119)**	**0.4752(0.0223)**
Ours$_\alpha$	0.3833(0.0389)	8.78%(0.0089)	0.8398(0.0064)	0.4555(0.0139)
Ours$_\beta$	0.4125(0.0319)	8.95%(0.0077)	0.8417(0.0059)	0.4489(0.0182)
eICU/24 h after eICU admission	Clinical time series imputation		In-hospital mortality prediction	
Metrics	MAE	MRE	AUROC	AUPRC
GRU-D	3.9791(0.2008)	52.11%(0.0262)	0.7455(0.0107)	0.3178(0.0190)
BRITS	3.6879(0.3782)	48.30%(0.0726)	0.7139(0.0101)	0.2511(0.0111)
GRUI-GAN	9.1031(0.0130)	119.29%(0.0016)	0.7298(0.0094)	0.3013(0.0141)
E^{2}GAN	7.5746(0.0141)	99.20%(0.0018)	0.7317(0.0155)	0.2973(0.0253)
E^{2}GAN-RF	6.7108(0.0127)	90.38%(0.0015)	0.7402(0.0131)	0.3045(0.0227)
STING	7.1447(0.0651)	93.56%(0.0083)	0.7197(0.0154)	0.2873(0.0182)
MTSIT	1.6192(0.1064)	21.20%(0.0139)	0.7215(0.0071)	0.2992(0.0115)
MIAM	1.1726(0.3103)	15.35%(0.0406)	0.7262(0.0179)	0.2659(0.0148)
Ours	**0.5365(0.0612)**	**7.02%(0.0079)**	**0.7626(0.0117)**	**0.3388(0.0211)**
Ours$_\alpha$	0.6792(0.0716)	8.89%(0.0093)	0.7501(0.0143)	0.3325(0.0151)
Ours$_\beta$	0.5923(0.0514)	7.75%(0.0067)	0.7533(0.0104)	0.3303(0.0175)
MIMIC-III/48 h after ICU admission	Clinical time series imputation		In-hospital mortality prediction	
Metrics	MAE	MRE	AUROC	AUPRC
GRU-D	1.4535(0.0806)	86.47%(0.0482)	0.8746(0.0026)	0.5143(0.0077)
BRITS	1.3802(0.1295)	82.21%(0.0768)	0.8564(0.0040)	0.4445(0.0189)
GRUI-GAN	1.7523(0.0030)	104.50%(0.0018)	0.8681(0.0077)	0.5123(0.0166)
E^{2}GAN	1.7436(0.0036)	103.98%(0.0022)	0.8705(0.0043)	0.5091(0.0120)
E^{2}GAN-RF	1.6122(0.0027)	102.34%(0.0017)	0.8736(0.0031)	0.5186(0.0095)
STING	1.6831(0.0068)	100.46%(0.0035)	0.8668(0.0123)	0.5232(0.0236)
MTSIT	0.4503(0.0465)	30.42%(0.0314)	0.8171(0.0114)	0.4308(0.0189)
MIAM	1.3158(0.0003)	78.20%(0.0002)	0.8327(0.0024)	0.4460(0.0061)
Ours	**0.4396(0.0588)**	**6.23%(0.0073)**	**0.8831(0.0149)**	**0.5328(0.0347)**
Ours$_\alpha$	0.7096(0.0532)	8.85%(0.0066)	0.8671(0.0093)	0.5161(0.0151)
Ours$_\beta$	0.5786(0.0429)	7.47%(0.0056)	0.8709(0.0073)	0.5114(0.0176)
eICU/48 h after eICU admission	Clinical time series imputation		In-hospital mortality prediction	
Metrics	MAE	MRE	AUROC	AUPRC
GRU-D	5.8071(0.2132)	44.53%(0.0164)	0.7767(0.0141)	0.3210(0.0182)
BRITS	5.5546(0.5497)	42.59%(0.0421)	0.7285(0.0114)	0.2510(0.0097)
GRUI-GAN	14.0750(0.0301)	107.96%(0.0021)	0.7531(0.0167)	0.2897(0.0201)
E^{2}GAN	12.9694(0.0195)	99.47%(0.0015)	0.7605(0.0063)	0.3014(0.0137)
E^{2}GAN-RF	11.8138(0.0161)	91.52%(0.0011)	0.7763(0.0057)	0.3101(0.0125)
STING	12.0962(0.0806)	92.79%(0.0062)	0.7453(0.0182)	0.2805(0.0190)
MTSIT	2.8150(0.2105)	21.58%(0.0161)	0.7418(0.0091)	0.3078(0.0120)
MIAM	2.1146(0.4012)	16.23%(0.0414)	0.7574(0.0127)	0.2776(0.0105)
Ours	**0.9412(0.0930)**	**7.21%(0.0071)**	**0.7907(0.0123)**	**0.3417(0.0217)**
Ours$_\alpha$	1.1099(0.1064)	8.51%(0.0081)	0.7732(0.0100)	0.3311(0.0265)
Ours$_\beta$	0.9930(0.0817)	7.61%(0.0062)	0.7790(0.0117)	0.3335(0.0178)

0.1. For the imputation task, the dimension size of $W_v^{(l)}$, $W_t^{(l)}$, $W_v^{(n)}$, and $W_t^{(n)}$ are 28.

The performance of contrastive learning heavily relies on data augmentation. We augment the observed value v with random time shifts and reversion. For example, given the observed value $v = [v_1, v_2, \cdots, v_T]$, we are able to obtain $v_{shift} = [v_{1+n}, v_{2+n}, \cdots, v_{T+n}]$ and $v_{reverse} = [v_T, v_{T-1}, \cdots, v_1]$ from random time shift and reversion, and n is the number of data points to shift.

4.4 Evaluation Metrics

We use the mean absolute error (MAE) and the mean relative error (MRE) between predicted and real-valued values as the evaluation metrics for imputation performance. We use the area under the receiver operating characteristic curve (AUROC) and the area under the precision-recall curve (AUPRC) as the evaluation metrics for prediction performance. We report the mean and standard deviation of the evaluation metrics after repeating all the approaches ten times.

5   Experimental Results

Table 2 presents the experimental results of all approaches on imputation and prediction tasks from MIMIC-III and eICU datasets. Together these results suggest that our approach achieves the best performance in both imputation and prediction tasks. For example, for the clinical time series imputation of MIMIC-III (24 h after ICU admission), the MAE and MRE of Ours are 0.3563 and 8.16%, smaller than 0.3988 and 38.44% achieved by the best baseline (i.e., MTSIT). For the in-hospital mortality prediction of MIMIC-III (24 h after ICU admission), the AUROC and AUPRC of Ours are 0.8533 and 0.4752, larger than 0.8461 and 0.4513 achieved by the best baseline (i.e., GRU-D).

As Table 2 shows, the RNN-based approach (i.e., GRU-D and BRITS) outperforms the GAN-based approach (i.e., GRUI-GAN, E^2GAN, E^2GAN-RF, and STING) in the imputation task. From the prediction results of the MIMIC-III dataset, we can see that the transformer-based approaches (i.e., MTSIT and MIAM) resulted in lower values of AUROC and AUPRC. From the prediction results of the eICU dataset, no significant difference between the transformer-based approach and other approaches was evident.

Ours outperforms its variants $Ours_\alpha$ and $Ours_\beta$. This result confirms the effectiveness of the network construction with enhanced imputation and prediction performance.

6   Conclusion

This paper presents a novel contrastive learning-based imputation-prediction network to carry out in-hospital mortality prediction tasks using EHR data. This prediction makes timely warnings available to ICU health professionals so that early interventions for patients at risk could take place. The proposed approach explicitly considers patient similarity by stratification of EHR data and successfully integrates contrastive learning into the network architecture. We empirically show that the proposed approach outperforms all the baselines by conducting clinical time series imputation and in-hospital mortality prediction on the publicly available MIMIC-III and eICU datasets.

Acknowledgement. This research is partially funded by the ARC Centre of Excellence for Automated Decision-Making and Society (CE200100005) by the Australian Government through the Australian Research Council.

Ethical Statement. The experimental datasets used for this work are obtained from the publicly available Medical Information Mart for Intensive Care (MIMIC-III) dataset and the eICU Collaborative Research dataset. These data were used under license. The authors declare that they have no conflicts of interest. This article does not contain any studies involving human participants performed by any of the authors.

References

1. Cao, W., Wang, D., Li, J., Zhou, H., Li, L., Li, Y.: Brits: bidirectional recurrent imputation for time series. In: Advances in Neural Information Processing Systems, vol. 31 (2018)
2. Che, Z., Purushotham, S., Cho, K., Sontag, D., Liu, Y.: Recurrent neural networks for multivariate time series with missing values. Sci. Rep. **8**(1), 1–12 (2018)
3. Chen, T., Kornblith, S., Norouzi, M., Hinton, G.: A simple framework for contrastive learning of visual representations. In: International Conference on Machine Learning, pp. 1597–1607. PMLR (2020)
4. Cho, K., et al.: Learning phrase representations using RNN encoder-decoder for statistical machine translation. arXiv preprint arXiv:1406.1078 (2014)
5. Cui, S., Wang, J., Gui, X., Wang, T., Ma, F.: Automed: automated medical risk predictive modeling on electronic health records. In: 2022 IEEE International Conference on Bioinformatics and Biomedicine (BIBM), pp. 948–953. IEEE (2022)
6. Goodfellow, I., et al.: Generative adversarial networks. Commun. ACM **63**(11), 139–144 (2020)
7. Groenwold, R.H.: Informative missingness in electronic health record systems: the curse of knowing. Diagn. Prognostic Res. **4**(1), 1–6 (2020)
8. Harutyunyan, H., Khachatrian, H., Kale, D.C., Ver Steeg, G., Galstyan, A.: Multitask learning and benchmarking with clinical time series data. Sci. Data **6**(1), 1–18 (2019)
9. Johnson, A.E., et al.: MIMIC-III, a freely accessible critical care database. Sci. Data **3**(1), 1–9 (2016)
10. Khosla, P., et al.: Supervised contrastive learning. Adv. Neural. Inf. Process. Syst. **33**, 18661–18673 (2020)
11. Kingma, D.P., Ba, J.: Adam: a method for stochastic optimization. arXiv preprint arXiv:1412.6980 (2014)
12. Le-Khac, P.H., Healy, G., Smeaton, A.F.: Contrastive representation learning: a framework and review. IEEE Access **8**, 193907–193934 (2020)

13. Lee, Y., Jun, E., Choi, J., Suk, H.I.: Multi-view integrative attention-based deep representation learning for irregular clinical time-series data. IEEE J. Biomed. Health Inform. **26**(8), 4270–4280 (2022)
14. Li, J., Shang, J., McAuley, J.: Uctopic: unsupervised contrastive learning for phrase representations and topic mining. arXiv preprint arXiv:2202.13469 (2022)
15. Li, M., Li, C.G., Guo, J.: Cluster-guided asymmetric contrastive learning for unsupervised person re-identification. IEEE Trans. Image Process. **31**, 3606–3617 (2022)
16. Li, R., Ma, F., Gao, J.: Integrating multimodal electronic health records for diagnosis prediction. In: AMIA Annual Symposium Proceedings, vol. 2021, p. 726. American Medical Informatics Association (2021)
17. Luo, Y., Cai, X., Zhang, Y., Xu, J., et al.: Multivariate time series imputation with generative adversarial networks. In: Advances in Neural Information Processing Systems, vol. 31 (2018)
18. Luo, Y., Zhang, Y., Cai, X., Yuan, X.: E2GAN: end-to-end generative adversarial network for multivariate time series imputation. In: Proceedings of the 28th International Joint Conference on Artificial Intelligence, pp. 3094–3100. AAAI Press (2019)
19. Ma, L., et al.: Adacare: explainable clinical health status representation learning via scale-adaptive feature extraction and recalibration. In: Proceedings of the AAAI Conference on Artificial Intelligence, vol. 34, pp. 825–832 (2020)
20. Ma, L., et al.: Distilling knowledge from publicly available online EMR data to emerging epidemic for prognosis. In: Proceedings of the Web Conference 2021, pp. 3558–3568 (2021)
21. Ma, L., et al.: Concare: personalized clinical feature embedding via capturing the healthcare context. In: Proceedings of the AAAI Conference on Artificial Intelligence, vol. 34, pp. 833–840 (2020)
22. McCombe, N., et al.: Practical strategies for extreme missing data imputation in dementia diagnosis. IEEE J. Biomed. Health Inform. **26**(2), 818–827 (2021)
23. Mulyadi, A.W., Jun, E., Suk, H.I.: Uncertainty-aware variational-recurrent imputation network for clinical time series. IEEE Trans. Cybern. **52**(9), 9684–9694 (2021)
24. Ni, Q., Cao, X.: MBGAN: an improved generative adversarial network with multi-head self-attention and bidirectional RNN for time series imputation. Eng. Appl. Artif. Intell. **115**, 105232 (2022)
25. Oh, E., Kim, T., Ji, Y., Khyalia, S.: Sting: self-attention based time-series imputation networks using GAN. In: 2021 IEEE International Conference on Data Mining (ICDM), pp. 1264–1269. IEEE (2021)
26. Pang, B., et al.: Unsupervised representation for semantic segmentation by implicit cycle-attention contrastive learning. In: Proceedings of the AAAI Conference on Artificial Intelligence, vol. 36, pp. 2044–2052 (2022)
27. Pereira, R.C., Abreu, P.H., Rodrigues, P.P.: Partial multiple imputation with variational autoencoders: tackling not at randomness in healthcare data. IEEE J. Biomed. Health Inform. **26**(8), 4218–4227 (2022)
28. Pollard, T.J., Johnson, A.E., Raffa, J.D., Celi, L.A., Mark, R.G., Badawi, O.: The eICU collaborative research database, a freely available multi-center database for critical care research. Sci. Data **5**(1), 1–13 (2018)
29. Sheikhalishahi, S., Balaraman, V., Osmani, V.: Benchmarking machine learning models on multi-centre eicu critical care dataset. PLoS ONE **15**(7), e0235424 (2020)
30. Shi, Z., et al.: Deep dynamic imputation of clinical time series for mortality prediction. Inf. Sci. **579**, 607–622 (2021)

31. Tan, Q., et al.: Data-GRU: dual-attention time-aware gated recurrent unit for irregular multivariate time series. In: Proceedings of the AAAI Conference on Artificial Intelligence, vol. 34, pp. 930–937 (2020)
32. Vaswani, A., et al.: Attention is all you need. In: Advances in Neural Information Processing Systems, pp. 5998–6008 (2017)
33. Wang, W., Zhou, T., Yu, F., Dai, J., Konukoglu, E., Van Gool, L.: Exploring cross-image pixel contrast for semantic segmentation. In: Proceedings of the IEEE/CVF International Conference on Computer Vision, pp. 7303–7313 (2021)
34. Wang, Y., Min, Y., Chen, X., Wu, J.: Multi-view graph contrastive representation learning for drug-drug interaction prediction. In: Proceedings of the Web Conference 2021, pp. 2921–2933 (2021)
35. Xu, D., Sheng, J.Q., Hu, P.J.H., Huang, T.S., Hsu, C.C.: A deep learning-based unsupervised method to impute missing values in patient records for improved management of cardiovascular patients. IEEE J. Biomed. Health Inform. **25**(6), 2260–2272 (2020)
36. Yang, C., An, Z., Cai, L., Xu, Y.: Mutual contrastive learning for visual representation learning. In: Proceedings of the AAAI Conference on Artificial Intelligence, vol. 36, pp. 3045–3053 (2022)
37. Yıldız, A.Y., Koç, E., Koç, A.: Multivariate time series imputation with transformers. IEEE Signal Process. Lett. **29**, 2517–2521 (2022)
38. Yuan, X., et al.: Multimodal contrastive training for visual representation learning. In: Proceedings of the IEEE/CVF Conference on Computer Vision and Pattern Recognition, pp. 6995–7004 (2021)
39. Zang, C., Wang, F.: SCEHR: supervised contrastive learning for clinical risk prediction using electronic health records. In: Proceedings of IEEE International Conference on Data Mining, vol. 2021, pp. 857–866 (2021)
40. Zhang, Y., Zhou, B., Cai, X., Guo, W., Ding, X., Yuan, X.: Missing value imputation in multivariate time series with end-to-end generative adversarial networks. Inf. Sci. **551**, 67–82 (2021)

Weak Supervision and Clustering-Based Sample Selection for Clinical Named Entity Recognition

Wei Sun[1,2(✉)], Shaoxiong Ji[3,4(✉)] (iD), Tuulia Denti[2], Hans Moen[3], Oleg Kerro[2], Antti Rannikko[2], Pekka Marttinen[3], and Miika Koskinen[2]

[1] KU Leuven, Leuven, Belgium
sun.wei@kuleuven.be
[2] HUS Helsinki University Hospital, Helsinki, Finland
[3] Aalto University, Espoo, Finland
{hans.moen,pekka.marttinen}@aalto.fi
[4] University of Helsinki, Helsinki, Finland
shaoxiong.ji@helsinki.fi

Abstract. One of the central tasks of medical text analysis is to extract and structure meaningful information from plain-text clinical documents. Named Entity Recognition (NER) is a sub-task of information extraction that involves identifying predefined entities from unstructured free text. Notably, NER models require large amounts of human-labeled data to train, but human annotation is costly and laborious and often requires medical training. Here, we aim to overcome the shortage of manually annotated data by introducing a training scheme for NER models that uses an existing medical ontology to assign weak labels to entities and provides enhanced domain-specific model adaptation with in-domain continual pretraining. Due to limited human annotation resources, we develop a specific module to collect a more representative test dataset from the data lake than a random selection. To validate our framework, we invite clinicians to annotate the test set. In this way, we construct two Finnish medical NER datasets based on clinical records retrieved from a hospital's data lake and evaluate the effectiveness of the proposed methods. The code is available at https://github.com/VRCMF/HAM-net.git.

Keywords: Named Entity Recognition · Distant Supervision · Sample Selection · Clinical Reports

1 Introduction

Although Electrical Health Records (EHR) are trending towards structured data, documentation in plain text remains popular in clinical work. As a result, text documents contain valuable information, which highlights the need for automatic information extraction and data structuring techniques for research and management purposes or to facilitate the clinician's work. Electrical Health Records (EHR) are nowadays widely adopted by healthcare institutes and medical service providers. EHRs are created and maintained by healthcare service

G. De Francisci Morales et al. (Eds.): ECML PKDD 2023, LNAI 14174, pp. 444–459, 2023.
https://doi.org/10.1007/978-3-031-43427-3_27

providers and consist of various information and data types related to patients' healthcare. This includes narrative free-text reports, laboratory results, demographics, diagnosis codes, and images. During hospitalization, patients' information is synchronically updated to the EHR system where clinicians can query the EHR system to obtain relevant medical information about patients. However, most clinical notes are in free-text format. Named Entity Recognition (NER) is a subtask of Natural Language Processing (NLP), aiming to detect and assign labels to pre-defined categories or concepts as they appear in the text, such as diseases, medicines, symptoms, anatomical structures, or procedures. NER is based on supervised learning. Thus, a substantial amount of training data consisting of input text and label sequences are required. To provide reliable token-level predictions, high-quality manually annotated data by clinical experts is necessary, which implies considerable human effort. Earlier, NER systems have been trained for different languages, such as for English text, such as n2c2[1], RadGraph [8], MalwareTextDB [14], and CoNLL2003 [18], and for smaller languages such as Finnish[2], but to our knowledge, no NER dataset for medical Finnish exists.

One solution to tackle the scarcity of manually labeled training data is to adopt distant supervision methods to generate labels for training samples based on external knowledge sources. In this framework, earlier approaches include, e.g., knowledge-based distant supervision, transfer learning from pretrained models, and dictionary-based methods, to name a few. For example, Zirikly et al. [25] and Wang et al. [22] leverage the transfer learning to project the label knowledge from resource-rich languages (English) into the low-resource one. Korkontzelos et al. [10] and Shang et al. [20] establish NER datasets based on in-domain dictionaries. It is necessary to generate entity-level supervision signals for training data and capitalize on domain-specific dictionaries and language knowledge.

We propose a novel NER framework called Hybrid Annotation Mechanism Network (HAM-net) to predict medical entities from clinical documents in an extremely low-resource scenario. We fuse a Finnish medical dictionary[3] and a dependency parser for Finnish[4] to enhance the annotation mechanism.

Considering the characteristics of medical-related NLP algorithms, we perform domain-specific continual pertaining (DCP) to resolve in-domain adaptation problems. Much research literature shows that language models suffer from performance degeneration on downstream tasks without taking in-domain adaptation into account [7,9]. Currently, advanced language models, such as Bidirectional Encoder Representations from Transformers (BERT) [5] and Longformer [3], incorporate biomedical and clinical knowledge through pre-training on large-scale biomedical and clinical corpus [13]. We deploy domain-specific continual pretraining with the masked language modeling (MLM) objective on an enormous Finnish medical text from the data lake of the hospital. To endow our

---

[1] https://n2c2.dbmi.hms.harvard.edu/.

[2] https://turkunlp.org/fin-ner.html.

[3] https://finto.fi/mesh/en/.

[4] http://turkunlp.org/Turku-neural-parser-pipeline/.

framework with better domain specification, we perform domain-specific continual pretraining to obtain domain-aware model parameters to initialize the NER model.

To validate the HAM-net in different medical documents, we retrieve patient clinical records from the data lake of the hospital and divide them into four text clusters based on frequent medical specialties to establish NER datasets. Also, we develop the **S**ample **S**election **M**odule (SSM) to choose the most informative data points as validation samples for better evaluation. The experiments show that the SSM is better than random selection, such that the validation samples generated by our module better represent the whole datasets.

Our contributions are illustrated in the following aspects:

- This paper proposes a novel framework to deal with the NER task in an extremely low-resource scenario, i.e., extract customized medical entities from clinical notes without human-annotated data.
- We integrate a Finnish medical dictionary and a Finnish language parsing pipeline to construct the **H**ybrid **A**nnotation **M**echanism (HAM) module for providing weakly labeled data.
- We design the **S**ample **S**election **M**odule (SSM) to select the representative samples for human annotation, which enables the reliable evaluation of our weakly supervised HAM-net and effectively reduces the annotation cost.

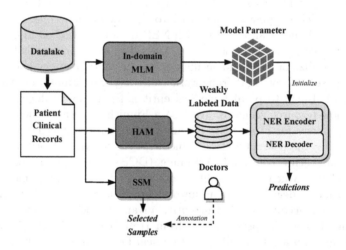

Fig. 1. Overall architecture of HAM-net. The texts in patient clinical records from the hospital data lake are written in a low-resource language (Finnish).

2   Related Work

Medical NER detects medically meaningful entities in unstructured documents and classifies them into predefined labels, such as drug dosages, diseases, medical devices, and anatomical structures. Most early medical NER works utilize feature engineering techniques and machine learning algorithms to resolve medical NER tasks [17,19,21]. Deep learning-based NER approaches have recently achieved state-of-the-art (SOTA) performance across NER tasks because of the semantic composition and continuous real-valued vector representations through nonlinear processing provided by deep neural networks [12]. For example, in the clinical setting, Wu et al. [23] used the convolutional and recurrent neural networks to encode the input sentences while the sequential labels were generated by a task-specific layer, i.e., a classification layer.

Acquiring high-quality training data for deep learning models in the medical setting can be difficult because human annotation is labor-intensive and expensive. As a classical supervised learning task, the medical-named entity recognition task requires a substantial amount of entity-level supervision signal, e.g., anatomical structure and drug dosage, to learn the transformation function between input data and our desired targets from the training dataset. Two common weak supervision schemes, i.e., incomplete and inaccurate supervision, are extensively studied in research communities [24] to resolve the data scarcity problem. Incomplete supervision approaches select a small set of training samples from a dataset, and then human encoders assign labels to selected samples for training the model. Ferreira et al. [6] leverage active learning strategies to select the most informative samples on a clinical multi-label classification, i.e., international classification disease (ICS) coding task. Inaccurate supervision approaches generate weakly labeled data by assigning many training samples with supervision signals provided by outside resources, such as dictionaries, knowledge graphs, and databases. Nesterov et al. [16] leverage Medical Dictionary for Regulatory Activities (MedDRA), a subset of UMLS, to construct a knowledge base as annotation resources. The weakly labeled data generated by a rule-based model is fed into a BERT model to generate entity-level predictions.

3   Method

This section introduces our proposed framework, i.e., **H**ybrid **A**nnotation **M**echanism Network (HAM-net). It consists of a hybrid annotation mechanism (HAM) and a **S**ample **S**election **M**odule (SSM). The overall architecture of HAM-net is shown in Fig. 1. We retrieve Finnish patient clinical records from the hospital data lake and deploy our framework in a real-world scenario. Domain-specific Masked Language Modeling (MLM) is performed on a large-scale clinical corpus from the data lake to learn medical knowledge that provides the HAM-net with in-domain adaptation. The HAM automatically assigns weak labels to training samples. The SSM selects the most informative data points as validation samples, and doctors annotate the selected samples. The NER model uses weakly labeled data to train a model identifying and classifying entities into pre-defined labels.

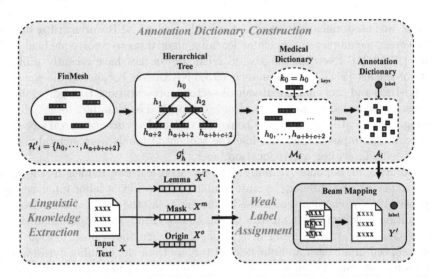

Fig. 2. Overall architecture of HAM-net. The patient clinical records from the hospital data lake are Finnish text. Annotation Dictionary is constructed based on the FinMesh ontology. Linguistic information, i.e., lemmatization and annotation mask, is derived from the Finnish neural parsing pipeline and human-defined rules. We leverage medical information from ontology and linguistic information to assign labels for given input entities.

3.1   Hybrid Annotation Mechanism

The **H**ybrid **A**nnotation **M**echanism (HAM) is divided into three steps as shown in Fig. 2, i.e., annotation dictionary construction, linguistic knowledge extraction, and weak label assignment. Firstly, we retrieve medical terms from the Finnish Medical Subject Heading (FinMesh) ontology and utilize parent-child relationships between subjects to establish hierarchical graphs. Each hierarchical graph consists of a root node and non-root nodes, which are used to construct a medical dictionary, i.e., the root node for the key and all non-root nodes for the terms. Based on clinicians' suggestions, we merge "key-item" pairs in the medical dictionary to provide an annotation dictionary with six pre-defined labels. Secondly, we integrate linguistic knowledge of sequential input extracted by the Finnish neural parsing pipeline and human-defined rules to provide tokenized words, annotation masks, and lemmatization to facilitate the following entity-level annotation. Thirdly, we design a beam-mapping algorithm that assigns weak labels to entities for establishing NER training datasets.

Annotation Dictionary Construction. Assume a collection of medical subjects related to a top-level concept, e.g., kudokset (tissue), is denoted as $\mathcal{H}'_i = \{h_i\}_{i=0}^{a+b+c+2}$, where a, b, and c represents each branch's depth in a hierarchical tree. Each medical subject stores relevant information, including their parent and child subjects, medical concepts in different languages (Finnish, Swedish, and English), preferred labels, alternative concepts, and related subjects.

We define the hierarchical graph for the concept as $\mathcal{G}_h^i = (\mathcal{H}', \mathcal{E})$ where relevant medical subjects $\mathcal{H}'$ are the graph's vertices and $\mathcal{E}$ represents the edges or association rules of the hierarchical graph, i.e., parent-child relations between subjects. The edges are $\mathcal{E} \rightarrow \{\{h_i, h_j\} | h_i, h_j \in \mathcal{H}_i'$ and $i \neq j\}$ while the association rules of the hierarchical graph (refer to the Fig. 2) is defined as follows:

- $h_0 \rightarrow h_1 \rightarrow \cdots \rightarrow h_{a+2}$,
- $h_0 \rightarrow h_2 \rightarrow \cdots \rightarrow h_{a+b+2}$,
- $h_0 \rightarrow h_2 \rightarrow \cdots \rightarrow h_{a+b+c+2}$.

To construct a medical dictionary $\mathcal{M}_i$, we flatten the hierarchical graph $\mathcal{G}_h^i$ by pooling all vertices or subjects in the graph (except the top-level vertex h_0). Retrieved subjects are regarded as the dictionary's terms, and the top-level vertex represents the dictionary's key, so that the medical dictionary is denoted to $\mathbf{M}_i(k_0) = \{h_i\}_{i=0}^{a+b+c+2}$. We regard the top-level vertex h_0 as a key of the medical dictionary k_0.

An annotation dictionary A_j (where $j \in \{1, 2, \cdots, 6\}$) is provided by merging related hierarchical graphs based on clinicians' suggestions, and the annotation dictionary is referred to as $A_j = \{\mathcal{M}_1(k_0^1), \mathcal{M}_2(k_0^2), \cdots, \mathcal{M}_m(k_0^m)\}$ where m is the number of related hierarchical graphs.

Annotation Masking and Lemmatization. Let X be a sentence with n tokens in a clinical document from the data lake. The sentence is denoted as $X = \{X_i\}_{i=1}^n$. The Finnish neural parser pipeline reads the sentence X and provides tokenized words (X^o), tokens' lemmatization (X^l), part of speech (POS), morphological tags, and dependency parsing. Firstly, we provide an annotation mask (X^m) to avoid the label assignment over entities with no specific meaning, by leveraging the following pre-defined rules:

- Set X_i^m as "False" if the POS of X_i does not belong to [*"NOUN"*, *"VERB"*, *"ADJ"*, *"ADV"*].
- Set X_i^m as "False" if the X_i is a unit, e.g., *"cm"*, *"kg"*, *"sec"*, to name a few.
- Remove all Finnish stop words provided by stopwords-fi[5].

Secondly, the pipeline lemmatizes the token X_i and returns the original format of the token. The reason for extracting tokens' lemmatization is that tokens in the clinical notes have different formats, such as past tense, plural, or misspellings, which might affect the string mapping during the entity-level annotation. Finally, the generated vectors, i.e., X^o, X^l, and X^m, align with the lengths of input sentence X to prevent dislocation mapping when the vectors participate in the following label assignment.

---

[5] https://github.com/stopwords-iso/stopwords-fi.

Weak Label Assignment. We develop an algorithm called *beam mapping* to assign weak labels to entities in the sentence. We adopt *BIO* scheme to define the entity boundaries. BIO stands for the beginning, inside, and outside of a textual segmentation. For example, NER systems assign ['O', 'O', 'B-medical-condition', 'I-medical-condition'] for a given sequence ['He', 'has', 'prostate', 'cancer']. The algorithm iterates through all tokens in the sentence X and generates *BIO* scheme labels, i.e., a combination of tokens can be annotated, within the receptive windows Win containing a list of w position shifting, Win $\in [s_1, s_2, \cdots, s_w]$, where s_w is a token at w position of a given sequence. For example, "prostate cancer" should be annotated as "B-Medical-condition" and "I-Medical-condition" rather than "B-Anatomical-structure" and "B-Medical-conditional" because it is plausible to treat the phrase "prostate cancer" as a unit instead of splitting them up.

Assume the *beam mapping* algorithm provides labels to tokens ranging from X_i to X_{i+s_j} where $j \in \{1, 2, \cdots, w\}$. Firstly, we check the i_{th} element in the annotation mask X^m and see whether X_i^m is True because we directly assign "O" to the X_i without executing the algorithm on the position i if the mask item is *False*. Secondly, a token mapping function generates the candidate labels on the lemmatizations of tokens $\{X_i^l\}_{i=i}^{i=i+s_j}$ by mapping each item in the annotation dictionary A to the lemmatizations. During the mapping, the algorithm selects candidates, i.e., terms in the annotation dictionary A_j, if the number of input tokens and lengths of each token equal the dictionary's terms. We denote z selected candidates as $C = \{C_i\}_{i=1}^{z}$ and calculate Levenshtein distance between the input string and the candidate to estimate the similarity between two strings for choosing the most matched candidate. Merge the input list $\{X_i^l\}_{i=i}^{i=i+s_j}$ separated by the space character to provide the input string $S_{i:i+s_j}$. The Levenshtein distance between two strings $(a$ and $b)$ is shown as follows:

$$
\text{lev}(a, b) = \begin{cases} |a| & \text{if } |b| = 0, \\ |b| & \text{if } |a| = 0, \\ \text{lev}\left(\text{tail}(a), \text{tail}(b)\right) & \text{if } a[0] = b[0] \\ 1 + \min \begin{cases} \text{lev}\left(\text{tail}(a), b\right) \\ \text{lev}\left(a, \text{tail}(b)\right) & \text{otherwise,} \\ \text{lev}\left(\text{tail}(a), \text{tail}(b)\right) \end{cases} \end{cases} \tag{1}
$$

where the tail(.) is to retrieve all elements in a string except the first one. Thirdly, we get the best-matched terms for the tokens $\{X_i\}_{i=i}^{i=i+s_j}$ based on the distances. The weak labels $\{Y_i'\}_{i=i}^{i=i+s_j}$ is provided by leveraging the indexes of the best candidates to look up the annotation dictionary A. The annotation rules for the BIO scheme are shown as follows:

– If the first label is empty, i.e., $Y_i' = $ "O", we re-run the algorithm on the position $i + 1$.
– If the first label is not empty, the weak labels $\{Y_i'\}_{i=i}^{i=i+s_j}$ are:
  • The first element is the beginning of the text segment, $Y_i' = $ "B-lb".
  • The rest elements are the inside of the text segment, $\{Y_i'\}_{i=i+1}^{i=i+s_j} = $ "I-lb".

where "lb" is an arbitrary label from the annotation dictionary A. The weakly labeled data for the sentence X with n tokens can be represented as $\{(X_i, Y_i')\}_{i=1}^n$.

3.2 NER Backbone Network

We use the weakly labeled data provided by the HAM as input samples to train a NER model. Also, the weakly labeled data contains inherent label noise of distant supervision approaches, affecting predictions' reliability. The noise stability property [2] shows that the noise will gradually attenuate when the noise propagates through a deep neural network. Therefore, a trained NER model, i.e., HAM-net, identifies and classifies entities into labels in a low-latency way. The label noise can be suppressed by the deep neural network or additional noise-suppressed approaches.

We leverage the word embedding technique to provide the word embedding matrix $\mathbf{X}_i \in \mathbb{R}^{d_e \times n}$ of the i_{th} sentence with n tokens. The input data is denoted as $\{(\mathbf{X}_i, \mathbf{Y}_i')\}_{i=1}^N$ where N is the total number of sentences and the $\mathbf{Y}_i' \in \mathbb{R}^{1 \times n}$ is to store the indexes of labels. We load the domain-specific model obtained with continual pretraining to initialize the encoder whose mapping function is denoted as $\mathcal{F}'(.)$. The vector $\mathbf{X}_i$ is encoded as:

$$\mathbf{Z}_i' = \text{Softmax}(\mathbf{O}'\mathcal{F}'(\mathbf{X}_i)), \tag{2}$$

where $\mathbf{O}' \in \mathbb{R}^{d_m \times d_h}$ is the weight matrix of the fully-connected layer and d_m is the dimension of predefined label space. $\mathbf{Z}' \in \mathbb{R}^{d_m \times n}$ represents the encoder's output.

We also consider a CRF layer as the decoder of the NER model, denoted as $f(\mathbf{Z}_i', j, \mathbf{Y}_{j-1}', \mathbf{Y}_j')$ where j is the position of the label to predict, $\mathbf{Y}_{j-1}'$ represents the label for the $(j-1)_{th}$ token of the input sequence $\mathbf{X}$, and $\mathbf{Y}_j'$ is the label for the j_{th} token of the input sequence $\mathbf{X}$. The conditional probability vectors of the i_{th} sentence is denoted as:

$$P(\mathbf{Y}_i'|\mathbf{Z}_i', \lambda) = \frac{1}{G(\mathbf{Z}')} \exp \sum_{j=1}^n \lambda_j f_j(\mathbf{Z}_i', j, \mathbf{Y}_{i,j-1}', \mathbf{Y}_{i,j}')), \tag{3}$$

$$G(\mathbf{Z}') = \exp \sum_{i=1}^N \sum_{j=1}^n \lambda_j f_j(\mathbf{Z}_i', j, \mathbf{Y}_{i,j-1}', \mathbf{Y}_{i,j}), \tag{4}$$

where the λ_j is the learn-able weight of j_{th} CRF feature function. The $G(\mathbf{Z}')$ represents the normalization factor of the CRF feature functions. The overall training loss of the HAM-net is:

$$\mathcal{L}(\mathbf{Z}', \lambda, \mathbf{Y}') = \sum_{i=1}^N \log P(\mathbf{Y}_i'|\mathbf{X}_i', \lambda) - \sum_{j=1}^m \frac{\lambda_j^2}{2\sigma^2}, \tag{5}$$

We train the model until convergence and use the Viterbi algorithm [11] to generate a label sequence for a new input sentence in the inference stage.

3.3   Sample Selection Module

To validate the effectiveness of our data annotation mechanism and NER model, we need the test set with a small set of samples annotated by clinicians. However, human annotation is expensive and labor-intensive, especially for doctors to assign entity-level labels to the test samples. To mitigate this problem, we developed the **S**ample **S**election **M**odule (SSM) to select samples that largely represent the datasets when constructing the test set. Compared with the random selection, the distributions of test samples provided by the SSM are closer to the distributions of each dataset. We provide the details about the SSM module as follows.

Note a set of g sentences $\phi \in \{\phi_1, \phi_2, \cdots, \phi_g\}$ from an arbitrary dataset. Firstly, we use the Finnish sentence transformer[6] to embed sentences $\{\phi_i\}_{i=1}^{g}$ into vectors $\{\varPhi_i\}_{i=1}^{g}$, where the i_{th} vector is $\varPhi_i \in \mathbb{R}^{1 \times d_s}$. The principal component analysis (PCA) [1] projects the high-dimension vector $\varPhi_i \in \mathbb{R}^{1 \times d_s}$ into a low-dimension vector $\hat{\varPhi}_i \in \mathbb{R}^{1 \times d_r}$ for dimensionality reduction while retraining the main patterns of the vectors. Secondly, we segment data points into different clusters by applying the Kmeans++ algorithm on the dimension-reduced vectors $\{\hat{\varPhi}_i\}_{i=1}^{g}$. For simplicity, we assume the vectors are in the same cluster, and the center point of the cluster is referred to as $\hat{\varPhi}_i^c \in \mathbb{R}^{1 \times d_r}$. Note that the center point might not be one of the vectors $\{\hat{\varPhi}_i\}_{i=1}^{g}$. The Euclidean distance between the center point $\hat{\varPhi}^c$ and the i_{th} vector $\hat{\varPhi}_i$ is denoted as follows:

$$d(\hat{\varPhi}^c, \hat{\varPhi}_i) = \sqrt{\sum_{j=1}^{n} (\hat{\varPhi}^c[j] - \hat{\varPhi}_i[j])^2}, \qquad (6)$$

where $\hat{\varPhi}^c[j]$ is the i_{th} element in the vector $\hat{\varPhi}^c$. We refer to the reciprocal of the normalized distances as the data sampling probabilities so that the sampling probability for the i_{th} data point is denoted as:

$$p(i) = \frac{\text{inv}_p(i)}{\sum_{j=1}^{g} \text{inv}_p(j)}, \qquad \text{inv}_p(i) = \frac{1}{d(\hat{\varPhi}^c, \hat{\varPhi}_i)}. \qquad (7)$$

We sample the data point from the cluster with the probabilities p as a part of the test sample. After traversing all clusters, we obtain a collection of test samples that can better represent the whole dataset.

4   Experiments

4.1   Dataset

We conduct experiments on these two real-world datasets, namely medical radiology and medical surgery. We retrieve patient clinical records from the hospital's data lake to build the basic medical corpus. Following the clinicians' suggestions,

---

[6] https://huggingface.co/TurkuNLP/sbert-cased-finnish-paraphrase.

we split the medical corpus into four text sets based on the medical specialties, i.e., "RTG (radiology reports)", "KIR (surgery text)", "SAD (radiotherapy documents)", "OPER (procedures notes)". The detailed specialty information can be found in the Kela - the Social Insurance Institution in Finland[7]. We combine the RTG and SAD sets into the medical radiology dataset, and the KIR and OPER sets into the medical surgery dataset. We only keep the main body of documents as a medical corpus for each clinical document and split some documents into sentences when constructing these two medical datasets. To better explore the model performance variation on different datasets, we truncate and maintain datasets at the same scale to eliminate the effect of data size.

Table 1. Numbers of weakly labeled entities based on four medical specialties. "B-X" and "I-X" represents the beginning and inside of a clinical term. To ensure anonymity, we represent values lower than 10 in the results as "<10".

Medical Specialty	Stru		Meas		Cond		Devi		Proc		Medi		O
	B-X	I-X	B-X	I-X	B-X	I-X	B-X	I-X	B-X	I-X	I-X	B-X	
KIR	10002	23	3689	27	10705	189	1773	11	13756	101	2984	14	142002
SAD	6993	<10	2722	33	10602	273	913	<10	14292	108	3494	11	123220
RTG	8623	64	1957	<10	8204	138	1219	<10	6740	22	1674	<10	99083
OPER	12784	61	2663	<10	7913	74	2696	<10	8577	40	2457	<10	137150

We leverage the SSM module and HAM scheme for each medical specialty to construct a human-annotated testing set and machine-annotated training set, respectively. We select 1000 sentences from both datasets based on the dataset sentence ratios, i.e., the number of sentences in each dataset over the number of sentences in all datasets. The number of sentences in different human-annotated datasets is 214 (KIR), 192 (RTG), 210 (SAD), and 192 (OPER). The rest of the sentences are used to construct the machine-annotated datasets by applying the HAM scheme mentioned in Sect. 3.1. Weakly labeled datasets generated by the HAM and clinician-annotated data are divided into training, validation, and test sets according to the predefined ratio, i.e., 7:2:1. For simplicity, we denote predefined NER labels as "Anatomical Structure (Stru)", "Body Function and Measurement (Meas)", "Medical Condition (Cond)", "Medical Device (Devi)", "Medical Procedure (Proc)", and "Medication (Medi)". Table 1 shows the statistical summary.

4.2 Baselines and Setup

We compare the three zero-shot baselines with different token classification layers and two variants of our proposed method. Three baselines are ZS-BERT (i.e., a Zero-Shot BERT-based model), ZS-BERT-LSR (i.e., Zero-Shot BERT with Label Smoothing Regularization), and ZS-BERT-CRF (i.e., Zero-Shot BERT

---

[7] https://tinyurl.com/3ybbdyjr.

with Conditional Random Field). We equip two token classification layers, i.e., softmax-based linear layers (Linear) and conditional random fields (CRF). The BERT model is pretrained over the collected corpus. All baselines are in the zero-shot setting and summarized as follows:

- ZS-BERT: A BERT model encodes input documents, and the linear layer decodes features into entity labels.
- ZS-BERT$_{LSR}$: Overall architecture is the same as the ZS-BERT, except the loss function is adjusted by the LSR.
- ZS-BERT$_{CRF}$: A CRF rather than a linear layer follows a BERT model to generate entity labels.

Accordingly, two variants of our proposed methods are HAM-Linear and HAM-LSR. **HAM-Linear** replaces the CRF layer of the HAM-net with a linear layer to generate token-level predictions; 2) **HAM-LSR** is the same as the HAM-Linear except for the model optimization part. The HAM-LSR leverages the label smoothing regularization (LSR) over the cross-entropy loss function.

We manually tune the hyper-parameter, select the best model evaluated on the validation set and report the results on the clinician-annotated test set. We use the base configuration of the BERT model to encode input sequences. The batch size is 1. The maximum length of the input is 512. We set the drop rate of all dropout layers as 0.03. The learning rate is $1e^{-5}$. We trained our neural network with mixed precision, i.e., FP16, to accelerate the training speed. We apply the early stopping strategy by monitoring the validation loss while the patience round is 5. The optimal PCA dimension for four datasets is ten, and the number of clusters is 2.

4.3   Main Results

To compare with baseline models, we report the model's results on the precision, recall, and F1 scores. Table 2 reports the performance of all models.

Table 2. Experimental results, i.e., precision (P), recall (R) & F1 scores in %, on the medical surgery and medical radiology datasets.

Models	Medical Surgery Dataset			Medical Radiology Dataset		
	P (%)	R (%)	F1 (%)	P (%)	R (%)	F1 (%)
ZS-BERT	8.87	13.77	10.78	8.55	11.64	9.86
ZS-BERT$_{LSR}$	8.87	13.74	10.78	8.56	11.65	9.87
ZS-BERT$_{CRF}$	8.14	11.68	9.59	7.94	10.01	8.85
HAM-Linear	32.34	8.84	13.53	24.31	9.91	13.50
HAM-LSR	31.31	8.48	13.06	23.70	9.04	12.92
HAM	**33.37**	**9.20**	**13.74**	**25.38**	**10.04**	**14.19**

Medical Surgery Dataset: Our model outperforms all baselines across evaluation metrics. The HAM achieved better scores compared with the best linear-decoding model, i.e., HAM-Linear. The HAM outperforms the HAM-LSR by 2.06, 0.72, and 0.68% points on precision, recall, and F1 scores.

Medical Radiology Dataset: Our model improves all evaluation scores on the medical radiology dataset. Compared with the HAM-Liner, the HAM improves the precision, recall, and F1 scores by 1.04, 0.13, and 0.69% points, respectively. The HAM also outperforms the HAM-LSR with 1.68, 1.00, and 1.27% points on all evaluation metrics.

4.4   The Effect of Sample Selection Module

We leverage Davies Bouldin scores [4] to find the optimal combination of the PCA projection dimension and clustering number. Figure 3 shows the distributions of Davies Bouldin scores with different PCA projection dimensions and clustering numbers on four datasets. From the figure, we can observe that cluster numbers largely affect the Davies Bouldin scores while the lower values indicating better clustering. Besides, we use different clustering algorithms, i.e., bisecting k-means and ward agglomerative clustering algorithm, to plot distributions of Davies Bouldin scores. The distributions show the same patterns as the k-means algorithm.

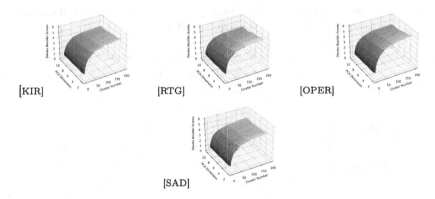

Fig. 3. Davies Bouldin scores by different PCA projection dimensions and the number of clusters.

To compare the random selection and SSM module, we exploit the Jensen-Shannon divergence [15] to measure the distribution distances between the full and selected datasets. Assume the distribution of the full dataset is P and the selected dataset is Q so that the Jenson-Shannon divergence is shown as follows:

$$\mathrm{JSD}(P \parallel Q) = \frac{1}{2}D(P \parallel M) + \frac{1}{2}D(Q \parallel M). \tag{8}$$

Table 3. Jensen-Shannon divergence between original label distributions and selected labels' distribution provided by different selection methods.

Method	KIR	RTG	OPER	SAD
Random	0.292	0.285	0.300	0.298
SSM	0.275	0.278	0.285	0.275

The SSM and random selection algorithms have been performed ten times and averaged across all results. Table 3 shows that the SSM significantly outperforms the random selection approach because the label distribution of the SSM is closer to the entire dataset.

4.5   The Effect of Continual Pretraining

We conduct an ablation experiment to study the effectiveness of domain-specific continual pretraining. Table 4 shows the results of the baselines and HAM with or without the domain-specific continual pretraining. We can observe that continual pretraining improves all scores on two medical NER datasets, validating that continual pretraining is important for the domain-specific application in this study.

Table 4. Comparison of the evaluation results of the model with or without the domain continual pertaining (DCP) on two medical NER datasets.

Models	DCP	Medical Surgery Dataset			Medical Radiology Dataset		
		P (%)	R (%)	F1 (%)	P (%)	R (%)	F1 (%)
ZS-BERT	✗	6.04	6.50	6.26	6.43	6.30	6.36
	✓	8.87	13.77	10.78	8.55	11.64	9.86
$ZS\text{-}BERT_{LSR}$	✗	6.04	6.49	6.26	6.43	6.29	6.36
	✓	8.87	13.74	10.78	8.56	11.65	9.87
$ZS\text{-}BERT_{CRF}$	✗	7.56	9.84	8.55	8.29	9.72	8.95
	✓	8.14	11.68	9.59	7.94	10.01	8.85
HAM-Linear	✗	33.50	4.46	7.82	20.83	4.95	7.98
	✓	32.34	8.84	13.53	24.31	9.91	13.50
HAM-LSR	✗	24.95	3.24	5.69	23.06	5.96	9.30
	✓	31.31	8.48	13.06	23.70	9.04	12.92
HAM	✗	34.00	4.43	7.80	21.79	5.16	8.32
	✓	33.37	9.20	13.74	25.38	10.04	14.19

4.6 Discussion

One key limitation of this paper is that the experimental results of our model are not superior in terms of those evaluation scores. This is mainly because the training of our models uses weakly annotated labels. Automated annotated labels with distant supervision methods naturally cannot achieve superior performance over evaluation metrics in many cases. However, the proposed HAM method paves the way for training NER models without human-annotated data. In our experiments, we leverage the domain-specific continual pretraining to improve the model performance further. Developed NER systems requiring limited or zero supervision can be deployed to extremely low-resource scenarios, such as resource-restrained language and medical NLP applications. The medical NER task in extremely low-resource scenarios is very challenging. Future work can combine the proposed HAM and semi-supervised methods to build more reliable entity recognition systems. Our study used clinical notes in Finnish as a case study. However, our proposed method can be replicated in other languages. Taking English as an example, we can use the English MeSH as the ontology and the corresponding preprocessing techniques for English in our hybrid annotation mechanism to generate weakly supervised labels.

5 Conclusion

This paper developed a novel framework, Hybrid Annotation Mechanism Network (HAM-net), to extract entity-level medical information from the clinical text in an extremely low-resource scenario. We design the Hybrid Annotation Mechanism (HAM) to detect and classify entities in documents into predefined labels by utilizing the distant supervision signals from the Finnish medical subject headings. The weakly labeled data produced by the HAM module is further used to train a NER model based on contextualized representations and domain-specific continual pretraining. Due to the scarcity of annotated evaluation data, we developed the Sample Selection Module (SSM) to select the samples which can better represent the original datasets than the random selection approach. The proposed SSM method can effectively select more representative samples, thus reducing the annotation cost. The experimental results show that our framework can be adapted to train neural models and establish a strong baseline for future studies when there are no explicit supervision signals provided by human experts. And domain-specific continual pretraining can help to improve the performance of NER models trained with weakly annotated data.

Acknowledgment. This work was supported by the Academy of Finland (Flagship programme: Finnish Center for Artificial Intelligence FCAI, and grants 336033, 352986) and EU (H2020 grant 101016775 and NextGenerationEU). We wish to acknowledge HUS Acamedic for providing secure computing resources. We also acknowledge the computational resources provided by the Aalto Science-IT project and CSC - IT Center for Science, Finland for prototyping our methods on synthetic data.

Ethical Statement. The study was based on approval of HUS Helsinki University Hospital (HUS/12199/2022). Data was analyzed on HUS Acamedic that is a certified data analytics platform and meets the requirements (General Data Protection Regulation, Finlex 552/2019) for processing sensitive healthcare data.

References

1. Abdi, H., Williams, L.J.: Principal component analysis. Wiley Interdiscip. Rev. Comput. Stat. **2**(4), 433–459 (2010)
2. Arora, S., Ge, R., Neyshabur, B., Zhang, Y.: Stronger generalization bounds for deep nets via a compression approach. In: International Conference on Machine Learning, pp. 254–263. PMLR (2018)
3. Beltagy, I., Peters, M.E., Cohan, A.: Longformer: the long-document transformer. arXiv preprint arXiv:2004.05150 (2020)
4. Davies, D.L., Bouldin, D.W.: A cluster separation measure. IEEE Trans. Pattern Anal. Mach. Intell. **2**, 224–227 (1979)
5. Devlin, J., Chang, M.W., Lee, K., Toutanova, K.: Bert: pre-training of deep bidirectional transformers for language understanding. arXiv preprint arXiv:1810.04805 (2018)
6. Ferreira, M.D., Malyska, M., Sahar, N., Miotto, R., Paulovich, F., Milios, E.: Active learning for medical code assignment. arXiv preprint arXiv:2104.05741 (2021)
7. Gururangan, S., et al.: Don't stop pretraining: adapt language models to domains and tasks. In: ACL (2020)
8. Jain, S., et al.: Radgraph: extracting clinical entities and relations from radiology reports. arXiv preprint arXiv:2106.14463 (2021)
9. Jiang, H., Zhang, D., Cao, T., Yin, B., Zhao, T.: Named entity recognition with small strongly labeled and large weakly labeled data. arXiv preprint arXiv:2106.08977 (2021)
10. Korkontzelos, I., Piliouras, D., Dowsey, A.W., Ananiadou, S.: Boosting drug named entity recognition using an aggregate classifier. Artif. Intell. Med. **65**(2), 145–153 (2015)
11. Lafferty, J.D., McCallum, A., Pereira, F.C.N.: Conditional random fields: probabilistic models for segmenting and labeling sequence data. In: Proceedings of the Eighteenth International Conference on Machine Learning, ICML 2001, pp. 282–289. Morgan Kaufmann Publishers Inc., San Francisco (2001)
12. Li, J., Sun, A., Han, J., Li, C.: A survey on deep learning for named entity recognition. IEEE Trans. Knowl. Data Eng. **34**(1), 50–70 (2020)
13. Li, Y., Wehbe, R.M., Ahmad, F.S., Wang, H., Luo, Y.: Clinical-longformer and clinical-bigbird: transformers for long clinical sequences. arXiv preprint arXiv:2201.11838 (2022)
14. Lim, S.K., Muis, A.O., Lu, W., Ong, C.H.: Malwaretextdb: a database for annotated malware articles. In: Proceedings of the 55th Annual Meeting of the Association for Computational Linguistics (Volume 1: Long Papers), pp. 1557–1567 (2017)
15. Manning, C., Schutze, H.: Foundations of Statistical Natural Language Processing. MIT Press, Cambridge (1999)
16. Nesterov, A., Umerenkov, D.: Distantly supervised end-to-end medical entity extraction from electronic health records with human-level quality. arXiv preprint arXiv:2201.10463 (2022)

17. Rindflesch, T.C., Tanabe, L., JN, W., et al.: Extraction of drugs, genes and relations from the biomedical literature. In: Pacific Symposium on Bio2 Computing, vol. 5, p. 5172528 (2000)
18. Sang, E.F., De Meulder, F.: Introduction to the CoNLL-2003 shared task: language-independent named entity recognition. arXiv preprint CS/0306050 (2003)
19. Settles, B.: Biomedical named entity recognition using conditional random fields and rich feature sets. In: Proceedings of the International Joint Workshop on Natural Language Processing in Biomedicine and its Applications (NLPBA/BioNLP), pp. 107–110 (2004)
20. Shang, J., Liu, L., Ren, X., Gu, X., Ren, T., Han, J.: Learning named entity tagger using domain-specific dictionary. arXiv preprint arXiv:1809.03599 (2018)
21. Tsuruoka, Y., Tsujii, J.: Boosting precision and recall of dictionary-based protein name recognition. In: Proceedings of the ACL 2003 Workshop on Natural Language Processing in Biomedicine, vol. 13, pp. 41–48. Citeseer (2003)
22. Wang, M., Manning, C.D.: Cross-lingual projected expectation regularization for weakly supervised learning. Trans. Assoc. Comput. Linguist. 2, 55–66 (2014)
23. Wu, Y., Jiang, M., Xu, J., Zhi, D., Xu, H.: Clinical named entity recognition using deep learning models. In: AMIA Annual Symposium Proceedings, vol. 2017, p. 1812. American Medical Informatics Association (2017)
24. Zhou, Z.H.: A brief introduction to weakly supervised learning. Natl. Sci. Rev. 5(1), 44–53 (2018)
25. Zirikly, A., Hagiwara, M.: Cross-lingual transfer of named entity recognizers without parallel corpora. In: Proceedings of the 53rd Annual Meeting of the Association for Computational Linguistics and the 7th International Joint Conference on Natural Language Processing (Volume 2: Short Papers), pp. 390–396 (2015)

Fairness-Aware Processing Techniques in Survival Analysis: Promoting Equitable Predictions

Zhouting Zhao[✉] and Tin Lok James Ng

School of Computer Science and Statistics, Trinity College Dublin, Dublin, Ireland
{zhaozh,ngja}@tcd.ie

Abstract. As machine learning (ML) systems are becoming pervasive in high-stakes applications, the issue of ML fairness is receiving increasing attention. A large variety of fair ML solutions have been developed to ensure that bias and inaccuracies in the data and model do not lead to decisions that treat individuals unfavorably on the basis of sensitive characteristics. While most of the fair ML literature focus on classification and regression setting, fairness of survival analysis for time-to-event outcomes are under-explored. In contrast to existing fair survival analysis solutions which typically incorporate fairness constraints in the learning mechanisms, we propose several pre-processing and post-processing approaches. Due to the model-agnostic nature of pre-processing and post-processing methods, they may offer more flexible fairness intervention. Additionally, pre-processing and post-processing methods tend to be more intuitive and explainable compared to in-processing methods. We carry out experimental studies with medical and non-medical data sets to evaluate the proposed fairness methods.

Keywords: Fair Survival Analysis · Pre-Processing · Post-Processing

1 Introduction

Nowadays, artificial intelligence (AI) and machine learning (ML) algorithms play a significant role in decision-making processes. Automated systems are commonly used in various domains, including commercial and government applications, for tasks such as autonomous driving, application screening, crime prediction, recommendations, and candidate ranking [25,26]. The growing use of AI and ML raises concerns about ensuring unbiased and fair models as algorithms are involved in making increasingly sensitive decisions across various domains [24,34].

Survival analysis is a versatile statistical method for analyzing time-to-event data, widely used in diverse fields such as healthcare, insurance, criminal justice, customer retention, and employee turnover [12,18]. In the context of Covid-19, survival analysis has become crucial for assessing patient outcomes, identifying risk factors for severe illness or death, and studying the pandemic's economic

G. De Francisci Morales et al. (Eds.): ECML PKDD 2023, LNAI 14174, pp. 460–476, 2023.
https://doi.org/10.1007/978-3-031-43427-3_28

impact, such as time-to-default for affected firms [32]. However, it is essential to ensure that these predictions are made in a fair and equitable manner. The Covid-19 pandemic has highlighted the importance of fair distribution of limited medical resources, like hospital beds, ventilators, and vaccines, while biased survival analysis models may lead to unfair resource allocations and unequal access to care. Fairness is also vital in other fields, like insurance, where biased models can result in discriminatory pricing based on factors like age, gender, and medical history, disproportionately affecting marginalized individuals. In criminal justice, survival analysis helps predict recidivism and determine sentence lengths. Biased models could perpetuate existing inequalities and lead to unequal treatment. Therefore, it is essential to investigate the fairness of survival analysis models in these contexts to ensure that they do not perpetuate biases and discrimination.

A growing literature in the emerging field of ethical machine learning have proposed mechanisms to ensure that algorithmic decision systems do not lead to unfair outcomes. An ever increasing array of fairness metrics have been proposed in the literature to quantify fairness for classification problems. Fairness metrics can be broadly classified into group-based fairness metrics and individual fairness metrics. Group-based fairness metrics are based on the notion of protected or sensitive variables and on (un)privileged groups: groups that are disproportionately (less) more likely to be positive classified. Statistical/demographic parity [9,20] is one of the most popular group-based fairness metric. This metric defines fairness as an equal probability of being classified with the positive label. As compared to group-based metrics, individual fairness metrics do not focus on comparing two or more groups as defined by a sensitive variable, but consider the outcome for each individual.

A major focus of machine learning fairness research is to develop techniques to mitigate the unfairness in the data and models. Unfairness mitigation methods can be classified into 1) pre-processing approaches which generally perform transformations on the data with the aim to remove discrimination from the data; 2) in-processing approaches which often incorporating one or more fairness metrics or their proxies into the model objective functions; and 3) post-processing approaches which apply transformations to model output to improve prediction fairness. A detailed review of fairness metrics and mitigation methods can be found in [5,13,24]. Compared to in-processing approaches, a key advantage of pre- and post-processing approaches is that they do not modify the machine learning models explicitly, and hence are more flexible.

Recently, algorithmic fairness in survival analysis has generated mild interests in the literature [16,22,28,31]. A range of fairness metrics have been proposed including fairness metrics based on hazard function [22], more general survival function [28], and predictive performance based fairness metrics [31]. Previous research on fair survival analysis has primarily focused on in-processing techniques. For example, [22] proposed Fair Cox Proportional Hazards models to promote equitable allocation of healthcare resources using a penalized maximum likelihood estimation approach. Similarly, [28] uses pseudo value-based objective functions and incorporate fairness metrics as constraints.

While in-processing based fair survival analysis approaches have shown promising results, pre-processing and post-processing approaches offer a more flexible and efficient way to address fairness concerns in survival predictions, thanks to their model-agnostic nature. A critical research question is whether and to what extent existing pre-processing and post-processing methods, initially developed for binary classification or regression tasks, can be adapted and applied to the context of survival analysis. By investigating this research question, we aim to expand the arsenal of fairness techniques available for survival analysis. This will provide practitioners and researchers with a wider range of options to mitigate potential biases and promote fairness in survival predictions.

Our contributions are summarized below:

1. We adapt and extend several pre-processing and post-processing approaches from classification and regression context to survival analysis, which are model-agnostic, flexible, intuitive and explainable.
2. We conduct experimental studies with medical and non-medical data sets to assess whether and to what extent the proposed methods improve fairness.
3. We assess the trade-offs among proposed methods in terms of group fairness, individual fairness, and predictive performance.

The rest of the article is structure as follows: Sect. 2 introduces background and related works on survival analysis and fairness metrics in survival analysis. The proposed pre-processing and post-processing methods are presented in Sect. 3. Experimental setting and six data sets are introduced in Sect. 4, and experimental results are presented and discussed in Sect. 5. Section 6 concludes the work with a discussion of future research directions.

2   Background and Related Work

2.1   Survival Analysis

Survival analysis encompasses statistical techniques that model time-to-event data while utilizing incomplete information from censored data [35]. Right censoring or loss-to-follow-up, occurs when an individual's survival time is not directly observed but is known to exceed a certain value [15].

Time-to-event data can be represented as triplets $\{t_i, e_i, \mathbf{z}_i\}_{i=1}^N$ where N is the total number of observation units, t_i is the observed event time for unit i (i.e. e_i is an event indicator, where $e_i = 1$ if event occurred, and $e_i = 0$ indicates the observation is censored), and $\mathbf{z}_i$ is a vector of observed covariates. Special modeling techniques are required due to the presence of censoring as time-to-event can not be observed when censoring occurs before the event of interest. A key objective of survival analysis is to estimate the distribution of event times conditional on covariates $\mathbf{z}$ defined by the survival probability $S(t|\mathbf{z}) = P(T > t|\mathbf{z})$. For each $\mathbf{z}$, $S(t|\mathbf{z})$ is a non-increasing function of t with $S(0|\mathbf{z}) = 1$ and $S(t|\mathbf{z}) \to 0$ as $t \to \infty$. The hazard function, $h(t|\mathbf{z})$, defined as

$$h(t|\mathbf{z}) := \lim_{\delta t \to 0} \frac{P(t \le T + \delta t | T \ge t, \mathbf{z})}{\delta t},$$

is another commonly used function which represents the instantaneous failure rate.

The cox proportional hazards model is a classical semi-parametric method for modeling time-to-event data [6]. The model assumes that the dependency of hazard function on covariates is time-invariant and multiplicative. Parametric models, such as the accelerated failure time model [36], provide an alternative approach to proportional hazards model. These models assume that the (logarithm of) survival times follow a theoretical distribution. Commonly used distributions for parametric model include normal, exponential, and Weibull distributions.

Machine learning methods have gained popularity in modeling time-to-event data due to their ability to capture non-linear relationships and make accurate predictions. Neural network based methods [8,29] relax the assumptions of traditional regression based approaches whereby complex and nonlinear dependency of hazard functions on covariates can be captured implicitly and the effect of covariates can vary over time. More recently, there has been increasing interest in modeling survival data using deep neural network approaches [21,23]. Desipte their popularity, the lack of interpretability of deep neural network models and the requirement of large sample size are major shortcomings.

Within the array of machine learning methods, the ensemble learning approach, particularly the Random Survival Forest (RSF), has been employed for modeling survival data. Random Survival Forest (RSF), proposed by [17], is a non-parametric ensemble estimation method that extends the concept of Random Forest [4] to survival data. The method uses an ensemble of survival trees, each built using a bootstrap sample drawn from the training set, with the remaining out-of-bag observations utilized for validation. For each bootstrap sample, a full-size survival tree is grown using a specific splitting criterion without pruning. At each internal node, a subset of candidate covariates is randomly selected from all covariates to determine the optimal split that minimizes the risk or maximizes the separation between nodes. The tree-growing process continues until a stopping condition is met, such as reaching a minimum node size or a maximum tree depth.

Given this backdrop, the focus of our work lies in the use of both semi-parametric (CPH) and non-parametric (RSF) models in the context of survival data analysis. By applying these models, we strive to provide a comprehensive examination of our proposed fairness-aware processing techniques in diverse modeling contexts.

2.2 Fairness Metrics in Survival Analysis

Compared to the wealth of literature on fairness in classification and regression, fairness in survival analysis is an under-explored field. Several fairness metrics have been proposed for survival analysis recently [22,28,31]. These metrics extend the fairness metrics for classification and regression and address the unique challenges of censoring in time-to-event data. Two fairness metrics, individual fairness, and group fairness, for survival models are considered. Both fairness metrics were originally proposed by [22] which are only applicable for hazard-based survival models. These metrics were later extended by [28] to both hazard and non-hazard-based models. At any time t, individual fairness is defined as,

$$F_I(t) = \sum_{i=1}^{N} \sum_{j=i+1}^{N} \max(0, \left| \hat{S}(t|\mathbf{z}_i) - \hat{S}(t|\mathbf{z}_j) \right| - \alpha D(\mathbf{z}_i, \mathbf{z}_j)) \qquad (1)$$

where $\hat{S}(t|\mathbf{z}_i)$ is the predicted survival probability at time t for subject i and $D(\mathbf{z}_i, \mathbf{z}_j))$ measures the distance (e.g., cosine or Euclidean distance) between the covariates of subject i and j, and α is a scale factor which can be adjusted to ensure that survival probability predictions and distance distances are similarly scaled.

Let $\mathcal{A}$ be the set of values in the sensitive attribute, group fairness is defined as

$$F_G(t) = \max_{\mathbf{a} \in \mathcal{A}} \left| E_\mathbf{a}(\hat{S}(t|\mathbf{Z})) - E(\hat{S}(t|\mathbf{Z})) \right| \qquad (2)$$

where $E_\mathbf{a}$ is the expectation w.r.t. the covariates distribution $p_\mathbf{a}$ for group $\mathbf{a}$:

$$E_\mathbf{a}(\hat{S}(t|\mathbf{Z})) := \int \hat{S}(t|\mathbf{z})p_\mathbf{a}(\mathbf{z})d\mathbf{z},$$

and E is the expectation w.r.t. the population covariates distribution p:

$$E(\hat{S}(t|\mathbf{Z})) := \int \hat{S}(t|\mathbf{z})p(\mathbf{z})d\mathbf{z}.$$

That is, $E_\mathbf{a}(\hat{S}(t|\mathbf{Z}))$ and $E(\hat{S}(t|\mathbf{Z}))$ measure the expected predicted survival probability for group $\mathbf{a}$ and the population, respectively. We note that both $p_\mathbf{a}$ and p can be estimated based on the sample and hence both $E_\mathbf{a}(\hat{S}(t|\mathbf{Z}))$ and $E(\hat{S}(t|\mathbf{Z}))$ can be estimated. The group fairness definition measures the maximum deviation between the average of group survival predictions and the average of population survival predictions.

We note from (1) and (2) that both definitions of fairness are functions of time t and $0 \le F_I(t), F_G(t) \le 1$ for all t. One may summarize individual (group) fairness using a single metric:

$$F_I^{(p)} := \left(\frac{1}{T} \int_0^T |F_I(t)|^p dt \right)^{1/p} = \left(\frac{1}{T} \int_0^T F_I(t)^p dt \right)^{1/p} \qquad (3)$$

where T is the end time and

$$F_I^{(\infty)} := \max_{t \in [0,T]} \{|F_I(t)|\} = \max_{t \in [0,T]} \{F_I(t)\}. \qquad (4)$$

$F_G^{(p)}$ and $F_G^{(\infty)}$ are analogously defined.

3   Methodology

We describe several pre-processing and post-processing mitigation methods which aim to improve the group fairness metric in Eq. (2). We apply, adapt, and extend pre-processing and post-processing mitigation methods developed for classification and regression to the survival analysis context. The training set is represented as $\mathcal{D} = \{(t_i, e_i, \mathbf{z}_i)\}_{i=1}^{N}$ where t_i is the event time, e_i is the event type, and $\mathbf{z}_i$ is a vector of attributes which consists of a vector of non-sensitive attributes $\mathbf{x}_i$, and a vector of sensitive attributes $\mathbf{a}_i$. Thus, we also write $\mathcal{D} = \{(t_i, e_i, \mathbf{x}_i, \mathbf{a}_i)\}_{i=1}^{N}$. While our focus is on the group fairness metric, potential trade-offs between group fairness, individual fairness, and predictive performance will be investigated in the experimental studies.

3.1   Pre-processing Methods

We consider four pre-processing mitigation methods, namely, *disparate impact remover, data augmentation with identical copies, correlation remover*, and *sampling* methods.

Disparate Impact Remover
The disparate impact remover [9] modifies the distributions of the ordinal non-sensitive features in a way that preserves the original ranks. Recall that $\mathcal{A}$ is the set of values of sensitive attributes, for each non-sensitive ordinal feature k a "median" distribution $F_{\mathcal{A},k}$ is defined in terms of its quantile function:

$$F_{\mathcal{A},k}^{-1}(u) := \text{median}_{\mathbf{a} \in \mathcal{A}} F_{\mathbf{a},k}^{-1}(u),$$

where $F_{\mathbf{a},k}$ is the distribution of the feature k restricted to sub-population with sensitive attributes $\mathbf{a}$. For each individual i and each non-sensitive ordinal feature k, the algorithm applies the following transformation:

$$\tilde{x}_{i,k} = F_{\mathcal{A},k}^{-1}(F_{\mathbf{a}_i,k}(x_{i,k})).$$

This algorithm is further extended to allow *partial repair* to balance the trade-offs between classification accuracy and fairness of the resulting data.

Data Augmentation with Identical Copies
Motivated by disparate impact remover which ensures that the distributions of features for all values of the sensitive attributes $a \in \mathcal{A}$ are similar (identical), we consider a simple strategy to ensure that the training subsets for all values of the sensitive attributes are identical. For each training instance $(t_i, e_i, \mathbf{x}_i, \mathbf{a}_i)$, $|\mathcal{A}| - 1$ identical copies $(t_i, e_i, \mathbf{x}_i, \mathbf{a})$ for $\mathbf{a} \in \mathcal{A}, \mathbf{a} \neq \mathbf{a}_i$ are created. The resulting training set is $|\mathcal{A}|$ times as large as the original one.

Sampling
A sampling based mitigation method for binary classification with a single binary sensitive attribute was proposed by [19]. The method divides the data set into four groups based on the sensitive attribute and class label: deprived community

with positive class label, deprived community with negative class label, favored community with positive class label, and favored community with negative class label. The expected size of each group is computed under the assumption of independence between class label and sensitive attribute. Each of the four groups is then sampled separately until the expected group size is reached.

We extend the sampling approach to time-to-event data. We perform quantile binning of the event times $(0, t^{(1)}], (t^{(1)}, t^{(2)}], \ldots, (t^{(m-1)}, t^{(m)}]$ where m is the number of bins and $t^{(m)}$ is the maximum event time in the data set. We then partition the data set into groups based on event times (the bin the event time belongs to), event types (censored or observed), and sensitive attributes. This leads to a total of $m \times 2 \times |\mathcal{A}|$ number of groups. We compute the expected group size under the assumption that the sensitive attribute is independent of event types and event times

$$P_{exp}(e_i = 1, t_i \in (t^{(k)}, t^{(k+1)}], \mathbf{a}_i = \mathbf{a}) = \frac{|\{(t_i, e_i, \mathbf{x}_i, \mathbf{a}_i) \in \mathcal{D} : e_i = 1, t_i \in (t^{(k)}, t^{(k+1)}]\}|}{|\mathcal{D}|}$$
$$\times \frac{|\{(t_i, e_i, \mathbf{x}_i, \mathbf{a}_i) \in \mathcal{D} : \mathbf{a}_i = \mathbf{a}\}|}{|\mathcal{D}|}.$$

Each group is then sampled individually until its expected group size is reached.

We consider two alternative sampling approaches, over-sampling and under-sampling. Suppose $\mathcal{A} = \{a^{(1)}, \ldots, a^{(J)}\}$ are the set of all possible values of the sensitive attributes. For an arbitrary combination of event time bin $(t^{(k)}, t^{(k+1)}]$ and event type e, we compute

$$n^{(j)} := |\{(t_i, e_i, \mathbf{x}_i, \mathbf{a}_i) : t_i \in (t^{(k)}, t^{(k+1)}], e_i = e, \mathbf{a}_i = \mathbf{a}^{(j)}\}|, \quad j = 1, \ldots, J.$$

The over-sampling approach involves randomly over sampling each minority group until the group size reaches $\max_j n^{(j)}$. The under-sampling approach randomly sample each group (apart from the group with the smallest size) until the grou size reaches $\min_j n^{(j)}$.

We illustrate the sampling methods using the NAFLD1 data set (Table 1). We consider gender as a sensitive attribute with two levels (Male and Female). The event times are divided into four bins which result in a total of 16 groups. The expected group size for each group is calculated based on the independence assumption. We note that under this approach the gender ratio is the same for every combination of event time bin and event type. The number of observations based on the under-sampling and over-sampling approaches are also provided in the table.

Correlation Remover
One limitation of the three pre-processing methods introduced is that $\mathcal{A}$ must be discrete and its size needs to be relatively small. In comparison, the correlation remover method allows both continuous and discrete and multi-dimensional sensitive attributes.

The method aims to project away the linear dependence between non-sensitive and sensitive attributes while retaining as much details as possible from the original data. Let $\mathbf{x}_i \in \mathbb{R}^q$ and $\mathbf{a}_i \in \mathbb{R}^p$ be the vectors of non-sensitive and sensitive attributes for subject i, respectively. Let $\beta \in \mathbb{R}^{p \times q}$ be the coefficient

Table 1. Sampling Methods on NAFLD1 [1] Dataset. This table shows the sampling results for the NAFLD1 dataset, where gender is the sensitive attribute. The dataset is split into eight groups based on the 25%, 50%, and 75% quantiles of the survival time distribution and the event type (censored or observed). The table displays the number of samples in each sub-group before and after applying resampling to reach the group size.

Event Time Bin	Event Type	Gender Identity	No. Actual	Expected Size	No. Under-sample	No. Over-sample
(0, 1145]	0	M	1055	972	1055	1135
		F	1135	1217	1055	1135
	1	M	170	142	151	170
		F	151	178	151	170
(1145, 2318]	0	M	999	1032	999	1325
		F	1325	1292	999	1325
	1	M	98	84	91	98
		F	91	105	91	98
(2318, 3330]	0	M	950	1041	950	1395
		F	1395	1303	950	1395
	1	M	78	75	78	89
		F	89	93	78	89
(3330, 7142]	0	M	1054	1054	1054	1320
		F	1320	1320	1054	1320
	1	M	59	62	59	80
		F	80	77	59	80

matrix to be estimated. The correlation remover method solves the following optimization problem:

$$\hat{\beta} := \operatorname{argmin}_{\beta} \sum_{i=1}^{N} ||\mathbf{x}_i - (\mathbf{a}_i - \bar{\mathbf{a}})^T \beta||^2,$$

where $\bar{\mathbf{a}}$ denotes the mean vector of sensitive attributes, and $||\cdot||$ is the L_2 norm. The residual vectors $\hat{\epsilon}_i \in \mathbb{R}^q$ are then obtained from

$$\hat{\epsilon}_i = \mathbf{x}_i - (\mathbf{a}_i - \bar{\mathbf{a}})^T \hat{\beta}.$$

Intuitively, $(\mathbf{a}_i - \bar{\mathbf{a}})^T \hat{\beta}$ captures the part of $\mathbf{x}_i$ that can be linearly explained by the sensitive attributes $\mathbf{a}_i$ whereas $\hat{\epsilon}_i$ captures the part of $\mathbf{x}_i$ that cannot be linearly explained by the sensitive attributes. The transformed non-sensitive features are given by

$$\tilde{\mathbf{x}}_i = \alpha \hat{\epsilon}_i + (1 - \alpha)\mathbf{x}_i,$$

where $\alpha \in [0, 1]$ is a tuning parameter.

3.2   Post-processing Methods

Post-processing by Controlling for Sensitive Attributes

This method was introduced by [27] in a linear regression setting and later extended to general regression and applied to insurance pricing by [38]. This method first fits a model with both sensitive and non-sensitive attributes as predictors. The fitted model is then averaged across the values of sensitive attributes in the population.

This approach can be naturally extended to survival analysis. Let $\hat{S}(\cdot|\mathbf{x}, \mathbf{a})$ denote the estimated survival model. The post-processed model $\tilde{S}(\cdot|\mathbf{x}, \mathbf{a})$ is given by

$$\tilde{S}(t|\mathbf{x}, \mathbf{a}) = \frac{1}{N} \sum_{i=1}^{N} \hat{S}(t|\mathbf{x}, \mathbf{a}_i).$$

Thus, the sensitive attributes are used in the model training, and are averaged out in the prediction phase. This approach directly ensures that for any time t and non-sensitive attributes $\mathbf{x}$, the prediction is same for all values of sensitive attributes $\mathbf{a}$, $\tilde{S}(t|\mathbf{x}, \mathbf{a}) = \tilde{S}(t|\mathbf{x}, \mathbf{a}')$ for all $\mathbf{a}, \mathbf{a}' \in \mathcal{A}$.

4   Experiments

We evaluate the pre-processing and post-processing methods presented in Sect. 3 using several medical and non-medical data sets. The experimental section is organized as follows: we first introduce the data sets and their characteristics (refer to Table 2). Subsequently, we describe the baseline and experimental implementations of the processing techniques discussed in the methodology section. Finally, we present the evaluation protocols for our experiment. Some related materials are available at https://github.com/noorazhaoz/EquiSurv.

4.1   Dataset

We use six datasets in our study: (1) FLChain [7], a stratified random sample exploring the link between serum FLC and mortality, with 7874 individuals;

Table 2. Overview of the Datasets

Dataset	Size	%. Censored	No. Variables	incl. No. Numerical	Gender Ratio M:F	Response Variable
FLChain	7874	72.45%	9	4	1:1.23	mortality
Whas	481	48.23%	9	3	1:1.48	mortality
Nafld1	17549	92.22%	5	4	1:1.14	mortality
Tumor	776	51.67%	7	2	1:1.46	mortality
Employee Turnover	1129	49.42%	13	6	1:3.09	resignation
Customer Subscription	63815	20.34%	9	3	1:0.74	un-subscription

(2) WHAS [14], the Worcester Heart Attack Study Dataset with 481 patients; (3) Tumor [3], a dataset with information on 776 patients treated for cancer in the stomach region; (4) Nafld1 [1], a dataset from a population study on non-alcoholic fatty liver disease, containing 17,549 individuals; (5) Employee Turnover [37], a dataset with 1129 samples predicting the probability of employees leaving their job; (6) Customer Subscription [10], a dataset from Kaggle with a randomly selected subset of 63,815 samples (20% of the original dataset, 330,512 cases in total) to reduce the computational complexity while maintaining the dataset's diversity. For all six data sets, we consider gender as the sensitive attribute with two levels (Female and Male).

The summary statistics of the data sets, including the sample size, percentage of censored cases, number of covariates, number of numerical covariates, gender ratio and response variables are presented in Table 2. We note from Table 2 that the chosen data sets have sample size ranging from 481 to 63815, percentage of censored cases ranging from 20.34% to 92.22%, and male-to-female ratio from 1:0.74 to 1:3.09. The response variables differ across data sets while mortality for medical data sets represents the occurrence of death, resignation for the employee dataset indicates termination of employment; and un-subscription for the customer subscription dataset refers to customers discontinuing their service or product subscription. This information offers a comprehensive overview of each dataset's characteristics, providing context for our fairness analysis in survival models.

4.2   Implementation and Baseline

Evaluation of the seven proposed pre-processing and post-processing methods are performed by using 80% of each data set as training sets and reserving the remaining 20% as test sets. Random survival forest and CPH model with an elastic net penalty [30] is used as the prediction model for all seven methods.

Consequently, the experimental results offer valuable insights into the performance of our fairness-aware techniques across both ensemble learning methodologies, such as the Random Survival Forest, and traditional statistical models like CPH. The Random Survival Forest (RSF) and Cox Proportional Hazards (CPH) models, devoid of any pre-processing or post-processing methods, are adopted as the baselines for our analysis. We have fine-tuned the hyperparameters to ascertain optimal performance from this baseline approach.

4.3   Evaluation Protocols

We evaluate the model performance and fairness of the seven proposed methods along with the baseline. We aim to assess: 1) whether and to what extent the proposed methods improve group fairness and 2) the trade-offs between group fairness, individual fairness and model performance.

Performance Evaluation. The following performance evaluation metrics are used: *concordance index* (C-Index) [2], *Brier score* [11], and *area under the curve*

(AUC) [33]. These performance metrics are designed to assess the accuracy of survival predictions.

Fairness Evaluation. Both group and individual fairness are measured to assess the success of the proposed methods in enforcing the fairness of survival predictions. For each of the methods, we measure how group and individual fairness vary over time using the fairness definitions in (2) and (1). For the computation of individual fairness, we adhere to the methodology outlined by [28], employing cosine as the distance metric and setting the scale parameter α to **0.01**. Average group and individual fairness, $F_G^{(1)}$ and $F_I^{(1)}$, over time are also computed.

5   Results and Discussion

Table 3 displays the performance and fairness measures of the pre- and post-processing methods along with the baseline on the six data sets described in Sect. 4.1. Average group and individual fairness are reported in the table. Superior performance is indicated by higher values of AUC and C-index, and lower values of Brier Score. Improved fairness is represented by lower values of Group Fairness and Individual Fairness. The optimal results for each metric are emphasized in boldface, while group fairness measures inferior to the baseline model are underlined.

We observe from Table 3 that the measured (averaged) individual fairness for all eight methods are similar in both survival models - Random Survival Forest (RSF) and Cox Proportional Hazards (CPH). This is expected since the pro-processing and post-processing methods are designed to improve group fairness. We also observe that the over-sampling, under-sampling, and post-processing methods consistently outperform the baseline method in terms of (averaged) group fairness, with the exception of the under-sampling technique for the Employee data set. Since the Employee data set exhibits a highly skewed gender ratio, the under-sampling strategy massively reduces its sample size and hence leads to worse performance. On the other hand, disparate impact remover does not lead to any improvement in group fairness for most data sets. This is likely due to the fact that the majority of the features of the chosen data sets are categorical.

5.1   Temporal Variation of Fairness

To investigate the temporal variations in fairness metrics, evenly spaced time points are selected to compute the prevailing group fairness and individual fairness values. These values, derived from the Random Survival Forest (RSF) model, along with their respective time points, are subsequently utilized to generate graphical representations, illustrating the progression of group and individual fairness over time. For FLChain and Employee data sets, We observe from Fig. 1(a) and 1(b) that disparate impact remover consistently under-performs relative to other methods in terms of group fairness whereas it consistently achieves

Table 3. Performance and Fairness Metrics of Various Techniques

Dataset	Techniques	RSF Performance AUC↑	Brier Score↓	C-index↑	RSF Fairness Group↓	Individual↓	CPH Performance AUC↑	Brier Score↓	C-index↑	CPH Fairness Group↓	Individual↓
FLChain	W/O	**0.8216**	0.1052	0.7939	0.0061	0.1077	0.8181	0.0967	0.7980	0.0052	0.0996
	DI Remover	0.8159	**0.0960**	**0.7949**	0.0115	0.0846	0.8096	**0.0960**	0.7907	0.0118	**0.0728**
	Correlation Remover	0.8180	0.1019	0.7937	0.0047	0.1018	0.8169	**0.0960**	0.7968	**0.0019**	0.0969
	Data Augmentation	0.8175	0.1078	0.7880	0.0058	0.1113	0.8141	0.0977	0.7938	0.0145	0.0991
	Sampling - Expected size	0.8211	0.1057	0.7938	0.0059	0.1080	0.8181	0.0967	0.7981	0.0052	0.0996
	Sampling - Oversampling	0.8219	0.1060	0.7938	0.0065	0.1095	0.8179	0.0964	0.7979	0.0037	0.1011
	Sampling - Undersampling	0.8170	0.1054	0.7915	0.0004	0.1055	0.8140	0.0967	0.7940	0.0105	0.0946
	Post-Processing	0.8192	0.1061	0.7939	0.0051	0.1071	0.8136	0.0979	0.7934	0.0151	0.0999
Whas	W/O	0.8617	0.1797	0.7703	0.0479	0.1120	0.8634	0.1653	0.7857	0.0228	0.1382
	DI Remover	0.8605	0.1787	0.7734	0.0541	0.1122	0.8642	0.1638	**0.7897**	0.0471	0.1398
	Correlation Remover	0.8599	**0.1780**	**0.7746**	0.0562	0.1137	**0.8670**	**0.1640**	0.7885	0.0458	0.1409
	Data Augmentation	0.8591	0.1779	0.7651	0.0414	0.1267	0.8605	0.1653	0.7848	0.0116	0.1385
	Sampling - Expected size	0.8620	0.1794	0.7685	0.0470	0.1117	0.8636	0.1657	0.7851	0.0221	0.1378
	Sampling - Oversampling	0.8617	0.1849	0.7663	0.0346	0.1123	0.8524	0.1726	0.7888	0.0058	0.1388
	Sampling - Undersampling	0.8624	0.1853	0.7694	0.0176	0.0953	0.8192	0.1786	0.7352	0.0419	0.1439
	Post-Processing	**0.8644**	0.1783	0.7703	0.0360	0.1102	0.8592	0.1657	0.7820	0.0104	**0.1375**
Tumor	W/O	0.6898	0.1889	0.6411	0.0103	0.0576	**0.6950**	0.1838	0.6351	0.0142	0.0863
	DI Remover	**0.7068**	**0.1858**	0.6429	0.0105	0.0586	0.6853	**0.1857**	0.6201	0.0104	0.0795
	Correlation Remover	0.6901	0.1897	**0.6459**	0.0060	0.0600	0.6873	0.1856	0.6268	0.0060	0.0863
	Data Augmentation	0.6812	0.1923	0.6274	0.0016	0.0640	0.6897	0.1848	0.6273	0.0016	0.0850
	Sampling - Expected size	0.6804	0.1920	0.6389	0.0098	0.0578	0.6797	0.1925	0.6329	0.0225	0.0888
	Sampling - Oversampling	0.6890	0.1776	0.6365	0.0092	0.0616	0.6933	0.1823	**0.6399**	0.0216	0.0938
	Sampling - Undersampling	0.6613	0.2272	0.6208	0.0020	**0.0543**	0.6577	0.2265	0.6113	0.0030	**0.0836**
	Post-Processing	0.6884	0.1879	0.6411	0.0004	0.0580	0.6872	0.1851	0.6270	0.0023	0.0857
Nafld1	W/O	**0.8091**	0.0703	**0.7906**	0.0216	0.0711	**0.8064**	0.0496	**0.7926**	0.0149	0.0380
	DI Remover	0.7990	0.0718	0.7784	0.0042	0.0648	0.8054	0.0498	0.7915	0.0093	**0.0327**
	Correlation Remover	0.7867	0.0747	0.7666	0.0130	0.0753	0.8049	0.0499	0.7910	0.0079	0.0401
	Data Augmentation	0.7902	0.0725	0.7712	0.0047	0.0717	0.8020	0.0496	0.7879	0.0065	0.0376
	Sampling - Expected size	0.7902	0.0736	0.7679	0.0045	0.0708	0.8050	0.0497	0.7911	0.0089	0.0381
	Sampling - Oversampling	0.7927	0.0699	0.7706	0.0015	0.0719	0.8052	**0.0491**	0.7911	0.0093	0.0366
	Sampling - Undersampling	0.7836	0.0545	0.7775	0.0095	0.0548	0.8018	0.0522	0.7882	0.0004	0.0453
	Post-Processing	0.7805	**0.0502**	0.7710	0.0031	0.0416	0.8004	**0.0504**	0.7865	0.0019	0.0377
Employee Turnover	W/O	0.7414	0.1388	0.6590	0.0143	0.0349	0.7105	0.1350	0.6420	0.0342	0.0610
	DI Remover	0.7291	0.1398	0.6426	0.0167	0.0353	0.7081	0.1352	0.6389	0.0413	0.0606
	Correlation Remover	0.7323	0.1397	0.6459	0.0140	0.0346	0.7058	**0.1348**	0.6380	0.0507	0.0622
	Data Augmentation	0.7400	**0.1377**	**0.6712**	0.0069	0.0436	0.7126	0.1350	0.6439	0.0288	0.0611
	Sampling - Expected size	0.7386	0.1397	0.6636	0.0146	0.0342	0.7048	0.1370	0.6374	0.0385	0.0604
	Sampling - Oversampling	0.7202	0.1388	0.6380	0.0058	0.0399	0.7052	0.1349	0.6307	0.0203	0.0663
	Sampling - Undersampling	0.6232	0.1591	0.5609	0.0203	0.0271	0.6347	0.1630	0.5741	0.0567	0.0744
	Post-Processing	0.7423	0.1390	0.6602	0.0088	0.0346	**0.7127**	0.1351	**0.6441**	0.0270	0.0607
Customer Subsription	W/O	0.7268	0.1722	0.6543	0.0126	0.0836	0.7278	0.1740	0.6618	0.0094	0.0667
	DI Remover	0.7265	0.1721	0.6546	0.0127	0.0838	0.7278	0.1740	0.6618	0.0094	0.0667
	Correlation Remover	0.7270	0.1719	0.6552	0.0107	0.0830	0.7278	0.1740	0.6618	0.0096	0.0668
	Data Augmentation	0.7277	0.1714	0.6564	0.0096	0.0824	0.7275	0.1741	0.6617	0.0082	0.0666
	Sampling - Expected size	0.7268	0.1722	0.6542	0.0127	0.0836	0.7278	0.1740	0.6618	0.0093	0.0667
	Sampling - Oversampling	0.7266	0.1720	0.6553	0.0122	0.0837	0.7294	0.1559	0.6617	0.0060	0.1094
	Sampling - Undersampling	0.7246	**0.1556**	**0.6586**	0.0012	0.1024	**0.7305**	0.1542	**0.6621**	0.0173	0.0783
	Post-Processing	**0.7286**	0.1833	0.6543	0.0104	0.0892	0.7228	**0.1319**	0.6617	0.0072	**0.0571**

better individual fairness. We observe similar pattern in Fig. 1(c) and Fig. 1(d). This is consistent with the finding in the binary classification fairness literature that group and individual fairness tends to be inversely related. However, under-sampling method outperforms all other methods in terms of both group and individual fairness (Fig. 1(e) and Fig. 1(f)).

5.2 Trade-Offs

We showcase the trade-offs among group fairness, individual fairness, and prediction performance by presenting a graph (Fig. 2) that illustrates the variations in each metric upon applying diverse processing techniques to a total of six datasets, compared to the baseline scores.

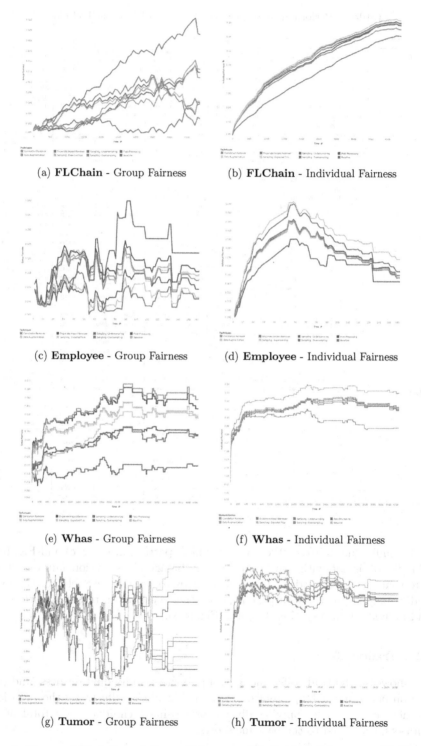

(a) **FLChain** - Group Fairness

(b) **FLChain** - Individual Fairness

(c) **Employee** - Group Fairness

(d) **Employee** - Individual Fairness

(e) **Whas** - Group Fairness

(f) **Whas** - Individual Fairness

(g) **Tumor** - Group Fairness

(h) **Tumor** - Individual Fairness

Fig. 1. Temporal Variation of Group Fairness and Individual Fairness on FLChain, Employee, Whas, and Tumor Data sets. **y-axis: the values of fairness. x-axis: Time.**

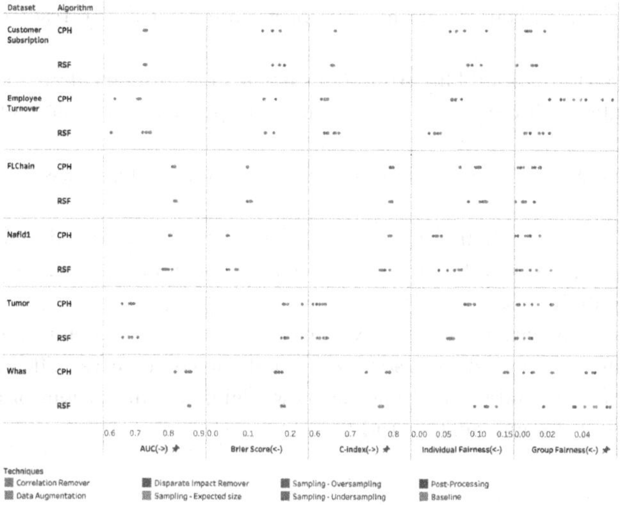

Fig. 2. Comparative Analysis of Group Fairness, Individual Fairness, and Prediction Performance Across Datasets Using Various Processing Techniques. **y-axis: Evaluation Metrics. x-axis: Data sets**

The graph indicates that our processing techniques do not adversely impact the performance metrics and individual fairness in both survival models; in fact, some of them exceed the baseline scores. Consequently, our processing techniques entail trade-offs between group fairness and model performance, as well as between group fairness and individual fairness.

We strongly recommend selecting the processing technique based on the specific attributes of each dataset, such as size, distribution, and data imbalance.

6 Conclusion and Future Works

In this research, we proposed and validated several pre-processing and post-processing methods to improve the fairness in survival analysis, considering both semi- and non-parametric models. We have experimentally demonstrated that the proposed methods generally lead to improvement in group fairness while achieving similar level of predictive performance and individual fairness as the baseline method. Compared to the commonly employed in-processing approach in fair survival analysis literature, our model-agnostic methods offer more flexibility. One potential future research direction is to develop fair survival analysis approaches with time varying covariates. Another interesting research topic is to develop fairness metrics and mitigation methods for survival analysis in the presence of competing risk events.

Ethical Statement. This research aims to explore the discrimination mitigation processing techniques (both pre-processing and post-processing) in time-to-event analysis.

The following ethical considerations have been addressed in the research design and procedures:

1. Voluntary participation: This study does not involve primary data collection.

2. Confidentiality: All data used in this study are publicly available and are properly cited.

3. Potential for harm: There is minimal risk or potential harm associated with this study.

4. Gender consideration: This study investigates potential biases and unfairness associated with using gender as a feature in survival analysis and proposes several approaches to address the unfairness.

5. Results communication: The study's results will serve academic purposes exclusively and will be reported in academic journals or conferences. The results will be presented accurately and without bias, acknowledging any limitations or ethical dilemmas encountered throughout the study.

References

1. Allen, A.M., Therneau, T.M., Larson, J.J., Coward, A., Somers, V.K., Kamath, P.S.: Nonalcoholic fatty liver disease incidence and impact on metabolic burden and death: a 20 year-community study. Hepatology **67**(5), 1726–1736 (2018)

2. Antolini, L., Boracchi, P., Biganzoli, E.: A time-dependent discrimination index for survival data. Stat. Med. **24**(24), 3927–3944 (2005)

3. Bender, A., Scheipl, F.: Pammtools: piece-wise exponential additive mixed modeling tools. arXiv preprint arXiv:1806.01042 (2018)

4. Breiman, L.: Random forests. Mach. Learn. **45**, 5–32 (2001)

5. Caton, S., Haas, C.: Fairness in machine learning: a survey. arXiv preprint arXiv:2010.04053 (2020)

6. Cox, D.R.: Regression models and life-tables. J. Roy. Stat. Soc.: Ser. B (Methodol.) **34**(2), 187–202 (1972)

7. Dispenzieri, A., et al.: Use of nonclonal serum immunoglobulin free light chains to predict overall survival in the general population. In: Mayo Clinic Proceedings, vol. 87, no. 6, pp. 517–523. Elsevier (2012)

8. Eleuteri, A., Tagliaferri, R., Milano, L., De Placido, S., De Laurentiis, M.: A novel neural network-based survival analysis model. Neural Netw. **16**(5–6), 855–864 (2003)

9. Feldman, M., Friedler, S.A., Moeller, J., Scheidegger, C., Venkatasubramanian, S.: Certifying and removing disparate impact. In: Proceedings of the 21th ACM SIGKDD International Conference on Knowledge Discovery and Data Mining, pp. 259–268 (2015)

10. Ganapaneni, S.: DSPP1 [data set]. Kaggle (2022). https://www.kaggle.com/datasets/gsagar12/dspp1

11. Graf, E., Schmoor, C., Sauerbrei, W., Schumacher, M.: Assessment and comparison of prognostic classification schemes for survival data. Stat. Med. **18**(17–18), 2529–2545 (1999)

12. Harrison, T., Ansell, J.: Customer retention in the insurance industry: using survival analysis to predict cross-selling opportunities. J. Financ. Serv. Mark. **6**, 229–239 (2002)

13. Hort, M., Chen, Z., Zhang, J.M., Sarro, F., Harman, M.: Bia mitigation for machine learning classifiers: a comprehensive survey. arXiv preprint arXiv:2207.07068 (2022)
14. Hosmer, D.W., Lemeshow, S., May, S.: Regression modeling of time to event data. New York (1999)
15. Hougaard, P.: Fundamentals of survival data. Biometrics **55**(1), 13–22 (1999)
16. Hu, S., Chen, G.H.: Distributionally robust survival analysis: a novel fairness loss without demographics. In: Machine Learning for Health, pp. 62–87. PMLR (2022)
17. Ishwaran, H., Kogalur, U.B., Blackstone, E.H., Lauer, M.S.: Random survival forests. Ann. Appl. Stat. **2**(3), 841–860 (2008)
18. Jin, Z., Shang, J., Zhu, Q., Ling, C., Xie, W., Qiang, B.: RFRSF: employee turnover prediction based on random forests and survival analysis. In: Huang, Z., Beek, W., Wang, H., Zhou, R., Zhang, Y. (eds.) WISE 2020. LNCS, vol. 12343, pp. 503–515. Springer, Cham (2020). https://doi.org/10.1007/978-3-030-62008-0_35
19. Kamiran, F., Calders, T.: Data preprocessing techniques for classification without discrimination. Knowl. Inf. Syst. **33**(1), 1–33 (2012)
20. Kamishima, T., Akaho, S., Asoh, H., Sakuma, J.: Fairness-aware classifier with prejudice remover regularizer. In: Flach, P.A., De Bie, T., Cristianini, N. (eds.) ECML PKDD 2012. LNCS (LNAI), vol. 7524, pp. 35–50. Springer, Heidelberg (2012). https://doi.org/10.1007/978-3-642-33486-3_3
21. Katzman, J.L., Shaham, U., Cloninger, A., Bates, J., Jiang, T., Kluger, Y.: Deep-surv: personalized treatment recommender system using a cox proportional hazards deep neural network. BMC Med. Res. Methodol. **18**(1), 1–12 (2018)
22. Keya, K.N., Islam, R., Pan, S., Stockwell, I., Foulds, J.: Equitable allocation of healthcare resources with fair survival models. In: Proceedings of the 2021 SIAM International Conference on Data Mining (SDM), pp. 190–198. SIAM (2021)
23. Lee, C., Zame, W., Yoon, J., Van Der Schaar, M.: Deephit: a deep learning approach to survival analysis with competing risks. In: Proceedings of the AAAI Conference on Artificial Intelligence, vol. 32, no. 1 (2018)
24. Mehrabi, N., Morstatter, F., Saxena, N., Lerman, K., Galstyan, A.: A survey on bias and fairness in machine learning. ACM Comput. Surv. (CSUR) **54**(6), 1–35 (2021)
25. Pagano, T.P., et al.: Bias and unfairness in machine learning models: a systematic literature review. arXiv preprint arXiv:2202.08176 (2022)
26. Pessach, D., Shmueli, E.: Algorithmic fairness. arXiv preprint arXiv:2001.09784 (2020)
27. Pope, D.G., Sydnor, J.R.: Implementing anti-discrimination policies in statistical profiling models. Am. Econ. J. Econ. Pol. **3**(3), 206–231 (2011)
28. Rahman, M.M., Purushotham, S.: Fair and interpretable models for survival analysis. In: Proceedings of the 28th ACM SIGKDD Conference on Knowledge Discovery and Data Mining, pp. 1452–1462 (2022)
29. Ripley, R.M., Harris, A.L., Tarassenko, L.: Non-linear survival analysis using neural networks. Stat. Med. **23**(5), 825–842 (2004)
30. Simon, N., Friedman, J., Hastie, T., Tibshirani, R.: Regularization paths for cox's proportional hazards model via coordinate descent. J. Stat. Softw. **39**(5), 1 (2011)
31. Sonabend, R., Pfisterer, F., Mishler, A., Schauer, M., Burk, L., Vollmer, S.: Flexible group fairness metrics for survival analysis. arXiv preprint arXiv:2206.03256 (2022)
32. Türk, U., Sap, S.: The effect of the Covid-19 on sharing economy: survival analysis of Airbnb listings. Bus. Manag. Stud. Int. J. **9**(1), 215–226 (2021)

33. Uno, H., Cai, T., Tian, L., Wei, L.J.: Evaluating prediction rules for T-year survivors with censored regression models. J. Am. Stat. Assoc. **102**(478), 527–537 (2007)

34. Verma, S.: Weapons of math destruction: how big data increases inequality and threatens democracy. Vikalpa **44**(2), 97–98 (2019)

35. Wang, P., Li, Y., Reddy, C.K.: Machine learning for survival analysis: a survey. ACM Comput. Surv. (CSUR) **51**(6), 1–36 (2019)

36. Wei, L.J.: The accelerated failure time model: a useful alternative to the cox regression model in survival analysis. Stat. Med. **11**(14–15), 1871–1879 (1992)

37. Wijaya, D.: Employee turnover dataset [data set]. Kaggle (2020). https://www.kaggle.com/datasets/davinwijaya/employee-turnover. Original data from: Babushkin, Edward. (2017). Employee Turnover: How to Predict Individual Risks of Quitting [Blog post]. https://edwvb.blogspot.com/2017/10/employee-turnover-how-to-predict-individual-risks-of-quitting.html

38. Xin, X., Huang, F.: Anti-discrimination insurance pricing: regulations, fairness criteria, and models. Fairness Criteria, and Models (2022)

BeeTLe: A Framework for Linear B-Cell Epitope Prediction and Classification

Xiao Yuan[(✉)]

Georgia Institute of Technology, Atlanta, USA
xyuan8@gatech.edu

Abstract. The process of identifying and characterizing B-cell epitopes, which are the portions of antigens recognized by antibodies, is important for our understanding of the immune system, and for many applications including vaccine development, therapeutics, and diagnostics. Computational epitope prediction is challenging yet rewarding as it significantly reduces the time and cost of laboratory work. Most of the existing tools do not have satisfactory performance and only discriminate epitopes from non-epitopes. This paper presents a new deep learning-based multi-task framework for linear B-cell epitope prediction as well as antibody type-specific epitope classification. Specifically, a sequenced-based neural network model using recurrent layers and Transformer blocks is developed. We propose an amino acid encoding method based on eigen decomposition to help the model learn the representations of epitopes. We introduce modifications to standard cross-entropy loss functions by extending a logit adjustment technique to cope with the class imbalance. Experimental results on data curated from the largest public epitope database demonstrate the validity of the proposed methods and the superior performance compared to competing ones.

Keywords: Amino acid sequence · Transformer · Class imbalance · Multi-task learning

1 Introduction

In our adaptive immune system, B cells play a critical role by producing antibodies that detect, neutralize and help eliminate the pathogens, such as viruses. Antibodies can recognize and bind to antigens, which are usually proteins, on the pathogens. These bound regions are called epitopes and they can be divided into linear and conformational epitopes. Although the majority of the B-cell epitopes are conformational, much attention is concentrated on the identification of linear epitopes, which consist of a contiguous sequence of amino acids (residues). The reason is that linear epitopes can be used to design peptide-based vaccines and replace infectious antigens in antibody production and diagnostic assay development [41]. Since experimental epitope mapping is time-consuming, costly, and laborious, computational prediction methods are desirable to reduce the number of potential epitope candidates for experimental validation [45].

G. De Francisci Morales et al. (Eds.): ECML PKDD 2023, LNAI 14174, pp. 477–494, 2023.
https://doi.org/10.1007/978-3-031-43427-3_29

With the ever-increasing data of verified epitopes, machine learning-based approaches are developed to distinguish epitopes from non-epitopes given the peptides (short chain of amino acids). Methods using classical machine learning require manual feature engineering on the primary sequence of peptides. Their mediocre performances indicate the challenge of B-cell epitope prediction [11]. Recently, several methods use embeddings derived from language models trained on large datasets of protein sequences to improve accuracy [3,6,7]. However, working with these huge models and neural embeddings is computationally expensive, especially for researchers with limited resources.

Antibodies can be classified into different types of immunoglobulins (Ig), each with different functions. Also, studies have shown that particular antigens induce specific types of antibodies [42]. For instance, IgA is vital against viral infections, IgE is involved in allergy, and IgM is linked to inflammation and autoimmunity. It is relevant to characterize epitopes potentially inducing specific classes of antibodies for applications like developing processing methods that mitigate food allergenicity. Only a few methods have been developed for Ig type-specific epitope classification, using classical machine learning [17,22].

In this work, we propose a new deep learning-based unified framework for the tasks of (non-)epitope prediction and Ig type-specific epitope classification. Unlike most existing tools that first compute sequence-level features for each peptide and then train a classifier, our end-to-end framework accepts variable-length sequences as input, encodes features at the residue level, and learns representations of peptides for classification. To our knowledge, no previous research has developed and trained Transformer-based networks for epitope prediction. We also incorporate cost-sensitive learning into our framework and design objective functions that handle the data imbalance, which is often overlooked in prior works. Experiments on data comprising over 120000 peptides obtained from the Immune Epitope Database (IEDB) [51] show results exceeding state-of-the-art baselines in terms of prediction performance. Our framework achieves high predictive capacity with an area under the curve (AUC) of 86% and outperforms the best baseline by 6% in accuracy. Ablation studies demonstrate the usefulness of different components in the framework. More specifically, the main contributions of our work are summarized below.

- We propose a simple encoding method for amino acids, leveraging the eigen decomposition of an amino-acid scoring matrix.
- We extend a logit adjustment technique and design a general loss function to address the class imbalance in binary and multiclass classifications.
- A neural network based on Transformer is developed for peptide classification, without relying on large language models.
- B-cell epitope data are collected and processed to create new redundancy-reduced datasets for benchmarking, concerning possible false negatives.

2   Related Work

2.1   B-Cell Epitope Prediction

Most of the machine learning-based methods designed to predict and classify B-cell epitopes are for linear epitopes rather than conformational epitopes, because of the more readily available data on protein primary sequence and by contrast the scarcity of data on protein three-dimensional structure. These methods vary from support vector machines (SVM) [3,17,46], tree-based methods [21,22,34], to neural networks [6,7,30,53]. No matter what kind of approaches they use, the key point is how to extract appropriate features from the epitope sequences as input for machine learning. The features used include the amino acid composition of the peptide [3,17,22,30,34,46] and propensity scales that depict the physicochemical properties of residues, including hydrophilicity, flexibility, surface accessibility, etc. [21,34]. Some models have the limitation that they only process fixed-length sequences [17,30,46]. Besides, some do not address the similarity between sequences before splitting training and test sets [17,22,30].

Given the analogy between amino acid sequences and human languages, natural language processing (NLP) techniques are applied in many biological property prediction tasks [33,37,48,49]. With sufficient data, deep neural networks can automatically learn meaningful features, thus reducing the need for hand-crafted features [25]. Recurrent neural networks (RNN), with long short-term memory (LSTM) [19] as a representative, are dominant in NLP because their chain-like structures allow them to process over sequences without pre-specified constraints on the sequence lengths. In recent years, Transformer models have become the state of the art by using attention and eliminating the need for recurrent layers, thus overcoming the sequential bottleneck of RNNs [50]. There is great interest in learning protein representation using language modeling, of which the paradigm is pre-training a large model in a self-supervised way on a large corpus of text, and then fine-tuning it in a supervised way for specific tasks [9]. Following the successful applications in protein property prediction, some studies use embeddings from protein language models as features to train classifiers for epitope prediction [3,6,7], which require a large demand of computing resources and time. Moreover, pre-trained models for proteins may not be an optimal solution for peptides, which are typically much shorter than proteins.

2.2   Imbalanced Learning

In data mining, the imbalance problem occurs when the distribution of classes (labels) is not uniform. This poses a challenge for the prediction on minority classes and makes learning biased toward majority classes, especially when the distribution is highly skewed. Fundamental approaches to coping with imbalance can be broadly divided into re-sampling and re-weighting. Re-sampling modifies the datasets, for example by under-sampling or over-sampling [23]. It is also used by existing epitope prediction methods [17,30]. The drawbacks of re-sampling are that under-sampling incurs information loss in the majority classes, while over-sampling increases the training workload and can lead to overfitting for the minority classes. Alternatively, re-weighting modifies the model, for example by changing the loss function. The core idea is to adjust the weights of different samples in the loss, such as the misclassified ones and the under-represented ones [8,29]. A recent paper proposed a strategy that modifies the inside of the logarithm in the standard cross-entropy loss and presented a statistical grounding for the strategy [35].

3   Methods

3.1   Task Definition and Solution Overview

Given a linear peptide, which can be represented as a linear sequence of amino acids, our task contains two subtasks. The major one is to predict whether the peptide is an epitope or non-epitope and the minor one is to classify an epitope according to the specific class of Ig it potentially binds to. In addition, a score between 0 and 1 inclusive is given to indicate the probability of the peptide being an epitope. This allows users to choose different thresholds for determining epitopes, which is a common practice in epitope prediction.

The problem is framed as a binary classification for (non-)epitope prediction and a multiclass classification for Ig-specific epitope prediction. We preprocess B-cell epitope data from the IEDB for model training and evaluation. A rough overview of the proposed framework is shown in Fig. 1. Raw peptide sequences are firstly tokenized at the residue level and then converted to numeric vectors by the encoder as input for the neural network. These numeric representations are passed through a bidirectional LSTM (BiLSTM) layer followed by two Transformer encoder blocks. Aggregated via an attention mechanism, the representations are classified using fully connected feedforward neural networks (FFNN). The whole model is jointly trained in a supervised manner for both epitope and Ig binding predictions, being aware of class imbalance.

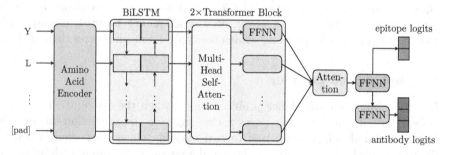

Fig. 1. A general illustration of our framework. The input peptide has been tokenized. The network is trained by optimizing logit-adjusted losses.

3.2   Tokenization and Encoding

Like sentences in natural languages, a peptide can be represented as a sequence of characters, each representing a residue. Since machine learning models can only work directly with numbers, the raw sequences have to be transformed into numerical form before being fed to models. We follow the standard way in NLP to tokenize peptide sequences and convert tokens into integers indices. A vocabulary of size 20 is used, which contains tokens corresponding to the 20 kinds of standard amino acids. In addition, a [unk] token and a [pad] token are added to the vocabulary. A peptide is tokenized, i.e., split into residues, with uncertain amino acids in the raw sequence being replaced by [unk] token. For a batch of peptides of varying lengths, [pad] token is added at the end of shorter sequences to ensure they have the same length as the longest sequence in the batch so that models can process the input in batches.

Many protein prediction methods use one-hot encoding to encode the residues. The problem with this binary representation is that it does not reflect the biological similarities between different amino acids. We propose an alternative encoding method that exploits similarity scoring matrices based on observed alignments of proteins. Generally, an amino-acid scoring matrix is a symmetric matrix of size 20×20, the entries of which are in the form of $\log \frac{q_{ij}}{p_i p_j}$, where q_{ij} is the substitution frequency of two amino acids in a homologous sequence, and p_i and p_j are the background frequencies [39]. The ratio provides a measure of the probability of two amino acids appearing in an alignment with a biological sense relative to appearing by chance, and therefore it captures the biological similarities between amino acids. We choose the widely used BLOSUM62 matrix and take the exponential of it, denoted by B. Note that B is positive definite and eigen decomposition factorizes B into the product of $U \Sigma U^{\top}$, where U is orthonormal and Σ is a diagonal matrix of eigenvalues (all positive). We propose the following encoding matrix E in which each row represents an amino acid:

$$E = U\sqrt{\Sigma}. \tag{1}$$

With this representation, the dot product of amino acid vectors corresponds to their biological similarity. We find this idea analogous to some works in NLP, in which word embedding methods maximize the dot product of similar words and implicitly factorize pointwise mutual information matrices [27, 36]. An advantage is that we can perform truncated decomposition by selecting only the top eigenvalues to get a lower-dimensional representation. We leverage the whole Σ since the dimension is not high. An additional dimension is added for the [unk] token, which is represented by a one-hot vector orthogonal to other amino acid tokens. The [pad] token is represented by a zero vector. Consequently, a peptide of length l is encoded as a matrix with size $l \times 21$. With this encoding, we intend to inject some biological heuristics to help the downstream learning.

3.3   Neural Networks

In this section, we depict the architecture of the neural network model, following a forward propagation through the model. The BiLSTM [16] layer combines two LSTM layers, one which processes the sequence in the forward direction, and one which processes the sequence in the backward direction. An LSTM layer can be regarded as multiple copies of the same LSTM cell, each passing information encoded in the hidden state from one step to the next. This chain-like structure is naturally applicable to sequential data. In particular, LSTM augments the hidden state with a memory cell state and gates that control this state. This leads to additive rather than multiplicative updates to the hidden states to alleviate the vanishing gradient problem in ordinary RNNs [19]. For each residue, the hidden state vectors computed by the forward and backward layers are concatenated as the output of BiLSTM, hence taking into account the contextual information in the sequence. In our implementation, the [pad] tokens are not involved in computation and do not affect the output of other tokens.

Next, a Transformer encoder [50] takes the output of BiLSTM as input. Since the output of BiLSTM already encodes the ordering information in the sequence, positional encoding in the original Transformer model is not needed. A Transformer encoder is a stack of multiple Transformer blocks, each of which is made up of multi-headed self-attention and FFNN. Self-attention [5] enables the model to attend other relevant residues in the sequence when processing each residue, which may lead to improved representations of context. Multi-headed attention expands the model's capacity to capture different relationships. The outputs of the self-attention layer are fed to a position-wise FFNN layer, such that the same FFNN is separately applied to each residue. For both self-attention layer and FFNN layer, residual connection [18] is used, followed by layer normalization [2]. The trainable parameters of each Transformer block are initialized according to Xavier uniform distribution [12]. Let d denote the size of an output vector of a residue. The output of the Transformer encoder has the same size of $l \times d$ as the input for a sequence of length l.

Attention mechanisms are often used in NLP to provide more flexibility in the context representation at the sentence or document level [54]. To acquire a sequence-level representation vector for the whole peptide based on the output of the previous module, we introduce an attention layer as a pooling layer to aggregate the information encoded in the residue vectors. Let vector $\mathbf{r_i} \in \mathbb{R}^d$ denotes the ith residue in a peptide of length l, the peptide vector $\mathbf{p}$ is computed as a weighted sum of the residue vectors as follows:

$$\alpha_i = \frac{\exp(\mathbf{q}^\top \mathbf{r_i}/\sqrt{d})}{\sum_{j=1}^l \exp(\mathbf{q}^\top \mathbf{r_j}/\sqrt{d})}, \tag{2}$$

$$\mathbf{p} = \sum_{i=1}^l \alpha_i \mathbf{r_i}. \tag{3}$$

That is, we use scaled dot-product attention [50] and compute the attention weights using the softmax function. The query vector $\mathbf{q}$ is initialized such that its elements follow the standard normal distribution, scaled to avoid large variance in the products, and is jointly learned during the training. We implement the attention layer using masks to ignore padded positions in the sequence. The peptide vector **p** is used as features for epitope classification in the subsequent classifier. The classifier contains two heads of two-layer FFNNs for (non-)epitope and Ig-specific classification, respectively. Rectified linear unit (ReLU) activation [13] is used in the FFNNs.

3.4 Loss Functions

Our data may exhibit an imbalanced label distribution. It is desirable to learn a model that minimizes the balanced error, which averages each of the per-class errors, instead of the naïve misclassification error. We modify the standard cross-entropy losses, based on a logit adjustment technique [35] and focal loss [29]. Both are originally proposed to address the imbalance problem in visual recognition.

One of the logit adjustment techniques is adding offsets to the logits in the loss function during training. We illustrate the intuition behind the logit-adjusted loss here. Suppose the unnormalized output (logits) of the model for all classes are $\mathbf{z} = [z_0, z_1, ..., z_{C-1}]^\top$, where C is the number of classes. Given a sample with instance x and class label y following distribution $\mathbb{P}$, the loss $\mathbb{E}_{(x,y)\sim\mathbb{P}}[\ell(\mathbf{z}, y)]$ is minimized during training. The standard softmax cross-entropy for a sample (x, y) is defined as $\ell(\mathbf{z}, y) = -\log(S(z_y)) = -\log(\exp(z_y)/\sum_{i=0}^{C-1}\exp(z_i))$, where S denotes the softmax function. One may view $S(z_y) \propto \exp(z_y)$ as an estimate of $\mathbb{P}(y|x)$, where $\mathbb{P}(y|x) \propto \mathbb{P}(x|y)\mathbb{P}(y)$ (Bayes' Theorem). However, to reduce the balanced error, balanced class-probability $\mathbb{P}_{\texttt{bal}}(y|x) \propto \mathbb{P}(x|y) \cdot \frac{1}{C}$ instead of the standard $\mathbb{P}(y|x)$ should be used in Bayes-optimal prediction. Noticing $\mathbb{P}_{\texttt{bal}}(y|x) \propto \mathbb{P}(y|x)/\mathbb{P}(y)$, the following logit-adjusted softmax cross-entropy loss was proposed in [35]:

$$\ell_{\texttt{softmax}}(\mathbf{z}, y) = -\log\frac{\exp(z_y + \tau\log\pi_y)}{\sum_{i=0}^{C-1}\exp(z_i + \tau\log\pi_i)}, \tag{4}$$

where π_y are empirical class frequencies used to estimate priors $\mathbb{P}(y)$, and $\tau \geq 0$ is a scaling parameter. In this way, the model directly estimates $\mathbb{P}_{\texttt{bal}}(y|x)$ using z_y, while it can still be trained with cross-entropy loss. Note that the prediction is still $\arg\max_y z_y$ as usual.

The original logit adjustment is for softmax loss in multiclass classification. We extend it to modify sigmoid loss and generalize it for binary and multi-label classification. In binary classification, suppose the logit for sample (x, y) is z. Sigmoid is equivalent to softmax when $C = 2$ and $\mathbf{z} = [0, z]^\top$, in that $\sigma(z) = 1/(1 + e^{-z}) = e^z/(e^z + e^0) = S(z)$ and $1 - \sigma(z) = S(0)$, where σ denotes the sigmoid function. Given this connection, following the idea on softmax loss, we can derive the logit-adjusted sigmoid cross-entropy loss for binary classification:

$$\ell_{\texttt{binary}}(z, y) = -y\log(\sigma(z + \tau\log\frac{\pi}{1-\pi})) - (1-y)\log(1 - \sigma(z + \tau\log\frac{\pi}{1-\pi})), \tag{5}$$

where π is the empirical positive class frequency. Here we add the logarithm of odds to the logit, in contrast to adding the logarithm of probability in logit-adjusted softmax. In the balanced scenario ($\pi = 0.5$), it becomes the standard sigmoid loss.

We can treat multiclass classification as multiple one-vs-all binary classification tasks, i.e. multi-label classification, and thus use sigmoid loss. Unlike softmax loss, sigmoid loss does not assume mutual exclusiveness among each class. This aligns well with real-world data, where different classes might have some overlaps. Using the same notation as Eq. (4), for convenience, we define adjusted logits z_i^* as:

$$z_i^* = \begin{cases} z_i + \tau \log \frac{\pi_i}{1-\pi_i} & \text{if } i = y \\ -z_i - \tau \log \frac{\pi_i}{1-\pi_i} & \text{otherwise.} \end{cases} \tag{6}$$

The logit-adjusted sigmoid cross-entropy loss for multiclass classification is:

$$\ell_{\text{sigmoid}}(\mathbf{z}, y) = -\frac{1}{C} \sum_{i=0}^{C-1} \log \frac{1}{1 + \exp(-z_i^*)}. \tag{7}$$

Another approach is training with standard sigmoid loss and then adjusting the logits to predict. The scaling parameter may be tuned in a post-hoc way, without training with different τ. Similar to the procedure in [35], we instead predict:

$$\arg \max_y z_y - \tau \log \frac{\pi_y}{1 - \pi_y}. \tag{8}$$

Furthermore, we apply focal loss [29] to Eqs. (4) and (7). Denote $p_y = S(z_y + \tau \log \pi_y)$, the focal softmax loss can be written as:

$$\ell_{\text{focal-softmax}}(\mathbf{z}, y) = -(1 - p_y)^\gamma \log p_y, \tag{9}$$

and denote $p_i^* = \sigma(z_i^*)$, the focal sigmoid loss can be written as:

$$\ell_{\text{focal-sigmoid}}(\mathbf{z}, y) = -\frac{1}{C} \sum_{i=0}^{C-1} (1 - p_i^*)^\gamma \log p_i^*, \tag{10}$$

where $\gamma \geq 0$ is a focusing parameter. Intuitively, since the modulating factor $(1-p)^\gamma$ becomes smaller when p is closer to 1, this focal term reduces the relative loss for well-classified samples, putting emphasis on the difficult samples. The losses defined above are quite flexible. When $\gamma = 0$ and $\tau = 0$, they are equivalent to the standard cross-entropy. Typically, we set $\gamma = 1$ and $\tau = 1$.

We adopt the proposed loss functions in our task. The total cost function is defined as $L = \alpha_p L_p + \alpha_{ig} L_{ig}$, where L_p is (non-)epitope classification loss and L_{ig} is Ig-specific classification loss, averaging over all training samples. The coefficient can be set according to the relative importance of the subtasks in practice, e.g., setting $\alpha_{ig} = 0$ for only training epitope prediction. We use AdamW [32] with AMSGrad [44] as the optimization algorithm to minimize the total loss L. The learning rate is scheduled such that during training it increases linearly from zero to a specified value in the warmup period [14], followed by a cosine decay [31]. The purpose of this dynamic learning rate is to reduce the instability at the early stage of optimization, avoid oscillation and help the model converge to a local minimum near the end of optimization. Regularization techniques such as dropout [47] and weight decay are applied to prevent overfitting.

4   Data and Experiments

4.1   Datasets and Preprocessing

The IEDB catalogs experimental data on B-cell and T-cell epitopes studied in humans and other species in the context of infectious disease, allergy, autoimmunity, etc., curated from the scientific literature [51]. To our knowledge, it is the most comprehensive epitope database containing the largest number of experimentally verified (non-)epitopes. We downloaded all B-cell epitope data for cleansing, which contains over 1.3 million entries of B-cell assays, associated with around 0.6 million epitopes. Note that there is a many-to-one relationship between assay and epitope. The data were processed in several steps as below.

We extracted linear peptides whose sequence contains only one-letter symbols, discarding peptides that contain modified residues. Peptides of length not larger than 25 were selected. The upper limit was set to reduce noise caused by the curation into IEDB, as long peptides could be epitope containing regions instead of exact epitopes. We counted the number of assays with positive and negative outcomes for each peptide. Following the instruction of IEDB, peptides having at least one positive measurement are defined as epitopes, and peptides having only negative measurements are defined as non-epitopes. Note that an epitope can have some negative assays. We further grouped epitopes by the type of antibodies they bind to in positive assays. Among the five major types of antibodies, there is no data on IgD. IgG is the predominant type that most epitopes induce. A few epitopes induce more than one type among IgA, IgE, and IgM. We labeled epitopes that specifically induce one of these three types but not the other two, while others were not used in the Ig prediction subtask.

Taking into account the homology between sequences, we utilized CD-HIT [10], a tool that uses a greedy incremental clustering algorithm and outputs the longest representative sequence for each cluster. We clustered epitopes and non-epitopes respectively using an identity threshold of 0.8 and removed redundant sequences. The sequences in non-epitopes that are similar to epitopes were further removed using the same threshold. There are several benefits of reducing redundancy. First, it ensures training and test sets do not have near identical sequences after splitting. Second, it reduces the bias of overrepresented sequences in training. Third, many short peptides are removed, especially in non-epitopes. It is beneficial since research shows that short peptides give false negative results in experiments, which confound computational epitope prediction [43].

We filtered the peptides of the organism severe acute respiratory syndrome coronavirus 2 (SARS-CoV-2) to create a COVID dataset for a case study of our framework. In the rest of the data, there are 64019 non-epitopes and 64940 epitopes, among which there are 443 IgA epitopes, 1450 IgE epitopes, and 7715 IgM epitopes. 5000 non-epitopes were randomly sampled, and 5000 epitopes were stratified sampled according to the Ig label frequencies, resulting in a hold-out test set of size 10000. We performed the same sampling to create a validation set of size 10000. The remaining data constitute the training set.

4.2   Baselines and Ablation Studies

For the (non-)epitope prediction subtask, we choose several recently published machine learning-based methods as baselines, which not only have sufficient implementation details but also state improvement over major methods. We also use the publicly available dataset of NetBCE [53] for comparison. The dataset was compiled from the IEDB but curated with different criteria from ours to select epitopes and reduce homology, resulting in 97784 non-epitopes and 27095 epitopes, having a ratio of 3.6 between the numbers. Other public datasets are not used since they are either not reduced or contain much fewer peptides.

DLBEpitope [30] uses dipeptide composition as the feature vector for peptides. Dipeptide composition is represented by a vector of length 400, specifying the fractions of all possible combinations of amino acid pairs in a peptide. The classifier is an FFNN with four hidden layers. RMSprop algorithm [15] is used to optimize the cross-entropy.

EpiDope [7] combines neural networks and a protein language model. Besides a widely used module composed of an embedding, a BiLSTM, and a linear layer, the architecture also involves a pre-trained model. The outputs of these two modules are concatenated and fed to an FFNN for classification. The model is trained as a whole with the weights of the language module being frozen.

NetBCE [53] applies one-hot encoding on the residues and uses a neural network to extract representations and classify peptides, with cross-entropy optimized by Adam [24] algorithm. The model contains a convolutional neural network (CNN) to capture the pattern in the sequences, followed by a BiLSTM layer to catch long-range dependencies. The CNN module is composed of a convolution [26], a batch normalization [20], and a max pooling layer.

Classical machine learning-based methods are also compared. LBtope [46] is the first method that uses validated non-epitopes in training. It uses SVM on composition-based features. iBCE-EL [34] is a framework that contains several classifiers on the amino acid compositions and the physicochemical properties. For a fair comparison, we select their best model, extremely randomized tree, and use within ensemble learning, a variant of random forest, as a baseline.

For the Ig-specific epitope classification subtask, we choose IgPred [17] and AbCPE [22] as the baselines. They are used to predict the antibody class based on the input epitope sequences that are experimentally verified. IgPred trains SVM using the radial basis function kernel while AbCPE trains AdaBoost classifier on the dipeptide composition features of the epitope sequences. We improve the performance by replacing AdaBoost with XGBoost [4] and use it instead for comparison. Class weights are computed to account for the imbalance.

We conduct ablation studies to investigate the contributions of different parts to the overall performance of our framework. We experiment with different sequence models. Particularly, besides the hybrid model, we also try a two-layer BiLSTM and a four-layer Transformer encoder with positional encoding being applied to the input. Also, our proposed encoding method and loss functions are compared with conventional methods. All the models in this part are trained for 100 epochs, using the AdamW optimizer with a warmup period of 200 steps.

In epitope prediction, the AUC of receiver operating characteristic (ROC), summarizing the tradeoff between sensitivity and specificity, is used in nearly all the papers for performance evaluation. Therefore we select AUC as the main metric for the (non-)epitope prediction subtask. For the imbalanced Ig-specific prediction subtask, balanced accuracy (Acc), i.e. the average of recall in each class, is used as the metric. We try to attain a comparable AUC for epitope prediction when comparing different loss functions.

We perform hyperparameter tuning and monitor the performance on the validation set during training to avoid overfitting and underfitting. Hyperparameters include learning rate, batch size, weight decay coefficient, dropout probability, hidden dimension size, number of heads in Transformer, etc. We evaluate the models on the test set. The results are averaged across five runs with different initialization of model parameters using different random seeds. All models are implemented in PyTorch [38] and scikit-learn [40]. Experiments are done in Ubuntu 20.04 with Intel Xeon 2.20 GHz CPU or NVIDIA Tesla P100 GPU.

5   Results and Analysis

Table 1 shows that our model achieves better performance than baselines. Traditional models require manually designed and computed features, yet still do not perform better than other sequence-based models. The primary structure, i.e. the linear sequence of amino acids, of a peptide greatly determines the high-level structures and functions of the peptide. It is analogous to how the arrangements of words define the semantic meaning of a sentence in a context-dependent way. Therefore, it is reasonable that employing NLP techniques can help understand the information encoded in peptides. Unlike NetBCE, we do not use CNN in our models. The rationale is that compared to self-attention in Transformer, convolution has a limited receptive field, which depends on the kernel size, and does not flexibly adapt to the input content due to the static weights of the filter.

Table 1. Performance (%) of baselines and our model for epitope prediction and Ig-specific classification. Models are ordered by publication dates.

Model	Our dataset			NetBCE dataset	
	AUC	Acc	Acc (Ig)	AUC	Acc
LBtope [46]	78.84	71.80	-	81.70	61.93
IgPred [17]	-	-	70.14	-	-
iBCE-EL [34]	80.38	73.05	-	83.17	64.76
DLBEpitope [30]	76.39	69.04	-	82.94	69.92
EpiDope [7]	81.62	73.19	-	83.44	70.72
AbCPE [22]	-	-	70.27	-	-
NetBCE [53]	82.41	72.80	-	84.00	68.65
Ours	**85.80**	**77.29**	**72.21**	**86.10**	**74.81**

Table 2 shows the results of ablation studies regarding our proposed model and its variants on the test set. Our simple encoding method for amino acids yields an improvement in performance for all three architectures, compared to the conventional method that uses an embedding layer with learnable weights. Incorporating this additional biological information is helpful in downstream learning.

Table 2. Performance (%) of different models and encodings in ablation studies.

Architecture	Residue encoding	AUC	Acc	Acc (Ig)
BiLSTM×2	✗	84.04	75.58	67.00
BiLSTM×2	✓	85.06	76.23	69.86
Transformer×4	✗	84.99	76.57	66.98
Transformer×4	✓	85.76	77.17	68.06
BiLSTM+Transformer×2	✗	85.27	76.73	70.73
BiLSTM+Transformer×2	✓	85.80	77.29	72.21

Interestingly, the hybrid architecture performs better than pure LSTM and pure Transformer encoder. Typically, Transformer needs a lot of data to overcome its relative lack of inductive bias. This could explain why a pure Transformer encoder does not perform well on Ig-specific epitope classification. For a fair comparison, all of our sequence-based models are constructed such that they cost roughly the same training time. Generally, the time complexity for a recurrent layer is $O(ld^2)$, while the time complexity for a Transformer block is $O(l^2d)$, where l is the sequence length and d is the hidden dimension size [50]. Fortunately, l is small in our task, with an average of approximately 15, and we use $d = 64$ in LSTM layers and $d = 128$ in Transformer blocks.

Table 3 shows the performance of our best model on the test set with different loss functions in Ig-specific epitope classification, which has an imbalance ratio of approximately 17. The standard cross-entropy losses have a strong bias towards the majority class IgM. Logit adjustment technique is conducive for both standard sigmoid and softmax loss. Focal loss further balances the per-class accuracy, though it does not affect the balanced accuracy very much. Overall, our proposed

Table 3. Accuracies (%) of Ig-specific classification with different loss functions.

Loss function	Balanced	IgA	IgE	IgM
softmax	68.74	64.71	47.99	93.52
logit-adjusted softmax	70.78	70.59	51.79	89.98
focal logit-adjusted softmax	71.20	70.59	53.12	89.90
sigmoid	68.79	60.78	52.08	93.49
logit-adjusted sigmoid	72.01	68.63	56.25	91.13
focal logit-adjusted sigmoid	72.21	74.12	55.00	87.51

logit-adjusted sigmoid loss (Eqs. (7) and (10)) achieves better performance than logit-adjusted softmax loss. Also, it is versatile in that it is applicable to binary ($C = 1$), multiclass, and multi-label classification. Alternatively, we can apply the post-hoc approach and predict as per (8). Figure 2 shows the effect of tuning the parameter. With suitable tuning, the accuracy is on par with using the logit-adjusted loss.

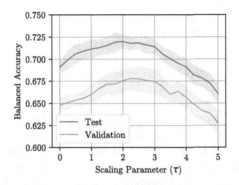

Fig. 2. Post-hoc adjustment with varying scaling parameter on the logits of Ig-specific classification. The models are trained using standard sigmoid loss.

6   Application and Discussion

We further demonstrate the validity of our framework in application on the small hold-out COVID dataset, which contains 497 non-epitopes and 1180 epitopes, and show the ROC curves in Fig. 3. Three recently published frameworks called EpiDope [7], EpitopeVec [3], and BepiPred-3.0 [6] are used for comparison, all of which use embeddings produced by language models, with AUC ranging from 63% to 78% reported in their papers. We directly input the COVID dataset to these tools. For the tools outputting scores per residue, we average to obtain a score for the peptide and compute the AUC. A decrease in performance is observed for all four frameworks compared to the reported AUC on their test sets. A possible explanation is that epitopes from different organisms could have different underlying data distributions, making a general model trained on a variety of species underperform on specific organisms [1]. Nevertheless, our framework still significantly outperforms the other three. Without a high computational cost incurred by the large models, the inference time is only 5 s on this dataset, while other tools using language models typically take over minutes.

The experimental results show that our framework is promising as a pre-screening tool for prioritizing targets for laboratory investigation. Our lightweight model can be trained on hundreds of thousands of sequences in moderate time, spending a couple of hours on CPU. Thus, it is friendly to researchers

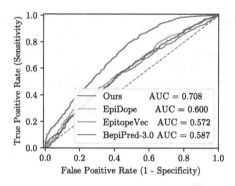

Fig. 3. ROC curves of different tools for epitope prediction on the COVID dataset.

having limited resources such as only CPU or low-end GPU. Moreover, based on the effectiveness and flexibility of the proposed methods, we believe our framework has the potential to be applied to other peptide classification problems. With the increasing availability of sequence and structure data, the information of antibodies can be incorporated in the future to model antigen-antibody interactions. Such studies will provide insights into the ligand-receptor interactions during immune response [28] and benefit the research on individualized immunotherapy [52].

7   Conclusion

This paper presents a deep learning-based multi-task framework, which is called BeeTLe, for linear B-cell epitope prediction and antibody type-specific epitope classification using Transformer and LSTM encoders. It involves a simple yet effective residue encoding method, a model whose backbone combines recurrent layers and attention mechanisms to learn feature representations for peptides, and modified cross-entropy loss functions to address the imbalance problem. A large dataset with potential false-negative epitopes being reduced is curated for benchmarking. We implement and deploy a command-line tool to facilitate the use and extension of our work. The code and the data are open-source at https://github.com/yuanx749/bcell.

Acknowledgements. The author sincerely thanks all the reviewers for their constructive feedback, and Jiarong Liang for the valuable discussions on the concepts and tools in immunology.

Ethical Statement. In this work, we develop a novel computational framework for predicting and classifying B-cell epitopes. The datasets we used are constructed from a publicly available database downloaded from the IEDB website. We do not require ethical approval during the research. Our work does not involve collecting personal data. The major implication will be in the medical domain such as vaccine production and diagnostics development. With that being said, we are aware that some medical applications may need to process personal data. Although the IEDB database does not involve sensitive data such as information on patients, it could be interesting for the community to investigate if the immunology data have a bias in race or gender.

References

1. Ashford, J., Reis-Cunha, J., Lobo, I., Lobo, F., Campelo, F.: Organism-specific training improves performance of linear B-cell epitope prediction. Bioinformatics **37**(24), 4826–4834 (2021). https://doi.org/10.1093/bioinformatics/btab536
2. Ba, J.L., Kiros, J.R., Hinton, G.E.: Layer normalization. arXiv preprint arXiv:1607.06450 (2016)
3. Bahai, A., Asgari, E., Mofrad, M.R., Kloetgen, A., McHardy, A.C.: EpitopeVec: linear epitope prediction using deep protein sequence embeddings. Bioinformatics **37**(23), 4517–4525 (2021). https://doi.org/10.1093/bioinformatics/btab467
4. Chen, T., Guestrin, C.: XGBoost: A scalable tree boosting system. In: Proceedings of the 22nd ACM SIGKDD International Conference on Knowledge Discovery and Data Mining, pp. 785–794 (2016). https://doi.org/10.1145/2939672.2939785
5. Cheng, J., Dong, L., Lapata, M.: Long short-term memory-networks for machine reading. In: Proceedings of the 2016 Conference on Empirical Methods in Natural Language Processing, pp. 551–561 (2016). https://doi.org/10.18653/v1/D16-1053
6. Clifford, J., Høie, M.H., Deleuran, S., Peters, B., Nielsen, M., Marcatili, P.: Bepipred-3.0: improved B-cell epitope prediction using protein language models. Protein Sci. **31**, e4497 (2022). https://doi.org/10.1002/pro.4497
7. Collatz, M., Mock, F., Barth, E., Hölzer, M., Sachse, K., Marz, M.: EpiDope: a deep neural network for linear B-cell epitope prediction. Bioinformatics **37**(4), 448–455 (2021). https://doi.org/10.1093/bioinformatics/btaa773
8. Cui, Y., Jia, M., Lin, T.Y., Song, Y., Belongie, S.: Class-balanced loss based on effective number of samples. In: 2019 IEEE/CVF Conference on Computer Vision and Pattern Recognition (CVPR), pp. 9260–9269. IEEE (2019). https://doi.org/10.1109/CVPR.2019.00949
9. Devlin, J., Chang, M.W., Lee, K., Toutanova, K.: Bert: pre-training of deep bidirectional transformers for language understanding. In: Proceedings of the 2019 Conference of the North American Chapter of the Association for Computational Linguistics: Human Language Technologies, Volume 1 (Long and Short Papers), pp. 4171–4186 (2019). https://doi.org/10.18653/v1/N19-1423
10. Fu, L., Niu, B., Zhu, Z., Wu, S., Li, W.: CD-HIT: accelerated for clustering the next-generation sequencing data. Bioinformatics **28**(23), 3150–3152 (2012). https://doi.org/10.1093/bioinformatics/bts565
11. Galanis, K.A., Nastou, K.C., Papandreou, N.C., Petichakis, G.N., Pigis, D.G., Iconomidou, V.A.: Linear B-cell epitope prediction for in silico vaccine design: a performance review of methods available via command-line interface. Int. J. Mol. Sci. **22**(6), 3210 (2021). https://doi.org/10.3390/ijms22063210
12. Glorot, X., Bengio, Y.: Understanding the difficulty of training deep feedforward neural networks. In: Proceedings of the Thirteenth International Conference on Artificial Intelligence and Statistics, pp. 249–256. JMLR Workshop and Conference Proceedings (2010)
13. Glorot, X., Bordes, A., Bengio, Y.: Deep sparse rectifier neural networks. In: Proceedings of the Fourteenth International Conference on Artificial Intelligence and Statistics, pp. 315–323. JMLR Workshop and Conference Proceedings (2011)

14. Goyal, P., et al.: Accurate, large minibatch SGD: training ImageNet in 1 hour. arXiv preprint arXiv:1706.02677 (2017)
15. Graves, A.: Generating sequences with recurrent neural networks. arXiv preprint arXiv:1308.0850 (2013)
16. Graves, A., Schmidhuber, J.: Framewise phoneme classification with bidirectional LSTM and other neural network architectures. Neural Netw. **18**(5–6), 602–610 (2005). https://doi.org/10.1016/j.neunet.2005.06.042
17. Gupta, S., Ansari, H.R., Gautam, A., Raghava, G.P.: Identification of B-cell epitopes in an antigen for inducing specific class of antibodies. Biol. Direct **8**(1), 1–15 (2013). https://doi.org/10.1186/1745-6150-8-27
18. He, K., Zhang, X., Ren, S., Sun, J.: Deep residual learning for image recognition. In: 2016 IEEE Conference on Computer Vision and Pattern Recognition (CVPR), pp. 770–778. IEEE (2016). https://doi.org/10.1109/CVPR.2016.90
19. Hochreiter, S., Schmidhuber, J.: Long short-term memory. Neural Comput. **9**(8), 1735–1780 (1997). https://doi.org/10.1162/neco.1997.9.8.1735
20. Ioffe, S., Szegedy, C.: Batch normalization: accelerating deep network training by reducing internal covariate shift. In: International Conference on Machine Learning, pp. 448–456. PMLR (2015)
21. Jespersen, M.C., Peters, B., Nielsen, M., Marcatili, P.: BepiPred-2.0: improving sequence-based B-cell epitope prediction using conformational epitopes. Nucleic Acids Res. **45**(W1), W24–W29 (2017). https://doi.org/10.1093/nar/gkx346
22. Kadam, K., Peerzada, N., Karbhal, R., Sawant, S., Valadi, J., Kulkarni-Kale, U.: Antibody class (es) predictor for epitopes (AbCPE): a multi-label classification algorithm. Front. Bioinform. **1**, 709951 (2021). https://doi.org/10.3389/fbinf.2021.709951
23. Kang, B., et al.: Decoupling representation and classifier for long-tailed recognition. In: International Conference on Learning Representations (2020)
24. Kingma, D.P., Ba, J.: Adam: a method for stochastic optimization. In: International Conference on Learning Representations (2015)
25. LeCun, Y., Bengio, Y., Hinton, G.: Deep learning. Nature **521**(7553), 436–444 (2015). https://doi.org/10.1038/nature14539
26. LeCun, Y., et al.: Backpropagation applied to handwritten zip code recognition. Neural Comput. **1**(4), 541–551 (1989). https://doi.org/10.1162/neco.1989.1.4.541
27. Levy, O., Goldberg, Y.: Neural word embedding as implicit matrix factorization. In: Proceedings of the 27th International Conference on Neural Information Processing Systems-Volume 2. pp. 2177–2185 (2014)
28. Li, S., et al.: Structure-aware interactive graph neural networks for the prediction of protein-ligand binding affinity. In: Proceedings of the 27th ACM SIGKDD Conference on Knowledge Discovery and Data Mining, pp. 975–985 (2021). https://doi.org/10.1145/3447548.3467311
29. Lin, T.Y., Goyal, P., Girshick, R., He, K., Dollár, P.: Focal loss for dense object detection. In: 2017 IEEE International Conference on Computer Vision (ICCV), pp. 2999–3007. IEEE (2017). https://doi.org/10.1109/ICCV.2017.324
30. Liu, T., Shi, K., Li, W.: Deep learning methods improve linear B-cell epitope prediction. BioData Min. **13**(1), 1–13 (2020). https://doi.org/10.1186/s13040-020-00211-0
31. Loshchilov, I., Hutter, F.: SGDR: stochastic gradient descent with warm restarts. In: International Conference on Learning Representations (2017)
32. Loshchilov, I., Hutter, F.: Decoupled weight decay regularization. In: International Conference on Learning Representations (2019)

33. Ma, Y., et al.: Identification of antimicrobial peptides from the human gut microbiome using deep learning. Nat. Biotechnol. **40**(6), 921–931 (2022). https://doi.org/10.1038/s41587-022-01226-0
34. Manavalan, B., Govindaraj, R.G., Shin, T.H., Kim, M.O., Lee, G.: iBCE-EL: a new ensemble learning framework for improved linear B-cell epitope prediction. Front. Immunol. **9**, 1695 (2018). https://doi.org/10.3389/fimmu.2018.01695
35. Menon, A.K., Jayasumana, S., Rawat, A.S., Jain, H., Veit, A., Kumar, S.: Long-tail learning via logit adjustment. In: International Conference on Learning Representations (2021)
36. Mikolov, T., Sutskever, I., Chen, K., Corrado, G., Dean, J.: Distributed representations of words and phrases and their compositionality. In: Proceedings of the 26th International Conference on Neural Information Processing Systems-Volume 2, pp. 3111–3119 (2013)
37. Ofer, D., Brandes, N., Linial, M.: The language of proteins: NLP, machine learning and protein sequences. Comput. Struct. Biotechnol. J. **19**, 1750–1758 (2021). https://doi.org/10.1016/j.csbj.2021.03.022
38. Paszke, A., et al.: Pytorch: an imperative style, high-performance deep learning library. In: Proceedings of the 33rd International Conference on Neural Information Processing Systems, pp. 8026–8037 (2019)
39. Pearson, W.R.: Selecting the right similarity-scoring matrix. Curr. Protoc. Bioinf. **43**(1), 3–5 (2013). https://doi.org/10.1002/0471250953.bi0305s43
40. Pedregosa, F., et al.: Scikit-learn: machine learning in Python. J. Mach. Learn. Res. **12**, 2825–2830 (2011)
41. Potocnakova, L., Bhide, M., Pulzova, L.B.: An introduction to B-cell epitope mapping and in silico epitope prediction. J. Immunol. Res. **2016**, 6760830 (2016). https://doi.org/10.1155/2016/6760830
42. Punt, J.: Kuby Immunology, eighth edn. W. H. Freeman and Company (2019)
43. Rahman, K.S., Chowdhury, E.U., Sachse, K., Kaltenboeck, B.: Inadequate reference datasets biased toward short non-epitopes confound B-cell epitope prediction. J. Biol. Chem. **291**(28), 14585–14599 (2016). https://doi.org/10.1074/jbc.M116.729020
44. Reddi, S.J., Kale, S., Kumar, S.: On the convergence of Adam and beyond. In: International Conference on Learning Representations (2018)
45. Sanchez-Trincado, J.L., Gomez-Perosanz, M., Reche, P.A.: Fundamentals and methods for T- and B-cell epitope prediction. J. Immunol. Res. **2017**, 2680160 (2017). https://doi.org/10.1155/2017/2680160
46. Singh, H., Ansari, H.R., Raghava, G.P.: Improved method for linear B-cell epitope prediction using antigen's primary sequence. PLoS One **8**(5), e62216 (2013). https://doi.org/10.1371/journal.pone.0062216
47. Srivastava, N., Hinton, G., Krizhevsky, A., Sutskever, I., Salakhutdinov, R.: Dropout: a simple way to prevent neural networks from overfitting. J. Mach. Learn. Res. **15**(1), 1929–1958 (2014)
48. Teufel, F., et al.: SignalP 6.0 predicts all five types of signal peptides using protein language models. Nat. Biotechnol. **40**(7), 1023–1025 (2022). https://doi.org/10.1038/s41587-021-01156-3
49. Thumuluri, V., Almagro Armenteros, J.J., Johansen, A.R., Nielsen, H., Winther, O.: DeepLoc 2.0: multi-label subcellular localization prediction using protein language models. Nucleic Acids Res. **50**(W1), W228–W234 (2022). https://doi.org/10.1093/nar/gkac278

50. Vaswani, A., et al.: Attention is all you need. In: Proceedings of the 31st International Conference on Neural Information Processing Systems, pp. 6000–6010 (2017)
51. Vita, R., et al.: The immune epitope database (IEDB): 2018 update. Nucleic Acids Res. **47**(D1), D339–D343 (2019). https://doi.org/10.1093/nar/gky1006
52. Widrich, M., et al.: Modern hopfield networks and attention for immune repertoire classification. In: Proceedings of the 34th International Conference on Neural Information Processing Systems, pp. 18832–18845 (2020)
53. Xu, H., Zhao, Z.: NetBCE: an interpretable deep neural network for accurate prediction of linear B-cell epitopes. Genomics Proteomics Bioinform. **20**, 1002–1012 (2022). https://doi.org/10.1016/j.gpb.2022.11.009
54. Yang, Z., Yang, D., Dyer, C., He, X., Smola, A., Hovy, E.: Hierarchical attention networks for document classification. In: Proceedings of the 2016 Conference of the North American Chapter of the Association for Computational Linguistics: Human Language Technologies, pp. 1480–1489 (2016). 10.18653/v1/N16-1174

Human-Computer Interaction

Ordinal Regression for Difficulty Prediction of StepMania Levels

Billy Joe Franks$^{(\boxtimes)}$ ⬥, Benjamin Dinkelmann ⬥, Marius Kloft ⬥, and Sophie Fellenz ⬥

University of Kaiserslautern-Landau, Kaiserslautern, Germany
`billy.franks@rptu.de`

Abstract. StepMania is a popular open-source clone of a rhythm-based video game. As is common in popular games, there is a large number of community-designed levels. It is often difficult for players and level authors to determine the difficulty level of such community contributions. In this work, we formalize and analyze the difficulty prediction task on StepMania levels as an ordinal regression (OR) task. We standardize a more extensive and diverse selection of this data resulting in five data sets, two of which are extensions of previous work. We evaluate many competitive OR and non-OR models, demonstrating that neural network-based models significantly outperform the state of the art and that StepMania-level data makes for an excellent test bed for deep OR models. We conclude with a user experiment showing our models' super-human performance.

Keywords: Ordinal regression · StepMania · Difficulty prediction

1 Introduction

Video game designers commonly order game levels in ascending order of difficulty. The first levels act as tutorials, while the later levels challenge the players. Games that rely heavily on community contributions lack communication present in game studios, leading to a more haphazard design and inconsistent game-level difficulties. Portal 2, Super Mario Maker, Happy Wheels, and Roblox are examples that profit heavily from community-created game levels. In this work, we focus on StepMania, a rhythm-based video game in which players step onto a keypad on the floor to the rhythm of a song. A level is represented by a sequence of directional inputs that must be hit at a specific time (see Fig. 1).

As difficulties are commonly represented as natural numbers (or ordinals), estimating the difficulty of video game levels is a natural ordinal regression (OR) task. OR has a long history dating back to at least the 18th century [15]. It is commonly applied in the social sciences for modeling human preferences, as it allows for the representation of ordinal relationships. More recently, [2] raised

---

B. J. Franks and B. Dinkelmann—Equally contributions.

G. De Francisci Morales et al. (Eds.): ECML PKDD 2023, LNAI 14174, pp. 497–512, 2023.
https://doi.org/10.1007/978-3-031-43427-3_30

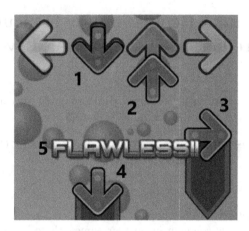

Fig. 1. This example of StepMania play shows the basic steps tap (1 and 2) and hold (3 and 4). Steps that coincide with notes of certain levels, like a quarter (2–4) or an eight (1), have unique colors. Different steps can also be combined, requiring the player to hit two or more keys simultaneously. Depending on how accurately in time a step is hit, the player receives feedback (5).

greater interest from a machine learning (ML) perspective, while the use of deep learning started with its advent around the 2000s [1]. Outside of the social sciences, OR also has applications in computer vision and natural language processing, which commonly require deep learning. Examples include age estimation [19], sentiment analysis [21], or depth estimation [10]. However, it has not yet been applied to the difficulty prediction of video game levels.

There is a huge potential for applying ML methods such as OR on video games other than StepMania, but so far, the number of publicly available labeled data sets is limited. Crawling the largest repository of StepMania data, StepMania Online[1], results in 602 GB of labeled data. More data can also be found on various platforms frequented by avid StepMania-level creators and players. So far, only level generation [9,23], and difficulty prediction [5,24] have been applied to this data. However, other tasks or subtasks of the former utilizing this data may also be interesting. Examples include detecting salient events in music, anomaly detection, and early anomaly detection. StepMania data is, in essence, extensively labeled sound data, and we encourage using it as such.

Our Contributions. We propose using OR to predict the difficulties of StepMania levels. Our contributions include the following:

- We provide the first analysis of deep OR methods on the task of difficulty prediction on StepMania data, resulting in a new state of the art. (Sect. 5.1)
- We increase the number of standardized data sets and expand upon previous data sets, provide a fundamental description of the data, and extensive

---

[1] https://search.stepmaniaonline.net/.

data analysis about StepMania data and the relationships between different StepMania data sets. (Sects. 4, 5.2 and 5.3)

- Finally, we demonstrate that OR models can improve human labels. For this, we evaluate each model considered here on its accuracy on user rankings of pairs of StepMania levels. (Sect. 5.4)

2   Related Work

We cover related work starting with previous work on StepMania and closely related data. Then, OR surveys and OR taxonomies are discussed from an ML and social sciences perspective.

2.1   StepMania and Related Data

[9] first investigated ML on StepMania data. They used ML for the task of level generation or learning to choreograph. [23] improved upon this previous work by blending more challenging and less challenging levels, creating levels of intermediary difficulty. [13] transferred this general approach to another rhythm game, Taiko no Tatsujin.

[24] first investigated the task of level difficulty analysis or difficulty prediction of StepMania levels. They clustered levels based on automatically extracted hand-picked features and found the resulting clusters to correlate with difficulty levels. [5] built on this idea by combining features calculated for a level by Step-Mania with the count and required speed of specific patterns occurring in the levels to predict the level difficulty using a classification approach.

Broadening the perspective from just StepMania levels to musical charts, which are very similar data, [22] distinguished four difficulty levels for piano pieces, from beginner to virtuoso. Musical features, including playing speed, chord ratio, and fingering difficulty, were automatically extracted and then separately classified and aggregated via human-validated decision rules. Similarly, [7] also extracted features from symbolic music charts but used various regression methods to relate these features to nine different difficulty levels. Finally, [11] developed a hybrid approach by combining the top-5 features from [7] with a deep convolutional NN based on piano roll representation of the music.

In contrast to existing work, we apply methods from OR to the difficulty prediction of StepMania levels. For this reason, we also list related work on OR.

2.2   Ordinal Regression Surveys

[12] conducted a comprehensive survey and experimental study of various OR models. [25] recently provided a taxonomy of OR models and applied these to a case study about public fear of nuclear energy. Similarly, [4] describe OR in detail from a social sciences perspective.

Contemporary research shows that OR methods generally outperform their non-OR counterparts on OR problems. [19] compare previous shallow and deep non-OR models with shallow and deep OR models and demonstrate the superiority of OR on age estimation data and the need for deep models in this field. [10] compare previous deep convolutional non-OR approaches against a deep OR approach, again demonstrating deep OR superiority. [21] provide the first application of OR combined with four ML models to a sentiment analysis task.

2.3 Difficulty Prediction in Games

Difficulty prediction is frequently studied in the area of player modeling [18, 20, 27]. From a player modeling perspective, the goal is to model a level's difficulty given a particular player. To this end, data of humans interacting with the game is commonly required [14]. In stark contrast, we are not interested in individual players but in the game difficulty in the context of a given community of players. The predicted difficulty should be consistent with other difficulty scores for levels in the same community. In StepMania, there is extensive training data for this approach. Therefore, we choose to model the difficulty of game levels directly instead of using the indirect route via the modeling of players.

3 StepMania Difficulty as Ordinal Regression

We first describe the problem setting. Then, we argue conceptually why OR is the superior approach for our problem. Lastly, we describe a selection of OR methods that we consider most relevant to the analysis performed herein. More details and the code can be found in the supplementary material[2].

We want to train an ML model that estimates the difficulty of a StepMania level, our data sequence $x_i = (x_i^{(1)}, \ldots, x_i^{(d)})$ of length d. We specify the $x_i^{(j)}$ in the experiments (Sect. 5). StepMania level difficulties are natural numbers and our labels $y_i \in \{1, \ldots, K\}$. We aim for the smallest possible prediction errors. Let $\hat{y}$ be a model's prediction. We assign a cost $c(\hat{y}, y) := |\hat{y} - y|$ to a prediction with label y. Training a model that minimizes this cost is an OR problem.

Readers might wonder why OR is separate from standard classification or regression. Later in the experiments, we will consider these as non-OR baselines. However, it is notable that both classification and regression do not inherently fit the metric present in OR, i.e., the cost function c. Usual classification approaches will minimize the negative log-likelihood (NLL). Based on this, the classifier loss function is independent of the ordering of labels, meaning an off-by-one error is treated the same as an entirely wrong prediction. Regression might seem more suitable than classification. However, the whole-valued nature of our labels complicates this approach. Training a regular regressor minimizing mean absolute error (MAE) without rounding to the nearest integer will result in the regressor not taking the rounding threshold into account.

In the following, we describe the OR methods considered in this work, chosen based on previous studies [12] and their compatibility with deep architectures.

---

[2] https://github.com/benjamin-dinkelmann/difficulty-estimation-stepmania/.

NNRank. [6] proposed using a set of binary classifiers to solve OR problems. A model predicts $K - 1$ binary classifiers, where the i-th binary classifier predicts the probability that $i < y$. In this sense, the target of an input is a vector of $y - 1$ ones followed by $K - y$ zeros, i.e., for $y = 4$, the target is $t = (1, 1, 1, 0, \ldots, 0)$.

RED-SVM. [16] introduced the reduction-based support vector machine (SVM) for OR. They propose to reduce multiple binary classifiers (as in NNRank) to just one binary classifier. For an input x, target y, and a category k, this classifier decides whether $k < y$. In practice, one data point (x, y) is transformed into $K - 1$ data points $((x, 1), 1 < y), ((x, 2), 2 < y), \ldots, ((x, K - 1), K - 1 < y)$. An SVM is then trained on this data. In the original SVM formulation, this translates to learning a linear (or kernelized) regressor and $K - 1$ thresholds.

Laplace. [8] proposed using soft labels. Instead of learning to predict a classification target vector $t = (0, \ldots, 0, 1, 0, \ldots, 0)$, they propose learning a smoothed target vector using a distance metric $\phi(y, i)$,

$$t_i = \frac{\exp^{-\phi(y,i)}}{\sum_{k=1}^{K} \exp^{-\phi(y,k)}}. \tag{1}$$

These targets are discretely sampled common probability distributions normalized by the denominator. For $\phi(y, i) = |y - i|$, the distribution is a Laplace distribution, and for $\phi(y, i) = \|y - i\|^2$, the distribution is normal. The cross-entropy between target and softmax predictions of a model is then used as training loss.

Binomial. With soft labels as distributions in mind, we also propose using a Poisson binomial distribution with $K + 3$ Bernoulli trials, mean $(K + 3)p = y + 1$, and variance 1 as a target. More specifically, we choose $y + 1$ Bernoulli trials with probability p_1 and $K - y + 2$ Bernoulli trials with probability p_2, where

$$p_1 := \frac{y + 1}{K + 3} + \sqrt{\frac{(K - y + 2)^2}{(K + 3)^2} - \frac{(K - y + 2)}{(y + 1)(K + 3)}} \tag{2}$$

$$p_2 := \frac{y + 1}{K + 3} - \sqrt{\frac{(y + 1)^2}{(K + 3)^2} - \frac{(y + 1)}{(K - y + 2)(K + 3)}}. \tag{3}$$

These choices of p_1 and p_2 result in a mean of $y + 1$ and a variance of 1 if the variance of a binomial with $p = \frac{y+1}{K+3}$ is larger or equal to one. This is guaranteed by considering $K + 3$ Bernoulli trials instead of $K - 1$. We discuss this in greater detail in the supplementary material.

4 StepMania Level Data

StepMania[3] is an open-source game engine with over 100 contributors initially developed as a clone of Konami's arcade game series Dance Dance Revolution

---

[3] https://www.stepmania.com/.

(DDR). StepMania has become the engine for multiple games based on DDR, including In the Groove, Pump It Up Pro, and others. In StepMania, a player may choose a song and a difficulty level to "play". This starts a game level in which the player must step onto four arrows, left, right, up, and down, to a certain rhythm on a controller on the floor, which is typically called a pad. Usually, this rhythm is in line with the chosen song playing in the background. The act of playing resembles dancing, where DDR likely got its name. Levels appear in combination with songs and it is most common for authors to distribute songs in packs, which is a collection of multiple songs. Most packs are created by a single individual or a small group working closely together, guaranteeing a homogeneous difficulty interpretation of levels in a pack.

Each song is associated with a music file and a background image or video. An SM (for StepMania) file encodes the level data in a custom ASCII-based file format. SM is an elementary file format used in StepMania and other rhythm games. A newer file format SSC with more design features has been established from StepMania version 5 (previously known as StepMania Spinal Shark Collective fork) and onward. Even though SSC contains more options for level design, more songs are available in the SM format (newer levels usually encode both SM and SSC), so we will use this format for this work. An SM file starts with header information followed by encoding at least one level. The header contains features that are consistent across levels, such as the title, artist, and tempo changes. A sequence then describes a level by dividing the song into measures (from musical notation), encoding which inputs are required at what time. Each measure can be split into 4–192 equidistant parts that define the granularity in which notes can be assigned. Together with the tempo, this defines the maximum speed at which inputs may need to be entered and the possible rhythmic complexity.

From an ML perspective, there are a few complications with this data. Packs are created for personal enjoyment rather than ML purposes, leading to categories with very few or no samples. Additionally, multiple levels per song with different labels may be available. These different levels for the same song are correlated both naturally and intentionally by the design process of the authors. This needs to be considered when splitting data into training and test sets. These issues are addressed in the experiments (Sect. 5).

Packs of songs for StepMania are freely available online, facilitating easy access to labeled data. StepMania Online[4] is one of these repositories, searchable by pack name but also song names or authors. Crawling the packs available there results in 602 GB of data, although this also includes the music file and, in some cases, background videos, which we discard in our analysis. We also consider packs that are released in other communities. Zenius-I-vanisher[5], for instance, has a relatively active community. Another notable community that was very influential in the proliferation, organization of conventions, and tournament-play of StepMania is DDRIllini[6].

---

[4] https://search.stepmaniaonline.net/.

[5] https://zenius-i-vanisher.com.

[6] https://ddrillini.club/.

Table 1. Overview of all data sets with statistics. Statistics shown are the number of packs used for construction, the number of songs included, the number of levels included, and the minimum and maximum difficulty available in each data set. [1] indicates expanded previous data sets. [2] indicates newly proposed data sets.

Name	#Packs	#Songs	#Levels	Min-Max
ITG[1]	4	297	1,469	1–14
fraxtil	3	90	450	1–15
Gpop[2]	12	542	2,710	1–18
Gulls[2]	7	70	260	2–14
Speirmix[2]	1	267	1,185	1–15

Some prolific individuals or groups create multiple packs, which we collate into more extensive data sets with consistent themes. This is how the following data sets were chosen. Table 1 provides an overview of all data sets.

ITG. [9] introduced the In The Groove (ITG) data set made up of 133 songs or 652 levels from multiple authors, which combine the packs ITG1 and ITG2. We expand this ITG data set by adding ITG3 and ITGRebirth, yielding 297 songs and 1,469 levels. ITG primarily contains electronic indie music. In contrast to the other data sets, ITG originates from the game studio Roxor Games and has been slightly modified by the StepMania community over time. Thus ITG is not purely a community contribution.

Fraxtil. [9] also introduced the fraxtil data set, which combines three packs from one level author, known as fraxtil, and contains 90 songs and 450 levels. fraxtil primarily contains electronic music.

Gpop. We propose Gpop, encompassing 542 songs and 2,710 levels from twelve packs. The levels are almost exclusively created by creator Gpop. Gpop features mostly Japanese pop and Vocaloid music.

Gulls. We propose Gull's Arrows, which consists of seven packs by creator Gamergull with ten songs each, for a total of 70 songs and 260 levels. The songs in this data set include mostly electronic music and some video game soundtracks.

Speirmix. Lastly, we propose using Ben Speirs' Speirmix Galaxy, consisting of 267 songs and 1,185 levels written chiefly by the creator Ben Speir. The genre of Speirmix mainly focuses on modern music, featuring many pop songs from the 2000 s and 2010 s.

Notably, the distinctions in StepMania-play are more complicated than they may have appeared. The StepMania community is split into multiple, overlapping, groups. The differences between these groups vary from the type of controller used to the design style of levels. Examples include (1) ITG, a common synonym for StepMania. (2) DDR, which is based on the original DDR style levels. (3) Keyboard play, which uses a computer keyboard as a controller. (4) Pump it Up, which uses a controller with up-right, down-right, down-left, up-left, and center keys. (5) Rhythm Horizon, a newer development, which uses all directions mentioned so far. Additionally, these communities have been split into different genres at different times. Currently, there are three such sub-genres for StepMania play. These groups referred to themselves as (1) Tech, which includes players focussing on accuracy in their play. (2) Stamina, which includes players that focus on long levels with continuous streams, i.e., continuous single steps with no breaks. (3) Modding, which includes players that play levels where reading is the main difficulty, meaning that each level's visuals are modified to such an extent that the required arrows are significantly harder to detect on screen. This work focuses primarily on pad-play (as opposed to keyboard play) and tech levels. The data sets also primarily feature older content starting around 2005. We expect the methodology proposed here to also function on data from most other groups. However, Modding levels would need entirely different approaches, most likely including extracting video to determine the difficulty of levels.

5   Experiments

Data Sets. As mentioned previously, the data sets are unbalanced, with some difficulty levels being rare. We first deal with small categories by joining adjacent difficulty categories until every remaining category accounts for at least 2 percent of all levels. We balance the data sets as part of the training procedure and evaluation protocol described later.

Secondly, the data sets described here must be split into train and test sets. We do not use regular cross-validation since multiple levels of the same song are correlated. Instead, we use Monte Carlo cross-validation with rejection sampling. Specifically, we choose 20% of songs (with all their respective levels) as a test set and the remainder as the train set. We reject samples until all difficulties are present in both sets. This results in an approximate 80–20 train-test split with each label present in both sets. We repeat this Monte Carlo cross-validation process 100 times yielding 100 different train-test splits for each data set.

Feature Extraction. From the SM files, we extract the level sequences. We encode each sequence element as a 19-dimensional feature vector $x_i^{(j)} \in \mathbb{R}^{19}$. This vector contains the tempo (1 feature), a note-level encoding (7 features), level progress in time (1 feature), level progress in sequence length (1 feature), time since the last element (1 feature), a one-hot encoding of the step direction in case of a tap (4 features) and hold (4 features), for a total of 19 features. Due to their rarity, we ignore all other potential features of the level sequence, like tempo changes, mines, or other effects. Find a more detailed description in the supplement.

Compared Methods. As our baselines, we evaluate PATTERN proposed by [5] as a non-deep non-OR method and a classification and regression model as deep non-OR methods. We compare all methods from Sect. 3 to these baselines.

Model Architecture. For PATTERN, we use a three-layer multilayer perceptron with a hidden size of 32. This model only uses a feature vector instead of a time series. Building on the recent success in sequence processing with transformers [3,26], we use the encoder of a transformer as the backbone to all deep models. Specifically, we use three layers of dimensionality 64 with four attention heads. Before applying the encoder, a small convolutional layer of kernel size two projects the 19 input features to the embedding dimension. Then, we add a positional encoding [26]. Global average pooling reduces the time series to a single vector before each model's head. We ensemble eight random sub-samples of length 60 from each input sequence to produce a prediction.

A model's head depends on the chosen method. We train PATTERN and the classifier with NLL. The regressor is trained using MAE. NNRank consists of $K - 1$ logits trained with NLL. We evaluate each data point for every threshold in RED-SVM and train the binary classifier with NLL. The target is a discrete distribution for Laplace, so we use cross-entropy between the target and a softmax multi-class head. For Binomial, we do the same as for Laplace, except that we replace the Laplace target distribution with a Poisson binomial distribution. Find more details in the supplement.

Training. We train each model on the training set for 200 epochs with a batch size of 128, AdamW [17] as the optimizer with a weight decay of 5e-2, and a learning rate of $lr = \frac{\#levels}{1500} \cdot 10^{-4}$ to adapt for data set size. Due to the unbalanced data sets, we use a weighted random sampler to select data points, resulting in each difficulty being drawn with equal probability. We train one model for each method on each training set of all 100 train-test splits of each data set. This results in a total of 3,500 models.

5.1 Evaluating our Methods on StepMania-Level Difficulty Prediction

Metrics. Due to the unbalanced data sets, we consider a class-weight-normalized version of the MAE as our metric. We refer to our metric as the weighted absolute error (WAE). The WAE of a model f on a data set D with data points (x, y) and K classes is defined as

$$\text{WAE}_D(f) = \frac{1}{K} \sum_{(x,y)\in D} \frac{1}{w_y}|y - f(x)|, \text{ with } w_y = |\{\mathbf{x}|(\mathbf{x}, y) \in D\}|. \quad (4)$$

Notably, for a balanced data set, WAE and MAE are equal.

We evaluate each of the 3,500 trained models using WAE and compute the mean and standard deviation across the 100 Monte Carlo cross-validation samples. The results can be found in Table 2a. The supplementary material contains additional evaluations for other metrics, including MAE.

5.2 Difficulty Across Data Sets

Readers might wonder whether the different data set's labels are consistent when compared to one another. They are not consistent. See the confusion matrix in

Table 2. OR and classification models outperform feature-extraction-based PATTERN and regression models. This table shows WAE performance rounded to the third nearest digit for different models on all StepMania data sets averaged over 100 models trained on separate Monte Carlo cross-validation splits. Lower values are better. The smallest value in each column is **bold**. According to a standard 5% significance t-test, all values in a column insignificantly higher than the best value are <u>underlined</u>.

(a) Trained and evaluated on the same data set.						
		ITG	fraxtil	Gpop	Gulls	Speirmix
non OR	PATTERN	0.457±0.043	0.736±0.092	0.460±0.028	0.695±0.101	0.297±0.037
	Classification	**0.366±0.033**	0.480±0.080	**0.342±0.027**	0.273±0.063	0.274±0.046
	Regression	0.379±0.030	0.489±0.058	0.356±0.025	0.284±0.064	0.278±0.043
OR	NNRank	0.372±0.033	**0.444±0.065**	0.344±0.025	0.275±0.066	0.268±0.047
	RED-SVM	0.368±0.030	0.481±0.058	0.349±0.024	**0.262±0.057**	0.268±0.043
	Laplace	0.367±0.029	0.455±0.070	0.342±0.026	0.270±0.067	0.269±0.051
	Binomial	0.368±0.031	0.448±0.072	0.344±0.027	0.264±0.069	**0.265±0.047**
(b) Trained on separate data sets from the one being evaluated.						
		ITG	fraxtil	Gpop	Gulls	Speirmix
non OR	PATTERN	0.717±0.16	0.618±0.179	0.717±0.167	0.549±0.126	0.670±0.129
	Classification	<u>0.461±0.060</u>	0.477±0.058	<u>0.488±0.060</u>	**0.379±0.085**	0.510±0.060
	Regression	0.483±0.048	<u>0.469±0.078</u>	<u>0.480±0.080</u>	0.411±0.122	0.562±0.103
OR	NNRank	**0.455±0.046**	<u>0.461±0.065</u>	<u>0.469±0.064</u>	<u>0.403±0.107</u>	**0.472±0.089**
	RED-SVM	0.465±0.046	**0.452±0.074**	**0.465±0.072**	0.387±0.104	0.546±0.095
	Laplace	0.475±0.057	<u>0.458±0.074</u>	<u>0.469±0.069</u>	0.388±0.108	0.529±0.095
	Binomial	0.475±0.057	<u>0.457±0.071</u>	0.471±0.066	<u>0.395±0.103</u>	0.498±0.080

Fig. 2, where Binomial was trained on Speirmix but evaluated on Gulls, for a visualization that difficulties can be offset significantly. More confusion matrices can be found in the supplementary material. With this in mind, we evaluated for each data set pair (A, B) how a model trained on A performs on B. Difficulties from B are adjusted based on the pooling defined for A.

Specifically, for each pair of data sets (A, B) and method M, all 100 models trained on A for method M are evaluated on the entire data set B and averaged. This would produce a $5 \times 5 \times 7$ tensor of evaluations. To make these evaluations easier to compare to Table 2a, we present for a data set B and method M the mean and standard deviation of method M trained on all data sets but B. Table 2b contains this evaluation. Find the entire tensor of evaluations in the supplementary material.

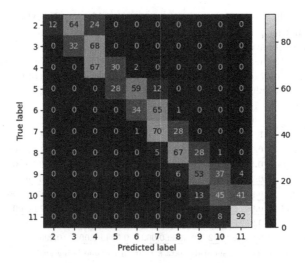

Fig. 2. Difficulty depends on subjective perceptions of level creators. This confusion matrix shows that there is often an offset of up to one category if a model trained on one dataset (here Speirmix) is evaluated on another dataset (here Gulls). The confusion matrix is averaged and category-normalized. The model was trained with the Binomial loss.

5.3   Difficulty Prediction as a Ranking Problem

As shown in the previous section, the previous evaluations are structurally biased because the given difficulty levels are inconsistent between data sets. However, viewing the data sets as ranking problems will avoid this bias. Specifically, instead of evaluating whether a data point x is predicted as label y, we evaluate for a pair of data points x, x' with $y < y'$ whether the prediction of x' is larger than x. Moving from OR models to ranking models is simple, as OR predictions can be compared to get ranking predictions. From a data set D with data points (x, y) we construct a new data set $D' := \{((x, x'), sign(y - y'))|(x, y), (x', y') \in D)\}$. The sign function can then be considered $+1$, -1, or 0 for equal labels affecting data set construction. We present the results here, assuming a separate label 0 for equal labels.

On this data set D', we can then measure accuracy. A slight inaccuracy might occur if either the data set or the predictions claim that a pair of data points is equal since the difficulties still do not align. For this reason, we will only consider the accuracy for pairs that agree or disagree without equality. To avoid confusion with previous experiments, we will refer to this metric as the agreement of the ranking predictions with the ranked labels or just agreement. We repeat both previous experiments using agreement. Models trained on a train set are evaluated on their respective test set (all pairs are drawn just from the test set), and models trained on all other data sets are evaluated on the one data set can be found in Table 3.

Table 3. Generalization is near perfect when considering StepMania difficulty prediction as a ranking problem. This table shows agreement of different models on all StepMania data sets averaged over 100 models trained on separate Monte Carlo cross-validation splits. Higher values are better. The largest value in each column is **bold**. According to a standard 5% significance t-test, all values in a column insignificantly lower than the best value are underlined.

(a) Trained and evaluated on the same data set.

		ITG	fraxtil	Gpop	Gulls	Speirmix
non OR	PATTERN	0.988±0.003	0.981±0.005	0.990±0.001	0.971±0.009	0.995±0.001
	Classification	**0.992±0.002**	0.991±0.003	0.994±0.002	0.996±0.003	0.995±0.002
	Regression	0.992±0.002	0.992±0.003	0.994±0.001	0.996±0.003	0.996±0.002
OR	NNRank	0.992±0.002	**0.992±0.003**	**0.994±0.001**	**0.997±0.002**	**0.996±0.002**
	RED-SVM	0.992±0.002	0.992±0.003	0.994±0.001	0.997±0.003	0.995±0.002
	Laplace	0.992±0.002	0.992±0.003	0.994±0.001	0.996±0.003	0.996±0.002
	Binomial	0.992±0.002	0.992±0.003	0.994±0.002	0.996±0.003	0.996±0.002

(b) Trained on separate data sets from the one being evaluated.

		ITG	fraxtil	Gpop	Gulls	Speirmix
non OR	PATTERN	0.980±0.006	0.985±0.009	0.978±0.008	0.990±0.005	0.992±0.005
	Classification	0.988±0.004	0.991±0.002	0.990±0.003	0.995±0.002	0.995±0.000
	Regression	0.989±0.002	0.992±0.001	0.992±0.001	0.995±0.001	0.996±0.000
OR	NNRank	**0.990±0.002**	0.993±0.001	0.992±0.001	0.995±0.002	**0.996±0.000**
	RED-SVM	0.989±0.002	0.993±0.001	0.992±0.001	**0.995±0.001**	0.996±0.000
	Laplace	0.989±0.004	0.993±0.001	0.991±0.002	0.995±0.002	0.996±0.000
	Binomial	0.988±0.004	0.993±0.001	0.991±0.002	0.995±0.002	0.996±0.000

5.4 Does ML Improve the Original Difficulties?

We expect the labels created by authors for StepMania levels to be noisy. With this motivation in mind, we evaluate whether the predictions of the models considered here improve upon the labels from the original authors using user feedback. Since StepMania players need context to rate levels, we decided to use the previously mentioned ranking approach to evaluate agreement.

Experimental Setup. We provide a participant with two songs and ask them which is more difficult. In essence, we ask the players to label a pair of StepMania levels (a, b) with a binary label (rank$(a) >$ rank(b)?).

We are left with a choice of which pairs to evaluate. Given the large number of possible pairs and the expected low number of user evaluations, we choose the pairs carefully. Specifically, we choose pairs for which different models or the original labels disagree.

Similarly to the previous experiment, while our model predictions might indicate that two StepMania levels have the same difficulty, players will always consider one level easier. As with the previous experiment, we disregard equal predictions entirely from the evaluation, i.e., the data set only includes pairs for which the predictions are not equal since players will always disagree with equality.

Table 4. Most models improve upon the original labels of each data set, except for ITG. This table shows the agreement with user evaluations on various data sets of models trained on other data sets.

		ITG	fraxtil	Gpop	Gulls	Speirmix
non OR	Original	**0.675**	0.470	0.257	0.607	0.388
	PATTERN	0.507	0.545	0.499	0.309	0.649
	Classification	0.322	0.659	**0.726**	**0.721**	0.746
	Regression	0.435	0.675	0.718	0.682	0.736
OR	NNRank	0.384	0.664	0.716	0.701	0.734
	RED-SVM	0.446	**0.678**	0.712	0.680	0.744
	Laplace	0.418	0.669	0.713	0.702	**0.747**
	Binomial	0.409	0.667	0.711	0.692	0.743 .

Conducting this experiment, we collected 217 human labels containing 105 unique pairs. Most pairs were evaluated more than once, and different players sometimes disagreed on what order they should have. We assigned each ordered pair a correctness value between 0 and 1, corresponding to the average support for this ordering. This correctness is reflected in the agreement. Table 4 shows models evaluated on a separate data set from the one they were trained on. The results evaluating a model trained and evaluated on the same data set can be found in the supplement.

6 Discussion and Conclusion

According to Table 2a, all OR methods, as well as just a basic classification approach, perform very well. However, no one method can be determined to be the best. In contrast to the varied results among the OR methods and classification, a basic regression approach and the PATTERN method from [5] perform poorly. The PATTERN method performs subpar in all experiments, likely because it is limited to only a couple of static features extracted from the level sequences. Regression performs close to the better methods, even though it is significantly outperformed in most experiments. We do not know why classification generally performs well, whereas regression does not.

Viewing StepMania data as a ranking task instead of an OR task demonstrates a near-perfect generalization as shown in Table 3. Comparing Tables 2a to 2b, however, highlights that these methods do not generalize from one data set to another when viewed naively. From this, we can follow that the poorer performance in Table 2b is due to labeling inconsistencies among authors of these packs. Figure 2 exemplifies this by demonstrating an offset of up to one between the difficulty scales of the Speirmix and Gulls data sets.

Finally, considering Table 4, we demonstrate that all OR models can unify different StepMania packs into one difficulty ranking. Except for ITG, all methods improve upon the original authors labeling. The better performance of the original labels for ITG is likely due to the ITG packs originating from a professional game studio instead of private individuals. We found that most errors made as part of Table 4 are because the model is oblivious to some StepMania-level features. The models investigated herein are limited by the feature extraction performed on the SM files. Some rare design elements were entirely ignored. Specifically, we ignored (1) mines, which require the player to step off of a direction not to trigger it, (2) tempo changes, which change the tempo during play, (3) warps, which skip ahead in a level, (4) stops, which stop the progress of the song for a predetermined time, and many more. These effects do affect the difficulty of StepMania levels. However, due to their rarity, they can lead to overfitting during training. Additionally, higher difficulties might also be caused by salient events in the music, which were not considered herein, being hard to detect, or by a level's steps being aligned not with the lead beat but with some salient events in the background.

Using all available StepMania data simultaneously during training is a significant challenge due to the labels not aligning, which is left as future work. The OR models considered here are not created equal, considering their practical use. RED-SVM specifically learns a regressor, which can be used to rank even where other methods consider a pair equal. This, in addition to its generally good performance, is why we suggest using RED-SVM to construct a unifying difficulty estimator for StepMania. Assuming RED-SVM is trained in a multi-task fashion on a large set of StepMania packs, each sharing a regressor but with separate thresholds, the final regressor can produce difficulty estimates on any of the trained scales. Additionally, scales can be hand-designed using standard StepMania levels as a reference. Considering that most levels are for mid-level play, a finer scale could split these mid-difficulty levels.

Based on our experiments, we conclude that StepMania-level difficulties are noisy and that ML models can help remove this noise and define a standard difficulty scale. Given its complexity, we also conclude that StepMania data should provide an excellent future test bed for deep OR models.

Acknowledgements. The authors acknowledge support by the Carl-Zeiss Foundation, the DFG awards KL 2698/2-1, KL 2698/5-1, BU 4042/2-1 and BU 4042/1-1, and the BMBF awards 01|S20048, 01|S18051A, 03|B0770E, and 01|S21010C.

Ethical Implications. This work focuses on applications in the entertainment industry. Specifically, the focus is improving the entertainment achieved when playing StepMania, a video game involving physical and mental exertion. The prediction of difficulty is closely related to reducing the churn in games, that is, the rate at which players stop playing a game for various reasons. While not the focus of this work, this does mean there is a chance that this work can be used to make rhythm-based video games more addictive.

Beyond the user experiment performed in Table 4, this work does not involve the use of personal data. For Table 4, we merely collected for pairs of songs played by a particular player which of the two was more difficult. This data is entirely anonymous, and for each rated pair, it is no longer possible to determine which player was the participant rating the pair.

References

1. Agarwal, A., Davis, J.T., Ward, T.: Supporting ordinal four-state classification decisions using neural networks. Inf. Technol. Manage. **2**(1), 5–26 (2001)
2. Armstrong, B.G., Sloan, M.: Ordinal regression models for epidemiologic data. Am. J. Epidemiol. **129**(1), 191–204 (1989)
3. Brown, T., et al.: Language models are few-shot learners. Adv. Neural. Inf. Process. Syst. **33**, 1877–1901 (2020)
4. Bürkner, P.C., Vuorre, M.: Ordinal regression models in psychology: a tutorial. Adv. Methods Pract. Psychol. Sci. **2**(1), 77–101 (2019)
5. Caronongan, A.P., Marcos, N.A.: Predicting chart difficulty in rhythm games through classification using chart pattern derived attributes. In: Alfred, R., Iida, H., Haviluddin, H., Anthony, P. (eds.) Computational Science and Technology. LNEE, vol. 724, pp. 193–205. Springer, Singapore (2021). https://doi.org/10.1007/978-981-33-4069-5_17
6. Cheng, J., Wang, Z., Pollastri, G.: A neural network approach to ordinal regression. In: 2008 IEEE International Joint Conference on Neural Networks (IEEE World Congress on Computational Intelligence), pp. 1279–1284. IEEE (2008)
7. Chiu, S.C., Chen, M.S.: A study on difficulty level recognition of piano sheet music. In: 2012 IEEE International Symposium on Multimedia, pp. 17–23. IEEE (2012)
8. Diaz, R., Marathe, A.: Soft labels for ordinal regression. In: Proceedings of the IEEE/CVF Conference on Computer Vision and Pattern Recognition, pp. 4738–4747 (2019)
9. Donahue, C., Lipton, Z.C., McAuley, J.: Dance dance convolution. In: International Conference on Machine Learning, pp. 1039–1048. PMLR (2017)
10. Fu, H., Gong, M., Wang, C., Batmanghelich, K., Tao, D.: Deep ordinal regression network for monocular depth estimation. In: Proceedings of the IEEE Conference on Computer Vision and Pattern Recognition, pp. 2002–2011 (2018)
11. Ghatas, Y., Fayek, M., Hadhoud, M.: A hybrid deep learning approach for musical difficulty estimation of piano symbolic music. Alex. Eng. J. **61**(12), 10183–10196 (2022)
12. Gutiérrez, P.A., Perez-Ortiz, M., Sanchez-Monedero, J., Fernandez-Navarro, F., Hervas-Martinez, C.: Ordinal regression methods: survey and experimental study. IEEE Trans. Knowl. Data Eng. **28**(1), 127–146 (2015)
13. Halina, E., Guzdial, M.: Taikonation: Patterning-focused chart generation for rhythm action games. In: The 16th International Conference on the Foundations of Digital Games (FDG) 2021, pp. 1–10 (2021)
14. Hooshyar, D., Yousefi, M., Lim, H.: Data-driven approaches to game player modeling: a systematic literature review. ACM Comput. Surv. (CSUR) **50**(6), 1–19 (2018)
15. Jian, H., van den Brink, H.M., Groot, W.: College Education and Social trust, Ph.D. thesis, Maastricht University (1727)
16. Lin, H.T., Li, L.: Reduction from cost-sensitive ordinal ranking to weighted binary classification. Neural Comput. **24**(5), 1329–1367 (2012)
17. Loshchilov, I., Hutter, F.: Decoupled weight decay regularization. In: International Conference on Learning Representations (2019)
18. Missura, O., Gärtner, T.: Player modeling for intelligent difficulty adjustment. In: Gama, J., Costa, V.S., Jorge, A.M., Brazdil, P.B. (eds.) DS 2009. LNCS (LNAI), vol. 5808, pp. 197–211. Springer, Heidelberg (2009). https://doi.org/10.1007/978-3-642-04747-3_17

19. Niu, Z., Zhou, M., Wang, L., Gao, X., Hua, G.: Ordinal regression with multiple output CNN for age estimation. In: Proceedings of the IEEE Conference on Computer Vision and Pattern Recognition, pp. 4920–4928 (2016)
20. Roohi, S., Relas, A., Takatalo, J., Heiskanen, H., Hämäläinen, P.: Predicting game difficulty and churn without players. In: Proceedings of the Annual Symposium on Computer-Human Interaction in Play, pp. 585–593 (2020)
21. Saad, S.E., Yang, J.: Twitter sentiment analysis based on ordinal regression. IEEE Access 7, 163677–163685 (2019)
22. Sébastien, V., Ralambondrainy, H., Sébastien, O., Conruyt, N.: Score analyzer: automatically determining scores difficulty level for instrumental e-learning. In: 13th International Society for Music Information Retrieval Conference (ISMIR 2012), pp. 571–576 (2012)
23. Tsujino, Y., Yamanishi, R.: Dance dance gradation: a generation of fine-tuned dance charts. In: Clua, E., Roque, L., Lugmayr, A., Tuomi, P. (eds.) ICEC 2018. LNCS, vol. 11112, pp. 175–187. Springer, Cham (2018). https://doi.org/10.1007/978-3-319-99426-0_15
24. Tsujino, Y., Yamanishi, R., Yamashita, Y.: Characteristics study of dance-charts on rhythm-based video games. In: 2019 IEEE Conference on Games (CoG), pp. 1–4. IEEE (2019)
25. Tutz, G.: Ordinal regression: a review and a taxonomy of models. Wiley Interdisc. Rev. Comput. Stat. 14(2), e1545 (2022)
26. Vaswani, A., et al.: Attention is all you need. In: Advances in Neural Information Processing Systems, vol. 30 (2017)
27. Yannakakis, G.N., Spronck, P., Loiacono, D., André, E.: Player Modeling. In: Lucas, S.M., Mateas, M., Preuss, M., Spronck, P., Togelius, J. (eds.) Artificial and Computational Intelligence in Games, Dagstuhl Follow-Ups, vol. 6, pp. 45–59. Schloss Dagstuhl-Leibniz-Zentrum fuer Informatik, Dagstuhl, Germany (2013). https://doi.org/10.4230/DFU.Vol6.12191.45

Double Machine Learning at Scale to Predict Causal Impact of Customer Actions

Sushant More$^{(\boxtimes)}$ [ID], Priya Kotwal [ID], Sujith Chappidi [ID], Dinesh Mandalapu [ID], and Chris Khawand [ID]

Amazon, Seattle, WA, USA
{morsusha,kotwalp,jcchappi,mandalap,khawandc}@amazon.com

Abstract. Causal Impact (CI) measurement is broadly used across the industry to inform both short- and long-term investment decisions of various types. In this paper, we apply the double machine learning (DML) methodology to estimate average and conditional average treatment effects across 100s of customer action types for ecommerce and digital businesses and 100s of millions of customers that can be used in decisions supporting those busiensses. We operationalize DML through a causal machine learning library. It uses distributed computation on Spark and is configured via a flexible, JSON-driven model configuration approach to estimate causal impacts at scale (i.e., across hundred of actions and millions of customers). We outline the DML methodology and implementation. We show examples of average treatment effect and conditional average treatment effect (i.e., customer-level) estimates values along with confidence intervals. Our validation metrics show a 2.2% gain over the baseline methods and a $2.5X$ gain in the computational time. Our contribution is to advance the scalable application of CI, while also providing an interface that allows faster experimentation, ability to onboard new use cases, and improved accessibility of underlying code for partner teams.

Keywords: Double Machine Learning · Potential Outcomes · Heterogeneous treatment effect · Invserse propenity weighting · Placebo tests

1 Introduction

Causal Impact (CI) is a measure of the incremental change in a customer's outcomes (usually spend or profit) from a customer event or action (e.g, signing up for a paid membership). Business leaders commonly use some version of CI values as important signals for driving various decisions, such as marketing content ranking or capital investments.

The CI values are leveraged by partner teams to understand and improve the value they generate through customer behaviors. Some examples include customer actions such as 'first purchase in category X', 'first stream in service Y',

© The Author(s), under exclusive license to Springer Nature Switzerland AG 2023
G. De Francisci Morales et al. (Eds.): ECML PKDD 2023, LNAI 14174, pp. 513–528, 2023.
https://doi.org/10.1007/978-3-031-43427-3_31

or 'sign up for program Z'[1]. For many of these customer actions, we are unable to conduct A/B experiments due to practical or legal constraints. We instead use observational data, effectively leveraging rich customer data to isolate causal relationships in the absence of a randomized experiment.

In this paper, we provide results for average treatment effects and conditional average treatment effects (i.e., customer-level CI values) estimated using a variant on the Double Machine Learning (DML) methodology [1]. The paper is arranged as follows. In Sect. 2, we give a brief overview of the use of causal measurement. In Sect. 2.1, we introduce an example of a conventional regression-and-propensity-adjustment system used for calculating CI values. We discuss the shortcomings of the traditional method and the advantages of moving to DML.

Section 3 covers the details of our DML implementation for calculating CI values. Our contributions include improving the robustness of CI estimates through inverse propensity weighting, adding the ability to produce heterogeneous CI values, implementing customer-level confidence intervals with various assumptions, and making available the JSON Machine Learning interface to accelerate experimentation. We present results in Sect. 4 for a few customer actions and conclude with the takeaways and ideas for future work in Sect. 6.

2 Causal Impact Estimation in Industry

Causal impact estimation drives a large number of business decisions across industry. This includes multiple organizations such as retail, search, devices, streaming services, and operations. To this end, most companies have invested in developing and deploying models that vend CI values for the cutsomer actions under consideration. In the next section, we give an overview of the traditional potential-outcome based model which is widely used in the industry for CI estimation. This will be the baseline model.

2.1 CI: P-Score Binning and Regression Adjustment Framework

CI framework applies the principles of observational causal inference. We rely on it because A/B testing is not possible to evaluate the impact of certain treatments due to practical constraints (e.g., the treatment is not effectively assignable, or would be too expensive to assign at scale). Observational causal inference methods rely on eliminating potential confounders through adjustment on observed variables. Under a "selection on observables" assumption, we believe we can estimate the causal effect correctly on average. Applied to the customer's next 365 days of spending, for example, the CI value represents the incremental spending that a customer makes because of participating in a certain action compared to the counterfactual case where they didn't take that particular action. The formal framework for this kind of counterfactual reasoning is the "potential outcomes" framework, sometimes known as the Neyman-Rubin causal framework [3–5].

---

[1] We use placeholder X,Y,Z to maintain business confidentiality.

There are many procedures aimed at estimating potential outcomes. One example estimator is a combination of propensity score stratification and regression adjustment:

1. Propensity binning. Group the customer based on their propensity to participate in the action. This is done based on features that relate to recency, frequency, and the monetary behavior of customers along with their other characteristics such as their tenure type.
2. Regression adjustment. In each of the groups, we build a regression model on the control customers with customer-spend as the target. The trained model is applied on the treatment customers to predict the counterfactual spend (how much would customer have spent if they didn't participate in the action). The difference between the predicted counterfactual and the actual spend is the CI value. We take a weighted average across different groups to get the final CI value for the customer action.

In addition, we require the CI model to be able to scale to the business use case. For instance, we may want generate CI values for hundreds of customer actions in an automated way. In the rest of the paper, we refer to this estimation procedure as "CI-PB" (short for "propensity binning") and the DML-based estimator as "CI-DML".

3   CI: DML Framework

Note that one of the challenges in validating the causal estimates is posed by the *Fundamental Problem of Causal Inference* [2]. The lack of observable ground truth makes it difficult to validate the output of a causal model, but well-constructed procedures can at least provide some guarantees of causally interpretable estimates under certain assumptions. The Double/Debiased Machine learning (DML) method proposed by Chernozhukov et al. [1] leverages the predictive power of modern Machine Learning (ML) methods in a principled causal estimation framework that is free of regularization bias asymptotically.

For treatment D, features X, we express the outcome Y as an additively separable function of D and arbitrary function of features X:

$$Y = D\beta + g(X) + \epsilon \tag{1}$$

DML's estimation strategy is motivated by writing out the residualized representation of Eq. (1) and its parts:

$$\tilde{Y} = Y - E(Y|X) \tag{2}$$
$$\tilde{D} = D - E(D|X) \tag{3}$$
$$\tilde{Y} = \tilde{D}\beta + \tilde{\epsilon} \tag{4}$$

We use ML models to estimate $E(Y|X)$ and $E(D|X)$. The residuals from outcome equation (Eq. (3)) are regressed on residuals from propensity equation

(Eq. (4)) to obtain the causal parameter β. We use ML models to predict $E(Y|X)$ and $E(D|X)$. We leverage K-fold sample splitting so that training and scoring of the ML models happens on different folds. We use a 3-fold sample split and follow the "DML2" approach [1] where we pool the residuals outcome and propensity residuals across all the folds to fit a single, final regression of the residualized outcome on the residualized treatment (Eq. (4)).

3.1   Inverse Propensity Treatment Weighting

We use a weighted ordinary least squares to solve the residual regression equation (Eq. (4)). Where the weights are determined by the Inverse Propensity Treatment Weighting (IPTW or IPW) [12]. Our IPTW weights correspond to the Horvitz-Thompson (HT) weight [13], in which the weight for each unit is the inverse of the probability of that unit being assigned to the observed group. In Table 1 we define the weights that balance the distributions of covariates between comparison groups for two widely used estimands, the Average Treatment Effect (ATE) and Average Treatment Effect on the Treated (ATT). Weighting helps achieve additional robustness, bringing us closer to a conventional Doubly Robust estimator. Applying these weights when conducting statistical tests or regression models helps reduce impact of confounders over and above what we get from the regression adjustment [14]. Secondly, the weights allow us to target the estimand; we prefer the ATT since it represents the treatment effects for those customers actually treated historically who are marginally closer to those who will be treated next. We refer to the customer-level counterparts of ATE, ATT estimands as HTE and HTT respectively.

Table 1. IPW weights for different estimands. D is the treatment assignment and $\hat{e}(X)$ is the treatment propensity, $E(D|X)$.

Estimand	IPW weight
Average treatment effect (ATE)	$\dfrac{D}{\hat{e}(X)} + \dfrac{1-D}{1-\hat{e}(X)}$
Average treatment effect on the treated (ATT)	$D + (1-D)\dfrac{\hat{e}(X)}{1-\hat{e}(X)}$

3.2   Common Support and Propensity Score Trimming

For many treatments, propensity distribution has significant mass near 1 for the treated group and near 0 for the control group (see an example histogram in Fig. 1). Scores near the boundary can create instability in weighting methods. In addition, these scores often represent units for whom we cannot make an adequate treatment-control comparison. We limit analysis to the common support region, where propensity score distributions overlap between treated and untreated samples.

We also use trimming to exclude customers whose estimated propensity is outside of the range $[\alpha, 1 - \alpha]$. We experimented with different thresholds on

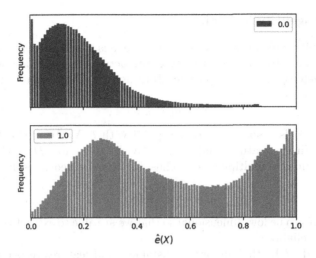

Fig. 1. Representiative propensity scores distribution for control (top panel) and treatment (bottom panel) groups.

various customer actions and observed that $\alpha = 0.001$ with rescaled propensity scores works the best.

Normalizing and Rescaling Weights. When using the IPW, we normalize the weights by rescaling the propensity scores for each customer i as in Eq. (5).

$$\hat{e}(X_i)_{\text{scaled}} = \left(\frac{\overline{D}}{\overline{\hat{e}(X)}} \right) * \hat{e}(X_i) \tag{5}$$

$\overline{D}$ and $\overline{\hat{e}(X)}$ in Eq. (5) are the averages of treatment assignment and propensity score respectively taken over both the treatment and control population combined. Propensity trimming and rescaling reduces variance, leads to more stable estimates, and tighter confidence intervals as seen in Fig. 2.

trimming boundary	CI-PO ATT	CI-DML ATT	CI-DML confidence interval	outcome model: R-squared	propensity model: ROC-AUC
(0.001, 0.999)	230.29	239.93	(224.47, 255.39)	0.52	0.79
(0.005, 0.995)	230.29	236.64	(222.31, 250.96)	0.52	0.79
no trimming and rescaling	230.29	844.13	(-243.58, 1931.84)	0.52	0.79

Fig. 2. Effect of propensity scores trimming and rescaling on estimated CI for a certain customer action.

3.3   Heterogeneity in DML

CI-DML implements a version of the heterogenous effects modeling proposed in [6], by leveraging the treatment-feature interactions in the final stage of DML to identify heterogenous (customer-level) responses. The general form of Eq. (4) can be written as

$$\tilde{Y} = h(X, \tilde{D}) + \tilde{\epsilon} \,. \tag{6}$$

In fact, Eq. (4) is a special case of Eq. (6) with $h(X, \tilde{D}) = \tilde{D}\beta$. We interact treatment with the features and define $h(X, \tilde{D}) \equiv \psi(X) * \tilde{D}\beta$, where '$*$' represents element-wise multiplication. Thus, the heterogeneous residual regression becomes:

$$\tilde{Y} = \psi(X) * \tilde{D}\beta + \tilde{\epsilon} \tag{7}$$

We want $\psi(X)$ to be low-dimensional so that we are able to extract the coefficient β in Eq. (7) reliably.

Let N and M be the number of customers and features respectively. If the dimension of $\psi(X)$ is $N \times K$, we want $K \ll M$. In our use case, M is typically 2000 and K is typically around 20. To get the low-dimensional representation, $\psi(X)$ we proceed as follows:

1. We project the original features onto an orthogonal space through Principal Component Analysis (PCA).
2. We run a K-means clustering algorithm on the highest-signal Principal Components. Dimension reduction from PCA helps to reduce dimensionality-related problems when computing Euclidean distance for K-means clustering.
3. We calculate the K cluster scores for each customer, as $\psi_{i,c} = \dfrac{1/d_{i,c}}{\sum_{k=1}^{K} 1/d_{i,k}}$

    where $d_{i,c}$ is the distance of customer i's value from centroid of cluster c (see schematic in Fig. 3).

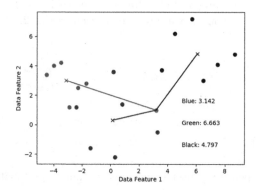

Fig. 3. Schematic for calculation of distance from cluster centroids. The red dot is represented by three features which is the distance from centroids from blue, green, and black clusters. (Color figure online)

Once we have calculated the distance features $\psi(X)$ for each customer, we interact them with the propensity residuals and fit a linear regression model using IPW (refer Sect. 3.1) to extract the coefficients β in Eq. (7). The heterogenous estimates are given by

$$h = \psi(X)\beta \,. \tag{8}$$

E.g., for $K = 3$, $h = \psi_1\beta_1 + \psi_2\beta_2 + \psi_3\beta_3$.

A schematic of CI-DML workflow is shown in Fig. 4.

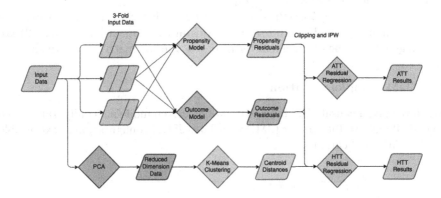

Fig. 4. Schematic of the CI-DML modeling framework.

3.4 Confidence Intervals in DML

One of the disadvantages of CI-PB is that generating confidence intervals requires bootstrapping around the multi-step process and is computationally expensive. Obtaining confidence intervals in CI-DML is straightforward. For a single ATT parameter estimate, we obtain the confidence interval simply by calculating the variance of the estimate of β in Eq. (4). We also estimate Huber-White heteroscedasticity consistent standard errors [7,8]. For the ATT case, the steps for calculating variance of the coefficient $\hat{\beta}$ are as follows:

$$Var(\beta) = H\hat{\Sigma}H'. \tag{9}$$

For a customer, 'p':

$$\hat{\sigma}_p^2 = \hat{U}_p^2 = (\tilde{Y}_p - \tilde{D}_p\hat{\beta})'(\tilde{Y}_p - \tilde{D}_p\hat{\beta}) \,, \tag{10}$$

where $\hat{\beta}$ is the value of coefficient from solving Eq. (4). Note that $\tilde{Y}_p$ and $\tilde{D}_p$ are scalars. Σ in Eq. (9) is a diagonal matrix with the squared prediction error $\hat{\sigma}_p^2$ for each customer on its diagonal and H in Eq. (9) is defined as

$$H = (\tilde{D}' * W\tilde{D})^{-1}\tilde{D}' * W \tag{11}$$

where W are the IPW weights as defined in Sect. 3.1.

We compute the confidence intervals on the causal estimate β using $Var(\beta)$.

Customer-Level Confidence Intervals. CI-DML also provides the ability to obtain customer-level confidence intervals. From Eq. (8), we can write

$$Var(h) = Var(\psi\beta) = \sum_k \psi_k^2 Var(\beta_k) + \sum_{k \neq l} \psi_k \psi_l Cov(\beta_k, \beta_l). \qquad (12)$$

We calculate variance of the heterogeneous coefficients following similar approach as in Eqs. 9, 10 and 11. The only difference is we replace $\tilde{D}_p \to \psi(X_p) * \tilde{D}_p$ in Eq. (10) and $\tilde{D} \to \psi(X) * \tilde{D}$ in Eq. (11).

For the ATT case, $Var(\beta)$ is a scalar whereas for the HTT case, $Var(\beta)$ is a $K \times K$ matrix. The first and second terms in the summation in Eq. (12) are the diagonal and the off-diagonal terms of the $Var(\beta)$ matrix respectively.

3.5 DML Implementation

We developed a causal ML library with JSON driven modeling configuration (see Fig. 5). JSON ML Interpreter (JMI) translates JSON configuration to executable Python ML application.

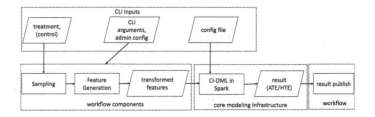

Fig. 5. JSON-Machine Learning Stage Interpreter modeling stages

The main advantages of JMI approach are:

Flexibility: Business questions from various domains cannot always be addressed through a single unified configuration of a causal model. We address this in our system where users can invoke different causal analysis frameworks (DML, Causal Forests) and prediction algorithm type (regression, classification, clustering).

Scalability: CI-DML utilizes distributed implementation of algorithms and file system via Apache Spark which helps causal modeling at the big-data scale (100 millions customers, multiple targets, and time horizons)

Persistence: CI-DML inherits SparkML serialization and deserialization methods to persist and instantiate fitted models for live or batch inference.

Compatibility: In addition to Spark, interfaces to adapt ML libraries from scikit-learn, tensorflow, and MXNet, and other communities can be onboarded using the configurable abstraction support by JMI.

In the system, we dockerize the JMI Causal ML library which is platform agnostic and has the flexibility to extend and utilize different compute engines like AWS EMR, Sagemaker or AWS Batch based on the use case and will abstract the computation information from the user. Dockerization also helps version control and the build environment via standard software development tooling.

4 Results

Next we present the results for CI-DML. The target variable we focus on is customer spending, but our framework on can be leveraged to obtain the causal impact on any other target variable of interest (e.g., net profit, units bought etc.). For every CI run, we produce both the population-level ATT values (Eq. (4)) and the customer-level HTT (Eq. (8)) values.

We compared the CI-PB and CI-DML results for 100+ customer actions. As noted earlier, two major advantages of CI-DML are the availability of customer grain results (aka. HTT) and confidence intervals. In Fig. 6, we present population-level (ATT) and customer-level values for selected representative customer actions[2]. The reported confidence intervals are for both homoscedastic and heteroscedastic error variances. To get a sense of the level of variance in customer-grain results, we report the percentage of customers where the customer-level confidence interval crosses zero. We also report the out-of-sample fit metrics for outcome and propensity models in DML.

Action	CI-PO (ATT)	CI-DML (ATT)	CI-DML (HTT mean)	CI-DML confidence interval (homoscedastic)	CI-DML confidence interval (heteroscedastic)	%customer-level conf. intervals crossing zero (heteroscedastic)	R-squared (outcome model)	ROC-AUC (propensity model)
Action 1	230.3	235.0	229.1	(233.9, 243.5)	(220.1, 249.9)	0.001	0.523	0.790
Action 2	186.5	197.3	181.2	(192.2, 200.0)	(178.0, 216.6)	1.99	0.499	0.818
Action 3	116.3	108.9	103.8	(92.5, 101.9)	(87.2, 130.6)	16.37	0.472	0.943
Action 4	180.6	186.5	229.8	(185.3, 195.9)	(161.9, 211.1)	5.96	0.153	0.957
Action 5	125.7	117.0	160.9	(173.4, 180.7)	(154.2, 218.3)	36.70	0.663	0.869
Action 6	12.3	21.0	21.1	(16.4, 24.4)	(9.0, 33.0)	76.95	0.748	0.885
Action 7	7.6	19.1	6.4	(14.1, 24.2)	(-1.7, 36.4)	83.17	0.738	0.913
Action 8	146.8	138.7	137.9	(129.8, 147.6)	(109.1, 160.8)	20.88	0.674	0.946
Action 9	89.3	86.5	101.1	(82.9, 93.1)	(61.0, 112.1)	45.63	0.726	0.903
Action 10	383.7	298.9	291.3	(295.5, 306.4)	(285.1, 312.6)	0.14	0.671	0.854

Fig. 6. CI values and confidence intervals for selected customer actions.

Our takeaways from the analysis of 100+ actions are:

1. Population-level CI-PB and CI-DML values are aligned for 86% of actions.

---

[2] We anonymize actions to preserve business confidentiality.

2. When the customer-level CI values are aggregated up, they are generally aligned with the population-level CI-DML values.
3. The difference between the CI-PB and CI-DML values are larger either when the data is noisy and/or we have a small sample size. For such cases, we also see large confidence intervals and the mean of HTT values is farther away from the CI-DML ATT values.
4. The homoscedastic confidence intervals are tighter than the heteroscedastic confidence interval as expected. However, the homoscedastic confidence intervals likely under-predict the variance. We recommend business stakeholders to use the heteroscedasticity-robust confidence intervals.
5. The customer-level confidence intervals are economically reasonable. The percentage of customer-level confidence interval crossing zero increases for data with lower participation and is small for customer actions with a long history.
6. The ML model metrics shown in Fig. 6 are using ridge regression for the outcome model and logistic regression for the propensity model. We noticed that the model metrics as well as the CI values are relatively insensitive to the choice of ML model at the outcome/propensity stage. Accordingly, we leverage ridge and logistic models due to their favorable compute time.

4.1   Hyperparameter Tuning

The hyperparameters (e.g., regularization strength) in the outcome and propensity model are chosen based on the out-of-sample performance. For the HTT estimates, the two main hyperparameters are the number of principal components and the number of clusters.

We choose the number of principal components (PC) based on the percentage of variance explained. We find that around 300 PC, about 80% of the variance is explained (Fig. 7). The amount of variance explained grows much slowly as we add more number of PC. To avoid sparsity issues in the downstream K-means calculation, we choose the number of PC components to be 300.

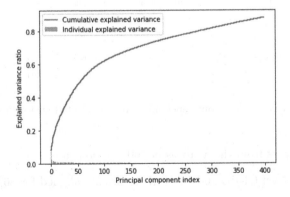

Fig. 7. Amount of variance explained as a function of principal components.

Choosing the number of clusters is less straightforward. Standard tools such as elbow method and Silhouette score do not yield a clear answer for the optimal cluster choice. In the current work, we choose 20 clusters, since we do not see much change in any form of out of sample fit statistics beyond 20. We also find that the mean of HTT values is robust with respect to the choice for number of clusters. In future work, we aim to make this choice in a more data-driven way (e.g., by evaluating how output scores perform in a downstream use case measured through A/B tests), since there may be important variation in the quality of output for decisions that is not picked up by conventional fit statistics.

4.2   Spread of Customer-Level CI Values

So far, we have only looked at the mean of customer-level values in Fig. 6. In Fig. 8, we look at the customer-level CI scores for an example customer action. We see that most of the customers have CI value close to the average HTT value. We see that there are few customers with a low CI value which shifts the mean to the left.

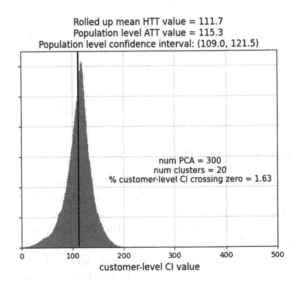

Fig. 8. Spread of customer-level CI values. The red line is the mean of customer-level CI values. (Color figure online)

5   Validation

5.1   Placebo Tests

Placebo tests help us understand the relative ability of competing causal estimates to account for selection bias. Selection bias occurs when customers who take an action (e.g., stream video) have unobserved characteristics not included in the model that makes them systematically more or less likely to take the action (e.g., high income, low age etc.). In placebo tests, we take the treatment group customers and simulate as though they took the action a year before the actual date. This is achieved by shifting the event date by one year and recalculating the features based on the shifted event date. The CI estimated in this set up is the "placebo error". Since, this is a fake event, a model with a lower placebo error than another on the same underlying data suggests that it has smaller contribution from selection bias in its estimate. Running placebo tests on all events is computationally expensive, so we selected a few events for placebo analysis. The results are shown in Fig. 9.

Customer Action	Placebo CI-PO	Placebo CI-DML	% Improvement
Action A	191.1	190.7	0.22
Action B	327.6	320.9	2.05
Action C	100.2	98.8	1.40
Action D	204.2	192.7	5.67
Action E	23.7	21.9	7.56
Action F	315.7	390.8	1.86
Action G	143.5	137.3	4.29
Action H	615.5	602.8	2.07
Action I	272.5	269.9	0.94

Fig. 9. Placebo results for selected customer actions for CI-PB and CI-DML model.

The key takeaways from Fig. 9 are:

- Selection bias is inherently event-dependent. When averaged across the selected customer actions, we see a 2.24% improvement in placebo estimates when going from CI-PB to CI-DML.
- Selection bias is primarily impacted by the modeling features. As CI-PB and CI-DML use the same features, we did not expect big improvements in placebo tests. The consistent improvement across the events shows that double machine learning methodology is better able to adjust for observables even when the same features are used.

5.2   Confidence Interval Comparison

One of the major wins in CI-DML is that we provide heteroskedasticity-consistent confidence intervals at both a customer and aggregate level for every CI analysis in a scalable and lower-cost fashion. We compare the uncertainty estimates (specifically the width of confidence intervals) from CI-DML with the bootstrap results in CI-PB for a few events in Fig. 10.

Action	CI-PO	confidence interval width CI-PO (bootstrap)	confidence interval width CI-DML (heterosckedastic)	% diff. in conf. interval over CI-PO point estimate
Action I	201.4	15.6	10.4	2.6
Action II	271.9	21.5	27.7	-2.3
Action III	123.7	8.2	11.5	-2.6
Action IV	80.0	39.3	20.2	23.9
Action V	340.5	41.6	56.6	-4.4
Action VI	180.4	7.0	7.7	-0.4
Action VII	221.6	11.4	10.5	0.4
Action VIII	209.2	10.8	8.2	1.3
Action IX	619.8	17.6	29.9	-2.0
Action X	268.0	12.6	10.3	0.8

Fig. 10. CI-PB bootstrap vs. CI-DML confidence interval width comparison

We find confidence interval width to be comparable among the two approaches. On average, the CI-DML width (scaled with CI-PB point estimate) is 1.5% smaller when compared to bootstrap-based confidence interval. A bootstrap-enabled CI-PB run takes about 2.5X more time than a CI-DML run. Bootstrap also does not scale for events with large number of customers. As CI-DML approach for confidence intervals is based on a closed form implementation, we do not have any scalability issues. In addition, note that bootstrapping has theoretical limitations when used for matching estimators [16].

6 Conclusion and Future Work

In this work, we introduced a state-of-the-art methodology used for calculating CI values. We noted that a DML based framework eliminates bias, allows us to extract heterogeneity in CI values, and provides a scalable way to construct heteroscedastic confidence intervals. We also made a case for using IPW and common support to refine the CI estimates. We demonstrated how leveraging PCA followed by K-means clustering allowed us to introduce customer-level heterogeneity. Using JSON based config allows flexibility to experiment with a wide variety algorithms and can take us from experimentation to production in minimal steps.

We presented results for few anonymized customer actions across different domains. Both the population-level and customer-level results for the customer actions we have looked at so far are aligned with the CI-PB results and our expectations, but we now can take advantage of convenient calculation of confidence intervals, estimates of heterogeneous treatment effects, and greater scalability.

Note that estimation of heterogeneous or context-aware treatment effects is an active area of research with wide applications ranging from marketing to health care. Distribution of treatment effects across different subgroups, or as a function of specific individual-level characteristics provides researchers with additional insights about the treatment/ intervention analyzed. Our work showcases a scalable real-world application for extracting average as well heterogeneous causal effects which we believe will be of interest to the broader scientific community.

6.1   Future Work

Validating the causal estimates is challenging due to lack of ground truth. In the current work, we relied on the model fit metrics in the DML steps, placebo tests, and on bridging the CI-DML and CI-PB outputs. In the future, we plan to include metrics which focus on the validation of heterogeneous treatment effects. Examples of these include metrics based on Generic Machine Learning [17] and empirically calibrated Monte Carlo resampling techniques [18].

Ethical Implication. The data presented in the paper is completely anonymized. It cannot be used for inference of personal information of any kind.

The method presented in this paper falls in the domain of observational causal inference. Observational causal inference methods are used to gauge impact of things already happened. The inference methods by itself do not aid in any wrong doing. But in the unfortunate case of bad things happening to an individual (e.g., unfair economic policy/ smoking/ abuse), the causal methods can help identify the impact and help guide the recovery methods. In that sense, work presented here can be used to seek justice for the victim.

Of course, as a society we want to make sure that we do not subject individuals to an unscrupulous treatment to extract the causal impact of that treatment. Because the impact of such treatment could be adverse in some cases. But again the work presented here is used to analyze the aftermath of an action/ treatment. The type of treatments a person can be subjected to is outside the scope of current work.

Appendix

A   Sample JSON Config

We show a snippet of JSON config in Fig. 11. We can swap the specified models in the outcome and propensity step with any ML model. Likewise we can easily configure pre/post-processing steps and hyperparameters through JSON files.

```json
{
    "macros": {
        "FEATURE_COLS":                {"regex": "^pre_.+$"},
        "STANDARDIZED_FEATURE_COLS":   {"regex": "^standardized_pre_.+$"},
        "OUTCOME_COLS":                {"regex": "^post_.+$"},
        "TREATMENT_COLS":              {"regex": "^treatment_.+$"}
    },

    "stages": [
        "standardizer", "propensity_model", "propensity_metrics", "outcome_model",
        "outcome_metrics", "residualer"
        ],

    "standardizer": {
        "module": "sklearn.preprocessing.StandardScaler",
        "with_mean": true, "with_std": true, "inference": "transform",
        "featureCols":    "FEATURE_COLS",
        "predictionCols": {"reference": "featureCols", "format": "standardized_%s"}
    },

    "propensity_model": {
        "module": "sklearn.linear_model.LogisticRegression",
        "fit_intercept": true, "solver": "sag", "n_jobs": -1, "inference": "probability",
        "featureCols": "STANDARDIZED_FEATURE_COLS", "targetCols": "TREATMENT_COLS",
        "predictionCols": {"reference": "targetCols", "format": "propensity_%s"}
    },

    "propensity_metrics": {"include": "configuration/metrics/propensity_sklearn.json"},

    "outcome_model": {
        "module": "sklearn.linear_model.Ridge",
        "alpha": 0.01, "fit_intercept": true, "normalize": false, "solver": "cholesky",
        "featureCols": "STANDARDIZED_FEATURE_COLS", "targetCols": "OUTCOME_COLS",
        "predictionCols": {"reference": "targetCols", "format": "prediction_%s"}
    },

    "outcome_metrics": {"include": "configuration/metrics/outcome_sklearn.json"},

    "residualer": {
        "module": "transformers.BinaryOperatorPandas", "operator": "-",
        "leftOperandCols": ["OUTCOME_COLS", "TREATMENT_COLS"],
        "rightOperandCols": [{"regex": "^prediction_.+$"}, {"regex": "^propensity_.+$"}],
        "resultCols":    {"reference": "leftOperandCols", "format": "residual_%s"}
    }
}
```

Fig. 11. A sample JSON config where we are using Ridge regression for the outcome model and the logistic regression for the propensity model.

References

1. Chernozhukov, V., et al.: Double/debiased machine learning for treatment and structural parameters. Economet. J. **21**(1), C1–C68 (2018). https://doi.org/10.1111/ectj.12097
2. Sekhon, J.: The Neyman-Rubin Model of Causal Inference and Estimation via Matching Methods. The Oxford Handbook of Political Methodology (2007)

3. Holland, P.W.: Statistics and causal inference. J. Am. Stat. Assoc. **81**(396), 945–960 (1986). https://doi.org/10.1080/01621459.1986.10478354

4. Neyman, J.: Sur les applications de la theorie des probabilites aux experiences agricoles: essai des principes. Master's thesis, excerpts reprinted in English. Stat. Sci. **5**, 463–472 (1923)

5. Rubin, D.: Causal inference using potential outcomes. J. Am. Stat. Assoc. **81**(396), 945–960 (2005). https://doi.org/10.1080/01621459.1986.10478354

6. Chernozhukov, V., Goldman, M., Semenova, V., Taddy, M.: Orthogonal Machine Learning for Demand Estimation: High Dimensional Causal Inference in Dynamic Panels. ArXiv:1712.09988 [Stat] (2017)

7. Huber, P.J.: The behavior of maximum likelihood estimates under nonstandard conditions. In: Proceedings of the Fifth Berkeley Symposium on Mathematical Statistics and Probability, vol. 5, pp. 221–233 (1967)

8. White, H.: A heteroskedasticity-consistent covariance matrix estimator and a direct test for heteroskedasticity. Econometrica **48**(4), 817–838 (1980)

9. Horvitz, D.G., Thompson, D.J.: A generalization of sampling without replacement from a Finite Universe. J. Am. Stat. Assoc. **47**(260), 663–685 (1952)

10. Nie, X., Wager, S.: Quasi-oracle estimation of heterogeneous treatment effects. ArXiv:1712.04912 [Econ, Math, Stat] (2017)

11. Kennedy, E.H.: Optimal doubly robust estimation of heterogeneous causal effects. ArXiv:2004.14497 [math.ST] (2020)

12. Robins, J.M., Mark, S.D.: Estimating exposure effects by modelling the expectation of exposure conditional on confounders. Biometrics **48**, 479–495 (1992). MR1173493

13. Ruth, C., et al.: Long-Term Outcomes Of Manitoba's Insight Mentoring Program: A Comparative Statistical Analysis. Manitoba Centre for Health Policy, Winnipeg, MB (2015)

14. Austin, P.C., Stuart, E.A.: Moving towards best practice when using inverse probability of treatment weighting (IPTW) using the propensity score to estimate causal treatment effects in observational studies. Stat. Med. **34**, 3661–3679 (2015)

15. Hirano, K., Imbens, G.W.: Estimation of causal effects using propensity score weighting: an application to data on right heart catheterization. Health Serv. Outcomes Res. Method. **2**, 259–278 (2001)

16. Abadie, A., Imbens, G.: On the failure of bootstrap for matching estimators. Econometrica **76**(6), 1537–1157 (2008)

17. Victor, C., Demirer, M., Duflo, E., Fernandez-Val, I.: Generic machine learning inference on heterogenous treatment effects in randomized experiments. aXiv:1712.04802v6 [stat.ML] (2022)

18. Knaus, M.C., Lechner, M., Strittmatter, A.: Machine learning estimation of heterogeneous causal effects: empirical monte carlo evidence. Economet. J. **24**(1), 134–161 (2021)

Graph-Enhanced Multi-Activity
Knowledge Tracing

Siqian Zhao$^{(\boxtimes)}$ and Shaghayegh Sahebi

Computer Science, University at Albany - SUNY, Albany, NY 12222, USA
{szhao2,ssahebi}@albany.edu

Abstract. Knowledge tracing (KT), or modeling student knowledge state given their past activity sequence, is one of the essential tasks in online education systems. Research has demonstrated that students benefit from both assessed (e.g., solving problems, which can be graded) and non-assessed learning activities (e.g., watching video lectures, which cannot be graded), and thus, modeling student knowledge from multiple types of activities with knowledge transfer between them is crucial. However, current approaches to multi-activity knowledge tracing cannot capture coarse-grained between-type associations and are primarily evaluated by predicting student performance on upcoming assessed activities (labeled data). Therefore, they are inadequate in incorporating signals from non-assessed activities (unlabeled data). We propose Graph-enhanced Multi-activity Knowledge Tracing (GMKT) that addresses these challenges by jointly learning a fine-grained recurrent memory-augmented student knowledge model and a coarse-grained graph neural network. In GMKT, we formulate multi-activity knowledge tracing as a semi-supervised sequence learning problem and optimize for accurate student performance and activity type at each time step. We demonstrate the effectiveness of our proposed model by experimenting on three real-world datasets.

Keywords: Educational data mining · Knowledge tracing · Knowledge transfer · Multi-activity · Transition-aware · Graph neural network

1 Introduction

The proliferation of large-scale online learning systems has facilitated distance education and provided students with access to a vast array of courses and diverse learning materials. One of the essential tasks in these systems is knowledge tracing (KT), which aims to model student knowledge based on their past interactions with the learning materials. Traditionally, KT models have focused on modeling assessed learning activities, such as solving problems and quizzes, and predicting students' performance in them [11,12,14,24,27]. However, recent research has recognized that students learn from both assessed and non-assessed learning activities, such as watching video lectures and studying worked examples [3,22].

G. De Francisci Morales et al. (Eds.): ECML PKDD 2023, LNAI 14174, pp. 529–546, 2023.
https://doi.org/10.1007/978-3-031-43427-3_32

Therefore, recently, multi-activity KT models [2,8,41,42] have emerged to incorporate students' learning history of both assessed and non-assessed types of learning materials, resulting in more accurate predictions of students' future performance. However, these models still do not fully utilize the observations from non-assessed learning activities and cannot model long-range associations and complex knowledge transitions between learning materials.

More specifically, similar to their traditional counterparts, current multi-activity KT models are formulated as supervised sequence learning problems that predict students' future performance in non-assessed activities. Although these models incorporate non-assessed learning activities as input, they are not explicitly considered in the model's objective function, and therefore, they are not fully involved in optimization and training process. In effect, the non-assessed activities are underrepresented and their impact on student knowledge growth is diluted by these models. Moreover, similar to most modern KT models, multi-activity KTs are formulated as a form of recurrent neural network or tensor factorization models with Markovian assumptions that represent learning materials in fine-grained latent-concept spaces. Thus, the long-range and coarse-grained associations between learning materials are lost in these models. Furthermore, most multi-activity KTs represent all learning activity types in the same latent space and do not explicitly model student knowledge transfers when students transition between different activity types. These models overlook essential aspects of KT by ignoring processes by which student knowledge is attained, transferred, and materialized when transitions happen between various activity types.

To solve these challenges, we propose Graph-enhanced Multi-activity Knowledge Tracing (GMKT). GMKT fully represents both assessed and non-assessed learning activity and incorporates the complex, long-range associations among them. In GMKT, we represent the fine-grained learning material associations by developing a knowledge transfer layer, and the coarse-grained long-range associations by constructing a multi-activity graph neural network (GNN [15]) layer. We develop a transition-aware recurrent network for GMKT's knowledge transfer layer that traces student knowledge over different learning material types and learns knowledge transfer patterns among them using transition-specific knowledge transfer weight matrices. In GMKT's graph neural network layer, we construct a multi-activity transition graph according to the global transitions between learning materials and learn coarse-grained learning material representations by discovering transition-aware propagation and association matrices between them. Moreover, we formulate multi-activity KT as a semi-supervised learning problem and introduce a new activity-type learning objective for GMKT that uses the student's choice of learning activity type as an additional signal in training the model. To summarize, the main contributions of this work are:

- We propose two transition-aware multi-activity recurrent and graph neural networks in GMKT that jointly represent fine-grained and long-range coarse-grained associations between different types of learning materials.

- We formulate the multi-activity knowledge tracing, with a novel perspective, as a semi-supervised sequence learning task and add an activity type objective to GMKT's optimization problem to fully discern the signals from non-assessed learning activities.
- We demonstrate the effectiveness of GMKT on three real-world datasets by comparing it with 15 baseline methods from various research lines, conducting ablation studies, and performing sensitivity analysis.
- We showcase the efficacy of GMKT's transition-aware knowledge transfer by analyzing knowledge transfer weight matrices between different material types.

2 Related Work

Knowledge Tracing: KT approaches mainly rely on the predefined association between learning material and knowledge concepts or components [5,11,13,26], such as BKT [11] and Regression-based KT methods [5,6,13,18,26]. These approaches measure student knowledge of learning material by quantifying student mastery level of the set of knowledge concepts [13,18,19,21]. Later, models like DKT and DKVMN have been proposed to learn the underlying latent concepts of the learning materials [14,17,24,27,30,32,39], since predefined mapping between materials and concepts is typically labeled by human experts, which is costly and impractical for nowadays large-scale online education systems.

All these methods focus on assessed learning materials and do not model students' non-assessed learning activities. Zhang et al. and Choi et al. suggest including non-assessed activities as additional features in modeling student knowledge [8,40]. However, these models do not explicitly measure a student's knowledge state when interacting with non-assessed materials. To the best of our knowledge, there are only a few multi-activity KT approaches that explicitly model student knowledge from multi-type students' learning activities, including MA-Elo [2], MA-FM [1], MVKM [41], DMKT [34], TAMKOT [42]. However, except TAMKOT, these methods either require a predefined mapping between the learning materials and concepts, or explicitly represent the dynamics of knowledge transfer among different learning activities. Moreover, including TAMKOT, none of the methods mentioned above consider the global neighborhood-based transitions and have an activity-type learning objective.

Graph Neural Network: More recently, GNN [15] is widely used to learn and represent the structural information of a graph. It has been shown success in various domains [28,29,35,37]. Existing GNN-based KT methods include GKT [23], GIKT [36], PEBG [20], SKT [33], and DGEKT [12]. Except for DGEKT building graphs through learning activities, these GNN-based methods all create graphs between learning materials or knowledge concepts, neglecting the global transition-structured information from student activity sequences. Additionally, all of the previous GNN-based methods focus on single-type learning material, while we propose to build graphs for multi-type materials.

3   Problem Formulation

In this work, our goal is to model and trace student knowledge by practicing both assessed and non-assessed learning activities. Assuming that there are two types of learning materials, one assessed (e.g., questions) and one non-assessed (e.g., video lectures), we represent a student's whole trajectory of activities as a sequence of tuples, $\{\langle i_1, d_1 \rangle, ..., \langle i_t, d_t \rangle\}$, where each tuple $\langle i_t, d_t \rangle$ indicates a student's activity at time step t. Here, $d_t \in \{0, 1\}$ is a binary indicator that represents the learning activity type at time step t, with 0 denoting assessed and 1 denoting non-assessed type, and i_t indicates the learning material being interacted with. Specifically, we formulate i_t as: $i_t = \begin{cases} (q_t, r_t) & \text{if } d_t = 0 \\ l_t & \text{if } d_t = 1 \end{cases}$, where (q_t, r_t) represents the student's interaction with the assessed material q_t at time step t, with performance r_t, and l_t represents the non-assessed material that the student interacted with at time step t. Conventionally, knowledge tracing is evaluated by the task of performance prediction in the target student's upcoming assessed learning activity q_{t+1}, based on their past assessed activity records $\{(q_1, r_1), \ldots, (q_t, r_t)\}$. Here, given a student's past assessed and non-assessed learning activity history, $\{\langle i_1, d_1 \rangle, \ldots, \langle i_t, d_t \rangle\}$, we aim to predict their upcoming performance on the assessed material q_{t+1} at time step $t + 1$.

4   Graph-Enhanced Multi-Activity Knowledge Tracing

Our model, Graph-enhanced Multi-activity Knowledge Tracing (GMKT), comprises four key layers, including (1) The embedding layer for encoding each student activity into a latent concept feature space; (2) The multi-activity transition graph layer that incorporates the coarse-grained long-range patterns among learning materials; (3) The recurrent knowledge transfer layer that captures student knowledge and fine-grained transfers as students transition between different activities; and (4) The prediction layer that generates a prediction of a student's upcoming performance on an assessed material. We introduce the details of each layer in the next sections and show GMKT's architecture in Fig. 1.

Notations. We use lowercase letters, boldface lowercase letters, and boldface capital letters to respectively denote scalars (q_t), vectors($\boldsymbol{q}_t$), and matrices ($\boldsymbol{A}^q$).

4.1   Embedding Layer

The embedding layer is designed to learn the embedding of each learning activity i_t, which is then used as input for capturing the students' knowledge state and transfer from the latent concept space. To do this, GMKT learns the latent representation of the material (q_t and l_t) and the student response (r_t) for activity i_t. Assuming two learning material types, questions and video lectures, we embed each material type separately. This design allows for a more flexible representation by allowing different embedding sizes for each material type. Specifically, GMKT learns two underlying latent embedding matrices $\boldsymbol{A}^q \in \mathbb{R}^{N^Q \times d_q}$

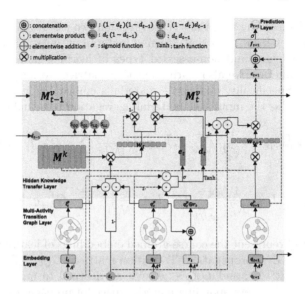

Fig. 1. The architecture of the GMKT model. The solid and dashed lines are identical. Different line types are used to clarify between lines that cross/fall over each other.

and $\boldsymbol{A}^l \in \mathbb{R}^{N^L \times d_l}$ to respectively map all questions and lectures to their specified latent spaces. Here, N^Q and N^L are the number of questions and video lectures, and d_q and d_l are the respective latent embedding sizes. To incorporate student performance outcomes in assessed activities, GMKT maps r_t into a higher-dimensional performance latent space. We consider two scenarios for r_t, namely, binary outcomes (e.g., correctness in solving a question) and numerical outcomes (e.g., normalized exam scores between 0 and 1). For the binary case, we learn an embedding matrix $\boldsymbol{A}^r \in \mathbb{R}^{2 \times d_r}$ to map r_t, where d_r is the performance embedding size. For the numerical case, we use $\boldsymbol{A}^r \in \mathbb{R}^{d_r}$, and apply a linear mapping function $f(r_t) = r_t \boldsymbol{A}^r$ to the performance r_t.

4.2 Multi-Activity Transition Graph Layer

Student learning activity sequences can provide coarse-grained insights into relationships between different learning materials. Observing students interacting with materials consecutively may indicate that they are similar or related. To capture such coarse-grained aggregate information, we construct a multi-activity transition graph $\mathcal{G} = (\mathcal{V}, \mathcal{E})$, where $\mathcal{V}$ consists of all assessed and non-assessed learning materials as nodes, and $\mathcal{E}$ represents the undirected edges between materials that correspond to transitions between materials in a student's sequence. An edge exists between two materials if a student from the training sessions has interacted with them consecutively. For example, given a student's sequence $\{\langle (question_1, 0), 0 \rangle, \langle lecture_4, 1 \rangle, \langle (question_2, 1), 0 \rangle, ... \}$, edges between $question_1$ and $lecture_4$, as well as $question_2$ and $lecture_4$, are added to graph.

To update a learning material's representation, we use propagation matrices to integrate the embedding of that learning material with its neighboring materials. Having assessed and non-assessed types of learning materials and their different contributions, we also learn transition matrices to map the two types to each other. Specifically, taking the material's embedding q_t or l_t from the embedding layer as the input, the material aggregation is formulated as:

$$q_t^p = V_Q^\top \left[q_t + \frac{1}{|\mathcal{N}_{q_t}^Q|} \sum_{i \in \mathcal{N}_{q_t}^Q} G_{QQ}^\top q_i + \frac{1}{|\mathcal{N}_{q_t}^L|} \sum_{j \in \mathcal{N}_{q_t}^L} G_{QL}^\top l_j \right] + b_Q \tag{1}$$

$$l_t^p = V_L^\top \left[l_t + \frac{1}{|\mathcal{N}_{l_t}^L|} \sum_{i \in \mathcal{N}_{l_t}^L} G_{LL}^\top l_i + \frac{1}{|\mathcal{N}_{l_t}^Q|} \sum_{ij \in \mathcal{N}_{l_t}^Q} G_{LQ}^\top q_j \right] + b_L \tag{2}$$

where q_t^p and l_t^p represent the coarse-grained embeddings of learning material q_t and l_t after the GNN propagation. Transition matrices $G_{QQ} \in \mathbb{R}^{d_q \times d_q}$, $G_{QL} \in \mathbb{R}^{d_l \times d_q}$, $G_{LL} \in \mathbb{R}^{d_l \times d_l}$, and $G_{LQ} \in \mathbb{R}^{d_q \times d_l}$ are learned to map each material type's embeddings to corresponding material space for propagation. $\mathcal{N}_{**}^*$ denotes the set of neighbors from type * for the material **. For example, $\mathcal{N}_{q_t}^L$ denotes all the lecture neighbors ("L") of question ("Q") q_t. $V_Q^\top \in \mathbb{R}^{d_q \times d_q}$ and $V_L^\top \in \mathbb{R}^{d_l \times d_l}$ are weight matrices for propagation, $b_Q \in \mathbb{R}^{d_q}$ and $b_L \in \mathbb{R}^{d_l}$ are bias terms.

In this layer, in addition to the coarse-grained associations, the neighborhood-based propagation enables the discovery of long-range relationships between materials that cannot be easily captured in the recurrent knowledge transfer layer of the architecture.

4.3   Knowledge Transfer Layer

We design the knowledge transfer layer to accurately learn the dynamic student knowledge state and the fine-grained material representations. To do so, similar to dynamic key-value memory networks (DKVMN) [39], we employ a static key matrix $M^k \in \mathbb{R}^{N \times d_k}$ to represent N latent concept features and a dynamic value matrix $M_t^v \in \mathbb{R}^{N \times d_v}$ to track the student's mastery state in them. Each vector in the static key matrix corresponds to a concept characterized by d_k latent concept features, while each vector in the dynamic value matrix is a d_v-size memory slot to monitor the student's updated knowledge state (mastery levels) of the corresponding concept over time steps.

Unlike DKVMN, GMKT further models different activity types and the transitions among them. As the way knowledge transfers between different material types can vary depending on the order of the transition, we learn a unique knowledge transfer pattern for each transition between every two distinct material types. To model these transition-specific transfer patterns, we incorporate current and previous activity types as additional inputs. GMKT uses a set of indicators to activate corresponding knowledge transfer weight at each time t. Having two material types, questions ("Q") and lectures ("L"), four transition indicators at each time t are formulated based on material types d_t and d_{t-1}:

$$s_{QQ} = (1-d_t)(1-d_{t-1}) \quad s_{QL} = d_t(1-d_{t-1}) \quad s_{LQ} = (1-d_t)d_{t-1} \quad s_{LL} = d_t d_{t-1} \tag{3}$$

At each time step t, only one of the above transition indicators is equal to 1, while the rest are 0. For example, $s_{QL} = 1$ and $s_{QQ} = s_{LQ} = s_{LL} = 0$ indicate that the student has transitioned from attempting a question at time $t-1$ to watching a video lecture at time t. Then, the transition indicators s_{**} are utilized to activate the corresponding transition-specific weight matrices $\boldsymbol{T}_{**}$ for updating the student's knowledge state $\boldsymbol{M}_t^v$. Consequently, GMKT first computes the attention weight vector $\boldsymbol{w}_t$, which represent the correlation between learning material (q_t or l_t) and each of the N latent concepts. The coarse-grained embedding of the material ($\boldsymbol{q}_t^p$ or $\boldsymbol{l}_t^p$) from Eq. 1 and 2, and the static key matrix $\boldsymbol{M}^k$ are used to compute $\boldsymbol{w}_t \in \mathbb{R}^N$ as follows:

$$w_t(i) = softmax\left(\left[(1-d_t) \cdot \boldsymbol{R}_q^{\mathsf{T}} \boldsymbol{q}_t^p + d_t \cdot \boldsymbol{R}_l^{\mathsf{T}} \boldsymbol{l}_t^p\right]^{\mathsf{T}} \boldsymbol{M}^k(i)\right) \tag{4}$$

where $w_t(i)$ is the i-th element in the attention weight vector $\boldsymbol{w}_t$, and the Softmax function $softmax(m_i) = e^{m_i}/\sum_j e^{m_j}$ is to ensure that the attention weights sum to one. $\boldsymbol{R}_q \in \mathbb{R}^{d_q \times d_k}$ and $\boldsymbol{R}_l \in \mathbb{R}^{d_l \times d_k}$ are used to map question and lecture activity embedding to the concept feature space of $\boldsymbol{M}^k$ in size d_k.

Then, at each time step t, the student's knowledge state is updated based on the learning activity i_t ((q_r, r_t) or l_t), using the *erase-followed-by-add* mechanism to modify the memory value matrix $\boldsymbol{M}_t^v$. It involves erasing previous redundant information before adding new information to $\boldsymbol{M}_t^v$ and is formulated as follows:

Erase:

$$e_t = \sigma\left((1-d_t) \cdot \boldsymbol{E}_q^{\mathsf{T}}[\boldsymbol{q}_t^p \oplus \boldsymbol{r}_t] + d_t \cdot \boldsymbol{E}_l^{\mathsf{T}} \boldsymbol{l}_t^p + \boldsymbol{b}_e\right) \tag{5}$$

$$\tilde{\boldsymbol{M}}_t^v(i) = \left[s_{QQ} \cdot \boldsymbol{T}_{QQ} \boldsymbol{M}_{t-1}^v + s_{LL} \cdot \boldsymbol{T}_{LL} \boldsymbol{M}_{t-1}^v + s_{QL} \cdot \boldsymbol{T}_{QL} \boldsymbol{M}_{t-1}^v + s_{LQ} \cdot \boldsymbol{T}_{LQ} \boldsymbol{M}_{t-1}^v\right](i) \cdot \left[\boldsymbol{1} - w_t(i)e_t\right] \tag{6}$$

Add:

$$d_t = Tanh\left((1-d_t) \cdot \boldsymbol{D}_q^{\mathsf{T}}[\boldsymbol{q}_t^p \oplus \boldsymbol{r}_t] + d_t \cdot \boldsymbol{D}_l^{\mathsf{T}} \boldsymbol{l}_t^p + \boldsymbol{b}_d\right) \tag{7}$$

$$\boldsymbol{M}_t^v(i) = \tilde{\boldsymbol{M}}_t^v(i) + w_t(i)\boldsymbol{d}_t \tag{8}$$

Here, σ and $Tanh$ are Sigmoid and Tanh activation functions. The erase vector $\boldsymbol{e}_t \in [0,1]^{d_v}$ is formulated to remove redundant knowledge information from $\boldsymbol{M}_{t-1}^v$. The add vector $\boldsymbol{d}_t \in \mathbb{R}^{d_v}$ is formulated to capture the new knowledge that the student acquires at time t. $\tilde{\boldsymbol{M}}_t^v(i)$ and $\boldsymbol{M}_t^v(i)$ indicates the i-th knowledge slot of $\boldsymbol{M}_t^v$ after erasing and adding process. We acknowledge that knowledge transfer can differ for the four possible transitions among different learning material types, therefore, separate transfer weight matrices are utilized. These matrices are activated by using the four different transition indicators s_{**}, namely $\boldsymbol{T}_{QQ}$, $\boldsymbol{T}_{QL}$, $\boldsymbol{T}_{LQ}$, and $\boldsymbol{T}_{LL} \in \mathbb{R}^{d_v \times d_v}$. For example, when the student switches from watching video lectures to solving questions, $\boldsymbol{T}_{LQ}$ represents knowledge transfer from the previous student knowledge state M_{t-1}^v to the current state and it is activated since $s_{LQ} = 1$. In addition, $(1 - d_t)$ and (d_t) are used to determine whether the learning activity i_t is a question or a lecture attempt. They are used to activate the corresponding matrices E_q and $D_q \in \mathbb{R}^{(d_q + d_r) \times d_v}$, E_l and $D_l \in \mathbb{R}^{d_l \times d_v}$ for mapping the learning activity embedding to concept feature space of value matrix. b_e and $b_d \in \mathbb{R}^{d_v}$ represent the bias terms.

In this layer, representing student knowledge and learning material concepts in fine-grained latent features and the transition-aware transfer matrices allow for more precise student performance prediction and capture more detailed associations between consequent learning materials in a sequence.

4.4   Prediction Layer

In this layer, GMKT predicts the performance of a student on a given question q_{t+1} at the next time $t + 1$, based on their knowledge state of the q_{t+1}'s concepts.

$$w_{t+1}(i) = softmax([R_q^\mathsf{T} q_{t+1}^p]^\mathsf{T} M^k(i)) \tag{9}$$

$$c_{t+1} = \sum_{i=1}^{N} w_{t+1}(i)\big[(1 - d_t) \cdot M_t^v T_{QQ} + d_t \cdot M_t^v T_{LQ}\big](i) \tag{10}$$

$$f_{t+1} = Tanh(W_f^\mathsf{T}[c_{t+1} \oplus q_{t+1}] + b_f) \tag{11}$$

Initially, the correlation between question q_{t+1} and each of the N latent concepts is determined by computing the attention weight vector w_{t+1} (Eq. 9). The read content c_{t+1} is then retrieved to summarize the student's knowledge state of question q_{t+1} by using the weighted sum of all memory slots in the value matrix M_t^v and w_{t+1} (Eq. 10). Here, $(1 - d_t)$ and d_t are used to indicate whether the knowledge transfer from time t to $t + 1$ for predicting the performance of q_{t+1} is from a question or a lecture. Next, the concatenation of c_{t+1} and the next question's embedding vector q_{t+1}, is passed through a fully connected layer with a Tanh activation function to obtain a summary vector f_{t+1}(equation 11), where $W_f \in \mathbb{R}^{(d_v + d_q) \times d_s}$ and $b_f \in \mathbb{R}^{d_s}$ is the weight matrix and the bias term, with d_s is the summary vector size. Finally, another fully connected layer with the Sigmoid activation function is used upon f_{t+1} to predict the student's performance p_{t+1}:

$$p_{t+1} = \sigma(W_p^\mathsf{T} f_{t+1} + b_p) \tag{12}$$

where a scalar p_{t+1} represents the probability of the student correctly answering the next question q_{t+1}, $W_p \in \mathbb{R}^{d_s \times 1}$ and $b_p \in \mathbb{R}$ are weight matrix and bias term.

4.5   Optimization and Objective Function

Similar to traditional KT models, we aim to minimize the following binary cross-entropy loss between actual and estimated student performance r_t and p_t:

$$\mathcal{L} = -\sum_{t} \big(r_t \log p_t + (1 - r_t) \log(1 - p_t)\big) \tag{13}$$

But, unlike previous KT models, our goal is to also learn from the unlabeled data (non-assessed activities). To do so, we propose an additional objective to accurately estimate the type of the next material. Accordingly, we propose a read content of learning material type c_t^o to summarize a student's behavior state of material type at each time t by using an attention weight vector, denoted by w_t^o:

$$w_t^o(i) = softmax([(1 - d_t) \cdot \boldsymbol{O}_q^\mathsf{T} \boldsymbol{q}_t^p + d_t \cdot \boldsymbol{O}_l^\mathsf{T} l_t^p]^\mathsf{T} \boldsymbol{M}^k(i)) \tag{14}$$

$$c_t^o = \sum_{i=1}^{N} w_t^o(i) \boldsymbol{M}_t^v(i) \tag{15}$$

where $w_t^o(i)$ is the i-th element of w_t^o, and $\boldsymbol{O}_q \in \mathbb{R}^{d_q \times d_k}$ and $\boldsymbol{O}_l \in \mathbb{R}^{d_l \times d_k}$ and two weight matrices to map question and lecture embeddings. We then model the type of material the student will interact with at time $t + 1$ using Eq. 16:

$$\boldsymbol{p}_{t+1}^o = \sigma(d_t \cdot \boldsymbol{W}_{oq}^T c_t^o + (1 - d_t) \cdot \boldsymbol{W}_{ol}^T c_t^o + b_o) \tag{16}$$

where p_{t+1}^o represents the probability that the next learning material student will interact be a question. $\boldsymbol{W}_{oq}$ and $\boldsymbol{W}_{ol} \in \mathbb{R}^{d_v \times 1}$ are two weight matrices, $b_o \in \mathbb{R}$ is the bias term. Finally, the activity-type objective function $\mathcal{L}^o$ is formulated as a binary cross-entropy loss between p_t^o and the actual material type d_t:

$$\mathcal{L}^o = -\sum_t (d_t \log p_t^o + (1 - d_t) \log (1 - p_t^o)) \tag{17}$$

Eventually, we minimize a combination of the performance objective function $\mathcal{L}$ Eq. 13) and the activity-type objective function $\mathcal{L}^o$ (Eq. 17) with a regularization term to learn the parameters of GMKT, as shown in Eq. 18:

$$\mathcal{L}_{total} = \mathcal{L} + \lambda_o \mathcal{L}^o + \lambda_\theta ||\theta||^2 \tag{18}$$

We use λ_o to balance between the contribution of student performance objective and activity-type objective. θ represents the set of all trainable parameters in GMKT, and the term $||\theta||^2$ corresponds to the regularization, while λ_θ denotes the hyperparameter that determines the weight of this regularization term.

5 Experiments

We evaluate GMKT through two sets of experiments. First, we compare GMKT's student performance predictive ability with baseline KT methods and perform ablation studies and sensitivity analysis of the model's components. Then, we compare transition weight matrices to examine knowledge transfer between learning material types. Our code and supplementary material are available on GitHub[1].

---

[1] https://github.com/persai-lab/2023-ECML-PKDD-GMKT.

Table 1. Descriptive statistics of datasets.

Dataset	#Stu-dents	#Assessed Materials	#Assessed Activities	Assessed Responses Mean	Assessed Responses STD	#Correct Assessed Responses	#Incorrect Assessed Responses	#Non-assessed Materials	#Non-assessed Activities
EdNet	1000	11249	200931	0.5910	0.2417	118747	82184	8324	150821
Junyi	2063	3760	290754	0.6660	0.2224	193664	97090	1432	69050
MORF	686	10	12031	0.7763	0.2507	N/A	N/A	52	41980

5.1 Datasets

We use three real-world datasets for our experiments. Table 1 provides an overview of the general statistics for each dataset.

EdNet[2] [9]: This dataset is collected from Santa[3], a multi-platform AI tutoring service that was designed to provide Korean students with a platform to practice for TOEIC[4] English testing. Every time, students choose a bundle that includes a set of problems to practice, and optional corresponding problem explanations to read. We use the preprocessed data introduced in [42] for our experiments, which use problems (assessed) and their associated problem explanations (non-assessed) as two types of learning materials.

Junyi[5] [10]: This dataset is sourced from a Chinese e-learning website that teaches math to students. The website covers eight math areas with varying difficulty levels. For our experiments, we use the preprocessed data made available in [7,42], with problems (assessed) and hints (non-assessed) as two distinct learning material types. Each problem may be associated with multiple hints. During practice, students have the option to request hints for solving problems.

MORF [4]: This dataset comprises data from an online course "Educational Data Mining" offered on Coursera[6] and accessed from the MOOC Replication Framework (MORF) platform[7]. The course consists of modules covering various topics, such as "classification". During the course, students are expected to watch several video lectures per module and complete an assignment, containing multiple problems. However, only coarse-grained assignment-level data is available. Thus, we treat each submission of an assignment as one assessed activity and consider the overall score as the activity response. For our experiments, the two material types are assignments (assessed) and video lectures (non-assessed).

5.2 Baselines

To evaluate our proposed method on student performance prediction task, we compare it with six state-of-the-art assessed-only supervised KT models and

---

[2] https://github.com/riiid/ednet.
[3] https://www.aitutorsanta.com/.
[4] https://www.ets.org/toeic.
[5] https://pslcdatashop.web.cmu.edu/DatasetInfo?datasetId=1275.
[6] https://www.coursera.org/.
[7] https://educational-technology-collective.github.io/morf/.

three multi-activity KT models. In addition, to ensure a fair comparison, we also extend the six assessed-only supervised KT models to handle both assessed and non-assessed activities and also include a multi-layer perceptron (MLP) baseline that can handle both types of activities. We denoted these extended models by "original model name +M". Overall, we evaluated our method against 15 baselines, consisting of eight deep learning-based models and one tensor factorization model among the original nine baselines. Notably, to ensure fairness, we refrain from comparing with GNN-based KT models mentioned in Sect. 2, as they require the predefined mapping between materials and concepts, whereas we learn the underlying latent concept. For baselines that originally used the knowledge concept of each question as inputs (e.g., DKT), we used each question as a knowledge component. The assessed supervised KT baselines are:

DKT [27] employs recurrent neural networks to model the knowledge state of students, and is the first deep learning-based KT method.

DKVMN [39] modifies MANN that utilizes a static key matrix to represent knowledge concepts and a dynamic value matrix to update student knowledge.

DeepIRT [38] extends DKVMN by incorporating the one-parameter logistic item response theory, which provides better interpretability of KT.

SAKT [24] applies a self-attentive mechanism to model the inter-dependencies between student interactions and improve the effectiveness of KT.

SAINT [8] is a transformer-based method and is an encoder-decoder model that employs deep self-attentive layers to separately encode exercises and responses.

AKT [14] is a context-aware KT model that utilizes a monotonic attention mechanism to summarize the impact of past student activity performance on the current activity's knowledge state.

The baseline methods support both assessed and non-assessed activities are:

DKT+M [40], **DKVMN+M**, **SAINT+M** [8], **AKT+M** and **AKT+M** are variants of DKT, DKVMN, SAINT, SAKT, and AKT. in these extended models, non-assessed learning activities embedding are summarized as an additional feature, with the problem embedding as the model input.

MLP+M [16] is a simple multi-layer perceptron that takes the embedding of a student's three most recent assessed activities and three non-assessed activities as input to predict student knowledge of a concept.

MVKM [41] can model student knowledge acquisition from multi-type learning activities. It is a method based on multi-view tensor factorization that constructs separate tensors for student activities from each learning material type but cannot explicitly capture the knowledge transition between material types.

DMKT [34] is based on DKVMN and models distinct read and write operations for assessed and non-assessed learning material types. However, it lacks the ability to explicitly model knowledge transfer between assessed and non-assessed learning materials. Moreover, it requires a fixed number of non-assessed learning activities between every two assessed ones, making it less flexible in modeling the student knowledge from the complete activity sequence.

TAMKOT [42] is a transition-aware KT model that builds based on LSTM. It learns multiple knowledge transfer matrices to explicitly model the knowledge transfer between different activity types. However, it does not consider the global neighborhood-based transitions its knowledge modeling layer is LSTM-based, and its objective function only considers students' assessed activities.

5.3 Experiment Setup

We adopt 5-fold student stratified cross-validation, following standard KT experiments [27,34]. In each fold, 80% of students' sequences are randomly chosen as the training set, while the remaining 20% of students' sequences are used as the test set. For hyperparameter tuning, we separate 20% of students from training set and use their sequences as the validation set. We conduct a coarse-grained grid search to find the best hyperparameters, which are reported in Table 2.

5.4 Student Performance Prediction

In student performance prediction experiments, we report the mean results across five folds of each method and present the paired t-test p-values that compare each baseline to GMKT. For datasets where student performance is binary (correctness), such as EdNet and Junyi, we evaluate model performance using Area Under Curve (AUC). For datasets where student performance is numeric values (scores), such as MORF, we normalize student assignment scores within the range of $[0, 1]$ using the assignment's maximum possible score. We then use Root Mean Squared Error (RMSE) to evaluate model prediction performance.

Comparison with Baselines: GMKT's results along with the baselines are presented in Table 3. We only run MVKM on MORF dataset due to its limitations in handling high-dimensional data with large computational time costs.

We first observe that GMKT outperforms all baseline methods, particularly in Junyi and MORF datasets, highlighting the importance of modeling both assessed and non-assessed activities for accurate student knowledge representation. The results demonstrate GMKT's effectiveness in capturing knowledge transfer between different material types and improving multi-activity student knowledge tracing through neighborhood-based and transition-aware representation learning. We also observe that the difference between GMKT and the second-best baseline is more significant in Junyi and MORF datasets. A potential explanation could be contrast in material associations and transition variability between different datasets. Contrary to GMKT which uses a complex key-value structure and neighborhood-based material representations, the second-best baseline (TAMKOT) models knowledge transfer between assessed and non-assessed materials using a simple LSTM-like structure. Hence, while the complex structure of GMKT is needed for more complex datasets, TAMKOT's performance could be adequate for the less complex ones. Particularly, in EdNet, related problems are bundled together, each problem is associated with one explanation, and students follow similar transitions between materials within bundles. So, the enhanced graph structure and complex knowledge representation may not provide much additional information in this dataset. Comparing

Table 2. Best learned hyperparameters

Dataset	d_q	d_r	d_l	d_k	d_v	d_s	N	λ_o	λ_θ
EdNet	64	32	32	32	32	32	8	0.1	0.05
Junyi	32	32	32	64	64	32	32	0.1	0.05
MORF	32	16	8	32	32	32	8	0.05	0.03

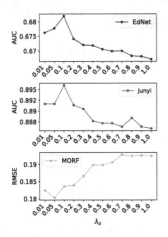

Fig. 2. Performance w.r.t. λ_o

Table 3. Student performance prediction results. The best and second-best results are in bold and underlined. ∗∗ and ∗ represent paired t-test $p-values < 0.05$ and < 0.1, compared to GMKT.

Methods	EdNet	Junyi	MORF
	AUC	AUC	RMSE
DKT	0.6393**	0.8623**	0.1990**
DKVMN	0.6296**	0.8558**	0.1995**
SAKT	0.6334**	0.8053**	0.1975**
SAINT	0.5205**	0.7951**	0.2190**
AKT	0.6393**	0.8093**	0.2417**
DeepIRT	0.6290**	0.8498**	0.1946**
DKT+M	0.6372**	0.8652*	0.1942**
DKVMN+M	0.6343**	0.8513**	0.2071**
SAKT+M	0.6323**	0.7911**	0.1981**
SAINT+M	0.5491**	0.7741**	0.2007**
AKT+M	0.6404**	0.8099**	0.2226**
MLP+M	0.6102**	0.7290**	0.2428**
MVKM	–	–	0.1936*
DMKT	0.6394**	0.8561**	<u>0.1856*</u>
TAMKOT	<u>0.6786</u>	<u>0.8745**</u>	0.1857*
GMKT	**0.6819**	**0.8960**	**0.1802**

GMKT to other two multi-activity methods, MVKM and DMKT, it shows that GMKT significantly outperforms both of them in all datasets. This again highlights the importance of explicitly modeling knowledge transfer and activity-type transitions, as well as incorporating graph-structured information in knowledge modeling.

Moreover, the results indicate that the multi-activity variants of assessed-only methods do not consistently improve prediction performance compared to their original formulations. For instance, SAKT+M performs worse than SKAT on EdNet and Junyi datasets, while DKVMN+M performs worse than DKVMN on MORF dataset. These suggest that simply adding non-assessed activities as additional features sometimes has a negative impact on performance prediction. Nonetheless, it can improve performance when knowledge transfer between assessed and non-assessed materials is adequately modeled, like GMKT.

Ablation Studies: We conduct two sets of ablation studies to validate the impact of coarse-grained representations (the multi-activity transition graph layer) and the type objective. First, we remove the GNN component from GMKT, referred to as GMKT-G. Second, we remove the type objective term, $\lambda_o \mathcal{L}^o$, from $\mathcal{L}_{total}$, in Eq. 18 (GMKT-O). According to the results in Table 4, removing either of these components has decreased performance in all datasets,

Table 4. Ablation study results

Methods	EdNet AUC	Junyi AUC	MORF RMSE
GMKT-G	0.6759	0.8909	0.1888
GMKT-O	0.6761	0.8911	0.1867
GMKT	**0.6819**	**0.8960**	**0.1802**

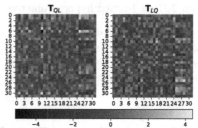

Fig. 3. Heatmaps for weight matrices T_{QL} and T_{LQ} for MORF dataset.

Table 5. Spearman correlation coefficients with p-values between T_{QL} and T_{LQ}

	EdNet	Junyi	MORF
Correlation	0.0357	-0.0128	-0.0504
p-value	0.2531	0.4120	0.1072

indicating that neighborhood-based representations and the type objective are both necessary and can provide the most significant improvement when used together. Comparing GMKT-G and GMKT-O, we observe similar results in EdNet and Junyi. Whereas, for MORF dataset, GMKT-O outperforms GMKT-G, meaning that neighborhood-based similarities are more important than the type objective in MORF. A potential reason can be the material complexity in MORF. Each problem covers one topic in EdNet and Junyi, but each MORF assignment has multiple problems and video lectures cover multiple concepts. So, more coarse-grained representation can provide richer information about materials in MORF.

Sensitivity Analysis: To have a deeper understanding of the impact of the type objective on student performance prediction, we perform a sensitivity analysis by changing λ_o in Eq. 18 while fixing all other hyperparameters to the best-learned values. The experiment results in Fig. 2 show that prediction performance initially improves, but gradually decreases after reaching a certain λ_o for all datasets. This demonstrates that while adding the type objective helps in achieving higher performance, a balance is necessary between the objective function components. Additionally, while the best λ_o varies slightly for each dataset (0.1 for EdNet and Junyi and 0.05 for MORF), the overall range for optimal λ_o is small and GMKT can robustly use a similar λ_o for different datasets.

5.5 Knowledge Transfer Modeling

In this set of experiments, we focus on examining the knowledge transfer between assessed materials to non-assessed ones. Specifically, we compare the transition weight matrices T_{QL} and T_{LQ} in Eq. 6 to determine if the knowledge transfer from assessed to non-assessed materials differs from that of non-assessed to assessed materials. These matrices represent the weight of knowledge transfer from one memory slot to another when a student switches from one material type to another. We flatten these matrices and calculate the Spearman correlation coefficient [31] between them. The resulting correlation coefficient and p-value are presented in Table 5, indicating that there is no significant correlation between T_{QL} (assessed to non-assessed) and T_{LQ} (non-assessed to assessed), as the correlations are small and the p-values are greater than 0.1 for all datasets. This implies that transition weights in T_{QL} and T_{LQ} are mostly different. To further investigate, we plot the heatmap of T_{QL} and T_{LQ} for the MORF dataset in Fig. 3(Heatmaps for the Junyi and Ednet are in the supplementary material due to space limitations). A z-score normalization [25] is performed to T_{QL} and T_{LQ} for better visualization. As evident from the heatmap, weight matrices are considerably different from each other, indicating that knowledge transfer weights depend on the order of transition between material types. Thus, modeling knowledge transfer between different material types is sufficient.

6 Conclusions

We focused on multi-activity knowledge tracing, modeling student knowledge as they transition between various types of materials. We developed GMKT, a model with a transition-aware dynamic knowledge transfer network and a transition-aware graph neural network that captures both fine-grained and coarse-grained associations between materials. We also proposed a semi-supervised learning approach that considers both student performance and activity type objectives. Our experimental results on three real-world datasets showed that explicitly modeling transition-aware knowledge transfers, capturing coarse-grained associations by the transition-aware GNN, and adding the activity type objective, are crucial for accurately representing student knowledge and predicting their performance. Our analysis showed that student knowledge transfers between assessed and non-assessed activities depend on transition order, indicating that transition-aware models are essential for multi-activity knowledge tracing.

Acknowledgements. This paper is based upon work supported by the National Science Foundation under Grant No. 2047500.

Ethical Statement. This research paper aims to assess students' knowledge states through their learning activities. It can assist students or instructors in better understanding student learning, which can be used to plan students' study plans to improve students' learning efficiency, recommend useful learning materials to students, and detect knowledge gaps in students. The research team has given careful consideration to the ethical implications of collecting and processing student personal data, and the potential inference of student personal information in our work. We ensured that all data used adhered to relevant laws and regulations, and relied on the publicly available datasets that ensure to maintain the anonymity and confidentiality of any personal information that could be inferred from the data. Furthermore, we have considered the broader impact of our research on society and aimed to ensure that it has a positive impact. As a part of broader impact, we strive to make all the developed code via this research publicly available. We acknowledge that ethical considerations are crucial in scientific research, and we have taken all necessary measures to ensure that our work meets the highest ethical standards. In summary, we confirm that our work follows ethical guidelines and standards set by the scientific community.

References

1. Abdi, S.: Learner models for learnersourced adaptive educational systems (2022)
2. Abdi, S., Khosravi, H., Sadiq, S., Darvishi, A.: Open learner models for multi-activity educational systems. In: Roll, I., McNamara, D., Sosnovsky, S., Luckin, R., Dimitrova, V. (eds.) AIED 2021. LNCS (LNAI), vol. 12749, pp. 11–17. Springer, Cham (2021). https://doi.org/10.1007/978-3-030-78270-2_2
3. Agrawal, R., Christoforaki, M., Gollapudi, S., Kannan, A., Kenthapadi, K., Swaminathan, A.: Mining videos from the web for electronic textbooks. In: Glodeanu, C.V., Kaytoue, M., Sacarea, C. (eds.) ICFCA 2014. LNCS (LNAI), vol. 8478, pp. 219–234. Springer, Cham (2014). https://doi.org/10.1007/978-3-319-07248-7_16
4. Andres, J.M.L., Baker, R.S., Siemens, G., Gašević, D., Spann, C.A.: Replicating 21 findings on student success in online learning. Technol. Instruct. Cogn. Learn. **10**(4), 313–333 (2016)
5. Cen, H., Koedinger, K., Junker, B.: Learning factors analysis – a general method for cognitive model evaluation and improvement. In: Ikeda, M., Ashley, K.D., Chan, T.-W. (eds.) ITS 2006. LNCS, vol. 4053, pp. 164–175. Springer, Heidelberg (2006). https://doi.org/10.1007/11774303_17
6. Cen, H., Koedinger, K., Junker, B.: Comparing two IRT models for conjunctive skills. In: Woolf, B.P., Aïmeur, E., Nkambou, R., Lajoie, S. (eds.) ITS 2008. LNCS, vol. 5091, pp. 796–798. Springer, Heidelberg (2008). https://doi.org/10.1007/978-3-540-69132-7_111
7. Chang, H.-S., Hsu, H.-J., Chen, K.-T.: Modeling exercise relationships in e-learning: a unified approach. In: EDM, pp. 532–535 (2015)
8. Choi, Y., et al.: Towards an appropriate query, key, and value computation for knowledge tracing. In: Proceedings of the 7th ACM Conference on Learning at Scale, pp. 341–344, New York, NY, USA. ACM (2020)
9. Choi, Y., et al.: EdNet: a large-scale hierarchical dataset in education. In: Bittencourt, I.I., Cukurova, M., Muldner, K., Luckin, R., Millán, E. (eds.) AIED 2020. LNCS (LNAI), vol. 12164, pp. 69–73. Springer, Cham (2020). https://doi.org/10.1007/978-3-030-52240-7_13
10. CMU DataShop. Junyi dataset. https://pslcdatashop.web.cmu.edu/Project?id=244, 2015
11. Corbett, A.T., Anderson, J.R.: Knowledge tracing: modeling the acquisition of procedural knowledge. User Model. User-Adapted Interact. **4**(4), 253–278 (1994)
12. Cui, C., et al.: DGEKT: a dual graph ensemble learning method for knowledge tracing. arXiv preprint arXiv:2211.12881 (2022)
13. Drasgow, F., Hulin, C.L.: Item response theory. In: Handbook of Industrial and Organizational Psychology, pp. 577–636 (1990)
14. Ghosh, A., Heffernan, N., Lan, A.S.: Context-aware attentive knowledge tracing. In: Proceedings of the 26th ACM SIGKDD International Conference on Knowledge Discovery & Data Mining, pp. 2330–2339, New York, NY, USA. ACM (2020)

15. Gori, M., Monfardini, G., Scarselli, F.: A new model for learning in graph domains. In: Proceedings 2005 IEEE International Joint Conference on Neural Networks, vol. 2, pp. 729–734. IEEE (2005)

16. Haykin, S.: Neural networks: a comprehensive foundation. Prentice Hall PTR (1994)

17. Jordan, M.I., Kearns, M.J., Solla, S.A.: Advances in Neural Information Processing Systems 10. In: Proceedings of the 1997 Conference, vol. 10. MIT Press (1998)

18. Lan, A.S., Waters, A.E., Studer, C., Baraniuk, R.G.: Sparse factor analysis for learning and content analytics. J. Mach. Learn. Res. (JMLR) **15**(57), 1959–2008 (2014)

19. Liu, Q., et al.: EKT: exercise-aware knowledge tracing for student performance prediction. IEEE Trans. Knowl. Data Eng. **33**(1), 100–115 (2019)

20. Liu, Y., Yang, Y., Chen, X., Shen, J., Zhang, H., Yu, Y.: Improving knowledge tracing via pre-training question embeddings. arXiv preprint arXiv:2012.05031 (2020)

21. Long, T., Liu, Y., Shen, J., Zhang, W., Yu, Y.: Tracing knowledge state with individual cognition and acquisition estimation. In: Proceedings of the 44th International ACM SIGIR Conference on Research and Development in Information Retrieval, pp. 173–182 (2021)

22. Najar, A.S., Mitrovic, A., McLaren, B.M.: Adaptive support versus alternating worked examples and tutored problems: which leads to better learning? In: Dimitrova, V., Kuflik, T., Chin, D., Ricci, F., Dolog, P., Houben, G.-J. (eds.) UMAP 2014. LNCS, vol. 8538, pp. 171–182. Springer, Cham (2014). https://doi.org/10.1007/978-3-319-08786-3_15

23. Nakagawa, H., Iwasawa, Y., Matsuo, Y.: Graph-based knowledge tracing: modeling student proficiency using graph neural network. In: IEEE/WIC/ACM International Conference on Web Intelligence, pp. 156–163 (2019)

24. Pandey, S., Karypis, G.: A self-attentive model for knowledge tracing. In: Proceedings of the 12th International Conference on Educational Data Mining, pp. 384–389. International Educational Data Mining Society (2019)

25. Patro, S., Sahu, K.K.: Normalization: a preprocessing stage. arXiv preprint arXiv:1503.06462 (2015)

26. Pavlik, P.I., Cen, H., Koedinger, K.R.: Performance factors analysis-a new alternative to knowledge tracing, Online Submission (2009)

27. Piech, C.: Deep knowledge tracing. In: Proceedings of the 28th International Conference on Neural Information Processing Systems, vol. 1, pp. 505–513, Cambridge, MA, USA. MIT Press (2015)

28. Qi, X., Liao, R., Jia, J., Fidler, S., Urtasun, R.: 3D graph neural networks for RGBD semantic segmentation. In: Proceedings of the IEEE International Conference on Computer Vision, pp. 5199–5208 (2017)

29. Qu, Y., Bai, T., Zhang, W., Nie, J., Tang, J.: An end-to-end neighborhood-based interaction model for knowledge-enhanced recommendation. In: Proceedings of the 1st International Workshop on Deep Learning Practice for High-Dimensional Sparse Data, pp. 1–9 (2019)

30. Sahebi, S., Lin, Y.-R., Brusilovsky, P.: Tensor factorization for student modeling and performance prediction in unstructured domain. Int. Educ. Data Min. Soc. (2016)

31. Spearman, C.: The proof and measurement of association between two things (1961)

32. Thai-Nghe, N., Horváth, T., Schmidt-Thieme, L.: Factorization models for forecasting student performance. In: Educational Data Mining 2011. Citeseer (2010)

33. Tong, S., et al.: Structure-based knowledge tracing: an influence propagation view. In: 2020 IEEE International Conference on Data Mining (ICDM), pp. 541–550. IEEE (2020)

34. Wang, C., Zhao, S., Sahebi, S.: Learning from non-assessed resources: deep multi-type knowledge tracing. Int. Educ. Data Min. Soc. (2021)

35. Wang, X., He, X., Cao, Y., Liu, M., Chua, T.-S.: KGAT: knowledge graph attention network for recommendation. In: Proceedings of the 25th ACM SIGKDD International Conference on Knowledge Discovery & Data Mining, pp. 950–958 (2019)

36. Yang, Y., et al.: GIKT: a graph-based interaction model for knowledge tracing. In: Hutter, F., Kersting, K., Lijffijt, J., Valera, I. (eds.) ECML PKDD 2020. LNCS (LNAI), vol. 12457, pp. 299–315. Springer, Cham (2021). https://doi.org/10.1007/978-3-030-67658-2_18

37. Yao, L., Mao, C., Luo, Y.: Graph convolutional networks for text classification. In: Proceedings of the AAAI Conference on Artificial Intelligence, vol. 33, pp. 7370–7377 (2019)

38. Yeung, C.K.: Deep-IRT: make deep learning based knowledge tracing explainable using item response theory. In: Proceedings of the 12th International Conference on Educational Data Mining, pp. 683–686. International Educational Data Mining Society (2019)

39. Zhang, J., Shi, X., King, I., Yeung, D.-Y.: Dynamic key-value memory networks for knowledge tracing. In: Proceedings of the 26th International Conference on World Wide Web, pp. 765–774, New York, NY, USA. ACM (2017)

40. Zhang, L., Xiong, X., Zhao, S., Botelho, A., Heffernan, N.T.: Incorporating rich features into deep knowledge tracing. In: Proceedings of the 4th ACM Conference on Learning at Scale, pp. 169–172, New York, NY, USA. ACM (2017)

41. Zhao, S., Wang, C., Sahebi, S.: Modeling knowledge acquisition from multiple learning resource types. In: Proceedings of The 13th International Conference on Educational Data Mining, pp. 313–324. International Educational Data Mining Society (2020)

42. Zhao, S., Wang, C., Sahebi, S.: Transition-aware multi-activity knowledge tracing. In: 2022 IEEE International Conference on Big Data (Big Data), pp. 1760–1769. IEEE (2022)

Knowledge Distillation with Graph Neural Networks for Epileptic Seizure Detection

Qinyue Zheng[1], Arun Venkitaraman[1(✉)], Simona Petravic[2],
and Pascal Frossard[1]

[1] Signal Processing Laboratory LTS4, EPFL, Lausanne, Switzerland
{qinyue.zheng,pascal.frossard}@epfl.ch, arun.venkitaraman@gmail.com
[2] Embark Studios, Stockholm, Sweden
petravic.s@gmail.com

Abstract. Wearable devices for seizure monitoring detection could significantly improve the quality of life of epileptic patients. However, existing solutions that mostly rely on full electrode set of electroencephalogram (EEG) measurements could be inconvenient for every day use. In this paper, we propose a novel knowledge distillation approach to transfer the knowledge from a sophisticated seizure detector (called the teacher) trained on data from the full set of electrodes to learn new detectors (called the student). They are both providing lightweight implementations and significantly reducing the number of electrodes needed for recording the EEG. We consider the case where the teacher and the student seizure detectors are graph neural networks (GNN), since these architectures actively use the connectivity information. We consider two cases (a) when a single student is learnt for all the patients using preselected channels; and (b) when personalized students are learnt for every individual patient, with personalized channel selection using a Gumbel-softmax approach. Our experiments on the publicly available Temple University Hospital EEG Seizure Data Corpus (TUSZ) show that both knowledge-distillation and personalization play significant roles in improving performance of seizure detection, particularly for patients with scarce EEG data. We observe that using as few as two channels, we are able to obtain competitive seizure detection performance. This, in turn, shows the potential of our approach in more realistic scenario of wearable devices for personalized monitoring of seizures, even with few recordings.

Keywords: Personalized seizure detection · Graph neural networks · Knowledge distillation

This work is supported by the PEDESITE project (data.snf.ch/grants/grant/193813). This work was done by the third author when she was a research intern in the same lab as the other authors at EPFL.

G. De Francisci Morales et al. (Eds.): ECML PKDD 2023, LNAI 14174, pp. 547–563, 2023.
https://doi.org/10.1007/978-3-031-43427-3_33

1   Introduction

Epilepsy is a neurological disorder that is characterized by recurring, unprovoked seizures caused by surges of electrical activity in the brain and affects nearly three million people [26]. About one-third of the patients do not respond to treatment by drugs [17]. Hence, real-time seizure monitoring is crucial for improving the patients' quality of life, for example, by alerting caregivers that their assistance is needed once a seizure occurs. A continuous monitoring of the electroencephalogram (EEG) is useful in identifying and even predicting seizures in critically ill patients [19], particularly with the use of deep-learning approaches [1,12,21,23,27] The monitoring is usually performed in a hospital environment over the course of several days, which makes it infeasible to monitor patients long-term in non-ambulatory settings. Wearable devices could overcome the need of specialised intrusive medical equipment and hospital environment and enable real-time seizure monitoring on a daily basis. Existing measurement devices [3] that use EEG head caps with over 20 wired electrodes are however uncomfortable and difficult to wear over prolonged intervals and lighter and more discrete wearables are desirable for patients. Previous studies have attempted to reduce the number of EEG electrodes needed for seizure detection [8,9,28] with promising results. However, these solutions typically involve training detection systems from scratch for the new setting and fail to incorporate the already existing historical EEG data of the patient recorded with many electrodes. Due to the nature of the disorder itself, seizure data is sparse in the number of available seizures and difficult to collect, and it is thus important to meaningfully use previous data. Further, it is known that the signals from the different regions of the brain (captured through the EEG electrodes) are not independent and exhibit strong inter-channel dependencies that could be viewed as a brain graph or a network. Hence, we ask the question:

How to transfer information gained from a full set of channels/graph to settings with a reduced number of channels/subgraph while actively using the connectivity information?

In this paper, we address this question by developing a novel approach for knowledge distillation (KD) with graph neural networks (GNNs) applied to seizure detection. Our motivation for the use of GNNs comes from the observation that they have been used extensively in applications with graph-structured data, and more recently have shown to result in promising seizure detection performance [22,30]. More specifically, we propose a seizure detection model that consists of three interconnected blocks. Firstly, we have the knowledge distillation block, whereby we transfer the knowledge from a pre-trained seizure detection model to obtain a model that is lightweight and uses only a reduced set of input channels and the corresponding subgraph. Secondly, a channel selection block, which takes the full multi-channel input and retains the signal only on a reduced set of channels that are either pre-selected or learned in a fully data-driven manner. Lastly, we have the GNN-based seizure detection model that classifies the multi-channel EEG input, from a reduced set of channels/electrodes and the corresponding subgraph, into seizure or non-seizure segments.

Our goal is to also investigate the influence of two important aspects in seizure detection performance with reduced channels: (i) prior knowledge (through the use of the teacher model), and (ii) personalization/patient-specific detection. The specific contributions of our paper are as follows:

- We propose new GNN models for epileptic seizure detection that build on knowledge distillation to generate models that are both lightweight and work on subgraphs of reduced channels. To the best of our knowledge, this is the first KD approach dedicated to obtaining subgraph GNNs with reduced channels.
- We propose two different models for seizure detection with reduced channels, namely one with pre-selected (clinically motivated) channels and one with data-driven channels obtained from Gumbel-softmax channel selection.
- By applying our approach on pre-trained GNN that uses a full electrode set, we obtain personalized (patient-specific) and global (non-patient-specific) GNN models that are both lightweight (using only $\approx 3\%$ of the parameters of the teacher) and requires only a reduced subset of electrodes (requiring as low as only 10% of the original electrodes).
- We demonstrate the results of our approach on the TUH Seizure Corpus, which is one of the most popular and diverse datasets for epileptic seizures.
- We show empirically that the combination of personalization and KD could significantly improve seizure detection in cases of very scarce data, and in cases when the measurements from the less-informative electrodes.

Finally, it could be noted that epilepsy seizure detection is a very active research problem. In particular, there has been a steady increase in the number of graph-based approaches, and particularly GNNs applied to the problem of seizure detection and classification [5,22,30]. However, to the best of our knowledge, no prior works exist that tackle the problem of channel reduction with GNNs and KD, particularly for seizure detection. While KD has been used in multiple settings related to GNNs [4,6,7,15,31–33], it has not been employed to the task of data-driven subgraph identification, which is the main objective in this paper.

2   Preliminaries

We now briefly review some of the basic concepts from GNNs and KD.

Graph Neural Networks. Graph Neural Networks (GNNs) refer to a class of deep learning models designed for graph-structured data [24]. GNNs learn the representations of the nodes/channels in a graph and predict the labels or properties of nodes/edges by actively using the underlying graph structure. Due to the graph structure, GNNs naturally provide an aspect of interpretability or explainability. GNNs have been shown to significantly outperform the use of CNNs or other non-graph approaches in many applications. While study and development of GNNs is an active research area, we consider the specific case of Graph convolutional networks (GCNs) in our work, since they form one of the simplest and most popular GNNs that directly generalize the convolution operation from CNNs to a graph setting [16]. A multi-layer GCN has the layer-wise propagation rule in the hidden layers:

$$H^{(l+1)} = \sigma(AH^{(l)}\Theta^{(l)}) \tag{1}$$

where $H^l \in \mathbb{R}^{N \times D}$ is the hidden node features at l-th layer; H^0 denoting the input, σ a non-linear activation function such as ReLU or sigmoid, A the adjacency matrix, and $\Theta(l)$ being the weight matrix in the l-th layer that is learned from the data for a given task. Put simply, the graph convolution operation takes the weighted sum of the features of the neighbors of a node and applies a non-linear activation function to produce the updated features for the node. This operation is repeated for each layer, allowing the model to learn more complex representations of the graph structure and node features. The final output of a GCN is typically obtained by applying a linear layer to the features of the nodes in the final layer. Finally, depending on whether the task is regression or classification, the parameters of the GNN are learned by minimizing a loss function, respectively.

Knowledge Distillation. Knowledge distillation (KD) [11] refers to transferring knowledge from a large/sophisticated pre-trained neural network (known as the *teacher* network) to a smaller network (known as the *student* network). The student represents a lightweight model derived from the teacher while enforcing the performance to be similar to that of the teacher. A distillation loss is used during training to guide the student to replicate the teacher's behavior as closely as possible. Different types of knowledge can be transferred, but the most straightforward one is response-based KD, which refers to the response of the output layer of the teacher. A widely used example of this is the class probability called as *soft targets* defined using a softmax function as

$$p(z_i, T) = \exp(z_i/T)/\sum_j \exp(z_j/T), \tag{2}$$

where p_i is the probability of belonging to class i, z is the vector of logits (outputs of the last layer of the teacher to a given input). The temperature T controls the contribution of each soft target to the knowledge. When T is equal to 1, we get the standard softmax function, but as T increases, the probability distribution is softened. The distillation loss can be seen as comparing the class probabilities obtained from the teacher and the student. It enforces the distribution of the outputs produced by the student to be close to that of the teacher. The Kullback-Leibler (KL) divergence is therefore often used as the distillation loss function, and minimizing this loss during training makes the logits of the student get closer to the logits of the teacher [10].

Let z_t and z_s denote the representation produced by the teacher and student models, respectively, for the same input. Then, the final loss function used to train the student is a weighted average of the two terms and is defined as

$$L_S = (1 - \delta)L_D(p(z_t, T), p(z_s, T)) + \delta L_{CE}(y, p(z_s, 1)),\qquad(3)$$

where L_D is the distillation loss function, $p(z_t, T)$ are the teacher soft targets, $p(z_s, T)$ are the student soft targets, $p(z_s, 1)$ are the student soft targets obtained when the softmax temperature is set to 1, i.e. using normal softmax function, L_{CE} is the cross entropy loss function, y are the ground truth labels, and α is the weighting factor. The parameter δ represents the relative weight given to the teacher's knowledge over the new training data corresponding to the student training – the higher δ, the lesser the model relies on the teacher for the training of the student. We shall consider KD as part of our approach later in Sect. 3.

3   KD with GNNs for Seizure Detection

3.1   Proposed Model

We first propose our approach to design a global seizure detection student GNN that works on data with reduced nodes/channels and the corresponding subgraph, obtained using KD from a teacher GNN that operates on the complete node set. Let D denote the number of nodes/channels in the full measurement. Let A denote the adjacency matrix of the graph capturing the inter-channel connectivity. The adjacency matrix could be obtained in different ways like a correlation matrix, functional connectivity, or simply the matrix that captures the physical proximity of the electrodes on the scalp. In our work, we use the latter.

Let $\mathbf{x} \in \mathbb{R}^{D \times T}$ denote the input signal consisting of the recordings/measurements from all the D channels for T time samples. Let us consider a GNN with parameters θ and let $z_\theta(\mathbf{x}, A)$ denote the output of the last layer or the logits learned by the GNN, where $A \in \mathbb{R}^{D \times D}$ denotes the graph between the channels. Further, let us use subscripts t and s for the teacher and student GNNs, respectively: $z_{\theta_t}(\cdot, A)$ and $z_{\theta_s}(\cdot, A)$ denote the output layers from the teacher and student GNNs, respectively. The teacher network is learnt by minimizing the following binary cross entropy function $BCE(\cdot, \cdot)$ between the class label y and the model prediction $f_{\theta_t}^t(\mathbf{x})$

$$\mathcal{L}_{CE}(\theta_t) = \mathbb{E}_{\mathbf{x}}\left(BCE(y, z_{\theta_t}(\mathbf{x}, A))\right),\qquad(4)$$

with respect to θ_t, where $\mathbb{E}$ denotes the expected value obtained by averaging over all training samples $\mathbf{x}$. We use the BCE function since we consider here only the seizure versus non-seizure classification problem. In order to train the student GNN from the pre-trained teacher, we minimize a regularized BCE cost, where the regularization term is given by the distillation loss that minimizes the KL divergence between the soft output of the teacher and student GNNs:

$$\mathcal{L}_D(\theta_t*, \theta_s) = \mathbb{E}_{\mathbf{x}}\left(KL(p(z_{\theta_t*}(\mathbf{x}, A), T), p(z_{\theta_s}(\mathbf{x}, A), T))\right),\qquad(5)$$

where $\theta_t *$ denotes the parameters of the pre-trained teacher and $p(z, T)$ is as defined in (2). Then, the student network is trained by minimizing the loss

$$L_S(\theta_s) \triangleq (1 - \delta)\mathcal{L}_D(\theta_t *, \theta_s) + \delta \mathcal{L}_{BCE}(\theta_s). \tag{6}$$

Our formulation so far uses the same input for both the student and teacher, and hence, the same number of input channels. This is because the KD formulation assumes that the input to both the student and the teacher are of the same class, as we discussed in the Preliminaries. However, our ultimate goal is to transfer knowledge to a student that uses the measurements from a reduced set of nodes/channels $\mathbf{x}^d$ with $d < D$, and not $\mathbf{x}$. In other words, we wish to train a student model that works on a subgraph A' of the original graph A. We achieve this by modifying the graph used by the student by deleting the edges from the full graph with an adjacency matrix A as follows:

$$A' = W^\top A W, \tag{7}$$

where $W \in \mathbb{R}^{D \times d}$ denotes the selection matrix which is a permutation of the matrix given by concatenation of an identity matrix of dimension d with an all-zero matrix of size $(D - d) \times d$ — retains only the subgraph of d-size subset of the channels.[1] The input $\mathbf{x}_d$ is then given by $\mathbf{x}_d = W^\top \mathbf{x} \in \mathbb{R}^d$, corresponding to the nodes of the subgraph defined by W. This in turn means that we must use $z_{\theta_s}(\mathbf{x}_d, A')$ and not $z_{\theta_s}(\mathbf{x}, A)$ in the total loss function in (6). Further, in order for the hidden nodes corresponding to the deleted channels to not be pooled in the GNN, we also multiply the output of each hidden layer of the GNN by W. This in turn means that in practice the student GNN working on D nodes can be fed with zeroes at test time on the discarded channels, corresponding to having only the reduced set of measurement channels as input for seizure detection. We note that, while the specific application setting used in this work is that of scalp EEG channels, our proposed approach can be applied also to other multi-channel settings such as fMRI, where there is knowledge of connectivity across channels/measurements. The use of GNNs also makes our approach inherently interpretable in terms of connectivity of the brain regions.

We consider three different instances of our model in this work: (a) **G**lobal **S**tudent GNN with **P**re-**S**elected channel reduction (GS-PS) model, (b) **G**lobal **S**tudent GNN with **d**ata-**d**riven channel reduction (GS-DD) model, and (c) **P**ersonalized **S**tudent with **D**ata-**D**riven channel reduction (PS-DD) model. We describe them next.

3.2   GS-PS Model

We first consider the case when the reduced electrodes are preselected, or known already. In particular, we chose the four channels of T3, T4, T5, and T6 of the 19 channels from the T-20 montage [14] as the reduced electrode set. This is

---

[1]   In general, A' may not necessarily be a connected graph, unless specifically regularized to be so.

motivated by input from neuroscientists that these temporal channels can be relatively more indicative channels for seizure in general [9]. In this case, the W matrix from Eq. (7) corresponds to a diagonal matrix with ones only at the indices corresponding to T3, T4, T5, and T6. We also validate the choice of these channels through the following experiment. We conduct an experiment where a new model with the same architecture as the teacher (keeping the full electrode channels) is trained to learn relevance weights w for each electrode: this was simply achieved by applying a learnable diagonal matrix $M \in \mathbb{R}^{D \times D}$ to the input before the GNN such that the effective input to the GNN was defined as $\mathbf{x}'_M = M \cdot \mathbf{x} \in \mathbb{R}^{D \times D}$. We notice that the weights assigned to the temporal and some of the occipital electrodes were the highest, in particular, T2,T3,T4, and T5, were given large weights. A more practical reason for the choice of temporal channels is the development of wearable sensors: many state-of-the-art wearable sensors are of the behind the ear type, corresponding to these four temporal channels [9,28]. We apply the proposed GS-PS model for seizure detection by training on the data from training patients and applying it to detect seizures on new test patients. In this case, the subgraph is pre-determined.

3.3 GS-DD Model

We next consider the case of learning a student with channel reduction achieved in a completely data-driven manner. We propose to use a Gumbel-softmax channel selection block akin to the approach pursued in [29]. Our proposed GS-DD model consists of two connected blocks, first, the Gumbel-softmax block that selects the subset of channels/electrodes, followed by the GNN block that produces a label as shown in Fig. 1. The details of the Gumbel-softmax block are given next.

The Gumbel-softmax EEG channel selection block was first proposed by Strypsteen and Bertrand [29], where channel selection was acheived through a learnable layer in the Deep Neural Network (DNN) in an end-to-end differentiable manner. The Gumbel-softmax layer represents a relaxation of the discrete selection operation that allows for differentiation [13,18,29]. Let x_n indicate the feature vector derived from channel n, and x_{new_i} indicate the ith channel in the reduced set of channels. During training, the output of each selection neuron k is given by $x_{new_k} = w_k^T X$, with w_k sampled from the concrete distribution given by [18]:

$$w_{nk} = \frac{\exp((\log \alpha_{nk} + G_{nk})/\beta)}{\sum_{j=1}^{N} \exp((\log \alpha_{jk} + G_{jk})/\beta)}, \tag{8}$$

with G_{nk} independent and identically distributed samples from the Gumbel distribution and $\beta \in (0, +\infty)$ the temperature parameter of the concrete distribution. The effective subset of input node features is computed as $X_{new} = w^T X$. The temperature parameter β controls the extent of this relaxation from the one-hot selection: as β approaches 0, the distribution becomes more discrete, the sampled weights converge to one-hot vectors. The continuous relaxation allows w

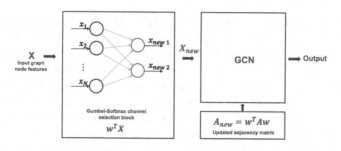

Fig. 1. Proposed approach

to be jointly optimized with model parameters, and to match the channel selection to the target model. The most pertinent EEG channels are thereby selected without prior expert knowledge or the need for manual feature selection. The learnable parameters α of this distribution are jointly optimized with the other network weights. At the end of training, the selection layer is made to select discrete channels by hard-thresholding the entries of w_k so that they select only

K channels as $w_{nk} = \begin{cases} 1 & \text{if } n = \arg\max_j \alpha^*_{jk} \\ 0 & \text{otherwise,} \end{cases}$, where α^* is the learned matrix

after training. We note that during test time, the Gumbel-softmax block takes the form of a fixed linear matrix multiplication W that acts to select the electrode channels. We also note that unlike the pre-selected case presented in Sect. 3.2, GS-DD model learns a *data-driven subgraph*.

In order to obtain a data-driven channel selection, we use the Gumbel-softmax channel selection block as part of our GNN pipeline shown in Fig. 1. In particular, we apply the GNN on the reduced subgraph obtained by selecting only a subset of input EEG channel signals X_{new} and that uses the adjacency matrix A_{new} corresponding to the selected channels. As discussed above, the Gumbel-softmax block is parameterized by a learnable matrix $\alpha \in \mathbb{R}^{N \times K}$, where N is the total number of electrodes, and K is the number of electrodes we wish to keep after reduction. When being fed a sample X, the selection block samples a weight matrix $W \in \mathbb{R}^{N \times K}$ from the concrete distribution following Equation (8). This can be viewed as a softmax operation, which produces a weight matrix whose elements sum to one as continuous relaxation of one-hot vectors. In our experiments, we use a similar method as in paper [29]. During training, we set $\beta(t) = \beta_s(\beta_e/\beta_s)^B$, decreasing in an exponential manner where B is the total number of training epochs. In particular, $\beta(t)$ is the temperature parameter at epoch t, β_s and β_s are respectively the starting and ending β. In our settings, $\beta_s = 100$, $\beta_e = 0.001$. In this setting, we start from $\beta = 100$ with β approaching 0. Intuitively, this would allow us to have a relaxed selection at the beginning of the training and approach the one-hot selection at the end. As we noted before, while the complete set of electrodes is indeed used during training of the student GNN, this is not the case during test time as the W matrix will be set to ones and zeros, thereby not requiring any measurements from the non-selected electrodes.

Channel Consolidation. We note that, though we force the weight matrix to select a reduced set of channels, it is possible that a given channel is chosen multiple times since we have not actively enforced that there is no duplication. In order to discourage duplicate channels, we minimize the total loss regularized with the penalty given by [29]: $\Omega(P) = \lambda \sum_{n=1}^{N} \text{ReLU}(\sum_{k=1}^{K} p_{nk} - \tau)$, where $\text{ReLU}(\cdot)$ is the rectified linear unit, λ is the weight of the regularization loss, and τ the threshold parameter. During training, we set $\tau(t) = \tau_s(\tau_e/\tau_s)^B$, decreasing in an exponential manner. In our settings, $\tau_s = 3$, $\tau_e = 1.1$. λ is set to be 5 to control the strength of the regularization. Then, we learn the GS-DD model with the regularized student loss, to obtain a seizure detection model that is global and applicable to any patient.

3.4 PS-DD Model

Epileptic seizures vary significantly between individuals and personalized models could be beneficial in taking into account their unique patterns and characteristics. This motivates us to extend our previous model to a personalized setting to for simultaneous electrode reduction and seizure detection for every single patient. As with the GS-PS and GS-DD models proposed in Sects. 3.2 and 3.3, our aim here is to arrive at light-weight models for seizure detection that use only a subset of electrode channels using KD, but personalized to the patient. As with GS-DD model, we let the channels be selected in a data driven manner. Our hypothesis is that *both knowledge-distillation and personalized models have an important role* to play in improving the seizure detection performance, *particularly in the cases when the available data is scarce.* The PS-DD model is in its essence the same as the GS-DD model in the architecture, with the crucial difference that the model is now trained in a patient-specific manner. This means that the PS-DD model also learns a *data-driven subgraph for every patient.*

4 Numerical Experiments

4.1 Settings

Dataset. We apply our models for the task of seizure detection on the data from the Temple University Hospital EEG Seizure Data Corpus (TUSZ) [20], which is one of the most popularly used, and diverse datasets that consists of over 100 patients of a wide range of ages (8-80) with different seizure types, e.g., focal seizure, tonic seizure, generalized non-specific seizure, and myoclonic seizure for long durations. The data is in the form of 19 channel EEG recordings in the 10–20 electrode placement system. As our work deals with the problem of seizure detection, no distinction is made between seizure types and all seizures were grouped into one class, resulting in a binary classification problem. The selected

Table 1. Three bands of patients.

Data Bands	# of Segments N	# of Patients	Batch Size	Epoch
Rare Data	$4 \leq N < 20$	65	2	20
Mid Data	$20 \leq N < 100$	53	16	100
Rich Data	$N \geq 100$	33	64	100

seizure (ictal) segments ranged between 5 and 60 s in length. Corresponding interictal segments of the same length were selected that ended one minute before seizure onset, following the methodology pursued in [9]. This resulted in a balanced dataset of 50% seizures and 50% nonseizure segments. The segments are taken sequentially without overlap. All selected segments were then split into five-second windows. The TUH dataset has two separate sets of recordings for `train` and for `dev`, which correspond to different set of patients for training and test, respectively. Similarly to the literature, we use only the patients from `train` for training models, and the test patients from `dev` for testing the learnt models on which the performance is reported. Finally, we have a total of 14382 samples for training and 4529 samples for testing, each sample being a 5-second window of multi-channel EEG signal.

Data Preprocessing. As customary in EEG signal processing, each sample is then filtered with a Butterworth bandpass filter of order 5 between 0.5 and 50 Hz to remove the artifacts and noise. Similarly to [25], the features were calculated for each EEG channel: energy of the signal filtered in frequency bands (from 0.5 Hz to 30 Hz with a bandwidth of 3 Hz and from 30 Hz to 50 Hz with a bandwidth of 10 Hz), Hjorth complexity and mobility, decorrelation time, L2-norm of the approximation and detail coefficients obtained from a six-level wavelet decomposition using a Daubechies db4 wavelet, log amplitudes of the non-negative frequency components. This results in 647 features in total for each sample/window. The features are then normalized component-wise and taken as input $\mathbf{x}$ to the GNN along with the distance based adjacency matrix.

Training Data. In order to train the teacher, no distinction is made between patients or segments and the entire training data is used to train the teacher. All the samples from all the test patients are used as test data. For training the global models of GS-PS and GS-DD, we use the data of all training patients during training and data from all test patients for testing. On the other hand, since the PS-DD model is trained for each patient separately, the training and test data segments are obtained by splitting the *segments* of the given patient randomly. Further, in order to understand the effect of personalization, we divide the patients into three bands based on the amount of data segments they possess as shown in Table 1. 80% of the personal segments go into the training set, the rest of 20% go into the test set.

Model Training. We use a two-layer GCN network with 32 hidden nodes in each hidden layer as the teacher model. It is trained with a batch size of 64 and a learning rate of 10^{-5}. The student network in all three cases of GS-PS, GS-DD, and PS-DD, is a lightweight model with just one-layer GCN of only 1 hidden node. We note that the number of parameters to learn in the student is *just* 3% of that of the teacher. Each of the three models is trained and tested both with and without KD in order to determine the contribution of the teacher knowledge. As described in Eq. (6), the KL divergence loss is used as the distillation loss function and the binary cross-entropy loss is used for the student loss function. We set $T = 5$, and δ values are set to $0.1, 0.5, 0.8$, where the hyperparameters in the total loss are obtained by performing 5-fold cross-validation. For GS-DD, we consider the case of $K = 4$ channels to compare the performance with that of GS-PS using the four temporal channels. For the PS-DD model, we use $K = 2$ electrodes for every patient. We also consider a non-graph baseline classifier using CNN to compare with our methods: A two-layer CNN is used for the teacher model and trained using only the training patients. For the convolutional layers we perform 2D convolutions with kernel size $(1, 80)$, $(5, 40)$, and stride $(1, 4)$, $(1, 4)$ respectively, with batch-norm and ReLU activation function. We also perform 2D max pooling at the end of each layer, with pooling kernel size $(1, 3)$, stride $(1, 1)$. As with our approach, we learn personalized student models using KD (called CNN PS-DD model) with the student CNNs having a single hidden layer.

Evaluation Metrics. Following [2,5], we evaluate the performance of the three models using two standard metrics used in evaluating seizure detection: F1-score and the Area Under the Receiver Operating Characteristic (AUROC). In all the cases, the performance is averaged over the different test patients.

4.2 Detection Performance Results

We now report the performance of the different approaches.

Non-graph CNN Baseline. The results of CNN teacher and CNN PS-DD (personalized student) models are reported in Table 2. We observe that while the highest test F1 and AUROC are reached when $\delta = 0.5$, showing that personalization and knowledge distillation help improve the test performance with lightweight and channel-compressed models.

GS-PS Model. The performance of the teacher and the global student with the pre-selected temporal channels is presented in Table 2. In the pre-selected student, we observe that KD significantly improves the performance in terms of the f1-score that tends to be comparable to that of the teacher.

Table 2. Test Results with Different Models

Model		w/o KD		w/ KD					
Channel	Personalization	–		$\delta = 0.1$		$\delta = 0.5$		$\delta = 0.8$	
Selection		f1	auroc	f1	auroc	f1	auroc	f1	auroc
GCN Teacher	–	0.689	0.781	–	–	–	–	–	–
GS-PS	×	0.401	0.755	0.683	0.766	–	–	–	–
GS-DD	×	0.690	0.763	0.695	0.761	0.697	0.763	0.693	0.764
PS-DD	✓	0.788	0.814	0.755	0.777	0.784	0.829	**0.795**	**0.829**
CNN Teacher	–	0.626	0.629	–	–	–	–	–	–
CNN PS-DD	✓	0.689	0.741	0.654	0.703	**0.699**	**0.774**	0.675	0.747

GS-DD Model. Unlike in the temporal channel pre-selection case, we see that the performance remains relatively constant to the different levels of KD. This is probably because the Gumbel-softmax selection already results in a high performance, and the teacher does not offer notable improvement.

PS-DD Model. In the case of a personalized student GNN with only two electrodes (that we call PS-DD 2), we observe that the performance improves as δ is increased, meaning more emphasis is given to the patient's data over the teacher's knowledge, with the highest performance obtained at $\delta = 0.8$. On the other hand, we also observe that completely relying on the patient's data and not using the teacher ($\delta = 1$) reduces the performance. Further, we note that the performance of the student even without teacher's knowledge ($\delta = 1$) is generally much better than that of the teacher or the global student. This in turn supports our intuition and hypothesis that personalization also plays a significant role in improving seizure detection performance. In the two plots in Fig. 2, we depict the distributions of test F1 and AUROC of all test patients in the circumstances with or without KD, respectively for the PS-DD model. The averaged performances are indicated in numbers in the figures. The dashed red/green lines show the general performances of models without personalization. When trained on the general population, we obtain the test F1 of models with and without KD as 0.7 and 0.4, respectively, whereas after personalization the average test F1 scores are improved by 16% and 50% to around 0.8, corresponding to with and without KD, respectively. This shows that by tackling the diversity in EEG seizure data on a large population, personalization has the potential to improve seizure detection. The average test AUROC is improved by 8% to above 0.8. The detailed results are reported in Table 2. We also note that in general that our graph-based approach significantly outperforms the non-graph CNN approach, showing the relevance of the connectivity information. However, the average performance of our approach with KD is only slightly higher than the average performance without KD in both metrics. This in turn motivated us to look into the performance in the three data bands individually next.

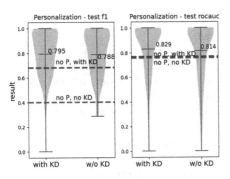
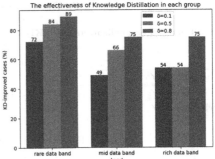

Fig. 2. The effectiveness of personalization: With personalization (P), both test F1 and test AUROC are significantly improved on average.

Fig. 3. The effectiveness of Knowledge Distillation (KD) in different bands

4.3 Performance Analysis

To better understand the effectiveness of our models, we do a detailed performance analysis by further dividing patients into three bands based on the number of seizure segments (rare-data band, mid-data band, rich-data band) and delve into the performances, respectively as shown in Table 1. In Table 3, we report the seizure detection results when the model training relies differently on the new patient data to different levels given by $\delta = 0.1$, $\delta = 0.5$ and $\delta = 0.8$, respectively, in (6). The setting of $\delta = 0.8$ corresponds to the case where the student training relies more heavily on unseen patient-specific data than the teacher. Figure 3 shows the differences in the percentages of cases in each band where KD boosted the model performance (in terms of test F1 and test AUROC). Overall, when $\delta = 0.1$, KD helps 72% (47 out of 65) patients in the rare-data band improve their model testing performances. The number of patients that benefit from KD increases when δ goes to 0.8, which explains the superior performance of PS-DD with $\delta = 0.8$ as seen in Table 2. In contrast, only 49% (26 out of 53) patients in the mid-data band and 54% (18 out of 33) patients benefit from the teacher when $\delta = 0.1$. In general, we observe that patients with scarce data benefit the most from KD. This gives us the motivation to further delve into the rare-data band case.

In the rare-data band, we notice that we constantly encounter four patients with the lowest performance that bias the overall performance significantly. It turns out that these four cases correspond to the patients with the least training data. We refer to these cases as the four "extremes" in our experiments. Since the TUSZ dataset is rather diverse and we wish to see the averaged performance without a strong bias, we chose to exclude the extremes out and recompute the performance metrics. We notice from Table 4, that the performance improves overall by excluding the extremes, and the best performance is obtained when $\delta = 0.8$. This indicates that the effectiveness of KD in personalized settings

Table 3. PS-DD Test Results on Different Bands

Data Bands	Personalization	w/o KD		w/ KD					
		−		$\delta = 0.1$		$\delta = 0.5$		$\delta = 0.8$	
		f1	auroc	f1	auroc	f1	auroc	f1	auroc
Rare Data	✓	0.786	0.791	0.783	0.783	0.790*	0.816*	**0.798***	**0.827***
Mid Data	✓	**0.791**	**0.837**	0.726	0.756	0.774	0.819	0.786	0.833
Rich Data	✓	0.790	0.821	0.749	0.800	0.786	**0.829**	**0.801***	0.828*

Table 4. PS-DD Test Results on Rare-Data Bands

Model		Extremes ×		Extremes ✓	
δ	Personalization	f1	auroc	f1	auroc
0.1	✓	0.794	0.806	0.783	0.783
0.5	✓	0.813	0.860	0.790	0.816
0.8	✓	**0.832**	**0.871**	0.798	0.827
1 (no KD)	✓	0.816	0.833	0.786	0.791

widely varies with the amount of data each patient possesses, and potentially across the patient types (since the dataset includes different types of seizures that we do not currently account for) and also varies with the change of the weight of student loss δ. In our experiments, $\delta = 0.8$ gave the best scores on average. A more exhaustive approach would be to compute personalized models with personalized δ, but that is beyond the scope of the current work.

Effectiveness of KD When Lacking Informative Channels/Signals. To further test the effectiveness of both personalization and KD in epileptic seizure detection in a more lack-of-information case, we select to keep only signals from channels FP1 and FP2 that belong to the frontal region, which are typically known to be the least informative regions for epileptic seizure detection. The Gumbel-softmax channel selection block is not involved in this section. The experiment is conducted on the rare data band, with the hypothesis that the combination of personalization and KD can help compensate for the adverse situation brought by a) lack of informative channels, and b) lack of data. With only personalization but no KD, 53.8% (35 out of 65) patients' test F1 and AUROC score still exceed 0.65, yielding fairly good performances. In the rest of not ideal personalized situations, 90% (27 out of 30 patients) benefit from the teacher. With even the less informative channels, we get 53.8% of the cases with rather promising results. For the rest of the cases, the integrated application of personalization and KD has been observed to be effective for detecting epileptic seizures. We thus see that the combination leverages the strengths of both techniques to provide highly accurate results in scarce data scenarios.

5 Conclusions and Future Work

We proposed an approach to transfer the knowledge from a pre-trained GNN-based seizure detection to the case when the number of measurement electrodes is reduced. We showed that it is possible to obtain models that are (i) light-weight (requiring just a 3% of the sophisticated network), and (ii) work with reduced electrodes (requiring as low as only 10% of the original electrodes), yet offer superior performance in seizure-detection, particularly in the personalized setting. The approach resulted in patient-specific choice of the reduced set of electrodes. Our experiments demonstrated the merit of both knowledge distillation and personalization, particularly when dealing with patients with scarce data. We observe that there is a trade-off between the use of prior information (teacher) and patient-specific data: although teacher-knowledge is necessary, the relative importance should be higher on the patient-specific data for maximum performance. We believe that these results show that our approach can provide meaningful insights and guidelines in the practical setting where there is need to move from full scalp electrode measurements to reduced form factor measurements, such as personalized wearable devices. We have currently restricted our analysis to a relatively simple GNN teacher model and used the graph given by physical placement of electrodes. The quality of the teacher and the graph used both translate into the quality of the student model, and hence, we believe that a more sophisticated GNN could be employed to further improve overall performance. In the future, it would also be interesting to look into multi-class seizure classification and identify the different types of seizures.

Ethical statement. We hereby draw the attention of the reviewers that in our experimental work we have made use of only the publicly available dataset: Temple University Hospital EEG Seizure Data Corpus (TUSZ). This dataset to the best of our knowledge has been anonymized and great care has been taken by the providers of the dataset during the acquisition, processing, and reporting of the dataset.

Additionally, to the best of our knowledge, we do not envision any ethical issues stemming from the use of our work by any third party. We are aware that in general personalized models could potentially have information that could be deemed as sensitive. But we do not directly foresee this being an issue with our model given that we make use of no personal information or identity of the patients/data in our work.

References

1. Ahmedt-Aristizabal, D., Fernando, T., Denman, S., Petersson, L., Aburn, M.J., Fookes, C.: Neural memory networks for seizure type classification. In: 2020 IEEE Engineering in Medicine & Biology Society (EMBC), pp. 569–575. IEEE (2020)
2. Asif, U., Roy, S., Tang, J., Harrer, S.: Seizurenet: multi-spectral deep feature learning for seizure type classification. In: Kia, S.M., et al. (eds.) Machine Learning in Clinical Neuroimaging and Radiogenomics in Neuro-oncology, pp. 77–87. Springer International Publishing, Cham (2020)

3. Blom, J.L., Anneveldt, M.: An electrode cap tested. Electroencephalogr. Clin. Neurophysiol. **54**(5), 591–4 (1982)
4. Chen, Y., Bian, Y., Xiao, X., Rong, Y., Xu, T., Huang, J.: On self-distilling graph neural network. CoRR abs/2011.02255 (2020), https://arxiv.org/abs/2011.02255
5. Covert, I.C., et al.: Temporal graph convolutional networks for automatic seizure detection. In: Machine Learning for Healthcare Conference, pp. 160–180. PMLR (2019)
6. Deng, X., Zhang, Z.: Graph-free knowledge distillation for graph neural networks. In: Zhou, Z. (ed.) Proceedings of the Thirtieth International Joint Conference on Artificial Intelligence, IJCAI 2021, Virtual Event / Montreal, Canada, 19–27 August 2021, pp. 2321–2327. ijcai.org (2021). https://doi.org/10.24963/ijcai.2021/320
7. Feng, K., Li, C., Yuan, Y., Wang, G.: Freekd: Free-direction knowledge distillation for graph neural networks. In: Zhang, A., Rangwala, H. (eds.) KDD '22: The 28th ACM SIGKDD Conference on Knowledge Discovery and Data Mining, Washington, DC, USA, August 14–18, 2022, pp. 357–366. ACM (2022). https://doi.org/10.1145/3534678.3539320
8. Fürbass, F., et al.: Automatic multimodal detection for long-term seizure documentation in epilepsy. Clin. Neurophysiol.**128**(8), 1466–1472 (2017). https://doi.org/10.1016/j.clinph.2017.05.013, https://www.sciencedirect.com/science/article/pii/S1388245717301980
9. Gabeff, V., et al.: Interpreting deep learning models for epileptic seizure detection on EEG signals. Artif. Intell. Medicine **117**, 102084 (2021). https://doi.org/10.1016/j.artmed.2021.102084, https://doi.org/10.1016/j.artmed.2021.102084
10. Gou, J., Yu, B., Maybank, S.J., Tao, D.: Knowledge distillation: a survey. Int. J. Comput. Vision **129**, 1789–1819 (2021)
11. Hinton, G., Vinyals, O., Dean, J.: Distilling the knowledge in a neural network. arXiv preprint arXiv:1503.02531 (2015)
12. Iešmantas, T., Alzbutas, R.: Convolutional neural network for detection and classification of seizures in clinical data. Med. Biol. Eng. Comput. **58**(9), 1919–1932 (2020)
13. Jang, E., Gu, S., Poole, B.: Categorical reparameterization with gumbel-softmax. arXiv preprint arXiv:1611.01144 (2016)
14. Jasper, H.H.: The ten-twenty electrode system of the international federation. Electroencephalogr. Clin. Neurophysiol. **10**, 370–375 (1958)
15. Joshi, C.K., Liu, F., Xun, X., Lin, J., Foo, C.: On representation knowledge distillation for graph neural networks. CoRR abs/2111.04964 (2021), https://arxiv.org/abs/2111.04964
16. Kipf, T.N., Welling, M.: Semi-supervised classification with graph convolutional networks. arXiv preprint arXiv:1609.02907 (2016)
17. Kwan, P., Brodie, M.J.: Definition of refractory epilepsy: defining the indefinable? Lancet Neurol. **9**(1), 27–29 (2010). https://doi.org/10.1016/S1474-4422(09)70304-7
18. Maddison, C.J., Mnih, A., Teh, Y.W.: The concrete distribution: A continuous relaxation of discrete random variables. arXiv preprint arXiv:1611.00712 (2016)
19. Maganti, R.K., Rutecki, P.: EEG and Epilepsy Monitoring. Continuum (Minneapolis, Minn.) **19**(3), 598–622 (2013). https://doi.org/10.1212/01.CON.0000431378.51935.d8
20. Obeid, I., Picone, J.: The Temple University Hospital EEG Data Corpus. Front. Neurosci. **10** (2016). https://doi.org/10.3389/fnins.2016.00196

21. Raghu, S., Sriraam, N., Temel, Y.e.a.: EEG based multi-class seizure type classification using convolutional neural network and transfer learning. Neural Netw. **124**, 202–212 (2020)
22. Rahmani, A., Venkitaraman, A., Frossard, P.: A meta-gnn approach to personalized seizure detection and classification. CoRR abs/2211.02642 (2022). https://doi.org/10.48550/arXiv.2211.02642
23. Roy, S., Asif, U., Tang, J., Harrer, S.: Seizure type classification using eeg signals and machine learning: Setting a benchmark. In: 2020 IEEE Signal Processing in Medicine and Biology Symposium (SPMB), pp. 1–6. IEEE (2020)
24. Scarselli, F., Gori, M., Tsoi, A.C., Hagenbuchner, M., Monfardini, G.: The graph neural network model. IEEE Trans. Neural Netw. **20**(1), 61–80 (2008)
25. Schiratti, J.B., Le Douget, J.E., Le Van Quyen, M., Essid, S., Gramfort, A.: An ensemble learning approach to detect epileptic seizures from long intracranial EEG recordings. In: 2018 IEEE International Conference on Acoustics, Speech and Signal Processing (ICASSP), pp. 856–860 (2018). https://doi.org/10.1109/ICASSP.2018.8461489
26. Shafer, M.P.O.: What Is Epilepsy? (2014). https://www.epilepsy.com/learn/about-epilepsy-basics
27. Siddiqui, M.K., Morales-Menendez, R., Huang, X., Hussain, N.: A review of epileptic seizure detection using machine learning classifiers. Brain Inform. **7**(1), 1–18 (2020)
28. Sopic, D., Aminifar, A., Atienza, D.: e-Glass: a wearable system for real-time detection of epileptic seizures. In: 2018 IEEE International Symposium on Circuits and Systems (ISCAS), pp. 1–5 (2018). https://doi.org/10.1109/ISCAS.2018.8351728
29. Strypsteen, T., Bertrand, A.: End-to-end learnable eeg channel selection for deep neural networks with gumbel-softmax. J. Neural Eng. **18**(4), 0460a9 (2021)
30. Tang, S., et al.: Self-Supervised Graph Neural Networks for Improved Electroencephalographic Seizure Analysis. In: Proceedings on the International Conference on Learning Representations (2022)
31. Yang, Y., Qiu, J., Song, M., Tao, D., Wang, X.: Distilling Knowledge from Graph Convolutional Networks. In: Proceedings of the IEEE/CVF Conference on Computer Vision and Pattern Recognition, pp. 7074–7083 (2020)
32. Zhang, C., Liu, J., Dang, K., Zhang, W.: Multi-Scale Distillation from Multiple Graph Neural Networks. Proceedings of the AAAI Conference on Artificial Intelligence **36**(4), 4337–4344 (2022). https://doi.org/10.1609/aaai.v36i4.20354
33. Zhou, S., et al.: Distilling Holistic Knowledge with Graph Neural Networks. In: Proceedings of the IEEE/CVF International Conference on Computer Vision, pp. 10387–10396 (2021)

Recommendation and Information Retrieval

OptMSM: Optimizing Multi-Scenario Modeling for Click-Through Rate Prediction

Xing Tang[1], Yang Qiao[1], Yuwen Fu[1], Fuyuan Lyu[2], Dugang Liu[3(✉)], and Xiuqiang He[1(✉)]

[1] FiT, Tencent, Shenzhen, China
{shawntang,sunnyqiao,evenfu,xiuqianghe}@tencent.com
[2] School of Computer Science, McGill University, Montreal, Canada
[3] Guangdong Laboratory of Artificial Intelligence and Digital Economy (SZ), Shenzhen University, Shenzhen, China
dugang.ldg@gmail.com

Abstract. A large-scale industrial recommendation platform typically consists of multiple associated scenarios, requiring a unified click-through rate (CTR) prediction model to serve them simultaneously. Existing approaches for multi-scenario CTR prediction generally consist of two main modules: i) a scenario-aware learning module that learns a set of multi-functional representations with scenario-shared and scenario-specific information from input features, and ii) a scenario-specific prediction module that serves each scenario based on these representations. However, most of these approaches primarily focus on improving the former module and neglect the latter module. This can result in challenges such as increased model parameter size, training difficulty, and performance bottlenecks for each scenario. To address these issues, we propose a novel framework called OptMSM (**Opt**imizing **M**ulti-**S**cenario **M**odeling). First, we introduce a simplified yet effective scenario-enhanced learning module to alleviate the aforementioned challenges. Specifically, we partition the input features into scenario-specific and scenario-shared features, which are mapped to specific information embedding encodings and a set of shared information embeddings, respectively. By imposing an orthogonality constraint on the shared information embeddings to facilitate the disentanglement of shared information corresponding to each scenario, we combine them with the specific information embeddings to obtain multi-functional representations. Second, we introduce a scenario-specific hypernetwork in the scenario-specific prediction module to capture interactions within each scenario more effectively, thereby alleviating the performance bottlenecks. Finally, we conduct extensive offline experiments and an online A/B test to demonstrate the effectiveness of OptMSM.

Keywords: CTR prediction · Multi-scenario modelling · Hypernetwork

---

X. Tang, Y. Qiao and Y. Fu—Contributed equally to this work.

G. De Francisci Morales et al. (Eds.): ECML PKDD 2023, LNAI 14174, pp. 567–584, 2023.
https://doi.org/10.1007/978-3-031-43427-3_34

1   Introduction

Click-through rate (CTR) prediction is a crucial component in online recommendation platform [3,5,19,23], which aims to predict the probability of candidate items being clicked and return top-ranked items for each user. In practice, a business is usually divided into different scenarios based on different user groups or item categories [4,6,20], and the resource overhead of customizing a proprietary CTR prediction model for each scenario is too high. Therefore, designing and deploying a unified CTR prediction model to efficiently serve all scenarios is a realistic challenge for a large-scale industrial recommendation platform. Taking the Tencent Licaitong financial recommendation platform used in the online experiment as an example, as shown in Fig. 1, these scenarios include the homepage (HP), balanced investment portfolio page (BIP), and aggressive investment portfolio page (AIP). Specifically, HP is the first page that each user interacts with, where the users usually browse the items without specific intent. The categories of items are mixed. The BIP and AIP pages list the items with corresponding categories for the users with different specific intents, respectively. We focus on how to effectively utilize all the user interactions in multiple scenarios to obtain a desired CTR prediction model.

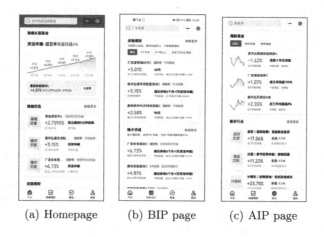

(a) Homepage   (b) BIP page   (c) AIP page

Fig. 1. The scenarios in Tencent Licaitong financial recommendation platform.

Different from single-scenario modeling [35], multi-scenario modeling (MSM) for CTR prediction is proposed in previous works to address the above goals. Existing works for MSM usually adopt the idea of multi-task learning to model the relationship between different scenarios [17,26,36]. They usually contain two main modules, i.e., the scenario-aware learning module and the scenario-specific prediction module. The former is used to learn versatile scenario-aware representations, where scenario-shared and scenario-specific information are captured simultaneously. The latter uses a scenario-specific architecture to predict the corresponding scenario based on scenario-aware representations. Obviously, the scenario-aware learning module carries more learning burden during training, and most of the existing works focus on improving the effectiveness of this module in modelling the multi-functional representations, where increasingly complex architectures are proposed [2,11,13,25,31,34,37]. Although these works have shown promising results, these complex architectures also increase both the model complexity and the training cost, which becomes an obstacle to generalization to more business scenarios. On the other hand, improvements for scenario-specific prediction modules are usually neglected in previous works, i.e., they only utilize simple fully-connected layers as the architecture of the predictor, which may lead to performance bottlenecks within each scenario.

In this paper, to address the above problems, we propose a novel **Opt**imizing **M**ulti-**S**cenario **M**odelling (OptMSM) framework. We propose a novel scenario-enhanced learning module to alleviate the first problem. Specifically, we incorporate scenario priors to partition the input feature set into scenario-specific and scenario-shared features, mapped to an embedding encoding specific information and a set of embeddings encoding shared information. After introducing adaptive gating and orthogonality constraints on the latter to facilitate the separation of shared information corresponding to each scene, it is combined with the former to obtain the multifunctional representation. Since neither adaptive gating nor orthogonality constraints require additional learnable parameters, and the separate modelling of feature sets eases the learning burden, the scenario-enhanced learning module provides an effective and efficient way to obtain the desired representations. Inspired by the effectiveness of feature interactions in single-scenario modelling, we then develop a scenario-specific hypernetwork to deal with the second problem, which generates adaptive network parameters based on scenario-aware representations. In this way, scenario-aware representations can fully interact with scenario-specific predictors to further improve performance. Moreover, as shown in Sect. 4.2, our framework can also be effectively integrated with existing multi-scenario models to improve performance.

2   Related Work

In this section, we briefly review some related works on two topics, including single-scenario modelling and multi-scenario modelling for CTR prediction.

Single-Scenario Modeling for CTR Prediction. Traditional CTR prediction aims to leverage the user interactions within a specific scenario to train an effective model for this scenario [5,16,19,22]. Most existing works on this topic focus on improving the modelling of feature interactions to enhance the performance of models, and many representative methods have been proposed. For example, DeepFM combines factorization machine and deep network layer to model the feature interactions [8], DCN [29] and DCN-V2 [30] develop a novel cross-network layer to further characterize the explicit feature interactions, and APG [33] proposes an adaptive parameter generation network for deep CTR prediction models, which can enhance the representation of feature interactions per instance with a larger parameter space. In addition, some recent works have introduced various automated machine learning ideas to efficiently find a suitable feature interaction architecture, such as AutoFIS [14] and OptInter [15]. Overall, previous works have shown that the design of feature interaction architecture is an important factor in improving the performance of single-domain CTR models, which is neglected in multi-scenario modelling for CTR prediction.

Multi-Scenario Modeling for CTR Prediction. Multi-scenario CTR modelling aims to leverage all the user interactions in different scenarios to train one or more models to serve these scenarios simultaneously [7,11,13,24,25,31,37], where the key question is how to use shared-specific information to learn the versatile scenario-aware representations, and then use a scenario-specific architecture for per-scenario prediction. A lot of work has been proposed to improve the effectiveness of scenario-aware representation learning. For example, STAR [25] designs a novel topological dependency to fully exploit the relationship between different scenarios. SAR-Net [24] introduces a scenario-aware attention module to extract scenario-specific user features, and a corresponding gating mechanism is designed to fuse them with shared information. CausalInt [31] introduces the priors on causal graphs to efficiently extract shared information and reduce negative transfer. However, these methods will significantly increase the model parameter size and training difficulty. Furthermore, ignoring the improvement of scenario-specific predictor architectures will lead to performance bottlenecks.

3   Preliminary

In this section, we first give a formal definition of the multi-scenario CTR prediction task. Given a set of scenarios $S = \{s^m\}_{m=1}^M$ and a set of training instance $\{(\mathbf{x}, y, s^m)\}_{n=1}^N$, where $\mathbf{x} \in \mathbf{X}$ is the feature vector, $y \in \{0,1\}$ is the label, and $m \in \{1, \cdots, M\}$ is the scenario indicator corresponding to each instance. The multi-scenario CTR prediction task needs to perform CTR prediction on these M related scenarios,

$$\hat{y} = \mathcal{F}(\mathbf{x}, y, s^m), \tag{1}$$

where $\mathcal{F}$ is the multi-scenarios model and $\hat{y}$ is the predicted label. Further, we can decompose this task into two stages, i.e., scenario-aware representation learning $f(\cdot)$ and scenario-specific prediction $g(\cdot)$,

$$\begin{aligned} \mathcal{R}^{s^m} &= f(\mathbf{x}, s^m \mid \mathbf{W}), \\ \hat{y} &= g(\mathcal{R}^{s^m} \mid \{\mathbf{W}^{s^m}\}), \end{aligned} \tag{2}$$

where $\mathbf{W}$ and $\{\mathbf{W}^{s^m}\}$ are weight parameters of the two stages, respectively. Therefore, the optimization objective for multi-scenario CTR prediction can be formalized as,

$$\mathcal{L}_{msm} = \sum_{n=1}^N \ell(y_n, \hat{y}_n), \tag{3}$$

where ℓ is an arbitrary loss function, such as a cross-entropy loss.

4   The Proposed Framework

The proposed framework for optimizing multi-scenario modelling, or OptMSM for short, is shown in Fig. 2. The OptMSM consists of three steps. First, the input feature partition module incorporates the scenario priors to partition the input features. Then, the scenario-enhanced learning module models the disentangled representation corresponding to each scenario from the scenario-shared features. Finally, after combining scenario-specific information and disentangled representation, a scenario-aware representation interaction module is used to explore the interactions within each scenario to enhance predictive performance. We will describe each module in detail based on the training process.

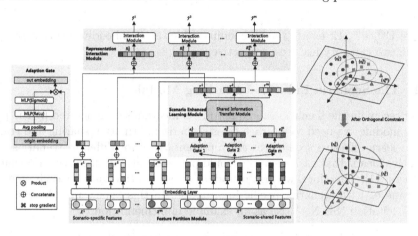

Fig. 2. The architecture of our OptMSM framework.

4.1   The Input Features Partition Module

To ease the model's learning burden for scenario-aware representations, we propose to divide the input features into two groups and model them separately, including scenario-specific features $\mathbf{x}^m$ and scenario-shared features $\mathbf{x}_c$, i.e. $\mathbf{x} = \{\mathbf{x}^m, \mathbf{x}_c\}$. An example of different categories of input features is listed in Table 1. It can be observed that some features are specific to certain scenarios, such as *scenario id*, while others are shared among all scenarios, such as *gender*. Note that previous modelling paradigms do not differentiate input feature categories. Therefore, scenario-specific features are difficult to transfer across scenarios during learning scenario-aware representations, and scenario information is hard to capture in the final prediction. Hence, the intuitive motivation for this module is to resolve these issues. In addition, the model needs more effort to reasonably balance the modeling of two categories of features. Next, we transform scenario-specific and scenario-shared features into corresponding low-dimensional embeddings and feed them into the following modules for further modeling.

$$\mathbf{e}^m = \mathbf{E}^m(\mathbf{x}^m) \quad \& \quad \mathbf{e}_c = \mathbf{E}(\mathbf{x}_c), \tag{4}$$

Table 1. An example of features included in the online financial recommendation platform used in the experiments.

Feature Category	Example
User Common Features	*gender, age, user behaviors, etc.*
Item Common Features	*item category, item price, etc.*
Context Common Features	*time, market condition*
User Scenario-specific Features	*user behaviors in scenarios*
Item Scenario-specific Features	*item statistics, item appearance in scenarios, etc.*
Context Scenario-specific Features	*scenario id, item position in scenarios, etc.*

where $\mathbf{E}^m$, $\mathbf{e}^m$, $\mathbf{E}$, $\mathbf{e}_c$ are the embedding tables and embeddings corresponding to the two category features, respectively.

4.2 The Scenario Enhanced Learning Module

After receiving the scenario-shared feature embeddings $\mathbf{e}_c$ generated by the previous module, we need to leverage cross-scenario information sharing and transfer to learn effective scenario-aware representations for different scenarios. An intuitive idea is that each scenario should pay extra attention to scenario-shared features [11]. Therefore, we first introduce an adaptation gate for each scenario to refine $\mathbf{e}_c$ with scenario-specific information. In this paper, we take Squeeze-and-Excitation (SE-Net) [10] as an example implementation,

$$
\begin{aligned}
\mathbf{z}^m &= \sigma(W^m[average(\mathbf{e}_{c1}), ..., average(\mathbf{e}_{ci})] + b^m), \\
\mathbf{e}_c^m &= concat([z_1^m * \mathbf{e}_{c1}, ..., z_i^m * \mathbf{e}_{ci}]),
\end{aligned}
\tag{5}
$$

where $\mathbf{z}^m = (z_1^m, z_2^m, \cdots, z_i^m)$ is the refined weight vector for scenario m, W^m and b^m are the corresponding learnable parameters, and i is the number of scenario-shared features. Note that adaptive gates can be implemented differently, such as an attention layer [27] or a perceptual layer [24], and the SE-Net block will be a lightweight approach for our purposes. Next, a built-in shared information transfer module aims to utilize the information synergy among all the scenarios to further distinguish different concerns of different scenarios on scenario-shared information. The issues for this module focus on how to transfer and what to transfer.

How to Transfer. A range of scenario-aware learning architectures have been explored in previous works on multi-scenario modeling, and they are easily integrated into this module. Here are some examples to illustrate the process:

- *shared network:* The shared network aims to extract commonality from all the scenarios and can be expressed as follows,

$$
r_{shared} = \mathbf{MLP}_{shared}(\mathbf{e}_c^m),
\tag{6}
$$

where $\mathbf{MLP}_{shared}$ is the multilayer perception network shared by all the scenarios. Note that multiple similar $\mathbf{MLP}_{shared}$ are used in MMOE, the parameters of $\mathbf{MLP}_{shared}$ are shared without explicit output in STAR, and the output of multiple $\mathbf{MLP}_{shared}$ are used as a shared expert component in PLE.

- *scenario-specific network*: The scenario-specific network aims to squeeze out scenario-specific information from shared information, in which only scenario-specific data are used,

$$r^m_{scenario} = \mathbf{MLP}^m(\mathbf{e}^m_c), \tag{7}$$

where $\mathbf{MLP}^m$ is the scenario-specific network. Note that the number of $\mathbf{MLP}^m$ can be set according to the plugged module, e.g., 0 in MMOE, equal to the number of scenarios in STAR, and a predefined value in PLE.

- *transferring layer*: In some previous works, different methods are introduced to jointly model the above two networks. For example, STAR proposes the FCN topology dependence, and PLE introduces the gated network. To illustrate the transfer process, we use FCN as an example,

$$r^m_{transfer} = FCN(\mathbf{e}^m_c) = (W_{shared} \otimes W^m) \cdot \mathbf{e}^m_c + b_{shared} + b^m, \tag{8}$$

where $\{W_{shared}, b_{shared}\}$ and $\{W^m, b^m\}$ are parameters in $\mathbf{MLP}_{shared}$ and $\mathbf{MLP}^m$, respectively, and $\otimes$ denotes element-wise multiplication.

Finally, this module will generate representations for all the scenarios, denoted as $\{r^m \mid m \in [1, M]\}$.

What to Transfer. Note that the scenario-aware representations are learned based on the model that mixes samples from all the scenarios. As a result, negative transfer often occurs, which perturbs the scenario-aware representations and misleads subsequent top-level predictions. A critical issue to mitigate the negative transfer effect is disentangling the representations between different scenarios. Inspired by the disentangled representation learning [21], we propose an explicit orthogonality constraint on the representation obtained above as an auxiliary loss to achieve this goal. Note that the number of samples in all the scenarios is usually unbalanced, and it is difficult to deal with the constraints of cross-sample representations. Therefore, we propose a strategy for enhanced learning. More specifically, for a sample b, we generate its representations in all the scenarios, i.e., $\{r^1_b, \cdots, r^m_b\}$. Only one representation corresponding to the real scenario will be used for prediction in subsequent layers, while the others are used as *contrastive representations* to compute the orthogonality constraint. Orthogonal constraints will make these representations perpendicular to each other to ensure independence and successfully disentangle scenario-specific information. Note that the idea behind this strategy is similar to contrastive loss [28]. Formally, the loss can be expressed as follows,

$$\mathcal{L}_{orth} = \sum_{\substack{i \neq j \\ b \in B}} < r^i_b, r^j_b > , \quad < r^i_b, r^j_b > = \frac{r^i_b \cdot r^j_b}{\|r^i_b\|_2 \cdot \|r^j_b\|_2} \tag{9}$$

where $\| \cdot \|_2$ refers to the l_2 norm, and B is the size of the mini-batch. Note that although the loss is conducted on C_m^2 pairs, it can be efficiently implemented in a vectorized manner at the mini-batch level and avoids loops.

4.3 The Scenario-Aware Representation Interaction Module

Although we get the disentangled scenario-aware representation, we still need to augment the representation with prior scenario-specific features in Eq.(4). On the one hand, scenario-specific information has a solid induction to the corresponding scenario, which helps the final prediction. On the other hand, considering complex interactions has been shown to benefit the performance of single-scenario CTR modeling. Therefore, to give the prediction more perception of prior information, we design a hypernetwork adaptively generating scenario-aware parameters [2,9], which provides a full representation interaction. We give a detailed illustration of this module as shown in Fig. 3.

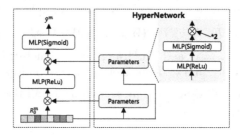

Fig. 3. The scenario-aware hypernetwork for parameters generation.

To preserve the priors, we only concatenate the prior scenario-specific features embeddings $\mathbf{e}^m$ with disentangled scenario-aware representation r^m,

$$\mathcal{R}_0^m = r^m \oplus \mathbf{e}^m. \tag{10}$$

We then adopt a two-layer perception to generate parameters from the representations, i.e.,

$$\begin{aligned} \mathbb{R}_{0l} &= Relu(w_0 \mathcal{R}_0^m + b_0), \\ \mathbb{R}_{1l} &= 2 \star \sigma(w_1 \mathbb{R}_{0l} + b_1), \end{aligned} \tag{11}$$

where σ is sigmoid function, $\mathbb{R}_{1l}$ has the same shape as $\mathcal{R}_l^m$, and l is is the current layer number. Setting the coefficient to 2 in Eq.(11) is to scale the mean of sigmoid output to 1. After parameters are generated, we interact $\mathbb{R}_{1l}$ with each layer in each scenario-specific predictor,

$$\mathcal{R}_l^m = \mathcal{R}_l^m \otimes \mathbb{R}_{1l}, \ l \in \{0, \cdots, L-1\} \tag{12}$$

where $\mathcal{R}_l^m$ is the latent output of layer l in the scenario m, and $L-1$ is the number of layers in each scenario. Finally, the final score for m-th scenario can be get,

$$\hat{y}^m = \sigma(W_{L-1} R_{L-1}^m + b_{L-1}), \tag{13}$$

where W_{n-1}, b_{n-1} is the parameters of classifier. After combining Eq.(3), (9) and (13), We can get the final optimization objective,

$$\mathcal{L} = \mathcal{L}_{msm} + \lambda \cdot \mathcal{L}_{orth}, \tag{14}$$

where λ is a hyper-parameter controlling the orthogonality constraint.

5 Experiments

In this section, we conduct comprehensive experiments with the aim of answering the following five key questions.

- **RQ1**: Could OptMSM achieve superior performance compared with mainstream multi-scenario models?
- **RQ2**: Could OptMSM transfer to more multi-scenario models?
- **RQ3**: How does each module of OptMSM contribute to the final results?
- **RQ4**: Does OptMSM really get the optimal scenario-aware representation?
- **RQ5**: How does OptMSM perform in real-world recommendation scenarios?

5.1 Experiment Setup

Datasets. We conduct our offline experiments on three datasets, including two publicly multi-scene CTR benchmark datasets (Ali-CCP and AliExpress) and a private product dataset. Ali-CCP[1] is collected from the traffic log of Tabao, and we divide logs into three scenarios according to the *scenario id*. AliExpress[2] is collected from the AliExpress search system, which contains user behaviours from five countries. We consider each country as an advertising scenario and select four countries in our experiments following the setting of previous work [38]. The real product dataset comes from the financial business scenario of Tencent Licaitong, and we collect consecutive 4 weeks of user feedback logs from four scenarios, respectively. For Ali-CCP, following previous work [32], we use all the single-valued categorical features and take 10% of the train set as the validation set to verify models. For AliExpress, we split the training set and test set according to the settings in the original paper [13]. For the production dataset, we keep data on the last day as the test set, and the rest as the training and validation sets. Table 2 summarize the statistics for these datasets. We can observe that the data distribution in Ali-CCP and Production is obviously unbalanced.

Comparison Models. To verify the effectiveness of our proposed framework, we compare OptMSM with the following models. **Mix**: The model with a 3-layer fully-connected network is trained with a mixture of samples from all Scenarios; **S-B**: We share the embedding table across scenarios, and each scenario-specific network is the same as Mix, i.e., shared bottom model; **MMoE** [17]: We adopt a

---
[1] https://tianchi.aliyun.com/dataset/408.
[2] https://tianchi.aliyun.com/dataset/74690.

Table 2. Statistics of datasets used in offline experiments. For impression and click, the percentages in each scenario are given in brackets.

Dataset	#Scenarios	#Impression	#Click
Ali-CCP	3	85,316,519 (0.75/37.79/61.46)	3,317,703 (0.84/38.91/60.25)
AliExpress	4	103,814,836 (17.07/26.04/30.51/26.38)	2,215,494 (17.02/24.49/38.15/20.34)
Production	4	823,972,400 (68.96/3.93/8.05/19.06)	59,466,088 (47.38/7.21/14.09/31.32))

shared Mixture-of-Experts model, where each expert is a 3-layer fully-connected network and the number of experts equals $2 * \#scenarios$; **HMOE** [13]: Except for explicit relatedness in the label space introduced by HMOE, the other settings are the same as MMOE; **PLE** [26]: The core module of PLE is CGC (Customized Gate Control), which consists of scenario-specific experts and shared experts. We keep the number of the former the same as MMOE with two additional shared experts; **STAR** [25]: This model consists of a centered network shared by all scenarios and the scenario-specific network for each scenario. The architectures of all networks are the same as Mix; and **PEPNet** [2]: This model adopts personalized prior information to enhance embedding and parameter personalization, and only has scenario-specific towers for predictions.

Implementation Details and Evaluation Settings. All models are implemented on Tensorflow [1] and trained with Adam optimizer [12]. We tune learning rate from $[10^{-2}, 10^{-3}, 10^{-4}, 10^{-5}]$, $L2$ weight from $[10^{-3}, 10^{-4}, 10^{-5}, 10^{-6}]$, and dropout rate from [0.1, 0.2, 0.3, 0.4]. The batch sizes for each dataset are set as 2048, 2048, and 512, respectively. The embedding dimensions are set as 20, 10, and 10. Besides, the hidden layers of the fully connected network are fixed to [256, 128, 32]. Following the previous works [8,25], we use two common metrics in CTR prediction, i.e., AUC (Area Under ROC) and Logloss (based on cross-entropy).

5.2   RQ1: Overall Performance

We show the overall performance of our OptMSM and other baselines in Table 3. We summarize our observations below: 1) OptMSM generally outperforms baselines in most scenarios in three datasets. Specifically, OptMSM performs consistently well in three scenarios in the Ali-CCP dataset and improves significantly in the first sparse scenario. In the other two datasets, our OptMSM performs better in most scenarios to different degrees. Although OptMSM achieves the second performance in some scenarios, note that the difference is within 0.1%, which is also acceptable considering OptMSM gains statistical improvements in other scenarios; 2) On the whole, MSM can boost performance in all scenarios compared with the model trained with mixed data. However, this model

Table 3. The overall performance over three datasets. The boldface and underline indicate the highest score of all the models and baselines. ⋆ indicates significant level p-value < 0.05.

	Scenario	Metric	Mix	S-B	MMOE	HMOE	PLE	STAR	PepNet	OptMSM
Ali-CCP	S1	AUC	0.5921	0.5899	0.5955	<u>0.5979</u>	0.5943	0.5924	0.5941	**0.6023**⋆
		Logloss	0.1838	0.1855	0.1811	<u>0.1801</u>	0.1811	0.1906	0.1922	**0.1782**⋆
	S2	AUC	0.6166	0.6202	0.6183	0.6214	0.6198	<u>0.6246</u>	0.6203	**0.6257**⋆
		Logloss	0.1673	0.1663	0.1657	0.1662	<u>0.1657</u>	0.1715	0.1724	**0.1648**⋆
	S3	AUC	0.6141	0.6164	0.6151	<u>0.6183</u>	0.6165	0.6175	0.6168	**0.6231**⋆
		Logloss	0.1641	0.1600	0.1596	0.1601	<u>0.1596</u>	0.1601	0.1693	**0.1587**⋆
AliExpress	NL	AUC	0.7256	0.7253	0.7257	<u>0.7261</u>	0.7256	0.7257	0.7258	**0.7286**⋆
		Logloss	0.1087	0.1086	0.1081	0.1080	0.1079	0.1084	<u>0.1078</u>	**0.1077**
	FR	AUC	0.7247	0.7256	0.7258	0.7260	0.7263	0.7258	**<u>0.7266</u>**	0.7256
		Logloss	0.1010	0.1013	0.1009	0.1007	0.1008	0.1009	<u>0.1006</u>	**0.1004**
	ES	AUC	0.7272	0.7276	0.7281	0.7285	0.7279	0.7277	<u>0.7290</u>	**0.7301**⋆
		Logloss	0.1211	0.1210	0.1207	0.1207	0.1208	0.1211	<u>0.1204</u>	**0.1201**
	US	AUC	0.7084	0.7059	0.7082	0.7084	0.7084	0.7073	<u>0.7088</u>	**0.7108**⋆
		Logloss	0.1015	0.1008	0.1008	0.1006	0.1006	0.1007	**<u>0.1004</u>**	0.1005
Production	S1	AUC	0.8718	0.8853	0.8866	0.8811	0.8872	<u>0.8875</u>	0.8866	**0.8890**⋆
		Logloss	0.0951	0.0914	0.0954	0.0982	0.0958	<u>0.0862</u>	0.0956	**0.0848**⋆
	S2	AUC	0.8997	0.9065	0.9069	0.9004	**<u>0.9077</u>**	0.9069	0.9068	0.9071
		Logloss	**0.0246**	0.0248	0.0256	0.0259	0.0258	0.0259	0.0317	0.0247
	S3	AUC	0.8414	0.8478	0.8491	0.8502	0.8496	<u>0.8515</u>	0.8507	**0.8524**⋆
		Logloss	0.0361	0.0288	0.0286	0.0286	0.0288	<u>0.0276</u>	0.0340	**0.0273**
	S4	AUC	0.8665	0.8765	0.8759	<u>0.8774</u>	0.8768	0.8756	0.8773	**0.8808**⋆
		Logloss	0.0569	0.0584	0.0581	0.0586	0.0585	<u>0.0575</u>	0.0654	**0.0538**⋆

performs slightly better than others in scenarios with sparse training samples. For example, the Mix model performs better in Ali-CCP S1 and Production S2. The possible reason for this is that samples in other scenarios are far more than these two scenarios and can directly help prediction in these two scenarios; and 3) PEPNet performs consistently better in AliExpress compared with other baselines while achieving relatively poor performance in other skewed datasets. Note that the distribution of AliExpress is more balanced than the other two datasets. Hence, this comparison directly verifies the effectiveness of information priors in some datasets and indirectly reflects that positive transfer is important when spares scenarios exist.

5.3   RQ2: Transferability Analysis

In this subsection, we investigate the transferability of our framework. We introduce FCN as our shared information transfer module in our framework. Here we extend our framework to other operation modules to illustrate whether our framework really optimizes the key factors for these modules. As shown in Fig. 4, we extend our OptMSM with transfer operations, including FCN, MoE, and CGC. Compared with the corresponding model, OptMSM improves its performance in all the scenarios, further validating the effectiveness of our design opti-

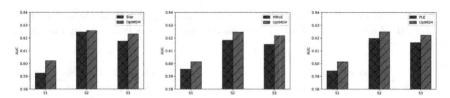

Fig. 4. Transferable analysis of OptMSM with different operation on Ali-CCP.

Table 4. Training cost comparison on the Ali-CCP.

Model	Star	OptMSM(FCN)	MMoE	OptMSM(MoE)	PLE	OptMSM(CGC)
Cost (s)	684	716 (+4.68%)	692	724 (+4.62%)	941	982 (+4.36%)

mizing module. To investigate whether the additional optimization will bring a lot of computation cost, we report the training time of these models in Table 4. Notably, the increment of training time of OptMSM is acceptable.

5.4   RQ3 and RQ4: Ablation Study

In this subsection, we validate the contribution of each component of OptMSM. We conduct a series of ablation studies over the datasets by examining the AUC after removing each component. The results are summarized in Table 5 and 6. The observations are summarized as follows: (1) All three components play important roles in optimizing different architectures, proving our optimizing framework's effectiveness. (2) In both datasets, removing orthogonal constraints generally suffers from the most decrement in AUC, which means the disentangled representation is effective. (3)Because of the significant improvement of PEPNet in AliExpress, removing hypernetwork in AliExpress is harmful to our framework, which indicates that our framework optimizing scenario-specific prediction module is useful. As the disentangled representation is a key factor in our OptMSM, we further illustrate visual results by comparing the t-SNE [18] representations with and without orthogonal constraint in Fig. 5. Note that our constraint is effective in explicitly disentangling representation.

5.5   RQ5: Online Experiments

In this subsection, we report the online experiment results of our OptMSM in a financial product recommender system for four consecutive weeks, and the results further verify the effectiveness of our OptMSM. Firstly, we briefly present the recommender system overview, shown in Fig. 6. This system has two main components: Online Service and Offline Training respectively. When users access any scenarios, a rank list request will be sent to the online service. Meanwhile, the user's attributes and contextual features will also be sent to the ranker, which utilizes the offline model to predict the score. In offline

Table 5. Ablation study on OptMSM with FCN for Ali-CCP. w/o means removing the corresponding component, and the relative decrement is reported in the brackets.

Model	S1	S2	S3
OptMSM	0.6023	0.6257	0.6231
w/o priors	0.6014 (−0.15%)	0.6247 (−0.16%)	0.6222 (−0.14%)
w/o constraint	0.6010 (−0.22%)	0.6246 (−0.18%)	0.6219 (−0.19%)
w/o hypernetwork	0.6016 (−0.12%)	0.6249 (−0.13)	0.6223 (−0.13%)

Table 6. Ablation study on OptMSM with CGC for AliExpress. w/o means removing the corresponding component, and the relative decrement is reported in the brackets.

Model	NL	FR	ES	US
OptMSM	0.7290	0.7268	0.7312	0.7117
w/o priors	0.7288 (−0.03%)	0.7260 (−0.11%)	0.7302 (−0.14%)	0.7112 (−0.07%)
w/o constraint	0.7277 (−0.18%)	0.7263 (−0.07%)	0.7301 (−0.15%)	0.7108 (−0.13%)
w/o hypernetwork	0.7280 (−0.14%)	0.7265 (−0.04)	0.7302 (−0.14%)	0.7107 (−0.14%)

Fig. 5. Visualization results on the representation in AliExpress. Left: with orthogonal constraint; Right: without orthogonal constraint.

training, the ranker leverages behaviour historical logs, and the trainer trains the model based on the logs daily. Our OptMSM trains a unified model here to serve multiple scenarios. We deploy the OptMSM on four scenarios in this financial product recommender platform, which serves millions of daily active users. And the model is trained in a single cluster, where each node contains 96-core Intel(R) Platinum 8255C CPU, 256GB RAM, and 8 NVIDIA TESLA A100 GPU cards. Besides using Click Through Rate (CTR)(i.e. $\frac{\#click}{\#impression}$), a commonly-used online evaluation metric, we also use purchase amount per mille (PAPM), defined as $\frac{\#purchase\_amount}{\#impression} \times 1000$. Briefly, our OptMSM improve the overall performance, achieving **+1.42%**, **+1.76%**, **+1.26%** and **+0.84%** lift on CTR, and **+6.58%**, **+7.10%**, **+5.82%** and **+6.90%** lift on PAPM over 4 scenarios. The daily improvements are illustrated in Fig. 7.

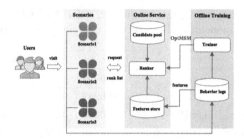

Fig. 6. Overview of the financial product recommender system.

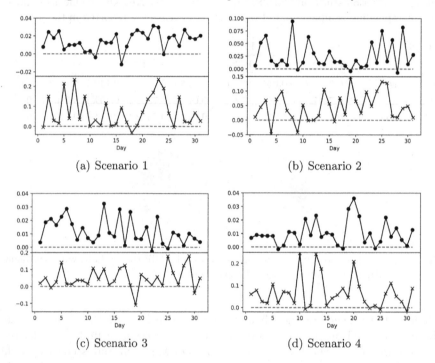

(a) Scenario 1   (b) Scenario 2

(c) Scenario 3   (d) Scenario 4

Fig. 7. Online relative improvement ratios in four scenarios in consecutive four weeks. (Upper is the CTR improvement, Bottom is the PAPM improvement).

6   Conclusion

In this paper, we propose a framework named OptMSM, which can optimize multi-scenario modeling with disentangled representation and scenario-specific interaction. First, we partition input features into two separate feature sets incorporating scenario priors, including scenario-specific and scenario-shared features. Then we design a scenario-enhanced learning module with plugged scenario-shared information transfer. With orthogonal constraints on both scenario-aware representation and contrastive representations, we obtain the disentangled representation. Finally, the scenario-specific interaction module adopts hypernetwork to make the scenario-specific information and scenario-aware representation fully interact. Compelling results from both offline evaluation and online A/B experiments validate the effectiveness of our framework.

References

1. Abadi, M., et al.: Tensorflow: A system for large-scale machine learning. In: Proceedings of the 12th USENIX Conference on Operating Systems Design and Implementation, pp. 265–283. OSDI'16, USENIX Association, USA (2016)
2. Chang, J., Zhang, C., Hui, Y., Leng, D., Niu, Y., Song, Y.: Pepnet: Parameter and embedding personalized network for infusing with personalized prior information. arXiv preprint arXiv:2302.01115 (2023)
3. Chapelle, O., Manavoglu, E., Rosales, R.: Simple and scalable response prediction for display advertising. ACM Trans. Intell. Syst. Technol. 5(4), 61 (dec 2015)
4. Chen, W., Hsu, W., Lee, M.: Making recommendations from multiple domains. In: The 19th ACM SIGKDD International Conference on Knowledge Discovery and Data Mining, KDD 2013, pp. 892–900. ACM, Chicago, IL, USA (2013). https://doi.org/10.1145/2487575.2487638
5. Cheng, H., et al.: Wide & deep learning for recommender systems. In: Proceedings of the 1st Workshop on Deep Learning for Recommender Systems, DLRS@RecSys 2016, pp. 7–10. ACM, Boston, MA, USA (2016)
6. Feng, J., et al.: Learning to collaborate: Multi-scenario ranking via multi-agent reinforcement learning. In: Proceedings of the 2018 World Wide Web Conference, pp. 1939–1948. WWW '18, International World Wide Web Conferences Steering Committee, Republic and Canton of Geneva, CHE (2018). https://doi.org/10.1145/3178876.3186165
7. Gu, Y., et al..: Self-supervised learning on users' spontaneous behaviors for multi-scenario ranking in e-commerce. In: Proceedings of the 30th ACM International Conference on Information & Knowledge Management, pp. 3828–3837. CIKM '21, Association for Computing Machinery, New York, NY, USA (2021). https://doi.org/10.1145/3459637.3481953
8. Guo, H., Tang, R., Ye, Y., Li, Z., He, X.: Deepfm: A factorization-machine based neural network for CTR prediction. In: 26th International Joint Conference on Artificial Intelligence, IJCAI 2017, pp. 1725–1731. ijcai.org, Melbourne, Australia (2017)
9. Ha, D., Dai, A.M., Le, Q.V.: Hypernetworks. In: International Conference on Learning Representations (2017)
10. Hu, J., Shen, L., Sun, G.: Squeeze-and-excitation networks. In: Proceedings of the IEEE Conference on Computer Vision and Pattern Recognition (CVPR) (June 2018)
11. Jiang, Y., et al.: Adaptive domain interest network for multi-domain recommendation. In: Proceedings of the 31st ACM International Conference on Information & Knowledge Management, pp. 3212–3221. CIKM '22, Association for Computing Machinery, New York, NY, USA (2022). https://doi.org/10.1145/3511808.3557137

12. Kingma, D.P., Ba, J.: Adam: A method for stochastic optimization. In: Bengio, Y., LeCun, Y. (eds.) 3rd International Conference on Learning Representations, ICLR 2015, San Diego, CA, USA, May 7–9, 2015, Conference Track Proceedings (2015)

13. Li, P., Li, R., Da, Q., Zeng, A., Zhang, L.: Improving multi-scenario learning to rank in e-commerce by exploiting task relationships in the label space. In: CIKM '20: The 29th ACM International Conference on Information and Knowledge Management, pp. 2605–2612. ACM, Virtual Event, Ireland (2020). https://doi.org/10.1145/3340531.3412713

14. Liu, B., et al.: Autofis: Automatic feature interaction selection in factorization models for click-through rate prediction. In: KDD '20: The 26th ACM SIGKDD Conference on Knowledge Discovery and Data Mining, pp. 2636–2645. ACM, USA (2020)

15. Lyu, F., et al.: Memorize, factorize, or be naive: Learning optimal feature interaction methods for CTR prediction. In: 38th IEEE International Conference on Data Engineering, ICDE 2022, pp. 1450–1462. IEEE, Kuala Lumpur, Malaysia (2022). https://doi.org/10.1109/ICDE53745.2022.00113

16. Lyu, F., et al.: Feature representation learning for click-through rate prediction: A review and new perspectives. CoRR abs/2302.02241 (2023). https://doi.org/10.48550/arXiv.2302.02241

17. Ma, J., Zhao, Z., Yi, X., Chen, J., Hong, L., Chi, E.H.: Modeling task relationships in multi-task learning with multi-gate mixture-of-experts. In: Proceedings of the 24th ACM SIGKDD International Conference on Knowledge Discovery & Data Mining, pp. 1930–1939. KDD '18, Association for Computing Machinery, New York, NY, USA (2018). https://doi.org/10.1145/3219819.3220007

18. Van der Maaten, L., Hinton, G.: Visualizing data using T-SNE. J. Mach. learn. Res. **9**(11) (2008)

19. Naumov, M., et al.: Deep learning recommendation model for personalization and recommendation systems. CoRR abs/1906.00091 (2019)

20. Niu, X., Li, B., Li, C., Tan, J., Xiao, R., Deng, H.: Heterogeneous graph augmented multi-scenario sharing recommendation with tree-guided expert networks. In: Proceedings of the 14th ACM International Conference on Web Search and Data Mining, pp. 1038–1046. WSDM '21, Association for Computing Machinery, New York, NY, USA (2021). https://doi.org/10.1145/3437963.3441729

21. Ranasinghe, K., Naseer, M., Hayat, M., Khan, S., Khan, F.S.: Orthogonal projection loss. In: Proceedings of the IEEE/CVF International Conference on Computer Vision (ICCV), pp. 12333–12343 (October 2021)

22. Rendle, S.: Factorization machines. In: ICDM 2010, The 10th IEEE International Conference on Data Mining, pp. 995–1000. IEEE Computer Society, Sydney, Australia (2010)

23. Richardson, M., Dominowska, E., Ragno, R.: Predicting clicks: estimating the click-through rate for new ads. In: Proceedings of the 16th International Conference on World Wide Web, WWW 2007, pp. 521–530. ACM, Banff, Alberta, Canada (2007). https://doi.org/10.1145/1242572.1242643

24. Shen, Q., Tao, W., Zhang, J., Wen, H., Chen, Z., Lu, Q.: Sar-net: A scenario-aware ranking network for personalized fair recommendation in hundreds of travel scenarios. In: Proceedings of the 30th ACM International Conference on Information & Knowledge Management, pp. 4094–4103. CIKM '21, Association for Computing Machinery, New York, NY, USA (2021). https://doi.org/10.1145/3459637.3481948

25. Sheng, X., et al.: One model to serve all: Star topology adaptive recommender for multi-domain CTR prediction. In: CIKM '21: The 30th ACM International Conference on Information and Knowledge Management, pp. 4104–4113. ACM, Virtual Event, Queensland, Australia (2021). https://doi.org/10.1145/3459637.3481941

26. Tang, H., Liu, J., Zhao, M., Gong, X.: Progressive layered extraction (ple): A novel multi-task learning (mtl) model for personalized recommendations. In: Proceedings of the 14th ACM Conference on Recommender Systems, pp. 269–278. RecSys '20, Association for Computing Machinery, New York, NY, USA (2020). https://doi.org/10.1145/3383313.3412236

27. Vaswani, A., et al.: Attention is all you need. In: Guyon, I., Luxburg, U.V., Bengio, S., Wallach, H., Fergus, R., Vishwanathan, S., Garnett, R. (eds.) Advances in Neural Information Processing Systems. vol. 30. Curran Associates, Inc. (2017)

28. Wang, F., et al.: Cl4ctr: A contrastive learning framework for ctr prediction. In: Proceedings of the Sixteenth ACM International Conference on Web Search and Data Mining, pp. 805–813. WSDM '23, Association for Computing Machinery, New York, NY, USA (2023). https://doi.org/10.1145/3539597.3570372.

29. Wang, R., Fu, B., Fu, G., Wang, M.: Deep & cross network for ad click predictions. In: Proceedings of the ADKDD'17. ADKDD'17, Association for Computing Machinery, Canada (2017)

30. Wang, R., et al.: Dcn v2: Improved deep & cross network and practical lessons for web-scale learning to rank systems. In: Proceedings of the Web Conference 2021, pp. 1785–1797. WWW '21, Association for Computing Machinery, New York, NY, USA (2021). https://doi.org/10.1145/3442381.3450078

31. Wang, Y., et al.: Causalint: Causal inspired intervention for multi-scenario recommendation. In: Proceedings of the 28th ACM SIGKDD Conference on Knowledge Discovery and Data Mining, pp. 4090–4099. KDD '22, Association for Computing Machinery, New York, NY, USA (2022). https://doi.org/10.1145/3534678.3539221

32. Xi, D., et al.: Modeling the sequential dependence among audience multi-step conversions with multi-task learning in targeted display advertising. In: Proceedings of the 27th ACM SIGKDD Conference on Knowledge Discovery & Data Mining, pp. 3745–3755. KDD '21, Association for Computing Machinery, New York, NY, USA (2021). https://doi.org/10.1145/3447548.3467071

33. Yan, B., et al.: APG: Adaptive parameter generation network for click-through rate prediction. In: Oh, A.H., Agarwal, A., Belgrave, D., Cho, K. (eds.) Advances in Neural Information Processing Systems (2022)

34. Zhang, Q., Liao, X., Liu, Q., Xu, J., Zheng, B.: Leaving no one behind: A multi-scenario multi-task meta learning approach for advertiser modeling. In: Proceedings of the Fifteenth ACM International Conference on Web Search and Data Mining, pp. 1368–1376. WSDM '22, Association for Computing Machinery, New York, NY, USA (2022). https://doi.org/10.1145/3488560.3498479

35. Zhang, W., Qin, J., Guo, W., Tang, R., He, X.: Deep learning for click-through rate estimation. In: Proceedings of the Thirtieth International Joint Conference on Artificial Intelligence, IJCAI-21, pp. 4695–4703. International Joint Conferences on Artificial Intelligence Organization, Montreal, Quebec, Canada (8 2021). https://doi.org/10.24963/ijcai.2021/636, survey Track

36. Zhang, Y., Yang, Q.: A survey on multi-task learning. IEEE Trans. Knowl. Data Eng. **34**(12), 5586–5609 (2022). https://doi.org/10.1109/TKDE.2021.3070203

37. Zhang, Y., Wang, X., Hu, J., Gao, K., Lei, C., Fang, F.: Scenario-adaptive and self-supervised model for multi-scenario personalized recommendation. In: Proceedings of the 31st ACM International Conference on Information & Knowledge Management. p. 3674–3683. CIKM '22, Association for Computing Machinery, New York, NY, USA (2022). https://doi.org/10.1145/3511808.3557154

38. Zou, X., et al.: Automatic expert selection for multi-scenario and multi-task search. In: Proceedings of the 45th International ACM SIGIR Conference on Research and Development in Information Retrieval, pp. 1535–1544. SIGIR '22, Association for Computing Machinery, New York, NY, USA (2022). https://doi.org/10.1145/3477495.3531942

PDF-VQA: A New Dataset for Real-World VQA on PDF Documents

Yihao Ding[1], Siwen Luo[1], Hyunsuk Chung[3], and Soyeon Caren Han[1,2(✉)]

[1] Unversity of Sydney, Sydney, NSW, Australia
{yihao.ding,siwen.luo,caren.han}@sydney.edu.au
[2] The University of Western Australia, Perth, WA, Australia
caren.han@uwa.edu.au
[3] FortifyEdge, Sydney, NSW, Australia

Abstract. Document-based Visual Question Answering examines the document understanding of document images in conditions of natural language questions. We proposed a new document-based VQA dataset, PDF-VQA, to comprehensively examine the document understanding from various aspects, including document element recognition, document layout structural understanding as well as contextual understanding and key information extraction. Our PDF-VQA dataset extends the current scale of document understanding that limits on the single document page to the new scale that asks questions over the full document of multiple pages. We also propose a new graph-based VQA model that explicitly integrates the spatial and hierarchically structural relationships between different document elements to boost the document structural understanding. The performances are compared with several baselines over different question types and tasks (The full dataset is released in https://github.com/adlnlp/pdfvqa).

Keywords: Document Understanding · Document Information Extraction · Visual Question Answering

1 Introduction

With the rise of digital documents, document understanding received much attention from leading industrial companies, such as IBM [35] and Microsoft [31,32]. Visual Question Answering (VQA) on visually-rich documents (i.e. scanned document images or PDF file pages) aims to examine the comprehensive document understandings in conditions of the given questions [13]. A comprehensive understanding of a document includes structural understanding [18,25,26] and content understanding [6,7].

The existing document VQA mainly examines the understanding of the document in terms of contextual understanding [21,29] and key information extraction [10,24]. Their questions are designed to ask about certain contents on a

---

Y. Ding and S. Luo—Co-First Authors.

© The Author(s), under exclusive license to Springer Nature Switzerland AG 2023
G. De Francisci Morales et al. (Eds.): ECML PKDD 2023, LNAI 14174, pp. 585–601, 2023.
https://doi.org/10.1007/978-3-031-43427-3_35

document page. For example, the question "What is the income value of consulting fees in 1979?" expects the specific value from the document contents. Such questions examine the model's ability to understand questions and document textual contents simultaneously.

Apart from the contents, the other important aspect of a document is its structured layout which forms the content hierarchically. Including such structural layout understandings in the document, the VQA task is also critical to improve the model's capabilities in understanding the documents from a high level. Because in real-world document understandings, apart from querying about certain contents, it is common to query a document from a higher level. For example, a common question would be "What is the figure on this page about?" and answering such a question requires the model to recognize the figure element and understand that the figure caption, which is structurally associated with the figure, should be extracted and returned as the best answer.

Additionally, the existing document VQA limits the scale of document understanding to a single independent document page [21,29]. But most document files of human's daily work are multi-page documents with successively logical connections between pages. It is a more natural demand to holistically understand the full document file and capture the connections of textual contents and their structural relationships across multiple pages rather than the independent understanding of each page. Thus, it is significant to expand the current scale of page-level document understanding to the full document-level.

In this work, we propose a new document VQA dataset, PDF-VQA, that contains questions to comprehensively examine document understandings from the aspects of 1)document element recognition 2) and their structural relationship understanding 3) from both page-level and full document-level. Specifically, we set up three tasks for our dataset with questions that target different aspects of document understanding. The first task mainly aims at the document elements recognition and their relative positional relationship understandings on the page-level, the second task focuses on the structural understanding and information extraction on the page level, and the third task targets the hierarchical understanding of document contents on the full document level. Moreover, we adopted the automatic question-answer generation process to save human annotation time and enrich the dataset with diverse question patterns. We have also explicitly annotated the relative hierarchical and positional relationships between document elements. As shown in Table 1, our PDF-VQA provides the hierarchically logical relational graph and spatial relational graph, indicating the different relationship types between document elements. This graph information can be used in model construction to learn the document element relationships. We also propose a graph-based model to give insights into how those graphs can be used to gain a deeper understanding of document element relationships from different aspects.

Our contributions are summarized as 1) We propose a new document-based VQA dataset to examine the document understanding of comprehensive aspects, including the document element recognition and the structural layout

Table 1. Summary of conventional document-based VQA. Answer type abbreviations are MCQ: Multiple Choice; Ex: Extractive; Num: Numerical answer; Y/N: yes/no; Ab: Abstractive. Datasets with a tick mark in Text Info. the column provides the textual information/OCR tokens on the image/document page ROI. LR graph: logical relational graph; SR graph: spatial relational graph.

Dataset	Source	Q. Coverage	Answer Type	Img. #	Q. #	Text Info.	Relation Info.
TQA [15]	Science Diagrams	diagram contents	MCQ	1K	26K	✓	✗
DVQA [13]	Bar charts	chart contents	Ex, Num, Y/N	300K	3.4M	✓	✗
FigureQA [14]	Charts	chart contents	Y/N	180K	2.4M	✗	✗
PlotQA [22]	Charts	chart contents	Ex, Num, Y/N	224K	29M	✓	✗
LEAFQA [3]	Charts	chart contents	Ex, Num, Y/N	250K	2M	✗	✗
DocVQA [21]	Single Doc Page	doc contents	Ex	12K	50K	✓	✗
VisualMRC [29]	Webpage Screenshot	page contents	Ab	10K	30K	✓	✗
InfographicVQA [20]	Infographic	graph contents	Ex, Num	5.4K	30K	✓	✗
PDF-VQA TaskA	Single Doc Page	doc elements	Ex, Num, Y/N	12k	81K	✓	LR graph SR graph
PDF-VQA TaskB	Single Doc Page	doc structure	Ex	12K	54K	✓	
PDF-VQA TaskC	Entire Doc	doc contents	Ex	1147	5.7K	✓	

understanding; 2) We are the first to boost the scale of document VQA questions from the page-level to the full document level; 3) We provide the explicit annotations of spatial and hierarchically logical relation graphs of document elements for the easier usage of relationship features for future works; 4) We propose a strong baseline for PDF-VQA by adopting the graph-based components.

2   Related Work

VQA is firstly proposed by [1] which categorizes the image source of the VQA task into three types: realistic/synthetic photos, scientific charts, and document pages. ***VQA with realistic or synthetic photos*** is widely known as the conventional VQA [1,8,11,12,19]. These realistic photos contain diverse object types and the questions of the conventional VQA query about the recognition of objects and their attributes and the positional relationship of the objects. The later proposed scene text VQA problem [2,23,27,30] involves realistic photos with scene texts, such as the picture of a restaurant with its brand name. The questions of scene text VQA query about recognising the scene texts associated with objects in the photos. ***VQA with scientific charts*** [3,13,14,22] contain the scientific-style plots, such as bar charts. The questions usually query trend recognition, value comparison, and the identification of chart properties. ***VQA with document pages*** involves images of various document types. For example, the screenshots of web pages that contain short paragraphs and diagrams [29], info-graphics [20], and single document pages of scanned letters/reports/forms/invoices [21]. These questions usually query the textual contents of a document page, and most answers are text spans extracted from the document pages.

VQA tasks on document pages are related to Machine Reading Comprehension (MRC) tasks in terms of questions about the textual contents and answered by extractive text spans. Some research works [21,29] also consider it as an MRC task, so it can be solved by applying language models on the texts extracted from

Table 2. Data Statistics of Task A, B, and C. The numbers in *Image* row for Task A/B refer to the number of document pages but the entire document number for Task C.

Task	Type	Train	Valid	Test	Total
Task A	Image	8,593	1,280	2,464	12,337
	Question	59,688	7,247	14,150	81,085
Task B	Image	8,593	1,280	2,464	12,337
	Question	37,428	5,660	10,784	53,872
Task C	Document	800	115	232	1,147
	Question	3,951	581	1,121	5,653

the document pages. However, input usage is the main difference between MRC and VQA. Whereas MRC is based on pure texts of paragraphs and questions, document-based VQA focuses on the processing of image inputs and questions. Our PDF-VQA is based on the document pages of published scientific articles, which requires the simultaneous processing of PDF images and questions. We compare VQA datasets of different attributes in Table 1. While the questions of previous datasets mainly ask about the specific contents of document pages or the certain values of scientific charts/diagrams, our PDF-VQA dataset questions also query the document layout structures and examine the positional and hierarchical relationships understandings among the recognized document elements.

3   PDF-VQA Dataset

Our PDF-VQA dataset contains three subsets for three different tasks to mainly examine the different aspects of document understanding: Task A) Page-level Document Element Recognition, B) Page-level Document Layout Structure Understanding, and C) Full Document-level Understanding. Detailed dataset statistics are in Table 2.

Task A aims to examine the document element recognition and their relative spatial relationship understanding on the document page level. Questions are designed into two types to verify the existence of the document elements and count the element numbers. Both question types examine relative spatial relationships and understandings between different document elements. For example, "Is there any table *below* the'Results' section?" in Fig. 1 and "How many tables are on this page?". Answers are yes/no and numbers from a fixed answer space.

Task B focuses on understanding the document layout structures spatially and logically based on the recognized document elements on the document page level and extracting the relevant texts as answers to the questions. There are two main question types: structural understanding and object recognition. The structural understanding questions relate to examining spatial structures from both relative positions or human reading order. For example, "What is the *bottom* section about?" requires understanding the document layout structures from

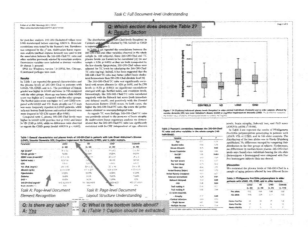

Fig. 1. PDF-VQA sample questions and document pages for Task A, B, and C.

the relative bottom position and "What is the *last* section about?" requires identifying the last section based on the human reading order of a document. The object recognition questions explicitly contain a specific document element in the questions and require to recognition of the queried element first, such as the question "What is the bottom table about?" in Fig. 1. Answering these two types of questions require a logical understanding of the hierarchical relationships of document elements. For instance, based on the textual contents, the section title would be a logically high-level summarization of its following section and is regarded as the answer to "What is the last section about?". Similarly, a table caption is logically associated with a table; table caption contents would best describe a table.

Task C questions have a sequence of answers extracted from multi-pages of the full document. It enhances the document understanding from the page to the full document level. Answering a question in Task C requires reviewing the full document contents and identifying the contents hierarchically related to the queried item in the question. For example, the question "Which section does describe Table 2 ?" in Fig. 1 requires the identification of all the sections of the full document that have described the queried table. The answers to such questions are the texts of the corresponding section titles extracted as the high-level summarization of the identified sections. Identifying the items at the higher-level hierarchy of the queried item is defined as the parent relation understanding the question in PDF-VQA. Oppositely, Task C also contains the questions of identifying the items at the lower-level hierarchy of the queried item, and such questions are defined as the child relation understanding. For example, a question, "What does the 'Methods' section about?" requires extracting all the subsection titles as the answer.

The detailed question type distribution of each task is shown in Table 3.

3.1   Data Source

Our PDF-VQA dataset collected the PDF version of visually-rich documents from the PubMed Central (PMC) Open Access Subset[1]. Each document file has a corresponding XML file that provides the structured representations of textual contents and graphical components of the article[2]. We applied the pre-trained Mask-RCNN [35] over the collected document pages to get the bounding boxes and categories for each document element. The categories initially consisted of five common PDF document element types: *title, text, list, figure,* and *table*. We then labelled the *text* elements that are positionally closest to the tables and figures into two additional categories *table caption* and *figure caption* respectively.

3.2   Relational Graphs

Visually rich documents of scientific articles consist of fixed layout structures and hierarchically logical relationships among the sections, subsections and other elements such as tables/figures and table/figure captions. Understanding such layout structures and relationships is essential to boost the understanding of this type of document. The graph has been used as an effective method to represent the relationships between objects in many tasks [4,18,33,34]. Inspired by this, for each document, we annotated the hierarchically *logical relational* graph (LR graph) and *spatial relational* graph (SR graph) to explicitly represent the logical and spatial relationships between document elements respectively. Those two graphs can be directly used by any deep-learning mechanisms to enhance the feature representation. In Sect. 6, we propose a graph-based model to enlighten how such relational information can solve the PDF-VQA questions. The SR graph indicates the relative spatial relationships between document elements based on their absolute geometric positions with their bounding box coordinates. For each document element of a single document page, we identify its relative spatial relationships with all the other document elements among eight spatial types: *top, bottom, left, right, top-left, top-right, bottom-left* and *bottom-right*. The LR graph indicates the potential affiliation between document elements by identifying the parent object and their children's objects based on the hierarchical structures of document layouts. We follow [18] to annotate the parent-child relations between the document elements in a single document page to generate the LR graph. The graph of the full document of multiple pages are augmented by the graphs of its document pages.

3.3   Question Generation

Visually rich documents of scientific articles have consistent spatial and logical structures. The associated XML files of these documents provide detailed logical

---

[1] https://www.ncbi.nlm.nih.gov/pmc/tools/openftlist/.

[2] It follows the XML schema module provided by the Journal Archiving and Interchange Tag Suite created by the National Library of Medicine (NLM) https://dtd.nlm.nih.gov/.

Table 3. Ratio and exact number of various question types of Task A, B and C.

Tasks	Question Type	Percentage	Total
Task A	Counting	17.74	14,387
	Existence	82.26	66,698
Task B	Structural Understanding	88.58	47,722
	Object Recognition	11.42	6,150
Task C	Parent Relationship Understanding	79.71	4,506
	Child Relationship Understanding	20.29	1,147

structures between semantic entities. Based on this structural information and the pre-defined question template, we applied an automatic question-generation process to generate large-scale question-answer pairs efficiently. For example, the question *"How many tables are above the 'Discussion'?"* is generated from the question template *"How many ⟨E1⟩ are ⟨R⟩ the '⟨E2⟩'?"* by filling the masked terms ⟨E1⟩, ⟨R⟩ and ⟨E2⟩ with document element label ("table"), positional relationship ("above") and title name extracted from document contents ("Discussion") respectively. We prepare each question template with various language patterns to diversify the questions. For instance, the above template can also be written as *"What is the number of ⟨E1⟩ are ⟨R⟩ the '⟨E2⟩'?"*. We have 36, 15, and 15 question patterns for Task A, B, and C, respectively. We limit the parameter values of the document element label to only *title, list, table, figure* as asking for the number/existence/position of *text* elements would be less valuable. The parameter values include four document element labels, eight positional relationships (*top, bottom, left, right, top-left, top-right, bottom-left* and *bottom-right*), ordinal form (*first, last*) and the texts from document contents (e.g. section title, references, etc.). We also replace some parameter values with their synonyms, such as *"on the top of"* for *"above"*.

To automatically generate the ground truth answers to our questions, we first represent each document page (for Task A and B)/the full document (for Task C) with all the document elements and the associated relations from the two relational graphs as in Sect. 3.2. We then apply the functional program, which is uniquely associated with each question template and contains a sequence of functions representing a reasoning step, over such document(page) representations to reach the answer. For example, the functional program for question *"How many tables are above of the 'Discussion'?"* consists of a sequence of functions *filter-unique → query-position → filter-category → count* to filter out the document elements that satisfy the asked positional relationships and count the numbers of them as the ground-truth answer.

Moreover, we conduct the question balancing from answer-based and question-based aspects to avoid question-conditional biases and balance the answer distributions. Firstly, we conduct an answer-based balancing by downsampling questions based on the answer distribution. We identify the QA pairs with large ratios, divide identified questions into groups based on the patterns,

Fig. 2. The top 4 words of questions in Task A, B and C.

and reduce QA pairs with large ratios until the answer distributions are balanced. After that, we further conducted the question-based balancing to avoid duplicated question types. To achieve this, we smooth over the distributions of parameter values filled in the question templates by removing the questions with large proportions of certain parameter values until the balanced distribution of parameter value combinations. Since the parameter values of Task C question templates are almost unique, as all of them are the texts from document contents, we did not conduct the balancing over Task C. After the balancing, Task A questions are down-sampled from 444,967 to 81,085, and Task B questions are down-sampled from 246,740 to 53,872.

4   Dataset Analysis and Evaluation

4.1   Dataset Analysis

The average number of questions per document page/document in Task A, B, and C are 6.57, 4.37, and 4.93. The average question length for Task A, B and C are 25, 10 and 15, respectively. A sunburst plot showing each task's top 4 question words is shown in Fig. 2. We can see that Task A question priors are more diverse to complement the simplicity of document element and position recognition questions and to prevent the model from memorizing question patterns. For Task B and C, question priors distribute over "What", "When", "Can you", "Which". And we also specifically design questions in a declarative sentence with "Name out the section..." in Task C. 13.43%, 0.24% and 29.38% of the questions in Task A, B, and C are unique questions. This unique question ratio seems low compared to other document-based VQA datasets. This is because, rather than only aiming at the textual understanding of certain page contents, our PDF dataset targets more the spatial and hierarchically structural understandings of document layouts. Our questions are generally formed to ask about the document structures from a higher level and thus contain less unique texts that are associated with the specific contents of each document page. Answers for Task A questions are from the fixed answer space that contains eight possible answers: "yes", "no", "0", "1", "2", "3", "4" and "5". Answers for Task B and C are texts retrieved from the document page/entire document. We also analyzed the top 15 frequent question patterns in Task A, B and C as shown in Fig. 3 to show the common questions of each question type in each task. We used a placeholder "X" to replace the different figures, table numbers or section titles that would exist in the questions to present the common question patterns in this analysis.

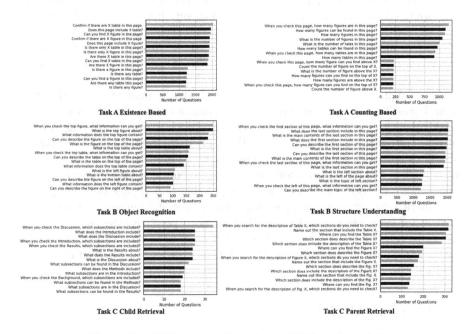

Fig. 3. Top 15 Frequency Questions of Task A, B and C.

Table 4. Positive rates (**Pos(%)**) and Fleiss Kappa Agreement (**Kappa**) of human evaluation.

Perspective	Task A		Task B		Task C	
	Pos(%)	Kappa	Pos(%)	Kappa	Pos(%)	Kappa
Relevance	98.46	94.02	91.67	77.07	100	100
Correctness	99.49	98.12	89.44	72.56	94.55	80.93
Meaningfulness	96.94	88.97	93.61	77.67	99.27	97.34

4.2 Human Evaluation

To evaluate the quality of automatically generated question-answer pairs, we invited ten raters, including deep-learning researchers and crowd-sourcing workers. Firstly, to determine the relevance between the question and the corresponding page/document, we define the *Relevance* criteria. Correspondingly, we define

Correctness to determine whether the auto-generated answer is correct to the question. In addition, we ask raters to judge whether our QA pairs are meaningful and possibly appear in the real world by using *Meaningfulness* criteria[3]. After we collect the raters' feedback, we calculate the positive rate of each perspective and apply Fleiss Kappa to measure the agreements between multiple raters, as can be seen in Table 4. All three tasks achieve decent positive rates with substantial or almost perfect agreements. For Task A, *Relevance* and *Correctness* can reach positive rates with nearly perfect agreements. Few raters gave negative responses regarding the *Meaningfulness* of questions about the existence of tables or figures, while those questions are crucial to understanding the document layout for any upcoming table/figure contents understanding questions. In Task B, all three perspectives achieve high positive rates with substantial agreements. The disagreements about Task B mainly come from the questions with no specific answer (N/A), some raters thought those questions were incorrect and meaningless, but these questions are crucial to understanding the commonly appearing real-world cases. Because it is possible that a page does not contain the queried elements in the question, and no specific answer is a reasonable answer for such cases. Finally, for Task C, both positive rates and agreement across three perspectives are notable. In addition, except for three perspectives, raters agree most of the questions in Task C need cross-page understanding (the positive rate is 82.91%).

5   Baseline Models

We experimented with several baselines on our PDF-VQA dataset to provide a preliminary view of different models' performances. We choose the vision-and-language models that have proved good performances on VQA tasks and a language model as listed in Table 5. We followed the original settings of each baseline but only made modifications on the output layers to suit different PDF-VQA tasks[4].

6   Proposed Model: LoSpa

In this paper, we introduce a strong baseline, Logical and Spatial Graph-based model (*LoSpa*), which utilizes logical and spatial relational information based on logical (LR) and spatial (SR) graphs introduced in Sect. 3.2.

Input Representation: We treat questions as sequential plain text inputs and encode them by BERT. For document elements of given document page I such as *Title*, *Text*, *Figure*, we use pre-trained ResNet-101 backbones to extract visual

---

[3] More details and human evaluation survey examples can be found in Appendix B https://github.com/adlnlp/pdfvqa/blob/main/Appendix.pdf.

[4] The detailed baseline model setup can be found in Appendix D https://github.com/adlnlp/pdfvqa/blob/main/Appendix.pdf.

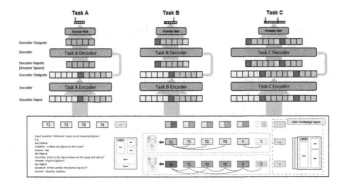

Fig. 4. Logical and Spatial Graph-based Model Architecture for three tasks. Task A, B and C use the same relational information to enhance the object representation but different model architectures in the decoding stage.

representations $X_v \in \mathbb{R}^{N \times d_f}$ and use [CLS] token from BERT as the semantic representation $X_s \in \mathbb{R}^{N \times d_s}$ for the texts of each document element.

Relational Information Learning: We construct two graphs: logical graph $\mathcal{G}_l = (\mathcal{V}_l, \mathcal{E}_l)$ and spatial graph $\mathcal{G}_s = (\mathcal{V}_s, \mathcal{E}_s)$ for each document page. For the logical graph $\mathcal{G}_l$, based on [18], we define the semantic feature as node representation $\mathcal{V}_l$ and the existence of parent-child relation between document elements (extracted from the logical relational graph annotation in our dataset) as binary edge values $\mathcal{E}_l$ $\{0, 1\}$. Similarly, for spatial graph $\mathcal{G}_s$, we follow [18] to use the visual features of document elements as node representation $\mathcal{V}_s$ and the distance with two nearest document elements to weight edge value $\mathcal{E}_s$.

For each document page I, we take $X_s \in \mathbb{R}^{N \times d_s}$ and $X_v \in \mathbb{R}^{N \times d_f}$ as the initial node feature matrix for $\mathcal{G}_l$ and $\mathcal{G}_s$ respectively. These initial node features are fed into a two-layer Graph Convolution Network (GCN) and trained by predicting each node category. After the GCN training, we extract the first layer hidden states as the updated node representations $X'_s \in \mathbb{R}^{N \times d}$ and $X'_v \in \mathbb{R}^{N \times d}$ that has augmented the relational information between document elements for $\mathcal{G}_s$ and $\mathcal{G}_f$ respectively, where $d = 768$. For each aspect feature, we conduct separated linear transformations to the initial feature matrices (X_v/X_s) and the updated feature matrices (X'_s/X'_v). Inspired by [18], we apply the element-wise max-pooling over them. The pooled features X''_s and X''_v are the final semantic and visual representations of nodes enhanced by logical and spatial relations, respectively. Finally, we concatenate semantic and visual features of each document element, yielding relational information enriched multi-modal object representations $O_1, O_2, ..., O_N$.

QA Prediction: We sum up the object features $O_1, O_2, ..., O_N$ with positional embedding to integrate the information of document elements orders, which are inputs into multiple transformer encoder layers together with the results of the sequence of question word features $q_1, q_2, ..., q_T$. We pass the encoder outputs into the transformer decoders and apply a pointer network upon the decoder output to predict the answers. We apply a one-step decoding process each time using the word embedding w_i of one answer from the fixed answer space as the decoder input. Let the z_i^{dec} be the decoder output for the decoder input w_i; we then conduct the score $y_{t,i}$ between z_i^{dec} and the answer word embedding w_i following $y_{t,i} = (w_i)^T z_t^{dec} + b_i^{dec}$, where $i = 1, ..., C$, and C are the total answer numbers of the fixed answer space for each task. We apply a softmax function over all the scores $y_1, ..., y_C$ and choose the answer word with the highest probability as the final answer for the current image-question pair. We treat Task B and C as the same classification problem as Task A, where the answers are fixed to 25 document element index numbers for Task B and 400 document element index numbers for Task C. The index numbers for document elements start from 0 and increase following the human-reading order (i.e. top to bottom, left to right) over a single document page (for Task B) and across multiple document pages (for Task C). OCR tokens are extracted from the document element with the corresponding predicted index number for the final retrieved answers for Task B and C questions. We use the Sigmoid function for Task C questions with multiple answers and select all the document elements whose probability has passed 0.5.

7   Experiments

7.1   Performance Comparison

We compare the performances of baseline models and our proposed relational information-enhanced model over three tasks of our PDF-VQA dataset in Table 5. All the models process the questions in the same way as the sequence of question words encoded by pretrained BERT but differ in other features' processing. The three large vision-and-language pretrained models (VLPMs): VisualBERT, ViLT and LXMERT, achieved better performances than other baselines with inputting only question and visual features. The better performance of VisualBERT than ViLT indicates that object-level visual features are more effective than image patch representations on the PDF-VQA images with segmented document elements. Among these three models, LXMERT, which used the same object-level visual features and the additional bounding box features, achieved the best results over Task A and B, indicating the effectiveness of bounding box information in the cases of PDF-VQA task. However, its performance on Task C is lower than VisualBERT. This might be because Task C inputs the sequence of objects (document elements) from multiple pages. The bounding box coordinates are independent on each page and therefore cause noise during training. Surprisingly, LayoutLM2, pretrained on document understanding datasets, achieved much lower accuracy than the three VLPMs. This might be because LayoutLM2 used token-level visual and bounding box features, which are ineffective for the whole document element identification. Compared to LayoutLM2 used the token-level contextual features, M4C, as a non-pretrained model, inputting object-level bounding box, visual and contextual features achieved higher performances. Such results further indicate that the object-level features are more effective for our PDF-VQA tasks. The object-level contextual features of each document element are represented as the [CLS] hidden states from the pretrained BERT model inputting the OCR token sequence extracted from each document element.

Our proposed *LoSpa* achieves the highest performance compared to all baselines, demonstrating the effectiveness of our adopted GCN-encoded relational features. Overall, all models' performances are the highest on Task A among all tasks due to the relatively simple questions associated with object recognition and counting. The performances of all the models naturally dropped on Task B when the ability of contextual and structural understanding are simultaneously required. Performances on Task C are the lowest for all models. It indicates the difficulty of document-level questions and produces massive room for improvement for future research on this task.

Table 5. Performance Comparison over Task A, B, and C. Acronym of feature aspects: Q: Question features; B: Bounding box coordinates; V: Visual appearance features; C: Contextual features; R: Relational Information.

	Feature Aspects					Task A		Task B		Task C	
Model	Q.	B.	V.	C.	R.	Val.	Test	Val.	Test	Val.	Test
VisualBERT [17]	✓	✗	✓	✗	✗	92.72	92.34	82.00	79.43	21.55	18.52
ViLT [16]	✓	✗	✓	✗	✗	90.82	91.31	54.36	53.45	10.21	9.87
LXMERT [28]	✓	✓	✓	✗	✗	94.34	94.41	86.61	86.36	16.37	14.41
BERT [5]	✓	✗	✗	✓	✗	82.35	81.87	22.41	23.64	–	–
LayoutLM2 [31]	✓	✓	✓	✓	✗	83.27	83.49	22.70	23.73	–	–
M4C [9]	✓	✓	✓	✓	✗	87.89	87.98	56.80	55.29	12.14	13.77
Our LoSpa	✓	✓	✓	✓	✓	**94.98**	**94.55**	**91.10**	**90.64**	**30.21**	**28.99**

Table 6. Validating the effectiveness of proposed logical-relation (LR) and spatial-relation (SR) based graphs.

Configurations	Task A		Task B		Task C	
	Val.	Test	Val.	Test	Val.	Test
None	94.17	94.12	90.02	89.59	27.13	27.71
Logical Relation (LR)	94.59	93.72	90.97	**90.67**	29.22	27.91
Spatial Relation (SR)	94.58	94.27	90.39	90.02	28.11	27.90
LR&SR	**94.98**	**94.55**	**91.10**	90.64	**30.21**	**28.99**

7.2   Relational Information Validation

To further demonstrate the influences of relational information on document VQA tasks, we perform the ablation studies on each task, as shown in Table 6. For all three tasks, adding both aspects of relational information can effectively improve the performance of our *LoSpa* model. Firstly, Spatial relation (SR) enhanced models can make the models of all three tasks more robust. Regarding logical relation (LR), it can lead to more apparent improvements on Task B since Task B involves more questions that require understanding document structure more comprehensively. Moreover, since the graph representation of two relation features is trained on the training set, most of the test set performance is lower than the validation set during the QA prediction stage.

7.3   Breakdown Results

We conduct the breakdown performance comparison over different question types of each task as shown in Table 7. Generally, all models' performances on Existence/Structural Understanding/Parent Relation Understanding questions are slightly better than Counting/Object Recognition/Child Relation Understanding questions in tasks A, B and C, respectively, due to their larger question numbers when training. Overall, all models' performances are stable on different question types of each task and follow the same performance trend as on all questions in Table 5. However, M4C's performance on Object Recognition is much lower than its performance on the Structural Understanding questions. This indicates that M4C is more powerful in recognizing the contexts and identifying the semantic structures between document elements. However, it does not have enough capacity to identify the elements and related semantic elements simultaneously. Also, the LXMERT's performances on Parent Relation Understanding questions are much better than those on Child Relation Understanding questions. This is because answers to parent questions are normally located on the same page as the queried elements. In contrast, answers to child questions are normally distributed over several pages, which is impacted by the independent

Table 7. Task A, B and C performance on different question types. Same as the overall performance shown previously, the metric of Task A/B is F1 and Task C is Accuracy.

Model	Task A				Task B				Task C			
	Existence		Counting		Struct-UD		Obj-Reg		Parent		Child	
	Val.	Test	Val.	Test	Val.	Test	Val.	Test	Val.	Test	Val.	Test
VisualBERT [17]	94.11	91.62	92.52	92.45	83.24	80.86	71.49	70.30	21.55	19.91	19.64	18.52
ViLT [16]	92.34	93.40	90.62	91.01	53.41	51.97	59.54	61.66	11.04	10.21	8.75	8.79
LXMERT [28]	96.02	94.59	94.10	94.38	86.65	86.86	86.46	83.15	26.66	23.57	8.56	9.51
BERT [5]	86.25	86.04	81.80	81.31	30.42	30.55	21.37	22.33	–	-	–	–
LayoutLM2 [31]	87.22	85.78	82.70	83.19	33.18	31.80	21.55	22.63	–	–	–	–
M4C [9]	90.78	89.15	87.51	87.87	60.74	60.29	21.29	20.39	13.63	14.34	12.21	9.89
Our LoSpa	**97.40**	**95.73**	**94.39**	**94.63**	**91.61**	**91.14**	**86.66**	**87.29**	**33.14**	**29.87**	**29.11**	**28.74**

bounding box coordinates of each page. The stable performances of M4C over the two question types of task C also indicate that using contextual features would eliminate such issues. Our *LoSpa*, incorporating relational information between document elements, achieves stable performances over both question types in Task C.

8   Conclusion

We proposed a new document-based VQA dataset to comprehensively examine the document understanding in conditions of natural language questions. In addition to contextual understanding and information retrieval, our dataset questions also specifically emphasize the importance of document structural layout understanding in terms of comprehensive document understanding. This is also the first dataset that introduces document-level questions to boost the document understanding to the full document level rather than being limited to one single page. We enriched our dataset by providing a Logical Relational graph and a Spatial Relational graph to annotate the different relationship types between document elements explicitly. We proved that such graph information integration enables outperforming all the baselines. We hope our PDF-VQA dataset will be a useful resource for the next generation of document-based VQA models with an entire multi-page document-level understanding and a deeper semantic understanding of vision and language.

Ethical Consideration. This study was reviewed and approved by the ethics review committee of the authors' institution and conducted in accordance with the principles of the Declaration. Written informed consent was obtained from each participant.

References

1. Antol, S., et al.: Vqa: visual question answering. In: Proceedings of the IEEE international Conference on Computer Vision, pp. 2425–2433 (2015)
2. Biten, A.F., et al.: Scene text visual question answering. In: Proceedings of the IEEE/CVF International Conference on Computer Vision, pp. 4291–4301 (2019)
3. Chaudhry, R., Shekhar, S., Gupta, U., Maneriker, P., Bansal, P., Joshi, A.: Leaf-qa: locate, encode & attend for figure question answering. In: Proceedings of the IEEE/CVF Winter Conference on Applications of Computer Vision, pp. 3512–3521 (2020)
4. Davis, B., Morse, B., Price, B., Tensmeyer, C., Wiginton, C.: Visual FUDGE: form understanding via dynamic graph editing. In: Lladós, J., Lopresti, D., Uchida, S. (eds.) ICDAR 2021. LNCS, vol. 12821, pp. 416–431. Springer, Cham (2021). https://doi.org/10.1007/978-3-030-86549-8_27
5. Devlin, J., Chang, M.W., Lee, K., Toutanova, K.: Bert: pre-training of deep bidirectional transformers for language understanding. In: Proceedings of the 2019 Conference of the North American Chapter of the Association for Computational Linguistics: Human Language Technologies, vol. 1 (Long and Short Papers), pp. 4171–4186 (2019)

6. Ding, Y., et al.: V-doc: visual questions answers with documents. In: Proceedings of the IEEE/CVF Conference on Computer Vision and Pattern Recognition, pp. 21492–21498 (2022)

7. Ding, Y., et al.: Form-nlu: Dataset for the form language understanding. arXiv preprint arXiv:2304.01577 (2023)

8. Goyal, Y., Khot, T., Summers-Stay, D., Batra, D., Parikh, D.: Making the v in vqa matter: Elevating the role of image understanding in visual question answering. In: Proceedings of the IEEE Conference on Computer Vision and Pattern Recognition, pp. 6904–6913 (2017)

9. Hu, R., Singh, A., Darrell, T., Rohrbach, M.: Iterative answer prediction with pointer-augmented multimodal transformers for textvqa. In: Proceedings of the IEEE/CVF Conference on Computer Vision and Pattern Recognition, pp. 9992–10002 (2020)

10. Huang, Z., et al.: Icdar 2019 competition on scanned receipt ocr and information extraction. In: 2019 International Conference on Document Analysis and Recognition (ICDAR), pp. 1516–1520. IEEE (2019)

11. Hudson, D.A., Manning, C.D.: Gqa: a new dataset for real-world visual reasoning and compositional question answering. In: Proceedings of the IEEE/CVF Conference on Computer Vision and Pattern Recognition, pp. 6700–6709 (2019)

12. Johnson, J., Hariharan, B., Van Der Maaten, L., Fei-Fei, L., Lawrence Zitnick, C., Girshick, R.: Clevr: a diagnostic dataset for compositional language and elementary visual reasoning. In: Proceedings of the IEEE Conference on Computer Vision and Pattern Recognition, pp. 2901–2910 (2017)

13. Kafle, K., Price, B., Cohen, S., Kanan, C.: Dvqa: Understanding data visualizations via question answering. In: Proceedings of the IEEE Conference on Computer Vision and Pattern Recognition, pp. 5648–5656 (2018)

14. Kahou, S.E., Michalski, V., Atkinson, A., Kádár, Á., Trischler, A., Bengio, Y.: Figureqa: an annotated figure dataset for visual reasoning. arXiv preprint arXiv:1710.07300 (2017)

15. Kembhavi, A., Seo, M., Schwenk, D., Choi, J., Farhadi, A., Hajishirzi, H.: Are you smarter than a sixth grader? textbook question answering for multimodal machine comprehension. In: Proceedings of the IEEE Conference on Computer Vision and Pattern Recognition, pp. 4999–5007 (2017)

16. Kim, W., Son, B., Kim, I.: Vilt: vision-and-language transformer without convolution or region supervision. In: International Conference on Machine Learning, pp. 5583–5594. PMLR (2021)

17. Li, L.H., Yatskar, M., Yin, D., Hsieh, C.J., Chang, K.W.: Visualbert: a simple and performant baseline for vision and language. arXiv preprint arXiv:1908.03557 (2019)

18. Luo, S., Ding, Y., Long, S., Poon, J., Han, S.C.: Doc-gcn: heterogeneous graph convolutional networks for document layout analysis. In: Proceedings of the 29th International Conference on Computational Linguistics, pp. 2906–2916 (2022)

19. Luo, S., Han, S.C., Sun, K., Poon, J.: REXUP: I reason, I extract, I update with structured compositional reasoning for visual question answering. In: Yang, H., Pasupa, K., Leung, A.C.-S., Kwok, J.T., Chan, J.H., King, I. (eds.) ICONIP 2020. LNCS, vol. 12532, pp. 520–532. Springer, Cham (2020). https://doi.org/10.1007/978-3-030-63830-6_44

20. Mathew, M., Bagal, V., Tito, R., Karatzas, D., Valveny, E., Jawahar, C.: Infographicvqa. In: Proceedings of the IEEE/CVF Winter Conference on Applications of Computer Vision, pp. 1697–1706 (2022)

21. Mathew, M., Karatzas, D., Jawahar, C.: Docvqa: a dataset for vqa on document images. In: Proceedings of the IEEE/CVF Winter Conference on Applications of Computer Vision, pp. 2200–2209 (2021)

22. Methani, N., Ganguly, P., Khapra, M.M., Kumar, P.: Plotqa: reasoning over scientific plots. In: Proceedings of the IEEE/CVF Winter Conference on Applications of Computer Vision, pp. 1527–1536 (2020)

23. Mishra, A., Shekhar, S., Singh, A.K., Chakraborty, A.: Ocr-vqa: Visual question answering by reading text in images. In: 2019 International Conference on Document Analysis and Recognition (ICDAR), pp. 947–952. IEEE (2019)

24. Park, S., et al.: Cord: a consolidated receipt dataset for post-ocr parsing. In: Workshop on Document Intelligence at NeurIPS 2019 (2019)

25. Rausch, J., Martinez, O., Bissig, F., Zhang, C., Feuerriegel, S.: Docparser: hierarchical document structure parsing from renderings. In: Proceedings of the AAAI Conference on Artificial Intelligence, vol. 35, pp. 4328–4338 (2021)

26. Shen, Z., Zhang, R., Dell, M., Lee, B.C.G., Carlson, J., Li, W.: LayoutParser: a unified toolkit for deep learning based document image analysis. In: Lladós, J., Lopresti, D., Uchida, S. (eds.) ICDAR 2021. LNCS, vol. 12821, pp. 131–146. Springer, Cham (2021). https://doi.org/10.1007/978-3-030-86549-8_9

27. Singh, A., et al.: Towards vqa models that can read. In: Proceedings of the IEEE/CVF Conference on Computer Vision and Pattern Recognition, pp. 8317–8326 (2019)

28. Tan, H., Bansal, M.: Lxmert: learning cross-modality encoder representations from transformers. In: Proceedings of the 2019 Conference on Empirical Methods in Natural Language Processing and the 9th International Joint Conference on Natural Language Processing (EMNLP-IJCNLP), pp. 5100–5111 (2019)

29. Tanaka, R., Nishida, K., Yoshida, S.: Visualmrc: machine reading comprehension on document images. In: Proceedings of the AAAI Conference on Artificial Intelligence, vol. 35, pp. 13878–13888 (2021)

30. Wang, X., et al.: On the general value of evidence, and bilingual scene-text visual question answering. In: Proceedings of the IEEE/CVF Conference on Computer Vision and Pattern Recognition, pp. 10126–10135 (2020)

31. Xu, Y., et al.: Layoutlmv2: Multi-modal pre-training for visually-rich document understanding. In: Proceedings of the 59th Annual Meeting of the Association for Computational Linguistics and the 11th International Joint Conference on Natural Language Processing, vol. 1: Long Papers, pp. 2579–2591 (2021)

32. Xu, Y., Li, M., Cui, L., Huang, S., Wei, F., Zhou, M.: Layoutlm: pre-training of text and layout for document image understanding. In: Proceedings of the 26th ACM SIGKDD International Conference on Knowledge Discovery & Data Mining, pp. 1192–1200 (2020)

33. Zhang, P., et al.: VSR: a unified framework for document layout analysis combining vision, semantics and relations. In: Lladós, J., Lopresti, D., Uchida, S. (eds.) ICDAR 2021. LNCS, vol. 12821, pp. 115–130. Springer, Cham (2021). https://doi.org/10.1007/978-3-030-86549-8_8

34. Zhang, Z., Ma, J., Du, J., Wang, L., Zhang, J.: Multimodal pre-training based on graph attention network for document understanding. arXiv preprint arXiv:2203.13530 (2022)

35. Zhong, X., Tang, J., Yepes, A.J.: Publaynet: largest dataset ever for document layout analysis. In: 2019 International Conference on Document Analysis and Recognition (ICDAR), pp. 1015–1022. IEEE (2019)

Future Augmentation with Self-distillation in Recommendation

Chong Liu[1], Ruobing Xie[1], Xiaoyang Liu[2], Pinzheng Wang[3], Rongqin Zheng[4],
Lixin Zhang[1], Juntao Li[3(✉)], Feng Xia[1], and Leyu Lin[1]

[1] WeChat, Tencent, Beijing, China
{nickcliu,ruobingxie}@tencent.com
[2] OPPO, Shenzhen, China
[3] Soochow University, Suzhou, China
ljt@suda.edu.cn
[4] Tencent, Shenzhen, China

Abstract. Sequential recommendation (SR) aims to provide appropriate items a user will click according to the user's historical behavior sequence. Conventional SR models are trained under the next item prediction task, and thus should deal with two challenges, including the data sparsity of user feedback and the variability and irregularity of user behaviors. Different from natural language sequences in NLP, user behavior sequences in recommendation are much more personalized, irregular, and unordered. Therefore, the current user preferences extracted from user historical behaviors may also have correlations with the next-k (i.e., future clicked) items besides the classical next-1 (i.e., current clicked) item to be predicted. Inspired by this phenomenon, we propose a novel Future augmentation with self-distillation in recommendation (FASRec). It considers future clicked items as augmented positive signals of the current clicks in training, which addresses both data sparsity and behavior irregularity and variability issues. To denoise these augmented future clicks, we further adopt a self-distillation module with the exponential moving average strategy, considering soft labels of self-distillation as confidence for more accurate augmentations. In experiments, FASRec achieves significant and consistent improvements on both offline and online evaluations with different base SR models, confirming its effectiveness and universality. FASRec has been deployed on a widely-used recommendation feed in Tencent. The source codes are in https://github.com/FASRec/FASRec.

Keywords: Future augmentation · Self-distillation · Recommendation

1 Introduction

Personalized recommendation attempts to recommend appropriate items for users according to their interests [28]. User historical behaviors are essential

---

C. Liu and R Xie—Equal contributions.

G. De Francisci Morales et al. (Eds.): ECML PKDD 2023, LNAI 14174, pp. 602–618, 2023.
https://doi.org/10.1007/978-3-031-43427-3_36

information to predict users' current preferences in personalized recommendation [37]. Therefore, sequential recommendation (SR), which focuses on the sequential modeling of user historical behaviors to capture user preferences, has been widely explored and deployed in real-world systems. A classical SR task takes a user's historical behavior sequence as the input, and outputs an item for the current recommendation. *Next item prediction* is a classical training objective and evaluation task in SR [14]. Due to the similar paradigm with language modeling in NLP, lots of sequential models including GRU, CNN, and Transformer have also been verified in SR to learn from behavior sequences [8,24,38].

Fig. 1. An example of the variability and irregularity in real-world sequential behaviors.

Different from the sequential modeling in NLP, sequential recommendation has the following two major challenges: (1) *The data sparsity of user feedback on items*. Each user has his/her own personalized interests and behavioral patterns, while the number of positive signals for a user merely equals the number of the user's historical behaviors in SR (nearly 10 in our datasets). Moreover, the tokens to be predicted in recommendation (i.e., items) are often million-level in practice, which are far more than words in NLP. Hence, it is hard to build good personalized sequential models for all users via the sparse user-item interactions. (2) *The variability and irregularity of users' behaviors*. Besides the personalized sequential patterns, users usually have multiple interests that switch or evolve frequently, which makes the sequential behavior modeling less predictable. Moreover, in practical systems (especially for article or video feeds), similar items having the same topic are usually deduplicated or dispersed via various strategies considering the diversity to avoid over-exposure. In this case, SR models are more difficult to find strict logical connections between adjacent clicked behaviors for next item prediction. Sometimes the effect of the current user interest may be *delayed* due to some diversification strategies (e.g., recommending items of other interests), and then *reawakened* at certain future clicked (next-k) items. The unpredictable randomness of user sequential behaviors and the delayed positive feedback increase the difficulty of sequential modeling.

Figure 1 displays a typical example to reveal the variability and irregularity of real-world user behaviors. We observe that this user mainly has two interested topics: *cat* and *football*, and interacts with them casually. Due to the switched interests, even the golden clicked item *football1* does not seem to perfectly match the current user interest of *cat* learned from historical behaviors of [*cat1→cat2*]. Instead, the user interest revealed by [*cat1→cat2*] does function and lead to future clicks (i.e., the fourth clicked item *cat3*). Based on this common observation, we assume that user preferences may be delayed and the current historical behaviors will possibly have a long-term impact on future clicks. Hence, an intuitive idea to make full use of this assumption is to conduct **future augmentations as labels**, training SR models via the **next-k item prediction** task besides the conventional *next item prediction*. However, simply regarding all next-k clicked items as augmented positive signals of the current prediction will inevitably bring in a large amount of noise (e.g., the next-3 item *football2* in Fig. 1 is noisy). The key challenge of future augmentation is how to select *high-quality* future clicks related to the current historical behaviors as additional training labels.

To address the above challenges, we propose a novel **Future augmentation with self-distillation in recommendation (FASRec)** to take advantage of the future information. Specifically, FASRec extends the classical next item prediction objective, where the next-k items are sampled as the positive augmented labels besides the current clicked items. We explore two classical sampling strategies for future augmentation. To denoise these augmented future clicks, we design a *self-distillation mechanism* that provides more informative soft labels to cooperate with the original hard labels as confidence-aware supervised signals in training. We further adopt the *exponential moving average (EMA)* strategy [26] to ensemble historical teachers for more effective and stable training. The advantages of FASRec are summarized as follows: (1) Future augmentation provides more labels for sufficient training against data sparsity. (2) Data augmentation from future clicked items enables the model to capture more accurate but delayed user preferences, which helps to better understand the variable and irregular user behaviors. (3) The self-distillation with EMA also helps to alleviate the noises caused by false positive augmentations from irrelevant future clicked items with the current historical behaviors. (4) FASRec is effective, universal, and easy-to-deploy with different base SR models and even other augmentation strategies, which is welcomed by the industry.

In experiments, we adopt our FASRec with different base sequential recommendation models on three public datasets. All FASRec models achieve significant and consistent improvements over corresponding baselines, which confirms their effectiveness and universality. We also deploy FASRec on a widely-used recommender system to verify its power in online scenarios. Moreover, we conduct extensive ablation tests, model analyses and explorations for a better understanding. The contributions of this work are concluded as follows:

– In this work, we propose a novel future augmentation with self-distillation framework for SR. To the best of our knowledge, we are the first to conduct future augmentation with self-distillation in recommendation.

- We explore different future augmentation sampling and self-distillation methods. FASRec is effective, universal, and easy-to-deploy in real-world systems.
- We achieve significant improvements on both offline and online evaluations with four representative sequential models on three datasets. Moreover, FASRec has been deployed on a popular real-world recommender system of Tencent for more than 6 months, affecting millions of users.

2   Related Works

Sequential Recommendation (SR). Recently, deep learning methods spring up in SR, including RNN [8], CNN [25], GNN [19], and Transformer [24]. Lots of SR model variants involve hierarchical structures [18,23], ranking loss designs [7,25], external behaviors and information [1,32]. Attention-based methods also achieve great successes [4,46]. Recently, there are also some works that adopt pre-trained models for sequential recommendation [6,10,11,33,43]. GRU4Rec [8] first brings the powerful RNN model into SR. SASRec [14] introduces a stacking self-attention. BERT4Rec [24] is inspired by Transformer. CL4SRec [37] is one of the SOTA models that further enhances SR with contrastive learning. These four classical SR models are regarded as the base SR model in FASRec.

Data Augmentation in Recommendation. Recently, contrastive learning (CL) [2] with augmentation has been verified in recommendation [12,20,30]. For user augmentation, CL4SRec [37] adopts crop, mask, and reorder to build augmentations of historical behavior sequences. [31] and [34] consider user behavior sequences in two behavior types or domains as natural user augmentations. Some works [40,42] consider contextual information to learn user representations inspired by the two-way data augmentation in NLP. Some efforts aim to build item augmentations via mask or dropout [22,29,35,45]. In this work, we purposefully consider the next-k items (natural high-quality positive item augmentations) as additional training labels, which are ignored by most existing methods.

Self-distillation. Knowledge distillation (KD) is a powerful tool to transfer knowledge from teachers to students [9]. Different from KD, self-distillation directly distills knowledge within the model itself [5,39,44]. [41] focuses on distillation between samples of the same class labels. Some studies apply outputs from a single model (of different portions) to enhance itself [44]. [15] uses the model at the last epoch as the teacher to soften hard targets. Besides, some researches focus on building better teachers for self-distillation [26]. [16] conducts self-distillation to filter and reuse false negative samples. There are very few works that adopt self-distillation in recommendation. [13] adopts self-distillation with a graph auto-encoder to enhance feature representations. In FASRec, we first adopt self-distillation to denoise augmented labels in future clicks.

3 Methodology

3.1 Preliminary

Notions. We first introduce some key notations in this work. Sequential recommendation attempts to predict the next interacted (often clicked) item according to the user's historical behavior sequence. Let $s_n = \{v_1, \cdots, v_t, \cdots, v_n\}$ represent the historical behavior sequence, where v_i represents the i-th clicked item. In training, given the *historical behavior sequence* $s_t = \{v_1, \cdots, v_t\}$ at time $t+1$, SR models should predict the probability of the *current clicked item* v_{t+1} being clicked, formulated as $P(v_{t+1}|s_t)$. Items in s_n after v_{t+1} are viewed as the *future clicked items* (which are the sources of the training label augmentation in FASRec). Since our FASRec framework has no constraints on model structures, we apply FASRec to four representative backbones to calculate $P(v_{t+1}|s_t)$, i.e., SASRec [14], GRU4Rec [8], BERT4Rec [24], and CL4SRec [37]. Commonly, we randomly sample negative items v_{t+1}^- for each positive item v_{t+1}, and adopt a classical cross entropy loss L_{ori} for all users u as the original training loss:

$$L_{ori} = \sum_u \sum_{t=1}^{n-1} (-\log(P(v_{t+1}|s_t)) - \log(1 - P(v_{t+1}^-|s_t))). \tag{1}$$

Overall Framework. Fig. 2 illustrates the overall framework of FASRec. In training, the base SR model Seq_Enc($\cdot$) takes the user's historical behavior sequence $s_t = \{v_1, \cdots, v_t\}$ at $t+1$ as input and outputs a user representation as $u = \text{Seq\_Enc}(s_t)$, which is utilized to predict the current clicked item v_{t+1}. FASRec conducts future augmentation to extend the original positive label v_{t+1} from future clicked items $\{v_{t+2}, \cdots, v_n\}$. To alleviate additional noises, we adopt a self-distillation module with EMA to generate soft labels of these augmented items as confidence, which are combined with their hard labels for training.

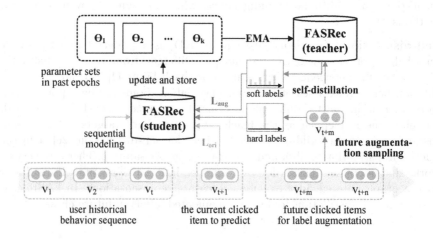

Fig. 2. The overall structure of FASRec.

3.2 Future Augmentation

We believe that future clicked items are natural high-quality augmentations of the current clicked item. Here, we propose two future augmentation sampling methods to extend target items, i.e., equal probability and exponential decay. (a) For the *equal probability* method, we randomly sample v_{t+m} of s_n ($1 \leq m \leq n-t$) with an equal probability $1/(n-t)$. (b) For the *exponential decay* method, we sample v_{t+m} with the positional decayed probability p_{t+m} as follows:

$$p_{t+m} = \begin{cases} (1-\beta)^{m-1} * \beta, \ 1 \leq m < n - t, \\ (1-\beta)^{m-1}, \quad m = n - t. \end{cases} \quad (2)$$

β is a hyper-parameter. Next, we consider v_{t+m} as an augmented positive item for the current state, replacing v_{t+1} with v_{t+m} as an additional training label.

3.3 Self-distillation with EMA

To avoid extra noise brought by future augmentation, we involve self-distillation to reweight our newly augmented positive samples v_{t+m}. Specifically, we rely on self-distillation to provide more reliable and stable soft labels for these augmentations. We introduce two methods to obtain our teacher model: (a) *Best in the past* [27], which directly adopts the previous model with the best performance upon the validation set during the past epochs as the teacher of the current epoch. (b) *EMA* [26], which combines the model parameters over recent training steps with varied weights to generate the teacher model. Formally, the parameters $\theta_T(t)$ of the teacher at t is generated from the last teacher's parameters $\theta_T(t-1)$ and the current model's parameters $\theta(t)$ with a decay rate d as:

$$\theta_T(t) = d\theta_T(t-1) + (1-d)\theta(t). \quad (3)$$

Next, we combine the predicted probability $P_T(v_{t+m}|s_t)$ of the teacher (i.e., soft label) with the hard label y with a weight α, and obtain the final label $\hat{y}$ as:

$$\hat{y} = \alpha P_T(v_{t+m}|s_t) + (1-\alpha)y. \quad (4)$$

$y = 1$ for positive samples v_{t+m} and $y = 0$ for random negative samples v_{t+m}^-. α is the soften weight. Finally, similar to Eq. (1), the augmented loss L_{aug} is as:

$$L_{aug} = \sum_u \sum_{t=1}^{n-1} \sum_{v_{t+m}} (-\hat{y}\log(P(v_{t+m}|s_t)) - (1-\hat{y})\log(1 - P(v_{t+m}^-|s_t))). \quad (5)$$

In this way, we adopt an ensemble of historical models to lead the learning with augmentations, which can alleviate extra noise and improve label quality.

3.4 Model Training and Online Deployment

We have deployed FASRec on a widely-used real-world recommendation feed used by millions of users. FASRec cooperates with an online best-performing SR model (i.e., BERT4Rec [24]) in matching with other modules unchanged. Due to anonymity, more details of the online system will be given in the final version. In offline training, we conduct a two-stage training paradigm as in Algorithm 1. In the first warmup stage, FASRec is only optimized on the original positive samples via L_{ori}. In the second augmentation stage, FASRec is updated via the augmented loss L_{aug} (note that the current clicked item v_{t+1} could also be sampled in this stage for a more stable training). Empirically, the warmup stage takes nearly 1/3 of the entire training epochs. In this case, we can ensure the quality of teachers to improve the accuracy of soft labels for augmented items.

Algorithm 1. Training Algorithm of FASRec.

Input: Training data $\mathcal{D} = \{s_t\}$.
Output: Model parameters θ of FASRec.
1: Initialize model parameters θ.
2: **while** $\mathcal{L}_{ori}$ descending rapidly **do**
3:　　For each $s_t \sim \mathcal{D}$, sample v_{t+1}^-.
4:　　Calculate $P(v_{t+1}|s_t)$ and $P(v_{t+1}^-|s_t)$ via the base SR model with θ.
5:　　$g \leftarrow \nabla_\theta \mathcal{L}_{ori}$, $\theta \leftarrow GradientUpdate(\theta, g)$.
6: **end while**
7: **while** not converged **do**
8:　　For each $s_t \sim \mathcal{D}$, sample future augmentations v_{t+m} and negative samples v_{t+m}^-.
9:　　Get the teacher's parameters θ_T as Eq. (3).
10:　　Get soft labels $P_T(v_{t+m}|s_t)$ and $P_T(v_{t+m}^-|s_t)$ via the teacher.
11:　　Get final labels $\hat{y}$ of v_{t+m} and v_{t+m}^- as Eq. (4).
12:　　Get $P(v_{t+m}|s_t)$ and $P(v_{t+m}^-|s_t)$ from the current student model with θ.
13:　　$g \leftarrow \nabla_\theta \mathcal{L}_{aug}$, $\theta \leftarrow GradientUpdate(\theta, g)$.
14: **end while**

3.5 Discussions on FASRec and Other Future-Involved Models

Some works claim that they have used "future" information in recommendation. [17] adopts historical behaviors of other users as supplements to the current user. [36] uses future clicks as features to enhance the discriminator so as to spur the generator to better recommend. [40,42] focus on using the past-future two-way information in historical behavior modeling to build better user representations for prediction. To some extent, the masked item prediction task [24] could also be regarded as a certain future-involved strategy, among which CL4SRec [37] is one of the SOTA models that adopts three types of augmented historical sequences.

Different from these models, FASRec uses future clicked items as *augmented training labels* with the original historical behaviors. It focuses more on the ignored long-term correlations to address the issue of behavioral variability and irregularity in practice. We deliberately design a simple and model-agnostic form of positive label augmentation, making it more flexible to cooperate with different base models. Very occasionally, some future augmentation cases (predicting v_{t+m} via s_t) could be generated in CL4SRec if all and only items after v_t are masked, while the proposed self-distillation with EMA enables a more accurate and motivated future augmentation. In Sect. 4.2, we have verified that our FAS-Rec could also cooperate well with CL4SRec and achieve further improvements.

4   Experiments

In this section, we conduct extensive experiments to answer five research questions related to FASRec's offline performance with different base models (RQ1), online performance (RQ2), effects of different components (RQ3), model parameters (RQ4), and future augmentation strategies (RQ5).

4.1   Datasets and Experimental Settings

Dataset. We evaluate our FASRec models on three widely-used public datasets, namely *Yelp*, *Amazon Beauty*, and *Amazon Sports*. (a) **Yelp.** This dataset is a classical business recommendation dataset collected from the Yelp platform[1]. Following [47], we utilize the data after January 1st, 2019. It has nearly 30 thousand users and 316 thousand click behaviors on 20 thousand items. (b) **Amazon Beauty.** This dataset is collected from a famous E-commerce system Amazon [21] with items having the *Beauty* category. It has nearly 52 thousand users and 395 thousand click behaviors on 57 thousand items. (c) **Amazon Sports.** This dataset is collected from the *Sports* category in Amazon. It has 26 thousand users, 18 thousand items, and 296 thousand click behaviors. Following classical settings [14], we select the second most recent user-item interactions of all users as the valid set and select the most recent interactions as the test set, with all other interactions viewed as the train set.

Competitors. FASRec is a universal training framework that brings in additional supervision via future augmentations. Different SR models could be easily used as the base SR models in FASRec. Therefore, we implement several classical SR models as the corresponding baselines to their enhanced versions armed with FASRec: (a) **GRU4Rec** [8]. GRU4Rec is a classical SR model that adopts GRU for the sequential behavior modeling in recommendation. (b) **SASRec** [14]. SASRec is a representative SR model that introduces a stacking multi-head self-attention to behavior interaction modeling. (c) **BERT4Rec** [24]. BERT4Rec uses the powerful transformer for sequential modeling. It further considers the masked token prediction task besides next item prediction, which could also be viewed as a future-involved strategy. (d) **CL4SRec** [37]. CL4SRec is one of the

---

[1] https://www.yelp.com/dataset.

SOTA CL-based SR models. It adds additional CL tasks based on three historical sequence augmentations, which also benefit from the "future" information in
behavior modeling. It is a very relevant and strong baseline since it also adopts
augmentations. We should highlight that all baselines share the same training
instances and features as used in FASRec for fair comparisons.

Parameter Settings. In experiments, all our models and baselines are optimized by Adam with the learning rate set as 0.001. The batch sizes are 128 for
all models. The maximum length of historical sequence is set as 50. In FASRec,
we select the equal probability strategy for simplicity. Both the augmented items
and randomly sampled negative samples are weighted by our self-distillation.
We conduct a grid search for hyper-parameter selection. We have evaluated the
soften weight α among $\{0.1, 0.3, 0.5, 0.7, 0.9\}$ and the decay rate d of EMA among
$\{0.1, 0.3, 0.5, 0.7, 0.9, 0.99, 0.999\}$. FASRec models achieve the best performance
when $\alpha = 0.7$ and $d = 0.999$. For other hyper-parameters of the base SR models
in FASRec, we follow the best original model settings in their corresponding
papers (e.g., behavior dimension sizes and model structures). Sect. 4.5 and Sect.
4.6 show detailed analyses on the selection of parameters and strategies.

4.2   Effectiveness and Universality of FASRec (RQ1)

This subsection aims to verify the effectiveness and universality of FASRec on
different datasets with various base SR models. Specifically, we randomly sample
99 items as negative samples for each positive sample in the test set as [14].
Similarly, we adopt two classical evaluation metrics, namely hit rate@k (HR@k)
and NDCG@k (N@k), with $k = \{1, 5, 10, 20\}$. The results are shown in Table 1,
from which we can observe that:

(1) All FASRec models significantly outperform their corresponding baselines on
   all metrics in three datasets, verifying the effectiveness of FASRec in SR. We
   have conducted significance tests of FASRec on all baselines and the significance level is $p < 0.05$. The advantages of FASRec over baselines mainly
   come from the following two points: (a) the augmentation of positive labels
   from future clicked items helps to address the sparsity issue. It successfully
   captures users' delayed interests, alleviating the information loss caused by
   the variability and irregularity of user behaviors. (b) Self-distillation with
   EMA can effectively denoise the augmented future clicks, enabling more precise training. FASRec has advantages over other future-involved models with
   behavior augmentations (e.g., CL4SRec), which inevitably bring in noises.
   EMA also helps to generate better teachers and soft labels. Section 4.4 gives
   further analyses on these components of FASRec.
(2) All FASRec models have consistent improvements with different base SR models on all datasets and metrics. The improvements are larger with smaller k in
   HR and NDCG. It confirms that our future augmentation with self-distillation
   is universal and robust in different scenarios and can cooperate well with
   different base models. Note that FASRec could even earn improvements on

Table 1. Results on three datasets with four base SR models. The improvements of FASRec are significant over all corresponding baselines (paired t-test with p<0.05).

Dateset	Model	HR@1	HR@5	HR@10	HR@20	N@5	N@10	N@20
Yelp	GRU4Rec	0.1882	0.5246	0.7069	0.8687	0.3602	0.4194	0.4607
	+FASRec	0.2086	0.5448	0.7292	0.8829	0.3810	0.4407	0.4797
	BERT4Rec	0.2830	0.6124	0.7545	0.8682	0.4545	0.5005	0.5294
	+FASRec	0.3041	0.6545	0.7929	0.8995	0.4869	0.5318	0.5590
	SASRec	0.2620	0.6281	0.7758	0.8742	0.4525	0.5004	0.5255
	+FASRec	0.2842	0.6398	0.7863	0.9022	0.4688	0.5163	0.5458
	CL4SRec	0.2715	0.6243	0.7809	0.9031	0.4551	0.5059	0.5371
	+FASRec	0.2809	0.6350	0.7930	0.9114	0.4651	0.5148	0.5461
	Avg Improv	**7.56%**	**3.58%**	**2.79%**	**2.34%**	**4.68%**	**4.07%**	**3.81%**
Beauty	GRU4Rec	0.1103	0.2929	0.4024	0.5305	0.2048	0.2402	0.2724
	+FASRec	0.1237	0.3217	0.4332	0.5641	0.2261	0.2619	0.2949
	BERT4Rec	0.1890	0.3796	0.4829	0.5941	0.2892	0.3225	0.3506
	+FASRec	0.2100	0.3988	0.4978	0.6108	0.3087	0.3407	0.3693
	SASRec	0.1930	0.3881	0.4854	0.6030	0.2951	0.3265	0.3562
	+FASRec	0.2162	0.4121	0.5127	0.6213	0.3191	0.3515	0.3790
	CL4SRec	0.2044	0.3940	0.4903	0.6049	0.3028	0.3340	0.3628
	+FASRec	0.2240	0.4238	0.5239	0.6334	0.3284	0.3608	0.3883
	Avg Improv	**11.22%**	**7.16%**	**5.80%**	**4.22%**	**8.43%**	**7.59%**	**6.76%**
Sports	GRU4Rec	0.1037	0.2866	0.4111	0.5597	0.1969	0.2371	0.2745
	+FASRec	0.1159	0.3074	0.4315	0.5817	0.2132	0.2531	0.2909
	BERT4Rec	0.1468	0.3684	0.4858	0.6305	0.2607	0.2986	0.3351
	+FASRec	0.1858	0.4015	0.5260	0.6559	0.2976	0.3376	0.3705
	SASRec	0.1630	0.3967	0.5178	0.6429	0.2849	0.3240	0.3555
	+FASRec	0.1788	0.4143	0.5344	0.6705	0.3014	0.3402	0.3746
	CL4SRec	0.1707	0.3908	0.5144	0.6517	0.2858	0.3257	0.3604
	+FASRec	0.1854	0.4089	0.5345	0.6727	0.3014	0.3416	0.3763
	Avg Improv	**14.16%**	**6.33%**	**5.09%**	**3.87%**	**8.42%**	**7.42%**	**6.58%**

CL4SRec, which is a SOTA CL-based SR model that conducts data augmentations on user historical behaviors. It indicates that our future augmentation could cooperate well with other augmentation-enhanced methods to further improve the performance. FASRec is a plug-and-play and developer-friendly method to bring in more supervised signals without external information. It is convenient to adopt our FASRec on most SR models in practice (refer to Sect. 4.3 for online tests).

Table 2. Online A/B tests on a real-world recommendation system (p<0.05).

Metrics	CTR	ACN
FASRec (online)	+1.63%	+2.01%

4.3   Online A/B Test (RQ2)

We also conduct an online evaluation on a widely-used feed recommender system of Tencent to verify FASRec in practical scenarios. The original matching module of this online system contains multi-channel matching models including a BERT4Rec channel. We adopt FASRec with BERT4Rec and add it as an additional matching channel with other modules of this system unchanged following classical settings. We mainly focus on two metrics: (a) CTR, and (b) average click numbers per capita (ACN). We have conducted the online evaluation for 5 days, affecting nearly 1.3 million users. In Table 2, we observe that FASRec achieves significant improvements over the original system without FASRec on both CTR and ACN metrics. It shows that our future augmentation with self-distillation could not only provide more accurate items, but also guide users to consume more items in our online systems. Currently, FASRec has been deployed online for more than 6 months and has been verified by millions of users.

4.4   Ablation Study (RQ3)

We conduct an ablation test to reveal the power of different components in FAS-Rec. Specifically, we build 4 ablation versions of FASRec (SASRec) on Amazon Beauty in Table 3. We find that: (1) The final FASRec significantly outperforms all its ablation versions, while these ablation versions still perform better than the baseline SASRec. We also find that the improvements are consistent across different datasets and base SR models. (2) FASRec w/o self-distillation merely adopts the hard labels for augmented future items, while this aggressive future augmentation not only captures missing delayed clicks, but also inevitably brings in noises and errors that may mislead the model training. Self-distillation is verified to be an effective denoising technique for augmentation. (3) FASRec achieves better results than FASRec w/o EMA (i.e., with the *Best in the past* strategy), which indicates that EMA is a better teacher. Figure 3 shows the training trends with different self-distillation strategies. We have also verified the effectiveness of the warmup stage, since the teacher's quality is essential in future augmentation. (4) To demonstrate the effectiveness of *future* information, we adopt the self-distillation module only on the original next-1 clicked item to provide soft labels without augmented future clicks (i.e., the third ablation version). This ablation has worse results, which confirms the existence of delayed interests and the necessity of adding confident future augmentations as labels. Future clicks are high-quality label augmentations of the current next item prediction.

Table 3. Results of ablation study. All improvements are significant (p<0.05).

Amazon Beauty	HR@1	HR@5	HR@10	HR@20	N@5	N@10	N@20
FASRec (SASRec)	**0.2162**	**0.4121**	**0.5127**	**0.6213**	**0.3191**	**0.3515**	**0.3790**
w/o self-distillation	0.2032	0.3927	0.4947	0.6064	0.3026	0.3355	0.3637
w/o EMA	0.2095	0.4031	0.5065	0.6177	0.3105	0.3438	0.3719
w/o future augmentation	0.2060	0.4037	0.5001	0.6071	0.3100	0.3411	0.3682
w/o all	0.1930	0.3881	0.4854	0.6030	0.2951	0.3265	0.3562

4.5 Model Analyses (RQ4)

Analysis on Soften Weight α. We first analyze the effects of different soften weights α in hard/soft label combination. The left two figures in Fig. 4 show the results of FASRec (SASRec) with different α. We discover that the performance first increases and then decreases with the soften weight growing, achieving the best results when $\alpha = 0.7$ (too large α may result in overfitting). It reveals the importance of jointly combining hard and soft labels in future augmentation.

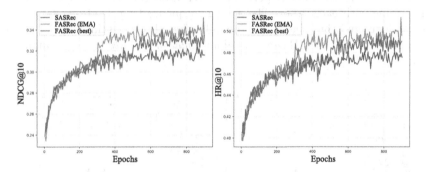

Fig. 3. Training trends of two self-distillation strategies *EMA* and *best in the past (best)* over SASRec. L_{aug} is activated after 300 epochs in our two-stage training.

Analysis on Decay Rate d **of EMA.** We also explore deeper into EMA and test different decay rates d of our EMA in the right two figures of Fig. 4. We find that the decay rate should be large (e.g., larger than 0.9) for relatively good results. Note that FASRec has a warmup stage (where only the original next-1 items are used for training). Hence, the historical teachers' parameters of EMA are relatively high-quality. Therefore, FASRec is not that sensitive to d.

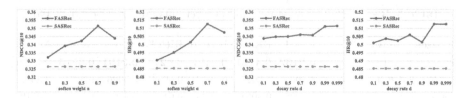

Fig. 4. Results of parameter analyses on Amazon Beauty. The left two figures show NDCG@10 and HR@10 results with different soften weights α, while the right two figures show NDCG@10 and HR@10 results with different decay rates d of EMA.

4.6   Explorations on Different Augmentation Strategies (RQ5)

We further conduct explorations on various future augmentation strategies on Amazon Beauty for more stable and effective training.

Effects of Different Future Sampling Strategies. We propose two straight-forward future sampling strategies in FASRec, i.e., *equal probability* and *exponential decay*. Figure 5 shows the performance trends of two strategies and SASRec, where both FASRec models perform better than the base SR model but are comparable with each other. The average sequence lengths of our datasets are not too long, and thus the equal probability based future sampling can perform well. Based on Occam's Razor, we adopt *equal probability* to select augmented clicks.

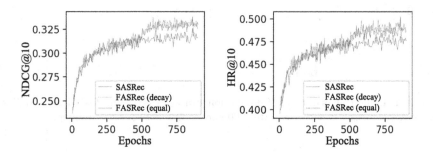

Fig. 5. Training trends of different future sampling strategies.

Effects of Different Augmentation Triggers. In FASRec, future augmentation is triggered for all positive instances. We attempt to investigate whether some positive instances need future augmentation more. Specifically, we design two types of augmentation triggers: (a) *large_loss*, which conducts augmentation for positive instances that have top larger losses than others (indicating this instance is noisy or under-optimized), and (b) *large_variance*, which conducts augmentation for instances having top instable performance following [3] (implying the conflicts between historical behaviors and clicked items). Table 4 gives the results of two augmentation triggers with different augmentation ratios (ratio = 1.0 equals the final FASRec). Figure 6 shows the trends of two triggers with ratio = 0.5. In general, the final FASRec (augmentation for all instances) has the best performance. However, both augmentation triggers have more stable trends from Fig. 6. The augmentation trigger is a promising exploration direction.

Table 4. Results of adopting the *large_loss* and *large_variance* augmentation triggers on positive instances with different augmentation ratios on Amazon Beauty.

aug ratio	*large_loss* trigger				*large_variance* trigger			
	0.1	0.3	0.5	1.0	0.1	0.3	0.5	1.0
HR@5	0.4108	0.4124	0.4083	0.4121	0.4101	0.4102	0.4125	0.4121
HR@10	0.5095	0.5097	0.5088	0.5127	0.5044	0.5081	0.5106	0.5127
N@5	0.3168	0.3181	0.3175	0.3191	0.3145	0.3174	0.3176	0.3191
N@10	0.3486	0.3494	0.3501	0.3515	0.3449	0.3490	0.3492	0.3515

Effects of Historical Behavior Based Augmentation Cooperating with Future Augmentation. We also combine our future augmentation with conventional historical behavior based augmentations to see whether they could cooperate well with each other. For simplicity, we build historical behavior based augmentations via random cropping with CL. Figure 7 gives the results of 4 combinations. We find that FASRec+CL achieves the overall best results, and combining two augmentations makes the performance more stable.

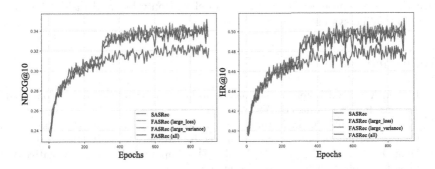

Fig. 6. Training trends of different augmentation triggers.

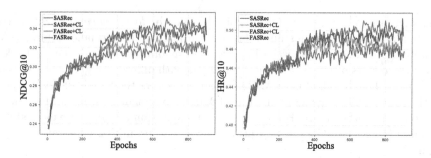

Fig. 7. Training trends of combining future augmentation with other augmentations.

5   Conclusion and Future Work

In this work, we propose an effective, universal, and easy-to-deploy future augmentation with self-distillation framework to address data sparsity and behavior irregularity issues in sequential recommendation via additional future augmented labels. FASRec achieves significant and consistent improvements on multiple datasets with different base SR models, and is also verified in online. It provides a promising and low-cost training framework to multiply high-quality supervised signals in real-world systems. FASRec has been deployed on a widely-used recommender system and affects lots of users.

In the future, we attempt to explore better future augmentation strategies, augmentation triggers, and combination methods to collect more accurate positive signals. We will also try to discover other types of high-quality, ubiquitous, but ignored positive and negative signals in practice to fight against sparsity.

Ethical Statement This work focuses on personalized recommendation. For offline evaluation, we conduct experiments on three classical public recommendation datasets. For online deployment, all sensitive information (e.g., user information) is preprocessed via data masking to protect user privacy. All user information (e.g., user historical behaviors) is collected and used in the online system with the users' consent. The trained model will only be used inside the corresponding online system.

References

1. Beutel, A., et al.: Latent cross: making use of context in recurrent recommender systems. In: Proceedings of WSDM (2018)
2. Chen, T., Kornblith, S., Norouzi, M., Hinton, G.: A simple framework for contrastive learning of visual representations. In: Proceedings of ICML (2020)
3. Ding, J., Quan, Y., Yao, Q., Li, Y., Jin, D.: Simplify and robustify negative sampling for implicit collaborative filtering (2020)
4. Fan, Z., et al.: Sequential recommendation via stochastic self-attention. In: Proceedings of WWW (2022)

5. Furlanello, T., Lipton, Z., Tschannen, M., Itti, L., Anandkumar, A.: Born again neural networks. In: Proceedings of ICML (2018)
6. Geng, S., Liu, S., Fu, Z., Ge, Y., Zhang, Y.: Recommendation as language processing (rlp): a unified pretrain, personalized prompt & predict paradigm (p5). In: Proceedings of RecSys (2022)
7. Hidasi, B., Karatzoglou, A.: Recurrent neural networks with top-k gains for session-based recommendations. In: Proceedings of CIKM (2018)
8. Hidasi, B., Karatzoglou, A., Baltrunas, L., Tikk, D.: Session-based recommendations with recurrent neural networks. In: Proceedings of ICLR (2016)
9. Hinton, G., Vinyals, O., Dean, J., et al.: Distilling the knowledge in a neural network. arXiv preprint arXiv:1503.02531 (2015)
10. Hou, Y., Mu, S., Zhao, W.X., Li, Y., Ding, B., Wen, J.R.: Towards universal sequence representation learning for recommender systems. In: Proceedings of KDD (2022)
11. Hou, Y., et al.: Large language models are zero-shot rankers for recommender systems. arXiv preprint arXiv:2305.08845 (2023)
12. Huang, J., et al.: Adversarial learning data augmentation for graph contrastive learning in recommendation. In: Proceedings of DASFAA (2023)
13. Huang, Z., Lin, Z., Gong, Z., Chen, Y., Tang, Y.: A two-phase knowledge distillation model for graph convolutional network-based recommendation. Inter. J. Intell. Syst. (2022)
14. Kang, W.C., McAuley, J.: Self-attentive sequential recommendation. In: Proceedings of ICDM (2018)
15. Kim, K., Ji, B., Yoon, D., Hwang, S.: Self-knowledge distillation with progressive refinement of targets. In: Proceedings of ICCV (2021)
16. Liu, X., et al.: Ufnrec: utilizing false negative samples for sequential recommendation. In: Proceedings of SDM (2023)
17. Lu, Y., et al.: Future-aware diverse trends framework for recommendation. In: Proceedings of WWW (2021)
18. Ma, C., Kang, P., Liu, X.: Hierarchical gating networks for sequential recommendation. In: Proceedings of KDD (2019)
19. Ma, C., Ma, L., Zhang, Y., Sun, J., Liu, X., Coates, M.: Memory augmented graph neural networks for sequential recommendation. In: Proceedings of AAAI (2020)
20. Ma, J., Zhou, C., Yang, H., Cui, P., Wang, X., Zhu, W.: Disentangled self-supervision in sequential recommenders. In: Proceedings of KDD (2020)
21. McAuley, J., Targett, C., Shi, Q., Van Den Hengel, A.: Image-based recommendations on styles and substitutes. In: Proceedings of SIGIR (2015)
22. Nie, P., et al.: Mic: model-agnostic integrated cross-channel recommender. In: Proceedings of CIKM (2022)
23. Quadrana, M., Karatzoglou, A., Hidasi, B., Cremonesi, P.: Personalizing session-based recommendations with hierarchical recurrent neural networks. In: Proceedings of RecSys (2017)
24. Sun, F., et al.: Bert4rec: sequential recommendation with bidirectional encoder representations from transformer. In: Proceedings of CIKM (2019)
25. Tang, J., Wang, K.: Personalized top-n sequential recommendation via convolutional sequence embedding. In: Proceedings of WSDM (2018)
26. Tarvainen, A., Valpola, H.: Mean teachers are better role models: weight-averaged consistency targets improve semi-supervised deep learning results. In: Proceedings of NeurIPS (2017)
27. Vu, D.Q., Le, N., Wang, J.C.: Teaching yourself: a self-knowledge distillation approach to action recognition. IEEE Access (2021)

28. Wang, R., et al.: Dcn v2: improved deep & cross network and practical lessons for web-scale learning to rank systems. In: Proceedings of WWW (2021)

29. Wei, Y., et al.: Contrastive learning for cold-start recommendation. In: Proceedings of MM (2021)

30. Wu, J., et al.: Self-supervised graph learning for recommendation. In: Proceedings of SIGIR (2021)

31. Wu, Y., et al.: Multi-view multi-behavior contrastive learning in recommendation. In: Proceedings of DASFAA (2022)

32. Wu, Y., et al.: Selective fairness in recommendation via prompts. In: Proceedings of SIGIR (2022)

33. Wu, Y., et al.: Personalized prompts for sequential recommendation. arXiv preprint arXiv:2205.09666 (2022)

34. Xie, R., Liu, Q., Wang, L., Liu, S., Zhang, B., Lin, L.: Contrastive cross-domain recommendation in matching. In: Proceedings of KDD (2022)

35. Xie, R., Qiu, Z., Zhang, B., Lin, L.: Multi-granularity item-based contrastive recommendation. In: Proceedings of DASFAA (2023)

36. Xie, R., Zhang, S., Wang, R., Xia, F., Lin, L.: A peep into the future: adversarial future encoding in recommendation. In: Proceedings of WSDM (2022)

37. Xie, X., et al.: Contrastive learning for sequential recommendation. In: Proceedings of ICDE (2022)

38. Xu, C., et al.: Recurrent convolutional neural network for sequential recommendation. In: Proceedings of WWW (2019)

39. Xu, T.B., Liu, C.L.: Data-distortion guided self-distillation for deep neural networks. In: Proceedings of AAAI (2019)

40. Yuan, F., et al.: Future data helps training: modeling future contexts for session-based recommendation. In: Proceedings of WWW (2020)

41. Yun, S., Park, J., Lee, K., Shin, J.: Regularizing class-wise predictions via self-knowledge distillation. In: Proceedings of CVPR (2020)

42. Zhang, H., et al.: Disentangling past-future modeling in sequential recommendation via dual networks. In: Proceedings of CIKM (2022)

43. Zhang, J., Xie, R., Hou, Y., Zhao, W.X., Lin, L., Wen, J.R.: Recommendation as instruction following: A large language model empowered recommendation approach. arXiv preprint arXiv:2305.07001 (2023)

44. Zhang, L., Song, J., Gao, A., Chen, J., Bao, C., Ma, K.: Be your own teacher: improve the performance of convolutional neural networks via self distillation. In: Proceedings of ICCV (2019)

45. Zhou, C., Ma, J., Zhang, J., Zhou, J., Yang, H.: Contrastive learning for debiased candidate generation in large-scale recommender systems. In: Proceedings of KDD (2021)

46. Zhou, G., et al.: Deep interest network for click-through rate prediction. In: Proceedings of KDD (2018)

47. Zhou, K., et al.: S3-rec: self-supervised learning for sequential recommendation with mutual information maximization. In: CIKM (2020)

Cooperative Multi-agent Reinforcement Learning for Inventory Management

Madhav Khirwar[✉], Karthik S. Gurumoorthy, Ankit Ajit Jain,
and Shantala Manchenahally

Walmart, Bengaluru, India
{madhav.khirwar,karthik.gurumoorthy,ankit.ajit.jain,
shantala.manchenahally}@walmart.com

Abstract. With Reinforcement Learning (RL) for inventory management (IM) being a nascent field of research, approaches tend to be limited to simple, linear environments with implementations that are minor modifications of off-the-shelf RL algorithms. Scaling these simplistic environments to a real-world supply chain comes with a few challenges, such as minimizing the computational requirements of the environment, specifying agent configurations that are representative of dynamics at real-world stores and warehouses, and specifying a reward framework that encourages desirable behavior across the whole supply chain. In this work, we present a system with a custom GPU-parallelized environment that consists of one warehouse and multiple stores, a novel architecture for agent-environment dynamics incorporating enhanced state and action spaces, and a shared reward specification that seeks to optimize for a large retailer's supply chain needs. Each vertex in the supply chain graph is an independent agent that, based on its own inventory, able to place replenishment orders to the vertex upstream. The warehouse agent, aside from placing orders from the supplier, has the special property of also being able to constrain replenishment to stores downstream, which results in it learning an additional allocation sub-policy. We achieve a system that outperforms standard inventory control policies such as a base-stock policy and other RL-based specifications for one product, and lay out a future direction of work for multiple products.

Keywords: Multi-Agent Reinforcement Learning · Shared Reward · Inventory Management · Allocation Policy

1 Introduction

Inventory management (IM) is the process of overseeing and controlling the flow of goods from the point of acquisition to the point of sale. The goal of IM is to ensure that an organization has the right products, in the right quantities, at the right time, and at the right place to meet customer demand while minimizing operation costs. A retail giant may consist of hundreds of stores dispersed through a vast geographic area, with each offering thousands of products. For

© The Author(s), under exclusive license to Springer Nature Switzerland AG 2023
G. De Francisci Morales et al. (Eds.): ECML PKDD 2023, LNAI 14174, pp. 619–634, 2023.
https://doi.org/10.1007/978-3-031-43427-3_37

each store, the inventory for these products is supplied by the warehouse to which it is mapped to in the supply chain topology (refer Fig. 1a). The warehouses in turn receive their replenishment from a dedicated supplier. The replenishment orders are fulfilled by trailers at regular intervals of time. Stores and warehouses are responsible for maintaining enough product inventory to cover for unexpected delays in replenishment for a few time periods.

The process of managing inventory involves various trade-offs, including maintaining inventory levels at the store and minimizing costs associated with holding inventory. Some key concepts in IM are: stock-out, holding costs, and lead time [15]. A stock-out at a store or warehouse occurs if the inventory for a particular product at the store goes to 0. This is undesirable as it not only leads to lost sales but also poor customer experience. Holding costs are incurred by stores and warehouses to maintain on-hand inventory of products. These are comprised of quantities such as electricity costs for the store, refrigeration costs for food items, and storage area maintenance costs. Since these costs scale with the amount of inventory being kept on-hand, it is suboptimal for a store or warehouse to keep the maximum possible amount of inventory on-hand. Lead time refers to the time it takes for a supplier or warehouse to deliver a replenishment order to a warehouse or store, respectively.

In this work, we demonstrate that our proposed system is able to successfully manage inventory for a single product across a simulated supply chain that mimics the complexities of its real-world counterpart. We discuss scaling the products by including results for 10 products, and propose future research directions to address challenges associated with simultaneously managing inventory for thousands of products. For simplicity, we study the setting consisting of one warehouse replenishing the needs of all the stores mapped to it. In supply chain networks that do not have inter-warehouse constraints and suppliers capacity is unbounded, our work is readily generalizable to the multi-warehouse set-up mapped either to the same supplier or receive their replenishment from multiple suppliers. For this paper, we define an inventory management problem as: *Given the distribution of demand for each product at each store, find optimal replenishment quantities for each product at each store and at the warehouse, such that over a specified number of time periods, system-wide profit is maximized (equivalently, cost is minimized).*

1.1   Reinforcement Learning for IM

Previous literature makes a case for an RL-based approach to building IM solutions over traditional optimization approaches, as RL systems have the ability to consider long-term trajectories of the future, which day-to-day heuristic optimization systems lack [8,19,21,26]. In fact, this enables RL systems to operate without an additional demand forecasting model, as they implicitly learn to predict customer demand during training. We demonstrate this property in our experiments, where the inventory policies learned by RL agents are superior compared to optimization methods such as base-stock policy (BSP) [1], without requiring an additional demand forecasting model.

Multi-agent RL (MARL) is a machine learning framework that uses multiple agents to learn and adapt. MARL may be a better choice for IM in a supply chain than heuristics-based optimization approaches, which often assume static supply chain properties like constant demand or fixed lead times for procurement. In a supply chain, product demand can fluctuate, and supplier delays and transportation issues can affect lead times. MARL algorithms can learn and adapt to environmental changes in real time without these assumptions (when trained on historical data) [25]. This makes them more resilient to supply chain uncertainty and variability. Unlike traditional optimization methods, MARL algorithms can be implemented in a decentralized manner, with each supply chain agent making decisions based on local information. This improves supply chain flexibility, as minor changes to a supply chain's topology do not require the entire system to be re-trained from scratch.

1.2   Contributions

The main contributions of this paper are: (i) a novel multi-agent architecture for IM where the warehouse agent has enhanced state and action spaces enabling it to effectively learn an allocation policy, especially when it does not have sufficient inventory to meet all the store requests, (ii) a novel reward specification to encourage system-wide cooperation where all agents in the supply chain share the same reward that is calculated for each time period based on the dynamics of the supply chain as a whole, and (iii) a CuPy-parallelized environment that can process all products in constant time, subject to GPU constraints. Henceforth, we refer to our enhanced warehouse, shared reward, multi-agent RL system as Cooperative MARL (CMARL).

2   Related Work

RL techniques frame the IM problem as a Markov Decision Process, with the state space being the current levels of inventory and the action space being the replenishment quantity for each item to be ordered at each time step. This approach has been gaining popularity in small-scale proof-of-concept environments in recent years. For instance, [19] extends deep Q-networks (DQN) to solve a decentralized variant of the beer game problem [2] and finds that a DQN agent learns a near-optimal policy when other supply chain participants follow a BSP. For a single product, a technique based on semi-Markov average reward to manage inventory decisions across a supply chain is studied in [5]. The usage of Q-learning [11] to minimize an operating cost target is proposed in [9] for managing inventory of a single product, and the results are compared against stock-based and age-based policies. Again, for a single product on a linear four-echelon supply chain, the authors in [8] compare different operations research methods with the proximal policy optimization (PPO) algorithm in environments with and without backlogged orders. Their experiments indicate that PPO outperforms BSP in both environments. An application of the vanilla policy gradient (VPG) algorithm to address a 2-echelon supply chain with stochastic and seasonal demand is discussed in [21]. The quantity of products to ship is determined by considering the inventory present in the warehouses. In all experiments, VPG performed better than the (s, Q)-policy employed as a baseline. A single agent RL (SARL) approach to optimize inventory flow across a 2-echelon supply chain is discussed in [25], where the authors compare their neuro-dynamic policies to an order-up-to policy, benchmark PPO against the VPG and the A3C algorithms, and conclude that PPO performs the best for managing the inventory. The works in [3,13] propose a multi-product MARL approach on a linear supply chain with one warehouse and one store, where each inventory for each product is managed by a separate RL agent. The former approach is shown to surpass baseline heuristics for up to 220 products, and the latter leverages a shared resource structure for holding inventory to outperform other MARL frameworks for up to 100 products.

The method that is closest to our CMARL and implements a MARL system for IM across a 2-echelon supply chain with 3 stores and one warehouse is [26]. However, there are fundamental differences in the specifications of RL agents with regard to environment dynamics, action spaces, reward structure, and training structure between the two methods. While [26] assumes the lead times between the warehouse and stores are zero, which is unrealistic as replenishment orders need to be transported and processed, our CMARL system explicitly encodes the notion of lead time in the environment dynamics. Having a single action policy across all products, with all weight parameters shared as in [26], results in training time increasing linearly with respect to the number of products. It could reduce performance across multiple products due to catastrophic forgetting [6]. Our experimental results (refer Fig. 4b) indicate that having individual action space for each product has higher reward values alongside the ability to simultaneously train for all products. Unlike [26] both the warehouse and store agents in CMARL share the system-wide cooperative reward which we demonstrate to be superior, as it avoids sacrificing supply chain-wide optimal agent policies for those where agents could compete for local rewards.

In our proposed CMARL approach, we enhance our warehouse agent with an extended observation space also consisting of past store actions, and an extended action space to explicitly learn an allocation sub-policy when it has limited inventory to meet all the stores' requests. This allows all our agents to be trained simultaneously, unlike [26], which employs a phased training approach and rests on assumptions of unbounded warehouse capacity so that the requested replenishment quantities for all products are always available in the warehouse, while exclusively training the store agents in the first phase. Once every store has converged to a locally optimal policy, only then is the warehouse set to have a finite shelf capacity, and is trained conditioned on converged store agents. However, since store agent behavior that is locally optimal may not be globally optimal across a supply chain, this phased training routine results in the warehouse agent being conditioned on a set of subpar policies. Also in [26], while the warehouse agent has access to replenishment requests from store agents at the current time period, it does not have access to past replenishment requests. This lack of information results in the warehouse only being able to make a binary decision on whether to replenish a store, and cannot intelligently allocate a constrained amount of inventory to stores which our system can achieve. Our CMARL system is able to successfully emulate a divergent supply chain, going beyond the linear supply chains described in most other operations research literature.

3   MARL for Inventory Management

A Markov Decision Process (MDP) is defined as a tuple $(\mathcal{S}, \mathcal{A}, \mathcal{T}, \mathcal{R}, \gamma)$ where $\mathcal{S}$ is the state space, $\mathcal{A}$ is the action space, $\mathcal{T}$ is the set of transition probabilities between states, $\mathcal{R}$ is the set of rewards associated with each state, and γ is a discount factor. At each time step, the MDP can be completely described by its state $s \in \mathcal{S}$, which is used by an agent to select an action $a \in \mathcal{A}$. According to the set of transition probabilities, the MDP will reach a new state $s' \in \mathcal{S}$ in the next time period: $\mathcal{T}(s' \in \mathcal{S} | s \in \mathcal{S}, a \in \mathcal{A}) : \mathcal{S} \times \mathcal{A} \to \mathcal{S}$. A RL agent learns a stochastic policy π that prescribes the probability of each action a that can be taken in state s, as $\pi(a|s) : \mathcal{S} \times \mathcal{A} \to [0, 1]$.

We define a generalization of MDP to a multi-agent setting with the tuple $(\mathcal{U}, \mathbf{S}, \mathbf{A}, \mathbf{T}, \mathbf{R}, \gamma)$. Here, $\mathcal{U} = \{u | 1 \le u \le |\mathcal{U}|\}$ is the set of agents in the environment, $\mathbf{S}$ is the Cartesian product of the state spaces of all agents $u \in \mathcal{U}$: $\mathbf{S} = \mathcal{S}_1 \times \mathcal{S}_2 \times \cdots \times \mathcal{S}_{|\mathcal{U}|}$, $\mathbf{A}$ is the Cartesian product of the action spaces of all agents $u \in \mathcal{U}$: $\mathbf{A} = \mathcal{A}_1 \times \mathcal{A}_2 \times \cdots \times \mathcal{A}_{|\mathcal{U}|}$, $\mathbf{T}$ denotes transition probabilities between $\mathbf{S}$ and $\mathbf{A}$: $\mathbf{T}(s' \in \mathbf{S} | s \in \mathbf{S}, a \in \mathbf{A})$, $\mathbf{R}$ is the Cartesian product over each agent's reward function: $\mathbf{R} = \mathcal{R}_1 \times \mathcal{R}_2 \times \cdots \times \mathcal{R}_{|\mathcal{U}|}$, and γ is a scalar discount factor. At each time step t, all agents synchronously take actions $\mathbf{a} \in \mathbf{A}$. The goal of each agent in the environment is to maximize its long-term reward by finding its own optimal policy $\pi_u : \mathcal{S}_u \to \mathcal{A}_u$ [27].

3.1   MARL Implementation

In the context of our supply chain, $\mathcal{U} = \mathcal{V} \cup \{wh\}$ is the set of vertices with each vertex being either the warehouse agent (wh), or the store agent $v \in \mathcal{V}$ as shown in Fig. 1a. While there is a hierarchy present in this supply chain, all agents execute synchronously. Each agent has its own individual policy, state and action spaces, and no agent can directly access the state space of another.

3.2   Store Agents

Let the vector $\mathbf{x}_v(t) = [x_v(t, 1), \dots, x_v(t, K)]$ denote the on-hand inventory of the K products, and $\mathbf{r}_v(t) = [r_v(t, 1), \dots, r_v(t, K)]$ be the accepted reorder quantity (defined below) at time step t for the store agent $v \in \mathcal{V}$. Its state space is defined as: $\mathcal{S}_v = \{\mathbf{x}_v(t)\} \cup \{\mathbf{r}_v(t-i)\}_{i=1}^{l_v}$, where l_v is the lead time to transfer products from the warehouse to store v. Since actions taken by an agent v during time period t only affect the reward at time period $t + l_v$ after its corresponding lead time l_v, we preserve the Markov property [14] by accounting for the delay

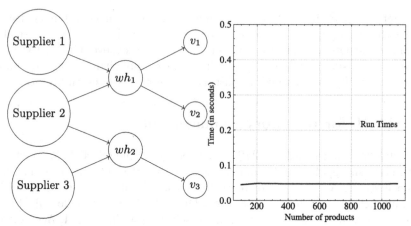

(a) Example supply chain topology (wh are warehouses, v are stores).

(b) Step time up to 1000 products.

Fig. 1. Environment Dynamics.

with a history of past replenishment orders included in the observation space (as described in Sect. 3). Thus, similar to TEXPLORE [7], agents are able to capture correlations between actions at time t and corresponding rewards at time $t + l_v$.

Each store agent learns a policy that performs an action $\mathcal{A}_v$ of placing replenishment orders $\hat{\mathbf{r}}_v(t) = [\hat{r}_v(t, 1), \ldots, \hat{r}_v(t, K)]$ to the warehouse at t for all the K products. We assume that both store and warehouse agents place orders in batches of units, where the action space is quantized into n possible actions for each product, i.e., $\hat{r}_v(t, k) \in \{0, 1, \ldots, n\}$. The value n is empirically deduced from historical data.

3.3 Warehouse Agent

The warehouse agent jointly learns two sub-policies. First, its own replenishment policy for placing replenishment requests $\hat{\mathbf{r}}_{wh}(t)$ from its supplier. Second, an allocation policy for distributing its on-hand inventory to the stores $v \in \mathcal{V}$. In situations when the warehouse does not have sufficient inventory to meet all the store requests, the accepted reorder quantity $\mathbf{r}_v(t)$ that the warehouse learns to allocate to the stores could be lesser than the store's requested quantity $\hat{\mathbf{r}}_v(t)$.

The warehouse state space is extended to include replenishment order quantities $\hat{\mathbf{r}}_v(t)$ from all the stores in the last m time periods, as it enables the warehouse to learn the allocation policy. Additionally, the state space includes its own inventory $\mathbf{x}_{wh}(t)$ as well as the replenishment orders $\hat{\mathbf{r}}_{wh}(t)$ placed in the last m time periods to optimally learn a replenishment policy for itself. Here $m = \max_{u \in \mathcal{U}} l_u$ is the maximum of all lead times in the network. Its state and actions spaces are:

$$\mathcal{S}_{wh} = \{\mathbf{x}_{wh}(t)\} \cup \{\hat{\mathbf{r}}_{wh}(t-i)\}_{i=1}^m \cup \{\{\hat{\mathbf{r}}_v(t-i)\}_{i=1}^m | v \in \mathcal{V}\}, \qquad (1)$$

$$\mathcal{A}_{wh} = \{\hat{\mathbf{r}}_{wh}(t)\} \cup \{\mathbf{r}_v(t) | v \in \mathcal{V}\}. \qquad (2)$$

In Fig. 2b of Sect. 6, we observe that when the store replenishment order quantities $\hat{\mathbf{r}}_v(t)$ are excluded from the warehouse state space in Eq. 1, labelled LimWh-ShRwd, its ability to learn the allocation policy $\mathbf{r}_v(t)$ for each store agent degrades with lower reward value. By additionally observing $\hat{\mathbf{r}}_v(t)$, labelled EnWh-ShRwd, the warehouse agent is able to prioritize replenishment to relevant stores. To the best of our knowledge, our work is the first to introduce this specific multi-agent architecture for IM with enhanced state and action spaces for the warehouse agent.

Demand $\hat{\mathbf{r}}_{wh}(t)$ is always met since the supplier is assumed to have infinite capacity, i.e. $\hat{\mathbf{r}}_{wh}(t) = \mathbf{r}_{wh}(t)$. Ideally, the warehouse should have enough inventory to fulfill all the store requests $\hat{\mathbf{r}}_v(t)$. The mechanism for penalizing the system when the warehouse replenishes a lesser amount $\mathbf{r}_v(t) \leq \hat{\mathbf{r}}_v(t)$ to the stores is described in Sect. 5.

4   Environment for Inventory Management

The environment is implemented as a set of tables that keep track of quantities $\mathbf{x}(t), \mathbf{s}(t), \hat{\mathbf{s}}(t), \mathbf{r}(t), \hat{\mathbf{r}}(t)$ and internal tables to keep a log of replenishment order status. These tables are implemented with CuPy [17] which leverages CUDA Toolkit libraries [16] such as cuBLAS, cuRAND, and cuSOLVER to execute matrix operations on a GPU. This allows updates to the environment tables to execute in constant time (subject to GPU constraints) as shown in Fig. 1b. While the environment can handle an arbitrary number of products, our MARL algorithm implementation converges during training for up to $K = 10$ products, as discussed in Sect. 6. We strongly believe the same environment can still be used for our future work when we seek to implement MARL for managing inventory of thousands of products.

A single episode in our environment starts with initial inventory levels at warehouse and store vertices for each product, and executes for $T = 30$ time periods. Each time period may be analogous to a day of sales, where each agent places its respective replenishment order, which is received after an associated lead time. Also, at each time period, a certain portion of the inventory is sold at the stores according to the customer demand sampled from a demand distribution corresponding to each product.

4.1   Dynamics at Stores

At each time t, customer demand $\hat{\mathbf{s}}_v(t) = [\hat{s}_v(t, 1), \ldots, \hat{s}_v(t, K)]$ for all the K products is sampled from a product-specific demand distribution. Bounded on $\mathbf{x}_v(t)$ the amount of actual inventory sold is: $\mathbf{s}_v(t) = \min(\hat{\mathbf{s}}_v(t), \mathbf{x}_v(t))$, where the min() function operates element-wise on each product.

At the end of each time period when the store vertex v receives accepted replenishment orders $\mathbf{r}_v(t - l_v)$ placed l_v time periods ago, its inventory gets updated as: $\mathbf{x}_v(t+1) = \mathbf{x}_v(t) - \mathbf{s}_v(t) + \mathbf{r}_v(t - l_v)$. Based on $\mathbf{x}_v(t)$ and replenishment history $\{\mathbf{r}_v(t-i)\}_{i=1}^{l_v}$, store v places a replenishment order $\hat{\mathbf{r}}_v(t)$ to the warehouse. We do not need to explicitly model the future demand, as the agent implicitly predicts it based on its learned policy and past demand. We demonstrate this property in Fig. 2b of Sect. 6, where an *oracle* implementation that can see the true customer demand, $\hat{\mathbf{s}}_v(t + l_v)$, l_v lead time period ahead does not outperform CMARL. The environment enforces that the inventory $\mathbf{x}_v(t)$ is always less than the maximum shelf capacity $\mathbf{c}_v$ of the corresponding product at all times, by setting $\mathbf{x}_v(t) = \min(\mathbf{x}_v(t), \mathbf{c}_v)$ element-wise. Inventory that cannot be held on the shelves gets discarded and not realized as sales. However, they need to be procured and stored at the warehouse to be allocated to the stores. Any discarded inventory proportionately penalizes the shared reward, defined subsequently in Eq. (7), by incurring procurement and inventory holding costs at the warehouse without generating any sales revenue. Hence, the stores implicitly avoid placing replenishment requests that would result in exceeding their shelf capacity.

4.2   Dynamics at Warehouse

Based on the store replenishment requests $\hat{\mathbf{r}}_v(t)$, the warehouse uses its allocation sub-policy to decide on the accepted replenishment order $\mathbf{r}_v(t)$. At the end of time t, when the warehouse receives its own replenishment $\mathbf{r}_{wh}(t - l_{wh})$ placed l_{wh} lead time periods ago, its inventory gets updated as:

$$\mathbf{x}_{wh}(t + 1) = \mathbf{x}_{wh}(t) - \left(\sum_{v \in \mathcal{V}} \mathbf{r}_v(t)\right) + \mathbf{r}_{wh}(t - l_{wh}).$$

Based on its available inventory, the warehouse places a replenishment order $\hat{\mathbf{r}}_{wh}(t)$ to its supplier which is always accepted, as the supplier has no inventory constraint. The maximum shelf capacity is again enforced by the environment by setting $\mathbf{x}_{wh}(t) = \min(\mathbf{x}_{wh}(t), \mathbf{c}_{wh})$ element-wise, where the vector $\mathbf{c}_{wh}$ represents the shelf capacities of each of the products at the warehouse. Any inventory discarded due to shelf capacity constraints, though procured by the warehouse when placing its replenishment request $\hat{\mathbf{r}}_{wh}(t - l_{wh})$, is not utilized in allocating to the stores $\mathbf{r}_v(t)$. The system-wide reward defined in Eq. (7) gets penalized proportionally because the cost of procuring this additional inventory is not realized as stores sales. Hence, the warehouse agent will implicitly minimize placing surplus replenishment requests that cannot be held on its shelves.

5   Reward Structure

Since the desired goal is maximizing the system-wide reward (profit across the entire supply chain), situations where agents compete for reward are undesirable. To ensure that the agents are fully cooperative, a shared reward structure is imposed, where each agent is rewarded for choosing actions that benefit the system as a whole. This is as opposed to the separate, local reward formulations for store and warehouse agents as specified in [26]. Sharing rewards can help the learning process converge faster and reach a more optimal solution [20], and reduce the risk of suboptimal behavior like pursuing individual goals at the cost of the system-wide goal [18]. Our results in Fig. 2b confirm this advantage of a shared reward structure over individual rewards, and are discussed in Sect. 6. Our shared reward function consists of the following components:

Sales Revenue. As described in Sect. 4.1, each store sells a certain portion of its inventory $s_v(t)$ based on customer demand $\hat{s}_v(t)$. The total revenue made by all the stores is:

$$P_r(t) = \sum_{k=1}^{K} \sum_{v \in \mathcal{V}} [s_v(t, k) \times \theta_{\text{SP}}(k, v)], \tag{3}$$

where $\theta_{SP}(k, v)$ is the selling price of a single unit of the kth product at v. In most large retailers' supply chains, the transfer of inventory from the warehouse to stores does not incur an intermediary sale. Thus, we do not explicitly model sales at the warehouse and set its sales revenue to zero.

Inventory Holding Cost. Each unit of on-hand inventory at the stores and warehouse typically incurs maintenance costs associated with refrigeration, cleaning, electricity etc. Sans this cost, it would be optimal for both warehouse and stores to keep their inventories stocked to near full-capacity at all times by always placing maximal allowed replenishment orders. To discourage such behavior, we introduce a penalty for holding inventory, defined as:

$$P_h(t) = \sum_{k=1}^{K} \sum_{v \in \mathcal{V} \cup wh} [x_v(t, k) \times \theta_h(k, v)], \tag{4}$$

where $\theta_h(k, v)$ is the cost of holding one unit of kth product at v.

Procurement Cost. As mentioned before, the warehouse procures its replenishment $r_{wh}(t - l_{wh})$ placed l_{wh} lead time ago from the supplier. The total procurement cost is:

$$P_p(t) = \sum_{k=1}^{K} [r_{wh}(t - l_{wh}, k) \times \theta_{CP}(k, wh)], \tag{5}$$

where $\theta_{\text{CP}}(k, wh)$ is the cost of procuring a single unit of product k. In most retailers' supply chains, the inventory transfer from the warehouse to stores does not incur an intermediary sale, as they are internal to the organization. Hence, we do not associate procurement cost with the stores.

Unfulfilled Penalty. We impose an unfulfilled order penalty when the inventory at the warehouse is insufficient to meet the sum of replenishment requests from stores, and when stores do not have enough inventory to satisfy customer demand. This penalty is formulated as:

$$P_u(t) = \theta_u \sum_{k=1}^{K} \text{ReLU} \left(\sum_{v \in \mathcal{V}} \hat{r}_v(t, k) - x_{wh}(t, k) \right) + \theta_u \sum_{k=1}^{K} \sum_{v \in \mathcal{V}} [\hat{s}_v(t, k) - s_v(t, k)],$$

$$(6)$$

where θ_u is a hyperparameter for this penalty, and ReLU() is the Rectified Linear Unit function defined as: $\text{ReLU}(x) = \max(0, x)$.

Shared Reward Specification. The rewards and penalties in Eqs. 3–6 are used to calculate a total reward for each time period in an episode, defined as:

$$P(t) = P_r(t) - (P_p(t) + P_h(t) + P_u(t)). \qquad (7)$$

This expression can also optionally include transportation and labor costs. We exclude them as our experiments deal with a small number of products.

6   Experimental Results

We implement all RL agents with proximal policy optimization (PPO) [23] over vanilla policy gradient (VPG) as the former is known to have better sample efficiency, improved training stability, more effective exploration of the action space, and robustness to high-dimensional state spaces [10,11,22,24,27]. A single product is assumed to have a Poisson distribution, with mean parameter $10 \leq \mu \leq 1000$. Each system is trained for $100,000$ episodes on an 8-core vCPU and a single NVIDIA Tesla P4 GPU. We set $\theta_u \gg \theta_h$, as this is experimentally determined to minimize stockout occurrences while keeping inventory stable.

6.1   Linear Supply Chain

We first consider a linear supply chain with 2 vertices $\mathcal{U} = \{wh, v\}$ consisting of one warehouse and one store that deals with a single product. We compare CMARL against inventory control policies such as base-stock policy (BSP) [1] and the single-agent RL (SARL). In the BSP and SARL implementations, the action and observation spaces are global and combined for both the warehouse and the store. The action space is the set of *all* vertices' requested replenishment quantities at time t: $\mathcal{A} = \{\hat{\mathbf{r}}_{wh}(t), \hat{\mathbf{r}}_v(t)\}$. Likewise, the observation space is the set of all vertices' on-hand inventories and their past accepted replenishment orders: $\mathcal{S} = \{\mathbf{x}_{wh}(t)\} \cup \{\mathbf{r}_{wh}(t-i)\}_{i=1}^{l_{wh}} \cup \{\mathbf{x}_v(t)\} \cup \{\mathbf{r}_v(t-i)\}_{i=1}^{l_v}$. The BSP is implemented following the approach described in [8].

For all the 3 approaches, we compute the rewards using Eq. 7 and plot them in Fig. 2a. The reward from SARL (over 450) is higher compared to the BSP, the latter of which does not exceed 300. This result is supported by [8,19,21,26]

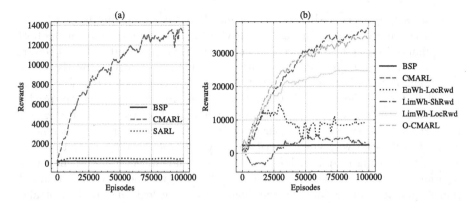

Fig. 2. Training rewards for: (a) linear supply chain, (b) divergent supply chain with 10 stores, both with 1 product.

where SARL, with enough training, is the superior choice to optimization-based approaches. However, our proposed CMARL framework far outperforms SARL with more than over 30 times the rewards. The proposed MARL system also reached and surpassed the rewards reaped by the SARL framework in a fraction of the time it took for the latter to reach its maximal value. This is likely because in a multi-agent environment, agents can have different roles and behaviors, leading to a more diverse and efficient exploration of the state space compared to a single agent. As observed in [12,29], the presence of multiple agents allows for an increase in the effective sample size, leading to faster convergence.

6.2   Divergent Supply Chain

Single Product. We now scale the environment to a divergent topology with one warehouse vertex and 10 store vertices, and start with a discussion of our experiments on a single product. An upper bound for the reward for the BSP can be set at $10 \times 360 = 3,600$. This is because a divergent supply chain with $|\mathcal{V}|$ stores can be modelled as $|\mathcal{V}|$ linear supply chains with constraints at warehouse vertices. Removing these constraints allows for a larger set of possible behaviors in each of the $|\mathcal{V}|$ linear supply chains, thereby increasing potential rewards. Over the course of training, the average reward reaches over 35,000 which is approximately 10 times that of the projected reward for base-stock policy, as shown in Fig. 2b.

We study multiple variants of our MARL system by: (i) limiting the observation space of the warehouse agent defined in Eq. (1) to only its past replenishment actions, and excluding the stores' replenishment requests (LimWh), and (ii) having independent localized reward for each agent as opposed to a system-wide shared reward (LocRwd). Specifically, we investigate 5 different MARL configurations: (i) CMARL a.k.a. EnWh-ShRwd, (ii) EnWh-LocRwd, (iii) LimWh-ShRwd, (iv) LimWh-LocRwd, and (v) Oracle implementation of CMARL (O-CMARL) where the store agents at time t see the actual customer demand, $\hat{s}_v(t + l_v)$, l_v lead time periods ahead and make replenishment requests $\hat{r}_v(t)$ accordingly. As seen in Fig. 2b, our CMARL system that implements both the enhanced observation space for the warehouse agent, and a shared reward structure has the highest reward values. It is not outperformed by the oracle implementation either, implying that we do not explicitly need a forecasting model to foresee the future demand. The agents are able to implicitly predict it based on their learned policy and past demand. The worst performing configuration is the system-wide shared reward without an enhanced warehouse agent (LimWh-ShRwd) which distributes rewards equally, and does not give the system any strong signal on how to improve behavior. As a result, allocation decisions are made essentially at random when the warehouse cannot fulfill all replenishment requests and the warehouse fails from learning an efficient allocation policy. Similarly, having an enhanced warehouse with individual rewards (EnWh-LocRwd) for each agent results in the warehouse agent converging to locally advantageous policies much faster than store agents, as it has access to more information about the environment than store agents.

A system where the MARL uses neither an enhanced warehouse agent nor a shared reward (LimWh-LocRwd) avoids these issues, as although agents compete for reward they converge to policies more or less at similar rates with respect to each other. Hence, it is the second-best performer as a system. However, this still produces suboptimal behavior as depicted in Fig. 3b, where the inventory levels for each time period are tracked by running the environment for one test episode after the agents policies are converged in the training phase. In the LimWh-LocRwd configuration in Fig. 3b, the warehouse agent converges to a policy where it simply keeps placing maximal replenishment requests from its supplier, and store agents are erratic with their replenishment requests, resulting in frequent stock-outs (as their inventories frequently go to zero). In contrast, the proposed CMARL system manages inventory much better. This is seen in Fig. 3a, where the warehouse in the CMARL system has a relatively stable inventory that isn't continuously increasing or decreasing. This implies a lowered holding cost as the leftover inventory after sales is minimized, while still fulfilling all orders with inventories never reaching 0 to have stockouts.

Multiple Products. To extend CMARL to supply chains of retailers that deal in multiple products, we experiment with up to 10 products. As described in Sect. 3, each agent's action and observation spaces increase linearly with respect to the number of products in the supply chain. This, along with our particular GPU-parallelized environment implementation discussed in Sect. 4, enables training agent policies for multiple products simultaneously, thereby avoiding training time overhead, and allows us to independently capture variations in demand distributions for each product individually. Figure 4a shows continuously increasing training rewards for a supply chain that manages inventory of 10 products at each vertex, implying system-wide convergence to optimal policies by agents.

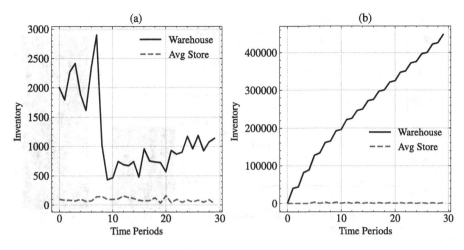

Fig. 3. Warehouse and average store inventories for 30 time periods with (a) CMARL, and (b) LimWh-LocRwd for a supply chain with 10 stores, 1 product.

In contrast, an implementation that shares policy parameters across products such as in [26] needs to be trained separately for each product, which increases training time by a factor of K. It also results in a relative inability to capture large variations between product types, leading to reduced overall performance. As a motivating example, a perishable item such as a fruit has fundamental differences with an electronic device such as a television in trading volume, shelf life, and customer demand, so much so that sharing parameters of an inventory management policy for the two is seldom the ideal choice. To emphasize this property, we implemented a variant of CMARL (ShPol-CMARL) with an action and observation space for each agent that can only handle a single product at a time as input, and train it sequentially for each of the 10 products by sharing policy parameters between different products. Figure 4b shows a comparison between rewards for a single episode, between our CMARL system with independent action and state dimensions for each of the 10 products as described in Sect. 3 and 4, and the shared policy variant (ShPol-CMARL). We notice CMARL to achieve double the reward of ShPol-CMARL. For the experiments in Fig. 4, each one of the Poisson distributions governing product demand had a different value for μ. Our current implementation of CMARL is unable to handle beyond 10 products for reasons described in the next section.

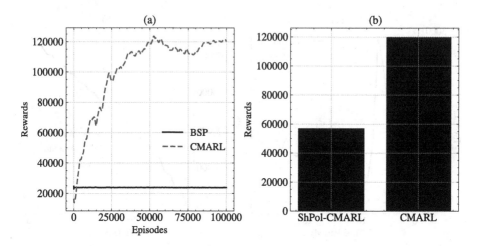

Fig. 4. (a) Training rewards and (b) Test Reward for one episode for a divergent supply chain with 10 stores, 10 products.

7 Conclusion and Future Work

We presented a system with a MARL formulation of the IM problem implemented with a GPU-parallelized environment that consists of one warehouse and multiple stores. Our agent-environment dynamics for the warehouse agent with enhanced observation and action space enables it to effectively learn an allocation sub-policy. Additionally, the shared reward formulation in CMARL encourages cooperation between agents to jointly optimize for a retailer's supply chain needs. We demonstrated that for managing inventory of a single product, CMARL outperforms optimization BSP approaches, single agent RL, as well as other MARL configurations with individual reward structure and limited warehouse observation space. Our experimental results indicate that having individual action/observation space dimensions corresponding to each product, instead of sharing a single policy across all products as done in [26], leads to superior reward values alongside the ability to simultaneously train for all products. Our synchronous training of both warehouse and store agents does not require (perhaps unrealistic) assumptions of unlimited warehouse capacity while exclusively training the store agents as performed in phases [26].

For our system, incorporating individual observation and action dimensions for each product in terms of increased reward value, results in the combinatorial explosion of agent's action and observation spaces with increasing numbers of products. This in turn limits the capacity of our current CMARL framework to handle over 10 products, while an IM system for a large retailer requires the ability to handle thousands of products. Our future directions of research include investigating extensions that are equipped to deal with large action spaces such as those proposed in [4], as well as alternatives such as Branching Deep Q-Networks [28].

Ethical Impact. We do not foresee any scenario where our work would put a certain demographic or a specific organization to a systematic disadvantage. We do not use any personal data in our experiments. We do not anticipate our algorithm to be used in policing or military applications. Our work is only focused on developing a RL-based solution to effectively manage inventory and optimize costs in a multi-echelon supply chain system.

References

1. Anbazhagan, N., Wang, J., Gomathi, D.: Base stock policy with retrial demands. Appl. Math. Model. **37**(6), 4464–4473 (2013)
2. D'Atri, A., et al.: From supply chains to supply networks: The beer game evolution. IFAC Proc. Volumes **42**(4), 1316–1321 (2009)
3. Ding, Y., et al.: Multi-agent reinforcement learning with shared resource in inventory management. CoRR abs/2212.07684 (2022)
4. Farquhar, G., Gustafson, L., Lin, Z., Whiteson, S., Usunier, N., Synnaeve, G.: Growing action spaces. In: Proceedings of the 37th International Conference on Machine Learning, vol. 119, pp. 3040–3051. PMLR (2020)
5. Giannoccaro, I., Pontrandolfo, P.: Inventory management in supply chains: a reinforcement learning approach. Int. J. Prod. Econ. **78**(2), 153–161 (2002)
6. Goodfellow, I.J., Mirza, M., Xiao, D., Courville, A., Bengio, Y.: An empirical investigation of catastrophic forgetting in gradient-based neural networks. arXiv preprint arXiv:1312.6211 (2013)
7. Hester, T., Stone, P.: Texplore: real-time sample-efficient reinforcement learning for robots. Mach. Learn. **90**, 385–429 (2013)
8. Hubbs, C.D., Perez, H.D., Sarwar, O., Sahinidis, N.V., Grossmann, I.E., Wassick, J.M.: Or-gym: a reinforcement learning library for operations research problem. CoRR abs/2008.06319 (2020)
9. Kara, A., Dogan, I.: Reinforcement learning approaches for specifying ordering policies of perishable inventory systems. Expert Syst. Appl. **91**, 150–158 (2018)
10. Konda, V., Tsitsiklis, J.: Actor-critic algorithms. In: Advances in Neural Information Processing Systems, vol. 12 (1999)
11. Lillicrap, T.P., et al.: Continuous control with deep reinforcement learning. arXiv preprint arXiv:1509.02971 (2015)
12. Lowe, R., Wu, Y.I., Tamar, A., Harb, J., Pieter Abbeel, O., Mordatch, I.: Multi-agent actor-critic for mixed cooperative-competitive environments. In: Advances in Neural Information Processing Systems, vol. 30 (2017)
13. Meisheri, H., et al.: Scalable multi-product inventory control with lead time constraints using reinforcement learning. Neural Comput. Appl. **34**(3), 1735–1757 (2022)
14. Miller, D.R.: Markov processes. In: Gass, S.I., Harris, C.M. (eds.) Encyclopedia of Operations Research and Management Science, pp. 486–490. Springer, New York (2001). https://doi.org/10.1007/1-4020-0611-X_582
15. Mittal, M., Shah, N.H.: Optimal Inventory Control and Management Techniques. IGI Global, Hershey (2016)
16. NVIDIA, Vingelmann, P., Fitzek, F.H.: Cuda, release: 10.2.89 (2020). https://developer.nvidia.com/cuda-toolkit

17. Okuta, R., Unno, Y., Nishino, D., Hido, S., Loomis, C.: Cupy: a numpy-compatible library for NVIDIA GPU calculations. In: Proceedings of Workshop on Machine Learning Systems (LearningSys) in the Thirty-first Annual Conference on Neural Information Processing Systems (NIPS) (2017)
18. Omidshafiei, S., Pazis, J., Amato, C., How, J.P., Vian, J.: Deep decentralized multi-task multi-agent reinforcement learning under partial observability. In: International Conference on Machine Learning, pp. 2681–2690. PMLR (2017)
19. Oroojlooyjadid, A., Nazari, M., Snyder, L.V., Takáč, M.: A deep q-network for the beer game: deep reinforcement learning for inventory optimization. Manuf. Serv. Oper. Manag. **24**(1), 285–304 (2022)
20. Panait, L., Luke, S.: Cooperative multi-agent learning: the state of the art. Auton. Agent. Multi-Agent Syst. **11**, 387–434 (2005)
21. Peng, Z., Zhang, Y., Feng, Y., Zhang, T., Wu, Z., Su, H.: Deep reinforcement learning approach for capacitated supply chain optimization under demand uncertainty. In: 2019 Chinese Automation Congress (CAC), pp. 3512–3517. IEEE (2019)
22. Schulman, J., Levine, S., Abbeel, P., Jordan, M., Moritz, P.: Trust region policy optimization. In: Proceedings of the 32nd International Conference on Machine Learning, vol. 37, pp. 1889–1897. PMLR (2015)
23. Schulman, J., Wolski, F., Dhariwal, P., Radford, A., Klimov, O.: Proximal policy optimization algorithms. arXiv preprint arXiv:1707.06347 (2017)
24. Silver, D., Lever, G., Heess, N., Degris, T., Wierstra, D., Riedmiller, M.: Deterministic policy gradient algorithms. In: Proceedings of the 31st International Conference on Machine Learning, vol. 32, pp. 387–395. PMLR (2014)
25. Stranieri, F., Stella, F.: A deep reinforcement learning approach to supply chain inventory management. CoRR abs/2204.09603 (2022)
26. Sultana, N.N., Meisheri, H., Baniwal, V., Nath, S., Ravindran, B., Khadilkar, H.: Reinforcement learning for multi-product multi-node inventory management in supply chains. CoRR abs/2006.04037 (2020)
27. Sutton, R.S., Barto, A.G.: Reinforcement Learning: An Introduction. MIT Press, Cambridge (2018)
28. Tavakoli, A., Pardo, F., Kormushev, P.: Action branching architectures for deep reinforcement learning. In: Proceedings of the AAAI Conference on Artificial Intelligence, vol. 32 (2018)
29. Yang, Y., et al.: Q-value path decomposition for deep multiagent reinforcement learning. In: Proceedings of the 37th International Conference on Machine Learning, vol. 119, pp. 10706–10715. PMLR (2020)

LtrGCN: Large-Scale Graph Convolutional Networks-Based Learning to Rank for Web Search

Yuchen Li[1], Haoyi Xiong[2](✉), Linghe Kong[1](✉), Shuaiqiang Wang[2], Zeyi Sun[3], Hongyang Chen[3], Guihai Chen[1], and Dawei Yin[2]

[1] Shanghai Jiao Tong University, Shanghai, China
{yuchenli,linghe.kong}@sjtu.edu.cn, gchen@cs.sjtu.edu.cn
[2] Baidu Inc., Beijing, China
haoyi.xiong.fr@ieee.org, yindawei@acm.org
[3] Zhejiang Lab, Hangzhou, China
sunzeyi@zhejianglab.com, dr.h.chen@ieee.org

Abstract. While traditional Learning to Rank (LTR) models use query-webpage pairs to perform regression tasks to predict the ranking scores, they usually fail to capture the structure of interactions between queries and webpages over an extremely large bipartite graph. In recent years, Graph Convolutional Neural Networks (GCNs) have demonstrated their unique advantages in link prediction over bipartite graphs and have been successfully used for user-item recommendations. However, it is still difficult to scale-up GCNs for web search, due to the (1) extreme sparsity of links in query-webpage bipartite graphs caused by the expense of ranking scores annotation and (2) imbalance between queries (billions) and webpages (trillions) for web-scale search as well as the imbalance in annotations. In this work, we introduce the **Q**-subgraph and **W**-subgraph to represent every query and webpage with the structure of interaction preserved, and then propose **LtrGCN**—an LTR pipeline that samples **Q**-subgraphs and **W**-subgraphs from all query-webpage pairs, learns to extract features from **Q**-subgraphs and **W**-subgraphs, and predict ranking scores in an end-to-end manner. We carried out extensive experiments to evaluate **LtrGCN** using two real-world datasets and online experiments based on the A/B test at a large-scale search engine. The offline results show that **LtrGCN** could achieve Δ NDCG$_5 = 2.89\%$–3.97% compared to baselines. We deploy **LtrGCN** with realistic traffic at a large-scale search engine, where we can still observe significant improvement. **LtrGCN** performs consistently in both offline and online experiments.

This work was supported in part by National Key R&D Program of China (No. 2021ZD0110303), NSFC grant 62141220, 61972253, U1908212, 62172276, 61972254, the Program for Professor of Special Appointment (Eastern Scholar) at Shanghai Institutions of Higher Learning, Shanghai Science and Technology Development Funds 23YF1420500, Open Research Projects of Zhejiang Lab No. 2022NL0AB01.

G. De Francisci Morales et al. (Eds.): ECML PKDD 2023, LNAI 14174, pp. 635–651, 2023.
https://doi.org/10.1007/978-3-031-43427-3_38

Keywords: Learning to Rank · Graph Convolutional Networks · Web Search

1 Introduction

Large-scale Learning to Rank (LTR) is a central part of real-world information retrieval problems, such as web search and content recommendations. Given a query of web search, the search engine first retrieves relevant webpages from the database and sorts the webpages by the ranking scores predicted by LTR models. While traditional LTR models transform ranking into regression problems of various types, they usually fail to capture the structural information over the interactions between billions of queries and trillions of webpages. These interactions indeed characterize how all these queries and webpages connect each other in a large bipartite graph of the web. To provide a better search experience, it is inevitable to incorporate such structural information in LTR.

On the other hand, in recent years, Graph Neural Networks, such as Graph Convolutional Neural Networks (GCN) [18], have been used for user-item recommendations and demonstrated their unique advantages in modeling the problem as link prediction over bipartite graphs [10]. Similar to LTR based on query-webpage pairs, the user-item recommendation also needs to rank items (e.g., products or contents) subject to the given profile of every user. However, it is difficult to directly adopt GCNs for LTR tasks at web-scale, due to the sparsity and imbalanced issues as follows. First of all, as shown in Fig. 1, *links are extremely sparse in the query-webpage bipartite graph* extracted from LTR training datasets, as labeling query-webpage pairs by professional annotators is expensive and time-consuming (difficult to scale-up). Furthermore, *from the webpages' perspectives, edges between queries and webpages are severely imbalanced*—it is quite common to link a query to dozens of webpages with both high and low relevant scores, while a webpage hardly links to any queries, especially to the queries that the webpage is less relevant or low-ranked, in the annotations. Apparently, either sparsity or imbalance issue would significantly downgrade the performance of GCN models [29]. Therefore, to tackle the above two challenges, there needs a non-trivial extension on the GCN-based model for handling LTR at web-scale.

In this work, we propose **LtrGCN** to tackle the above two issues and adopt GCNs for LTR tasks in a pipeline as follows. Given all query-webpage pairs in the LTR training dataset, **LtrGCN** first leverages two advanced sampling strategies to generate the **Q**-subgraph and **W**-subgraph for every query and webpage. Then, **LtrGCN** leverages GCNs to extract feature vectors from the **Q**-subgraph and **W**-subgraph as the representation of the query-webpage pair for ranking score prediction. The feature extraction and ranking score prediction are optimized in an end-to-end manner, so as to enable discriminative feature extraction while preserving structural information in the bipartite graph. As sparsity and imbalance issues are addressed, **LtrGCN** can work with the training datasets, where it is sufficient that only a small proportion of query-webpage pairs are labeled by experts. Furthermore, we conduct extensive experiments to evaluate

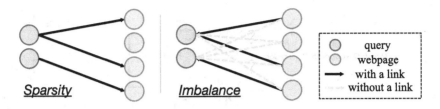

Fig. 1. Sparsity and Imbalance Issues in the Query-Webpage Bipartite Graph.

LtrGCN using two real-world datasets (offline), and launch online experiments based on an A/B test at a large-scale search engine. The offline results show that **LtrGCN** could achieve the best performance on both datasets compared to baselines. As for the online evaluation, we deploy **LtrGCN** with realistic traffic at a large-scale search engine, where we still observe significant improvement. **LtrGCN** performs consistently in both offline and online experiments. Our main contributions are summarized as follows:

- We study the problem of the extreme sparsity of links in query-webpage bipartite graphs caused by the expense of ranking score annotation and the imbalance between queries and webpages for web-scale search. To the best of our knowledge, this work is the first to investigate sparsity and imbalance in query-webpage bipartite graphs for large-scale industrial LTR tasks.
- We propose **LtrGCN** consisting of three steps: (1) *Q-subgraph Generation via Self-tuned Labeling* that annotates all unlabeled query-webpage pairs and assigns every query webpages with ranking scores to generate **Q**-subgraphs, (2) *W-subgraph Generation via Negative Sampling* that find irrelevant queries for every webpage to construct **W**-subgraphs, (3) *Learning to Rank based on GCN with Q-subgraphs and W-subgraphs* that learns the representations of query-webpage pairs from **Q**-subgraphs and **W**-subgraphs and predicts ranking scores in an end-to-end manner.
- We carry out extensive offline experiments on a public LTR dataset and a real-world dataset collected from a large-scale search engine. We also deploy **LtrGCN** at the search engine and implement a series of online evaluations. The experiment results show that, compared to the state-of-the-art in webpage ranking, **LtrGCN** could achieve the best performance on both offline datasets. Furthermore, **LtrGCN** obtains significant improvements in online evaluations under fair comparisons.

2   Methodology

2.1   Task Formulation

Given a set of search queries $\mathcal{Q} = \{q_1, q_2, \dots\}$ and all archived webpages $\mathcal{D} = \{d_1, d_2, \dots\}$, for each query $q_i \in \mathcal{Q}$, the search engine could retrieve a

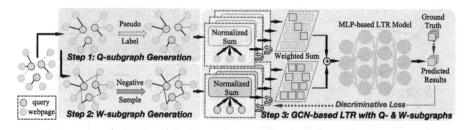

Fig. 2. The framework of **LtrGCN** consisting of three steps: (1) *Q-subgraph Generation via Self-tuned Labeling*, (2) *W-subgraph Generation via Negative Sampling*, and (3) *GCN-based LTR with Q-subgraphs and W-subgraphs*.

set of relevant webpages denoted as $D_i = \{d_j^i\}_{j=1}^{|D_i|} \subset \mathcal{D}$. Through professional labeling, a set of ranking scores $\boldsymbol{y}_i = \{y_j^i\}_{j=1}^{|D_i|}$ for q_i is established to characterize the relevance of the webpage $d_j^i \in D_i$ to the search query q_i. In this paper, we follow the settings in [26] and scale the relevant score from 0 to 4 to represent levels of relevance (i.e., {**bad-0, fair-1, good-2, excellent-3, perfect-4**}). We denote a set of query-webpage pairs with ranking score annotations as triples $\mathcal{S} = \{(q_1, D_1, \boldsymbol{y}_1), (q_2, D_2, \boldsymbol{y}_2), (q_3, D_3, \boldsymbol{y}_3), \dots\}$. We aim to learn an LTR scoring function $f : \mathcal{Q} \times \mathcal{D} \to [0, 4]$, which could be approximated through minimizing the following ranking loss:

$$\mathcal{L} = \frac{1}{|\mathcal{S}|} \sum_{i=1}^{|\mathcal{S}|} \left(\frac{1}{|D_i|} \sum_{j=1}^{|D_i|} \ell(\boldsymbol{y}_j^i, f(q^i, d_j^i)) \right), \tag{1}$$

where ℓ represents the loss of the ranking prediction for query q_i with returned webpage d_j^i against the ground truth label $\boldsymbol{y}_j^i$. Note that, **LtrGCN** is flexible with standard loss functions (i.e., pointwise, pairwise, and listwise). As annotators can barely label a small number of query-webpage pairs due to the limited budgets, the key problem of LTR is thus to incorporate the unlabeled query-webpage pairs denoted as set $\mathcal{S}' = \{(q_1', D_1'), (q_2', D_2'), \dots\}$.

2.2   Overall Framework of LtrGCN

As illustrated in Fig. 2, **LtrGCN** consists of three steps: (1) *Q-subgraph Generation via Self-tuned Labeling*, (2) *W-subgraph Generation via Negative Sampling*, and (3) *Learning to Rank based on GCN with Q-subgraphs and W-subgraphs*. Specifically, in Step (1), **LtrGCN** first annotates all unlabeled query-webpage pairs with *pseudo* ranking scores and then assigns every query webpages with high ranking scores and also webpages with low scores to generate **Q**-subgraphs from the training set. Then, in Step (2), **LtrGCN** proposes a *negative sampling strategy* to find irrelevant queries for every webpage to construct **W**-subgraphs. Eventually, in Step (3), given **Q**-subgraphs and **W**-subgraphs for every high-ranked query-webpage pair, **LtrGCN** learns the representations of query-webpage pairs using a Light Graph Convolution Network (LightGCN) [12] and enables LTR in an end-to-end manner.

2.3   Q-subgraph Generation via Self-tuned Labeling

As mentioned above, to leverage GCN for ranking, there needs to feed the model with **Q**-subgraphs and **W**-subgraphs. Given query-webpage pairs that are sparsely annotated with ranking scores in the training set, **LtrGCN** adopts a labeling approach [23] that first annotates every unlabeled query-webpage pair with a *pseudo* ranking score and then assigns every query webpages with high ranking scores and also webpages with low scores, so as to generate **Q**-subgraphs from the training set at full-scale. Thus, there needs the learning to predict *pseudo* ranking scores with labeled/unlabeled samples in the training set.

LtrGCN first gets every possible query-webpage pair from query and webpage datasets as (q_i, d_i^j) for $\forall q_i \in \mathcal{Q}$ and $\forall d_i^j \in D_i \subset \mathcal{D}$. For each query-webpage pair (q_i, d_i^j), **LtrGCN** further extracts an m-dimensional feature vector $\boldsymbol{x}_{i,j}$ representing the features of the jth webpage under the ith query. Then, the labeled and unlabeled sets of feature vectors can be presented as $\mathcal{M} = \{(\boldsymbol{x}_{i,j}, \boldsymbol{y}_j^i) | \forall (q_i, D_i, \boldsymbol{y}) \in \mathcal{S}$ and $\forall d_j^i \in D_i\}$ and $\mathcal{M}' = \{\boldsymbol{x}_{i,j} | \forall (q_i, D_i) \in \mathcal{S}'\}$. Given the labeled feature set $\mathcal{M}$ and the unlabeled feature set $\mathcal{M}'$, **LtrGCN** further takes a two-step strategy to accomplish the pseudo-label generation via multi-loss learning as follows.

First, **LtrGCN** trains an LTR model with the listwise loss function as:

$$\mathcal{L}_{List} = -\frac{1}{|\mathcal{M}|} \sum_{i=1}^{|\mathcal{M}|} \left(\frac{1}{|D_i|} \sum_{j=1}^{|D_i|} \text{softmax}(\boldsymbol{y}_j^i) \times \log\left(\text{softmax}\, f(q^i, d_j^i)\right) \right). \quad (2)$$

The listwise-based LTR model is denoted as Rank^{List}. **LtrGCN** trains Rank^{List} using both $\mathcal{M}$ and $\mathcal{M}'$ through self-training, where Rank^{List} is first trained using $\mathcal{M}$ through supervised learning. Then, Rank^{List} predicts the ranking score for each feature vector in $\mathcal{M}'$ and pseudo-labels the feature vector with the prediction result. After that, **LtrGCN** combines $\mathcal{M}$ with pseudo-labeled data $\mathcal{M}^P$ and retrains Rank^{List} using the *combined data* $\mathcal{M}^C$.

Given the $\mathcal{M}^C$, $\mathcal{M}$ and $\mathcal{M}'$, **LtrGCN** (1) trains an LTR model with the pointwise loss function as:

$$\mathcal{L}_{Point} = \frac{1}{|\mathcal{M}^C|} \sum_{i=1}^{|\mathcal{M}^C|} \left(\frac{1}{|D_i|} \sum_{j=1}^{|D_i|} |f(q^i, d_j^i) - \boldsymbol{y}_j^i|^2 \right). \quad (3)$$

The pointwise-based LTR model is denoted as Rank^{Point}. **LtrGCN** first trains Rank^{Point} with $\mathcal{M}^C$ and predicts pseudo-labels for each feature vector in $\mathcal{M}'$ using trained Rank^{Point}. Then, **LtrGCN** updates $\mathcal{M}^P$ with the prediction results of Rank^{Point} and combines $\mathcal{M}$ with $\mathcal{M}^P$ to conduct $\mathcal{M}^C$. **LtrGCN** further retrains Rank^{List} using $\mathcal{M}^C$ and predicts ranking scores for each feature vector in $\mathcal{M}'$ using trained Rank^{List}. Finally, **LtrGCN** updates $\mathcal{M}^P$ with the prediction results of R^{List} and combines $\mathcal{M}$ with $\mathcal{M}^P$ to obtain $\mathcal{M}^C$. **LtrGCN** repeats the above steps with $\mathcal{T}$ rounds and returns $\mathcal{M}^C$.

With *pseudo* ranking scores predicted for all unlabeled samples, **LtrGCN** builds a **Q**-subgraph for every query with the (*pseudo*) ranking scores greater than **2 (good)**. Specifically, to build the **Q**-subgraph, **LtrGCN** randomly picks up a webpage that the query-webpage is with the ranking score lower than **1 (fair)**, and forms the three items (i.e., *the query, a highly-ranked webpage of the query, a low-ranked webpage of the query*) into a **Q**-subgraph.

2.4   W-subgraph Generation via Negative Sampling

Though **Q**-subgraph Generation step could generate ranking scores for every query-webpage pair in the training dataset, it is still difficult to construct **W**-subgraphs using predicted scores at full-scale. While every query connects to the webpages with high/low *pseudo* ranking scores, a webpage usually only connects to one or very limited highly-relevant queries and the number of webpages is much larger than that of effective queries from a webpages' perspective. Thus, there needs to find irrelevant queries for every webpage. To build **W**-subgraphs for a webpage, **LtrGCN** leverages a *negative sampling strategy*. Given a webpage, **LtrGCN** retrieves all query-webpage pairs, builds a **W**-subgraph for every query-webpage with the ranking scores higher than **2 (fair)**. Specifically, **LtrGCN** randomly picks up a query that does not connect to the webpage as the irrelevant query, then forms the three (i.e., *the webpage, a query where the webpage is highly ranked, and an irrelevant query*) into a **W**-subgraph. Specifically, for a query q^i, **LtrGCN** randomly chooses the webpage from the other query to conduct the negative samples and assigns the relevant score as 0 or 1 to represent poor relevance. Through this negative sampling method, **LtrGCN** could build **W**-subgraphs for a webpage.

2.5   GCN-Based LTR with Q-subgraphs and W-subgraphs

Given **Q**-subgraphs and **W**-subgraphs for every high-ranked query-webpage pair, in this step, **LtrGCN** learns the representations of query-webpage pairs with a GCN and enables learning to rank (LTR) in an end-to-end manner.

In the initial step, given the **Q**-subgraph and **W**-subgraph, **LtrGCN** extracts the feature vector of each query and webpage. Specifically, the feature of query q_i and webpage d_j^i is denoted as $z_{q^i}^{(n=0)}$ and $z_{d_j^i}^{(n=0)}$, where n indicates the feature output from the nth GCN layer. Next, the GCN-based encoder utilizes the query-webpage interaction graph to propagate the representations as:

$$
\begin{aligned}
z_{q^i}^{(n+1)} &= \sum_{d_j^i \in \mathcal{N}_{q^i}} \frac{1}{\sqrt{|\mathcal{N}_{q^i}|}\sqrt{|\mathcal{N}_{d_{j,i}}|}} z_{d_j^i}^{(n)}, \\
z_{d_j^i}^{(n+1)} &= \sum_{q^i \in \mathcal{N}_{d_j^i}} \frac{1}{\sqrt{|\mathcal{N}_{q^i}|}\sqrt{|\mathcal{N}_{d_{j,i}}|}} z_{q^i}^{(n)},
\end{aligned}
\tag{4}
$$

where $\mathcal{N}_{q^i}$ and $\mathcal{N}_{d_{j,i}}$ represent the set of webpages that are relevant to query q^i and the set of queries that are relevant to webpage d_j^i, respectively. Moreover, $\dfrac{1}{\sqrt{|\mathcal{N}_{q^i}|}\sqrt{|\mathcal{N}_{d_{j,i}}|}}$ is the normalization term used to prevent the scale of representations from increasing as a result of graph convolution operations. After N layers graph convolution operations, **LtrGCN** combines the representations generated from each layer to conduct the final representation of query q^i and webpage d_j^i as follows:

$$z_{q^i} = \sum_{n=0}^{N} \beta_n z_{q^i}^{(n)}; \ z_{d_j^i} = \sum_{n=0}^{N} \beta_n z_{d_j^i}^{(n)}, \tag{5}$$

where $\beta_n \in [0, 1]$ is a hyper-parameter to balance the weight of each layer representation. Then, **LtrGCN** combines z_{q^i} and $z_{d_j^i}$ to conduct the learned query-webpage pair representation as $z_{i,j}$.

Given the learned vector $z_{i,j}$, **LtrGCN** adopts a Multi-Layer Perception (MLP)-based model with a fully-connected layer to calculate the predicted score $s_{i,j}$. The whole process can be formulated as: $s_{i,j} = f_\theta(z_{i,j})$, where θ is the set of discriminative parameters. Against the ground truth, **LtrGCN** leverages the discriminative loss function, which is defined as:

$$\mathcal{L}_{Disc} = \frac{1}{|\mathcal{Q}|} \sum_{i=1}^{|\mathcal{Q}|} \left(\frac{1}{|D_i|} \sum_{j=1}^{|D_i|} \ell_{LTR}\left(y_j^i, f_\theta(z_{i,j})\right) \right), \tag{6}$$

where ℓ_{LTR} represents the standard LTR loss function (i.e., pointwise, pairwise and listwise).

3 Deployment of LtrGCN

In this section, we introduce the deployment settings of **LtrGCN** at a large-scale industrial search engine. As illustrated in Fig. 3, we present the overall workflow of the real-world deployment and the three-stage design of the search engine as follows: (1) *Webpage Collection*, (2) *Webpage Storage and Indexing*, and (3) *Retrieval and Ranking*.

Webpage Collection. To efficiently navigate the vast expanse of webpages available on the internet, the search engine employs high-performance crawlers known as Web Crawlers. These crawlers play a vital role in collecting and downloading webpages. The Web Crawler operates by systematically scanning a comprehensive list of links, and actively searching for new webpages and updates to existing ones. It selects and stores valid links containing the desired content, creating a downloading list. Utilizing real-time web traffic data, the Web Crawler initiates the downloading process, ensuring timely retrieval of information.

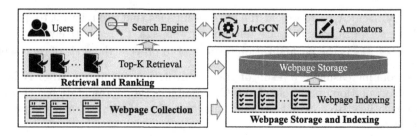

Fig. 3. The overview of the large-scale search engine with **LtrGCN** deployed.

Webpage Storage and Indexing. The search engine stores downloaded webpages in distributed archival storage systems and create efficient indices for high-performance search. These storage systems utilize elastic resources across multiple regional data centers, reducing storage costs. The indexing system balances indexing workloads and achieves superb I/O efficiency through novel key-value operations and in-memory computation. This combination allows search engines to effectively manage large volumes of web content and provide fast and accurate search results.

Retrieval and Ranking. Given a search query, the search engine first retrieves all relevant webpages from the dataset and sorts top-K relevant webpages. Specifically, the search engine adopts a pre-trained language model based semantic retrieval algorithms to enhance the conventional retrieval approach. Then, the search engine pairs each webpage with the query to conduct a query-webpage pair and uses **LtrGCN** to accomplish ranking tasks. To ensure **LtrGCN** can satisfy the rapid shift of internet interest, the search engine periodically picks up new queries and relevant webpages, hires people to annotate scores and re-trains **LtrGCN** with labeled data.

4   Experiments

In this section, we first detail experimental settings. Then, we introduce the results of the offline experiments. Finally, extensive online experiments further demonstrate the effectiveness of **LtrGCN** at a real-world search engine.

4.1   Experimental Settings

Datasets. To demonstrate the effectiveness of our proposed model, we present extensive experiments on a common-used public dataset, MSLR-Web30K [26] and a real-world dataset collected from a large-scale commercial web search engine. **MSLR-Web30K** contains about 30,000 queries and 3,771,125 query-webpage pairs. Each query-webpage pair is represented as a 136-dimensional real-valued feature vector associated with a relevance label with a scale from 0 (irrelevant) to 4 (perfectly relevant). In our experiments, we perform the five-fold cross-validation [26] and report the average results across five folds.

Collected Dataset contains 15,000 queries and over 770,000 query-webpage pairs from a large-scale industrial search engine. In our dataset, each query-webpage pair is also represented as a 120-dimensional real-valued feature vector associated with a relevant score. We randomly split the real-world dataset into a training set (9,000 queries), a validation set (3,000 queries), and a test set (3,000 queries). All features are standardized before being fed into the ranking models in our experiments.

Evaluation Metric. To evaluate the performance of **LtrGCN**, we utilize **Normalized Discounted Cumulative Gain (NDCG)** [15], which is widely adopted in LTR tasks. The NDCG score for the query could be computed as follows:

$$\text{NDCG}_N = \frac{1}{Z} \sum_{i=1}^{N} \frac{2^{y_i} - 1}{\log_2(1 + i)}, \tag{7}$$

where Z is a normalization factor that is the ideal order of Discounted Cumulative Gain [14], and y_i is the ranking score of the ith webpage. Additionally, the value of NDCG ranges between $[0, 1]$, and a higher NDCG_N indicates a better LTR model. *In our experiments, we consider the NDCG of the top 5 and 10 results (i.e., $NDCG_5$ and $NDCG_{10}$) for research and business purposes.*

Interleaving [9] is a widely used metric for evaluating the performance of an industrial search engine. In interleaved comparison, two results generated from different systems are delivered to users whose click-through actions would be attributed to the system that delivers the corresponding results.

Good vs. Same vs. Bad (GSB) [41] is an online pairwise metric evaluated by professional annotators. In manual comparison, two results produced by the new system and the legacy system are provided to human experts that are required to judge which result is better.

Loss Functions and Competitor Systems. To evaluate the effectiveness of our proposed model comprehensively, we adopt different state-of-the-art ranking loss functions as follows: **Root Mean Square Error (RMSE)** is a widely used *pointwise* loss. **RankNet** [6] and **LambdaRank** [5] are two popular *pairwise* losses for neural LTR tasks both in research and industry. More particular, LambdaRank multiplies actual gradients with the change in NDCG by swapping the rank positions of the two candidates. **ListNet** [7] and **ListMLE** [36] are two *listwise* losses, which calculate the probability of the ideal permutation based on the ground truth. **ApproxNDCG** [27] and **NeuralNDCG** [25] are two *listwise* loss functions that directly optimize the metric.

For offline experiments, we compare **LtrGCN** with the state-of-the-art ranking models to conduct comprehensive comparisons as follows: **MLP** is a commonly used ranking model. **Context-Aware Ranker (CAR)** [24] is a Trans-

Table 1. Performance on MSLR-Web30k under various ratios of labeled data.

Methods	5%		10%		15%		20%	
	$NDCG_5$	$NDCG_{10}$	$NDCG_5$	$NDCG_{10}$	$NDCG_5$	$NDCG_{10}$	$NDCG_5$	$NDCG_{10}$
RMSE	35.26	38.02	39.12	41.95	43.31	45.65	46.04	48.86
RankNet	34.51	37.43	38.52	41.32	42.54	45.08	45.32	47.89
LambdaRank	35.84	38.50	39.65	42.47	43.69	46.23	46.57	49.56
ListNet	34.90	37.94	38.71	41.76	42.85	45.40	45.63	48.42
ListMLE	33.85	36.95	37.90	40.84	41.88	44.43	44.72	47.26
ApproxNDCG	34.29	37.20	38.32	41.01	42.37	44.70	45.26	47.50
NeuralNDCG	35.36	38.26	39.50	42.10	43.60	45.97	46.39	49.20
CAR_{RMSE}	35.89	38.82	40.24	43.02	44.16	46.51	46.96	49.78
$CAR_{RankNet}$	36.04	38.94	40.46	43.27	44.32	46.62	47.03	49.84
$CAR_{LambdaRank}$	35.83	38.79	40.05	42.84	44.03	46.39	46.83	49.62
$CAR_{ListNet}$	35.52	38.54	39.80	42.60	43.84	46.19	46.59	49.38
$CAR_{ListMLE}$	36.17	39.03	40.61	43.45	44.45	46.81	47.12	49.90
$CAR_{ApproxNDCG}$	35.48	38.47	39.68	42.48	43.72	46.04	46.45	49.26
$CAR_{NeuralNDCG}$	35.66	38.64	39.87	42.70	43.90	46.25	46.72	49.53
XGBoost	33.63	36.94	37.68	40.81	41.67	44.46	44.53	47.28
LightGBM	35.14	38.12	39.63	42.32	43.38	45.98	46.05	49.39
+RMSE	35.62	38.64	39.49	42.29	43.64	46.05	46.42	49.21
+RankNet	35.64	38.67	39.22	42.48	43.98	46.48	46.73	49.24
+LambdaRank	35.96	38.72	40.24	42.75	44.01	46.62	46.95	49.92
+ListNet	36.13	38.87	40.47	43.03	44.26	46.73	47.02	50.14
+ListMLE	36.05	38.91	40.35	42.86	44.15	46.58	46.71	50.03
+ApproxNDCG	36.33	**39.08**	40.94	43.36	44.60	47.01	47.28	50.43
+NeuralNDCG	**36.52**	39.07	**41.16**	**43.62**	**44.72**	**47.35**	**47.49**	**50.76**

former [31]-based ranking model. **XGBoost** [8] and **LightGBM** [17] are two tree-based ranking models with pairwise and listwise loss, respectively.

Considering the high expense of deploying ranking models and the prior experience, we only compare our proposed model with the aforementioned models without including more previous ranking models [2,3,16]. *For online experiments, we only report the improvement between* **LtrGCN** *and the* **legacy system**.

4.2   Offline Experimental Results

Comparative Results. Tables 1 and 2 illustrate offline experimental results of **LtrGCN** compared with baselines on MSLR-Web30K and Collected Dataset on $NDCG_5$ and $NDCG_{10}$. *We use the name of each loss to present MLP with the loss and "+" to represent "LtrGCN+".* Intuitively, we could observe that **LtrGCN** outperforms all baselines on two datasets. Specifically, **LtrGCN**+ApproxNDCG obtains the best performance on $NDCG_{10}$ with 5% labeled data on MSLR-Web30K, which gains 1.88% improvements compared with the base model with

Table 2. Performance on Collected Dataset under various ratios of labeled data.

Methods	5%		10%		15%		20%	
	NDCG$_5$	NDCG$_{10}$	NDCG$_5$	NDCG$_{10}$	NDCG$_5$	NDCG$_{10}$	NDCG$_5$	NDCG$_{10}$
RMSE	50.12	53.42	54.45	57.86	57.62	61.34	59.64	64.76
RankNet	49.76	53.07	54.08	57.37	57.41	60.92	59.38	64.25
LambdaRank	51.19	54.24	55.38	58.62	58.38	62.05	61.30	65.28
ListNet	50.48	53.61	54.91	58.04	58.05	61.41	59.92	64.82
ListMLE	49.24	52.46	53.42	56.70	56.61	60.25	58.67	63.68
ApproxNDCG	49.50	52.75	53.73	57.02	57.08	60.61	59.05	64.01
NeuralNDCG	51.05	53.89	55.19	58.31	58.24	61.82	61.21	64.97
CAR$_{RMSE}$	51.24	53.71	55.42	58.78	58.16	62.08	61.43	65.42
CAR$_{RankNet}$	51.36	53.82	55.49	58.81	58.33	62.15	61.49	65.58
CAR$_{LambdaRank}$	51.60	54.08	55.76	59.13	58.73	62.19	61.62	65.89
CAR$_{ListNet}$	51.68	54.14	55.85	59.24	58.84	62.27	61.75	65.92
CAR$_{ListMLE}$	51.47	53.96	55.52	58.90	58.50	62.12	61.56	65.70
CAR$_{ApproxNDCG}$	51.72	54.17	55.93	59.32	59.02	62.32	61.91	66.08
CAR$_{NeuralNDCG}$	51.98	54.38	56.02	59.43	59.17	62.39	62.04	66.12
XGBoost	50.70	53.19	54.91	58.36	58.16	61.75	61.43	64.75
LightGBM	51.53	53.94	55.74	59.05	58.87	62.28	62.15	65.98
+RMSE	50.68	53.86	54.66	58.35	57.94	61.65	60.13	65.10
+RankNet	50.83	53.92	54.92	58.42	58.23	61.69	60.56	65.19
+LambdaRank	51.34	54.47	55.82	59.06	58.87	62.27	61.62	65.61
+ListNet	51.62	54.60	55.95	59.23	59.06	62.36	61.87	65.88
+ListMLE	51.32	54.23	55.70	59.04	58.62	61.82	61.50	65.43
+ApproxNDCG	52.05	54.57	56.17	59.60	59.39	62.42	62.23	66.17
+NeuralNDCG	**52.16**	**54.79**	**56.36**	**59.78**	**59.62**	**62.53**	**62.64**	**66.29**

ApproxNDCG. **LtrGCN** with NeuralNDCG achieves the best performance on MSLR-Web30K with the other settings. Moreover, **LtrGCN** with NeuralNDCG obtains the best performance against all competitors. Specifically, **LtrGCN+** NeuralNDCG achieves the improvement with 1.11%, 1.17%, 1.38% and 1.43% that MLP with NeuralNDCG on NDCG$_5$ on Collected Dataset. The performance of our model improves consistently with the label ratio increasing. We also compared **LtrGCN** with LightGCN [12], which cannot be trained at all with "Out of Memory" flagged, due to the sparsity issue.

Ablation Studies. In this study, we conduct a series of ablation studies to investigate the effectiveness of the three steps of **LtrGCN**. Specifically, **LtrGCN** w/o *Q-subgraph Generation via Self-tuned Labeling (QGSL)* is the model that replaces *QGSL* with a pointwise-based self-trained LightGBM to pseudo data. As for **LtrGCN** w/o *W-subgraph Generation via Self-tuned Labeling*, it fails to train the model due to the sparsity issue. **LtrGCN** w/o *GCN-based LTR with Q-subgraphs and W-subgraphs (GLQW)* is the proposed model that directly utilizes the MLP-based LTR model on the combined data. **LtrGCN**

Table 3. Ablation studies of **LtrGCN**+NeuralNDCG on NDCG$_5$ under various ratios of labeled data on two datasets.

Methods	MSLR-Web30K				Collected Dataset			
	5%	10%	15%	20%	5%	10%	15%	20%
+NeuralNDCG	**36.52**	**41.16**	**44.72**	**47.49**	**52.16**	**56.36**	**59.62**	**62.64**
+NeuralNDCG w/o $QGSL$	35.71	40.34	43.87	46.65	51.29	55.48	59.12	61.78
+NeuralNDCG w/o $GLQW$	35.48	40.19	43.70	46.54	51.50	55.65	59.35	61.91
+NeuralNDCG w/o MLM	35.92	40.43	44.12	46.90	51.47	55.74	59.48	62.12

Table 4. Ablation studies of **LtrGCN**+ApproxNDCG on NDCG$_{10}$ under various ratios of labeled data on two datasets.

Methods	MSLR-Web30K				Collected Dataset			
	5%	10%	15%	20%	5%	10%	15%	20%
+ApproxNDCG	**39.08**	**43.36**	**47.01**	**50.43**	**54.57**	**59.60**	**62.42**	**66.17**
+ApproxNDCG w/o $QGSL$	37.84	42.15	45.76	49.24	53.21	58.23	61.01	64.74
+ApproxNDCG w/o $GLQW$	38.12	42.40	46.15	49.36	53.39	58.57	61.28	65.62
+ApproxNDCG w/o MLM	38.05	42.37	45.98	49.39	53.40	57.92	61.17	64.93

w/o *MLP-based LTR Model* (*MLM*) is the proposed model that utilizes an MLP model with two layers following $GLQW$.

As shown in Tables 3 and 4, we sample the ablation study results of **LtrGCN** with NeuralNDCG on NDCG$_5$ and **LtrGCN** with ApproxNDCG on NDCG$_{10}$ under four ratios of labeled data. Intuitively, we could observe that the three steps contribute to positive improvements for **LtrGCN** under all settings. Specifically, $GLQW$ gains the improvement with 1.04%, 0.97%, 1.02% and 0.95% on NDCG$_5$ for **LtrGCN**+NeuralNDCG on MSLR-Web30K. Similarly, $QGSL$ improves the performance of **LtrGCN** with ApproxNDCG on NDCG$_{10}$ with 1.36%, 1.37%, 1.41% and 1.43% on Collected Dataset. All results of ablation studies demonstrate the effectiveness of the three steps for **LtrGCN**.

4.3   Online Experimental Results

Interleaving and Manual Evaluation. Table 5 illustrates performance improvements on Δ_{AB} and ΔGSB. We first find that **LtrGCN** trained under 20% labeled data achieves substantial improvements for the online system on two metrics, which demonstrates the practicability and effectiveness of our proposed model. Specifically, the proposed model achieves the most significant improvement with 0.26% and 3.00% on Δ_{AB} and ΔGSB for random queries, respectively. Also, we observe that the proposed model outperforms the *legacy system* for long-tail queries whose search frequencies are lower than 10 per week. Particularly, the largest advantages of Δ_{AB} and ΔGSB are 0.41% and 6.50%.

Table 5. Performance improvements of online evaluation.

Model	Δ_{AB}		ΔGSB	
	Random	Long-Tail	Random	Long-Tail
The Legacy System	–	–	–	–
LtrGCN+ApproxNDCG	0.14%	0.35%	2.50%	5.00%
LtrGCN+NeuralNDCG	**0.26%**	**0.41%**	**3.00%**	**6.50%**

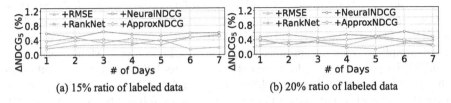

(a) 15% ratio of labeled data   (b) 20% ratio of labeled data

Fig. 4. Online comparative performance (ΔNCDG$_5$) of **LtrGCN** for 7 days (*t*-test with $p < 0.05$ over the baseline).

Online A/B Test. To further verify the effectiveness of **LtrGCN**, we conduct a series of online A/B test with real-world web traffic and compare it with the *legacy system* at a large-scale search engine. According to offline experimental results, we deploy the trained **LtrGCN** under four ratios of labeled data with 5% real-world web traffic, which contains millions of queries per day. The online A/B tests last for 7 days. Due to the page limit, we only report the performance of trained models under 15% and 20% labeled data. Figure 4 illustrates the comparison of **LtrGCN** with the *legacy system* on ΔNCDG$_5$. **LtrGCN** could boost the performance compared with the online *legacy system* all day, which demonstrates that **LtrGCN** is practical for improving the performance of the large-scale search engine. Moreover, we could observe that the trained **LtrGCN** with NeuralNDCG under 15% and 20% labeled data achieves the most significant improvement with 0.64% and 0.60%. The improvement reveals the effectiveness of **LtrGCN**. Eventually, it could be observed that **LtrGCN** performs stably on all days. Online performance is consistent with offline experiment results.

5   Related Work

Learning-to-rank (LTR) techniques generally pertain to machine learning methods that are utilized to solve ranking problems, which are crucial in various applications, such as search engine and recommendation system. Based on the loss function, LTR models could be divided into three types: pointwise [20], pairwise [5,16] and listwise [7,25,27,36]. The pointwise loss formulates the LTR problem into a regression task. The pairwise loss converts two documents into a document pair to treat LTR tasks as binary classification problems. The listwise loss treats the whole document list as a sample and directly optimizes the evaluation metrics [28], such as NDCG [15]. Recently, deep models have been widely employed in LTR tasks, achieved by minimizing various ranking loss functions in an end-to-end manner [4,22,32,39]. However, deep techniques have led to the study of learning to rank using implicit user feedback, but biases cause unsatisfied performance, so unbiased learning to rank has been proposed to mitigate these biases [30,34,38]. *In this work, we focus on solving practical LTR problems in the industrial scenario.*

In recent years, the modeling graph structure is highlighted by the developed Graph Convolutional Networks (GCN). Existing GCN methods could be categorized into two families [35,40]: spectral GCN and spatial GCN. Spectral GCN leverages graph spectral representations to define graph convolutions, such as SGCN [33], JK-Net [37] and MixHop [1]. Spatial GCN models suggest mini-batch graph training on spatially connected neighbours [42]. Many works have studied the problem of node representation and re-defined graph convolution in the spatial domain, such as GraphSage [11] and ASGCN [13]. It is important to note that several recent attempts offer comprehensive insights on GNNs [19,21]. Moreover, some outstanding works pay more attention to avoiding the unnecessary complexity of GCN, such as SGCN [33] and LightGCN [12]. *In this work, we leverage a GCN-based encoder to learn the representations of query-webpage pairs for the downstream LTR task.*

6   Conclusion

In this work, we design, implement and deploy a GCN-based LTR model **LtrGCN** at a large-scale industrial search engine to address the problem of extreme sparsity of links in query-webpage bipartite graphs and imbalance between queries and webpages for web-scale search. Specifically, **LtrGCN** utilizes two advanced sampling strategies to generate the **Q**-subgraphs and **W**-subgraphs from all query-webpage pairs in the first two steps. Then, **LtrGCN** leverages GCNs to extract feature vectors from **Q**-subgraphs and **W**-subgraphs for LTR as the representation of the query-webpage pair or ranking score prediction. The feature extraction and ranking scores prediction are optimized in an end-to-end manner, so as to enable discriminative feature extraction while preserving structural information in the bipartite graph. To demonstrate the effectiveness of **LtrGCN**, we conduct extensive offline and online experiments compared with a large number of baseline methods. Offline experiment results show that **LtrGCN** could achieve significant performance compared with other competitors. Furthermore, **LtrGCN** significantly boosts the online ranking performance at the industrial search engine, which is consistent with offline results.

Ethical Statement. The authors declare that they have listed all conflicts of interest. This article does not contain any studies with human participants or animals performed by any of the authors. All research and analysis presented in this paper will adhere to ethical principles of honesty, integrity, and respect for human dignity. Sources of information will be cited accurately and fully, and any potential conflicts of interest will be disclosed. Informed consent will be obtained from human subjects involved in the research, and any sensitive or confidential information will be handled with the utmost discretion. Data they used, the data processing and inference phases do not contain any user personal information. This work does not have the potential to be used for policing or the military. The rights and welfare of all individuals involved in this research project will be respected, and no harm or discomfort will be inflicted upon them. This paper strives to maintain high ethical standards and promote the advancement of knowledge in an ethical and responsible manner.

References

1. Abu-El-Haija, S., et al.: Mixhop: higher-order graph convolutional architectures via sparsified neighborhood mixing. In: Proceedings of the 36th International Conference on Machine Learning, ICML, pp. 21–29 (2019)
2. Ai, Q., Bi, K., Guo, J., Croft, W.B.: Learning a deep listwise context model for ranking refinement. In: The 41st International ACM SIGIR Conference on Research and Development in Information Retrieval, SIGIR, pp. 135–144 (2018)
3. Ai, Q., Wang, X., Bruch, S., Golbandi, N., Bendersky, M., Najork, M.: Learning groupwise multivariate scoring functions using deep neural networks. In: Proceedings of the 2019 ACM SIGIR International Conference on Theory of Information Retrieval, SIGIR, pp. 85–92 (2019)
4. Bruch, S., Zoghi, M., Bendersky, M., Najork, M.: Revisiting approximate metric optimization in the age of deep neural networks. In: Proceedings of the 42nd International ACM SIGIR Conference on Research and Development in Information Retrieval, SIGIR, pp. 1241–1244 (2019)
5. Burges, C.J.C., Ragno, R., Le, Q.V.: Learning to rank with nonsmooth cost functions. In: Proceedings of the Twentieth Annual Conference on Neural Information Processing Systems, Vancouver, British Columbia, NeurIPS, pp. 193–200 (2006)
6. Burges, C.J.C., et al.: Learning to rank using gradient descent. In: Machine Learning, Proceedings of the Twenty-Second International Conference, ICML, pp. 89–96 (2005)
7. Cao, Z., Qin, T., Liu, T., Tsai, M., Li, H.: Learning to rank: from pairwise approach to listwise approach. In: Machine Learning, Proceedings of the Twenty-Fourth International Conference, ICML, pp. 129–136 (2007)
8. Chen, T., Guestrin, C.: XGBoost: a scalable tree boosting system. In: Proceedings of the 22nd ACM SIGKDD International Conference on Knowledge Discovery and Data Mining, SIGKDD, pp. 785–794 (2016)
9. Chuklin, A., Schuth, A., Zhou, K., Rijke, M.D.: A comparative analysis of interleaving methods for aggregated search. ACM Trans. Inf. Syst. (TOIS) **33**(2), 1–38 (2015)
10. Gao, C., Wang, X., He, X., Li, Y.: Graph neural networks for recommender system. In: The Fifteenth ACM International Conference on Web Search and Data Mining, WSDM, pp. 1623–1625 (2022)
11. Hamilton, W.L., Ying, Z., Leskovec, J.: Inductive representation learning on large graphs. In: Advances in Neural Information Processing Systems 30: Annual Conference on Neural Information Processing Systems, NeurIPS, pp. 1024–1034 (2017)
12. He, X., Deng, K., Wang, X., Li, Y., Zhang, Y., Wang, M.: LightGCN: simplifying and powering graph convolution network for recommendation. In: Proceedings of the 43rd International ACM SIGIR Conference on Research and Development in Information Retrieval, SIGIR, pp. 639–648 (2020)

13. Huang, W., Zhang, T., Rong, Y., Huang, J.: Adaptive sampling towards fast graph representation learning. In: Advances in Neural Information Processing Systems 31: Annual Conference on Neural Information Processing Systems 2018, NeurIPS, pp. 4563–4572 (2018)
14. Järvelin, K., Kekäläinen, J.: Cumulated gain-based evaluation of IR techniques. ACM Trans. Inf. Syst. **20**(4), 422–446 (2002)
15. Järvelin, K., Kekäläinen, J.: IR evaluation methods for retrieving highly relevant documents. SIGIR Forum **51**(2), 243–250 (2017)
16. Joachims, T.: Training linear SVMs in linear time. In: Proceedings of the Twelfth ACM SIGKDD International Conference on Knowledge Discovery and Data Mining, SIGKDD, pp. 217–226 (2006)
17. Ke, G., et al.: LightGBM: a highly efficient gradient boosting decision tree. In: Advances in Neural Information Processing Systems 30: Annual Conference on Neural Information Processing Systems, NeurIPS, pp. 3146–3154 (2017)
18. Kipf, T.N., Welling, M.: Semi-supervised classification with graph convolutional networks. In: 5th International Conference on Learning Representations, ICLR (2017)
19. Klicpera, J., Bojchevski, A., Günnemann, S.: Predict then propagate: graph neural networks meet personalized pagerank. In: 7th International Conference on Learning Representations, ICLR (2019)
20. Li, P., Burges, C.J.C., Wu, Q.: Mcrank: learning to rank using multiple classification and gradient boosting. In: Advances in Neural Information Processing Systems 20, Proceedings of the Twenty-First Annual Conference on Neural Information Processing Systems, NeurIPS, pp. 897–904 (2007)
21. Li, Q., Han, Z., Wu, X.: Deeper insights into graph convolutional networks for semi-supervised learning. In: Proceedings of the Thirty-Second AAAI Conference on Artificial Intelligence, AAAI, pp. 3538–3545 (2018)
22. Li, Y., Xiong, H., Kong, L., Zhang, R., Dou, D., Chen, G.: Meta hierarchical reinforced learning to rank for recommendation: a comprehensive study in moocs. In: Joint European Conference on Machine Learning and Knowledge Discovery in Databases, ECML PKDD, pp. 302–317 (2022)
23. Li, Y., et al.: Coltr: semi-supervised learning to rank with co-training and over-parameterization for web search. IEEE Trans. Knowl. Data Eng. (2023)
24. Pobrotyn, P., Bartczak, T., Synowiec, M., Białobrzeski, R., Bojar, J.: Context-aware learning to rank with self-attention. arXiv preprint arXiv:2005.10084 (2020)
25. Pobrotyn, P., Białobrzeski, R.: NeuralNDCG: direct optimisation of a ranking metric via differentiable relaxation of sorting. arXiv preprint arXiv:2102.07831 (2021)
26. Qin, T., Liu, T.Y.: Introducing letor 4.0 datasets. arXiv preprint arXiv:1306.2597 (2013)
27. Qin, T., Liu, T., Li, H.: A general approximation framework for direct optimization of information retrieval measures. Inf. Retr. **13**(4), 375–397 (2010)
28. Qiu, Z., Hu, Q., Zhong, Y., Zhang, L., Yang, T.: Large-scale stochastic optimization of NDCG surrogates for deep learning with provable convergence. In: International Conference on Machine Learning, ICML, pp. 18122–18152 (2022)
29. Shi, M., Tang, Y., Zhu, X., Wilson, D.A., Liu, J.: Multi-class imbalanced graph convolutional network learning. In: Proceedings of the Twenty-Ninth International Joint Conference on Artificial Intelligence, IJCAI, pp. 2879–2885 (2020)
30. Vardasbi, A., de Rijke, M., Markov, I.: Cascade model-based propensity estimation for counterfactual learning to rank. In: Proceedings of the 43rd International ACM SIGIR Conference on Research and Development in Information Retrieval, SIGIR, pp. 2089–2092 (2020)

31. Vaswani, A., et al.: Attention is all you need. In: Advances in Neural Information Processing Systems 30: Annual Conference on Neural Information Processing Systems, NeurIPS, pp. 5998–6008 (2017)

32. Wang, R., et al.: DCN V2: improved deep & cross network and practical lessons for web-scale learning to rank systems. In: WWW '21: The Web Conference 2021, Virtual Event / Ljubljana, Slovenia, WWW, pp. 1785–1797 (2021)

33. Wu, F., Jr, A.H.S., Zhang, T., Fifty, C., Yu, T., Weinberger, K.Q.: Simplifying graph convolutional networks. In: Proceedings of the 36th International Conference on Machine Learning, ICML, pp. 6861–6871 (2019)

34. Wu, X., Chen, H., Zhao, J., He, L., Yin, D., Chang, Y.: Unbiased learning to rank in feeds recommendation. In: The Fourteenth ACM International Conference on Web Search and Data Mining, WSDM, pp. 490–498 (2021)

35. Wu, Z., Pan, S., Chen, F., Long, G., Zhang, C., Yu, P.S.: A comprehensive survey on graph neural networks. IEEE Trans. Neural Netw. Learn. Syst. **32**(1), 4–24 (2021)

36. Xia, F., Liu, T., Wang, J., Zhang, W., Li, H.: Listwise approach to learning to rank: theory and algorithm. In: Machine Learning, Proceedings of the Twenty-Fifth International Conference, ICML, pp. 1192–1199 (2008)

37. Xu, K., Li, C., Tian, Y., Sonobe, T., Kawarabayashi, K., Jegelka, S.: Representation learning on graphs with jumping knowledge networks. In: Proceedings of the 35th International Conference on Machine Learning, ICML, pp. 5449–5458 (2018)

38. Yan, L., Qin, Z., Zhuang, H., Wang, X., Bendersky, M., Najork, M.: Revisiting two tower models for unbiased learning to rank. In: Proceedings of the 45th International ACM SIGIR Conference on Research and Development in Information Retrieval, SIGIR, pp. 2410–2414 (2022)

39. Yang, T., Ying, Y.: AUC maximization in the era of big data and AI: a survey. ACM Comput. Surv. **55**(8), 172:1–172:37 (2023)

40. Zhang, Z., Cui, P., Zhu, W.: Deep learning on graphs: a survey. IEEE Trans. Knowl. Data Eng. **34**(1), 249–270 (2022)

41. Zhao, S., Wang, H., Li, C., Liu, T., Guan, Y.: Automatically generating questions from queries for community-based question answering. In: Fifth International Joint Conference on Natural Language Processing, IJCNLP, pp. 929–937 (2011)

42. Zhou, J., et al.: Graph neural networks: a review of methods and applications. AI Open **1**, 57–81 (2020)

Prototype-Guided Counterfactual Explanations via Variational Auto-encoder for Recommendation

Ming He[(⊠)], Jiwen Wang, Boyang An, and Hao Wen

Beijing University of Technology, Beijing, China
heming@bjut.edu.cn, {wangjiwen,boyangan,bearwen}@emails.bjut.edu.cn

Abstract. Counterfactual reasoning has recently achieved impressive performance in the explainability of recommendation. However, existing counterfactual explainable methods ignore the realism of explanations and consider only the sparsity and proximity of explanations. Moreover, the huge counterfactuals space causes a time-consuming search process. In this study, we propose Prototype-Guided Counterfactual Explanations (PGCE), a novel counterfactual explainable recommendation framework to overcome the above issues. At its core, PGCE leverages a variational auto-encoder generative model to constrain the modification of features to generate counterfactual instances that are consistent with the distribution of real data. Meanwhile, we constructed a contrastive prototype for each user in a low-dimensional latent space, which can guide the search direction towards the optimal candidate instance space, thus, speed up the search process. For evaluation, we compared our method with several state-of-the-art model-intrinsic methods on three real-world datasets, in addition to the latest counterfactual reasoning-based method. Extensive experiments show that our model is not only able to efficiently generate realistic counterfactual explanations but also achieve state-of-the-art performance on other popular explainability evaluation metrics.

Keywords: Recommender systems · Explainable recommendation · Counterfactual explanation

1 Introduction

Due to the explosive growth of information, recommender systems have been playing an increasingly significant role in many online services, such as search engines (Yahoo, Bing, etc.), e-commerce (Amazon, JD, etc.), and social networks (Twitter, Facebook, etc.). It is fairly well-accepted that high-quality explanations for the recommended content can help improve the performance of recommendations, while being actionable toward improving the underlying models [33]. Explainable recommendation attempts to develop models that generate not only high-quality recommendations but also intuitive explanations [31].

Existing methods for explainable recommendation can be divided into two categories, model-intrinsic and model-agnostic [16]. The model-intrinsic methods

G. De Francisci Morales et al. (Eds.): ECML PKDD 2023, LNAI 14174, pp. 652–668, 2023.
https://doi.org/10.1007/978-3-031-43427-3_39

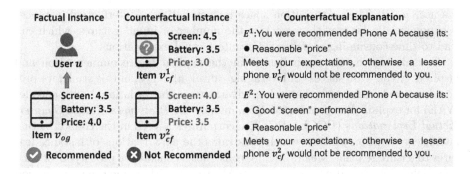

Fig. 1. Toy examples of counterfactual explanations based on unrealistic counterfactual instance (above) and realistic counterfactual instance (below), respectively.

develop interpretable models, whose decision mechanism is transparent [34]. The model-agnostic methods consider the underlying recommendation model as a black-box and provide explanations after the recommendation decision has been made. Despite effectiveness to some extent, existing methods are still limited because the explanation is built with correlation, and correlation does not imply causation [25]. Moreover, extracting correlations from the observed data without the support of causal inference may lead to the wrong explanations [8].

Recently, some studies have considered the explainable recommendations based on counterfactual reasoning from the causal perspective. A *counterfactual explanation* is a necessary perturbation in input features that cause the recommended items to be removed from the recommendation list. Existing methods mainly take into account sparsity and proximity. Sparsity requires that the perturbation involves as few features as possible, and proximity requires that the counterfactual instances formed after the perturbation are as relevant as possible to the user's interest. However, these methods cannot effectively address the following two challenges: (i) Perturbing each input feature independently without considering the data-generating process can sometimes lead to infeasible counterfactual instances. We use a toy example in Fig. 1 for illustration. A recommendation system recommends a factual phone instance v_{og} to user u. To explain this recommendation, the counterfactual explanation model perturbs the original instance v_{og} to generate a counterfactual instance v_{cf} that will not be recommended to user u anymore. However, a counterfactual instance v_{cf}^1 generated by perturbing only the price-performance feature (i.e., the Price) is not consistent with the real situation. In fact, features that are strongly correlated with the Price should be changed at the same time, such as the Battery or the Screen. Consequently, the distribution difference between the unrealistic counterfactual data and the factual data leads to a counterfactual explanation E^1 that is equally unrealistic. On the contrary, a counterfactual instance v_{cf}^2 that fits the real data distribution implies that its corresponding counterfactual explanation E^2 is realistic and therefore more understandable and persuasive to the user u. (ii) The perturbation space for generating counterfactual instances is exponentially large with respect to the number of input features, which can lead to time-consuming searches for counterfactual explanations.

Considering the above challenges in the explainable recommendation and inspired by the wide success of leveraging causal inference, in this study, we proposed a novel framework that takes advantage of the variational auto-encoder (VAE) for explainable recommendation, namely the *Prototypes-Guided Counterfactual Explanations* (PGCE). PGCE incorporates a VAE in the counterfactual instance generation process, which constrains the perturbations of instance features to ensure realism. Meanwhile, we construct a contrastive prototype for each user, defined in the latent space of the VAE, to explicitly guide the perturbation quickly toward an optimal candidate instance space and avoid the senseless perturbations. Through our formulated counterfactual learning framework, PGCE aims to extract realistic explanations for the recommendation faster to ensure it can be used in real-life settings.

The key contributions of this study are summarized as follows:

- We proposed the counterfactual explanation model PGCE within the constraints of the variational autoencoder, which is able to generate counterfactual instances that are closer to the real data distribution enabling us obtain realistic explanations.
- To the best of our knowledge, this is the first work leveraging contrastive prototypes for explainable recommendation, which can explicitly guide the search direction to make PGCE capable of searching the optimal candidate counterfactual instance space efficiently.
- Based on three real-world datasets, we have conducted extensive experiments to evaluate our model's effectiveness. The results reveal that PGCE can significantly advance state-of-the-art.

2   Related Work

2.1   Explainable Recommendation

Research on explainable recommendations can be divided into two categories: model-intrinsic and model-agnostic. As for model-intrinsic approaches, various types of explainable recommendation models have been proposed, ranging from traditional recommenders, such as collaborative filtering [11,23], factorization models [3,28,34]; up to modern recommenders, such as deep learning models [5,7,14], knowledge graph models [18,36]. However, these methods require mixing recommendation mechanisms with specific interpretable components, limiting their application to specific recommendation models. The model-agnostic approaches can provide explanations after the recommendation decision is made, thus, can be flexibly applied in different recommendation models. Examples include [24] that proposed an explainable tree-based model for the ranking list, [22] that proposed a sparse linear model to approximate a complex model around a sample and thus explain which feature of the sample contributed to its recommendation, and [6] that employed influence functions to measure the effect of training points on the predictions of black-box models and provided intuitive neighbor-style explanation based on the most influential training data. However, these existing methods are built with correlation, which may not reflect the true causes of interaction. *In this study, we consider explainable recommendations from the causal perspective by using counterfactual reasoning.*

2.2 Counterfactual Explanations

Counterfactual reasoning naturally can be applied to explainable AI research, such as natural language processing [2,30,32] and computer vision [1,10,27]. In the recommender systems domain, there are some study that aim to provide counterfactual explanations for recommendations. Ghazimatin et al. [9] proposed PRINCE, which uses a polynomial-time optimal algorithm for finding the minimal set of a user's actions from an exponential search space, based on random walks over heterogeneous information graph. Inspired by [9], Tran et al. [26] proposed ACCENT, which extends the influence function [6] to generate counterfactual explanations for neural recommenders. Considering that finding concise counterfactual explanations is a hard search problem, Kaffes et al. [12] used normalized length and the importance of a candidate to guide the search of counterfactual explanations. Zhong et al. [37] proposed a counterfactual explanation method enhanced by SHAP [17] for generating easily understandable explanations. Xu et al. [31] extracted counterfactual explanations through a perturbation model and a causal rule mining model. While these works mentioned above generate counterfactual explanations based on user information, Tan et al. [25] proposed CountER, which aims to find an counterfactual item with minimal distance to the original item to reverse the recommendation result for generating counterfactual explanations based on item aspects. Wang et al. [29] proposed CERec, a reinforcement learning-based counterfactual explainable recommendation framework over a collaborative knowledge graph to generate counterfactual explanations on the item side. Counterfactual explanation models are independent of recommendation models, therefore they are model-agnostic.

Our proposed model differs from the above mentioned study on two key points: *1) These previous studies search for counterfactual explanations simply considering sparsity and proximity, while we take into account the realism of the explanation. 2) Previous studies performed heuristic search on the user side by measuring the quality of candidate counterfactuals, while we explicitly guide the counterfactual search direction on the item side by using contrastive prototypes.*

3 Proposed Model

3.1 Preliminary

In this study, we denoted a user set with m users as $\mathcal{U} = \{u_1, u_2, \ldots, u_m\}$ and an item set with n items as $\mathcal{V} = \{v_1, v_2, \ldots, v_n\}$. Each user u is associated with a list of recommendations, and we take the top-k recommended items denoted as $\mathcal{R}(u,k)$. We say $v \in \mathcal{R}(u,k)$ if item v belongs to the top-k items recommended to user u. Compared with using the isolated features from either the user or the item, the textual review features are a better source of explanation because it is the explicit interaction between the user and the item that can help to build more informative explanations [38]. Following the same method as in [25,34], we extract (Feature, Opinion, Sentiment) triplets from the textual reviews by the sentiment analysis toolkit[1] built in [35]. For example, in the *Electronics* domain, the extracted features would include *screen, battery, price*, etc. We further denoted a r-dimensional feature space as $\mathcal{F} = \{f_1, f_2, \ldots, f_r\} \subseteq \mathbb{R}^r$.

Then, we construct the user-feature attention matrix $X \in \mathbb{R}^{m \times r}$ and the item-feature quality matrix $Y \in \mathbb{R}^{n \times r}$. Each element $X_{i,k} \in X$ measures to what extent a user cares about the product feature, and each element $Y_{j,k} \in Y$ measures the quality of an item for the corresponding product feature. More specifically, suppose $t_{i,k}$ is the frequency that user u_i mentioned feature f_k, $t_{j,k}$ is the frequency that item v_j is mentioned on feature f_k, and $s_{j,k}$ is the average of the sentiment of feature f_k in those $t_{j,k}$ mentions. We defined X and Y as:

$$
\begin{aligned}
X_{i,k} &= \begin{cases} 0, \text{if user } u_i \text{ did not mention feature } f_k \\ 1 + (N-1)\left(\frac{2}{1+\exp{(-t_{i,k})}} - 1\right), \text{else} \end{cases} \\
Y_{j,k} &= \begin{cases} 0, \text{if item } v_j \text{ is not reviewed on feature } f_k \\ 1 + \frac{N-1}{1+\exp{(-t_{j,k} \cdot s_{j,k})}}, \text{else} \end{cases}
\end{aligned}
\tag{1}
$$

where the choice of N is 5 in many real-world five stars based reviewing systems. The elements in the matrices X and Y are rescaled into the range of $[1, N]$ by reformulating the sigmoid function.

3.2 Counterfactual Explanation

This subsection shows the proposed model, with its architecture of as illustrated in Fig. 2. For a given black-box recommendation model F, if an item $\mathbf{v}$ is among the top-k items recommended to user $\mathbf{u}$, i.e., $\mathbf{v} \in \mathcal{R}(\mathbf{u}, k)$, then we look for a counterfactual instance $Y_{cf} = Y_{og} + \Delta$, where $Y_{og} \in Y$ is the item $\mathbf{v}$'s original quality vector and $\Delta = \{\delta_0, \delta_1, \ldots, \delta_r\} \in \mathcal{F}$ is the perturbation vector for Y_{og}, such that if item $\mathbf{v}$'s quality vector change to Y_{cf} from Y_{og}, then it will be removed from the top-k list, i.e., $\mathbf{v} \notin \mathcal{R}(\mathbf{u}, k)$. Intuitively, a counterfactual instance Y_{cf} should be closed to the original instance Y_{og} but not belong to the top-k list, which implies optimizing the following objective function:

$$
\underset{\Delta}{minimize} \; L_{pred}(Y_{cf}) + L_{dist}(Y_{cf})
\tag{2}
$$

where $L_{pred}(Y_{cf})$ encourages the counterfactual instance Y_{cf} to be removed from the top-k list while ensuring the proximity of Y_{cf}. We define it as a hinge loss:

$$
L_{pred}(Y_{cf}) = \eta \cdot max(0, F(Y_{cf}, \mathbf{u}) - F(Y_{k+1}, \mathbf{u}) + \alpha)
\tag{3}
$$

---

[1] https://github.com/evison/Sentires/.

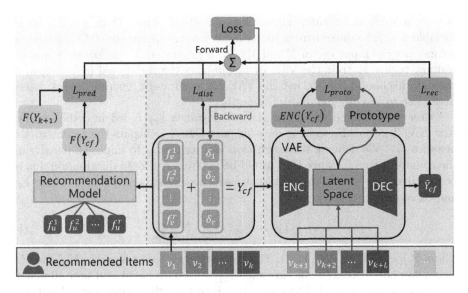

Fig. 2. The overall architecture of our proposed model. In the figure, $(f_u^1, f_u^2, \ldots, f_u^r)$ and $(f_v^1, f_v^2, \ldots, f_v^r)$ are the feature attention vector of the user who requires an explanation and the feature quality vector of the item to be explained, respectively, while $(\delta_1, \delta_2, \ldots, \delta_r)$ is the counterfactual explanation the model is searching for.

where $F(Y_{cf}, \mathbf{u})$ is the ranking score of Y_{cf} to user $\mathbf{u}$, $F(Y_{k+1}, \mathbf{u})$ is the ranking score of the $k+1$'s item in user $\mathbf{u}$'s original recommendation list, and $\alpha \geq 0$ controls the required margin on the ranking score to flip a recommendation. In this way, item $\mathbf{v}$ will be removed from the top-k list when Y_{cf} ranked lower than Y_{k+1}. The other term $L_{dist}(Y_{cf})$ encourages minimizing the distance between Y_{cf} and Y_{og} to generate sparse counterfactual instance, which takes a weighted sum of the two factors:

$$L_{dist}(Y_{cf}) = \beta \cdot \|Y_{cf} - Y_{og}\|_1 + \|Y_{cf} - Y_{og}\|_2^2$$
$$= \beta \cdot \|\Delta\|_1 + \|\Delta\|_2^2 \tag{4}$$

where $\mathcal{L}_1$-norm $\|\Delta\|_1$ is used to constrain the number of features involved in the perturbation vector Δ due to $\mathcal{L}_0$-norm $\|\Delta\|_0$ being nonconvex and $\mathcal{L}_2$-norm $\|\Delta\|_2^2$ to constrain the perturbation magnitude of the vector Δ on the features.

While the objective function (2) can generate counterfactual instances, Y_{cf} does not necessarily respect the real data distribution resulting in counterfactual instances out of the distribution. Item features do not exist in a vacuum. They come from a data-generating process that constrains their modification [19]. In this case, we can consider a VAE trained on dataset $D = \{Y_j\}_{j=1}^m$, where $Y_j \in \mathcal{F}$ is item-feature quality vector. More specifically, the VAE is composed of an encoder $(\mu, \sigma) = ENC(\mathcal{Y})$ and a decoder $\tilde{y} = DEC(z)$. The $ENC(\cdot)$ projects an item-feature quality vector $\mathcal{Y} \in \mathbb{R}^r$ onto a d-dimensional latent space $\mathbb{R}^d$, and extracts the variational information for the vector, i.e., mean and variance of the latent variables under independent Gaussian distribution. Then, given a latent variable $z \in \mathbb{R}^d$ sampled from the Gaussian distribution, the $DEC(\cdot)$ tries to reconstruct the input vector $\mathcal{Y}$ and $\tilde{\mathcal{y}} \in \mathbb{R}^r$ is generated. We follow the standard training regime to train the VAE by maximizing the variational lower bound of the data likelihood [13] so that the VAE can accurately generate reconstructed data close to the original data distribution.

After pre-training, the counterfactual instance Y_{cf} is fed into the encoder part $ENC(\cdot)$ of VAE, and the decoder part $DEC(\cdot)$ outputs the reconstructed instance $\tilde{Y}_{cf}$. We define a reconstruction loss term L_{rec} to impose a penalty on the counterfactual instance that would be far from real data distribution due to perturbing each feature independently, which equals the distance between Y_{cf} and its reconstruction $\tilde{Y}_{cf}$:

$$L_{rec}(Y_{cf}) = \lambda \cdot \|Y_{cf} - \tilde{Y}_{cf}\|_2^2 \tag{5}$$

where $\tilde{Y}_{cf} = DEC(ENC(Y_{cf}))$. The reconstruction error between Y_{cf} and $\tilde{Y}_{cf}$ represents how successful the instance Y_{cf} is reconstructed and how similar it is to the training data D. Therefore, L_{rec} is to have the counterfactual instance Y_{cf} conform to the training data distribution.

The vast counterfactual space lead to a time-consuming search process. Fortunately, the decision boundary of the recommendation model F can be a way of partitioning the instance space (containing factual and counterfactual instances). According to the definition of counterfactual explanation, suitable counterfactual instances should be closer to the decision boundary. Since user $\mathbf{u}$ are almost uninterested in instances far away from the decision boundary, the counterfactual explanations generated from these instances will not be persuasive, whereas instances close to the decision boundary but not in fact recommended imply the critical reason why the original item Y_{og} was recommended. Therefore, we consider using the semantic information of factual instances close to the decision boundary to guide the search direction for counterfactual instances.

Specifically, since measuring the distance between instances in a low dimensional latent space can better capture the instance semantics [15], we defined a contrastive prototype for user $\mathbf{u}$ based on the d-dimensional latent space $\mathbb{R}^d$, which equals to the mean encoding of the L items that are nearest to the top-k recommendation list $\mathcal{R}(\mathbf{u}, k)$ but not recommended:

$$Proto := \frac{1}{L} \sum_{l=k+1}^{k+L} ENC(Y_l) \tag{6}$$

where L is a hyperparameter that represents the number of items used to compute the prototype. In the top-k recommendation scenario, L equals to the number of recommended items k, avoiding the bias introduced by other items that are not of interest to the user, and $Y_l \in Y$ is the l-th item quality vector in the original list of recommendations. If we consider that these L encoded items $ENC(Y_l)$ $(l = k+1, \ldots, k+L)$ define a cluster of the most desirable but not yet recommended items, then $Proto \in \mathbb{R}^d$ is the center of the cluster, which represents the optimal candidate counterfactual instance space. Intuitively, it should be given priority when generating counterfactual instances for Y_{og}. Now, the prototype loss L_{proto} can be defined as:

$$L_{proto}(Y_{cf}) = \gamma \cdot \|ENC(Y_{cf}) - Proto\|_2^2 \qquad (7)$$

where $ENC(Y_{cf}) \in \mathbb{R}^d$ is the encoding of the counterfactual instance Y_{cf}. As a result, L_{proto} explicitly guides the search toward the optimal candidate counterfactual instance space around $Proto$ and avoids the senseless perturbations, speeding up the counterfactual search process.

To summarize, a counterfactual instance $\hat{Y}_{cf} = Y_{og} + \hat{\Delta}$ is found by optimizing the following objective function:

$$\hat{\Delta} \leftarrow \underset{\Delta}{minimize}\ L_{pred}(Y_{cf}) + \beta \cdot \|\Delta\|_1 + \|\Delta\|_2^2 + L_{rec}(Y_{cf}) + L_{proto}(Y_{cf}) \quad (8)$$

where the hyper-parameters $(\eta, \alpha, \beta, \lambda, \gamma)$ are the weights of the loss terms.

4   Experiments

4.1   Experimental Setup

Recommendation Model. The experiments aim to validate the effectiveness of the model-agnostic counterfactual explanation model PGCE, so we choose a simple deep neural network to implement the black-box recommendation model. The recommendation model consists of a fusion layer and three fully connected layers with {512, 256, 1} neurons respectively, which connect the user and item feature vectors as input and finally output the ranking score of the item. We take the last five interactions from each user to construct the testing set, and use all previous interactions from each user as the training set.

Variational Autoencoder Model. The VAE model consists of an encoder and a decoder, which are both deep neural networks with three fully connected layers containing {1024, 1024, *latent size*} and {1024, 1024, *original size*} neurons, respectively, and the original item feature as the input to the encoder while the decoder outputs the reconstructed item feature. The original size and latent size are the dimensions of the item feature in the real space and the latent space, respectively. We optimize the model using the Adam optimizer with a learning rate of 0.001. We freeze the parameters of the trained VAE model and the recommendation model to recommend items and generate explanations.

Datasets. We choose the real-world review dataset in the Amazon[2] e-commerce system, which helps to better construct the feature quality data for items. The Amazon dataset [20] contains 29 category product sub-datasets, and we adopt

---

[2] https://nijianmo.github.io/amazon/.

Table 1. Summary of the datasets. Density is computed by $\#Reviews/(Users \cdot Items)$.

Dataset	#Users	#Items	#Reviews	#Features	Density
CDs and Vinyl	8,119	52,193	245,391	230	0.058%
Electronic	2,832	19,816	53,295	105	0.095%
Cell Phones	251	1,918	4,454	88	0.835%

three datasets of different scales, *CDs and Vinyl*, *Electronic* and *Cell Phones*, to evaluate the proposed model. We remove all users with less than ten reviews so that the profiles are big and balanced enough for learning discriminative user models. A brief summary of the datasets is shown in Table 1.

Baselines. Since our model aims to solve the issue of nonrealism of counterfactual explanations, it is generating multi-feature explanations at the item side. Therefore, we compare PGCE against four feature-based baselines.

- **EFM** [34] extracts explicit item features from user reviews, and then aligns the latent factors of matrix factorization with the item features to provide explainable recommendations.
- **MTER** [28] integrates two companion learning tasks user preference modeling for recommendation and opinionated content modeling for explanation. However, this model is not suitable for model-oriented evaluation since the user prediction scores are not directly predicted based on item features.
- **A2CF** [4] leverages a residual feed-forward neural network to model the user-item preferences and item-item relationships, and then generates explainable recommendations by analyzing the features users currently care about.
- **CountER** [25] is a state-of-the-art model with insights into counterfactual reasoning, which formulates a joint optimization problem to generate feature-based counterfactual explanations on the item side for recommendations.

Initialization. We generated explanations for the top-5 recommendation list of each user. The prototype is calculated for each user based on the L items behind the top-k list, and we set L equal to 5. The $\mathcal{L}_1$-norm $\|\Delta\|_1$ and $\mathcal{L}_2$-norm $\|\Delta\|_2^2$ are of the same scale, thus, we set β to 1. We set the hyper-parameters α to 0.2 following the suggestions in [25]. Since our model additionally incorporates constraint terms, we set θ to 400 in order to keep the relative weight of L_{pred} terms to generate explanations for more items. The L_{rec} work on the whole feature space while L_{proto} operates on the dimensionality-reduced latent space, therefore, we set the hyper-parameters λ and γ to 1 and 10, respectively.

Evaluation Metrics. We adopted the following metrics for evaluation.

- **User & Model-oriented Evaluation.** A user's true review of an item can serve as the ground-truth reason why the user purchased the item [33]. The

Precision measures the percentage of features in generated explanation that is really liked by the user, the **Recall** measures how many percentages of features liked by the user are really included in the explanation, and the F_1 score is the harmonic mean between the two. Additionally, the **PN** and **PS** measure the necessity and sufficiency of an explanation, respectively, and F_{NS} score is the harmonic mean between the two. A detailed definition of all the above metrics can be referred to [25].

- **Fidelity.** The fidelity [21] as a measure to evaluate model-agnostic explainable recommendation methods, which is defined as the percentage of explainable items in the recommended items:

$$Fidelity = \frac{|explainable\ items \cap recommended\ items|}{|recommended\ items|} \quad (9)$$

- **Realism.** The realism implies that the perturbations applied to each feature of the original instance should be well-balanced without causing the counterfactual instance to be far away from the real data distribution:

$$Realism = \frac{\|\Delta\|_2^2}{\|\Delta\|_0} \quad (10)$$

where the denominator $\|\Delta\|_0$ is the number of the perturbed features, and the numerator $\|\Delta\|_2^2$ is the magnitude of that perturbation. A lower value indicates that the counterfactual instance lies closer to the data manifold.

- **Speed.** The speed is measured by the mean time required until a satisfactory counterfactual instance is found. It should be noted that since realism and speed are defined for counterfactual perturbation, it is not applicable to evaluate the model-intrinsic methods.

Personalized Explanation. In the generation of counterfactual explanations, although the recommendation model can discriminate users' preferences to predict their ratings of counterfactual instances, it does not explicitly consider users' linguistic preferences to generate more personalized explanations. Specifically, we define the linguistic mask $M_u = \{m_1, m_2, \ldots, m_r\}$ for the user **u**, where $m_i = 1$ if element $X_{u,i} \neq 0$ in the user-feature attention matrix X and $m_i = 0$ otherwise. Then, we apply the mask M_u on the perturbation vector Δ to generate an explanation by choosing features only from the user **u**'s linguistic preference space. It means that let the Δ in equation (8) be equal to $\Delta \odot M_u$.

4.2   Experimental Results

Table 2 summarizes the results of the fidelity and realism evaluations of the counterfactual explanation. To ensure a fair comparison, we compare the original model and the masked version separately. First, we can see that our model achieves the same good fidelity as the baseline, which indicates that counterfactual reasoning can generate explanations for the majority of recommended items. Moreover, we can observe that with or without the mask, our model performs better than the baseline in terms of realism on all datasets. In detail, our model has an average improvement of 5.15% and 21.54% on the realism than the baseline with and without the mask, respectively, which indicates that the perturbation on item features by our model take into account the correlation between features, rather than aimlessly perturbing each feature independently. As a result, the counterfactual instances are closer to the real data distribution and the counterfactual explanations have better performance on realism.

Table 2. Fidelity and Realism evaluation of the counterfactual explanations. The fidelity numbers in the table are percentage numbers with '%' omitted.

Model		CDs and Vinyl		Electronic		Cell Phones	
		Fidelity	Realism	Fidelity	Realism	Fidelity	Realism
With Mask	CountER	93.80	1.21	81.80	1.78	85.20	1.87
	PGCE	93.87	1.15	81.84	1.67	85.20	1.79
Without Mask	CountER	94.20	0.95	98.00	0.93	99.92	1.10
	PGCE	94.55	0.78	98.21	0.69	100	0.87

Then we report the speed evaluation of the counterfactual explanation in Fig. 3. To fairly validate the role of the contrastive prototype in the counterfactual search process, we remove the reconstruction loss term L_{rec} (denoted by "PGCE-R") and prototype loss term L_{proto} from PGCE (denoted by "PGCE-P"), respectively. We can see that the PGCE-R and PGCE have better performance than their baseline speed on all datasets. In detail, the PGCE-R has average improvement of 7.87% and 12.93% than the countER with and without the mask, respectively. Meanwhile, the PGCE has the average improvement of 6.40% and 9.30% than the PGCE-P with and without the mask, respectively. This indicates that the contrastive prototype successfully guides the search direction toward the optimal counterfactuals space it represents and thus speeds up the search process. Another interesting observation is that compared to baselines, our model achieves a greater performance improvement on realism and speed when there is no mask. The reason is that the perturbed feature space is limited when applying a linguistic mask to the perturbation vector Δ, indicating that PGCE has more advantages when the counterfactual search space increases.

Finally, we reported the user-oriented and model-oriented evaluations of the explanations generated by the PGCE and the baselines, with the experimental results shown in Tables 3 and 4, respectively. For the user-oriented evaluation, we can see that on all datasets, the explanation generated by the masked PGCE model outperforms all baselines in terms of F_1 scores and has a 5.02% average improvement over the best performance of the baseline models. This indicates

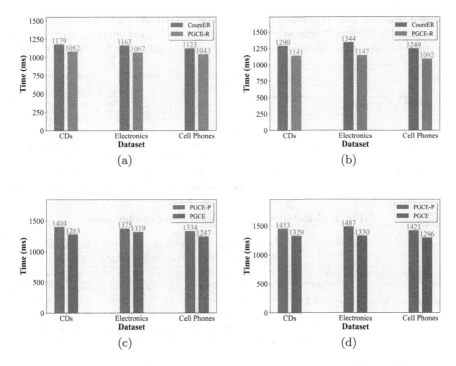

Fig. 3. Speed evaluation of the counterfactual explanation model. (a) and (b) show the comparison between CountER and PGCE-R under with and without a mask, respectively. (c) and (d) show the comparison between PGCE-P and PGCE under with and without a mask, respectively.

the model PGCE that considering personalized linguistic preference from the user's perspective can generate more agreeable explanations. Additionally, we note that compared to CountER, which also belongs to the counterfactual explanation method, our model has a significant improvement on recall (on average 16.29% and 21.49% with and without the mask, respectively) while it is slightly decreasing on precision (on average 0.85% and 2.04% with and without the mask, respectively). The underlying reason is that the explanations generated by PGCE contain more necessary item features to ensure realism. Therefore, more item features that users like are included resulting in a significant improvement on Recall, despite the slight sacrifice on Precision. Similarly, because the linguistic mask constrains the selection of perturbed features, the masked PGCE model suffers little on precision compared to its original version.

For the model-oriented evaluation, we can see that on all datasets, the explanation generated by the PGCE outperforms all baselines in terms of PS, PN, and F_{NS} scores and has 7.05%, 2.49%, and 5.24% average improvement over the best performance of the baselines, respectively, which indicates that the PGCE model correctly explains the essential mechanism of the recommendation model. Additionally, we observe that although the model-intrinsic explanation

Table 3. User-oriented evaluation of the explanations. Pr and Re in the table represent the evaluation metrics Precision and Recall, respectively. The marker (m) represents the mask version of the model. The best result on each column is highlighted in bold.

Model		CDs and Vinyl			Electronic			Cell Phones		
		Pr%	Re%	F1%	Pr%	Re%	F1%	Pr%	Re%	F1%
Model-Intrisic Explanation	EFM	17.39	32.94	20.50	19.80	56.56	27.48	12.53	30.48	17.81
	MTER	14.41	39.28	19.74	10.54	27.24	13.42	12.50	25.00	16.67
	A2CF	19.39	57.84	26.62	18.07	53.72	25.32	16.05	28.29	18.76
Counterfactual Explanation	CountER	16.21	33.55	19.96	17.42	45.72	22.13	19.13	47.70	25.05
	CountER(m)	**20.95**	68.98	30.00	**25.68**	45.78	29.73	**21.72**	42.82	26.97
	PGCE	15.79	39.48	20.83	16.97	**57.74**	23.75	18.95	**57.48**	26.30
	PGCE(m)	20.62	**82.08**	**31.36**	25.57	53.26	**31.45**	21.60	48.62	**28.25**

Table 4. Model-oriented evaluation of the explanations.

Model		CDs and Vinyl			Electronic			Cell Phones		
		PN%	PS%	F_{NS}%	PN%	PS%	F_{NS}%	PN%	PS%	F_{NS}%
Model-Intrisic Explanation	EFM	47.65	87.35	61.66	29.65	84.67	43.92	52.66	87.98	65.88
	A2CF	49.12	91.52	63.93	59.47	81.66	68.82	56.45	80.97	66.52
Counterfactual Explanation	CountER	80.89	88.60	84.57	97.08	96.24	96.66	99.52	98.48	99.00
	CountER(m)	72.47	67.72	70.01	77.96	89.26	83.23	86.62	91.78	89.13
	PGCE	**95.46**	**96.31**	**95.97**	**98.80**	**97.39**	**98.21**	**99.84**	**99.52**	**99.64**
	PGCE(m)	81.11	76.04	79.12	80.39	90.81	85.31	88.66	93.60	91.03

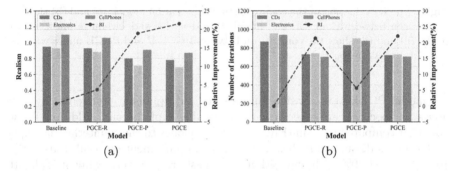

(a)   (b)

Fig. 4. Ablation Studies on constraint terms L_{rec} and L_{proto}. (a) and (b) show the Realism and Speed for the different variant models, respectively.

has decreased by 12.43% average on PS compared to the counterfactual explanation, it still has an acceptable performance of 86.19% on average, which shows that the model-intrinsic explanation is indeed highly correlated with the recommendation result. However, the model-intrinsic explanation has a dramatic decrease of 104.24% average on PN, which indicates that it is not the necessary factor for the recommendation model to make the decision, while the counterfactual explanation generated from the causal perspective is capable of revealing the true cause for recommending the original item.

4.3 Ablation Study

In this section, we first discussed the influence of the two additional constraint terms L_{rec} and L_{proto} on realism, with models without linguistic masks as an example. Particularly, we used the variant models PGCE-R and PGCE-P to see how their performance changes on realism. The results are shown in Fig. 4(a). We made three observations: 1) PGCE-R has a slight average improvement of 3.71% on realism, the reason being that L_{proto} can guide the perturbation toward the nearest contrastive prototype. The contrastive prototype is defined as the mean encoding in the latent space of several real items, which is, to some extent, consistent with the real data distribution. 2) PGCE-P has a significant improvement of 18.91% on realism because the L_{rec} is to have counterfactual instance Y_{cf} respect the real data distribution. 3) The combination of L_{rec} and L_{proto} makes the PGCE model further improve by 21.54% on realism, which indicates that our model combines the advantages of both PGCE-P and PGCE-R to achieve the best experimental result on the three different datasets.

In addition, in order to conduct a horizontal comparison of speed on the four models, we redefined the speed as the number of iterative updates required until a satisfactory counterfactual instance is found. The results are shown in Fig. 4(b). Similarly, we made three observations: 1) PGCE-R has a significant improvement of 21.39% on speed owing to the fact that L_{proto} explicitly guides the search direction toward the optimal counterfactual instance space. 2) PGCE-P has an average improvement of 5.64% on speed, the reason may be that the additional constraint term L_{rec} has filtered out-of-distribution counterfactual instances. 3) PGCE shows an average improvement of 22.05% on speed over the baseline, while the performance gain compared to PGCE-P is marginal. This indicates that our model PGCE is able to find satisfactory counterfactual explanations faster mainly owing to the role of the contrastive prototype.

5 Conclusions

In this study, we proposed PGCE, a novel counterfactual explainable recommendation framework. Particularly, we used a generative model VAE that fits the real data distribution to discover realistic counterfactual instances. In addition, we constructed a contrastive prototype to speed up the search process in the vast counterfactuals space. The experimental results show that PGCE is not only able to efficiently generate realistic explanations, but also achieves state-of-the-art performance on other popular explainability evaluation metrics.

Acknowledgements.. This work is supported by the Project of Construction and Support for High-level Teaching Teams of Beijing Municipal Institutions.

Ethical Statement. Firstly, the experimental data were all obtained from the publicly desensitised Amazon Review Data, and therefore did not involve the collection, processing or inference of private personal information. Secondly, there is no potential use of our research work for the police or the military. Thirdly, this paper does not contain any studies with animals performed by any of the authors. Finally, informed consent was obtained from all individual participants included in the study. All procedures performed in studies involving human participants were in accordance with the ethical standards of the institutional and/or national research committee.

References

1. Akula, A.R., Wang, S., Zhu, S.C.: Cocox: generating conceptual and counterfactual explanations via fault-lines. In: Proceedings of the 34rd AAAI Conference on Artificial Intelligence, pp. 2594–2601 (2020)
2. Alvarez-Melis, D., Jaakkola, T.S.: A causal framework for explaining the predictions of black-box sequence-to-sequence models. In: Conference on Empirical Methods in Natural Language Processing, pp. 412–421 (2017)
3. Chen, J., Zhuang, F., Hong, X., Ao, X., Xie, X., He, Q.: Attention-driven factor model for explainable personalized recommendation. In Proceedings of the 41st International ACM SIGIR Conference on Research and Development in Information Retrieval, pp. 909–912 (2018)
4. Chen, T., Yin, H., Ye, G., Huang, Z., Wang, Y., Wang, M.: Try this instead: personalized and interpretable substitute recommendation. In Proceedings of the 43rd International ACM SIGIR Conference on Research and Development in Information Retrieval, pp. 891–900 (2020)
5. Chen, X., et al.: Sequential recommendation with user memory networks. In: Proceedings of the Eleventh ACM International Conference on Web Search and Data Mining, pp. 108–116 (2018)
6. Cheng, W., Shen, Y., Huang, L., Zhu, Y.: Incorporating interpretability into latent factor models via fast influence analysis. In Proceedings of the 25th ACM SIGKDD International Conference on Knowledge Discovery and Data Mining, pp. 885–893 (2019)
7. Costa, F.S.D., Ouyang, S., Dolog, P., Lawlor, A.: Automatic generation of natural language explanations. In: Proceedings of the 23rd International Conference on Intelligent User Interfaces Companion, pp. 1–2 (2018)
8. Gao, C., Zheng, Y., Wang, W., Feng, F., He, X., Li, Y.: Causal inference in recommender systems: a survey and future directions. arXiv abs/2208.12397 (2022)
9. Ghazimatin, A., Balalau, O., Roy, R.S., Weikum, G.: Prince: provider-side interpretability with counterfactual explanations in recommender systems. In: Proceedings of the 13th International Conference on Web Search and Data Mining, pp. 196–204 (2020)
10. Goyal, Y., Wu, Z., Ernst, J., Batra, D., Parikh, D., Lee, S.: Counterfactual visual explanations. In: International Conference on Machine Learning, pp. 2376–2384 (2019)
11. Herlocker, J.L., Konstan, J.A., Riedl, J.: Explaining collaborative filtering recommendations. In: Proceedings of the 2000 ACM Conference on Computer Supported Cooperative Work, pp. 241–250 (2000)
12. Kaffes, V., Sacharidis, D., Giannopoulos, G.: Model-agnostic counterfactual explanations of recommendations. In: Proceedings of the 29th ACM Conference on User Modeling, Adaptation and Personalization, pp. 280–285 (2021)
13. Kingma, D.P., Welling, M.: Auto-encoding variational Bayes. arXiv preprint arXiv:1312.6114 (2013)

14. Li, C., Quan, C., Peng, L., Qi, Y., Deng, Y., Wu, L.: A capsule network for recommendation and explaining what you like and dislike. In: Proceedings of the 42nd International ACM SIGIR Conference on Research and Development in Information Retrieval, pp. 275–284 (2019)

15. Li, O., Liu, H., Chen, C., Rudin, C.: Deep learning for case-based reasoning through prototypes: a neural network that explains its predictions. In: Proceedings of the 32rd AAAI Conference on Artificial Intelligence, pp. 3530–3537 (2018)

16. Lipton, Z.C.: The mythos of model interpretability. Commun. ACM, 36–43 (2018)

17. Lundberg, S.M., Lee, S.I.: A unified approach to interpreting model predictions. In: Conference on Neural Information Processing Systems, pp. 4768–4777 (2017)

18. Ma, W., et al.: Jointly learning explainable rules for recommendation with knowledge graph. In Proceedings of the 28th International Conference on World Wide Web, pp. 1210–1221 (2019)

19. Mothilal, R.K., Sharma, A., Tan, C.: Explaining machine learning classifiers through diverse counterfactual explanations. In: Proceedings of the 2020 Conference on Fairness, Accountability, and Transparency, pp. 607–617 (2020)

20. Ni, J., Li, J., McAuley, J.: Justifying recommendations using distantly-labeled reviews and fine-grained aspects. In: Proceedings of the 2019 Conference on Empirical Methods in Natural Language Processing and the 9th International Joint Conference on Natural Language Processing, pp. 188–197 (2019)

21. Peake, G., Wang, J.: Explanation mining: post hoc interpretability of latent factor models for recommendation systems. In: Proceedings of the 24th ACM SIGKDD International Conference on Knowledge Discovery and Data Mining, pp. 2060–2069 (2018)

22. Ribeiro, M.T., Singh, S., Guestrin, C.: "why should I trust you?": Explaining the predictions of any classifier. In: Proceedings of the 22nd ACM SIGKDD International Conference on Knowledge Discovery and Data Mining, pp. 1135–1144 (2016)

23. Sarwar, B.M., Karypis, G., Konstan, J.A., Riedl, J.: Item-based collaborative filtering recommendation algorithms. In: Proceedings of the 10th International Conference on World Wide Web, pp. 285–295 (2001)

24. Singh, J., Anand, A.: Posthoc interpretability of learning to rank models using secondary training data. arXiv abs/1806.11330 (2018)

25. Tan, J., Xu, S., Ge, Y., Li, Y., Chen, X., Zhang, Y.: Counterfactual explainable recommendation. In Proceedings of the 30th ACM International Conference on Information and Knowledge Management, pp. 1784–1793 (2021)

26. Tran, K.H., Ghazimatin, A., Saha Roy, R.: Counterfactual explanations for neural recommenders. In: Proceedings of the 44th International ACM SIGIR Conference on Research and Development in Information Retrieval, pp. 1627–1631 (2021)

27. Van Looveren, A., Klaise, J.: Interpretable counterfactual explanations guided by prototypes. In: Machine Learning and Knowledge Discovery in Databases. Research Track: European Conference, pp. 650–665 (2021)

28. Wang, N., Wang, H., Jia, Y., Yin, Y.: Explainable recommendation via multi-task learning in opinionated text data. In: Proceedings of the 41st International ACM SIGIR Conference on Research and Development in Information Retrieval, pp. 165–174 (2018)

29. Wang, X., Li, Q., Yu, D., Xu, G.: Reinforced path reasoning for counterfactual explainable recommendation. arXiv abs/2207.06674 (2022)

30. Wu, T., Ribeiro, M.T., Heer, J., Weld, D.S.: Polyjuice: generating counterfactuals for explaining, evaluating, and improving models. In: Annual Meeting of the Association for Computational Linguistics, pp. 6707–6723 (2021)

31. Xu, S., et al.: Learning causal explanations for recommendation. In: CEUR Workshop Proceedings (2021)
32. Yang, L., Kenny, E.M., Ng, T.L.J., Yang, Y., Smyth, B., Dong, R.: Generating plausible counterfactual explanations for deep transformers in financial text classification. In: International Conference on Computational Linguistics, pp. 6150–6160 (2020)
33. Zhang, Y., Chen, X., et al.: Explainable recommendation: a survey and new perspectives. Found. Trends Inf. Retr. **14**(1), 1–101 (2020)
34. Zhang, Y., Lai, G., Zhang, M., Zhang, Y., Liu, Y., Ma, S.: Explicit factor models for explainable recommendation based on phrase-level sentiment analysis. In: Proceedings of the 37th International ACM SIGIR conference on Research and development in information retrieval, pp. 83–92 (2014)
35. Zhang, Y., Zhang, H., Zhang, M., Liu, Y., Ma, S.: Do users rate or review?: Boost phrase-level sentiment labeling with review-level sentiment classification. In: Proceedings of the 37th International ACM SIGIR Conference on Research and Development in Information Retrieval, pp. 1027–1030 (2014)
36. Zhang, Y., Xu, X., Zhou, H., Zhang, Y.: Distilling structured knowledge into embeddings for explainable and accurate recommendation. In: Proceedings of the 13th International Conference on Web Search and Data Mining, pp. 735–743 (2020)
37. Zhong, J., Negre, E.: Shap-enhanced counterfactual explanations for recommendations. In: Proceedings of the 37th ACM/SIGAPP Symposium on Applied Computing, pp. 1365–1372 (2022)
38. Zhou, Y., Wang, H., He, J., Wang, H.: From intrinsic to counterfactual: on the explainability of contextualized recommender systems. arXiv abs/2110.14844 (2021)

PCDF: A Parallel-Computing Distributed Framework for Sponsored Search Advertising Serving

Han Xu[1], Hao Qi[2], Yaokun Wang[2], Pei Wang[1](✉), Guowei Zhang[2],
Congcong Liu[2], Junsheng Jin[2], Xiwei Zhao[2], Zhangang Lin[2], Jinghe Hu[2],
and Jingping Shao[2]

[1] Beijing, China
xhbj66@gmail.com, wangpei102595@gmail.com
[2] JD.com, Beijing, China
{qihao1,wangkunyao,jinjunsheng1,zhaoxiwei,
linzhangang,hujinghe,shaojingping}@jd.com, cliubh@connect.ust.hk

Abstract. Traditional online advertising systems for sponsored search follow a cascade paradigm with retrieval, pre-ranking, ranking, respectively. Constrained by strict requirements on online inference efficiency, it tend to be difficult to deploy useful but computationally intensive modules in the ranking stage. Moreover, ranking models currently used in the industry assume the user click only relies on the advertisements itself, which results in the ranking stage overlooking the impact of organic search results on the predicted advertisements (ads). In this work, we propose a novel framework PCDF (Parallel-Computing Distributed Framework), allowing to split the computation cost into three parts and to deploy them in the pre-module in parallel with the retrieval stage, the middle-module for ranking ads, and the post-module for re-ranking ads with external items. Our PCDF effectively reduces the overall inference latency compared with the classic framework. The whole module is end-to-end offline training and adapt for the online learning paradigm. To our knowledge, we are the first to propose an end-to-end solution for online training and deployment on complex CTR models from the system framework side.

Keywords: Parallel and Distributed Mining · Advertising System · Online Serving

1 Introduction

CTR prediction is the core task of advertising systems, predicting the probability of the users' click events on a certain item. A typical paradigm in online

---

H. Xu and H. Qi—Equal contribution.

G. Zhang—The author made a lot of contributions to this work.

G. De Francisci Morales et al. (Eds.): ECML PKDD 2023, LNAI 14174, pp. 669–683, 2023.
https://doi.org/10.1007/978-3-031-43427-3_40

advertising systems is to retrieve a subset of advertisements relevant to the users from a large corpus by a candidate generation network [1], and then rank these candidates through a ranking network [1,2], leaving only a few items to present to the user.

Driven by the advancement of deep learning, large-scale deep neural networks are usually employed as ranking models in recommendation systems to achieve good system performance. However, complex models are difficult to deploy under extremely low system latency constraints in real-time recommendation systems. Many existing works focus on improving the effectiveness and efficiency of recommender systems [2–13]. Recent works [14–17] reduce computational latency and improve system efficiency by using two-stage modeling methods. Although these methods reduce the computation cost in the ranking stage, maintaining data consistency between the two-stage brings the challenge to the online serving system, and the ranking model doesn't fully exploit the rich information contained in the features generated in the one-stage model. Furthermore, these methods are not suitable for the online learning paradigm, which further impairs the accuracy of prediction. The above methods concentrate on pre-reducing online inference time through model design in the ranking stage but ignore the rationality of the overall framework.

From the system deployment side, many existing recommendation systems decompose models and data to benefit from data parallelism and model parallelism [18–20]. However, the acceleration revenue of the above two strategies reaches a bottleneck since model computing complexity keeps growing. Pipeline parallelism [7] has been a handful solution to simplify the design of algorithms and facilitate deployment, but many recommendation frameworks applied pipeline parallelism suffer from the unbalanced load.

Given the above limitations, in this paper, we rethink the challenges of deploying complex models in e-commerce search platform, from a system design perspective and take user long-term behavior modeling and organic search information modeling as the case study. Unlike other methods that design training-inference inconsistent models to reduce online computational complexity, we adopt end-to-end training and maintain training-inference consistency to achieve good performance. More specifically, We split the precision ranking model into three modeling stages: pre-modeling, middle-modeling, and post-modeling, and perform parallel computing for pre-modeling and post-modeling with other modules in the recommendation system. Benefiting from the parallel framework, the latency of the whole ranking model can be reduced even if adding a complex target-independent module. The main contributions of this work are summarized as follows:

- We propose a novel Parallel-Computing Distribution Framework(PCDF) from the perspective of system framework design. To the best of our knowledge, PCDF is the first systematic solution for deploying computationally expensive target-independent modules in online advertising serving.
- A new pipeline parallelism recommendation inference strategy is proposed, which split the deep rank stage into three modeling stages: pre-modeling,

in-modeling, and post-modeling; the above three-stage deep rank process is carried out in a pipeline parallelism way by one single deep rank model. Computing power cost in the ranking stage is explicitly reduced by applying PCDF. This further brings space for the advertising systems to apply more complex deep models to reach better performance.

- We introduce a hands-on practice of the PCDF framework on both offline training and online deployment for CTR prediction on a real-world advertising platform.
- The modeling for Long-term user historical behavior and externalities is deployed as a task and conduct comprehensive offline and online experiments to validate our solution's rationality. We achieve a 5% improvement on CTR and 5.1% improvement on RPM in the online A/B test. And there is almost no increase in inference time in the whole ranking system.

2   Related Work

2.1   Latency Optimization

There are generally several methods for optimizing the performance of online inference. On the model side, two common methods are model pruning and model quantization with low-precision inference. Model pruning reduces model size by removing unnecessary weights or neurons, which speeds up inference. Model quantization converts floating-point model parameters to integers or uses lower bit-width data representation to accelerate inference [21–24]. However, these methods may lead to a reduction in model parameters, which can decrease the model's accuracy and performance. Achieving optimal results requires significant experimentation and computational resources to adjust parameters. On the framework side, parallel computing distributes the model or data across different nodes for parallel modeling training, however, the parallel computing approach does not conform to the paradigm of online learning and is rarely used in model inference.

Once the traditional three stages have been carried out in e-commerce search platform, a post-processing module is typically deployed. This module is utilized for the reordering of strategies between items, as well as for handling new strategies resulting from different business practices. Due to system latency limitations, it is generally difficult to deploy complex models in the post-processing stage. In order to cut down on the latency it takes to run the post-processing module, optimization methods such as edge computing are used to eliminate latency from the edge to the server [25, 26]. Additionally, performance-enhancing algorithmic strategies are applied to decrease computation cost [27, 28].

To address the aforementioned issues, we propose a pipelined parallel framework that divides the model inference process into three stages: pre-modeling, middle-modeling, and post-modeling. Through pipeline parallelism and parallel computing, we successfully deployed complex models without increasing model latency. This approach improved model inference accuracy and achieved good online performance benefits.

3   Methodology

In this section, we explain the motivation behind the PCDF (Parallel Computing Distributed Framework) framework and introduce its design considerations. We then provide a detailed overview of the architecture of the deployment framework, summarized the online serving framework of the e-commerce sponsored search system, and introduce our proposed PCDF. Next, we briefly explain how the models, including behavior modeling and external information modeling, are applied in PCDF to demonstrate that PCDF provides scalable, efficient, and easy-to-use deployment solutions for machine learning models.

3.1   Preliminaries

CTR Task. The CTR prediction is to predict the probability that a user clicks an item. After retrieving hundreds of candidate items at the retrieval stage, a ranking module is employed to make a prediction between user u and every item x from candidate items X. In general, a CTR prediction model involves four kinds of features:

$$CTR = f(L_u^{1:T_l}, S_u^{1:T_s}, x_u, x_t, x_c) \tag{1}$$

where $L_u^{1:T_l}$ and $S_u^{1:T_s}$ are long and short historical behaviors respectively, x_u, x_t, x_c corresponds to user profile, target item profile and contexts. As shown in Fig. 1(a), the user request R_u from upstreams is handled by a retrieval Module for hundreds of items I_R this user u might be interested in. Followed by predictions on all items made by Pre Rank Module and Deep Rank Module. Each module has a Feature extract process, to process all Module required features ($L_u^{1:T_l}, S_u^{1:T_s}, x_u, x_t, x_c$). Since Rank Modules require the candidate items responded from Retrieval Module, the whole process is serialized.

E-commerce Search Platform. A practical e-commerce search platform that recommends multiple products to online users, usually through two separate systems, the Organic Search System (OS) and the Sponsored Search Advertisement System (AS). To present a mix of search and advertising listings, the organic results The list is first generated by the OS, and then the AS assigns the correct ad on the correct ad slot [29]. In this paper, we mainly focus on the search advertising system, which follows a three-stage design with recall, rough sorting, and sorting. Specifically, a large number of items and Ads that are relevant to the user are first retrieved from the query, which is then sent to a predictive model that estimates various ad quality metrics, such as click-through rate. These candidate ads are then ranked by the metrics generated and advertiser bids. The winning bid after these auction advertisements will ultimately be presented to consumers along with organic search results [2,14,30].

3.2   Design Considerations and Motivation

1) Strict Online Serving Latency. The major target for designing a real-time recommendation system is to reach peak recommendation accuracy under strict

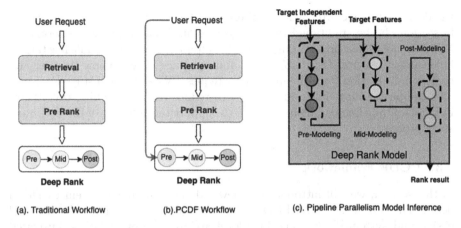

Fig. 1. Illustration of traditional recommendation workflow and PCDF workflow, traditional recommendation workflow illustrated in fig.(a) includes three stages: retrieval, pre ranking, and deep ranking. The deep ranking stage includes three aspects of work: target-independent pre preprocessing, model estimation, and post-processing. PCDF workflow illustrated in fig.(b) adds a pre-computing stage to move the target-independent processing of the fine ranking stage forward in parallel with the recall and pre ranking, which reduces the burden of the deep ranking stage. in fig(c), the deep ranking model is split into three stages: pre-modeling, mid-modeling, and post-modeling, which can be performed in parallel to support target-independent and target-dependent feature computation, as well as post-processing.

constraints of latency. Generally speaking, as prediction accuracy increases with model complexity, the trade-off between prediction accuracy and system latency has to been made, due to the limitation of latency. In our scenario with heavy throughput, there are lots of optimization work, including multi-thread, data parallelism, and tensorflow op parallelism to keep system latency under 60ms which is the system latency of our recommendation system.

2) Deployment Costs. Given that GPU has a good acceleration effect on many models, currently mainstream recommendation system will use GPU for inference acceleration while the cost of GPU resources is higher than that of CPU. Many recommendation system architectures deploy CPU resources and GPU resources together, however, it is difficult to accurately adjust the allocation ratio of GPU computing resources, bandwidth, and CPU computing resources; with the iterative changes of the model, an unbalanced load of CPU and GPU leads to higher deployment costs leading to high costs for large-scale commercial recommendation system.

We formulate Large-scale Distributed Real-Time Prediction (RTP) system in Fig. 1(a), which consists of three core components: Retrieval module, Pre Rank Module, and Deep Rank Module. The computation latency is generally unsatisfying if complex model is performed on thousands of advertisements in the retrieval stage [2]. Thus complex model is usually deployed and performed in the deep rank stage after ads are filtered in the retrieval stage. As introduced in section3.1, the traditional three-stage recommendation process is serialized. However, not all features are only accessible after the retrieval Module like target-independent features ($L_u^{1:T_l}$, $S_u^{1:T_s}$, x_u and x_c) since we can know the user and context information from the initial user request. We propose a stage-level parallel computing idea shown in Fig. 1(b) to reduce online reasoning time. Show in Fig. 1(c), pipeline parallelism is used to support the splitting of the deep rank stage process.

3.3   PCDF Framework

In this section, we will introduce our newly designed ranking system PCDF in detail. The core idea behind PCDF is to take into consideration of both model design and system design. The high-level architecture of PCDF is illustrated in Fig. 2. PCDF consists of two components: the training component(shown in the left, which contains model online learning, Feature Engineering, and model detachment module) uses Tensorflow to train the model serving for online server, and data used for training model comes from user and target features.

Deep Ranking Model in PCDF. As shown in Fig. 2, model designed for online serving is divided into three sub-models (pre-model, mid-model, post-model) and deployed on an online server, where the online serving component recommends items to users based on their preferences in real-time. Specifically, when a front-end user requests recommended targets, it obtains task-independent features and sends the processed features to the pre-processing model. After the pre-processing stage is completed, the captured information is sent back to the deep ranking module. These processes run in parallel with

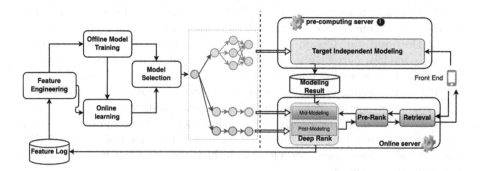

Fig. 2. Illustration of online advertising system. Typically it consists of three important components: real-time serving module, offline model training, and model deploy module. Left is the feature log module and Model training module, after model training, the new model will be split and deployed in a real-time server. The same model will perform different calculations at different stages to achieve a staged pipeline model inference process.

the retrieval module's call. Once the deep ranking module receives feedback from the pre-ranking and pre-processing modules, it reprocesses the features to obtain item features and sends all the results to the ranking module in the deep ranking model. As the main ranking stage, the mid-model and post-model rank all candidate items based on item features, user features, context features, and externalities in e-commerce sponsored search.

Shown in Fig. 1(c), we design a pipeline parallelism strategy that allows the same model to provide modeling services for different stage modeling processes in the deep ranking stage. Firstly, pre-modeling is used to model target-independent features in the first stage. Then, the outputs of pre-modeling along with target features are sent to the mid-modeling process to obtain prediction scores. Finally, a post-modeling is applied to process the mid-modeling results and externality. Next, we will introduce how PCDF is deployed in the online learning and serving manner. In industry, online learning refers to updating the model parameters in real-time through online requests during the online service stage, in order to adapt to the dynamic distribution of data.

Training. As shown on the left side of Fig. 2, after the target-independent modeling is finished, feature engineering is performed on the feature log with hadoop [31], including fusing the outputs of the pre-computing server with other features related to candidate items. In the way that all modules in the ranking model are jointly learning to optimize the deep ranking task, the parameters of the part for the target-independent model are synchronously updated with other parts through training in an end-to-end way.

The model training process adopts the online learning paradigm to update the model. With the continuous generation of data streams, the model can dynamically update its parameters to adapt to the new data distribution as new data arrives. During this process, the model's training and inference are performed alternately, and the model can continuously learn and improve from new data. The model selection module will prioritize the selection of different model and push it to the real-time recommendation system to start providing services. Joint learning enables the information of target-independent features fully utilized, compared to the two-stage models [17,30]. Besides, the end-to-end model updated all parameters synchronously, which keeps consistency during online learning.

Pipeline Parallelism Servering. Deep Ranking stage on the right of Fig. 2 is divided into three stages: pre-modeling, mid-modeling, and post-modeling. **1) Pre-modeling.** target independent pre-modeling process is deployed in pre-computing module❶ and triggered simultaneously with retrieval process by front end user request. The results of pre-modeling are cached by redis [32]. **2) Mid-modeling.** After the processes of the retrieval and pre-ranking stage are completed, the pre-modeling result in the cache is fetched and sent to the mid-modeling module along with pre rank result, mid-modeling module predicts all targets score. **3) Post-modeling.** a post-modeling stage is added, for different business scenarios, the sorting strategies could be quite different. The post-modeling stage performs personalized post-processing on the predicted items to meet business requirements, again, the pre-modeling result cached in redis is fetched as input parameters for post-modeling. The key used for storing pre-modeling results could be user id or request session id; the cached data life-cycle is configurable according to recommended accuracy and system cost.

Design of Flexible Ranking Model. Unlike the previous modeling, which reduces computing power cost by restricting model architecture and thus causes loss of model performance, PCDF allows applying arbitrary complex architecture of deep models to ensure the best model performance. For example, in our real system, we take transformer based models [33] as our user behavior model architecture in pre-stage. Figure 4 illustrates the results from pre-stage sent to pos-model in fully connected layer with the concatenation of other features as inputs. Other model for user behavior and model for other features independent with Ads, are also applicable, which we leave readers for further trying. In post-stage, the output from middle model is fused with the external items and compute the final score for the candidate items.

Multi-thread is also used for better concurrency performance, each thread accepts several user requests and business strategies will be applied to each request. Finally, a cache is used to reduce feature search latency and network communication costs.

3.4   Deployment

In this section, we give hands-on practice of the PCDF framework on online deployment in the industry.

As mentioned above in Sect. 3.3, the model is split into three branches when online serving: long-term behavior sequence module deployed in pre-modeling module, the rest candidate item-dependent models deployed in mid-modeling module and modeling external information in pos-modeling module.

Although three sub-models are responsible for different tasks and are called sequentially, we export one dynamic computation graph and deploy the whole graph on the same server. The Prediction Server can choose the PCDF or CTR branch output corresponding to the request. Specifically, the Prediction Server can know the rank stage from the requests sent by the interface Server. This deployment method naturally supports online learning since there is actually only one serving computation graph. Furthermore, deployment on the same machine contributes to consistency and enables easy management of all model versions, e.g., rollback or model structure updating.

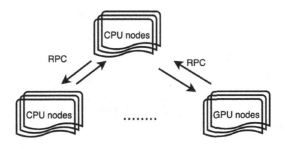

Fig. 3. CPU and GPU Isolation.

Isolation of CPU and GPU Computing Resources. As mentioned in Sect. 3.2, it's hard to balance CPU resources and CPU resources in large-scale recommendation systems. To reduce the difficulty of deployment, we treated recommendation processes as computationally intensive and io-intensive, shown in Fig. 3. We designed a distributed computing architecture that isolates CPU resources from GPU resources and split them to different nodes. RPC (Remote Procedure Call) is applied to exchange data between GPU nodes and CPU nodes. Using appropriate computing graph splitting strategy, hash operation and request unpacking are handled by CPU nodes while model inference is performed on GPU nodes. As the model changes, CPU and GPU computing resources are adjusted independently. This distributed recommendation system architecture can greatly alleviate waste of computing resources in large industrial scenarios. Our hands-on practice shows that resource utilization increases from 35% to 65%. It is expected that as the model calculation distribution continues to change, the resource utilization rate will be further improved.

Other Optimization Trick. Apart from pipeline parallelism mentioned in Sect. 1, which is good at accelerating target-independent modeling, we also apply various data parallelism optimizations that may fit most recommendation processes. In our system, the target item's score ranking process is independent of each other. That means score computing could be processed in parallel with each other. At the front-end use request level, each request will be split into several inference sub-requests; each sub-request handles part of targets, after all sub-request processes are finished, results will be merged and ranked by score. The trade-off will be made when split user request since RPC is used in our recommendation system, too many RPC network communications means sub-requests have more chance get failed.

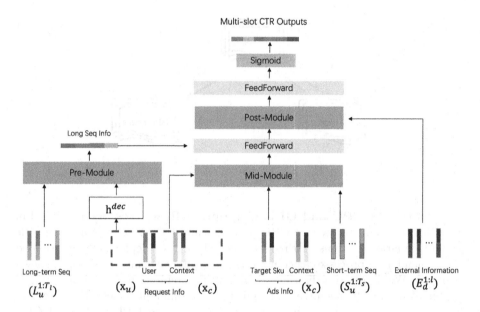

Fig. 4. Network Architecture of the CTR Model

4   Experiments

We carefully compare the prediction latency of the baseline and our proposed framework at varying lengths of behavioral sequences. Furthermore, we compare the proposed search framework with several state-of-the-art works in modeling long-term behaviors on an industrial dataset. Finally, we conduct an A/B online test to verify the performance of PCDF.

4.1   The Impact of the Sequence Length

For validating the newly designed framework's effectiveness, we conduct the prediction latency experiments carefully in our online advertising system.

Experimental Settings. For comparison of the impact of behavior lengths between the baseline and our new framework, we adopt precisely the same model in Sect. 3.3 and denote *Baseline* and *PCDF* as the deployment method mentioned in Sect. 3.2 respectively. Precisely, the **Baseline** deploys the whole CTR model in Deep Rank module while **PCDF** deploys long-term modeling in pre-computing module and the rest in Ranking module. Both the baseline and PCDF deployed the same hardware environment. Retrieval server runs on a machine with 1 Intel Xeon CPU E5-2683 and 8GB RAM, and deep rank module Server runs on a machine with 1 Intel Xeon Gold 6267C CPU and 128GB RAM; The connection bandwidth between each service is 10Gbps.

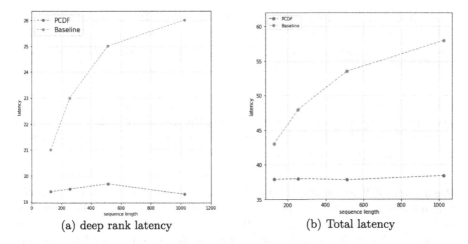

(a) deep rank latency   (b) Total latency

Fig. 5. Illustration of system latency, **(a)** shows that baseline CTR prediction latency increase as behavior sequences increases, while PCDF remains stable, **(b)** shows total latency of deep ranking stage, the latency trend is consistent with **(a)**

Prediction Latency Results. *PCDF* achieve better performance on latency compared with *Baseline*, demonstrating its high efficientness. Figure 5a gives the overall latency of the *PCDF* and *Baseline* in the ranking stage under different behavior lengths. With an increase in the length of behavior sequences, the overall latency of *Baseline* shows an upward trend, where the latency increases by 15 ms when the length goes up from 128 to 1024. In contrast, the latency in the ranking stage of *PCDF* remains stable at about 38ms, even though the length reaches 1024. It is noted that the predictor latency of *Baseline* is about 58 ms, which is not acceptable considering our strict online latency.

The results show that the latency of the baseline in the ranking stage keeps increasing with increasing sequence length, while the latency of PCDF is stable. It is noticed that about 60ms prediction latency in the original framework when length at 1024, shown in Fig. 5b, is unable to deploy under the constraint of extremely low system latency. Therefore, PCDF provides a solution and enables our complex modules like long-term user behavior modeling deployment.

4.2 Experiments on Industrial Dataset

Competitive Models. **SIM** [30] is a CTR prediction model, which proposes a search unit to extract user interests from long-term user behavior sequences in a two-stage manner. SIM(hard) is the SIM that searches top-k behavior items by category id in the first stage. We follow previous work to compare SIM(hard) as the performance is almost the same as they deploy SIM(hard) online. **ETA** [34] applies LSH to encode target items and user behavior sequences into binary codes and then calculates the Hamming distance of the items to select top-k similar items for subsequent target attention in an end-to-end manner.

Experimental Settings. For all the baselines and PCDF, we use the same features as input and adopt the same model structure except for the long-term user behavior modeling module. All models use the same length of long-term user behaviors.

Industrial Dataset. We select consecutive 15-day samples for training and the next two days for evaluation and testing, the number of training examples is about 10 billion. The recent 50 behaviors are selected as short-term sequences, and the recent 1,024 behaviors are selected as long-term sequences.

Result on Offline Experiment. The evaluation results are shown in Table 1. For industrial dataset, we report the result of baselines and PCDF. The best performance is highlighted in bold. Results show that PCDF consistently outperforms all baselines on the industrial dataset. Specifically, it achieves improvements over the strongest baselines in terms of AUC by 2.51%, 1.60%. This validates the effectiveness of our module for modeling long-term historical behaviors for CTR prediction task. Note that SIM(hard) performs worst in the baseline models due to the loss of information caused by user behavior retrieval according to category.

Table 1. Performance comparison of PCDF to other methods on modeling long-term behavior sequence

Model	AUC
SIM(hard)	0.7290
ETA	0.7355
PCDF	**0.7473**

4.3   Online A/B Test

The PCDF is deployed in our real display advertising system with a long-term behavior sequence module with a length of 1024 and modeling the external information.

A strict online A/B test is conducted. Table 2 shows online experimental results using the proposed PCDF framework while the original framework without long-term behavior module and post-module as a benchmark. Compared to the benchmark, the PCDF achieves 5% CTR and 5.1% RPM (Revenue Per Mille) gain. Note that 5.1% improvement on RPM is nontrivial improvement given that all other components of our base model have already been highly optimized and this leads to additional millions of revenues per day.

Finally, we analyze the efficiency of the proposed PCDF in online serving. The comparison of latency is also examined at the peak of queries per second (QPS), as shown in Table 2. Adding long-term behavior modeling and post-modelling almost brings no extra inference time compared with the base model, proving the stability and effectiveness of our proposed framework.

We tested the performance of the pre-model and the post-model online respectively. Among them, the effect of the long-term behavior modeling in the pre-module achieves 3% CTR and 3.1% RPM gain and the post-module modeling of organic search information achieves 2% CTR and 2% RPM gain, respectively. All of them have little to no time-consuming addition to the overall ranking stage.

Table 2. Online effectiveness and efficiency of the proposed framework on A/B test

	CTR	RPM	latency in ranking stage
PCDF Framework	+5.00%	+5.10%	+0.4 ms

5 Conclusions

In this paper, we propose an efficient framework PCDF for deploying complex models and utilizing personalized externalities in CTR prediction for practical e-commerce sponsored search systems. The framework is designed for online learning through joint training and online distributed deployment, without increasing extra online inference time for complex computation modules. We comprehensively present the rationale behind our deployment, offer practical experience and conduct various experiments to demonstrate the superiority of our proposed PCDF. To the best of our knowledge, our work represents the first systematic solution to address the unacceptable efficiency of computationally intensive modules in CTR prediction, thus creating a new research direction.

References

1. Jiang, B., et al.: Dcaf: a dynamic computation allocation framework for online serving system. arXiv preprint arXiv:2006.09684 (2020)
2. Covington, P., Adams, J., Sargin, E.: Deep neural networks for Youtube recommendations. In: Proceedings of the 10th ACM Conference on Recommender Systems, pp. 191–198 (2016)
3. Crankshaw, D., Wang, X., Zhou, G., Franklin, M.J., Gonzalez, J.E., Stoica, I.: Clipper: a low-latency online prediction serving system. In: NSDI, vol. 17, pp. 613–627 (2017)
4. Dean, J., et al.: Large scale distributed deep networks. Advances in neural information processing systems 25 (2012)
5. Grbovic, M., Cheng, H.: Real-time personalization using embeddings for search ranking at airbnb. In: Proceedings of the 24th ACM SIGKDD International Conference on Knowledge Discovery & Data Mining, pp. 311–320 (2018)
6. Ke, L., et al.: Recnmp: accelerating personalized recommendation with near-memory processing. In: 2020 ACM/IEEE 47th Annual International Symposium on Computer Architecture (ISCA), pp. 790–803. IEEE (2020)

7. Narayanan, D., et al.: Pipedream: generalized pipeline parallelism for DNN training. In: Proceedings of the 27th ACM Symposium on Operating Systems Principles, pp. 1–15 (2019)

8. Liu, C., et al.: Position awareness modeling with knowledge distillation for CTR prediction. In: Proceedings of the 16th ACM Conference on Recommender Systems, pp. 562–566 (2022)

9. Zhu, J., Liu, C., Wang, P., Zhao, X., Lin, Z., Shao, J.: Confidence ranking for CTR prediction. In: Companion Proceedings of the ACM Web Conference 2023, pp. 437–441 (2023)

10. Liu, C., Teng, F., Zhao, X., Lin, Z., Hu, J., Shao, J.: Always strengthen your strengths: a drift-aware incremental learning framework for CTR prediction. arXiv preprint arXiv:2304.09062 (2023)

11. Liu, C., Li, Y., Zhao, X., Peng, C., Lin, Z., Shao, J.: Concept drift adaptation for CTR prediction in online advertising systems. arXiv preprint arXiv:2204.05101 (2022)

12. Zhu, J., et al.: Dynamic parameterized network for CTR prediction. arXiv preprint arXiv:2111.04983 (2021)

13. Liu, C., Li, Y., Zhu, J., Zhao, X., Peng, C., Lin, Z., Shao, J.: Rethinking position bias modeling with knowledge distillation for CTR prediction. arXiv preprint arXiv:2204.00270 (2022)

14. Goel, S., Langford, J., Strehl, A.: Predictive indexing for fast search. Advances in neural information processing systems 21 (2008)

15. Krishnappa, D.K., Zink, M., Griwodz, C., Halvorsen, P.: Cache-centric video recommendation: an approach to improve the efficiency of youtube caches. ACM Trans. Multimed. Comput. Commun. Appl. (TOMM) 11(4), 1–20 (2015)

16. Pi, Q., Bian, W., Zhou, G., Zhu, X., Gai, K.: Practice on long sequential user behavior modeling for click-through rate prediction. In: Proceedings of the 25th ACM SIGKDD International Conference on Knowledge Discovery & Data Mining, pp. 2671–2679 (2019)

17. Qin, J., Zhang, W., Wu, X., Jin, J., Fang, Y., Yu, Y.: User behavior retrieval for click-through rate prediction. In: Proceedings of the 43rd International ACM SIGIR Conference on Research and Development in Information Retrieval, pp. 2347–2356 (2020)

18. Minakova, S., Tang, E., Stefanov, T.: Combining task- and data-level parallelism for high-throughput CNN inference on embedded CPUs-GPUs MPSoCs. In: Orailoglu, A., Jung, M., Reichenbach, M. (eds.) SAMOS 2020. LNCS, vol. 12471, pp. 18–35. Springer, Cham (2020). https://doi.org/10.1007/978-3-030-60939-9_2

19. Pujol, R., Tabani, H., Kosmidis, L., Mezzetti, E., Abella Ferrer, J., Cazorla, F.J.: Generating and exploiting deep learning variants to increase heterogeneous resource utilization in the nvidia xavier. In: 31st Euromicro Conference on Real-Time Systems (ECRTS 2019), vol. 23 (2019)

20. Kang, D., Oh, J., Choi, J., Yi, Y., Ha, S.: Scheduling of deep learning applications onto heterogeneous processors in an embedded device. IEEE Access 8, 43980–43991 (2020)

21. Polino, A., Pascanu, R., Alistarh, D.: Model compression via distillation and quantization. arXiv preprint arXiv:1802.05668 (2018)

22. Zhou, Y., Moosavi-Dezfooli, S.M., Cheung, N.M., Frossard, P.: Adaptive quantization for deep neural network. In: Proceedings of the AAAI Conference on Artificial Intelligence, vol. 32 (2018)

23. Lin, T., Stich, S.U., Barba, L., Dmitriev, D., Jaggi, M.: Dynamic model pruning with feedback. arXiv preprint arXiv:2006.07253 (2020)

24. Jiang, Y., et al.: Model pruning enables efficient federated learning on edge devices. IEEE Trans. Neural Networks Learn. Syst. (2022)

25. Gong, Y., et al.: Edgerec: recommender system on edge in mobile taobao. In: Proceedings of the 29th ACM International Conference on Information & Knowledge Management, pp. 2477–2484 (2020)

26. Pustokhina, I.V., Pustokhin, D.A., Gupta, D., Khanna, A., Shankar, K., Nguyen, G.N.: An effective training scheme for deep neural network in edge computing enabled internet of medical things (iomt) systems. IEEE Access **8**, 107112–107123 (2020)

27. Pei, C., et al.: Personalized re-ranking for recommendation. In: Proceedings of the 13th ACM Conference on Recommender Systems, pp. 3–11 (2019)

28. Feng, Y., Gong, Y., Sun, F., Ge, J., Ou, W.: Revisit recommender system in the permutation prospective. arXiv preprint arXiv:2102.12057 (2021)

29. Chen, C., et al.: Extr: click-through rate prediction with externalities in e-commerce sponsored search. In: Proceedings of the 28th ACM SIGKDD Conference on Knowledge Discovery and Data Mining, pp. 2732–2740 (2022)

30. Pi, Q., et al.: Search-based user interest modeling with lifelong sequential behavior data for click-through rate prediction. In: Proceedings of the 29th ACM International Conference on Information & Knowledge Management, pp. 2685–2692 (2020)

31. Hadoop (2022). https://hadoop.apache.org

32. Redis (2022). https://redis.io

33. Vaswani, A., et al.: Attention is all you need. Advances in neural information processing systems 30 (2017)

34. Chen, Q., Pei, C., Lv, S., Li, C., Ge, J., Ou, W.: End-to-end user behavior retrieval in click-through rateprediction model. arXiv preprint arXiv:2108.04468 (2021)

A Vlogger-augmented Graph Neural Network Model for Micro-video Recommendation

Weijiang Lai[1,2], Beihong Jin[1,2(✉)], Beibei Li[3], Yiyuan Zheng[1,2], and Rui Zhao[1,2]

[1] State Key Laboratory of Computer Science, Institute of Software, Chinese Academy of Sciences, Beijing, China
[2] University of Chinese Academy of Sciences, Beijing, China
`Beihong@iscas.ac.cn`
[3] College of Computer Science, Chongqing University, Chongqing, China

Abstract. Existing micro-video recommendation models exploit the interactions between users and micro-videos and/or multi-modal information of micro-videos to predict the next micro-video a user will watch, ignoring the information related to vloggers, i.e., the producers of micro-videos. However, in micro-video scenarios, vloggers play a significant role in user-video interactions, since vloggers generally focus on specific topics and users tend to follow the vloggers they are interested in. Therefore, in the paper, we propose a vlogger-augmented graph neural network model VA-GNN, which takes the effect of vloggers into consideration. Specifically, we construct a tripartite graph with users, micro-videos, and vloggers as nodes, capturing user preferences from different views, i.e., the video-view and the vlogger-view. Moreover, we conduct cross-view contrastive learning to keep the consistency between node embeddings from the two different views. Besides, when predicting the next user-video interaction, we adaptively combine the user preferences for a video itself and its vlogger. We conduct extensive experiments on two real-world datasets. The experimental results show that VA-GNN outperforms multiple existing GNN-based recommendation models.

Keywords: Recommender Systems · Micro-video Recommendation · Graph Neural Networks · Contrastive Learning

1 Introduction

Micro-video streaming platforms are hubs for uploading and watching micro-videos. In recent years, micro-video apps such as TikTok, Kwai, etc. attract a huge number of users, who spend most of their spare time watching diversified micro-videos. This also promotes more people to become vloggers, producing and publishing more micro-videos. With the increase in the number of micro-videos, the micro-video recommendation in the app becomes indispensable to users.

© The Author(s), under exclusive license to Springer Nature Switzerland AG 2023
G. De Francisci Morales et al. (Eds.): ECML PKDD 2023, LNAI 14174, pp. 684–699, 2023.
https://doi.org/10.1007/978-3-031-43427-3_41

Currently, some deep neural network models have been proposed for the micro-video recommendation, including ranking models and recall models. A few of the ranking models leverage multi-modal information including visual, acoustic, and textual features to achieve the recommendation [1–4], thus being costly in terms of time and computational power. On the other hand, existing models for recalling micro-videos are relatively few in number [5,6]. What is worse, existing micro-video recommendation models only exploit interactions between users and micro-videos for modeling and totally ignore the vlogger information.

We argue that vloggers play important roles in micro-video recommendation. Firstly, the vlogger of a micro-video can be treated as an attribute of the micro-video, since the vlogger potentially reflects the style of the micro-video. Meanwhile, a vlogger can also be treated as an attribute of a user, since the vloggers a user follows reveal the user's preferences. Taken together, treating vloggers as the auxiliary information of users or videos cannot adequately reflect the dynamic relationships among users, vloggers, and micro-videos. Secondly, the "Follow" function permits a user to find micro-videos newly published by followed vloggers. Thus, users are more likely to interact with the videos published by vloggers they follow. These user-video interactions may result from either user preferences for videos themselves or user preferences for their vloggers, the latter factor is overlooked by existing recommendation models.

For taking the effect of vloggers on recommendation into consideration, in the paper, we construct a heterogeneous graph with users, micro-videos, and vloggers as nodes, and propose a model named **VA-GNN** (**V**logger-**A**ugmented **G**raph **N**eural **N**etworks) to exploit the complex semantic relationships among users, vloggers, and micro-videos. VA-GNN learns node embeddings from two different views, and set up meta-paths to build the connection between individual views in the original heterogeneous graph, thus improving the performance of micro-videos recommendations.

Our contribution can be summarized as follows.

- We model the relationships among users, micro-videos, and vloggers in a tripartite graph and capture and combine user preferences for micro-videos themselves and vloggers so as to take full advantage of user-video interactions, user-vlogger interactions, and vlogger-video publishing relationships.
- We generate two embeddings for each node in the graph, using embedding propagation over the video view and the vlogger view, as well as the propagation along meta-paths which are formed by random walk across two views. Moreover, we employ cross-view contrastive learning to keep consistency between the two embeddings of the same node.
- We conduct extensive experiments on two real-world datasets. The experimental results show VA-GNN outperforms the other five models, in terms of Recall and NDCG.

2   Related Work

Our work is related to the research in three topics: GNN-based recommendation, contrastive learning for recommendation, and micro-video recommendation.

GNN-Based Recommendation. GNNs are the neural networks that capture the dependence in a graph via message passing between nodes of the graph. They have been adopted by some recommendation models to perform different recommendation tasks, including the item recommendation [7] [8] [9], social recommendation [10], session recommendation [11], bundle recommendation [12], and cross-domain recommendation [13].

Taking the item recommendation as an example, NGCF [7] models the user-item interactions as a bipartite graph and performs graph convolutions to update embeddings of nodes. Then the learned embeddings of nodes are used for the item recommendation. Further, LightGCN [8] is proposed as a lightweight version of NGCF, which removes the nonlinear activation function and the feature transformation matrix in NGCF but has better performance than NGCF. Moreover, GTN [9] is also a GNN model on the user-item bipartite graph but it can identify the reliability of the interactions, thus improving the performance.

Contrastive Learning for Recommendations. Contrastive learning is a branch of self-supervised learning. It has obtained great achievements in the fields of computer vision [14] and NLP [15], and also helps improve the performance of recommendation models [16].

Some sequential recommendation models, e.g., CL4SRec [17] and DuoRec [18], have been combined with contrastive learning. Typically, they generate the augmented sequences for the original sequence and then design an auxiliary task to pull positive sequence pairs closer to each other and push negative sequence pairs away from each other.

Contrastive learning is also applied to GNN-based recommendation models. Some models, e.g., SGL [19] and PCRec [20], design perturbations in the structure of the original graph to obtain augmented graphs, and then with the aid of any GNN-based encoder, the contrastive learning task will drive embeddings of the same node existing in augmented graphs closer. Some models, e.g., EGLN [21] and BiGI [22], construct the contrastive loss to keep the consistency between the local and global graphs. Further, SimGCL [23] adds uniform noise directly to the embeddings of nodes in the graph, which develops a new way to obtain self-supervised signals.

Micro-Video Recommendation. Existing micro-video recommendation models have many model structures, including attention-based structures, CNNs, or GNNs. For example, Wei et al. [2] construct a user-item bipartite graph for each modality and generate modal-specific representations of users and micro-videos.

Some micro-video recommendation models have supplemented the contrastive learning component in their models. For example, CMI [5] learns user multi-interests in micro-videos from historical interaction sequences and proposes a contrastive multi-interest loss to minimize the difference between interests extracted from two augmented views of the same interaction sequence. PDM-Rec [6] applies a multi-head self-attention mechanism to learn sequence embeddings and proposes contrastive learning strategies to reduce the interference from micro-video positions in interaction sequences.

Compared to the existing work, our work models the relationship among users, micro-videos, and vloggers in a heterogeneous graph, and combines GNNs with contrastive learning for micro-video recommendation for the first time.

3   Problem Formulation

We use $\mathcal{U}, \mathcal{V}, \mathcal{P}$ to denote the set of users, micro-videos, and vloggers, and define the user-video interaction matrix, user-vlogger interaction matrix, and vlogger-video publishing matrix as $X_{|\mathcal{U}| \times |\mathcal{V}|} = \{x_{uv} \mid u \in \mathcal{U}, v \in \mathcal{V}\}$, $Y_{|\mathcal{U}| \times |\mathcal{P}|} = \{y_{up} \mid u \in \mathcal{U}, p \in \mathcal{P}\}$ and $Z_{|\mathcal{P}| \times |\mathcal{V}|} = \{z_{pv} \mid p \in \mathcal{P}, v \in \mathcal{V}\}$, respectively. If there is at least one explicit interaction (e.g., liking/thumb-up) between user u and micro-video v, then $x_{uv} = 1$, otherwise, $x_{uv} = 0$. Similarly, $y_{up} = 1$ indicates that user u interacts with vlogger p, for example, user u follows vlogger p. Moreover, $z_{pv} = 1$ indicates that vlogger p publishes video v.

Our goal is to design a recommendation model to predict the probability of interaction between any user $u \in \mathcal{U}$ and any candidate micro-video $v \in \mathcal{V}$ based on the user-video interaction matrix $X_{|\mathcal{U}| \times |\mathcal{V}|}$, user-vlogger interaction matrix $Y_{|\mathcal{U}| \times |\mathcal{P}|}$ and vlogger-video publishing matrix $Z_{|\mathcal{P}| \times |\mathcal{V}|}$.

4   Our Model

We propose a model named VA-GNN, whose architecture is shown in Fig. 1. VA-GNN is composed of the following components: heterogeneous graph construction, embedding propagation, cross-view contrastive learning, prediction, and multi-task learning, which are detailed below.

4.1   Heterogeneous Graph Construction

To explicitly model the relationships between users, micro-videos, and vloggers, we construct a heterogeneous graph $\mathcal{G} = (\mathcal{U} \cup \mathcal{V} \cup \mathcal{P}, \mathcal{E})$, where nodes consist of user nodes $u \in \mathcal{U}$, micro-videos $v \in \mathcal{V}$ and vlogger nodes $p \in \mathcal{P}$, edges are $\mathcal{E}$ consisting of user-video interaction edges (u, v) with $x_{uv} = 1$, user-vlogger interaction edges (u, p) with $y_{up} = 1$, vlogger-video publishing edges (p, v) with $z_{pv} = 1$.

We use $\mathbf{e}_u \in \mathbf{E}_{\mathcal{U}}$, $\mathbf{e}_v \in \mathbf{E}_{\mathcal{V}}$, $\mathbf{e}_p \in \mathbf{E}_{\mathcal{P}}$ to denote the embeddings of user $u \in \mathcal{U}$, micro-video $v \in \mathcal{V}$ and vlogger $p \in \mathcal{P}$, respectively, where $\mathbf{E}_{\mathcal{U}} \in \mathbb{R}^{d \times |\mathcal{U}|}$, $\mathbf{E}_{\mathcal{V}} \in \mathbb{R}^{d \times |\mathcal{V}|}$, $\mathbf{E}_{\mathcal{P}} \in \mathbb{R}^{d \times |\mathcal{P}|}$, and d is the dimension of embeddings.

4.2   Video-View Embedding Propagation

In order to capture the high-order collaborative signals between users and micro-videos and learn more expressive user and micro-video embeddings, we exploit

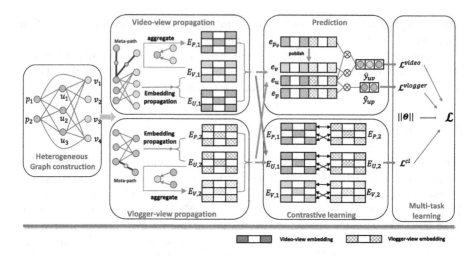

Fig. 1. Architecture of model VA-GNN.

graph neural networks to propagate item-view information on the constructed heterogeneous graph based on user-video interactions.

Meanwhile, we use the random walk to build the 'user-vlogger-user' meta-path and 'user-vlogger-video' meta-path to capture the impact of vlogger on users and micro-videos. Specifically, we construct a meta-path of length 3 by starting from a user u and walking with probability q_1 to a vlogger p interacted by u. Then we walk with probability q_2 to another user u' interacted by p or $1 - q_2$ to a video v published by p, involving the nodes at the end of the meta-path in the embedding propagation of the item-view. Here, we adopt a simple but effective embedding propagation operation, as shown follows.

$$\mathbf{e}_{u,1}^{(l)} = \sum_{v \in \mathcal{V}_u} \frac{1}{\sqrt{|\mathcal{V}_u|}\sqrt{|\mathcal{U}_v|}} \mathbf{e}_{v,1}^{(l-1)}, \tag{1}$$

$$\mathbf{e}_{v,1}^{(l)} = \sum_{u \in \mathcal{U}_v} \frac{1}{\sqrt{|\mathcal{U}_v|}\sqrt{|\mathcal{V}_u|}} \mathbf{e}_{u,1}^{(l-1)}, \tag{2}$$

$$\mathbf{e}_{u,1}^{(0)} = \mathbf{e}_u, \quad \mathbf{e}_{v,1}^{(0)} = \mathbf{e}_p, \tag{3}$$

where $\mathcal{V}_u$ denote micro-video neighbors and the 'user-vlogger-user' meta-path endpoints of user u. $\mathcal{U}_v$ denote user neighbors and the 'user-vlogger-video' meta-path endpoints of micro-video v. $\mathbf{e}_{u,1}^{(l)}$ and $\mathbf{e}_{v,1}^{(l)}$ denote the item-view embeddings of user u and micro-video v at the l-th propagation step.

For a vlogger, we aggregate the item-view embeddings of all the videos he/she published and obtain his/her item-view embedding, as follows.

$$\mathbf{e}_{p,1}^{(l)} = \mathbf{aggregate}\left(\mathbf{e}_{v,1}^{(l)} \mid v \in \mathcal{V}_p\right) \tag{4}$$

where $\mathcal{V}_p$ denotes the micro-video neighbors of vlogger p, i.e., the set of videos vlogger p published. Here, we directly take average pooling as the aggregator.

After iteratively performing embedding propagation for L steps, we obtain L embeddings for each user/video/vlogger node. We average the L embeddings of each node to generate its final item-view embedding, as follows.

$$\mathbf{e}_{u,1} = \frac{1}{L}\sum_{l=0}^{L}\mathbf{e}_{u,1}^{(l)}, \quad \mathbf{e}_{v,1} = \frac{1}{L}\sum_{l=0}^{L}\mathbf{e}_{v,1}^{(l)}, \quad \mathbf{e}_{p,1} = \frac{1}{L}\sum_{l=0}^{L}\mathbf{e}_{p,1}^{(l)}, \tag{5}$$

where $\mathbf{e}_{u,1}, \mathbf{e}_{v,1}$, and $\mathbf{e}_{p,1}$ are item-view embeddings of user u, micro-video v and vlogger p, respectively.

4.3 Vlogger-View Embedding Propagation

The videos published by the same vlogger usually fall in the same category. Thus, vlogger-view user preferences can reflect user preferences for certain video categories. For example, a vlogger who is a basketball coach mostly publishes videos about basketball skills, and users who follow the vlogger have a high probability of favoring basketball and are highly likely to be interested in other vloggers and micro-videos about basketball.

Therefore, in order to learn the implied characteristics of each vlogger and capture vlogger-view user preferences, we perform vlogger-view embedding propagation based on user-vlogger interactions and calculate vlogger-view embeddings of users and vloggers. Similarly, we use the random walk to build the 'user-video-user' meta-path to capture the impact of micro-videos on users and vloggers, involving the nodes at the end of the meta-path in the embedding propagation of the video-view. As shown follows.

$$\mathbf{e}_{u,2}^{(l)} = \sum_{p\in\mathcal{P}_u}\frac{1}{\sqrt{|\mathcal{P}_u|}\sqrt{|\mathcal{U}_p|}}\mathbf{e}_{p,2}^{(l-1)}, \tag{6}$$

$$\mathbf{e}_{p,2}^{(l)} = \sum_{u\in\mathcal{U}_p}\frac{1}{\sqrt{|\mathcal{U}_p|}\sqrt{|\mathcal{P}_u|}}\mathbf{e}_{u,2}^{(l-1)}, \tag{7}$$

$$\mathbf{e}_{u,2}^{(0)} = \mathbf{e}_u, \mathbf{e}_{p,2}^{(0)} = \mathbf{e}_p, \tag{8}$$

where $\mathbf{e}_{u,2}^{(l)}$ and $\mathbf{e}_{p,2}^{(l)}$ denote the vlogger-view embeddings of user u and vlogger p in the l-th layer, respectively. $\mathcal{P}_u$ denote the neighbor vlogger nodes of user u. $\mathcal{U}_p$ denote the neighbor user nodes and the 'user-video-user' meta-path endpoints of vlogger p.

We calculate vlogger-view embeddings of micro-videos by aggregating the vlogger-view embeddings of their user neighbors. For example, the vlogger-view embedding of micro-video v is calculated as Eq. 9. For simplicity, we employ mean pooling as the aggregation function.

$$\mathbf{e}_{v,2}^{(l)} = \mathtt{aggregate}\left(\mathbf{e}_{u,2}^{(l)} \mid u \in \mathcal{U}_v\right) \tag{9}$$

Similar to the final video-view embedding calculation in Sect. 4.2, we take the average of the K vlogger-view embeddings of each node as the final vlogger-view embedding, as shown as follows.

$$\mathbf{e}_{u,2} = \frac{1}{L} \sum_{l=0}^{L} \mathbf{e}_{u,2}^{(l)}, \quad \mathbf{e}_{v,2} = \frac{1}{L} \sum_{l=0}^{L} \mathbf{e}_{v,2}^{(l)}, \quad \mathbf{e}_{p,2} = \frac{1}{L} \sum_{l=0}^{L} \mathbf{e}_{p,2}^{(l)}. \tag{10}$$

4.4   Cross-view Contrastive Learning

After performing video-view and vlogger-view embedding propagation, we obtain pairwise embeddings from two different views for each user, micro-video, and vlogger, which are supposed to keep consistency. For example, user embeddings at video-view and vlogger-view both imply user preferences.

Here, we facilitate embedding learning by conducting contrastive learning that mines the consistency between embeddings from different views of the same entity. Specifically, we treat the video-view and vlogger-view embeddings of the same user/video/vlogger as a positive pair, the embeddings of different users/videos/vloggers as negative pairs, and construct a cross-view contrastive learning loss as follows.

$$\mathcal{L}_{user}^{cl} = \frac{1}{|\mathcal{U}|} \sum_{u \in \mathcal{U}} -\log \frac{\exp\left(\mathbf{sim}\left(\mathbf{e}_{u,1}, \mathbf{e}_{u,2}\right)/\tau\right)}{\sum_{u' \in \mathcal{U}} \exp\left(\mathbf{sim}\left(\mathbf{e}_{u,1}, \mathbf{e}_{u',2}\right)/\tau\right)}, \tag{11}$$

$$\mathcal{L}_{video}^{cl} = \frac{1}{|\mathcal{V}|} \sum_{v \in \mathcal{V}} -\log \frac{\exp\left(\mathbf{sim}\left(\mathbf{e}_{v,1}, \mathbf{e}_{v,2}\right)/\tau\right)}{\sum_{v' \in \mathcal{V}} \exp\left(\mathbf{sim}\left(\mathbf{e}_{v,1}, \mathbf{e}_{v',2}\right)/\tau\right)}, \tag{12}$$

$$\mathcal{L}_{vlogger}^{cl} = \frac{1}{|\mathcal{P}|} \sum_{p \in \mathcal{P}} -\log \frac{\exp\left(\mathbf{sim}\left(\mathbf{e}_{p,1}, \mathbf{e}_{p,2}\right)/\tau\right)}{\sum_{p' \in \mathcal{P}} \exp\left(\mathbf{sim}\left(\mathbf{e}_{p,1}, \mathbf{e}_{p',2}\right)/\tau\right)}, \tag{13}$$

where $\mathbf{sim}(\cdot)$ is the cosine similarity function, τ is the temperature parameter, which is a hyper-parameter.

The final contrastive loss is obtained by calculating the average of the three contrastive learning losses, as follows.

$$\mathcal{L}^{cl} = \frac{1}{3} \left(\mathcal{L}_{user}^{cl} + \mathcal{L}_{video}^{cl} + \mathcal{L}_{vlogger}^{cl}\right). \tag{14}$$

4.5   Prediction

We concatenate user embeddings from two different views and obtain the final embedding of user u as $\mathbf{e}_u = \mathbf{e}_{u,1} \| \mathbf{e}_{u,2}$, where $\|$ denotes vector concatenation and $\mathbf{e}_u \in \mathbb{R}^{2d}$. In the same way, final embeddings of micro-video v and vlogger p are $\mathbf{e}_v = \mathbf{e}_{v,1} \| \mathbf{e}_{v,2}$ and $\mathbf{e}_p = \mathbf{e}_{p,1} \| \mathbf{e}_{p,2}$, respectively. The predicted preference score between user u and vlogger p can be calculated as follows.

$$\hat{y}_{up} = \mathbf{e}_u^T \mathbf{e}_p. \tag{15}$$

Despite the target being micro-video itself, user preferences for vloggers who publish the video also play important roles in user-video interaction prediction. For example, in a situation where the target video does not fit well with the video-view preferences of a user, the user is still highly likely to interact with the video if he/she already follows the vlogger who published the video. Therefore, it is necessary to take user preferences for the vlogger of the target video into consideration when predicting the interaction score. Thus, we combine the user preference score for the video itself and the user preference score for its vlogger to obtain the final user-video interaction score as follows.

$$\hat{y}_{uv} = w \times \mathbf{e}_u^T \mathbf{e}_v + (1 - w) \times \mathbf{e}_u^T \mathbf{e}_{p_v}, \tag{16}$$

where $w \in (0, 1)$ is the weight of user preferences for the video v itself, p_v denotes the vlogger who published the video v.

It is reasonable that if the content of a video is highly consistent with the focus of its vlogger, the video itself and its vlogger play comparable roles in interaction prediction since users like/dislike the video and its vlogger at the same time. But if the two are somewhat divergent, either the video itself or its vlogger plays a more important role. Motivated by that, we build a gate based on the correlation between the video and its vlogger to adaptively calculate weights of preferences at two different views as follows.

$$w = \sigma(\mathbf{e}_v^T Q \mathbf{e}_{p_v}), \tag{17}$$

where $Q \in \mathbb{R}^{2d \times 2d}$ is model parameter to be trained.

4.6   Multi-task Learning

We train our model by optimizing the multiple tasks, i.e., a micro-video recommendation task, a vlogger recommendation task, and a contrastive learning task.

For the micro-video recommendation task, we construct a BPR (Bayesian Personalized Ranking) loss as follows.

$$\mathcal{L}^{video} = - \sum_{(u,v,v^-) \in S} \ln \sigma \left(\hat{y}_{uv} - \hat{y}_{uv^-} \right), \tag{18}$$

where σ is the sigmoid function, $S = \{(u, v, v^-) \mid (u, v) \in \mathcal{Y}^+, (u, v^-) \in \mathcal{Y}^-\}$ denote the pairwise training data with negative sampling, $\mathcal{Y}^+$ and $\mathcal{Y}^-$ denote observable and unobservable user-video interactions, respectively.

In order to make the most of user-vlogger interaction data and capture vlogger-view user preferences more accurately, we leverage the vlogger recommendation task as an auxiliary task to train the model. Similarly, the training data of user-vlogger interactions can be denoted as $S' = \{(u, p, p') \mid (u, p) \in \mathcal{Z}^+, (u, p') \in \mathcal{Z}^-\}$, where $\mathcal{Z}^+$ denotes the set of observable positive user-vlogger pairs, and $\mathcal{Z}^-$ denotes the set of unobservable negative user-vlogger pairs, we construct vlogger recommendation loss as follows.

$$\mathcal{L}^{vlogger} = - \sum_{(u,p,p^-)\in S'} \ln \sigma \left(\hat{y}_{up} - \hat{y}_{up^-} \right). \tag{19}$$

Finally, we train the model by multi-task learning, and the final loss function is as follows.

$$\mathcal{L} = \mathcal{L}^{video} + \lambda_1 \mathcal{L}^{vlogger} + \lambda_2 \mathcal{L}^{cl} + \lambda_3 \|\Theta\|, \tag{20}$$

where $\lambda_1, \lambda_2, \lambda_3$ are hyper-parameters that balance each loss function, and $\|\Theta\|$ is the regularization term of the model parameters.

5   Experiments

5.1   Experimental Settings

Datasets. We conduct experiments on two real-world datasets, i.e., one public dataset and one industrial dataset.

- **WeChat-Channels:** This dataset is released by WeChat Big Data Challenge 2021. The dataset contains 14-day user interactions from WeChat-Channels, a popular micro-video platform in China.
- **TakaTak:** This dataset is collected from TakaTak, a micro-video streaming platform for Indian users. The dataset contains user behaviors in four weeks.

Both two datasets include user-video interactions, user-vlogger interactions, and vlogger-video publishing relationships.

We preprocess the datasets to clean user-video and user-vlogger positive interactions. We define posting comment, reading comments, liking, sharing, and so on as explicit positive feedback to videos. For the WeChat-Channels dataset, only the interactions which indicate explicit positive feedback from a user or the watching loop greater than 1.5 or the watching time greater than 60 s are retained. For the TakaTak dataset, the interactions with explicit positive feedback or completion rate greater than 1.8 or watching time greater than 15 s are defined as positive interactions. We also remove users and micro-videos with less than 5 interactions and remove vloggers who publish less than 3 micro-videos. As a result, the ratio of positive user-video interactions to non-positive ones approximately is equal to 1:3 for both datasets.

As for user-vlogger interactions, we treat following and entering the homepage as explicit positive behaviors and define a user-vlogger interaction if there exists an explicit positive interaction between them or the user interacts with more than two micro-videos published by the vlogger. Further, we remove users and vloggers with less than 5 interactions and obtain the final user-vlogger interactions.

The statistics of the processed user-video interactions and user-vlogger interactions are shown in Table 1.

After sorting user interactions in ascending order by timestamp, we use the leave-one-out method to divide a dataset into train/validation/test sets. For each user, the last interaction is used for testing, the interaction before the last one is used for validation, and the remaining interactions are used for training.

Table 1. Statistics of the datasets

Dataset	#Users	#Micro-videos	#Vloggers	#User-video Interactions	#User-vlogger Interactions
WeChat	19739	25976	2088	1490633	34450
TakaTak	14571	13133	912	1661032	262548

Metrics. We adopt *Recall@K* and *NDCG@K* as metrics of performance evaluation, where Recall focuses on whether the recommended micro-videos are hit or not and NDCG focuses on the ranking of the recommended micro-videos. We set K to 10, 20, and 50.

Competitors. To evaluate the performance of our model, we choose the following models as the competitors.

- **NGCF** [7]: a GNN-based recommendation model. Based on the idea of collaborative filtering, the model explicitly models the high-order connectivity between users and micro-videos through GNN, which is beneficial to embedding learning.
- **LightGCN** [8]: a GNN-based recommendation model. The model finds that the nonlinear activation function and feature transformation matrix in NGCF degrade the performance, and it only utilizes simple weighting and aggregation methods.
- **GTN** [9]: a GNN-based recommendation model. The model considers that not all user interactions are reliable and designs graph neural networks to capture interaction reliability.
- **SGL** [19]: a recommendation model that introduces contrastive learning to GNN. The model generates contrastive views by employing node drop (ND), edge drop (ED), or random walk (RW), and then adds a contrastive loss to align the embeddings of positive pairs.
- **SimGCL** [23]: a recommendation model that integrates with a contrastive learning task. The model gives up the data augmentation at the graph level in SGL and proposes an augmentation method at the embedding level, that is, to construct positive pairs by adding uniform noise to the embeddings.

Implementation Details. For all the competitors, we adopt the implementations of open-source code. The hyperparameters of competitors are tuned based on their original papers. For a fair comparison, we initialize all the model parameters with a normal distribution, set the embedding size to 64, and set the batch size to 4096.

Our model is implemented by PyTorch. We use a random negative sample method and set the number of negative samples to 1 for the BPR loss. We use Adam with a learning rate of 0.001 to optimize our model. For the other hyperparameters, we tune λ_1, λ_2 and τ within $\{0.01, 0.05, \ldots, 5, 10\}$,

{0.0001,0.0005,...,1,5} and {0.01,0.05,...,1,5}, respectively. The model reaches the optimal performance on the WeChat-Channels dataset with λ_1, λ_2, and τ set to 5, 0.0005, and 0.5 and on the TakaTak dataset with λ_1, λ_2, and τ set to 5, 0.05, and 0.05.

We train the model with an early stopping strategy. That is, we stop training the model if Recall@10 does not increase on the validation set for 10 epochs consecutively. We adopt model parameters achieving the best performance on the validation set for testing. Our model is not allowed to recommend micro-videos that have been watched by the user. Our implementation code is available at https://github.com/laiweijiang/VAGNN.git.

5.2   Performance Comparison

The performance of all models on two datasets is listed in Table 2. From the results, we have the following observations.

Our model achieves the best performance and outperforms all the competitors on all datasets in terms of all metrics, indicating the superiority of our model. We attribute this result to that we effectively model the complex relationship among users, micro-videos, and vloggers, and utilize contrastive learning to further enhance the performance of the model. LightGCN outperforms NGCF in all datasets, which is consistent with the claim in [8]. However, the performance of the GTN model is lower than LightGCN, presumably because we removed users, micro-videos, and vloggers with few interactions during the data processing stage. It may also remove some noise data simultaneously, which is not beneficial for GTN.

Our model outperforms LightGCN by a large margin. For example, our model outperforms LightGCN by 14.06% and 30.13% on Recall@10 in WeChat-Channels and TakaTak datasets, respectively. Compared to LightGCN which conducts embedding propagation on the user-video bipartite graph, we perform embedding propagation on the user-video-vlogger tripartite graph. The experimental results show that vloggers do contain extensive information, such as the implied user preferences, in the micro-video scenario. Mining the information related to vloggers helps our model enhance the quality of embedding.

The three SGL variants and SimGCL outperform LightGCN in most metrics. Besides, SimGCL and SGL-ND are the second-best models on WeChat-Channels and TakaTak datasets, respectively, which demonstrates the effectiveness of contrastive learning in graph recommendation models. However, SimGCL only has the average performance on TakaTak, and also SGL-ND shows mediocre performance on WeChat-Channels. The reason might be that in the data augmentation phase, the approach of adding uniform noise by SimGCL and the approach of randomly dropping nodes and surrounding edges by SGL-ND greatly change the original embedding and graph structure, respectively, resulting in unstable performance on different datasets. On the contrary, VA-GNN adopts cross-view contrastive learning that directly relies on the structure of the graph, thus benefiting stably from contrastive learning.

Table 2. Recommendation performance on two datasets.

WeChat-Channels

Model	Recall			NDCG		
	@10	@20	@50	@10	@20	@50
NGCF	0.0382	0.0698	0.1356	0.0185	0.0264	0.0393
LightGCN	0.0441	0.0742	0.1413	0.0221	0.0296	0.0428
GTN	0.0433	0.0721	0.1385	0.0214	0.0286	0.0417
SGL-ED	0.0451	0.0751	0.1454	0.0222	0.0297	0.0435
SGL-ND	0.0441	0.0723	0.1404	0.0220	0.0291	0.0425
SGL-RW	0.0452	0.0752	0.1451	0.0225	0.0300	0.0438
SimGCL	<u>0.0470</u>	<u>0.0801</u>	<u>0.1518</u>	<u>0.0233</u>	<u>0.0317</u>	<u>0.0458</u>
VA-GNN	**0.0503**	**0.0826**	**0.1545**	**0.0248**	**0.0330**	**0.0471**
Improv. (%)	7.02	3.12	1.78	6.44	4.10	2.84

TakaTak

Model	Recall			NDCG		
	@10	@20	@50	@10	@20	@50
NGCF	0.0437	0.0810	0.1769	0.0204	0.0298	0.0487
LightGCN	0.0478	0.0867	0.1837	0.0227	0.0324	0.0514
GTN	0.0461	0.0852	0.1779	0.0224	0.0321	0.0504
SGL-ED	0.0481	0.0885	0.1809	0.0229	0.0330	0.0511
SGL-ND	<u>0.0497</u>	<u>0.0903</u>	<u>0.1840</u>	<u>0.0241</u>	<u>0.0341</u>	<u>0.0527</u>
SGL-RW	0.0467	0.0881	0.1833	0.0226	0.0329	0.0516
SimGCL	0.0471	0.0863	0.1823	0.0229	0.0327	0.0516
VA-GNN	**0.0622**	**0.0987**	**0.1870**	**0.0320**	**0.0411**	**0.0585**
Improv. (%)	25.15	9.30	1.63	32.78	20.53	11.01

5.3 Ablation Study

We evaluate the effectiveness of designed modules through the ablation study. We construct five variants as shown in Table 3, where variant A is VA-GNN without contrastive loss. Variant B is VA-GNN without the vlogger recommendation loss. Variant C is VA-GNN without video-view embedding propagation. Variant D is VA-GNN without vlogger-view embedding propagation. The variant E is VA-GNN that predicts interaction scores without considering user preferences for the vlogger of the target video, i.e., predicting the user-video interaction score between user u and video v as $\hat{y}_{uv} = \mathbf{e}_u^T \mathbf{e}_v$. The results on two datasets are shown in Table 3.

From the results, we find that variants C and D have a substantial decline in performance, compared to VA-GNN, indicating that embedding propagations over video-view and vlogger-view are critical in modeling and mining the relationship among users, micro-videos and vloggers. The performance of variant

Table 3. Ablation study.

WeChat-Channels

Model	Recall			NDCG		
	@10	@20	@50	@10	@20	@50
VA-GNN	**0.0503**	**0.0826**	**0.1545**	**0.0248**	**0.0330**	**0.0471**
(A) w/o CL loss	0.0470	0.0778	0.1492	0.0235	0.0312	0.0453
(B) w/o vlogger loss	0.0424	0.0732	0.1439	0.0214	0.0291	0.0430
(C) w/o video-view	0.0240	0.0421	0.0921	0.0114	0.0159	0.0257
(D) w/o vlogger-view	0.0443	0.0725	0.1313	0.0226	0.0296	0.0412
(E) w/o $\hat{y}_{up}$	0.0477	0.0811	0.1518	0.0238	0.0322	0.0461

TakaTak

Model	Recall			NDCG		
	@10	@20	@50	@10	@20	@50
VA-GNN	**0.0622**	**0.0987**	**0.1870**	**0.0320**	**0.0411**	**0.0585**
(A) w/o CL loss	0.0605	0.0980	0.1791	0.0303	0.0396	0.0555
(B) w/o vlogger loss	0.0488	0.0838	0.1721	0.0226	0.0314	0.0487
(C) w/o video-view	0.0349	0.0662	0.1371	0.0155	0.0233	0.0372
(D) w/o vlogger-view	0.0465	0.0817	0.1662	0.0215	0.0303	0.0469
(E) w/o $\hat{y}_{up}$	0.0463	0.0837	0.1727	0.0222	0.0315	0.0490

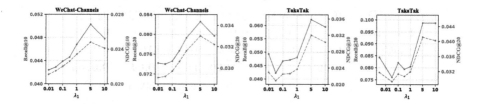

Fig. 2. Sensitivity of vlogger loss weight λ_1 on two datasets.

E is comparable to LightGCN but shows a significant decrease compared to VA-GNN. This indicates that user preferences for a micro-video originate from both the micro-video itself and the vlogger who publishes the video. Therefore, combining the user preference score for the video itself and the user preference score for its vlogger to predict the final user-video interaction score can effectively improve the model performance. Further, the performance of variant B shows that learning from positive user-vlogger pairs can substantially improve the model performance. Finally, the variant model (A) shows a slight performance decline, compared to VA-GNN, this indicates that contrastive learning can boost the performance of the model a bit.

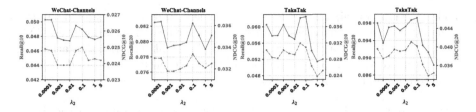

Fig. 3. Sensitivity of contrastive loss weight λ_2 on two datasets.

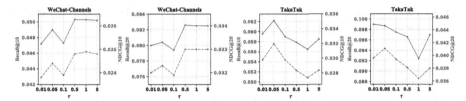

Fig. 4. Sensitivity of the temperature τ on two datasets.

5.4 Hyperparameter Sensitivity Analysis

We conduct experiments on two datasets to observe the impact of different values of hyperparameters (i.e., vlogger loss weight λ_1, contrastive loss weight λ_2 and the temperature τ) on the performance. Figures 2, 3, and 4 show the performance changes with the change of these hyperparameters, respectively.

From Fig. 2, we find that the model performance increases sharply when the value of λ_1 is set from 0.01 to 5 and achieves the maximum when λ_1 is 5, and then decreases slowly when λ_1 is set from 5 to 10. Obviously, choosing an appropriate λ_1 has a large impact on the performance. From Fig. 3, we find the choice of λ_2 is directly related to the dataset. On the WeChat-Channels dataset, the model performs best with λ_2 of 0.0005, on the WeChat-Channels dataset, the model performs best with λ_2 of 0.1 on the TakaTak dataset.

The temperature controls the sensitivity of hard samples and the tolerance of similar samples. In general, a low temperature is beneficial for mining hard negative samples, but a quite low value may damage the semantic structure. From Fig. 4, we can find that a high or low τ has different impacts on different datasets. Besides, TakaTak dataset is more sensitive to the temperature than WeChat-Channels dataset, and deviating from the best setting will degrade the performance remarkably. That is because the effect of temperature will be magnified by λ_2. λ_2 on TakaTak dataset needs to be set relatively large to achieve good performance. Therefore, changes in temperature on TakaTak dataset can obviously affect the performance.

6 Conclusion

The popularity of micro-video apps benefits from a large number of micro-videos produced by plenty of different vloggers. Inspired by this characteristic, VA-GNN models the relationship among users, micro-videos, and vloggers, and mines user preferences for micro-videos as well as vloggers for recommendations. VA-GNN also incorporates contrastive learning into graph neural networks, thus achieving the best micro-video recommendation performance on two real-world datasets while comparing to five existing models.

Acknowledgment. This work was supported by the National Natural Science Foundation of China under Grant No. 62072450 and the 2021 joint project with MX Media.

Ethical Statements. Hereby, we consciously assure that the data used in the experiments are desensitized and do not contain personal privacy.

References

1. Li, Y., Liu, M., Yin, J., Cui, C., Xu, X.-S., Nie, L.: Routing micro-videos via a temporal graph-guided recommendation system. In: Proceedings of the 27th ACM International Conference on Multimedia, pp. 1464–1472 (2018)
2. Wei, Y., Wang, X., Nie, L., He, X., Hong, R., Chua, T.-S.: MMGCN: multi-modal graph convolution network for personalized recommendation of micro-video. In: Proceedings of the 27th ACM International Conference on Multimedia, pp. 1437–1445 (2019)
3. Liu, S., Chen, Z., Liu, H., Hu, X.: User-video co-attention network for personalized micro-video recommendation. In: The World Wide Web Conference, pp. 3020–3026 (2019)
4. Jiang, H., Wang, W., Wei, Y., Gao, Z., Wang, Y., Nie, L.: What aspect do you like: Multi-scale time-aware user interest modeling for micro-video recommendation (2020)
5. Li, B., Jin, B., Song, J., Yu, Y., Zheng, Y., Zhuo, W.: Improving micro-video recommendation via contrastive multiple interests. In: Proceedings of the 45th International ACM SIGIR Conference on Research and Development in Information Retrieval, pp. 2377–2381 (2022)
6. Yu, Y., Jin, B., Song, J., Li, B., Zheng, Y., Zhuo, W.: Improving micro-video recommendation by controlling position bias. In: ECML PKDD 2022: Machine Learning and Knowledge Discovery in Databases - European Conference (2022)
7. Wang, X., He, X., Wang, M., Feng, F., Chua, T.-S.: Neural graph collaborative filtering. In: Proceedings of the 42nd international ACM SIGIR conference on Research and development in Information Retrieval, pp. 165–174 (2019)
8. He, X., Deng, K., Wang, X., Li, Y., Zhang, Y., Wang, M.: Lightgcn: simplifying and powering graph convolution network for recommendation. In: Proceedings of the 43rd International ACM SIGIR Conference on Research and Development in Information Retrieval, pp. 639–648 (2020)
9. Fan, W., Liu, X., Jin, W., Zhao, X., Tang, J., Li, Q.: Graph trend filtering networks for recommendation. In: Proceedings of the 45th International ACM SIGIR Conference on Research and Development in Information Retrieval, pp. 112–121 (2022)
10. Junliang, Yu., Yin, H., Li, J., Wang, Q., Hung, N.Q.V., Zhang, X.: Self-supervised multi-channel hypergraph convolutional network for social recommendation. In: Proceedings of the Web Conference 2021, pp. 413–424 (2021)

11. Shu, W., Tang, Y., Zhu, Y., Wang, L., Xie, X., Tan, T.: Session-based recommendation with graph neural networks. In: Proceedings of the AAAI Conference on Artificial Intelligence 33, pp. 346–353 (2019)

12. Chang, J., Gao, C., He, X., Jin, D., Li, Y.: Bundle recommendation with graph convolutional networks. In: Proceedings of the 43rd International ACM SIGIR Conference on Research and Development in Information Retrieval, pp. 1673–1676 (2020)

13. Zhao, C., Li, C., Fu, C.: Cross-domain recommendation via preference propagation graphnet. In: Proceedings of the 28th ACM International Conference on Information and Knowledge Management, pp. 2165–2168 (2019)

14. Chen, T., Kornblith, S., Norouzi, M., Hinton, G.E.: A simple framework for contrastive learning of visual representations. In: Proceedings of the 37th International Conference on Machine Learning, ICML 2020, 13–18 July 2020, Virtual Event, pp. 1597–1607 (2020)

15. Gao, T., Yao, X., Chen, D.: Simcse: simple contrastive learning of sentence embeddings. In: Proceedings of the 2021 Conference on Empirical Methods in Natural Language Processing, EMNLP 2021, Virtual Event/Punta Cana, Dominican Republic, 7–11 November, 2021, pp. 6894–6910 (2021)

16. Ma, Y., He, Y., Zhang, A., Wang, X., Chua, T.-S.: Crosscbr: cross-view contrastive learning for bundle recommendation. arXiv preprint arXiv:2206.00242, 2022

17. Xie, X., et al.: Contrastive learning for sequential recommendation. In: 2022 IEEE 38th International Conference on Data Engineering, pp. 1259–1273 (2022)

18. Qiu, R., Huang, Z., Yin, H., Wang, Z.: Contrastive learning for representation degeneration problem in sequential recommendation. In: Proceedings of the Fifteenth ACM International Conference on Web Search and Data Mining, pp. 813–823 (2022)

19. Wu, J., et al.: Self-supervised graph learning for recommendation. In Proceedings of the 44th International ACM SIGIR Conference on Research and Development in Information Retrieval, pp. 726–735 (2021)

20. Wang, C., Liang, Y., Liu, Z., Zhang, T., Philip, S.Yu.: Pre-training graph neural network for cross domain recommendation. In: 2021 IEEE Third International Conference on Cognitive Machine Intelligence, pp. 140–145 (2021)

21. Yang, Y., Wu, L., Hong, R., Zhang, K., Wang, M.: Enhanced graph learning for collaborative filtering via mutual information maximization. In: Proceedings of the 44th International ACM SIGIR Conference on Research and Development in Information Retrieval, pp. 71–80 (2021)

22. Cao, X., Lin, X., Guo, S., Liu, L., Liu, T., Wang, B.: Bipartite graph embedding via mutual information maximization. In: Proceedings of the 14th ACM International Conference on Web Search and Data Mining, pp. 635–643 (2021)

23. Yu, J., et al.: Are graph augmentations necessary? simple graph contrastive learning for recommendation. In: Proceedings of the 45th International ACM SIGIR Conference on Research and Development in Information Retrieval, pp. 1294–1303 (2022)

Author Index

G. De Francisci Morales et al. (Eds.): ECML PKDD 2023, LNAI 14174, pp. 701–703, 2023.
https://doi.org/10.1007/978-3-031-43427-3

Printed in the United States
by Baker & Taylor Publisher Services